PEARSON CUSTOM BUSINESS RESOURCES

Compiled by

Pearson Learning Solutions

New York   Boston   San Francisco
London   Toronto   Sydney   Tokyo   Singapore   Madrid
Mexico City   Munich   Paris   Cape Town   Hong Kong   Montreal

Senior Vice President, Editorial and Marketing: Patrick F. Boles
Editor: Ana Díaz-Caneja
Development Editor: Abbey Lee Briggs
Operations Manager: Eric M. Kenney
Production Manager: Jennifer Berry
Art Director: Renée Sartell
Cover Designer: Renée Sartell

Cover Art: Courtesy of EyeWire/Getty Images and PhotoDisc/Getty Images. Photodisc, "Globe surrounded by business people on computer monitors," courtesy of Photodisc/Getty Images. Dave Cutler (Artist), "Man Dropping Coins Into Glass Jar," courtesy of David Cutler/Images.com. Dave Cutler (Artist), "Three Coins in Glass Jar," courtesy of David Cutler/Images.com. Dean Turner, "Stock Vector: Global Finance" Courtesy of Dean Turner/iStockphoto. Hal Bergman, "Refinery Silhouette" Courtesy of Hal Bergman/iStockphoto. Dan Barnes, "Cargo Container Ship Aerial View" Courtesy of Dan Barnes/iStockphoto. Franc Podgorsek, "Stock Numbers" Courtesy of Franc Podgorsek/iStockphoto. "Customer in Line at Grocery Store" Courtesy of Digital Vision Photography/Veer Inc. Owaki-Kulla, "Pumping Gas" Courtesy of Flirt Photography/Veer Inc. Lynn Johnson, "Yunnan Province, People's Republic of China" Courtesy of Lynn Johnson/Getty Images, Inc. Thomas Bendy, "Student Typing" Courtesy of Thomas Bendy/iStockphoto.

This special edition published in cooperation with Pearson Learning Solutions.

Printed in the United States of America.

Please visit our web site at *www.pearsoncustom.com*.

Attention bookstores: For permission to return any unsold stock, contact us at *pe-uscustomreturns@pearson.com*.

Pearson Learning Solutions, 501 Boylston Street, Suite 900, Boston, MA 02116
A Pearson Education Company
www.pearsoned.com

ISBN 10: 1-256-17894-2
ISBN 13: 978-1-256-17894-1

Editorial Advisory Board

Contents

1 Creative Use of Advertising and Promotion
Norman M. Scarborough 1

2 Global Marketing Strategies
Norman M. Scarborough 43

3 Pricing and Credit Strategies
Norman M. Scarborough 83

4 Sources of Debt Financing
Norman M. Scarborough 113

5 Sources of Equity Financing
Norman M. Scarborough 147

6 E-Commerce and Entrepreneurship
Norman M. Scarborough 181

7 Supply Chain Management
Norman M. Scarborough 223

8 Location, Layout, and Physical Facilities
Norman M. Scarborough 263

9 Staffing and Leading a Growing Company
Norman M. Scarborough 309

10 Managing Inventory
Norman M. Scarborough 349

11 Management Succession and Risk Management Strategies in the Family Business
Norman M. Scarborough 383

12 The Legal Environment: Business Law and Government Regulation
Norman M. Scarborough 423

13 Ethics and Social Responsibility: Doing the Right Thing
Norman M. Scarborough 461

14 Management Succession and Risk Management Strategies in the Family Business
Norman M. Scarborough 497

Index 537

Creative Use of Advertising and Promotion

Learning Objectives

Upon completion of this chapter, you will be able to:

1. Define your company's unique selling proposition (USP).
2. Explain the differences among promotion, publicity, personal selling, and advertising.
3. Describe the advantages and disadvantages of the various advertising media.
4. Identify four basic methods for preparing an advertising budget.
5. Describe practical methods for stretching an entrepreneur's advertising budget.

Advertising is salesmanship mass produced. No one would bother to use advertising if he could talk to all of his prospects face-to-face. But he can't.

—Morris Hite

The man who stops advertising to save money is like the man who stops the clock to save time.

—Anonymous

From Chapter 10 of *Effective Small Business Management: An Entrepreneurial Approach*, 10/e. Norman M. Scarborough.

Advertising is not just a business expense; it is an investment in a company's future. Without a steady advertising and promotional campaign, a small business's customer base soon dries up. Advertising can be an effective means of increasing sales by telling customers about a business and its goods or services, by improving the image of the firm and its products, and by persuading customers to purchase its goods or services. A mega-budget is not a prerequisite for building an effective advertising campaign. With a dose of creativity and ingenuity, a small company can make its voice heard above the clamor of its larger competitors—and stay within a limited budget! A company's promotional strategy, which comprises advertising, publicity, and personal selling, must deliver the same clear, consistent, and compelling message about the business and its products or services. Customers respond best to a positive message that is delivered consistently by each component of the strategy. One goal of a company's promotional strategy is to create brand equity, which is measured by customer loyalty and customers' willingness to pay a premium for its products and services.

Developing an effective advertising program has become more challenging for business owners recently. Because of media overflow, overwhelming ad clutter, increasingly fragmented audiences, a plethora of advertising options, and more skeptical consumers, companies have had to become more innovative and creative in their advertising campaigns. Rather than merely turning up the advertising volume on their campaigns, companies are learning to change their frequencies, trying out new approaches in different advertising media.

A company's promotional efforts must differentiate its products and services from those of competitors. Some of the most effective advertisers have enhanced their brand loyalty by emphasizing in their promotional strategies the unique customer benefits that their products or services provide. For example, Nordstrom department stores are defined by friendly customer service, Volvo is known for automotive safety, and FedEx is recognized for guaranteed overnight delivery. One of the first steps is to carefully and thoughtfully define the message that a company's promotional campaign will emphasize by defining its *unique selling proposition*.

Define Your Company's Unique Selling Proposition (USP)

1. Define your company's unique selling proposition (USP).

Entrepreneurs should build their advertising messages on a **unique selling proposition (USP)**, a key customer benefit or a product or service that sets it apart from its competition. To be effective, a USP must actually *be* unique—something the competition does not (or cannot) provide—and compelling enough to encourage customers to buy. One technique is to replace your company's name and logo in one of your advertisements with those of your top competitor. Does the ad still make sense? If so, the ad is not based on your company's unique selling proposition! Unfortunately, many business owners never define their companies' USPs, and the result is an uninspiring "me-too" message that cries out "buy from us" without offering customers any compelling reasons to do so.

A successful USP answers the critical question every customer asks: "What's in it for me?" A successful USP should express in no more than 10 words what a business can do for its customers. Can your product or service save your customers time or money, make their lives easier or more convenient, improve their self-esteem, or make them feel better? If so, you have the foundation for building a USP. The most effective ads are *not* just about a company's products and services; instead, they focus on the company's customers and how its products and services can improve their lives.

The most effective USPs are simple, concrete, believable, emotional, and easy to communicate to prospective customers. The best way to identify a meaningful USP is to describe the primary benefits a product or service offers customers and then to list other secondary benefits it provides. Most businesses have no more than three primary benefits. Smart entrepreneurs look beyond the physical characteristics of their products or services, recognizing that sometimes the most powerful foundation for a USP is the *intangible* or *psychological* benefit a product or service offers customers—for example, safety, security, acceptance, status, prestige, and others. The key is to identify a gap that customers typically experience and then explain how your company's product or service can fill it. Before creating advertisements, entrepreneurs should develop a brief list of the facts that support the company's USP—for example, 24-hour service; a fully trained, experienced staff; industry awards won; and others. The final step is to consolidate the gap-filling benefits the company offers into a single statement, the USP.

Profile

Zappos

Customers already appreciate the shopping convenience that Zappos, the online shoe company, offers; however, the potential gap that customers may experience is "What if the shoes don't fit or aren't comfortable?" Zappos eliminates those concerns with its USP: "365 day return policy, free shipping both ways." The result is that Zappos, which founder Tony Hseih recently sold to Amazon.com, has a base of 8 million customers and annual sales that exceed $1 billion![1]

The USP becomes the heart of a company's advertising message because it has the ability to cut through all of the advertising clutter. For instance, the owner of a quaint New England bed and breakfast came up with a four-word USP that captures the essence of the escape her business offers guests from their busy lives: "Delicious beds, delicious breakfasts." Sheila Paterson, cofounder of Marco International, a marketing consulting firm, says her company's USP is "Creative solutions for impossible marketing problems."[2]

By focusing a company's advertising message on these top benefits and the facts that support them, entrepreneurs can communicate their USPs to their target audiences in meaningful, attention-getting ways. Building a firm's marketing message around a USP spells out for customers the benefits they can expect if they buy the company's product or service and why they should do business with a company rather than with its competition. However, a company must be able to *deliver* on its USP; otherwise, the advertising effort is futile!

Table 1 describes a six-sentence advertising strategy designed to create powerful ads that focus on a USP.

Creating a Promotional Strategy

2. Explain the differences among promotion, publicity, personal selling, and advertising.

The terms *advertising* and *promotion* are often confused. **Promotion** is any form of persuasive communication designed to inform consumers about a product or service and to influence them to purchase these goods or services. It includes publicity, personal selling, and advertising.

Publicity

Publicity is any commercial news covered by the media that boosts sales but for which the small business does not pay. "[Publicity] is telling your story to the people you want to reach—namely the news media, potential customers, and community leaders," says the head of a public relations firm. "It is not haphazard . . . It requires regular and steady attention."[3] Publicity has power; because it is from an unbiased source, a news feature about a company or a product appearing in a newspaper or magazine has more impact on people's buying decisions than an advertisement does. Exposure in any medium raises a company's visibility and boosts sales, and, best of all, publicity is free! It does require some creativity and effort, however.

TABLE 1 A Six-Sentence Advertising Strategy

Does your advertising deliver the message you want to the audience you are targeting? If not, try stating your strategy in six sentences:

1. *Primary purpose.* What is the primary purpose of this ad? "The purpose of Rainbow Tours' ads is to get people to call for or download a free video brochure."
2. *Primary benefit.* What USP can you offer customers? "We will stress the unique and exciting places our customers can visit."
3. *Secondary benefits.* What other key benefits support your USP? "We will also stress the convenience and value of our tours and the skill and experience of our tour guides."
4. *Target audience.* At whom are we aiming the ad? "We will aim our ads at adventurous male and female singles and couples, 21 to 34, who can afford our tours."
5. *Audience reaction.* What response do you want from your target audience? "We expect our audience to download or call to request our video brochure."
6. *Company personality.* What image do we want to convey in our ads? "Our ads will reflect our innovation, excitement, conscientiousness, and our warm, caring attitude toward our customers."

Source: Adapted from Jay Conrad Levinson, "The Six-Sentence Strategy," *Communication Briefings,* December 1994, p. 4. Reprinted by permission from Communication Briefings. ©Briefing Media Group LLC.

Profile

Jody Hall and Vérité Coffee

After working at Starbucks for 12 years, Jody Hall saw firsthand the value of publicity and decided to emphasize it when she launched her own Seattle-based coffee shop, Vérité Coffee. In addition to selling coffee, Hall included a unique gourmet cupcake bakery in her store, which has generated articles in both the *Los Angeles Times* and *Food & Wine* magazine. During elections, Hall hands out free cupcakes to voters, advertising the offer in local papers with catchy slogans such as "Legalize Frostitution." Hall also generated publicity for Vérité Coffee by donating 1,000 cupcakes to the local zoo for an elephant's birthday party and to auctions at local schools. Her efforts have paid off; Vérité Coffee generates sales of more than $1 million, and several local supermarkets have approached her about carrying her company's products.[4]

The following tactics can help entrepreneurs stimulate publicity for their companies:

- *Write an article that will interest your customers or potential customers.* One investment advisor writes a monthly column for the local newspaper on timely topics such as "Retirement Planning," "Minimizing Your Tax Bill," and "How to Pay for College." Not only do the articles help build her credibility as an expert, but they also have attracted new customers to her business.
- *Sponsor an event designed to attract attention.* Even local events, for which sponsorships can be quite inexpensive, garner press coverage for sponsors.
- *Involve celebrities "on the cheap."* Few small businesses can afford to hire celebrities as spokespersons for their companies. Some companies have discovered other ways to get celebrities to promote their products, however. For instance, when Karen Neuburger, owner of Karen Neuburger's Sleepwear, learned that Oprah Winfrey is a "pajama connoisseur," she sent the talk show host a pair of her pajamas. The move paid off; Neuburger has appeared on Oprah's popular television show on three separate occasions.[5]
- *Contact local TV and radio stations and offer to be interviewed.* Many local news or talk shows are looking for guests to talk about topics of interest to their audiences (especially in January and February). Even local shows can reach new customers.
- *Publish a newsletter.* With a personal computer and desktop publishing software, any entrepreneur can publish a professional-looking newsletter. Freelancers can offer design and editing advice. Use the newsletter to reach present and potential customers.
- *Contact local business and civic organizations and offer to speak to them.* A powerful, informative presentation can win new business. (Be sure your public speaking skills are up to par first! If not, consider joining Toastmasters.)
- *Offer or sponsor a seminar.* Teaching people about a subject you know a great deal about builds confidence and goodwill among potential customers. The owner of a landscaping service and nursery offers a short course in landscape architecture and always sees sales climb afterwards!
- *Write news releases and fax or e-mail them to the media.* The key to having a news release picked up and printed is finding a unique angle on your business or industry that would interest an editor. Keep it short, simple, and interesting. E-mail press releases should be shorter than printed ones—typically four or five paragraphs rather than one or two pages—and they should include a link to the company's Web site.

Profile

Richard Mori and Mori Books

When New Hampshire switched to a new toll road system, the state declared all outstanding highway toll tokens worthless. Sensing a public relations opportunity, Richard Mori, owner of Mori Books in Amherst, offered to redeem the outdated tokens at double their face value for up to half the price of any book in his store and sent out press releases announcing the deal. Within days, newspapers and television and radio stations across New Hampshire were featuring Mori's business. The exposure led to a 25 percent increase in sales.[6]

- *Volunteer to serve on community and industry boards and committees.* You can make your town a better place to live and work and raise your company's visibility at the same time.
- *Sponsor a community project or support a nonprofit organization or charity.* Not only will you be giving something back to the community, but you will also gain recognition,

goodwill, and, perhaps, customers for your business. Appearance Plus, a dry cleaning business in Cincinnati, Ohio, received the equivalent of thousands of dollars worth of advertising from the publicity generated by its Coats for Kids campaign. Customers donated winter coats and blankets, which the company cleaned for free and then distributed to the needy.[7]

■ *Promote a cause.* By engaging in **cause marketing**, entrepreneurs can support and promote a nonprofit cause or charity that is important to them and raise the visibility of their companies in the community at the same time. The key is choosing a cause that is important to your customers. One marketing expert offers the following formula for selecting the right cause: Mission statement + personal passion + customer demographics = ideal cause.[8] REI, a retailer of outdoor gear, generates goodwill among its customers and publicity for its business by donating both money and employees' time to worthy outdoor nonprofit programs such as Big City Mountaineers, which leads wilderness adventures for urban teens, and conservation causes such as the Continental Divide Trail Alliance and the Leave No Trace Center for Outdoor Ethics.[9]

IN THE ENTREPRENEURIAL
SPOTLIGHT   One Small Company's 10 Seconds of Fame

Netflix revolutionized the video rental industry with its "keep a video as long as you want with no late fee" policy and its fast, convenient delivery. Lloyd Lapidus and Greg Pippo, the founders of Bag Borrow or Steal (now called Avelle) applied that same philosophy to the $5 billion women's handbag industry, allowing fashionistas to keep pace with rapid changes in designer handbag styles and avoid the guilt associated with buying them and shortly retiring them to the back of the closet. Lapidus and Pippo recognized that designer bags are as much status symbols for women as sleek sports cars are for men, but that trendy bags have a very short fashion life. The entrepreneurs also saw an increased desire for luxury goods among shoppers, even those whose budgets do not match their high-end tastes. Writers call the trend "masstige," prestige for the masses, and companies such as Bag Borrow or Steal that lease exclusive merchandise make it affordable. One reporter says, "The devil may wear Prada, but she can also borrow it—and exchange it—through Bag Borrow or Steal."

Launched in 2004 in Seattle, Washington, Bag Borrow or Steal offers women unlimited access to more than 4,000 styles of bags from more than 100 designers, including Louis Vuitton, Gucci, Fendi, Jimmy Choo, Vera Wang, Coach, Balenciaga, and others, for as little as $13 per week. Fashion divas lease upscale designer bags, many of which sell for thousands of dollars, for a few days, a week, a month, or even longer at a fraction of their selling prices. For instance, customers can lease a Louis Vuitton clutch that sells for $1,300 for just $65 a week. A beige Chanel bag that sells for $3,500 rents for $120 per week. Bag Borrow or Steal refurbishes all bags to like-new condition

before leasing them. A customer who falls in love with a particular bag also can purchase it at a discount. Customers who pay a $10 monthly fee to become members earn discounts on bag rental rates (insurance and postage extra).

For the first 4 years of its existence, Bag Borrow or Steal experienced a solid, if not stellar, growth rate. Mike Smith, CEO of the 75-employee company, then learned that Hollywood movie producer/writer/director Michael Patrick King had incorporated a line about Bag Borrow or Steal into the script of *Sex and the City: The Movie*, the original film based on the hit HBO series of the same name. In the scene, Louise (played by Jennifer Hudson), the assistant to Carrie Bradshaw (played by Sarah Jessica Parker), has an affinity for high-end handbags and admits that she does not buy them; instead, she rents them from Bag Borrow or Steal. Companies often pay millions of dollars for product placement or a mention like the one in the 10-second scene from *Sex and the City*, but Bag Borrow or Steal paid nothing. Smith says that the small company could not have been able to afford that kind of publicity. Executives at New Line Cinema, the movie studio that produced the film, contacted Smith and Chief Marketing Officer Jody Watson 6 months before the film's release, which gave the small company enough time to maximize the benefit of the publicity that was coming its way.

On its Web site, Bag Borrow or Steal offered visitors the opportunity to watch the movie trailer, launched a YouTube sweepstakes to win tickets to the premiere, and created a "Sex and the City" shop in which customers could browse through handbags inspired by the four main characters in

Sex and the City: The Movie, mentioned Bag Borrow or Steal, a small company that leases designer handbags to women. The company's 10 seconds of fame resulted in its customer base tripling.

Source: Bobby Bank\Getty Images-WireImage.com

the film. Visitors could take a quiz to discover which of the movie's characters they were most like—and then shop for bags connected to that character. Bag Borrow or Steal also added a new line of sunglasses and jewelry to its line of rental merchandise. "Companies don't get a gift like this every day," says Watson.

After the release of *Sex and the City: The Movie*, which grossed more than $415 million worldwide, membership at Bag Borrow or Steal tripled to 1.5 million customers. Despite ramping up its inventory in the weeks before the film's release, demand for rental bags was so overwhelming that Bag Borrow or Steal had to place some customers on waiting lists. For 7 straight days following the release, the small company set sales records. Magazines and television networks across the country featured stories on the small company. "It's a Cinderella story for us," says Watson.

1. Bag Borrow or Steal was fortunate enough to have an opportunity for top-tier publicity fall in its lap. What steps can entrepreneurs take to garner publicity for their small companies?
2. Select a small business with which you are familiar. Work with a team of your classmates to generate ideas for generating publicity for the company.

Sources: Based on Simona Covel, "Bag Borrow Or Steal Lands the Role of a Lifetime," *Wall Street Journal*, May 27, 2008, p. B7; Wendy Kaufman, "Women Turn to Online Rentals for Handbags," *National Public Radio*, December 5, 2005, *www.npr.org/templates/story/story.php?storyId=5038856;* Stuart Elliott, "'Sex and the City' and Its Lasting Female Appeal," *New York Times*, March 17, 2008, *www.nytimes.com/2008/03/17/business/media/17adco.html;* "Bag Borrow or Steal," Hambrick Group, *www.hambrickgroup.com/clientListBagBorrow.html;* Lauren Folino, "Fashion Entrepreneurs Capitalizing on High-End Rentals," *Inc.*, December 4, 2009, *www.inc.com/news/articles/2009/12/designer-fashion-rental.html.*

Personal Selling

Advertising often marks the beginning of a sale, but personal selling usually is required to close the sale. **Personal selling** is the personal contact between salespeople and potential customers that comes from sales efforts. Effective personal selling gives a small company an advantage over its larger competitors by creating a feeling of personal attention. Personal selling deals with the salesperson's ability to match customer needs to the company's goods and services. Top salespeople:

- *Are enthusiastic and are alert to opportunities.* Star sales representatives demonstrate deep concentration, high energy, and drive.
- *Are experts in the products or services they sell.* They understand how their product lines or services can help their customers.

- *Concentrate on their best accounts.* They focus on customers with the greatest sales potential first. They understand the importance of the 80/20 rule: Approximately 80 percent of their sales comes from about 20 percent of their customers.
- *Plan thoroughly.* On every sales call, the best representatives act with a purpose to close the sale.
- *Use a direct approach.* They get right to the point with customers.
- *Approach the sales call from their customers' perspectives.* They have empathy for their customers and know their customers' businesses and their needs. Rather than sell the features of a product or service, they emphasize the benefits those features offer their customers.
- *Offer proof of the benefits their product or service provides.* The best salespeople provide tangible evidence such as statistics, facts, and testimonies from other customers about how their product or service will benefit the customer.
- *Are good listeners.* They ask questions and listen. By listening, sales representatives are able to identify customers' "hot buttons," key issues that drive their purchase decisions. "Questions are the key to selling," says one experienced salesperson. "Nobody ever listened themselves out of a sale!"[10]
- *Use past success stories.* They encourage customers to express their problems and then present solutions using examples of past successes.
- *Leave sales material with clients.* The material gives the customer the opportunity to study company and product literature in more detail.
- *See themselves as problem solvers, not just vendors.* Their perspective is "How can I be a valuable resource for my customers?" In fact, smart salespeople take the time to ask their existing customers, "Is there anything I am not doing that I could be doing to serve you better?" A study by Cahners Research found that sales representatives who understand the business needs and pressures that their customers face are 69 percent more likely to close a sale.[11]
- *Measure their success not just by sales volume but by customer satisfaction.* The key to sustaining sales for the long term is to build a corps of satisfied customers.

One extensive study found that just 20 percent of all salespeople have the ability to sell and are selling the "right" product or service and that that 20 percent make 80 percent of all sales. The study also concluded that 55 percent of sales representatives have "absolutely no ability to sell"; the remaining 25 percent have sales ability but are selling the wrong product or service.[12]

A study by Cahners Research found that it takes an average of 5.12 sales calls to close a deal.[13] Common causes of sales rejections include the representative's failure to determine customers' needs, talking too much, and neglecting to ask for the order. Given the high cost of making a sales call (an average of nearly $400), those missed opportunities are quite costly. Figure 1 shows how sales representatives spend their time. (Note that they spend less than 25 percent of their time engaged in active selling!)

FIGURE 1
How Sales Representatives Spend Their Time

Source: Pace Productivity Inc., 2008.

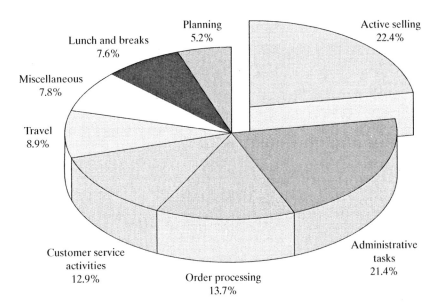

Planning 5.2%

Active selling 22.4%

Lunch and breaks 7.6%

Miscellaneous 7.8%

Travel 8.9%

Customer service activities 12.9%

Order processing 13.7%

Administrative tasks 21.4%

Entrepreneurs can improve their sales representatives' "closing averages" by following some basic guidelines:

- *Hire the right people.* A successful sales effort starts well before a sales representative calls on a potential customer. The first step is hiring capable salespeople who demonstrate empathy for customers, are motivated, persistent, and focused.
- *Train sales representatives.* Too often, business owners send sales representatives out into the field with little or no training and then wonder why they cannot produce. Training starts with teaching salespeople every aspect of the products or services they will be selling before moving on to teach them how to build relationships with customers. Training must also include the two most important selling skills of all: listening to the customer and closing the sale. Many business owners find that role playing exercises are an effective sales training technique.
- *Develop a selling system.* To be successful, sales representatives must develop an effective selling system. To build a winning selling system, entrepreneurs can take the following steps:
  1. *Prepare.* The best sales representatives know that what they do *before* they make a sales call significantly influences their success. In fact, the top complaint about sales representatives among buyers is a salesperson who is unprepared. Unfortunately, according to a study by Knowledge Anywhere, nearly 63 percent of sales representatives spend less than 20 minutes preparing for a sales call.[14] Smart salespeople take the time to research their customers (most often using the Internet) and to learn about the companies where their customers work.
  2. *Approach.* Establish rapport with the prospect. Customers seldom buy from salespeople they dislike or distrust.
  3. *Interview.* Get the prospect to do most of the talking; the goal is to identify his or her needs, preferences, and problems. The key is to *listen* and then to ask follow-up questions that help determine exactly what the customer wants. Norm Brodsky, founder of six companies, including a highly successful records storage business, says, "When I call on a prospect for the first time, I don't even talk about our company. I spend the whole visit just trying to learn all I can about the people I'm dealing with. I look to build rapport and understand how the customer likes to do business."[15]
  4. *Demonstrate, explain, and show.* Make clear the features and benefits of your product or service and point out how they meet the prospect's needs or solve his problems.
  5. *Validate.* Prove the claims about your product or service. If possible, offer the prospect names and numbers of other satisfied customers (with their permission, of course). Testimonials really work.
  6. *Negotiate.* Listen for objections from the prospect. Objections can be the salesperson's best friend; they tell him or her what must be "fixed" before the prospect will commit to an order. The key is to determine the *real* objection and confront it.
  7. *Close.* Ask for a decision. Good sales representatives know when the prospect flashes the green light on a sale. They stop talking and ask for the order.
- *Be empathetic.* The best salespeople look at the sale from the customer's viewpoint, not their own! Doing so encourages the sales representative to stress *value* to the customer.
- *Set multiple objectives.* Before making a sales call, salespeople should set three objectives:
  1. *The primary objective* is the most reasonable outcome expected from the meeting. It may be to get an order or to learn more about a prospect's needs.
  2. *The minimum objective* is the very least the salesperson will leave with. It may be to set another meeting or to identify the prospect's primary objections.
  3. *The visionary objective* is the most optimistic outcome of the meeting. This objective forces the salesperson to be open-minded and to shoot for the top.
- *Monitor sales efforts and results.* Selling is just like any other business activity and must be controlled. At a minimum, entrepreneurs should know the following numbers for their companies:
  1. Actual sales versus projected sales
  2. Sales generated per call made
  3. Average cost of a sales call

4. Total sales costs

5. Sales by product, salesperson, territory, customer, and so on

6. Profit contribution by product, salesperson, territory, customer, and so on

Advertising

Advertising is any sales presentation that is nonpersonal in nature and is paid for by an identified sponsor. A company's target audience and the nature of its message determine the advertising media it will use. However, the process does not end with creating and broadcasting an ad. Entrepreneurs also must evaluate an ad campaign's effectiveness. Did it accomplish the objectives it was designed to accomplish? Immediate-response ads can be evaluated in a number of ways. For instance, a business owner can include coupons that customers redeem to get price reductions on products and services. Dated coupons identify customer responses over certain time periods. Some firms use "hidden offers," statements hidden somewhere in an ad that offer customers special deals if they mention an ad or bring in a coupon from it. For example, Scott Fiore, owner of the Herbal Remedy, an all-natural pharmacy in Littleton, Colorado, uses a "bring this ad in for 10 percent off" message in his print ads so he can track each ad's success rate and adjust his advertising expenditures accordingly.

Business owners can also gauge an ad's effectiveness by measuring the volume of store traffic generated. Effective advertising should increase store traffic, which boosts sales of advertised and nonadvertised items. Of course, if an advertisement promotes a particular bargain item, the owner can judge its effectiveness by comparing sales of the items to preadvertising sales levels. Remember: The ultimate test of an ad is whether it increases sales!

Ad tests enable entrepreneurs to determine the most effective methods of reaching their target customers. An owner can design two different ads (or use two different media or broadcast times) that are coded for identification and see which one produces more responses. For example, a business owner can use a split run of two different ads in a local newspaper; that is, he can place one ad in part of the paper's press run and another ad in the remainder of the run. Then he can measure the response level to each ad to compare its effectiveness. Table 2 offers 12 tips for creating an effective advertising campaign.

The remainder of this chapter will focus on selecting advertising media, developing an advertising plan, and creating an advertising budget. Figure 2 illustrates the characteristics of a successful ad.

Selecting Advertising Media

3. Describe the advantages and disadvantages of the various advertising media.

Entrepreneurs quickly discover that a wide array of advertising media are available, including newspapers, magazines, radio, television, direct mail, the Web, as well as many specialty media. One of the most important decisions an entrepreneur must make is which media to use to disseminate the company's message. The medium used to transmit the message influences the customer's perception—and reception—of it. The right message broadcast in the wrong medium will miss its mark. Before selecting the vehicle for the message, entrepreneurs should consider several important questions:

- *How large is my company's trading area?* How big is the geographic region from which the firm will draw its customers? The size of this area influences the choice of media.
- *Who are my target customers and what are their characteristics?* Determining a customer profile often points to the appropriate medium to use to get the message across most effectively.
- *With which media are my target customers most likely to interact?* Until he knows who his target audience is, a business owner cannot select the proper advertising media to reach it.
- *What budget limitations do I face?* Every business owner must direct the firm's advertising program within the restrictions of its operating budget. Certain advertising media cost more than others.
- *Which media do my competitors use?* Is it helpful for a business owner to know the media his competitors use, although he should *not* automatically assume that they are

TABLE 2 12 Tips for Effective Advertising

1. *Plan more than one advertisement at a time.* An advertising campaign is likely to be more effective if it is developed from a comprehensive plan for a specific time period. A piecemeal approach produces ads that lack continuity and a unified theme.

2. *Set long-run advertising objectives.* One cause of inadequate planning is the failure to establish specific objectives for the advertising program. If an entrepreneur never defines what is expected from advertising, the program is likely to lack a sense of direction.

3. *Use advertisements, themes, and vehicles that appeal to diverse groups of people.* Although personal judgment influences every business decision, business owners cannot afford to let bias interfere with advertising decisions. For example, you should not use a particular radio station simply because you like it. What matters is whether the company's target customers listen to the station.

4. *View advertising expenditures as investments not as expenses.* In an accounting sense, advertising is a business expense, but money spent on ads tends to produce sales and profits over time that might not be possible without advertising. An effective advertising program generates more sales than it costs. You must ask, "Can I afford *not* to advertise?"

5. *Use advertising that is different from your competitors' advertising.* Some managers tend to "follow the advertising crowd" because they fear being different from their competitors. "Me-too" advertising frequently is ineffective because it fails to create a unique image for the firm. Don't be afraid to be different!

6. *Choose the media vehicle that is best for your business even if it's not "number one."* It is not uncommon for several media within the same geographic region to claim to be "number one." Different media offer certain advantages and disadvantages. Entrepreneurs should evaluate each according to its ability to reach their target audiences most effectively.

7. *Consider using someone else as the spokesperson on your TV and radio commercials.* Although being your own spokesperson may lend a personal touch to your ads, the commercial may be seen as nonprofessional or "homemade." The ad may detract from the company's image rather than improve it.

8. *Limit the content of each ad.* Some entrepreneurs think that to get the most for their advertising dollar, they must pack their ads full of facts and illustrations. Overcrowded ads confuse customers and are easy to ignore. Simple, well-designed ads that focus on your USP are much more effective.

9. *Devise ways of measuring your ads' effectiveness that don't depend on just two or three customers' responses.* Measuring the effectiveness of advertising is an elusive art at best. But the opinions of a small unrepresentative sample of customers, whose opinions may be biased, is not a reliable gauge of an ad's effectiveness. The techniques described earlier offer objective measurements of an ad's ability to produce results.

10. *Don't simply drop an ad because nothing happens immediately.* Some ads are designed to produce immediate results, but many ads require more time because of the lag effect they experience. One of advertising's rules is: It's not the size; it's the frequency. The head of one advertising agency claims, "The biggest waste of money is stop-and-start advertising." With advertising, patience is essential, and entrepreneurs must give an advertising campaign a reasonable time to produce results. One recent study concluded that sales increases are most noticeable 4 to 6 months after an advertising campaign begins. One advertising expert claims that successful advertisers "are not capricious ad-by-ad makers; they're consistent ad campaigners."

11. *Emphasize the benefits that the product or service provides to the customer.* Too often, ads emphasize only the features of the products or services a company offers without mentioning the benefits they provide customers. Customers really don't care about a product's or service's "bells and whistles"; they are much more interested in the *benefits* those features can give them! Their primary concern is "What's in it for me?"

12. *Evaluate the cost of different advertising medium.* Remember the difference between the absolute and relative cost of an ad. The medium that has a low absolute cost may actually offer a high relative cost if it does not reach your intended target audience. Evaluate the cost of different media by looking at the cost per thousand customers reached. Remember: No medium is a bargain if it fails to connect you with your intended customers.

Sources: Adapted from Sue Clayton, "Advertising," *Business Start-Ups*, December 1995, pp. 6–7; *Marketing for Small Business*, The University of Georgia Small Business Development Center: Athens, Georgia, 1992, p. 69; "Advertising Leads to Sales," *Small Business Reports*, April 1988, p. 14; Shelly Meinhardt, "Put It in Print," *Entrepreneur*, January 1989, p. 54; Danny R. Arnold and Robert H. Solomon, "Ten 'Don'ts' in Bank Advertising;" *Burroughs Clearing House*, vol.16, no. 12, September 1980, pp. 20–24, 43; Howard Dana Shaw, "Success with Ads," *In Business*, November–December 1991, pp. 48–49; Jan Alexander and Aimee L. Stern, "Avoid the Deadly Sins in Advertising;" *Your Company*, August/September 1997, p. 22.

the best choice. An approach that differs from the traditional one may produce better results.

- *How important is repetition and continuity of my advertising message?* Generally, an ad becomes effective only after it is repeated several times, and many ads must be continued for some time before they produce results. Some experts suggest that an ad must be run at least six times in most mass media before it becomes effective.
- *How does each medium compare with others in its audience, its reach, and its frequency?* **Audience** measures the number of paid subscribers a particular medium attracts. This is called *circulation* in most print media, such as newspapers and magazines.

FIGURE 2
**Characteristics of a
Successful Ad**

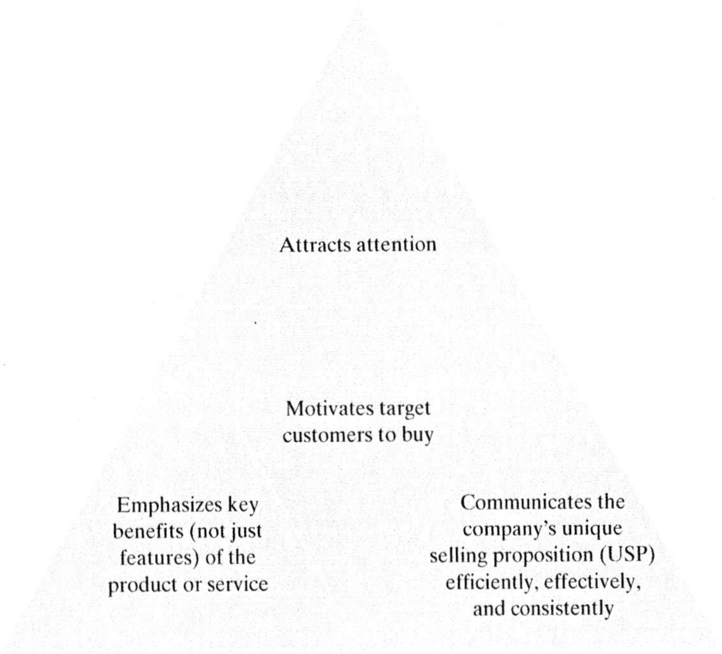

Attracts attention

Motivates target
customers to buy

Emphasizes key
benefits (not just
features) of the
product or service

Communicates the
company's unique
selling proposition (USP)
efficiently, effectively,
and consistently

Reach is the total number of people exposed to an ad at least once in a period of time, usually 4 weeks. **Frequency** is the average number of times a person is exposed to an ad in that same time period.

▪ *What does the advertising medium cost?* The entrepreneur must consider two types of advertising costs: absolute and relative. **Absolute cost** is the actual dollar outlay a business owner must make to place an ad in a particular medium for a specific time period. An even more important measure is an ad's **relative cost**, the ad's cost per potential customer reached. Relative cost is most often expressed as **cost per thousand (CPM)**, the cost of the ad per 1,000 customers reached. Suppose an entrepreneur decides to advertise his product in one of two newspapers in town. The *Sentinel* has a circulation of 21,000 and charges $1,200 for a quarter-page ad. The *Independent* has a circulation of 18,000 and charges $1,300 for the same space. Reader profiles of the two papers suggest that 25 percent of *Sentinel* readers and 37 percent of *Independent* readers are potential customers. Using this information, the entrepreneur computes the following relative costs:

	Sentinel	Independent
Circulation	21,000	18,000
Percentage of readers who are potential customers	× 25%	× 37%
Potential customers reached	5,250	6,660
Absolute cost of ad	$1,200	$1,300
Relative cost of ad (CPM)	$1,200/5,250 = .22857, or $228.57 per thousand potential customers reached	$1,300/6,660 = .19520, or $195.20 per thousand potential customers reached

Although the *Sentinel* has a larger circulation and a lower absolute cost for running the ad, the *Independent* offers this entrepreneur a better advertising deal because of its lower cost per thousand potential customers (CPM) reached. It is important to note that this technique does not give a reliable comparison across media; it is a meaningful comparison only *within* a single medium. Differences among the format, presentation, and coverage of ads in different media are so vast that cross-comparisons are not meaningful.

Traditional Versus Online Advertising Expenditures by Small Businesses in Local Markets

Source: Based on *The Local Commerce Monitor*, The BIA/Kelsey Group, 2009.

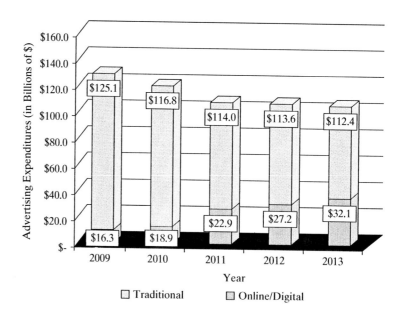

Media Options

The world of advertising is undergoing seismic changes. The lines that once separated the various advertising media are now blurring. Features that once were unique to a specific medium now operate across multiple media. Video, once the distinctive signature of television, now appears on companies' Web sites, in e-mail ads, on YouTube, on smart phones, and other devices. Traditional methods of advertising are not as effective as they once were because of increased advertising clutter, the growth in the time that customers spend online, and intense competition for buyers' attention. Small businesses are steadily shifting their advertising expenditures away from traditional media such as newspapers, television, direct mail, radio, magazines, and directories toward digital media such as e-mail campaigns, search engines, online and mobile device ads, and others (see Figure 3). According to *The Local Commerce Monitor* by BIA/Kelsey, 77 percent of small businesses now use digital or online advertising media, compared to 69 percent that use traditional advertising media.[16]

Entrepreneurs are looking to supplement or even replace traditional methods of advertising with inexpensive online tools and innovative, sometimes offbeat, techniques that capture buyers' attention.

Choosing advertising media is no easy task because each has particular advantages, disadvantages, and costs. Figure 4 gives a breakdown of U.S. business advertising expenditures by medium. Let's examine the features of various advertising media.

Advertising Expenditures by Medium

Source: Advertising Age, McCann-Erickson Inc., 2009.

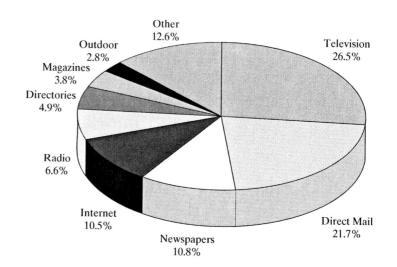

WORD-OF-MOUTH ADVERTISING. Perhaps the most effective and certainly the least expensive form of advertising is **word-of-mouth advertising** whereby satisfied customers recommend a business to friends, family members, and acquaintances. Unsolicited testimonials are powerful; because they are impartial, they score high on importance and credibility among potential customers. According to the Media Myth and Realities survey, 47 percent of U.S. consumers say that advice from family members and friends is a significant source of information about the products and services they buy.[17]

The best way for a company to generate positive word-of-mouth advertising is to provide superior quality and service, giving customers a reason to talk about the company in a positive way. A stellar experience leads to loyal customers who become walking advertisements for the company. In an age of social networking, the quality of the experience customers have with a business has more impact than any form of advertising. Word-of-mouth advertising can make or break a business because *dissatisfied* customers also speak out against businesses that treat them poorly. To ensure that the word-of-mouth advertising a company generates is positive, business owners must actually do what they want their customers to say they do.

ENTREPRENEURIAL
Profile

Shelly Hwang and Young Lee and Pinkberry

When Shelly Hwang and Young Lee opened Pinkberry, a shop that sells all-natural, nonfat yogurt in West Hollywood, California, in a location that was less than ideal, they knew that they would have to rely on word-of-mouth advertising to build a customer base. Their yogurt, which comes in plain and green tea flavors with 18 toppings, ranging from kiwi and mango to fruity pebbles and carob chips, is served in a modern environment with upscale Italian furniture, Scandinavian light fixtures, and hip European music. Everything about Pinkberry resonates with the entrepreneurs' target customers, and the result was rampant word-of-mouth advertising. "When residents tasted the yogurt, their mouths were like machine guns," says Lee. "They talked about it; they brought their friends. Business has been just phenomenal from the first month." Word-of-mouth advertising has been so effective for Pinkberry that Hwang and Lee are planning to open other locations in California, Arizona, New York, and Texas.[18]

A customer endorsement is an effective way of converting the power of word of mouth to an advertising message. Of course, unpaid and unsolicited endorsements are the most valuable. Online, those endorsements often come from customer-generated product reviews. Today, customers tend to rely more on customer reviews for information about a product or service than on the company's own descriptions.[19] The lesson: Make sure that your Web site includes a section for customer endorsements and reviews.

The Holy Grail of word-of-mouth advertising is "buzz." Buzz occurs when a product is hot and everyone is talking about it. From the mood rings of the 1970s to Apple's iPods, buzz drives the sales of many products. The Internet has only magnified the power of buzz to influence a product's sales. Buzz on the Web has become a powerful force in influencing the popularity of a firm's products or services. What can business owners do to start a buzz about their companies or their products or services? Sometimes buzz starts on its own, leaving a business owner struggling to keep up with the fury it creates. More often than not, however, business owners can give it a nudge by creating interest, mystique, and curiosity in a product or service. Creating buzz does not have to be expensive, but it does require being different. Consider the following tips:

- *Make your business buzz-worthy.* If your company has nothing to set it apart, customers have no incentive to create buzz about it. Does your company sell a novel product, have a unique marketing approach, offer stellar customer service, use a wacky logo, or anything else that can set it apart? If so, that can be the basis for buzz.
- *Promote your company to "influencers" in your market.* Influencers are high-profile customers who are on the front edge of every trend. They are the first to wear the hottest athletic shoe, master the coolest video game, or make the hippest restaurant their new hangout; they also are willing to tell their friends. Promoting your company's products and services to influencers increases the likelihood that your company will be the subject of buzz.
- *Make it easy for satisfied customers to spread the word about your company.* Ask customers periodically to tell a friend about your business and their positive experience with it. Put a "tell-a-friend" link on every page of your company's Web site. Reward customers who refer customers to your business by offering them something special in return.

Entrepreneur Lauren Luke uses YouTube videos to create buzz for her line of cosmetics, By Lauren Luke.

Source: TLA/Newscom

- *Use the Web to encourage viral marketing and amplify your company's word-of-mouth advertising.* One of the easiest ways to accomplish this is through e-mail because it is so easy for people to pass along to their friends. Another technique is to publicize news about your company on a blog and to include links to your company's Web site. Entrepreneurs also can use social media sites such as Facebook, Twitter, and others to engage customers and encourage buzz.
- *Tap into the power of YouTube.* Video-oriented Web sites such as YouTube, which draws 96.1 million unique viewers per month, can be a powerful tool for creating buzz for a company's products and services.[20] Videos on YouTube often become viral and are an important source of buzz for small companies.

ENTREPRENEURIAL
Profile

Laura Luke and By Lauren Luke

Thanks to the makeup tutorials that Lauren Luke began posting on YouTube to help her sell makeup on eBay, the 28-year-old single mother has become one of the United Kingdom's most popular YouTube stars, with 68 million views and 277,000 subscribers. In addition to the practical makeup tips Luke offers, the unscripted, unedited, genuine nature of her videos (viewers often hear her three dogs snoring in the background or her son watching cartoons) resonates with women of all ages—from preteens to octogenarians. Although not professionally trained, Luke's appeal is her knowledge, sincerity, and girl-next-door looks. "I'm definitely not a makeup artist," she says. "I've had no professional training. I'm more everybody's best friend they'd love to have in their bedroom playing makeup and giving tips." Building on her YouTube popularity, Luke now has her own line of cosmetics, By Lauren Luke. She also writes a popular newspaper column, has published a book, and has even helped develop a video game, Super Model Makeover by Lauren Luke.[21]

SPONSORSHIPS AND SPECIAL EVENTS. Although sponsorships and special events are a relatively new promotional medium for small companies, a growing number of small businesses are finding that sponsoring special events attracts a great deal of interest and provides a lasting impression of the company in customers' minds. As customers become increasingly harder to reach through any single advertising medium, companies of all sizes are finding that sponsoring special events—from wine tastings and beach volleyball tournaments to fitness walks and barbeque festivals—is an excellent way to reach their target audiences. North American businesses spend nearly $17 billion a year on event sponsorships.[22]

The costs of sponsorships vary and can meet a variety of budgets. Sponsoring a hole at a charitable golf outing may cost as little as $100, but landing the name of your business or product on the hood of a car driven by a NASCAR racer may reach as much as $7 million. Sponsorships and participation in special events can be very cost-effective if the entrepreneur supports events where attendees are potential customers. Local festivals and events gain the sponsor a great deal of positive public relations. Support for charity functions enhances the sponsor's community image, boosts sales, and often attracts new customers.

Profile

*George Cigale and
Tutor.com*

George Cigale, CEO of Tutor.com, a company based in New York City that sells online educational services, invests a significant portion of the company's promotional budget as a sponsor for the American Library Association's annual conference. Because public libraries are one of the company's primary customers, the conference gives Cigale and his employees the opportunity to spend quality time with an important group of their target customers. The sponsorship costs Tutor.com $10,000, and Cigale spends an additional $50,000 on travel and lodging for employees to attend and to sponsor a breakfast for the more than 300 librarians who attend the event. The sponsorship has paid off for Tutor.com. A librarian that Cigale met at the conference hired the company to create a pilot program for the California library system, a job that has generated $3 million a year in revenue.[23]

Small companies do not have to rely on other organizations' events to generate advertising opportunities; they can create their own special events. The owner of Quadrille Quilting in North Haven, Connecticut, partnered with the owners of two other quilting shops to create Shop Hops, an event in which customers buy "passports" to all three stores that entitle them to refreshments and special prizes. The first Shop Hop, which took place on a Super Bowl weekend, generated an entire month's sales in just one day for Quadrille Quilting.[24]

Creativity and uniqueness are essential ingredients in any special event promotion, and entrepreneurs excel at those. The following tips will help entrepreneurs get the greatest promotional impact from event sponsorships:

- *Do not count on sponsorships for your entire advertising campaign.* Sponsorships are most effective when they are part of a coordinated advertising effort. Most sponsors spend no more than 10 percent of their advertising budgets on sponsorships.
- *Look for an event that is appropriate for your company and its products and services.* The owner of a small music store in an upscale mountain resort sponsors a local jazz festival every summer during the busy tourist season and generates lots of business among both residents and tourists. Ideally, an event's audience should match the sponsoring company's target audience. Otherwise, the sponsorship will be a waste of money.
- *Research the event and the organization hosting it before agreeing to become a sponsor.* How well attended is the event? What is the demographic profile of the event's visitors? Is it well organized?
- *Try to become a dominant (or, ideally, the only) sponsor of the event.* A small company can be easily lost in a crowd of much larger companies sponsoring the same event. If sole sponsorship is too expensive, make sure that your company is the only one from its industry sponsoring the event.
- *Clarify the costs and level of participation required for sponsorship up front.* Doing so avoids unexpected surprises that can break a small company's advertising budget.
- *Get involved.* Do not simply write a check for the sponsorship fee and then walk away. Find an event that is meaningful to you, your company, and its employees and take an active role in it. Your sponsorship dollars will produce a higher return if you do.

In some cases the line between advertising and publicity has become blurry. In recent years, entrepreneurs have begun to explore new methods of getting their products or services in front of their target customers in a more subtle fashion. Many companies are engaged in product placement strategies in which their products or services appear in television shows, movies, video games, and other media that their target customers are likely to see.

After the portable CT scanner made by NeuroLogica, a small company in Danvers, Massachusetts, appeared on the 300th episode of *ER*, traffic to its Web site increased 60 percent. The company also received 10 inquiries from hospital administrators who had seen the $330,000 machine on the television show, far above the normal two or three inquiries each month. The scanner also became the topic of discussion on several *ER*-related blogs, and fans of the show posted video clips on YouTube. "I was shocked to see how much exposure we received," says NeuroLogica's director of sales, David Webster. "My friends in the industry could not believe that we did not pay for it."[25]

Product placement is effective because it relies on highly sophisticated yet subtle brand exposure. One of the earliest and most successful cases of product placement occurred in the 1982 movie classic *E.T.: The Extra-Terrestrial*, in which the main character (E.T., the alien) discovers an affinity for Reese's Pieces. After the movie's premiere, sales of Reese's Pieces increased 65 percent![26]

TELEVISION. In advertising dollars spent, television ranks first in popularity of all media. Although the cost of national TV ads precludes their use by most small businesses, local spots can be an extremely effective means of broadcasting a small company's message. A 30-second commercial on network television may cost more than $500,000 (a 30-second spot during the Super Bowl sells for $2.5 million to $3 million, up from $600,000 in 1987), but a 30-second spot on local cable television, which now is in 61.5 percent U.S. homes, may go for as little as $10 in small markets.[27]

Jason Apfel launched FragranceNet.com, an online retailer of brand name fragrances and beauty products, in 1995. "At first, we just had an 800 number that customers could call to order fragrances over the phone," he says. "Then the Internet came along." An early Internet adopter, Apfel initially set up a static Web page designed to prompt customers to call the company's toll-free number and was amazed at the results. "The phone started ringing off the hook," he recalls. Apfel then set up an e-commerce site and, in 2001, began using search engine marketing with tools such as Google AdWords. "We've seen a 20 percent year-on-year increase in our conversion rate," says Apfel. In 2007, looking to expand the company's customer base, Apfel turned to television, a medium that FragranceNet.com had used before without much success. This time, however, Apfel used Google TV Ads to decide which cable networks across the nation to use and which programs to target while placing caps on costs. Apfel used the tool to locate programs that were relevant to the company's product line and that attracted the highest concentrations of its target customers. "We don't have $20 million to throw at a campaign and hope it works," he says. After the cable television ads ran, FrangranceNet.com saw a 35 percent increase in the number of visitors to its Web site and a corresponding increase in sales.[28]

Television advertising offers a number of distinct advantages:

- *Broad coverage.* Television ads provide extensive coverage of a sizeable region, and they reach a significant portion of the population. Television reaches 90.2 percent of adults every day, exceeding the reach of all other major advertising media.[29] In fact, the average household spends 8 hours and 14 minutes each day tuned in to television.[30] The typical adult sees 26 commercial breaks a day, for a total of 73 minutes of advertisements.[31]
- *Ability to focus on a target audience.* Because many cable channels focus their broadcasting in topical areas—from home and garden or food to science or cartoons—cable television

offers advertisers the ability to reach specific target markets much as radio ads do. Because an inverse relationship exists between time spent in television viewing and education level, television ads overall are more likely to reach people with lower educational levels.

- *Visual advantage.* The primary benefit of television is its capacity to present the advertiser's product or service visually. With TV ads, entrepreneurs are not limited to mere descriptions of a product or service; instead, they can demonstrate their uses and show firsthand their advantages. For instance, a small retail store selling a hydraulic log splitter can design a television commercial to show how easily the machine works. The ability to use sight, sound, and motion makes TV ads a powerful selling tool.

- *Flexibility.* Television ads can be modified quickly to meet the rapidly changing conditions in the marketplace. Advertising on TV is a close substitute for personal selling. Like a sales representative's call, television commercials can use "hard sell" techniques, attempt to convince through logic, appeal to viewers' emotions, persuade through subtle influence, or use any number of other strategies. In addition, advertisers can choose the length of the spot (30-second ads are most common), its time slot, and even the program during which to broadcast the ad.

- *Design assistance.* Few entrepreneurs have the skills to prepare an effective television commercial. Although professional production firms might easily charge $50,000 to produce a commercial, the television station from which an entrepreneur purchases air time often will help to design and produce an ad very inexpensively.

Television advertising also has several disadvantages:

- *Brief exposure.* Most television ads are on the screen for only a short time and require substantial repetition to achieve the desired effect. One of the realities is that television viewers often avoid or ignore the commercial messages.

- *Clutter.* By the age of 65, the average person has seen more than 2 million television commercials, and more ads are on the way![32] With so many television ads beaming across the airwaves, a small company's advertising message easily can become lost in the shuffle.

- *"Zapping" and "zipping."* "**Zappers**," television viewers who flash from one channel to another during commercials, and "**zippers**," those who use digital video recording devices such as TiVo to fast-forward through commercials, pose a real threat to TV advertisers. Zapping can cut deeply into an ad's reach, and 36 percent of U.S. households now own a DVR device (compared to just 12.3 percent in 2007).[33] One study reported that 85 percent of DVR users zip through all or most commercials when watching a show.[34] Zapping and zipping prevent TV advertisers from reaching the audiences they hope to reach.

- *Fragmented audience.* As the number of channels available proliferates, the question of where to advertise becomes more difficult to answer. The average household in the United States now receives 130 television channels, up from just 33 in 1990![35] This dramatic increase in the number of channels available has fragmented the audience that an ad run on a single channel reaches.

- *Costs.* TV commercials can be expensive to create. A professionally done 30-second ad (the most common length of a television ad) can cost several thousand dollars to develop, even before an entrepreneur purchases airtime. Advertising agencies and professional design firms offer design assistance—sometimes at hefty prices—leading many small business owners to hire less expensive freelance ad designers or turn to the stations on which they buy air time for help with their ads. Table 3 offers some suggestions for developing creative television commercials.

Using Television Creatively. Although television ads are not affordable for every small business, many entrepreneurs have found creative ways to use the power of television advertising without spending a fortune. Two popular methods include infomercials and home shopping networks. **Infomercials** (also called **direct-response television**) come in two lengths: short form, which are 2- to 3-minute pitches, and long form, 30-minute full-length television commercials packed with information, testimonials, and a sales pitch asking for an immediate response. The length of these ads allows entrepreneurs to demonstrate and explain their products in detail and to show customers the benefits of using them, a particularly important consideration for a new or complex product. Producing and airing a half-hour infomercial can be expensive, often costing $300,000 to $1 million, depending on its production quality, format, content, celebrity involvement, and

TABLE 3 Guidelines for Creative TV Ads

- *Keep it simple.* Avoid confusing the viewer by sticking to a simple concept.
- *Have one basic idea.* The message should focus on a single, important benefit to the customer. Why should people buy from your business?
- *Make your point clear.* The customer benefit should be obvious and easy to understand.
- *Make it unique.* To be effective, a television ad must reach out and grab the viewer's attention. Take advantage of television's visual experience.
- *Get viewers' attention.* Unless viewers watch the ad, its effect is lost.
- *Involve the viewer.* To be most effective, an ad should portray a situation to which the viewer can relate. Common, everyday experiences are easiest for people to identify with.
- *Use emotion.* The most effective ads evoke an emotion from the viewer—a laugh, a tear, or a pleasant memory.
- *Consider production values.* Television offers vivid sights, colors, motions, and sounds. Use them to your advantage!
- *Prove the benefit.* Television allows an advertiser to prove a product's or service's customer benefit by actually demonstrating it.
- *Identify your company well and often.* Make sure your store's name, location, and product line stand out. The ad should portray your company's image.

Source: Adapted from *How to Make a Creative Television Commercial*, Television Bureau of Advertising.

broadcast schedule. Short-form infomercials cost about $15,000 to $20,000 to produce. Because most infomercials ask for an immediate response from viewers, entrepreneurs can gauge their success at landing customers, sometimes within minutes of airing them and almost always within 1 week. Products such as the ShamWow, Snuggie, and PedEgg have reached millions of units in sales with the help of infomercials.

ENTREPRENEURIAL Profile

Roger Fredericks and Fredericks Golf

Roger Fredericks, founder of Fredericks Golf has used 30-minute infomercials to sell instructional golf DVDs since 2005. Aired on the Golf Channel, Fredericks' infomercials typically generate $3,000 in sales for every $1,000 that he spends. Fredericks says that his company has sold $7 million in golf DVDs and that the infomercials have made him a celebrity, giving him opportunities to speak at golf clinics and conferences across the country and filling his instructional classes 6 months in advance.[36]

Only 1 in 10 products that rely on infomercials succeeds.[37] To become an infomercial star, a product should meet the following criteria:

- Be unique and of good quality.
- Solve a common problem.
- Be easy to use and easy to demonstrate.
- Appeal to a mass audience.
- Have an "aha! factor" that makes customers think "What a great idea!"

Shopping networks such as QVC and the HSN, which reach nearly 100 million homes, offer entrepreneurs another route to television. Time on these networks is free, but getting a product accepted is difficult; only a small percentage of the products reviewed by QVC or HSN are featured on the show. Shopping networks look for high-quality products that have "demonstration appeal" and are typically priced between $15 and $50 (although there are exceptions). Landing a product on one of these networks may be a challenge, but entrepreneurs who do often sell thousands of units in a matter of minutes.

ENTREPRENEURIAL Profile

Sean "Diddy" Combs and Sean John and HSN

Entrepreneur Sean "Diddy" Combs recently set a new sales record on HSN when he appeared on the network 3 weeks before Christmas with a line of scents from his Sean John line of fragrances, including one for women. Viewer response was so overwhelming that Combs sold the entire collection of 5,600 units at $60 each in just 15 minutes.[38]

RADIO. Radio permits advertisers to reach specific audiences over large geographic areas. By choosing the appropriate station, program, and time for an ad, a small company can reach virtually any target market.

Radio advertising offers several advantages:

- *Extensive reach.* Radio's nearly universal presence gives advertisements in this medium a major advantage. Nearly every home and car in the United States is equipped with a radio, which means that radio ads receive a tremendous amount of exposure in the target market. Although the myriad of entertainment options available has reduced the time that customers spend with all advertising media, the average adult spends 18.5 hours each week listening to the radio. According to the Radio Advertising Bureau, radio reaches 71 percent of adults each day and 93 percent of customers each week![39]

- *Audience delivery.* Radio commercial breaks retain on average 92 percent of the lead-in listening audience, which means fewer commercial zappers than television ads experience.[40]

- *Market segmentation.* Radio advertising is flexible and efficient because advertisers can choose stations aimed at a specific market within a broad geographic region. Radio stations design their formats to appeal to specific types of audiences. (Ever notice how the stations you listen to are not the same ones your parents listen to?) AM stations, which once ruled the airways, now specialize mainly in "talk formats" such as call-in, news, religion, sports, and automotive shows. On the FM dial, country, urban contemporary, classical, classic rock, rhythm and blues, Hispanic, and "oldies" stations have listener profiles that give entrepreneurs the ability to pinpoint practically any advertising target.

- *Flexibility and timeliness.* Radio commercials have short closing times and can be changed quickly. Small firms that sell seasonal merchandise or advertise special sales or events can change their ads on short notice to match changing market conditions.

- *Friendliness.* Radio ads are more "active" than ads in printed media because they use the spoken word to influence customers. Vocal subtleties used in radio ads are impossible to convey through printed media. Spoken ads can suggest emotions and urgency, and they lend a personalized tone to the message.

Radio advertisements also have some disadvantages:

- *Poor listening.* Radio's intrusiveness into the public life almost guarantees that customers will hear ads, but they may not listen to them. Listeners are often engaged in other activities while the radio is on and may ignore the message.

- *Need for repetition.* Listeners usually do not respond to radio ads after a single exposure to them. Radio ads must be broadcast repeatedly to be effective. Consistency in radio ads is the key to success.

- *Limited message.* Radio ads are limited to 1 minute or less, which requires that business owners keep their messages simple, covering only one or two points. In addition, radio spots do not allow advertisers to demonstrate their products or services. Although listeners can hear the engine purr, they can't see the car; spoken messages can only describe the product or service.

Buying Radio Time. Business owners can zero in on a specific advertising target by using the appropriate radio station. Stations follow various formats—from rap to rhapsodies—to appeal to specific audiences. Radio advertising time is usually sold in 15-, 30-, and 60-second increments. Many radio stations now offer 5-second spots called "adlets" and even super-short 1- or 2-second "blinks" that are designed to increase the awareness of a brand among listeners.

Fixed spots are guaranteed to be broadcast at the times specified in the owner's contract with the station. Preemptible spots are cheaper than fixed spots, but the advertiser risks being preempted by an advertiser willing to pay the fixed rate for a time slot. Floating spots are the least expensive, but the advertiser has no control over broadcast times. Many stations offer package plans, using flexible combinations of fixed, preemptible, and floating spots. Table 4 offers a guide to producing effective radio copy.

Radio rates vary depending on the time of day the ads are broadcast and, like television, there are prime-time slots known as drive-time spots. Although exact hours may differ from station to station, the following classifications are common (listed in descending order of cost):

Class AA: Morning drive time—6 A.M. to 10 A.M.

Class A: Evening drive time—4 P.M. to 7 P.M.

TABLE 4 Guidelines for Effective Radio Copy

- *Mention the business often.* This is the single most important and inflexible rule in radio advertising. Also make sure listeners know how to find your business. If the address is complicated, use landmarks.
- *Stress the benefit to the listener.* Don't say "Dixon's has new fall fashions." Say "Dixon's fall fashions make you look fabulous."
- *Use attention-getters.* One key to a successful radio ad is grabbing listeners' attention from the start and holding it. Radio gives the options of music, sound effects, and unusual voices. Crack the barrier with sound.
- *Zero in on your audience.* Know to whom you're selling. Radio's selectivity attracts the right audience. It's up to you to communicate in the right language.
- *Keep the copy simple and to the point.* Don't try to impress listeners with vocabulary. "To be or not to be" may be the best-known phrase in the language . . . and the longest word has just three letters.
- *Sell early and often.* Don't back into the selling message. At most, you've got 60 seconds. Make the most of them. Don't be subtle.
- *Write for the ear.* Forget the rules of grammar; write conversationally.
- *Prepare your copy.* Underline words you want to emphasize so that the announcer knows how the ad should read.
- *Triple space.* Type clean, legible copy. Make sure the announcer rehearses the ad.
- *Use positive action words.* Use words such as *now* and *today*, particularly when you're writing copy for a sale. Radio has qualities of urgency and immediacy. Take advantage of them by including a time limit or the date the sale ends.
- *Put the listener in the picture.* Radio's theater of the mind means you don't have to talk about a new car. With sounds and music, you can put the listener behind the wheel.
- *Focus the spot on getting a response.* Make it clear what you want the listener to do. Don't try to get a mail response. Use phone numbers or a Web site address only, and repeat the number or Web address at least three times. End the spot with the phone number or the Web address.
- *Don't stay with a loser.* Direct-response ads produce results right way—or not at all. Don't stick with a radio spot that is not generating sales. Change it.

Sources: Kim T. Gordon, "Turn It Up," *Entrepreneur*, January 2004, pp. 80–81; *Radio Basics*, Radio Advertising Bureau.

Class B: Home worker time—10 A.M. to 4 P.M.

Class C: Evening time—7 P.M. to Midnight

Class D: Nighttime—Midnight to 6 A.M.

Some stations may have different rates for weekend time slots.

NEWSPAPERS. Traditionally, the local print newspaper has been the medium that most small companies rely on to get their messages across to customers. Both the circulation and the number of newspapers in the United States are declining, however, and the share of advertising dollars the medium attracts has fallen below 11 percent. However, newspapers provide several advantages to small business advertisers:

- *Targeted geographic coverage.* Newspapers are geared to a specific geographic region, and they reach potential customers across all demographic classes. Local newspapers, in particular, provide extensive coverage of a company's immediate trading area.
- *Flexibility.* A business can change its newspaper advertisements on very short notice. Entrepreneurs can select the size of the ad, its location in the paper, and the days on which it runs. For instance, auto repair shops often advertise their tune-up specials in the sports section on weekends, and party shops display their ads in the entertainment section as the weekend approaches.
- *Timeliness.* Papers almost always have very short closing times, the publication deadline prior to which the advertising copy must be submitted. Many newspapers allow advertisers to submit their copy as late as 24 hours before the ad runs.
- *Communication potential.* Newspaper ads can convey a great deal of information by employing attractive graphics and copy. Properly designed, they can be very effective in attracting attention and persuading readers to buy.
- *Low costs.* Newspapers normally offer advertising space at low absolute cost and, because of their blanket coverage of a geographic area, at low relative cost as well.
- *Prompt responses.* Newspaper ads typically produce a relatively quick customer response. A newspaper ad is likely to generate sales the very next day, and advertisers who use coupons can track the response to an ad. This advantage makes newspapers an ideal medium for promoting special events such as sales, grand openings, or the arrival of a new product.

▨ *Popularity of free newspapers.* Most communities have at least one free (to readers) newspaper, and their reach can be significant, an important consideration for advertisers. Studies show that 60 percent of consumers say that they read a free paper at least once a week.[41]

Newspaper advertisements also have disadvantages:

▨ *Wasted readership.* Because newspapers reach a wide variety of people, at least a portion of an ad's coverage is wasted on readers who are not potential customers. This nonselective coverage makes it more difficult for newspapers to reach specific target markets than ads in other media.

▨ *Reproduction limitations.* The quality of reproduction in newspapers is limited, especially when it is compared with that of magazines and direct mail. Recent technology advances, however, are improving the quality of reproduction in newspaper ads.

▨ *Lack of prominence.* One frequently cited drawback of newspapers is that they carry so many ads that a small company's message might be lost in the crowd. The typical newspaper is 62 percent advertising. This disadvantage can be overcome by increasing the size of the ad or by adding color to it. Color can increase the reading of ads by as much as 80 percent over black-and-white ads. Studies show that two-color ads do "pull" better than black-and-white ones, but only by a small margin.[42] The *real* increase in ad recall and response comes from using full four-color ads. Bold headlines, illustrations, and photographs also increase an ad's prominence.

▨ *Proper ad placement in the newspaper can increase an ad's effectiveness.* The best locations are on a right-hand page, near the right margin, above the half-page mark, or next to editorial articles. The most-read sections in the typical newspaper are the front page and the comics.

▨ *Declining readership.* Newspaper circulation as a percentage of U.S. households has dropped from 98 percent in 1970 to less than 40 percent today as readers have migrated to the Internet.[43] In fact, more people now get national and international news from the Internet than from a newspaper.[44] Print newspaper ads are more effective with older adults and those with higher education and income. They are less effective with younger adults; studies show that just 32 percent of adults aged 18 to 34 read a daily newspaper.[45]

▨ *Short ad life.* The typical newspaper is soon discarded and, as a result, an ad's life is extremely short. Business owners can increase the effectiveness of their ads by giving them greater continuity. Spot ads can produce results, but maintaining a steady flow of business requires some degree of continuity in advertising.

Buying Newspaper Ads. Newspapers typically sell ad space by lines and columns or inches and columns. For instance, a 4-column × 100-line ad occupies four columns and 100 lines of space 14 lines = 1 column inch. For this ad, a business owner pays the rate for 400 lines. If the newspaper's line rate is $3.50, this ad would cost $1,400 (400 lines × $3.50 per line). Most papers offer discounts for bulk, long-term, and frequency contracts and full-page ads. Advertising rates vary from one paper to another, depending on factors such as circulation and focus. Entrepreneurs should investigate the circulation statements, advertising rates, and reader profiles of a newspaper to see how well it matches the company's target audience before selecting one as an advertising medium.

INTERNET ADVERTISING. Just as the Internet has become a common tool for conducting business, it also has become a popular medium for advertisers. Internet advertising is growing rapidly because advertisers recognize that that is where their target customers are spending more of their time and because advertisers can track the effectiveness of their advertising campaigns. By 2013, U.S. companies are expected to spend $37.2 billion on online advertising (see Figure 5).

The blurring line between television and the Internet provides opportunities for small businesses to reach customers with inexpensive video ads. The Web's multimedia capabilities make it an ideal medium for companies to demonstrate their products and services with full motion, color, and sound and to get customers involved in the demonstration. Businesses that normally use direct mail can bring the two-dimensional photos and product descriptions in their print catalogs to life in video, avoid the expense of mailing them, and attract new customers that traditional mailings might miss.

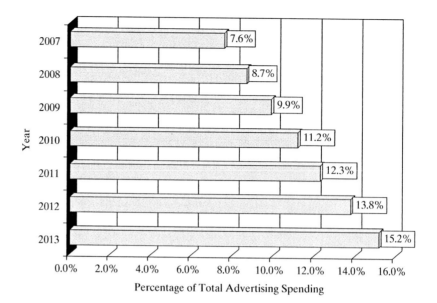

ENTREPRENEURIAL

Profile

Wendy Chatelain and Antoine's

The fifth-generation owners of Antoine's, the legendary New Orleans restaurant founded in 1840, recently decided to branch out from the print and radio ads they had relied on for many years and create on online video. Working with online video production company TurnHere, Wendy Chatelain, sales and marketing manager of the nation's oldest family-owned restaurant, created a short video starring one of Antoine's third-generation waiters and featuring the famed restaurant's rich history and outstanding menu, including its flaming baked Alaska dessert. The ad, which Antoine's posted on its online Yellow Pages ad, its Web site, and on YouTube, cost just $1,000 to shoot, edit, and upload. The ad's results—300 new customers in just 1 month— exceeded Chatelain's expectations.[46]

Online advertisements take five basic forms: banner ads, display ads, contextual ads, pay-per-click ads, and e-mail ads. **Banner ads** are small rectangular ads that reside on Web sites, much like roadside billboards, touting a company's product or service. When site visitors click the banner ad, they go straight to the advertiser's homepage. One measure of a banner ad's effectiveness is the number of impressions it produces. An **impression** occurs every time an ad appears on a Web page, whether or not the user clicks on the ad to explore it. Another common way of judging the effectiveness of banner ads is the **click-through rate**, which is calculated by dividing the number of times customers actually click on the banner ad by the number of impressions for that ad. For instance, if an ad is displayed 1,000 times and 12 customers actually click the ad and go to the advertiser's Web site, the ad's click-through rate is 1.2 percent (12 ÷ 1,000). Banner ads suffer from a very low click-through rate—less than 0.5 percent compared to an average click-through rate of 15 percent for search engines.[47] The cost of a banner ad to an advertiser depends on the number of prospects who actually click on it.

Banner ads do not have to be expensive to be effective. Many small business owners increase the exposure their banner ads receive by joining a banner exchange program, which is similar to an advertising cooperative. In a banner exchange program, member companies can post their banners on each other's sites. These programs work best for companies selling complementary products or services. For instance, a small company that sells gourmet food products over the Web could exchange banner ads with a company that uses the Web to sell fine wines or upscale kitchen tools and appliances.

The primary disadvantage of banner ads is that Web users can easily ignore them. These ads have become such a part of the landscape of the Web that users tend to ignore them. Web designers search for the best page placement for banner ads and the "bells and whistles" that will attract browsers and encourage them to click through.

A form of Web advertising that is more difficult to ignore is **display ads**, which include both pop-up, interstitial ads, and contextual ads. A **pop-up ad** appears spontaneously in a separate window, blocking the site behind it. It is designed to grab consumers' attention for the few nanoseconds it takes them to close the window. One danger of such ads is that Internet users do not like them, perceiving them as an annoying intrusion. A slight variation on this ad is the "pop-under" ad, which immediately goes behind the active screen but stays open until the browser window is closed. An **interstitial ad** is an ad page that appears for a short time before a user-requested page appears. These ads are also called transition ads, splash pages, and flash pages.

Contextual ads are ads on Web sites that are correlated to a particular user's interests or on-line behavior. For instance, a user searching for sports information might see an ad for athletic shoes or T-shirts, and one searching for vitamins might see an ad for green tea or herbal remedies. To catch the attention of Web users, many advertisers, particularly those companies that aim their products at young customers, are using video ads rather than traditional display ads.

Pay-per-click ads require companies to bid on top-ranking search engine listings using key words that they expect Internet users to type into a search engine when they are interested in purchasing a particular product or service. The higher a company's bid is for a key word, the more prominent is the location of its ad on the results that the search engine returns. Companies pay for an ad only when a prospect actually clicks on it. Entrepreneurs who advertise on the Internet should consider making pay-per-click ads a part of their advertising strategies. Compete's Online Shopper Intelligence Study found that 61 percent of Internet shoppers use a search engine as their first stop for locating the products and services they are interested in purchasing.[48] According to a study by Goldstein Group Communications, companies allocate 11 percent of their marketing budgets to search engine marketing and landing highly placed spots on popular search engines.[49] Google, Yahoo!, and Bing are the leading search engines, and advertisers who want to increase the odds of reaching their target audiences should advertise on all three.

To calculate the maximum amount a company can afford to bid on a key word, use the following formula:

$$\text{Maximum keyword bid} = \text{Conversion rate} \times \text{Profit per sale}$$

Online conversion rates vary by industry, but the average conversion rate is about 3.2 percent. That means that for every 1,000 visitors to a company's site, 32 of them actually make a purchase. For a company that has a conversion rate of 3.2 percent and an average profit per order of $12, the maximum amount the owner should bid on a key word is:

$$\text{Maximum keyword bid} = 3.2\% \times \$12 = 38.4 \text{ cents}$$

Used properly, pay-per-click ads can drive customers to a company's Web site even before the search engines discover it and include it in their search results. Pay-per-click ads also allow advertisers to test the effectiveness of different ads by running several variations at once (e.g., one version might include a discounted price and another might include a free accessory).

These ads are efficient because advertisers pay for an ad only when a customer actually clicks on it. **Click fraud**, which occurs when a person or a computer program generates ad clicks even though they have no interest in the advertiser's product or service, is a danger to entrepreneurs who use pay-per-click ads. The click fraud rate on search engines ranges from 13 to 18 percent, with an average of 14.7 percent.[50]

E-mail is the most common application on the Internet, and e-mail advertising capitalizes on that popularity. The Radicati Group estimates that Internet users have more than 3.1 billion e-mail accounts![51] **E-mail advertising**, whereby companies broadcast their advertising messages by e-mail, is growing rapidly because it is effective and inexpensive. E-mail advertising takes two forms: permission e-mail and spam. As its name suggests, **permission e-mail** involves sending e-mail ads to customers with their permission; **spam** is unsolicited commercial e-mail. The Radicati Group also estimates that despite modern antispam technology, 19 percent of all delivered e-mail messages are spam.[52] Because most e-mail users see spam as a nuisance, they often view companies that use it in a negative fashion. Smart entrepreneurs do *not* rely on spam in their marketing strategies. Permission e-mail, however, can be an effective and money-saving advertising tool. Permission e-mail messages often produce very high response rates. According to Epsilon, a marketing services company, the average open rate for e-mail ads is 22 percent, and the average click-through rate is 5.9 percent.[53]

Building an e-mail address list simply requires attention to the basics of marketing. The goal is to encourage potential buyers to share their e-mail addresses. The reward may be a white paper report, a one-time discount, a special offer, a special report, a sweepstakes entry, or a drawing for a prize. Once a small company obtains potential customers' e-mail addresses, the next step is to send messages that are useful and interesting to them. The message must be geared to their interests and should highlight the product's unique selling proposition. Many companies have success with e-mail ad campaigns that produce immediate results and are very inexpensive to conduct.

ENTREPRENEURIAL
Profile

Josh Molinari and Anthony Green and Fajita Grill

When Josh Molinari and Anthony Green launched Fajita Grill, a quick-serve restaurant that sells fresh Southwestern-style food at two locations in Oswego and Fulton, New York, they wanted to build a large base of loyal customers as fast as possible and could not afford to wait for word-of-mouth advertising to take effect. Marketing director Abby Weaver experimented with traditional advertising media but had only limited success, which prompted her to turn to e-mail ads. She worked with e-mail marketing company Constant Contact to build an e-mail list of nearly 3,300 customers and to create clever ad campaigns that tell customers about special events, remind them of the benefits of their "Frequent Eater" cards, and offer discount coupons. "I can e-mail a coupon at 10 A.M., and by 11:30 there are people in line, coupon in hand," says Weaver. In addition to the high (and measurable) response rate, Weaver enjoys the flexibility and speed of e-mail ad campaigns. "I don't need a designer," she says. "I don't have to wait for a printer or the Postal Service to get it delivered. I can hit 'send' at 10 A.M. and watch how many people open the e-mail and where they click on the Fajita Grill Web site." Because of the informational reports that Weaver receives after each ad goes out, Fajita Grill constantly fine-tunes its e-mail campaign and has an impressive e-mail ad open rate of 43.8 percent.[54]

LESSONS FROM THE STREET-SMART ➤ entrepreneur

E-Mail Ads That Produce Results

When John and Jennifer Nugent opened the Colorado Wine Company in Pasadena, California, their goal was to remove much of the mystique and highbrow attitude that some people associate with wine. "We wanted to create an environment where anyone, no matter what level of wine knowledge they had, could enter the store, receive personal service and recommendations, try a sip or two of the daily selections at the bar, and leave feeling more comfortable and educated about wine," says Jennifer. The store, which also features a wine bar, specializes in wines, sakes, Champagnes, and beers from around the world, most of which are priced at $25 or less. To drive business to their store, the Nugents created a whimsical e-mail newsletter that covers a multitude of topics in an engaging manner. In addition to describing wine specials and arrivals and offering profiles of the wineries that supply the company, the newsletter includes fun topics such as "wine paraphernalia that makes us uncomfortable and/or scared" and invitations to upcoming wine tastings such as the popular "White Trash" tasting that pairs various wines with cheap convenience food. One recent newsletter, titled "Beans Don't Burn on the Grill, the Nearness of You, and What Pairs Best with a Roman Candle?" invited customers to attend a 1980's theme music night at the shop.

The Nugents use the newsletter to reinforce the casual, fun image of the store, to foster a sense of community among its customers, and to build a connection with them. "We're a small shop, and people like to visit because it's like a living room," says John. "We want the newsletter to feel the same way." The number of newsletter subscribers has increased from just a few hundred to several thousand and continues to grow rapidly. "After a broadcast, we usually spend half the next day returning e-mail," says John.

Businesses spend $2 billion a year on e-mail marketing campaigns and experts expect that number to grow by an impressive 18.5 percent each year for the next 5 years. What makes e-mail marketing appealing, especially to entrepreneurs, is that it is inexpensive, measurable, and it works! According to a study by the Direct Marketing Association, every $1 that companies spend on e-mail marketing produces a return of $45.06. Entrepreneurs who want to reproduce the success that the Colorado Wine Company has created using an e-mail advertising campaign should consider the following tips from The Street-Smart Entrepreneur:

Make a concerted effort to collect customers' (and potential customers') e-mail addresses.

Every contact that anyone in your company has with a customer presents an opportunity to collect another e-mail address. Seize them! Ensure that everyone in the company understands the importance of building an accurate and reliable e-mail list.

Make sure the e-mail's subject line is short, meaningful, and to-the-point.

Without the right subject line, e-mail recipients may never open the e-mail. One rule of thumb suggests that the subject line should not exceed 40 characters, including spaces. The best subject lines suggest the product's or service's USP. For example, "Fresh lunch FAST—just $5.99!" in the subject line of an e-mail expresses several product features to potential customers. Other subject line words that result in responses include "new," "save," "you," "instant," and "free."

Make sure your e-mails' look and feel are consistent with your company's overall image.

Every component of a company's advertising campaign should have a look and feel that is consistent with its brand, even though the ads may appear in many diverse media. The design of a company's e-mail ads should rely on the same colors, themes, slogans, and look as its ads in other media.

Send e-mails when customers are most likely to make their purchases.

Proper timing of e-mail ads can improve customer response rates dramatically. Friday is the day of the week on which recipients are most likely to read e-mails. January, July, August, and December are the months in which customers are least likely to pay attention to e-mail ads (although there are exceptions). A study by marketing research firm Atlas reports that lunch time and the late evening were the times of day that resulted in the highest response rates to e-mail ads in general. Companies must time their e-mail ads to correspond to their customers' demand for their products and services.

Write copy that produces the results you seek.

Start by concentrating on one idea. Before writing any copy, develop a mental picture of your target customer. Give him or her a name and try to envision how your company's product or service can benefit him or her. This will help you keep your ad copy focused on the USP you put in the subject line of the e-mail. When appropriate, consider including an endorsement from an existing customer (perhaps with a photo) to add credibility to your claims. Be sure to provide clearly visible links to your company's Web site at several places in the e-mail ad, including at the top and the bottom of the page. Always include a prominent call to action: How do you want the customer to respond?

Incorporate social networking links and video into e-mails.

Adding "Become a fan on Facebook" or "Follow us on Twitter" links to e-mails encourages customers to engage your company in other media and to promote it to their friends. The E-mail Marketing Trends Survey reports that 53.8 percent of small business owners say that including video in e-mails increases their company's click-through and open rates. Buttons that allow customers to download videos, forward them to friends, or post them on their Facebook pages encourage the viral nature of the Web to expand their advertising efforts many times over.

Use value-added items to increase your campaign's response rate.

In the typical inbox, there are dozens (if not more) of messages competing for the person's attention. One way to boost your campaign's response rate is to offer recipients something of value—for example, a coupon, a newsletter, or a white paper. Betsy Harper, CEO of Sales and Marketing Search, an executive search firm that specializes in sales and marketing positions, says that publishing a monthly e-mail newsletter that includes hiring trends and tips has improved her company's visibility, reputation, and sales. Recently, says Harper, "within 2 minutes (literally!) of sending our e-mail newsletter, I got an e-mail from a fellow in New York. He asked me to call him right away about filling a senior sales position. We talked, signed an agreement to work together the very next day, and started the search. We finished the search in record time and received a $22,000 fee."

Always comply with the CAN-SPAM Act.

The CAN-SPAM Act, a law that sets the rules for commercial e-mail, establishes requirements for commercial messages, gives recipients the right to opt out of e-mails, and spells out tough penalties for violators.

Sources: Based on: "E-mail Success Stories: How 11 Companies Are Pushing the (Electronic) Envelope," *Marketing Profs,* 2009, pp. 3–4; Lisa Barone, "E-mail Marketing Success Is About Relevance," *Small Business Trends,* June 18, 2009, *http://smallbiztrends.com/2009/06/email-marketing-success.html;* Peter Prestipino and Mike Phillips, "E-mail Marketing's Future . . . Right Now," *Website,* November 2009, pp. 26–29; Michelle Keegan, "Real Life Small Business Newsletter Tips," Constant Contact, *www.constantcontact.com/learning-center/hints-tips/volume10-issue2.jsp;* Gail Goodman, "Writing Compelling Promotional Copy," Constant Contact, *www.constantcontact.com/learning-center/hints-tips/ht-2006-07.jsp;* David Kesmodel, "More Marketers Place Web Ads by Time of Day," *Wall Street Journal,* June 23, 2006, pp. B1, B3; Ivan Levison, "Five Common E-mail Mistakes and How to Avoid Them," *Levison Letter,* vol. 17, no. 2, April 2002, *www.levison.com/email-advertising.htm;* "You've Got the Power," *Marketing Profs,* vol. 1, no. 23, May 22, 2008; 2010 E-mail Marketing Trends Survey, GetResponse, 2010, *www.getresponse.com/documents/core/reports/2010_Email_Marketing_Trends_Survey.pdf,* p. 5.

MAGAZINES. Another advertising medium available to the small business owner is magazines. Today, customers have more than 20,600 magazine titles from which to choose. Magazines have a wide reach, and their readers tend to be more educated and have higher incomes than consumers of other advertising media, such as television.[55]

Magazines offer several advantages for advertisers:

- *Long life spans.* Magazines have a long reading life because readers tend to keep them longer than other printed media. Few people read an entire magazine at one sitting. Instead, most pick it up, read it at intervals, and come back to it later. The result is that each magazine ad has a good chance of being seen several times.
- *Multiple channels of engagement.* More than 15,200 magazines have associated Web sites, which gives them the ability to engage customers across two channels. Magazine Web site usage is growing faster than Web usage overall.[56]
- *Multiple readership.* The average magazine has a readership of 3.9 adults, and each reader spends about 1 hour and 33 minutes with each copy. Many magazines have a high "pass-along" rate; they are handed down front reader to reader. For instance, the in-flight magazines on jets reach many readers in their lifetimes.
- *Target marketing.* Within the past 20 years, magazines have become increasingly focused. Advertisers can select magazines aimed at customers with specific interests—from wooden boats and black-and-white photography to container gardening and body-building. By selecting the appropriate special-interest periodical, small business owners can reach those customers with a high degree of interest in their goods or services. Once business owners define their target markets, they can select magazines whose readers most closely match their customer profiles. For instance, *House and Garden* magazine reaches a very different audience than *Rolling Stone*.
- *Ad quality.* Magazine ads usually are of high quality. Photographs and drawings can be reproduced very effectively, and high-quality color ads are readily available. In fact, consumers rank magazine ads ahead of ads in all other media on creating a positive impression.[57] Advertisers can choose the location of their ads in a magazine and can design creative ads that capture readers' attention. The most effective locations for magazine ads are the back cover, the inside front cover, and the inside back cover. Multiple page spreads also increase ad recall among readers.[58]

Magazines also have several disadvantages:

- *Costs.* Magazine advertising rates vary according to their circulation rates; the higher the circulation, the higher the rate. Thus, local magazines, whose rates are often comparable to newspaper rates, may be the best bargain for small businesses.
- *Long closing times.* Another disadvantage of magazines is the relatively long closing times they require. For a weekly periodical, the closing date for an ad may be several weeks before the actual publication date, making it difficult for advertisers to respond quickly to changing market conditions.
- *Lack of prominence.* Another disadvantage of magazine ads arises from their popularity as an advertising vehicle. The effectiveness of a single ad may be reduced because of a lack of prominence; 46.2 percent of the typical magazine content is devoted to advertising.[59] Proper ad positioning, therefore, is critical to an ad's success. Research shows that readers "tune out" right-hand pages and look mainly at left-hand pages.
- *Declining circulation rates.* Circulation rates for most magazines have declined over the last decade. According to the Pew Research Center for the People and the Press, 23 percent of adults say they are regular magazine readers, down from 33 percent in 1994.[60]

SPECIALTY ADVERTISING. As advertisers have shifted their focus to "narrowcasting" their messages to target audiences and away from "broadcasting," specialty advertising has grown in popularity. This category includes all customer gift items such as pens, shirts, caps, and umbrellas that are imprinted with a company's name, address, telephone number, Web site, and slogan. Specialty items are best used as reminder ads to supplement other forms of advertising and help to create goodwill among existing and potential customers.

Specialty advertising offers several advantages:

- *Reaching select audiences.* Advertisers have the ability to reach specific audiences with well-planned specialty items.
- *Personalized nature.* By carefully choosing a specialty item, business owners can "personalize" their advertisements. When choosing advertising specialties, business owners should use items that are unusual, related to the nature of the business, and meaningful to customers. For instance, a small software company generated a great deal of recognition by giving existing and potential customers flash memory sticks imprinted with its company logo and Web address.
- *Versatility.* The rich versatility of specialty advertising is limited only by the business owner's imagination. Advertisers print their logos on everything from pens and golf balls to key chains and caps.

The following are the disadvantages of specialty advertising:

- *Potential for waste.* Unless entrepreneurs choose the appropriate specialty item for their businesses, they will be wasting time and money.
- *Cost.* Some specialty items can be quite expensive. In addition, some owners have a tendency to give advertising materials to anyone—even to those people who are not potential customers. Proper distribution of give-away items is an important aspect of enhancing the effectiveness of and controlling the cost of specialty advertising.

POINT-OF-PURCHASE ADS. In-store advertising has become popular as a way of reaching the customer at a crucial moment—the point of purchase. Research suggests that consumers make 74 percent of all buying decisions at the point of sale.[61] Self-service stores are especially well suited for in-store ads because they remind people of the products as they walk the aisles. These in-store ads are not just simple signs or glossy photographs of the product in use. Some businesses use in-store music interspersed with household hints and, of course, ads. Another technique involves shelves that contain tiny devices that sense when a customer passes by and triggers a prerecorded sales message. Some self-service stores use floor graphics, point-of-purchase ads that transform their floors into advertising space.

OUT-OF-HOME ADVERTISING. Out-of-home, or outdoor, advertising is one of the oldest forms of advertising in existence. Archeological evidence shows that merchants in ancient Egypt chiseled advertising messages on stone tablets and placed them along major thoroughfares. Out-of-home advertising remains popular today; advertisers spend nearly $6 billion on this medium annually.[62] The United States is a highly mobile society, and out-of-home advertising takes advantage of this mobility. Out-of-home advertising is popular among small companies, especially retailers, because well-placed ads serve as reminders to shoppers that the small business is nearby and ready to serve their needs. Very few small businesses rely solely on out-of-home advertising; instead, they supplement other advertising media with out-of-home ads such as billboards and transit ads. With a creative out-of-home ad campaign, a small company can make a big impact with only a small budget.

ENTREPRENEURIAL
Profile

Rob Bennett and Bennett Infinity

Rob Bennett, owner of Bennett Infinity in Lehigh Valley, Pennsylvania, saw his inventory of luxury cars building up and knew that he had to do something to attract customers and boost sales. Although Bennett never had used out-of-home advertising, he realized that the medium was ideal for reaching his target audience: upscale, well-educated professionals who enjoy driving. Research showed that although these buyers are affluent, they are value-conscious in their purchases. Bennett launched an outdoor ad campaign that emphasized the low monthly lease payments that were available on the most popular luxury models, concentrating the ads in upscale areas near his dealership. In the first 4 weeks, Bennett Infinity's sales jumped from an average of just two cars per week to seven cars per week! The initial campaign was such a hit that Bennett conducted a follow-up ad campaign that proved to be even more successful.[63]

Innovative out-of-home ads remind shoppers that a small business is nearby, ready to serve their needs.

Source: Outdoor Advertising Association of America, Inc.

Outdoor advertising offers certain advantages to a small business:

- ▧ *High exposure.* Out-of-home advertising offers a high-frequency exposure, especially among people who commute to work. The average one-way commute to work in the United States is just over 25 minutes.[64] Most people tend to follow the same routes in their daily travels, and billboards are there waiting for them when they pass by.

Source: www.CartoonStock.com

"Then, for some reason, sales dropped right off."

- ▧ *Broad reach.* The typical billboard reaches an adult 29 to 31 times each month. The nature of outdoor ads makes them effective devices for reaching a large number of potential customers within a specific area. Not only has the number of cars on the road increased, but the number of daily vehicle trips people take has also climbed. In addition, the people outdoor ads reach tend to be younger, wealthier, and better educated than the average person.

28

▓ *Attention-getting.* The introduction of new technology such as 3-D, fiber optics, digital and LCD displays, and other creative special effects to out-of-home advertising has transformed billboards from flat, passive signs to innovative, attention-grabbing promotions that passersby cannot help but notice.

▓ *Flexibility.* Advertisers can buy out-of-home advertising units separately or in a number of packages. Through its variety of graphics, design, and unique features, outdoor advertising enables a small advertiser to match his or her message to the particular audience.

▓ *Cost efficiency.* Out-of-home advertising offers one of the lowest costs per thousand customers reached of all advertising media. The CPM for out-of-home ads is $2.26, compared to $4.54 for radio, $5.50 for newspaper ads, $6.98 for magazine ads, and $5.99 to $10.25 for television commercials.[65]

Out-of-home ads also have several disadvantages:

▓ *Brief exposure.* Because billboards are immobile, the reader is exposed to the advertiser's message for only a short time—typically only 1 or 2 seconds. As a result, the message must be short and to the point.

▓ *Limited ad recall.* Because customers often are zooming past out-of-home ads at high speed, they are exposed to an advertising message very briefly, which limits their ability to retain the message.

▓ *Legal restrictions.* Outdoor billboards are subject to strict regulations and to a high degree of standardization. Many cities place limitations on the number and type of signs and billboards allowed along the roadside. More than a dozen cities have banned digital billboards in the name of traffic safety.[66]

▓ *Lack of prominence.* A clutter of billboards and signs along a heavily traveled route tends to reduce the effectiveness of a single ad that loses its prominence among the crowd of billboards.

Using Out-of-Home Ads. Consumers are spending more time in their cars than ever before (18.5 hours per week), and out-of-home advertising is an effective way to reach them.[67] Technology has changed the face of out-of-home advertising dramatically in recent years. Computerized printing techniques that render truer, crisper, and brighter colors; billboard extensions; and three-dimensional effects have improved significantly the quality of standard billboards (known as posters or bulletins in the industry). New vinyl surfaces accept print-quality images and are extremely durable. Digital billboards, giant computer screens that rotate messages every 6 to 10 seconds, allow companies to create vibrant, eye-catching ads that really capture viewers' attention at reasonable cost.

Because the outdoor ad is stationary and the viewer is in motion, a small business owner must pay special attention to its design. An outdoor ad should:

▓ Allow viewers to identify the product and the company clearly and quickly.

▓ Use a simple background. The background should not compete with the message.

▓ Rely on large illustrations that jump out at the viewer.

▓ Include clear, legible fonts. All lowercase or a combination of uppercase and lowercase letters works best. Very bold or very thin typefaces become illegible at a distance. Select simple fonts that are easy to read from a distance.

▓ Use black-and-white designs. Research shows that black-and-white outdoor ads are more effective than color ads. If color is important to the message, pick color combinations that contrast both hue and brightness—for example, black on yellow.

▓ Emphasize simplicity. Short copy and short words are best. Don't try to cram too much onto a billboard. Because of their brief window of exposure, ads with just 3 to 5 words are most effective, and ads containing more than 10 words are ineffective.

▓ Use illumination so that passersby can read them at night. By using illuminated billboards, advertisers can increase the reach of outdoor ads by 16 percent.[68]

▓ Be located on the right-hand side of the highway.

Two of the latest trends in outdoor advertising are Internet-connected digital boards and billboards that send messages to customers' cell phones. With digital billboards, ad content is virtually unlimited; advertisers can include eye-catching graphics and streaming media in their ads. (Giant digital billboards, called spectaculars, are common in New York's Times Square, where much of the traffic includes pedestrians, whose travel speeds are slower than cars.) Digital billboard ads, which cost between $1,200 and $10,000 per month, offer advertisers great flexibility. For instance, a restaurant could change the messages it displays to advertise its breakfast offerings in the morning, lunch specials at mid-day, and dinner menu in the afternoon and evening.

The latest outdoor ads include a computer chip that interacts with a cell phone's Web browser, which enables advertisers to send messages to passersby's cell phones. For instance, a movie theater's smart billboard could send messages stating starting times for feature films it is running to interested customers' cell phones.

TRANSIT ADVERTISING. A variation of out-of-home advertising is transit advertising, which includes advertising signs on the inside and outside of the public transportation vehicles such as trains, buses, and subways throughout the country's urban areas. The medium is likely to grow as more cities look to public transit systems to relieve traffic congestion.

Transit ads offer a number of advantages:

- *Wide coverage.* Transit advertising offers advertisers mass exposure to a variety of customers. The message literally goes to where the people are.
- *Repeat exposure.* Transit ads provide lengthy and repeated exposure to a message, particularly for inside cards, the ads that appear inside the vehicle.
- *Low cost.* Even small businesses with limited budgets can afford transit advertising.
- *Flexibility.* Transit ads come in a wide range of sizes, numbers, and duration. With transit ads, an owner can select an individual market or any combination of markets across the country.

Transit ads also have several disadvantages:

- *Generality.* Although entrepreneurs can choose the specific transit routes on which to advertise, they cannot target a particular segment of the market through transit advertising as effectively as they can with other media. The effectiveness of transit ads depends on the routes that public vehicles travel and on the people they reach, which, unfortunately, the advertiser cannot control. Overall, transit riders tend to be young, affluent, and culturally diverse.
- *Limited appeal.* Unlike many media, transit ads are not beamed into the potential customer's residence or business. The result is that customers cannot keep them for future reference.
- *Brief message.* Transit ads do not permit advertisers to present a detailed description or a demonstration of the product or service for sale. Although inside ads have a relatively long exposure (the average ride lasts 22.5 minutes), outside ads must be brief and to the point.

DIRECT MAIL. Direct mail has long been a popular method of direct marketing and includes tools such as letters, postcards, catalogs, discount coupons, brochures, and other items that are mailed to homes or businesses. The earliest known catalogs were printed by fifteenth-century printers. Although Internet sales have surpassed direct mail catalog sales, companies still sell virtually every kind of product imaginable through direct mail, from Christmas trees and lobsters to furniture and clothing (the most popular mail-order purchase). Nearly 20,000 U.S. companies send 20 billion direct mail catalogs to stay-at-home shoppers, who purchase $102 billion in goods each year.[69]

Direct mail offers some distinct advantages to entrepreneurs:

- *Flexibility.* An advantage of direct mail is that businesses can tailor the message to the target audience. Rather than send a blanket mail blast to 100,000 addresses, advertisers can target 5,000 high-potential customers with a mailing. An advertiser's presentation to customers can be as simple or as elaborate as necessary. One custom tailor shop achieved a great deal of success with fliers it mailed to customers on its mailing list when it included a swatch of material from the fabric for the upcoming season's suits. With direct mail, the tone of the message can be personal, creating a positive psychological effect. In addition, advertisers control the timing of their campaigns, sending ads when they are most appropriate.
- *Reader attention.* With direct mail, an advertiser's message does not have to compete with other ads for the reader's attention. Most people enjoy getting mail, and the U.S.

30

Postal Service estimates that 85 percent of households open and read daily some or all of the direct mail that they receive.[70] Unlike many e-mail messages, direct mail gets a recipient's undivided attention at least for a moment. If the message is on the mark and sent to the right audience, direct mail ads can be a powerful advertising tool.

- *Rapid feedback.* Direct mail advertisements produce quick results. In most cases, an ad will generate sales within 3 or 4 days after customers receive it. Business owners should know whether a mailing has produced results within a relatively short time period.
- *Measurable results and testable strategies.* Because they control their mailing lists, direct marketers can readily measure the results their ads produce. In addition, direct mail allows advertisers to test different ad layouts, designs, and strategies (often within the same "run") to see which one "pulls" the greatest response. The best direct marketers are always fine-tuning their ads to make them more effective. Table 5 offers guidelines for creating direct mail ads that really work.
- *Effectiveness.* The right message targeted at the right mailing list can make direct mail one of the most efficient forms of advertising. Direct mail to the right people produces results.

Direct-mail ads also suffer from several disadvantages:

- *Inaccurate mailing lists.* The key to the success of the entire mailing is the accuracy of the customer list. Using direct mail ads with a poor mailing list is a guaranteed waste of money. Experienced direct mail marketers cite the 60-30-10 rule, which says that 60 percent of a campaign's success depends on the quality of the list, 30 percent on the offer, and 10 percent on the creativity of the ad.[71] Make sure the mailing list you use is accurate and up-to-date.
- *Clutter.* The average household in the United States receives about 900 pieces of direct mail each year.[72] With that volume of direct mail, it can be difficult for an advertisement to get customers' attention.
- *High relative costs.* Relative to the size of the audience reached, the cost of designing, producing, and mailing an advertisement via direct mail is high. Rising paper and postage costs pose real threats to companies that use direct mail. However, if a mailing is well planned and properly executed, it can produce a high percentage of returns, making direct mail one of the least expensive advertising methods in terms of results.
- *High throwaway rate.* Often called junk mail, direct-mail ads become "junk" when an advertiser selects the wrong audience or broadcasts the wrong message. According to the Direct Mail Association, the average response rate for a direct mail campaign is 3.7 percent.[73] By supplementing traditional direct-mail pieces with toll-free (800) numbers, links to Web sites, and carefully timed follow-up phone calls, companies have been able to increase their response rates.

How to Use Direct Mail. The key to a direct mailing's success is the right mailing list. Even the best direct-mail ad will fail if sent to the "wrong" customers. Owners can develop lists themselves, using customer accounts, telephone books, city and trade directories, and other sources, including companies that sell complementary but not competing products, professional organizations' membership lists, business or professional magazines' subscription lists, and mailing list brokers who sell lists for practically any need. Advertisers can locate list brokers through *The Direct Marketing List Source* from the Standard Rate and Data Service found in most public libraries. In a world in which the average U.S. adult receives 41 pounds of direct mail each year, the key to success with a direct mail campaign is to get your ad noticed, and the right mailing list is the ideal starting point.

ENTREPRENEURIAL
Profile

Michael Greco and Dartmouth Pharmaceuticals

Dartmouth Pharmaceuticals, launched in 1991 as a maker of cold and allergy medications, developed a line of all-natural skin and nail care products called Elon Essentials, but annual sales were a measly $5,000. To pump up sales, CEO Michael Greco decided to send direct mail ads to dermatologists. To increase the probability that the busy doctors would look at the ads, Greco sent them by priority mail. The direct mail campaign helped Dartmouth increase sales of its Elon Essentials line to more than $1.5 million in just a few years, and the company is now gearing up to add a national sales force to sell its products.[74]

TABLE 5 **Guidelines for Creating Direct Mail Ads That Really Work**

In many industries, a successful direct mail campaign is one that produces a response rate of at least 2.5 percent, which means that *97.5 percent* of the customers who received the ad did *not* respond to it! What steps can entrepreneurs take to improve the results of their direct mail campaigns?

Realize that repetition is one key to success.

Experts estimate that customers must receive at least three direct mail pieces per month from a business before they really notice the ad.

Provide meaningful incentives.

Direct mail succeeds by getting prospects to respond to a written offer. To do that, a direct mail ad must offer potential customers something of value—a free sample, a special price, a bonus gift, or anything that a company's target customers value. Twenty percent of prospects who do not open the direct mail ads they receive say that they have no reason to open them. Make sure your offer gives them a reason!

Write copy that will get results.

Try the following proven techniques:

- Promise readers your most important benefit in the headline or first paragraph.
- Use short "action" words and paragraphs and get to the point quickly.
- Make the copy look easy to read with lots of "white space."
- Use eye-catching words such as *free, you, save, guarantee, new, profit, benefit, improve,* and others.
- Consider using computerized "handwriting" somewhere on the page or envelope; it attracts attention.
- Forget grammatical rules; write as if you were speaking to the reader.
- Repeat the offer three or more times in various ways.
- Back up claims and statements with proof and endorsements whenever possible.
- Ask for the order or a response.
- Ask attention-getting questions such as "Would you like to lower your home's energy costs?" in the copy.
- Use high-quality copy paper and envelopes (those with windows are best) because they stand a better chance of being opened and read. Brown envelopes that resemble government correspondence work well.
- Envelopes that resemble bills almost always get opened.
- Address the envelope to an individual, not "Occupant."
- Avoid mailing labels, which shout "direct mail ad piece." The best campaigns print addresses directly on the envelopes.
- Use stamps if possible. They get more letters opened than metered postage.
- Use a postscript (P.S.)—always; they are the most often read part of a printed page. Make sure the P.S. contains a "hook" that will encourage the recipient to read on. This is the perfect place to restate the offer's unique selling proposition.
- Include a separate order form that passes the following "easy" test:
    - *Easy to find.* Consider using brightly colored paper or a unique shape.
    - *Easy to understand.* Make sure the offer is easy for readers to understand. Marketing expert Paul Goldberg says, "Confuse 'em and you lose 'em."
    - *Easy to complete.* Keep the order form simple and unconfusing.
    - *Easy to pay.* Direct mail ads should give customers the option to pay by whatever means is most convenient.
    - *Easy to return.* Including a postage-paid return envelope (or at a minimum a return envelope) will increase the response rate.
- **Build and maintain a quality mailing list over time.** The right mailing list is the key to a successful direct mail campaign. You may have to rent lists to get started, but once you are in business use every opportunity to capture information about your customers. Constantly focus on improving the quality of your mailing list.

Test your campaigns and track their results.

"Testing is everything," says the founder of a company that used direct mail ads as part of a marketing strategy that led his company to $10 million in annual sales. Monitoring the response rate from each mailing is essential for knowing which ads and which lists actually produce results.

Sources: Adapted from *What's in the Mailbox? The Impact of One-to-One Marketing on Consumer Response,* Winterberry Group, January 2007, p. 7; "Direct Mail Tips for Manufacturers' Letters," Koch Group, *www.kochgroup.com/directmail.html;* Kim T. Gordon, "Copy Right," *Business Start-Ups,* June 1998, pp. 18–19; Paul Hughes, "Profits Due," *Entrepreneur,* February 1994, pp. 74–78; "Why They Open Direct Mail, " *Communications Briefings,* December 1993, p. 5; Ted Lammers, "The Elements of Perfect Pitch," *Inc.,* March 1992, pp. 53–55: "Special Delivery," *Small Business Reports,* February 1993, p. 6; Gloria Green and James W. Peltier, "How to Develop a Direct Mail Program," *Small Business Forum,* Winter 1993/1994, pp. 30–45; Susan Headden, "The Junk Mail Deluge," *U.S. News & World Report,* December 8, 1997, pp. 40–48; Joanna L. Krotz, "Direct-Mail Tips for Sophisticated Marketers," Microsoft Small Business Center, *www.microsoft.com/smallbusiness/resources/marketing/customer_service_acquisition/ direct_mail_tips_for_sophisticated_marketers.mspx.*

DIRECTORIES. Directories may seem old-fashioned compared to newer high-tech tools, but both are valuable ways for businesses to reach commercial or industrial customers. Directories are an important medium for reaching those customers who have already made purchase decisions. The directory simply helps these customers locate the specific product or service they have decided to buy. Directories include telephone books, industrial guides, buyer guides, annuals, catalog files, and yearbooks that list various businesses and the products they sell.

Directories offer several advantages to advertisers:

- *Prime prospects.* Directory listings reach customers who are prime prospects because they have already decided to purchase an item. The directory just helps them find what they are looking for.
- *Long life.* Directory listings usually have long lives. A typical directory may be published annually.

However, there are certain disadvantages to using directories:

- *Lack of flexibility.* Listings and ads in many directories offer only a limited variety of design features. Business owners may not be as free to create unique ads as in other printed media.
- *Ad clutter.* In many directories, ads from many companies are clustered together so closely that no single ad stands out from the rest.
- *Obsolescence.* Because directories are commonly updated only annually, some of their listings become obsolete. This is a problem for a small firm that changes its name, location, or phone number.

When choosing a directory, the small business owner should evaluate several criteria:

- *Completeness.* Does the directory include enough listings that customers will use it?
- *Convenience.* Are the listings well organized and convenient? Are they cross-referenced?
- *Evidence of use.* To what extent do customers actually use the directory? What evidence of use does the publisher offer?
- *Age.* Is the directory well established and does it have a good reputation?
- *Circulation.* Do users pay for the directory or do they receive complimentary copies? Is there an audited circulation statement?

TRADE SHOWS. Trade shows provide manufacturers and distributors with a unique opportunity to advertise to a preselected audience of potential customers who are inclined to buy. Thousands of trade shows take place each year, and carefully evaluating and selecting the right shows can produce profitable results for a business owner. Trade show success does *not* depend on how much an exhibitor spends; instead, success is a function of planning, preparation, and follow-up.

Trade shows offer the following advantages:

- *A natural market.* Trade shows bring together buyers and sellers in a setting in which exhibitors can explain and demonstrate their products. Comparative shopping is easy, and the buying process is efficient for customers.
- *Pre-selected audience.* Trade exhibits attract potential customers with a genuine interest in the goods or services on display. There is a high probability that trade show attendees will make a purchase. A study by Exhibit Surveys reports that 53 percent of trade show attendees plan to purchase at least one of the products on display within 1 year.[75]
- *New customer market.* Trade shows offer exhibitors a prime opportunity to reach new customers and to contact people who are not accessible to sales representatives.
- *Cost advantage.* As the cost of making a field sales call continues to escalate, companies are realizing that trade shows are an economical method of generating leads and making sales presentations.

However, trade shows do have certain disadvantages:

- *Increasing costs.* The cost of exhibiting at trade shows is rising. Registration fees, travel and setup costs, sales salaries, and other expenditures may be a barrier to some small firms.
- *Wasted effort.* A poorly planned exhibit ultimately costs the small business more than its benefits are worth. Too many firms enter exhibits in trade shows without proper preparation, and they end up wasting their time, energy, and money on unproductive activities.

To avoid these disadvantages, entrepreneurs should:

- Research trade shows to find the ones that will put you in front of the best prospects for your product or service.
- Establish objectives for every trade show. Do you want to generate 100 new sales leads, make new product presentations to 500 potential customers, or make $5,000 in sales?
- Communicate with key potential customers *before* the show; send them invitations or invite them to stop by your booth for a special gift.
- Plan your display with your target audience in mind and make it memorable. Be sure your exhibit shows your company and its products or services in the best light. Do everything to maximize the visibility of your exhibit and keep the display neat.
- Staff your booth with knowledgeable salespeople. Attendees appreciate meeting face-to-face with knowledgeable and friendly staff.
- Do something to attract a crowd to your booth. Demonstrate your product or service so that customers can see it in action, sponsor a drawing for a prize, or set up an interactive display. Drawing a crowd creates "buzz" for your company among attendees.
- Learn to distinguish between serious customers and "tire-kickers."
- Make it easy for potential customers to get information about your company and its products and services. Distribute literature that clearly communicates the benefits of your products or services.
- Project a professional image at all times. Salespeople who man the booth should engage prospects in conversation and should ask qualifying questions.
- Follow up promptly on sales leads. The most common mistake trade show participants make is failing to follow up on the sales leads the show generated. If you are not going to follow up leads, why bother to attend the show in the first place?

Few small businesses rely on a single advertising medium to communicate their advertising messages to potential customers, choosing instead to employ **cross-channel advertising strategies** whereby they communicate with potential customers using a variety of media. For instance, Gary Lindsey, head of marketing at The Parent Company, a consumer product business that targets young parents, says that although the company is primarily Web-based, it relies heavily on direct mail catalogs and e-mail marketing to drive sales. "There's real return on investment from those catalogs," says Lindsey. "People love shopping on the Internet, but there is something powerful when you combine print and Internet."[76]

▶ ENTREPRENEURSHIP IN ACTION ▶

A "Gorilla" Marketing Strategy

Located halfway between Los Angeles and Las Vegas on a desolate stretch of highway just off of Interstate 15 near the famous Route 66, passersby might mistake Peggy Sue's 50's Diner as just another kitschy restaurant aimed at tourists. But there's far more to this small business than meets the eye. The diner was originally built in 1954 with just three booths and nine counter stools, but in 1987 Champ and Peggy Sue Gabler took over and began revitalizing the diner and its advertising strategy. They expanded the original diner to a 60-seat restaurant. Thanks to family recipes from Peggy Sue's grandmother and great 1950s music, the diner became a popular destination for local residents, truck drivers, passing tourists, and soldiers from a nearby military post.

By the early 1990s, Peggy Sue's was generating $280,000 in annual sales, a respectable figure given that the economy was experiencing a recession. The Gablers decided that the diner could do much better, however, and invested $600,000 from their own savings and an SBA-guaranteed loan to quadruple the diner's capacity and add a juke-boxed theme façade, a 3,000-square-foot 50's-style five-and-dime store, soda and ice cream fountains, a pizza parlor, and a large collection of 1950s memorabilia. Upon entering the diner, visitors can learn about their futures from a Magic Elvis Fortune Telling Machine, where "The King tells all." Waitresses dress in real waitress uniforms and are prone to call their guests "Hon." The menu, which includes breakfast, lunch, and dinner, features items such as the Buddy Holly bacon cheeseburger, a Mickey Mouse

The juke-boxed themed facade of Peggy Sue's 50's Diner invites customers to step back to a simpler time.

Source: ©America/Alamy

club sandwich, the Fabian French dip, and the Fats Domino meat loaf special.

The Gablers ramped up their advertising, renting space on billboards along nearby highways and launching a radio advertising campaign. Within 2 years, sales had increased to nearly $1 million. Sales have continued to grow steadily, reaching $3 million a year. Recently, however, sales have remained flat, and the Gablers decided once again that it was time to shake things up. Champ rented a large billboard just outside of Las Vegas that cost $1,600 more per month than any of Peggy Sue's other billboard locations. "Big casinos pay top dollar to advertise in that area," he says. "And here is our [billboard], saying nothing more than our name and 'Hungry? 90 miles.'" The Gablers also added a "dinersaur" park next to the restaurant, complete with larger-than-life dinosaur sculptures made of sheet metal that cost $40,000 to build and install. A 12-foot-tall sheet metal statue of King Kong also is part of the diner's "gorilla" marketing strategy. "Forty thousand cars a day

pass the back of our property [on Interstate 15]," says Champ. "We're not sure how long it will take to get a return on our new monsters, but they have created another marketing strategy in trying times."

1. Visit the Web site of Peggy Sue's 50's Diner *(www.peggysuesdiner.com)* and use a search engine to locate visitors' photos of the diner and its "dinersaur" park. Evaluate the advertising plan that the Gablers have developed for the diner.

2. Are there other advertising media and techniques described in this chapter that you would suggest the Gablers consider using to boost Peggy Sue's 50's Diner's sales and profits? Explain.

Sources: Based on Maggie Overfelt, "Gorilla Marketing," *FSB*, June 2008, pp. 49–50; "About Us, Peggy Sue's 50's Diner" *www.peggysuesdiner.com;* Spencer Cross, "Because You Know You've Always Wondered . . . Yermo's 'Peggy Sue's 50's Diner' Isn't Half Bad," *Los Angeles Met Blogs*, November 25, 2008, *http://la.metblogs.com/2008/11/25/because-you-know-youve-always-wonderedyermos-peggy-sues-50s-diner-isnt-half-bad/.*

How to Prepare an Advertising Budget

4. Identify four basic methods for preparing an advertising budget.

One of the most challenging decisions confronting a small business owner is how much to spend on advertising. The amount entrepreneurs want to spend and the amount they can afford to spend usually differ significantly. Entrepreneurs can use the following four methods to create an advertising budget: *what-is-affordable, matching competitors, percentage of sales,* and *objective and task.*

With the what-is-affordable method, business owners see advertising as a luxury. They view it completely as an expense rather than as an investment that generates sales and profits in the future. As the name implies, entrepreneurs who use this method spend whatever their companies can afford on advertising. Too often, business owners determine their advertising budgets after they have funded all of the other budget items. The result is an advertising budget that is inadequate for getting the job done. This method also fails to relate the marketing communications budget to the marketing communications objective.

Another approach is to match the advertising budget of the company's competitors, either in a flat dollar amount or as a percentage of sales. This method assumes that a company's advertising needs and strategies are the same as those of its competitors, which is rarely the case. Although competitors' actions can be helpful when establishing a floor for marketing communications expenditures, relying on this technique can lead to blind imitation instead of a budget suited to a small company's circumstances.

The most commonly used method of establishing an advertising budget is the simple percentage-of-sales approach. This method relates advertising expenditures to actual sales results. Tying advertising expenditure to sales rather than to profits creates greater consistency in advertising because most companies' sales tend to fluctuate less than profits. One rule of thumb for establishing an advertising budget is spending 10 percent of projected sales the first year of business, 7 percent the second year, and at least 5 percent in each successive year. Relying totally on broad rules like these can be dangerous, however. They may not be representative of a small company's advertising needs.

The objective-and-task method is the most difficult and least used technique for establishing an advertising budget. It also is the method most often recommended by advertising experts. With this method, an entrepreneur links advertising expenditures to specific business objectives. The objective-and-task method builds up an advertising budget from the bottom up by analyzing what it will cost to accomplish an entrepreneur's business objectives. For example, suppose that an entrepreneur wants to boost sales of a particular product 10 percent by attracting local college students. He may determine that a nearby rock radio station would be the best advertising medium to use. Then he must decide on the number and frequency of the ads and estimate their costs. Entrepreneurs follow this process for each advertising objective.

Once they establish their advertising objectives and budgets, many entrepreneurs find it useful to use a calendar to plan the timing of their advertising campaigns and expenditures across the year. Figure 6 illustrates three common advertising scheduling strategies.

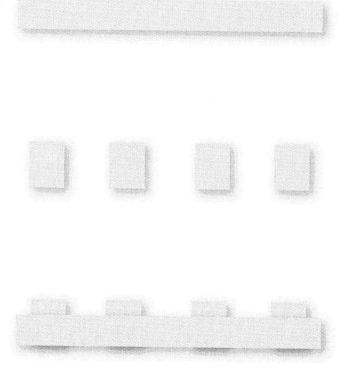

FIGURE 6
Advertising Scheduling Strategies

Continuous—Small business spends its advertising budget consistently across time. Ideal for companies whose products or services are in demand year-round—e.g., grocery stores and drug stores.

Flighting—Small business concentrates its ad expenditures in carefully timed batches. Ideal for companies that experience peaks and valleys in the demand for their products or services—e.g., vacation rental companies.

Pulsing—Small business makes some expenditures consistently across the year but concentrates the rest of its ad expenditures in carefully timed pulses. Ideal for companies that must keep their names in front of customers year-round but experience peaks and valleys in the demand for their products or services—e.g., landscape services.

How to Advertise Big on a Small Budget

5. Describe practical methods of stretching a small business owner's advertising budget.

The typical small business does not have the luxury of an unlimited advertising budget. Most cannot afford to hire a professional ad agency. This does not mean, however, that a small company should assume a second-class advertising posture. Most advertising experts say that, unless a small company spends more than $10,000 to $15,000 a year on advertising, it probably doesn't need an ad agency. For most, hiring freelance copywriters and artists on a per-project basis is a much better bargain. With a little creativity and a dose of ingenuity, small business owners can stretch their advertising dollars and make the most of what they spend. Four useful techniques are cooperative advertising, shared advertising, stealth advertising, and publicity.

COOPERATIVE ADVERTISING. With **cooperative advertising**, a manufacturing company shares the cost of advertising with a retailer if the retailer features its products in those ads. Both the manufacturer and the retailer get more advertising per dollar by sharing expenses. Cooperative advertising not only helps small businesses stretch their advertising budgets, but it also offers another source of savings: the free advertising packages that many manufacturers supply to retailers. These packages usually include photographs and illustrations of the product as well as professionally prepared ads to use in different media.

SHARED ADVERTISING. With **shared advertising**, a group of similar businesses forms a syndicate to produce generic ads that allow the individual businesses to dub in local information. The technique is especially useful for small businesses that sell relatively standardized products or services such as legal assistance, autos, and furniture. Because the small firms in the syndicate pool their funds, the result usually is higher-quality ads and significantly lower production costs.

STEALTH ADVERTISING. Guerrilla marketing principles are offbeat, low-cost techniques for marketing a small company's goods and services. In advertising, these techniques are called **stealth advertising**, which includes innovative ads that do not necessarily look like traditional ads and often are located in unexpected places. Ads now appear on electrical outlets in airport terminals, on eggs (gently printed directly onto the shells with lasers), clothes hangers from laundries, in urinals in public restrooms (using a device called Wizmark that plays sounds and pictures when a guest arrives), and other unusual places.[77] One consumer products company achieved success with a campaign that involved painting manhole covers in New York City to look like steaming hot cups of coffee. Bamboo Lingerie attracted a great deal of attention for its brand by stenciling on New York City sidewalks the message "From here it looks like you could use some new underwear" and its name and logo.[78]

OTHER WAYS TO SAVE. Other cost-saving suggestions for advertising expenditures include the following:

- *Repeat ads that have been successful.* In addition to reducing the cost of ad preparation, repetition may create a consistent image in a small firm's advertising program.
- *Use identical ads in different media.* If a billboard has been an effective advertising tool, an owner should consider converting it to a newspaper or magazine ad or a direct mail flier.
- *Hire independent copywriters, graphic designers, photographers, and other media specialists.* Many small businesses that cannot afford a full-time advertising staff buy their advertising services à la carte. They work directly with independent specialists and usually receive high-quality work that compares favorably with that of advertising agencies without paying a fee for overhead.
- *Concentrate advertising during times when customers are most likely to buy.* Some small business owners make the mistake of spreading an already small advertising budget evenly—and thinly—over a 12-month period. A better strategy is to match advertising expenditures to customers' buying habits.

Chapter Review

1. Define your company's unique selling proposition (USP).
   - Branding a company's products or services depends on communicating the correct *unique selling proposition* (USP), a key customer benefit or a product or service that sets a business apart from its competition.
   - The USP answers the customer's ultimate question: "What's in it for me?"
2. Explain the differences among promotion, publicity, personal selling, and advertising.
   - Promotion is any form of persuasive communication designed to inform consumers about a product or service and to influence them to purchase these goods or services. It includes publicity, personal selling, and advertising.
   - Publicity is any commercial news covered by the media that boosts sales but for which the business does not pay.
   - Personal selling is the personal contact between salespeople and potential customers that comes from sales efforts.
   - Advertising is any sales presentation that is nonpersonal in nature and is paid for by an identified sponsor. A company's target audience and the nature of its message determine the advertising media it will use.
3. Describe the advantages and disadvantages of various advertising media.
   - The medium used to transmit an advertising message influences the customer's perception—and reception—of it.
   - Media options include word-of-mouth, sponsorships and special events, television, radio, newspapers, the Internet, magazines, specialty advertising, point-of-purchase ads, out-of-home advertising, transit advertising, direct mail, directories, and trade shows.
4. Identify four basic methods for preparing an advertising budget.
   - Establishing an advertising budget presents a real challenge to the small business owner.
   - The four basic methods of preparing an advertising budget are what is affordable, matching competitors, percentage of sales, and objective and task.
5. Describe practical methods for stretching a business owner's advertising budget.
   - Despite their limited advertising budgets, small businesses do not have to take a second-class approach to advertising. Three techniques that can stretch a small company's advertising dollars are cooperative advertising, shared advertising, and stealth advertising.

Discussion Questions

1. What are the three elements of promotion? How do they support one another?
2. What factors should a small business manager consider when selecting advertising media?
3. What is a unique selling proposition? What role should it play in a company's advertising strategy?
4. One company sent an e-mail that stated the following USP: "Combining the strategy, business processes, implementation, and technical support skills of a CRM systems integrator with the data management, analytic, and marketing skills of a database marketing service provider to deliver and operate a close-looped marketing and sales environment." How do you rate the effectiveness of this USP? Explain. What are the characteristics of an effective USP?
5. Review the advantages and disadvantages of the following advertising media:
   a. Word of mouth
   b. Sponsorships and special events
   c. Television
   d. Radio
   e. Newspapers
   f. Internet advertising
   g. Magazines
   h. Specialty advertising
   i. Direct mail
   j. Out-of-home advertising
   k. Transit advertising
   l. Directories
   m. Trade shows

6. Assume you are a small business owner who has an advertising budget of $1,500 to invest in a campaign promoting a big July 4th "blowout" sale. Where would you be most likely to invest your advertising budget if you were trying to reach customers in the 25–45 age range with higher than average disposable income who are likely to be involved in boating activities in a local resort town? Explain. How would you generate free publicity to extend your advertising budget?

7. What are fixed spots, preemptible spots, and floating spots in radio advertising?

8. Describe the characteristics of an effective out-of-home advertisement.

9. Briefly outline the steps in creating an advertising plan. What principles should the small business owner follow when creating an effective advertisement?

10. Describe the common methods of establishing an advertising budget. Which method is most often used? Which technique is most often recommended? Why?

11. What techniques can small business owners use to stretch their advertising budgets?

12. Use a search engine to locate the most recent "E-mail Marketing Trends Survey." Using the information in it, work with a team of your classmates to select a local small business with which you are familiar to design an effective e-mail advertising campaign. What are the advantages and the disadvantages of using e-mail as an advertising medium?

Business Plan Pro

A coordinated and consistent advertising and promotion effort is essential to an entrepreneur's success. Companies that fail to maintain a high profile among their target customers are soon forgotten. As an entrepreneur, your job is to leverage the advertising and promotion ideas from the chapter. Review the concepts and company examples in the chapter to determine whether they provide insight and ideas that may work to promote your business. How do you anticipate promoting your business? Which advertising media do you plan to use? Why?

On the Web

If you anticipate using the Web to promote your business, you will want to invest time to determine how best to do that. Search for similar businesses on the Internet. Identify three favorite sites. Note the appearance, layout, and navigation tools on these sites. What do you find attractive? What do you find distracting? Use this to develop ideas about how your site should look and what it should accomplish for your business.

In the Software

Determine how much you plan to invest in your advertising and promotional activities. Will you use newspapers, radio, television, sponsorships, or other media? What role will publicity play in promoting your business? Include estimates of the cost of your advertising and promotional activities in your business plan. Once again, reviewing sample plans may help to get ideas of where you want to invest your advertising budget. You also will need to do some additional research to help determine how much your advertising and promotional efforts are going to cost. Once you have come up with some preliminary figures, go to the marketing section and develop your unique selling proposition. Review other information to test for consistency throughout the plan.

Building Your Business Plan

Continue to build your business plan with the new information you have acquired. Step back to assess whether you have a solid understanding of your market and whether your business plan effectively communicates that understanding.

Endnotes

1. Larry Dignan, "5 Looming Questions About the Amazon-Zappos Deal," ZDNet, July 23, 2009, *www.zdnet.com/blog/btl/5-looming-questions-about-the-amazon-zappos-deal/21591.*
2. Lin Grensing-Pophal, "Who Are You?" *Business Start-Ups*, September 1997, pp. 38–44.
3. Meg Whittemore, "PR on a Shoestring," *Nation's Business*, January 1991, p. 31.
4. Sara Wilson, "Learning from the Best: Coffee 101," *Entrepreneur*, March 2006, p. 64.
5. Debra Phillips, "Fast Track," *Entrepreneur*, April 1999, p. 42.
6. Elaine Appleton Grant, "A Token Strategy," *Inc.*, May 2006, *www.inc.com/magazine/20060501/priority-promos.html.*
7. Joanna L. Krotz, "'Cause Marketing' Tips: Boost Business by Giving Back," Microsoft Small Business Center, *www.microsoft.com/smallbusiness/resources/marketing/advertising_branding/cause_marketing_tips_boost_business_by_giving_back.mspx.*
8. Peggy Linial, "Small Business and Cause Related Marketing: Getting Started," Cause Marketing Forum, *www.causemarketingforum.com/framemain.asp?ID=189.*
9. Catharine Livingston and Gordy Megrose, "Adventure Altruism: Giving Large," *Outside Online*, January 2006, *http://outside.away.com/outside/altruism.html.*
10. Barry Farber, "Sales Shape-Up," *Entrepreneur*, August 2006, p. 72.
11. Barbara K. Mednick, "Behavior Counts in Sales," *Minneapolis St. Paul Star Tribune*, May 28, 2004, *www.startribune.com/working.*
12. "Most Salespeople Can't Sell," *Small Business Reports*, September 1990, p. 10.
13. Eric Anderson and Bob Trinkle, *Outsourcing the Sales Function: The Real Cost of Field Sales* (Mason, OH: Thomson Publishing, 2005), p. 8.
14. "Salespeople Don't Prep Enough for Calls," *Sales & Marketing Management's Performance Newsletter*, December 12, 2005, p. 2.

15. Norm Brodsky, "Keep Your Customers," *Inc.*, September 2006, pp. 57–58.
16. Steve Marshall, "Local Commerce Monitor Wave XIII," BIA/Kelsey, August 2009, *www.kelseygroup.com/research/local-commerce-monitor.asp*.
17. "Survey Reveals Media Channel Lines Continue to Blur," Media Myth and Realities, Ketchum, January 12, 2009, *www.ketchum.com/media_myths_and_realities_2008_survey_news_release*.
18. Sara Wilson, "All Systems Yo," *Entrepreneur*, February 2007, p. 38; "About Us," Pinkberry, *www.pinkberry.com*.
19. Dave Kissel, "Shaping the 90 Percent," *Media Myths and Realities*, Ketchum Perspectives, 2009, *http://ketchumperspectives.com/archives/2009_i1/90percent.php*.
20. "Online Video Viewership Rises 1.3%," Marketing Charts, April 10, 2010, *www.marketingcharts.com/direct/online-video-viewership-rises-13-12779/nielsen-online-brands-unique-viewers-mar-10-apr-2010jpg/*.
21. Maria Ricapito, "Lauren Luke's Next Project," *Vanity Fair*, March 3, 2010, *www.vanityfair.com/online/beauty/2010/03/lauren-lukes-next-project.html;* Deborah Song, "Putting Her Best Face Forward," *Entrepreneur*, August 28, 2009, *www.entrepreneur.com/startingabusiness/successstories/article203188.html*.
22. Ryan McCarthy, "Blessed Events: How to Make a Sponsorship Pay Off," *Inc.*, April 2008, pp. 48–50.
23. Solano Avenue Events and News, *www.solanoavenueassn.org/scut_past/scut04_7.html*.
24. Kim T. Gordon, "Tips for Event Sponsorship," *Entrepreneur*, March 2006, *www.entrepreneur.com/magazine/entrepreneur/2006/march/83672.html*.
25. Adam Bluestein, "Prime-Time Exposure," *Inc.*, March 2008, pp. 66–68.
26. "And Now a Word from Our Sponsor . . ." Media Awareness Network, *www.media-awareness.ca/english/resources/educational/teachable_moments/word_from_our_sponsor.cfm*.
27. "TV Basics," Television Bureau of Advertising, 2010, *www.tvb.org/rcentral/mediatrendstrack/tvbasics/12_ADS-Natl.asp;* Emily Fredrix, "Super Bowl Ad Prices Dip, But Still Pricey," *CBS News*, January 11, 2010, *www.cbsnews.com/stories/2010/01/11/sportsline/main6082591.shtml*.
28. "Sweet Smell of Success," Google AdWords, *www.google.com/adwords/tvads/success/fragrancenet.html*.
29. "Adults Reached Yesterday by Major Media," Television Bureau of Advertising, *www.tvb.org/nav/build_frameset.aspx*.
30. "Consumers Allocate High Percentage of Total Daily Media Hours to Television," Television Bureau of Advertising, *www.tvb.org/nav/build_frameset.aspx*.
31. "TV Viewers Watch Commercials," *Marketing Charts*, May 14, 2010, *www.marketingcharts.com/television/tv-viewers-watch-commericals-12877/*.
32. "Television and Health," *The Sourcebook for Teaching Science*, *www.csun.edu/science/health/docs/tv&health.html*.
33. Andrew Hayes, "Increased DVR Usage Is Good News for Marketing Research Companies," Bernett Research, May 4, 2010, *www.bernett.com/Bernett-Marketing-Research-Blog/?Tag=DVR%20Usage*.
34. Darren Murph, "DVR Owners Do Indeed Skip Ads, Study Affirms," *Switched*, August 7, 2008, *www.switched.com/2008/08/07/dvr-owners-do-indeed-skip-ads-study-affirms/*.
35. "TV Universe Expands, Share of Channels Tuned Does Not," *Media Daily News*, July 21, 2009, *www.mediapost.com/publications/?fa=Articles.showArticle&art_aid=110159*.
36. Shelly Banjo, "As Seen (Often) on TV," *Wall Street Journal*, May 11, 2009, *http://online.wsj.com/article/SB1000142405297020447500457412682096329560.html*.
37. Ibid.
38. Ismael AbduSalaam, "Diddy Breaks Record with Shopping Channel Appearance," *AllHipHop*, December 2, 2009, *http://allhiphop.com/stories/news/archive/2009/12/02/22051224.aspx*.
39. *Radio Marketing Guide*, Radio Advertising Bureau, 2009, *www.rab.com/public/marketingGuide/rabRmg.html*.
40. Ibid.
41. "Advertisers Chase News Consumers," *Sales and Marketing Management's Manage Smarter Newsletter*, March 5, 2007, p. 1.
42. "What Makes Products Sell?" *Communication Briefings*, July 1997, p. 6.
43. Martin Langeveld, "Newspapers Take a Bus Plunge: Circulation Plummets 10.6%," *Nieman Journalism Lab*, October 26, 2009, *www.niemanlab.org/2009/10/newspapers-take-a-bus-plunge-circulation-plummets-10-6-percent/*.
44. "Internet Overtakes Newspapers as News Outlet," The Pew Research Center for the People and the Press, December 23, 2008, *http://people-press.org/report/479/internet-overtakes-newspapers-as-news-source*.
45. The State of the News Media: An Annual Report on American Journalism, Project for Excellence in Journalism, 2009, *www.stateofthemedia.org/2009/narrative_newspapers_audience.php*.
46. Evelyn Nussenbaum, "Instant Infomercials," *FSB*, December 2008–January 2009, pp. 37–38.
47. Ralph F. Wilson, "Use Banner Ads to Promote Your Web Site," *Web Marketing Today*, March 9, 2009, *www.wilsonweb.com/articles/bannerad.htm;* "Study: Click-Through Rates Lower Than Expected," *Marketing Vox*, February 27, 2009, *www.marketingvox.com/study-click-through-rates-lower-than-expected-043342/*.
48. "Online Shoppers Rely on Search Engines," *Marketing Charts*, February 23, 2010, *www.marketingcharts.com/interactive/online-shoppers-rely-on-search-engines-12056/*.
49. "Marketing Budget Survey: How Do I Plan for 2010?" Goldstein Group Communications, Solon, OH, 2009, p. 2.
50. *Click Fraud Report, Q1 2010*, Click Forensics, April 2010, p. 3.
51. E-mail Security Market, 2010–2014, Executive Summary, Radicati Group, Palo Alto, CA, 2010, pp. 2–3.
52. E-mail Security Market, 2010-2014, Executive Summary, Radicati Group, Palo Alto, CA, 2010, pp. 2–3.
53. Q3 2009 North America E-mail Trends and Benchmarks Results, Epsilon, Irving, TX, December 2009, p. 2.
54. "Innovative Southwestern Restaurant Sizzles," Constant Contact, *www.constantcontact.com/email-marketing/customer-examples/fajita-grill.jsp*.
55. *The Magazine Handbook*, Magazine Publishers of America (New York: Author, 2009), pp. 8, 9, 57.
56. Ibid., pp. 7, 10.
57. Ibid., p. 31.
58. *The Magazine Handbook: A Comprehensive Guide 2006/07*, Magazine Publishers of America (New York: Author, 2007) p. 23.
59. *The Magazine Handbook* (2009), p. 13.
60. *The State of the News Media 2009: An Annual Report on American Journalism*, Pew Project for Excellence in Journalism, *www.stateofthemedia.org/2009/narrative_magazines_audience.php?media=9&cat=2*.
61. POPAI Library, Point-of-Purchase Advertising International, *www.popai.com/Content/NavigationMenu/Resources/Research/Research.htm*.
62. "Facts & Figures," Outdoor Advertising Association of America, *www.oaaa.org/marketingresources/factsandfigures.aspx*.
63. "Case Studies: Bennett Infiniti Inc.," Outdoor Advertising Association of America, *www.oaaa.org/images/upload/research/200312916163668014966.pdf*.
64. American Fact Finder, U.S. Census Bureau, *http://factfinder.census.gov/servlet/ADPTable?_bm=y&-geo_id=01000US&-qr_name=ACS_2005_EST_G00_DP3&-gc_url=null&-ds_name=&-_lang=en&-redoLog=false*.
65. "U.S. Advertising CPM, by Media," *eMarketer*, February 2009, *www.emarketer.com/Results.aspx?N=785*.
66. Larry Copeland, "More Cities Ban Digital Billboards," *USA Today*, March 24, 2010, *www.usatoday.com/news/nation/2010-03-22-visual-soup_N.htm*.
67. *Arbitron National In-Car Study* (New York: 2009), p. 5.
68. *Arbitron National In-Car Study* (New York: December 2003), p. 2, *www.oaaa.org/pdf/Incarstudy_summary.pdf*.
69. Hamilton Davison, "The U.S. Catalog Mailing Industry—Today and Tomorrow," American Catalog Mailers Association, January 31, 2008, pp. 3, 8.
70. "Staying Power," *Direct Mail News*, December 1, 2008, pp. 17–19.
71. "Direct Mail Tips for Manufacturers' Letters," Koch Group, *www.kochgroup.com/directmail.html*.
72. "Advertising Mail and the Environment," Mail Moves America, December 15, 2008, *www.mailmovesamerica.org/environmentmyth.php*.
73. Amanda Ferrante, "New DMA Response Rate Study Shows E-mail Still Strong for Conversion Rates," *DemandGen*, March 16, 2009, *www.demandgenreport.com/home/archives/feature-articles/183-new-dma-response-rate-study-shows-email-still-strong-for-conversion-rates.html*.
74. "Success Stories: Dartmouth Pharmaceuticals," U.S. Postal Service, *www.usps.com/directmail/dartmouthpharmaceuticals.htm;* "Company Info," Dartmouth Pharmaceuticals, *www.ilovemynails.com/elonhome.html*.
75. Skip Cox, "The Unique Value of Exhibitions in Accelerating the Sales Process," Exhibition Surveys, presented at the Exhibition and Convention Executives Forum, June 15, 2006, *www.exhibitsurveys.com/files/File/whitepapers/AcceleratingSalesProcess.pdf*.

76. "'Dead Tree Medium' No Longer: For Many Marketers, Print Outperforms Digital," *Knowledge@Wharton*, March 19, 2008, *http://knowledge.wharton.upenn.edu/article.cfm?articleid=1919&CFID=19193179&CFTOKEN=81243060&jsessionid=a830557b30537714f7f0107e5da2e19272f2.*

77. Max Chafkin, "Ads and Atmospherics: Outdoor Campaigns Are Suddenly Hip," *Inc.*, February 2007, pp. 39–41; Jennifer Pollack, "Can Your Banner Ad Do This?" *Fast Company*, July–August 2006, p. 51; Sara Wilson, "Hawking on Eggshells," *Entrepreneur*, February 2007, p. 75.

78. Steven Heller, "Going Overground," *Metropolis*, March 14, 2007, *www.metropolismag.com/cda/story.php?artid=2557.*

Global Marketing Strategies

Learning Objectives

Upon completion of this chapter, you will be able to:

1 Explain why "going global" has become an integral part of many small companies' strategies.
2 Describe the nine principal strategies small businesses can use to go global.
3 Explain how to build a successful export program.
4 Discuss the major barriers to international trade and their impact on the global economy.
5 Describe the trade agreements that have the greatest influence on foreign trade.

You can't do business in the world today unless you are a global citizen. We live in a world that is so small now that the "community" is the people on the planet.

—Margaret Lee

It is easier to go to the moon than it is to enter the world of another civilization. Culture—not space—is the greatest distance between two people.

—Jamake Highwater

Until recently, the world of international business was much like the world of astronomy before Copernicus, who revolutionized the study of the planets and the stars with his theory of planetary motion. In the sixteenth century, his Copernican system replaced the Ptolemaic system, which held that the earth was the center of the universe, with the sun and all the other planets revolving around it. The Copernican system, however, placed the sun at the center of the solar system with all of the planets, including the earth, revolving around it. Astronomy would never be the same.

In the same sense, business owners across the globe were guilty of having Ptolemaic tunnel vision when it came to viewing international business opportunities. Like their pre-Copernican counterparts, owners saw an economy that revolved around the nations that served as their home bases. Market opportunities stopped at their homeland's borders. Global trade was only for giant corporations that had the money and the management to tap foreign markets and enough resources to survive if the venture flopped. That scenario no longer holds true in the twenty-first century. Indeed, a survey by consulting firm Grant Thornton of medium-size businesses reports that 56 percent of CEOs view globalization as an opportunity for their companies; just 19 percent of CEOs see it as a threat.[1]

Fifteen years ago, if a company was considered to be multinational, everyone knew that it was a giant corporation; today, that is no longer the case. The global marketplace is as much the territory of small, upstart companies as it is that of giant multinational corporations. Powerful, affordable technology, the Internet, increased access to information on conducting global business, and the growing interdependence of the world's economies have made it easier for companies of all sizes, many of which had never before considered going global, to engage in international trade.

ENTREPRENEURIAL
Profile
Ethan Siegel: Orb Audio

Ethan Siegel, founder of Orb Audio, and his wife, Lelenya

Source: Alex Quesada/*New York Times*-Maps and Graphics

In 2003, Ethan Siegel and a friend launched Orb Audio, a New York City–based company that makes high-end, orb-shaped speakers for home theater and stereo systems. The business, which generates most of its sales online, grew slowly, but in 2008, when the value of the U.S. dollar dropped against foreign currencies, Siegel saw a dramatic increase in inquiries from customers from other countries. Spotting an opportunity, Siegel began targeting customers in Canada, Australia, Great Britain, and Finland with country-specific Web pages and Internet ads on sites that are popular with customers in those countries. International sales at Orb Audio now comprise 35 percent of total sales. The growth in international sales has more than offset the decline in domestic sales for the company, which generates more than $5 million in revenue per year. Orb Audio now has customers around the globe, including places as far away as Zimbabwe, Africa, and Easter Island, located 2,300 miles off the coast of Chile and home to the famous moai stone statues.[2]

Just a few years ago, military might governed world relationships; today, commercial trade and economic benefit have become the forces that drive global interaction. Since 1948, the value of world merchandise exports has risen from $58.0 billion to $12.5 *trillion*.[3] Countries at every stage of development are reaping the benefits of increased global trade. Forecasts show that the economies of emerging markets such as China and India will expand faster than those of mature markets such as the United States and Germany. Consulting firm Grant Thornton has created an emerging-markets opportunity index that reflects countries' population and economic growth, involvement in world trade, and other factors. The countries that top the list are China, India, Russia, Mexico, and Brazil.[4] The International Monetary Fund estimates that China, where economic growth has been among the fastest in the world, will boast the largest gross domestic product (GDP) in the world by 2030.[5] The message is clear: Global markets present a tremendous opportunity for small companies that are prepared to market to them.

Political, social, cultural, technological, and economic changes continue to sweep the world, creating a new world order—and a legion of both threats and opportunities for businesses of all sizes. Market economies are replacing centralized economies in countries where only decades ago private ownership of productive assets was unthinkable. Technology advances have cut the cost of long-distance communications and transactions so low that conducting business globally often costs no more than doing business locally. Even the smallest companies are using their Web sites to sell in foreign markets at minimal costs. Small businesses are buying raw materials and services from all over the globe, wherever the deals are best. Jack Stack, CEO of Springfield Remanufacturing Corporation, a Springfield, Missouri–based company that refurbishes automotive engines and parts, was surprised when he learned that the company was purchasing parts from suppliers in 56 different countries! "Here we were, minding our business in Springfield, Missouri," says Stack, "and suddenly we discover that we've gone global."[6] Entrepreneurs are seeing new markets emerge in countries around the world as the ranks of their middle classes surge. These business owners realize that the size of these fast-growing markets is small today compared to their potential in the near future. Changes such as these are creating instability for businesses of *any* size going global, but they also are creating tremendous opportunities for those small companies ready to capitalize on them. One writer explains why entrepreneurs, with their unique perspective on risk taking, stand ready to embrace going global:

> Globalizing is risky. The risks include potential spoilers such as an unfamiliar language, an alien business landscape, untested partners, and political volatility. Still, the chance to try new things in new places is like a jumper cable to the entrepreneurial engine. Like the Internet companies of a decade ago, company owners [who go global] are working out the rules as they go, drawing lessons from the failures and the successes alike. They see the scale of battle growing, and they are girding for it.[7]

Expanding a business beyond its domestic borders actually enhances a small company's overall performance. Several studies have concluded that small companies that export earn more money, grow faster, create higher paying jobs, and are more likely to survive than their purely domestic counterparts.

Why Go Global?

1. Explain why "going global" has become an integral part of many small companies' strategies.

Small companies can no longer consider themselves to be strictly domestic businesses in this hotly competitive global environment. "In the global economy, the competitor six time zones away is potentially as serious a threat as the competitor six blocks away," says one expert.[8] For companies across the world, going global is a matter of survival, not preference. No matter where a company's home base is, competitors are forcing it to think globally. "There are an awful lot of people in the rest of the world who think they are pretty good at doing your business," warns Lester Thurow.[9] Companies that fail to see the world as a global marketplace risk being blindsided in their markets both at home and abroad. "Just being part of the domestic market and depending on that source of revenue isn't cutting it anymore," says Maryann Stein, director of a development agency in Erie, Pennsylvania, that helps small companies break into global markets. "We haven't really had to explore other markets because U.S. companies have been OK just selling domestically. That's not the case anymore."[10]

Failure to cultivate global markets can be a lethal mistake for modern businesses—whatever their size. In short, to thrive in the twenty-first century, small businesses must take their place in the world market. Today, the potential for doing business globally for businesses of all sizes means that where a company's goods and services originate or where its headquarters is located is insignificant. To be successful, companies must consider themselves to be businesses without borders.

Brad Oberwager:
Sundia Inc.

Dan Hoskins, general manager and founder of Sundia, a company that sells fruit and fruit juices to upscale grocery stores around the world. Sundia's founder, Brad Oberwager, established the company as a global business from the outset.

Source: ZUMA Press

Brad Oberwager, chairman and founder of Sundia, a company that sells cut fruit and fruit juices to upscale grocery stores around the world, operates the business from an office in the basement of his home in San Francisco, California, but employs workers across the United States, India, and the Philippines. From the outset, Oberwager set up Sundia to be a micro-multinational business, and he relies on Web-based business systems to coordinate the company's far-flung activities. For instance, suppose that a customer in Europe orders several cases of watermelon–pomegranate juice (which is processed in Washington from fruit grown in Mexico and California) by calling Sundia's San Francisco telephone number. The call is forwarded to a customer service center in the Philippines, where a representative takes the order and submits it to a warehouse that is closest to the customer, in this case, London. The warehouse ships the order to the customer and notifies the accounting department, which is housed in India. The accounting department generates a customer invoice, sends it to company headquarters in San Francisco, which forwards the invoice to the customer in Europe. In less than 2 years, Oberwager's global strategy has made Sundia the largest watermelon brand in the world and the fastest growing produce brand in the United States.[11]

Going global can put a tremendous strain on a small company, but entrepreneurs who take the plunge into global business can reap many benefits, including the ability to offset sales declines in the domestic market, increase sales and profits, improve the quality of their products to meet the stringent demands of foreign customers, lower the manufacturing cost of their products by spreading fixed costs over a larger number of units, and enhance their competitive positions to become stronger businesses. In a recent study conducted by CompTIA of small and medium-size businesses that export, 64 percent of owners say that doing business globally has made their companies significantly more competitive. In addition, 86 percent of these business owners say that their companies' export sales are growing faster than their domestic sales.[12]

Unfortunately, many entrepreneurs have not learned to view their companies from a global perspective. Indeed, learning to *think globally* may be the first—and most threatening—obstacle an entrepreneur must overcome on the way to creating a truly global business. One British manager explains:

> If you are operating in South America, you'd better know how to operate in conditions of hyperinflation. If you're operating in Africa, you'd better know a lot about government relations and the use of local partners. If you're operating in Germany, you'd better understand the mechanics of codetermination and some of the special tax systems that one finds in that country. If you're operating in China, it's quite useful in trademark matters to know how the People's Court of Shanghai works. . . . If you're operating in Japan, you'd better understand the different trade structure.[13]

Gaining a foothold in newly opened foreign markets or maintaining a position in an existing one is no easy task, however. Until an entrepreneur develops the attitude of operating a truly global company rather than a domestic company that happens to be doing business abroad, achieving success in international business is difficult. That attitude starts at the top in the executive's office. Success in the global economy also requires constant innovation; staying nimble enough to use speed as a competitive weapon; maintaining a high level of quality and constantly improving it; being sensitive to foreign customers' unique requirements; adopting a more respectful attitude toward foreign habits and customs; hiring motivated, multilingual employees; and retaining a desire to learn constantly about global markets. In short, the path to success requires businesses to become "insiders" who see the world as their market rather than just "exporters."

Before venturing into the global marketplace, an entrepreneur should consider six questions:

1. Is there a profitable market in which our company has the potential to be successful over the long run? Table 1 shows a country-screening matrix designed to help entrepreneurs decide which countries offer the best opportunities for their products.
2. Do we have and are we willing to commit adequate resources of time, people, and capital to a global campaign?
3. Are we considering going global for the right reasons? Are domestic pressures forcing our company to consider global opportunities?
4. Do we understand the cultural differences, history, economics, values, opportunities, and risks of conducting business in the countries we are considering?
5. Do we have a viable exit strategy for our company if conditions change or the new venture does not succeed?
6. Can we afford *not* to go global?

TABLE 1 A Country-Screening Matrix

For an entrepreneur considering launching a global business venture, getting started often is the hardest step. "The world is such a big place! Where do I start?" is a typical comment from entrepreneurs considering global business. The following matrix will help you narrow your options. Based on preliminary research, select three to five countries that you believe have the greatest market potential for your products. Then, use the following factors to guide you as you conduct more detailed research into these countries and their markets. Rate each factor on a scale of 1 (lowest) to 5 (highest). Based on your ratings, which country has the highest score?

Market factor	Country 1 Rating	Country 2 Rating	Country 3 Rating
Demographic/physical environment			
Population size, growth, density			
Urban and rural distribution			
Climate and weather variations			
Shipping distance			
Product-significant demographics			
Physical distribution and communication network			
Natural resources			
Political environment			
System of government			
Political stability and continuity			
Ideological orientation			
Government involvement in business			
Attitudes toward foreign business (trade restrictions, tariffs, nontariff barriers, bilateral trade agreements)			
National economic and developmental priorities			
Economic environment			
Overall level of development			
Economic growth: GNP, industrial sector			
Role of foreign trade in the economy			
Currency: inflation rate, availability, controls, stability of exchange rate			
Balance of payments			
Per capita income and distribution			
Disposable income and expenditure patterns			
Social/cultural environment			
Literacy rate, educational level			
Existence of middle class			
Similarities and differences in relation to home market			
Language and other cultural considerations			

(*continued*)

TABLE 1 Continued

Market access

   ▩ Limitations on trade: high tariff levels, quotas
   ▩ Documentation and import regulations
   ▩ Local standards, practices, and other nontariff barriers
   ▩ Patents and trademark protection
   ▩ Preferential treaties
   ▩ Legal considerations for investment, taxation, repatriation, employment, code of laws

Product potential

   ▩ Customer needs and desires
   ▩ Local production, imports, consumption
   ▩ Exposure to and acceptance of product
   ▩ Availability of linking products
   ▩ Industry-specific key indicators of demand
   ▩ Attitudes toward products of foreign origin
   ▩ Competitive offerings

Local distribution and production

   ▩ Availability of intermediaries
   ▩ Regional and local transportation facilities
   ▩ Availability of manpower
   ▩ Conditions for local manufacture

Total Score

Source: Adapted from "International Business Plan," *Breaking into the Trade Game: A Small Business Guide,* U.S. Small Business Administration Office of International Trade (Washington, DC: 2001), *www.sba.gov/oit/info/Guide-To-Exporting/trad6.html.*

▶ ENTREPRENEURSHIP IN ACTION ▶

Stay at Home or Go Abroad?

Joan Denizot came up with the idea for her business when she realized that other people faced the same problem that she did. Denizot, 52, is one of the millions of Americans struggling to lose weight with the help of an exercise regimen. For Denizot, one of the most appealing forms of exercise is cycling. While recovering from gastric bypass surgery, Denizot tried cycling but quickly realized that every bicycle she tried out was too small for her full figure. "I'd get on bikes, and the tires would flatten," she says.

Denizot searched the Internet for plus-sized bikes but found very little. "They talked about how much the bike and all of its parts weighed but never about how much weight the bike would carry," she recalls. "Even bikes that were built for 'large riders' went up to only 225 pounds." She considered finding someone to build a custom bicycle that would be sturdy enough for her frame, but she wanted to help others like her to get outside, exercise, and become healthier. That's when she decide to launch Super Sized Cycles.

The company, which is based in Vermont, currently sells about 100 bicycles per year through its Web site (*www.supersizedcycles.com*) and generates sales of $104,000. Sales have increased each of the 5 years that the company has been in business, but Denizot's business earns a modest profit and can afford to pay her only a very small salary. Super Sized Cycles offers six bicycle models that range in price from $669 for the entry-level model to $3,395 for a tricycle version with a small electric motor. Because of their strong steel frames and broad, sturdy tires, the bikes can accommodate riders up to 6 feet, 7 inches tall and who weigh up to 550 pounds. The company's best-selling models are A New Leaf and Time of Your Life, both of which Denizot designed herself. They sell for $2,070 each.

Depending on the specific model, Denizot pays $400 to $500 for bicycle frames, which are made in Iowa and shipped to Vermont, where the company's master assembler, Timothy Mathewson, builds each bike to the customer's specifications, which adds another $1,250 to her costs. Although Super Sized Cycles' gross profit margin is low, Denizot says that some potential customers balk at the company's prices. Taking the advice of a private investor who helped finance Super Sized Cycle's start up, Denizot outsourced production of 70 New Leaf bicycles to a manufacturer in Taiwan as a test.

She was pleased with the quality of the bicycles manufactured by the Taiwanese company and was even more pleased with the price she paid. Denizot says that, despite one-time costs associated with placing the order, she would be able to purchase fully assembled bicycles designed to her specifications for just $550, allowing her to offer customers lower prices and increase her company's profit margin. Denizot is caught in a quandary. She sees many advantages of keeping production in the United States: fast delivery times, the ability to oversee quality easily, and the ability to provide extraordinary customer service thanks to the technical skills of her "bike guru," Timothy Mathewson. She also likes the idea of keeping manufacturing jobs in the United States. "There's a lot to be said for helping a community and creating jobs here," she says, "but I need to be competitive, and I need to make a quality product."

1. Should Denizot keep production of her company's bicycles in the United States or outsource production to the manufacturer in Taiwan? Explain. What other recommendations can you offer her?
2. If Denizot were to outsource production to Taiwan, what steps do you suggest she take to maintain the quality of her products and protect her designs from piracy?

Sources: Based on John Grossman, "Make Bikes in the U.S., or Go Abroad to Cut Costs?" *New York Times*, June 2, 2010, *www.nytimes.com/2010/06/03/business/smallbusiness/03sbiz.html*; "About Us," Super Sized Cycles, *www.supersizedcycles.com/index.php?l=page_view&p=about_us*.

Going Global: Strategies for Small Businesses

2. Describe the nine principal strategies small businesses can use to go global.

The globalization of business actually *favors* small businesses because it creates an abundance of niche markets that are ideal for small companies to serve. "In this global economy, the competitive edge is swiftness to market and innovation," says John Naisbitt, trend-spotting author of *The Global Paradox*, and those characteristics are the hallmarks of entrepreneurs.[14] Their agility and adaptability gives small firms the edge in today's highly interactive, fast-paced global economy. "The bigger the world economy, the more powerful its smallest players," concludes Naisbitt.[15]

Becoming a global business depends on instilling a global culture throughout the organization that permeates *everything* the company does. Entrepreneurs who conduct international business successfully have developed a global mind-set for themselves and their companies. As one business writer explains:

The global [business] looks at the whole world as *one market*. It manufactures, conducts research, raises capital, and buys supplies wherever it can do the job best. It keeps in touch with technology and market trends around the world. National boundaries and regulations tend to be irrelevant, or a mere hindrance. [Company] headquarters might be anywhere.[16]

As cultures across the globe become increasingly interwoven, companies' ability to go global will determine their degree of success. Small companies pursuing a global presence have nine principal strategies available: creating a presence on the Web, relying on trade intermediaries, establishing joint ventures, engaging in foreign licensing arrangements, franchising, using countertrading and bartering, exporting products or services, establishing international locations, and importing and outsourcing (see Figure 1).

FIGURE 1
Nine Global Strategies

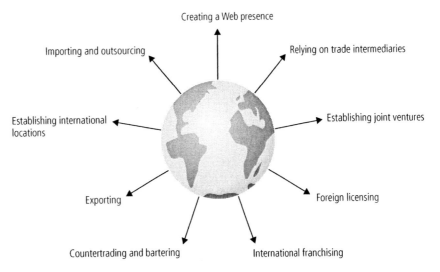

Creating a Web presence

Relying on trade intermediaries

Importing and outsourcing

Establishing joint ventures

Establishing international locations

Foreign licensing

Exporting

Countertrading and bartering

International franchising

Creating a Presence on the Web

Approximately 96 percent of the world's consumers live outside the United States, and the simplest and least expensive way for a small business to begin to reach them is to establish a Web site. The Web gives small businesses tremendous marketing potential all across the globe without having to incur the expense of opening international locations. With a well-designed Web site, a small company can extend its reach to customers anywhere in the world—without breaking the budget! A Web site is available to anyone, anywhere in the world and provides 24-hour-a-day exposure to a company's products or services, making global time differences meaningless.

Establishing a presence on the Web is an essential ingredient in the strategies of small companies trying to reach customers outside the borders of the United States. Although Internet usage varies greatly by region of the world (see Figure 2), the number of Internet users is growing extremely fast—nearly 400 percent worldwide since 2000. Another important factor for U.S. entrepreneurs to note is that 86 percent of the estimated 1.8 billion Internet users worldwide live *outside* of North America.[17]

FIGURE 2A

Internet Users Worldwide

Source: "Internet Usage Statistics: The Big Picture," Internet World Stats 2009, *www.internetworldstats.com/stats.htm.*

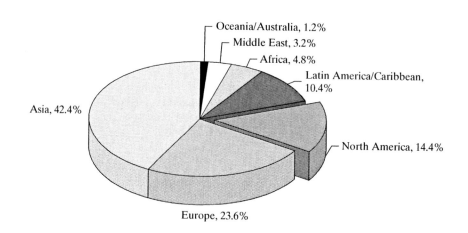

FIGURE 2B

Internet Penetration Rate by World Region

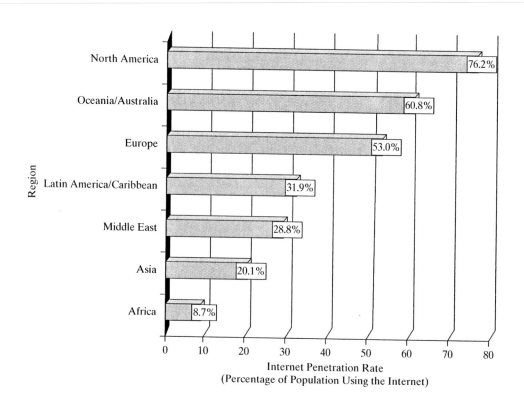

Before the advent of the Internet, small businesses usually took incremental steps toward becoming global businesses. They began selling locally, and, then, after establishing a reputation, expanded regionally, and perhaps nationally. Only after establishing themselves domestically did small businesses begin to think about selling their products or services internationally. The Web makes that business model obsolete because it provides small companies with a low-cost global distribution channel that they can utilize from the day they are launched. Designed properly, a Web site can be an engaging marketing tool.

Profile

Greg Jackson: Carolina Classic Boats

Shortly after starting his company, Greg Jackson created a Web site for his boat- and auto-brokering business, Carolina Classic Boats and Cars (*www.carolina-classic-boats.com*), which specializes in buying, selling, and trading antique wooden boats made from the 1920s to the 1950s by manufacturers such as Chris Craft, Gar Wood, Atlas, Hacker Craft, and Riva. Jackson recently added classic cars to his product line of "big-boy toys." Although Jackson operates his business in Clinton, South Carolina, a small town of fewer than 10,000 residents, his company operates globally with the help of the Web site, where customers can see photographs and read detailed descriptions of the boats and cars they are considering. Jackson has bought, sold, and shipped classic boats and cars all over the world, from Europe to Australia. "As long as I have a cell phone and a laptop, it doesn't matter where I am," he says.[18]

Entrepreneurs who do not want to take the time to set up their own Web sites can still sell to international customers through the Internet giant eBay, which has a wide global reach of 90 million active users. eBay handles an average of $2,000 worth of transactions every second, and 54 percent of all eBay transactions take place outside the United States.[19] eBay's international sales are growing twice as fast as its domestic sales.

Profile

Lanny and Deena Morton: Sports Closeouts

In 2002, Lanny Morton spotted 20 baseball bats priced at just $40 each. His girlfriend and, now wife, Deena, encouraged him to buy them and resell them on eBay. Morton had to borrow $800 to make the purchase and quickly resold the bats for $1,300 on eBay. Recognizing a potential business, Deena invested $1,300 to purchase more discount sporting goods, which the pair sold for $2,600. Soon, Lanny and Deena had a successful eBay business selling quality sporting goods at discount prices. They used their 1,400 square-foot home in Glendale, Arizona, as their warehouse (with boxes of items often stacked to the ceiling in almost every room) until their business, Sports Closeouts, outgrew the space. "We started out on the living room floor," recalls Lanny, "writing labels and shipping out 10 or 15 items at a time. Eventually, the product just consumed the house." The Mortons have created their own Web site (*www.sportscloseouts.com*) but still sell items on eBay. Now operating out of a 7,200 square-foot warehouse, Sports Closeouts sells to customers across the globe and generates more than $4 million in annual revenue.[20]

Rather than merely counting on international customers to find their Web sites, small companies can take a proactive approach by translating their sites into other languages. Business owners can determine which countries to target by using Web analytics reports to identify the countries in which their existing online customers live. Hiring someone who understands the nuances of the language and the culture of the target countries to translate a site is the safest strategy and avoids embarrassing cultural blunders.

Relying on Trade Intermediaries

Another alternative for low-cost and low-risk entry into international markets is to use a trade intermediary. Trade intermediaries are domestic agencies that serve as distributors in foreign countries for domestic companies of all sizes. They rely on their networks of contacts, their

IN THE ENTREPRENEURIAL SPOTLIGHT

Building a Global Business in the Middle of a War Zone

During his regular evening reading time, Bill McNeely came across several articles about the iPhone's short battery life, and the inspiration for a business struck him. "I saw a big market and not that many players," he says. Although McNeely has no technical background, he had a simple idea that he was confident would work: a sleek, external battery that snaps onto the bottom of an iPhone, extending its battery life. All he needed was someone to design the battery and manufacture it for him. He went to Alibaba.com, a Web site that serves as a marketplace for importers, exporters, and suppliers from more than 240 countries, and within a few weeks found a reliable Chinese manufacturer that would transform his idea into a real product. He then went to Elance, a Web site that allows entrepreneurs to hire and manage freelance employees, and found a graphic designer to create the packaging for his iPhone battery, which he calls the 3GPower2. McNeely used the Web to find a consultant with a Harvard Business School degree to help him with his business plan, and an article in the *New York Times* led him to a Web designer, who helped him create his company's Web site, *www.3GPower2.com*.

With a total investment of $6,000, McNeely had 3GPower2 up and running as a global business in less than 3 months, something not all that unusual for modern entrepreneurs. However, one fact makes McNeely's accomplishments noteworthy: He built his company while managing the logistical operations of a police training base in one of the most dangerous places in the world: Kunduz, Afghanistan, a city mired in battle with the Taliban. The camp where McNeely works trains Afghan police and is under constant threat of attack from terrorists. Recently, a rocket launched by the Taliban landed only a few hundred feet from the base. "I've been through some pretty rough stuff," admits McNeely. He recalls the day when he was working for a defense contractor in southern Afghanistan when terrorists attacked his convoy, killing several drivers and destroying McNeely's SUV. Somehow McNeely survived the attack. His goal is to build his business to the point where he can retire from his job with the defense contractor and go back home to Texas to operate 3GPower2 full-time.

In the meantime, McNeely's wife, Suzy, handles the day-to-day operations of the business, including shipping, from the couple's home in Temple, Texas. Bill McNeely spends a great deal of time making Skype calls at night and on weekends to Suzy about 3GPower2. Currently, the McNeelys are focusing on search engine optimization techniques to boost the company's placement in search engines and on creating a coupon through Groupon (*www.groupon.com*).

1. How does the Internet enable entrepreneurs to create global businesses at start up? Has this always been the case?
2. What lessons can you draw from Bill McNeely's experience launching 3GPower2?

Source: Based on Jason Del Rey, "Report from the War Zone," *Inc.*, April 2010, pp. 25–26.

extensive knowledge of local customs and markets, and their experience in international trade to market products effectively and efficiently all across the globe. Trade intermediaries serve as export departments for small businesses. Although a broad array of trade intermediaries is available, the following are ideally suited for small businesses:

EXPORT MANAGEMENT COMPANIES (EMCS). **Export management companies (EMCs)** are an important channel of foreign distribution for small companies just getting started in international trade or for those lacking the resources to assign their own people to foreign markets. Most EMCs are merchant intermediaries, working on a buy-and-sell arrangement with small domestic companies. They provide small businesses with a low-cost, efficient, independent international marketing department, offering services ranging from market research on foreign countries and advice on patent protection to arranging financing and handling shipping. More than 1,000 EMCs operate across the United States, and many of them specialize in particular products or product lines. The chief advantage of using an EMC is that a small business's products get international exposure without having to tie up its own resources.

ENTREPRENEURIAL
Profile
*Steven Meier and
David Cisneros: Western
Export Services*

Western Export Services (WES), an export management company in Denver, Colorado, founded by Steven Meier and David Cisneros, specializes in selling food and beverage products from U.S.-based small and medium-size companies in markets across the globe. Recently named "Exporter of the Year," WES represents food and beverage suppliers from across the United States in the Pacific Rim, the Middle East, Latin America, and Europe.[21]

The greatest benefits that EMCs offer small companies are ready access to global markets and an extensive knowledge base on foreign trade, both of which are vital for entrepreneurs who are inexperienced in conducting global business. In return for their services, EMCs usually earn an extra discount on the goods they buy from their clients or, if they operate on a commission rate, a higher commission than domestic distributors earn on what they sell. EMCs charge commission rates of about 10 percent on consumer goods and 15 percent on industrial products. Although EMCs rarely advertise their services, finding one is not difficult. The Federation of International Trade Associations (FITA) provides useful information for small companies about global business and trade intermediaries on its Web site (*http://fita.org*), including a *Directory of Export Management Companies*. Industry trade associations and publications and the U.S. Department of Commerce's Export Assistance Centers* also can help entrepreneurs to locate EMCs and other trade intermediaries.

EXPORT TRADING COMPANIES (ETCs). Another tactic for getting into international markets with a minimum of cost and effort is through an export trading company (ETC). ETCs have been an important vehicle in international trade throughout history. The Hudson's Bay Company and the East India Company were dominant powers in world trade in the sixteenth, seventeenth, and eighteenth centuries.

Export trading companies are businesses that buy and sell products in a number of countries, and they typically offer a wide range of services, such as exporting, importing, shipping, storing, distributing, and others, to their clients. Unlike EMCs, which tend to focus on exporting, ETCs usually perform both import and export trades across many countries' borders. However, like EMCs, ETCs lower the risk of exporting for small businesses. Some of the largest trading companies in the world are based in the United States and Japan. In fact, many businesses that have navigated successfully Japan's complex system of distribution have done so with the help of ETCs.

In 1982, Congress passed the Export Trading Company Act to allow producers of similar products to form ETC cooperatives without the fear of violating antitrust laws. The goal was to encourage U.S. companies to export more goods by allowing businesses in the same industry to band together to form export trading companies.

MANUFACTURER'S EXPORT AGENTS (MEAs). **Manufacturer's export agents (MEAs)** act as international sales representatives in a limited number of markets for various noncompeting domestic companies. Unlike the close, partnering relationship formed with most EMCs, the relationship between an MEA and a small company is a short-term one, in which the MEA typically operates on a commission basis.

EXPORT MERCHANTS. **Export merchants** are domestic wholesalers who do business in foreign markets. They buy goods from many domestic manufacturers and then market them in foreign markets. Unlike MEAs, export merchants often carry competing lines, which means they have little loyalty to suppliers. Most export merchants specialize in particular industries—office equipment, computers, industrial supplies, and others.

RESIDENT BUYING OFFICES. Another approach to exporting is to sell to a **resident buying office**, a government-owned or privately-owned operation established in a country for the purpose of buying goods made there. Many foreign governments and businesses have set up

*A searchable list of the Export Assistance Centers is available at the Export.gov Web site (*www.export.gov/eac/index.asp*).

buying offices in the United States. Selling to them is just like selling to domestic customers because the buying office handles all the details of exporting.

FOREIGN DISTRIBUTORS. Some small businesses work through foreign distributors to reach international markets. Small domestic companies export their products to these distributors who handle all of the marketing, distribution, and service functions in the foreign country.

In 2007, when Peter Cole took over Gamblin Artists Colors, a company that makes handcrafted oil paints, varnishes, and other artists' supplies, international sales accounted for less than 5 percent of the company's revenue. Cole realized that foreign markets represented a significant opportunity for the company's high-quality products and traveled to several countries that basic market research helped managers select as prime targets. Logging more than 80,000 miles in less than 1 year, Cole established relationships with foreign distributors in Israel, Australia, Mexico, Great Britain, and Spain. Gamblin Artists Colors now generates more than $5 million in annual sales, and international sales account for 10 percent (and growing) of the total.[22]

THE VALUE OF USING TRADE INTERMEDIARIES. Trade intermediaries such as these are becoming increasingly popular among businesses attempting to branch out into world markets because they make that transition much faster and easier. Most small business owners simply do not have the knowledge, resources, or confidence to go global alone. Intermediaries' global networks of buyers and sellers allow their small business customers to build their international sales much faster and with fewer hassles and mistakes. Entrepreneurs who are inexperienced in global sales and attempt to crack certain foreign markets quickly discover just how difficult the challenge can be. However, with their know-how, experience, and contacts, trade intermediaries can get small companies' products into foreign markets quickly and efficiently. The primary disadvantage of using trade intermediaries is that doing so requires entrepreneurs to surrender control over their foreign sales. Maintaining close contact with intermediaries and evaluating their performance regularly help to avoid major problems, however.

The key to establishing a successful relationship with a trade intermediary is conducting a thorough screening to determine which type of intermediary—and which one in particular—will best serve a small company's needs. The 50 World Trade Centers (most of which are affiliated with the U.S. government) and the Export Assistance Centers located in more than 100 cities across the United States and in 80 countries around the world offer valuable advice and assistance to small businesses wanting to get started in conducting global business. In addition, entrepreneurs can find reliable intermediaries by using their network of contacts in foreign countries and by attending international trade shows while keeping an eye out for potential candidates. Table 2 describes various resources that can help entrepreneurs locate trade intermediaries.

Joint Ventures

Joint ventures, both domestic and foreign, lower the risk of entering global markets for small businesses. They also give small companies more clout in foreign lands. In a **domestic joint venture**, two or more U.S. small businesses form an alliance for the purpose of exporting their goods and services abroad. For export ventures, participating companies get antitrust immunity, allowing them to cooperate freely. The businesses share the responsibility and the costs of getting export licenses and permits, and they split the venture's profits. Establishing a joint venture with the right partner has become an essential part of maintaining a competitive position in global markets for a growing number of industries.

In a **foreign joint venture**, a domestic small business forms an alliance with a company in the target nation. The host partner brings to the joint venture valuable knowledge of the local market and the customs and the tastes of local customers, making it much easier to conduct business in the foreign country. "For a small business, a far less risky approach to selling goods or services in a distant market is to work through local partners who understand the market and often have built-in distribution channels," says Edward Wes, a partner in a law firm that specializes in international business.[23] Forming a joint venture with a local company also is the best way for a business to negotiate the maze of government regulations in some countries. Some foreign countries

TABLE 2 Resources for Locating a Trade Intermediary

Trade intermediaries make doing business around the world much easier for small companies, but finding the right one can be a challenge. Fortunately, several government agencies offer a wealth of information to businesses interested in reaching into global markets with the help of trade intermediaries. Entrepreneurs looking for help in breaking into global markets should contact the International Trade Administration, the U.S. Commerce Department, and the Small Business Administration first to take advantage of the following services:

- *Agent/Distributor Service (ADS).* Provides customized searches to locate interested and qualified foreign distributors for a product or service. (Search cost, $250 per country)
- *Commercial Service International Contacts (CSIC) List.* Provides contact and product information for more than 82,000 foreign agents, distributors, and importers interested in doing business with U.S. companies.
- *Country Directories of International Contacts (CDIC) List.* Provides the same kind of information as the CSIC List but is organized by country.
- *Industry Sector Analyses (ISAs).* Offer in-depth reports on industries in foreign countries, including information on distribution practices, end-users, and top sales prospects.
- *International Market Insights (IMIs).* Include reports on specific foreign market conditions, upcoming opportunities for U.S. companies, trade contacts, trade show schedules, and other information.
- *Trade Opportunity Program (TOP).* Provides up-to-the-minute, prescreened sales leads around the world for U.S. businesses, including joint venture and licensing partners, direct sales leads, and representation offers.
- *International Company Profiles (ICPs).* Commercial specialists will investigate potential partners, agents, distributors, or customers for U.S. companies and will issue profiles on them.
- *Commercial News USA.* A government-published magazine that promotes U.S. companies' products and services to 400,000 business readers in 176 countries at a fraction of the cost of commercial advertising. Small companies can use *Commercial News USA* to reach new customers around the world for as little as $499.
- *Gold Key Service.* For a small fee, business owners wanting to export to a specific country can use the Department of Commerce's Gold Key Service, in which experienced trade professionals arrange meetings with prescreened contacts whose interests match their own.
- *Platinum Key Service.* The U.S. Commercial Service's Platinum Key Service is more comprehensive than its Gold Key Service, offering business owners long-term consulting services on topics such as building a global marketing strategy, deciding which countries to target, and how to reach customers in foreign markets.
- *Matchmaker Trade Delegations Program.* This program helps small U.S. companies establish business relationships in major markets abroad by introducing them to the right contacts.
- *Multi-State/Catalog Exhibition Program.* The Department of Commerce presents companies' product and sales literature to hundreds of interested business prospects in foreign countries for as little as $450.
- *Trade Fair Certification Program.* This service promotes U.S. companies' participation in foreign trade shows that represent the best marketing opportunities for them.
- *Globus and National Trade Data Bank (NTDB).* With the NTDB (*http://www.wand.com/ntdb/*), small companies have access to leads on trading partners (both suppliers and customers) around the world.
- *International Trade Library.* At the Bureau of National Affairs Web site (*http://www.bna.com/products/corplaw/itlw.htm*), entrepreneurs can access the International Trade Library, where they can learn about managing currency exchange risks, find country-specific market research, read Country Commercial Guides, and access a treasure trove of information on doing business globally. The Global Business Opportunity Leads section helps entrepreneurs locate leads and make business contacts for conducting international business.
- *Economic Bulletin Board (EBB).* Provides online trade leads and valuable market research on foreign countries compiled from a variety of federal agencies.
- *U.S. Export Assistance Centers.* The Department of Commerce has established 19 export assistance centers (USEACs) in major metropolitan cities around the country to serve as one-stop shops for entrepreneurs who need export help. Visit *www.sba.gov/aboutsba/sbaprograms/internationaltrade/useac/index.html* for more information.
- *Trade Information Center.* The center helps locate federal export assistance, provides export assistance, and offers a 24-hour automated fax retrieval system that gives entrepreneurs free information on export promotion programs, regional market information, and international trade agreements. Call USA-TRADE.

(continued)

TABLE 2 Continued

- *Office of International Trade.* Through the Office of International Trade, the Small Business Administration works with other government and private agencies to provide a variety of export development assistance, how-to publications, online courses, and information on foreign markets.
- *Export-U.com.* This Web site (*www.export-u.com*) offers free export Webinars to business owners on topics that range from the basics, "Exporting 101," to more advanced topics, such as export financing arrangements. The site also provides links to many useful international trade Web sites.
- *U.S. Commercial Service.* The U.S. Commercial service, a division of the International Trade Administration (*www.trade.gov*), provides many of the services listed in this table. Its Web site (*www.buyusa.gov/home/*) is an excellent starting point for entrepreneurs who are interested in exporting.
- *Export.gov.* This Web site (*www.export.gov*) from the U.S. Commercial Service is an excellent gateway to a myriad of resources for entrepreneurs who are interested in learning more about exporting. The site includes market research, trade events, trade leads, and much more.
- *Federation of International Trade Associations (FITA).* The FITA Global Trade Portal (*www.fita.org*) is an excellent source for international import and export trade leads and events and provides links to about 8,000 Web sites related to international trade.

place limitations on how joint ventures operate. Some nations, for example, require domestic (host) companies to own at least 51 percent of the venture. Sometimes, says one international manager, "the only way to be German in Germany, Canadian in Canada, and Japanese in Japan is through alliances."[24] When Subway, one of the leading franchises in the world, enters foreign markets with one of its sandwich shops, it often looks for a local company with which to form a joint venture. "Nobody knows an area like a local partner," says Don Fertman, a director of international development at Subway.[25]

The most important ingredient in the recipe for a successful joint venture is choosing the right partner. A productive joint venture is much like a marriage, requiring commitment, trust, and understanding. In addition to picking the right partner(s), a second key to creating a successful alliance is to establish common objectives. Defining *exactly* what each party in the joint venture hopes to accomplish at the outset minimizes the opportunity for misunderstandings and disagreements later on. One important objective should always be to use the joint venture as a learning experience, which requires a long-term view of the business relationship. Issues to address *before* entering into a joint venture include:

- What contributions will each party make?
- Who will be responsible for making which decisions?
- How much control will each party have over the joint venture's direction?
- How will the earnings from the joint venture be allocated?
- How long will the joint venture last? Under what circumstances can the parties terminate the relationship?

ENTREPRENEURIAL Profile

Bombardier Inc.: Joint Ventures with Sifang Locomotive, Rolling Stock, and Shenyang Aircraft Corporation

Bombardier Inc., a Quebec, Canada-based company that manufactures aircraft and trains, used a joint venture as part of its strategy to enter the Chinese market. Recognizing that China's decision to invest 3.2 trillion yuan in upgrading its infrastructure, including railways and airports (97 new airports by 2020), presented a tremendous business opportunity for both its aircraft and train divisions, Bombardier forged joint ventures with Chinese companies, one in the rail industry and the other in the aircraft industry. Bombardier will partner with Sifang Locomotive and Rolling Stock Ltd. to build its new ZEFIRO 380 trains that can go nearly 240 miles per hour. The company also has created a joint venture with China's Shenyang Aircraft Corporation to build its Q400 turboprop and C series regional aircraft. Thanks to these joint ventures, Bombardier forecasts call for China to become the company's third largest market behind North America and Europe.[26]

Unfortunately, most joint ventures fail. That makes it essential for the companies in an alliance to establish a contingency plan for getting out in case the joint venture doesn't work. Common problems leading to failure include improper selection of partners, incompatible management styles, failure to establish common goals, lack of flexibility, and failure to trust one another. What can entrepreneurs do to avoid these pitfalls in joint ventures?

- Understand their partner's reasons and objectives for joining the venture.
- Select a partner that shares their company's values and standards of conduct.
- Spell out in writing exactly how the venture will work, what each partner's responsibilities are, and where decision-making authority lies.
- Select a partner whose skills are different from but compatible with those of their own companies.
- Prepare a "prenuptial agreement" that spells out what happens in case of a "business divorce."

Foreign Licensing

Rather than sell their products or services directly to customers overseas, some small companies enter foreign markets by licensing businesses in other nations to use their patents, trademarks, copyrights, technology, processes, or products. In return for licensing its assets, a small company collects royalties from the sale of its foreign licenses. Licensing is a relatively simple way for even the most inexperienced business owners to extend their reach into global markets. Licensing is ideal for companies whose value lies in its intellectual property, unique products or services, recognized name, or proprietary technology. Although many businesses consider licensing only their products to foreign companies, the licensing potential for intangibles such as processes, technology, copyrights, and trademarks often is greater. Some entrepreneurs earn more money from licensing their know-how for product design, manufacturing, or quality control than they do from actually selling their finished goods in a highly competitive foreign market with which they are not familiar. Foreign licensing enables a small business to enter foreign markets quickly, easily, and with virtually no capital investment. Risks to the company include the potential loss of control over its manufacturing and marketing processes and creating a competitor if the licensee gains too much knowledge and control. Securing proper patent, trademark, and copyright protection beforehand can minimize those risks, however.

International Franchising

Franchising has become a major export industry for the United States. A survey by the International Franchise Association reports that 52 percent of U.S.-based franchisors have an international presence, and more domestic franchisors are looking to expand abroad.[27] Franchises are attracted to international markets, where they find it easier to increase sales and profits because the domestic market has become increasingly saturated with outlets and is much tougher to wring growth from than in the past. As a growth strategy, international franchising works best for experienced franchisors. Both the cost and the complexity of franchising increase as the distance between franchisor and franchisees increases. Before committing to global expansion, franchisors should meet the following criteria:

The International Franchise Association reports that 52 percent of U.S.-based franchisors have an international presence. Pictured here are McDonald's and KFC outlets in Dubai, United Arab Emirates.
Source: vario images GmbH & Co. KG/Almay Images

- Sufficient financial and managerial resources to devote to globalization
- A solid track record of success in the United States
- Adequate trademark protection for the franchise's brand
- Time-tested training, support, and reporting procedures that help franchisees succeed[28]

International franchisors sell virtually every kind of product or service imaginable—from fast food to child day care—in global markets. In some cases, the products and services sold in international markets are identical to those sold in the United States. However, most franchisors have learned that they must adapt their products and services to suit local tastes and customs. Fast-food chains operating in other countries often must make adjustments to their menus to please locals' palates.

ENTREPRENEURIAL
Profile

*McDonald's and
Domino's Pizza*

In Japan, McDonald's (known as "Makudonarudo") outlets sell koroke burgers (made of mashed potatoes and cabbage), rice burgers, and katsu burgers (cheese wrapped in a roast pork cutlet topped with katsu sauce and shredded cabbage) in addition to their traditional American fare. In the Philippines, the McDonald's menu includes a spicy Filipino-style burger, spaghetti, and chicken with rice. In Germany, McDonald's restaurants sell McBeer, and in Great Britain they offer British Cadbury chocolate sticks. Some McDonald's outlets in Canada sell poutine, French fries topped with cheese curds and gravy, and the McHomard, a sandwich made of chunks of lobster meat on a roll. Domino's Pizza operates more than 3,500 restaurants in 60 international markets, where local managers have developed pizza flavors such as shrimp, squid, broccoli, fried garlic, and cheese (Japan), lamb and pickled ginger (India), tuna and sweet corn (England), crab, shrimp, onions, and peapods, (Taiwan), and reindeer sausage (Iceland) to cater to customers' preferences.

Although franchise outlets span the globe, Europe is the primary market for U.S. franchisors, with Pacific Rim countries and Canada following. Because they are the most populous nations on earth, China and India are becoming franchising "hot spots." These markets are most attractive to franchisors because they offer large middle-class populations, rising personal incomes, significant numbers of young consumers with purchasing power and a fascination with Western products, growing service economies, and spreading urbanization. Because the franchise industry is nascent in both China and India, the potential for growth is tremendous, and U.S. franchisors are taking note. Many franchisors are laying the groundwork to enter these markets, whose unique cultures pose challenges to foreign companies who do business there.

Growth potential is the primary attraction of international markets. Franchisors that decide to expand internationally should take these steps:

1. *Identify the country or countries that are best suited to the franchisor's business concept.* Factors to consider include a country's business climate, demographic profile, level of economic development, rate of economic growth, degree of legal protection, language and cultural barriers, and market potential. Franchisors making their first forays into global markets should consider focusing on a single nation where cultural barriers are minimal (such as Canada) or a small group of similar nations.

2. *Generate leads for potential franchisees.* Franchisors looking for prospective franchisees in foreign markets have many tools available to them, including international franchise trade shows, their own Web sites, trade missions, and brokers. Many franchisors have had success with trade missions, such as those sponsored by trade groups such as the International Franchise Association, the U.S. Department of Commerce's Gold Key Program, or various state programs. These trade missions are designed to introduce franchisors to qualified franchise candidates in target countries. Some franchisors rely on brokers who have extensive business contacts in specific countries.

3. *Select quality candidates.* Just as in any franchise relationship, the real key to success is choosing the right franchisee. Because of the complexity and cost of international franchising, selecting quality franchisees is essential to success.

4. *Structure the franchise deal.* Franchisors can structure international franchise arrangements in a variety of ways, but three techniques are most popular: direct franchising, area development, and master franchising.

- **Direct franchising**, which is common in domestic franchise deals, involves selling single-unit franchises to individual operators in foreign countries. Although dealing with individual franchisees makes it easier for the franchisor to maintain control, it also requires more of the franchisor's time and resources.

- **Area development** is similar to direct franchising except that the franchisor allows the franchisee to develop multiple units in a particular territory, perhaps a province, a county, or even an entire nation. A successful area development strategy depends on a franchisor selecting and then supporting quality franchisees.

- **Master franchising** is the most popular strategy for companies entering international markets. In a master franchising deal, a franchisor sells to a franchisee the right to develop subfranchises within a broad geographic area or, sometimes, an entire foreign country. In short, master franchising turbo charges a franchisor's growth. Many franchisors use this method to open outlets in international markets more quickly and efficiently because their master franchisees understand local laws and the nuances of selling in local markets. Although master franchising simplifies a franchisor's expansion into global markets, it gives franchisors the least amount of control over their international franchisees.

Countertrading and Bartering

As business becomes increasingly global, companies are discovering that attracting customers is just one part of the battle. Another problem global businesses face when selling to some countries is that their currencies are virtually worthless outside their borders, so getting paid in a valuable currency is a real challenge! Companies wanting to reach these markets must countertrade or barter. A **countertrade** is a transaction in which a company selling goods and services in a foreign country agrees to help promote investment and trade in that country. The goal of the transaction is to help offset the capital drain from the foreign country's purchases. As entrepreneurs enter more developing nations, they will discover the need to develop skill at implementing this global trading strategy.

Countertrading does suffer from numerous drawbacks. Countertrade transactions can be complicated, cumbersome, and time consuming. They also increase the chances that a company will get stuck with useless merchandise that it cannot move. They can lead to unpleasant surprises concerning the quantity and quality of products required in the countertrade. Still, countertrading offers one major advantage: Sometimes it's the only way to make a sale!

Entrepreneurs must weigh the advantages against the disadvantages for their companies before committing to a countertrade deal. Because of its complexity and the risks involved, countertrading is not the best choice for a novice entrepreneur looking to break into the global marketplace.

Bartering, the exchange of goods and services for other goods and services, is another way of trading with countries lacking convertible currency. In a barter exchange, a company that manufactures electronics components might trade its products for the coffee that a business in a foreign country processes, which it then sells to a third company for cash. Barter transactions require finding a business with complementary needs, but they are much simpler than countertrade transactions.

ENTREPRENEURIAL
Profile

Howard Dahl: Amity Technology

Howard Dahl, owner of Amity Technology, a North Dakota–based manufacturer of farm equipment, was part of the first wave of entrepreneurs to enter Russia after the communist regime in the former Soviet Union collapsed. Conducting business in those early years was challenging, and Dahl's company often relied on bartering. "[The Russians] would trade rapeseed, which you could use to make vegetable oil, for our machinery," he says. "We would then sell the seeds to a German agribusiness in a back-to-back transaction." Dahl is glad that he didn't give up the Russian export market; today, exports to Russia account for 40 percent of Amity Technology's total sales.[29]

3. Explain how to build a
successful export program.

Exporting

For years, small businesses in the United States could afford the luxury of conducting business at home in the world's largest market, never having to venture outside its borders. However, a growing number of small companies, realizing the incredible profit potential that exporting offers, are making globalization an ever-expanding part of their marketing plans. Approximately 95 percent of the world's population lives outside the United States, and more than 75 percent of the world's purchasing power lies outside the borders of the United States. Companies that export can tap into that purchasing power.[30] A recent study by CompTIA reports that small and medium-size companies that export generate, on average, 12 percent of their revenues from exports.[31]

Large companies continue to dominate export sales, however. Less than 1 percent of the nearly 30 million businesses in the United States export their goods and services.[32] Although small companies with fewer than 100 employees account for 90.7 percent of the 266,500 U.S. businesses that export goods and services, they generate only 21.0 percent of the nation's export sales.[33] Their impact is significant, however; small companies generate $1.1 billion each day in export sales.

Experts estimate that at least twice as many small companies are capable of exporting but are not doing so.[34] One of the biggest barriers facing companies that have never exported is not knowing where or how to start (see Figure 3). Paul Hsu, whose company sells ginseng across the globe, explains, "Exporting starts with a global mind-set, which unfortunately, is not all that common among owners of small- and medium-sized businesses in the United States. Most entrepreneurs in the United States envision markets only within domestic and sometimes even state borders, while foreign entrepreneurs look at export markets first."[35]

Breaking the psychological barrier to exporting is the first—and most difficult—step in setting up a successful program. The U.S. Chamber of Commerce's Trade Roots initiative, an international trade leadership program that networks more than 3,000 local U.S. chambers of commerce, is a useful resource for entrepreneurs looking to launch into global business. The program provides information on the benefits and methods for its members' who want to engage in international trade but aren't sure where to start. The U.S. Commercial Service's *Export Programs Guide* provides entrepreneurs with a comprehensive list of federal programs designed to help U.S. exporters. Another valuable source of information are the U.S. Export Assistance Centers (*www.sba.gov/oit/export/useac.html*), which serve as single contact points for information on the multitude of federal export programs that are designed to help entrepreneurs who want to start exporting. Entrepreneurs who want to learn more about exporting should investigate *A Basic Guide to Exporting* (*www.unzco.com/basicguide/*), which is published by the Department of Commerce and Unz and Company. The U.S. government export portal, *www.export.gov*, gives entrepreneurs access to valuable information about exporting in general (finance, shipping, documentation, and others), as well as details on individual nations (market research, trade

FIGURE 3
Small Business Exporting Survey, 2010

Source: NSBA/SBEA Small Business Exporting Survey, 2010.

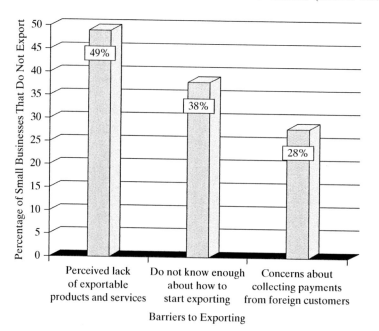

Barriers to Exporting

agreements, statistics, and more). Learning more about exporting and realizing that it is within the realm of possibility for small companies—even *very* small companies—is the first, and often most difficult, step in breaking the psychological barrier to exporting.

The next challenge is to create a sound export strategy. In fact, a study of 346 small exporting companies by Pierre-André Julien and Charles Ramangahahy found that small companies with well-defined export strategies outperformed those that merely dabbled in exporting.[36] What steps must entrepreneurs take to build a successful export strategy?

1. *Recognize that even the tiniest companies and least experienced entrepreneurs have the potential to export; help is available.* Size and experience are not prerequisites for a successful export program.

In 1985, when John and Nancy Kleppe launched J&N Enterprises, a company that sells the Gas Trac, a portable combustible gas detector, in the spare bedroom of their home in Union, Indiana, they had no intention of operating their tiny business globally. J&N Enterprises grew over time, and in 2003, the company moved into a new high-tech 14,000-square-foot building in nearby Valparaiso. With the help of state agencies, president Scott Kleppe, the couple's son, attended a trade show in China, which led to orders that increased the company's sales by 22 percent. Today, J&N Enterprises exports its expanded product line to 16 countries, including Australia, Korea, Mexico, and Turkey and recently was named the Indiana Exporter of the Year by the U.S. Small Business Administration.[37]

2. *Analyze your product or service.* Is it special? New? Unique? High quality? Priced favorably due to lower costs or exchange rates? Does it appeal to a particular niche? In which countries would there be sufficient demand for it? In many foreign countries, products from the United States are in demand because they have an air of mystery about them! Exporters quickly learn the value foreign customers place on quality. Ron Schutte, president of Creative Bakers of Brooklyn, a company that makes presliced cheesecakes for restaurants, saw an opportunity to sell in Japan. The only modification Schutte made to his high-quality cheesecakes was reducing the portion size from 4.5 ounces to 2.25 ounces to accommodate Japanese diners' smaller appetites.[38]

3. *Analyze your commitment.* Are you willing to devote the time and the energy to develop export markets? Does your company have the necessary resources to capitalize on market opportunities? In any international venture, patience is essential. One expert estimates that penetrating a foreign market requires at least 3 years.[39] Laying the groundwork for an export operation can take from 6 to 8 months (or longer), but entering foreign markets isn't as tough as most entrepreneurs think. "One of the biggest misconceptions people have is that they can't market overseas unless they have a big team of lawyers and specialists," says one export specialist. "That just isn't true."[40] Table 3 summarizes key issues managers must address in the export decision.

4. *Research markets and pick your target.* The average small or medium-size business exports to eight countries (see Figure 4).[41] Before investing in a costly sales trip abroad, however, entrepreneurs should make a trip to the local library or visit the Web sites of the Department of Commerce and the International Trade Administration. Exporters can choose from a multitude of guides, manuals, books, statistical reports, newsletters, videos, and other resources to help them research potential markets. Armed with research, small business owners can avoid wasting time and money on markets with limited potential for their products and can concentrate on those with the greatest promise. According to the Economist Intelligence Unit, the fastest growing economies outside the United States between 2006 and 2020 will be China, India, Brazil, and Russia. Asian economies in particular will be attractive markets for small exporters, increasing their share of global GDP from 35 percent today to 43 percent in 2020.[42] India alone has a rapidly expanding middle class the size of the entire U.S. population that is becoming increasingly well-educated, making it an attractive export target.[43]

Research also shows export entrepreneurs whether they need to modify their existing products and services to suit the tastes and preferences of their foreign target customers. Sometimes foreign customers' lifestyles, housing needs, body sizes, traditions, and cultures require exporters to make alterations to their product lines. When Peter Cole, CEO of Gamblin Artists Colors, the

TABLE 3 **Management Issues in the Export Decision**

I. Experience

1. With what countries has your company already conducted business (or from what countries have you received inquiries about your product or service)?
2. What product lines do foreign customers ask about most often? Prepare a list of sales inquiries for buyer by product and by country.
3. Is the trend of inquiries or sales increasing or decreasing?
4. Who are your primary domestic and foreign competitors?
5. What lessons has your company learned from past export experience?

II. Management and Personnel

1. Who will be responsible for the export entity's organization and staff? (Do you have an export "champion"?)
2. How much top management time
   a. Should you allocate to exporting?
   b. Can you afford to allocate to exporting?
3. What does management expect from its exporting efforts? What are your company's export goals and objectives?
4. What organizational structure will your company require to ensure that it can service export sales properly? (Note the political implications, if any.)
5. Who will implement the plan?

III. Production Capacity

1. To what extent is your company using its existing production capacity? Is there any excess? If so, how much?
2. Will filling export orders hurt your company's ability to make and service domestic sales?
3. What will additional production for export markets cost your company?
4. Are there seasonal or cyclical fluctuations in your company's workload? When? Why?
5. Is there a minimum quantity foreign customers must order for a sale to be profitable?
6. To what extent would your company need to modify its products, packaging, and design specifically for its export targets? Is your product quality adequate for foreign customers?
7. What pricing structure will your company use? Will the prices be competitive?
8. How will your company collect payment on its export sales?

IV. Financial Capacity

1. How much capital will your company need to begin exporting? Where will it come from?
2. How will you allocate the initial costs of your company's export effort?
3. Does your company have other expansion plans that would compete with an exporting effort?
4. By what date do you expect your company's export program to pay for itself?
5. How important is establishing a global presence to your company's future success?

Source: Adapted from *A Basic Guide to Exporting* (Washington, DC: U.S. Department of Commerce, 1986), p. 3.

FIGURE 4
Number of Countries to Which Small Businesses Export

Source: Elizabeth Clark, *Small and Medium-Sized Exporting Companies: A Statistical Handbook*, International Trade Administration, Office of Trade and Industry Information (Washington, DC: 2005), p. 19.

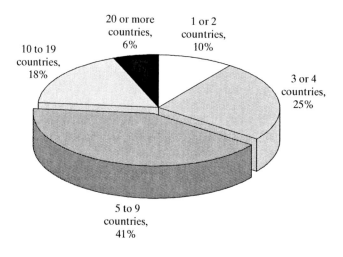

20 or more countries, 6%

1 or 2 countries, 10%

10 to 19 countries, 18%

3 or 4 countries, 25%

5 to 9 countries, 41%

TABLE 4 Questions to Guide International Market Research

- Is there an overseas market for your company's products or services?
- Are there specific target markets that look most promising?
- Which new markets abroad are most likely to open up or expand?
- How big is the market your company is targeting, and how fast is it growing?
- What are the major economic, political, legal, social, technological, and other environmental factors affecting this market?
- What are the demographic and cultural factors affecting this market: e.g., disposable income, occupation, age, gender, opinions, activities, interests, tastes, and values?
- Who are your company's present and potential customers abroad?
- What are their needs and desires? What factors influence their buying decisions: price, credit terms, delivery terms, quality, brand name, etc.?
- How would they use your company's product or service? What modifications, if any, would be necessary to sell to your target customers?
- Who are your primary competitors in the foreign market?
- How do competitors distribute, sell, and promote their products? What are their prices?
- What are the best channels of distribution for your product?
- What is the best way for your company to gain exposure in this market?
- Are there any barriers such as tariffs, quotas, duties, or regulations to selling your product in this market? Are there any incentives?
- Are there any potential licensing or joint venture partners already in this market?

Source: Adapted from *A Basic Guide to Exporting* (Washington, DC: Department of Commerce, 1986), p. 11.

company that makes handcrafted oil paints, varnishes, and other artists' supplies, began exporting to Australia, he quickly realized the importance of modifying the size of the products. "In Australia, they want larger sizes of paints—sizes we had not contemplated for the U.S. market," says Cole. "People tend to paint bigger and thicker."[44]

Japan is the second largest international market for coffee retailer Starbucks. Since entering Japan in 1996, Starbucks has customized its menu to appeal to local customers' tastes. For instance, menu additions include a Sakura Steamer (steamed milk infused with a flavored syrup), a Roasted Green Tea Latte, and a Sakura steamed bun filled with red bean paste.[45] Making modifications such as these often spells the difference between success and failure in the global market. In other cases, products destined for export need little or no modification. Experts estimate that one-half of exported products require little modification; one-third require moderate modification; only a few require major changes. Table 4 offers questions to guide entrepreneurs as they conduct export research.

5. Develop a distribution strategy. Should you use an export intermediary or sell directly to foreign customers? As you learned earlier in this chapter, many small companies just entering international markets prefer to rely on trade intermediaries or a joint venture partner to break new ground. Using intermediaries or joint ventures often makes sense until an entrepreneur has the chance to gain experience in exporting and to learn the ground rules of selling in foreign lands. Figure 5 illustrates the various distribution strategies that micro-size companies (those with less than $1 million in annual sales) and small companies (those with annual sales between $1 million and $20 million) use to export their products and services.

6. Find your customer. Small businesses can rely on a host of export specialists to help them track down foreign customers. (Refer to Table 2 for a list of some of the resources available from the government.) The U.S. Department of Commerce and the International Trade Administration should be the first stops on an entrepreneur's agenda for going global. These agencies have market research available through the U.S. Commercial Service Web site (*www.buyusa.gov*) that can help entrepreneurs locate the best target markets for its products or services and specific customers within those markets. Industry Sector Analysis (ISA), International Market Insights (IMIs), and Customized Market Analysis (CMA) are just some of the reports and services that global entrepreneurs find most useful. These agencies also have knowledgeable staff specialists experienced in the details of global trade and in the intricacies of foreign cultures. Through the Platinum Key Service, Commercial Service agents consult with companies as they build their global strategies, evaluate markets, and decide how to reach foreign markets.

One of the most efficient and least expensive ways for entrepreneurs to locate potential customers for their companies' products and services is to participate in a trade mission. These

FIGURE 5

Export Distribution Strategies

Source: Small and Medium-Size Business Export Insights and Opportunities, CompTIA, 2010, p. 8.

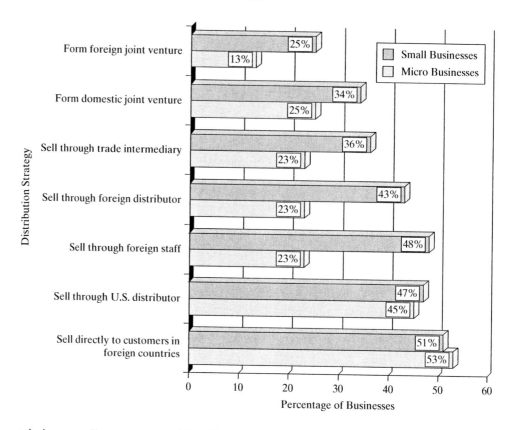

missions usually are sponsored by either a federal or a state economic development agency or an industry trade association for the purpose of cultivating international trade by connecting domestic companies with potential trading partners overseas. A trade mission may focus on a particular industry or may cover several industries but target a particular country. "We set up meetings for them with distributors, suppliers, manufacturers, customers, accountants, law firms, the whole gamut, to be able to provide them with the necessary resources to get into that market," says Christian Bartley, president of the World Trade Center Wisconsin, an organization that regularly sponsors trade missions to foreign countries for Wisconsin entrepreneurs who are interested in exploring export markets.[46] Fourteen small companies participated in a recent trade mission to China sponsored by Automation Alley, an organization that specializes in trade missions for high-tech companies. The trip resulted in 15 sales contracts from Chinese companies and added nearly $18.5 million in export sales to the participating companies' revenue streams. "As a direct result of the China Trade Mission, we signed up four highly qualified distributors," says Lee King, a top manager at Numatics Inc., one of the trade mission participants. "We have generated $500,000 in sales and, as a result of exporting, we have hired 15 more employees."[47]

7. *Find financing.* One of the biggest barriers to small business exports is lack of financing. The trouble is that bankers and other sources of capital don't always understand the intricacies of international sales and view financing them as highly risky ventures. In addition, among major industrialized nations, the U.S. government spends the least per capita to promote exports.

ENTREPRENEURIAL Profile

Cindy Lowry: Blossom Bucket

Cindy Lowry started Blossom Bucket as a part-time business, making simple crafts for decorating homes and selling them at trade shows. Before long, sales accelerated, and Lowry became a full-time entrepreneur. At one trade show, Lowry landed $200,000 in orders, many of them from foreign customers, for a new line of holiday ornaments that one of her friends had designed. "I went to three banks for financing," she says, "and none of them would lend me any money. [They said] that orders are not money. You can cancel an order." Lowry turned to the only source of capital she could find: credit cards. "I got as many credit cards as I could and filled those orders," she says. "Now we are off and running."[48]

Access to adequate financing is a crucial ingredient in a successful export program because the cost of generating foreign sales often is higher and collection cycles are longer. Several federal, state, and private programs are operating to fill this export financing void, however. Loan programs from the Small Business Administration include its Export Working Capital program (90 percent loan guarantees up to $1,500,000), Export Express (a streamlined approach to obtaining SBA-guaranteed financing up to $250,000), and International Trade Loan program (75 percent loan guarantees up to $1,500,000). In addition, the Export-Import Bank (*www.exim.gov*), the Overseas Private Investment Corporation, and a variety of state-sponsored programs offer export-minded entrepreneurs both direct loans and loan guarantees. (Recall that the *Export Programs Guide* provides a list of the 20 government agencies that help companies to develop their export potential.) The Export-Import Bank, which has been financing the sale of U.S. exports for more than 70 years, provides small exporters with export credit insurance and loans through its working capital line of credit and a variety of pre-export loan programs. The Bankers Association for Foreign Trade (*www.baft.org/jsps/*) is an association of 150 banks around the world that matches exporters needing foreign trade financing with interested banks.

ENTREPRENEURIAL
Profile

Craig Matheson:
Web Press

Web Press, a maker of newspaper-printing equipment founded in 1968 and based in Kent, Washington, had generated orders from customers in Europe, Mexico, and Nigeria but needed financing because of the longer collection periods involved in export sales. When the company's bank balked at extending credit on export sales, CEO Craig Matheson worked with the Export Finance Assistance Center of Washington to secure a line of credit from another bank that carried a guarantee from the SBA's Export Working Capital Program. Web Press has since closed export deals with customers in Vietnam, Costa Rica, and Canada.[49]

8. *Ship your goods.* Export novices usually rely on international freight forwarders and custom-house agents—experienced specialists in overseas shipping—for help in navigating the bureaucratic morass of packaging requirements and paperwork demanded by customs. These specialists, also known as *transport architects,* are to exporters what travel agents are to passengers and normally charge relatively small fees for a valuable service. They move shipments of all sizes to destinations all over the world efficiently, saving entrepreneurs many headaches. Good freight forwarders understand U.S. export regulations, foreign import requirements, shipping procedures (such as packing, labeling, documenting, and insuring goods), customs processes, and maintaining proper records for paying tariffs. In addition, because they work for several companies, freight forwarders can aggregate payloads to negotiate favorable rates with shippers. "[A freight forwarder] is going to be sure that his client conforms with all the government regulations that apply to export cargo," explains the owner of an international freight forwarding business. "He acts as an agent of the exporter, and, in most circumstances, is like an extension of that exporter's traffic department." The Johnston Sweeper Company, a manufacturer of street sweepers, ships its 20,000-pound pieces of equipment worldwide with the help of an international freight forwarder.[50]

Exporters can find an online directory of more than 400 freight forwarders located in 120 countries at Freightbook (*www.freightbook.net*). Another useful resource is the National Customs Brokers and Forwarders Association of America (*www.ncbfaa.org*), which represents more than 800 freight forwarders and customs brokers. Table 5 features common international shipping terms and their meaning.

9. *Collect your money.* Collecting foreign accounts can be more complex than collecting domestic ones; however, by picking their customers carefully and checking their credit references closely, entrepreneurs can minimize bad-debt losses. Businesses engaging in international sales can use four primary payment methods (ranked from least risk to most risky): cash in advance, a letter of credit, a bank (or documentary) draft, and an open account. The safest method of selling to foreign customers is to collect cash in advance of the sale. This is the safest option for the seller because it eliminates the risk of collection problems and provides immediate cash flow. However, requiring cash payments up front may severely limit a small company's base of foreign customers.

One tool that small exporters can use to minimize the risk of bad-debt losses on foreign sales is export credit insurance, which protects a company against the nonpayment of its open accounts due to commercial and political problems. The cost of export credit insurance usually is a very

TABLE 5 **Common International Shipping Terms and Their Meaning**

Shipping Term	Seller's Responsibility	Buyer's Responsibility	Shipping Method(s) Used
FOB ("Free on Board") Seller	Deliver goods to carrier and provide export license and clean onboard receipt. Bear risk of loss until goods are delivered to carrier.	Pay shipping, freight, and insurance charges. Bear risk of loss while goods are in transit.	All
FOB ("Free on Board") Buyer	Deliver goods to the buyer's place of business and provide export license and clean onboard receipt. Pay shipping, freight, and insurance charges.	Accept delivery of goods after documents are tendered.	All
FAS ("Free Along Side") Vessel	Deliver goods alongside ship. Provides an "alongside" receipt.	Provide export license and proof of delivery of the goods to the carrier. Bear risk of loss once goods are delivered to the carrier.	Ship
CFR ("Cost and Freight")	Deliver goods to carrier, obtain export licenses, and pay export taxes. Provide buyer with clean bill of lading. Pay freight and shipping charges. Bear risk of loss until goods are delivered to buyer.	Pay insurance charges. Accept delivery of goods after documents are tendered.	Ship
CIF ("Cost, Insurance, and Freight")	Same as CFR plus pay insurance charges and provide buyer with insurance policy.	Accept delivery of goods after documents are tendered.	Ship
CPT ("Carriage Paid to . . .")	Deliver goods to carrier, obtain export licenses, and pay export taxes. Provide buyer with clean transportation documents. Pay shipping and freight charges.	Pay insurance charges. Accept delivery of goods after documents are tendered.	All
CIP ("Carriage and Insurance Paid to . . .")	Same as CPT plus pay insurance charges and provide buyer with insurance policy.	Accept delivery of goods after documents are tendered.	All
DDU ("Delivered Duty Unpaid")	Obtain export license, pay insurance charges, and provide buyer documents for taking delivery.	Take delivery of goods and pay import duties.	All
DDP ("Delivered Duty Paid")	Obtain export license and pay import duty, pay insurance charges, and provide buyer documents for taking delivery.	Take delivery of goods.	All

Source: Adapted from *Guide to the Finance of International Trade*, edited by Gordon Platt (HBSC Trade Services, Marine Midland Bank, and the Journal of Commerce), *http://infoserv2.ita.doc.gov/efm/efm.nsf/503d177e3c63f0b48525675900112e24/6218a8703573b32985256759004c41f3/$FILE/Finance_.pdf*, pp. 6–10. Reprinted with permission by the Journal of Commerce.

small percentage of the sale that the company is insuring. Private insurers and the Export-Import Bank offer export credit insurance. The Export-Import Bank provides nearly $3 billion in export credit insurance annually to small businesses. Applied Fabric Technologies (AFT), a company based in Orchard Park, New York, that specializes in products to contain oil spills, regularly uses export credit insurance to lower the risk associated with its foreign sales. A customer in Liberia placed an order with AFT and insisted on "net 30" credit terms from the receipt of the merchandise, risky terms on an international sale, especially for a small company. Rather than pass up the sale, AFT purchased an export credit insurance policy through the Export-Import Bank. The company has since used a similar strategy on sales to customers in Taiwan, South Africa, Australia, and Egypt.[51]

Financing foreign sales often involves special credit arrangements such as letters of credit and bank (or documentary) drafts. A **letter of credit** is an agreement between an exporter's bank and the foreign buyer's bank that guarantees payment to the exporter for a specific shipment of goods. In essence, a letter of credit reduces the financial risk for the exporter by substituting a bank's creditworthiness for that of the purchaser (see Figure 6). A **bank draft** is a document the seller draws on the buyer, requiring the buyer to pay the face amount (the purchase price of

FIGURE 6
A Letter of Credit

Seller   Buyer

Foreign buyer agrees to buy products; seller agrees to ship goods if buyer arranges a letter of credit.

Seller ships goods to buyer according to letter of credit's terms and submits shipping documents to bank issuing letter of credit.

Seller's bank   Buyer's bank

Letter of credit

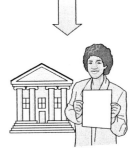

Buyer requests that his bank grant a letter of credit, which assures exporter payment if she presents documents proving goods were actually shipped. Bank makes out letter of credit to seller and sends it to seller's bank (called the confirming bank).

Buyer's bank makes payment to seller's (confirming) bank. Confirming bank then pays seller amount specified in letter of credit.

the goods) either on sight (a sight draft) or on a specified date (a time draft) once the goods are shipped. Rather than use letters of credit or drafts, some exporters simply sell to foreign customers on open account. In other words, they ship the goods to a foreign customer without any guarantee of payment. This method is the riskiest because collecting a delinquent account from a foreign customer is even more difficult than collecting past-due payments from a domestic customer. The parties to an international deal should always come to an agreement in advance on an acceptable method of payment.

Establishing International Locations

Once established in international markets, some small businesses set up permanent locations there. Establishing an office or a factory in a foreign land can require a substantial investment that reaches beyond the budgets of many small companies. In addition, setting up an international office can be an incredibly frustrating experience. In some countries, business infrastructures are in disrepair or are nonexistent. Getting a telephone line installed can take months in some places, and finding reliable equipment to move goods to customers is nearly impossible. Securing necessary licenses and permits from bureaucrats often takes more than filing the necessary paperwork; in some nations, bureaucrats expect payments to "grease the wheels of justice." In fact, the Foreign Corrupt Practice Act, passed in 1977, considers bribing foreign officials to be a criminal act. One study by the World Bank of "grease payments" for the purpose of minimizing the red tape imposed by foreign regulations concludes that the payments do not work; in fact, companies that actually used them experienced greater government scrutiny and red tape in their international transactions.[52] In another study, risk management company Simmons & Simmons reports that 35.4 percent of companies said that they had refused to make investments in certain countries because of the nation's reputation for corruption.[53] Finally, finding the right person to manage an international office is crucial to success; it also is a major challenge, especially for small businesses. Small companies usually have lean management staffs and cannot afford to send key people abroad without running the risk of losing their focus.

Small companies that establish international locations can reap significant benefits. Start-up costs are lower in some foreign countries (but not all!), and lower labor costs can produce significant savings as well. In addition, by locating in a country a business learns firsthand how its culture influences business and how it can satisfy customers' demands most effectively. In essence, the business becomes a local corporate citizen.

Importing and Outsourcing

In addition to selling their goods in foreign markets, small companies also buy goods from distributors and manufacturers in foreign markets. In fact, the intensity of price competition in many industries—from textiles and handbags to industrial machinery and computers—means that more companies now shop the world market, looking for the lowest prices they can find. Because labor costs in countries such as China and India are far below those in other nations, businesses there offer goods and services at very low prices. Increasingly, these nations are home to well-educated, skilled workers that are paid far less than comparable workers in the United States or Western Europe. For instance, a computer programmer in the United States might earn $100,000 a year, but in India a computer programmer doing the same work earns $25,000 a year or less. As a result, many companies either import goods or outsource work directly to manufacturers in countries where costs are far lower than they would be domestically. According to TPI, a leading outsourcing consulting firm, global outsourcing is a $424 billion per year industry (up from $232 billion in 2000).[54]

Valerie Johnson, founder of Big Feet Pajamas.

Source: John Gurzinski/The New York Times/ Redux

ENTREPRENEURIAL Profile

Valerie Johnson: Big Feet Pajama Company

Valerie Johnson left a corporate career to pursue her entrepreneurial dream and launched the Big Feet Pajama Company in 2005 in the basement of her Las Vegas, Nevada, home. Her company, which makes more than 50 styles of footed pajamas for men, women, and children and generates annual sales of more than $1 million, includes among its customers celebrities such as Taylor Swift and Niecy Nash. One of Johnson's first challenges was to locate a company to manufacture her pajama designs. She turned to Alibaba.com, a Web site that connects importers, exporters, and suppliers from more than 240 countries, to screen potential suppliers. Johnson narrowed her choices to three factories before boarding a plane to make onsite visits. The factory she chose "was not the least expensive," she says, "but I was confident in the quality and efficiency of its operation and how it treated employees."[55]

Entrepreneurs who are considering importing goods and service or outsourcing their service or manufacturing jobs to foreign countries should follow these steps:

- *Make sure that importing or outsourcing is right for your business.* Even though foreign manufacturers often can provide items at significant cost savings, using them may not always be the best business decision. Entrepreneurs sometimes discover that achieving the lowest price may require a trade-off of other important factors, such as quality and speed of delivery. When Patrick Kruse, owner of Ruff Wear, a business that sells dog booties, began outsourcing many of his company's products to Chinese factories, he discovered that the quality of the goods was poor. "We actually had to refuse some shipments, which really hurt our business," he says.[56] In addition, some foreign manufacturers require sizeable minimum orders, perhaps $200,000 or more, before they will produce a product.
- *Establish a target cost for your product.* Before setting off on a global shopping spree, entrepreneurs first should determine exactly what they can afford to spend on manufacturing a product and make a profit on it. Given the low labor costs of many foreign manufacturers, products that are the most labor intensive make good candidates for outsourcing.
- *Do your research before you leave home.* Investing time in basic research about the industry and potential suppliers in foreign lands is essential before setting foot on foreign soil. Useful resources are plentiful, and entrepreneurs should use them. Refer to Table 2 for a

list of some of the most popular sources of information on foreign countries and the companies that are based there.

- *Be sensitive to cultural differences.* When making contacts, setting up business appointments, or calling on prospective manufacturers in foreign lands, make sure you understand what is acceptable business behavior and what is not. Once again, this is where your research pays off; be sure to study the cultural nuances of doing business in the countries you will visit.

- *Do your groundwork.* Once you locate potential manufacturers, contact them to set up appointments, and go visit them. Preliminary research is essential to finding reliable sources of supply, but "face time" with representatives from various companies allows entrepreneurs to judge the intangible factors that can make or break a relationship. After months of online research, Cathy Raff, founder of My Stone Company, a business that markets religious jewelry and The Friendship Stone, flew to South Africa to evaluate several mines that were potential suppliers of the stones her company used. "I needed to go meet the people I would be working with," says Raff, who also flew to China to select the factory that produces the embroidered suede pouches that hold her company's products. "Outsourcing is the best way to go because you can get really high quality work from these countries at much lower rates," she says.[57]

- *Protect your company's intellectual property.* A common problem that many entrepreneurs have encountered with outsourcing is "knockoffs." Some foreign manufacturers see nothing wrong with agreeing to manufacture a product for a company and then selling their own "knockoff" version of it. Securing a nondisclosure agreement and a contract that prohibits such behavior helps, but experts say that securing a patent for the item in the source country itself (not just the United States) is a good idea.

- *Select a manufacturer.* Using quality, speed of delivery, level of trust, degree of legal protection, costs, and other factors as criteria, select the manufacturer that can do the best job for your company. Be aware that delivery times may be longer—sometimes much longer—for outsourced goods. Items that domestic suppliers can supply within a week or two may take months to arrive from some foreign countries.

- *Provide an exact model of the product you want manufactured.* Providing a manufacturer with an actual model of the item to be manufactured will save lots of time, mistakes, and problems. One entrepreneur learned this lesson the hard way when he submitted a rough prototype of a product to a Chinese factory with which he had contracted for production. When the first shipment of the products arrived, he was shocked to see that they were exact duplicates—including imperfections and flaws—of the prototype that he had submitted!

- *Stay in constant contact with the manufacturer and try to build a long-term relationship.* Communication is a key to building and maintaining a successful relationship with a foreign manufacturer. Weekly teleconferences, e-mails, and periodic visits are essential to making sure that your company gets the performance you expect from a foreign manufacturer.

Going global by employing one or more of these nine strategies can put tremendous strain on a small company, but the benefits of cracking international markets can be significant. Not only does going global offer attractive sales and profit possibilities, but it also strengthens the company's competitive skills and enhances its overall reputation. Pleasing tough foreign customers also keeps companies on their competitive toes.

Barriers to International Trade

4. Discuss the major barriers to international trade and their impact on the global economy.

Governments have always used a variety of barriers to block free trade among nations in an attempt to protect businesses within their own borders. The benefit of protecting their own companies, however, comes at the expense of foreign businesses, which face limited access to global markets. Ultimately, customers in nations that restrict free trade pay the price in the form of higher prices and smaller supplies of goods available. Numerous trade barriers—both domestic and international—restrict the freedom of businesses in global trading. Despite these barriers, international trade has grown to more than $14.2 trillion.[58]

Domestic Barriers

Sometimes the biggest barriers potential exporters face are right here at home. Three major domestic roadblocks are common: attitude, information, and financing. Perhaps the biggest barrier to small businesses exporting is the attitude that "I'm too small to export. That's just for big corporations." The first lesson of exporting is "Take nothing for granted about who can export and what you can and cannot export." The first step to building an export program is recognizing that the opportunity to export exists.

Another reason entrepreneurs neglect international markets is a lack of information about how to get started. The key to success in international markets is choosing the correct target market and designing the appropriate strategy to reach it. That requires access to information and research. Although a variety of government and private organizations make volumes of exporting and international marketing information available, many small business owners never use it. A successful global marketing strategy also recognizes that not all international markets are the same. Companies must be flexible and willing to make adjustments to their products and services, promotional campaigns, packaging, and sales techniques.

Another significant obstacle is the lack of export financing available. A common complaint among small exporters is that they lose export business simply because they cannot get the financing to support it. Financial institutions that serve small companies often do not have experience in conducting international business and simply deny loans for international transactions as being too risky.

International Barriers

Domestic barriers are not the only ones export-minded entrepreneurs must overcome. Trading nations also erect obstacles to free trade. Two types of international barriers are common: tariff and nontariff.

Source: (2009) Thaves. Reprinted by permission. Newspaper dist. by UF.

TARIFF BARRIERS. A **tariff** is a tax, or duty, that a government imposes on goods and services imported into that country. Imposing tariffs raises the price of the imported goods—making them less attractive to consumers—and protects the makers of comparable domestic products and services. Established in the United States in 1790 by Alexander Hamilton, the tariff system generated the majority of federal revenues for about 100 years. Today, the *Harmonized Tariff Schedule*, which sets tariffs for products imported into the United States, includes 37,000 categories of goods. The United States imposes tariffs on thousands of items, ranging from brooms and fish fillets to costume jewelry and fence posts. The average tariff on goods imported into the United States is just 1.3 percent, but the U.S. International Trade Commission estimates that eliminating tariffs would expand U.S. exports by $5.5 billion and increase imports by $13.1 billion.[59] After sales of tires exported to the United States from China tripled in just 4 years and several U.S. tire factories closed, the U.S. government imposed a 35 percent tariff on auto and light truck tires. The result was a significant decrease in the supply of low-end tires, those priced between $50 and $60 each, which caused prices to increase by 20 to 25 percent.[60]

Nations across the globe rely on tariffs to protect local manufacturers of certain products. For instance, Japan's tariffs average 5.4 percent, and those in China average 10 percent. If a small company's products are subject to those tariffs, exporting to that nation becomes much more difficult because remaining price competitive with products made by local manufacturers is virtually impossible.

NONTARIFF BARRIERS. Many nations have lowered the tariffs they impose on products and services brought into their borders, but they rely on other nontariff structures as protectionist trade barriers.

Quotas. Rather than impose a direct tariff on certain imported products, nations often use quotas to protect their industries. A **quota** is a limit on the amount of a product imported into a country. The United States imposes quotas on sugar imports from 40 countries, limiting the amount of sugar they can sell in the United States each year.[61] The result of these trade restrictions is that in the United States sugar sells for 56 cents per pound, but the international market price is just 23 cents per pound, 59 percent lower. Other countries impose quotas on everything from shoes to movies in an attempt to protect domestic industries. For instance, China allows only 20 foreign films to be released each year. In addition, foreigners can invest in Chinese cinemas, but they can own no more than 49 percent of the joint venture.[62]

Embargoes. An **embargo** is a total ban on imports of certain products or all products from a particular nation. The motivation for embargoes is not always economic but can involve political differences, environmental disputes, terrorism, and other issues. For instance, the United States imposes embargoes on products from nations it considers to be adversarial, including Cuba, Iran, Iraq, and North Korea, among others. An embargo on trade with Cuba, begun in 1962, still exists today. In other cases, embargoes originate from cultural differences or health reasons. Many countries, including the United States, imposed embargoes on live birds from nations where avian influenza outbreaks occurred.

Dumping. In an effort to grab market share quickly, some companies have been guilty of **dumping** products, selling large quantities of them in foreign countries below cost. The United States has been a dumping target for steel, televisions, shoes, and computer chips in the past. More than 60 nations now have antidumping laws. Under the U.S. Antidumping Act, a company must prove that the foreign company's prices are lower here than in the home country and that U.S. companies are directly harmed. In response to a complaint from U.S.-based companies, the U.S. International Trade Commission ruled that Chinese honey producers were dumping thousands of tons of honey illegally in the United States at unfairly low prices and, as a result, were damaging the ability of U.S. producers to compete. "It's been a struggle for many [beekeepers] to survive," says John Talbert, owner of Sabine Creek Honey Farm in Josephine, Texas. The ITC imposed tariffs of 200 percent and more on honey imported from China.[63]

Piracy. Another barrier to conducting business globally is the threat that counterfeit and pirated products pose to businesses and their customers. The OECD estimates that the proportion of counterfeit and pirated goods in world trade has increased from 1.85 percent in 2000 to 1.95 percent today. Counterfeit and pirated goods cost the U.S. economy $250 billion per year.[64] Pirates and counterfeiters ply their illegal, unethical trade to almost every kind of product, from designer handbags and smartphones to birth control pills and industrial equipment. Not only do counterfeit products erode the profitability of the companies that make the "genuine" articles, but they also can be dangerous or even deadly to consumers who purchase them.

Political Barriers

Entrepreneurs who go global quickly discover a labyrinth of political tangles. Although many American business owners complain of excessive government regulation in the United States, they are often astounded by the complex web of governmental and legal regulations and barriers they encounter in foreign countries.

Companies doing business in politically risky lands face the very real dangers of government takeovers of private property; attempts at coups to overthrow ruling parties; kidnappings, bombings, and other violent acts against businesses and their employees; and other threatening events. Companies' investments of millions of dollars may evaporate overnight in the wake of a government coup or the passage of a law nationalizing an industry (giving control of an entire industry to the government). In 2005, Jeff Ake, owner of Equipment Express, was kidnapped by militants in Iraq while installing bottling equipment that his La Porte, Indiana, company manufactured. His kidnappers called his wife to demand a ransom, and a video of Ake being held at gunpoint appeared on Arabic television network Al-Jazeera. His wife and four children still do not know what happened to Ake.[65]

Business Barriers

U.S. companies doing business internationally quickly learn that business practices and regulations in foreign lands can be quite different from those in the United States. Simply duplicating the practices they have adopted (and have used successfully) in the domestic market and using them in foreign markets is not always a good idea. Perhaps the biggest shock comes in the area of human resources management, where international managers discover that practices common in the United States, such as overtime, women workers, and employee benefits, are restricted, disfavored, or forbidden in other cultures. Business owners new to international business sometimes are shocked at the wide range of labor costs they encounter and the accompanying wide range of skilled labor available. In some countries, what appear to be "bargain" labor rates turn out to be excessively high after accounting for the quality of the labor force and the mandated benefits their governments impose—from company-sponsored housing, meals, and clothing to required profit sharing and extended vacations. For instance, in most European nations, workers are accustomed to 4 to 6 weeks of vacation compared to 2 weeks in the United States.

In 2003, Harry Tsao and Talmadge O'Neill launched Smarter.com, a comparison-shopping Web site, in Monrovia, California. The entrepreneurs thought that by hiring software engineers in China they could keep their operating costs low. They opened a branch in Shanghai to handle the back office of their e-commerce operation and hired 10 engineers at bargain salaries. Then Tsao and O'Neill discovered that companies operating in China must pay exorbitant payroll taxes, an unforeseen technicality that cost their fledgling company an unexpected $26,000. "I had no choice," recalls Tsao. "I had to take on those costs."[66]

In many nations, labor unions represent workers in almost every company, yet they play a very different role from the unions in the United States. Although management–union relations are not as hostile as in the United States and strikes are not as common, unions can greatly complicate a company's ability to compete effectively.

Cultural Barriers

The **culture** of a nation includes the beliefs, values, views, and mores that its inhabitants share. Differences in cultures among nations create another barrier to international trade. The diversity of languages, business philosophies, practices, and traditions make international trade more complex than selling to the business down the street. Entrepreneurs wanting to do business in international markets must have a clear understanding and appreciation of the cultures in which they plan to do business. Consider the following examples:

- A U.S. entrepreneur, eager to expand into the European Community, arrives at his company's potential business partner's headquarters in France. Confidently, he strides into the meeting room, enthusiastically pumps his host's hand, slaps him on the back, and says "Tony, I've heard a great deal about you; please, call me Bill." Eager to explain the benefits of his product, he opens his briefcase and gets right down to business. The French executive politely excuses himself and leaves the room before negotiations ever begin, shocked by the American's rudeness and ill manners. Rudeness and ill manners? Yes—from the French executive's perspective.

- Another American business owner flies to Tokyo to close a deal with a Japanese executive. He is pleased when his host invites him to play a round of golf shortly after he arrives. He plays well and manages to win by a few strokes. The Japanese executive invites him to play again the next day, and again he wins by a few strokes. Invited to play another round the following day, the American asks, "But when are we going to start doing business?" His host, surprised by the question, says, "But we *have* been doing business."

■ The CEO of a successful small company is in China negotiating with several customers on deals, any of which would be significant to the company. On the verge of closing one deal, the CEO sends in his place to the negotiation a young sales representative, thinking that the only thing that remained is to sign the contract. At the meeting, the manager of the Chinese company remarks, "Ah, you are about the same age as my son." Much to the U.S. entrepreneur's surprise, the deal falls through.[67]

When American businesspeople enter international markets for the first time, they often are amazed at the differences in foreign cultures' habits and customs. In the first scenario described, for instance, had the entrepreneur done his homework, he would have known that the French are very formal (back slapping is *definitely* taboo!) and do not typically use first names in business relationships (even among long-time colleagues). In the second scenario, a global manager would have known that the Japanese place a tremendous importance on developing personal relationships before committing to any business deals. Thus, he would have seen the golf games for what they really were: an integral part of building a business relationship. In the final scenario, the U.S. entrepreneur did not understand that status (*shehui dengji*) is extremely important to the Chinese. The Chinese executive would consider negotiating a deal with an executive whose rank in the organization did not at least equal his to be a great insult. That particular deal was doomed the minute the lower-level salesperson walked into the room.

Understanding and heeding these often subtle cultural differences is one of the most important keys to international business success. "There's more to business than just business," says one writer, "particularly when confronting the subtleties of deeply ingrained cultural customs, conventions, and protocols that abound in today's global marketplace."[68] Conducting a business meeting with a foreign executive in the same manner as one with an American businessperson could doom the deal from the outset. Business customs and behaviors that are acceptable—even expected—in this country may be taboo in others.

Entrepreneurs who fail to learn the differences in the habits and customs of the cultures in which they hope to do business are at a distinct disadvantage. When it comes to conducting international business, a lack of understanding of cultures and business practices can be as great a barrier to structuring and implementing a business transaction as an error in the basic assumptions of the deal. Consider, for instance, the American who was in the final stages of contract negotiations with an Indonesian company. Given the size of the contract and his distance from home, the American business executive was nervous. Sitting across from his Indonesian counterpart, the American propped his feet up. Obviously angered, the Indonesian business owner stormed out of the room, refused to sign the contract, and left the American executive totally bewildered. Only later did he discover that exposing the soles of one's shoes to an Indonesian is an insult. Profuse apologies and some delicate negotiations salvaged the deal.[69]

An American businesswoman in London was invited to a party hosted by an advertising agency. Unsure of her ability to navigate the streets and subways of London alone, she approached a British colleague who was driving to the party and asked him, "Could I get a ride with you?" After he turned bright red from embarrassment, he regained his composure and politely said, "Lucky for you I know what you meant." Unknowingly, the young woman had requested a sexual encounter with her colleague, not a lift to the party![70]

Inaccurate translations of documents into other languages often pose embarrassing problems for companies conducting international business.

ENTREPRENEURIAL
Profile
Interactive Magic

Interactive Magic, a North Carolina software company, had introduced several computer games in Germany that had been quite successful. Executives at the small company expected that their newest release, "Capitalism," would be the best selling game yet. After the game hit store shelves in Germany, however, managers discovered that the instructions told customers to use a nail file to get the game running on their computers. In the translation from English to German, the word *file* somehow lost its electronic meaning and became a beauty accessory![71]

Mistranslated ads have left foreign locals scratching their heads, wondering why a company's advertising message would say that. For example, when an ad for KFC that was supposed to say "Finger lickin' good" was translated into Chinese, it came out as "Eat your fingers off." An ad for the Parker Pen Company that was supposed to say "Avoid embarrassment" in Spanish actually said "Avoid pregnancy," leaving Parker Pen executives quite embarrassed themselves.[72]

The accompanying "Lessons from the Street-Smart Entrepreneur" feature shows the importance of learning about a nation's culture before conducting business there.

LESSONS FROM THE STREET-SMART ➤ entrepreneur

The Secret Language of International Business

When U.S. businesspeople enter international markets for the first time, they often are amazed at the differences in foreign cultures' habits and customs. Understanding and heeding these often subtle cultural differences is one of the most important keys to international business success. The maze of cultural variables from one country to another can be confusing, but with proper preparation and a little common sense any manager can handle international transactions successfully. In short, before you pack your bags, do your homework. In most cases, conducting international business successfully requires managers to have unlimited patience, a long-term commitment, and a thorough knowledge of the local market, business practices, and culture. The key for entrepreneurs is learning to be sensitive to the business cultures in which they operate. Consider these pointers from the Street-Smart Entrepreneur:

■ Patience is a must for doing business in Spain. Like the French, Spaniards want to get to know business associates before working with them. In the United States, business comes before pleasure, but in Spain business is conducted after dinner, when the drinks and cigars are served. "I've known American businessmen who have shocked their Spanish host by pulling out their portfolios and charts before dinner is even served," says one expert. In Spain, women should avoid crossing their legs; it is considered unladylike. Men usually cross their legs at the knees.

■ In India, entrepreneurs who rush in to close a deal quickly often find that the deal never materializes. As in Spain, businesspeople in India prefer to get to know prospective business partners before doing business with them. Indian culture also is far less focused on time than American business is. Entrepreneurs should not be surprised or angered if meetings, dinners, and other events do not start promptly at the appointed hour. Dress codes in India tend to be conservative. Entrepreneurs should avoid

using a person's first name until they are invited to do so; in some parts of India, doing so is considered rude. In restaurants, do not order beef. Although some Indians eat beef, many are vegetarian.

■ In Great Britain, businesspeople consider it extremely important to conduct business "properly" with formality and reserve. Boisterous behavior such as backslapping or overindulging in alcohol and ostentatious displays of wealth are considered ill-mannered. The British do not respond to hard-sell tactics but do appreciate well-mannered executives. Politeness and impeccable manners are useful tools for conducting business successfully in Great Britain.

■ In Mexico, making business appointments through a well-connected Mexican national will go a long way to assuring successful business deals. "People in Mexico do business with somebody they know, they like, or they're related to," says one expert. Because family and tradition are top priorities for Mexicans, entrepreneurs who discuss their family heritages and can talk knowledgeably about Mexican history are a step ahead. In business meetings, making extended eye contact is considered impolite.

■ In China, entrepreneurs will need an ample dose of the "three Ps": patience, patience, patience. Nothing in China—especially business—happens fast! In conversations and negotiations, periods of silence are common; they are a sign of politeness and contemplation. The Chinese view personal space much differently than Americans; in normal conversation, they will stand much closer to their partners. Before doing business with someone, especially foreigners, Chinese businesspeople look to build a personal relationship (renji hexie) that demonstrates trust and harmony. Doing so often involves invitations to sporting events, sight-seeing, long dinners that involve talking about everything but business, and home visits, all of which may take months. Be careful when selecting gifts for your Chinese hosts. Clocks, umbrellas, white flowers, and handkerchiefs are inappropriate gifts because of their association with separation and death. A traditional part of Chinese culture involves haggling over the terms of a deal, and Chinese negotiators are very good at it! Howard Schultz, CEO of Starbucks, the coffee retailer, says that China, where Starbucks has nearly 400 stores and plans for hundreds more, "is a complicated market that requires significant discipline and thoughtfulness."

- American entrepreneurs doing business in the Pacific Rim should avoid hard-sell techniques, which are an immediate turnoff to Asian businesspeople. Harmony, patience, and consensus make good business companions in this region. It is also a good idea to minimize the importance of legal documents in negotiations. Although getting deals and trade agreements down in writing always is advisable, attempting to negotiate detailed contracts (as most U.S. businesspeople tend to do) would insult most Asians, who base their deals on mutual trust and benefits.

- Japanese executives conduct business much like the British: with an emphasis on formality, thoughtfulness, and respect. Greeting a Japanese executive properly includes a bow and a handshake—showing respect for both cultures. In many traditional Japanese businesses, exchanging gifts at the first meeting is appropriate. Also, a love of golf (the Japanese are crazy about the game) and a willingness to participate in karaoke are real pluses for winning business in Japan. Don't expect to hear Japanese executives say "no," even during a negotiation; they don't want to offend or to appear confrontational. Instead of saying "no," a Japanese negotiator will say, "It is very difficult," "Let us think about that," or "Let us get back to you on that." Similarly, a "yes" from a Japanese executive doesn't necessarily mean that. It could mean, "I understand," "I hear you," or "I don't understand what you mean, but I don't want to embarrass you."

- In Japan and South Korea, exchanging business cards, known in Japan as *meishi*, is an important business function (unlike Great Britain, where exchanging business cards is less popular). A Western executive who accepts a Japanese companion's card and then slips it into his pocket or scribbles notes on it has committed a major blunder. Tradition there says that a business card must be treated just as its owner would be—with respect. Travelers should present their own cards using both hands with the card positioned so the recipient can read it. (The flip side should be printed in Japanese, an expected courtesy.)

1. What steps should an entrepreneur take to avoid committing cultural blunders when conducting global business?
2. Select a foreign country in which you are interested. Use the Internet to learn about other tips for conducting business there in a way that shows respect for the culture and its people. Prepare a one-page report on your findings.

Sources: Based on Mariko Sanchanta, "Starbucks Plans Big Expansion in China," *Wall Street Journal*, April 14, 2010, p. B10; John L. Graham and N. Mark Lam, "The Chinese Negotiation," *Harvard Business Review*, October 2003, pp. 82–91; Laura Fortunato, "Japan: Making It in the USA," *Region Focus*, Fall 1997, p. 15; David Stamps, "Welcome to America," *Training*, November 1996, p. 30; Barbara Pachter, "When in Japan, Don't Cross Your Legs," *Business Ethics*, March–April 1996, p. 50; Tom Dunkel, "A New Breed of People Gazers," *Insight*, January 13, 1992, pp. 10–14; M. Katherine Glover, "Do's and Taboos," *Business America*, August 13, 1990, pp. 2–6; Deidre Sullivan, "An American Businesswoman's Guide to Japan," *Overseas Business*, Winter 1990, pp. 50–55; Stephanie Barlow, "Let's Make a Deal," *Entrepreneur*, May 1991, p. 40; "Worldy Wise," *Entrepreneur*, March 1991, p. 40; David Altany, "Culture Clash," *IndustryWeek*, October 2, 1998, pp. 13–20; Edward T. Hall, "The Silent Language of Overseas Business," *Harvard Business Review*, May–June 1960, pp. 5–14; John S. McClenahen, Andrew Rosenbaum, and Michael Williams, "As Others See U.S.," *IndustryWeek*, January 8, 1990, pp. 80–82; James Bredin, "Japan Needs to be Understood," *IndustryWeek*, April 20, 1992, pp. 24–26; David L. James, "Don't Think About Winning," *Across the Board*, April 1992, pp. 49–51; "When in Japan," *Small Business Reports*, January 1992, p. 8; Bernie Ward, "Other Climates, Other Cultures," *Sky*, March 1992, pp. 72–86; Roger E. Axtell, *Gestures: The Do's and Taboos of Body Language Around the World*, New York: John Wiley & Sons, 1991; Suzanne Kreiter, "Customs Differ Widely from Those in the U.S.," *Greenville News*, September 26, 1993, p. 15D; Bradford W. Ketchum, "Going Global: East Asia-Pacific Rim," *Inc.* (Special Advertising Section), May 20, 1997; Valerie Frazee, "Getting Started in Mexico," *Global Workforce*, January 1997, pp. 16–17; Shawna McAlearny, "Business Mistakes: 11 Cultural Faux Pas You Should Never Make in China," *CIO*, April 21, 2009, *www.cio.com/article/490168/Business_Mistakes_11_Cultural_Faux_Pas_You_Should_Never_Make_in_China*; Shawna McAlearny, "Business Mistakes: 10 Cultural Faux Pas You Should Never Make in India," *CIO*, April 17, 2009, *www.cio.com/article/489763/Business_Mistakes_10_Cultural_Faux_Pas_You_Should_Never_Make_in_India*.

International Trade Agreements

5. Describe the trade agreements that have the greatest influence on foreign trade.

In an attempt to boost world trade, nations have created a variety of trade agreements over the years. Although hundreds of agreements are paving the way for free trade across the world, the following stand out with particular significance: the World Trade Organization (WTO), the North American Free Trade Agreement (NAFTA), and the Dominican Republic-Central American Free Trade Agreement (CAFTA-DR).

World Trade Organization

The World Trade Organization (WTO) was established in January 1995 and replaced the General Agreement on Tariffs and Trade (GATT), the first global tariff agreement, which was created in 1947 and designed to reduce tariffs among member nations. The WTO, currently with 153 member countries, is the only international organization that establishes rules for trade among nations. Its member countries represent more than 97 percent of all world trade. The rules and agreements of the WTO, called the **multilateral trading system**, are the result of negotiations among its members. The WTO actively implements the rules established by the Uruguay Round negotiations of General Agreement on Tariffs and Trade from 1986 to 1994 and continues to negotiate additional trade agreements.

Through the agreements of the WTO, members commit themselves to nondiscriminatory trade practices. These agreements spell out the rights and obligations of each member country. Each member country receives guarantees that its exports will be treated fairly and consistently in other member countries' markets. The WTO's General Agreement on Trade in Services (GATS) addresses specific industries, including banking, insurance, telecommunications, and tourism. In addition, the WTO's intellectual property agreement, which covers patents, copyrights, and trademarks, defines rules for protecting ideas and creativity across borders.

In addition to the development of agreements among members, the WTO is involved in the resolution of trade disputes among members. The WTO system is designed to encourage dispute resolutions through consultation. If this approach fails, the WTO has a multi-stage procedure that culminates in a ruling by a panel of experts.

The North American Free Trade Agreement

The North American Free Trade Agreement (NAFTA) created the world's largest free trade zone among Canada, Mexico, and the United States. A **free trade zone** is an association of countries that have agreed to eliminate trade barriers—both tariff and nontariff—among partner nations. Under the provisions of NAFTA, these barriers were eliminated for trade among the three countries, but each remained free to set its own tariffs on imports from nonmember nations.

NAFTA forged a unified U.S.–Canada–Mexico market of 456.5 million people with a total annual output of more than $17 trillion of goods and services. This important trade agreement binds together the three nations on the North American continent into a single trading unit stretching from the Yukon to the Yucatan. NAFTA has made trade less cumbersome and more profitable for companies of all sizes and has opened export opportunities for many businesses. Today, Canada and Mexico are the largest trading partners for companies in the United States.

The Dominican Republic-Central America Free Trade Agreement

The Dominican Republic-Central America Free Trade Agreement (CAFTA-DR) is to Central America what NAFTA is to North America. The agreement, which took effect on August 2, 2005, is designed to promote free trade among the United States and six Central American countries: Costa Rica, El Salvador, Guatemala, Honduras, Dominican Republic, and Nicaragua. U.S. exports to these seven nations are $20 billion a year.[73]

In addition to reducing tariffs among these nations, CAFTA-DR protects U.S. companies' investments and intellectual property in the region, simplifies the export process for U.S. companies, and provides easier access to Central American markets.

ENTREPRENEURIAL

Profile

*Maureen Coughlin:
Clabber Girl*

Lower tariffs and the elimination of other trade barriers through CAFTA-DR allowed Clabber Girl, a small company in Terre Haute, Indiana, to increase export sales of its line of baking powder, baking soda, corn starch, and gourmet cookie mixes to Central America. The company worked with a variety of trade agencies to develop customers in Central America and has since expanded its export program to include South America and Asia. "Because of reduced tariffs on our products, buyers in this region are more interested in importing our products," says Maureen Coughlin, the company's export sales manager. "We find that free trade agreement countries cultivate stronger import–export trade relations."[74]

Conclusion

For a rapidly growing number of small businesses, conducting business on a global basis will be the key to future success. A small company going global exposes itself to certain risks, but, if planned and executed properly, a global strategy can produce huge rewards. To remain competitive, businesses of all sizes must assume a global posture. Global effectiveness requires managers to be able to leverage workers' skills, company resources, and customer know-how across borders and throughout cultures across the world. Managers also must concentrate on maintaining competitive cost structures and a focus on the core of every business—the *customer*! Robert G. Shaw, CEO of International Jensen Inc., a global maker of home and automobile stereo speakers, explains the importance of retaining that customer focus as his company pursues its global strategy: "We want [our customers] to have the attitude of [our] being across the street. If we're going to have a global company, we have to behave in that mode—whether [the customer is] across the street—or 7 miles, 7 minutes, or 7,000 miles away."[75]

Few businesses can afford the luxury of limiting their target markets to the boundaries of their home country's borders. The manager of one global business, who discourages the use of the word *domestic* among his employees, says, "Where's 'domestic' when the world is your market?"[76] Although there are no sure-fire rules for going global, small businesses wanting to become successful international competitors should observe these guidelines:

- Make yourself at home in all three of the world's key markets—North America, Europe, and Asia. This triad of regions is forging a new world order in trade that will dominate global markets for years to come. Small companies that focus on business opportunities in the fast-growing economies of Brazil, Russia, India, and China are likely to benefit most because forecasts call for these four nations to account for 44 percent of global GDP by 2050.[77]
- Appeal to the similarities within the various regions in which you operate but recognize the differences in their specific cultures. Although the European Union is a single trading bloc composed of 27 countries with a combined population of 498 million people, smart entrepreneurs know that each country has its own cultural uniqueness and do not treat them as a unified market.
- Be willing to commit the necessary resources to make your global efforts successful. Going global requires an investment of time, talent, money, and patience.
- Develop new products for the world market. Make sure your products and services measure up to world-class quality standards.
- Use the many resources available, such as the U.S. Commercial Service and the International Trade Administration, to research potential markets and to determine the ideal target market for your products.
- Familiarize yourself with foreign customs and languages; constantly scan, clip, and build a file on the cultures of countries where you are likely to do business—their lifestyles, values, customs, and business practices.
- Learn to understand your customers from the perspective of *their* culture, not your own. Bridge cultural gaps by being willing to adapt your business practices to suit their preferences and customs.
- "Glocalize." Make global decisions about products, markets, and management, but allow local employees to make tactical decisions about packaging, advertising, and service. Building relationships with local companies that have solid reputations in a region or a country can help overcome resistance, lower risks, and encourage residents to think of them as local companies.
- Make positive and preferably visible contributions to the local community. A company's social responsibility does not stop at the borders of its home country. Seattle-based Starbucks enhances its reputation in the Chinese communities in which it does business by donating coffee and snacks for local celebrations such as the Autumn Moon Festival. Once, when a group of protesters approached the U.S. Embassy in Beijing, they stopped at a nearby Starbucks café to buy coffee. Rather than being the object of a protest, the branch actually saw sales climb![78]
- Train employees to think globally, send them on international trips, and equip them with state-of-the-art communications technology.

- Hire local managers to staff foreign offices and branches.
- Do whatever seems best wherever it seems best, even if people at home lose jobs or responsibilities.
- Consider using partners and joint ventures to break into foreign markets you cannot penetrate on your own.
- Be patient. International business often takes time to cultivate. "Selling to the world does not happen overnight," says Laurel Delaney, an international business expert and author. "It is a slow process that requires thought, discipline, and lots of hard work. However, go global today, and you could fulfill your own version of the American dream."[79]

By its very nature, going global can be a frightening experience for an entrepreneur considering the jump into international markets. Most of those who have already made the jump, however, have found that the benefits outweigh the risks and that their companies are much stronger because of it.

Chapter Review

1. Explain why "going global" has become an integral part of many entrepreneurs marketing strategies.
   - Companies that move into international business can reap many benefits, including offsetting sales declines in the domestic market; increasing sales and profits; extending their products' life cycles; lowering manufacturing costs; improving competitive position; raising quality levels; and becoming more customer-oriented.
2. Describe the nine principal strategies for going global.
   - Perhaps the simplest and least expensive way for a small business to begin conducting business globally is to establish a site on the World Wide Web. Companies wanting to sell goods on the Web should establish a secure order and payment system for online customers.
   - Trade intermediaries such as export management companies, export trading companies, manufacturer's export agents, export merchants, resident buying offices, and foreign distributors can serve as a small company's "export department."
   - In a domestic joint venture, two or more U.S. small companies form an alliance for the purpose of exporting their goods and services abroad. In a foreign joint venture, a domestic small business forms an alliance with a company in the target area.
   - Some small businesses enter foreign markets by licensing businesses in other nations to use their patents, trademarks, copyrights, technology, processes, or products.
   - Over the last decade, a growing number of franchises have been attracted to international markets to boost sales and profits as the domestic market has become increasingly saturated with outlets and much tougher to wring growth from. International franchisors sell virtually every kind of product or service imaginable in global markets. Most franchisors have learned that they must modify their products and services to suit local tastes and customs.
   - Some countries lack a hard currency that is convertible into other currencies, so companies doing business there must rely on countertrading or bartering. A countertrade is a transaction in which a business selling goods in a foreign country agrees to promote investment and trade in that country. Bartering involves trading goods and services for other goods and services.
   - Although small companies account for 91 percent of the companies involved in exporting, they generate only 21 percent of U.S. export sales. However, small companies, realizing the incredible profit potential it offers, are making exporting an ever-expanding part of their marketing plans.
   - Once established in international markets, some small businesses set up permanent locations there. Although they can be very expensive to establish and maintain, international locations give businesses the opportunity to stay in close contact with their international customers.

3. Explain how to build a thriving export program.
   - Building a successful export program takes patience and research. Steps include: realize that even the tiniest firms have the potential to export; analyze your product or service; analyze your commitment to exporting; research markets and pick your target; develop a distribution strategy; find your customer; find financing; ship your goods; and collect your money.
4. Discuss the major barriers to international trade and their impact on the global economy.
   - Three domestic barriers to international trade are common: the attitude that "we're too small to export," lack of information on how to get started in global trade, and a lack of available financing.
   - International barriers include tariffs, quotas, embargoes, dumping, and political business, and cultural barriers.
5. Describe the trade agreements that have the greatest influence on foreign trade.
   - Created in 1947, the General Agreement on Tariffs and Trade (GATT), the first global tariff agreement, was designed to reduce tariffs among member nations and to facilitate trade across the globe.
   - The World Trade Organization (WTO) was established in 1995 and replaced GATT. The WTO has 153 member nations and represents more than 97 percent of all global trade. The WTO is the governing body that resolves trade disputes among members.
   - The North American Free Trade Agreement (NAFTA) created a free trade area among Canada, Mexico, and the United States. The agreement created an association that knocked down trade barriers, both tariff and nontariff, among these partner nations.
   - The Dominican Republic-Central America Free Trade Agreement (CAFTA-DR) is designed to promote free trade among the United States and six Central American countries.

Discussion Questions

1. Why must entrepreneurs learn to think globally?
2. What forces are driving small businesses into international markets?
3. Outline the nine strategies that small businesses can use to go global.
4. Describe the various types of trade intermediaries small business owners can use. Explain the functions they perform.
5. What is a domestic joint venture? A foreign joint venture? What advantages does taking on an international partner through a joint venture offer? What are the disadvantages?
6. What mistakes are first-time exporters most likely to make? Outline the steps a small company should take to establish a successful export program.
7. What are the benefits of establishing international locations? What are the disadvantages?
8. Describe the barriers businesses face when trying to conduct business internationally. How can a small business owner overcome these obstacles?
9. What is a tariff? A quota? What impact do they have on international trade?

10. Thirty furniture makers in the United States recently asked the U.S. International Trade Commission (ITC) to impose high tariffs on Chinese makers of wooden bedroom furniture for dumping their products in the U.S. market at extremely low prices. The U.S. manufacturers claimed that the Chinese imports single-handedly sent their industry into a deep tailspin. The Chinese factory owners contend that their low-cost furniture is the result of taking a labor-intensive product and building it with low-priced workers in high-tech modern factories. Identify the stakeholders in this trade dispute. What are the consequences for each stakeholder likely to be if the ITC were to impose tariffs on Chinese furniture? What impact do tariffs have on international trade? If you served on the ITC, what factors would you consider in making your decision? How would you vote in this case? Explain.
11. What impact have the WTO and NAFTA had on small companies wanting to go global? What provisions are included in these trade agreements?
12. What advice would you offer an entrepreneur interested in launching a global business effort?

Are there global opportunities for your business? If so, include them as an "opportunity" in your SWOT analysis. Review the other sections that will benefit from incorporating these global plans into your business plan strategy. For example, you may need to address your global strategy in the marketing strategy and the Web site sections of your business plan. You may need to include additional expenses in the financial section of your business plan relating to your global strategy.

On the Web

A number of Web resources are available that may assist you with developing global strategies. You will find several of those links at the Companion Web site at *www.pearsonhighered.com/scarborough*.

In the Software

If you plan to employ a global strategy, make certain that you have addressed that intent in your business plan. International activity of any kind will have implications to several sections of your business plan, including your products and services, market analysis, strategy, implementation, Web plans, management, and financial sections.

This is also an excellent time to review your entire plan, paying specific attention to the summary sections at the beginning of each major section. You may have used these areas for notes and now is a good time to review what you

have written in each of these sections. Make certain the summaries provide a brief overview of what each section contains. Those sections include:

- Company
- Product and Services
- Market Analysis
- Strategy and Implementation
- Web Plan
- Management Plan
- Financial Plan

These initial introductory statements will add flow to your plan. You may also want to review each section to avoid redundancy and optimize the efficiency of your overall plan.

Building Your Business Plan

As you near the final stages of creating your business plan, have others review your plan. Do they understand the "story" your business plan is telling? Do they follow your rationale? Do they have questions that the plan should address? Based on their comments, assess whether the plan is successful at communicating your message. If there are deficiencies, make the necessary changes to improve your plan.

Endnotes

1. "International Business Owners Survey 2006: Key Findings," Grant Thornton, June 2006, *www.internationalbusinessreport.com/main/index1.php?page=14&lang=en&id=120811&country_id=0*; "U.S. Business Embraces Global Growth," *Sales & Marketing Management's Performance Newsletter*, October 15, 2006, p. 1.
2. Ian Mount, "Tips for Increasing Sales in International Markets," *New York Times*, April 21, 2010, *www.nytimes.com/2010/04/22/business/smallbusiness/22sbiz.html*.
3. "International Trade Statistics 2009: World Merchandise Exports by Region and Selected Economy," World Trade Organization, *www.wto.org/english/res_e/statis_e/its2009_e/its09_toc_e.htm*.
4. "Emerging Markets: Leading the Way to Recovery," International Business Report, Grant Thornton, 2010, p. 5.
5. Ibid., p. 3.
6. Jack Stack with Bo Burlingham, "My Awakening," *Inc.*, April 2007, pp. 93–97.
7. Leigh Buchanan, "Going Global," *Inc.*, April 2007, p. 91.
8. Ted Miller, "Can America Compete in the Global Economy?" *Kiplinger's Personal Finance Magazine*, November 1991, p. 8.
9. Bernard Wysocki, Jr., "Going Global in the New World," *Wall Street Journal*, September 21, 1990, p. R3.
10. Matt Glynn, "Setting Sites on Small Business Exports," *Buffalo News*, April 21, 2010, *www.buffalonews.com/2010/04/20/1025651/setting-sights-on-small-business.html*.
11. Michael V. Copeland, "The Mighty Micro-Multinational," *Business 2.0*, July 2006, pp. 106–114.
12. "Small and Medium Size Businesses Export Insights and Opportunities: Executive Summary," CompTIA, January 2010, pp. 3, 4.
13. "Globesmanship," *Across the Board*, January–February 1990, p. 26.
14. Michael Barrier, "Why Small Looms Large in the Global Economy," *Nation's Business*, February 1994, p. 9; Vivian Pospisil, "Global Paradox: Small Is Powerful," *IndustryWeek*, July 18, 1994, p. 29.
15. Michael Barrier, "A Global Reach for Small Firms," *Nation's Business*, April 1994, p. 66.
16. Jeremy Main, "How to Go Global—And Why," *Fortune*, August 28, 1989, p. 70.
17. "Internet Usage Statistics: The Big Picture," Internet World Stats 2009, *www.internetworldstats.com/stats.htm*.
18. Joey Holleman, "Classic Wooden Boats Ready to Fulfill Dreams," *The State*, March 14, 2010, *www.thestate.com/2010/03/14/1198132/classic-wooden-boats-ready-to.html*.
19. "Who We Are," eBay, *www.ebayinc.com/who*; Rick Aristotle Munarriz, "Lights Out eBay," The Motley Fool, January 24, 2008, *www.fool.com/investing/general/2008/01/24/lights-out-ebay.aspx*.
20. "Sports Closeouts Equal Millions," *Rich Couples*, June 14, 2007, *www.richcouples.com/sport-closeouts-equal-millions/*; "eBay Success Story: From $800 to $3.3 Million in 3 Years," Fox News, March 28, 2007, *www.youtube.com/watch?v=eTnf2cJUxLQ*.
21. "Think Global," Kentucky World Trade Center, July 14, 2006, *www.kwtc.org/enews/071406/eleven.htm*; "About Us," IMPEX, *www.rgrana.com/about.htm*; "About Arch Environmental," Arch Environmental, *www.aeec.com/Help/About.aspx*.
22. Ian Mount, "Tips for Increasing Sales in International Markets," *New York Times*, April 21, 2010, *www.nytimes.com/2010/04/22/business/smallbusiness/22sbiz.html*.
23. Jennifer LeClaire, "How to Take Your Small Business Global," *E-Commerce Times*, June 20, 2006, *www.ecommercetimes.com/story/50910.html?wlc=1276800833*.
24. Joseph E. Pattison, "Global Joint Ventures," *Overseas Business*, Winter 1990, p. 25.
25. Polly Larson, "Opening Doors to Emerging Markets," International Franchise Association, *www.ifa.org/intl/News/Prjf6.asp*.
26. Scott Deveau, "Bombardier Joint Venture Wins Big in China," *Financial Post*, September 28, 2009, *www.financialpost.com/news-sectors/story.html?id=2042464*.
27. David J. Kaufman, "What a Ride!" *Entrepreneur*, May 2007, pp. 108–113.
28. William Edwards, "International Expansion: Do Opportunities Outweigh Challenges?" *Franchising World*, February 2008, *www.franchise.org/Franchise-News-Detail.aspx?id=37992*.
29. Howard Dahl, "How I Did It," *Inc.*, April 2007, pp. 102–105.
30. Rich Laden, "International Trade a Key for Local Businesses, Chamber Speaker Says," *Colorado Springs Gazette*, May, 18, 2010, *www.gazette.com/articles/international-99007-trade-local.html*.
31. *Small and Medium Size Business Export Insights and Opportunities*, CompTIA, January 2010, p. 3.
32. Ian Mount, "Tips for Increasing Sales in International Markets," *New York Times*, April 21, 2010, *www.nytimes.com/2010/04/22/business/smallbusiness/22sbiz.html*.
33. *A Profile of U.S. Exporting Companies, 2006–2007*, U.S. Census Bureau, U.S. Department of Commerce, Washington, DC: April 9, 2009, p. 6.
34. Geoff Williams, "It's a Small World After All," *Entrepreneur*, May 2004, pp. 39–43; Joshua Kurlantzick, "Stay Home?" *Entrepreneur*, February 2003, pp. 58–59; *Small and Medium-Sized Exporting*

Companies: A Statistical Handbook, International Trade Administration, Office of Trade and Industry Information (Washington, DC: 2005), p. 1.

35. Paul C. Hsu, "Profiting from a Global Mind-Set," *Nation's Business*, June 1994, p. 6.

36. David Newton, "Shipping News," *Entrepreneur*, February 2004, p. 22.

37. "Success Stories: J&N Enterprises," Indiana Small Business Development Center, *www.isbdc.org/default.aspx?action=SuccessStories&id=29*.

38. Jan Alexander, "To Sell Well Overseas, Customize," *Your Company*, Fall 1995, p. 15.

39. Joshua Kurlantzick, "Stay Home?" *Entrepreneur*, February 2003, pp. 58–59.

40. Frances Huffman, "Hello, World!" *Entrepreneur*, August 1990, p. 108.

41. *Small and Medium Size Business Export Insights and Opportunities*, CompTIA, January 2010, p. 6.

42. "Foresight 2020: Economic, Industry, and Corporate Trends," Economist Intelligence Unit, *The Economist*, 2006, p. 7.

43. Lee Smith, "Modern India," Special Advertising Section, *Fortune*, April 12, 2010, pp. S1–S12.

44. Ian Mount, "Tips for Increasing Sales in International Markets," *New York Times*, April 21, 2010, *www.nytimes.com/2010/04/22/business/smallbusiness/22sbiz.html*.

45. Mariko Sanchanta, "Starbucks Plans Big Expansion in China," *Wall Street Journal*, April 14, 2010, p. B10.

46. Eric Decker, "The Art of the Trade Mission," *Small Business Times*, June 8, 2007, *www.biztimes.com/news/2007/6/8/the-art-of-the-trade-mission*.

47. "Trade Missions Testimonials," Automation Alley, *www.automationalley.com/autoalley/International+Business+Center/Trade+Missions/Testimonials.htm*; "Past Missions," Automation Alley, *www.automationalley.com/autoalley/International+Business+Center/Trade+Missions/Past+Missions/China2002.htm*.

48. Marcia Pledger, "Woman Builds Craft Hobby into Multimillion Dollar Importing Business," *Everything Cleveland*, November 19, 2009, *www.cleveland.com/business/index.ssf/2009/11/post_19.html*.

49. "Success Stories," Export Finance Center of Washington, *www.efacw.org/success-stories/*; "News," Web Press, *www.webpresscorp.com/News2.html*.

50. Charlotte Mulhern, "Fast Forward," *Entrepreneur*, October 1997, p. 34.

51. Matt Glynn, "Setting Sites on Small Business Exports," *Buffalo News*, April 21, 2010, *www.buffalonews.com/2010/04/20/1025651/setting-sights-on-small-business.html*.

52. Daniel Kaufmann and Shang-Jin Wei, "Does 'Grease Money' Speed Up the Wheels of Commerce?" World Bank, *www.worldbank.org/wbi/governance/pdf/grease.pdf*.

53. *International Business Attitudes to Corruption*, Simmons & Simmons, 2006, p. 7.

54. Clemmie Newton-Taylor, "Trends in the Global Outsourcing Market," *Executive View*, June 9, 2010, *www.executiveview.com/knowledge_centre.php?id=11693*.

55. "The Growing Company: Big Feet Pajamas," Advertising Insert, *Fast Company*, June 2009, p. 18; "Company Overview," Alibaba.com, *http://news.alibaba.com/specials/aboutalibaba/index.html?tracelog=24581_foot_company_info*.

56. Mark Henricks, "The New China?" *Entrepreneur*, February 2006, pp. 17–18.

57. Michelle Wu, "How I . . . Hopscotched the Globe to Build My Business," *Wall Street Journal*, January 15, 2010, *http://online.wsj.com/article/SB10001424052748704281204575002943447096122.html*.

58. "International Trade Statistics 2009," World Trade Organization, *www.wto.org/english/res_e/statis_e/its2009_e/its09_toc_e.htm*.

59. *The Economic Effects of Significant U.S. Import Restraints, Sixth Update*, United States International Trade Commission (Washington, DC: February 2009), pp. ix–x.

60. Edmund L. Andrews, "U.S. Adds Tariffs on Chinese Tires," *New York Times*, September 11, 2009, *www.nytimes.com/2009/09/12/business/global/12tires.html*; Timothy Aeppel, "Tariff on Tires to Cost Consumers," *Wall Street Journal*, September 14, 2009, p. A3.

61. Bob Meyer, "Sugar Import Quota Increase Being Considered," *Brownfield Ag News for America*, April 14, 2010, *http://brownfieldagnews.com/2010/04/14/sugar-import-quota-increase-being-considered/*; Mattie Duppler, "Sickeningly Sweet—Sugar Quotas and Obama's Protectionism," *Americans for Tax Reform*, August 25, 2009, *www.atr.org/sickeningly-sweet-sugar-quotas-obamas-protectionism-a3758*.

62. Chi-Chi Zhang, "China: Theaters Must Meet Domestic Movie Quota," *ABC News*, January 27, 2010, *http://abcnews.go.com/Entertainment/wireStory?id=9672337*.

63. Eric Berger, "Honey from China Adds to U.S. Beekeepers' Woes," *Spartanburg Herald-Journal*, May 16, 2010, p. A4.

64. *Magnitude of Counterfeiting and Piracy of Tangible Products: An Update*, Organization for Economic Cooperation and Development, November 2009, pp. 1–2.

65. Jason Hanna, "Five Years After Iraq Abduction, Family Tries Making Own Closure," *CNN*, April 11, 2010, *www.cnn.com/2010/LIVING/04/11/missing.iraq.ake.altaie/index.html*.

66. Michelle Tsai, "Shanghai Surprises: The Perils of Opening an Office in China," *Inc.*, March 2007, pp. 47–49.

67. John L. Graham and N. Mark Lam, "The Chinese Negotiation," *Harvard Business Review*, October 2003, p. 87.

68. Stephen J. Simurda, "Trade Secrets," *Entrepreneur*, May 1994, p. 120.

69. Edward T. Hall, "The Silent Language of Overseas Business," *Harvard Business Review*, May–June 1960, pp. 5–14.

70. Lawrence Van Gelder, "It Pays to Watch Words, Gestures While Abroad," *Greenville News*, April 7, 1996, p. 8E.

71. Anton Piëch, "Speaking in Tongues," *Inc.*, June 2003, p. 50.

72. Anton Piëch, "Lost in the Translation," *Inc.*, June 2003, *www.inc.com/magazine/20030601/25511.html*.

73. "CAFTA-DR," Office of the United States Trade Representative, *www.ustr.gov/trade-agreements/free-trade-agreements/cafta-dr-dominican-republic-central-america-fta*.

74. "Indiana Food Supplier Doubles International Business Thanks to Food Export Midwest Programs and Services," Food Export USA, 2009, *www.foodexportusa.org/success/story19.htm*; "Free Trade Agreements Open Door to Foreign Markets," *Global Food Marketer*, May–June 2008, p. 1.

75. John S. McClenahen, "Sound Thinking," *IndustryWeek*, May 3, 1993, p. 28.

76. Jeremy Main, "How to Go Global—And Why," *Fortune*, August 28, 1989, p. 70.

77. "Businesses Capitalising on Opportunities in the World's Fastest Growing Economies," Grant Thornton, February 2007, *www.internationalbusinessreport.com/main/index1.php?page=131&lang=en&id=114557&country_id=0*.

78. Orit Gadiesh and Jean-Marie Pean, "Think Globally, Market Locally," *Wall Street Journal*, September 9, 2003, p. B2.

79. Jennifer LeClaire, "How to Take Your Small Business Global," *E-Commerce Times*, June 20, 2006, *www.ecommercetimes.com/story/50910.html?wlc=1276800833*.

Pricing and Credit Strategies

Learning Objectives

Upon completion of this chapter, you will be able to:

1 Explain why pricing is both an art and a science.
2 Discuss the relationships among pricing, image, competition, and value.
3 Describe effective pricing strategies for both new and existing products and services.
4 Explain the pricing techniques used by retailers.
5 Explain the pricing techniques used by manufacturers.
6 Explain the pricing techniques used by service firms.
7 Describe the impact of credit on pricing.

Price is what you pay. Value is what you get.

—Warren Buffett

The real price of everything, what everything really costs to the

man who wants to acquire it, is the toil and trouble of acquiring it.

—Adam Smith

Pricing: A Creative Blend of Art and Science

1. Explain why pricing is both an art and a science.

One of the most challenging, yet most important, decisions entrepreneurs must make involves pricing their products and services. Studies by the consulting firm Accenture indicate that increasing prices by just 1 percent can produce an 11 percent increase in a company's profit, a result that is much greater than that produced by a comparable 1 percent decrease in costs.[1] "There's nothing you can do as quickly to improve profitability—and nothing you can do as quickly to destroy profitability—as change your pricing," says one consultant who specializes in pricing.[2] Prices that are too high can drive customers away and hurt a small company's sales. Pricing products and services too low, a common tendency among first-time entrepreneurs, robs a business of its ability to earn a profit, leaves customers with the impression that the business's goods and services are of inferior quality, and threatens the business's long-term success.

ENTREPRENEURIAL
Profile

Ilana Eberson:
The NYC Business
Networking Group

Ilana Eberson, founder of the NYC Business Networking Group, a New York City–based business networking company, wondered why her young company was struggling financially, given her $50 per hour fee. When she worked with a consultant to determine how much of her time she donated to her clients without charge (including free follow-up work, travel time, and support services), Eberson discovered that her hourly fee was closer to $7 per hour! She tightened her pricing policy, turned down jobs from potential customers who balked at her prices, eliminated the money-losing practices that she had fallen into, and, in the process, turned around her company.[3]

Determining the most appropriate price for a product or service requires entrepreneurs to consider how the following factors interact to provide clues about the proper price to charge:

- The total cost associated with providing the product or service
- Target customers' characteristics, including their buying power and their perceptions of the product or service
- The current and anticipated market forces that determine supply and demand
- The pricing strategies of competitors and their competitive behavior
- The company's anticipated sales volume and the impact of that production volume on unit cost
- The entrepreneur's desired image for the company and customers' expectations regarding product or service quality and price
- Normal cycles or seasonality in the market
- Customers' sensitivity to price changes
- Psychological factors that influence customers' perceptions of price and quality
- Substitute products or services that are available to customers
- Traditional and expected credit terms and discount policies

Notice that some of the factors, such as costs and competitors' prices, are relatively easy to quantify, but others, such as customers' sensitivity to price changes and desired image, are much less tangible. This is where the creative blending of art and science comes into play that leads to a final pricing decision. In pure economic terms, **price** is the monetary value of a good or service; it is a measure of what a customer must give up to obtain a good or service. For shoppers, price is a reflection of value. Customers often look to a product's or service's price for clues about value. Consider the following examples, which illustrate the sometimes puzzling connection between price and perceived value:

- From a tiny shop in Florence, Italy, Stefano Bemer handcrafts some of the finest shoes in the world. Bemer, who decided to enter the shoemaking business when the cobbler in his small town died, makes both ready-to-wear and custom shoes for customers around the globe. Materials range from the mundane (traditional leather) to the exotic (shark, ostrich, stingray, crocodile, toad, and hippopotamus). Prices for a pair of ready-to-wear shoes range from $1,200 to $2,600, and a pair of custom shoes, which require between 38 and 45 hours of work and two fittings, sells for $3,350 to $4,100. Despite these lofty prices, Bemer has a waiting list of customers and delivery times of 2 to 3 months.[4]

Shoemaker Stefano Bemer, whose handmade shoes sell for $1,200 to $4,100 per pair.

Source: Laif

For sporting clays shooters and hunters, the ultimate in gear is a custom-made shotgun. Companies such as Holland & Holland, Boss, William Evans, and Purdey offer some of the finest custom shotguns in the world. Skilled craftsmen who specialize in particular components build each part of the gun, which is a one-of-a-kind work of art. "It's built completely for you, not anybody else," says one appreciative customer. At Purdey, building a shotgun to a customer's measurements and specifications requires dozens of artisans and at least 2 years. The company makes just 80 to 90 guns per year. Purdey's over-and-under (the arrangement of the barrels) models start at $110,000, but custom engraving (e.g., a photorealistic etching of a dog or bird in flight), gold inlays, special woods, checkering, and other features easily can add another $100,000 to the price. "When I shoot with my Purdey, I feel like an orchestra conductor waving my baton," says one customer, who owns six Purdeys and has two more under construction.[5]

As you can see, setting higher prices sometimes can *increase* the appeal of a product or service ("If you charge more, you must be worth it").

Entrepreneurs must develop a keen sensitivity to both the psychological and economic impact of their pricing decisions. A product's or service's price must exceed the cost of providing it, and it must be compatible with customers' perceptions of value. "Pricing is not just a math problem," says one business writer. "It's a psychology test."[6] The psychology of pricing is an art much more than it is a science. It focuses on creating value in the customer's mind but recognizes that value is what the customer perceives it to be. At the outset, the goal is not necessarily to determine the ideal *price*, but an ideal *price range*. This **price range** is the area between the **price floor** that is established by a company's total cost to produce the product or provide the service and the **price ceiling**, which is the most the target customers are willing to pay (see Figure 1). The final price within this range depends on the image the company wants to create in the minds of its customers.

FIGURE 1
Acceptable Price Range

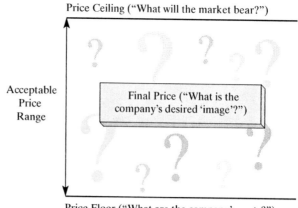

Price Ceiling ("What will the market bear?")

Acceptable Price Range

Final Price ("What is the company's desired 'image'?")

Price Floor ("What are the company's costs?")

The price floor depends on a company's cost structure, which can vary considerably from one business to another, even though they may be in the same industry. Although their cost structures may be different from their competitors', many entrepreneurs play follow-the-leader with their prices, simply charging what their competitors do on similar or identical products or services. Although this strategy simplifies the pricing decision, it can be very dangerous. Determining the price floor for a product or service requires entrepreneurs to have access to timely, accurate information about the cost of producing or selling a product or providing a service.

The price ceiling depends on entrepreneurs' ability to understand their customers' characteristics and buying behavior, the benefits that the product or service offers customers, and the prices of competing products. The best way to learn about customers' buying behavior is to conduct ongoing market research and to spend time with customers, listening to the feedback they offer. Small companies with effective pricing strategies tend to have a clear picture of their target customers and how their companies' products and services fit into their customers' perception of value. A company that begins losing valued customers who complain that its prices are too high has bumped into the price ceiling, and the owner should consider cutting prices.

An entrepreneur's goal is to position the company's prices within this acceptable price range that falls between the price floor and the price ceiling. The final price that entrepreneurs set depends on the desired image they want to create for their products or services: discount (bargain), middle-of-the road (value), or prestige (luxury). A prestige pricing strategy is not necessarily better or more effective than a no-frills, value pricing strategy. What matters most is that the company's pricing strategy matches the image the owner wants to create for the product or service.

Entrepreneurs often find themselves squeezed by rising operating and raw material costs but are hesitant to raise prices because they fear losing customers. Businesses faced with rising operating and raw material costs should consider the following strategies:

- *Communicate with customers.* Let your customers know what's happening. Danny O'Neill, owner of The Roasterie, a wholesale coffee business that sells to upscale restaurants, coffeehouses, and supermarkets, operates in a market in which the cost of raw material and supplies can fluctuate wildly due to forces beyond his control. When coffee prices nearly doubled in just 3 months, O'Neill was able to pass along the rising costs of his company's raw material to customers without losing a single one. He sent his customers a six-page letter and copies of newspaper articles about the increases in coffee prices. The approach gave the Roasterie credibility and helped show customers that the necessary price increases were beyond his control.[7]
- *Rather than raise the price of the good or service, include a surcharge.* Price increases tend to be permanent, but if higher costs are the result of a particular event (e.g., a hurricane that disrupted the nation's ability to process oil and resulted in rapidly rising fuel costs), a company can include a temporary surcharge. If the pressure on its costs subsides,

the company can eliminate the surcharge. When fuel prices began climbing rapidly, John Bunch, owner of a fishing guide service in St. James City, Florida, added a $50 fuel surcharge to his charter boat fishing rates, which start at $375 for 4 hours.[8]

■ *Rather than raise prices, consider eliminating customer discounts, coupons, and "freebies."* Eliminating discounts, coupons, and other freebies is an invisible way of raising prices that can add significantly to a small company's profit margin. Borders, the large bookstore chain, recently restructured its generous discount program because it had begun to cut too deeply into the company's profitability. Loyal customers still earn discounts (as do loyal customers at Borders' competitors), but the discounts are smaller and expire faster.[9]

■ *Offer products in smaller sizes or quantities.* As food costs soared, many restaurants introduced "small plates," reduced portions that enabled them to keep their prices in check. In the quick-service sector, mini-burgers billed as "fun food" and offered in bundles became a popular item on many menus.

■ *Focus on improving efficiency everywhere in the company.* Although raw materials costs may be beyond a business owner's control, other costs within the company are not. One way to cope with the effects of a rapid increase in costs is to find ways to cut costs and to improve efficiency in other areas. These improvements may not totally offset higher raw materials costs, but they can dampen their impact. Rather than raise prices, the owners of Jen-Mor Florists, a family-run flower shop in Dover, Delaware, decided to cut the number of deliveries to the edge of their territory to just one per day to reduce the company's delivery expenses.[10]

■ *Consider absorbing raw material cost increases to keep accounts with long-term importance to the company.* Saving a large account might be more important than keeping pace with rising costs. Companies that absorb the rising cost of raw materials often find ways to cut costs in other areas and to operate more efficiently.

■ *Emphasize the value your company provides to customers.* Unless a company reminds them, customers can forget the benefits and value its products offer. "If you provide great value to your customers, a little price increase isn't going to scare them away," says Elizabeth Gordon, a small business consultant.[11]

■ *Raise prices incrementally and consistently rather than rely on large periodic increases.* Companies that raise prices incrementally are less likely to experience resistance due to customers' sticker shock.

■ *Shift to less expensive raw materials, if possible.* When seafood and beef prices increased, many restaurants added more chicken dishes to their menus. When gold prices tripled within a 4-year period, jeweler John Christian, based in Austin, Texas, began creating more designs in silver and gold, all-silver, and even steel to keep costs and prices under control. The company also launched a separate line of products called Carved Creations priced well below the average $750 price for the John Christian line. Within 2 years, Carved Creations accounted for 30 percent of the company's sales.[12]

■ *Anticipate rising materials costs and try to lock in prices early.* It pays to keep tabs on raw materials prices and to be able to predict cycles of inflation. Entrepreneurs who can anticipate rising prices may be able to make purchases early or lock in long-term contracts before prices take off. After Hurricane Katrina devastated the Gulf Coast and disrupted the production of gasoline, fuel prices skyrocketed both for motorists and for airlines. Because Southwest Airlines had locked in contracts for fuel at pre-Katrina prices, the low-cost carrier was able to post impressive profits even though the rest of the industry's fuel cost had climbed 57 percent.[13]

Three Powerful Pricing Forces: Image, Competition, and Value

Price Conveys Image

2. Discuss the relationships among pricing, image, competition, and value.

A company's pricing policy can be a powerful tool for establishing a brand and for creating a desired image among its target customers. Whether they are seeking an image of exclusivity or one that reflects bargain basement deals, companies use price to enhance their brands. Some companies emphasize low prices, whereas others establish high prices to convey an image of quality, exclusivity, and prestige, all of which appeal to a particular market segment. For example, price reflects the notion of perceived value nowhere better than in the Swiss watch industry. Companies such as Bulgari, Rolex, Cartier, Patek Philippe, Blanepain, and Corum are legendary brands of ultrapremium handmade watches that sell from $5,000 to $395,000. Bulgari created a limited edition of just 24 ASIOMA Multi-Complications Tourbillon watches and priced them at $134,000 each.[14] Manufactured by Maîtres du Temps, is one of the most complex watches in the world, featuring nearly 700 moving parts (it weighs nearly half a pound), and sells for $395,000.[15] Some of these timepieces keep time no better than an inexpensive quartz-driven watch, but their owners are buying more than just a watch. Owning one of these watches is a mark of financial success. Value for some products does not reside solely in their superior technical performance but in their scarcity and uniqueness and the resulting image ("wow" factor) they create for the buyer. Although entrepreneurs must recognize the extremely limited market for ultraluxury items such as these, the ego-satisfying ownership of limited-edition watches, shoes, handbags, cars, jewelry, and other items is the psychological force that supports a premium price strategy.

Too often, small companies underprice their products and services, believing that low prices are the only way they can gain an advantage in the marketplace. According to management consulting firm McKinsey and Company, 80 to 90 percent of the pricing mistakes that companies make involve setting prices that are too low.[16] Companies that fall into this trap fail to recognize the extra value, convenience, service, and attention that they give their customers—things that many customers are willing to pay extra for. These entrepreneurs forget that price is just *one* element of the marketing mix and that for many customers it is not the most important factor. A study by Accenture reports that 73 percent of customers in the United States say that they have switched service providers because of poor service; only 47 percent say they have switched because another company offered lower prices.[17]

The secret to setting prices properly is understanding a company's target market, the customer groups at which it aims its goods or services. Target market, business image, and price are closely related.

Profile

Jan Ryde: Hästens

Hästens, a fifth-generation family-owned business founded in Kopping, Sweden, and owned by Jan Ryde, has been making beds that are renowned for their quality, comfort, and durability since 1852. Hästens beds, which are made from all-natural materials, including cotton, horsehair, flax, down, and wool (no foam, no latex, no chemicals), take 4 days to construct by hand and are designed to last at least 30 years. The springs are made from heat-treated steel and are mounted in individual fabric pockets so that they move independently of one another and conform to the curves of a person's body without affecting the surrounding springs. To prove the durability of its beds, Hästens tests them under conditions that they are likely to encounter (kids using them as trampolines) as well as those they are not (dragging them down dirt roads). Aimed at upscale customers who are connoisseurs of the finest life has to offer, Hästens beds range in price from $3,500 for the Naturally model to $70,000 for the King Vividus. Its most popular model is the 2000T, which sells for $27,500.[18]

Competition and Prices

An important part of setting appropriate prices is tracking competitors' prices regularly; however, the prices that competitors are charging is just *one* variable in the pricing mix (and often not the most important one at that). When setting prices, entrepreneurs should take into account their competitors' prices, but they should *not* automatically match or beat them. Businesses that offer customers extra quality, value, service, or convenience can charge higher prices as long as customers recognize the "extras" they are getting. In other words, companies that successfully implement a differentiation strategy can charge higher prices for their products and services.

Profile

Sarah Lurie:
Iron Core Kettlebells

Sarah Lurie, founder of Iron Core Kettlebells

Source: Jack Smith/New York Times-Maps and Graphics

After spending 8 years as a Wall Street trader, Sarah Lurie returned to college in Arizona to finish her degree. While in school, Lurie discovered kettlebells, a traditional Russian technique of using iron weights in a swinging motion, and incorporated them into her exercise and bodybuilding routine. (A kettlebell looks like a bowling ball with a suitcase handle attached and weighs from 9 to 88 pounds.) After earning a master's degree in economics, she used $50,000 of her personal savings and a business credit card to launch Iron Core Kettlebells gym, a facility devoted to the unusual exercise equipment, in San Diego. Over time, the costs of operating her business increased, and Lurie knew that it was time to raise prices. Since opening, she had kept a close eye on her competitors' prices but recognized that her gym offered customers something unique: short, intense workouts with unusual equipment that produce impressive results. Lurie, a certified Russian Kettlebell Challenge Instructor, author of *Kettlebells for Dummies,* and the star of a series of kettlebell exercise videos, confidently raised her prices 30 percent. Only a handful of customers left because of the price increase. Lurie, who has opened a second Iron Core location, says, "If you're providing such great value to your customers that they can't live without you, a little price increase isn't going to scare them away."[19]

Two factors are vital to determining the effects of competition on a small firm's pricing policies: the location of the competitors and the nature of the competing goods. In most cases, unless a company can differentiate the quality and the quantity of extras it provides, it must match the prices charged by nearby competitors for identical items. For example, if a self-service station charges a nickel more for a gallon of gasoline than the self-service station across the street charges, customers will simply go across the street to buy. Without the advantage of a unique business image—quality of goods sold, value of service provided, convenient location, favorable credit terms—a small company must match local competitors' prices or lose sales. Before matching any competitor's price change, however, entrepreneurs should consider their rivals' strategies. The competition may be establishing its prices using a unique set of criteria and a totally different strategy.

The nature of competitors' goods also influences a small company's pricing policies. Entrepreneurs must recognize those products that are direct substitutes for those they sell and strive to keep prices in line with them. For example, the local sandwich shop should consider the hamburger restaurant, the taco shop, and the roast beef shop as competitors because they all serve fast foods. Although none of them offer the identical menu of the sandwich shop, they are all competing for the same quick-meal dollar.

Whenever possible, entrepreneurs should avoid head-to-head price competition with other firms that can more easily offer lower prices because of their lower cost structures. Most locally owned drugstores cannot compete with the prices of large national drug chains. However, many local drugstores operate successfully by using nonprice competition by offering personal service, free delivery, credit sales, and other extras that the chains have eliminated. Nonprice competition can be an effective strategy for a small business in the face of larger, more powerful enterprises, because there are many dangers in experimenting with prices. For instance, price shifts cause fluctuations in sales volume that the small firm may not be able to tolerate. In addition, frequent price changes may damage the company's image and its customer relations.

One of the deadliest games a small business can get into with competitors is a price war. Price wars eradicate profit margins, force companies out of business, and scar an entire industry for years. The retail book industry has been marred by price wars. Although dominated by large retailers such as online giant Amazon.com and chain stores such as Barnes & Noble, the industry is home to more than 23,000 small, independent booksellers whose annual sales average just $1.5 million. In an attempt to gain market share, Walmart, with annual sales of more than $400 billion, launched a price war, offering new-release books that normally sell between $28 and $35 for just $8.99, a price that Amazon.com quickly matched. Because publishers sell the books to retailers for $14 to $17.50, the price war eliminated profit margins on books for both giant retailers. The battle between the retail leviathans also had a devastating effect on the entire industry, particularly locally owned, independent booksellers, some of whom were forced to close because they could not one compete with prices that were below their costs![20]

Price wars usually begin when one competitor believes that it can achieve a higher volume through lower price or that it can exert enough pressure on competitors' profits to drive them out of business. In most cases, entrepreneurs overestimate the power of price cuts to increase sales sufficiently to improve net profitability.

ENTREPRENEURIAL Profile

McDonald's

McDonald's infamous "Campaign 55," in which it planned to lower the price of a different sandwich to 55 cents each month, launched another volley in an ongoing fast-food price war that no company seemed to be winning. The 55-cent price was a throwback to the prices in 1955, the year McDonald's was founded. The company kicked off the campaign by selling Big Macs (which cost around 40 cents to make) for 55 cents and hoped to increase store traffic and boost sales on other menu items enough to offset the lower margin on the sandwich. Unfortunately, the increased traffic never materialized, and same-store sales fell 6 percent from the year before. In less than 2 months, amid complaints from its franchisees, McDonald's abandoned the promotion.[21]

In a price war, a company may cut its prices so severely that it is impossible to achieve the volume necessary to offset the lower profit margins. If a company that has a 25 percent gross profit margin cuts prices by 10 percent, it would have to *triple* its sales volume just to break even. Even when price cuts work, their effects are often temporary. Customers lured by the lowest price usually have almost no loyalty to a business. The lesson: The best way to survive a price war is to stay out of it by emphasizing the unique features, benefits, and value your company offers its customers!

Focus on Value

Ultimately, the "right" price for a product or service depends on one factor: the value that it provides customers. There are two aspects of value, however. Entrepreneurs may recognize the *objective* value of their products and services, which is the price customers would be willing to pay if they understood perfectly the benefits that a product or service delivers for them. Unfortunately, few, if any, customers can see a product or a service's true objective value; instead, they see only its *perceived* value, which determines the price they are willing to pay for it. "Customers see value in more than product and price," says Jim Barnes, a business owner, consultant, and author. "They spend where they believe they get the best total value, and that does not mean always opting for the lowest price." Small companies that find creative ways to add value to their products and services—for instance, by making it easy for customers to buy from them (Barnes calls these "I'll-look-after-that-for-you" moments), impressing them with stellar service, and providing unexpected extras (such as an electronics retailer consolidating a customer's various remote controls into one when installing a new television)—do not have to resort to price cuts as often as companies that fail to do these things. By offering extra value, these companies encourage their customers to look beyond mere price to determine value. "We must offer the customer something that allows us to earn the prices we charge," concludes Barnes. "We must go above and beyond, creating new and different forms of value that will compensate for the pressure on customers to obtain more for less."[22]

Businesses that underprice their products and services or that run constant sales and discount price promotions may be short-circuiting the value proposition they are trying to communicate to their customers. Customers may respond to price cuts, but companies that rely on them to boost sales risk undermining the perceived value of their products and services. In addition, once customers grow accustomed to buying products and services during special promotions, the habit can be difficult to break. They simply wait for the next sale. Many retailers now face this problem as customers accustomed to buying items on sale postpone buying them until the next special sale arrives. The result has been fluctuating sales and a diminished value of those stores' brands.

In some economic conditions, companies have little choice but to offer lower-priced products. Techniques that companies can use to increase customers' perception of value, and essentially lower their prices with less risk of diminishing their brands, include offering coupons and rebates that are not as closely connected to the product as direct price cuts. Limited-time discounts used

"I'm getting the fire-breathing dragon
with wings. He wanted $200, but I
talked him down to fifty bucks."

sparingly also increase sales without causing long-term damage to a brand. Another strategy that some companies have used successfully is to launch a **fighter brand**, a less expensive, no-frills version of a company's flagship product that is designed to confront lower-priced competitors head-on, satisfy the appetites of value-conscious customers, and preserve the image of the company's premium product. Rather than lower the price of its Pentium computer chip, Intel introduced the lower-cost Celeron chip to stave off rival AMD's line of value-priced chips.

The good news is that companies can influence customers' perceptions of value through marketing and other efforts. "The price you get for a product is a function of what it's truly worth—and how good a job you do communicating that value to the end user," says one entrepreneur.[23] Indeed, setting a product's or a service's price is another way a company can communicate value to its customers. For most shoppers, three reference points define a fair price: the price they have paid for the product or service in the past, the prices competitors charge for the same or similar product or service, and the costs a company incurs to provide the product or service. The price that customers have paid in the past for an item serves as a baseline reference point, but people often forget that inflation causes a company's costs to rise from year to year. Therefore, it is important for business owners to remind customers periodically that they must raise prices to offset the increased cost of doing business. "Over time, costs always go up," says Norm Brodsky, owner of a successful document storage company. "I'd rather raise prices a little every year or with every new contract than be forced to demand a big increase down the road."[24]

As we have seen already, companies often find it necessary to match competitors' prices on the same or similar items unless they can establish a distinctive image in customers' minds. One of the most successful strategies for companies facing direct competition is to differentiate their products or services by adding value for customers and then charging for it. For instance, a company might offer faster delivery, a longer product warranty, extra service, or something else that adds value to an item for its customers and allows the business to charge a higher price.

Perhaps the least understood of the three reference points is a company's cost structure. Customers often underestimate the costs businesses incur to provide products and services, whether it is a simple cotton T-shirt on a shelf in a beachfront shop or a life-saving drug that may have cost hundreds of millions of dollars and many years to develop. They forget that business owners must make or buy the products they sell, market them, pay their employees, and cover a host of other operating expenses, ranging from health care to legal fees.

Enhancing Your Company's Pricing Power

As the economy slowed in a recent recession, businesses of all sizes and across a myriad of industries began offering price discounts to encourage customers to buy their goods and services. Fast-casual restaurants such as Applebee's and Ruby Tuesday offered a selection of dinner specials priced at two for $20. Quick-service restaurants expanded their value menus and introduced bundled items at rock-bottom prices. Subway's $5 footlong sandwiches were a hit, appealing to a broad base of customers.

Many of these companies then realized that they had created a challenging problem: How do we raise prices when the economy improves? Once customers become accustomed to value deals, how does a business change customers' perceptions of the relationship between price and value? The following pricing-power matrix can help:

The horizontal axis of the matrix measures the extent to which customers view a product or service as a necessity or as a discretionary purchase. The vertical axis describes a product's or service's level of uniqueness, which ranges from an undifferentiated commodity to a completely unique item. Where on the matrix does your company's product or service fall?

The best quadrant for a company to operate in is the upper-left corner, a unique necessity, a situation in which customers have a high need for a product or service that is unique and highly differentiated from competing products and services. An individual's favorite brand of shampoo or the blades that fit a person's razor are good examples. These products have the greatest degree of pricing power, even during economic downturns.

The lower-right quadrant is discretionary commodities. With a discretionary commodity, a company's products or services are very similar to those of competitors and customers do not have to have them or can postpone their purchases of them, at least for a while. The airline industry finds itself in this unenviable position because many customers can choose alternative methods of travel, postpone their trips, or choose a less expensive flight on a competing airline.

The remaining two quadrants offer in-between positions of pricing power. In the lower-left corner are products and services that, although necessities, offer little opportunity for differentiation. Light bulbs and lumber are good examples, and companies that produce them often end up matching competitors' prices because customers see them as the same.

The upper-right quadrant contains products and services that are unique but highly discretionary; customers simply do not have to have them. Companies that operate in this sector do not have maximum pricing power. Luxury cars such as Rolls-Royce are good examples. During a recent economic downturn, for instance, Rolls-Royce introduced the $245,000 Ghost, a smaller, more "affordable" car (at least compared to the rest of its line, including the $380,000 Phantom) that is, in the Rolls-Royce tradition, built by hand. It offers amenities such as night-vision

The Pricing-Power Matrix

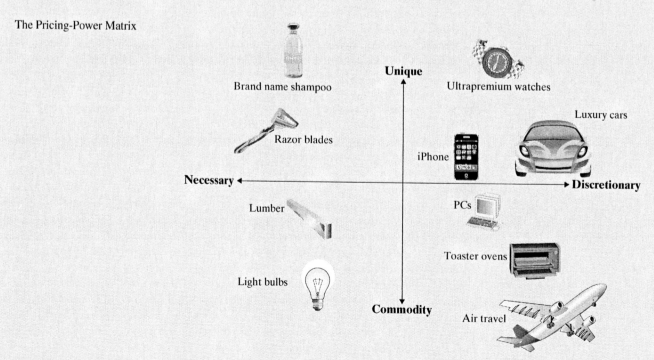

92

cameras, inch-thick lamb's wool carpet, and a cashmere head liner. Apple, which is also located in this quadrant, recently cut the price of its entry-level iPhone in half and introduced a next-generation model to maintain sales in the face of competing smartphones and more frugal customers.

Companies have the ability to move from one quadrant to a more desirable one by executing the proper strategy. The following questions can help entrepreneurs to determine their strategic options to increase their pricing power:

1. Can you offer a product or service that your customers consider a necessity? Doing so enhances a small company's pricing power.
2. Can you offer an "affordable luxury"? Even in austere economic conditions, customers often are willing to splurge on small luxuries such as gourmet chocolates, premium ice cream, and luxury muffins. These affordable luxuries give companies a great deal of pricing power.

3. What steps can you take to differentiate your company's products or services from those of competitors? The greater the degree of differentiation of a company's products and services, the less price sensitive customers tend to be and the more pricing power a company has.
4. Can you offer customers something that will save them money? If so, your company has the ability to increase its pricing power.
5. Can you reduce the role of price in customers' buying decisions by, for example, offering superior customer service? Most small companies have the ability to de-emphasize the role that price plays in customers' buying decisions.

Sources: Based on Geoff Colvin, "Yes, You Can Raise Prices," *Fortune*, March 2, 2009, p. 20; Sara Wilson, "When to Lower Your Price Point," *Entrepreneur*, April 2009, pp. 28–29; Hannah Elliott, "Stealth Wealth," *Forbes*, January 18, 2010, p. 62; Dan Neil, "Rolls Royce Builds a Real Car," *Wall Street Journal*, April 10–11, 2010, p. W6; Yukari Iwatani Kane, "To Sustain iPhone, Apple Halves Price," *Wall Street Journal*, June 9, 2009, p. B1.

Pricing Strategies and Tactics

3. Describe effective pricing strategies for both new and existing products and services.

The number of variations in pricing strategies and tactics is limitless. The wide variety of options is exactly what allows entrepreneurs to be so creative with their pricing. This section will examine some of the more commonly used tactics under a variety of conditions. Pricing always plays a critical role in a firm's overall strategy; pricing policies must be compatible with a company's total marketing plan.

New Product Pricing: Penetration, Skimming, or Sliding

Most entrepreneurs approach setting the price of a new product with a great deal of apprehension because they have no precedent on which to base their decisions. If a new product's price is too high, it is in danger of failing because of low sales volume. However, if its price is too low, the product's sales revenue might not cover costs. Establishing a price that is too low is far more dangerous. Not only does the company forego revenues and profits, but it also limits the product's perceived value in the eyes of its target customers.

When pricing any new product, an entrepreneur must satisfy three objectives:

1. ***Get the product accepted.*** No matter how unique a product is, its price must be acceptable to a company's potential customers. The price a company can charge depends, in part, on the type of product it introduces:
   - **Revolutionary products** are so new that they transform an industry. Companies that introduce these innovative products usually have the ability to charge prices that are close to the price ceiling, although they may have to educate customers about the product's benefits.
   - **Evolutionary products** involve making enhancements and improvements to products that are already on the market. Companies that introduce these products do not have the ability to charge premium prices unless they can use the enhancements they have made to differentiate their products from those of competitors. Establishing a price that is too low for an evolutionary product can lead to a price war.
   - **Me-too products** are products that companies introduce just to keep up with competitors. Because they offer customers nothing new or unique, me-too products offer companies the least amount of pricing flexibility. Achieving success with these products means focusing on cost control and targeting the right market segments.

2. ***Maintain market share as competition grows.*** If a new product is successful, competitors will enter the market, and a small company must work to expand or at least maintain its market share. Continuously reappraising a product's price in conjunction with special advertising and promotion techniques helps the company maintain market share.

3. *Earn a profit.* A small company must establish a price for the new product that is higher than its cost. Entrepreneurs should not introduce a new product at a price below cost because it is much easier to lower the price than to increase it once the product is on the market. Pricing their products too low is a common and often fatal mistake for new businesses; entrepreneurs are tempted to underprice their products and services when they enter a new market to ensure its acceptance.

Entrepreneurs have three basic strategies to choose from in establishing a new product's price: penetration, skimming, and life cycle pricing.

PENETRATION. When a company introduces a new product into a market in which customers are price sensitive, a **penetration pricing strategy** enables the business to build market share quickly and establish itself as the market leader. In other words, it sets the price just above total unit cost to develop a wedge in the market and quickly achieve a high volume of sales. The resulting low profit margins may discourage other competitors from entering the market with similar products.

A penetration pricing strategy is ideal when introducing relatively low-priced goods into a market in which no elite segment and little opportunity for differentiation exists. This strategy works best when customers' switching costs (the cost of switching to a lower-priced competitor's product) is high (e.g., video game consoles). Penetration pricing also works when a company's competitors are locked into high cost structures that result from the channels of distribution they use, labor agreements, or other factors. For instance, since its inception Southwest Airlines has relied on its lower cost structure to compete with older, "legacy" carriers by emphasizing low prices.

Entrepreneurs must recognize that penetration pricing is a long-range strategy; until a company achieves customer acceptance for the product, profits are likely to be small. When a young college student launched a carpet cleaning business to help pay for his education, he decided to be the low-cost provider in his area. Although he landed plenty of work for his part-time business, he found that his company generated very little profit after deducting the expenses of doing business. Realizing that his customers would be willing to pay more for quality work, he raised his prices and began earning a reasonable profit.[25]

A danger of a penetration pricing strategy is that it attracts customers who know no brand loyalty. Companies that garner customers by offering low introductory prices must wonder what will become of their customer bases if they increase their prices or if a competitor undercuts their prices. If a penetration pricing strategy succeeds and the product achieves mass-market penetration, sales volume increases, economies of scale result in lower unit cost, and the company earns attractive profits. The objective of the penetration strategy is to achieve quick access to the market to generate high sales volume as soon as possible.

SKIMMING. A **skimming pricing strategy** often is used when a company introduces a unique product into a market with little or no competition. Sometimes a company uses this tactic when introducing a product into a competitive market that contains an elite group that is willing and able to pay a premium price. A company sets a higher-than-normal price in an effort to quickly recover the initial developmental and promotional costs of the product. The idea is to set a price well above the product's total unit cost and to promote the product heavily to appeal to the segment of the market that is not sensitive to price. This pricing tactic often reinforces the unique, prestigious image of a company and projects a high quality picture of the product. A skimming strategy works well when a company has a mature product, loyal customers, a reputation for quality, and few competitors.

ENTREPRENEURIAL
Profile

*Sylvie Chantecaille:
Chantecaille*

When Sylvie Chantecaille, owner of the cosmetic company that bears her name, launched a new biodynamic lifting cream aimed at female baby boomers who are fighting the aging process, she priced the product at $295 for 1.7 ounces. "Can we really sell it for that much?" Chantecaille recalls thinking as she pondered her pricing decision. Her concern was unfounded; her company sells more than 20,000 units of the special cream each year through exclusive department stores, such as Neiman Marcus and Barneys New York, and small, upscale cosmetic shops. Encouraged by customers' response, Chantecaille recently introduced a 1.7-ounce Nano Gold Energizing Cream that sells for $420.[26]

LIFE CYCLE PRICING. A variation of the skimming pricing strategy is **life cycle pricing**. Using this technique, the firm introduces a product at a high price. Then, as the product moves through its life cycle, the company relies on technological advances, the learning curve effect, and economies of scale to lower its cost and to reduce the product's price faster than its competitors can. By beating other businesses in a price decline, the company discourages competitors and, over time, becomes a high-volume producer. High-definition television sets are a prime example of a product introduced at a high price that quickly cascaded downward as companies forged important technological advances and took advantage of economies of scale. When they were first introduced in 1998, high-definition TVs sold for $10,000; today, high-definition sets that have more features are priced at $500 or less. Life cycle pricing assumes that competition will emerge over time. Even if no competition arises, companies almost always lower the product's price to attract a larger segment of the market. In a sliding strategy, the initial high price contributes to the rapid return of start-up or development costs and generates a pool of funds to finance expansion and technological advances.

Table 1 offers useful tips for avoiding common pricing mistakes.

Pricing Techniques for Established Products and Services

Entrepreneurs have a variety of pricing techniques or tactics available to them to apply to established products and services.

ODD PRICING. Although studies of consumer reactions to prices are mixed and generally inconclusive, many entrepreneurs use the technique known as **odd pricing**. They set prices that end in odd numbers (frequently 5, 7, or 9), because they believe that an item selling for $12.69 appears to be much cheaper than an item selling for $13.00. Psychological techniques such as odd pricing are designed to appeal to certain customer interests, but research on their effectiveness is mixed. Some studies show no benefits from using odd pricing, but others have concluded that the technique can produce significant increases in sales.

TABLE 1 **Tips for Avoiding Pricing Mistakes**

Tip #1. Be careful with cost-plus pricing. When companies base their prices on costs rather than on customers' perception of value, the result is almost always prices that are either too low or too high.

Tip #2. Recognize that "me-too" pricing gives a company no pricing power. A much better strategy is to differentiate your company's products or services by creating additional value for customers or by targeting market niches.

Tip #3. Realize that you cannot achieve the same profit margin across every product line your company sells. The profit margin for paper clips is likely to be quite different from the profit margin for printers.

Tip #4. Recognize that your customer base is made up of different customer segments and that some of them are more sensitive to price than others. Even if a company sells a single product or service, its value proposition differs among its different customer segments. That means that by adding extra value to its offerings aimed at customers who are willing to pay for it, a company can charge higher prices.

Tip #5. Do not put off raising prices out of fear of a customer backlash. If your costs of providing a product or service go up and you never raise prices, your profit margins shrink until you can no longer stay in business. Perpetually absorbing cost increases by holding prices the same is the pricing equivalent of sticking your head in the sand. The outcome is certain: business failure.

Tip #6. Do not compensate sales representatives solely on sales volume. Doing so encourages them to sell at any price, particularly low prices that destroy the company's profitability. Create profit-based incentives for your sales force.

Tip #7. Avoid launching a price war. As you learned in this chapter, no one "wins" a price war, and one can devastate an industry's profits for years.

Tip #8. Realize that although discounts have their place in a company's pricing strategy, they can be as addictive as drugs. "Companies that get hooked on discounts do little more than drive down their value proposition, sometimes past the point of no return," says one pricing consultant. If you decide to use discounts, use them sparingly, briefly, and creatively.

Tip #9. Recognize that some customers are more valuable to your business than others. Customers who always demand the lowest prices and the highest level of service often are a company's least profitable customers. Do not waste a disproportionate amount of time and energy catering to them; instead, identify your company's most profitable customers, focus on serving them well, and attract more customers like them.

Tip #10. Remember that price is just one variable in the sales equation. Costs, customers' perception of value, and image are important factors as well. Use them!

Sources: Based on "Eradicate Pricing Errors," *Sales & Marketing Management*, August 5, 2009, p. 1; Steve McKee, "How to Discount (If You Insist)," *BusinessWeek*, August 14, 2009, www.businessweek.com/smallbiz/content/aug2009/sb20090814_425078.htm.

PRICE LINING. **Price lining** is a technique that greatly simplifies the pricing function. Under this system, the manager stocks merchandise in several different price ranges or price lines. Each category of merchandise contains items that are similar in appearance, quality, cost, performance, or other features. Many lined products appear in sets of three—good, better, and best—at prices designed to satisfy different market segment needs and incomes. Apple revised pricing for its industry-leading iTunes music downloads, moving from a flat 99 cents per song to a lined pricing strategy, with songs available for 69 cents, 99 cents, or $1.29. Price lining can boost a store's sales because it makes goods available to a wide range of shoppers, simplifies the purchase decision for customers, and allows them to keep their purchases within their budgets.

DYNAMIC PRICING. For many businesses, the pricing decision has become more challenging because the Web gives customers access to incredible amounts of information about the prices of items ranging from cars to computers. Increasingly, customers are using the Web to find the lowest prices available. To maintain their profitability, companies have responded with **dynamic (or customized) pricing**, in which they set different prices on the same products and services for different customers using the information they have collected about their customers. Rather than sell their products at fixed prices, companies using dynamic pricing rely on fluid prices that may change based on supply and demand and on which customer is buying or when a customer makes a purchase. For instance, a first-time customer making a purchase at an online store may pay a higher price for an item than a regular customer who shops there frequently pays for that same item.

Dynamic pricing is not a new concept. The standard practice in ancient bazaars involved merchants and customers haggling until they came to a mutually agreeable price, which meant that different customers paid different prices for the same goods. Although the modern version of dynamic pricing often involves sophisticated market research or the Internet, the goal is the same: to charge the right customer the right price at the right time. For example, travelers can use Priceline and similar Web sites to purchase last minute airline tickets at significant discounts (e.g., a round-trip ticket from New York to Los Angeles for just $250 rather than for the full-fare price of $750). Travelers benefit from lower prices, and the airlines are able to generate revenue from seats that otherwise would have gone unsold.

LEADER PRICING. **Leader pricing** is a technique in which the small retailer marks down the customary price (i.e., the price consumers are accustomed to paying) of a popular item in an attempt to attract more customers. The company earns a much smaller profit on each unit because the markup is lower, but purchases of other merchandise by customers seeking the leader item often boost sales and profits. In other words, the incidental purchases that consumers make when shopping for the leader item boosts sales revenue enough to offset a lower profit margin on the leader. Grocery stores often use leader pricing. For instance, during the holiday season, stores often use turkeys as a price leader, knowing that they will earn higher margins on the other items shoppers purchase with their turkeys.

GEOGRAPHIC PRICING. Small businesses whose pricing decisions are greatly affected by the costs of shipping merchandise to customers across a wide range of geographic regions frequently employ one of the **geographic pricing** techniques. For these companies, shipping costs constitute a substantial portion of the cost of doing business and often cut deeply into already narrow profit margins. One type of geographic pricing is **zone pricing**, in which a company sells its merchandise at different prices to customers located in different territories. For example, a manufacturer might sell at one price to customers east of the Mississippi and at another to those west of the Mississippi. The U.S. Postal Service's parcel post charges are a good example of zone pricing. A small business must be able to show a legitimate basis (e.g., difference in selling or transportation costs) for the price discrimination or risk violating Section 2 of the Clayton Act.

Another variation of geographic pricing is the **uniform delivered pricing**, a technique in which a company charges all of its customers the same price regardless of their location, even though the cost of selling or transporting merchandise varies. The company calculates freight charges for each region in which it sells and combines them into a uniform fee. The result is that local customers subsidize the firm's charge for shipping merchandise to distant customers.

A final variation of geographic pricing is **F.O.B. factory**, in which the small company sells its merchandise to customers on the condition that they pay all shipping costs. Using this technique, a company can set a uniform price for its product and let each customer cover the freight cost.

DISCOUNTS. Many small businesses use **discounts**, or **markdowns**, reductions from normal list prices, to move stale, outdated, damaged, or slow-moving merchandise. A seasonal discount is a price reduction designed to encourage shoppers to purchase merchandise before an upcoming season. For instance, many retail clothiers offer special sales on winter coats in late summer. Some companies grant discounts to special groups of customers, such as senior citizens or college students, to establish a faithful clientele and to generate repeat business. One study suggests that for items other than luxury goods, placing discount signs close to merchandise displays and promoting dollar discounts rather than percentage discounts increases the probability of making a sale.[27]

As tempting as discounts are to businesses when sales are slow, they also carry risks. Because price is an important signal of quality and image to customers, businesses that turn to discounts too often create the impression that they may be lowering their quality standards, thereby diluting the value of their brand and image in the marketplace. "For the sake of a short-term increase in sales, you can wreck the long-term value of your brand," says Rafi Mohammed, author of *The Art of Pricing*.[28] Many restaurants, from quick-service chains to fast-casual outlets, relied heavily on price discounts in an attempt to attract customers during a recent recession. For many, however, the increased traffic that the discounts generated failed to offset the impact of price cuts, resulting in the same lower total revenues they were trying to avoid. In addition, when the economy improved, many restaurants had difficulty weaning customers from their discount price expectations. "They've trained customers to eat $5 footlong sandwiches," says one industry analyst about a popular chain's discounts.[29] As the economy improved, restaurants reduced their use of discount coupons and introduced new, higher-priced menu items.[30]

Recent research suggests that using a **steadily decreasing discount (SDD)**, a limited duration discount that declines over time, is superior to a standard (hi-lo) discount, a common tactic in which a company offers frequent discounts off of its standard prices. When one company used a hi-lo discount of 20 percent for 3 days before returning the items to full price, sales increased by 75 percent. For the same items, a steadily decreasing discount of 30 percent the first day, 20 percent the second day, and 10 percent the third day (which yielded an average discount of 20 percent), produced an increase in sales of 200 percent. The researchers conclude that the SDD is more effective because it creates a sense of urgency, especially among wary or indecisive customers.[31]

Multiple unit pricing is a promotional technique that offers customers discounts if they purchase in quantity. Many products, especially those with a relatively low unit value, are sold using multiple pricing. For example, instead of selling an item for 50 cents, a small company might offer five for $2.

BUNDLING. Many small businesses have discovered the marketing benefits of **bundling**, grouping together several products or services, or both, into a package that offers customers extra value at a special price. Rather than cut into their already thin profit margins with price discounts during a recent recession, some restaurants used a bundling strategy, offering customers value-priced groupings of items. Dairy Queen (DQ) introduced its Sweet Deals menu, which offers customers a choice of nine items—two for $3, three for $4, and four for $5. Within just a few months, sales had increased, and the Sweet Deals menu accounted for 7 percent of the company's sales. More important, DQ's BrandIndex score, a rating that tracks customers' perceptions of a company's value, had increased by 1.7 percentage points and was among the industry's highest.[32]

Optional-product pricing involves selling the base product for one price but selling the options or accessories at a much higher percentage markup. Automobiles are often sold at a base price with each optional price separately. In many cases, the car is sold with some of the options bundled together.

ENTREPRENEURIAL
Profile

Don and Joseph Saladino: Drive 495

Drive 495, an upscale fitness and golf center in New York's SoHo District started by brothers Don and Joseph Saladino, offers three simulation bays where urban golfers can practice their swings on 31 famous courses from around the world, including Pebble Beach and St. Andrews. Drive 495 uses optional-product pricing; standard 1-year memberships start at $5,000, an annual membership with unlimited golf and fitness lessons costs $25,000, and a lifetime membership with unlimited lessons for 1 year is $100,000.[33]

Captive-product pricing is the granddaddy of all pricing tactics, in which the basic product is useless without the appropriate accessories. King Gillette, the founder of the company that manufactures Gillette razors, taught the business world that the *real* money is not in the razor (the product) itself, but in the blades (the accessory). Today, we see the same pricing strategy used by Nintendo and other electronic game system manufacturers that have a very small profit margin on the product but substantially higher margins on the game cartridges. When Nintendo launched its popular Wii game system, the company's strategy was to sell a simpler game system with games that players could enjoy without having to invest dozens of hours to learn them. This strategy enabled Nintendo to introduce its game system at a price of just $249, well below the $500 price tag on Sony's PlayStation 3 and Microsoft's $400 Xbox 360. Nintendo's real money-maker, however, is the games that it sells to Wii owners, which are priced at $50 each (still below the $60 price tag on most PlayStation games). Nintendo's pricing strategy worked, and sales of Wii stations and games outstripped those of Sony's and Microsoft's products.[34]

By-product pricing is a technique in which the revenues from the sale of by-products allow a firm to be more competitive in its pricing of the main product. For years, owners of sawmills considered bark chips to be a nuisance. Today they package them and sell them as ground cover to homeowners, gardeners, and landscapers. Zoos across the globe offer one of the most creative examples of byproduct pricing, packaging once-worthless exotic animal droppings and marketing it as fertilizer under the clever name "Zoo Doo."

SUGGESTED RETAIL PRICES. Many manufacturers print suggested retail prices on their products or include them on invoices or in wholesale catalogs. Small business owners frequently follow these suggested retail prices because doing so eliminates the need to make a pricing decision. Nonetheless, following prices established by a distant manufacturer may create problems for the small firm. For example, a haberdasher may try to create a high-quality, exclusive image through a prestige pricing policy, but manufacturers may suggest discount outlet prices that are incompatible with the small firm's image. Another danger of accepting the manufacturer's suggested price is that it does not take into consideration a small company's cost structure or competitive situation. A recent controversial U.S. Supreme Court decision overturned a nearly 100-year-old ruling and allows manufacturers to set and enforce minimum prices that retailers must charge for the manufacturer's products as long as doing so does not reduce competition. However, more than 30 states are considering passing new antitrust laws that explicitly ban all minimum price agreements in an attempt to preempt the court's decision.[35]

FOLLOW-THE-LEADER PRICING. Some businesses make no effort to be price leaders in their immediate geographic areas and simply follow the prices that their competitors establish. Maintaining a follow-the-leader pricing policy may not be healthy for a small business because it robs the company of the opportunity to create a distinctive image in its customers' eyes.

A small company's pricing strategy must be compatible with its marketing objectives, its marketing mix, and its cost structure. In addition, the pricing strategy must be consistent with the competitive realities of the marketplace and the shifting forces of supply and demand. The forces that shape the pricing decision can change rapidly and, therefore, a company's pricing strategy is never completely fixed. Pricing decisions must take into account a company's cost, the special value the product or service creates for buyers, and the pricing tactics of competitors.

The underlying forces that dictate how a business prices its goods or services vary greatly among industries. The next three sections will investigate pricing techniques used in retailing, manufacturing, and service firms.

IN THE ENTREPRENEURIAL
SPOTLIGHT   When the Price Is *Not* Right

When the economy slowed, Jason Robbins, CEO of ePromos Promotional Products, a New York City–based company that sells a variety of promotional products, corporate gifts, and trade show giveaways, resisted using discounts to sustain the 10-year-old company's sales growth. "We always wanted to be the service leader," explains Robbins.

"Our fear was that once you get people hooked on cheap prices, they wouldn't pay full price again." However, after reaching $25 million in annual sales, the company's revenue began declining rapidly. "Everything just froze," says Robbins. He and his team of employees began considering price cuts to kick-start sales. The principal question was,

"How can we use discounts judiciously to rejuvenate sales without sending a signal to customers that our company is just another low-price competitor?"

Robbins eventually decided to offer a limited-time $50 discount to first-time buyers and to mark down prices on 3,000 of the 13,000 items that ePromos sells. To minimize the impact on the company's 25 percent gross profit margin, however, Robbins reduced the prices only on those items on which the company received rebates from manufacturers for meeting sales goals. Robbins also understood the power of offering free shipping for increasing sales at online companies and offered customers free shipping. Even though sales were down for the year, the pricing moves halted the free-fall in the company's revenue, and ePromos weathered the storm far better than many of its competitors. "We believe we maintained our position as a high-service competitor and didn't damage our reputation," Robbins says.

By refusing to engage in a price war with competitors and offering limited discounts only on certain items, Robbins was able to generate sales without portraying his company as a discount seller. When his company's sales began to decline due to a faltering economy, Robbins knew that he had to re-evaluate ePromos' pricing strategy. What are the signs that mean it is time to consider changing your company's pricing strategy?

1. *Unit sales growth slows or declines.* When sales volume stalls or declines, the market may be saturated, the economy may be struggling, competitors could be stealing away your customers, or your prices are out of line with customers' perceived value of your products and services.
2. *Discounts fail to increase sales.* The reason that companies offer price discounts is to increase sales, ideally by a greater percentage than the discount. If a discount fails to produce results, continuing to offer it is a recipe for disaster. "Price cutting usually is not the best strategy for a small business—especially a business that serves a target market that cares more about value and service than paying the lowest possible price," explains one business writer. "Not only does discounting generally fail to help you acquire

new customers, but it may also result in your making less money from the customers you already have."
3. *Competitors introduce new products or services.* Innovations by competitors can change—sometimes dramatically—the price–value equation in the market. "If the competition has leapfrogged you on value, you may not be able to maintain your current pricing strategy," explains one pricing expert.
4. *Low-cost competitors enter the market.* When a market is experiencing high growth, it often attracts new entrants. If those new competitors have lower cost structures and utilize penetration pricing strategies, their entry can muddle the entire industry's pricing structure. When faced with this situation, some companies engage in a price war, but others take different approaches, such as introducing fighter brands or moving into less-price-sensitive niche markets.
5. *Gross profit margin declines.* "Creating a Solid Financial Plan," that a company's gross profit margin equals (Sales − Cost of goods sold) ÷ Sales. The only ways to repair a gross profit margin that is too low is to either reduce the company's cost of goods sold or to increase its prices.

1. Explain the dangers of using discounting as a pricing strategy for increasing sales.
2. Use the Web to research price wars. What conditions usually prompt price wars? What impact do price wars have on an industry and the companies in it? What are the typical outcomes in a price war?
3. Many small companies compete successfully without focusing on providing the lowest prices, even in industries in which customers view product or service prices as important purchasing criteria. What tactics do these companies use to compete successfully without relying on the lowest prices?

Sources: Based on Ryan McCarthy, "Pricing: How Low Can You Really Go?" *Inc.*, March 2009, pp. 91–92; Vincent Ryan, "The Price Is Wrong," *CFO*, December 2009, p. 52; Rosalind Resnick, "Hold the Line on Price," *Washington Post*, March 9, 2009, *www.washingtonpost.com/wp-dyn/content/article/2009/03/11/AR2009031103668.html*; "About Us," ePromos, *www.epromos.com/AboutePromos/AboutUs.jsp*.

Pricing Techniques for Retailers

4. Explain the pricing techniques used by retailers.

Because retail customers have become more price conscious and the Internet has made prices more transparent, retailers have changed their pricing strategies to emphasize value. This value–price relationship allows for a wide variety of highly creative pricing and marketing practices. Delivering high levels of recognized value in products and services is one key to retail customer loyalty. To justify paying a higher price than those charged by competitors, customers must perceive a company's products or services as giving them greater value.

Markup

The basic premise of a successful business operation is selling a good or service for more than it costs to produce it. The difference between the cost of a product or service and its selling price is called **markup** (or **markon**). Markup can be expressed in dollars or as a percentage of either cost or selling price:

$$\text{Dollar markup} = \text{Retail price} - \text{Cost of the merchandise}$$

$$\text{Percentage (of retail price) markup} = \frac{\text{Dollar markup}}{\text{Retail price}}$$

$$\text{Percentage (of cost) markup} = \frac{\text{Dollar markup}}{\text{Cost of unit}}$$

For example, if a man's shirt costs $15, and the manager plans to sell it for $25, the markup is as follows:

$$\text{Dollar markup} = \$25 - \$14 = \$11$$

$$\text{Percentage (of retail price) markup} = \frac{\$11}{\$25}$$

$$= 44\%$$

$$\text{Percentage (of cost) markup} = \frac{\$11}{\$14}$$

$$= 78.6\%$$

The cost of merchandise used in computing markup includes not only the wholesale price of the merchandise but also any incidental costs (e.g., selling or transportation charges) that the retailer incurs.

Once entrepreneurs have a financial plan in place, including sales estimates and anticipated expenses, they can compute their companies' initial markup. The **initial markup** is the *average* markup required on all merchandise to cover the cost of the items, all incidental expenses, and a reasonable profit.

$$\text{Initial markup} = \frac{\text{Operating expenses} + \text{Reductions} + \text{Profits}}{\text{Net sales} + \text{Reductions}}$$

Operating expenses are the cost of doing business, such as rent, utilities, and depreciation; reductions include markdowns, special sales, employee discounts, and the cost of stockouts. For example, if a small retailer forecasts sales of $980,000, operating expenses of $540,000, and $24,000 in reductions, and she expects a profit of $58,000, the initial markup percentage is:

$$\text{Initial markup percentage} = \frac{\$540,000 + \$24,000 + \$58,000}{\$980,000 + \$24,000}$$

$$= 62\%$$

Any item in the store that carries a markup of at least 62 percent covers costs and meets the owner's profit objective. Any item that carries a markup less than 62 percent reduces the company's net income.

Once an entrepreneur determines the initial markup percentage, he or she can compute the appropriate retail price to achieve that markup using the following formula:

$$\text{Retail price} = \frac{\text{Dollar cost}}{(1 - \text{Initial markup percentage})}$$

For instance, applying the markup 62 percent to an item that cost the retailer $17.50 gives the following retail price:

$$\text{Retail price} = \frac{\$17.50}{(1 - 62\%)} = \$45.99$$

The owner establishes a retail price of $45.99 for the item using a 62 percent markup.

Finally, a retailer must verify that the computed retail price is consistent with the company's overall image. Is the final price congruent with the company's strategy? Is it within an acceptable price range? How does it compare with the prices charged by competitors? Perhaps most important, are the customers willing and able to pay this price?

Pricing Techniques for Manufacturers

5. Explain the pricing techniques used by manufacturers.

For manufacturers, the pricing decision requires the support of accurate, timely accounting records. The most commonly used pricing technique for manufacturers is **cost-plus pricing**. Using this method, manufacturers establish a price composed of direct materials, direct labor, factory overhead, selling and administrative costs, plus the desired profit margin. Figure 2 illustrates the components of cost-plus pricing.

The primary advantage of the cost-plus pricing method is its simplicity. Given the proper cost accounting data, computing a product's final selling price is relatively easy. In addition, because this technique adds a profit onto the top of the firm's costs, a manufacturer is likely to achieve the desired profit margin. This strategy does not encourage manufacturers to use their resources efficiently, however. Because manufacturers' cost structures vary so greatly, cost-plus pricing also fails to consider the competition adequately. Finally, cost-plus pricing fails to recognize the important relationships among price, value, and image. "The price that consumers are willing to pay has little to do with manufacturing costs," says pricing expert Rafi Mohammed. He says that a better pricing strategy is to capture "the value of a product, not simply mark up its costs."[36] Despite its drawbacks, the cost-plus method of establishing prices remains prominent in industries such as construction and printing.

Direct Costing and Pricing

One requisite for a successful pricing policy in manufacturing is a reliable cost accounting system that can generate timely reports to determine the costs of processing raw materials into finished goods. The traditional method of product costing is called **absorption costing** because all manufacturing and overhead costs are absorbed into the finished product's total cost. Absorption costing includes direct materials and direct labor, plus a portion of fixed and variable factory overhead costs, in each unit manufactured. Full-absorption financial statements are used in published annual reports and in tax reports and are very helpful in performing financial analysis. However, full-absorption statements are of little help to a manufacturer when determining prices or the impact of price changes.

A more useful technique for managerial decision making is **variable** (or **direct**) **costing**, in which the cost of the products manufactured includes only those costs that vary directly with the quantity produced. In other words, variable costing encompasses direct materials, direct labor, and factory overhead costs that vary with the level of the company's output of finished goods. Factory overhead costs that are fixed (e.g., rent, depreciation, and insurance) are *not* included in the costs of finished items. Instead, they are considered to be expenses of the period.

A manufacturer's goal when establishing prices is to discover the cost combination of selling price and sales volume that exceeds the variable costs of producing a product and contributes enough to cover fixed costs and earn a profit. Full-absorption costing clouds the true relationships among price, volume, and costs by including fixed expenses when calculating unit cost. Direct costing, however, yields a constant unit cost of the product no matter what the volume of production is. The result is a clearer picture of the price–volume–costs relationship.

FIGURE 2
Components of Cost-Plus Pricing

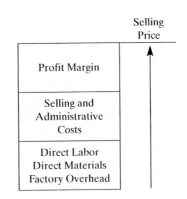

TABLE 2 Full-Absorption Versus Direct-Cost Income Statement

Full-Absorption Income Statement

Sales Revenue		$ 790,000
Cost of Goods Sold		
Materials	250,500	
Direct Labor	190,200	
Factory Overhead	120,200	560,900
Gross Profit		$ 229,100
Operating Expenses		
General & Administrative	66,100	
Selling	112,000	
Other	11,000	
Total Operating Expenses		189,100
Net Income (before taxes)		$ 40,000

Direct-Cost Income Statement

Sales Revenue (100%)		$ 790,000
Variable Costs		
Materials	250,500	
Direct Labor	190,200	
Variable Factory Overhead	13,200	
Variable Selling Expenses	48,100	
Total Variable Costs (63.5%)		502,000
Contribution Margin (36.5%)		288,000
Fixed Costs		
Fixed Factory Overhead	107,000	
Fixed Selling Expenses	63,900	
General and Administrative	66,100	
Other Fixed Expenses	11,000	
Total Fixed Expenses (31.4%)		248,000
Net Income (before taxes)(5.1%)		$ 40,000

The starting point for establishing product prices is the direct-cost income statement. As Table 2 indicates, the direct-cost statement yields the same net income as does the full-absorption income statement. The only difference between the two statements is the format. The full-absorption statement allocates costs such as advertising, rent, and utilities according to the activity that caused them, but the direct-cost income statement separates expenses into fixed and variable costs. Fixed expenses remain constant regardless of the production level, but variable expenses fluctuate according to production volume.

When variable costs are subtracted from total revenues, the result is the manufacturer's **contribution margin,** the amount remaining that contributes to covering fixed expenses and earning a profit. Expressing this contribution margin as a percentage of total revenue yields the firm's contribution percentage. Computing the contribution percentage is a critical step in establishing prices through the direct-costing method. This manufacturer's contribution percentage is 36.5 percent, which is calculated as follows:

$$\text{Contribution percentage} = 1 - \frac{\text{Variable expenses}}{\text{Revenues}}$$

$$= 1 - \frac{\$502,000}{\$790,000} = 36.5\%$$

Computing a Break-Even Selling Price

A manufacturer's contribution percentage tells what portion of total revenue remains after covering variable costs to contribute toward meeting fixed expenses and earning a profit. This manufacturer's contribution percentage is 36.5 percent, which means that variable costs absorb 63.5 percent of total revenues. In other words, variable costs represent 63.5 percent $(1.00 - 0.365 = 0.635)$ of the product's selling price. Suppose that this manufacturer's variable costs include the following:

Material	$2.08/unit
Direct labor	$4.12/unit
Variable factory overhead	$0.78/unit
Total variable cost	$6.98/unit

The minimum price at which the manufacturer would sell the item is $6.98. Any price below that would not cover variable costs. To compute the break-even selling price for his product, an entrepreneur uses the following equation:

$$\text{Break-even selling price} = \frac{\text{Profit} + \left(\dfrac{\text{Variable cost}}{\text{per unit}} \times \dfrac{\text{Quantity}}{\text{produced}}\right) + \dfrac{\text{Total}}{\text{fixed cost}}}{\text{Quantity produced}}$$

To break even, the manufacturer assumes $0 profit. Suppose that its plans are to produce 50,000 units of the product and that fixed costs will be $110,000. The break-even selling price is as follows:

$$\text{Break-even selling price} = \frac{\$0 + (\$6.98/\text{unit} \times 50,000 \text{ units}) + \$110,000}{50,000 \text{ units}}$$

$$= \frac{\$459,000}{50,000 \text{ units}}$$

$$= \$9.18 \text{ per unit}$$

Thus, $2.20 ($9.18/unit − $6.98/unit) of the $9.18 break-even price goes toward meeting fixed production costs. But suppose the manufacturer wants to earn a $50,000 profit. Then the required selling price is calculated as follows:

$$\text{Selling price} = \frac{\$50,000 + (6.98/\text{unit} \times 50,000 \text{ units}) + \$110,000}{50,000 \text{ units}}$$

$$= \frac{\$509,000}{50,000 \text{ units}}$$

$$= \$10.18/\text{unit}$$

Now the manufacturer must decide whether customers will purchase 50,000 units at $10.18. If the manufacturer thinks they won't, managers must decide either to produce a different, more profitable product or lower the selling price by lowering either its cost or its profit target. Any price above $9.18 will generate some profit, although less than that desired. In the short run, the manufacturer could sell the product for less than $9.18 if competitive factors dictate, but *not* below $6.98 because a price below $6.98 would not cover the variable costs of production.

Because the manufacturer's capacity in the short run is fixed, pricing decisions should be aimed at using resources most efficiently. The fixed cost of operating the plant cannot be avoided, and the variable costs can be eliminated only if the firm ceases to offer the product. Therefore, the selling price must be at least equal to the variable costs (per unit) of making the product. Any price above that amount contributes to covering fixed costs and providing a reasonable profit.

Of course, over the long run the manufacturer cannot sell below total costs and continue to survive. A product's selling price must cover total product costs—both fixed and variable—and generate a reasonable profit.

▶ ENTREPRENEURSHIP IN ACTION ▶

Guitars and Pearls: A Lesson in Pricing

Founded in 1833, C. F. Martin & Company is the oldest guitar maker in the world. Now in its sixth generation of family ownership, the company's acoustic guitars have a reputation for being among the highest quality, best sounding instruments on the market, and many stars—past and current, ranging from the King of Rock and Roll, Elvis Presley; the Singing Cowboy, Gene Autry; to Sting and Steve Miller—play nothing but a Martin. The company makes 52,000 guitars each year. Although employees use modern equipment in the manufacturing process, much of the work performed in the 300 steps required to build a guitar at 60 different workstations is done by the hands of highly skilled and experienced workers. Workers hand tune each guitar to make sure that its sound is just right. Prices for the most popular Martin guitars range from $2,000 to $3,000, but the company makes highly specialized limited edition models such as the D-100 Deluxe made of Brazilian rosewood, which sells for $110,000.

When a faltering economy caused consumers to pull back their spending and Martin's sales to decline, CEO Chris Martin was hesitant to reduce the company's prices because he feared diluting the company's reputation as a maker of fine guitars. "We needed something so we wouldn't have to lay people off," he says. To devise a strategy for dealing with declining sales, Chris Martin looked back at the company's rich history and took note of how his great-grandfather managed to get Martin through the Great Depression: He introduced a lower-cost guitar made of mahogany without any inlay or frills and priced it at

$20 to $30, a fraction of the price of the company's standard model that had beautiful wood, fancy inlays, and lots of features. The moderately priced models played an important role in the company's ability to survive the Depression and carried the company until the economy became stronger and Martin began producing its higher-end guitars once again.

In 2009, Martin introduced the Series 1 guitar, a solid wood guitar (no laminates) that, like its Depression-era predecessor, lacks inlays and extra features and sells for less than $1,000, which is considered a "sweet spot" in the industry. "For the money, they're very good instruments," says one long-time Martin retailer. "It was really smart of Martin to come out with [the Series 1] in the current economy. They are filling a niche quite well." Indeed, the company sold out of its entire first production run of 8,000 Series 1 guitars within 1 month. Production costs are considerably lower for the Series 1 because "we have fewer man-hours in each instrument," says Chris Martin. The strategy was successful because Martin could produce Series 1 guitars using the same basic production process and already had a network of distributors in place to sell them.

Although Jeremy Shepherd, founder of Pearl Paradise, an online retailer of pearls, is in a completely different industry, he faces many of the same challenges that Chris Martin did. As the economy slowed, Shepherd noticed that sales of high-end pearl jewelry began to decline. He had built his company by selling high-quality pearl necklaces and bracelets priced between $1,000 and $5,000. About 40 percent of the company's sales occurred during the last

Chris Martin is the sixth generation CEO of C. F. Martin & Company, a company that makes quality guitars, most of which are priced between $2,000 and $3,000. Martin is pictured holding his daughter, Claire Francis Martin, perhaps the seventh generation CEO of the company.

Source: Tim Shaffer/New York Times-Maps and Graphics

quarter of the year. As the crucial Christmas season drew near, Shepherd noticed that although traffic on the company's Web site had increased, the company's sales had declined. Customers were purchasing fewer high-end items, opting instead for pearl jewelry priced at less than $1,000. Shepherd and his employees began discussing their options for getting the company's sales back on track.

1. Visit the Web sites of C. F. Martin & Company (*www.martinguitar.com*) and Pearl Paradise (*www.pearlparadise.com*). Search online for more information on these companies. How are the two companies similar, particularly with regards to the

quality of the products they sell and the pricing strategies they use?

2. What course of action do you recommend that Shepherd take to improve sales at Pearl Paradise without damaging his company's reputation as a retailer of quality pearl jewelry and an expert in pearls? Explain.

Sources: Based on Timothy Appel, "Guitar Maker Revives No-Frills Act from the '30s," *Wall Street Journal*, July 6, 2009, pp. B1–B2; Ryan McCarthy, "Prices: How Low Can You Really Go?" *Inc.*, March 2009, pp. 91–92; "Famous Martin Owners," C. F. Martin & Company, *www.martinguitar.com/artists/famous.php*.

Pricing Techniques for Service Businesses

6. Explain the pricing techniques used by service firms.

Service businesses must establish their prices on the basis of the materials used to provide the service, the labor employed, an allowance for overhead, and a profit. As in a manufacturing operation, a service firm must have a reliable and accurate accounting system to track the total costs of providing the service. Most service firms base their prices on an hourly rate, usually the actual number of hours required to perform the service. For most firms, labor and materials constitute the largest portion of the cost of the service. To establish a reasonable and profitable price for service, the small business owner must know the cost of materials, direct labor, and overhead for each unit of service. Using these basic cost data and a desired profit margin, an owner of a small service firm can determine the appropriate price for the service.

Consider a simple example for pricing a common service—television repair. Ned's TV Repair Shop uses the direct-costing method to prepare an income statement for exercising managerial control (see Table 3). Ned estimates that he and his employees spend about 9,250 hours in the actual production of television repair service. The total cost per productive hour for Ned's TV Repair Shop is as follows:

$$\text{Total cost per hour} = \frac{\$104,000 + 68,000}{9,250 \text{ hours}} = \$18.59/\text{hour}$$

Now Ned must add in an amount for his desired profit. He expects a net operating profit margin of 18 percent on sales. To compute the final price, he uses the following equation:

$$\text{Price per hour} = \text{Total cost per productive hour} \div (1 - \text{net profit target as \% of sales})$$

$$= \$18.59 \div (1 - .18)$$

$$= \$22.68/\text{hour}$$

TABLE 3 **Direct-Cost Income Statement, Ned's TV Repair Shop**

Sales Revenue		$199,000
Variable Expenses		
Labor	52,000	
Materials	40,500	
Variable Factory Overhead	11,500	
Total Variable Expenses		104,000
Fixed Expenses		
Rent	2,500	
Salaries	38,500	
Fixed Overhead	27,000	
Total Fixed Expenses		68,000
Net Income		$ 27,000

A price of $22.68 per hour will cover Ned's costs and generate the desired profit. Smart service shop owners compute the cost per production hour at regular intervals throughout the year because they know that rising costs can eat into their profit margins very quickly. Rapidly rising labor costs and materials prices dictate that the service firm's price per hour be computed even more frequently. As in the case of the retailer and the manufacturer, Ned must evaluate the pricing policies of competitors and decide whether his price is consistent with the firm's image.

Of course, the price of $22.68 per hour assumes that all jobs require the same amount of materials. If this is not a valid assumption (and it probably is not), Ned must recalculate the price per hour without including the cost of materials.

$$\text{Cost per productive hour} = \frac{\$172{,}000 - \$40{,}500}{9{,}250 \text{ hours}}$$

$$= \$14.22/\text{hour}$$

Adding in the desired 18 percent net operating profit on sales yields:

$$\text{Price per hour} = \$14.22/\text{hour} \div (1 - .18)$$

$$= \$17.34/\text{hour}$$

Under these conditions Ned would charge $17.34 per hour plus the actual cost of materials used and a markup on the cost of materials. For instance, a repair job that takes 4 hours to complete would have the following price:

Cost of service (4 hours × $17.34/hour)	$ 69.36
Cost of materials	$ 41.00
Markup on materials (60%)	$ 24.60
Total price	$134.96

Because services are intangible, their pricing offers more flexibility than do tangible products. One danger that entrepreneurs face is pricing their services too low because prospective customers' perceptions of a service are influenced heavily by its price. In other words, establishing a low price for a service actually may harm a service company's sales!

Reid Carr, founder of Red Door Interactive, a San Diego–based company that specializes in Web services, prices each project that his company takes on by estimating the number of hours it will take to complete, multiplying that number by an hourly rate, and then including some "wiggle room" for unforeseen cost overruns. If the flow of work slows, Carr allows his employees to work on pro bono projects to raise the visibility of his company and to show the quality of work his employees create. "Pro bono work is free advertising," explains Carr.[37]

The Impact of Credit on Pricing

7. Describe the impact of credit on pricing.

In today's business environment, linking a company's pricing strategy with its credit strategy has become essential because many customers expect to "pay with plastic" rather than with cash. Consumers crave convenience when they shop, and one of the most common conveniences they demand is the ability to purchase goods and services on credit. Small businesses have three options for selling to customers on credit: credit cards, installment credit, and trade credit.

Credit Cards

Nearly 181 million Americans have credit cards. The average credit card holder has 4.4 credit cards but uses only two of them regularly. Shoppers use credit cards for more than 20 billion transactions a year to purchase nearly $2 trillion worth of goods and services annually.[38] The message

Shoppers purchase nearly $2 trillion worth of goods and services using credit cards each year. Accepting credit and debit cards increases a small company's customer base and leads to higher sales.

Source: Deklofenak/Shutterstock

is clear: Customers expect to make purchases with credit cards, and small companies that fail to accept credit cards run the risk of losing sales to competitors who do. Research shows that customers who use credit cards make purchases that are 112 percent higher than if they had used cash.[39] Accepting credit cards broadens a small company's customer base and closes sales that it would lose if customers had to pay in cash.

Companies that accept credit cards incur additional expenses for offering this convenience, however. Businesses must pay to use the system—typically 1 to 6 percent of total credit card charges, which they, in turn, must factor into the prices of their products or services. They also pay a transaction fee of 5 to 50 cents per charge (the average fee is 10 cents) and must purchase or lease equipment to process transactions. Fees operate on a multistep process. On a $100 Visa or MasterCard purchase at a typical business, a processing bank buys the credit card slip from the retailer for $97.71. The processing bank collects a processing fee of 40 cents and sells the slip to the bank that issued the card for about $98.11. The remaining $1.89 discount is called the interchange fee, which is what the processing bank passes along to the issuing bank. The prices entrepreneurs charge must reflect the higher costs associated with credit card transactions.

DEBIT CARDS. Consumers in the United States carry more than 507 million debit cards that act as electronic checks, automatically deducting the purchase amount immediately from a customer's checking account. Shoppers conduct more than 36 billion debit card transactions each year.[40] As customers' use of debit cards grows, small businesses also are equipping their stores to handle debit card transactions. The equipment is easy to install and to set up, and the cost to the company is negligible. The payoff can be big, however, in the form of increased sales and decreased losses from bad checks.

E-COMMERCE AND CREDIT CARDS. When it comes to online business transactions, the most common method of payment is the credit card. Internet vendors are constantly challenged by the need to provide secure methods of transacting business in a safe environment. Many shoppers are suspicious of online transactions for reasons of security and privacy. Therefore, online merchants must be sure to ensure their customers' privacy and the security of their credit card transactions by using computer encryption software.

Online merchants also face another obstacle: credit card fraud. Because they lack the face-to-face contact with their customers, online merchants face special challenges to avoid credit card fraud. According to a study by the Merchant Risk Council, online merchants lose 1.2 percent of their annual revenue, about $3.3 billion, to fraud each year.[41] Because small and mid-sized companies are less likely than large businesses to use high-tech online fraud detection tools, they are more likely to be victims of e-commerce fraud.[42] The following steps can help online merchants reduce the probability that they will become victims of credit card fraud:

- Use an address verification system (AVS) to compare every customer's billing information on the order form with the billing information in the bank or credit card company's records.
- Require customers to provide the CVV2 number from the back of the credit card. Although crooks can get access to this number, it can help screen out some fraudulent orders.
- Check customers' Internet Protocol (IP) addresses. If an order contains a billing address in California, but the IP address from which the order is placed is in China, chances are that the order is fraudulent.
- Monitor activity on the Web site with the help of a Web analytics software package. Many packages are available, and analyzing log files can help online entrepreneurs to pinpoint the sources of fraud.
- Verify large orders. Large orders are a cause for celebration, but only if they are legitimate. Check the authenticity of large orders, especially if the order is from a first-time customer.
- Post notices on the Web site that your company uses antifraud technology to screen orders. These notices make legitimate customers feel more confident about placing their orders and crooks trying to commit fraud tentative about running their scams.
- Contact the credit card company or the bank that issued the card. If you suspect that an order may be fraudulent, contact the company *before* processing it. Taking this step could save a small company thousands of dollars in losses.[43]

Installment Credit

Small companies that sell big-ticket consumer durables—major appliances, cars, and boats—frequently rely on installment credit. Because very few customers can purchase these items in a single lump-sum payment, small businesses finance them over time. The time horizon may range from just a few months up to 25 or more years. Most companies require the customer to make an initial down payment for the merchandise and then finance the balance for the life of the loan. The customer repays the loan principal plus interest on the loan. One advantage of installment loans for a small business is that the owner retains a security interest as collateral on the loan. If the customer defaults on the loan, the owner still holds the title to the merchandise. Because installment credit absorbs a small company's cash, many entrepreneurs rely on financial institutions such as banks and credit unions to provide the installment credit. When a business has the financial strength to "carry its own paper," the interest income from the installment loan contract often yields more than the initial profit on the sale of the product. For some businesses, such as auto dealerships and furniture stores, financing is an important source of revenue and profit.

Trade Credit

Many small companies, especially those that sell to other businesses, offer their customers trade credit; that is, they create customer charge accounts. The typical small business invoices its credit customers monthly. To speed collections, some offer cash discounts if customers pay their balances early; others impose penalties on late payers. Before deciding to use credit as a competitive weapon, the small business owner must make sure that the company's cash position is strong enough to support that additional pressure.

Trade credit can be a double-edged sword. Small businesses must be willing to grant credit to purchasers to get and keep their business, but they must manage credit accounts carefully to make sure that their customers pay in full and on time.

Chapter Review

1. Explain why pricing is both an art and a science.
   - Pricing requires a knowledge of accounting to determine the firm's cost; strategy to understand competitors' behaviors; and psychology to understand customers' behaviors.

2. Discuss the relationships among pricing, image, competition, and value.
   - Company pricing policies offer potential customers important information about the firm's overall image. Accordingly, when developing a marketing approach to pricing, business owners must establish prices that are compatible with what their customers expect and are willing to pay. Too often, small business owners *underprice* their goods and services, believing that low prices are the only way they can achieve a competitive advantage. They fail to identify the extra value, convenience, service, and quality they give their customers—all things many customers are willing to pay for.
   - An important part of setting appropriate prices is tracking competitors' prices regularly; however, what the competition is charging is just one variable in the pricing mix. When setting prices, business owners should take into account their competitors' prices, but they should not automatically match or beat them. Businesses that offer customers extra quality, value, service, or convenience can charge higher prices as long as customers recognize the "extras" they are getting. Two factors are vital to studying the effects of competition on the small firm's pricing policies: the location of the competitors and the nature of the competing goods.
3. Describe effective pricing strategies for both new and existing products and services.
   - Pricing a new product is often difficult for the small business owner, but it should accomplish three objectives: getting the product accepted, maintaining market share as the competition grows, and earning a profit.
   - Three major pricing strategies are generally used to introduce new products into the market: penetration, skimming, and sliding down the demand curve.
   - Pricing techniques for existing products and services include odd pricing, price lining, leader pricing, geographic pricing, opportunistic pricing, discounts, multiple pricing, bundling, and suggested retail pricing.
4. Explain the pricing techniques used by retailers.
   - Pricing for the retailer means pricing to move merchandise. Markup is the difference between the cost of a product or service and its selling price.
   - Some retailers use retail price, but others put a standard markup on all their merchandise; more frequently, they use a flexible markup.
5. Explain the pricing techniques used by manufacturers.
   - A manufacturer's pricing decision depends on the support of accurate cost-accounting records. The most common technique is cost-plus pricing, in which the manufacturer charges a price that covers the cost of producing a product plus a reasonable profit. Every manufacturer should calculate a product's break-even price, the price that produces neither a profit nor a loss.
6. Explain the pricing techniques used by service firms.
   - Service firms often suffer from the effects of vague, unfounded pricing procedures and frequently charge the going rate without any idea of their costs. A service firm must set a price based on the cost of materials used, labor involved, overhead, and a profit. The proper price reflects the total cost of providing a unit of service.
7. Describe the impact of credit on pricing.
   - Offering customer credit enhances a small company's reputation and increases the probability, speed, and magnitude of customers' purchases. Small firms offer three types of customer credit: credit cards, installment credit, and trade credit (charge accounts).

Discussion Questions

1. Stuart Frankel, a Subway franchisee, came up with the idea for Subway's "$5 footlong" to combat slow weekend sales at his restaurants. It was such a hit that Subway introduced the idea to all of its 33,000 outlets, and in 1 year it generated $3.8 billion in sales. One marketing consultant asks, "Is the $5 footlong just a flash in the pan, or is it a function of consumer price points and price elasticity that affect all markets?" What do you think?

2. What does the price of a good or service represent to the customer? Why is a customer orientation to pricing important?
3. How does pricing affect a small firm's image?
4. What competitive factors must the small firm consider when establishing prices?
5. Describe the strategies a small business could use when setting the price of a new product. What objectives should the strategy seek to achieve?

6. Define the following pricing techniques: odd pricing, price lining, leader pricing, geographic pricing, and discounts.

7. Why do many small businesses use the manufacturer's suggested retail price? What are the disadvantages of this technique?

8. What is markup? How is it used to determine prices?

9. What is follow-the-leader pricing? Why is it risky?

10. What is cost-plus pricing? Why do so many manufacturers use it? What are the disadvantages of using it?

11. Explain the difference between full-absorption costing and direct costing. How does absorption costing help a manufacturer determine a reasonable price?

12. Explain the techniques a small service firm can use to set an hourly price.

13. What is the relevant price range for a product or service?

14. What advantages and disadvantages does offering trade credit provide to a small business?

15. What are the most commonly used methods to purchase online using credit? What accounts for consumer uncertainty when giving credit card information online as opposed to via the telephone?

16. What advantages does accepting credit cards provide a small business? What costs are involved?

Business Plan Pro

Determining an "ideal" price for a product or service is challenging. Setting a price that is too low can generate high sales volume but also can reduce profit margins and possibly impede the company's ability to generate a positive cash flow. Setting a price that is too high may send potential customers to competitors, and sales may never materialize. Pricing is both an art and a science. The first step is to determine what it costs to provide your product or service to customers; the second step is to establish a price that covers total costs, generates a profit, and creates the desired image for your business. Setting the price of your products and services and knowing your company's break-even point is a fundamental element of your business plan. Resources and information are available within Business Plan Pro that may help you better understand the impact that pricing will have on your business.

On the Web

Conduct some competitive pricing research on the Web. Search for products and services that are similar to those that you are offering and list their price points. Check to see that you are making parallel comparisons of these products. For example, are you considering the entire price, which may include shipping, handling, complementary products, and other attributes that will influence the final price to the customer? Do you consider these businesses to be direct competitors? If not, why?

What does this information tell you about your price point? Is your price strategy consistent with your business strategy?

In the Software

Open your business plan and locate the "Break-Even" section under "Financial Plan." Follow the instructions and enter the information that will enable you to determine your break-even point. This will require you to have estimated figures for your fixed costs, variable costs, and prices. Once you have entered that information, look at the break-even point shown in units and revenue. Is this break-even point realistic? How long would you expect it would take to reach your break-even point? Is this time frame acceptable? Now increase your price by 10 percent. How does this change your break-even point? The software is an excellent tool to experiment with your break-even by entering different price points and costs to see the impact price will have on the break-even point when you will begin making a profit.

Building Your Business Plan

Go to the "Sales Forecast" table under the "Sales Strategy" section. An optional wizard will appear that you may select to help you through the process, or you can enter your information directly on the worksheet. If you have not done so yet, enter your price information in that section. Work through the rest of the table as you estimate your direct unit costs. The instructions and examples will assist you through that process.

Endnotes

1. Christopher T. Heun, "Dynamic Pricing Boosts Bottom Line," *Information Week*, October 29, 2001, *www.informationweek.com/story/showArticle.jhtml?articleID=6507202.*

2. Vincent Ryan, "Price Fixing," *CFO*, December 2009, p. 50.

3. Norm Brodsky, "Rule No. 1: Never Work for Chump Change," *Inc.*, March 2010, pp. 31–32.

4. Gary Walther, "The Sole of Stefano Bemer," *Forbes Life*, October 27, 2008, pp. 56–57.

5. Eric Arnold, "Aim High," *Forbes*, December 28, 2009, p. 86.

6. Howard Scott, "The Tricky Art of Raising Prices," *Nation's Business*, February 1999, p. 32.

7. Rick Bruns, "Tips for Coping with Rising Costs of Key Commodities," *Fast Company*, December 1997, pp. 27–30.

8. Rick Brooks, "More Businesses Slap on Fuel Fees," *Wall Street Journal*, May 4, 2006, pp. D1, D2; GiddyUp Fishing Charters, *www.captgiddyup.net/.*

9. Jeffrey A. Trachtenberg, "Borders Slashes Buyer Rewards, Cuts Discounts," *Wall Street Journal*, March 28, 2007, pp. D1, D4.

10. "Gas Prices Could Affect the Price of Pizzas, Flowers," *Greenville News*, April 29, 2006, p. 3A.

11. C. J. Prince, "Is the Price Right," *Entrepreneur*, November 2008, *www.entrepreneur.com/magazine/entrepreneur/2008/november/198068.html*.

12. Malika Zouhali-Worrall, "Ring in the Profits," *FSB*, December 2009/January 2010, p. 15.

13. Kate Dubose Tomassi, "Southwest Best Prepared for Rising Fuel Prices," *Forbes*, July 19, 2006, *www.forbes.com/markets/2006/07/19/southwest-airlines-markets06.html*.

14. Stacy Meichtry, "What Your Time Is Really Worth," *Wall Street Journal,* April 7–8, 2007, pp. P1, P4, and P5; Adam McCollum, "The Big Time," *Forbes Life*, September 18, 2006, *http://members.forbes.com/fyi/2006/0918/114.html*.

15. Adam McCollum, "Maîtres du Temps Chapter One," *Forbes Life*, October 27, 2008, p. 33.

16. Michael V. Marn, Eric V. Roegner, and Craig C. Zawada, "Pricing New Products," *McKinsey Quarterly*, Number 3, 2003, *www.mckinseyquarterly.com/article_abstract.aspx?ar=1329&l2=16&l3=19&srid=190&gp=0*.

17. Barbara Lyon, "Customer Service, Not Price, Remains Top Cause of Customer Churn, Accenture Study Finds," Accenture, November 18, 2008, *http://newsroom.accenture.com/article_print.cfm?article_id=4769article_id=4769*.

18. Greg Hardesty, "Luxury Mattress Is the Stuff of Dreams," *Greenville News*, August 15, 2009, p. 3D; "History," Hästens, *www.hastens.com/en/THE-EXPERIENCE/History/*.

19. C. J. Prince, "Is the Price Right?" *Entrepreneur*, November 2008, p. 55; Erin Chambers, "Career Reinvention: Wall Street Trader Turned Fitness Guru," *Wall Street Journal*, May 8, 2008, *http://online.wsj.com/article/SB121018652707174445.html*; "Our Story," Iron Core, *www.ironcorekettlebells.com/story/*.

20. "ABA Asks Department of Justice to Investigate Bookseller Price Wars," *Bookselling This Week*, October 22, 2009, *http://news.bookweb.org/news/aba-asks-department-justice-investigate-bestseller-price-wars*; Veronica G. Rodriguez, "Bookstores," Small Business Development Center National Information Clearing House, May 2007, pp. 1–5.

21. Richard Gibson, "Big Price Cut at McDonald's Seems a McFlop," *Wall Street Journal*, May 9, 1997, pp. B1, B2; Richard Gibson, "Prices Tumble on Big Macs, but Fries Rise," *Wall Street Journal*, April 25, 1997, pp. B1, B2; Cliff Edwards, "Some McDonald's Franchisees Quietly Boosting Prices to Offset Cost of Promotion," *Greenville News*, April 26, 1997, p. 8D.

22. Jim Barnes, "Stop Cutting Prices! Retain Customers with Four Types of Experiential Value," Customer Think, April 24, 2009, *www.customerthink.com/article/retain_customers_with_four_types_experiential_value*.

23. Allison Stein Wellner, "Is It Time to Raise Prices?" *Inc.*, June 2005, p. 80.

24. Norm Brodsky, "Dealing with Cost Hikes," *Inc.*, August 2005, p. 49.

25. Gladys Edmunds, "Price Is Right? Not If It's Too Low," *USA Today*, June 8, 2005, *www.usatoday.com/money/smallbusiness/columnist/edmunds/2005-06-08-price_x.htm*.

26. Lisa Sefcik, "About Chantecaille," *Live Strong*, October 4, 2009, *www.livestrong.com/article/25297-chantecaille/*; Rachel Dodes and Cheryl Lu-Lien Tan, "What Price Beauty? Costly Face Creams Lift Prices, Spirits," *Wall Street Journal*, December 19, 2006, pp. A1, A12.

27. "New Study on Retail Discounting: What Works for Some Products Might Be a Bust for Others," Kelley School of Business, Indiana University, November 18, 2009, *http://info.kelley.iu.edu/news/page/normal/12630.html*.

28. Josh Hyatt, "And in This Corner, the Price-Fighter," *CFO*, December 2008, p. 29.

29. Lisa Baertlein, "Subway's $5 Deal a Hard Habit to Break," *Reuters*, September 17, 2009, *www.reuters.com/article/idUSTRE58G6NG20090917*.

30. "NPD: Restaurants Likely to Wean Customers Off Discounts/Deals," *Fast Casual*, May 20, 2010, *www.fastcasual.com/article.php?id=18348*.

31. "Don't Let This One Get Away," *Get to the Point: Customer Insight*, January 20, 2010, pp. 1–2.

32. Mark Brandeau, "Chains Mull Benefits of Value Menus, Combo Deals," *Nation's Restaurant News*, February 23, 2009, *www.nrn.com/breakingNews.aspx?id=363398&menu_id=1368*.

33. "City Swingers," *Forbes Life*, September 2006, p. 30; "Swing Set," *Men's Vogue*, April 2007, *www.mensvogue.com/health/regimen/articles/2007/04/drive_495*.

34. Hiroshi Suzuki, "Nintendo's Japan Wii Sales Double Those of Sony PlayStation 3," *Bloomberg News*, April 2, 2007, *www.bloomberg.com/apps/news?pid=conewsstory&refer=conews&tkr=NTDOY:US&sid=a_A5anLn.xE8*; Brian Bremmer, "Will Nintendo's Wii Strategy Score?" *Business Week*, September 20, 2006, *www.businessweek.com/globalbiz/content/sep2006/gb20060920_163780.htm*; Kathleen Sanders and Matt Casamassina, "U.S. Wii Price, Launch Date Revealed," *IGN Entertainment*, September 13, 2006, *http://wii.ign.com/articles/732/732669p1.html*; "Playing a Different Game," *Economist*, October 26, 2006, *www.economist.com/business/displaystory.cfm?story_id=8080787*.

35. Joseph Pereira, "State Law Targets 'Minimum Pricing,'" *Wall Street Journal*, April 28, 2009, p. D1.

36. Rafi Mohammed, "Apple's iPad Can Capitalize on Fragmented Marketplace," *The Wrap*, February 8, 2010, *www.thewrap.com/blog-entry/apples-ipad-can-capitalize-fragmenting-marketplace-14006*.

37. David Worrell, "Time Well Spent," *Entrepreneur*, June 2006, p. 63.

38. Ben Woolsey and Matt Schulz, "Credit Card Statistics, Industry Facts, Debt Statistics," *CreditCards.com*, May 13, 2010, *www.creditcards.com/credit-card-news/credit-card-industry-facts-personal-debt-statistics-1276.php#issuervolume*.

39. "Credit Counseling Statistics," Consumer Credit Counseling Service, *http://creditcounselingbiz.com/credit_counseling_statistics.htm*.

40. Ben Woolsey and Matt Schulz, "Credit Card Statistics, Industry Facts, Debt Statistics," *CreditCards.com*, May 13, 2010, *www.creditcards.com/credit-card-news/credit-card-industry-facts-personal-debt-statistics-1276.php#issuervolume*.

41. "Merchant Risk Council Announces Annual e-Commerce Fraud Survey Results," Merchant Risk Council, March 10, 2010, *www.merchantriskcouncil.org/index.cfm?fuseaction=Feature.showFeature&FeatureID=137*.

42. "Merchants Hit Back at E-Commerce Fraud," CyberSource, November 17, 2009, *www.cybersource.com/news_and_events/view.php?page_id=1798*.

43. Michael Bloch, "Preventing Credit Card Chargebacks—Anti-Fraud Strategies," Taming the Beast, *www.tamingthebeast.net/articles2/card-fraud-strategies.htm*.

Sources of Debt Financing

Always borrow from pessimists. They never expect to get it back.

—Anonymous

The best source of money is not to need it.

—Therese Flaherty

Learning Objectives

Upon completion of this chapter, you will be able to:

1. Describe the various sources of debt capital and the advantages and disadvantages of each.
2. Explain the types of financing available from nonbank sources of credit.
3. Identify the sources of government financial assistance and the loan programs these agencies offer.
4. Describe the various loan programs available from the Small Business Administration.
5. Discuss state and local economic development programs.
6. Discuss methods of financing growth and expansion internally with bootstrap financing.
7. Explain how to avoid becoming a victim of a loan scam.

Debt financing involves the funds that a small business owner borrows and must repay with interest. Small companies in the United States rely heavily on debt capital to start and feed their growing businesses. The U.S. Small Business Administration (SBA) estimates that lenders make $700 billion worth of loans of less than $1 million to small companies each year. Add to that amount loans from family members and friends and credit card borrowing, and total small business borrowing approaches $1 trillion a year.[1] Lenders of capital are more numerous than investors, but small business loans can be just as difficult (if not more difficult) to obtain, especially given the recent turbulence in the financial markets. Small businesses are facing a credit crunch; the crises on Wall Street have severely limited credit on Main Street. A recent survey by the National Federation of Independent Businesses (NFIB) reports that just 50 percent of small business owners who attempted to borrow money received at least most of the capital they sought, down from 89 percent just 3 years before.[2] The NFIB also reports that capital spending by small businesses, which is fueled by their access to financing, is hovering just above a 35-year low.[3] When entrepreneurs do not have access to credit, they cannot make capital investments, and their companies do not grow as fast, hire as many employees, and generate as much in sales—and the entire economy suffers.

The government's attempt to increase the availability of credit through the Troubled Asset Relief Program (TARP), which the Treasury Department launched at the pinnacle of the financial meltdown, failed to improve access to credit, especially for small companies, according to a report from the Congressional Oversight Panel.[4]

ENTREPRENEURIAL
Profile

*Frank and Ingrid
Brown: The Villager*

Frank and Ingrid Brown, owners of The Villager, a gallery in Auburn, Alabama, that sells affordable artwork from more than 150 artists from across the United States, needed capital to expand their business, which currently has 20 employees. They approached a bank for a loan backed by a guarantee from the U.S. Small Business Administration's 7(a) loan program, but the bank rejected their application. The Browns then applied for the maximum $35,000 loan through America's Recovery Capital (ARC) loan program, which Congress passed in response to the banking crisis as a way to provide financing to viable but struggling small companies. After completing volumes of paperwork, the Browns received a loan, but for just $14,000. "We couldn't get any answers for why we didn't get the full amount," says Frank, who says that the small loan was hardly worth the effort required to complete the application process. The Browns also are frustrated because their local bank extended their business a $10,000 line of credit, just 20 percent of the amount they had requested. "People like us hire people," says Frank, "but without the capital it needs to grow, The Villager isn't bringing on new staffers."[5]

Although entrepreneurs who borrow capital maintain complete ownership of their businesses, they must carry it as a liability on the balance sheet as well as repay it with interest at some point in the future. In addition, because lenders consider small businesses to be greater risks than bigger corporate customers, small companies must pay higher interest rates because of the risk–return trade-off—the higher the risk, the greater the return demanded. Most small firms pay the **prime rate**, the interest rate banks charge their most creditworthy customers, *plus* two or more percentage points. Still, the cost of debt financing often is lower than that of equity financing because debt financing does not require entrepreneurs to dilute their ownership interest in the company.

The need for debt capital can arise from a number of sources, but financial experts identify the following reasons business owners should consider borrowing money:[6]

- *Increasing the company's workforce and/or inventory to boost sales.* Sufficient working capital is the fuel that feeds a company's growth.
- *Gaining market share.* Businesses often need extra capital as their customer bases expand and they incur the added expense of extending credit to customers.
- *Purchasing new equipment.* Financing new equipment that can improve productivity, increase quality, and lower operating expenses often takes more capital than a growing company can generate internally.

- *Refinancing existing debt.* As companies become established, they can negotiate more favorable borrowing terms compared to their start-up days, when entrepreneurs take whatever money they can get at whatever rate they can get. Replacing high-interest loans with loans carrying lower interest rates improves cash flow significantly.
- *Taking advantage of cash discounts.* Suppliers sometimes offer discounts to customers who pay their invoices early. "Purchasing, Quality Management, and Vendor Analysis," business owners should take advantage of cash discounts in most cases.
- *Buying the building in which the business is located.* Many entrepreneurs start out renting the buildings that house their businesses; however, if location is crucial to their success, it may be wise to purchase the location.
- *Establishing a relationship with a lender.* If a business has never borrowed money, taking out a loan and developing a good repayment and credit history can pave the way for future financing. Smart business owners know that bankers who understand their businesses play an integral role in their companies' ultimate success.
- *Retiring debt held by a "nonrelationship" creditor.* Entrepreneurs find that lenders who have no real interest in their companies' long-term success or do not understand their businesses can be extremely difficult to work with. They prefer to borrow money from lenders who are willing to help them achieve their business mission and goals.
- *Foreseeing a downturn in business.* Establishing access to financing before a business slowdown hits insulates a company from a serious cash crisis and protects it from failure.

Entrepreneurs seeking debt capital face an astounding range of credit options varying greatly in complexity, availability, and flexibility. Not all of these sources of debt capital are equally favorable, however. By understanding the various sources of capital—both commercial and government lenders—and their characteristics, entrepreneurs can greatly increase the chances of obtaining a loan.

Figure 1 shows the financing strategies that small business owners use for their companies. We now turn to the various sources of debt capital.

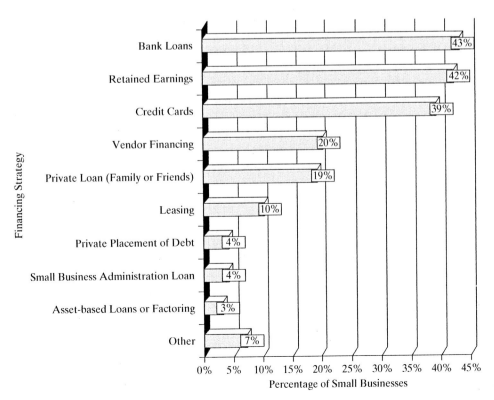

FIGURE 1
Small Business Financing Strategies

Source: 2010 Mid-Year Economic Report, National Small Business Association, p. 8.

IN THE ENTREPRENEURIAL
SPOTLIGHT A Tale of Two Borrowers

Aaron's Automotive

Tari Dudley had a plan to open a woman-friendly auto repair shop in Fort Worth, Texas, and operate it with her son-in-law, Aaron Phelps, who had owned a swimming pool cleaning business. Dudley had $47,000 in collateral, including a $30,000 certificate of deposit, and an excellent credit rating. Neither Dudley nor Phelps had operated a repair shop before, but Phelps had worked on cars all of his life and recently had returned to school to become a certified mechanic.

However, when Dudley applied for a $250,000 loan at the bank where she had been a customer for 24 years, the loan officer did not bother to hand her an application; instead, he wrote her name and phone number on a small adhesive note. "That was it," says Dudley, who suspects that the loan officer threw away the note as soon as she left the bank. She then applied for a loan at two community banks, both of which were impressed with her plan for an auto repair shop aimed at women. After 3 weeks, however, both rejected Dudley's loan request.

Like many entrepreneurs, Dudley is caught square in the middle of a severe credit crunch. Government officials are encouraging banks to lend money; bankers say they want to lend money but claim that government policies discourage them from doing so.

After striking out at banks, Dudley turned to a private investor, who promised to put up $30,000 but later backed out. Undeterred by the inability to get capital, Dudley and Phelps decided to forge ahead with their repair shop, confident that it would be successful. Dudley emptied her 401(k) retirement account and invested the severance pay she received from her former job, and Phelps and his wife contributed their savings account. They also scaled back their start-up costs, holding off on the purchase of an $80,000 piece of diagnostic equipment until their business becomes cash flow positive. They opened their repair shop, Aaron's Automotive ("the woman-friendly shop") with two employees and rely on a credit card with a $12,000 limit to cover their monthly deficits. They charge $80 per hour for labor, an amount that is below what most auto dealerships in the area charge. Customers are beginning to discover the business, but Dudley and Phelps do not have the money to advertise. "We're keeping our head above water," says Dudley. As the entrepreneurs fill small bags with candy, business cards, and pens bearing the Aaron's Automotive logo to deliver to prospective customers, Dudley says, "It's all about cash flow. I can't put out a big sign because we don't have the money. I can't advertise. So we're putting candy in bags."

Gorman Mechanical

Michael Mushegan, a graduate of the University of Arizona with a degree in finance, wanted to purchase Gorman Mechanical, a company in Azle, Texas, that installs and services commercial and residential heating and air conditioning units in the Dallas–Fort Worth area. Mushegan was familiar with the industry because he had grown up in it; his family operated a similar business in Arizona. Mushegan applied for a loan to purchase Gorman Mechanical, which had been in business for nearly 10 years and was profitable, at the bank where he was a customer. When the loan officer did not ask detailed questions about the business, the loan, and how he would use the money, Mushegan knew that his chances of getting financing were slim. Then he learned about SBA-guaranteed loans and discovered that a large bank, Wells Fargo, was one of the most active SBA lenders in the nation. Mushegan applied for an SBA-backed loan at Wells Fargo. "[Bankers told me] that industry experience is crucial and that my credit rating was outstanding, which also was extremely important," he says.

With an SBA loan guarantee, Wells Fargo approved Mushegan's loan application. After putting up 15 percent of the purchase price using his own money and investments from family, he took over Gorman Mechanical and became a business owner for the first time.

1. One of these businesses received a bank loan and the other did not. Describe the differences between the two companies that led to one entrepreneur receiving the financing he needed and the other one failing to qualify for a loan.
2. What steps would you have recommended to Tari Dudley to increase the probability of qualifying for a loan?
3. Suppose that Dudley had approached you for help after being turned down by three banks. What other sources of capital would you have suggested she use?

Source: Based on Barry Shlacter, "Small Businesses Continue to Feel Lending Pinch," *Fort Worth Star-Telegram*, December 27, 2009, *www.finreg21. com/news/small-businesses-continue-feel-lending-pinch-4.*

Sources of Debt Capital

Commercial Banks

1. Describe the various sources of debt capital and the advantages and disadvantages of each.

Commercial banks are the very heart of the financial market, providing the greatest number and variety of loans to small businesses. Commercial banks provide 50 percent of the dollar value of all loans to small businesses.[7] For small business owners, banks are lenders of *first* resort, especially as their companies grow. The typical loan amount is small; more than 88 percent of all small business bank loans are for less than $100,000 (see Figure 2). The average micro business loan (those less than $100,000) is $6,820, and the average small business loan (those between $100,000 and $1 million) is $245,775.

ENTREPRENEURIAL
Profile

Blanca and Robert Welborn: Med-National

Med-National, a company founded in 1987 by Blanca and Robert Welborn in San Antonio, Texas, that provides medical and dental services to the Department of Defense, applied for a $300,000 loan from several local banks with which the company had done business in the past. The company needed the financing to hire 20 doctors, dentists, and support staff to secure two contracts with the U.S. Army. Even though Med-National generates nearly $6 million in annual sales, has been profitable since its inception, and has an excellent credit rating, the banks refused the loan request. After nearly a year, the Welborn's persistence finally paid off when they secured the $300,000 loan they needed from one of the nation's largest small business lenders, Wells Fargo. Despite the Welborn's success, lack of access to credit has slowed their company's growth. "If we could borrow money more easily, we would be hiring even more people," says Robert.[8]

Banks tend to be conservative in their lending practices and prefer to make loans to established small businesses rather than to high-risk start-ups. Small companies that are less than 3 years old are as much as 50 percent less likely to receive loans or lines of credit than older, more established businesses.[9] Because start-ups are so risky, bankers prefer to make loans to companies that have successful track records. Banks are concerned with a small company's operating past and scrutinize its records to project its position in the immediate future. They also want proof of a company's stability and its ability to generate adequate cash flows that ensure repayment of the loan. If they do make loans to a start-up venture, banks like to see significant investment from the owner, sufficient cash flows to repay the loan, ample collateral (such as compensating balances)

FIGURE 2

Commercial Bank Loans to Small Businesses by Size of Loan

Source: The Small Business Economy: A Report to the President, 2009, p. 74.

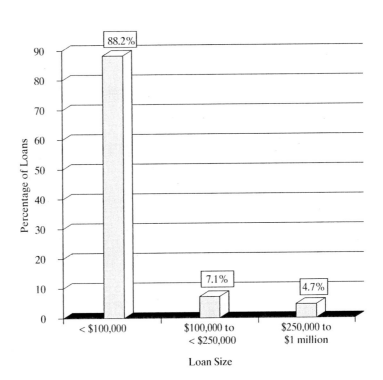

to secure it, or an SBA guarantee to insure it. Entrepreneurs should not overlook small community banks (those with less than $10 billion in assets) for loans. These small banks, which make up 98.7 percent of U.S. banking institutions, account for 52 percent of the dollar volume of all small business loans.[10] They also tend to be "small business–friendly" and are more likely than their larger counterparts to customize the terms of their loans to the particular needs of small businesses, offering, for example, flexible payment terms to match the seasonal pattern of a company's cash flow or interest-only payments until a piece of equipment begins generating revenue.

When evaluating a loan application, banks focus on a company's capacity to create positive cash flow because they know that's where the money to repay their loans will come from. The first question in most bankers' minds when reviewing an entrepreneur's business plan is "Can this business generate sufficient cash to repay the loan?" Even though they rely on collateral to secure their loans, the last thing banks want is for a borrower to default, forcing them to sell the collateral (often at "fire sale" prices) and use the proceeds to pay off the loan. *That's* why bankers stress cash flow when analyzing a loan request, especially for a business start-up. "Cash is more important than your mother," jokes one experienced borrower.[11]

Banks, as well as many other lenders, also require that entrepreneurs sign a personal guarantee for any loan they make to small businesses. By making a personal loan guarantee, an entrepreneur is pledging that he or she will be personally liable for repaying the loan in the event that the business itself cannot repay the loan. In the eyes of the law a sole proprietor or a general partner and the business are one and the same; therefore, for them, personal loan guarantees are redundant. However, because the owners of S corporations, corporations, and LLCs are separate from their businesses, they are not automatically responsible for the company's debts. Once the owners of these businesses sign a personal loan guarantee, however, they become liable for their companies' loans. (It is as if these individuals have "cosigned" the loan with the business.) Working with a partner, Rosalind Resnick launched NetCreations, an Internet marketing company, using money from various sources, including bank loans. The bank "required us to provide personal guarantees for [NetCreation's] credit line and equipment lease—loans that totaled $2 million," says Resnick. "It wasn't until our company went public that the bank let us off the hook [for those loans]."[12]

Short-Term Loans

Short-term loans, extended for less than 1 year, are the most common type of commercial loan banks make to small companies. These funds typically are used to replenish the working-capital account to finance the purchase of inventory, boost output, finance credit sales to customers, or take advantage of cash discounts. As a result, an owner repays the loan after converting inventory and receivables into cash. There are several types of short-term loans.

COMMERCIAL LOANS (OR TRADITIONAL BANK LOANS). The basic short-term loan is the commercial bank's specialty. Business owners typically repay the loan, which often is unsecured because secured loans are much more expensive to administer and maintain, as a lump sum within 3 to 6 months. In other words, the bank grants a loan to the small business owner without requiring him or her to pledge any specific collateral to support the loan in case of default. The owner repays the total amount of the loan at maturity. Sometimes the interest due on the loan is prepaid—deducted from the total amount borrowed. Until a small business is able to prove its financial strength and liquidity (cash flow) to the bank's satisfaction, it will probably not qualify for this kind of commercial loan.

LINES OF CREDIT. One of the most common requests entrepreneurs make of banks is to establish a **line of credit**, a short-term loan with a preset limit that provides much needed cash flow for day-to-day operations. With a commercial (or revolving) line of credit, business owners can borrow up to the predetermined ceiling at any time during the year quickly and conveniently by writing themselves a loan. Banks set up lines of credit that are renewable for anywhere from 90 days to several years, and they usually limit the open line of credit to 40 to 50 percent of a firm's present working capital, although they may lend more for highly seasonal businesses. Bankers may require a company to rest its line of credit during the year, maintaining a zero balance, as proof that the line of credit is not a perpetual crutch. Like commercial loans, lines of credit can be secured or unsecured. Small lines of credit often are unsecured, and large ones usually are secured by accounts receivable, inventory, equipment, or other business assets. A business typically pays a small handling fee (1 to 2 percent of the maximum amount of credit) plus interest on the amount borrowed—usually prime-plus-three points or more. Because banks prefer the security of established businesses, securing a line of credit can be difficult for some small companies, especially new ones. A study by the National Federation of Independent Businesses reports that the most difficult type of loan for small business owners to obtain is a line of credit; only 37.6 percent of the small companies that apply receive one.[13]

ENTREPRENEURIAL
Profile

Brad Glaberson: Cucina Fresca, Inc.

Brad Glaberson, founder of Cucina Fresca, Inc., a specialty foods company in Seattle, Washington, switched from the bank he had used for 10 years when his banker eliminated his company's $70,000 line of credit and converted the existing $38,000 balance to a term loan. Glaberson approached Foundation Bank, a small community bank in Seattle, and offered loan officers a tour of his operations, monthly financial reports, and access to all of his company's financial records as part of his loan application. Foundation Bank extended Cucina Fresca a $102,000 line of credit, which Glaberson used to launch a new product line called Lazy Lasagna.[14]

Table 1 shows one method for determining how large a line of credit a small company should seek.

FLOOR PLANNING. Floor planning is a form of financing frequently employed by retailers of "big-ticket items" that are easily distinguishable from one another (usually by serial number), such as automobiles, recreational vehicles, boats, and major appliances. For example, Thrifty

TABLE 1 How Large Should Your Line of Credit Be?

Determining how large a small company's line of credit should be is an important step for a growing business. As a company's sales grow, so will its inventory and accounts receivable balances, both of which tie up valuable cash. To avoid experiencing a cash crisis, many growing companies rely on a line of credit. How large should that line of credit be? The following formulas will help you answer that question:

$$\frac{\text{Average collection}}{\text{period ratio}} + \frac{\text{Average inventory}}{\text{turnover ratio}} - \frac{\text{Average payable}}{\text{period ratio}} = \frac{\text{Cash}}{\text{flow cycle}}$$

Cash flow cycle $\times$ Average daily sales $-$ Forecasted annual profit $=$ Line of credit requirement

Example: Suppose that Laramie Corporation has an average collection period ratio of 49 days and an average inventory turnover ratio of 53 days. The company's average payable period is 39 days, its annual sales are $5,800,000, and its net profit margin is 6.5 percent. What size line of credit should Laramie seek?

Average collection period ratio	49 days
Average inventory turnover ratio	53 days
Total	102 days
Minus average payable period ratio	39 days
Cash flow cycle	63 days
Annual sales	$5,800,000
Average daily sales (annual sales ÷ 365 days)	$ 15,890
Cash flow cycle	63 days
Times average daily sales	$ 15,890
Equals	$1,001,096
Minus forecasted profit (annual sales × net profit margin)	377,000
Equals line of credit requirement	$ 624,096

Laramie Corporation should seek a line of credit of $624,000.

Source: Adapted from George M. Dawson, "It Figures," *Entrepreneur Start-Ups,* December 2000, p. 27.

Car Sales makes a floor-plan financing program available to the network of franchised dealers that sell the used cars that are taken out of service from its Thrifty Car Rental system. Bombadier Capital, the provider of the floor plan, finances Thrifty Car Sales dealers' purchases of automobiles from Thrifty Car Rental and maintains a security interest in each car by holding its title as collateral.[15] Dealers pay interest on the loan monthly and repay the principal as the cars are sold. The longer a floor-planned item sits in inventory, the more it costs a business owner in interest expense. Banks and other floor planners often discourage retailers from using their money without authorization by performing spot checks to verify prompt repayment of the principal as items are sold.

Intermediate and Long-Term Loans

Banks primarily are lenders of short-term capital to small businesses, although they will make certain intermediate and long-term loans. Intermediate and long-term loans are extended for 1 year or longer and are normally used to increase fixed- and growth-capital balances. Commercial banks grant these loans for starting a business, constructing a plant, purchasing real estate and equipment, and other long-term investments. Loan repayments are normally made monthly or quarterly.

TERM LOANS. Another common type of loan banks make to small businesses is a **term loan**. Typically unsecured, banks grant these loans to businesses whose past operating history suggests a high probability of repayment. Some banks make only secured term loans, however. Term loans impose restrictions (called **covenants**) on the business decisions an entrepreneur makes concerning the company's operations. For instance, a term loan may set limits on owners' salaries, prohibit further borrowing without the bank's approval, or maintain certain financial ratios. An entrepreneur must understand all of the terms attached to a loan before accepting it.

INSTALLMENT LOANS. These loans are made to small firms for purchasing equipment, facilities, real estate, and other fixed assets. When financing equipment, a bank usually lends the small business from 60 to 80 percent of the equipment's value in return for a security interest in the equipment. The loan's amortization schedule typically coincides with the length of the equipment's usable life. When financing real estate (commercial mortgages), banks typically will lend up to 75 to 80 percent of the property's value and will allow a lengthier repayment schedule of 10 to 30 years.

Source: www.CartoonStock.com

CHARACTER LOANS. Banking regulatory changes intended to create jobs by increasing the credit available to small- and medium-sized companies now allow banks to make **character loans.** Rather than requiring entrepreneurs to prove their creditworthiness with financial statements, evaluations, appraisals, and tax returns, banks making character loans base their lending decisions on the borrower's reputation and reliability (i.e., "character").

The Lessons from the Street-Smart Entrepreneur feature describes how small business owners can maintain positive relationships with their bankers.

LESSONS FROM THE STREET-SMART **entrepreneur**

How to Maintain a Positive Relationship with Your Banker

Too often, entrepreneurs communicate with their bankers only when they find themselves in a tight spot and needing money. Unfortunately, that's not the best way to manage a working relationship with a bank. "Businesspeople have a responsibility to train their bankers in their businesses," says one lending advisor. "A good banker will stay close to the business, and a good business will stay close to the banker." A good banking relationship has the power to influence in a significant way the success of a small business.

How can business owners develop and maintain positive relationships with their bankers? The first step is picking the right bank and the right banker. Some banks are not terribly enthusiastic about making small business loans, whereas others target small businesses as their primary customers. Entrepreneurs should visit several banks—both small community banks and large national banks—and talk with a commercial loan officer about their banking needs and the bank's products and services. After finding the right banker, the entrepreneur must focus on maintaining effective communication. The best strategy is to keep bankers informed—*of both good news and bad.*

Karyn Korteling started her restaurant, Pastabilities, in downtown Syracuse, New York, when the city's downtown revitalization efforts were just underway. She knew that a quality restaurant located downtown could be successful by appealing to the 30,000 people who worked in the area. The menu of delicious pastas, pizzas, salads, and specialty dishes struck a chord with the lunch crowd, and soon Pastabilities also became a gathering spot for people heading out for a night on the town. Pastabilities has grown from a one-room lunch spot into a full-blown restaurant with three dining rooms, a full-service bar, and seasonal outdoor dining in a quaint plaza. Ready to add a second location but needing financing to make the move, Korteling has been meeting with her banker for several months to discuss the company's financial performance and expansion plans. She keeps her banker informed about the progress of her company (such as how she has trained her management team so that she can split her time between two locations) as well as the challenges it faces. She also asks for advice on some issues. "The more they know about you and your business, the better," she says.

What else can entrepreneurs do to manage their banking relationships?

- *Understand the factors that influence a banker's decision to lend money.* Bankers *want* to lend money to businesses; that's how they generate a profit. However, they want to lend money to businesses they believe offer a very high probability of repaying their loans on time. Bankers look for companies that are good credit risks and have clear plans for success.
- *Invite the banker to visit your company.* An on-site visit gives the banker the chance to see exactly what a company does and how it does it. It's also a great opportunity to show the bank where and how its money is put to use.
- *Make a good impression.* A company's physical appearance can go a long way toward making either a positive (or a negative) impression on a banker. Lenders appreciate clean, safe, orderly work environments and view sloppily maintained facilities (such as spills, leaks, and unnecessary clutter) as negatives.
- *Send customer mailings to the banker as well.* "Besides the numbers, we try to give our bankers a sense of our vision for the business," says Mitchell Goldstone, president of Thirty-Minute Photos Etc. Goldstone sends customer mailings to his bankers "so they know we're thinking about opportunities to generate money."
- *Send the banker samples of new products.* "I try to make my banker feel as if he's a partner," says Drew Santin, president of a product-development company. "Whenever we get a new machine, I go out of my way to show the banker what it does."

- *Show off your employees.* Bankers know that one of the most important components of building a successful company is a dedicated team of capable employees. Giving bankers the opportunity to visit with employees and ask them questions while touring a company can help alleviate fears that they are pumping their money into a high-risk "one-person show."
- *Know your company's assets.* Almost always interested in collateral, bankers will want to judge the quality of your company's assets—property, equipment, inventory, accounts receivable, and others. Be sure to point them out. "As you walk the lender through your business," says one experienced banker, "it's always a good idea to identify assets the banker might not think of."
- *Be prepared to personally guarantee any loans the bank makes to your business.* Even though many business owners choose the corporate form of ownership for its limited liability benefits, some are surprised when a banker asks them to make personal guarantees on business loans. It's a common practice, especially on small business loans.
- *Keep your business plan up-to-date and make sure your banker gets a copy of it.* Bankers lend money to companies that can demonstrate that they will use the money wisely and productively. They also

want to make sure that the company offers a high probability of repayment. The best way to provide bankers with that assurance is with a solid business plan.
- *Know how much money you need and how you will repay it.* When a banker asks "How much money do you need?" the correct answer is not "How much can I get?"

1. What advantages do entrepreneurs gain by communicating openly with their bankers?
2. Why do so few entrepreneurs follow Karyn Korteling's example when dealing with their bankers?
3. What are the consequences of an entrepreneur failing to communicate effectively with a banker?

Sources: Based on Emily Maltby, "Uptick Catches Entrepreneurs by Surprise," *Wall Street Journal*, December 8, 2009, p. B7; Keith Lowe, "Keep Your Banker Informed," *Entrepreneur*, April 1, 2002, *www.entrepreneur.com/article/0,4621,298380,00.html*; David Worrell, "Attacking a Loan," *Entrepreneur*, July 2002, *www.entrepreneur.com/article/0,4621,300734,00.html*; Maggie Overfelt, "How to Raise Cash During Crunch Time," *FSB*, March 2001, pp. 35–36; Jenny McCune, "Getting Banks to Say 'Yes'," Bankrate.com, March 19, 2001, *www.bankrate.com/brm/news/biz/Capital_borrowing/200010319a.asp*; Joan Pryde, "Lending a Hand with Financing," *Nation's Business*, January 1998, pp. 53–59; Joseph W. May, "Be Frank with Your Bank," *Profit*, November/December 1996, pp. 54–55; "They'll Up Your Credit If . . ." *Inc.*, April 1994, p. 99; Jane Easter Bahls, "Borrower Beware," *Entrepreneur*, April 1994, p. 97; Jacquelyn Lynn, "You Can Bank on It," *Business Start-Ups*, August 1996, pp. 56–61; Stephanie Barlow, "Buddy System," *Entrepreneur*, March 1997, pp. 121–125; Carlye Adler, "Secrets from the Vault," *FSB*, June 2001, p. 33.

Nonbank Sources of Debt Capital

2. Explain the types of financing available from nonbank sources of credit.

Although they are usually the first stop for entrepreneurs in search of debt capital, banks are not the only lending game in town. We now turn our attention to other sources of debt capital that entrepreneurs can tap to feed their cash-hungry companies.

Asset-Based Lenders

Asset-based lenders, which are usually smaller commercial banks, commercial finance companies, or specialty lenders, allow small businesses to borrow money by pledging otherwise idle assets such as accounts receivable, inventory, or purchase orders as collateral. This form of financing works especially well for manufacturers, wholesalers, distributors, and other companies with significant stocks of inventory, accounts receivable, equipment, real estate, or other assets. Even unprofitable companies whose income statements could not convince loan officers to make traditional loans can get asset-based loans. Because asset-based lenders focus more on collateral than on a company's credit rating, these cash-poor but asset-rich companies can use normally unproductive assets—accounts receivable, inventory, equipment, and purchase orders—to finance rapid growth and the cash crises that often accompany it. Even large companies such as Levi Strauss, Goodyear, and Rite Aid rely on asset-based loans.[16]

Like banks, asset-based lenders consider a company's cash flow, but they are much more interested in the quality of the assets pledged as collateral. The amount a small business can borrow through asset-based lending depends on the **advance rate**, the percentage of an asset's value that a lender will lend. For example, a company pledging $100,000 of accounts receivable might negotiate a 70 percent advance rate and qualify for a $70,000 asset-based loan. Advance rates can vary dramatically depending on the quality of the assets pledged and the lender. Because inventory is an illiquid asset (i.e., hard to sell), the advance rate on inventory-based loans is quite low, usually 10 to 50 percent. Steven Melick, CEO of the Sycamore Group, an e-business software developer, gets an 85 percent advance rate on his company's loans from GE Capital by pledging high-quality accounts receivable as collateral.[17] The most common types of asset-based financing are discounting accounts receivable, inventory financing, and purchase order financing.

DISCOUNTING ACCOUNTS RECEIVABLE. The most common form of secured credit is accounts receivable financing. Under this arrangement, a small business pledges its accounts receivable as collateral; in return, the lender advances a loan against the value of approved accounts receivable. The amount of the loan tendered is not equal to the face value of the accounts receivable, however. Even though the lender screens the firm's accounts and accepts only qualified receivables, it makes an allowance for the risk involved because some receivables will be uncollectible. A small business usually can borrow an amount equal to 55 to 85 percent of its receivables, depending on their quality. Generally, lenders do not accept receivables that are past due.

Profile
Seth Chapman: Weezabi LLC

When the University of Alabama received an invitation recently to play for a national championship in football, Weezabi LLC, a three-person company in Birmingham, Alabama, had to scramble to produce 60,000 Crimson Tide T-shirts. Unable to qualify for traditional financing, the tiny company, one of just a few licensed to produce Alabama merchandise, turned to asset-based financing for the capital it needed to purchase and print the T-shirts. "If it [weren't] for that loan, we would have missed the boat on all of this hot-market stuff," says owner Seth Chapman.[18]

INVENTORY FINANCING. Here, a small business loan is secured by its inventory of raw materials, work in process, or finished goods. If an owner defaults on the loan, the lender can claim the firm's inventory, sell it, and use the proceeds to satisfy the loan (assuming the bank's claim is superior to the claims of other creditors). Because inventory usually is not a highly liquid asset and its value can be difficult to determine, lenders are willing to lend only a portion of its worth, usually no more than 50 percent of the inventory's value. Most asset-based lenders avoid inventory-only deals; they prefer to make loans backed by inventory *and* more secure accounts receivable.

PURCHASE ORDER LOANS. Small companies that receive orders from large customers can use those purchase orders as collateral for loans. The customer places an order with a small business, which needs financing to fill the order. The small business pledges the future payment from the order as security for the loan, and the lender verifies the credit rating of the customer (not the small business) before granting the short-term loan, which often carries annual interest rates of 40 percent or more. Borrowers usually repay the loan within 60 days.

Profile
George Tarrab: Slider the UNscooter

Sales at Slider the UNscooter, a Simi Valley, California-based company that sells ride-on scooters, were outstripping the company's cash flow, but because the company was less than 2 years old, lenders were not willing to extend traditional financing. Owner George Tarrab landed orders from several major retailers but needed financing to manufacture the scooters to fill them. He turned to a lender that specializes in purchase order financing, which provided $200,000 in financing. Even though UNscooter incurred large fees on the purchase order loans, Tarrab says that the loan allowed his company to fill the orders, free up cash for marketing, and attract other high-volume customers. Even though most experts advise using purchase order loans as a last resort, Tarrab had little choice. "We had to get creative," he says.[19]

Asset-based financing is a powerful tool. A small business that could obtain a $1 million line of credit with a bank would be able to borrow as much as $3 million by using accounts receivable as collateral. It is also an efficient method of borrowing because entrepreneurs borrow only the money they need, when they need it. Asset-based borrowing is an excellent just-in-time method of borrowing, one that often is available within just hours. As bank credit has tightened, its popularity has increased.

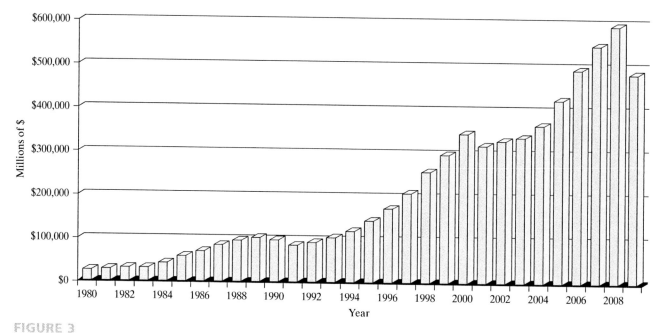

SOURCES OF DEBT FINANCING

FIGURE 3

Asset-Based Loans

Source: Commercial Finance Association.

However, asset-based loans are more expensive than traditional bank loans because of the cost of originating and maintaining them and the higher risk involved. To ensure the quality of the assets supporting the loans they make, lenders often monitor borrowers' assets, perhaps as often as weekly, making paperwork requirements on these loans intimidating, especially to first-time borrowers. Rates usually run from 2 to 8 percentage points (or more) above the prime rate. Because of this rate differential, small business owners should not use asset-based loans over the long term; their goal should be to establish their credit through asset-based financing and then to move up to a line of credit. Figure 3 shows the trend in asset-based borrowing since 1980.

Trade Credit

Because of its ready availability, trade credit is an extremely important source of financing to most entrepreneurs. In fact, 60 percent of small businesses use trade credit as a source of financing.[20] Trade credit involves convincing vendors and suppliers to sell goods and services without requiring payment up front. When banks refuse to lend money to a small business because they see it as a poor credit risk, an entrepreneur may be able to turn to trade credit for capital. Getting vendors to extend credit in the form of delayed payments (e.g., "net 30" credit terms) usually is much easier for small businesses than obtaining bank financing. Essentially, a company receiving trade credit from a supplier is getting a short-term, interest-free loan for the amount of the goods purchased.

Vendors and suppliers usually are willing to finance a small business owner's purchase of goods from 30 to 90 days, interest free. The key to maintaining trade credit as a source of funds is establishing a consistent and reliable payment history with every vendor.

ENTREPRENEURIAL
Profile

*Ed and Jennifer Foy:
eFashion Solutions*

In 2000, Ed and Jennifer Foy started eFashion Solutions, a company that provides e-commerce solutions for branded, well-known companies in the apparel, entertainment, and specialty retail industries, in Secaucus, New Jersey. The company performs a full range of services, including purchasing, merchandising, Web site design, marketing, business intelligence, customer service, order management, and order fulfillment for its clients. As their company grew, the Foys raised $24 million in equity capital and used a variety of traditional bank financing to support its operations. When the company's regular lender shut off access to credit because of the financial crisis, the Foys began using trade credit from their vendors. eFashion Solutions has been able to negotiate "net 60" credit terms with some vendors but takes advantage of cash discounts from other vendors that range from 1 to 10 percent for early payment.[21]

Equipment Suppliers

Most equipment suppliers encourage business owners to purchase their equipment by offering to finance the purchase over time. This method of financing is similar to trade credit but with slightly different terms. Usually, equipment vendors offer reasonable credit terms with only a modest down payment and the balance financed over the life of the equipment (often several years). In some cases, the vendor repurchases equipment for salvage value at the end of its useful life and offers the business owner another credit agreement on new equipment. Start-up companies often use trade credit from equipment suppliers to purchase equipment and fixtures such as counters, display cases, refrigeration units, machinery, and the like. It pays to scrutinize vendors' credit terms, however; they may be less attractive than those of other lenders.

Commercial Finance Companies

When denied bank loans, small business owners often look to commercial finance companies for the same types of loan. Commercial finance companies are second only to banks in making loans to small businesses and, unlike their conservative counterparts, are willing to tolerate more risk in their loan portfolios.[22] For instance, Chris Lehnes, a top manager at CIT Small Business Lending, says that his company regularly makes loans to small businesses with debt to equity ratios of 10:1 (10 times as much debt as equity), a situation that would send most bankers scurrying back to their vaults.[23] Of course, like banks, finance companies' primary consideration is collecting their loans, but finance companies tend to rely more on obtaining a security interest in some type of collateral, given the higher risk loans that make up their portfolios. Because commercial finance companies depend on collateral to recover most of their losses, they do not always require a complete set of financial projections of future operations as most banks do. However, this does *not* mean that they neglect to evaluate carefully a company's financial position, especially its cash balance, before making a loan. "We're looking at the projected cash flow—the ability of the business to repay us," says CIT's Lehnes. "We put a lot of weight on what the business has done in the past couple of years."[24]

Approximately 150 large commercial finance companies, such as AT&T Small Business Lending, UPS Capital, GE Capital Solutions, CIT Small Business Lending, and others, make a variety of loans to small companies, ranging from asset-based loans and business leases to construction and SBA loans. Dubbed "the Wal-Marts of finance," commercial finance companies usually offer many of the same credit options as commercial banks do, including intermediate and long-term loans for real estate and fixed assets as well as short-term loans and lines of credit.

ENTREPRENEURIAL
Profile
*Connie Kalitta:
Kalitta Air*

Connie Kalitta started Kalitta Air, an air cargo carrier, in 2000, and the company grew quickly to become a leading company in the air cargo market. Three years later, Kalitta wanted to expand his company to reach global markets, which required larger aircraft with greater cruising ranges. Kalitta turned to GE Capital, which provided the company with long-term financing for two Boeing 747-400 freighters, allowing the company to gain significant market share in air shipments to Asia.[25]

Finance companies offer small business borrowers faster turnaround times, longer repayment schedules, and more flexible payment plans than traditional lenders, all valuable benefits to cash-hungry small companies. However, because their loans are subject to more risks, finance companies charge higher interest rates than commercial banks. Their most common methods of providing credit to small businesses are asset-based—accounts receivable financing and inventory loans. Rates on loans from commercial finance companies are higher than those at banks—as high as 15 to 30 percent (including fees), depending on the risk a particular business presents and the quality of the assets involved. Because many of the loans they make are secured by collateral (usually the business equipment, vehicle, real estate, or inventory purchased with the loan), finance companies often impose more onerous reporting requirements, sometimes requiring weekly (or even daily) information on a small company's inventory levels or accounts receivable balances. However, entrepreneurs who cannot secure financing from traditional lenders because of their short track records, less-than-perfect credit ratings, or fluctuating earnings often find the loans they need at commercial finance companies.

In 1994, Mariusz Kolodziej left his native Poland and moved to New York City, where he opened Hudson Bakery, a small commercial bakery. Soon some of New York's finest restaurants and hotels were serving his breads, baguettes, rolls, Panini, and focaccias, and the company's reputation for distinctive, high-quality products and excellent service—and its sales—grew rapidly. In 2003, using a combination of retained earnings, bank financing, and loans and leases from a commercial finance company, Kolodziej moved production into a 50,000-square-foot bakery in North Bergen, New Jersey. Later, he opened a second bakery near Philadelphia to serve restaurants and hotels in that city. GE Capital provided Hudson Bakery with a $1.5 asset-based lease that enabled Kolodziej to acquire the equipment to outfit its new commercial bakeries.[26]

Savings and Loan Associations

Savings and loan associations (S&Ls) specialize in loans for real property. In addition to their traditional role of providing mortgages for personal residences, S&Ls offer financing on commercial and industrial property. In the typical commercial or industrial loan, the S&L will lend up to 80 percent of the property's value with a repayment schedule of up to 30 years. Minimum loan amounts are typically $50,000, but most S&Ls hesitate to lend money for buildings specially designed for a particular customer's needs. S&Ls expect the mortgage to be repaid from the company's future profits.

Stock Brokerage Houses

Stockbrokers also make loans, and many of them offer loans to their customers at lower interest rates than banks. These **margin loans** carry lower rates because the collateral supporting them—the stocks and bonds in the customer's portfolio—is of high quality and is highly liquid. Moreover, brokerage firms make it easy to borrow. Usually, brokers set up a line of credit for their customers when they open a brokerage account. To tap that line of credit, a customer simply writes a check or uses a debit card. Typically, a margin loan does not have a fixed repayment schedule; the debt can remain outstanding indefinitely, as long as the market value of the borrower's portfolio of collateral meets minimum requirements. Aspiring entrepreneurs can borrow up to 50 percent of the value of their stock portfolios, up to 70 percent of their bond portfolios, and up to 90 percent of the value of their government securities.

Using stocks and bonds as collateral on a loan can be risky. Brokers typically require a 30 percent cushion on margin loans. If the value of the borrower's portfolio drops, the broker can make a **margin call**; that is, the broker can call the loan and require the borrower to provide more cash and securities as collateral. Recent swings in the stock market have translated into margin calls for many entrepreneurs, requiring them to repay a significant portion of their loan balances within a matter of days—or hours. If an account lacks adequate collateral, the broker can sell some of the customer's portfolio to pay off the loan.

Insurance Companies

For many small businesses, life insurance companies can be an important source of business capital. Insurance companies offer two basic types of loans: policy loans and mortgage loans. **Policy loans** are extended on the basis of the amount of money paid through premiums into the insurance policy; with a policy loan, a business owner serves as his or her own bank, borrowing against the money accumulated in the investment portion of an insurance policy. It usually takes about 2 years for an insurance policy to accumulate enough cash surrender value to justify a loan against it. Once the cash value accumulates in a policy, an entrepreneur may borrow up to 95 percent of that value for any length of time. Interest is levied annually, but the entrepreneur determines the repayment rate, or repayment may be deferred indefinitely. However, the amount of insurance coverage is reduced by the amount of the loan. Policy loans typically offer very favorable interest rates, sometimes below the prime rate. Only insurance policies that build cash value—those that combine a savings plan with insurance coverage—offer the option of borrowing. These include whole life (permanent insurance), variable life, universal life, and many corporate-owned life insurance policies. Term life insurance, which offers only pure insurance coverage, has no borrowing capacity.

Insurance companies make **mortgage loans** on a long-term basis on real property worth a minimum of $500,000. They are based primarily on the value of the real property being purchased. The insurance company will extend a loan of up to 75 or 80 percent of the real estate's value and will allow a lengthy repayment schedule over 25 or 30 years so that payments do not strain the firm's cash flows excessively. Many large real estate developments such as shopping malls, office buildings, and theme parks rely on mortgage loans from insurance companies.

Credit Unions

Credit unions, nonprofit financial cooperatives that promote saving and provide loans to their members, are best known for making consumer and car loans. However, many are also willing to lend money to their members to launch businesses, especially since many banks have restricted loans to higher-risk start-ups. The first credit union in the United States was chartered in New Hampshire in 1909.[27] Today, more than 7,500 federally and state-chartered credit unions operate in the United States, and many of them make business loans, usually in smaller amounts than commercial banks typically make. In fact, the average credit union business loan is $181,000, but some credit unions have made business loans in the millions of dollars.[28] Because credit unions are exempt from federal income tax, they often charge lower interest rates than banks.

Today credit unions make more than $33.4 billion in small business loans to their members, nearly triple the $12.3 billion in small business loans they made in 2004.[29] Lending practices at credit unions are very much like those at banks, but they are subject to restraints that banks are not. For instance, credit unions are prohibited from making business loans that total more than 12.25 percent of their assets (a cap that Congress is considering increasing to 25 percent). Recent changes in legislation, however, exempt certain business loans from that limitation. In another move that favors entrepreneurs, the SBA recently opened its 7(a) loan programs to credit unions, providing even more avenues for entrepreneurs seeking financing. The Export-Import Bank also is exploring ways to work with credit unions that want to provide export financing to small businesses. Increasingly, entrepreneurs are turning to credit unions to finance their businesses' capital needs.

Gladys and Eustace Kumanja immigrated to the United States from Kenya in 1996 with the dream of one day opening a business of their own. Their dream became a reality when the Kumanjas opened Queen Bee Beauty Supply in Smyrna, Delaware, with the help of a $250,000 business loan from the American Spirit Federal Credit Union. Initially, the Kumanjas approached three commercial banks, but their applications were denied because the banks said that they lacked sufficient capital and business experience. The loan from the credit union, the result of the 2009 American Recovery and Investment Act designed to stimulate the economy, is supported by a 90 percent guarantee from the SBA.[30]

Entrepreneurs searching for a credit union near them can use the online database at the Credit Union National Association's Web site (*www.cuna.org*).

Bonds

Bonds, which are corporate IOUs, have always been a popular source of debt financing for large companies, but few small business owners realize that they can also tap this valuable source of capital. Although the smallest businesses are not viable candidates for issuing bonds, a growing number of small companies are finding the funding they need through bonds when banks and other lenders say no. Because of the costs involved, issuing bonds usually is best suited for companies generating annual sales between $5 million and $30 million and have capital requirements between $1.5 million and $10 million. Although they can help small companies raise much needed capital, bonds have certain disadvantages. The issuing company must follow the same regulations that govern businesses selling stock to public investors. Even if the bond issue is private, the company must register the offering and file periodic reports with the SEC.

Convertible bonds, bonds that give the buyer the option of converting the debt to equity by purchasing the company's stock at a fixed price in the future, have become more popular for small companies. In exchange for offering the option to convert the bond into stock, the small company issuing the convertible bonds gets the benefit of paying a lower interest rate on the bond than on a traditional bond. The conversion feature is valuable only if the company is successful and its value increases over time.

Small manufacturers needing money for fixed assets with long repayment schedules have access to an attractive, relatively inexpensive source of funds in **industrial development revenue** bonds (IDRBs). To issue IDRBs, a company must work with a local or state government agency, which issues the bonds on the company's behalf. The company, not the government entity, is responsible for repaying both the principal and the interest on the bond issue. Typically, the amount of money companies that issue IDRBs seek to raise is at least $2 million, but some small manufacturers have raised as little as $500,000 using a mini-bond program that offers a simple application process and short closing times. Each government entity has its own criteria, such as job creation, expansion of the tax base, and others that companies must meet to be eligible to issue mini-bonds. NGK Spark Plugs, a company founded in 1936 that produces spark plugs for automotive, marine, motorcycle, and small engines, issued $15 million in industrial revenue bonds with the help of the West Virginia Economic Development Agency to build an 85,000 square-foot factory in Sissonville, West Virginia, that created 80 new jobs.[31]

To open IDRBs up to even smaller companies, some states pool the industrial bonds of several small companies too small to make an issue alone. By joining together to issue composite industrial bonds, companies can reduce their issuing fees and attract a greater number of investors. The issuing companies typically pay lower interest rates than they would on conventional bank loans.

Private Placements

We saw how companies can raise capital by making private placements of their stock (equity). Private placements are also available for debt instruments. A private placement involves selling debt to one or a small number of investors, usually insurance companies or pension funds. Private placement debt is a hybrid between a conventional loan and a bond. At its heart, it is a bond, but its terms are tailored to the borrower's individual needs, as a loan would be.

Privately placed securities offer several advantages over standard bank loans. First, they usually carry fixed interest rates, rather than the variable rates banks often charge. Second, the maturity of private placements is longer than most bank loans: 15 years rather than 5. Private placements do not require hiring expensive investment bankers. Finally, because private investors can afford to take greater risks than banks, they are willing to finance deals for fledgling small companies.

Entrepreneur Mark Benioff started Salesforce.com, a company that provides customer relationship management applications to more than 72,500 businesses, in his apartment in San Francisco in 1999. The company, now a leader in the field of enterprise cloud computing, recently closed a $500 million private debt placement of 5-year notes that are convertible to company stock to fund its rapid growth and acquisitions of smaller companies.[32]

Small Business Investment Companies (SBICs)

The Small Business Investment Company program was started after Russia's successful launch of the first space satellite, Sputnik, in 1958. Its goal was to accelerate the United States' position in the space race by funding high-technology start-ups. Created by the 1958 Small Business Investment Act, **small business investment companies (SBICs)** are privately owned financial institutions that are licensed and regulated by the SBA. In a unique public–private partnership, the 307 SBICs operating across the United States use a combination of private capital and federally guaranteed debt to provide long-term venture capital to small businesses. In other words, SBICs operate like any other venture capital firm, but, unlike traditional venture capital firms, they use private capital and borrowed government funds to provide both debt and equity financing to small businesses.

Since 1958, SBICs have provided $57.2 billion in long-term debt and equity financing to more than 107,000 small businesses, adding many thousands of jobs to the U.S. economy.[33] Most SBICs prefer later-round financing over funding raw start-ups. Because of changes in their financial structure made a few years ago, however, SBICs now are better equipped to invest in start-up companies. On average, about 30 percent of SBIC investments go to companies that are less than 2 years old.[34] Funding from SBICs helped launch companies such as Apple, Federal Express, Whole Foods Market, Sun Microsystems, Outback Steakhouse, and Build-A-Bear Workshop.

SBICs must be capitalized privately with a minimum of $5 million, at which point they qualify for up to three dollars in long-term SBA loans for every dollar of private capital invested in small businesses, up to the ceiling of $150 million. As a general rule, SBICs may provide financial assistance only to small businesses with a net worth of less than $18 million and average after-tax earnings of $6 million during their past 2 years. However, employment and total annual sales standards vary from industry to industry. SBICs are limited to a maximum investment or loan amount of 30 percent of their private capital to a single client.

Operating as government-backed venture capitalists, SBICs provide both debt and equity financing to small businesses. Currently, the average amount of SBIC financing in a company is $649,000.[35] Because of SBA regulations affecting the financing arrangements an SBIC can offer, many SBICs extend their investments as loans with an option to convert the debt instrument into an equity interest later. Most SBIC loans are between $100,000 and $5 million. Although their interest rates can be high, the loan term is longer than most banks allow. Borrowers typically do not make installment payments; instead, the loan is due at an agreed-upon date. When they make equity investments, SBICs are prohibited from obtaining a controlling interest in the companies in which they invest (no more than 49 percent ownership). The most common methods of SBIC financing are straight debt instruments (24.5 percent), debt instruments combined with equity investments (29.8 percent), and equity-only investments (45.7 percent).[36]

ENTREPRENEURIAL
Profile

Mike Tie and Philip Williams: Paramount Building Solutions

Paramount Building Solutions, a company formed in Tempe, Arizona, in 2003 by Mike Tie and Philip Williams, provides janitorial services to leading retailers in the grocery and "big box" categories. To finance their expansion plans for their company, Tie and Williams worked with LaSalle Capital Group, a Chicago-based SBIC with an investment pool of $128 million. Using capital from LaSalle, Paramount expanded its footprint by acquiring Janitorial Management Services, a similar company that serves large retail customers in 14 states. Paramount, which recently received the Portfolio Company of the Year award from the National Association of Small Business Investment Companies, now has thousands of service locations across the United States. "In partnership with LaSalle and our other investors, we have grown Paramount from a small start-up business to a leading national player in the janitorial services industry," says Tie, the company's CEO.[37]

Small Business Lending Companies (SBLCs)

Small business lending companies (SBLCs) make only intermediate and long-term SBA-guaranteed loans. They specialize in loans that many banks would not consider and operate on a nationwide basis. For instance, most SBLC loans have terms extending for at least 10 years. The maximum interest rate for loans of 7 years or longer is 2.75 percent above the prime rate; for shorter-term loans, the ceiling is 2.25 percent above prime. Another feature of SBLC loans is the management expertise that SBLCs offer the companies to which they make loans. Corporations own most of the nation's SBLCs, which gives them a solid capital base.

Federally Sponsored Programs

Federally sponsored lending programs have suffered from budget reductions in the last several years. Current trends suggest that the federal government is reducing its involvement in the lending business, but many programs are still quite active and some are actually growing.

Economic Development Administration (EDA)

3. Identify the sources of government financial assistance and the loan programs these agencies offer.

The Economic Development Administration (EDA), a branch of the Commerce Department, offers a variety of grants, loan guarantees, and loans to create new businesses and to expand existing businesses in areas with below-average income and high unemployment. Focusing on economically distressed communities, the EDA finances long-term investment projects needed to stimulate economic growth and to create jobs by making loan guarantees. The EDA guarantees up to 80 percent of business loans between $750,000 and $10 million. Entrepreneurs apply for loans through private lenders, for whom an EDA loan guarantee significantly reduces the risk of lending. Start-up companies must supply 15 percent of the guaranteed amount in the form of equity, and established businesses must make equity investments of at least 15 percent of the guaranteed amount. Small businesses can use the loan proceeds for a variety of purposes, including supplementing working capital, purchasing equipment, buying land, and renovating buildings.

EDA business loans are designed to help replenish economically distressed areas by creating or expanding small businesses that provide employment opportunities in local communities. To qualify for a loan, a business must be located in a disadvantaged area and its presence must directly benefit local residents. Some communities experiencing high unemployment or suffering from the effects of devastating natural disasters have received EDA Revolving Loan Fund (RLF) grants to create loan pools for local small businesses. The EDA provides grants to a state or local agency, which makes loans at or below market rates to small companies that otherwise have difficulty borrowing money. Currently, 578 revolving loan funds with a capital base of $852 million are in operation. Loan amounts range from as little as $1,000 to more than $1 million, but most fall between $25,000 and $175,000.[38]

ENTREPRENEURIAL
Profile

Leroy Shatto: Shatto Milk Company

Tired of struggling to survive in the traditional dairy industry, Leroy Shatto, owner of Shatto Milk Company, wanted to differentiate his company by shifting to producing all-natural, hormone-free milk that the company would market to customers directly in old-fashioned glass bottles. Shatto used the revolving loan fund at the Mo-Kan Regional Council in St. Joseph, Missouri, to revamp his entire dairy operation and now produces high-quality, hormone-free milk. The SBA recently named Shatto Missouri's Small Business Owner of the Year.[39]

The EDA's Trade Adjustment Assistance for Firms (TAAF) program provides financial assistance to manufacturers and service companies that have been affected adversely by imports. Small companies work with one of 11 Trade Adjustment Assistance Centers to receive grants that cover 50 to 75 percent of the cost of projects (from market research and product development to e-commerce and inventory control) that are aimed at improving the company's competitive position. For instance, a family-owned business that produces a line of food items recently received a grant that allowed it to implement a lean manufacturing system, install sophisticated computer software that enables it to track production batches and inventory, and train workers. Because of the grant, the company has added 50 employees and has increased its sales by 20 percent.[40]

Department of Housing and Urban Development (HUD)

The Department of Housing and Urban Development (HUD) sponsors several loan programs to assist qualified entrepreneurs in raising needed capital. Community Development Block Grants (CDBGs) are extended to cities and towns that, in turn, lend or grant money to entrepreneurs to start small businesses that will strengthen the local economy. Grants are aimed at cities and towns in need of revitalization and economic stimulation. Some grants are used to construct buildings and plants to be leased to entrepreneurs, sometimes with an option to buy. Others are earmarked for revitalizing a crime-ridden area or making start-up loans to entrepreneurs or expansion loans to existing business owners. No ceilings or geographic limitations are placed on CDBG loans and grants, but projects must benefit low- and moderate-income families.

HUD also makes loan guarantees through its Section 108 provision of the Community Block Development Grant program. The agency has funded more than 1,200 projects since its inception in 1978. These loan guarantees allow a community to transform a portion of CDBG funds into federally guaranteed loans large enough to pursue economic revitalization projects that can lead to the renewal of entire towns. For instance, the city of Greenville, South Carolina, used Section 108 funds to renovate a public market designed to serve as an anchor in its West End section that was targeted for revitalization. Since its construction, 16 small businesses have located in the market, creating new jobs and stimulating economic growth in the area, and a new stadium modeled after Boston's Fenway Park is home to the local minor league baseball team.[41]

U.S. Department of Agriculture's Rural Business and Cooperative Program and Business Program

The U.S. Department of Agriculture (USDA) provides financial assistance to certain small businesses through its Rural Business-Cooperative Service (RBS). The RBS program is open to all types of businesses (not just farms) and is designed to create nonfarm employment opportunities in rural areas—those with populations below 50,000 and not adjacent to a city where densities exceed 100 people per square mile. Entrepreneurs in many small towns, especially those with populations below 25,000, are eligible to apply for loans through the RBS program, which makes almost $900 million in loan guarantees each year.

The RBS does make a limited number of direct loans to small businesses, but the majority of its activity is in loan guarantees. Through its Business and Industry (B&I) Guaranteed Loan Program, the RBS will guarantee as much as 80 percent of a commercial lender's loan up to $25 million (although actual guarantee amounts are almost always far less, usually between $200,000 and $1 million) for qualified applicants. Entrepreneurs apply for loans through private lenders, who view applicants with loan guarantees favorably because the agency's guarantee reduces the lender's risk dramatically.

Profile

Jasch and Kathleen Hamilton: Diamond Organics

Founded in 1998 by copreneurs Jasch and Kathleen Hamilton with the help of a $298,000 B&I loan guarantee from the USDA, Diamond Organics has become the largest online supplier of organic foods in the United States from its location in tiny Moss Landing, California. To fuel the company's current growth spurt and to launch a prepared food line called Kathleen's Kitchen, CEO Kathleen Hamilton is relying on another B&I guarantee of $2.9 million for a loan from Excel National Bank.[42]

To make a loan guarantee, the RBS requires much of the same documentation as most banks and most other loan guarantee programs. Because of its emphasis on developing employment in rural areas, the RBS requires an environmental impact statement describing the jobs created and the effect the business has on the area. The RBS also makes grants available to businesses and communities for the purpose of encouraging small business development and growth.

Small Business Innovation Research (SBIR) Program

Started as a pilot program by the National Science Foundation in the 1970s, the Small Business Innovation Research (SBIR) program has expanded to 11 federal agencies, ranging from NASA to the Department of Defense. The total SBIR budget across all 11 agencies is more than $2 billion annually. These agencies award cash grants or long-term contracts to small companies that want to initiate or to expand their research and development (R&D) efforts. SBIR grants give innovative small companies the opportunity to attract early stage capital investments *without* having to give up significant equity stakes or taking on burdensome levels of debt.

The SBIR process includes three phases. Phase I (project feasibility) grants, which determine the feasibility and commercial potential of a technology or product (called "proof of concept"), last for up to 6 months and have a ceiling of $100,000. Phase II (prototype development) grants, designed to develop the concept into a specific technology or product, run for up to 24 months and have a ceiling of $750,000. Approximately 40 percent of all phase II applicants receive funding. Phase III is the commercialization phase, in which the company pursues commercial applications of the research and development conducted in phases I and II and must use private or non-SBIR federal funding to bring a product to market.

Competition for SBIR funding is intense; only 17 percent of the small companies that apply receive funding. So far, nearly 108,400 SBIR awards totaling more than $25.2 billion (26 percent in phase I and 74 percent in phase II) have gone to more than 16,000 small companies, which traditionally have had difficulty competing with big corporations for federal R&D dollars. The government's dollars have been well invested. Nearly 45 percent of small businesses receiving phase II SBIR awards have achieved commercial success with their products.[43]

Profile

AeroTech Research, Inc.

AeroTech Research, Inc., a small company in Newport Beach, Virginia, received phase I and II grants from NASA to develop its Turbulence Prediction and Warning System (TPAWS) that improves pilots' awareness of weather conditions that create turbulence so that they can avoid it. Air turbulence is a problem for both military and commercial flights and is the leading cause of injuries in the airline industry. Turbulence has actually ripped engines from airplanes, broken wings, and caused passengers great anxiety. With the help of the SBIR grants, AeroTech created an enhanced radar warning system that alerts pilots to turbulence hotspots well in advance so that they can fly around them. AeroTech has installed TPAWS on more than 120 Delta commercial jets and is marketing the system to other airlines, both domestic and foreign.[44]

The Small Business Technology Transfer Program

The Small Business Technology Transfer (STTR) program complements the SBIR program. Whereas SBIR focuses on commercially promising ideas that originate in small businesses, the STTR allows small companies to exploit the commercially promising ideas that originate in universities, federally funded R&D centers, and nonprofit research institutions. Researchers at these institutions can join forces with small businesses to spin off commercially promising ideas while remaining employed at their research institutions. Five federal agencies award grants in two of three phases (up to $100,000 in phase I and up to $500,000 in phase II) to these research partnerships. The STTR's annual award budget is approximately $2 billion.

▶ ENTREPRENEURSHIP IN ACTION ▶

Where Do We Turn Now?

Tina Bean started Five Star Feeds, a business that sells livestock feed, pet food, and gardening supplies, in Port Arthur, Texas, in 2001 and has operated it at a profit since then. Bean applied for a business expansion loan at her bank and received $800,000, which she used to more than double the size of her store. With the expansion completed, she needs $150,000 to purchase the inventory—more pet supplies, jeans, boots, and Western-style clothing—to fill it, but the bank is balking at making the loan. The loan officer's response is "We'll cross that bridge when we get there," says Bean. "Well, I'm there. I can't open the store if I don't have anything to put in it." Until she can get the capital she needs to purchase the inventory, Bean says she is stuck.

Like Tina Bean, Matt and Marnie Brannon have been running their business, Midwest Fiat, for several years. Their company, located in Columbus, Ohio, sells vintage Italian car parts online and operates a service and restoration shop for Fiat autos. Matt started the business as a hobby, but it grew into a full-time business for him and his wife in 2004. "Our revenues have grown each year," he says, pointing out the company's excellent credit rating and its track record of success. The Brannons have the opportunity to purchase one of their main competitors, a move that would quadruple the company's revenue, expand its product line, and enable it to move into a larger space. "We need a loan to help us make the purchase and sustain the operating capital needed for the first 6 months of the expansion, which includes hiring five employees."

Until now, the Brannons have never borrowed money for their business, choosing instead to allow it to grow organically, using its earnings to fund its growth. "With a solid business plan and all of the documentation, financials, and records needed for the loan, we approached a national bank," says Matt. "The loan officer [said] it would be a slam dunk," he recalls. "In fact, he encouraged us to increase the request from $110,000 to $125,000." A month later, the loan officer contacted the Brannons and told them that the bank had denied their loan request. "He encouraged us to pursue a home-equity line of credit, but that would give us only half the amount we would need," says Matt. The Brannons have applied for a loan at two small community banks. "They're asking questions," he says. "I'm optimistic but nervous. They are taking a long time to make a decision, and we are on borrowed time at this point, having already missed the deadline our competitor gave us to take the offer."

1. What other sources of financing do you recommend Tina Bean and Matt and Marnie Brannon turn to for the financing they need for their businesses?
2. The Brannons had never borrowed money for their business before the opportunity to purchase a competitor suddenly emerged. What steps can entrepreneurs take to make sure that they have financing arrangements in place when such opportunities arise?

Sources: Based on Peter S. Goodman, "Credit Tightens for Small Businesses," *New York Times*, October 13, 2009, *www.nytimes.com/2009/10/13/business/smallbusiness/13lending.html*; Emily Maltby, "SOS: Send Loans Now," *CNNMoney*, July 27, 2009, *http://money.cnn.com/galleries/2009/smallbusiness/0903/gallery.loan_woes.smb/index.html.*

Small Business Administration (SBA)

4. Describe the various loan programs available from the Small Business Administration.

The Small Business Administration (SBA) has several programs designed to help finance both start-up and existing small companies that cannot qualify for traditional loans because of their thin asset bases and their high risk of failure. In its nearly 60 years of operation, the SBA has helped 20 million small companies through a multitude of programs get the financing they need for start up or for growth by making or guaranteeing $211 billion in loans.[45] In the wake of the upheaval in the financial markets, banks have tightened their lending standards, and many small businesses cannot qualify for loans. Although SBA loan programs account for less than 10 percent of all small business lending, tight credit conditions make them all the more important for small companies in search of capital.[46] "SBA programs help newer businesses and businesses that don't have a lot of collateral," says an executive at a bank that makes SBA-guaranteed loans.[47] About 35 percent of SBA-backed loans go to start-up companies.[48]

The SBA's $90.5 billion loan portfolio makes it the largest single financial backer of small businesses in the nation.[49] The SBA does *not* actually lend money to entrepreneurs directly; instead, entrepreneurs borrow money from a traditional lender (About 4,500 lenders in the United States make SBA loans), and the SBA guarantees a percentage of the loan to the lender in case the borrower defaults. To be eligible for SBA backing, a business must be within the agency's criteria that define a small business. In addition, some types of businesses, such as those engaged in gambling, pyramid sales schemes, or real estate investment, among others, are ineligible for SBA loans. The loan application process can take from 3 days to many months, depending on how well prepared the entrepreneur is and which bank is involved.

Express Programs

To speed up processing times, the SBA has created three "express" programs that give entrepreneurs responses to their loan applications within 36 hours.

THE SBA*EXPRESS* PROGRAM. With the **SBA*Express* Program**, participating lenders use their own loan procedures and applications to make loans of up to $350,000 to small businesses, streamlining the application process for SBA loan guarantees. Because the SBA guarantees up to 50 percent of the loan, banks are often more willing to make smaller loans to entrepreneurs who might otherwise have difficulty meeting lenders' standards. Lenders can charge up to 6.5 percent above the prime interest rate on SBA*Express* loans below $50,000 and up to 4.5 percent above prime on loans greater than $50,000. Loan maturities on these loans typically are 7 years. Mike Robillard, president of San Antonio Clippers in San Antonio, Texas, used an SBA*Express* loan to add two locations to his Sports Clips hair salon franchise operation. Robillard needed growth capital quickly to secure the best locations, a key to success in his industry. "We had to start laying out money quickly to lock down those locations," he says.[50]

PATRIOT EXPRESS PROGRAM. The SBA recently piloted the **Patriot Express Program**, which is designed to assist some of the nation's 25 million veterans and their spouses who want to become entrepreneurs. The loan ceiling is $500,000, and the SBA guarantees up to 90 percent (normally 85 percent) of the loan amount in case the borrower defaults. Like SBA*Express* loans, the turnaround time on loan applications is just 36 hours. Patriot Express loans carry interest rates that range from 2.25 to 4.75 percent above the prime interest rate. The average Patriot Express loan is $82,000.[51]

ENTREPRENEURIAL
Profile
*Jenny Housely:
Sorpresas Moments
of Celebration*

Jenny Housely, a military veteran, started Sorpresas Moments of Celebration, a business in Augusta, Georgia, that hosts birthday parties and other celebrations and offers preschool fine arts classes, with the help of a $25,000 loan guarantee from the Patriot Express Program. Even though she was armed with a business plan and assistance from a local Small Business Development Center, Housely still found attracting start-up capital to be a challenge. "It is difficult to get money from anyone because we are a new business," she says. Backed by the Patriot Express Program guarantee, Housely was able to acquire the loan from a Florida lender and start her company.[52]

COMMUNITY*EXPRESS* PROGRAM. In 1999, working with the National Community Reinvestment Coalition, the SBA created the Community*Express* loan program, which provides loans to entrepreneurs in communities that have experienced economic distress [those that are identified under the SBA's Historically Underutilized Business Zones (HUBZones) and the Community Reinvestment Act] and who are viewed as high-risk borrowers. The maximum loan amount is $250,000, with an SBA guarantee of 90 percent (normally 85 percent), and turnaround times on loan requests can be as fast as 36 hours. Community*Express* loans account for 9 percent of all SBA loans, up from just 1 percent in 2002.[53] Approximately 70 percent of Community*Express* loans go to minority entrepreneurs, and 40 percent go to start-up companies. Like Patriot Express loans, Community*Express* loans carry interest rates that range from 2.25 to 4.75 percent above the prime interest rate. The average Community*Express* loan is $27,000.[54] Recipients of Community*Express* loans also receive training and consulting services for their businesses.

SBA Loan Programs

7(A) LOAN GUARANTY PROGRAM. The SBA works with local lenders (both bank and nonbank) to offer a variety of loan programs designed to help entrepreneurs who cannot get capital from traditional sources to gain access to the financing they need to launch and grow their businesses. By far the most popular SBA loan program is the **7(A) loan guaranty program** (see Figure 4), which makes partial guarantees on loans up to $2 million to small businesses. Private lenders actually extend these loans to companies, but the SBA guarantees them in case the borrower defaults. Normally, the SBA guarantees 85 percent of loans up to $150,000 and 75 percent of loans above $150,000 up to the loan guarantee ceiling of $1,500,000. However, as part of the American Recovery and Reinvestment Plan, the SBA temporarily increased its guarantees to 90 percent (up to the $1.5 million guarantee cap) and eliminated all of the loan processing fees, which range from 2 percent to 3.75 percent. After Gary Skrla lost his corporate job, he secured an $879,000 loan from Seattle, Washington-based Fortune Bank with the help of a 7(a) guarantee to open Ace Hardware in Silver Lake, Washington. Skrla saved nearly $20,000 due to the elimination of the fees on the SBA's loan guarantees.[55]

The SBA does not actually lend any money to small businesses; it merely acts as an insurer, guaranteeing the lender a certain level of repayment in case the borrower defaults on the loan. Because the SBA assumes most of the credit risk, lenders are more willing to consider riskier deals that they normally would refuse.

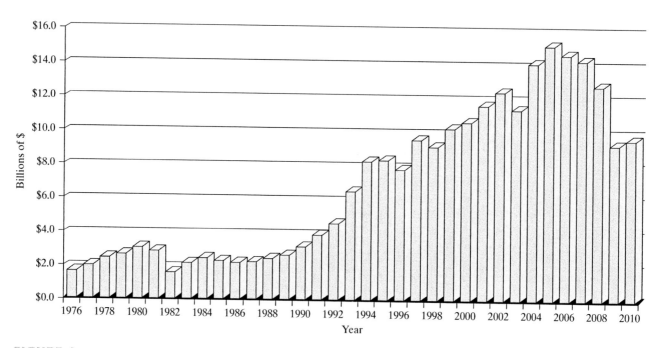

FIGURE 4

SBA 7(A) Guaranteed Loans

Source: U.S. Small Business Administration.

ENTREPRENEURIAL
Profile

Anamika Khanna and Tim Volkem: Kasa Indian Eatery

Anamika Khanna and Tim Volkem, founders of Kasa Indian Eatery.

Source: Kasa Indian Eatery

Anamika Khanna, a former brand manager for Kraft Foods, and Tim Volkem, a former attorney, used two SBA-guaranteed 7(a) loans totaling $700,000 and $300,000 of their money to open two Indian restaurants in San Francisco, California, in just 2 years. They used the first loan to start Kasa (which means "Royal Meal" in Sanskrit) Indian Eatery in the city's Castro neighborhood and a year later received a second SBA-guaranteed loan to open another location in the Marina district. The popular restaurants, which feature a menu built around recipes from Khanna's grandmother and the kati roll, a flaky, flatbread sandwich filled with fresh, high-quality ingredients, now employ 30 people.[56]

Qualifying for an SBA loan guarantee requires cooperation among the entrepreneur, the participating bank, and the SBA. The participating bank determines the loan's terms and sets the interest rate within SBA limits. Contrary to popular belief, SBA guaranteed loans do *not* carry special deals on interest rates. An entrepreneur negotiates interest rates with the participating bank, with a ceiling of prime plus 2.25 percent on loans of less than 7 years and prime plus 2.75 percent on loans of 7 to 25 years. Interest rates on loans of less than $25,000 can go up to prime plus 4.75 percent. The average interest rate on SBA-guaranteed loans is prime plus 2 percent (compared to prime plus 1 percent on conventional bank loans). The SBA normally assesses a one-time guaranty fee of between 2.5 and 3.5 percent for all loan guarantees, depending on the loan amount.

In a recent 5-year period, the SBA provided 7(a) guarantees on loans to an average of nearly 77,000 small businesses per year that would have had difficulty getting loans without the help of the SBA guarantee. The average 7(a) loan is $174,000, and the average duration of an SBA loan is 12 years—longer than the typical commercial small business loan. In fact, longer loan terms are a distinct advantage of SBA loans. At least half of all bank business loans are for less than 1 year. By contrast, SBA real estate loans can extend for up to 25 years (compared to just 10 to 15 years for a conventional loan), and working capital loans have maturities of 7 years (compared with 2 to 5 years at most banks). These longer terms translate into lower payments, which are better suited for young, fast-growing, cash-strapped companies.

ENTREPRENEURIAL
Profile

Ted Clarke and Pat Easter: Jet Stream Car Wash

Ted Clarke and Pat Easter, former fighter pilots and squadron mates in the Navy, became commercial airline pilots after their military careers, but both men wanted to own their own business. With the help of a 25-year SBA-guaranteed 7(a) loan from Business Loan Express, Clarke and Easter constructed Jet Stream Car Wash, a touchless car wash, in Bonney Lake, Washington, that operates 24 hours a day.[57]

THE CAPLINE PROGRAM. In addition to its basic 7(a) loan guarantee program (through which the SBA makes about 70 percent of its loans), the SBA provides guarantees on small business loans for start up, real estate, machinery and equipment, fixtures, working capital, exporting, and restructuring debt through several other methods. Approximately two-thirds of all SBA loan guarantees are for machinery and equipment or working capital. The **CAPLine Program** offers short-term capital to growing companies seeking to finance seasonal buildups in inventory or accounts receivable under five separate programs, each with maturities of up to 5 years: seasonal line of credit (provides advances against inventory and accounts receivable to help businesses weather seasonal sales fluctuations), contract line of credit (finances the cost of direct labor and materials costs associated with performing contracts), builder's line of credit (helps small contractors and builders finance labor and materials costs), standard asset-based line of credit (an asset-based revolving line of credit for financing short-term needs), and small asset-based line of credit (an asset-based revolving line of credit up to $200,000). CAPLine is aimed at helping cash-hungry small businesses by giving them a credit line to draw on when they need it. These loans are what small companies need most because they are so flexible, efficient, and, unfortunately, so hard for small businesses to get from traditional lenders.

SECTION 504 CERTIFIED DEVELOPMENT COMPANY PROGRAM. Established in 1980, the SBA's Section 504 program is designed to encourage small businesses to purchase fixed assets, expand their facilities, and create jobs. Section 504 loans provide long-term financing at fixed rates to small companies to purchase land, buildings, or equipment. Because they are designated for fixed asset purchases that provide basic business infrastructure to small companies that otherwise might not qualify, 504 loans are intended to serve as a catalyst for economic development. Three lenders play a role in every 504 loan: a bank, the SBA, and a **certified development company (CDC)**. A CDC is a nonprofit organization licensed by the SBA and designed to promote economic growth in local communities. Some 270 CDCs now operate across the United States and make more than 9,000 504 loans in an average year. An entrepreneur generally is required to make a down payment of just 10 percent of the total project cost. The CDC puts up 40 percent at a low, long-term, fixed rate, supported by an SBA loan guarantee in case the entrepreneur defaults. The bank provides long-term financing at market rates for the remaining 50 percent, which also is supported by an SBA guarantee. The major advantages of Section 504 loans are their fixed rates and terms, their 10- to 20-year maturities, and the low down payment required.

Despite a 10-year track record of success in business, John Fernandez, CEO of Daystar Desserts, a company in Ashland, Virginia, that makes cheesecakes and other desserts, struck out with three banks when he applied for a loan to fulfill a contractual obligation to purchase the building that his company had been renting for 5 years. Daystar, with 54 employees and $15 million in annual sales, was in solid financial shape, but a crumbling real estate market and turmoil in the financial markets stymied the company's attempts to secure a $2 million loan. Fernandez turned to the SBA's 504 loan program, and, with the agency's loan guarantee, Village Bank extended Daystar a $2 million loan. Because the loan came under the America's Recovery Capital program, Fernandez saved nearly $60,000 in loan fees. Fernandez, a trained chef, started Daystar in his home in 1998; today, the company is one of the leading suppliers of cakes in the Northeast.[58]

As attractive as they are, 504 loans are not for every business owner. The SBA imposes several restrictions on 504 loans:

- For every $50,000 ($100,000 for small manufacturers) the CDC lends, the project must create at least one new job or achieve a public policy goal such as rural development, expansion of exports, minority business development, and others.
- Machinery and equipment financed must have a useful life of at least 10 years.
- The borrower must occupy at least two-thirds of a building constructed with the loan, or the borrower must occupy at least half of a building purchased or remodeled with the loan.
- The borrower must qualify as a small business under the SBA's definition and must not have a tangible net worth in excess of $7 million or have an average net income in excess of $2.5 million after taxes for the preceding 2 years.

Because of strict equity requirements, existing small businesses usually find it easier to qualify for 504 loans than do start-ups. The average 504 loan is $586,000.[59]

MICROLOAN PROGRAM. The majority of entrepreneurs require less than $100,000 to launch their businesses. Indeed, research suggests that most entrepreneurs require less than $50,000 to start their companies. Unfortunately, loans of that amount can be the most difficult to get. Lending these relatively small amounts to entrepreneurs starting businesses is the purpose of the SBA's Microloan Program. Called **microloans** because they range from just a hundred dollars to as much as $35,000, these loans have helped thousands of people take their first steps toward entrepreneurship. Banks typically have shunned loans in such small amounts because they considered them to be unprofitable. In 1992, the SBA began funding microloans at 96 private, nonprofit lenders in 44 states in an attempt to "fill the void" in small loans to start-up companies, and the program has expanded from there. Since its inception, the SBA Microloan Program has made loans totaling more than $407 million to nearly 35,000 entrepreneurs![60]

Today, more than 170 authorized lenders make SBA-backed microloans. The average size of a microloan is $13,550, with a maturity of 3 years (the maximum term is 6 years), and interest rates that range between 8 and 13 percent. Lenders' standards are less demanding than those on conventional loans; in fact, about 37 percent of all microloans go to business start-ups.[61] All microloans are made as installment loans through nonprofit intermediaries such as Trickle Up and ACCION International that are approved by the SBA. The typical microloan recipient is a small company with five or fewer employees and collateral that bankers shun for traditional loans, for example, earthworms from a fish bait farmer in Ohio or a Minnesota grocery store's frozen fish inventory.[62] Although microloans are available to anyone, the SBA hopes to target those entrepreneurs who have the greatest difficulty getting start-up and expansion capital: women, minorities, and people with low incomes.

Profile

*Michael Golata
and Sam's Club*

Retailer Sam's Club, a division of Walmart, is working with a nonbank SBA lender, Superior Financial Group, to offer its small business members microloans of up to $25,000 through the SBA. "Access to capital is a major pain point for our [small business] members," says Catherine Corley, vice-president of membership. Michael Golata, a contractor for UPS who delivers emergency medical equipment to hospitals, had the opportunity to expand his business by bringing other delivery drivers into his business. Golata found a used Sprinter van for $12,500 and applied to two local banks for a loan, but both rejected his loan application. A commercial finance company was willing to lend him the money, but Golata balked at the 21 percent interest rate and $450 monthly payments. He learned about the microloans that Sam's Club was offering with Superior Financial Group and applied online for a $10,000 loan. The next day, Superior approved his loan with a 7.25 percent interest rate over 10 years. "I thought I was dreaming," says Golata, whose business with UPS immediately increased from $3,000 a week to $8,000.[63]

LOANS INVOLVING INTERNATIONAL TRADE. For small businesses going global, the SBA has the **Export Express Program**, which, like other express programs, offers quick turnaround times on applications for guarantees of 75 to 85 percent on loans up to $250,000 to help small companies develop or expand their export initiatives. Loan maturities range from 5 to 25 years, depending on the purpose of the loan.

The SBA also offers the **Export Working Capital (EWC) Program**, which is designed to provide working capital to small exporters by providing loan guarantees of 90 percent of the loan amount up to $1.5 million. The SBA works in conjunction with the Export-Import Bank to administer this loan guarantee program. Applicants file a one-page loan application, and the response time normally is 10 days or less. Small businesses must use loan proceeds to finance small business exports.

Profile

*James Dixon:
Thomasville Lumber
Company*

After a fire destroyed the Coastal Lumber Company's sawmill in Thomasville, Alabama, former employee James Dixon worked with a local bank to secure an Export Working Capital loan of $1 million to reopen the mill as Thomasville Lumber, purchase raw materials, and begin exporting lumber. Thomasville Lumber produces more than 20 million board feet of yellow pine lumber annually and exports 80 to 90 percent of it to Spain, Western Europe, Japan, and the Caribbean. The company, with export sales that exceed $10 million, employs more than 70 workers and received the Governor's Trade Excellence Award.[64]

The **International Trade Loan Program** is for small businesses that are engaging in international trade or that are being adversely affected by competition from imports. The SBA allows global entrepreneurs to combine loans from the Export Working Capital Program with those from the International Trade Program for a maximum guarantee of $1.75 million. The loan ceiling is $2 million, and maturities run up to 25 years.

DISASTER ASSISTANCE LOANS. As their name implies, **disaster assistance loans** are made to small businesses devastated by financial or physical losses from hurricanes, earthquakes, floods, tornadoes, and other disasters. Business physical disaster loans are designed to help companies repair or replace damage to physical property (buildings, equipment, inventory, etc.) caused by the disaster, and economic injury loans provide working capital for businesses throughout the disaster period. For businesses, the maximum disaster loan usually is $2 million, but Congress often raises

Workers clean up oil from the Deepwater oil spill in the Gulf of Mexico along a beach in Alabama. The SBA extended disaster loans to many small companies that suffered losses as a result of the spill.

Source: AP Photo/Dave Martin

that ceiling when circumstances warrant. Disaster loans carry below-market interest rates and long payback periods. Loans that exceed $14,000 require the entrepreneur to pledge some kind of collateral, usually a lien on the business property. In the aftermath of the Deepwater oil spill that dumped more than 200 million gallons of oil into the Gulf of Mexico, shutting down commercial and recreational fishing and decimating the tourist industry, the SBA granted disaster assistance loans to small businesses that suffered financial losses.[65]

State and Local Loan Development Programs

5. Discuss state and local economic development programs.

Just when many federally funded programs are facing cutbacks, state-sponsored loan and development programs are becoming more active in providing funds for business start-ups and expansions. Many states have decided that their funds are better spent encouraging small business growth rather than "chasing smokestacks"—trying to entice large businesses to locate in their boundaries. These programs come in many forms, but they all tend to focus on developing small businesses that create the greatest number of jobs and economic benefits. Entrepreneurs who apply for state and local funding must have patience and be willing to slog through some paperwork, however.

Although each state's approach to economic development and job growth is unique, one common element is some kind of small business financing program: loans, loan guarantees, development grants, venture capital pools, and others. One approach many states have had success with is **capital access programs (CAPs)**. First introduced in 1986 in Michigan, 22 states now offer CAPs that are designed to encourage lending institutions to make loans to businesses that do not qualify for traditional financing. Under a CAP, a bank and a borrower each pay an up-front fee (a portion of the loan amount) into a loan-loss reserve fund at the participating bank, and the state matches this amount. The reserve fund, which normally ranges from 6 to 14 percent of the loan amount, acts as an insurance policy against the potential loss a bank might experience on a loan and frees the bank to make loans that it otherwise might refuse. One study of CAPs found that 55 percent of the entrepreneurs who received loans under a CAP would not have been granted loans without the backing of the program.[66]

Even cities and small towns have joined in the effort to develop small businesses and help them grow. More than 7,500 communities across the United States operate **revolving loan funds (RLFs)** that combine private and public funds to make loans to small businesses, often at below-market interest rates. As money is repaid into the funds, it is loaned back out to other entrepreneurs. Full Spectrum Solutions, a company that produces a line of high-quality energy- and cost-saving light fixtures, recently received a $200,000 loan from the Jackson County (Mississippi) Economic Development Corporation's revolving loan fund. Full Spectrum used the loan to purchase the equipment and machinery and to hire new workers to manufacture its Everlast® Induction Lighting System.[67]

In addition to RLFs, more than 1,000 communities across the United States have created **community development financial institutions (CDFIs)** that designate at least some of their loan portfolios for entrepreneurs and small businesses. CDFIs operate through a variety of mechanisms, including microenterprise loan funds, community development loan funds, and others, and provide loans to people who do not meet traditional lenders' criteria. Because the loans that they make are higher risk, the interest rates that CDFIs charge are higher than those charged by traditional lenders.

Profile

*Anthony Viggiano:
Autotether*

When Anthony Viggiano's friend nearly died in a boating accident, he created a device called the Autotether that makes boating safer. Autotether is a wireless lanyard that automatically shuts off a boat's ignition if the driver falls overboard. The system also protects up to three passengers by sounding an alarm if one of them falls overboard. Because it is wireless and allows a boat's operator and passengers to move about freely, the Autotether offers significant improvements over standard kill switches. To accommodate growing demand for the product, Viggiano received a $250,000 loan from a CDFI, the Connecticut Development Authority, which provided Autotether with critical working capital and allowed the young company to hire 16 more employees.[68]

IN THE ENTREPRENEURIAL
SPOTLIGHT Alternative Sources of Financing

Although banks tend to be lenders of first resort for small businesses, accounting for the greatest volume of loans to small businesses, they are not the only lending game in town, as the following profiles illustrate.

Heart to Heart Gifts

Yi Ping Lai's business, Heart to Heart Gifts, an online store based in San Diego, California, sells toys, costumes, party decorations, and accessories priced from $6 to $100 for girls up to age 6. Recently, the company's sales passed the $1 million mark. Even though a recession caused sales to decline by nearly 50 percent, Yi says that the company remained profitable. Yet her bank cancelled Heart to Heart's $55,000 line of credit, saying that Yi and her company had become high credit risks. After many meetings with her bankers, Yi was able to get the line of credit reestablished, but only for $20,000. Yi is developing a new product line that will increase her company's sales, but without adequate financing her efforts are hampered. "I need that cash flow for my business," she says. Finally, Yi turned to a nonprofit community development corporation in San Diego, where a loan officer helped her obtain a $35,000 line of credit.

Lake Powell Furniture

Kip and Melissa Bennett became the owners of Lake Powell Furniture, a small furniture store in Page, Arizona, in 2003. Within a few years, their hard work paid off; sales had increased so much that the business had outgrown its existing location. Kip had spotted an ideal location for their store on a busy corner in downtown Page, and the building was for sale. All he needed was the financing to purchase the building and transform it into a furniture store. Kip began approaching banks about commercial property loans and found one willing to make a $500,000 loan. Unfortunately, the bank was a victim of the crisis in the financial markets, and Kip lost the $7,000 that he had put into the loan application.

At the recommendation of another business owner in Page, Kip approached Mercantile Commercial Capital, a nonbank lender that specializes in SBA 504 loans, which are designed to help small business owners purchase fixed assets such as buildings and equipment. Within a few months, the Bennetts received a $500,000 loan from Mercantile backed by an SBA guarantee. Despite an economic slowdown, they say that sales are on track to match their best year ever, an outcome that they say would not have been possible without their new, larger store.

Jackson Pianos

Joseph Jackson, owner of Jackson Pianos LLC, in St. Louis, Missouri, a company that tunes, repairs, refurbishes, and sells pianos, has seen his company's sales increase by 35 percent within the last year to exceed $500,000. His company has outgrown its existing space, but Jackson is having difficulty getting a loan to expand his business into a larger building. Jackson's bank rejected his loan application even though he has an excellent personal credit score and his company is profitable. He then turned to two large banks, but they also rejected his applications, saying that his company's cash flow was insufficient and that he should have more money tucked away in accounts. Even when Jackson reduced his loan request from $300,000 to $90,000, both banks again refused. "We've already missed our chance on a few buildings because of this," he says.

1. What advice can you offer business owners when banks refuse their loan applications?
2. Assume the role of consultant to Joe Jackson, owner of Jackson Pianos. What advice can you offer him about getting the financing he needs to support his company's expansion?

Sources: Based on Nick Carey, "Small U.S. Firms Face Credit Squeeze as Crisis Drags," *Reuters*, October 11, 2009, *www.reuters.com/article/idUSN1111766420091012*; "Start-up Stories: 'How We Got the Cash,'" *CNNMoney*, April 27, 2009, *http://money.cnn.com/galleries/2009/smallbusiness/0904/gallery.how_entrepreneurs_got_bank_loans.smb/2.html*; Emily Maltby, "Real Collateral Damage," *Wall Street Journal*, July 22, 2010, pp. B1, B6.

Internal Methods of Financing

6. Discuss methods of financing growth and expansion internally with bootstrap financing.

Small business owners do not have to rely solely on financial institutions and government agencies for capital. Instead, the business itself has the capacity to generate capital. Perhaps the least expensive form of capital is the company's retained earnings, the portion of its profits that the owner keeps in the company. Another method of "generating capital" is never to use it in the first place by managing the business frugally. Other types of **bootstrap financing** are available to virtually every small business and include factoring, leasing rather than purchasing equipment, and using credit cards.

Factoring Accounts Receivable

Rather than carry credit sales on its own books (some of which may never be collected), a small business can sell outright its accounts receivable to a factor. A **factor** buys a company's accounts receivable and pays for them in two parts. The first payment, which the factor makes immediately, is for 50 to 80 percent of the accounts' agreed-upon value, which is typically discounted at a rate of 3 to 5 percent of the value of the invoice. The factor makes the second payment of 15 to 18 percent, which makes up the balance less the factor's service fees, when the original customer pays the invoice. Because factoring is a more expensive type of financing than loans from either banks or commercial finance companies, many entrepreneurs view factors as lenders of last resort. However, for businesses that cannot qualify for those loans, factoring may be the only choice!

Begun by American colonists to finance their cotton trade with England, factoring has become an important source of capital for many small businesses that depend on fast billing turnaround across a multitude of industries ranging from hardware stores and pharmacies to pest control firms and staffing agencies (see Figure 5). Factoring deals are either with recourse or without recourse. Under deals arranged with recourse, a small business owner retains the responsibility for customers who fail to pay their accounts. The business owner must take back these uncollectible invoices. Under deals arranged without recourse, however, the owner is relieved of the responsibility of collecting them. If customers fail to pay their accounts, the factor bears the loss. Because the factoring company assumes the risk of collecting the accounts, it normally

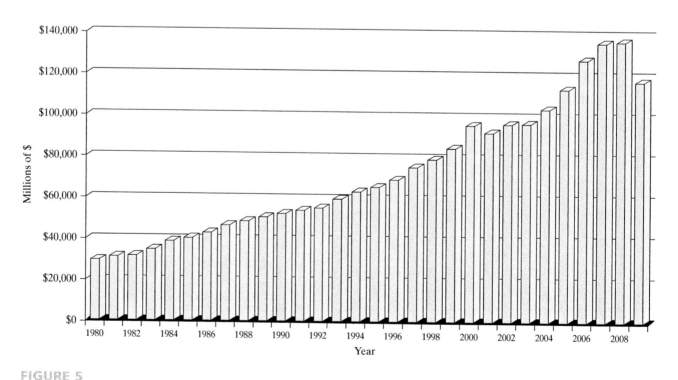

FIGURE 5

Factoring Volume

Source: "Annual Asset-Based Lending and Factoring Surveys 2009," Commercial Finance Association, May 17, 2010, p. 15.

screens the firm's credit customers, accepts those judged to be creditworthy, and advances the small business owner a portion of the value of the accounts receivable. Factors will discount anywhere from 2 to 40 percent of the face value of a company's accounts receivable, depending on a small company's:

- Customers' financial strength, credit ratings, and their ability to pay their invoices on time.
- Industry and its customers' industries because some industries have a reputation for slow payments.
- History and financial strength, especially in deals arranged with recourse.
- Credit policies.

The discount rate on deals without recourse usually is higher than on those with recourse because of the higher level of risk they carry for the factor.

Although factoring is more expensive than traditional bank loans (a 2 percent discount from the face value of an invoice due in 30 days amounts to an annual interest rate of 24.5 percent), it is a source of quick cash and is ideally suited for fast-growing companies, especially start-ups that cannot qualify for bank loans. "Factoring provides a business with immediate cash for accounts receivable because a business can sell receivables as soon as they are generated," explains the head of one factoring operation.[69] Small companies that sell to government agencies and large corporations, both famous for stretching out their payments for 60 to 90 days or more, also find factoring attractive because they collect the money from the sale (less the factor's discount) much faster. Taylor Pershing, CEO of a staffing company that provides employees for hospitals, relies on factoring as a source of financing. His company incurs payroll expenses for 50 employees up front but does not collect from its clients until later and uses factoring to fill the cash gap. "We sometimes wait 30, 60, or 90 days to get paid," he says. "Without factoring, I'd need at least $500,000 in cash on hand or a similar-sized revolving credit line to meet payroll."[70]

Leasing

Leasing is another common bootstrap financing technique. Today, small businesses can lease virtually any kind of asset—from office space and telephones to computers and heavy equipment. By leasing expensive assets, a small business owner is able to use them without tying up valuable capital for an extended period of time. In other words, entrepreneurs can reduce the long-term capital requirements of their businesses by leasing equipment and facilities, and they are not investing their capital in depreciating assets. Also, because no down payment is required and because the cost of the asset is spread over a longer time (lowering monthly payments), the company's cash flow improves.

Credit Cards

Unable to find financing elsewhere, many entrepreneurs have launched their companies using the fastest and most convenient source of debt capital available: credit cards! Because they cannot get financing anywhere else, many entrepreneurs launch their companies by charging their start-up expenses to credit cards. It is a common financing technique; nearly 58 percent of entrepreneurs use credit cards to cover the costs of starting their businesses, a significant increase from the 16 percent who used credit cards for start-ups in 1993.[71] Filmmaker Spike Lee financed one of his first movies, *Do the Right Thing*, with credit cards and launched his career as a director. Putting business start-up costs on credit cards charging 20 percent or more in annual interest is expensive, risky, and can lead to severe financial woes, however. A study by Robert Scott of Monmouth University and the Kauffman Foundation reports that taking on credit card debt reduces the likelihood that a start-up company will survive its first 3 years of operation. Every $1,000 increase in credit card debt results in a 2.2 percent increase in the probability that a company will fail.[72]

Unfortunately, some determined entrepreneurs have no other choice but to finance their companies with credit cards. Credit cards are a ready source of temporary financing that can carry a company through the start-up phase until it begins generating positive cash flow, but entrepreneurs must use them judiciously.

ENTREPRENEURIAL
Profile

*Shannon Cumberland:
Rosy Rings*

Shannon Cumberland launched Rosy
Rings in her kitchen by maxing out
five credit cards.
Source: Shannon Cumberland/Rosy Rings

Shannon Cumberland launched Rosy Rings, a company that sells handmade botanical candles, in her Denver, Colorado, kitchen by maxing out five credit cards. For Cumberland, the high-risk move paid off. Rosy Rings, now with more than $2 million in annual sales, manufactures more than 250,000 candles each year that are sold online and in 1,800 retail stores across the United States.[73]

Where *Not* to Seek Funds

7. Explain how to avoid becoming a victim of a loan scam.

Entrepreneurs searching for capital must be wary of con artists whose targets frequently include financially strapped small businesses. The swindle usually begins when the con artist scours an area for "DEs"—desperate entrepreneurs—in search of quick cash injections to keep their businesses going. Usually, the scam involves advance fees and follows one of two patterns (although a number of variations exist). Under one scheme, scammers guarantee a small business owner a loan from a nonexistent bank with false credentials. The con artist tells the owner that loan processing will take time and that in the meantime the owner must pay a percentage of the loan amount as an advance fee. Of course, the loan never materializes, and the small business owner loses the deposit, sometimes several thousands of dollars.

Another common scam begins with a "loan broker" who promises a capital-hungry small business owner an SBA loan if the owner pays a small processing fee. Again, the loan never appears, and the small business owner loses his or her deposit. Other scammers charge entrepreneurs excessive fees to help them apply for SBA loan guarantees.

Unfortunately, schemes by con artists preying on unsuspecting business owners who are in need of capital are more common when credit tightens. Scams most commonly involve the SBA's smallest loan programs, such as the SBA*Express* and Microloan programs. The Internet has made crooks' jobs easier. On the Web, they can establish a legitimate-looking presence, approach their targets anonymously, and vanish instantly—all while avoiding mail fraud charges if they happen to get caught. These con artists move fast, cover their trails well, and are extremely smooth. The best protection against such scams is common sense and remembering the adage, "If it sounds too good to be true, it probably is." Experts offer the following advice to business owners:

- Be suspicious of anyone who approaches you—unsolicited—with an offer for "guaranteed financing."
- Watch out for red flags that indicate a scam: "guaranteed" loans, up-front fees, and unsolicited pitches over the Web.
- Conduct a thorough background check on any lenders, brokers, or financiers with whom you intend to do business. Is the lender registered to do business in your state? Does the Better Business Bureau have a record of complaints against the company?
- Make sure you have an attorney review all loan agreements before you sign them.
- *Never* pay advance fees for financing, especially on the Web, unless you have verified the lender's credibility.

Chapter Review

1. Describe the various sources of debt capital and the advantages and disadvantages of each.
   - Commercial banks offer the greatest variety of loans, although they are conservative lenders. Typical short-term bank loans include commercial loans, lines of credit, discounting accounts receivable, inventory financing, floor planning, and character loans.
2. Explain the types of financing available from nonbank sources of credit.
   - Asset-based lenders allow small businesses to borrow money by pledging otherwise idle assets, such as accounts receivable, inventory, or purchase orders, as collateral.

- Trade credit is used extensively by small businesses as a source of financing. Vendors and suppliers commonly finance sales to businesses for 30, 60, or even 90 days.
- Equipment suppliers offer small businesses financing similar to trade credit, but with slightly different terms.
- Commercial finance companies offer many of the same types of loans that banks do, but they are more risk oriented in their lending practices. They emphasize accounts receivable financing and inventory loans.
- Savings and loan associations specialize in loans to purchase real property— commercial and industrial mortgages—with payback terms of up to 30 years.
- Stock brokerage houses offer loans to prospective entrepreneurs at lower interest rates than banks because they have high-quality, liquid collateral—stocks and bonds in the borrower's portfolio.
- Insurance companies provide financing through policy loans and mortgage loans. Policy loans are extended to the owner against the cash surrender value of insurance policies. Mortgage loans are made for large amounts and are based on the value of the land being purchased.
- Small business investment companies (SBICs) are privately owned companies licensed and regulated by the SBA that qualify for SBA loans to be invested in or loaned to small businesses.
- Small business lending companies (SBLCs) make only intermediate and long-term loans that are guaranteed by the SBA.

3. Identify the various federal loan programs aimed at small businesses.
   - The Economic Development Administration, a branch of the Commerce Department, makes loan guarantees to create and expand small businesses in economically depressed areas.
   - The Department of Housing and Urban Development extends grants (such as Community Development Block Grants) to cities that, in turn, lend and grant money to small businesses in an attempt to strengthen the local economy.
   - The Department of Agriculture's Rural Business-Cooperative Service loan program is designed to create nonfarm employment opportunities in rural areas through loans and loan guarantees.
   - The Small Business Innovation Research Program involves 11 federal agencies that award cash grants or long-term contracts to small companies wanting to initiate or to expand their research and development (R&D) efforts.
   - The Small Business Technology Transfer Program allows researchers at universities, federally funded R&D centers, and nonprofit research institutions to join forces with small businesses and develop commercially promising ideas.

4. Describe the various loan programs available from the Small Business Administration.
   - SBA loan activity is in the form of loan guarantees rather than direct loans. Popular SBA programs include the SBA*Express* Program, the Patriot Express Program, the Community*Express* Program, the 7(a) loan guaranty program, the CAPLine Program, the Microloan Program, the 504 Certified Development Company Program, several export loan programs, and the disaster loan program.

5. Discuss state and local economic development programs.
   - In an attempt to develop businesses that create jobs and economic growth, most states offer small business financing programs, usually in the form of loans, loan guarantees, and venture capital pools.
   - Many state and local loan and development programs, such as capital access programs and revolving loan funds, complement those sponsored by federal agencies.

6. Discuss valuable methods of financing growth and expansion internally with bootstrap financing.
   - Small business owners may also look inside their firms for capital. By factoring accounts receivable, leasing equipment instead of buying it, and using credit cards, owners can stretch their supplies of capital.

7. Explain how to avoid becoming a victim of a loan scam.
   - Entrepreneurs hungry for capital for their growing businesses can be easy targets for con artists running loan scams. Entrepreneurs should watch out for promises of "guaranteed" loans, up-front fees, and offers that seem too good to be true.

Discussion Questions

1. What role do commercial banks play in providing debt financing to small businesses? Outline and briefly describe the major types of short-term, intermediate, and long-term loans commercial banks offer.
2. What is trade credit? How important is it as a source of debt financing to small firms?
3. Explain how asset-based financing works. What is the most common method of asset-based financing? What are the advantages and disadvantages of using this method of financing?
4. What function do SBICs serve? How does an SBIC operate? What methods of financing do SBICs rely on most heavily?
5. Briefly describe the loan programs offered by the following:
   a. Economic Development Administration
   b. Department of Housing and Urban Development
   c. Department of Agriculture
   d. Local development companies
6. Explain the purpose and the methods of operation of the Small Business Innovation Research Program and the Small Business Technology Transfer Program.
7. Which of the SBA's loan programs accounts for the majority of its loan activity? How does the program work?
8. Explain the purpose and the operation of the SBA's Microloan Program.
9. How can a firm employ bootstrap financing to stretch its current capital supply?
10. What is a factor? How does the typical factor operate? Explain the advantages and the disadvantages of factoring. What kinds of businesses typically use factors?

Many entrepreneurs are reluctant to give up a percentage of ownership in their companies that equity capital requires and turn instead to debt capital as a source of funds. Almost every lending institution expects to see a quality business plan. A business plan adds credibility and is testimony that you have invested thought and time in your business idea. If you need debt capital for your venture, a business plan can help you clarify how much money you will need, formulate a financing strategy for acquiring the funds, and communicate to potential lenders why you are worth the risk.

On the Web

If you need start-up or growth capital for your venture, visit the Companion Web site at *www.pearsonhighered.com/scarborough* and review some equity financing options. Determine whether these sources may be useful as you explore financing opportunities. You will also find additional information regarding bootstrap and nontraditional funding.

Sample Plans

You should review sample plans in Business Plan Pro for companies that are seeking debt financing. Lenders will want to confirm that you have a sound business or business idea, that you are motivated enough to make the business successful, and that you will be able to make your payments on time! They also will want to know about any collateral that you have to bring to the table. Use each aspect of the financial section—the break-even analysis, projected profit and loss, projected cash flow, projected balance sheet, and business ratios—to tell your company's financial story to your lending audience.

In the Software

Open your plan in Business Plan Pro and go to the "Financial Plan" section. Your assumptions will state anticipated economic conditions, current short-term and long-term interest rates, expected tax rates, personnel expenses, cash expenses, sales on credit, or any areas that you hope to develop and confirm through further research. You will then assess the type and amount of debt financing that you will need. Will this be short- or long-term financing? Work through the finance section and review the numbers in your break-even point calculation, balance sheet, projected profit and loss statement, and cash flow forecast. This section also will enable you to review industry ratios and to compare them to your company's anticipated performance. These ratio comparisons may be helpful for lenders. Make certain this section clearly tells your financial story. Providing relevant information that will be meaningful to the potential lenders who will review your plan is critical.

Building Your Business Plan

The business plan will help to assess the amount of debt financing needed, describe the use of these funds, and make certain that you can live with the financial consequences of these decisions. This "financial road map" helps you to analyze your funding options. Expect potential lenders to review your pro forma statements and, like investors, to assess the qualifications of your management team, the industry's growth potential, your proposed exit strategy, and other factors as they assess the financial stability of your venture.

Endnotes

1. Mara Der Hovanesian, "Tapped Out?" *BusinessWeek*, Winter 2007, *www.businessweek.com/magazine/content/07_09/b4023443.htm*.
2. William J. Dennis, *Small Business Credit in a Deep Recession*, National Federation of Independent Businesses, February 2010, pp. 8–9.
3. Melissa Sharp, "Small Business Optimism Declines in June," National Federation of Independent Businesses, July 13, 2010, *www.nfib.com/press-media/press-media-item?cmsid=52004*.
4. Emily Maltby, "Bailout Missed Main Street, New Report Says," *Wall Street Journal*, May 14, 2010, p. B6.
5. Catherine Clifford, "Small Business Loans: 410 Billion Evaporates," *CNNMoney*, November 17, 2009, *http://money.cnn.com/2009/11/16/smallbusiness/small_business_loans_evaporate/*.
6. Cynthia E. Griffin, "Something Borrowed," *Entrepreneur*, February 1997, p. 26; Business Lenders Inc., *www.businesslenders.com/q&a.htm*.
7. *The Small Business Credit Crunch and the Impact of the TARP*, Congressional Oversight Panel, May 2010, p. 13.
8. Peter S. Goodman, "Credit Tightens for Small Businesses," *New York Times*, October 13, 2009, *www.nytimes.com/2009/10/13/business/smallbusiness/13lending.html*.
9. Conor Dougherty and Pu-Wing Tam, "Start-ups Chase Cash as Funds Trickle Back," *Wall Street Journal*, April 1, 2010, p. B1.
10. *Small Business and Micro Business Lending in the United States for Data Years 2007–2008*, U.S. Small Business Administration, Office of Advocacy, May 2009, p. 6.
11. Daniel M. Clark, "Banks and Bankability," *Venture*, September 1989, p. 29.
12. Rosalind Resnick, "Loan Woes," *Entrepreneur*, April 2007, p. 96.
13. Dennis, Jr., *Small Business Credit in a Deep Recession*, p. 1.
14. Emily Maltby, "Tightening the Credit Screws," *Wall Street Journal*, May 17, 2010, *http://online.wsj.com/article/NA_WSJ_PUB: SB10001424052748704784904575111250456800076.html*.
15. "Thrifty Names President of Thrifty Car Sales; Announces Strategic Alliances with Bank of America, APCO, Manheim, and Others," Dollar Thrifty Automotive Group, February 8, 2005, *www.dtag.com/phoenix.zhtml?c=71946&p=irol-newsArticle&ID=27723&highlight=*.
16. Tim Reason, "Borrowing Big Time," *CFO*, November 2003, pp. 87–94.
17. Juan Hovey, "Want Easy Money? Look for Lenders Who Say Yes," *FSB*, November 2000, pp. 41–44.
18. Kyle Stock, "Asset-Based Lending Grows in Popularity," *Wall Street Journal*, February 2, 2010, p. B5.
19. Carol Tice, "Can a Purchase Order Loan Keep Your Business Growing?" *Entrepreneur*, June 17, 2010, *www.entrepreneur.com/money/financing/article207058.html*.
20. Rebel Cole, *Bank Credit, Trade Credit, or No Credit: Evidence from the Surveys of Small Business Finances*, U.S. Small Business Administration, Office of Advocacy, June 2010, p. 21.
21. Emily Maltby, "Vendors Can Help Financing," *Wall Street Journal*, February 18, 2010, p. B5; Ina Steiner, "eFashion Solutions Powers Brands on eBay, *Fashion Vault*, Amazon.com," Auction Bytes, July 8, 2010, *www.auctionbytes.com/cab/abn/y10/m07/i08/s01*.
22. *Small Business and Micro Business Lending in the United States 2005*, p. 6.
23. David Worrell, "The Other Colors of Money," *Entrepreneur*, July 2004, p. 67.
24. Ibid.
25. "Case Studies: Kalitta Air," GE Capital, *www.gecapital.com/en/case-study-kalitta-air.html*.
26. "Customer Success Story: Hudson Bakery," GE Capital, *www.hudsonbread.com/media.html*; "Tactical Conquest," Hudson Bakery, *www.hudsonbread.com/media.html*.
27. John R. Walter, "Not Your Father's Credit Union," *Economic Quarterly*, Federal Reserve Bank of Richmond, Vol. 92, No. 4, Fall 2006, pp. 353–377.
28. Jorina Fontelera, "Where to Go When Banks Say No," *ThomasNet News*, June 9, 2009, *http://news.thomasnet.com/IMT/archives/2009/06/where-to-go-when-banks-say-no-alternative-funding-sources-for-entrepreneurs.html*.
29. *2009 Yearend Statistics for Federally Insured Credit Unions*, National Credit Union Administration, p. 7.
30. Chris Branch, "Delaware Business: Loan Big for Beauty Shop, Credit Union," *Delaware Online*, July 17, 2010, *www.delawareonline.com/article/20100717/BUSINESS/7170317/Delaware-business-Loan-big-for-beauty-shop-credit-union*.
31. "NGK Overview," NGK Spark Plugs, *www.ngksparkplugs.com/About_nGK/index.asp?mode=nml*; *West Virginia Economic Development Agency Annual Report 2008*, West Virginia Economic Development Agency, p. 9; "Success Stories," West Virginia Department of Commerce, *www.wvcommerce.org/business/successstories/default.aspx*.
32. Steven E. F. Brown, "Salesforce Wraps Up $500 Million Private Placement," *San Francisco Business Times*, January 19, 2010, *http://sanfrancisco.bizjournals.com/sanfrancisco/stories/2010/01/18/daily29.html*; "Company Milestones," Salesforce.com, *www.salesforce.com/ company/co_milestones.jsp*.
33. "America's Small Business Partners," National Association of Small Business Investment Companies, *www.nasbic.org*.
34. "History and Current Highlights," National Association of Small Business Investment Companies, *www.nasbic.org/?page=SBIC_Program_History*.
35. "SBIC Program Overview," National Association of Small Business Investment Companies, January 23, 2009, p. 2.
36. Ibid.
37. "Paramount 2009 Portfolio Company of the Year Award from NASBIC," Paramount Building Solutions, November 11, 2009, *www.paramountbldgsol.com/about/pressRelease.cfm?preID=16*; "Paramount Building Solutions Named Portfolio Company of the Year," LaSalle Capital Group, November 2009, *www.lasallecapitalgroup.com/PDFs/NASBIC-award.pdf*.
38. *Economic Development Administration Fiscal Year 2009 Annual Report*, Economic Development Administration, *www.eda.gov/PDF/EDA%20FY%202009%20Annual%20Report.pdf*.
39. "Revolving Loan Fund Innovative Practices: Mo-Kan Regional Council Revolving Loan Fund," *EDA Update*, September 2009, Vol. 2, No. 9, *www.planning.org/eda/newsletter/2009/sep.htm#4*.
40. "Trade Adjustment Assistance for Firms Case Studies," U.S. Economic Development Administration, *www.lasallecapitalgroup.com/PDFs/NASBIC-award.pdf*.
41. "Section 108 Case Studies," U.S. Department of Housing and Urban Development, *www.hud.gov/offices/cpd/communitydevelopment/programs/108/casestudies.cfm*.
42. *USDA Rural Development Progress Report 2009*, U.S. Department of Agriculture, pp. 22–23.
43. Charles Wessner, "An Assessment of the SBIR Program," National Research Council, *http://books.nap.edu/openbook.php?record_id= 11989&page=12*, pp. 91–107.
44. "SBIR/STTR Hallmarks of Success Videos: AeroTech Research Inc.," NASA Small Business Innovation Research Program, *http://sbir.nasa.gov/SBIR/video/aerotech.html*; "Steering Aircraft Clear of Choppy Air," *Tech Briefs*, January 1, 2006, *www.techbriefs.com/content/view/1238/118/*; "NASA Selects AeroTech to Quantify Benefits of Advanced Weather Avoidance Systems for Aircraft," *Federal Circle*, August 5, 2010, *http://thefederalcircle.com/nasa-selects-aerotech-to-quantify-benefits-of-advanced-weather-avoidance-systems-for-aircraft/*.
45. *Summary of Performance and Financial Information 2009 Fiscal Year*, U.S. Small Business Administration, February 22, 2010, p. 5.
46. Emily Maltby, "A Credit Crunch That Lingers," *Wall Street Journal*, June 21, 2010, *http://online.wsj.com/article/NA_WSJ_PUB: SB10001424052748704852004575257970246239874.html*.
47. Diana Ransom, "Status Report: Small Business Lending," *Wall Street Journal*, September 23, 2009, *http://online.wsj.com/article/NA_WSJ_PUB:SB125372460362634601.html*.
48. "2009 Recovery Act: Helping Small Business Start, Grow, and Succeed—Q&A for Small Business Owners," U.S. Small Business Administration, p. 2.
49. *Summary of Performance and Financial Information 2009 Fiscal Year*, U.S. Small Business Administration, February 22, 2010, p. 3.
50. Julie Monahan, "Quick Fix," *Entrepreneur*, April 2004, p. 27.
51. Michelle Samaad, "Patriot Express's $500 Million in Loans Helps Returning Military," *Credit Union Times*, July 1, 2010, *www.cutimes.com/News/2010/7/Pages/Patriot-Express-500-Million-in-Loans-Helps-Returning-Military-.aspx*.
52. Tim Rausch, "Federal Program Provides Loans for Small Businesses," *Augusta Chronicle*, October 18, 2009, *http://chronicle.augusta.com/ stories/2009/10/18/bus_552290.shtml*.

53. Raymund Flandez, "SBA Loan Cap Hits Minority Owners," *Wall Street Journal*, December 9, 2008, pp. B1, B7.
54. "The SBA's 7(a) Loan Program: A Flexible Tool for Commercial Lenders," *Community Development Insights*, Washington, D.C.: U.S. Department of the Treasury, September 2008, *www.occ.treas.gov/cdd/Insights-SBAs7(a).pdf*, p. 3.
55. "Success Story: Ace Hardware of Silver Lake," *Summary of Performance and Financial Information, 2009 Fiscal Year*, U.S. Small Business Administration, p. 21.
56. Tom Abate, "Small Business Facing Credit Crunch," *San Francisco Chronicle*, January 21, 2010, *www.sfgate.com/cgi-bin/article.cgi?f=/c/a/2010/01/20/BUOL1BKH26.DTL*; Joan M. Lang, "Kasa Indian Eatery," *Restaurant Business*, June 2009, p. 26.
57. "Spotlight on Success: Navy Pilots Aim for Business Success on Land," *BLX Lending Report*, Vol. 1, No. 1, *www.blxonline.com/Files/Public/BLX-Success-Story-Jet-Stream-Car-Wash.pdf*.
58. "Starved for Financing: Is There Relief in Sight for U.S. Small Businesses?" *Knowledge@Wharton*, October 28, 2009, *www.knowledgeatwharton.com.cn/index.cfm?fa=viewArticle&articleID=2135&languageid=1*; John Reid Blackwell, "Daystar Desserts CEO Chef Shares Recipe for Survival," *Richmond Times-Dispatch*, September 13, 2009, *www2.timesdispatch.com/business/2009/sep/13/cake13_20090912-192805-ar-30606/*.
59. Summary of Performance and Financial Information Fiscal Year 2009, Small Business Administration, *www.sba.gov/idc/groups/public/documents/sba_homepage/serv_aboutsba_perf_summ.pdf*, p.8.
60. "Microloan Program," U.S. Small Business Administration, *www.sba.gov/financialassistance/borrowers/guaranteed/mlp/index*.
61. *SBA Microloan Program: FY 2007*, Women Impacting Public Policy, *www.wipp.org/news_details.asp?story_id=204&memberonly=False*.
62. Gwendolyn Bounds, "Risky Businesses May Find Loans Even Scarcer," *Wall Street Journal*, April 13, 2004, p. B8.
63. Mae Anderson, "Sam's Club Will Offer Small Business Loans," *MSNBC*, July 6, 2010, *www.msnbc.msn.com/id/38103657/*; Stephanie Clifford, "Retailers Devise Novel Ways to Revive Sales," *New York Times*, July 4, 2010, *www.nytimes.com/2010/07/05/business/05loan.html*.
64. Brian Davis, "Lumber Company Builds Small Town Employment," Alabama International Trade Center, *www.aitc.ua.edu/success-stories*, p. 1; Arthur McLean, "Thomas Lumber Honored by Governor," *Thomasville Times*, March 29, 2007, *www.thethomasvilletimes.com/news/2007-03-29/Front_Page/Thomasville_Lumber_honored_by_Gov.html*.
65. Carol Chastang, "SBA Administrator Offers Economic Injury Assistance to Louisiana Small Businesses Affected by Deepwater BP Oil Spill," U.S. Small Business Administration, May 6, 2010, pp. 1–2.
66. Ziona Austrian and Zhongcai Zhang, "An Inventory and Assessment of Pollution Control and Prevention Financing Programs," Great Lakes Environmental Finance Center, Levin College of Urban Affairs, Cleveland State University, *www.csuohio.edu/glefc/inventor.htm#sba*.
67. "Full Spectrum Solutions Growing Green," Enterprise Group of Jackson, *www.enterprisegroup.org/economic-development-corporation*, p. 1.
68. "Success Stories: CDA Helps CT Businesses," Connecticut Development Authority, *www.ctcda.com/successStories/newsView.asp?NewsID=52*; "About Us," Autotether, *www.autotether.com/at/index.php?option=com_content&view=article&id=67&Itemid=81*.
69. Sean P. Melvin, "Hidden Treasure," *Entrepreneur*, February 2002, pp. 56–58.
70. "Success Stories," Keystone Capital, *www.keystonefactoring.com/success-stories/*.
71. Raymond J. Keating, *Credit Cards and Small Business: The Benefits, Opportunities, and Policy Debate*, Small Business and Entrepreneurship Council, March 2009, p. 11; Robert Scott, *The Use of Credit Card Debt by New Firms*, The Kauffman Firm Survey, August 2009, p. 2.
72. Robert Scott, *The Use of Credit Card Debt by New Firms*, The Kauffman Firm Survey, August 2009, pp. 2, 4.
73. Linda Dishman, "Play Your Cards Right," *Entrepreneur*, November 9, 2009, *www.entrepreneur.com/money/financing/article203940.html*.

Sources of Equity Financing

All it takes to start a company is one hundred thousand dollars . . .

and no "sense."

—Guy Jones, founder of River Runner Outdoor Center

The key for entrepreneurs is to find investors who are going to add

value to the company as it goes along.

—Rod Nelson

Learning Objectives

Upon completion of this chapter, you will be able to:

1. Explain the differences among the three types of capital small businesses require: fixed, working, and growth.
2. Describe the various sources of equity capital available to entrepreneurs, including personal savings, friends and relatives, angels, partners, corporations, venture capital, and public stock offerings.
3. Describe the process of "going public," as well as its advantages and disadvantages.
4. Explain the various simplified registrations, exemptions from registration, and other alternatives available to entrepreneurs who want to sell shares of equity to investors.

From Chapter 14 of *Effective Small Business Management: An Entrepreneurial Approach*, 10/e. Norman M. Scarborough.

Raising the money to launch a new business venture has always been a challenge for entrepreneurs. Capital markets rise and fall with the stock market, overall economic conditions, and investors' fortunes. These swells and troughs in the availability of capital make the search for financing look like a wild roller-coaster ride. Entrepreneurs, especially those in less glamorous industries or those just starting out, soon discover the difficulty of finding outside sources of financing. Many banks shy away from making loans to start-ups, venture capitalists are looking for ever-larger deals, private investors have grown cautious, and a public stock offering remains a viable option for only a handful of promising companies with good track records and fast-growth futures. The result has been a credit crunch for entrepreneurs looking for small to moderate amounts of start-up capital. Entrepreneurs and business owners who need between $100,000 and $3 million are especially hard hit because of the vacuum that exists at that level of financing.

In the face of this capital crunch, businesses' need for capital has never been greater. When searching for the capital to launch their companies, entrepreneurs must remember the following "secrets" to successful financing:

■ *Choosing the right sources of capital for a business can be just as important as choosing the right form of ownership or the right location.* It is a decision that will influence a company for a lifetime; therefore, entrepreneurs must weigh their options carefully and understand the consequences of the deal before committing to a particular funding source. Avoid the tendency to jump at the first check that comes your way; instead, consider the long-term impact on your business of accepting that check.

■ *The money is out there; the key is knowing where to look.* Entrepreneurs must do their homework *before* they set out to raise money for their ventures. Understanding which sources of funding are best suited for the various stages of a company's growth and then taking the time to learn how those sources work are essential to success.

■ *Creativity counts.* To find the financing their businesses demand, entrepreneurs must use as much creativity in attracting financing as they did in generating the ideas for their products and services.

ENTREPRENEURIAL
Profile

*Drue Kataoka and
Svetlozar Kazanjiev:
Aboomba*

As Drue Kataoka (left) and Svetlozar Kazanjiev planned their wedding, they drew inspiration from traditional wedding registries to create the world's first start-up registry to finance the launch of their business, Aboomba.

Source: Gary Reyes/Newscom

When Drue Kataoka and Svetlozar Kazanjiev began planning their wedding, they took a different approach to their wedding registry. Rather than list the typical household appliances that appear on most wedding registries, the couple created "The World's First Start-up Registry," listing items to help them launch their e-commerce site called Aboomba. They took elements from their business plan, such as "feed an engineer for a day ($273.97)," "Red Bull for a week ($52.41)," and "Amazon EC2 Cloud Web hosting for a week ($134.40)," and incorporated them into their start-up registry. Guests and others responded to the creative approach to raising capital, providing the couple with every item on their start-up registry at least three times over.[1]

■ *The Internet puts vast resources of information that can lead to financing at entrepreneurs' fingertips.* The Internet often offers entrepreneurs, especially those looking for relatively small amounts of money, the opportunity to discover sources of funds that they otherwise might miss. The Web site created for this text (*www.pearsonhighered.com/scarborough*) provides links to many useful sites related to raising both start-up and growth capital. The Internet also provides a low-cost, convenient way for entrepreneurs to get their business plans into potential investors' hands anywhere in the world. When searching for sources of capital, entrepreneurs must not overlook this valuable tool!

■ *Be thoroughly prepared before approaching potential lenders and investors.* In the hunt for capital, tracking down leads is tough enough; don't blow a potential deal by failing to be ready to present your business idea to potential lenders and investors in a clear, concise, convincing way. That, of course, requires a solid business plan.

■ *Looking for "smart" money is more important than looking for "easy" money.* Some entrepreneurs have little difficulty attracting investors' money. However, easy money is not always smart money. Even though it may be easy to acquire, money from the wrong investor can spell disaster for a small company. Entrepreneurs cannot overestimate the importance of making sure that the "chemistry" among themselves, their companies, and their funding sources is a good one. Too many entrepreneurs get into financial deals because they needed the money to keep their businesses growing only to discover that their plans do not match those of their financial partners.

ENTREPRENEURIAL
Profile

*Brian Carlton: New
Breed Wireless*

When Brian Carlton launched CEIG, a company that sells content and applications for mobile phones under the brand name New Breed Wireless, he accepted an offer from a private investor who put up $400,000, payable in two installments, in exchange for 25 percent of the company. The relationship was rocky from the beginning, and the investor made clear his expectations of the company's performance. When CEIG missed one benchmark 1 year into the deal, the investor refused to invest the second installment, and Carlton was forced to scramble for money to keep the company afloat. "That investor didn't understand how technology businesses grow," says Carlton, whose company ultimately received the remaining $200,000 from the investor. Wiser for the experience, Carlton has revised his capital searching strategy, relying on smaller amounts of money and screening carefully every potential investor. With his new approach, Carlton has raised $1.1 million from 25 investors and has retained 75 percent of the equity in his business.[2]

■ *Plan an exit strategy.* Although it may seem peculiar for entrepreneurs to plan an exit strategy for investors when they are seeking capital to *start* their businesses, doing so increases their chances of closing a deal. Investors do not put their money into a business with the intent of leaving it there indefinitely. Their goal is to get their money back—along with an attractive return on it. Entrepreneurs who fail to define potential exit strategies for their investors reduce the likelihood of getting the capital their companies need to grow.

Rather than rely primarily on a single source of funds as they have in the past, entrepreneurs must piece together capital from multiple sources, a method known as **layered financing**. They

ENTREPRENEURIAL
Profile

*Martin Eberhard, Marc
Tarppening, and Elon
Musk: Tesla Motors*

Elon Musk, CEO of Tesla Motors, poses with one of the company's high performance electric cars in New York City's Times Square following Tesla Motors' initial public offering.

Source: Mark Lennihan/AP Wide World Photos

Founded in 2003 by Silicon Valley engineers Martin Eberhard and Marc Tarppening and PayPal founder Elon Musk, Tesla Motors, a Palo Alto, California-based maker of sleek, high-performance electric cars, has relied on layered financing from a variety of sources to produce its first two all-electric cars, the Roadster and the Model S. The Roadster, which goes from zero to 60 miles per hour in just 3.7 seconds and travels 245 miles between charges, sells for $100,000. The Model S, a seven-passenger hatchback capable of hitting 60 miles per hour in 5.5 seconds, sells for about $50,000. To launch their company (which is named after Nikola Tesla, the inventor of alternating current), the cofounders invested some of their own money and turned to private investors, a "who's who" list of Silicon Valley entrepreneurs, including Google founders Sergey Brin and Larry Page, for capital. As it grew, the company also attracted millions of dollars of financing from a number of venture capital companies. Daimler, the parent company of Mercedes-Benz invested $50 million in return for 9 percent of the company's stock. Tesla also received a low-interest $465 million loan from the Department of Energy after being recognized as one of the nation's leading electric vehicle research companies. Because of the huge capital investment required to build a successful automotive company, Tesla's founders knew that an initial public offering (IPO) of the company's stock was necessary. Seven years after its launch, the company, which had not yet earned an annual profit, conducted a successful IPO that raised more than $226 million. Musk, now Tesla's CEO, already is developing plans for new models, including a crossover SUV, a delivery van, and a pickup truck.[3]

have discovered that raising capital successfully requires them to cast a wide net to capture the financing they need to launch their businesses. Much like assembling a patchwork quilt from using fabric from many different sources, financing a small business often requires entrepreneurs to find capital from many different sources.

For most entrepreneurs, raising the money to start or expand their businesses is a challenge that demands time, energy, creativity, and a measure of luck. "Raising money is a marathon, not a sprint," says one entrepreneur who has raised $4 million for her 4-year-old company.[4] This chapter and the next one will guide you through the myriad of financing options available to entrepreneurs, focusing on both sources of equity (ownership) and debt (borrowed) financing.

IN THE ENTREPRENEURIAL
SPOTLIGHT The Hunt for Capital

While majoring in business at the University of Arizona, Sean Conway, who suffers from attention deficit hyperactivity disorder (ADHD), had difficulty listening to lectures and taking notes simultaneously. Conway noticed that many students experienced the same problem, and he and Justin Miller, a junior at the University of Arizona, recognized a business opportunity. They decided to launch Notehall (www.notehall.com), a Web site that serves as a marketplace for students to buy and sell class notes and study guides, first targeting students on their campus. Their goal, however, was to harness the power of the Web and take the concept to other campuses around the world. Conway and Miller started Notehall with $70,000 from Conway's inheritance and Miller's bar mitzvah money.

To access class notes, users purchase credits through the site's virtual currency system and spend them to download files (100 credits cost $3; lecture notes cost 25 credits; and a complete study guide costs 100 credits). Students who post notes and study guides receive a commission (25 cents on lecture notes and $1 on a study guide) when they are downloaded. Notehall generates revenue by taking a commission on each download. "With the time it takes to make a study guide, let alone study, you can go to Notehall and find someone who's already made a study guide," says one enthusiastic user at the University of Arizona.

One year into business, the company was out of cash, and the 20-something entrepreneurs had no more money to invest. Conway convinced his grandfather to contribute $17,000 for marketing, which helped the young company reach nearly 8,000 students at the University of Arizona while Conway pitched the business to angel investors and venture capital firms. No one was interested in investing.

Desperate for capital, Conway submitted his business plan to DreamIt Ventures, an entrepreneurial boot camp in Philadelphia funded by four economic development organizations that provides promising entrepreneurs with office space, advisors, and the opportunity to meet

potential lenders and investors. Notehall was one of just 10 companies selected to participate in DreamIt for the summer. Conway's boot camp experience paid off. By the end of the program, Conway had convinced investors to put $500,000 into Notehall.

Conway's next move was to apply to become a contestant on ABC's *Shark Tank*, a television show that gives entrepreneurs the opportunity to pitch their business ideas to five angel investors who ask questions and then decide to invest or pass on each business opportunity. The show's producers accepted Notehall, and after a few tense minutes of grilling from the angel investors, Conway and D. J. Stephan, the company's marketing officer, struck a deal with investor Barbara Corcoran for $90,000 in exchange for 25 percent of Notehall.

Conway has expanded the management team at Notehall and has created an advisory board composed of both academicians and businesspeople. The company now reaches 33 colleges and generates sales of $900,000, up from just $40,000 in the previous year. Conway knows that to continue to expand, Notehall will need more capital to fuel its growth.

1. How typical is Notehall's struggle to raise capital? What advice can you give to an entrepreneur such as Sean Conway about raising capital to start a business? Which sources of funding do you recommend and in what sequence? Explain.

2. Is it ethical for students to make money selling notes taken from a professor's lecture? Critics of Notehall claim that some students may not have enough money to purchase notes on Notehall, which might put them at a disadvantage compared to those who can afford to purchase notes. Do you agree? Explain.

3. Visit the Web site for ABC's *Shark Tank* at http://abc.go.com/shows/shark-tank and watch an episode. (You can find Sean Conway and

Notehall cofounders (left to right) Justin Miller, Sean Conway and Fadi Chalfoun.

Source: NoteHall, 340 Bryant Street, Suite #104, San Francisco, CA 94107 (650)276-0409

D. J. Stephan's pitch for Notehall on episode 108.) At the site, you can also read more about the entrepreneurs who appear on the show and their businesses. Do you agree with the angels' decisions? In which of the businesses, if any, would you invest? What criteria did you use to evaluate each opportunity? What does this experience teach you about pitching your own idea to potential investors?

Sources: Based on Emily Maltby, "Need Funding? Better Get Creative," *Wall Street Journal*, October 15, 2009, p. B5; "America's Best Young Entrepreneurs: Notehall," *Bloomberg's Business Week*, http://images. businessweek.com/ss/09/10/1009_entrepreneurs_25_and_under/18.htm; "About Us," Notehall, www.notehall.com/index/about; Hank Stephenson, "Study Buddy," *Tucson Weekly*, May 7, 2009, www.tucsonweekly.com/ tucson/study-buddy/Content?oid=1180388.

Planning for Capital Needs

1. Explain the differences among the three types of capital small businesses require: fixed, working, and growth.

Becoming a successful entrepreneur requires one to become a skilled fund-raiser, a job that usually requires more time and energy than most business founders anticipate. In start-up companies, raising capital can easily consume as much as one-half of the entrepreneur's time and can take many months to complete. Most entrepreneurs are seeking less than $1 million (indeed, most need less than $100,000), which may be the toughest money to secure. Where to find this seed money depends, in part, on the nature of the proposed business and on the amount of money required. For example, the creator of a computer software firm would have different capital requirements than the founder of an ice cream shop. Although both entrepreneurs might approach some of the same types of lenders or investors, each would be more successful targeting specific sources of funds best suited to their particular financial needs and businesses.

Capital is any form of wealth employed to produce more wealth. It exists in many forms in a typical business, including cash, inventory, plant, and equipment. Entrepreneurs need three different types of capital.

Fixed Capital

Fixed capital is needed to purchase a business's permanent or fixed assets, such as buildings, land, computers, and equipment. Money invested in these fixed assets tends to be frozen because it cannot be used for any other purpose. Typically, large sums of money are involved in purchasing fixed assets, and credit terms usually are lengthy. Lenders of fixed capital expect the assets purchased to improve the efficiency, and thus the profitability, of the business and to create improved cash flows that ensure repayment.

Working Capital

Working capital represents a business's temporary funds; it is the capital used to support a company's normal short-term operations. Accountants define working capital as current assets minus current liabilities. The need for working capital arises because of the uneven flow of cash into and out of the business due to normal seasonal fluctuations. Credit sales, seasonal sales swings, or unforeseeable changes in demand create fluctuations in *any* small company's cash flow. Working capital normally is used to buy inventory, pay bills, finance credit sales, pay wages and salaries, and take care of any unexpected emergencies. Lenders of working capital expect it to produce higher cash flows to ensure repayment at the end of the production/sales cycle.

Growth Capital

Growth capital, unlike working capital, is not related to the seasonal fluctuations of a small business. Instead, growth capital requirements surface when an existing business is expanding or

TABLE 1 Equity Capital Sources at Various Stages of Company Growth

Characteristics	Start-Up	Early	Expansion	Profitability
	Business is in conceptual phase and exists only on paper.	Business is developing one or more products or services but is not yet generating sales.	Business is selling products or services and is generating revenue and is beginning to establish a customer base.	Company has established a customer base and is profitable.
Possible Sources of Funding	Likelihood of using each source: H = Highly likely; P = Possible; U = Unlikely			
Personal savings	H	H	H	H
Retained earnings	U	U	U	H
Friends and relatives	H	H	P	P
Angel investors	H	H	P	U
Partners	H	H	P	U
Corporate venture capital	P	H	H	H
Venture capital	U	P	H	H
Initial public offering (IPO)	U	U	P	H
Regulation S-B Offering	U	U	P	H
Small Company Offering Registration (SCOR)	U	P	P	H
Private placements	U	P	P	H
Intrastate offerings (Rule 147)	U	P	P	H
Regulation A	U	P	P	H

changing its primary direction. For example, a small manufacturer of silicon microchips for computers saw his business skyrocket in a short time period. With orders for chips rushing in, the growing business needed a sizable cash infusion to increase plant size, expand its sales and production workforce, and buy more equipment. During times of such rapid expansion, a growing company's capital requirements are similar to those of a business start-up. Like lenders of fixed capital, growth capital lenders expect the funds to improve a company's profitability and cash-flow position, thus ensuring repayment.

Although these three types of capital are interdependent, each has certain sources, characteristics, and effects on the business and its long-term growth that entrepreneurs must recognize. Table 1 shows the various stages of a company's growth and the sources of capital most suitable in each stage.

Sources of Equity Financing

2. Describe the various sources of equity financing available to entrepreneurs. including personal savings, friends and relatives, angels, partners, corporations, venture capital, and public stock offerings.

Equity capital represents the personal investment of the owner (or owners) in a business and is sometimes called *risk* capital because the investor assumes the primary risk of losing his or her funds if the business fails. For instance, private investor Victor Lombardi lost the $3.5 million he invested in a start-up called NetFax, a company that was developing the technology to send faxes over the Internet. However, when NetFax's patent application stalled, the company foundered. Just 3 years after its launch, NetFax ceased operations, leaving Lombardi's investment worthless.[5]

If a venture succeeds, however, founders and investors share in the benefits, which can be quite substantial. The founders of and early investors in Yahoo!, Sun Microsystems, FedEx, Intel, and Microsoft became multimillionaires when the companies went public and their equity investments finally paid off. To entrepreneurs, the primary advantage of equity capital is that it does not have to be repaid like a loan does. Equity investors are entitled to share in the company's earnings (if there are any) and usually to have a voice in the company's future direction.

The primary disadvantage of equity capital is that the entrepreneur must give up some—perhaps *most*—of the ownership in the business to outsiders. Although 50 percent of something is better than 100 percent of nothing, giving up control of your company can be disconcerting and dangerous. Many entrepreneurs who give up majority ownership in their companies in exchange for equity capital find themselves forced out of the businesses they started! Entrepreneurs are most likely to give up more equity in their businesses in the start-up phase than in any other.

We now turn our attention to nine common sources of equity capital.

Personal Savings

The *first* place entrepreneurs should look for start-up money is in their own pockets. It's the least expensive source of funds available! Entrepreneurs apparently see the benefits of self-sufficiency; the most common source of equity funds used to start a small business is the entrepreneur's pool of personal savings, a technique known as **bootstrapping**. The Global Entrepreneurship Monitor (GEM) study reports that in the United States, the average cost to start a business is $70,200 and that the typical entrepreneur provides 67.9 percent of the initial capital requirement.[6]

Lenders and investors *expect* entrepreneurs to put their own money into a business start-up. If an entrepreneur is not willing to risk his or her own money, potential investors are not likely to risk their money in the business either. Furthermore, failure to put up sufficient capital of their own means that entrepreneurs must either borrow excessive amounts of capital or give up significant shares of ownership to outsiders to fund their businesses properly. Excessive borrowing in the early days of a business puts intense pressure on its cash flow, and becoming a minority shareholder may dampen a founder's enthusiasm for making a business successful. Neither outcome presents a bright future for the company involved. Using their own money at start up allows entrepreneurs to minimize the debt their companies take on and to retain control of their companies' future.

Because they are not able to attract capital from outside sources, entrepreneurs often must bootstrap their companies, launching them with little or no money. It takes creativity, boldness, and a certain degree of brashness and moxie, but it works.

ENTREPRENEURIAL Profile

Vlad Shmunis and Vlad Vendrow: RingCentral

In 2003, Vlad Shmunis and Vlad Vendrow cofounded RingCentral, a company that uses cloud computing to offer small companies sophisticated Internet-based voice and fax services that require no special hardware or software, by bootstrapping it with their own money. By targeting small companies with services that were once available only to large corporations with sophisticated phone systems, such as virtual receptionists, call forwarding, multiple extensions, and transcribing voice mail into e-mail, for as little as $10 per month, their company grew quickly. "Customers were happy and recommended [our service] to their friends," says Shmunis, who earlier had launched a company called Ring Zero Systems. "We were always growing." Like most bootstrappers, the founders focused on keeping their costs low. "We ran this business out of a 1,000-square-foot office with 10 people," Shmunis says. "We kept building and building." Within 3 years, RingCentral had 20,000 customers, and its capital requirements were outstripping the company's ability to meet them. Only then did Shmunis and Vendrow look for outside financing. RingCentral negotiated two rounds of investments totaling $24 million from venture capital companies, but Shmunis and Vendrow maintained control of their company.[7]

Friends and Family Members

Although most entrepreneurs look to their own bank accounts first to finance a business, few have sufficient resources to launch their businesses alone. After emptying their own pockets, entrepreneurs should look to friends and family members who might be willing to invest in a business venture. Because of their relationships with the founder, these people are most likely to invest.

Profile

Dave and Catherine Cook: myYearbook

While flipping through their high school yearbooks, 17-year-old Dave Cook said to his 15-year-old sister, Catherine, "This is 2005. Why is anyone buying yearbooks anymore?" Soon they envisioned a social networking Web site where young people could post photos, stories, and other memorabilia. Over dinner one evening, the budding entrepreneurs described their idea to their older brother Geoff, who had started his own Internet company while in college in 1997 and sold it in 2002. "As soon as I heard the idea, I thought it was very cool and put in $250,000," says Geoff, who is now the company's CEO. "We got another $250,000 from an angel investor whom I had worked with on my previous company." In just 6 weeks, the Cooks used the money to launch myYearbook; hire staff (including programmers in India); set up headquarters in quaint New Hope, Pennsylvania; and market the company's Web site (*www.myyearbook.com*). Within months of the site's launch, thousands of teenagers had signed up as members. myYearbook has since landed $17.1 million in two rounds of venture capital to finance its rapid growth. The site has more than 20 million members worldwide, is one of the 30 most-trafficked Web sites, and generates annual sales of more than $20 million. myYearbook recently launched a new service, Chatter, which allows users to play games and connect with other users in their immediate geographic areas.[8]

The GEM study of entrepreneurial trends across the globe reports that family members and friends are the biggest source of external capital used to launch new businesses. Investments from family and friends are an important source of capital for entrepreneurs, but the amounts invested typically are small, often no more than just a few thousand dollars. Across the globe, the average amount that family members and friends invest in start-up businesses averages just $3,000.[9] In the United States alone, family members and friends invest an average of $27,715 in a typical small business start-up for an astonishing total of $100 billion per year![10]

Investments (or loans) from family and friends are an excellent source of seed capital and can get a start-up far enough along to attract money from private investors or venture capital companies. Inherent dangers lurk in family business investments and loans, however. A recent study reports a default rate of 14 percent on business loans from family and friends, compared to a default rate of 1 percent for bank loans.[11] Unrealistic expectations or misunderstood risks have destroyed many friendships and have ruined many family reunions. To avoid problems, an entrepreneur must honestly present the investment opportunity and the nature of the risks involved to avoid alienating friends and family members if the business fails. Smart entrepreneurs treat family members and friends who invest in their companies in the same way they would treat business partners. Some investments in start-up companies return more than friends and family members ever could have imagined. In 1995, Mike and Jackie Bezos invested $300,000 into their son Jeff's start-up business, Amazon.com. Today, Mike and Jackie own 6 percent of Amazon.com's stock, and their shares are worth billions of dollars![12]

Table 2 offers suggestions for structuring family and friendship financing deals.

Angels

After dipping into their own pockets and convincing friends and relatives to invest in their business ventures, many entrepreneurs still find themselves short of the seed capital they need. Frequently, the next stop on the road to business financing is private investors. These **private investors** (or **angels**) are wealthy individuals, often entrepreneurs themselves, who invest in business start-ups in exchange for equity stakes in the companies. Alexander Graham Bell, inventor of the telephone, used angel capital to start Bell Telephone in 1877. More recently, companies such as Google, Facebook, Apple, Starbucks, Amazon.com, and Costco relied on angel financing in their early years to finance growth.

In many cases, angels invest in businesses for more than purely economic reasons (often because they have experience and a personal interest in the industry), and they are willing to put money into companies in the earliest stages (often before a company generates any revenue), long before venture capital firms jump in. Angel financing is ideal for companies that have outgrown the capacity of investments from friends and family but are still too small to attract the interest of venture capital companies. For instance, after raising the money to launch Amazon.com from family and friends, Jeff Bezos turned to angels because venture capital firms were not interested in the business start-up. Bezos attracted $1.2 million from a dozen angels before landing $8 million from venture capital firms a year later.[13]

TABLE 2 Suggestions for Structuring Family and Friendship Financing Deals

Tapping family members and friends for start-up capital, whether in the form of equity or debt financing, is a popular method of financing business ideas. In a typical year, some 6 million individuals in the United States invest about $100 billion in entrepreneurial ventures. Unfortunately, these deals don't always work to the satisfaction of both parties. Even those that do can strain family relationships in the early, uncertain days of a company's tenuous existence. "[Family] relationships change when money enters the picture," says Meg Hirshberg, who with her husband, Gary, cofounded Stonyfield Farm. She recalls fretting over family gatherings at Thanksgiving in the now successful company's early days because her mother and her brothers had invested heavily in their start-up business, which Meg knew was a risky venture. "I knew that soon after our arrival, the conversation would turn to the fate of their cash," she says. "Their questions were sheathed in a kindness that barely covered the sharp blade of concern within. Profits? Not even close. Margins? Come on. Cash burn? Lots of that. I would sympathize with the turkey as slivers of explanations and excuses were sliced from our tender hides. In those early days, our carcass of a business felt cooked, too."

The following suggestions can help entrepreneurs avoid needlessly destroying family relationships and friendships:

- *Consider the impact of the investment on everyone involved.* Will it impose a hardship on anyone? Is the investor putting up the money because he or she wants to or because he or she feels obligated to? Can all parties afford the loan if the business folds? Convincing Aunt Sally to invest her retirement nest egg in a high-risk start-up is not the best financing strategy. Lynn McPhee used $250,000 from family members to launch Xuny, a Web-based clothing store. "Our basic rule of thumb was, if [the investment is] going to strap someone, we won't take it," she says.
- *Keep the arrangement strictly business.* The parties should treat all loans and investments in a business-like manner, no matter how close the friendship or family relationship, to avoid problems down the line. If the transaction is a loan exceeding $10,000, it must carry a rate of interest at least as high as the market rate; otherwise the IRS may consider the loan a gift and penalize the lender.
- *Educate "naïve" investors.* Family members and friends usually invest in a business because of their relationships with the founder, not because they understand the business itself. Take the time to explain to potential investors the basics of the business idea, how it will make money, and the risks associated with investing in it.
- *Settle the details up front.* Before any money changes hands, both parties must agree on the details of the deal. How much money is involved? Is it a loan or an investment? How will the investor cash out? How will the loan be paid off? What happens if the business fails?
- *Never accept more than investors can afford to lose.* No matter how much capital you may need, accepting more than family members or friends can afford to lose is a recipe for disaster—and perhaps financial hardship or even bankruptcy for the investors. In the early days of Stonyfield Farm, Meg Hirshberg was frightened because she knew that her mother had invested far more in the company than she could afford to lose. "I was terrified of how our potential failure might affect her retirement and her relationship with Gary and me," she recalls. Although Hirshberg's fears proved to be unfounded, they caused her much grief.
- *Create a written contract.* Don't make the mistake of closing a financial deal with just a handshake. The probability of misunderstandings skyrockets! Putting an agreement in writing demonstrates the parties' commitment to the deal and minimizes the chances of disputes from faulty memories and misunderstandings.
- *Treat the money as "bridge financing."* Although family and friends can help you launch your business, it is unlikely that they can provide enough capital to sustain it over the long term. Sooner or later, you will need to establish a relationship with other sources of capital if your company is to grow. Consider money from family and friends as a bridge to take your company to the next level of financing.
- *Develop a payment schedule that suits both the entrepreneur and the lender or investor.* Although lenders and investors may want to get their money back as quickly as possible, a rapid repayment or cash-out schedule can jeopardize a fledgling company's survival. Establish a realistic repayment plan that works for the parties without putting excessive strain on the young company's cash flow.
- *Have an exit plan.* Every deal should define exactly how investors will "cash out" their investments.
- *Keep everyone informed.* Entrepreneurs should keep investors informed about the company's progress, its successes and failures, and the challenges it faces. Investors want to know both good news and bad news.

Sources: Based on Meg Cadoux Hirshberg, "Brother Can You Spare a Dime?" *Inc.*, November 2009, pp. 45–46; Jenny McCune, "Tips for Feud-Free Financing from Friends and Family," *Bankrate*, July 24, 2000, *www.bankrate.com/brm/ news/biz/Capital_borrowing/20000724.asp*; Andrea Coombes, "Retirees as Venture Capitalists," CBS.MarketWatch.com, November 2, 2003, *http://netscape.marketwatch.com/news/story.asp?dist=feed&siteid= netscape&guid={1E1267CD-32A4-4558-9F7E-40E4B7892D01}*; Paul Kvinta, "Frogskins, Shekels, Bucks, Moolah, Cash, Simoleans, Dough, Dinero: Everybody Wants It. Your Business Needs It. Here's How to Get It," *Smart Business*, August 2000, pp. 74–89. Alex Markels, "A Little Help from Their Friends," *Wall Street Journal*, May 22, 1995, p. R10; Heather Chaplin, "Friends and Family," *Your Company*, September 1999, p. 26.

SOURCES OF EQUITY FINANCING

FIGURE 1
Angel Financing

Source: Center for Venture Financing, Whittemore School of Business, University of New Hampshire, *www.unh.edu/cvr*.

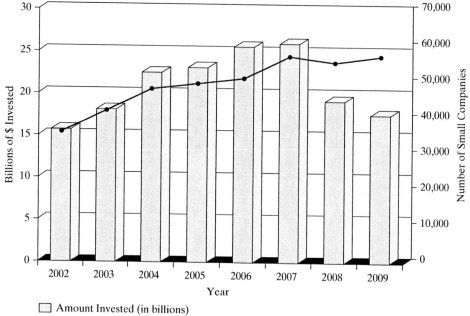

Angels are a primary source of capital for companies in the start-up stage through the growth stage, and their role in financing small businesses is significant. The Center for Venture Research at the University of New Hampshire estimates that nearly 260,000 angels invest $17.6 billion a year in 57,000 small companies, most of them in the start-up phase (see Figure 1).[14] Angels invest as much money in small companies as venture capital firms, but they put it into 20 times as many companies as venture capital firms. Because the angel market is so fragmented and, in many cases, built on anonymity, we may never get a completely accurate estimate of its investment in business start-ups. However, experts concur on one fact: Angels are a vital source of equity capital for small businesses.

Angels fill a significant gap in the seed capital market. They are most likely to finance start-ups with capital requirements in the $10,000 to $2 million range, well below the $3 million to $10 million minimum investments most professional venture capitalists prefer. Because they invest in the earliest stages of a business, angels also tolerate risk levels that would make venture capitalists shudder. In fact, 52 percent of angels' investments lose money, returning less than the angels' original investment. The potential for investing in big winners exists as well; 7 percent of angels' investments produce a return of more than 10 times their original investments.[15]

Lewis Gersh, an experienced angel investor, says that out of 10 companies that an angel invests in, 5 will fail, 2 will break even, and 2 will return two to three times the original investment. Just 1 company out of 10 will produce a significant return, "which means that every one of them has to have the potential of being a home run," says Gersh. Most angels consider a "home run" investment to be one that results in a return of 10 to 30 times the original investment in 5 to 7 years, somewhat lower than the returns that venture capital firms expect.[16] One angel investor, a retired entrepreneur, says that of the 31 companies he has invested in, "more than half have gone under, but four were home runs, returning 25 times my investment. The others gave me a small return or at least some of my money back."[17] Angel financing is important because angels often finance deals that venture capitalists will not consider.

ENTREPRENEURIAL
Profile

Shan Sinha and Alex DeNeui: Docverse

Chris Dixon, a serial entrepreneur and angel investor, has put money into 23 start-up companies. Although not all of them have been successful, some of Dixon's investments have been home runs, including Skype and Postini. Dixon also was an early investor in Docverse, a company whose software simplifies Web-based collaboration on Microsoft Office documents. Microsoft veterans Shan Sinha and Alex DeNeui launched Docverse in 2007 and attracted nearly $2 million from Dixon and other angel investors to build the company before selling it to Google for $25 million, producing an impressive return for themselves and their angel investors.[18]

Because angels prefer to maintain a low profile, the real challenge lies in *finding* them. Most angels are seasoned entrepreneurs themselves; on average, angel investors have founded 2.7 companies and have 14.5 years of entrepreneurial experience. They also are well educated; 99 percent have college degrees. Research also shows that 88 percent of angel investors are men (their average age is 57 years) who have been investing in promising small companies for 9 years. The typical angel invests an average of $50,000 in a company that is at the seed or start-up growth stages and makes an investment in one company per year.[19] The average time required to close an angel financing deal is 67 days.[20] Angels accept 14.5 percent of the investment proposals they receive.[21] When evaluating a proposal, angels look for a qualified management team ("We invest in people," says one angel), a business with a clearly defined niche, the potential to dominate the market, and a competitive advantage. They also want to see market research that proves the existence of a sizable and profitable customer base.

Because angels frown on "cold calls" from entrepreneurs they don't know, locating them boils down to making the right contacts. Asking friends, attorneys, bankers, stockbrokers, accountants, other business owners, and consultants for suggestions and introductions is a good way to start. "Angels are more likely to invest in a company that was referred to them by someone they know and trust," says Marianne Hudson, director of the angel initiative at the Kauffman Foundation.[22] Networking is the key. Angels almost always invest their money locally, so entrepreneurs should look close to home for them—typically within a 50- to 100-mile radius. Angels also look for businesses they know something about, and most expect to invest their knowledge, experience, and energy as well as their money in a company. In fact, the advice and the network of contacts that angels bring to a deal can sometimes be as valuable as their money!

ENTREPRENEURIAL Profile

Rich Aberman and Bill Clerico: WePay

When Rich Aberman and Bill Clerico started WePay, an online payment service that allows groups ranging from fraternities to owners of fantasy sports teams to collect, manage, and spend money, they relied on angel investor Max Levchin to help them build out their system and keep it secure. Chafkin, who cofounded online payment company PayPal, "built the PayPal fraud system," says Clerico. "That's why we aggressively sought him out." WePay raised $1.65 million in capital from angel investors.[23]

Angel investing has become more sophisticated, with investors pooling their resources to form angel networks and angel capital funds, dubbed *super angels*, that operate like mini versions of professional venture capital firms and draw on the investors' skills, experience, and contacts to help the start-ups in which they invest succeed. Veteran angel investor Mike Maples operates Floodgate, a super-angel fund that manages $35 million in angel capital and invests between $250,000 and $1 million in promising start-ups, including Twitter and Digg.[24]

Today, more than 300 angel capital networks operate in cities of all sizes across the United States (up from just 10 in 1996), with as many operating in other countries.[25] Entrepreneurs can find angel networks in their areas with the help of the Angel Capital Association's directory (*www.angelcapitalassociation.org*). With the right approach, an entrepreneur can attract more money and a larger network of advisors from an angel capital group than from individual investors. The typical angel capital group has 44 members, who invest $1.77 million each year in 6.3 companies, on average.[26]

ENTREPRENEURIAL Profile

Hans Severiens: Band of Angels

In 1994, Hans Severiens, a professional investor, created the Band of Angels, a group of about 130 angels (mostly Silicon Valley millionaires) who meet monthly in Portola Valley, California, to listen to entrepreneurs pitch their business plans. The Band of Angels reviews about 50 proposals each month before inviting a handful of entrepreneurs to make brief presentations at its monthly meeting. Interested members often team up with one another to invest in the businesses they consider most promising. The Band of Angels' average investment is $890,000, which usually nets the investors between 15 and 20 percent of a company's stock. Since its inception, the Band of Angels has invested more than $186 million in more than 200 promising young companies, most of them in the high-tech sector, including Symantec and Logitech. Nine of the companies have made initial public offerings, and 45 of them have been acquired by larger companies.[27]

Angels are an excellent source of "patient money," often willing to wait 5 to 7 years or longer to cash out their investments. They earn their returns through the increased value of the business, not through dividends and interest. For example, more than 1,000 early investors in Microsoft Inc. are now millionaires, and the original investors in Genentech Inc. (a genetic engineering company) have seen their investments increase more than 500 times.[28] Angels' return-on-investment targets tend to be lower than those of professional venture capitalists. Although venture capitalists shoot for 60 to 75 percent returns annually, angel investors usually settle for 20 to 50 percent (depending on the level of risk involved in the venture). A study by the Kauffman Foundation reports that the average return on angels' investments in small companies is 2.6 times the original investment in 3.5 years, which is the equivalent of an annual 27 percent internal rate of return.[29] Angel investors typically purchase 15 to 30 percent ownership in a small company, leaving the majority ownership to the company founder(s). They look for the same exit strategies that venture capital firms look for: either an initial public offering or a buyout by a larger company.

The accompanying Lessons from the Street-Smart Entrepreneur feature offers useful tips for attracting angel financing.

Tips for Attracting Angel Financing

John White and John Bellaud understand the importance of capital to a small business and know firsthand how hard raising capital can be for a small company. White and Bellaud are in the process of raising $14 million for their company, Joy Berry Enterprises, Inc., which distributes the works of Joy Berry, a popular author of more than 250 children's books. Berry's books, which teach children about responsibility and proper behavior through stories, music, and multimedia, have sold more than 85 million copies. White and Bellaud want to consolidate all of Berry's books in one publishing house with marketing muscle. They raised $600,000 from angel investors in the company's early days, but turbulence in the financial markets has squeezed the flow of capital to a trickle. White and Bellaud managed to scrape together $3 million in another round of angel investments, enough to license Berry's books and get them on the market, but they still need $11 million to secure intellectual property rights and implement their marketing plan.

Although they are an important source of small business financing, angels can be extremely difficult to locate. You won't find them listed under "angels" in the Yellow Pages of the telephone directory. Patience and persistence—and connections—pay off in the search for angel financing, however. How does an entrepreneur who needs financing find an angel to help launch or expand a company and make the deal work? Take the following tips from the Street-Smart Entrepreneur:

■ *Start looking for potential investors early—before you need the money.* Finding private investors takes a lot longer than most entrepreneurs think. Starting early is one key to success.

■ *Have a business plan ready.* Once you find potential private investors, don't risk them losing interest while you put together a business plan. Have the plan ready to go *before* you begin your search.

■ *Don't expect to raise all of the money at once.* Entrepreneurs often get capital for their businesses in fits and spurts. In one 2-year period, Joy Berry Enterprises raised money in five different rounds, sometimes in amounts as small as $200,000.

■ *Look close to home.* Most angels prefer to invest their money locally, so conduct a thorough search for potential angels within a 50- to 100-mile radius of your business.

■ *Canvass your industry.* Angels tend to specialize in particular industries, usually ones they know a lot about.

■ *Recognize that, in addition to the money they invest, angels also want to provide their knowledge and expertise.* Indeed, angels' experience and knowledge can be just as valuable as their money *if* entrepreneurs are willing to accept it.

■ *Remember that angels invest for more than just financial reasons.* Angels want to earn a good return on the money they invest in businesses, but there's usually more to it than that. Angels often invest in companies for personal reasons.

■ *Emphasize the skills and experience of the management team.* Angels, like venture capitalists, invest in people, not just good ideas.

■ *Join local philanthropic organizations, chambers of commerce, nonprofit organizations, and advisory* boards so that you can meet potential angels. Potential investors often are involved in these organizations.

■ *Ask business professionals such as bankers, lawyers, stockbrokers, accountants, and others for names of potential angels.* They know people who have the money and the desire to invest in business ventures.

■ *Network, network, network.* Finding angel financing initially is a game of contacts—getting an introduction to the right person from the right person.

■ *Investigate the investors and their past deals.* Never get involved in a deal with an angel you don't know or trust. Be sure you and your investors have a common vision of the business and the deal.

■ *Summarize the details of the deal in a letter of intent.* Although a letter of intent is not legally binding, it outlines the basic structure of the deal and exposes the most sensitive areas of negotiation so that there are no surprises. What role, if any, will the angel play in running the business? Angels can be a source of valuable help, but some entrepreneurs complain of angels' meddling.

■ *Talk about the risks up front.* Some entrepreneurs do everything they can to disguise the risks associated with their businesses from potential investors. Smart entrepreneurs disclose the risks early on. Don't dwell on the downside, but be honest about the risk of the investment.

■ *Keep the deal simple.* The simpler the deal is, the easier it will be to sell to potential investors. Probably the simplest way to involve angels is to sell them common stock.

■ *Be prepared to "pay to pitch."* Many angel networks charge entrepreneurs a few hundred dollars to pitch their ideas to a group of angels. If you have your pitch ready and can get before the right group of potential investors, your money is well spent.

■ *Nail down the angels' exit path.* Angels make their money when they sell their ownership interests. Ideally, the exit path should be part of structuring the deal. Will the company buy back the angels' shares? Will the company go public so the angels can sell their shares on the market? Will the owners sell out to a larger company? What is the time frame for doing so?

■ *Avoid intimidating potential investors.* Most angels are turned off by entrepreneurs with an attitude of "I have someone else who will do the deal if you don't." In the face of such coercion, many private investors simply walk away from the deal.

■ *Always be truthful.* Overpromising and underdelivering will kill a deal and spoil future financing opportunities.

■ *Develop alternative financing arrangements.* Never back an angel into a corner with "take this deal or leave it." Have alternative plans prepared in case the investor balks at the outset.

■ *Don't take the money and run.* Investors appreciate entrepreneurs who keep them informed—about how their money is being spent and the results it shows. Prepare periodic reports for them.

■ *Stick to the deal.* It is tempting to spend the money where it is most needed once it is in hand. Resist! If you promised to use the funds for specific purposes, do it. Nothing undermines an angel's trust as quickly as violating the original plan.

■ *Don't forget to "make the ask."* After pitching your idea to a potential angel investor, remember to ask for the investment. Otherwise, you're sure to be turned down.

Sources: Based on Rosalind Resnick, "The Art (and Journey) of Raising Funds," *Wall Street Journal*, July 13, 2010, *http://online.wsj.com/article/ NA_WSJ_PUB:SB10001424052748704288204575363052617468556.html*; David E. Gumpert, "Confessions of an Angel Investor," November 14, 2007, *Bloomberg Business Week*, November 14, 2007, *www.businessweek.com/ smallbiz/content/nov2007/sb20071114_582315.htm*.

Partners

Entrepreneurs can take on partners to expand the capital base of a business.

ENTREPRENEURIAL
Profile

Lan Tran Cao: Viet Café

After spending nearly 30 years in various IT jobs for major corporations, Lan Tran Cao decided to return to her first love—cooking. Raised in Saigon, Cao started cooking for the 13 members of her family when she was just 12 and then went on to study the art of cooking in France. Cao used her experience starting restaurants (she launched two of them while in college in Sydney, Australia) to open Viet Café in downtown Manhattan. She used money from her savings to finance most of the start-up costs of the restaurant, which serves traditional Vietnamese dishes such as lemongrass chicken rolls and roast lacquered duck. Starting a restaurant in New York City is extremely expensive, however, and Cao needed more capital. She decided to bring in a partner, who owns 30 percent of Viet Café, but Cao is both the chef and the CEO of the company.[30]

Before entering into any partnership arrangement, however, entrepreneurs must consider the impact of giving up some personal control over operations and of sharing profits with others. Whenever entrepreneurs give up equity in their businesses (through whatever mechanism), they run the risk of losing control over it. As the founder's ownership in a company becomes increasingly diluted, the probability of losing control of its future direction and the entire decision-making process increases.

Corporate Venture Capital

Large corporations are in the business of financing small companies. Today, about 13 percent of all venture capital deals involve corporate venture capital. The average investment that large corporations make in small companies is $3.52 million, an amount that represents 7.4 percent of total venture capital investments.[31] Approximately 300 large corporations across the globe, including Intel, Motorola, Cisco Systems, Chevron, Comcast, Nokia, UPS, Best Buy, and General Electric, have venture capital divisions that invest on average a total of $2.1 billion a year in young companies, most often those in the product development and sales growth stages. The large companies are looking not only for financial returns from the small companies in which they invest, but also for innovative products that can benefit them. Young companies get a boost from the capital injections large companies give them, but they also stand to gain many other benefits from the relationship. The right corporate partner may share technical expertise, distribution channels, marketing know-how, and provide introductions to important customers and suppliers. Another intangible yet highly important advantage that an investment from a large corporate partner gives a start-up is credibility, often referred to as "market validation." Doors that otherwise would be closed to a small company magically open when the right corporation becomes a strategic partner.

Foreign corporations also are interested in investing in small U.S. businesses. Often these corporations are seeking strategic partnerships to gain access to new technology, new products, or access to lucrative U.S. markets. In return, the small companies they invest in benefit from the capital infusion as well as from their partners' international experience and extensive network of connections. "What's most difficult for start-ups is finding customers and establishing a brand, but Intel Capital can help," says Arvind Sodhani, head of Intel's venture capital division, one of the largest and most active venture capital companies in the world.[32] Figure 2 shows recent trends in corporate venture capital.

ENTREPRENEURIAL
Profile

Craig McCaw and Intel Capital: Clearwire

In 2006, Intel Capital invested $600 million in Clearwire, a wireless broadband communications and networking company that was founded in 2003 by Craig McCaw. Intel's leading investment attracted venture capital investments from other corporations, including Motorola. In 2007, Clearwire made an initial public offering of 24 million shares of its stock at $25 per share and raised $600 million in capital. In 2008, Intel made a follow-on investment of $1 billion in Clearwire. Since 1991, Intel has invested more than $9 billion in more than 1,000 promising young companies not only in the United States but also in 45 countries around the world whose products or services align with its strategy.[33]

Venture Capital Companies

Venture capital companies (VCs) are private, for-profit organizations that raise money from investors to purchase equity positions in young businesses they believe have high-growth and high-profit potential, producing annual returns of 300 to 500 percent over 5 to 7 years. More than 700 venture capital firms operate across the United States today, investing in promising small companies in a variety of industries (see Figure 3). Companies in California's Silicon Valley and Boston's high-tech corridor attract about half of all venture capital investments.[34] Some colleges and universities have created venture funds designated to invest in promising businesses started by their students, alumni, faculty, and others. Business schools at the University of Michigan, the University of Maryland, the University of North Dakota, Cornell University, and, in a joint venture called the University Venture Fund, the University of

SOURCES OF EQUITY FINANCING

FIGURE 2
Corporate Venture Capital

Source: PricewaterhouseCoopers MoneyTree Report, 2010.

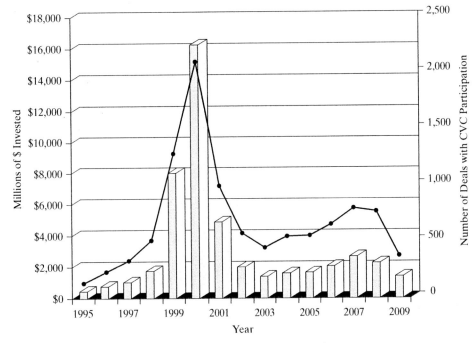

Pennsylvania, Brigham Young University, the University of Utah, and Westminster College operate venture capital funds that are comanaged by students, faculty, and sometimes professional venture capitalists.[35]

Venture capital firms, which provide about 7 percent of all funding for private companies, have invested billions of dollars in high-potential small companies over the years, including notable businesses such as Apple, Microsoft, Intel, and Outback Steakhouse. Clearwire, the wireless communications company, tops the list of companies backed by venture capital with a

FIGURE 3
Venture Capital Financing

Source: PricewaterhouseCoopers MoneyTree Report, 2009.

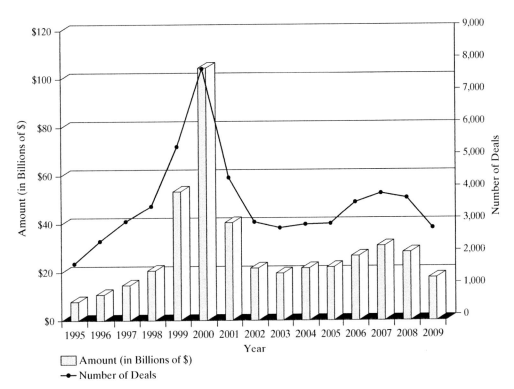

record $1.3 billion of equity capital raised.[36] Although companies in high-tech industries such as communications, computer software, energy, medical care, and biotechnology are the most popular targets of venture capital, a company with extraordinary growth prospects has the potential to attract venture capital, whatever its industry. Table 3 offers a humorous look at how venture capitalists decipher the language of sometimes overly optimistic entrepreneurs.

TABLE 3 Deciphering the Language of the Venture Capital Industry.

By nature, entrepreneurs tend to be optimistic. When screening business plans, venture capitalists must make an allowance for entrepreneurial enthusiasm. Here's a dictionary of phrases commonly found in business plans and their accompanying venture capital translations.

Exploring an acquisition strategy—Our current products have no market.

We're on a clear P2P (pathway to profitability)—We're still years away from earning a profit.

Basically on plan—We're expecting a revenue shortfall of 25 percent.

Internet business model—Potentially bigger fools have been identified.

A challenging year—Competitors are eating our lunch.

Considerably ahead of plan—Hit our plan in 1 of the last 3 months.

Company's underlying strength and resilience—We still lost money, but look how we cut our losses.

Core business—Our product line is obsolete.

Currently revising budget—The financial plan is in total chaos.

Cyclical industry—We posted a huge loss last year.

Entrepreneurial CEO—He is totally uncontrollable, bordering on maniacal.

Facing challenges—Our sales continue to slide, and we have no idea why.

Facing unprecedented economic, political, and structural shifts—It's a tough world out there, but we're coping the best we can.

Highly leverageable network—No longer works but has friends who do.

Ingredients are there—Given 2 years, we might find a workable strategy.

Investing heavily in R&D—We're trying desperately to catch the competition.

Limited downside—Things can't get much worse.

Long sales cycle—Yet to find a customer who likes the product enough to buy it.

Major opportunity—It's our last chance.

Niche strategy—A small-time player.

On a manufacturing learning curve—We can't make the product with positive margins.

Passive investor—Someone who phones once a year to see if we're still in business.

Positive results—Our losses were less than last year.

Refocus our efforts—We've blown our chance, and now we have to fire most of our employees.

Repositioning the business—We've recently written off a multimillion-dollar investment.

Selective investment strategy—The board is spending more time on yachts than on planes.

Solid operating performance in a difficult year—Yes, we lost money and market share, but look how hard we tried.

Somewhat below plan—We expect a revenue shortfall of 75 percent.

Expenses were unexpectedly high—We grossly overestimated our profit margins.

Strategic investor—One who will pay a preposterous price for an equity share in the business.

Strongest fourth quarter ever—Don't quibble over the losses in the first three quarters.

Sufficient opportunity to market this product no longer exists—Nobody will buy the thing.

Too early to tell—Results to date have been grim.

A team of skilled, motivated, and dedicated people—We've laid off most of our staff, and those who are left should be glad they still have jobs.

Turnaround opportunity—It's a lost cause.

Unique—We have no more than six strong competitors.

Volume-sensitive—Our company has massive fixed costs.

Window of opportunity—Without more money fast, this company is dead.

Work closely with the management—We talk to them on the phone once a month.

A year in which we confronted challenges—At least we know the questions even if we haven't got the answers.

Sources: Adapted from Scott Herhold, "When CEOs Blow Smoke," *e-company,* May 2001, pp. 125–127; Suzanne McGee, "A Devil's Dictionary of Financing," *Wall Street Journal,* June 12, 2000, p. C13; John F. Budd Jr., "Cracking the CEO's Code," *Wall Street Journal,* March 27, 1995, p. A20; "Venture-Speak Defined," *Teleconnect,* October 1990, p. 42; Cynthia E. Griffin, "Figuratively Speaking," *Entrepreneur,* August 1999, p. 26.

POLICIES AND INVESTMENT STRATEGIES. VCs usually establish stringent policies to govern their overall investment strategies.

Investment Size and Screening. The average venture capital firm's investment in a small company is $7.8 million. Depending on the size of the venture capital company and its cost structure, minimum investments range from $50,000 to $5 million. Investment ceilings, in effect, do not exist. Most firms seek investments in the $3 million to $10 million range to justify the cost of screening the large number of proposals they receive.

In a normal year, VCs invest in only 3,500 of the nearly 30 million small businesses in the United States! The venture capital screening process is *extremely* rigorous. The typical venture capital company invests in less than 1 percent of the business plans it receives. According to the Global Entrepreneurship Monitor, only about 1 in 1,000 businesses in the United States attracts venture capital during its existence.[37] The typical venture capital firm receives about 1,100 business plans each year. For every 100 business plans that the average venture capital firm receives, 90 of them are rejected immediately because they do not match the firm's investment criteria or requirements. The firm conducts a thorough due diligence investigation of the remaining 10 companies and typically invests in only 1 of them. The average time required to close a venture capital deal is 80 days, slightly longer than the time required to complete angel financing.[38]

Ownership. Most venture capitalists prefer to purchase ownership in a small business through common stock or convertible preferred stock. Although some venture capital firms purchase less than 50 percent of a company's stock, it is not uncommon for others to buy a controlling share of a company, leaving its founders with a minority share of ownership. Entrepreneurs must weigh the positive aspects of receiving needed financing against the disadvantages of owning a smaller share of the business. "Would you rather have 80 percent of a company worth zero or 50 percent of a company worth $500 million?" asks a partner at one venture capital firm.[39]

Stage of Investment. Most venture capital firms invest in companies that are either in the early stages of development (called early stage investing) or in the rapid-growth phase (called expansion stage investing); few invest in businesses that are only in the start-up phase (see Figure 4). According to the Global Entrepreneurship Monitor, only 1 in 10,000 entrepreneurs

Venture Capital by Stage of Company Growth

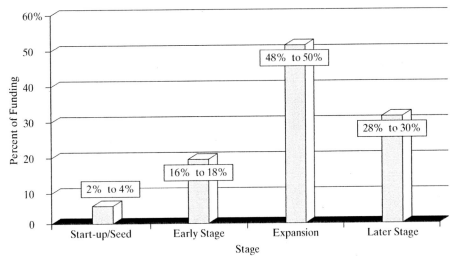

Start-up/Seed—This is the initial stage in which companies are just beginning to develop their ideas into products or services. Typically, these businesses have been in existence less than 18 months and are not yet fully operational.

Early Stage—These companies are refining their initial products or services in pilot tests or in the market. Even though the product or service is available commercially, it typically generates little or no revenue. These companies have been in business less than 3 years.

Expansion Stage—These companies' products or services are commercially available and are producing strong revenue growth. Businesses at this stage may not be generating a profit yet, however.

Later Stage—These companies' products or services are widely available and are producing ongoing revenue and, in most cases, positive cash flow. Businesses at this stage are more likely to be generating a profit. Sometimes these businesses are spin-offs of already established successful private companies.

worldwide receives venture capital funding at start up.[40] About 96 to 98 percent of all venture capital goes to businesses in the early, expansion, and later stages, although some venture capital firms are showing more interest in companies in the start up phase because of the tremendous returns that are possible by investing then.[41] Most venture capital firms do not make just a single investment in a company. Instead, they invest in a company over time across several stages, where their investments often total $10 to $15 million or more. To fuel its fast growth, Gilt Groupe, a company that conducts online sample sales of luxury branded merchandise to its members at discounts up to 70 percent, has landed $83 million in venture capital in three rounds of financing in just 3 years.[42]

Advice and Contacts. In addition to the money they invest, venture capital companies provide the small companies in their portfolios with management advice and access to valuable networks of contacts of suppliers, employees, customers, and other sources of capital. One of their goals in doing so is to strengthen the companies in which they have invested, thereby increasing their value. Former NBA star David Robinson's company, Admiral Capital Group, recently invested in Centerplate, an event catering business that focuses on sports venues, and plans to use his network of contacts to help the company expand, particularly into professional basketball events.[43]

Control. In exchange for the financing they receive from venture capitalists, entrepreneurs must give up a portion of their businesses, sometimes surrendering a majority interest and control of its operations. Most venture capitalists prefer to let the founding team of managers employ its skills to operate a business *if* they are capable of managing its growth. However, most venture capitalists join the boards of directors of the companies they invest in or send in new managers or a new management team to protect their investments. The term sheets they negotiate often include the right to determine the CEO. In other words, venture capitalists are *not* passive investors! A study of new business ventures by Harvard professor Noam Wasserman reports that only half of the companies' founders were in the CEO position after 3 years and that the likelihood of a founder being replaced increases significantly after a company receives capital from outside investors, especially venture capitalists.[44]

Some venture capitalists serve only as financial and managerial advisors, whereas others take an active role managing the company—recruiting employees, providing sales leads, choosing attorneys and advertising agencies, and making daily decisions—which can cause friction with the founding entrepreneur(s). The majority of these active venture capitalists say they are forced to step in because the existing management team lacked the talent and experience to achieve growth targets.

ENTREPRENEURIAL
Profile

Jason Brown: Cotton Comfort

As Jason Brown learned, a common complaint among entrepreneurs who accept venture capital is that their investors push too hard for too much growth too soon. Brown was just 26 years old when a group of venture capitalists offered to invest $5 million in Cotton Comfort, a small chain of clothing stores he had launched at age 20. He gave up 46 percent of his company in exchange for the capital investment and the investors' experience. Brown says that the venture capitalists pushed him to grow the company too fast, and when the economy slowed Cotton Comfort ran out of cash and folded. "I was too young to know that my job was to listen to what the VCs had to say but to know that they had only a chapter out of the novel of understanding about my business," says Brown, who went on to launch two more successful businesses.[45]

Investment Preferences. Venture capital funds are larger, more professional, and more specialized than they were 25 years ago. As the industry grows, more venture capital funds are focusing their investments in niches—everything from information technology services to biotechnology. Some will invest in almost any industry but prefer companies in particular stages, including the start-up phase. Traditionally, however, only about 2 to 4 percent of the companies receiving venture capital financing are in the start-up (seed) stage, when entrepreneurs are forming a company or developing a product or service. Most of the start-up businesses that attract venture capital today are in the biotechnology, software, IT services, energy, and medical device industries.

WHAT VENTURE CAPITALISTS LOOK FOR. Entrepreneurs must realize that it is very difficult for any small business, especially start-ups, to pass the intense screening process of a venture capital company and qualify for an investment. Two factors make a deal attractive to venture capitalists: high returns and a convenient (and profitable) exit strategy. "VCs spend a lot of time boiling down the characteristics of successful companies to their essence: team, market, and product," says David Pakman, an entrepreneur turned venture capitalist.[46] When evaluating potential investments, venture capitalists look for the following features.

Competent Management. Attracting venture capital takes more than just a good idea; it requires a management team that can transform an idea into a viable business. Venture capitalists believe in the adage "Money follows management." To them, the most important ingredient in the success of any business is the ability of the management team. They are looking for a team of managers that shares the same vision for the company and have the experience and the ability to make that vision a reality. "Our business is about investing in people who can get it done," explains Steve Domenik of venture capital fund Sevin Rosen. "The [business] idea is almost secondary."[47] From a venture capitalist's perspective, the ideal management team has experience, managerial skills, commitment, and the ability to build effective teams.

Competitive Edge. Investors are searching for some factor that will enable a small business to set itself apart from its competitors. This distinctive competence may range from an innovative product or service that satisfies unmet customer needs to a unique marketing or R&D approach. It must be something with the potential to make the business a leader in its field.

Growth Industry. Hot industries attract profits—and venture capital. Most venture capital funds focus their searches for prospects in rapidly expanding fields because they believe the profit potential is greater in these areas. Venture capital firms are most interested in young companies in industries that have enough growth potential to become at least $100 million businesses within 3 to 5 years. Venture capitalists know that most of the businesses they invest in will flop, so their winners have to be *big* winners.

Viable Exit Strategy. Venture capitalists not only look for promising companies with the ability to dominate a market, but they also want to see a plan for a feasible exit strategy, ideally to be executed within 3 to 5 years. A recent study by the National Venture Capital Association reports that the number one factor that venture capitalists say creates a nonfavorable environment for venture capital is difficulty in achieving successful exits.[48] Venture capital firms realize the return on their investments when the companies they invest in either make an initial public offering or sell out to a larger business. For instance, Dell recently purchased Equallogic, a company that developed highly efficient network data storage solutions for businesses, for $1.4 billion, creating a handsome payout for Equallogic's three founders and the venture capital companies that had invested in it. Paula Long, Peter Haden, and Paul Koning started Equallogic in Haden's attic in 2003, and within 3 years its sales had increased from $492,000 to more than $100 million.[49] "If your vision is to run a company and hand it over to your kids, VC funding is out of the question," says Mike Simon, CEO of LogMeIn, Inc., a software company that has raised $20 million in capital, half of it from venture capital firms.[50]

Intangible Factors. Some other important factors considered in the screening process are not easily measured; they are the intuitive, intangible factors the venture capitalist detects by gut feeling. This feeling might be the result of the small firm's solid sense of direction, its strategic planning process, the chemistry of its management team, or a number of other factors.

ENTREPRENEURIAL
Profile

Ofer Raz and Hod Fleishman: GreenRoad

In 2003, Ofer Raz and Hod Fleishman launched GreenRoad, a company whose software helps companies and individuals improve driving habits, reduce collisions, improve fuel economy, and reduce vehicle operating costs, and quickly realized that their company would require a significant investment to capitalize on the market opportunity that lay before it. The duo estimates that the cost of vehicle crashes in the United States alone is $235 billion, and that 90 percent of all crashes are the result of driver behavior. Their subscription-based service provides real-time feedback and driver coaching and is designed to reduce those costs and save lives by improving drivers' behavior. Customers who use the company's technology (including Ryder, Ericsson,

T-Mobile, LeFleur Transportation, and others) typically reduce the number of crashes by 50 percent and fuel consumption and emissions by up to 10 percent. After pitching their idea to many venture capital firms, Raz and Fleishman have received $42.5 million in financing across three rounds. Venture capitalists were impressed with the experience of the management team that Raz and Fleishman had assembled, the company's fast growth, and the size of the potential market. Representatives from the venture capital firms hold five of GreenRoad's board seats, but the company has the capital it needs to support continued R&D, product innovation, and a more concentrated sales and marketing effort.[51]

Despite its many benefits, venture capital is not suitable for every entrepreneur. "VC money comes at a price," warns one entrepreneur. "Before boarding a one-way money train, ask yourself if this is the best route for your business and personal desires because investors are like department stores the day after Christmas—they expect a lot of returns in a short period of time."[52]

IN THE ENTREPRENEURIAL
SPOTLIGHT   A Mint of an Idea

At age 25, Aaron Patzer held masters degrees in computer science and electrical engineering from Princeton and had a full-time job as a software engineer for an electronic design automation company. Like many young people, Patzer was creating a household budget and tracking his spending using one of the best-selling money management programs on the market, but he grew increasingly frustrated by its complexity, lack of flexibility, and inability to give him real-time information. "There's got to be a better way to do this," he recalls thinking. Convinced that he could create a money management tool that would be simple to use, Patzer, who says that his father read the *Wall Street Journal* to him as a toddler, quit his job and spent 14 hours a day for the next 7 months writing the software to drive Mint.com, an online financial planning Web site that allows users to create budgets, track their spending, and compare their spending habits to other people with similar lifestyles. In the early days, he financed the company out of his personal savings but realized that building a real business would take more cash than he had available.

Patzer pitched his business plan to a dozen angel investors and to some of the top venture capital firms in Silicon Valley, but none of them were interested in investing money in an unproven start-up. "Every single VC told me that I would fail because no one would trust a start-up with their financial information," he says. Despite the negative feedback, Patzer persisted in his quest for capital, eventually getting the opportunity to make a presentation about Mint.com to Josh Kopelman, cofounder of venture capital firm First Round Capital, at a networking event for entrepreneurs. "I had a server running on a laptop in the trunk of my car," recalls the always-prepared Patzer. "I ran out and got the laptop and fired up a demo."

Kopelman was impressed with the demonstration and asked Patzer to send him a business plan. Reading it, Kopelman says that he spotted "a really big market and someone who had really thought it out. [Patzer] saw an opportunity to solve a really big pain point for customers." Ten days later, First Round Capital, which, unlike most venture capital firms, focuses on small companies in the start-up and seed stages, invested $325,000 in Mint.com and lined up another $725,000 from other early stage VCs Felicis Ventures and Soft Tech VC. In less than 1 year, Mint.com had attracted 400,000 users, a signal of the success that was to come.

First Round Capital member Rob Hayes, who had extensive product development experience at Palm, joined the Mint.com board, and Kopelman became a board advisor. Guidance from Hayes, Kopelman, and others helped CEO Patzer avoid many mistakes that start-up companies make and to quickly resolve others. After Mint.com won the top award at a technical conference, a surge in traffic to its Web site caused the company's servers to crash, and engineers at Mint.com traced the problem to a flaw in its database technology. That evening, drawing on his extensive network of contacts, Kopelman contacted an executive at Mint.com's database provider and asked him to help solve the problem. "We were able to resolve the issue within 24 hours because of the connections Josh had," says Patzer.

As Mint.com continued to grow and its capital requirements increased, First Round Capital was there to help, investing more of its own money in subsequent rounds of venture capital for a total of more than $2.5 million and connecting Patzer and the management team with other venture capital firms. Patzer continued to rely on Kopelman, Hayes, and other advisors to help him navigate the challenges of building a company, and within 2 years Mint.com had 1.5 million users and was tracking $200 billion in transactions. Just 3 years after starting Mint.com, Patzer and his venture capital investors sold the company to Intuit, the leading producer of money management software for $170 million, producing an impressive rate of return for Patzer, First Round Capital, and all of the company's investors. Kopelman says that the Mint.com deal produced the highest return of any investment that First Round Capital has made. Patzer says that he is "eternally grateful" to Kopelman, Hayes, and First Round Capital. "They took a risk on a 25-year-old kid who didn't have a whole lot of experience," he says. His advice for other young entrepreneurs? "Stone-cold, iron-willed determination," he says. "It's going to be long hours and a lot of hard work, but if you have confidence in your product, you will succeed."

1. Early stage venture capital was an essential ingredient in Mint.com's success. Yet only 2 to 4 percent of all venture capital goes to companies in the seed and start-up phases. Why?

2. Suppose that an entrepreneur with a fast-growing business tells you that he has the opportunity to acquire an investment from a venture capital company and wants your advice. What questions would you ask him before offering him advice?

3. Refer to question 2. Explain the advantages and disadvantages that entrepreneurs experience when they accept venture capital.

Sources: Based on Spencer E. Ante, "Mint.com: Nurtured by SuperAngel VCs," *Bloomberg Business Week*, September 15, 2009, *www.businessweek. com/technology/content/sep2009/tc20090915_065038.htm*; Rieva Lesonsky, "Entrepreneurship: The Next Generation, Aaron Patzer, 29," *All Business*, June 2010, *www.allbusiness.com/banking-finance/banking-lending-credit-services-electronic/14562114-1.html*; "30 Under 30" America's Coolest Young Entrepreneurs, *Inc.*, 2008, *www.inc.com/30under30/2008/profile/ 5-patzer.html*; "Intuit to Acquire Mint.com," Mint.com, September 14, 2009, *www.mint.com/press/intuit-to-acquire-mint-com/*.

Public Stock Sale ("Going Public")

3. Describe the process of "going public," as well as its advantages and disadvantages.

In some cases, small companies can "go public" by selling shares of stock to outside investors. In an **initial public offering (IPO)**, a company raises capital by selling shares of its stock to the general public for the first time. A public offering is an effective method of raising large amounts of capital, but it can be an expensive and time-consuming process filled with regulatory nightmares. "An IPO can be a wonderful thing," says one investment banker, "but it's not all sweetness and light."[53] Once a company makes an initial public offering, *nothing* will ever be the same again. Managers must consider the impact of their decisions not only on the company and its employees but also on shareholders and the value of their stock.

Going public isn't for every business. In fact, most small companies do not meet the criteria for making a successful public stock offering. Since 2001, the average number of companies that make initial public offerings each year is 139, and only about 20,000 companies in the United States—less than 0.5 percent of the total—are publicly held. Few companies with less than $25 million in annual sales manage to go public successfully. It is extremely difficult for a start-up company with no track record of success to raise money with a public offering. Instead, investment bankers who underwrite public stock offerings typically look for established companies with the following characteristics:

- Consistently high growth rates.
- High profit potential. Strangely enough, profitability at the time of the IPO is not essential; since 2001, 47 percent of companies making IPOs had negative earnings.[54]
- Three to 5 years of audited financial statements that meet or exceed SEC standards. After the Enron and WorldCom scandals, investors are demanding impeccable financial statements.
- A solid position in a rapidly growing industry. In 1999, the median age of companies making IPOs was 4 years; today, it is 15 years.[55]
- A sound management team with experience and a strong board of directors.

Figure 5 shows the trend in the number of IPOs and the amount of capital raised.

FIGURE 5
IPOs

Source: Thomson Financial
Securities Data.

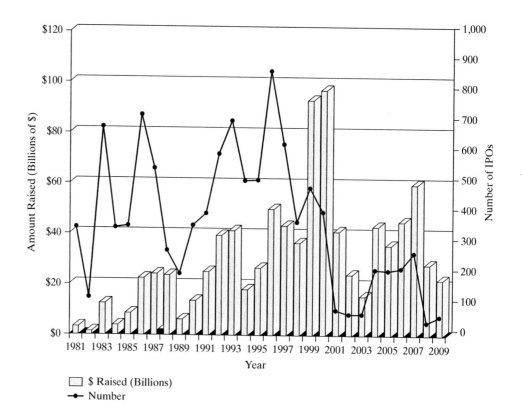

Entrepreneurs who are considering taking their companies public should first consider carefully the advantages and the disadvantages of an IPO. The *advantages* include the following:

ABILITY TO RAISE LARGE AMOUNTS OF CAPITAL. The biggest benefit of a public offering is the capital infusion the company receives. Since 2001, the average IPO has raised $250 million for the issuing company. After going public, the corporation has the cash to fund R&D projects, expand plant and facilities, repay debt, or boost working capital balances without incurring the interest expense and the obligation to repay that comes with debt financing. For instance, when Ancestry.com, the Web site that helps people research family histories and create family trees, went public, the sale of 7.4 million shares at $13.50 per share generated $100 million for the company (before subtracting the expenses of making the offering).[56]

IMPROVED CORPORATE IMAGE. All of the media attention a company receives during the registration process makes it more visible. In addition, becoming a public company in some industries improves its prestige and enhances its competitive position, one of the most widely recognized, intangible benefits of going public.

IMPROVED ACCESS TO FUTURE FINANCING. Going public boosts a company's net worth and broadens its equity base. Its improved stature and financial strength make it easier for the firm to attract more capital—both equity and debt—and to grow.

ATTRACTING AND RETAINING KEY EMPLOYEES. Public companies often use stock-based compensation plans to attract and retain quality employees. Stock options and bonuses are excellent methods for winning employees' loyalty and for instilling a healthy ownership attitude among them. Employee stock ownership plans (ESOPs) and stock purchase plans are popular recruiting and motivational tools in many small corporations, enabling them to hire top-flight talent they otherwise would not be able to afford.

USING STOCK FOR ACQUISITIONS. A company whose stock is publicly traded can acquire other businesses by offering its own shares rather than cash. Acquiring other companies with shares of stock eliminates the need to incur additional debt. When search engine giant Google purchased YouTube, the small company that popularized online video, for $1.65 million (Google's largest acquisition to date), it used Google stock rather than cash to complete the transaction. YouTube founders Chad Hurly, Steve Chen, and Jawed Karim had been considering an IPO for YouTube, but Google's offer was attractive enough to change their minds.[57]

LISTING ON A STOCK EXCHANGE. Being listed on an organized stock exchange, even a small regional one, improves the marketability of a company's shares and enhances its image. When a company's stock trades on an organized exchange, it has more clout in its market. Most small companies' stocks, however, do not qualify for listing on the nation's largest exchanges—the New York Stock Exchange (NYSE) and the American Stock Exchange (AMEX). However, the AMEX offers a market for small-company stocks, The Emerging Company Marketplace. Most small companies' stocks are traded on either the National Association of Securities Dealers Automated Quotation (NASDAQ) system's National Market System (NMS) and its emerging small-capitalization exchange or one of the nation's regional stock exchanges. The most popular regional exchanges include the Midwest (MSE), Philadelphia (PHLX), Boston (BSE), and Pacific (PSE).

The *disadvantages* of going public include the following:

DILUTION OF FOUNDER'S OWNERSHIP. Whenever entrepreneurs sell stock to the public, they automatically dilute their ownership in their businesses. Most owners retain a majority interest in the business, but they may still run the risk of unfriendly takeovers years later after selling more stock.

LOSS OF CONTROL. If enough shares are sold in a public offering, the company founder risks losing control of the company. If a large block of shares falls into the hands of dissident stockholders, they could vote the existing management team (including the founder) out.

LOSS OF PRIVACY. Taking their companies public can be a big ego boost for owners, but they must realize that their companies are no longer solely theirs. Information that was once private must be available for public scrutiny. The initial prospectus and the continuous reports filed with the Securities and Exchange Commission (SEC) disclose a variety of information about the company and its operations—from financial data and raw material sources to legal matters and patents to *anyone*—including competitors. Entrepreneurs who decide not to take their companies public most often cite the loss of privacy and loss of control as the primary reasons.

REGULATORY REQUIREMENTS AND REPORTING TO THE SEC. Operating as a publicly held company is expensive, especially since Congress passed the Sarbanes-Oxley Act in 2002. The SEC traditionally has required publicly held companies to file periodic reports with it, which often requires a more powerful accounting system, a larger accounting staff, and greater use of attorneys and other professionals. Created in response to ethical fiascoes involving Enron and WorldCom, Sarbanes-Oxley was designed to improve the degree of internal control and the level of financial reporting by publicly held companies. Critics contend that the cost of complying with the law is overbearing and point to Sarbanes-Oxley as one reason the number of IPOs has plunged. According to an SEC study, the median cost of complying with Sarbanes-Oxley to public companies with market values of less than $75 million is $365,900 per year.[58]

Paymaxx and CompuPay

The high cost of regulatory compliance dissuades many potential companies from going public. Paymaxx, founded in 1991, became one of the largest payroll provider companies in the United States, and the fast-growing company was considering an IPO to acquire the capital necessary to fuel its growth. Its founders made an abrupt U-turn in their plans when they discovered the cost of complying with Sarbanes-Oxley, choosing instead to sell the company to a larger payroll processing company, CompuPay.[59]

FILING EXPENSES. A public stock offering usually is an expensive way to generate funds to finance a company's growth. For the typical small company, the cost of a public offering is about 15 percent of the capital raised. On small offerings, costs can eat up as much as 40 percent of the capital raised, whereas on larger offerings, those above $25 million, only 10 to 12 percent will go to cover expenses. Once an offering exceeds $15 million, its relative issuing cost drops. The largest cost is the underwriter's commission, which is typically 6.5 to 7 percent of the proceeds on offerings less than $10 million and 13 percent on those over that amount. Critics claim that the underwriting fees that U.S. investment banks charge are the highest in the world, which, when combined with the reporting requirements of the Sarbanes-Oxley Act, dissuade companies, particularly small ones, from making IPOs in the United States. Research by Grant Thornton shows a decline in the proportion of small-company IPOs in recent years. From 1991 to 1997, IPOs that generated less than $50 million accounted for nearly 80 percent of all IPOs; today, that percentage had dropped to just 28 percent.[60]

ACCOUNTABILITY TO SHAREHOLDERS. The capital that entrepreneurs manage and risk is no longer just their own. The managers of a publicly held firm are accountable to the company's shareholders. Indeed, the law requires that managers recognize and abide by a relationship built on trust. Profit and return on investment become the primary concerns for investors. If the stock price of a newly public company falls, shareholder lawsuits are inevitable. Investors whose shares decline in value often sue the company's managers for fraud and the failure to disclose in the IPO prospectus the potential risks of their investments.

ENTREPRENEURIAL

Profile

Vonage

When VoIP provider Vonage went public, the offering price of its shares was $17, and the company set aside 13.5 percent of the 31.25 million shares it was offering for its customers. However, when Vonage shares fell to $14.85 on its first day of trading and then plummeted in the months that followed, more than 10,000 customers filed a lawsuit against Vonage, claiming that the company made false and misleading statements about its financial condition during the IPO. As part of its agreement with the issue's underwriters, Vonage had to pay $11.7 million to cover the cost of the shares for which disgruntled customers refused to pay when the stock price fell.[61]

PRESSURE FOR SHORT-TERM PERFORMANCE. In privately held companies, entrepreneurs are free to follow their strategies for success, even if those strategies take years to produce results. When a company goes public, however, entrepreneurs quickly learn that shareholders are impatient and expect results immediately. In publicly held companies, quarterly results matter. Founders are under constant pressure to produce short-term results, which can have a negative impact on a company's long-term strategy. The U.S. Chamber of Commerce has called the emphasis on the short term "one of the biggest threats to America's competitiveness."[62] David Klock, who took his once publicly held company Comp Benefits private, says, "I am glad we're private because [it gives us] the ability to make investments that may take two or three quarters to give a good return. That's difficult to do as a public company."[63]

LOSS OF FOCUS. As impatient as they can be, entrepreneurs often find the time demands of an IPO frustrating and distracting. Managing the IPO takes time away from managing the company. Working on an IPO can consume as much as 75 percent of top managers' time, robbing them of their ability to manage the business effectively. "The most common mistake [in an IPO] is the failure to understand the amount of time and effort that is required and the amount of distraction from the primary business," says one IPO expert.[64]

TIMING. Many factors that are beyond the company's control, such as declines in the overall stock market, economic recessions, industry shakeups, and potential investors' jitters, can quickly slam shut a company's "window of opportunity" for an IPO even after top managers have spent months and many thousands of dollars working on the offering. After 5 months of work with its lead underwriter, Credit Suisse, Smile Brands Group, a company that provides

" HUNTING AND GATHERING ISN't VERY PROFITABLE.
LET'S INVENT IPOs."

support services to dental practices, withdrew its proposed $132 million IPO, citing volatile and deteriorating market conditions that hampered the company's ability to sell its stock within the projected $16 to $18 price range.[65]

THE REGISTRATION PROCESS. Taking a company public is a complicated, bureaucratic process that usually takes several months to complete. Many experts compare the IPO process to running a corporate marathon, and both the company and its management team must be in shape and up to the grueling task. Making an IPO requires a coordinated effort from a team of professionals, including company executives, an accountant, a securities attorney, a financial printer, and at least one underwriter. The key steps in taking a company public follow.

Choose the Underwriter

The single most important ingredient in making a successful IPO is selecting a capable **underwriter** (or **investment banker**). The underwriter serves two primary roles: helping to prepare the registration statement for the issue and promoting the company's stock to potential investors. The underwriter works with company managers as an advisor in preparing the registration statement that must be filed with the SEC, promoting the issue in a road show, pricing the stock, and providing after-market support. Once the registration statement is finished, the underwriter's primary job is selling the company's stock through an underwriting syndicate of other investment bankers it develops.

ENTREPRENEURIAL
Profile

*Allen and Eugene
Stoltzfus and John
Fairfield: Rosetta Stone*

Rosetta Stone, a company founded in 1992 by Allen and Eugene Stoltzfus and John Fairfield that sells software that allows people to learn foreign languages using pictures and sounds in context rather than translations, recently made an initial public offering. The company, whose shares now trade on the New York Stock Exchange under the symbol "RST," selected Morgan Stanley and William Blair as its lead underwriters to manage the offering of 6.25 million shares at $18 per share (above the initial estimate of $15 to $17 per share) that generated $112 million to fuel the company's global expansion plans.[66]

Negotiate a Letter of Intent

To begin an offering, the entrepreneur and the underwriter must negotiate a **letter of intent**, which outlines the details of the deal. The letter of intent covers a variety of important issues, including the type of underwriting, its size and price range, the underwriter's commission, and any warrants and options included. It almost always states that the underwriter is not bound to the offering until it is executed—usually the day before or the day of the offering. However, the letter usually creates a binding obligation for the company to pay any direct expenses the underwriter incurs relating to the offer.

There are two types of underwriting agreements: firm commitment and best effort. In a **firm commitment agreement**, the underwriter agrees to purchase all of the shares in the offering and resell them to investors. This agreement *guarantees* that the company will receive the required funds, and most large underwriters use it. In a **best efforts agreement**, the underwriter merely agrees to use its best efforts to sell the company's shares and does not guarantee the company will receive the needed financing. The managing underwriter acts as an agent, selling as many shares as possible through the syndicate. Some best effort contracts are all or nothing—if the underwriter cannot sell all of the shares, the offering is withdrawn. Another version of the best efforts agreement is to set a minimum number of shares that must be sold for the issue to be completed. These methods are riskier because the company has no guarantee of raising the required capital.

The company and the underwriter must decide on the size of the offering and the price of the shares. To keep the stock active in the aftermarket, most underwriters prefer to offer a *minimum* of 400,000 to 500,000 shares. A smaller number of shares inhibits sufficiently broad distribution. Most underwriters recommend selling 25 to 40 percent of the company in the IPO. To keep interest in the issue high, the underwriter usually recommends an initial price between $10 and $20 per share, although some companies stock is priced higher. The underwriter establishes an estimated price range for the company's IPO in the underwriting agreement, but it does not establish the final price until the day before the offering takes place. Depending on anticipated demand for the company's shares, the condition of the market, and other factors, the actual price may be outside the estimated range. Since 2001, 55 percent of companies' offerings have been within the underwriter's estimated price range; 17 percent of them actually came in above the range.[67] For instance, in an IPO that generated $226 million for Tesla Motors, the maker of high-performance electric cars, lead underwriters estimated the offering price to be $14 to $16 per share, but because of strong demand for the issue, the actual offering price was $17 per share.[68]

Most letters of intent include a **lock-up agreement** that prevents the sale of insider shares, those owned by directors, managers, founders, employees, and other insiders, for 12 to 36 months. The sale of these shares early in a company's public life could send negative signals to investors, eroding their confidence in the stock and pushing its price downward.

Prepare the Registration Statement

After a company signs the letter of intent, the next task is to prepare the **registration statement** to be filed with the SEC and the prospectus to be distributed to potential investors. These documents describe both the company and the stock offering and disclose information about the risks of investing. It includes information on the use of the proceeds, the company's history, its financial position, its capital structure, the risks it faces, its managers, and many other details. The statements are extremely comprehensive and may take months to develop. To prepare them, entrepreneurs must rely on their team of IPO professionals.

File with the SEC

When the statement is finished (with the exception of pricing the shares, proceeds, and commissions, which cannot be determined until just before the issue goes to market), the company officially files the statement with the SEC and awaits the review of the Division of Corporate Finance. The division sends notice of any deficiencies in the registration statement to the company's attorney in a comment letter. The company and its team of professionals must address all of the deficiencies noted in the comment letter and prepare an amended registration statement. Finally, the company files the revised registration statement, along with a pricing amendment (giving the price of the shares, the proceeds, and the underwriter's commission).

Wait to Go Effective

While waiting for the SEC's approval, the managers and the underwriters are busy. The underwriters are building a syndicate of other underwriters who will market the company's stock. (No sales can be made prior to the effective date of the offering, however.) The SEC also limits the publicity and information a company may release during this **quiet period** (which officially starts when the company reaches a preliminary agreement with the managing underwriter and ends 90 days after the effective date).

Securities laws do permit a **road show**, a gathering of potential syndicate members sponsored by the managing underwriter. Its purpose is to promote interest among potential underwriters in the IPO by featuring the company, its management, and the proposed deal. The managing underwriter and key company officials barnstorm major cities such as New York, Boston, San Francisco, Chicago, Los Angeles, and sometimes foreign cities such as London and Hong Kong at a grueling pace. Company executives often make presentations to stockbrokers and institutional investors in two or three cities a day for 2 to 4 weeks. During the road show for Unica Corporation, a company that sells enterprise marketing management software, top managers courted potential underwriters in 12 cities in just 14 days! Their efforts were exhausting but productive: Unica sold 4.8 million shares of its stock and raised $48 million.[69]

On the last day before the registration statement becomes effective, the company signs the formal underwriting agreement. The final settlement, or closing, takes place a few days after the effective date for the issue. At this meeting the underwriters receive their shares to sell and the company receives the proceeds of the offering.

Typically, the entire process of going public takes from 60 to 180 days, but it can take much longer if the issuing company is not properly prepared for the process.

Meet State Requirements

In addition to satisfying the SEC's requirements, a company also must meet the securities laws in all states in which the issue is sold. These state laws (or "blue sky" laws) vary drastically from one state to another, and the company must comply with them.

Simplified Registrations and Exemptions

4. Explain the various simplified registrations, exemptions from registration, and other alternatives available to entrepreneurs wanting to sell shares of equity to investors.

The IPO process described previously (called an S-1 filing) requires maximum disclosure in the initial filing and costly compliance with federal regulations, discouraging most small businesses from using it. Fortunately, the SEC allows several exemptions from this full-disclosure process for small businesses. Many small businesses that go public choose one of these simplified options the SEC has designed for small companies. The SEC has established a number of simplified registration statements and exemptions from the registration process:

REGULATIONS S-B AND S-K. In 2009, the SEC eliminated Regulation S-B but transferred many of its provisions into Regulation S-K, a simplified registration process for small companies seeking to make initial or subsequent public offerings. Not only does this regulation simplify the initial filing requirements with the SEC, but it also reduces the ongoing disclosure and filings required of companies by giving them "smaller reporting company" status. Its primary goals are to open the doors to capital markets to smaller companies by cutting the paperwork and the costs of raising capital. To be eligible for the simplified registration process under Regulation S-K, a company must have annual revenues of less than $50 million or have outstanding publicly held stock ("public float") worth no more than $75 million. The goal of Regulation S-K's simplified registration requirements is to enable smaller companies to go public without incurring the expense of a full-blown registration.

REGULATION D (RULES 504, 505, AND 506). Regulation D rules minimize the expense and the time required to raise equity capital for small businesses by simplifying or eliminating the requirement for registering the offering with the SEC, which often takes months and costs many thousands of dollars. Under Regulation D, the whole process typically costs less than half of what a traditional public offering costs. The SEC's objective in creating Regulation D was to give small companies the same access to equity financing that large companies have via the stock market while bypassing many of the same costs and filing requirements. A Regulation D offering requires only minimal notification to the SEC. Offerings made under Regulation D do impose limitations and demand certain disclosures, but they only require a company to file a simple form (Form D) with the SEC within 15 days of the first sale of stock. Form D consists of fill-in-the-blank questions about the company, the issue, the use of the proceeds, and other pertinent matters.

Rule 504 is the most popular of the Regulation D exemptions because it is the least restrictive. It allows a company to sell shares of its stock to an unlimited number of investors without regard to their experience or level of sophistication. A business also can make multiple offerings under Rule 504 as long as it waits at least 6 months between them. However, Rule 504 does place a cap of $1 million in a 12-month period on the amount of capital a company can raise. Ligatt

Security International, a small cyber-security company in Norcross, Georgia, recently raised $147,000 under Rule 504 to finance its expansion.[70]

A Rule 505 offering has a higher capital ceiling ($5 million) than Rule 504 in a 12-month period but imposes more restrictions (no more than 35 nonaccredited investors, no advertising of the offer, and more stringent disclosure requirements).

Rule 506 imposes no ceiling on the amount that can be raised, but most companies that make Rule 506 offerings raise between $1 million and $50 million in capital. Like a Rule 505 offering, it limits the issue to no more than 35 nonaccredited investors and prohibits advertising the offer to the public. There is no limit on the number of accredited investors, however. Rule 506 also requires detailed disclosure of relevant information, but the extent depends on the size of the offering.

SECTION 4(6). Section 4(6) covers private placements and is similar to Regulation D, Rules 505 and 506. It does not require registration on offers up to $5 million if they are made only to accredited investors.

INTRASTATE OFFERINGS (RULE 147). Rule 147 governs intrastate offerings, those sold only to investors in a single state by a company doing business in that state. To qualify, a company must be incorporated in the state in which it makes the offering, conduct a significant percentage of its business in that state, and make offers and sales of the issue only to residents of that state. There is no ceiling on the amount of the offering, but only residents of the state in which the issuing company operates can invest. The maximum number of shareholders is 500, and a company's asset base cannot exceed $10 million.

REGULATION A. Regulation A, although currently not used often, allows an exemption for public stock offerings up to $5 million over a 12-month period. Regulation A imposes few restrictions, but it is more costly than the other types of exempted offerings because it requires a company to file a registration statement with the SEC (although its requirements are simpler than those for an S-1 offering). A Regulation A offering allows a company to sell its shares directly to investors.

A small company can sell its stock under Rule 504 of Regulation D, Rule 147, or Regulation A using a Small Corporate Offering Registration (SCOR) by also registering the offering at the state level. The ceiling on a SCOR offering is $1 million (except in Texas, where there is no limit), and the issuing price of the stock must be at least $1 per share. Before selling its stock, a company must file Form U-7, a disclosure document that resembles a business plan but also serves as a state securities offering registration, a disclosure document, and a prospectus. A company must register the offering in every state in which it will sell its stock to comply with the states' blue sky laws, although current regulations allow simultaneous registration in multiple states. Entrepreneurs using SCOR may advertise their companies' offerings and can sell them directly to any investor with no restrictions and no minimums.

DIRECT STOCK OFFERINGS. Many of the simplified registrations and exemptions discussed previously give entrepreneurs the power to sidestep investment bankers and sell their companies' stock offerings directly to investors and, in the process, save themselves thousands of dollars in underwriting fees. By going straight to Main Street rather than through underwriters on Wall Street, entrepreneurs cut out the underwriter's commission, many legal expenses, and most registration fees. Entrepreneurs willing to handle the paperwork requirements and to market their own shares can make direct public offerings (DPOs) for about 6 percent of the total amount of the issue, compared with 15 percent for a traditional stock offering, and raise as much or more money as a private placement generates.

Profile

Gary Steszewski:
CityMade, Inc.

CityMade, Inc., a company founded in 1999 that specializes in the sale of local gift items ranging from apparel and food to beverages and sports merchandise that are made in particular cities, recently launched a direct public offering. The company prepared its SCOR offering with the help of Direct Public Offerings Services, a company in Niagara Falls, New York, that helps small businesses make DPOs, and is offering 375,000 shares of common stock at $2 per share. With a minimum purchase of just $300, the DPO is aimed at small investors, many of whom are loyal customers. CityMade, which currently operates in 12 cities, including Boston, New York City, and Washington, DC plans to use the $750,000 of equity capital from the DPO to expand into 100 new cities within the next 5 years. "CityMade has positioned itself for aggressive growth over the next 3 years," says CityMade's president, Gary Steszewski. "We doubled our sales to $1.3 million in 3 years and project sales will more than double in the next 2 years."[71]

The Internet has opened a new avenue for direct public offerings and is one of the fastest-growing sources of capital for small businesses. Much of the Internet's appeal as a fund-raising tool stems from its ability to reach large numbers of prospective investors very quickly and at a low cost. Companies that make direct stock offerings on the Internet most often make them under either Regulation A or Regulation D and usually generate between $300,000 and $4 million for the company.

Direct public offerings work best for companies that have a single product or related product lines, a base of customers who are loyal to the company, good name recognition, and annual sales between $3 million and $25 million. The first company to make a successful DPO over the Internet was Spring Street Brewing, a microbrewery founded by Andy Klein. Klein raised $1.6 million in a Regulation A offering in 1996. Companies that make successful direct public offerings of their stock over the Web must meet the same standards as companies making stock offerings using more traditional methods. Experts caution Web-based fund seekers to make sure that their electronic prospectuses meet SEC and state requirements. Table 4 provides a brief quiz to help entrepreneurs determine whether their companies would be good candidates for a DPO.

Foreign Stock Markets

Some foreign stock markets offer entrepreneurs access to equity funds more readily than U.S. markets. The London Stock Exchange's AIM (Alternative Investment Market) is geared to small companies with its lower costs and less extensive reporting and regulatory requirements. "Smaller deals can get done on the AIM," says one securities attorney. "They're cheaper, and there are fewer requirements. The deals I've seen there could not have been done here." Similarly, stock exchanges in Canada (Toronto and Vancouver), Germany, Korea, Hong Kong, and Singapore are attracting small U.S. companies that are hungry for capital. These foreign exchanges encourage equity listings of small companies because the cost of offerings is about half that in the United States.

TABLE 4 Is a Direct Public Offering for You?

Drew Field, an expert in direct public offerings, has developed the following 10-question quiz to help entrepreneurs decide whether their companies are good candidates for a DPO.

1. Does your company have a history of consistently profitable operations under the present management?
2. Is your company's management team honest, socially responsible, and competent?
3. In 10 words or fewer, can you explain the nature of your business to laypeople who are new to investing?
4. Would your company excite prospective investors, making them want to share in its future?
5. Does your company have natural affinity groups, such as customers with strong emotional loyalty?
6. Do members of your natural affinity groups have discretionary cash to risk for long-term gains?
7. Would your company's natural affinity groups recognize your company's name and consider your offering materials?
8. Can you get the names, addresses, and telephone numbers of affinity group members, as well as some demographic information about them?
9. Can a high-level company employee spend half-time for 6 months as a DPO project manager?
10. Does your company have—or can you obtain—audited financial statements for at least the last 2 fiscal years?

The more questions you can answer with "yes," the more likely it is that a direct public offering could work for your company.

Sources: Drew Field Direct Public Offers, "Screen Test for a Direct Public Offering," *www.dfdpo.com/screen.htm*; Stephanie Gruner, "Could You Do a DPO?" *Inc.*, December 1996, p. 70.

▶ ENTREPRENEURSHIP IN ACTION ▶

Three Twins Ice Cream: We Need to Build a Factory

Neil Gottlieb spent several years working in corporate finance at Gap and Levi's, but his entrepreneurial aspirations finally lured him to start his own company. The Cornell University graduate was considering returning to graduate school but, remembering the delicious fresh orange sherbet his mother made in the family kitchen, he was inspired to start Three Twins Ice Cream in San Rafael, California. Having heard that the Business Planning Class at San Francisco's Renaissance Entrepreneurship Center was known as "The Mini MBA Program," Gottlieb enrolled and began developing the business plan for launching Three Twins Ice Cream, the name for which was inspired by his twin brother and sister-in-law, who also is a twin. Based on the research gathered for his business plan, Gottlieb was confident that a market existed for rich, premium ice cream made with all-natural, organic ingredients.

After graduating from the class, Gottlieb invested the $70,000 he had been saving since he began delivering newspapers as a boy and opened the first Three Twins Ice Cream store in a San Rafael shopping center. Manning the shop alone, Gottlieb worked 166 days in a row. He made ice cream every morning, sold it in the shop during the day, and cleaned up and did paperwork in the evenings. In addition to selling ice cream in the retail shop, Gottlieb sold pints of Three Twins Ice Cream to local restaurants, cafés, small retail outlets, and even farmers' markets, building name recognition for the brand and his small company. He made the ice cream from a carefully formulated mix that he purchased for $15 per gallon from a local organic dairy. Similar mixes made from nonorganic ingredients would have cost just $4 per gallon, but Gottlieb adhered to his company's "organic only" strategy. To be certified organic, "All of your inputs—the milk, cream, sugar, and flavorings—have to be organic," he explains. "Even the chemicals you use to clean and sanitize equipment have to be organic. You have to keep records of sanitation and production so you can show for any batch that you are in compliance."

The company's first store became a success, and Gottlieb opened two more retail stores, one in Napa Valley and one in San Francisco's Haight-Ashbury district. He pitched his company's ice cream to Whole Foods, and the upscale grocer began selling Three Twins Ice Cream at one of its San Francisco stores. Despite Gottlieb's success with retail stores and a growing wholesale business, his goal was to transform Three Twins Ice Cream into a national brand. "We don't want to be an artisanal brand selling $8 pints of ice cream," he says. "We want to be a national brand that sells really good ice cream." To realize that goal, however, Gottlieb knew that he had to build his own factory, where he could produce large quantities of ice cream at lower cost and expand the range of flavors the company offered. Currently, Three Twins has the ability to produce about 50,000 pints of ice cream per year.

Gottlieb began creating plans for a 4,200-square-foot certified-organic factory at a cost of about $2 million that would be capable of producing 2 million pints of ice cream per year. "The economics of the company are not sustainable without the factory," he says. Gottlieb found an ideal site in nearby Petaluma, California, and approached several lenders, but banks were embroiled in their own financial crisis and were not interested in making a large loan to a small start-up company. "No one's lending money right now," says Gottlieb. Financial projections show that once the factory is up and running, Three Twins could reduce the cost of making its ice cream enough to reduce its retail prices from $7 to $8 per pint to $5 per pint.

Gottlieb realizes that borrowing money from traditional lenders is not a likely prospect in the near future and that he must turn to alternative sources of financing.

1. Work with a small team of your classmates to brainstorm ideas for financing alternatives for Three Twins Ice Cream's capital needs.
2. Refer to question 1. Rank the list of financing sources that you have developed in order of priority. Briefly explain the advantages and the disadvantages of each.
3. What tips can you offer Gottlieb before he approaches the sources of financing you have listed?
4. Assuming that you have the financial means to invest in a small company, would you invest in Three Twins Ice Cream? Explain. If so, what questions would you ask before investing?

Sources: Based on Jessica Bernstein, "Sweet Success for Three Twins Ice Cream," *Marin Independent Journal,* July 5, 2010, *http://dailyme.com/story/2010070500001093/sweet-success-twins-ice-cream.html*; Loralee Stevens, "Organic Ice Cream Maker Three Twins Adds Production Plant," *North Bay Business Journal,* April 26, 2010, *www.northbaybusinessjournal.com/20581/organic-ice-cream-maker-three-twins-adds-production-plant/*; "Neal Gottlieb of Three Twins Ice Cream," Renaissance Entrepreneurship Center, 2010, *www.rencenter.org/index.php?option=com_content&view=article&id=222:neal-gotlieb&catid=41:general&Itemid=108*; Paul Jones, "Terra Linda Ice Cream Shop Opens Factory," *Marinscope Newspapers,* May 5, 2010, *www.marinscope.com/articles/2010/05/05/news_pointer/news/doc4be0d603d2f58277165007.txt.*

Founded in 1999 by Jay Shaw and Ray Ruff with the help of angel investors, NetDimensions has grown steadily into a global provider of performance, knowledge, and learning management systems to corporate human resource management departments. Needing capital for product development, working capital, and marketing, managers considered an initial public offering in the United States, but the cost of making a relatively small issue and the subsequent cost of complying with Sarbanes-Oxley caused them to turn to London's Alternative Investment Market, which lists more than 1,000 small companies. (The average market capitalization of the companies listed on AIM is $59 million, compared to $1.2 billion for companies that are listed on the NASDAQ OMX.) The company, then with annual sales of $3.5 million, made an IPO that raised £3 million ($4.75 million), netting the company £2.32 million ($3.68 million) after the expenses of the offering. Today NetDimensions, which is listed under the symbol "NETD" on AIM, has offices around the globe and serves more than 800 clients, many of them *Fortune* 500 companies.[72]

Securing capital to launch or to expand a small business is no easy task. However, entrepreneurs who understand the equity funding options that are available and are prepared to go after them stand a much better chance of getting the financing they seek than those who don't.

Chapter Review

1. Explain the differences among the three types of capital small businesses require: fixed, working, and growth.
   - Capital is any form of wealth employed to produce more wealth. Three forms of capital are commonly identified: fixed capital, working capital, and growth capital.
   - Fixed capital is used to purchase a company's permanent or fixed assets; working capital represents the business's temporary funds and is used to support the business's normal short-term operations; growth capital requirements surface when an existing business is expanding or changing its primary direction.
2. Describe the various sources of equity capital available to entrepreneurs, including personal savings, friends and relatives, angels, partners, corporations, venture capital, and public stock offerings.
   - The most common source of financing a business is the owner's personal savings. After emptying their own pockets, the next place entrepreneurs turn for capital is family members and friends. Angels are private investors who not only invest their money in small companies, but also offer valuable advice and counsel to them. Some business owners have success financing their companies by taking on limited partners as investors or by forming an alliance with a corporation, often a customer or a supplier. Venture capital companies are for-profit, professional investors looking for fast-growing companies in "hot" industries. When screening prospects, venture capital firms look for competent management, a competitive edge, a growth industry, and important intangibles that will make a business successful. Some owners choose to attract capital by taking their companies public, which requires registering the public offering with the SEC.
3. Describe the process of "going public," as well as its advantages and disadvantages.
   - Going public involves: (1) choosing an underwriter, (2) negotiating a letter of intent, (3) preparing the registration statement, (4) filing with the SEC, and (5) meeting state requirements.
   - Going public offers the advantages of raising large amounts of capital, better access to future financing, improved corporate image, and gaining listing on a stock exchange. Disadvantages include dilution of the founder's ownership, loss of privacy, the burden of reporting to the SEC, filing expenses, and accountability to shareholders.

4. Explain the various simplified registrations and exemptions from registration available to small businesses wanting to sell securities to investors.
- Rather than go through the complete registration process, some companies use one of the simplified registration options and exemptions available to small companies: Regulations S-B and S-K, Regulation D (Rule 504), Regulation D (Rule 505 and Rule 506) Private Placements, Section 4(6), Rule 147, Regulation A, Small Corporate Offering Registration (SCOR), direct stock offerings, and foreign stock markets.

Discussion Questions

1. Why is it so difficult for most small business owners to raise the capital needed to start, operate, or expand their ventures?

2. What is capital? List and describe the three types of capital a small business needs for its operations.

3. Define *equity financing*. What advantage does it offer over debt financing?

4. What is the most common source of equity funds in a typical small business? If an owner lacks sufficient equity capital to invest in the firm, what options are available for raising it?

5. What guidelines should entrepreneurs follow if friends and relatives choose to invest in their businesses?

6. What is an angel investor? Assemble a brief profile of the typical private investor. How can entrepreneurs locate potential angels to invest in their businesses?

7. What advice would you offer an entrepreneur on how to strike a deal with a private investor and avoid problems?

8. What types of businesses are most likely to attract venture capital? What investment criteria do venture capitalists use when screening potential businesses? How do these compare to the typical angel's criteria?

9. How do venture capital firms operate? Describe their procedure for screening investment proposals.

10. Summarize the major exemptions and simplified registrations available to small companies wanting to make public offerings of their stock.

Business Plan Pro

A business plan is an important instrument in the search for capital; therefore, one of the most common motivations for creating a business plan is to secure equity financing. The business plan can be an excellent communication tool to convince investors of a business's stability and convey its potential earning power. A business plan adds credibility to your vision and the investments that others may make in it. Think about the financial needs of your company. Do you need start-up funding beyond the amount that you can provide? Is your business going to need working capital? Does your business need additional financing for growth? If you have the need to raise capital for any purpose, your business plan can help you clarify those needs and formulate a strategy for raising capital.

Review some sample plans in Business Plan Pro and note the financial sections in them. If you are creating a start-up plan, you may want to review the following sample plans: Elsewares Promotional, Westbury Storage, Inc., and Southeast Health Plans. If you are going to be searching for financing for an ongoing business, these plans may be of interest: Coach House Bed & Breakfast, The Daily Perc, and Bioring SA. These diverse plans present financial information in ways that may give you ideas how to best communicate your company's financial needs and potential. Use approaches that fit your plan as you consider the elements that potential investors will find enticing so that they will want to learn more about the growth and earning potential of your business. Leverage each aspect of the financial section—the break-even analysis, projected profit and loss, projected cash flow, projected balance sheet, and business rations—to prove your company's attractiveness as an investment opportunity.

On the Web

If you need start-up or growth capital for your venture, visit the Companion Web Site at *www.pearsonhighered.com/scarborough* for this chapter and review these equity financing options. Determine whether these sources may be useful to you as you explore financing opportunities. You will also find additional information regarding bootstrap and nontraditional funding.

In the Software

Open your plan in Business Plan Pro and go to the "Financial Plan" section. You may want to begin this section by providing an overview of your financial situation and needs. State your assumptions about the existing financial environment. Your assumptions will help to identify general facts upon which you are basing your plan, such as anticipated economic conditions, short-term interest rates, long-term interest rates, expected tax rates, personnel expenses, cash expenses, sales on credit, and others. Let the software lead you through this section.

Next consider which of the following sources you plan to use as a source of equity capital:

- Friends and family members
- Private investors or "angels"
- Partners
- Corporate venture capitalist
- Venture capital companies
- Public stock sale
- Simplified registrations and exemptions

Building Your Business Plan

One of the most valuable aspects of developing the financial section of your business plan is to determine the amount of capital your business will need and to describe the use of that capital in the business. In addition, you must consider the implications of accepting capital from outside investors. There always are costs associated with using other people's money; make sure that you know what they are in your situation. Keep in mind that potential investors will also be assessing the qualifications of your management team, the industry's growth potential, the proposed exit strategy, and other factors as they assess the financial stability and potential of your business venture. A business plan is an effective way to expand your equity financing options and to help you strike a deal with the options that are best for your situation.

Endnotes

1. Jennifer Wang, "Dearly Beloved, Please Send Cash," *Entrepreneur*, December 2009, p. 76.
2. Elizabeth Holmes, "Show Me the Money—Maybe," *Wall Street Journal*, June 25, 2007, p. R6.
3. Antonio Perez, "U.S. Venture Capital Investments at Two-Year High," *Epoch Times*, July 18, 2010, www.theepochtimes.com/n2/content/view/39423/99999999/1/1/; Ben Oliver, "The Man Behind Tesla," *CAR*, March 5, 2010, p. 113; Mara Lemos-Stein, "Tesla Motors Files for IPO—So Much for Profits," *Wall Street Journal*, January 29, 2010, http://blogs.wsj.com/venturecapital/2010/01/29/tesla-motors-files-for-ipo-so-much-for-the-profits/; "Tesla History," Edmunds, www.edmunds.com/tesla/history.html; "About Tesla," Tesla Motors, www.teslamotors.com/about.
4. Mark Henricks, "The Money Market," *Entrepreneur*, July 2006, p. 72.
5. Silva Sansoni, "Burned Angels," *Forbes*, April 19, 1999, pp. 182–185.
6. *Global Entrepreneurship Monitor: National Entrepreneurship Assessment—United States of America, 2004–2005 Executive Report*, Global Entrepreneurship Research Association, 2006, p. 23.
7. Sramana Mitra, "Bootstrapped SaaS Gains Critical Mass," *Forbes*, April 16, 2010, www.forbes.com/2010/04/15/bootstrap-medallia-krawler-intelligent-technology-saas.html; Patrick Hoge, "Ringtones in the Cloud," *Portfolio*, June 9, 2010, www.portfolio.com/industry-news/technology/2010/06/09/startup-ringcentral-aims-internet-phone-service-at-small-businesses; Dalia Fahmy, "Financing, with Strings Attached," *New York Times*, January 29, 2009, www.nytimes.com/2009/01/29/business/smallbusiness/29sbiz.html.
8. "Social Media: An Interview with the Co-founder and CEO of myYearbook," ThinkEquity LLC, March 8, 2010, pp. 1–3; Neil Glassman, "myYearbook's Celebrity Chatter Launches with Miley Cyrus, Rihanna, Lady Gaga, and More," *Social Times*, June 11, 2010, www.socialtimes.com/2010/06/myyearbook-celebrity-chatter/; Henricks, "The Money Market," pp. 69–74; Sara Wilson, "Most Likely to Succeed," *Entrepreneur*, May 2007, p. 41.
9. *Global Entrepreneurship Monitor 2006 Financing Report*, Global Entrepreneurship Research Association, 2006, p. 8.
10. *Global Entrepreneurship Monitor: National Entrepreneurship Assessment—United States of America, 2004–2005 Executive Report*, Global Entrepreneurship Research Association, 2006, p. 22.
11. Stephen L. Rosenstein, "Use Caution with Family Loans for Your Business," *Baltimore Sun*, August 10, 2008, www.baltimoresun.com/business/bal-bz.ml.biztip10aug10,cs-bearstoday,6345879.column.
12. Paul Kvinta, "Frogskins, Shekels, Bucks, Moolah, Cash, Simoleans, Dough, Dinero: Everybody Wants It. Your Business Needs It. Here's How to Get It," *Smart Business*, August 2000, pp. 74–89.
13. Pamela Sherrid, "Angels of Capitalism," *U.S. News & World Report*, October 13, 1997, pp. 43–45.
14. Wright, "Angel Investor Market Holds Steady in 2009 but Changes Seen in Types of Deals UNH Center for Venture Research Finds."
15. Robert Wiltbank and Warren Boeker, "Returns to Angel Investors in Groups," Angel Capital Education Foundation, November 2007, www.angelcapitaleducation.org/dir_downloads/resources/RSCH_-_ACEF_-_Returns_to_Angel_Investor_in_Groups.pdf.
16. "Raising Funds," *Inc.*, November 2008, pp. 69–70.
17. Jeanne Lee, "Building Wealth," *FSB*, June 2006, p. 43.
18. Tomio Geron, "Filling Vacuum Left by VCs, 'Super Angels' Show Growing Influence," *VentureWire*, April 28, 2010, www.fis.dowjones.com/article.aspx?ProductIDFromApplication=32&aid=DJFVW00020100428e64s00002&r=Rss&s=DJFVW; Ira Sager, Kimberly Weisul, and Spencer Ante, "Tech Investing: How Smart Is the Smart Money?" *Bloomberg Business Week*, February 25, 2010, http://images.businessweek.com/ss/10/02/0225_angel_investors/2.htm.
19. Robert E. Wilbank and Warren Boeker, "Angel Performance Project," Angel Capital Education Foundation, November 2007, www.angelcapitalassociation.org/dir_downloads/resources/RSCH_-_ACEF_-_Returns_to_Angel_Investors_PPT.pdf; Wright, "Angel Investor Market Holds Steady in 2009 but Changes Seen in Types of Deals UNH Center for Venture Research Finds."
20. "What Is the Average Closing Time to Receive Financing?" *Jian Business Power Tools*, www.jian.com/library-of-business-information/f252/venture-capital/what-is-the-average-closing-time-it-takes-between-receiving-a.php.
21. Wright, "Angel Investor Market Holds Steady in 2009 but Changes Seen in Types of Deals UNH Center for Venture Research Finds."
22. Henricks, "The Money Market," p. 72.
23. Tomio Geron, "'Super Angels' Rise to Fore," *Wall Street Journal*, May 6, 2010, http://online.wsj.com/article/SB1000142405274870442350457521279267222699. html?KEYWORDS=Super+Angels+Rise+to+Fore&mg=com-wsj.
24. Ibid.; Bambi Francisco Roizen, "How to Get Funded by Super Angel Mike Maples," *Vator News*, May 13, 2010, http://vator.tv/news/2010-05-13-how-to-get-funded-by-super-angel-mike-maples.
25. "FAQ: The Value of Angel Investors and Angel Groups," Angel Capital Association, 2009, p. 1.
26. "ACA Member Landscape: 2009 Different Than 2008 (and Not)," Angel Capital Association, April 16, 2009, pp. 2, 3, and 7.
27. "Vital Statistics," Band of Angels, www.bandangels.com; Bonnie Azab Powell, "Angel Investors Fill Void Left by Risk Capital," *New York Times*, July 6, 2001, p. 28; Loren Fox, "Heaven Can't Wait," *Business 2.0*, March 20, 2001, pp. 123–124; Anne Ashby Gilbert, "Small Stakes in Small Business," *Fortune*, April 12, 1999, p. 162[H]; Sherrid, "Angels of Capitalism," pp. 43–45; John Heylar, "The Venture Capitalist Next Door," *Fortune*, November 13, 2000, pp. 293–312.
28. Bruce J. Blechmna, "Step Right Up," *Entrepreneur*, June 1993, pp. 20–25.
29. Wiltbank and Boeker, "Returns to Angel Investors in Groups."
30. Anne Fisher, "Changing Course," *Fortune*, November 27, 2006, p. 278.
31. *Corporate Venture Capital Group Investment Analysis 1995 Through Q1 2010*, National Venture Capital Association, 2010, p. 1.
32. "Intel Capital Featured in TopCapital," Intel, May 28, 2009, www.intel.com/capital/news/releases/090528_2.htm.
33. "Intel Capital Featured in TopCapital," Intel, May 28, 2009, www.intel.com/capital/news/releases/090528_2.htm; *Key Steps Before Talking to Venture Capitalists*, Intel Capital, 2009, p. 3; Stephen Lawson, "Clearwire IPO Jumps Up on Opening," *Network World*, March 8, 2007, www.networkworld.com/news/2007/030807-clearwire-ipo-jumps-up-on.html; Scott Austin, "The Top 10 Richest Venture-Backed

Companies of All Time," *Wall Street Journal*, June 1, 2010, *http://blogs.wsj.com/venturecapital/2010/06/01/the-top-10-richest-venture-backed-companies-of-all-time/*.

34. "Investments by Region," PricewaterhouseCoopers MoneyTree Survey, Q1 2010, *www.pwcmoneytree.com/MTPublic/ns/nav.jsp?page=region*.

35. David Worrell, "School Ties," *Entrepreneur*, November 2006, pp. 88–90.

36. Austin, "The Top 10 Richest Venture-Backed Companies of All Time."

37. William D. Bygrave with Mark Quill, *Global Entrepreneurship Monitor: 2006 Financing Report*, Global Entrepreneurship Research Association, 2006, p. 23.

38. Dee Power and Brian E. Hill, "Venture Capital Survey," *The Capital Connection*, 2008, *www.capital-connection.com/survey-close.html*.

39. Sharon Kahn, "The Venture Game," *FSB*, May 2009, pp. 60–95.

40. Mabel Brecrick-Okereke, "Report to U.N. Cautions that Focus on Venture Capital Can Hinder Entrepreneurial Economy," United Nations Association of the United States of America, *http://unusa.school.aol.com/newsroom/NewsReleases/ean_venture.asp*; Cara Cannella, "Where Seed Money Really Comes From," *Inc.*, August 2003, p. 26.

41. PricewaterhouseCoopers MoneyTree Survey, *www.pwcmoneytree.com/MTPublic/ns/nav.jsp?page=stage*; National Venture Capital Association, *www.nvca.org*.

42. Anthony Tjan, "Changing Fashion: An Interview with Gilt Groupe Founder Alexandra Wilkis Wilson," *Harvard Business Review*, March 5, 2010, *http://blogs.hbr.org/tjan/2010/03/on-a-recent-trip-to.html*; Colleen Debaise, "Luanching Gilt Groupe, A Fashionable Enterprise," *Wall Street Journal*, July 16, 2010, *http://online.wsj.com/ article/ SB10001424052748703792704575366842447271892.html*.

43. Jason Del Ray, "The Ticker," *Inc.*, September 200, p. 30.

44. Dan Bigman, "On the Hunt," *Forbes*, August 3, 2009, pp. 56–59; Michael J. Roberts and Noam T. Wasserman, "The Founding CEO's Dilemma: Stay or Go?" *Working Knowledge*, August 15, 2005, *http://hbswk.hbs.edu/item/4948.html*.

45. Dalia Fahmy, "Financing, With Strings Attached," *New York Times*, January 29, 2009, *www.nytimes.com/2009/01/29/business/smallbusiness/29sbiz.html*.

46. David Pakman, "Why Mint Matters: A Message to Entrepreneurs About Products," *Pakman's Blog: Disruption*, March 2, 2009, *http://dpakman.wordpress.com/2009/03/02/why-mint-matters-a-message-to-entrepreneurs-about-products/*.

47. Tracy T. Leteroff, "In Full Bloom," *Entrepreneur*, July 2006, p. 78.

48. *Results from the 2010 Global Venture Capital Survey*, National Venture Capital Association and Deloitte, July 13, 2010, p. 14.

49. Benjamin Kepple, "Equallogic Founders to be Honored," *New Hampshire Union Leader*, May 14, 2008, *www.unionleader.com/article.aspx?headline=EqualLogic+founders+to+be+honored&articleId=775baed8-e07f-4d16-ba43-45d2f75034fe*.

50. Henricks, "The Money Market," p. 72.

51. Gwen Moran, "Toward Safer, Greener Roads," *Entrepreneur*, May 2010, p. 65; "GreenRoad Company Overview," GreenRoad Technologies, *www.greenroad.com/company_overview.html*.

52. Dave Pell, "What's Old Is New Again," *FSB*, July/August 2000, p. 122.

53. Kvinta, "Frogskins, Shekels, Bucks, Moolah, Cash, Simoleans, Dough, Dinero," p. 87.

54. Jay Ritter, "Some Factoids About the 2009 IPO Market," University of Florida, April 14, 2010, p. 15.

55. Ibid., p. 8.

56. "Ancestry.com IPO Trades Higher," *Street Insider*, November 5, 2009, *www.streetinsider.com/Hot+List/Ancestry.com+(ACOM)+IPO+Trades+Higher/5079090.html*; "Ancestry.com Inc.," Hoover's IPO Central, 2010, *www.hoovers.com/company/Ancestrycom_Inc/rrcrkxi-1.html*.

57. Kevin Delaney, "Google Looks to Boost Ads with YouTube," *Wall Street Journal*, October 10, 2006, p. B1.

58. Tony Taylor, "A Going (Public) Concern," *GSA Business*, February 20, 2006, p. 15.

59. "CompuPay and PayMaxx Finalize Agreement," CompuPay, June 24, 2005, *www.compupay.com/about_compupay.cfm?subpage=426*; Lynn Stephens and Robert C. Schwartz, "The Chilling Effects of Sarbanes-Oxley: Myth or Reality?" *CPA Journal*, June 2006, *www.nysscpa.org/cpajournal/2006/606/infocus/p14.htm*.

60. David Weild and Edward Kim, *Market Structure Is Causing the IPO Crisis—and More*, Grant Thornton, June 2010, p. 10.

61. Darren Dahl, "Assessing Vonage's Grim IPO," *Inc.*, August 2006, p. 26; Shawn Young, "Vonage Customers Withholf Payment for IPO Shares," *Wall Street Journal*, August 2, 2006, p. B1; Shawn Young and Randy Smith, "How Vonage's High Profile IPO Stumbled on the Stock Market," *Wall Street Journal*, June 3–4, 2006, pp. A1, A6.

62. Joseph McCafferty, "The Long View," *CFO*, May 2007, p. 48.

63. Tim Reason, "Off the Street," *CFO*, May 2003, p. 58.

64. Joanna L. Ossinger, "Stock Answers," *Wall Street Journal*, June 25, 2007, p. R6.

65. Clare Baldwin, "NewPage, Smile Brands Withdraw IPOs as Stocks Sink," Fox Business, May 25, 2010, *www.foxbusiness.com/personal-finance/2010/05/25/update-newpage-smile-brands-withdraw-ipos-stocks-sink/*; "IPO Withdrawals—U.S.," IPO Home, Renaissance Capital, *www.renaissancecapital.com/IPOHome/Press/IPOWithdrawals.aspx*.

66. Andrew Ross Sorkin, "Rosetta Stone IPO Prices Above Estimate Range," *New York Times*, April 16, 2009, *http://dealbook.blogs. nytimes.com/2009/04/16/rosetta-stone-ipo-prices-above-estimate-range/*; "Our History," Rosetta Stone, *www.rosettastone.com/global/history*.

67. "IPO Pricings Compared to Range," IPO Home, Renaissance Capital, *www.renaissancecapital.com/ipohome/news/Tesla-Motors-prices-IPO-at-$17.00-above-the-range-8215.html*.

68. "Tesla Motors Prices at $17, Above the Range," IPO Home, Renaissance Capital, July 22, 2010, *www.renaissancecapital.com/ipohome/news/Green-Dot-sells-more-shares-and-prices-at-$36-above-the-range-8288.html*.

69. David M. Katz, "A Tough Act to Follow," *CFO*, March 2006, pp. 65–72; Unica Corporation, IPO Home, *www.ipohome.com/common/ipoprofile.asp?ticker=UNCA*.

70. Form D: Ligatt Security International, March 23, 2010, *http://attrition.org/errata/charlatan/gregory_evans/ligatt04/LIGATT-SEC-Form-D.pdf*.

71. Aria Munro, "New York's CityMade, Inc. Announces Direct Public Offering," *eNewsChannels*, April 16, 2009, *http://enewschannels.com/2009/04/16/enc6687_151018.php*; "CityMade Direct Public Offering," CityMade, *www.citymade.com/dpo.php*.

72. "NetDimensions Announces Intention to Float on AIM," NetDimensions, *www.netdimensions.com/company/view-news.php?NewsId=43*; "First Day of Dealings on AIM and Placing," *www.netdimensions.com/company/view-news.php?NewsId=44NetDimensions*; Chee Sing Chan, "Beating the Dotcom Bust," *Computerworld Hong Kong*, June 2010, p. 26; "Corporate Fact Sheet," NASDAQ OMX, 2009, p. 1; "Market Statistics," London Stock Exchange, June 2010, p. 2.

E-Commerce and Entrepreneurship

Like China, the Internet is a huge new market. It's up to you to

figure out what to do with it: use it as a prospecting tool, make

connections with people, add value for your existing customers.

—Larry Chase

In the mental geography of e-commerce, distance has been

eliminated. There is only one economy and one market.

—Peter Drucker

Learning Objectives

Upon completion of this chapter, you will be able to:

1 Describe the benefits of selling on the World Wide Web.
2 Understand the factors an entrepreneur should consider before launching into e-commerce.
3 Explain the 10 myths of e-commerce and how to avoid falling victim to them.
4 Explain the basic strategies entrepreneurs should follow to achieve success in their e-commerce efforts.
5 Learn the techniques of designing a killer Web site.
6 Explain how companies track the results from their Web sites.
7 Describe how e-businesses ensure the privacy and security of the information they collect and store from the Web.

E-commerce is creating a new economy, one that is connecting producers, sellers, and customers via technology in ways that have never been possible before. The result is a new method of doing business that is turning traditional methods of commerce and industry on their heads. Companies that ignore the impact of the Internet on their markets run the risk of becoming as relevant to customers as the rotary-dial telephone. The most successful small companies are embracing the Internet, not as merely another advertising medium or marketing tool, but as a mechanism for transforming their companies and changing *everything* about the way they do business. As these companies discover new, innovative ways to use the Internet and communications technology to connect with their suppliers and to serve their customers better, they are creating a new industrial order. In short, e-commerce has launched a revolution. Just as in previous revolutions in the business world, some old players are ousted, and new leaders emerge. The winners are discovering new business opportunities, new ways of serving their customers, and new methods of organizing and operating their businesses.

Perhaps the most visible changes are occurring in the world of retailing. Although e-commerce will not replace traditional retailing, no retailer, from the smallest corner store to industry giant Walmart, can afford to ignore the impact of the Web on their businesses. Companies can take orders at the speed of light from anywhere in the world and at any time of day. The Internet enables companies to collect more information on customers' shopping and buying habits than any other medium in history. This ability means that companies can focus their marketing efforts like never before—for instance, selling garden supplies to customers who are most likely to buy them and not wasting resources trying to sell to those who have no interest in gardening. The capacity to track customers' Web-based shopping habits allows companies to personalize their approaches to marketing and to realize the benefits of individualized (or one-to-one) marketing. Ironically, the same Web-based marketing approach that allows companies to get so personal with their customers also can make shopping extremely impersonal. Entrepreneurs who set up shop on the Web will likely never meet their customers face-to-face or even talk to them. Yet those customers, who can live anywhere in the world, visit the online store at all hours of the day or night and expect to receive individual attention. Making a Web-based marketing approach succeed requires a business to strike a balance, creating an e-commerce strategy that capitalizes on the strengths of the Web while meeting customers' expectations of convenience and service.

In this fast-paced world of e-commerce, size doesn't matter as much as speed and flexibility do. One of the Web's greatest strengths is its interactive, social nature and the ability to provide companies with instantaneous customer feedback, giving them the opportunity to learn and to make necessary adjustments. Businesses, whatever their size, that are willing to experiment with different approaches to reaching customers and are quick to learn and adapt will grow and prosper; those that cannot will fall by the wayside. The Internet continues to create a new industrial order, and companies that fail to adapt to it will soon become extinct.

E-commerce is redefining even the most traditional industries, such as the pizza business. Both Papa John's and Domino's have long since passed the $1 billion mark in online pizza sales. Online pizza sales are growing so fast that it took Papa John's 7 years to reach its first billion in online sales but only 2 years to achieve its second billion. Andy Freitas, a Papa John's franchisee in Washington, DC, says that in two of his outlets online sales account for more than 50 percent of total sales. On a recent Super Bowl Sunday (the busiest single day in the pizza business), Domino's, where online sales account for nearly 25 percent of total sales, took more than 160,000 orders online, and more than 1,000 customers *per minute* were placing online orders just before kickoff. Pizza Hut, the largest pizza chain in the United States, generates online sales of $2 billion a year.[1]

High-volume, low-margin commodity products tend to be best suited for selling on the Web. Although the most popular items purchased online vary from one country to another, the items that customers purchase most often online are computer hardware, clothing, and consumer electronics.[2] However, companies can—and do—sell practically anything over the Web, from antiques and pharmaceuticals to popcorn and drug-free urine.

Companies of all sizes are establishing a presence on the Web because that's where their customers are. The number of Internet users worldwide now stands at more than 1.9 billion, up from only 361 million at the end of 2000.[3] In the United States, people spend an average of 13.2 hours per week on the Internet (not including reading and sending e-mail, which adds 4.5 hours), nearly as much as they do watching television (14.0 hours per week).[4] Figure 1 shows how people in various countries compare in their time spent online.

FIGURE 1

Time Spent Online by Country (Hours per Week)

Source: Brian McRoberts, George H. Terhanian, Ken Allredge, and Carla Keppler, "Understanding the Role of the Internet in the Lives of Consumers: Digital Influence Index," Fleishman-Hillard and Harris Interactive, June 2010, p. 8.

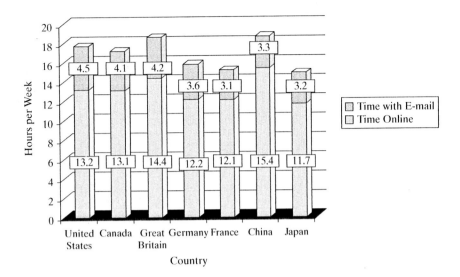

Consumers have adopted the Internet much more quickly than any other major innovation in the past. The Internet reached an audience of 50 million people in just 4 years, compared to 38 years for radio and 13 years for television. One of the Internet's most popular sites, Facebook, reached 50 million users in just 2 years.[5] Online sales now account for 7 percent of total retail sales in the United States, and experts forecast that they will reach $249 billion in 2014, which amounts to a 10 percent annual growth rate. In addition, Jupiter Research predicts that online research will influence 53 percent of total purchases by 2014, up from 27 percent in 2005 (see Figure 2).[6] Although the rapid growth rate of online sales will not last indefinitely, the Web represents a tremendous opportunity for both online and off-line sales that small businesses cannot afford to ignore.

Benefits of Selling on the Web

1. Describe the benefits of selling on the World Wide Web.

Although a Web-based sales strategy does not guarantee success, small companies that have established Web sites realize many benefits, including the following:

- ***The opportunity to increase revenues and attract new customers.*** For many small businesses, launching a Web site is the equivalent of opening a new sales channel. Companies that launch e-commerce efforts soon discover that their sites are generating additional sales from new customers.
- ***The ability of brick-and-mortar retailers to drive online customers into their stores and increase sales there.*** Owners of retail stores have discovered that setting up a Web site leads not only to increased online sales, but also to higher in-store sales. Some retailers offer customers the convenience of ordering products online and then picking them up in the store.

FIGURE 2

U.S. Online and Web-Influenced Retail Sales 2009–2014 (in Billions of $)

Source: Forrester Research Web Influenced Retail Sales Forecast, 2009.

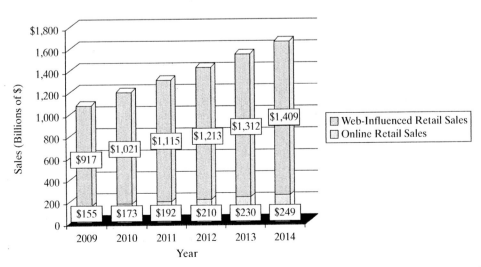

- ▣ ***The ability to expand their reach into global markets.*** The Web is the most efficient way for small businesses to sell their products to the millions of potential customers who live outside the borders of the United States.
- ▣ ***The ability to remain open 24 hours a day, 7 days a week.*** More than half of all retail sales occur after 6 P.M., when many traditional stores close. Extending the hours a brick-and-mortar store remains open can increase sales, but it also takes a toll on the business owner and the employees. With a Web site up and running, customers never have to worry about whether an online store is "open."
- ▣ ***The capacity to use the Web's interactive nature to enhance customer service.*** Although selling on the Web can be highly impersonal because of the lack of human interaction, companies that design their sites properly can create an exciting, interactive experience for their online visitors. Customers can contact a company at any time of the day, control the flow of information they get, and, in some cases, interact with company representatives in real time. In addition, technology now allows companies to "personalize" their sites to suit the tastes and preferences of individual customers.
- ▣ ***The power to educate and to inform.*** Far more than most marketing media, the Web gives entrepreneurs the power to educate and to inform customers. Women and members of Generation Y, especially, crave product information before they make purchases. The Web allows business owners to provide more detailed information to visitors than practically any other medium.
- ▣ ***The ability to lower the cost of doing business.*** The Web is one of the most efficient ways of reaching both new and existing customers. Properly designed and promoted, a Web site can reduce a company's cost of generating sales leads, providing customer support, and distributing marketing materials. For instance, sending customers an e-mail newsletter is much less expensive than paying the printing and postage costs of sending the same newsletter by "snail mail."
- ▣ ***The capacity to improve the efficiency of purchasing and inventory control processes.*** The Internet also has the potential to improve the efficiency of small companies' purchasing and inventory-control processes. In a study by BuyerZone, an online marketplace for business purchasing, more than 75 percent of small business owners say that using the Internet in their purchasing decisions allows them to save both money and time when making buying decisions.[7] By integrating its Web site and its inventory-control system, a company also can shorten its sales cycle and reduce its inventory costs. Linking its Web orders directly to suppliers enables a business to cut purchasing costs even more.
- ▣ ***The ability to spot new business opportunities and to capitalize on them.*** E-commerce companies are poised to give customers just what they want when they want it. As the number of dual-career couples rises and the amount of available leisure time shrinks, consumers are looking for ways to increase the convenience of shopping, and the Web is fast becoming the solution they seek. Increasingly, customers view shopping as an unpleasant chore that cuts into already scarce leisure time, and they are embracing anything that reduces the amount of time they must spend shopping. (One study of New York shoppers by Visa reports that 42 percent of people prefer to clean their bathrooms and 18 percent would rather visit the dentist than stand in a checkout line![8]) Entrepreneurs who tap into customers' need to buy goods more conveniently and with less hassle are winning the battle for market share.
- ▣ ***The power to track sales results.*** The Web gives businesses the power to track virtually any kind of activity on their Web sites, from the number of visitors to the click-through rates on their banner ads. With modern Web analytics tools, entrepreneurs can track not only the number of visitors to their sites, but also how they got there, how they maneuver around the site, and what they buy. Web entrepreneurs can experiment with different designs and layouts for their sites to determine their impact on the site's sales.
- ▣ ***The opportunity to build credibility and a brand identity among customers.*** Many entrepreneurs who operate off-line businesses have discovered that launching a Web site enhances their company's reputation among existing and potential customers. A well-designed Web site can help a small company differentiate itself from its competitors, especially those that lack Web sites. One business writer says, "A company that neglects its Web site may be committing commercial suicide. A Web site is increasingly becoming the gateway to a company's brand, products, and services—even if the firm does not sell online."[9]

ENTREPRENEURIAL
Profile

*Jesse and Anne Heap:
Pink Cake Box*

Anne Heap, co-owner of Pink Cake Box Bakery, works on an edible high-heel shoe that is part of a custom-made cake.

Source: Mike Derer/AP Wide World Photos

In 2005, Jesse and Anne Heap launched Pink Cake Box, a bakery in Denville, New Jersey, that specializes in custom-made cakes, cupcakes, and cookies. They immediately set up a Web site and started a blog that now reach tens of thousands of customers each month. Recognizing that the Web was a powerful yet low-cost way to connect with their customers, the Heaps devoted significant effort during start up to building a meaningful online presence. Still, "I don't think we realized how critical the Web would become to our business," admits Jesse. "It's been crucial to building the business and driving customer growth. The majority of our customers originate through the Web." The Pink Cake Box blog also has been an integral part of the company's success. "To differentiate ourselves, we used our blog to promote our cakes and offer customers and cake enthusiasts a constant stream of new cakes, contests, and videos," says Anne, the company's cake designer and pastry chef. "Our goal was to stay connected to our customers and to foster strong brand recognition." The rich content of the Pink Cake Box Web site, which includes photographs and videos of many of the company's astonishing cakes (which start at $250), customer testimonials, information about cake-making classes, and a link to the blog, has produced a site that is highly visible in search engines and that brings in customers. "The blog receives upwards of 120,000 unique visitors per month and drives a large percentage of our orders," says Jesse. The Heaps are developing plans to launch a retail shop and international versions of their Web site and blog. "It takes time to build a strong Web presence," says Jesse, "but once you gain momentum, the site's popularity will sustain your business."[10]

Source: www.CartoonStock.com

"Ya, right. Who needs a Web presence. I'll just compete in the global economy from here."

Factors to Consider Before Launching into E-Commerce

2. Understand the factors an entrepreneur should consider before launching into e-commerce.

Despite the many benefits the Web offers, not every small business owner has embraced e-commerce. According to a study by advertising and marketing firm Ad-ology, just 54 percent of small companies have Web sites, nearly double the percentage that were operating online in 2007.[11] Even more surprising, 46 percent of small business owners in a Discover Small Business Watch survey say that not every company needs a Web site![12] Why are so many small companies hesitant to use the Web as a business tool? For many entrepreneurs, the key barrier is not knowing where or how to start an e-commerce effort, whereas for others cost concerns are a major issue. Other roadblocks include the fear that customers will not use the Web site and the problems associated with ensuring online security.

Whatever the size of their companies, entrepreneurs are realizing that establishing a presence on the Web is no longer a luxury. "A Web site is your ticket to get into the game," says the CEO of one high-tech company. "If you don't have one, you might as well not even name your business."[13] Indeed, business owners who are not at least considering creating a Web presence or integrating the Web creatively into their operations are putting their companies at risk. However, before launching an e-commerce effort business owners should consider the following important issues:

- How a company exploits the Web's interconnectivity and the opportunities it creates to transform relationships with its suppliers and vendors, its customers, and other external stakeholders is crucial to its success.
- Web success requires a company to develop a plan for integrating the Web into its overall strategy. The plan should address issues such as site design and maintenance, creating and managing a brand name, marketing and promotional strategies, sales, and customer service.
- Developing deep, lasting relationships with customers takes on even greater importance on the Web. Attracting customers on the Web costs money, and companies must be able to retain their online customers to make their Web sites profitable.
- Creating a meaningful presence on the Web requires an ongoing investment of resources—time, money, energy, and talent. Establishing an attractive Web site brimming with catchy photographs of products is only the beginning.
- Measuring the success of its Web-based sales effort is essential to remaining relevant to customers whose tastes, needs, and preferences are always changing.

Doing business on the Web takes more time and energy than many entrepreneurs think. Answering the following questions helps entrepreneurs make sure they are ready to do business on the Web and avoid unpleasant surprises in their e-commerce efforts:

- What exactly do you expect a Web site to do for your company? Will it provide information only, reach new customers, increase sales to existing customers, generate sales from foreign customers, improve communication with customers, enhance customer service, or reduce your company's cost of operation?
- How much can you afford to invest in an e-commerce effort?
- What rate of return do you expect to earn on that investment?
- How long can you afford to wait for that return?
- How well suited are your products and services to sell on the Web?
- How will the "back office" of your Web site work? Will you tie your Web site directly into your company's inventory-control system?
- How will you handle order fulfillment? Can your current fulfillment system handle the increase in volume you are expecting?
- What impact, if any, will your Web site have on your company's traditional channels of distribution?
- What mechanism will your site use to ensure secure customer transactions?
- How will your company handle customer service for the site? What provisions will you make for returned items?
- How do you plan to promote the site to draw traffic to it?
- What information will you collect from the visitors to your site? How will you use it? Will you tell visitors how you intend to use this information?
- Have you developed a privacy policy? Have you posted that policy on your company's Web site for customers?
- Have you tested your site with real, live customers to make sure that it is easy to navigate and easy to order from?
- How will you measure the success of your company's Web site? What objectives have you set for the site?

IN THE ENTREPRENEURIAL
SPOTLIGHT   An E-Commerce Strategy That Fits

Warren Bennett had always enjoyed wearing fine suits, but his appreciation for a fine-fitting suit became the genesis of a business idea when he purchased several custom-made wool suits from the Tulsi Tailoring Family while performing volunteer work at a small school in Nepal. When Bennett returned to his home in the United Kingdom, he reconnected with an old school friend, David Hathiramani, who also appreciated well-made suits. The duo decided to combine their engineering and software training to create A Suit That Fits (ASTF), a company whose goal is to combine technology and fine tailoring to give customers custom-made suits at off-the-rack prices. Bennett and Hathiramani tested their business idea at the Hampstead Market, a small street market in London, and within 20 minutes had sold two suits. Recognizing that their idea had potential, they quickly created a Web site (*www.asuitthatfits.com*) and used credit cards to cover the start-up costs of their business.

To achieve the ideal fit, customers can go to one of the company's 22 measuring and fitting centers across the United Kingdom, have a tailor come to them for a custom fitting if they live in or around London, or use an innovative online measurement wizard that allows them to input their exact measurements. The Web-based Style Wizard offers customers complete control over the details of their suits—from the type of pockets to the color of the buttons—even if they cannot meet with a tailor in person. It also allows them to narrow the more than 40 billion possible suit combinations to the exact specifications they want. Nearly 85 percent of the company's existing customers go online to reorder. The suits—both men's and women's—are made in Kathmandu, Nepal, by a small group of expert tailors, with final adjustments made in London. Suit prices start at just £200 (about $310) an incredible bargain for a hand-tailored garment.

The fast-growing company now employs more than 30 people in London and 85 in Nepal. A Suit That Fits reflects the founders' ethical values and operates in a socially responsible manner. The company makes a concerted effort to live up to its mission statement: "A Suit That Fits believes in building long-term relationships through responsible business—achieving commercial success while incorporating ethical values and respect for people, communities, and the environment." The company's tailors in Nepal receive salaries that are 50 percent above the national average and receive incentive bonuses.

ASTF also donates 5 percent of its production costs to a school in Kathmandu, recently providing funding for a new science lab and a computer lab. At its London operation, ASTF works hard to keep employees engaged, providing them with a dedicated place to socialize and an "ideas wall," where anyone can post innovative ideas and suggestions for improvement. Bennett and Hathiramani also hold weekly team meetings to share information with their employees and to listen to their concerns. ASTF also donates sample suits to two charities in London that help homeless men find work.

The young entrepreneurs behind ASTF maximize the cost advantages that operating on the Web and sourcing their products to their connections in Nepal provide them. They also recognize the importance of using guerrilla marketing techniques, including using social networking sites such as Facebook and Twitter, to promote their business. "We want to think strategically about how we use social media and develop a consistent tone of voice across all customer touch points," says Hathiramani. ASTF usually ranks at the top on Google searches for "tailored suits." The company also has made suits for British celebrities and for Sultan Kosen, the world's tallest man, who stands 8 feet, 1 inch tall.

With its e-commerce strategy in place, ASTF, which generates nearly $3.1 million in annual sales, has a bright future. The company recently won Dell's Global Small Business Excellence Award, which awards $50,000 worth of Dell products and services to small companies that use technology in innovative ways to improve the customer experience and to grow. In just 3 years, ASTF has more than 20,000 customers, and the founders' goal is to use their Web site to add another 15,000 customers, most of them outside the United Kingdom, within 1 year. "We'll be putting our Dell prize to work to streamline productivity, reach more customers around the world, foster innovation, and build an infrastructure that can support our long-term growth," says Bennett. "The possibilities are endless."

1. How does the Internet allow small companies such as A Suit That Fits to achieve rapid growth and sales success so quickly? Do you think the company would have been as successful as it is without its e-commerce strategy? Explain.
2. Several competitors have entered the market, trying to duplicate ASTF's strategy. What steps do you

recommend Bennett and Hathiramani take to maintain their competitive advantage? How can they connect with their customers more effectively? What challenges does a company that makes tailor-made suits face by conducting a significant portion of its business online?

Sources: Based on "A Suit That Fits Business Income Doubles," *Telegraph*, January 19, 2010, *www.telegraph.co.uk/finance/businessclub/sales/7028017/*

A-Suit-That-Fits-business-income-doubles.html; Dan Martin, "British Start-Up Named World's Best Small Business," *Business Zone*, December 17, 2009, *www.businesszone.co.uk/topic/business-trends/tailoring-start-named-worlds-best-small-business*; "Label Spotlight: A Suit That Fits.com," *Commerce with a Conscience*, January 21, 2010, *www.commercewithaconscience.info/2010/01/21/label-spotlight-a-suit-that-fits/*; "2009 U.K. Winner: A Suit That Fits," Dell Entrepreneur Excellence Award, Dell Inc., September 2009, *www.dellhero.com/uk/country-winner.asp*; Dan Martin, "Back to the Floor: A Small Business in Action," *Business Zone*, April 13, 2010, *www.businesszone.co.uk/topic/business-trends/back-floor-small-business-action/27689.*

Ten Myths of E-Commerce

3. Explain the 10 myths of e-commerce and how to avoid falling victim to them.

Although many entrepreneurs have boosted their businesses with e-commerce, setting up shop on the Web is no guarantee of success. Scores of entrepreneurs have plunged unprepared into the world of e-commerce only to discover that there is more to it than merely setting up a Web site and waiting for the orders to start pouring in. Make sure that you do not fall victim to one of the following e-commerce myths.

Myth 1. If I Launch a Site, Customers Will Flock to It

Some entrepreneurs think that once they set up their Web sites, their expenses end there. Not true! Without promotional support, no Web site will draw enough traffic to support a business. With an estimated 600 billion Web pages already in existence and the number of new Web documents growing by 6 million per day, getting a site noticed has become increasingly difficult. Experts estimate that only about half of the Web's content is indexed and therefore retrievable by search engines.[14] Merely listing a site with popular Web search engines cannot guarantee that Web users will find a small company's site. Just like traditional retail stores seeking to attract customers, virtual companies have discovered that drawing sufficient traffic to a Web site requires promotion—and lots of it! "No one will know you're on the Web unless you tell them and motivate them to visit," explains Mark Layton, owner of a Web-based distributor of computer supplies and author of a book on e-commerce.[15]

Entrepreneurs with both physical and virtual stores must promote their Web sites at every opportunity by printing their URLs on everything related to their physical stores—on signs, in print and broadcast ads, in store windows, on shopping bags, on merchandise labels, and anywhere else their customers might see it. Virtual shop owners should consider buying ads in traditional advertising media as well as using banner ads, banner exchange programs, and cross-marketing arrangements with companies selling complementary products on their Web sites. Other techniques include creating some type of interactivity with customers, such as a Web-based newsletter, posting a video about the company's products on YouTube, writing articles that link to the company's site, hosting a chat room that allows customers to interact with one another and with company personnel, incorporating a bulletin board or customer-generated reviews, establishing a blog, or sponsoring a contest. For instance, one small pet store has had success promoting both its Web site and its retail store with Howl-O-Ween, an online photo contest featuring people's dogs dressed in Halloween costumes.

Blogs are easy to create, but they require regular updating with fresh content to attract visitors. BlogPulse, a company that tracks blogs, estimates that the Web hosts more than 143 million blogs.[16] Blogs with fresh, entertaining content and a soft-sell approach can be an effective way to draw potential customers to a company's Web site. Podcasts, video versions of blogs, are another attention-getting tool for a small company's Web site.

ENTREPRENEURIAL
Profile
Andrew Lock: GotBiz.TV

Andrew Lock, who launched a Web-based television business, GotBiz.TV, from his Utah home, got his start with a podcast aimed at entrepreneurs called "Help! My Business Sucks!" With a blend of clever humor, sharp wit, and business know-how, Lock's 10-minute podcasts offer entrepreneurs useful advice on a variety of topics. More than 100,000 viewers from around the world tune into Lock's online broadcast each week.[17]

The key to promoting a Web site successfully is networking, building relationships with customers, bloggers, social media, trade associations, online directories, and other Web sites a company's customers visit. "You need to create relationships with the businesses and people with whom you share common customers," says Barbara Ling, author of a book on e-commerce. "Then you need to create links between sites to help customers find what they are looking for."[18]

Myth 2. Online Customers Are Easy to Please

Customers who shop online today tend to be experienced Internet users whose expectations for their online shopping experiences are high and continue to rise. Experienced online shoppers tend to be unforgiving, quickly clicking to another site if their shopping experience is subpar or if they cannot find the products and information they want. Because Web shoppers are becoming more discriminating, companies are finding that they must improve their Web sites to attract and keep their customers.

To be successful online marketers, small companies must create Web sites with the features that appeal to experienced Web shoppers, such as simple navigation, customer reviews, rock-solid security, and quick access to product information, videos, and blogs. Many small businesses outsource most (sometimes all) of the activities associated with conducting business online to companies that specialize in e-commerce services. These companies prefer to focus on their core competencies—product design, marketing, extending a brand, manufacturing, and others—and hire other companies whose core competencies reside in e-commerce to handle Web site design, hosting, order processing, and order fulfillment ("pick, pack, and ship"). Rather than make constant investments in technology that may not produce a reasonable return, these small companies preserve their capital and their energy and focus them on the aspects of business that they do best. Other entrepreneurs prefer to keep the design and operation of their Web sites in house.

Myth 3. Making Money on the Web Is Easy

Promoters who hawk "get-rich-quick" schemes on the Web lure many entrepreneurs with the promise that making money on the Web is easy. It isn't. Doing business online can be quite lucrative, but it takes time and requires an up-front investment. As hundreds of new Web sites spring up every day, getting a company's site noticed requires more effort and marketing muscle than ever before.

Entrepreneurs engaging in e-commerce recognize the power that the Internet gives customers. Pricing, for example, is no longer as simple as it once was for companies. Auction sites such as eBay and Priceline.com mean that entrepreneurs can no longer be content to take into account only local competitors when setting their own prices. With the Web, price transparency is now the rule of the day. With a few mouse clicks, customers can compare the prices of the same or similar products and services from companies across the globe. In this wired and connected economy, the balance of power has shifted to customers, and new business models recognize this fact.

Myth 4. Privacy Is Not an Important Issue on the Web

The Web allows companies to gain access to almost unbelievable amounts of information about their customers. Many sites offer visitors "freebies" in exchange for information about themselves. Companies then use this information to learn more about their target customers and how to market to them most effectively. Concerns over the privacy of and the use of this information have become the topic of debate by many interested parties, including government agencies, consumer watchdog groups, customers, and industry trade associations.

Companies that collect information from their online customers have a responsibility to safeguard their customers' privacy, to protect it from unauthorized use, and to use it responsibly. That means that businesses should post a privacy statement on their Web sites, explaining to customers how they intend to use the information they collect. One of the surest ways to alienate online customers is to experience a security breach that allows their personal information to be stolen, to abuse the information collected from them by selling it to third parties, or to spam customers with unwanted solicitations. A recent survey by PayPal and comScore reports that 21 percent of online shoppers have abandoned their shopping carts because of security concerns.[19] BBBOnLine offers a useful resource center (*www.bbbonline.org/UnderstandingPrivacy/PMRC/*) that is designed to help small business owners who want to establish or upgrade their Web site's privacy policies.

Businesses that publish privacy policies and then adhere to them build trust among their customers, an important facet of doing business on the Web. According to John Briggs, director of e-commerce for the Yahoo! Network, customers "need to trust the brand they are buying and believe that their online purchases will be safe transactions. They need to feel comfortable that [their] personal data will not be sold and that they won't get spammed by giving their e-mail address. They need to know about shipping costs, product availability, and return policies up front."[20] Privacy *does* matter on the Web, and businesses that respect their customers' privacy will win their customers' trust. Trust is the foundation on which companies build the long-term customer relationships that are so crucial to Web success.

Myth 5. "Strategy? I Don't Need a Strategy to Sell on the Web! Just Give Me a Web Site, and the Rest Will Take Care of Itself."

Building a successful e-business is no different than building a successful brick-and-mortar business, and that requires a well-thought-out strategy. Building a strategy means that an entrepreneur must first develop a clear definition of the company's target audience and a thorough understanding of customers' needs, wants, likes, and dislikes. To be successful, a Web site must be appealing to the customers it seeks to attract just as a traditional store's design and décor must draw foot traffic. Before your Web site can become the foundation for a successful e-business, you must create it with your target audience in mind.

One goal of developing a strategy is to set a business apart from its competitors. The same is true for creating a strategy for conducting business online. It is just as important, if not more important, for an online business to differentiate itself from the competition if it is to be successful. Unlike customers in a retail store, who must exert the effort to go to a competitor's store if they cannot find what they want, online customers only have to make a mouse click or two to go to a rival Web site. Therefore, competition online is fierce, and to succeed a company must have a sound strategy.

ENTREPRENEURIAL Profile

Nick Swinmurn: Zappos

Zappos, the largest online shoe retailer, founded in 1999 by Nick Swinmurn after a frustrating and fruitless trip to a local mall in search of shoes, offers online customers a huge selection of shoes, including dress and athletic shoes for men and women, extra-wide shoes for hard-to-fit feet, and even "vegetarian" shoes made from materials other than leather. Zappos' strategy is simple: offer customers the greatest variety and selection of shoes possible to gain an edge over brick-and-mortar stores that are limited in the stock that they can carry and offer stellar customer service. Zappos, now owned by Amazon.com, stocks more than 90,000 styles in a wide array of sizes of more than 500 brands for a total inventory of nearly 2 million pairs of shoes. As part of Zappos' commitment to customer service, the company offers free expedited shipping (even on shoes that customers return) and a sophisticated warehouse system that provides shoppers real-time information on the availability of any particular shoe. Tony Hsieh, CEO and majority owner, says that Zappos' focus on its customers (evidenced by its free-shipping policy, which costs more than $100 million annually) is the reason that 65 percent of Zappos shoppers are repeat customers. Its strategy is working. The Las Vegas–based company reached $1 billion in sales in just 10 years.[21]

Myth 6. The Most Important Part of Any E-Commerce Effort Is Technology

Although understanding the technology of e-commerce is an important part of the formula for success, it is *not* the most crucial ingredient. What matters most is the ability to understand the underlying business and to develop a workable business model that offers customers something of value at a reasonable price while producing a reasonable return for the company. The entrepreneurs who are proving to be most successful in e-commerce are those who know how their industries work inside and out and then build an e-business around that knowledge. They know that they can hire Web designers, database experts, and fulfillment companies to create the technical aspects of their online businesses, but that nothing can substitute for a solid understanding of their industry, their target market, and the strategy needed to pull the various parts together. The key is seeing the Web for what it really is: another way to reach and serve customers with an effective business model and to minimize the cost of doing business.

Tony Hsieh, CEO of Zappos, the online shoe retailer, has created collaborative relationships with the company's vendors and suppliers using the Web, including giving them information that most retailers would never share about sales, inventory levels, and profits. Vendors work in tandem with Zappos' buyers via the Internet to manage inventory and generate sales and "have complete visibility into our business," says Fred Mossler, head of the company's merchandising team. "The benefits we've reaped from building relationships with our vendors are endless," he says. "They help us plan our business and make sure that we have enough of the right product at the right time. They help procure inventory on hot-selling items. Sometimes they provide unique items that can be found only on Zappos. They work closely with our marketing team to plan the right campaigns."[22]

Unfortunately, many entrepreneurs tackle e-commerce by focusing on technology first and then determine how that technology fits their business idea. "If you start with technology, you're likely going to buy a solution in search of a problem," says Kip Martin, program director of META Group's Electronic Business Strategies. Instead, he suggests, "Start with the business and ask yourself what you want to happen and how you'll measure it. *Then* ask how the technology will help you achieve your goals. Remember: Business first, technology second."[23]

Myth 7. On the Web, Customer Service Is Not as Important as It Is in a Traditional Retail Store

The Web offers shoppers the ultimate in convenience. With just a few mouse clicks, people can shop for practically anything anywhere in the world and have it delivered to their doorsteps within days. In fact, 78 percent of online customers say that they prefer shopping online because it is more convenient than other shopping methods.[24] As convenient as online shopping is, customers still expect high levels of service. Unfortunately, many e-commerce companies treat customer service as an afterthought, an attitude that costs businesses in many ways, including lost customers and a diminished public image. In one study, 79 percent of shoppers who had experienced a frustrating online shopping experience reported that they were not likely to return to the online store. The study also revealed 27 percent of shoppers said that they were less likely to shop at the retailer's physical store.[25]

The average conversion rate for e-commerce sites is just 3.2 percent.[26] In other words, out of 1,000 visitors to the typical company's Web site, just 32 of them actually make a purchase! Sites that are difficult to navigate, slow to load, offer complex checkout systems, or confuse shoppers will turn customers away quickly, never to return. Online merchants must recognize that customer service is just as important (if not more so) on the Web as it is in traditional brick-and-mortar stores.

There is plenty of room for improvement in customer service on the Web. Research by PayPal and comScore shows that 45 percent of Web shoppers who fill their online shopping carts abandon them without checking out and that the average value of the goods in their carts is $109.[27] The most common reasons for leaving a site without purchasing include the following: (1) shipping and handling charges were too high (46 percent), (2) the customer was simply comparison shopping (37 percent), (3) the total cost of the items was higher than the customer anticipated (36 percent), and (4) the customer wanted to either look for a coupon or to make the purchase off-line (27 percent). Even more alarming is the fact that 47 percent of the owners of e-businesses do not know their sites' shopping cart abandonment rate.[28]

When customers do abandon their online shopping carts, companies often can close a significant percentage of those sales by sending a prompt follow-up e-mail designed to win back the customer. One survey by Listrak, an e-mail marketing company, reports that just 11 percent of e-commerce companies send follow-up e-mails to customers who have abandoned their shopping carts.[29] The benefits from doing so can be significant, however. A study by Experian CheetahMail indicates that follow-up e-mails to customers who abandon their carts produce 20 times the transaction rates and revenue of their traditional e-mail marketing campaigns.[30]

Rockler Woodworking and Hardware, founded in 1954, sells specialty hardware, tools, and woodworking products through its 30 retail stores, a catalog, and its Web site (*www.rockler.com*), which the company has been operating since 1996. Recognizing the potential that abandoned online shopping carts represented, Rockler began sending automated e-mails to shoppers who left their carts without checking out. The e-mails, which contain no incentives (45 percent of companies that send follow-up e-mails offer some kind of incentive), recaptured so many of the company's lost sales that the initiative now accounts for 2 percent of Rockler's total sales![31]

The lesson for e-commerce entrepreneurs is simple: Devote time, energy, and money to developing a functional mechanism for providing superior customer service. Those who do will build a sizeable base of loyal customers who will keep coming back. Perhaps the most significant actions online companies can take to bolster their customer service efforts are to provide a quick, intuitive online checkout process, create a well-staffed and well-trained customer response team, offer a simple return process, and provide an easy order-tracking process so customers can check the status of their orders at any time.

LESSONS FROM THE STREET-SMART ➤ entrepreneur

How to Reduce Your Company's Shopping Cart Abandonment Rate

Nearly half of all online shoppers abandon their shopping carts without completing their transactions. This chapter points out the reasons customers abandon their carts. Sometimes they are merely window shopping or just change their minds, but, more often than not, the cause has more to do with a company's Web site, purchase process, or perceived lack of security or customer service. E-commerce entrepreneurs can reduce the likelihood that customers will leave their companies' Web sites frustrated and unlikely to return by taking the following tips from the Street-Smart Entrepreneur:

- Consider providing free shipping if a customer's order exceeds some minimum purchase. Research by Wharton professor David Bell shows that companies that want to fill relatively few orders should establish higher free-shipping thresholds; firms that want customers to visit regularly—perhaps so that they can sell ads on their site—should use lower shipping thresholds. More than 60 percent of online retailers say that providing free shipping (with conditions) is their most successful marketing tool.
- If you do not offer free shipping, provide multiple shipping methods and be sure to include a table that shows shoppers the cost of each shipping option—and do it early in the checkout process.
- Label the cart button "add to cart" rather than "buy now" or "purchase." "Buy now" and similar language creates in customers' minds the impression that their decision is irreversible. The reality is that the average delay between a customer's first visit to a site and the final purchase is 33 hours and 54 minutes.
- Reassure customers that their personal information is safe and that their transaction is secure. Security concerns cause 21 percent of Web shoppers to abandon their carts. Many customers look for sites that have been certified as secure by a reliable third-party service such as the Better Business Bureau, VeriSign, TRUSTe, McAfee, and others. Make sure that shoppers feel secure from their first click on your site.
- Make sure that your site presents an image of credibility. E-businesses must communicate their trustworthiness by providing highly visible privacy policies, customer satisfaction guarantees, exchange and return policies, and contact information. For small companies, including a telephone number and a physical address are important. Photographs of the owners and employees help, too.
- Reduce the number of steps required to complete the checkout process. Just as in regular retail stores, online customers appreciate a quick, efficient checkout process that is as simple as possible. A convoluted checkout process is an invitation to customers to abandon their shopping carts.
- Once shoppers have filled their carts, make sure that the "checkout" button is easy to find. Label it clearly and put it in a prominent location.
- Include a progress indicator on each checkout page. Clearly numbering the steps in the process and letting customers know where they are in that process improves customer-retention rates during checkout.

- Provide a link back to the items in the customers' shopping cart. This allows customers to return to the product page to make sure they have selected the correct item without losing their place in the check-out process.
- Allow customers to see whether an item is in stock on the product page. Customers become frustrated when they learn that an item is out of stock *after* having clicked through most or all of the checkout process.
- Include product photos in the shopping cart. Research shows that simply including product photos increases a company's conversion rate by as much as 10 percent.
- Make it easy for customers to change the contents of their shopping carts. The cart page should allow customers to change quantities, colors, sizes, and other options or to delete an item from the cart (believe it or not!) with just one mouse click.
- Give customers the option of calling to resolve problems they encounter during checkout. A toll-free line enables a company to track the number of problem-solving calls, which can point out flaws in the design of the Web site or the checkout process.
- Make it easy for customers to pay for their online purchases. Credit cards are the most popular online payment method (55 percent of all transactions), but many small online merchants do not generate enough revenue to justify the costs of gaining credit card merchant status. If a small company's credit card sales are no more than $250 per month, a credit card company charges about 35 percent of each transaction, compared to just 3 to 5 percent of monthly credit card sales of at least $7,500 per month. Electronic payment services such as Google's Checkout or PayPal, which is owned by eBay, allow customers to send payments to anyone with an e-mail address through their checking accounts or their credit cards. Customers who sign up for the free service can use their PayPal accounts to buy products online conveniently, and PayPal charges the company making the sale a fee that ranges from 1.9 to 2.9 percent of the transaction, depending on its monthly transaction volume. When a merchant signs on with PayPal, it simply adds PayPal's "Buy Now" button to its site, which customers click to pay with their PayPal accounts.

Kurt Denke and Pam Moore launched Blue Jeans Cable, a company that sells high-quality video and audio cables and connectors as a part-time, home-based, eBay business. Sales grew quickly, and in 2002 the copreneurs decided to launch their own Web site, but they needed a low-cost, convenient, and secure payment-processing system. "We looked at all kinds of payment processing solutions," recalls Denke. "The initial fees to set up a merchant [account] and payment processing gateway were just too much." Denke and Moore settled on PayPal, which charges no up-front or monthly fees, offers very competitive processing rates, and provides a free shopping cart tool. The couple frequently download their merchant sales report and analyze it to understand better their customers' buying habits. Denke and Moore's home-based business has "exceeded our wildest expectations," says Denke. Sales are rising fast, and 95 percent of Blue Jeans Cable's sales are processed through PayPal.

- Encourage user reviews and reward customers who provide them. User reviews can be an important selling tool online. When shoppers read about the positive experiences that customers have had with a company, they are more likely to make purchases.
- Incorporate a short survey of randomly chosen customers who abandon their shopping carts. The results can help you to improve their online shopping experience and lower your cart abandonment rates.

Sources: Based on Terry Jukes, "8 Best Practices for Reducing Shopping Cart Abandonment," E-Marketing and Commerce, February 12, 2009, *www.emarketingandcommerce.com/article/8-best-practices-reducing-shopping-cart-abandonment/1*; Bryan Eisenberg, "20 Tips to Minimize Shopping Cart Abandonment, Part 1," ClickZ, August 8, 2003, pp. 1–2; Bryan Eisenberg, "20 Tips to Minimize Shopping Cart Abandonment, Part 2," ClickZ, August 15, 2003, pp. 1–2; "Reasons Why Web Site Visitors Abandoned Their Shopping Carts," SeeWhy, June 3, 2010, *http://seewhy.com/blog/2010/06/03/reasons-why-website-visitors-abandoned-their-shopping-carts/*; "Digital Window Shopping: The Long Journey to 'Buy'" (Santa Clara, CA: McAfee, 2009), pp. 3–4; "Customer Case Study: Blue Jeans Cable," PayPal, 2006, *www.paypal.com/en_US/pdf/bluejeanscableCaseStudy.pdf*; Sally Lowery, "Got the Shopping Cart Blues?" Bronto Software Inc., 2009.

Myth 8. Flashy Web Sites Are Better Than Simple Ones

Businesses that fall into this trap pour significant amounts of money into designing flashy Web sites with all of the "bells and whistles." The logic is that to stand out on the Web a site really has to sparkle. That logic leads to a "more is better" mentality when designing a site. On the Web, however, "more" does *not* necessarily equate to "better." A Web site that performs efficiently and loads quickly is essential to online retail success. Although fancy graphics, photographs, music, bright colors, and spinning icons can attract attention, sites filled with "cornea gumbo" are distracting, slow to download, and generally ineffective. Sites that download slowly usually never have the chance to sell because customers click to another site. A study by Forrester Research and Akamai concludes that the new threshold for Web site download times is just 2 seconds and that 40 percent of online shoppers will wait no longer than 3 seconds for a Web site to load before moving on to another site.[32] A study by TagMan, a company that specializes in digital tracking and reporting, reports that a 1-second delay in a Web page loading results in 10 percent of users abandoning the page. "Businesses do not understand the impact of poor site performance," warns Brian Walker, an analyst at Forrester Research. "Customers not only will bail out on a session or a [shopping] cart, but they also may not return." Walker points out that the company's research shows that more than 25 percent of customers are less likely to shop at a company's brick-and-mortar store if they have a bad experience online.[33] The lesson: Keep the design of your site simple so that pages download in no more than 2 or 3 seconds and make sure that it performs effectively.

Myth 9. It's What's Up Front That Counts

Designing an attractive Web site is important to building a successful e-business. However, designing the back office, the systems that take over once a customer places an order on a Web site, is just as important as designing the site itself. If the behind-the-scenes support is not in place or cannot handle the traffic from the Web site, a company's entire e-commerce effort will come crashing down. Although e-commerce can lower many costs of doing business, it still requires a basic infrastructure somewhere in the channel of distribution to process orders, maintain inventory, fill orders, and handle customer service. Many entrepreneurs hoping to launch virtual businesses are discovering the need for a "click-and-mortar" approach to provide the necessary infrastructure to serve their customers. "The companies with warehouses, supply-chain management, and solid customer service are going to be the ones that survive," says Daryl Plummer, head of the Gartner Group's Internet and New Media division.[34]

To customers, a business is only as good as its last order, and many e-companies are not measuring up. Many small e-tailers' Web sites do not offer real-time inventory lookup, which gives online shoppers the ability to see whether an item they want to purchase is actually in stock. In addition, many have not yet linked their Web sites to an automated back office, which means that processing orders takes longer and that errors are more likely. As software to integrate Web sites with the back office becomes easier to use and more affordable, more small businesses will use them to offer these features.

ENTREPRENEURIAL
Profile

David Cox: Fragrances of Ireland

Fragrances of Ireland, a small company founded in 1983 in the village of Kilmacanogue, Ireland, by Brian Cox and Donald Pratt, sells a line of Irish perfumes, colognes, soaps, and toiletries across Ireland, the United Kingdom, Canada, and the United States. The fast-growing company sells its products in more than 300 stores in Ireland and the United Kingdom and on its Web site (*www.perfume.ie*) but was falling farther behind on its deliveries as volume increased. Current owner David Cox was struggling to manage the company's inventory because reports were inaccurate and outdated. Cox turned to Webgistix, an order fulfillment company, which helped the company implement a Web-based order fulfillment system that allows managers to view orders, check inventory levels, and generate customized reports anytime. Fragrances of Ireland's new system has enabled the company to gain control of its inventory and to speed up delivery times by getting orders out the same day that customers place them.[35]

Web-based entrepreneurs often discover that the greatest challenge their businesses face is not necessarily attracting customers on the Web but creating a workable order fulfillment strategy. Order fulfillment involves everything required to get goods from a warehouse into a customer's hands and includes order processing, warehousing, picking and packing, shipping, and billing. Some entrepreneurs choose to handle order fulfillment in-house with their own employees, whereas others find it more economical to hire specialized fulfillment houses to handle these functions. **Virtual order fulfillment** (or drop-shipping) suits many e-tailers perfectly. When a customer orders a product from its Web site, the company forwards the order to its wholesaler or distributor, which then ships the product to the customer with the online merchant's label on it.

Although e-tailers avoid the risks and problems associated with managing inventory, they lose control over delivery times and service quality. In addition, for some small businesses, finding a fulfillment house willing to handle a relatively small volume of orders at a reasonable price can be difficult. Major fulfillment providers that focus on small companies include Amazon.com, FedEx, UPS, DHL, ShipWire, Webgistix, and WeFulfillIT.com.

Myth 10. It's Too Late to Get on the Web

A common myth, especially among small business owners, is that those companies that have not yet moved onto the Web have missed a golden opportunity. One Internet entrepreneur who has launched two multimillion-dollar companies, compares e-commerce to the California gold rush in the mid-nineteenth century, "The [e-commerce] landscape looks like California must have looked in 1850. The gold rush is over, and the easy money is gone. However, much more gold was mined in California after 1850 than before; so it is with e-commerce. Enormous opportunities are still available online to those smart enough to take advantage of them."[36] The reality is that e-commerce is still very young, and companies are still figuring out how to succeed on the Web. For every e-commerce site that exists, many others have failed. An abundance of online business opportunities exists for those entrepreneurs insightful enough to spot them and clever enough to capitalize on them.

One fact of e-commerce that has emerged is the importance of speed. Companies doing business on the Web have discovered that those who reach customers first often have a significant advantage over their slower rivals. "The lesson of the Web is not how the big eat the small, but how the fast eat the slow," says a manager at a venture capital firm specializing in Web-based companies.[37] Succumbing to this myth often leads entrepreneurs to make a fundamental mistake once they finally decide to go online: They believe they have to have a "perfect" site before they can launch it. Few businesses get their sites "right" the first time. In fact, the most successful e-commerce sites are constantly changing, removing what does not work and adding new features to see what does. Successful Web sites are much like a well-designed flower garden, constantly growing and improving, yet changing to reflect the climate of each season. Their creators worry less about creating the perfect site at the outset than about getting a site online and then fixing it, tweaking it, and updating it to meet changing customer demands.

Strategies for E-Success

4. Explain the basic strategies entrepreneurs should follow to achieve success in their e-commerce efforts.

The typical Internet user in the United States spends an average of 13.2 hours a week online, almost as much time as the average person spends each week watching television. However, converting these Web users into paying customers requires a business to do more than merely set up a Web site and wait for the hits to start rolling in. Doing business from a Web site is like setting up shop on a dead-end street or a back alley. You may be ready to sell, but no one knows you are there! Building sufficient volume for a site takes energy, time, money, creativity, and, perhaps most important, a well-defined strategy. Many entrepreneurs choose to start their e-commerce efforts small and simply and then expand them as sales grow and their needs become more sophisticated. Others make major investments in creating full-blown, interconnected sites at the outset. The cost of e-commerce varies significantly, depending on the options that an entrepreneur chooses. Following are some guidelines for building a successful Web strategy for a small e-company.

Focus on a Niche in the Market

Like Curly, the crusty old trail boss in the movie *City Slickers*, who said that the secret to happiness was "one thing," many small businesses are finding success on the Web by focusing on one thing. Rather than try to compete head-to-head with the dominant players on the Web who have the resources and the recognition to squash smaller competitors, smart entrepreneurs focus on serving market niches. Smaller companies' limited resources usually are better spent serving niche markets than trying to be everything to everyone. The idea is to concentrate on serving a small corner of the market the giants have overlooked. Niches exist in every industry and can be highly profitable, given the right strategy for serving them. A niche can be defined in many ways, including by geography, by customer profile, by product, by product usage, and many others.

Like Curly, the crusty trail boss in *City Slickers* who said that the secret to happiness was "one thing," many small companies are finding success online by focusing on one thing—a market niche.

Source: Photos 12/Alamy Images

ENTREPRENEURIAL
Profile

James Hughes: Caledonian Creations

James Hughes launched Caledonian Creations, a company that specializes in making leather goods such as sporrans (the pouch worn from the belt on the front of a kilt), straps, kilt belts, and Celtic bags, when he was in his early twenties after his business plan helped him win financing from the Prince's Scottish Business Trust, a fund established by the Prince of Wales to help young people in the United Kingdom launch businesses. One disadvantage of a focus strategy is being so narrowly focused that attracting a large enough customer base can be a challenge. Without the power of the Web, it is unlikely that Caledonian Creations, with its highly specialized product line, would be able to survive from its location in Drymen, Scotland![38]

The Web allows small businesses to attract niche customers that would have been impossible to reach in sufficient volume without it. Because of its broad reach, the Web is the ideal mechanism for implementing a focus strategy because small companies can reach large numbers of customers with a common interest.

Develop a Community

On the Web, competitors are just a mouse click away. To attract customers and keep them coming back, e-companies have discovered the need to offer more than just quality products and excellent customer service. Many seek to develop a community of customers with similar interests, the nucleus of which is their Web site. The idea is to increase customer loyalty by giving customers the chance to interact with other like-minded visitors or with experts to discuss and learn more about topics they are passionate about. E-mail lists, chat rooms, customer polls ("What is your favorite sports drink?"), blogs, guest books, and message boards are powerful tools for building a community of visitors at a site because they give visitors the opportunity to have conversations about products, services, and topics that interest them.

Small businesses that are most successful at building a community enlist their most passionate customers as company evangelists. Companies that successfully create a community around their Web sites turn their customers into loyal fans who keep coming back and, better yet, invite others to join them.

Attract Visitors by Giving Away "Freebies"

One of the most important words on the Internet is "free." Many successful e-merchants have discovered the ability to attract visitors to their sites by giving away something free and then selling them something else. One e-commerce consultant calls this cycle of giving something away and then selling something "the rhythm of the Web."[39] The "freebie" must be something that customers value, but it does *not* have to be expensive nor does it have to be a product. In fact, one of the most common giveaways on the Web is *information.* (After all, that's what most people on the Web are after!) Creating a free online or e-mail newsletter with links to your company's site, of course, and to others of interest is one of the most effective ways of drawing potential customers to a site. Meaningful content presented in a clear, professional fashion is a must. Experts advise keeping online newsletters short—no more than about 600 words.

Catherine Bean and Megan Murphy started Bella ("Beautiful, Eclectic, Lovely, Luscious, and Affordable") of Cape Cod in 2004 by selling affordable, fashionable jewelry at home parties. The stay-at-home moms soon realized that the number of jewelry parties they could host was limited by their time, their schedules, and the short New England tourist season. They came up with the creative solution of holding Web-based virtual parties hosted by their online customers. To make their idea work, they needed an inexpensive yet effective way to promote their online parties to customers. Bean and Murphy created a newsletter packed with interesting stories about their jewelry, tips on how to care for it and wear it, and, of course, promotions about their parties and products. The virtual parties were a big hit with customers, and each party resulted in more customers on the company's contact list, which has grown from 1,500 people to nearly 8,100. The e-mail newsletter's open rate is an impressive 30 percent, and Bella's sales, especially in the "off season," have increased significantly.[40]

Make Creative Use of E-Mail, but Avoid Becoming a "Spammer"

Used properly and creatively, e-mail can be an effective, low-cost way to build traffic on a Web site. E-commerce companies cite e-mail as the most effective marketing technique (89 percent), followed by pay-per-click searches (80 percent) and search engine optimization (53 percent).[41] E-mail **click-through rates**, the percentage of recipients who open an e-mail and click the link to the company's Web site, average 6.0 percent.[42] Marketing e-mails sent on Wednesdays have the highest combination of open and click-through rates (see Figure 3). A survey by eROI shows that the best time of day to send marketing e-mails is mid-day, from 10 A.M. to 2 P.M.[43]

Just as with newsletters, an e-mail's content should offer something of value to recipients. Customers welcome well-constructed permission e-mail that directs them to a company's site for information or special deals, unlike unsolicited and universally despised e-mails known as spam. Unfortunately, getting legitimate e-mails noticed has become more challenging for business

FIGURE 3

E-Mail Open and Click-Through Rates by Day of the Week

Source: eROI, 2007.

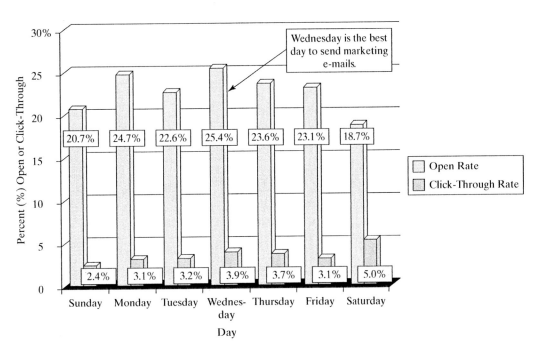

TABLE 1 Does Your E-Mail Measure Up to the Anti-Spam Test?

1. Is the content of your e-mail appropriate for your audience? Are recipients likely to be interested in the offers or articles you are sending? The biggest problem with sales-oriented e-mails and the primary cause of low open and click-through rates is irrelevant content.
2. Does the e-mail offer something of value to recipients—an invitation to a special sale, a free newsletter filled with useful information, or something similar? Sending frivolous e-mails that pack little or no value to customers is one surefire way to send your company's click-through rate plummeting.
3. Has your e-mail provider been blacklisted by spam-screening tools?
4. Have the recipients on your e-mail list opted into your e-mail list? Trolling Internet user lists for e-mail addresses is *not* an acceptable way to build a recipient list.
5. Does the subject line include your company's name? Is the subject line accurate and not misleading? Do *not* include "$$$" in the subject line, as so many spam messages do.
6. Is the e-mail readable? Some e-mails sent in HTML format can appear garbled and unreadable on some computers.
7. Is the frequency of the e-mail appropriate? Customers do not appreciate being hammered by 20 e-mails from a company in 1 week.
8. Is the timing of your e-mail appropriate? Monday mornings, when people are returning to work from the weekend and their inboxes are full of messages, is *not* the best time to send an e-mail.
9. Can recipients opt out of your e-mail list if they choose to?
10. Does the e-mail contain your company's valid mailing address? In 2003, Congress passed the CAN-SPAM Act, which did not ban spam but put limitations on how marketers can use e-mail as part of their marketing tools. This is one of the act's requirements.

owners because spam is on the rise. Symantec, a company that provides online security and software services, estimates that 89.8 percent of all e-mails sent are spam.[44]

Companies often collect visitors' e-mail addresses when they register to receive a "freebie." To be successful at collecting a sufficient number of e-mail addresses, a company must make clear to customers that they will receive messages that are meaningful to them and that the company will not sell e-mail addresses to others (which should be part of its posted privacy policy). Once a company has a customer's permission to send information in additional e-mail messages, it has a meaningful marketing opportunity to create a long-term customer relationship. Table 1 includes a spam test to which every company should submit its e-mail campaigns.

Make Sure Your Web Site Says "Credibility"

Many studies have concluded that trust and security issues are the leading inhibitors of online shopping. Unless a company can build customers' *trust* in its Web site, selling is virtually impossible. Visitors begin to evaluate the credibility of a site as soon as they arrive. In fact, one study says that Web users judge the credibility of a Web site within the first one-twentieth of a second (50 milliseconds)![45] "Windows of opportunity, especially in the online environment, close very quickly," says Jay Bower, president of Crossbow Group, a digital marketing company.[46] Does the site look professional? Are there misspelled words and typographical errors? If the site provides information, does it note the sources of that information? If so, are those sources legitimate? Are they trustworthy? Is the presentation of the information fair and objective, or is it biased? Has the site been updated recently? Does the company include a privacy policy posted in an obvious place?

One of the simplest ways to establish credibility with customers is to use brand names they know and trust. Whether a company sells nationally recognized brands or its own well-known private brand, using those names on its site creates a sense of legitimacy. People buy brand names they trust, and online companies can use that to their advantage. Another effective way to build customer confidence is by joining an online seal program such as TRUSTe or BBBOnLine. The online equivalent of the Underwriter Laboratories stamp or the Good Housekeeping Seal of Approval, these seals mean that a company meets certain standards concerning the privacy of customers' information and the resolution of customer complaints. A survey by *Consumer Reports* shows that 71 percent of customers say that it is important for a Web site they purchase from to display a trust or security seal.[47] Finally, providing a street address, an e-mail address, and a toll-free telephone number sends a subtle message to shoppers that a legitimate business is behind the

Web site. Many small companies include photographs of their brick-and-mortar stores and of their founders and employees to combat the Web's anonymity and to let shoppers know that they are supporting a friendly small business.

Consider Forming Strategic Alliances

Most small companies seeking e-commerce success lack the brand and name recognition that larger, more established companies have. Creating that sort of recognition on the Web requires a significant investment of both time and money, two things that most small companies find scarce. If building name recognition is one of the keys to success on the Web, how can small companies with their limited resources hope to compete? One option is to form strategic alliances with bigger companies that can help a small business achieve what it could not accomplish alone. One expert says, "The question is no longer, 'Should I consider an alliance?' Now the questions are 'What form should the alliance take?' and 'How do I find the right partner?'"[48]

One of the simplest ways to begin forging alliances online is through an **affiliate marketing program**. Also known as *referral* or *associate marketing*, this technique involves an online merchant paying a commission to another online business (the affiliate) for directing customers to the merchant's Web site. As social media have become more important, affiliate marketing has slipped in its popularity. According to the Affiliate Marketing Survey Report, just 15 percent of online merchants say that affiliate marketing drives a high volume of sales for their businesses.[49] Still, Forrester Research predicts that affiliate marketing revenues will increase from $1.9 billion in 2009 to $4 billion in 2014.[50]

Make the Most of the Web's Global Reach

The Internet has reduced dramatically the cost of launching a global business initiative; even the tiniest of businesses can engage in international business with a well-designed Web site. Still, despite the Web's reputation as an international marketplace, many Web entrepreneurs fail to utilize its global reach. Nearly 90 percent of the 1.9 billion people around the world who use the Internet live outside the United States. Only 27.7 percent of Web users speak English.[51] It does not make sense for entrepreneurs to limit their Web sites to just a small percentage of the world because of a language barrier. A top manager at Travelocity, a travel-planning Web site, says that whenever his company adds country-specific features to its site, sales in that country typically double![52]

ENTREPRENEURIAL
Profile
Diane Irvine: Blue Nile

At Blue Nile, a leading online retailer of diamonds and fine jewelry, global sales have proved to be the company's engine for growth, displaying far greater increases than domestic sales. Sales in foreign countries took off after Blue Nile created country-specific versions of its Web site with a local currency payment option in 35 nations. CEO Diane Irvine says that Blue Nile was able to expand at a very low cost without building stores or warehouses abroad. "It's all about the technology," she says.[53]

E-companies seeking to draw significant sales from foreign markets must design their sites with customers from other lands and cultures in mind. A common mechanism is to include several "language buttons" on the opening page of a site that take customers to pages in the language of their choice. Companies trying to establish a foothold in foreign markets by setting up Web sites dedicated to them run the same risk that companies setting up physical locations there do: offending international visitors by using the business conventions and standards they are accustomed to using in the United States. Business practices, even those used on the Web that are acceptable, even expected, in the United States, may be taboo in other countries. Color schemes can be important, too. Selecting the "wrong" colors and symbols on a site targeting people in a particular country can hurt sales and offend visitors. A little research into the subtleties of a target country's culture and business practices can save a great deal of embarrassment and money! Creating secure, simple, and reliable payment methods for foreign customers also increases sales.

When translating the content of their Web pages into other languages, entrepreneurs must use extreme caution. This is *not* the time to pull out their notes from an introductory Spanish course and begin their own translations. Hiring professional translation and localization services to convert a company's Web content into other languages minimizes the likelihood of a company unintentionally offending foreign customers.

Promote Your Web Site Online and Off-Line

E-commerce entrepreneurs have to use every means available—both online and off-line—to promote their Web sites and to drive traffic to them. Cross-promotions in which a physical store promotes the Web site and the Web site promotes the physical store can boost sales in both venues. In addition to using traditional online techniques, such as registering with search engines, creating banner ads, and joining banner exchange programs, Web entrepreneurs must promote their sites off-line as well. Ads in other media such as direct mail or newspapers that mention a site's URL will bring customers to it. It is also a good idea to put the company's Web address on *everything* a company publishes, from its advertisements and letterhead to shopping bags and business cards. A passive approach to generating Web site traffic is a recipe for failure. Entrepreneurs who are as innovative at promoting their e-businesses as they are at creating them can attract impressive numbers of visitors to their sites.

Ling Valentine, founder of Ling's Cars, and the military truck she uses to promote her company's Web site.

Source: LingsCars.com

Ling Valentine, owner of Ling's Cars, one of the most successful car-leasing operations in the United Kingdom, purchased a used six-wheel military truck and had her husband build a fake nuclear missile on top of it imprinted with her company's Web address, Lingscars.com, to promote her site. Ling uses the truck and missile as a movable billboard, placing it on busy highways, where millions of drivers see it every year. "My nuclear missile truck brings in loads of visitors every time I park it next to a motorway," says Valentine.[54]

Use Web 2.0 Tools to Attract and Retain Customers

The social aspects of the Internet that are evident on sites such as Facebook and Twitter have become part of companies' e-commerce efforts. Known as enterprise 2.0, these online selling techniques recognize that shoppers, especially young ones, expect to take a proactive role in their shopping experience by writing (and reading) product reviews, asking questions, posting comments in blogs, and engaging in other interactive behavior. According to the Pew Internet & American Life Project, 69 percent of adult Internet users have watched online videos, 33 percent read blogs, and 46 percent participate in social networking sites.[55] Simply inviting customers to post product reviews on a site can boost sales. A global study by Nielsen reports that 70 percent of online shoppers say that they trust customer reviews that are posted online when making a purchase decision, second only to reviews from people that they know (90 percent).[56]

Small businesses are responding to the opportunity to connect with their customers online by adding the following social media to their e-commerce strategies:

- **Mashups.** A mashup is a Web site or an application that combines content from multiple sources into a single Web service. For example, Twitzu is a mashup that allows users to manage invitations and responses to events. They invite their Twitter followers to an event—the grand opening of a new location, for example—and then receive responses from guests on Twitzu.
- **Really Simple Syndication (RSS). Really Simple Syndication** is an application that allows subscribers to aggregate content from their favorite Web sites into a single feed that is delivered automatically whenever the content is updated. RSS is ideal for companies whose customers are information junkies. "[RSS] is a must-have for any company Web site or blog because it allows people to track current news via their RSS feeds," says Louis Columbus, an expert on using social media.[57]

- **Social networking.** Many small businesses attract potential customers to their Web sites by adding a social networking component that allows visitors to engage in "conversation" with one another through bulletin boards, blogs, and links to social Web sites such as Facebook and Twitter. Tony Hsieh, CEO of online shoe retailer Zappos, uses his Twitter account to update more than 14,000 followers on news about the company and its products.[58] Other companies are finding that enabling customers to post their favorite products to their MySpace and Facebook profiles increases sales.

ENTREPRENEURIAL
Profile

Gina Drennon: Feather Your Nest

Gina Drennon, owner of Feather Your Nest, a specialty shop in Eureka Springs, Arkansas, that sells a unique collection of handmade and vintage gifts and decorations, has made her business stand out from the competition by actively engaging customers in a variety of online social media. Shoppers can find Feather Your Nest on Facebook and Twitter and can learn about what's happening behind the scenes by reading Drennon's blog. "I've seen our Web stats increase, followers increase, interactions increase, and most important, sales increase," she says. "I've made many meaningful connections with bloggers and magazine editors that have featured our products and our store, which brings us huge amounts of attention that you really cannot put a price on. At least half of the national press we've received is due to contacts we've made over social media."[59]

- **Wikis.** A **wiki** is a dynamic collection of Web pages that allows users to add to or edit their content. The most popular wiki is Wikipedia, the user-created online encyclopedia for which users provide the content. Some companies use wikis to encourage customers to participate in the design of their products, a process called **co-creation**.
- **Widgets.** Another tool that small companies use to attract attention on the Web is **widgets** (also known as *gadgets*), which are low-cost applications that appear like small television screens on Web sites, blogs, or computer desktops and perform specific functions. Entrepreneurs can create their own widgets or purchase them from developers and customize them, adding their own names, brands, and logos. Customers and visitors can download the widget to their desktops or perhaps post it to their own blogs or Facebook pages, where other Web users will see it. A popular widget not only drives customers to a site but can also improve a company's ranking on major search engines. "It's a great way to continually remind people that you exist," says Ivan Pope, CEO of widget developer Snipperoo.[60] Pizza retailer Papa John's developed a widget that allows customers to order a pizza from almost anywhere, including a Facebook page, a YouTube video, a Google search—even a cell phone.[61]

Develop an Effective Search Engine Optimization (SEO) Strategy

Because of the growing popularity of search engines among Internet shoppers, Web search strategies have become an essential part of online companies' promotion strategies. Because the sheer number of Web pages is overwhelming, it is no surprise that Internet shoppers use search engines extensively. A study by Compete shows that search engines are the most common tool that online shoppers use to find the products and services they want; 61 percent of shoppers say that they always or often use search engines when shopping online.[62] As a result, companies are devoting more of their marketing budgets to search engine listings that are focused on landing their Web sites at or near the top of the most popular search engines. For a company engaged in e-commerce, a well-defined search marketing strategy is an essential part of its overall marketing strategy.

One of the biggest challenges facing e-commerce entrepreneurs is maintaining the effectiveness of their search engine marketing strategies. Because the most popular search engines are constantly updating and refining their algorithms, the secretive formulas and methodologies search engines use to find and rank the results of Web searches, Web entrepreneurs also must evaluate and refine constantly their search strategies. Allan Keiter, owner of MyRatePlan.com, a company that helps customers compare cellular phone plans, traditionally had relied on natural listings on the search engine giant Google to direct customers to his company's Web site. His company almost always appeared in the top 10 results list for customers looking for information on calling plans. Then Google engineers changed the algorithm used to produce search results, and MyRatePlan.com virtually disappeared from its search results. Keiter watched helplessly as his company's revenues plunged by 20 percent.[63]

A company's Web search strategy must recognize the two basic types of search engine results: natural or organic listings and paid or sponsored listings. **Natural (or organic) listings** often arise as a result of "spiders," powerful programs search engines use to crawl around the Web, analyzing sites for keywords, links, and other data. Based on what they find, spiders index Web sites so that a search engine can display a listing of relevant Web sites when a person enters a keyword in the engine to start a search. Some search engines use people-powered searches rather than spider-powered ones to assemble their indexes. With natural listings, an entrepreneur's goal is to get his or her Web site displayed at or near the top of the list of search results. **Search engine optimization (SEO)** involves managing the content, keywords, titles, tags, features, and design of a Web site so that it appears at or near the top of Internet search results. The reason that SEO is so important: iProspect reports that 68 percent of search engine users click a link to a site that appears on the first page of the search results.[64] "The difference between being seen on page one and page two of search results can mean thousands, even millions, of dollars for a business in revenue," says Martin Falle, CEO of SEO Research, a search engine marketing company.[65] A useful resource for entrepreneurs is SEO Book, a search engine optimization site (*www.seobook.com*) that offers both free tools and more than 100 training modules on a variety of SEO topics for a fee.

Companies can use the following tips to improve their search placement results:

- Conduct brainstorming sessions to develop a list of keywords and phrases that searchers are likely to use when using a search engine to locate a company's products and services and then use those words and phrases on your Web pages. Usually, simple terms are better than industry jargon.
- Use Google's AdWords Keyword Tool to determine how many monthly searches users conduct globally and locally for a keyword or phrase. More specific, lower-volume keywords and phrases usually produce higher search rankings because they provide potential customers the more focused results they are seeking.
- Use relevant keywords in the title tags (meta tags, which are limited to 25 characters) and headlines of your Web pages. Most search engines are geared to pick them up. For best results, you should focus each page of your site on one specific keyword or phrase, which should appear in the page's title. Placing keywords in these critical locations can be tedious, but it produces better search results for the companies that take the time to do it.
- Visit competitors' sites for keyword ideas, but avoid using the exact phrases. Simply right-clicking a competitor's Web page and choosing "View Source" will display the keywords used in the meta tags on the site.
- Ask customers which words and phrases they use when searching for the products and services the company sells.
- Use data analysis tools to review Web logs to find the words and phrases (and the search engines) that have brought visitors to the company's Web site.
- Check blogs and bulletin boards related to the company's products and services for potential key terms.
- Don't forget about misspellings; people often misspell the words they type into search engines. Include them in your list.
- Hire services such as Wordtracker that monitor and analyze Web users' search engine tendencies.
- Block irrelevant results with "negative keywords," those that are excluded in a search.
- Place links to your Web site on high-profile Web sites. Search engines rank sites that have external links to high-volume sites higher than those that do not. John W. Tuggle, founder of Learn Guitar Now, an online company that sells guitar instruction, benefits from having one of the leading guitar makers, Gibson Guitars, post links to his Web site and several of his tutorial videos on its site. Before going online, Tuggle made just $19,000 a year giving guitar lessons and had to work a second job. With his online business, Tuggle now earns $100,000 a year, "and it just keeps going up," he says.[66]
- Start a blog. Well-written blogs not only draw potential customers to your site, but they also tend to attract links from other Web sites. Blogs also allow entrepreneurs to use keywords strategically and frequently, which moves their sites up in search engine rankings.

■ Post videos on your site. In addition to uploading them to video sites such as YouTube, companies can wait for organic listings to appear or they can submit their videos to search engines for listing. Forrester Research estimates that a properly submitted video is 50 times more likely to achieve a first-page listing on Google than any text-based page.[67]

Because organic listings can take months to materialize, many e-commerce companies rely on paid listings, which give them an immediate presence in search engines. **Paid, or sponsored, listings** are short text advertisements with links to the sponsoring company's Web site that appear on the results pages of a search engine when a user types in a keyword or phrase. Entrepreneurs use paid search listings to accomplish what natural listings cannot. Fortunately, just five search engines—Google, Yahoo!, Microsoft Bing, AOL, and Ask.com—account for 99 percent of the searches conducted in the United States.[68] Google, the most popular search engine with nearly 72 percent of all searches, displays paid listings as "sponsored links" at the top and down the side of each results page, and Yahoo! shows "sponsored results" at the top and the bottom of its results pages. Advertisers bid on keywords to determine their placement on a search engine's results page. On Google, an ad's placement in the search results is a function of the ad's relevance (determined by a quality score of 1 to 10 that Google assigns) and the advertiser's bid on the keyword. The ad that gets the most prominent placement (at the top) of the search engine's results page when a user types in that keyword on the search engine is the one with the highest combination of quality score and bid price. An advertiser pays only when a shopper clicks through to its Web site from the search engine. For this reason, paid listings also are called *pay-for-placement, pay-per-click,* or *pay-for-performance ads.* At one popular search engine, the average bid for keywords in its paid listings is 40 cents, but some words can bring as much as $100!* For small e-commerce companies, the average cost for a pay-per-click keyword has risen from 39 cents in 2004 to 52 cents today.[69] Although paid listings can be expensive, they allow advertisers to evaluate their effectiveness using the statistical reports the search engine generates. Pay-per-click advertisers can control costs by geo-targeting their ads, having them appear only in certain areas, and by setting a spending limit per day.

Using generic terms results in large numbers of searches but often produces very small conversion rates and very little in sales; normally, entrepreneurs get better results bidding on more precise, lower volume keywords. Rather than compete with much larger companies for 5 or 10 common keywords, a more effective strategy is to bid on 200 less popular keywords.

Profile

Tomima Edmark: Andra Group Inc.

Tomima Edmark, CEO of Andra Group Inc., a business that sells lingerie at HerRoom.com and men's underwear at HisRoom.com, has seen the return on her company's paid listings increase by at least 100 percent since shifting to this strategy. Andra Group now bids on about 36,000 keywords, including more specific terms, up from 12,000 words before. "For example, 'bra' is a generic term, and there's a ton of traffic on it, but not high conversion," says Edmark. "We have been able to find specific phrases with 'bra' in them [such as specific brands and sizes] that turned our bra campaign profitable."[70]

One problem facing companies that rely on paid listings to generate Web traffic is **click fraud**, which occurs when a company pays for clicks that are generated by someone with no interest in or intent to purchase a product or service. "Clickbots," programs that can generate thousands of phony clicks on a Web site, are a common source of click fraud. Experts estimate that the pay-per-click fraud rate is between 15 and 17.5 percent.[71] Web analytics software can help online merchants detect click fraud, which can be quite costly. Large numbers of visitors who leave within seconds of arriving at a site, computer IP addresses that appear from all over the world, and pay-per-click costs that rise without any corresponding increase in sales are clues that a company is a victim of click fraud.

---

*An online merchant's cost per sale = cost per click ÷ merchant's conversion rate. For example, a merchant with a 1 percent conversion rate who submits a keyword bid of 10 cents per click is paying $10 per sale ($0.10 ÷ 0.01 = $10).

IN THE ENTREPRENEURIAL
SPOTLIGHT A "Gilt"-Free Shopping Experience

It is noon on a typical weekday, and customers are waiting to pounce on the discounted merchandise as soon as the sale kicks off, eager to snap up a great deal on clothing from designers such as Rodarte, Derek Lam, Christian Louboutin, and others, because they know the best bargains go very quickly. Designer sample sales typically are by invitation only, and fashionistas work their list of contacts to finagle invitations to these private events, where they can purchase luxury brand merchandise at discounts of 50 to 70 percent. Shoppers line up around the block for the semi-annual Barneys Warehouse Sale in New York City and, because all sales are final, often strip down to their underwear between the racks to try on a $3,000 dress marked down to $600.

This particular sample sale has a different twist, however, because more than 100,000 customers will be attending, making this the most crowded store in the city. Except that there is no store. Gilt Groupe, founded in 2007 by Alexis Maybank and Alexandra Wilkis Wilson (who are known inside the company as A&A), runs "flash sales" entirely online. Access to Gilt's Web site is by invitation only (which gives it an air of exclusivity, exactly what the designers whose items are sold there are looking for), but, because the site has limited access, none of the sales or merchandise shows up in online searches. Landing an invitation to join is much easier than scoring an invitation to a brick-and-mortar New York sample sale, however. One of Gilt's 2 million customers (75 percent of whom are women) can issue an invitation or interested shoppers can contact the company's customer service department to receive one.

On its Web site, Gilt hosts about 70 sales each week and runs each one for just 36 hours before taking all of the merchandise down. "Whereas a department store might move a certain amount of product in a season, we can do it in 36 hours," says Amanda Graber, Gilt's public relations manager. The speed of the sales and the discreetness with which the company conducts them appeal to designers, some of whom were initially reluctant to offer their merchandise through Gilt. Thanks to the site's tremendous success and rapid growth rate, that reluctance has withered. "I have so many brands banging down our door, that I have to say 'no,'" says Wilkis Wilson. Gilt also boasts an incredible sell-through rate, the proportion of a designer's inventory that customers actually purchase. In the typical department store, the sell-through rate is about 65 percent across a 12-week season; at Gilt, the sell-through rate typically is 92 percent, which means Gilt customers tend to pick the virtual racks clean! "Most online shopping mirrors brick-and-mortar stores," says Susan Lyne, Gilt's CEO. "They're not taking advantage of what's uniquely possible online, the heightened sense of entertainment and competition. A big part of the Gilt promise is discovery: You come every day, and it's new every day." Recently, an ostrich feather jacket from Alessandro Dell'Aqua, originally priced at $3,175, sold for $618. Normally priced at $2,420, a Marc Jacobs leather bomber jacket sold for $548. Generating sales totally online means that Gilt has a tremendous cost advantage over its brick-and-mortar rivals, which incur the expense of operating physical locations.

Maybank and Wilkis Wilson have been friends since they were students at Harvard, where they met in a Portuguese class. After completing Harvard Business School, Maybank learned the ropes of e-commerce at eBay and AOL, and Wilkis Wilson embarked on a career as a merchandising executive at luxury brands Bulgari and Louis Vuitton. The two had been discussing ideas for starting a business and told Kevin Ryan, former CEO of DoubleClick and now a venture capitalist, about their ideas. According to Ryan, his "eureka" moment occurred one day when he saw a long line of women waiting in line to get into a Marc Jacobs sale on New York's 18th Street. "If there are 200 women who are willing to stand in this line," he recalls thinking, "that means that in the United States there are probably hundreds of thousands. But they don't live in New York, they're busy right now, and they just can't do that. We can bring the sale to them." The skills, experience, and networks of the three proved to be the ideal launching pad for Gilt Groupe. Ryan, who knew of a French company called Vente Privée that had achieved success in Europe with online designer fashion sales, invested some seed capital, and the Web site went live in late 2007.

Sales at Gilt have grown very rapidly. When Maybank and Wilkis Wilson launched the site, there were just 15,000 members, most of whom came through their network of contacts. Today, Gilt boasts more than 2 million members—and growing. Just 2 years after start-up, sales had reached $170 million, and 1 year later they were pushing $500 million. Gilt's success has convinced design houses to create clothing specifically for the site rather than merely selling overstocked merchandise. The company now works with more than 700 brands and has launched other sites such as Jettsetter, which offers travel deals; Gilt Fuse, which offers lower-priced brands such as American Apparel; and Gilt Man, which sells men's clothing. Since launching the Gilt Man site, the company's revenue from menswear has tripled. Some early Gilt members complain that the company has moved away from its original concept, including many brands whose names they do not recognize.

The Gilt Web site has a decidedly upscale look, with muted colors and no flashing "sale" signs and appeals to the company's target customers: upscale shoppers who are "aspirational" luxury buyers, people who are eager to purchase designer goods but cannot afford to pay full price for them. The key is to make sure that customers feel as though they are getting access to bargains that are not available to just anyone. The site also provides shoppers with extensive product descriptions and simple photographs of merchandise. "We deliver an incredible amount of information about the product," says Lyne, "and we have a direct line to our customers every day." The company also offers an iPad application for shoppers.

Gilt's management team is exploring an initial public offering for the company, which was valued at $400 million in its latest round of venture capital financing. Challenges do exist, however. "This is a pretty easy market to enter," admits Lyne, "but the operational aspects of it are incredibly complex. We change out the store every night. Receiving, sale preparation, and shipping and fulfillment are incredibly complex." Lyne is focusing on the company's e-commerce strategy. "We have to be thinking about what the Internet makes possible," she says. "Can we do something that drives the next wave of excitement in e-commerce? We need to get better at personalization. We need to be able to offer you different sales than we might offer somebody in Minneapolis or your mother."

1. What advantages does operating solely online offer Gilt Groupe? What are the disadvantages?
2. What advice can you offer the Gilt Groupe's management team as they continue to develop their e-commerce strategy? What steps can they take to stay connected to their customers and to keep their customers coming back?

Sources: Based on Mary Jo A Pham, "Gilt Groupe's Haute Sample Sales Expand," *Fortune*, June 25, 2010, *http://tech.fortune.cnn.com/2010/06/25/gilt-groupe-brings-you-the-online-sample-sale/*; Lauren Sherman, "By Invitation Only," *Forbes*, February 25, 2008, *www.forbes.com/forbes/2008/0225/070.html*; Andrew Rice, "What's a Dress Worth?" *New York Magazine*, February 24, 2010, *http://nymag.com/fashion/10/spring/63807/*.

Gilt Groupe founders Alexis Maybank (center) and Alexandra Wilkis Wilson (right) with CEO Susan Lyne (left).

Source: Ben Baker/Redux Pictures

Designing a Killer Web Site

5. Learn the techniques of designing a killer Web site.

Web users are not a patient lot. They sit before their computers, their fingers poised on their mouse buttons, daring any Web site to delay them with files that take too long to load. Slow-loading sites or sites that are confusing and poorly designed cause Web users to move on faster than a bolt of lightning can strike. With more than 234 million Web sites online and more added every day, how can an entrepreneur design a Web site that will capture and hold potential customers' attention long enough to make a sale? What can they do to keep customers coming back on a regular basis? There is no surefire formula for stopping online customers in their tracks, but the following suggestions will help.

Decide How to Bring Your Site to Life

Entrepreneurs who are not technologically savvy often turn to e-commerce hosting companies that provide one-stop services, including site design, built-in shopping carts, security filters, Web analytics, and, in some cases, credit card processing. Many of these services offer customizable templates that allow entrepreneurs to update and modify their sites very easily using "wizards." Other entrepreneurs choose to hire Web site designers to create a customized Web site or build their own sites. Whatever option they choose, entrepreneurs must pay a monthly hosting fee, which can be a flat amount, an amount per transaction, or a percentage of sales. When it comes

FIGURE 4 (a)

Percentage of Adult Internet Users.

Source: "Generations Online in 2009," Pew Internet and American Life Project, 2009.

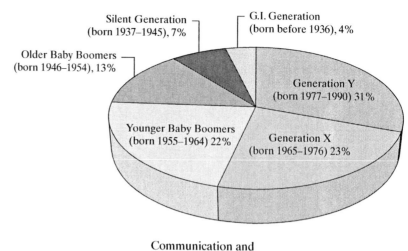

FIGURE 4 (b)

Online Activities by Generation

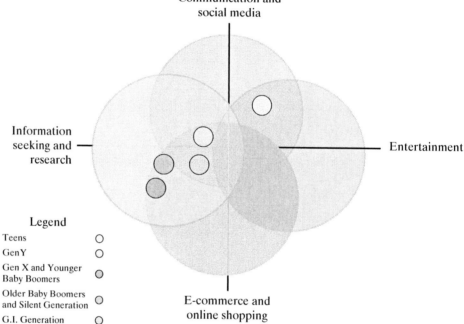

to e-commerce, the lesson for entrepreneurs is this: Focus your efforts on the core competencies that your company has developed, whether they reside in "traditional" business practices or online, and outsource all of the other aspects of doing business online to companies that have the expertise to make your e-commerce business successful.

Start with Your Target Customer

Before creating their Web sites, entrepreneurs must paint a clear picture of their target customers. Only then are they ready to design a site that will appeal to their customers. The goal is to create a design in which customers see themselves when they visit. Creating a site in which customers find a comfortable fit requires a careful blend of market research, sales know-how, and aesthetics. The challenge for a business on the Web is to create the same image, style, and ambiance in its online presence as in its off-line stores. Figure 4 shows the percentage of adults online by generation and the type of online experiences they seek.

Give Customers What They Want

Although Web shoppers are price conscious, they rank fast, reliable delivery high on their list of criteria in their purchase decisions. Studies also show that shoppers look for a large selection of merchandise available to them immediately. Remember that the essence of the selling on the Web is providing *convenience* to customers. A well-designed Web site is intuitive, leading customers to a series of actions that are natural and result in a sale. Sites that allow them to shop whenever

FIGURE 5

Features That Make U.S. Shoppers More Likely to Buy from a Web Site

Factors that Web shoppers say are most important when they are deciding whether to purchase from a Web site.

Source: Revolutionizing Web Site Design: The New Rules of Usability, Oneupweb, 2010, p. 11.

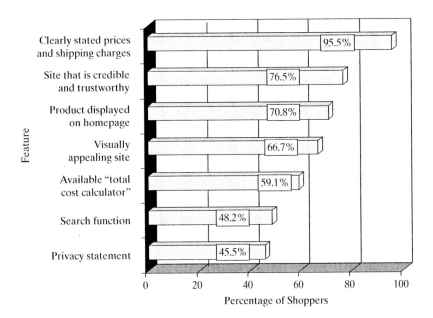

they want, to find what they are looking for easily, and to pay for it conveniently and securely will keep customers coming back. Clear photographs of merchandise with a feature that allows customers to rotate the image, change colors, and zoom in increase sales. Furniture maker Herman Miller's Web site not only makes it easy for shoppers to browse and to buy its products, but the site also offers research on the benefits of ergonomic designs and allows visitors to try various furniture layouts in rooms created with a special 3D design tool.[72] One of the reasons Amazon.com has become the largest online retailer is that its five-point strategy is designed to give online shoppers exactly what they want: low prices, wide selection, product availability, shopping convenience, and extensive information about the products it sells.[73]

Figure 5 shows the factors that Web shoppers say are most important when they are deciding whether to buy from a Web site.

Select an Intuitive Domain Name

Choose a domain name that is consistent with the image you want to create for your company and register it. Entrepreneurs should never underestimate the power of the right domain name or Universal Resource Locator (URL), which is a company's address on the Internet. It not only tells online shoppers where to find a company, but it also should suggest something about the company and what it does. Even the casual Web surfer could guess that the "toys.com" name belongs to a company selling children's toys. (It does; it belongs to eToys, Inc., which also owns "etoys.com," "e-toys.com," and several other variations of its name.) The ideal domain name should be:

- *Short.* Short names are easy for people to remember, so the shorter a company's URL is, the more likely potential customers are to recall it.
- *Memorable.* Not every short domain name is necessarily memorable. Some business owners use their companies' initials as their domain name (e.g., "*www.sbfo.com*" for Stanley Brothers Furniture Outlet). The problem with using initials for a domain name is that customers rarely associate the two, which makes a company virtually invisible on the Web.
- *Indicative of a company's business or business name.* Perhaps the best domain name for a company is one that customers can guess easily if they know the company's name. For instance, mail-order catalog company L.L.Bean's URL is "*www.llbean.com*," and New Pig, a maker of absorbent materials for a variety of industrial applications, uses "*www.newpig.com*" as its domain name. (The company carries this concept over to its toll-free number, which is 1-800-HOT-HOGS.)
- *Easy to spell.* Even though a company's domain name may be easy to spell, it is usually wise to buy several variations of the correct spelling simply because some customers are not likely to be good spellers!

Just because entrepreneurs come up with the perfect URL for their companies' Web sites does not necessarily mean that they can use it. Domain names are given on a first-come, first-served basis. Before business owners can use a domain name, they must ensure that some-one else has not already taken it. The simplest way to do that is to go to one of the accredited domain name registration services such as Network Solutions (*www.networksolutions.com*), NetNames (*www.netnames.com*), or Go Daddy (*www.godaddy.com*) to conduct a name search. Entrepreneurs who find the domain name they have selected already registered to someone else have two choices: They can select another name, or they can try to buy the name from the original registrant.

With more than 82 million ".com" domain names currently registered, finding a relevant, unregistered domain name can be a challenge, but several new top-level domain names recently became available: .aero (airlines), .biz (any business site), .coop (business cooperatives), .info (any site), .museum (museums), .name (individuals' sites), and .pro (professionals' sites).[74] Once an entrepreneur finds an unused name that is suitable, he or she must register it (plus any varia-tions of it)—and the sooner, the better! Registering is quite easy: Simply submit a form and pay the required fee to one of the registration services. Although not required, registering the domain name with the U.S. Patent and Trademark Office (USPTO) at a cost of $275 provides maximum protection for a company's domain name. The USPTO's Web site (*www.uspto.gov*) not only allows users to register a trademark online, but it also offers useful information on trademarks and the protection they offer.

Make Your Web Site Easy to Navigate

Research shows that the leading factor in convincing online shoppers to make a purchase from a Web site is its ease of navigation. The starting point for evaluating a site's navigability is to con-duct a user test. Find several willing shoppers, sit them in front of a computer, and watch them as they cruise through the company's Web site to make a purchase. It is one of the best ways to get meaningful, immediate feedback on the navigability of a site. Watching these test customers as they navigate the site also is useful. Where do they pause? Do they get lost in the site? Are they confused by the choices the site gives them? Is the checkout process too complex? Are the navi-gation buttons from one page of the site to another clearly marked, and do they make sense? "Eighty percent of visitors will leave [a Web site] if they can't find what they are looking for af-ter three pages," says Bryan Eisenberg, an e-commerce consultant.[75]

Successful Web sites recognize that shoppers employ different strategies to make a purchase. Some shoppers want to use a search tool, others want to browse through product categories, and still others prefer a company to make product recommendations. Effective sites accommodate all three strategies in their design.

Add Wish List Capability

Giving customers the ability to create wish lists of products and services they want and then con-nect other people to those lists not only boosts a company's sales but also increases its visibility.

Create a Gift Idea Center

Online retailers have discovered that one of the most successful tools for improving their conver-sion rates is to offer a gift idea center. A gift idea center is a section of a Web site that includes a variety of gift ideas where shoppers can browse for ideas based on price, gender, or category. Gift idea centers can provide a huge boost for e-tailers, particularly around holidays because they offer creative suggestions for shoppers looking for the perfect gift. Other variations of this approach that have proved to be successful for e-commerce entrepreneurs include suggested items pages, bargain basement sale pages, and featured sale pages.

Build Loyalty by Giving Online Customers a Reason to Return to Your Web Site

Just as with brick-and-mortar retailers, e-tailers that constantly have to incur the expense of attracting new customers find it difficult to remain profitable because of the extra cost required to acquire customers. One of the most effective ways to encourage customers to return to a site is to establish an incentive program that rewards them for repeat purchases. "Frequent buyer" programs that offer discounts or points toward future purchases, giveaways such as T-shirts em-blazoned with a company's logo, or special sales only for loyal customers are common elements of incentive programs. Incentive programs that are properly designed with a company's target customer in mind really work.

Establish Hyperlinks with Other Businesses, Preferably Those Selling Products or Services That Complement Yours

Listing the Web addresses of complementary businesses on your company's site and having them list your site's address on their sites offers customers more value and can bring traffic to your site that you otherwise would have missed. For instance, the owner of a site selling upscale kitchen gadgets should consider a cross-listing arrangement with sites that feature gourmet recipes, wines, and kitchen appliances.

Include an E-Mail Option, an Address, and a Telephone Number on Your Site

Customers appreciate the opportunity to communicate with your company, and you should give them many options for doing so. If you include e-mail access on your site, however, be sure to respond to it promptly. Nothing alienates customers faster than a company that is slow to respond or fails to respond to their e-mail messages. Also be sure to include an address and a toll-free telephone number for customers who prefer to write or call with their questions. Unfortunately, many companies either fail to include their telephone numbers on their sites or bury them so deeply within the sites' pages that customers never find them.

Offer Shoppers Online Order Tracking

Give shoppers the ability to track their orders online. Many customers who order items online want to track the progress of their orders. One of the most effective ways to keep a customer happy is to send an e-mail confirmation that your company received the order and another e-mail notification when you ship the order. The shipment notice should include the shipper's tracking number and instructions on how to track the order from the shipper's site. Order and shipping confirmations instill confidence in even the most Web-wary shoppers.

Offer Web-Only Specials

Give Web customers a special deal that you don't offer in any other advertising piece. Change your specials often (weekly, if possible) and use clever "teasers" to draw attention to the offer. Regular special offers available only on the Web give customers an incentive to keep visiting a company's site.

Look for Opportunities to Up-Sell and Cross-Sell

Sales clerks in brick-and-mortar retail stores quickly learn the art of up-selling, recommending more upscale products, and cross-selling, offering, for example, a customer who purchases a shirt the opportunity to purchase a matching tie as well. Online merchants can use the same tactic by displaying recommended items on product pages. Men's clothing retailer Jos. A Bank (*www.josabank.com*) employs this sales strategy extremely well when a customer places an item in a shopping cart by displaying a list of "matching apparel" on the product page.

Use the Power of Social Media

Make it easy for customers to connect with your company on social media such as Facebook, Twitter, and others by including social media sharing links and links to your company's social media pages on your Web site. Social media can be a powerful marketing tool.

Use Customer Testimonials

Customer testimonials about a company and its products and services lend credibility to a site, but the testimonials must be genuine and believable.

American Pearl, a company that sells pearls from its Fifth Avenue showroom in New York City and its Web site (*www.americanpearl.com*), reinforces the owners' extensive knowledge of and dedication to pearls with a Web page dedicated to customer testimonials. Explaining the importance of the testimonial page, Eddie Bakhash, whose father, Charlie, started the company in 1950, says, "We understand that purchasing an expensive strand of pearls for a loved one on the Internet can require courage." The highly successful company also instills confidence in customers by offering an unconditional 30-day, money-back guarantee.[76]

Follow a Simple Design

Catchy graphics and photographs are important to snaring customers, but designers must choose them carefully. Designs that are overly complex take a long time to download, and customers are likely to move on before they appear. The Web Site Garage (*http://thewebsitegarage.com*), a Web site maintenance company, offers companies a free 21-point inspection of their Web sites and a report that describes problems ranging from slow download speeds to search engine optimization and their potential solutions.

Specific design tips include:

- Avoid clutter, especially on your site's homepage. "The homepage is like a store's display window, minus the mannequins," explains a report on proper Web design.[77] The best designs are simple and elegant with a balance of both text and graphics. "The minimalist approach makes a site appear more professional," says one design expert.[78]
- Use less text on your site's homepage, landing pages, and initial product or service pages. Although including detailed, text-heavy content deeper in your site is acceptable and even desirable, incorporating too much text early on dissuades customers. Allow customers to drill down to more detailed product and service descriptions.
- Avoid huge graphic headers that must download first, prohibiting customers from seeing anything else on your site as they wait (or, more likely, *don't* wait). Use graphics judiciously so that the site loads quickly; otherwise, impatient customers will abandon the site.
- Include a menu bar at the top of every page that makes it easy for customers to find their way around your site.
- Make the site easy to navigate by including easy-to-follow navigation buttons at the bottom of pages that enable customers to return to the top of the page or to the menu bar. This avoids "the pogo effect," where visitors bounce from page to page in a Web site looking for what they need. Without navigation buttons or a site map page, a company runs the risk of customers getting lost in its site and leaving. Organizing a Web site into logical categories also helps.
- Minimize the number of clicks required for a customer to get to any particular page in the site. Long paths increase the likelihood of customers bailing out before they reach their intended destination.
- Incorporate meaningful content in the site that is useful to visitors, well organized, easy to read, and current. The content should be consistent with the message a company sends in the other advertising media it uses. Although a Web site should be designed to sell, providing useful, current information attracts visitors, keeps them coming back, and establishes a company's reputation as an expert in the field.
- Include a "frequently asked questions" (FAQ) section. Adding a searchable FAQ section to a site can reduce dramatically the number of telephone calls and e-mails customer service representatives must handle. FAQ sections typically span a wide range of issues—from how to place an order to how to return merchandise—and cover topics customers most often want to know about.
- Be sure to include privacy and return policies as well as product guarantees the company offers.
- Avoid fancy typefaces and small fonts because they are too hard to read.
- Be vigilant for misspelled words, typographical errors, and formatting mistakes; they destroy a site's credibility in no time and send customers fleeing to competitors' sites.
- Don't put small fonts on "busy" backgrounds; no one will read them!
- Use contrasting colors of text and graphics. For instance, blue text on a green background is nearly impossible to read.
- Be careful with frames. Using frames that are so thick that they crowd out text makes for a poor design.
- Test the site on different Web browsers and on different size monitors. A Web site may look exactly the way it was designed to look on one Web browser and be a garbled mess on another. Sites designed to display correctly on large monitors may not view well on small ones.
- Use your Web site to collect information from visitors, but don't tie up customers with a tedious registration process. Most will simply leave the site never to return. Offers for a free e-mail newsletter or a contest giveaway can give visitors enough incentive to register with a site.
- Incorporate a search function that allows shoppers to type in the items they want to purchase. Unlike in-store shoppers, who might browse until they find the item, online shoppers usually

want to go straight to the products they seek. Ideally, the search function acknowledges common misspellings of key terms, avoiding the dreaded "No Results Found" message.

- Include company contact information and an easy-to-find customer service telephone number.
- Avoid automated music that plays continuously and cannot be cut off.
- Make sure the overall look of the site is consistent and appealing. "When a site is poorly designed, lacks information, or cannot support customer needs, that [company's] reputation is seriously jeopardized," says one expert.[79]
- Remember: Simpler usually is better.

Assure Customers That Online Transactions Are Secure

If you are serious about doing business on the Web, make sure that your site includes the proper security software and encryption devices. Computer-savvy customers are not willing to divulge their credit card numbers on sites that are not secure. E-commerce companies should avoid storing their customers' credit card information (even though one-third of small companies do).[80] With attacks from hackers increasingly prevalent, the risk is just too high.

Post Shipping and Handling Charges Up Front

A common gripe among online shoppers is that some e-tailers fail to reveal their shipping and handling charges early in the checkout process. Responsible online merchants keep shipping and handling charges reasonable and display them early on in the buying process—before shoppers add items to a cart. When customers' orders qualify for free shipping, the site should automate this step rather than require customers to input a free shipping code.

Create a Fast, Simple Checkout Process

One sure-fire way to destroy an online company's conversion rate is to impose a lengthy, convoluted checkout process that requires customers to wade through pages of forms to fill out just to complete a purchase. When faced with a lengthy checkout process, customers simply abandon a site and make their purchases elsewhere. E-commerce experts suggest that the top performing sites require a maximum of five clicks to check out, but the fewer the steps required for customers to check out, the more successful will be the site at generating sales.[81]

Confirm Transactions

Order-confirmation e-mails, which a company can generate automatically, let a customer know that the company received the online order and can be an important first line of defense against online fraud. If the customer claims not to have placed the order, the company can cancel it and report the transaction and the credit card information as suspicious. Order confirmation e-mails should include shipping information and a tracking number that allows customers to view the status of their orders.

Keep Your Site Fresh

Customers want to see something new when they visit stores, and they expect the same when they visit virtual stores as well. Regularly add new content such as videos, blogs, customer testimonials, or information-rich articles to your site. Delete any hyperlinks that have disappeared, and keep the information on your Web site current. One sure way to run off customers on the Web is to continue to advertise your company's "Christmas Special" in August! Fresh information and new specials keep customers coming back.

Test Your Site Often

Smart e-commerce entrepreneurs check their sites frequently to make sure they are running smoothly and are not causing customers unexpected problems. A good rule of thumb is to check your site at least monthly—or weekly if its content changes frequently.

Consider Hiring a Professional Designer

Pros can do it a lot faster and better than you can. However, don't give designers free rein to do whatever they want to with your site. Make sure it meets your criteria for an effective site that can sell.

Entrepreneurs must remember that on the Web every company, no matter how big or how small, has the exact same screen size for its site. What matters most is not the size of your company, but how you put that screen size to use.

▶ ENTREPRENEURSHIP IN ACTION ▶

In Need of a Web Site Makeover

While attending Stanford University, Brian Spaly began using a girlfriend's sewing machine to alter his pants so that they fit better. Soon, Spaly's friends were asking for good-fitting pants of their own. Spaly and his roommate Andy Dunn spotted a business opportunity and launched Bonobos, an online company that sells pants that fit well with the help of a proprietary curved waistband that follows the body's natural shape and "some magic in the seat" that makes them "comfortable but not frumpy." Bonobos sells its pants only online (*www.bonobos.com*) at prices that range from about $110 to $200.

Bonobos is committed to customer service, and the company's Web site emphasizes convenience. "We hate shopping, too," explains one page. "You have to do it on your free time at the expense of things you actually enjoy." The company offers free shipping and the most accommodating return policy in the business: "any pant, any time, any reason." Bonobos even pays for the return shipping. The company generates about $170,000 in sales each month, but Spaly and Dunn believe that a redesigned Web site can generate a higher level of sales. A group of e-commerce experts reviewed Bonobos' Web analytics and discovered some interesting trends.

Finding Us

Typically, about half of the traffic on a company's Web site comes from search engines, with the remainder split evenly among referrals, affiliate sites, and direct traffic; that is, customers who type in the company's Web address. Bonobos, however, generates just 21 percent of its traffic from search engines and 50 percent from referring Web sites. About 25 percent of the company's customers go directly to its Web site. Bonobos invests a great deal of energy in generating publicity, but the analytics report suggests that the company is not scoring high placement in search engine results. The report shows that "Bonobos" is one of the most common keywords that customers use. Very few customers find the company by searching for "men's pants" or "pants that fit."

Conversion Rate

Like most e-commerce companies, Bonobos' conversion rate fluctuates from week to week. The Web analytics report shows that the site's current conversion rate typically falls between 1.8 and 3.0 percent, which is below average. Many factors influence a company's conversion rate, but Spaly and Dunn are convinced that theirs should be higher.

Shopping Cart Abandonment

Bonobos' shopping cart abandonment rate is 63 percent. One analyst points out that the site's checkout process asks for a coupon code early in the process and suspects that many customers abandon their carts to search for a discount coupon. Many of them never return to complete their transactions. The team of experts points out that if Bonobos could lower its cart abandonment rate by 10 percent, sales would increase by $20,000 per month.

Page Views and Bounce Rate

Web analytics show that the typical visitor to the Bonobos site views on average eight pages. However, the site's bounce rate, the percentage of visitors that leave the site after viewing just one page, is nearly 33 percent, well above the 20 percent that the experts consider "good." The bounce rate is one measure of the quality of a guest's visit. High bounce rates indicate that a site's landing pages simply are not relevant to visitors. If Bonobos can reduce its bounce rate to 20 percent, sales would increase by $10,000 per month. A high bounce rate coupled with a high number of page views per visit suggests that shoppers are not finding the products that they are looking for.

Navigation and Shopping

The team of experts questions the site's use of quirky names for various types of pants such as Snapdragons, Jive Cats, and Cracker Jacks on the homepage. To be effective, the online shopping experience must be intuitive, allowing customers to easily find the items they seek. "They should make it easier for a visitor to figure out where to find corduroy pants or weekend wear," says one expert. "A new customer is not going to know what 'Snapdragons' means." Improving the site's navigation and simplifying the shopping process can lead to greatly increased sales.

Global Reach

One of the greatest advantages to small companies that operate online is the ability to expand their reach globally at a low cost. Although Bonobos generates most of its sales from customers across North America, the site receives a considerable amount of traffic from shoppers in Australia. Bonobos can ship its pants internationally just as easily as it can locally, but the existing site lacks the ability to be customized for foreign customers and cultures. For instance, a customer in North America is most likely to use a search engine to look for "pants," but a shopper in Australia would use the term "trousers."

1. What suggestions can you make for improving Bonobos' search engine optimization (SEO) strategy?
2. Visit the Bonobos Web site and spend a few minutes exploring it. Work with a small team of your classmates to develop a list of ideas for

improving the site. Review each of the points described in this feature and incorporate specific suggestions for improving each area.

Source: Based on Max Chafkin, "Improving Your Sense of Style," *Inc.*, November 2008, pp. 35–37.

Tracking Web Results

6. Explain how companies track the results from their Web sites.

Web sites offer entrepreneurs a treasure trove of valuable information about how well their sites are performing—if they take the time to analyze it. **Web analytics**, tools that measure a Web site's ability to attract customers, generate sales, and keep customers coming back, help entrepreneurs to know what works—and what doesn't—on their sites. Online companies that use Web analytics have an advantage over those that do not. Their owners can review the data collected from their customers' Web site activity, analyze them, make adjustments to the Web site, and then start the monitoring process over again to see whether the changes improve the site's performance. In other words, Web analytics give entrepreneurs the ability to apply the principles of continuous improvement to their sites. In addition, the changes these e-business owners make are based on facts (the data from the Web analytics) rather than on mere guesses about how customers interact with a site. A variety of Web analytics software packages are available, but effective ones offer the following types of information:

- *Commerce metrics.* Basic analytics such as sales revenue generated, number of items sold, which products are selling best (and which are not), and others.
- *Visitor segmentation measurements.* These measurements provide entrepreneurs valuable information about online shoppers and customers, including whether they are return customers or new customers, how they arrived at the site (e.g., via a search engine or a pay-per-click ad), which search terms they used (if they used a search engine), and others.
- *Content reports.* This information tells entrepreneurs which products customers are looking for and which pages they view most often (and least often), how they navigate through the site, how long they stay, which pages they are on when they exit, and more. Using this information, an entrepreneur can get an idea of how effective the site's design is.
- *Process measurements.* These metrics help entrepreneurs to understand how their Web sites attract visitors and convert them into customers. Does the checkout process work smoothly? How often do shoppers abandon their carts? At what point in the process do they abandon them? These measures can lead to higher conversion rates for an online business.

Other common measures of Web site performance include the following:

- **Recency** is the length of time between a customer's visits to a Web site. The more frequently customers visit a site, the more likely they are to become loyal customers.
- The **click-through rate (CTR)** is the proportion of people who see a company's online ad and actually click on it to reach the company's Web site. Each time an ad is displayed is called an impression; therefore:

$$\text{CTR} = \text{Number of clicks} \div \text{Number of impressions}$$

For instance, if a company's ad is displayed 500 times in 1 day and 12 people clicked it, the CTR is $12 \div 500 = .024$, or 2.4 percent.
- The **cost per acquisition (CPA)** is the cost a company incurs to generate each purchase (or customer registration):

$$\text{CPA} = \text{Total cost of acquiring a new customer} \div \text{Number of new customers}$$

For example, if a company purchases an advertisement in an e-magazine for $200, and it yields 15 new customers, then the cost of acquisition is $200 \div 15 = \$13.33$.

■ The **conversion** (or **browse-to-buy**) **rate** is the proportion of visitors to a site who actually make a purchase. It is one of the most important measures of Web success and is calculated as follows:

Conversion rate = Number of customers who make a purchase ÷ Number of visitors to the site

Conversion rates vary dramatically across industries but usually range from 1 to 4 percent. The average conversion rate is 3.2 percent.[82] In other words, out of every 1,000 people who visit a Web site, on average, 32 of them actually make a purchase.

Ensuring Web Privacy and Security

Privacy

7. Describe how e-businesses ensure the privacy and security of the information they collect and store from the Web.

The Web's ability to track customers' every move naturally raises concerns over the privacy of the information companies collect. E-commerce gives businesses access to tremendous volumes of information about their customers, creating a responsibility to protect that information and to use it wisely. The potential for breaching customers' privacy is present in any e-business. To make sure they are using the information they collect from visitors to their Web sites legally and ethically and safeguarding it adequately, companies should take the following steps:

TAKE AN INVENTORY OF THE CUSTOMER DATA COLLECTED. The first step to ensuring proper data handling is to assess exactly the type of data the company is collecting and storing. How are you collecting the information? Why are you collecting it? How are you using it? Do visitors know how you are using the data? Should you get their permission to use the data in this way? Do you use all of the data you are collecting?

DEVELOP A COMPANY PRIVACY POLICY FOR THE INFORMATION YOU COLLECT. A **privacy policy** is a statement explaining the type of information a company collects online, what it does with that information, and the recourse customers have if they believe the company is misusing the information. *Every* online company should have a privacy policy, but many do not. A survey by TRUSTe, a provider of Internet privacy services, reports that 56 percent of small business's Web sites have no privacy policy. Of the small companies that do have privacy policies, 35 percent of the owners say that they simply cut the privacy policy from another company's Web site and pasted it onto their own.[83]

Several online privacy firms, including TRUSTe (*www.truste.org*), BBBOnline (*www.bbbonline.com*), and BetterWeb (*www.betterweb.com*), offer Web "seal programs," the equivalent of a Good Housekeeping seal of privacy approval. To earn a privacy seal of approval, a company must adopt a privacy policy, implement it, and monitor its effectiveness. Many of these privacy sites also provide online policy wizards, automated questionnaires that help e-business owners create comprehensive privacy statements.

POST YOUR COMPANY'S PRIVACY POLICY PROMINENTLY ON YOUR WEB SITE AND FOLLOW IT. Creating a privacy policy is not sufficient; posting it in a prominent place on the Web site (accessible from every page on the site) and then abiding by it make a policy meaningful. Whether a company has a privacy policy posted prominently often determines whether customers will do online business with it. A study by Carnegie Mellon University reports that shoppers are more likely to purchase from online merchants that have sound privacy policies and post them.[84] One of the worst mistakes a company can make is to publish its privacy policy online and then fail to follow it. Not only is this unethical, but it also can lead to serious damage awards if customers take legal action against the company.

Security

Concerns about security and fraud present the greatest obstacles to the growth of e-commerce. A study by Harris Interactive reports that 45 percent of Web users have terminated an order or abandoned a shopping cart because of security fears.[85] Indeed, cybercrime has become big business, costing consumers and companies $5.8 billion annually.[86] Determining the extent of online security breaches is difficult because many companies never report breaches of computer security to authorities. Every company with a Web site—no matter how small—is a potential target for hackers and others seeking to cause harm. Hackers and attackers have become more sophisticated, which makes Web site security a top priority for *every* company doing business online. In a recent WhiteHat Security study of 1,659 Web sites that researchers considered "serious" about security, 75 percent had at least one serious point of vulnerability that hackers could exploit.[87]

A company doing business on the Web faces two conflicting goals: to establish a presence on the Web so that customers can have access to its site and the information maintained there and to preserve a high level of security so that the business, its site, and the information it collects from customers are safe from hackers and intruders intent on doing harm. Companies have a number of safeguards available to them, but hackers with enough time, talent, and determination usually can beat even the most sophisticated safety measures. If hackers manage to break into a system, they can do irreparable damage—stealing programs and sensitive customer data, modifying or deleting valuable information, changing the look and content of sites, or crashing sites altogether. In the largest data breach to date, hackers broke into the database at one retail company and stole information that included more than 45 million debit and credit card numbers.[88] Web-hosting company Network Solutions discovered that despite layers of protection, hackers had breached the transaction data of more than 4,300 of its merchant Web sites, which exposed the credit card data of 574,000 shoppers.[89] In addition to the actual losses these scams cause, another real danger is that scams such as these erode customers' confidence in e-commerce, posing real threats to every online entrepreneur.

Security threats are real for companies of every size, and entrepreneurs must contend with that reality. To minimize the likelihood of invasion by hackers and viruses, e-companies rely on several tools, including virus detection software, intrusion detection software, and firewalls. The most basic level of protection is **virus detection software**, which scans computer drives for viruses, nasty programs written by devious hackers that are designed to harm computers and the information they contain. The severity of viruses ranges widely, from relatively harmless programs that put humorous messages on a user's screen to those that erase a computer's hard drive or cause the entire system to crash. Because hackers are *always* writing new viruses to attack computer systems, entrepreneurs must keep their virus detection software up-to-date and run it often. An attack by one virus can bring a company's entire e-commerce platform to a screeching halt in no time! One virus that was sent by e-mail with the subject line "I love you" infected computer systems across the globe, leaving companies with an estimated $15 billion in damages and downtime.

Intrusion detection software is essential for any company doing business on the Web. These packages constantly monitor the activity on a company's network server and sound an alert if they detect someone breaking into the company's computer system or if they detect unusual network activity. Intrusion detection software not only detects attempts by unauthorized users to break into a computer system while they are happening, but it also traces the hacker's location. Most packages also have the ability to preserve a record of the attempted break-in that will stand up in court so that companies can take legal action against cyber-intruders. Web security companies such as McAfee provide software such as ScanAlert that scans a small business's Web site daily to certify that it is "Hacker Safe." Online companies using the software are able to post a certification mark signifying that their sites are protected from unauthorized access.

A **firewall** is software that operates between the Internet and a company's computer network that allows authorized data from the Internet to enter a company's network and the programs and data it contains but keeps unauthorized data, such as viruses, spyware, and other malware out. The equivalent of the lock on a small company's front door, a firewall serves as the lock on its computer network's front door. Establishing a firewall is essential for any company operating on the Web, but entrepreneurs must make sure that their firewalls are set up properly. Otherwise, they are useless! Even with all of these security measures in place, it is best for a company to run its Web site on a separate server from the network that runs the business. If hackers break into the Web site, they still do not have access to the company's sensitive data and programs.

Increasing the security of a computer system requires using properly installed security tools, perhaps in multiple layers, and making sure that they function properly and are up-to-date. Even though 65 percent of small businesses store customer data on their computer systems, only 53 percent of small companies check their virus detection software and firewalls weekly to ensure that they are up-to-date (and 11 percent *never* check them).[90] The National Cyber Security Alliance (*http://staysafeonline.org*) and the Computer Security Institute (*www.gocsi.com*) offer articles, information, and seminars to help business owners maintain computer security. *Information Security Magazine* (which can be found at *http://searchsecurity.techtarget.com*) also offers helpful advice on maintaining computer security.

In e-commerce, just as in traditional retailing, sales do not matter unless a company gets paid! On the Web, customers demand transactions they can complete with ease and convenience, and the simplest way to allow customers to pay for e-commerce transactions is with credit cards. From a Web customer's perspective, however, one of the most important security issues is the security of his or her credit card information. To ensure the security of their customers' credit card information, online retailers typically use **secure sockets layer (SSL) technology** to encrypt customers' transaction information as it travels across the Internet. By using secure shopping cart features from storefront-building services or Internet service providers, even the smallest e-commerce stores can offer their customers secure online transactions.

Processing credit card transactions requires a company to obtain an Internet merchant account from a bank or financial intermediary. Setup fees for an Internet merchant account typically range from $500 to $1,000, but companies also pay monthly access and statement fees of between $40 and $80 plus a transaction fee of 10 to 60 cents per transaction. Once an online company has a merchant account, it can accept credit cards from online customers.

Online credit card transactions also pose a risk for merchants; online companies lose $3.3 billion a year to online payment fraud each year, 1.2 percent of their sales revenue (see Figure 6), about half of it from **chargebacks**, online credit card transactions that customers dispute.[91] Good customer service minimizes the number of legitimate chargebacks. Illegitimate chargebacks usually are the result of thieves stealing credit card numbers and then using them to make online purchases. Unlike credit card transactions in a retail store, those made online ("card not present" transactions) involve no signatures, and Internet merchants incur the loss (and usually a fine from the credit card company) when a customer disputes the transaction.

Jamon Robinson, president of Sun Tints, Inc., a company that sells automotive accessories online and from a store in Bountiful, Utah, was frustrated that 1 out of every 100 online purchases resulted in a chargeback. In an effort to combat the problem, Robinson signed up with BadCustomer.com, a Web site (*www.badcustomer.com*) that allows merchants to search for customers who have a history of chargebacks before completing a credit card sale. In the first 3 months of using the service, Robinson refused several credit card transactions and did not have any chargebacks.[92]

Losses to Online Fraud

Source: "Online Fraud Report: 11th Annual Edition," Cybersource Corporation, Mountain View, California: 2010, p. 4.

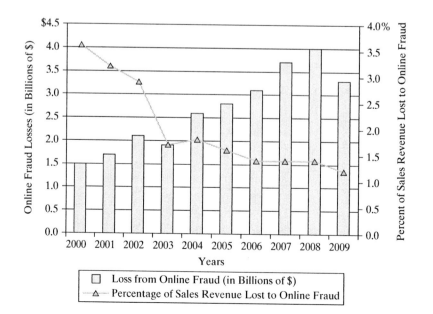

One way to prevent fraud is to ask customers for their card verification value (CVV, CID, or CVV2), the three-digit number above the signature panel on the back of the credit card, as well as their card number and expiration date. Online merchants also can subscribe to a real-time credit card processing service that authorizes credit card transactions, but the fees can be high. Sending confirmation e-mails that include the customer's shipping information after receiving an order also reduces the likelihood of a chargeback. In addition, using a shipper that provides the ability to track shipments so online merchants can prove that the customer actually received the merchandise can help minimize the threat of payment fraud.

Chapter Review

1. Describe the benefits of selling on the World Wide Web.
   - The opportunity to increase revenues
   - The ability to expand their reach into global markets
   - The ability to remain open 24 hours a day, 7 days a week
   - The capacity to use the Web's interactive nature to enhance customer service
   - The power to educate and to inform
   - The ability to lower the cost of doing business
   - The ability to spot new business opportunities and to capitalize on them
   - The power to track sales results
2. Understand the factors an entrepreneur should consider before launching into e-commerce.
   - How a company exploits the Web's interconnectivity and the opportunities it creates to transform relationships with its suppliers and vendors, its customers, and other external stakeholders is crucial to its success.
   - Web success requires a company to develop a plan for integrating the Web into its overall strategy. The plan should address issues such as site design and maintenance, creating and managing a brand name, marketing and promotional strategies, sales, and customer service.
   - Developing deep, lasting relationships with customers takes on even greater importance on the Web. Attracting customers on the Web costs money, and companies must be able to retain their online customers to make their Web sites profitable.
   - Creating a meaningful presence on the Web requires an ongoing investment of resources—time, money, energy, and talent. Establishing an attractive Web site brimming with catchy photographs of products is only the beginning.
   - Measuring the success of Web-based sales efforts is essential to remaining relevant to customers whose tastes, needs, and preferences are always changing.
3. Explain the 10 myths of e-commerce and how to avoid falling victim to them.
   - Myth 1. If I launch a site, customers will flock to it.
   - Myth 2. Online customers are easy to please.
   - Myth 3. Making money on the Web is easy.
   - Myth 4. Privacy is not an important issue on the Web.
   - Myth 5. "Strategy? I don't need a strategy to sell on the Web! Just give me a Web site, and the rest will take care of itself."
   - Myth 6. The most important part of any e-commerce effort is technology.
   - Myth 7. On the Web, customer service is not as important as it is in a traditional retail store.
   - Myth 8. Flashy Web sites are better than simple ones.
   - Myth 9. It's what's up front that counts.
   - Myth 10. It's too late to get on the Web.
4. Explain the basic strategies entrepreneurs should follow to achieve success in their e-commerce efforts.
   - Consider focusing on a niche in the market.
   - Develop a community of online customers.
   - Attract visitors by giving away "freebies."
   - Make creative use of e-mail, but avoid becoming a "spammer."
   - Make sure your Web site says "credibility."

- Consider forming strategic alliances with larger, more established companies.
- Make the most of the Web's global reach.
- Promote your Web site online and off-line.

5. Learn the techniques of designing a killer Web site.
   - Select a domain name that is consistent with the image you want to create for your company and register it.
   - Be easy to find.
   - Give customers want they want.
   - Establish hyperlinks with other businesses, preferably those selling products or services that complement yours.
   - Include an e-mail option and a telephone number on your site.
   - Give shoppers the ability to track their orders online.
   - Offer Web shoppers a special all their own.
   - Follow a simple design for your Web page.
   - Assure customers that their online transactions are secure.
   - Keep your site up-to-date.
   - Consider hiring a professional to design your site.

6. Explain how companies track the results from their Web sites.
   - Web sites offer entrepreneurs a treasure trove of valuable information about how well their sites are performing—if they take the time to analyze it. Web analytics, tools that measure a Web site's ability to attract customers, generate sales, and keep customers coming back, help entrepreneurs to know what works—and what doesn't—on their sites.

7. Describe how e-businesses ensure the privacy and security of the information they collect and store from the Web.
   - To make sure they are using the information they collect from visitors to their Web sites legally and ethically, companies should take the following steps:
     - Take an inventory of the customer data collected.
     - Develop a company privacy policy for the information you collect.
     - Post your company's privacy policy prominently on your Web site and follow it.
   - To ensure the security of the information they collect and store from Web transactions, companies should rely on virus and intrusion detection software and firewalls to ward off attacks from hackers.

Discussion Questions

1. How has the Internet and e-commerce changed the ways companies do business?
2. Explain the benefits a company earns by selling on the Web.
3. Discuss the factors entrepreneurs should consider before launching an e-commerce site.
4. What are the 10 myths of e-commerce? What can an entrepreneur do to avoid them?
5. What strategic advice would you offer an entrepreneur about to start an e-company?
6. What design characteristics make for a successful Web page?
7. Explain the characteristics of an ideal domain name.
8. Describe the techniques that are available to e-companies for tracking results from their Web sites. What advantages does each offer?

9. What steps should e-businesses take to ensure the privacy of the information they collect and store from the Web?
10. What techniques can e-companies use to protect their banks of information and their customers' transaction data from hackers?
11. How can online entrepreneurs evaluate the effectiveness of their Web sites?
12. When Matt Buchan and Alex Garcia purchased a struggling hair salon in Seattle, Washington, their turnaround strategy included using the Internet as a key component of their business and marketing strategies. What advice can you offer these entrepreneurs for integrating the Web into their hair salon to enhance their customers' experience?

Business Plan Pro

The Internet has transformed the way entrepreneurs operate, giving them the ability to sell their goods and services 24/7 and to reach customers around the world. Web-based businesses can connect with suppliers, provide higher levels of customer service, understand and respond to customer's preferences, and gain insight into their customers' online buying behavior to improve the experience. One of the initial questions asked in the initial Business Plan Pro wizard relates to your business Web site. What was your response to that question— yes or no? Use the contents of this chapter to review your decision. Think about the online presence that you would like your business to have. Is your Web site going to be an information only site, or do you plan to have a robust online store that is capable of conducting e-commerce? As you look through the list of the 10 myths mentioned in this chapter, ask yourself if you have fallen prey to any of these myths. What benefits do you expect to realize from your online presence?

On the Web

If you are planning to create a Web site that is for information-only purposes, go to sites that accomplish that goal. For example, you may want to visit *www.epinions.com*. Note the layout and navigation of the site and how it presents this information. If you plan to have a dynamic online store, Amazon.com's site was a pioneer in the evolution of online shopping. Go to *www.amazon.com* and take a fresh look at the site's attributes. What attributes on the site make it simple, efficient, and "safe" for new and returning buyers? Identify those qualities and explore how your site might also benefit from those attributes.

In the Software

Open your plan in Business Plan Pro and go to the "Web Summary" section. If you will create a Web site, click "View" and "Wizard" and change that decision. Business Plan Pro will update the outline of your business plan by adding a "Web Summary" section. Read the instructions within the software and click the sample plan link in the upper right-hand section of the instructions. Add content to this section. The following questions may help you as you build your e-commerce strategy:

- Have you registered a URL for your business? If not, how will you begin the process to secure and register a Web address?
- How would you assess the general level of comfort that your target market has with the Web? For example, are they a technologically savvy group that uses the Web as a part of their daily life, or is this group an older audience that is just learning how to leverage the power of the Web?
- List the objectives you hope to realize through your Web site.
- Is your site going to have an online store? If so, explore how to implement credit card or other online payment options. What are the costs associated with the method of accepting payments online that you have chosen?
- Who will design and update the site? Will you or someone in your organization, or will you outsource that work?
- How will you measure, track, and assess the performance of your site, and how often will that occur?
- Are you going to incorporate Web analytics tools and resources that may help you to measure your Web site's performance?
- Does your business plan demonstrate that you have planned and budgeted for your Web site based on the required resources to design, launch, and maintain your site?

Building Your Business Plan

The additions you have made regarding your Web site may be significant or minimal. Step back and review the information that you have captured in your plan to date. With these additions, does your plan continue to tell a consistent and coherent story about your business? Review and edit other sections that may be affected by your additions to the Web section. Some of those sections may include areas that relate to marketing promotions, communications, expenses, and revenues.

Endnotes

1. Bret Thorn, "Domino's Passes $1 Billion in Online Sales," *Nation's Restaurant News*, February 10, 2010, *www.nrn.com/article/dominos-passes-1-billion-online-sales*; "Pizza Hut Expects $2 Billion in Online Sales," I4UNews, April 20, 2010, *www.i4u.com/article33268.html*; Karl Flinders, "Web Takes a Bigger Slice of Domino's," February 16, 2010, *Computer Weekly, www.computerweekly.com/Articles/2010/02/16/240320/Web-takes-a-bigger-slice-of-Domino39s-Pizza.htm*; "Papa John's Surpasses $1 Billion in Online Pizza Sales," Fresh News, May 8, 2008, *www.freshnews.in/papa-johns-surpasses-1-billion-in-online-pizza-sales-26218*; "Online Ordering Leader Papa John's First to Surpass $2 Billion in Online Sales," *QSR*, May 3, 2010, *www.qsrmagazine.com/articles/wire/story/20100503006043en*.

2. Erick Schonfeld, "Forrester Forecast: Online Retail Sales Will Grow to $250 Billion by 2014," TechCrunch, March 8, 2010. *http://techcrunch.com/2010/03/08/forrester-forecast-online-retail-sales-will-grow-to-250-billion-by-2014/*.

3. "Internet Usage Statistics: The Internet Big Picture," Internet World Stats, 2009, *www.internetworldstats.com/stats.htm*.

4. Brian McRoberts, George H. Terhanian, Ken Allredge, and Carla Keppler, *Understanding the Role of the Internet in the Lives of Consumers: Digital Influence Index*, Fleishman-Hillard and Harris Interactive, June 2010, p. 8.

5. "Living in Exponential Times," Get to the Point: Marketing Inspiration, *Marketing Profs*, May 11, 2009, pp. 1–2.

6. Erick Schonfeld, "Forrester Forecast: Online Retail Sales Will Grow to $250 Billion by 2014," TechCrunch, March 8, 2010, *http://techcrunch. com/2010/03/08/forrester-forecast-online-retail-sales-will-grow-to-250-billion-by-2014/*; Don Davis, "Consumers Will Buy or Research Online Half of Purchases by 2014, Forrester Says," *Internet Retailer*, March 31, 2010, *www.internetretailer.com/2010/03/31/ consumers-will-buy-or-research-online-half-of-purchases-by-2014*.

7. "Business Purchasing Survey Shows 93 Percent of Small Businesses Value Internet for Research over Online Purchasing," BuyerZone, *www.buyerzone.com/corporate/about_buyerzone/pr051705.html*.

8. Nick Timiraos, "Facts," *Wall Street Journal*, December 23–24, 2006, p. A7.

9. "A Perfect Market," *Economist*, May 15, 2004, p. 4.

10. Kelly Heyboer, "Baking and Blogging: Speaking with Extreme Baker and Pink Cake Blogger Anne Heap," *Star Ledger*, March 4, 2009, *http://blog. nj.com/jerseyblogs/2009/03/baking_and_blogging_speaking_w. html*; Matt McGee, "A Small Marketing Success Story: Pink Cake Box," Search Engine Land, March 13, 2008, *http://searchengineland .com/a-small-business-marketing-success-story-pink-cake-box-13567*.

11. "Small Business Marketing Forecast 2010," Ad-ology, November 2009, p. 17.

12. Denise O'Berry, "Yes, You Do Need a Web Site for Your Small Business," *All Business*, December 17, 2009, *www.allbusiness.com/ company-activities-management/company-structures-ownership/ 13624856-1.html*.

13. Lauren Simonds, "Web Sites: They're Not Just for E-Commerce," *Small Business Computing*, February 15, 2007, *www.smallbusinesscomputing .com/news/article.php/3660186*.

14. Frank Fortunato, "Search Engine Strategy Expo Exposes Valuable Tips," *E-Commerce Guide*, May 1, 2007, *www.ecommerce-guide.com/ solutions/article.php/3675066*.

15. Robert McGarvey, "Connect the Dots," *Entrepreneur*, March 2000, pp. 78–85.

16. "BlogPulse Stats," BlogPulse, July 9, 2010, *www.blogpulse.com*.

17. Kristin Ladd, "Help! My Business Sucks!" *Entrepreneur*, September 3, 2009, *www.entrepreneur.com/startingabusiness/successstories/ article203244.html*; Richard Markosian, "Rage Against Businesses That Suck," *Utah Stories*, September 21, 2009, *www.utahstories.com/ help-my-business-sucks.html*.

18. Claire Tristram, "Many Happy Returns," *Small Business Computing*, May 1999, p. 73.

19. *Digital Window Shopping: The Long Journey to 'Buy*,' McAfee, Santa Clara, California: 2009, p. 3.

20. "Survival of the Fastest," *Inc. Technology*, No. 4, 1999, p. 57.

21. Fred Mossler and Tony Hsieh, "A Lesson from Zappos: Follow the Golden Rule," *Harvard Business Review*, June 4, 2010, *http://blogs. hbr.org/cs/2010/06/a_lesson_from_zappos_follow_th.html*; "The Zappos Story," Zappos.com, *www.zappos.com/about.zhtml*; Sidra Durst, "Shoe In," *Business 2.0*, December 2006, p. 54; "Beyond Their Years," *Entrepreneur*, November 2003, *www.entrepreneur.com/ article/0,4621,311420,00.html*; "Zappos.com on Pace to More Than Double Sales This Year," *Internet Retailer*, November 3, 2003, *www.internetretailer.com/dailynews.asp?id=10577*; Jane Bennett Clark, Robert Frick, Sean O'Neill, Ronaleen Roha, and Alison Stevenson, "Point Click Buy," *Kiplinger's*, June 2003, pp. 90–93.

22. Fred Mossler and Tony Hsieh, "A Lesson from Zappos: Follow the Golden Rule," *Harvard Business Review*, June 4, 2010, *http://blogs. hbr.org/cs/2010/06/a_lesson_from_zappos_follow_th.html*.

23. Steve Bennett and Stacey Miller, "The E-Commerce Plunge," *Small Business Computing*, February 2000, p. 50.

24. John Horrigan, "Online Shopping," February 13, 2008, Pew Internet and American Life Project, *www.pewinternet.org/Reports/2008/ Online-Shopping.aspx?r=1*.

25. "Akamai Reveals 2 Seconds as the New Threshold of Acceptability for E-Commerce Web Page Response Time," Akamai, September 14, 2009, *www.akamai.com/html/about/press/releases/2009/press_091409.html*.

26. Fiona Swerdlow, "2009 State of Retailing Online: Marketing Report," Shop.org, May 5, 2009, *http://blog.shop.org/2009/05/05/2009-state-of-retailing-online-marketing-report/*.

27. Melissa Campanelli, "Abandonment Issues," *E-Marketing and Commerce*, June 24, 2009, *www.emarketingandcommerce.com/blog/ abandonment-issues*.

28. "Why Do We Abandon Shopping Carts?" Vovici, January 2006, *www.vovici.com/efm-innovation/reference/website-visitors/ shopping-cart-abandonment-survey.asp*.

29. "E-mail Service Provider Listrak Conducts 'Shop and Abandon' Cart Study Using Internet Retailer 500 List," Listrak, August 13, 2009, *www.listrak.com/News/Listrak-Conducts-Abandon-Cart-Study/*.

30. "The Remarketing Report: Benchmark Data and Analysis on Connecting Web Behavior to E-mail Marketing," Experian CheetahMail, January 2010, p. 2.

31. "Case Studies: Rockler Automated Cart Abandonment Program Drives 2% of Sales," Blue Hornet Digital River, *www.bluehornet.com/ case-studies/full/rockler*; "E-mail Service Provider Listrak Conducts 'Shop and Abandon' Cart Study Using Internet Retailer 500 List," Listrak, August 13, 2009, *www.listrak.com/News/Listrak-Conducts-Abandon-Cart-Study/*.

32. "Akamai Reveals 2 Seconds as the New Threshold of Acceptability for E-Commerce Web Page Response Times," Akamai, September 14, 2009, *www.akamai.com/html/about/press/releases/2009/press_091409.html*; Kristina Knight, "Study: Consumers Abandon Slow-Loading Web Sites," *BizReport*, April 27, 2010, *www.bizreport.com/ 2010/04/study_consumers_abandon_slow_loading_websites.html#*; "TagMan Solves Slow Page Load/Audience Loss Problems with Introduction of New TagMan ServerTags," TagMan, May 10, 2010, *http://blog.tagman.com/2010/05/tagman-solves-slow-page-loadaudience-loss-problems-with-introduction-of-new-tagman-servertags/*.

33. "Web Site Performance Management," *Internet Retailer*, July 1, 2010, *www.internetretailer.com/2010/07/01/web-site-performance-management*.

34. Fred Vogelstein, "A Cold Bath for Dot-Com Fever," *U.S. News & World Report*, September 13, 1999, p. 37.

35. "The World Is Discovering Fragrances of Ireland Through Webgistix," Webgistix, Olean, New York, *www.webgistix.com/success_FOI.pdf*.

36. Greg Howlett, "Trade PPV for VLV: Visitor Lifetime Value Metric Makes Money," *E-Commerce Guide*, May 23, 2007, *www. ecommerce-guide.com/solutions/building/article.php/3679441*.

37. Bronwyn Fryer and Lee Smith, ".com or Bust," *Forbes Small Business*, December 1999–January 2000, p. 41.

38. "History," Caledonian Creations, *www.caledoniancreations.co.uk/ company/history.htm*.

39. Ralph F. Wilson, "The Five Mutable Laws of Web Marketing," *Web Marketing Today*, April 1, 1999, *www.wilsonweb.com/wmta/basic-principles.htm*, pp. 1–7.

40. "Bella of Cape Cod Offers a Lot of Bling for the Buck," Constant Contact, *www.constantcontact.com/email-marketing/customer-examples/bella-of-cape-cod.jsp*.

41. "E-Commerce Spending Will Rise 11% to $156 Billion This Year, Study Says," *Internet Retailer*, May 5, 2009, *www.internetretailer.com/ 2009/05/05/e-commerce-spending-will-rise-11-to-156-1-billion-this-year-s*.

42. "Epsilon Q4 2009 E-mail Trends and Benchmarks," Epsilon, Irving, Texas: February 2010, p. 2.

43. "Use of Testing in E-mail Marketing," eROI, 2009, p. 5; "Q3 E-mail Marketing Statistics," eROI, January 2008, p. 1.

44. "State of Spam and Phishing," Symantec, June 2010, p. 1.

45. Gitte Lindgaard, Gary Fernandes, Cathy Dudek, and J. Brown, "Attention Web Designers: You Have 50 Milliseconds to Make a Good Impression," *Journal of Behaviour and Information Technology*, March 2006, p. 115.

46. David Port, "How to Make Your Web Site Really Sell," *Entrepreneur*, September 2009, p. 84.

47. Phil Hochmuth, "Trust Marks: What's Behind the Label Counts," Yankee Group, Boston, Massachusetts: 2009, p. 3.

48. Jan Gardner, "10 Ideas for Growing Business Now," *Inc.*, October 29, 2001, *www2.inc.com/search/23629.html*.

49. "Affiliate Marketing Survey Report," e-Consultancy, 2008, *www.slideshare.net/econsultancy/affiliate-marketing-survey-report-2008-presentation-594947*.

50. Peter Figueredo, "Best-Kept Secrets of Affiliate Marketing Success," iMedia Connection, January 15, 2010, *www.imediaconnection. com/content/25634.asp*.

51. "The Top Ten Languages Used in the Internet," *Internet World Stats*, July 9, 2010, *www.internetworldstats.com/stats7.htm*.

52. Dylan Tweney, "Think Globally, Act Locally," *Business 2.0*, November 2001, pp. 120–121.

53. Don Davis, "Survivor: E-retail," *Internet Retailer*, April 2009, *www.internetretailer.com/2009/04/01/survivor-e-retail*; "Blue Nile Announces First Quarter 2010 Financial Results," Blue Nile, Inc., May 6, 2010, *www.internetworldstats.com/stats7.htm*.

54. Patrick Altoft, "5 Killer Ways to Promote Your Web Site Offline," Blogstorm, January 7, 2008, *www.blogstorm.co.uk/5-killer-ways-to-promote-your-website-offline/*; "Interview with 'Dragon Eater' Ling Valentine," Self Made Minds, January 31, 2008, *http://selfmademinds .com/200801/interview-with-dragon-eater-ling-valentine/*.

55. Kristin Purcell, "The State of Online Video," Pew Internet and American Life Project, June 3, 2010, *www.pewinternet.org/Reports/2010/State-of-Online-Video.aspx*; Aaron Smith, "New Numbers for Blogging and Blog Readership," Pew Internet and American Life Project, July 22, 2008, *www.pewinternet.org/Commentary/2008/July/New-numbers-for-blogging-and-blog-readership.aspx*; "Adults on Social Network Sites," Pew Internet and American Life Project, October 8, 2009, *www.pewinternet .org/Infographics/Growth-in-Adult-SNS-Use-20052009.aspx*.

56. "Global Advertising: Consumers Trust Real Friends and Virtual Strangers the Most," NielsenWire, July 7, 2009, *http://blog.nielsen.com/nielsenwire/consumer/global-advertising-consumers-trust-real-friends-and-virtual-strangers-the-most/print/*.

57. Louis Columbus, "Is Social Networking and Asset or a Liability for Your Company?" *CRM Buyer*, September 2, 2008, *www.crmbuyer.com/story/64352.html*.

58. Jessica E. Vascellaro, "Twitter Goes Mainstream," *Wall Street Journal*, October 27, 2008, pp. R1, R8.

59. Erica Swallow, "5 Small Business Social Media Success Stories," *Mashable*, June 2, 2010, *http://mashable.com/2010/06/02/small-business-social-media-success-stories/*.

60. Dan Briody, "Puppy Power," *Inc.*, November 2007, pp. 55–56.

61. Steve Coomes, "Pizza Chains 'Fan' Sales Flames by Adding Widgets to Social Networking Sites," *Nation's Restaurant News*, November 20, 2008, *www.nrn.com/article/pizza-chains-fan-sales-flames-adding-widgets-social-networking-sites*.

62. Jack Loechner, "Search Engines: The Shopper's Aid," Center for Media Research: Research Brief, March 4, 2010, *www.mediapost.com/publications/?fa=Articles.printFriendly&art_aid=123651*.

63. Justin Martin, "Get Right with Google," *FSB*, September 2006, pp. 70–78.

64. "iProspect Blended Search Results Study," iProspect, April 2008, p. 13.

65. James A. Martin, "Search Engine Optimization: SEO Tips for Small Business," *Small Business Computing*, September 29, 2009, *www.smallbusinesscomputing.com/buyersguide/article.php/3841381/Search-Engine-Optimization-SEO-Tips-for-Small-Business.htm*.

66. Ibid.

67. Nate Elliot, "The Easiest Way to a First-Page Ranking on Google," *Forrester Blogs*, January 8, 2009, *http://blogs.forrester.com/interactive_marketing/2009/01/the-easiest-way.html*.

68. "Top Search Engines for 2010," SEO Consultants Directory, July 2, 2010, *www.seoconsultants.com/search-engines/*.

69. Justin Martin, "Get Right with Google," *FSB*, September 2006, pp. 70–78; "E-Commerce Spending Will Rise 11% to $156 Billion This Year, Study Says," *Internet Retailer*, May 5, 2009, *www.internetretailer .com/2009/05/05/e-commerce-spending-will-rise-11-to-156-1-billion-this-year-s*.

70. "Lingerie e-Retailer Andra Group Uncovers Customers Ready to Buy," *Internet Retailer*, April 30, 2009, *www.internetretailer.com/2009/04/30/lingerie-e-retailer-andra-group-uncovers-customers-ready-to-buy*.

71. "Click Fraud Rises in Q1 2010," *Marketing Charts*, May 21, 2010, *www.marketingcharts.com/direct/click-fraud-rises-in-q1-2010-12972/*.

72. Herman Miller, *www.hermanmiller.com*; "Design Matters," *Fortune Tech Guide*, 2001, pp. 183–188.

73. "Santa's Helpers," *Economist*, May 15, 2004, pp. 5–8.

74. Max Chafkin, "Where Have All the Words Gone?" *Inc.*, July–August 2009, pp. 23–24.

75. Christopher Saunders, "How Do I: Attract and Keep Customers?" *E-Commerce Guide*, June 8, 2004, *www.ecommerce-guide.com/news/article.php/3365551*.

76. "About Us," American Pearl, *www.americanpearl.com/aboutus.html*.

77. *Revolutionizing Web Site Design: The New Rules of Usability*, OneupWeb, Traverse City, Michigan: 2010, p. 11.

78. Melissa Campanelli, "The Right Stuff," *Entrepreneur*, April 2007, p. 54.

79. Carol Stavraka, "There's No Stopping E-Business. Are You Ready?" *Forbes*, December 13, 1999, Special Advertising Section.

80. "2009 National Cyber Security Alliance/Symantec Small Business Study," National Cyber Security Alliance, 2009, pp. 3–4.

81. James Maguire, "The 'Mystery Shopping' Report," *E-Commerce Guide*, February 21, 2006, *www.e-commerce-guide.com/solutions/customer_relations/article.php/3586441*.

82. Fiona Swerdlow, "2009 State of Retailing Online: Marketing Report," Shop.org, May 5, 2009, *http://blog.shop.org/2009/05/05/2009-state-of-retailing-online-marketing-report/*.

83. "How to Reduce Shopping Cart Abandonment," TRUSTe, San Francisco: 2009, p. 3.

84. "Online Shoppers Will Pay Extra to Protect Privacy, Study Shows," PhysOrg.com, June 6, 2007, *www.physorg.com/news100357431.html*.

85. "Digital Window Shopping: The Long Journey to 'Buy,'" McAfee, Santa Clara, California: 2009, p. 5.

86. Methusela Cebrian Ferrer, "State of the Internet 2009: A Report on the Ever-Changing Threat Landscape," CA Internet Business Security Unit, CA Technologies, Islandia, New York: 2010, p. 1.

87. "WhiteHat Web Site Security Statistics Report, 9th Edition," WhiteHat Security, Santa Clara, California: Spring 2009, p. 5.

88. Larry Greenemeier, "Largest Data Breach Ever," *Information Week*, April 2, 2007, p. 21.

89. Pankaj Kumar, "E-Commerce Data Security 2010: Learning from 2009's Debacles," *CRMBuyer*, January 18, 2010, *www.crmbuyer.com/story/69129.html?wlc=1278516295*.

90. "2009 National Cyber Security Alliance/Symantec Small Business Study," National Cyber Security Alliance, 2009, pp. 3–4.

91. "Online Fraud Report, 11th Annual Edition," Cybersource Corporation, Mountain View, California: 2010, p. 4.

92. Emily Maltby, "Shady Shoppers Beware," *Wall Street Journal*, November 24, 2009, *http://online.wsj.com/article/SB10001424052748704533904574548210301039526.html#*.

Supply Chain Management

Without the right goods, sales are impossible.

—Anonymous

Quality in a product or service is not what the supplier puts in. It is what the customer gets out and is willing to pay for. Customers pay only for what is of use to them and gives them value. Nothing else constitutes quality.

—Peter Drucker

From Chapter 17 of *Effective Small Business Management: An Entrepreneurial Approach*, 10/e. Norman M. Scarborough.

This chapter discusses the activities involved in managing a small company's supply chain—purchasing, quality management, and vendor analysis. Although none of these is the most glamorous or exciting job an entrepreneur undertakes, they form an important part of the foundation that supports every small business. When entrepreneurs begin producing products or providing services, they quickly learn how much their products or services depend on the quality of the components and services they purchase from their suppliers. Today, success depends on higher levels of collaboration among the businesses that make up a company's supply chain. "Many businesses still regard the supply chain as the back end of their businesses, but the modern supply chain has a much bigger contribution to make," concludes one study of supply chain management. "It can help companies differentiate themselves from the competition and achieve greater sustainable growth."[1] Today, thriving companies operate as part of a seamless network of alliances and partnerships with customers, suppliers, and distributors. For many businesses, the quality of the supply chain determines their ability to satisfy their customers and to compete effectively. "Competition is not really company vs. company," says one expert, "but supply chain vs. supply chain."[2] In other words, supply chain management has become an important strategic issue rather than merely a tactical matter for companies. Several studies have found that companies that utilize best practice supply chain management tools outperform those with average supply chains. Top performing companies saw their revenues grow more than twice as fast and earn 33 percent more profit, while carrying one-third less inventory.[3]

Managing the supply chain has become more challenging, however, because the globalization of business makes supply chains longer and adds layers of complexity to supply chain activities. A recent study by FM Global and CFO Research Services reports that 67 percent of CFOs say that purchasing production inputs from foreign suppliers is at least "somewhat common" in their companies, and 62 percent say that global sourcing activity will increase over the next 3 years. Nearly 40 percent of these executives report that their companies' global purchasing patterns increase the level of risk in the supply chain.[4] Figure 1 shows the greatest risks that companies face in their supply chains. Purchasing goods and services from companies scattered across the globe means that entrepreneurs must manage the elements of their supply chains much more closely to avoid disruptions, inventory shortages, or, at the other extreme, excess inventories that they must discount to sell.

U.S. companies spend more than $20 trillion on goods and services each year, and small and medium-size businesses account for 45 percent of that total.[5] Selecting the right vendors and designing a fast and efficient supply chain influences a small company's ability to produce and sell quality products and services at competitive prices. These decisions have far-reaching effects for a business as well as a significant impact on its bottom line. Depending on the type of business involved, the purchasing function can consume anywhere from 25 to 85 cents of each dollar

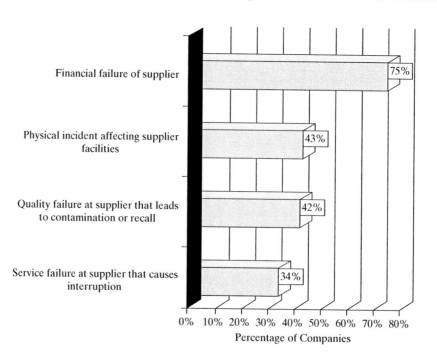

FIGURE 1
Supply Chain Risks

of sales. By shaving just 2 percent off of its cost of goods sold, a typical small company can increase its net income by more than 25 percent! A study of various industries by IBM determined that to match the bottom-line impact of a $1 savings in purchasing, a company must increase its sales revenue by an average of 19.7 percent.[6] To realize these savings, however, entrepreneurs must create a purchasing plan, establish well-defined measures of product or service quality, and select vendors and suppliers using a set of relevant, objective criteria.

When a company's supply chain breaks down, the result can be devastating in both immediate and future costs, such as recalling dangerous or defective products and lost sales from customers who turn to substitute products. Some of those lost customers never return, and, worse yet, the company's name and reputation are tarnished forever. For instance, Robert's American Gourmet, a company founded in 1986 by Robert Ehrlich that produces snack foods aimed at health-conscious customers, was forced to recall two of its snacks, Veggie Booty and Super Veggie Tings Crunchy Corn Sticks, after the FDA linked them to a salmonella outbreak that sickened 60 people in 19 states. An analysis traced the salmonella to a spray-on vegetable seasoning that a supplier imported from China. The products, which had accounted for more than 12 percent of the company's sales, were off of store shelves for 3 months, and Robert's American Gourmet's sales declined during the recall and for months afterward.[7]

Both manmade and natural disasters pose a threat to companies' supply chains. In a study of companies across a variety of industries conducted by the Aberdeen Group, 82 percent of managers say that their companies had experienced a supply disruption or outage within the previous 2 years.[8] Automakers BMW and Nissan were among the many companies whose supply chains were disrupted by the eruption of the Eyjafjallajökull volcano in Iceland. Nissan interrupted production at its Japanese factories of three models, the Cube, the Murano, and the Rogue, because the volcanic eruption halted cargo flights from a European supplier of air pressure sensors. BMW slowed production at three German plants and its sole North American plant in Greer, South Carolina, because the ash cloud prevented flights carrying supplies of transmissions. BMW scrambled to find alternative shipping routes but, in the meantime, the company lost many days of production of some of its most popular models, including the X5 and X6.[9] Minimizing problems from disruptions in a company's supply chains as a result of disasters and unexpected events requires a sound purchasing plan.

Creating a Purchasing Plan

1. Understand the components of a purchasing plan.

Purchasing involves the acquisition of needed materials, supplies, services, and equipment of the right quality, in the proper quantities, for reasonable prices, at the appropriate time, and from the right vendor. A major objective of purchasing is to acquire enough (but not too much) stock to ensure smooth, uninterrupted production or sales and to see that the merchandise is delivered on time. A purchasing plan must identify a company's quality requirements, its cost targets, and the criteria for determining the best supplier, considering such factors as reliability, service, delivery, and cooperation.

ENTREPRENEURIAL
Profile

McCormick and Company

McCormick and Company, a business that sells spices ranging from allspice to turmeric, literally spans the globe to purchase from hundreds of suppliers the raw materials it requires for its product line. For more than 100 years, company buyers have traveled to Uganda and Madagascar for vanilla; to China and Nigeria for ginger; to Yugoslavia and Albania for sage; and to India, Turkey, Pakistan, and Syria for cumin seed. McCormick makes significant investments to find suppliers that can deliver quality materials in a timely manner and engages in extensive testing and security practices to ensure the quality and the safety of the raw materials it purchases.[10]

A purchasing plan is closely linked to the other functional areas of managing a small business: production, marketing, sales, engineering, accounting, finance, and others. A purchasing plan should recognize this interaction and help integrate the purchasing function into the total organization. A small company's purchasing plan should focus on the five key elements of purchasing: quality, quantity, price, timing, and vendor selection (see Figure 2).

FIGURE 2
**Components of a
Purchasing Plan**

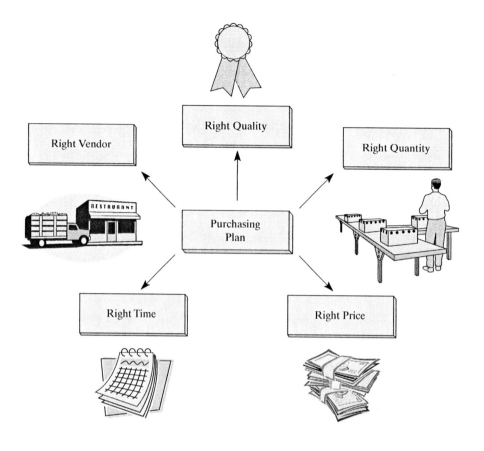

FIGURE 2
**Components of a
Purchasing Plan**

Quality

2. Explain the principles of total quality management (TQM) and Six Sigma and their impact on quality.

Not long ago businesses saw quality products and services as luxuries for customers who could afford them. Many companies mistakenly believed that producing or purchasing high-quality products and services was too costly. Today, business owners understand that quality goods and services are absolutely *essential* to remaining competitive. The benefits that companies earn by creating quality products, services, and processes come not only in the form of fewer defects, but also in lower costs, higher productivity, and higher customer retention rates. W. Edwards Deming, one of the founding fathers of the modern quality movement, always claimed that higher quality resulted in lower costs. Internally, companies with a quality focus report significant improvements in work-related factors such as increased employee morale, lower employee turnover, and enhanced quality of work life. Benefits such as these can result in a significant competitive advantage over rivals of *any* size.

Total quality companies believe in and manage with the attitude of continuous improvement, a concept the Japanese call *kaizen*. The kaizen philosophy holds that small improvements made continuously over time accumulate into a radically reshaped and improved process. When defective items do occur, managers and employees who are engaged in continuous improvement do not simply rework or repair them. Instead, they see defective items as an opportunity to improve the entire process. Their goal is to identify the root cause of the defects and to change the entire process so that the same problem does not occur again. Kaizen also encourages managers to focus on improving the entire system, not just its individual components. World-class organizations in the twenty-first century have made continuous improvement a fundamental element of their competitive strategies.

Quality has an impact on both costs and revenues. Improved quality leads to less scrap and rework time, lower warranty costs, and increased worker productivity. On the revenue side of the equation, quality improves the firm's reputation, attracts customers, and often allows a firm to charge higher prices. The bottom-line impact of quality is increased profitability.

LEAN PRINCIPLES. Originally applied to manufacturing, Lean principles also have produced significant quality improvements in both the retail and service sectors. The fundamental idea behind the Lean philosophy is to eliminate waste in a company's activities, whether they are in manufacturing, distribution, inventory control, customer service, human resources, or other areas, and to make a company lean (and efficient) in its operation. Lean is built on five principles:

1. *Value.* Companies must create products and services that add value from the customer's perspective.
2. *Value stream.* Businesses must identify the essential steps that allow them to create an efficient production or service workflow.
3. *Flow.* Companies must eliminate every step in the value stream that adds no value or creates delays, bottlenecks, and wasted effort. The goal is to create a smoothly flowing, efficient process that produces value for customers.
4. *Pull.* Companies produce only when customer demand pulls products and services through the system. Attempting to push them through the system results in inefficiency in the form of excess inventory, costs, and waste. Customer demand, the "pull" in the system, drives the entire supply chain.
5. *Perfection.* Companies should strive for perfection by eliminating waste and inefficiency everywhere it arises and by providing exactly the products and services customers want.

The principles of Lean are aimed at eliminating seven wastes. Figure 3 (a) shows the seven wastes in a manufacturing environment, and Figure 3 (b) shows the seven wastes in a service operation. Some experts have added an eighth waste to both lists: underutilization of people. Some companies treat their workers as if they know very little. World-class companies see their employees as a valuable source of ideas, creativity, and solutions, and they create systems that capture their employees' knowledge and apply it to the process of continuous improvement.

FIGURE 3 (a)
Seven Wastes of Manufacturing

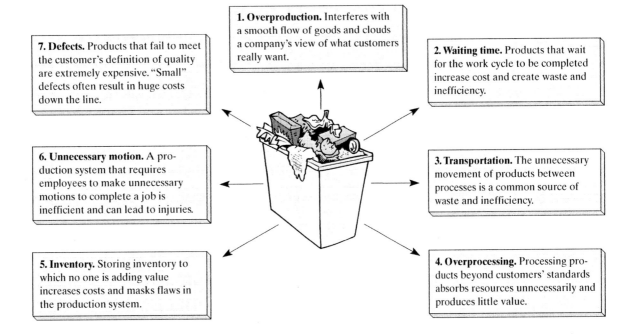

7. Defects. Products that fail to meet the customer's definition of quality are extremely expensive. "Small" defects often result in huge costs down the line.

1. Overproduction. Interferes with a smooth flow of goods and clouds a company's view of what customers really want.

2. Waiting time. Products that wait for the work cycle to be completed increase cost and create waste and inefficiency.

6. Unnecessary motion. A production system that requires employees to make unnecessary motions to complete a job is inefficient and can lead to injuries.

3. Transportation. The unnecessary movement of products between processes is a common source of waste and inefficiency.

5. Inventory. Storing inventory to which no one is adding value increases costs and masks flaws in the production system.

4. Overprocessing. Processing products beyond customers' standards absorbs resources unnecessarily and produces little value.

FIGURE 3 (b)
**Seven Wastes
of Service**

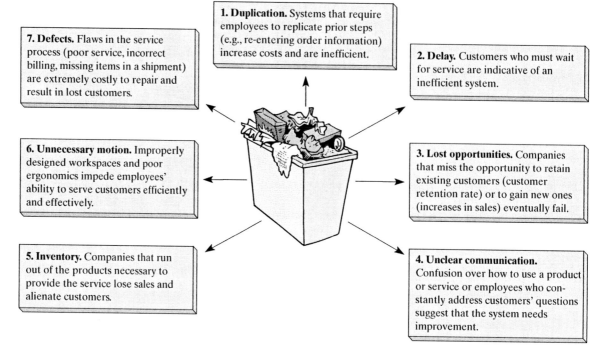

7. Defects. Flaws in the service process (poor service, incorrect billing, missing items in a shipment) are extremely costly to repair and result in lost customers.

1. Duplication. Systems that require employees to replicate prior steps (e.g., re-entering order information) increase costs and are inefficient.

2. Delay. Customers who must wait for service are indicative of an inefficient system.

6. Unnecessary motion. Improperly designed workspaces and poor ergonomics impede employees' ability to serve customers efficiently and effectively.

3. Lost opportunities. Companies that miss the opportunity to retain existing customers (customer retention rate) or to gain new ones (increases in sales) eventually fail.

5. Inventory. Companies that run out of the products necessary to provide the service lose sales and alienate customers.

4. Unclear communication. Confusion over how to use a product or service or employees who constantly address customers' questions suggest that the system needs improvement.

IN THE ENTREPRENEURIAL SPOTLIGHT   Lean Works Anywhere

Innovation always has been a key ingredient at Capel Incorporated, the oldest and largest privately owned rug manufacturer in the United States. Founded by Leon Capel, Sr., in 1917 in Troy, North Carolina, the company actually began life as the Gee-Haw Plowline Company, a manufacturer of plow lines used to guide mules and horses in the fields. Within a few years, the introduction of the motorized tractor made Capel's plow line business obsolete, but his ability to innovate saved the company. Capel used the materials from the plow lines to create a continuous yarn, which he then spun into the world's first continuous-yarn braided rug. Leon's sons eventually took over the family business and added their own innovations, including an air table that spun rugs as they were braided, minimizing the amount of manual handling and increasing workers' productivity. They also opened the company's first retail stores, which now number 11.

Capel is now in the hands of third-generation owner Richard Capel, who has introduced important innovations of his own. Perhaps Richard's most important contribution has been introducing Lean principles to the business, an idea that was inspired after he attended a workshop sponsored by North Carolina State University's Industrial Extension

Service on the Toyota Production System, on which many of the Lean principles are based.

Richard started with the company's manufacturing process, introducing workers to Lean principles and teaching them to spot the seven wastes. He set up a system to encourage employee ideas and solutions to production problems and established a "pull" system in which customer demand rather than production capacity determines production. Richard implemented a kanban inventory system that triggers orders for more materials only when they are needed, a move that allowed Capel to cut its investment in inventory while increasing the availability of materials.

The results of Capel's early efforts at Lean were impressive. With these basic changes, the company reduced its costs by $890,000 annually. Sales also increased because Capel could process and deliver customers' orders much faster and much more efficiently, which produced a total economic benefit to the company of more than $2 million. Performance improved so much that Capel began offering a Zip Ship program that allows 1-day turnaround on some orders.

Everyone at Capel was so impressed with the results of implementing Lean in the company's manufacturing process that managers decided to apply them to the corporate office. One of the first processes Lean teams addressed was setting up customer accounts, which took weeks to complete because of paperwork, credit checks, database setup, and other activities. The first step was to create a Value Stream Map (VSM), a Lean tool that displays every step required in a process. Mapping the account creation process enabled a team of employees to identify waste, inefficiency, and bottlenecks, just as it did when applied to manufacturing processes. "Once you visualize the problem areas, only then can you begin to resolve them," says Steve Laton, one of the members of the Lean team. The VSM helped the team identify the "ideal flow," which removed the non-value-added steps in the process. The new lean process creates customer accounts within 24 hours.

Buoyed by their success with Lean principles, Capel and his employees are developing plans to apply them in other areas of the business. "Lean works anywhere," says Richard.

1. What lessons can other small companies learn from Capel's experience of applying Lean principles?
2. Do you agree with Richard Capel's statement, "Lean works anywhere"? Explain.
3. Use the Internet to research Value Stream Mapping. Work with a local business owner to map one of the company's processes. Do you spot inefficiencies? How can you redesign the process to create the "ideal flow"?

Source: Based on "Capel Rugs of Troy Weaves Continuous Improvement," Industrial Extension Service, North Carolina State University, January 2010, *www.ies.ncsu.edu/_library/docs/capelrugs_lean.cfm.*

5S PRINCIPLES. Often used in conjunction with Lean, the 5S principles are simple but effective ways to improve quality by organizing the employees' work environment. The 5Ss are:

1. *Sort.* Companies sort items in the workplace into two categories—necessary and unnecessary—and eliminate everything that is unnecessary.
2. *Straighten.* Companies arrange the tools, equipment, and materials employees need to do their jobs in the most efficient manner, minimizing wasted motion and effort.
3. *Shine.* Once organized, employees keep their workspaces neat and clean.
4. *Systematize.* Businesses strive for continuous improvement in sorting, straightening, and shining by standardizing best-practice processes.
5. *Sustain.* Companies sustain their drive toward continuous improvement by encouraging the involvement of all employees, self-discipline, and creating a performance measurement system.

Bill Vogel, CEO of Vogel Wood Products, a Monona, Wisconsin-based maker of wood and laminate cabinetry, fixtures, and office systems for home and commercial use, knew that his 15-employee company was operating well below peak efficiency. "We were putting in tons of overtime to get orders out the door," he says. Vogel knew that competition in the industry was becoming fiercer and that his company had to undergo dramatic changes to gain a competitive edge. With the help of the Wisconsin Manufacturing Extension Partnership, Vogel and his employees embarked on a quality improvement journey using Lean manufacturing and 5S principles. The goal was to get every employee involved and to create a culture in which the customer comes first. The first step was to map the company's existing processes, including those in manufacturing, assembly, and the front office, so that they could identify areas of inefficiency and waste. Employees then focused on using 5S principles to create a clean, organized, and efficient workplace. "With Lean and 5S, the goal is to work more effectively, not harder," says Vogel. One team of employees came up with the idea of placing tools on carts that employees could move from one work station to another, reducing time wasted searching for the right tool. The changes allowed employees to identify and eliminate bottlenecks in the production process that Vogel says "unlocked the flow" of work. The company has reaped many benefits from the changes. In addition to improved employee morale, Vogel Wood Products cut its cycle time (the time from receiving an order to delivering it to the customer) in half, reduced its work-in-process inventory by 70 percent, reduced overtime and labor costs by more than 6 percent, and increased its profits by 4 percent. "The principles of Lean are simple," says sales manager Denita Ward. "The trick is to step back to see where basic changes can be made that result in real improvements."[12]

SIX SIGMA. Six Sigma relies on data-driven statistical techniques to improve the quality and the efficiency of any process and to increase customer satisfaction. The quality threshold that Six Sigma programs set is high: just an average of 3.4 defects per 1 million opportunities! Although initially used by large corporations, Six Sigma can be adapted to work in small businesses as well. The four key tenets of Six Sigma are:

1. *Delight customers with quality and speed.* Six Sigma recognizes that the customer's needs come first. The goal is to produce products that are of the highest quality in a process that is efficient and fast.
2. *Constantly improve the process.* Six Sigma builds on the concept of continuous improvement. According to W. Edwards Deming, most quality problems are the result of the *process* (which management creates) rather than the *employees* (who work within the process that management builds). The goal is to reduce the variation of the process, which is measured by the standard deviation (denoted by the Greek letter sigma).
3. *Use teamwork to improve the process.* Six Sigma counts on teams of employees working together to improve a process. People working together to share their knowledge can generate better solutions to quality problems than individuals can.
4. *Make changes to the process based on facts, not guesses.* To improve a process, employees must have quantifiable measures of results (e.g., quality of output) and of the process itself (e.g., how the process operated to produce those results).[11]

Table 1 explains the DMAIC process upon which the Six Sigma approach is built. For small companies, the goal of this process is to understand their core business processes better so that managers and employees can work together to make significant improvements to them over time.

TOTAL QUALITY MANAGEMENT. Under the total quality management (TQM) philosophy, companies define a quality product as one that conforms to predetermined standards that satisfy customers' demands. That means getting *everything*—from delivery and invoicing to installation and follow-up—right the first time. Although these companies know that they may never reach their targets of perfect quality, they never stop striving for perfection, recognizing that even a 99.9 percent level of quality is not good enough (see Table 2). The businesses that have effectively implemented these programs understand that the process involves a total commitment from strategy to practice and from the top of the organization to the bottom.

Rather than trying to inspect quality into products and services after they are completed, TQM instills the philosophy of doing the job right the first time. Although the concept is simple, implementing such a process is a challenge that requires a very different kind of thinking and very

TABLE 1 The Six Sigma DMAIC Approach

Principle	Process Improvement Technique
Define	Identify the problem. Define the requirements. Set the goal for improvement.
Measure	Validate the process problem by mapping the process and gathering data about it. Refine the problem statement and the goal. Measure current performance by examining the relevant process inputs, steps, and output to establish a baseline.
Analyze	Develop a list of potential root causes. Identify the vital few. Use data analysis tools to validate the cause-and-effect connections between root causes and the quality problem.
Improve	Develop potential solutions to remove root causes by making changes to the process. Test potential solutions and develop a plan for implementing those that are successful. Measure the results of the improved process.
Control	Establish standard measures for the new process. Establish standard procedures for the new process. Review performance periodically and make adjustments, as needed.

Source: Adapted from Andrew Spanyi and Marvin Wurtzel, "Six Sigma for the Rest of Us," *Quality Digest,* July 2003. Reprinted with permission.

TABLE 2 Why 99.9 Percent Quality Isn't Good Enough

Most companies willingly accept a certain percentage of errors and defects. Usually the range is 1 to 5 percent. In some companies, errors and defects are regarded as a routine part of daily operations. However, quality consultants say that even 99.9 percent isn't good enough.

What would be the result if some things were done right only 99.9 percent of the time? Consider the implications:

- Two unsafe landings at Chicago's O'Hare Airport per day.
- 16,000 lost pieces of mail per hour.
- 200,000 incorrectly filled drug prescriptions per year.
- 5,000 incorrect surgical procedures performed each week.
- 22,000 checks deducted from the wrong accounts every hour.
- 1,314 telephone calls misdirected every minute.
- 14 babies delivered to the wrong parents each day.
- 2,488,200 magazines published with the wrong covers every year.

If you are in the unlucky one-tenth of 1 percent, the error affects you 100 percent. In addition, unless a company strives for 100 percent product or service quality, there is little chance that it will ever achieve 99.9 percent quality.

Sources: Based on Lieca Brown, "Sigma Management," *Point of Beginning*, August 2001, p. 6; *On the Job Performance* (Chicago: Dartnell Corporation, 1997), p. 3; San Marino, "Is Good Enough' Good Enough?" *IndustryWeek*, February 3, 1997, p. 22.

different culture than most organizations are comfortable with. Because the changes TQM requires are so significant, patience is a must for companies adopting the philosophy. Consistent quality improvements rarely occur overnight. Yet, too many small business managers think, "We'll implement TQM today and tomorrow our quality will soar." TQM is *not* a "quick-fix," short-term program that can magically push a company to world-class-quality status overnight. Because it requires such fundamental, often drastic, changes in the way a company does business, TQM takes time both to implement and to produce results. Patience is a must. Although some small businesses that use TQM begin to see some improvements within just a matter of weeks, the *real* benefits take longer to realize. It takes at least 3 or 4 years before TQM principles gain acceptance among employees, and as many as 8 years are necessary to fully implement TQM in a company.

To implement TQM successfully, a small business owner must rely on these fundamental principles:

- *Employ benchmarking to achieve quality outcomes.* **Benchmarking** is the process of identifying world-class processes or procedures other companies (often in other industries) currently are using and building quality standards around these for your business. This search for best practices is ongoing. As part of their quality initiative, employees at Scotsman Ice Systems, a small company in Fairfax, South Carolina, that makes high-end commercial and residential ice machines and refrigerators, benchmark production processes of other manufacturing companies. To make sure that they do not miss anything, they have developed a benchmarking booklet that contains a list of key questions to take with them on benchmarking trips.[13]
- *Shift from a management-driven culture to a participative, team-based one.* Two basic tenets of TQM are employee involvement and teamwork. Business owners must be willing to push decision-making authority down the organization to where the real experts are. Teams of employees working together to identify and solve problems can be a powerful force in an organization of any size. Experience with TQM has taught entrepreneurs that the combined knowledge and experience of workers is much greater than that of only one person. Tapping into the problem-solving capabilities of the team produces profitable results.
- *Modify the reward system to encourage teamwork and innovation.* Because the team, not the individual, is the building block of TQM, companies often have to modify their compensation systems to reflect team performance. Traditional compensation methods pit one employee against another, undermining any sense of cooperation. Often they are based on seniority rather than on how much an employee contributes to the company. Compensation

systems under TQM usually rely on incentives, linking pay to performance. However, rather than tying pay to individual performance, these systems focus on team-based incentives. Each person's pay depends on whether the entire team (or, sometimes, the entire company) meets a clearly defined, measurable set of performance objectives.

- *Train workers constantly to give them the tools they need to produce quality and to upgrade the company's knowledge base.* One of the most important factors in making long-term, constant improvements in a company's processes is teaching workers the philosophy and the tools of TQM. Admonishing employees to "produce quality" or offering them rewards for high quality is futile unless a company gives them the tools and know-how to achieve that end. Managers must be dedicated to making their companies "learning organizations" that encourage people to upgrade their skills and give them the opportunities and incentives to do so. The most successful companies spend anywhere from 1 to 5 percent of their employees' time on training, most of it invested in workers, not managers. To give employees a sense of how the quality of their job fits into the big picture, many TQM companies engage in **cross-training,** teaching workers to do other jobs in the company.

- *Train employees to measure quality with the tools of statistical process control (SPC).* The only way to ensure gains in quality is to measure results objectively and to trace the company's progress toward its quality objectives. That requires teaching employees how to use statistical process control techniques such as fishbone charts, Pareto charts, control charts, and measures of process capability.* Without knowledgeable workers using these quantitative tools, TQM cannot produce the intended results.

- *Use Pareto's Law to focus TQM efforts.* One of the toughest questions managers face in companies embarking on TQM for the first time is "Where do we start?" The best way to answer that fundamental question is to use Pareto's Law (also called the 80/20 Rule), which states that 80 percent of a company's quality problems arise from just 20 percent of all causes. By identifying this small percentage of causes and focusing quality improvement efforts on them, a company gets maximum return for its effort. This simple yet powerful rule forces workers to concentrate resources on the most significant problems first, where payoffs are likely to be biggest, and helps build momentum for successful TQM effort.

- *Share information with everyone in the organization.* Asking employees to make decisions and to assume responsibility for creating quality necessitates that the owner share information with them. Employees cannot make sound decisions consistent with the company's initiative if managers are unwilling to give them the information they need to make those decisions.

- *Focus quality improvements on astonishing the customer.* The heart of TQM is customer satisfaction—better yet, customer astonishment. Unfortunately, some companies focus their quality improvement efforts on areas that never benefit the customer. Quality improvements with no customer focus (either internal or external customers) are wasted.

- *Don't rely on inspection to produce quality products and services.* The traditional approach to achieving quality was to create a product or service and then to rely on an army of inspectors to "weed out" all of the defects. Not only is such a system a terrible waste of resources (consider the cost of scrap, rework, and no-value-added inspections), but it gives managers no opportunity for continuous improvement. The only way to improve a process is to discover the cause of poor quality, fix it (the sooner the better), and learn from it so that workers can *avoid* the problem in the future. Using the statistical tools of the TQM approach allows a company to learn from its mistakes with a consistent approach to constantly improving quality.

- *Avoid using TQM to place blame on those who make mistakes.* In many firms, the only reason managers seek out mistakes is to find someone to blame for them. The result is a culture based on fear and the unwillingness of workers to take chances to innovate. The goal of TQM is to improve the processes in which people work, *not* to lay blame on

---

*To learn more about total quality management and the tools of statistical quality control, look in modern statistics or operations management textbooks or visit the following Web sites: *http://deming.eng.clemson.edu/pub/den/ deming_map.htm* and *http://search.bnet.com/search/Total+Quality+Management.html?t=13&s=0&o=0.*

workers. Searching out "the guilty party" doesn't solve the problem. The TQM philosophy sees each problem that arises as an opportunity for improving the company's system.

■ *Strive for continuous improvement in processes as well as in products and services.* There is no finish line in the race for quality. A company's goal must be to improve the quality of its processes, products, and services constantly, no matter how high it currently stands!

Many of these principles are evident in quality guru W. Edwards Deming's 14 points, a capsulized version of how to build a successful TQM approach (see Table 3).

Implementing a TQM program successfully begins at the top. If the owner or chief executive of a company doesn't actively and visibly support the initiative, the employees who must make it happen will never accept it. TQM requires change: change in the way a company defines quality, in the way it sees its customers, in the way it treats employees, and in the way it sees itself. Successful implementation also involves modification of the organization's culture.

Quantity: The Economic Order Quantity (EOQ)

3. Conduct economic order quantity (EOQ) analysis to determine the proper level of inventory.

The typical small business has its largest investment in inventory. However, an investment in inventory is not profitable because dollars spent return nothing until the inventory is sold. In a sense, a small company's inventory is its largest non-interest-bearing investment. Entrepreneurs must focus on controlling this investment and on maintaining proper inventory levels.

TABLE 3 Deming's 14 Points

Total quality management cannot succeed as a piecemeal program or without true commitment to its philosophy. W. Edwards Deming, the man most visibly connected to TQM, drove home these concepts with his 14 points, the essential elements for integrating TQM successfully into a company. Deming's message was straightforward. Companies must transform themselves into customer-oriented, quality-focused organizations in which teams of employees have the training, the resources, and the freedom to pursue quality on a daily basis. The goal is to track the performance of a process, whether manufacturing a clock or serving a bank customer, and to develop ways to minimize variation in the system, eliminate defects, and spur innovation. The 14 points are as follows:

1. *Constantly strive to improve products and services.* This requires total dedication to improving quality, productivity, and service—*continuously.*
2. *Adopt a total quality philosophy.* There are no shortcuts to quality improvement; it requires a completely new way of thinking and managing.
3. *Correct defects as they happen,* rather than relying on mass inspection of end products. Real quality comes from improving the process, not from inspecting finished products and services. At that point, it's too late. Statistical process control charts help workers detect when a process is producing poor-quality goods or services. Then they can stop it, make corrections, and get the process back on target.
4. *Don't award business on price alone.* Rather than choosing the lowest-cost vendor, businesses should work toward establishing close relationships with the vendors who offer the highest quality.
5. *Constantly improve the system of production and service.* Managers must focus the entire company on customer satisfaction, measure results, and make adjustments as necessary.
6. *Institute training.* Workers cannot improve quality and lower costs without proper training to erase old ways of doing things.
7. *Institute leadership.* The supervisor's job is not to boss workers around; it is to lead. The nature of the work is more like coaching than controlling.
8. *Drive out fear.* People often are afraid to point out problems because they fear the repercussions. Managers must encourage and reward employee suggestions.
9. *Break down barriers among staff areas.* Departments within organizations often erect needless barriers to protect their own turf. Total quality requires a spirit of teamwork and cooperation across the entire organization.
10. *Eliminate superficial slogans and goals.* These only offend employees because they imply that workers could do a better job if they would only try.
11. *Eliminate standard quotas.* They emphasize quantity over quality. Not everyone can move at the same rate and still produce quality.
12. *Remove barriers to pride of workmanship.* Most workers want to do quality work. Eliminating "de-motivators" frees them to achieve quality results.
13. *Institute vigorous education and retraining.* Managers must teach employees the new methods of continuous improvement, including statistical process control techniques.
14. *Take demonstrated management action to achieve the transformation.* Although success requires involvement of all levels of the organization, the impetus for change must come from the top.

These 14 interrelated elements contribute to a chain-reaction effect. As a company improves its quality, costs decline, productivity increases, the company gains additional market share due to its ability to provide high-quality products at competitive prices, and the company and its employees prosper.

Source: Deming, W. Edwards, *Out of the Crisis,* pp. 23–24, © 2000 Massachusetts Institute of Technology, by permission of The MIT Press.

COMPLAINTS

JUNIOR CHEMISTRY SET

ENTREPRENEURIAL
Profile

Peter Nygard: Nygard International

A few years ago, Peter Nygard, founder of Nygard International, a women's clothing manufacturer in Toronto, Ontario, was concerned about the high and increasing level of inventory in his warehouse. The company's inventory had ballooned to its highest level ever, and what concerned Nygard even more than the amount of stock was the imbalance of the inventory. Nygard was overstocked with out-of-style fashions but was running short of items that were popular. To solve the inventory problem, Nygard developed a purchasing plan designed to create a more efficient flow of goods from "the sheep and the silkworms to the consumer," he says. Nygard invested in software that tracked both actual and forecasted sales of specific products, and he shifted the company's ordering, manufacturing, shipping, and selling operations online. The company cut its manufacturing costs by one-third and reduced the time required to fill a customer's order from 3 weeks to just 1 day! Nygard estimates that making these changes in the company's supply chain has added about $10 million a year to his company's bottom line. In addition, he says, "We can gather information and make decisions based on what is actually selling with the snap of a finger as opposed to philosophizing or assuming."[14]

A primary objective of this portion of the purchasing plan is to generate an adequate turnover of merchandise by purchasing proper quantities. Tying up capital in extra inventory limits a company's working capital and exerts pressure on its cash flows. Also, a business risks the danger of being stuck with spoiled or obsolete merchandise, an extremely serious problem for many small businesses. Excess inventory also takes up valuable selling space that could be used for items with higher turnover rates and more profit potential. However, maintaining too little inventory can be extremely costly. An owner may be forced to reorder merchandise too frequently, escalating total inventory costs. In addition, inventory stockouts occur when customer demand exceeds a company's supply of merchandise, causing customer ill will. Persistent stockouts are inconvenient for customers, and many customers eventually abandon the store to shop elsewhere. Manufacturers that run out of inventory must shut down temporarily and incur huge costs. For instance, Toyota, which operates an extremely lean production process, was forced to shut down production when the factory that supplies all of its brake shoes was damaged by an earthquake. The supply shortage cost Toyota an estimated $200 million in revenue.[15] Carrying either too much or too little inventory both are expensive mistakes that lead to serious problems in other areas of the business.

The goal is to maintain enough inventory to meet customer orders and to satisfy production needs but not so much that storage costs and inventory investments are excessive. The analytical techniques used to calculate **economic order quantities (EOQs)** help business owners to determine the amount of inventory to purchase in an order or to produce in a production run to minimize total inventory costs. To compute the economic order quantity, a small business owner must first determine the three principal elements of total inventory costs: the cost of the units, the holding (or carrying) cost, and the setup (or ordering) cost.

Cost of Units

The cost of the units is simply the number of units demanded for a particular time period multiplied by the cost per unit. Suppose that a small manufacturer of lawnmowers forecasts demand for the upcoming year to be 100,000 mowers. He needs to order enough wheels at $4.15 each to supply the production department. He computes:

$$\text{Total annual cost of units} = D \times C$$

where:

$$D = \text{Annual demand (in units)}$$

$$C = \text{Cost of a single unit (\$)}$$

In this example,

$$D = 100{,}000\,\text{mowers} \times 4\,\text{wheels per mower} = 400{,}000\,\text{wheels}$$

$$C = \$4.15\,\text{per wheel}$$

Total annual cost of units $= D \times C$

$$= 400{,}00\,\text{wheels} \times \$4.15$$

$$= \$1{,}660{,}000$$

Holding (Carrying) Costs

An excessive inventory investment ties up a large amount of a company's cash unproductively in the form of holding costs. The typical costs of holding inventory include the costs of storage, insurance, taxes, interest, depreciation, damage or spoilage, obsolescence, and pilferage. The expense involved in physically storing the items in inventory is usually substantial, especially if inventories are large. An entrepreneur may have to rent or build additional warehousing facilities, pushing the cost of storing the inventory even higher. The company also may incur expenses in transferring items into and out of inventory. The cost of storage also includes the expense of operating the facility (e.g., heating, lighting, refrigeration), as well as the depreciation, taxes, and interest on the building. Most small business owners purchase insurance on their inventories to shift the risk of fire, theft, flood, and other disasters to an insurer. The premiums paid for this coverage also are included in the cost of holding inventory. In general, the larger a company's average inventory, the greater is its storage cost. For most companies, holding costs for an item range from 15 to 35 percent of its actual cost.

Depreciation costs represent the reduced value of inventory over time. Some businesses experience rapidly depreciating inventory. For example, an auto dealership's inventory is subject to depreciation because it must sell models left over from the previous year at reduced prices.

Spoilage, obsolescence, and pilferage also add to the costs of holding inventory. Some small firms, especially those that deal in trendy merchandise, assume an extremely high risk of obsolescence. For example, a fashion merchandiser with a large inventory of the latest styles may be left with worthless merchandise when styles change. In addition, unless the entrepreneur establishes sound inventory control procedures, the business will suffer losses from employee theft and shoplifting.

Let us return to the lawnmower manufacturer example to illustrate the cost of holding inventory:

$$\text{Total annual holding (carrying) costs} = \frac{Q}{2} \times H$$

where:

$$Q = \text{Quantity of inventory ordered}$$

$$H = \text{Holding cost per unit per year}$$

TABLE 4 Holding (Carrying) Costs

If Q Is ...	$Q/2$, Average Inventory, Is ...	$Q/2 \times H$, Holding Cost, Is ...
500	250	$312.50
1,000	500	625.00
2,000	1,000	1,250.00
3,000	1,500	1,875.00
4,000	2,000	2,500.00
5,000	2,500	3,125.00
6,000	3,000	3,750.00
7,000	3,500	4,375.00
8,000	4,000	5,000.00
9,000	4,500	5,625.00
10,000	5,000	6,250.00

The greater the quantity ordered, the greater is the inventory carrying costs. This relationship is shown in Table 4, assuming that the cost of carrying a single unit of inventory for 1 year is $1.25.

Setup (Ordering) Costs

The various expenses incurred in actually ordering materials and inventory or in setting up the production line to manufacture them determine the setup or ordering costs of a product. The costs of obtaining materials and inventory typically include preparing purchase orders; analyzing and choosing vendors; processing, handling, and expending orders; receiving and inspecting items; and performing all of the required accounting and clerical functions. Even if the small company produces its own supply of goods, it encounters most of these same expenses. Ordering costs are usually relatively fixed, regardless of the quantity ordered.

Setup or ordering costs are found by multiplying the number of orders made in a year (or the number of production runs in a year) by the cost of placing a single order (or the cost of setting up a single production run). In the lawnmower manufacturing example, the annual requirement is 400,000 wheels per year and the cost to place an order is $9.00, and the ordering costs are as follows:

$$\text{Total annual stepup (ordering) costs} = \frac{D}{Q} \times S$$

where:

D = Annual demand

Q = Quantity of inventory ordered

S = Setup (ordering) costs for a single run (or order)

The greater the quantity ordered, the smaller the number of orders placed. This relationship is shown in Table 5, assuming an ordering cost of $9.00 per order.

TABLE 5 Setup Cost

If Q is ...	D/Q, Number of Orders per Year, Is ...	$D/Q \times S$, Setup (Ordering) Cost, Is ...
500	800	$7,200.00
1,000	400	3,600.00
5,000	80	720.00
10,000	40	360.00

If carrying costs were the only expense involved in obtaining inventory, the business owner would purchase the smallest number of units possible in each order to minimize the cost of holding the inventory. For example, if the lawnmower manufacturer purchased just four wheels per order, carrying cost would be minimized:

$$\text{Carrying cost} = \frac{Q}{2} \times H$$

$$= \frac{4}{2} \times \$1.25$$

$$= \$2.50$$

but the ordering cost would be outrageous:

$$\text{Ordering cost} = \frac{D}{Q} \times S$$

$$= \frac{400,000}{4} \times \$9$$

$$= \$900,000$$

Obviously this is not the small manufacturer's ideal inventory solution.

Similarly, if ordering costs were the only expense involved in procuring inventory, the business owner would purchase the largest number of units possible in order to minimize the ordering cost. In our example, if the lawnmower manufacturer purchased 400,000 wheels per order, ordering cost would be minimized:

$$\text{Ordering cost} = \frac{D}{Q} \times S$$

$$= \frac{400,000}{400,000} \times \$9$$

$$= \$9$$

but carrying cost would be tremendously high:

$$\text{Carrying cost} = Q \times H$$

$$= \frac{400,000}{2} \times \$1.25$$

$$= \$250,000$$

A quick inspection shows that neither of those solutions minimizes the total cost of the manufacturer's inventory. Total cost is composed of the cost of the unit, carrying cost, and ordering costs:

$$\text{Total cost} = (D \times C) + \left(\frac{Q}{2} \times H \right) + \left(\frac{D}{Q} \times S \right)$$

These costs are illustrated in Figure 4. Notice that as the quantity ordered increases, the ordering costs decrease and the carrying costs increase.

The EOQ formula simply balances the ordering cost and the carrying cost of the small business owner's inventory so that total costs are minimized. Table 6 summarizes the total costs for various values of Q for our lawnmower manufacturer.

As Table 6 and Figure 4 illustrate, the EOQ formula locates the minimum point on the total cost curve, which occurs where the cost of carrying inventory ($Q/2 \times H$) equals the cost of ordering inventory ($D/Q \times S$). As we have seen, if a small business places the smallest number of orders possible each year, its ordering cost is minimized, but its carrying cost is maximized.

FIGURE 4
Economic Order Quantity

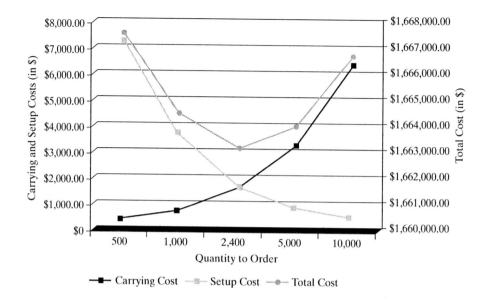

Conversely, if the company orders the smallest number of units possible in each order, its carrying cost is minimized, but its ordering cost is maximized. Total inventory cost is minimized when carrying cost and ordering cost are balanced.

Let us return to our lawnmower manufacturer and compute its economic order quantity, EOQ, using the following formula:

$$S = \$9.00 \text{ per order}$$

$$C = \$1.55 \text{ per wheel}$$

$$EOQ = \sqrt{\frac{2 \times D \times S}{H}}$$

$$= \sqrt{\frac{2 \times 400,000 \times \$9.00}{\$1.25}}$$

$$= 2,400 \text{ wheels}$$

To minimize total inventory cost, the lawnmower manufacturer should order 2,400 wheels at a time. Furthermore,

$$\text{Number of orders per year} = \frac{D}{Q}$$

$$= \frac{400,000}{2,400}$$

$$= 166.67 \text{ orders}$$

TABLE 6 Economic Order Quantity and Total Cost

If Q is . . .	$D \times C$, Cost of Units, Is . . .	$Q/2 \times H$, Carrying Cost, Is . . .	$D/Q \times S$, Ordering Cost, Is . . .	TC, Total Cost, Is . . .
500	$1,660,000	$312.50	$7,200.00	$1,667,512.50
1,000	1,660,000	625.00	3,600.00	1,664,225.00
2,400	**1,660,000**	**1,500.00**	**1,500.00**	**1,663,000.00**
5,000	1,660,000	3,125.00	720.00	1,663,845.00
10,000	1,660,000	6,250.00	360.00	1,666,610.00

This manufacturer will place approximately 167 orders this year at a minimum total cost of $1,663,000, computed as follows:

$$\text{Total cost} = (D \times C) + \left(\frac{Q}{2} \times H \right) + \left(\frac{D}{Q} \times S \right)$$

$$= (400,000 \times \$4.15) + (2,400/2 \times \$1.25) + (400,000/2,400 + \$9.00)$$

$$= \$1,660,000 + \$1,500 + \$1,500$$

$$= \$1,663,000$$

Economic Order Quantity with Usage

The preceding EOQ model assumes that orders are filled instantaneously; that is, fresh inventory arrives all at once. Because that assumption does not hold true for many small manufacturers, it is necessary to consider a variation of the basic EOQ model that allows inventory to be added over time rather than instantaneously. In addition, a manufacturer is likely to be taking items from inventory for use in the assembly process over the same time period. For example, the lawnmower manufacturer may be producing blades to replenish his supply, but at the same time assembly workers are reducing the supply of blades to make finished mowers. The key feature of this version of the EOQ model is that inventories are used while inventories are being added.

Using the lawnmower manufacturer as an example, we can compute the EOQ for the blades. To make the calculation, we need two additional pieces of information: the usage rate for the blades, U, and the factory's capacity to manufacture the blades, P. Suppose that the maximum number of lawnmower blades the company can manufacture is 480 per day. We know from the previous illustration that annual demand for mowers is 100,000 units (therefore, 100,000 blades). If the plant operates 5 days per week for 50 weeks (250 days), its usage rate is

$$U = \frac{100,000 \text{ units per year}}{250 \text{ days}} = 400 \text{ units per day}$$

It costs $325 to set up the blade manufacturing line and $8.71 to store one blade for 1 year. The cost of producing a blade is $24.85. To compute EOQ, we modify the basic formula:

$$EOQ = \sqrt{\frac{2 \times D \times S}{H \times \left(1 - \frac{U}{P} \right)}}$$

For the lawnmower manufacturer,

$$D = 100,000 \text{ blades}$$
$$S = \$325 \text{ per production run}$$
$$H = \$8.71 \text{ per blade per year}$$
$$U = 400 \text{ blades per day}$$
$$P = 480 \text{ blades per day}$$

$$EOQ = \sqrt{\frac{2 \times 100,000 \times \$325}{8.71 \times \left(1 - \frac{400}{480} \right)}}$$

$$= 6,691.50 \text{ blades} = 6,692 \text{ blades}$$

Therefore, to minimize total inventory cost, the lawnmower manufacturer should produce 6,692 blades per production run. In addition,

$$\text{Number of production runs per year} = \frac{D}{Q}$$

$$= \frac{100,000 \text{ blades}}{6,692 \text{ blades/run}}$$

$$= 14.9 \approx 15 \text{ runs}$$

The manufacturer will make 15 production runs during the year at a total cost of:

$$\text{Total cost} = (D \times C) + \left(\left(1 - \frac{U}{P}\right) \times \frac{Q}{2} \times H\right) + \left(\frac{D}{Q} \times S\right)$$

$$= (100{,}000 \times \$24.85) + \left(\left(1 - \frac{400}{480}\right) \times \frac{6{,}692}{2} \times \$8.71\right) + \left(\frac{100{,}000}{6.692} \times \$325\right)$$

$$= \$2{,}485{,}000 + \$4{,}857 + \$4{,}857$$

$$= \$2{,}494{,}714$$

Business owners must remember that the EOQ analysis is based on estimations of cost and demand. The final result is only as accurate as the input used. Consequently, this analytical tool serves only as a guideline for decision making. The final answer may not be the ideal solution because of intervening factors, such as opportunity costs or seasonal fluctuations. Knowledgeable entrepreneurs use EOQ analysis as a starting point in making a decision and then use managerial judgment and experience to produce a final ruling.

Price

For the typical small business owner, price is always a substantial factor when purchasing inventory and supplies. In many cases, an entrepreneur can negotiate price with potential suppliers on large orders of frequently purchased items. In other instances, perhaps when an entrepreneur purchases small quantities of items infrequently, he or she must pay list price. The typical entrepreneur shops around before ordering from the supplier that offers the best price. However, this does not mean that a business owner should always purchase inventory and supplies at the lowest price available. The best purchase price is the lowest price at which the owner can obtain goods and services *of acceptable quality*. As quality guru W. Edwards Deming said, "Price has no meaning without a measure of the quality being purchased."[16] Companies that are lured by low prices on key products or components from suppliers in foreign countries sometimes discover that shipping costs, customs fees, and the additional costs and challenges of coordinating long-distance shipments more than offset the goods' lower prices.

Recall that one of Deming's 14 points is *"Don't award business on price alone."* Without proof of quality, an item with the lowest initial price actually may produce the *highest* total cost. Deming condemned the practice of constantly switching suppliers in search of the lowest initial price because it increases the variability of a process and lowers its quality. Instead, he recommended that businesses establish long-term relationships built on mutual trust and cooperation with a single supplier.

When evaluating a supplier's price, small business owners must consider not only the actual price of goods and services, but also the selling terms accompanying them. In some cases, the selling terms can be more important than the price itself. Sometimes a vendor's terms might include some type of purchase discount. Vendors typically offer three types of discounts: trade discounts, quantity discounts, and cash discounts.

4. Differentiate among the three types of purchase discounts that vendors offer.

TRADE DISCOUNTS. Trade discounts are established on a graduated scale and depend on a small firm's position in the channel of distribution. In other words, trade discounts recognize the fact that manufacturers, wholesalers, and retailers perform a variety of vital functions at various stages in the channel of distribution and compensate them for providing these needed activities. Figure 5 illustrates a typical trade discount structure.

QUANTITY DISCOUNTS. Quantity discounts are designed to encourage businesses to order large quantities of merchandise and supplies. Vendors are able to offer lower prices on bulk purchases because the cost per unit is lower than for handling small orders. Quantity discounts normally exist in two forms: noncumulative and cumulative. Noncumulative quantity discounts are granted only if a certain volume of merchandise is purchased in a single order. For example, a wholesaler may offer small retailers a 3 percent discount only if they purchase 10 gross of Halloween masks in a single order. Table 7 shows a typical noncumulative quantity discount structure. Cumulative quantity discounts are offered if a firm's purchases from a particular vendor exceed a specified quantity or dollar value over a predetermined time period. The time frame

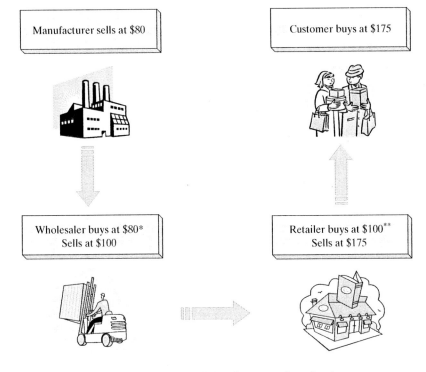

FIGURE 5
Trade Discount Structure

*Wholesale discount = 54% of suggested retail price.
** Retail discount = 43% of suggested retail price.

varies, but one year is most common. For example, a manufacturer of appliances may offer a small business a 3 percent discount on subsequent orders if its purchases exceed $10,000 per year.

Some small business owners who normally buy in small quantities and are unable to qualify for quantity discounts can earn such discounts by joining buying groups, purchasing pools, or buying cooperatives.

ENTREPRENEURIAL

Profile

Blue Hawk Cooperative

Blue Hawk Cooperative is an organization that allows small, independent heating, ventilation, and air conditioning (HVAC) dealers to earn discounts on items they purchase from more than 100 vendors. Founded in 2005 by Dan Bleier, owner of Able Distributors, an HVAC dealer in Chicago, Illinois, Blue Hawk provides quantity discounts to its 230 members (who have nearly 1,100 locations) by combining their purchasing power into one entity. Bleier started Blue Hawk as a way for his family-owned distributorship and other independent HVAC dealers to compete effectively with large chain stores whose volume purchases earned them significant discounts (and hence the ability to offer low prices). "We didn't have the volume to get the manufacturer rebates they could," he says. With the help of the cooperative, members receive discounts on their purchases of items ranging from electric motors to refrigerants. "Our Blue Hawk affiliation has boosted our buying power, enhanced our supplier relationships, and increased our customer satisfaction," says Don Chmura, vice president of purchasing for Refrigeration and Electric Supply Company, a distributor with eight locations in Little Rock, Arkansas.[17] According to the National Cooperative Business Association, more than 700 purchasing cooperatives like Blue Hawk operate in the United States.[18]

TABLE 7 **Noncumulative Quantity Discount Structure**

Order Size	Price
1–1,000 units	List price
1,001–5,000 units	List price – 2%
5,001–10,000 units	List price – 4%
10,001 units and above	List price – 6%

CASH DISCOUNTS. Cash discounts are offered to customers as an incentive to pay for merchandise promptly. Many vendors grant cash discounts to avoid being used as an interest-free bank by customers who purchase merchandise and then fail to pay by the invoice due date. To encourage prompt payment of invoices, many vendors allow customers to deduct a percentage of the purchase amount if they remit payment within a specified time. Cash discount terms "2/10, net 30" are common in many industries. This notation means that the total amount of the invoice is due 30 days after its date, but if the bill is paid within 10 days the buyer may deduct 2 percent from the total. A discount offering "2/10, EOM" (EOM means "end of month") indicates that the buyer may deduct 2 percent if the bill is paid by the tenth of the month after the purchase.

In general, it is sound business practice to take advantage of cash discounts. The money saved by paying invoices promptly is freed up for use elsewhere.

ENTREPRENEURIAL

Profile

Jeff Schreiber: Hansen Wholesale

When Jeff Schreiber, owner of Hansen Wholesale, a small distributor of home products, attended a January trade show, he purchased $40,000 of ceiling fans from a manufacturer. The contract gave Schreiber until July to pay for the fans, but the manufacturer also included a cash discount: If Schreiber paid before May 1, he could earn a 3 percent discount on the purchase. By paying in February, Schreiber could save another 1.5 percent of the purchase price. For Schreiber, who manages his company's cash flow meticulously, the decision was an easy one; he paid the invoice in February and saved $1,800. "Your money works better if you take advantage of the discounts," says Schreiber, who recently saved $15,000 in cash discounts for his company in just 1 year.[19]

Businesses incur an implicit (opportunity) cost of forgoing a cash discount. By failing to take advantage of a cash discount, a business owner is, in effect, paying an annual interest rate to retain the use of the discounted amount for the remainder of the credit period. For example, suppose the Print Shop receives an invoice for $1,000 from a vendor offering a cash discount of 2/10, net 30. Figure 6 illustrates this situation and shows how to compute the cost of forgoing the cash discount. Actually, it costs the Print Shop $20 to retain the use of its $980 for an extra 20 days. Translating this into an annual interest rate:

$$I = P \times R \times T$$

where

$$I = \text{Interest (\$)}$$
$$P = \text{Principle (\$)}$$
$$R = \text{Rate of interest (\%)}$$
$$T = \text{Time (number of days/360)}$$

To compute R, the annual interest rate,

$$R = \frac{I}{P \times T}$$

FIGURE 6
A Cash Discount

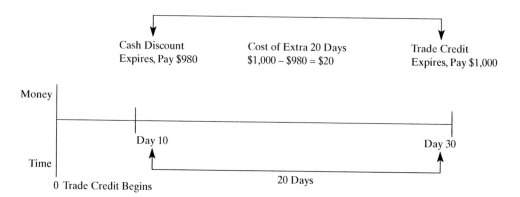

Cash Discount	Cost of Extra 20 Days	Trade Credit
Expires, Pay $980	$1,000 − $980 = $20	Expires, Pay $1,000

Money

Day 10   Day 30

Time

0 Trade Credit Begins   20 Days

TABLE 8 **Cost of Forgoing Cash Discounts**

Cash Discount Terms	Cost of Forgoing Cash Discounts (Annually)
2/10, net 30	36.735%
2/30, net 60	34.490%
2/10, net 60	13.693%
3/10, net 30	55.670%
3/10, net 60	22.268%

In our example,

$$R = \frac{\$20}{980 \times \frac{20}{360}}$$

$$= 36.735\%$$

The cost to the Print Shop of forgoing the cash discount is 36.735 percent per year! If there is $980 available on day 10 of the trade credit period, the entrepreneur should pay the invoice unless he is able to earn more than 36.735 percent on that money. If the entrepreneur does not have $980 on day 10 but can borrow it at less than 36.735 percent, he should do so to take advantage of the cash discount. Table 8 summarizes the cost of forgoing cash discounts offering various terms.

Although it is a good idea for business owners to take advantage of cash discounts, it is not a wise practice to stretch accounts payable to suppliers beyond the payment terms specified on the invoice. Letting payments become past due destroys the trusting relationship a small company has built with its vendors.

Timing—When to Order

5. Calculate a company's reorder point.

Timing the purchase of merchandise and supplies is also a critical element of a purchasing plan. Entrepreneurs must schedule delivery dates so that their companies do not lose customer good-will from stockouts. In addition, they must concentrate on maintaining proper control over the firm's inventory investment without tying up an excessive amount of working capital. There is a trade-off between the cost of running out of stock and the cost of carrying additional inventory.

When planning delivery schedules for inventory and supplies, owners must consider the **lead time** for an order, the time gap between placing an order and receiving it. In general, business owners cannot expect instantaneous delivery of merchandise. As a result, managers must plan reorder points for inventory items with lead times in mind. To determine when to order merchandise for inventory, entrepreneurs must calculate the reorder point for key inventory items. Developing a reorder point model involves determining the lead time for an order, the usage rate for the item, the minimum level of stock allowable, and the economic order quantity (EOQ). The **lead time** for an order is the time gap between placing an order with a vendor and actually receiving the goods. It may be as little as a few hours or as long as several weeks to process purchase requisitions and orders, contact the supplier, receive the goods, and add them to the company's inventory. Obviously, owners who purchase from local vendors encounter shorter lead times than those who rely on distant suppliers.

Profile

Seth Murray: Belle Baby Carriers

Seth Murray, founder of Belle Baby Carriers, opted to use local vendors and service companies to supply the components of his company's simple, comfortable baby carrier to ensure the quality of his product, which has proved popular with celebrities such as Jessica Alba, Julia Roberts, and Angelina Jolie. Murray considered outsourcing the components to suppliers in China but instead chose suppliers "within 30 miles" of his Boulder, Colorado, location. Although his company's costs are somewhat higher, Belle Baby Carriers places orders with local vendors as they come in, a practice that conserves cash, keeps inventory levels low, and allows the company to operate using Lean principles. In the meantime, Murray's competitors must pay for and wait for the arrival of large containers from Asia and deal with shipping costs and customs regulations. "We have a just-in-time mentality," says Murray. "We have constant communications with our suppliers, and we don't have to worry about shipping costs and import duties."[20]

Business owners can determine the usage rate for a particular product from past inventory and accounting records. They must estimate the speed at which the supply of merchandise will be depleted over a given time. The anticipated usage rate for a product determines how long the supply will last. For example, if an entrepreneur projects that she will use 900 units in the next 6 months, the usage rate is five units per day (900 units/180 days). The simplest reorder point model assumes that the firm experiences a linear usage rate; that is, depletion of the firm's stock continues at a constant rate over time.

Business owners must determine the minimum level of stock allowable. If a firm runs out of a particular item (i.e., incurs stockouts), customers soon lose faith in the business and begin to shop elsewhere. To avoid stockouts, many firms establish a minimum level of inventory greater than zero. In other words, they build a cushion, called **safety stock,** into their inventories in case demand runs ahead of the anticipated usage rate. If that occurs, the owners can dip into the safety stock to fill customer orders until a shipment of goods arrives.

To compute the reorder point for an item, the owner must combine this inventory information with the product's EOQ. The following example illustrates the reorder point technique:

$$L = \text{Lead time for an order} = 5\,\text{days}$$
$$U = \text{Usage rate} = 5\,\text{units per day}$$
$$S = \text{Safety stock (minimum level)} = 75\,\text{units}$$
$$\text{EOQ} = \text{Economic order quantity} = 540\,\text{units}$$

The formula for computing the reorder point is:

$$\text{Reorder point} = (L \times U) + S$$

In this example,

$$\text{Reorder point} = (5\,\text{days} \times 18\,\text{units/day}) + 75\,\text{units}$$
$$= 165\,\text{units}$$

This business owner should order 540 more units when inventory drops to 165 units. Figure 7 illustrates the reorder point situation for this small business.

The simple reorder technique makes assumptions that may not be valid in particular situations. First, the model assumes that the firm's usage rate is constant, but for most small businesses demand varies daily. Second, the model assumes that lead time for an order is constant when, in fact, few vendors deliver precisely within lead time estimates. Third, in this model, the owner never taps safety stock; however, late deliveries or accelerated demand often force owners to dip into their inventory reserves. More advanced models relax some of these assumptions, but the simple model can be a useful inventory guideline for making inventory decisions in a small company.

Another popular reorder point model assumes that the demand for a product during its lead time is normally distributed (see Figure 8). The area under the normal curve at any given point represents the probability that a particular demand level will occur. Figure 9 illustrates the application of this normal distribution to the reorder point model *without* safety stock. The model

FIGURE 7
Reorder Point Model

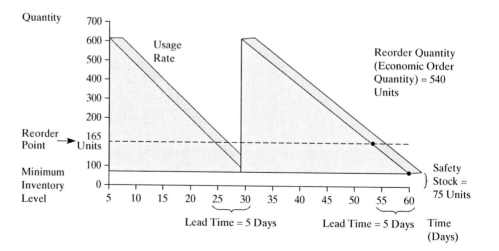

FIGURE 8
Demand During Leading

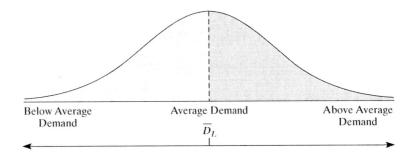

recognizes that three different demand patterns can occur during a product's lead time. Demand pattern 1 is an example of below-average demand during lead time; demand pattern 2 is an example of average demand during lead time; and demand pattern 3 is an example of an above-average demand during lead time.

If the reorder point for this item is normal for the product during lead time, 50 percent of the time demand will be below average (note that 50 percent of the area under the normal curve lies below average). Similarly, 50 percent of the time demand during lead time will exceed the average, and the firm will experience stockouts (note that 50 percent of the area under the normal curve lies above average).

To reduce the probability of inventory shortage, a business owner can increase the reorder point above $\overline{D}_L$ (average demand during the lead time). But how much should the owner increase the reorder point? Rather than attempt to define the actual costs of carrying extra inventory versus the costs of stockouts (remember the trade-off described earlier), this model allows the small business owner to determine the appropriate reorder point by setting a desired customer level. For example, the owner may want to satisfy 95 percent of customer demand for a product during lead time. This service level determines the amount of increase in the reorder point. In effect, these additional items serve as a safety stock:

$$\text{Safety stock} = SLF \times SD_L$$

where:

$$SLF = \text{Service level factor (the appropriate Z score)}$$

$$SD_L = \text{Standard deviation of demand during lead time}$$

Table 9 shows the appropriate service level factor (Z score) for some of the most popular target customer service levels.

FIGURE 9
Reorder Point Without Safety Stock

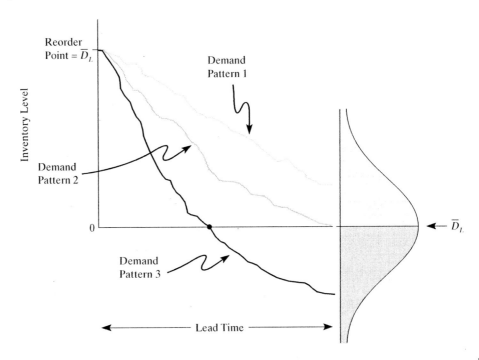

TABLE 9 **Service Level Factors and Z Scores**

Target Customer Service Level	Z Score*
99%	2.33
97.5%	1.96
95%	1.645
90%	1.275
80%	0.845
75%	0.675

*Any basic statistics book provides a table of areas under the normal curve, which gives the appropriate Z score for any service level factor.

▶ ENTREPRENEURSHIP IN ACTION ▶

Supply Chain Risk

Fifty years ago, business was more localized than it is today, and companies had more control over their supply chains and faced less risk of supply interruptions. If one supplier failed to deliver goods or materials, a company usually could find a nearby supplier to fill the order with very little delay. Today, a global economy means that supply chains are longer and more complex; companies all across the globe buy and sell products to other businesses, and the logistics of those deliveries must be choreographed as carefully as an elaborate dance. A glitch at any point in the process often causes ripples—and problems—throughout the remainder of the chain. Natural disasters, labor strikes, dangerous ingredients, faulty products, political instability, terrorism, piracy, and a host of other problems threaten companies' supply chains. A recent study by McKinsey and Company reports that 77 percent of executives say that the amount of supply chain risk their companies face has increased in the last 5 years. More than half of these executives admit that their companies have not addressed the factors that pose the greatest risk to their supply chains.

Just 2 weeks away from a major production run, Gigi Lee Chang, owner of Plum Organics (www.plumorganics.com), a New York City–based company with sales of more than $1 million that produces organic meals for children, received a call from her supplier of organic cheese. "We're out of organic parmesan cheese because there's a shortage of organic milk," the representative told Chang. The manager *thought* that a shipment of organic milk would arrive in time for the company to be able to produce the cheese for Plum Organics' production run, but he could not guarantee it. Chang was concerned and contacted another company about its organic cheese, but its organic parmesan had not fully aged. She was afraid that the cheese would affect the

taste of the finished product. She had a choice to make: Count on her regular supplier to get the shipment of organic milk and come through with the cheese or use the less-than-fully-aged parmesan from the other company. "You try to ask questions to figure out what the risk is, and when you make your bet, hopefully it's going to turn out," she says.

Julie Allison, owner of Eyebobs (*www.eyebobs.com*), a 10-employee company in Minneapolis, Minnesota, that markets stylish reading glasses, understands the importance of managing her company's supply chain. Allison travels to Italy, France, and China at least three times a year

Gigi Lee Chang, founder of Plum Organics.

Source: Amanda Edwards/Getty Images, Inc.-Liaison

to visit Eyebob's suppliers. When working with a new supplier, she tests the quality of the product and the supplier's delivery by placing small orders. To keep costs—and product prices—in check, Allison has introduced glasses with frames made from materials other than plastic, which is adversely affected by increases in petroleum prices. Eyebobs sells reading glasses with frames made from metal and bamboo. "The risks change," says Allison. "Every day you're learning something new."

1. Suppose that Gigi Lee Chang asks you to make a recommendation on the decision she faces

concerning the delivery of the organic cheese for her company's production run. What do you tell her? Explain your reasoning.

2. What steps can Chang and Allison take to manage the risks in the supply chains for their businesses?

Sources: Based on Denise Paulonis and Sabrina Norton, "Managing Global Supply Chains: McKinsey Global Survey Results," *The McKinsey Quarterly,* August 2008, *www.mckinseyquarterly.com/McKinsey_Global_Survey_Results_ Managing_global_supply_chains_2179;* Chris Penttila, "Risky Business," *Entrepreneur,* November 2008, pp. 17–18; Russ Banham, "Reducing Disruption in the Global Supply Chain," *Wall Street Journal,* April 21, 2009, p. A12.

Figure 10 shows the shift to a normally distributed reorder point model with safety stock. In this case, the manager has set a 95 percent customer service level; that is, the manager wants to meet 95 percent of the demand during lead time. The normal curve in the model without safety stock (from Figure 9) is shifted up so that 95 percent of the area under the curve lies above the zero inventory level. The result is a reorder point that is higher than the original reorder point by the amount of the safety stock:

$$\text{Reorder point} = \bar{D}_L + (SLF \times SD_L)$$

where

$\bar{D}_L$ = Average demand during lead time (original reorder point)

SLF = Service level factor (the appropriate Z score)

SD_L = Standard deviation of demand during lead time

FIGURE 10
Reorder Point with Safety Stock

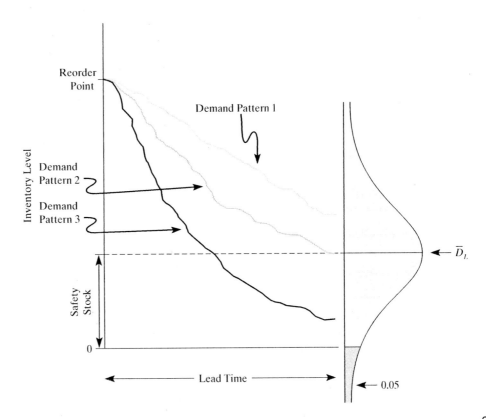

To illustrate, suppose that the average demand for a product during its lead time (1 week) is 325 units with a standard deviation of 110 units. If the desired service level is 95 percent, the service level factor (from Table 9) would be 1.645. The reorder point is:

$$\text{Reorder point} = 325 + (1.645 \times 110) = 325 + 181 = 506 \text{ units}$$

Figure 11 illustrates the shift from a system without safety stock to one with safety stock for this example. With a reorder point of 325 units ($\bar{D}_L$), this small business owner will experience inventory shortages during the lead time 50 percent of the time. With a reorder point of 506 units (i.e., a safety stock of 181 units), the business owner will experience inventory stockouts during the lead time only 5 percent of the time.

Managing the Supply Chain: Vendor Analysis and Selection

6. Develop a vendor rating scale.

Businesses have discovered that managing their supplies chains for maximum effectiveness and efficiency not only can increase their profitability but also can provide them with an important competitive advantage in the marketplace. Proper **supply chain management (SCM)** enables companies to reduce their inventories, get products to market much faster, increase quality, and

FIGURE 11

Shift from a No-Safety Stock System to a Safety Stock System

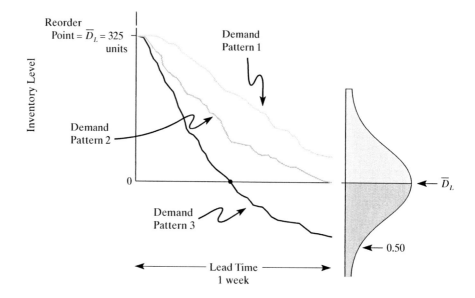

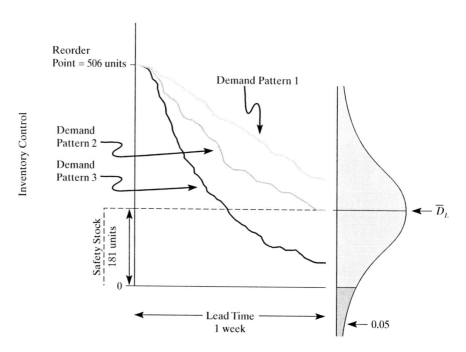

improve customer satisfaction. SCM requires businesses to forge long-term partnerships with reliable suppliers rather than to see vendors merely as "someone trying to sell me something." Doing so can produce an impressive payoff; experts note that implementing a successful SCM system yields an average savings of 15 percent by controlling unnecessary spending, negotiating lower prices, maintaining lower inventory levels, and reducing waste and inefficiency in the purchasing process, all of which save companies vast amounts of money.[21]

Companies are learning that to make SCM work they must share information with their suppliers and make their entire supply chains transparent to everyone involved in them. In the early days, that meant linking suppliers and companies as if they were parts of a single business on private data networks using electronic data interchange (EDI), which allowed companies and vendors to exchange orders and invoices electronically. The Internet takes EDI a step further. Web-based supply chain management, or **e-procurement**, allows companies to share information concerning production plans, shipment schedules, inventory levels, sales forecasts, and actual sales on a real-time basis with their vendors, enabling the companies to make instant adjustments to their orders and delivery schedules. Many studies have found a correlation between the amount of information shared among supply chain members and the efficiency of the entire chain. Costs are significantly lower for retailers, wholesalers, and manufacturers when they are connected in a supply chain network with open communication.[22]

With e-procurement, companies are connected via the Web to their customers and to their suppliers, which allows them to respond rapidly to changing buyer preferences by modifying in real time the inventory they purchase. In turn, suppliers can make the fast adjustments in production scheduling to produce the items that customers actually are buying. Companies "are starting to understand that the 'supply' side of the supply chain isn't worth a hill of beans if the 'demand' side is disconnected," says one industry expert.[23] A study by the consulting firm Aberdeen Group reports that companies that use e-procurement to connect seamlessly the members of their supply chains are able to reduce the prices that they pay for their purchases by 7 percent and cut the delivery time for their orders by 67 percent.[24] With these systems, valuable information flows from the small business selling suits to customers up the supply chain all the way to the sheep shearer harvesting wool!

A Web-based SCM process works like this: Software at a retail store captures data from sales as they happen and looks for underlying trends for use in calculating quantities of which products to purchase in the future. For instance, SCM software at a retail store may notice that sales of black low-rise jeans are selling more briskly than anticipated and forecasts the quantity of jeans the store should order. That information then goes up the supply chain to the jean maker. Taking into account delivery times and manufacturing speed, the software helps the jean maker create a detailed production plan for cutting, sewing, and shipping the garments on time. The software determines how much fabric the jean maker must have to produce the required number of black low-rise jeans and orders it from the textile producer. The software can track everything from the location of the raw materials in the production process to the quality of the finished product for everyone in the supply chain. "Supply chain analytics boost the bottom line because they produce greater efficiency, less scrap, better quality, and lower production costs and improve the top line through greater customer satisfaction," says a top manager at IDC, a research company that has studied the impact of SCM on companies' performance. "This is basic business made better."[25]

To function smoothly, a small company's supply chain should follow the "triple A's": agile, adaptable, and aligned.[26] An *agile* supply chain is one that is fast, flexible, and responsive to changes in demand. Agile supply chains are able to deal with the inevitable disruptions and fluctuations by creating strong partnerships with suppliers, adequate but not excessive levels of safety stock, contingency plans for catastrophic events, and an information system that provides everyone in the chain with timely information. Companies that sell products such as fashion merchandise or video games that have unpredictable demand, high costs associated with stockouts (and the resulting lost sales), and require large end-of-season markdowns to move leftover items require an agile supply chain. Companies that sell basic products such as groceries and cosmetics that have predictable demand, carry low profit margins, and require small end-of-season markdowns require supply chains that are lean and efficient. An *adaptable* supply chain is one that changes as a company's needs change and is able to accommodate a small company's growth. Adaptable supply chains are predictive and are able to anticipate changes in companies' buying and selling processes and help them to adapt to the changes in real time. A supply chain is properly *aligned* when all companies in it work together as a team to improve the chain's performance for the benefit of the entire group. In the past, some companies were hesitant to share information with the businesses in their supply chains. Success today requires that companies not only share information seamlessly but that they also synchronize their efforts to maximize efficiency throughout the entire chain. Agile, adaptable, aligned supply chains reduce costs and improve performance by increasing the speed at which companies get products into customers' hands, reducing excess inventory, and decreasing the use of price markdowns that erode companies' profit margins.

Profile

Seven Eleven Japan

Seven Eleven Japan (SEJ), the Japanese division of the convenience store chain, operates a supply chain characterized by the triple A's. SEJ uses real-time point-of-sale terminals in its stores that track sales constantly and monitor inventory levels. Satellite connections link stores with vendors, distribution centers, and shipping companies so that every element in the supply chain has access to relevant, timely information. The system is so agile that SEJ delivers products to its store three times a day and reconfigures their arrangement on shelves to appeal to different customer groups at different times. SEJ's supply chain proved its adaptability when an earthquake rocked a major city, closing roadways and eliminating normal distribution routes. To deliver the products its customers needed in the midst of a crisis, SEJ employed helicopters and motorcycles to navigate around the gridlock. SEJ aligns its suppliers' interests with its own by allowing them to make deliveries without requiring store managers to verify the contents of every delivery.[27]

If a company's supply chain is to conform to the triple A's, it must be built on the foundation of reliable vendors that can supply it with quality merchandise, equipment, supplies, and services at reasonable prices in a timely manner. Finding the right vendors sometimes can be a challenge.

Profile

Matthew Accarrino: SPQR

Some small business owners hire "foragers" to track down hard-to-find specialty items that the typical supply chain misses. When Matthew Accarrino, now head chef at SPQR, an upscale restaurant in San Francisco, worked at a famous restaurant outside of Rome, Italy, he and his staff visited local farmers for freshly picked ingredients for that evening's meals. "You differentiate yourself not only through cooking but also by accessing products that are unique to your restaurant," he says. Accarrino relies on that same philosophy at SPQR, but his busy schedule requires him to hire foragers to locate certain unique, hard-to-find items for the menu. Forager Erin Littlestar is the sustainability and sourcing manager (her nickname is the "sourceress") for Sweetgreen, a small chain of fast-casual restaurants in Washington, D.C. "I'm systematically going through the menu and looking at what's there that could be better," she says. She has tracked down a farmer who provides "a dozen different varieties of dates" and cream that is so good that the pastry chef churns her own butter with it.[28]

Selecting the right vendors or suppliers for a business has an impact well beyond simply obtaining goods and services at the lowest cost. Although searching for the best price is always an important factor, successful small business owners must consider other factors in vendor selection, such as reliability, reputation, quality, support services, speed, and proximity.

Vendor Certification

To add objectivity to the vendor selection process, many firms are establishing vendor certification programs, agreements to give one supplier the majority of their business if that supplier meets rigorous quality and performance standards. Today, businesses of all sizes and types are establishing long-term "partnering" arrangements with vendors that meet their certification standards. When creating a vendor certification program, entrepreneurs should remember the three Cs: *commitment, communication,* and *control. Commitment* to consistently meeting the company's quality standards must be paramount. No company can afford to do business with vendors that cannot meet its quality targets. Second, a company must establish two-way *communication* with vendors. Communication implies trust, and trust creates working relationships that are long-term and mutually beneficial. Treating suppliers like partners can reveal ways to boost quality and lower costs for both parties. Finally, a company must make sure that its vendors and suppliers have in place the *controls* that enable them to produce quality results and to achieve continuous improvements in their processes. In today's competitive marketplace, entrepreneurs expect all vendors to demonstrate that they operate processes built on continuous improvement.

Creating a vendor certification program requires entrepreneurs to develop a vendor rating scale that allows them to evaluate the advantages and disadvantages of each potential vendor. The scale allows entrepreneurs to score potential vendors on a measurement of the purchasing criteria that are most important to their companies' success. The first step to developing a scale is to determine the criteria that are most important to selecting a vendor (e.g., price, quality, prompt delivery). The next step is to assign weights to each criterion to reflect its relative importance. The third step involves developing a grading scale for comparing vendors on the criteria. Developing a usable scale requires that the owner maintain proper records of past vendor performances. Finally, the owner must compute a weighted total score for each vendor and select the vendor that scores the highest on the set of criteria. Consider the following example. Bravo Bass Boats, Inc., is faced with choosing from among several suppliers of a critical raw material. The company's owner has decided to employ a vendor rating scale to select the best vendor using the following procedure.

Step 1   *Determine important criteria.* The owner of Bravo has selected the following criteria:

    Quality
    Price
    Prompt delivery
    Service
    Assistance

Step 2   *Assign weights to each criterion to reflect its relative importance.*

Criterion	Weight
Quality	35
Price	30
Prompt delivery	20
Service	10
Assistance	5
Total	100

Step 3   *Develop a grading scale for each criterion.*

Criterion	Grading Scale
Quality	$\dfrac{\text{Number of acceptable lots from Vendor X}}{\text{Total number of lots from Vendor X}}$
Price	$\dfrac{\text{Lowest quoted price of all vendors}}{\text{Price offered by Vendor X}}$
Prompt Delivery	$\dfrac{\text{Number of on-time deliveries from Vendor X}}{\text{Total number of deliveries from Vendor X}}$
Service	A subjective evaluation of the quality of service offered by each vendor
Assistance	A subjective evaluation of the advice and assistance provided by each vendor

Step 4   *Compute a weighted score for each vendor.*

Criterion	Weight	Grade	Weighted Score (weight × grade)
Vendor 1			
Quality	35	9/10	31.5
Price	30	12.50/13.00	28.8
Prompt delivery	20	10/10	20.0
Service	10	8/10	8.0
Assistance	5	5/5	5.0
Total weighted score			93.3
Vendor 2			
Quality	35	8/10	28.0
Price	30	12.50/13.50	27.8
Prompt delivery	20	8/10	16.0
Service	10	8/10	8.0
Assistance	5	4.5	4.0
Total weighted score			83.8
Vendor 3			
Quality	35	7/10	24.5
Price	30	12.50/12.50	30.0
Prompt delivery	20	6/10	12.0
Service	10	7/10	7.0
Assistance	5	1/5	1.0
Total weighted score			74.5

Using this analysis of the three suppliers, Bravo should purchase the majority of this raw material from Vendor 1.

This vendor analysis procedure assumes that business owners have a working knowledge of their supplier network. Start-up companies seldom will, however. Owners of start-up companies must find suppliers and gather data to conduct a vendor analysis. One of the best ways to do that is to ask potential vendors for references. In some cases, industry trade associations have knowledge regarding the integrity of suppliers or vendors. Other sources for information on vendors include trade association and shows, the local chamber of commerce, and publications such as *McRAE's Blue Book* (*www.macraesbluebook.com*), which includes information on more than 1,000,000 industrial companies with more than 40,000 product listings, and the *Thomas Register of American Manufacturers* (*www.thomasnet.com*), which lists more than 67,000 industrial product categories. Both of these sources provide lists of products and services and the names, addresses, telephone numbers, and ratings of their manufacturers. Entrepreneurs whose product lines have an international flair may look to the *Thomas Global Register* for information on companies throughout the world dealing in practically every type of product or service. Web sites such as Alibaba (*www.alibaba.com*), Worldwide Brands (*www.worldwidebrands.com*), and Panjiva (*www.panjiva.com*) also are valuable tools that help entrepreneurs locate reliable suppliers across the globe for practically any product.

The Final Decision

Once business owners identify potential vendors and suppliers, they must decide which one (or ones) to do business with. Entrepreneurs should consider the following factors before making the final decision about the right supplier.

How to Manage Supply Chain Risk

Many small firms pay prices for goods and services that are too high and they find their purchasing options limited by a lack of competent suppliers. The broader the base of potential suppliers a business has, the more supply flexibility and security it has and the greater is its ability to get the best prices on its purchases. Use the following tips from the Street-Smart Entrepreneur to build meaningful, long-term relationships with the best suppliers:

1. *Establish your company's critical criteria for selecting a vendor.* What characteristics must the ideal vendor have? You must know up front what you are looking for in a vendor.

2. *Research thoroughly prospective vendors before you purchase anything from them.* The Internet is a useful tool for conducting a preliminary screening analysis.

3. *Interview prospective vendors with the same level of intensity that you interview prospective employees.* Both relationships influence how successful a company is at achieving quality objectives. "It's not easy to put aside the time," says James Walker, president of Octagon Research Solutions, a 60-person software company, "but for us, it's all about whether we can have a good relationship with [our vendors.]" Use the criteria you established in step 1 to establish a list of questions to ask potential vendors.

4. *Be assertive.* Ask tough questions and be a knowledgeable buyer. Don't allow suppliers to do their typical "sales pitches" before you have time to ask your questions.

5. *Check potential vendors' credit ratings.* Judging a potential vendor's financial strength and stability is important. Dealing with a vendor that is undergoing financial woes creates unnecessary complications for business owners.

6. *Get referrals.* Ask all potential vendors to supply a list of referrals of businesses that they have served over the last 5 years or more. Then make the necessary contacts.

7. *Visit potential vendors' businesses.* The best way to judge a vendor's ability to meet your company's needs is to see the operation firsthand. Nancy Connolly, president of Lasertone Corporation, a maker of copier and laser toner, insists on "a personal meeting between me and the president of the company," she says, before establishing a relationship with a vendor. The goal is to judge the level of the potential vendor's commitment to meeting Lasertone's needs.

8. *Evaluate potential suppliers' plans for dealing with risks and interruptions in their own supply chains.* Remember that if your vendor's supply of materials is interrupted, your supply also will be interrupted.

9. *Don't fixate on price.* Look for value in what they sell. If your only concern is lowest price, vendors will push their lowest-priced (and often lowest-quality) product lines.

10. *Ask "What if?"* The real test of a strong vendor—customer relationship occurs when problems arise. Smart entrepreneurs ask vendors how they will handle particular types of problems when they arise.

11. *Attend trade shows.* Work the room. A visit to a trade show is not a vacation; it's business. Find out whether the next booth has a valuable new vendor who has the potential to increase your company's profitability.

12. *Don't forget about local vendors.* Because of their proximity, local vendors can sometimes provide the fastest service. Solving problems often is easier because local vendors can make on-site service calls.

13. *Test a vendor before committing completely.* Susan Gilbert, owner of Café in the Park, a restaurant in San Diego, says, "Inventory is cash flow. When I'm dealing with a vendor, I need to know how quickly they can deliver, how quickly I can turn over the inventory, and keep it all tight." Rather than place an order for 100 Danish pastries with a new vendor, for instance, Gilbert starts with an order of a few dozen pastries to judge the vendor's performance.

14. *Find an appropriate balance between sole sourcing, which offers the benefits of economies of scale, and multisourcing, which reduces the risk of interrupted supplies.* Recall that a common strategy uses Pareto's Law, the 80/20 Rule.

15. *Work with the vendors.* Tell your suppliers what you like and don't like about their products and service. In many cases, they can resolve your concerns. Most vendors want to build long-term relationships with their customers. Give them a chance to do so.

16. *Do unto others . . .* Treat your vendors well. Be selective, but pay on time and treat them with respect.

1. Why do so many firms focus solely on selecting vendors that offer the lowest prices? What are the dangers of doing so?
2. Develop a list of 10 questions you would ask a potential vendor on a product you select.

Sources: Based on Nancy Germond, "Supply Chain Risk Management a Must as Global Sourcing Intensifies," *All Business*, June 11, 2010, *www.allbusiness.com/company-activities-management/management-risk-management/14609006-1.html*; Kelly L. Frey, "Selecting a Vendor: RFPs and Responses to RFPs," Baker, Donelson, Bearman, Caldwell, and Berkowitz, *www.bakerdonelson.com/Documents/Selecting%20a%20Vendor.pdf*; Allison Stein Wellner, "Finding the Right Vendor," *Inc.*, July 2003, pp. 88–95; Jan Norman, "How to Find Suppliers," *Business Start-ups*, October 1998, pp. 44–47; *Physical Risks to the Supply Chain: A View from Finance*, CFO Research Services and FM Global, February 2009, pp. 6–7.

NUMBER OF SUPPLIERS. One important question entrepreneurs face is "Should I buy from a single supplier or from several different sources?" Concentrating purchases at a single supplier (or sole sourcing) results in special attention from the supplier, especially if orders are substantial. Second, a business may be able to negotiate quantity discounts if its orders are large enough. Finally, a small company can cultivate a closer, more cooperative relationship with the supplier. Suppliers are more willing to work with companies that prove to be loyal customers. The result of this type of partnership can be better-quality goods and services. Stratsys, a company that makes plastic prototypes for the aerospace, automotive, and medical industries, purchases some of its most important raw materials from a single source. Company managers admit that doing so involves risk, but they believe that their company produces better quality products by eliminating the variability that multiple sources of supply would introduce into their production process.[29]

However, using a single vendor also has disadvantages. A company can experience shortages of critical materials if its only supplier suffers a catastrophe, such as bankruptcy, a fire, a strike, or a natural disaster.

ENTREPRENEURIAL

Profile

Caterpillar Inc.

Caterpillar Inc. narrowly avoided a devastating worldwide shutdown of its factories when a tornado severely damaged the sole plant in Oxford, Mississippi, that manufactures the steel cylinder couplings that link hydraulic hoses on almost every piece of equipment the company makes. Managers quickly took steps to get the damaged factory back online, scoured their warehouses for existing couplings, and transferred production to several new suppliers, including a metal-working company in Ontario, Canada, that had surplus capacity from a slowdown in the auto industry. The close call caused managers to add machinery in several of its factories that can produce couplings in an emergency.[30]

To offset the risks of sole sourcing, many companies rely on the 80/20 Rule. They purchase 80 percent of their supplies from their premier supplier and the remaining 20 percent from several "backup" vendors. Although this strategy may require a compromise on getting the lowest prices, it removes the risk of sole sourcing and lets a company's premier suppliers know that they have competition.

RELIABILITY. Business owners must evaluate a potential vendor's ability to deliver adequate quantities of quality merchandise when it is needed. One common complaint small businesses have against their suppliers is late delivery. Late deliveries or shortages cause lost sales and create customer ill will. Large customers often take precedence over small ones when it comes to service.

PROXIMITY. A supplier's physical proximity is an important factor when choosing a vendor. The cost of transporting merchandise can increase significantly the total cost of merchandise to a buyer. Foreign manufacturers also require longer delivery times, and because of the distance that shipments must travel, a hiccup anywhere in the distribution channel often results in late deliveries. In addition, entrepreneurs can solve quality problems more easily with nearby suppliers than with distant vendors.

Profile

*Jamey Bennett:
LightWedge*

When Jamey Bennett decided to start a company to sell the LightWedge, an idea he came up with when he was 17, he looked to foreign manufacturers to produce the sheet of clear acrylic that contained light-emitting diodes that softly illuminate a page, allowing one to read in bed without disturbing a sleeping partner. With orders in hand from bookseller Barnes & Noble and catalog retailer Levenger, Bennett purchased equipment and tooling for a factory in China's Guangdong Province. Things ran smoothly for a few months until Bennett introduced a LightWedge designed for paperbacks. The factory ignored Bennett's repeated requests to modify the original design, and he switched production to another Chinese factory where things quickly got worse. Bennett ordered 5,000 LightWedges, but only 2,000 arrived—4 months late—and many had lenses that were so scratched or marred by "some kind of mysterious goop" that they were unusable. Because of the problems, LightWedge lost an estimated $1.5 million in sales, and Bennett decided that it was time to bring production back to the United States. Today, a factory in Newport News, Virginia, manufactures the LightWedge, and although costs are 20 percent higher than they were in China, Bennett knows that he will get quality products delivered on time.[31]

Despite potential problems such as the ones that Jamey Bennett encountered, outsourcing purchases of materials and components to foreign manufacturers, particularly to those in Asia, Eastern Europe, and Mexico, is a growing trend. Even though the risks and complications of using foreign suppliers are substantial, many companies cannot resist the lure of the low prices they offer. In China, for example, the typical factory worker earns slightly more than $1 per hour, compared to wages that are 20 to 30 times that in the United States and Western Europe. Yet the poor transportation infrastructure in China can increase the cost and the complexity of getting a product to market. Many companies—from toy manufacturers to drug makers—also have experienced quality problems with Chinese suppliers.

SPEED. How fast can a supplier deliver products to your business? A speedy supply chain can be a competitive advantage for a company.

Profile

Zara

A successful retail operation depends on a smoothly functioning supply chain that is transparent, agile, adaptable, and aligned with members' best interests.

Source: Archimage/Alamy Images

Zara, a popular clothing chain owned by Spanish company Inditex, is known for its tightly controlled supply chain that zips the latest fashions at very affordable prices (the average item sells for $27) to its stores in 73 countries. The company's high-tech logistics system gets the latest designer styles from the drawing board to store shelves in less than 2 weeks, compared to an industry average of 9 months![32]

SERVICES. Entrepreneurs must evaluate the range of services vendors offer. Do salespeople make regular calls, and are they knowledgeable about their product line? Will sales representatives assist in planning store layout and in creating attractive displays? Will the vendor make convenient deliveries on time? Is the supplier reasonable in making repairs on equipment after installation and in handling returned merchandise? Are sales representatives able to offer useful advice on purchasing and other managerial functions? Is the supplier willing to take the time to help you solve problems that inevitably will crop up?

CPA Charles Ross uses payroll services company PayCycle to handle the payroll function for his own business as well as for many of his small business clients. PayCycle won Ross as a loyal customer after he discovered that he had entered a client's payroll information incorrectly, creating a problem that PayCycle remedied quickly. It was Friday afternoon, and the client's W-2 forms had to go out the following Monday, which meant that PayCycle had to recalculate an entire year's payroll. Even though it required almost a full day's work for someone at PayCycle over a weekend, the payroll service fixed the problem, and the forms went out on schedule on Monday. That level of service explains why Ross is a lifelong customer and why 90 percent of PayCycle's customers refer new customers to the company.[33]

COLLABORATION. The goal is to find a supplier that is eager to join forces with the intent of building a long-term partnership with your company. Other small companies make ideal candidates.

When NASA approached Scott Fischer, president of the Center for Systems Management (CSM), a Vienna, Virginia, company that provides training and consulting services for corporations and government agencies, about creating a video for an internal marketing campaign, Fischer knew that the job was beyond his company's ability. Wanting the chance to expand his work with the space agency, Fischer began looking for a company with which he could partner to create the video. He had to work quickly because NASA needed the video in just 45 days. Fischer and a team of employees selected Technovative Marketing, a seven-person marketing firm headed by Harriet Donnelly. Donnelly worked on the video herself and attended every meeting that Fischer had with NASA officials. (Donnelly assigns both a staff person and a senior manager to every Technovative project to make sure that clients always have two points of contact.) Because of the partnership that CSM and Technovative Marketing forged, the project turned out to be a huge success. NASA has enlisted CSM for similar projects, and, in turn, CSM is partnering with Technovative Marketing.[34]

PRICE NEGOTIATIONS. Small firms usually must pay market or list price for items that they purchase infrequently. This is not the case for goods purchased on a regular basis and that are essential components or supplies. An entrepreneur should have no hesitation about attempting to purchase the critical goods or services it needs at the best price and terms of sale. The terms of sale, as mentioned previously, can be a significant factor in the final price that the entrepreneur pays.

Legal Issues Affecting Purchasing

7. Describe the legal implications of the purchasing function.

When a small business purchases goods for a supplier, ownership passes from seller to buyer. But when do title and risk of loss to the goods pass from one party to the other? The answer is important because any number of things can happen to the merchandise after a customer orders it but before a company delivers it. When small business owners order merchandise and supplies from their vendors, they should know when the ownership of the merchandise—and the risk associated with it—shifts from supplier to buyer.

IN THE ENTREPRENEURIAL SPOTLIGHT
A (Supply) Chain Is Only as Strong as Its Weakest Link

Zoran Corporation is a designer of the chips that go into many of the electronic gizmos that are so prevalent today, including smartphones, digital cameras, television sets, printers, DVDs, DVRs, and others. Based in Sunnyvale, California, the company sits squarely in the middle of a complex supply chain that can be extremely challenging to manage because companies are hesitant to share sensitive sales information with other businesses. Sometimes Zoran does not know how customers use its specialized video- and audio-processing chips. One batch that the company thought was going into DVD players ended up in digital picture frames. Most of Zoran's customers are the anonymous factories located in Asia that produce consumer electronics for global giants such as Toshiba, Samsung, Sony, and many others.

Zoran does not actually manufacture the chips it designs. Instead the company subcontracts manufacturing to dozens of companies, such as Taiwan Semiconductor Manufacturing Company (TSMC), that specialize in chip-making. TSMC, in turn, purchases equipment used to etch circuits and bake chemicals onto semiconductors from companies such as Applied Materials in Santa Clara, California. Customer demand for electronic devices drives the entire supply chain, however. Thin profit margins and the rapid decline in the value of electronic components demand that companies keep their inventories lean and manage their supply chains carefully.

The accompanying figure shows how lengthy modern supply chains can be. Electronics retailers such as Best Buy place orders with Toshiba for DVD players 6 weeks before the items are to be stocked on stores' shelves, but the length and the complexity of the global supply chain means that acquiring all of the components and assembling them into finished players often takes as long as 12 weeks. Toshiba then places an order for the DVD players with the contract factories in Asia (many of which are in China), which, in turn, place orders for chips they need with Zoran. Zoran then orders its subcontractors, including TSMC, to make the chips to supply the orders from the contract factories in Asia.

Life of a DVD Player | How the tech supply chain makes the world's gadgets

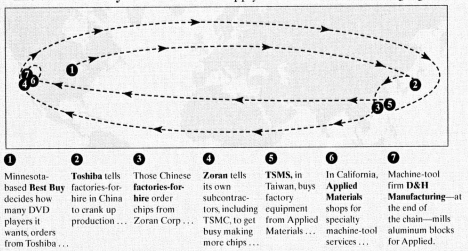

❶	❷	❸	❹	❺	❻	❼
Minnesota-based **Best Buy** decides how many DVD players it wants, orders from Toshiba ...	**Toshiba** tells factories-for-hire in China to crank up production ...	Those Chinese **factories-for-hire** order chips from Zoran Corp ...	**Zoran** tells its own subcontractors, including TSMC, to get busy making more chips ...	**TSMS,** in Taiwan, buys factory equipment from Applied Materials ...	In California, **Applied Materials** shops for specialty machine-tool services ...	Machine-tool firm **D&H Manufacturing**—at the end of the chain—mills aluminum blocks for Applied.

To produce the chips, TSMC and other factories order equipment and machinery from Applied Materials, which orders parts from machine tool shops such as D&H Manufacturing, a small precision machining company in Fremont, California. Hiccups at any point in the supply chain often ricochet through the entire chain, disrupting the smooth flow of goods from producer to consumer. For instance, an anticipated decrease in demand due to an economic slowdown led Best Buy to reduce the number of DVD players it ordered, which caused TSMC to cut back production in its factories to just 35 percent utilization and idle thousands of workers. Applied Materials, an equipment supplier to those factories, saw its sales plummet as well. Angelo Grestoni, owner of D&H Manufacturing, the machine shop, says that he was left holding a year's supply of some products rather than the normal 3 months' worth. "We've got millions of dollars of inventory we can't sell, and we're paying storage fees on it," he says.

1. What types of supply chain risks does Zoran face?
2. What steps can Zoran take to minimize the risks it faces?

Source: Based on Phred Dvorak, "Clarity Is Missing Link in Supply Chain," *Wall Street Journal*, May 18, 2009, pp. A1, A14.

Title

Before the Uniform Commercial Code (UCC) was enacted, the concept of title—the right to ownership of goods—determined where responsibility for merchandise fell. Today, however, the UCC has replaced the concept of title with three other concepts: identification, risk of loss, and insurable interest.

Identification

Before title can pass to the buyer, the goods must already be in existence and must be identifiable from all other similar goods. Specific goods already in existence are identified at the time the sales contract is made. For example, if Graphtech, Inc., orders a Model 477-X plotter, the goods are identified at the time the contract (oral or written) is made. Generic goods are identified when they are marked, shipped, or otherwise designated as the goods in the contract. For example, an order of fuel oil may not be identified until it is loaded into a transfer truck for shipment.

Risk of Loss

Risk of loss determines which party incurs the financial risk if the goods are damaged, destroyed, or lost while in transit. Risk of loss does *not* always pass with title. Three particular rules govern the passage of title and the transfer of risk or loss.

RULE 1: AGREEMENT. A supplier and a small business owner can agree to the terms under which title passes. Similarly, the two parties can agree (preferably in writing) to shift the risk of loss at any time during the transaction. In other words, any explicit agreement between buyer and seller determines when title and risk of loss will pass.

RULE 2: F.O.B. SELLER. Under a sales contract designated F.O.B. ("free on board") seller, title passes to the buyer as soon as the seller delivers the goods into the care of a carrier or shipper. In addition, an **F.O.B. seller contract** (also known as a **shipment contract**) requires that the buyer pay all shipping and transportation costs. For example, a North Carolina manufacturer sells 100,000 capacitors to a buyer in Ohio with terms "F.O.B. North Carolina." Under this contract, the Ohio firms pays all shipping costs, and title and risk of loss pass from the manufacturer as soon as the carrier takes possession of the shipment. If the goods are lost or damaged in transit, the buyer suffers the loss. Of course, the buyer can purchase insurance (see insurable interest below) and has legal recourse against the carrier if the carrier is at fault. If a contract is silent on shipping terms, the courts assume that the contract is a shipment contract (F.O.B. seller), and the buyer bears the risk of loss while the goods are in transit.

RULE 3: F.O.B. BUYER. A sales contract designated F.O.B. buyer requires that the seller deliver the goods to the buyer's place of business (or to a place that the buyer designates such as a warehouse). Title and risk of loss transfer to the small business when the goods are delivered to the business or to the designated destination. Also, an **F.O.B. buyer contract** (also called a **destination contract**) requires the seller to pay all shipping and transportation costs. In the example above, if the contract were "F.O.B. Ohio," the North Carolina manufacturer pays the cost of shipping the order, and title and risk of loss pass to the Ohio company when the shipment is delivered to its place of business. In this case, the seller bears any losses due to goods that are lost or damaged in transit.

Insurable Interest

Insurable interest ensures the right of either party to the sales contract to obtain insurance to protect against lost, damaged, or destroyed merchandise as long as that party has "sufficient interest" in the goods. In general, once goods are identified, the buyer has an insurable interest in them. The seller has a sufficient interest as long as the seller retains title to the goods. However, under certain circumstances both the buyer and the seller have insurable interests even after title has passed to the buyer.

Receiving Merchandise

Once the merchandise is received, the buyer must verify its identity and condition. When the goods are delivered, the owner should check the number of cartons unloaded against the carrier's delivery receipt to make sure that the shipment is complete. It is also a good idea to examine the boxes for damage; if shipping cartons are damaged, the carrier should note this on the delivery receipt. The owner should open all cartons immediately after delivery, inspect the merchandise for quality and condition, and check it against the invoices for discrepancies. If merchandise is damaged or faulty, the buyer should contact the supplier immediately and follow up with a written report. The owner should never destroy or dispose of damaged or flawed merchandise unless the supplier specifically authorizes it. Proper control techniques in receiving merchandise prevent the small business owner from paying for suppliers' and shippers' mistakes.

Selling on Consignment

Small business owners who lack the necessary capital to invest or are unwilling to assume the risk of investing in inventory may be able to sell goods on consignment. Selling on **consignment** means that the small business owner does not purchase the merchandise carried from the supplier (called the consignor); instead, the owner pays the consignor only for the merchandise actually sold. For providing the supplier with a market for his goods, the small business owner normally receives a percentage of the revenue on each item sold. The business owner (called the **consignee**) may return any unsold merchandise to the supplier (the **consignor**) without obligation. Under a consignment agreement, title and risk of loss do not pass to the consignee unless the contract specifies these terms. In other words, the supplier bears the financial costs of lost, damaged, or stolen merchandise. The small business owner who sells merchandise on a consignment basis realizes the following advantages:

- The owner does not have to invest money in these inventory items, but the merchandise on hand is available for sale.
- The owner does not pay the consignor until the item is sold.
- Because the consignment relationship is founded on the law of agency, the consignee never takes title to the merchandise and does not bear the risk of loss for the goods.
- The supplier normally plans and sets up displays for the merchandise and is responsible for maintaining them.

Before selling items on consignment, the small business owner and the supplier should create a written contract, which should include the following items:

- A list of items to be sold and their quantities
- Prices to be charged
- Location of merchandise in store
- Duration of contract
- Commission charged by the consignee
- Policy on defective items and rejects
- Schedule for payments to consignor
- Delivery terms and merchandise storage requirements
- Responsibility for items lost to pilferage and shoplifting
- Provision for terminating consignment contract

If managed properly, selling goods on consignment can be beneficial to both the consignor and the consignee.

Chapter Review

1. Understand the components of a purchasing plan.
   - The purchasing function is vital to every small business's success because it influences a company's ability to sell quality goods and services at reasonable prices. Purchasing is the acquisition of needed materials, supplies, services, and equipment of the right quality, in the proper quantities, for reasonable prices, at the appropriate time, and from the right suppliers.
2. Explain the principles of total quality management (TQM) and Six Sigma and their impact on quality.
   - The idea behind Lean principles is to eliminate waste in a company's activities using five principles: value, value stream, flow, pull, and perfection.

- 5S principles are simple but effective ways to improve quality in an organization:
  - Sort items into two categories, necessary and unnecessary, and eliminate everything that is unnecessary
  - Straighten and organize the tools employees use and their workspaces.
  - Shine all workspaces.
  - Systematize best-practice processes so that the company can apply them universally.
  - Sustain the drive toward continuous improvement.
- Six Sigma relies on quantitative tools to improve quality. At its core are four key tenets: Delight customers with quality and speed, constantly improve the process, use teamwork to improve the process, and make changes to the process based on facts, not guesses.
- Under the total quality management (TQM) philosophy, companies define a quality product as one that conforms to predetermined standards that satisfy customers' demands. The goal is to get delivery and invoicing to installation and follow-up right—the first time.
- To implement TQM successfully, a small business owner must rely on 10 fundamental principles: Shift from a management-driven culture to a participative, team-based one; modify the reward system to encourage teamwork and innovation; train workers constantly to give them the tools they need to produce quality and to upgrade the company's knowledge base; train employees to measure quality with the tools of statistical process control (SPC); use Pareto's Law to focus TQM efforts; share information with everyone in the organization; focus quality improvements on astonishing the customer; don't rely on inspection to produce quality products and services; avoid using TQM to place blame on those who make mistakes; and strive for continuous improvement in processes as well as in products and services.

3. Conduct economic order quantity (EOQ) analysis to determine the proper level of inventory.
  - A major goal of the small business is to generate adequate inventory turnover by purchasing proper quantities of merchandise. A useful device for computing the proper quantity is economic order quantity (EOQ) analysis, which yields the ideal order quantity, the amount that minimizes total inventory costs. Total inventory costs consist of the cost of the units, holding (carrying) costs, and ordering (setup) costs. The EO balances the costs of ordering and of carrying merchandise to yield minimum total inventory cost.

4. Differentiate among the three types of purchase discounts vendors offer.
  - Trade discounts are established on a graduated scale and depend on a small firm's position in the channel of distribution.
  - Quantity discounts are designed to encourage businesses to order large quantities of merchandise and supplies.
  - Cash discounts are offered to customers as an incentive to pay for merchandise promptly.

5. Calculate a company's reorder point.
  - There is a time gap between the placing of an order and actual receipt of the goods. The reorder point model tells the owner when to place an order to replenish the company's inventory.

6. Develop a vendor rating scale.
  - Creating a vendor analysis model involves four steps: Determine the important criteria (i.e., price, quality, prompt delivery, service, etc.); assign a weight to each criterion to reflect its relative importance; develop a grading scale for each criterion; and compute a weighted score for each vendor.

7. Describe the legal implications of the purchasing function.
  - Important legal issues involving purchasing goods involve title, or ownership of the goods; identification of the goods; risk of loss and when it shifts from seller to buyer; and insurable interests in the goods. The buyer and seller can have an insurable interest in the same goods at the same time.

Discussion Questions

1. What is purchasing? Why is it important for the small business owner to develop a purchasing plan?
2. What is TQM? How can it help small business owners achieve the quality goods and services they require?
3. One top manager claims that to implement total quality management successfully, "You have to change your company culture as much as your processes." Do you agree? Explain.
4. Visit the Web site of the National Institute of Standards and Technology (*www.quality.nist.gov*), the organization that grants the Malcolm Baldrige National Quality Award, the highest quality award in the United States. Research one of the companies that received the Baldrige Award and prepare a one-page summary of its quality initiative and the results that it produced.
5. List and briefly describe the three components of total inventory costs.
6. What is the economic order quantity? How does it minimize total inventory costs?
7. Should a small business owner always purchase products from the vendor with the lowest prices? Why or why not?
8. Briefly outline the three types of purchase discounts. Under what circumstances is each the best choice?
9. What is lead time? Outline the procedure for determining a product's reorder point.
10. Explain how an entrepreneur launching a company could locate suppliers and vendors.
11. What factors are commonly used to evaluate suppliers?
12. Explain the procedure for developing a vendor rating scale.
13. Explain briefly the three concepts that have replaced the concept of title. When do title and risk of loss shift under an FOB seller contract? An FOB buyer contract?
14. What should a small business owner do when merchandise is received?
15. Explain how a small business would sell goods on consignment. What should be included in a consignment contract?

Business Plan Pro

Entrepreneurs can improve the quality of the products and services they offer, control the cost of purchasing or producing those products and services, and enhance the level of service that they provide their customers through effective management of supply chains. The issues of purchasing, quality management, and vendor analysis cut across all of the functions of an organization and, in many cases, play a significant role in determining a company's ability to compete successfully. If your business is product-based, supply chain management issues will represent a significant part of your business and your business plan. Supply chain management factors are an important part of a product-based business plan.

On the Web

The Companion Web site at *www.pearsonhighered.com/ scarborough* offers additional information in the areas of supply chain management, including purchasing, quality management, and vendor analysis. Review these sites and determine whether these sources may be useful to you as you build your plan.

In the Software

Confirm that you have selected the "product" type of plan outline within Business PlanPro. You can do this by clicking on the "Plan Setup" icon and looking at the "Type of business" comments below. It will state, "I sell products" or "I sell services," depending on your choice. If you do sell products, select the proper choice to indicate whether you manufacture those products or purchase and resell them. The outline within Business PlanPro will automatically adjust to your choice. Complete the information in the "Product" section of your business plan. Make sure you also review your financial information regarding product and inventory expenses.

Building Your Business Plan

Once you have completed the "Product" section, step back and review your plan. By now, you have completed most of the sections in your plan, and it should tell a cohesive story about your business.

Endnotes

1. Gina Paglucia Morrison and Anca van Assendelft, *Charting a New Course: The Retail Merchandising-Supply Network*, IBM, November 1, 2006, p. 1.

2. Ian Mount and Brian Caulfield, "The Missing Link," *eCompany*, May 2001, p. 84.

3. Morrison and Assendelft, *Charting a New Course*, p. 1; "Rethinking the Purchasing Function," *McKinsey Quarterly Chart Focus Newsletter*, May 2008, p. 1.

4. *Physical Risks to the Supply Chain: The View from Finance*, CFO Research Services and FM Global, February 2009, p. 2.

5. "U.S. Commercial Spending Estimated at $20.3 Trillion in 2008," *Web CPA*, September 29, 2009, *www.webcpa.com/news/-51868-1.html*.

6. *Low-Cost Country Sourcing Can Benefit a Company's Bottom Line*, IBM, 2006, p. 6.

7. Helen Coster, "Tainted Booty," *Forbes*, April 21, 2008, pp. 84–86.

8. Beth Bacheldor, "Keeping Risks to a Minimum," *InformationWeek*, October 10, 2005, pp. 43–45.

9. Rudolph Bell, "Volcano Disrupts BMW Supply Chain to S.C," *The State*, April 20, 2010, *www.thestate.com/2010/04/20/1251405/volcano-disrupts-bmw-supply-chain.html*; "Iceland Volcano: Nissan and BMW Suspend Some Production," *BBC News*, April 20, 2010, *http://news.bbc.co.uk/2/hi/8631676.stm*.

10. Randy Myers, "The Spice Trade," *CFO*, June 2007, p. 74.

11. Joelle Dick, Caroline Kvitka, Aaron Lazenby, and Rich Schwerin, "Four Keys to Lean Six Sigma," *Profit*, November 2004, p. 9.

12. "Vogel Wood Slices Through Lead Times with Lean Transformation," Wisconsin Manufacturing Extension Partnership, *www.wmep.org/SuccessStories/vogel.aspx*.

13. Jill Jusko, "Scotsman Ice Systems: IW Best Plants Profile 2006," *IndustryWeek*, October 1, 2006, *www.industryweek.com/ReadArticle.aspx?ArticleID=12682*.

14. Mount and Caulfield, "The Missing Link," p. 84.

15. Doug Bartholomew, "Supply Chains at Risk," *IndustryWeek*, October 1, 2006, *www.industryweek.com/ReadArticle.aspx?ArticleID=12713*.

16. W. Edwards Deming, *Out of the Crisis*, MIT Press: Cambridge, Massachusetts, 2000, p. 32.

17. Donna Abernathy, "Purchasing Cooperatives Give Small Business an Edge," Business Know-How, 2010, *www.businessknowhow.com/money/purchasing-coop.htm*; Kelly Johnson and Suzette Rubio, "Blue Hawk Cooperative: The New Kid on the Block," *Supply House Times*, July 1, 2007, *www.supplyht.com/CDA/Articles/Feature_Article/BNP_GUID_9-5-2006_A_1000000000000131400*; "Testimonials," Blue Hawk Cooperative, *www.bluehawk.coop/membertestimonia.html*.

18. "Co-Op Types," National Cooperative Business Association, *www.ncba.coop/ncba/about-co-ops/co-op-types*.

19. Crystal Detamore-Rodman, "Cash In, Cash Out," *Entrepreneur*, June 2003, *www.entrepreneur.com/magazine/entrepreneur/2003/june/61916.html*.

20. David Worrell, "Paying for Quality over Quantity," *Entrepreneur*, October 2008, p. 53.

21. Connie Winkler, "Where Does the Money Go?" *CFO-IT*, Spring 2005, pp. 45–49.

22. "The Value of Sharing Information Up and Down the Supply Chain," *CIO*, January 28, 2005, *www.cio.com/article/1887/The_Value_of_Sharing_Information_Up_and_Down_the_Supply_Chain/1*; Imam Baihaqi and Nicholas Beaumont, "Information Sharing in Supply Chains: A Literature Review and Research Agenda," Monash University Department of Management Working Paper Series, June 2005, *www.buseco.monash.edu.au/mgt/research/working-papers/2005/wp45-05.pdf*.

23. Bob Evans, "Supply Chains Hit Home (Sweet Home)," *InformationWeek*, February 7, 2007, p. 68.

24. Brian Nadel, "Show Me the Money," Special Advertising Feature in *Fortune*, April 3, 2006, pp. S1–S5.

25. Ian Mount and Brian Caulfield, "The Internet-Based Supply Chain," *eCompany*, May 2001, p 85.

26. Hau Lee, "The Three A's of Supply Chain Excellence," *Electronics Supply and Manufacturing*, October 1, 2004, *www.my-esm.com/showArticle.jhtml?articleID=47903369*; Tracy Mayor, "The Supple Supply Chain," *CIO*, June 13, 2007, *www.cio.com/article/119301/*.

27. Hau L. Lee, "The Triple-A Supply Chain," BNet, *www.bnet.com/cp/the-triple-a-supply-chain/174992*.

28. Bret Thorn, "Search Party," *Nation's Restaurant News*, March 8, 2010, pp. 30–34.

29. Ian MacMillan, "A Few Good Suppliers," *CFO*, October 2004, p. 26.

30. Ilan Brat, "Rebulding After a Catastrophe," *Wall Street Journal*, May 19, 2008, pp. B1–B2.

31. John Turrettini, "Remade in America," *Forbes*, January 12, 2004, p. 190; "LightWedge," *Inc.*, September 2006, pp. 124–125.

32. Cecelie Rohwedder, "Zara Grows as Retail Rivals Struggle," *Wall Street Journal*, March 26, 2009, pp. B1, B5.

33. Michael Fitzgerald, "Turning Vendors into Partners," *Inc.*, August 2005, pp. 94–100.

34. Ibid.

Location, Layout, and Physical Facilities

The more alternatives, the more difficult the choice.

—Abbe' D'Allanival

Choices are the hinges of destiny.

—Pythagoras

Learning Objectives

Upon completion of this chapter, you will be able to:

1 Explain the stages in the location decision.
2 Describe the location criteria for retail and service businesses.
3 Outline the basic location options for retail and service businesses.
4 Explain the site selection process for manufacturers.
5 Discuss the benefits of locating a start-up company in a business incubator.
6 Describe the criteria used to analyze the layout and design considerations of a building, including the Americans with Disabilities Act.
7 Explain the principles of effective layouts for retailers, service businesses, and manufacturers.

I. Explain the stages in the location decision.

Few decisions that entrepreneurs make have as lasting and as dramatic an impact on their businesses as the choice of a location. Entrepreneurs who choose their locations wisely—with their customers' preferences and their companies' needs in mind—can establish an important competitive advantage over rivals who choose their locations haphazardly. Because the availability of qualified workers, tax rates, infrastructure, traffic patterns, quality of life, and many other factors vary from one site to another, the location decision is an important one that influences the growth rate and the ultimate success of a company. Thanks to widespread digital connectivity, mobile computing, extensive cellular coverage, and affordable air travel, entrepreneurs have more flexibility when choosing a business location than ever before.

The characteristics that make for an ideal location often vary dramatically from one company to another due to the nature of their business. In the early twentieth century, companies looked for ready supplies of water, raw materials, or access to railroads. For instance, West Virginia once was home to a thriving glassmaking industry because it provided entrepreneurs with ample supplies of quality sand (a key raw material), natural gas for heating glass furnaces, and inexpensive river transportation to get finished products to market.[1] Today, businesses are more likely to look for sites that are close to universities and offer high-speed Internet access and accessible interstate highways and airports. In fact, one study concluded that the factors that made an area most suitable for starting and growing small companies included access to dynamic universities, an ample supply of skilled workers, a nearby airport, a temperate climate, and a high quality of life.[2]

The key to finding a suitable location is identifying the characteristics that can give a company a competitive edge and then searching out potential sites that meet those criteria. For example, businesses that depend on face-to-face contact with customers must identify locations that attract high volumes of well-qualified walk-in customers. Although online sales continue to increase steadily, brick-and-mortar stores still dominate consumer sales, accounting for 93 percent of all retail sales.[3] One reason for the staying power of physical locations is the appeal of their real-world presence. An inviting physical location enables people to touch, feel, and experience the products and services a business offers. Potential buyers can pick up merchandise, try it on, and compare it side-by-side with other items. An optimal location also provides a gathering place where people can share experiences and one-on-one exchanges. The ability to look someone in the eye and ask questions or watch a demonstration appeals to human nature and provides a powerful sales tool for the business. Investing time in collecting and analyzing the data relevant to choosing a location pays off in increased customer traffic, higher sales, and greater efficiencies.

ENTREPRENEURIAL
Profile

Tony and John Calamunci: Johnny's Lunch

When Tony and John Calamunci began selling franchises based on the family-owned diner that their grandfather, Johnny Colera, started in Jamestown, New York, in 1936 (and that their parents still operate), they realized that opening outlets in areas in which large concentrations of their target customers lived was essential to their success. They hired an experienced franchise veteran, George Goulson, and worked with Pitney-Bowes' MapInfo to use the latest geospatial technology to determine the ideal locations for their restaurants, which sell budget-priced meals such as hot dogs, hamburgers, onion rings, and milkshakes. The Calamuncis started by defining their target customers, which they discovered includes people in the lower-middle to upper-middle income bracket who fall between the ages of 16 and 24 or over 60. Using the MapInfo software, they identified 72 types of neighborhoods that best matched the demographic and psychographic profile of Johnny's Lunch customers. The next step was to find locations that matched the 72 prototype neighborhoods. They identified 4,500 areas across the United States that held large concentrations of potential Johnny's Lunch customers (most of whom lived within 1 mile of the proposed location) and would be good locations for restaurants. "These models increase our ability to pick 'home-run' locations and avoid the site mistakes that can cripple a budding franchise," says Goulson. Johnny's Lunch is launching its franchising effort in and around Toledo, Ohio, which Goulson says is a microcosm of the United States. "Small restaurant owners like us can use location intelligence to prevent mistakes that could cripple franchising plans from the start. They can't afford not to invest in location intelligence."[4]

264

The location decision process resembles an inverted pyramid. The first level of the decision is the broadest, requiring an entrepreneur to select a particular region of the country. Then an entrepreneur must select the right state, then the right city, and, finally, the right site within the city (see Figure 1). The "secret" to selecting the ideal location lies in knowing the factors that are most important to a company's success and then finding a location that satisfies as many of them as possible, particularly those that are most critical. For instance, one of the most important location factors for high-tech companies is the availability of a skilled labor force, and their choice of location reflects this. If physically locating near customers is vital to a company's success, an entrepreneur's goal is to find a site that makes it most convenient for his or her target customers to do business with the company!

Selecting the Region

The first step in selecting the best location is to focus on selecting the right region. This requires entrepreneurs to look at the location decision from the "30,000-foot level," as if he or she were in an airplane looking down. In fact, in the early days of their companies, Sam Walton, founder of retail giant Walmart, and Ray Kroc, who built McDonald's into a fast-food legend, actually used private planes to survey the countryside for prime locations for their stores.

Which region of the country has the characteristics necessary for a new business to succeed? Above all, entrepreneurs must place their customers first when considering a location. As the experience of Johnny's Lunch suggests, facts and statistics, not speculation, lead entrepreneurs to the best locations for their businesses. Common requirements may include rapid growth in the

FIGURE 1
The Location Decision

Source: From Dale M. Lewison and M. Wayne DeLozier, *Retailing* (Columbus, OH: Merrill/Macmillan Publishing, 1984), p. 341.

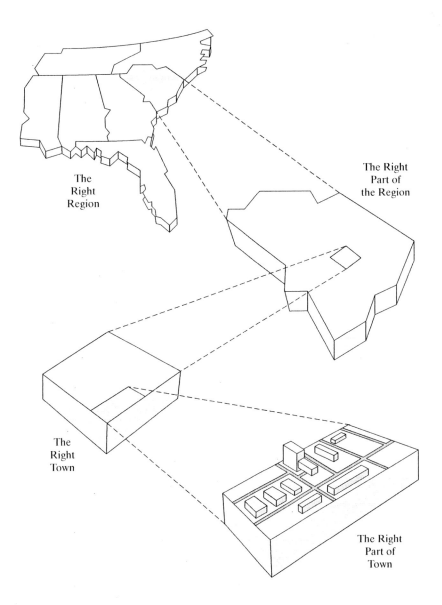

The
Right
Region

The Right
Part of
the Region

The
Right
Town

The Right
Part of
Town

population of a certain age group, rising disposable incomes, the existence of necessary infrastructure, a nonunion environment, and low costs. At the broadest level of the location decision, entrepreneurs prefer to locate in regions of the country that are experiencing substantial growth. Every year many popular business publications prepare reports on the various regions of the nation—which ones are growing, which are stagnant, and which are declining. Studying shifts in population and industrial growth gives entrepreneurs an idea of where the action is—and isn't. Questions to consider include: How large is the population? How fast is it growing? What is the makeup of the overall population? Which segments are growing fastest? Slowest? What is the trend in the population's income? Is it increasing or decreasing? Are other businesses moving into the region? If so, what kinds of businesses? Generally, entrepreneurs want to avoid dying regions; they simply cannot support a broad base of potential customers. A small company's customers are the people, businesses, and industries in an area, and if it is to be successful it must choose a location that is convenient to its customers.

One of the first stops entrepreneurs should make when conducting a regional evaluation is the U.S. Census Bureau. It provides a number of excellent sources of basic demographic and population data, including the *U.S. Statistical Abstract* and the *County and City Data Book*. The *U.S. Statistical Abstract* provides entrepreneurs looking for the right location with a multitude of helpful information, from basic population characteristics and projections to poverty rates and energy consumption. Each state also publishes its own statistical abstract, which provides the same type of data for its own population. The *County and City Data Book* contains useful statistics on the populations of all of the nation's 3,142 counties and 12,175 cities with populations of 25,000 or more (and even more data for cities with populations that exceed 100,000). *USA Counties* provides similar information and focuses only on the nation's counties. The *State and Metropolitan Area Data Book* includes more than 1,500 data items for individual states, counties, and metropolitan areas.

In addition to the print versions of its publications, the Census Bureau makes most of the information contained in its vast and valuable databases available to entrepreneurs researching potential sites through its easy-to-use Web site (*www.census.gov*). Entrepreneurs can use this Web site to locate vital demographic information for different potential locations, such as age, income, education level, employment level, occupation, ancestry, commuting times, housing data (house value, number of rooms, mortgage or rent status, number of vehicles owned, and so on), and many other characteristics. The Census Bureau's American FactFinder site (*http://factfinder.census.gov*) provides easily accessible demographic fact sheets and maps on nearly every community in the United States, including small towns. The Census Bureau's American Community Survey (*www.census.gov/acs/www/*) provides detailed information on the demographic and economic characteristics of areas with populations of at least 250,000 and of other selected areas with populations of at least 65,000. Both the American FactFinder and the American Community Survey allow entrepreneurs to produce easy-to-read, customizable maps of the information they generate in their searches. The U.S. Census Bureau also offers the Zip Code Tabulation Areas (ZCTA) Web site (*www.census.gov/geo/ZCTA/zcta.html*), which organizes the wealth of census data by zip code. The database of 33,178 ZCTAs across the United States allows users to create tables and plot maps of census data by zip code. With a little practice, entrepreneurs can prepare customized reports on the potential sites they are considering. These Web-based resources give entrepreneurs instant access to important site-location information that only a few years ago would have taken many hours of intense research to compile!

A variety of nongovernment resources also are available that can help entrepreneurs research potential locations. ZoomProspector (*www.zoomprospector.com*) is a useful Web site that gives entrepreneurs access to much of the same information that large companies use when selecting locations and allows them to search for the ideal location using a multitude of factors, including population size, job growth rate, number of patents issued, venture capital invested, education level, household incomes, and proximity to interstate highways, railroads, and airports. Once entrepreneurs locate a city that matches their customer profiles, they can find other cities across the United States that have similar profiles with a single mouse click. Entrepreneurs who are considering a particular region can create "heat maps" that display the areas that have the highest concentrations of people who have a particular characteristic, such as a bachelor's degree or the highest household incomes. Another useful online tool for entrepreneurs, ePodunk (*www.epodunk.com*), provides in-depth census-based information on more than 46,000 towns and cities of all sizes around the United States. ZIPskinny (*www.zipskinny.com*) is a Web site that provides census profiles and comparison communities using zip codes.

ENTREPRENEURIAL
Profile
Sharon Chan: Laurus Construction

Laurus Construction, a company in Costa Mesa, California, that builds and renovates commercial and residential buildings, uses ZoomProspector to identify potential new markets to enter. Managers use profiles of existing towns where the company has had success to spot other towns with similar characteristics. "I'm able to figure out which communities to rule out and which to pursue," says Vice President Sharon Chan. "It's almost like having a marketing company on tap."[5]

The Population Reference Bureau (*www.prb.org*) provides a detailed breakdown of the most relevant data collected from the most recent census reports. Its DataFinder database includes 244 variables for the United States and 132 variables for 210 other nations. The site also includes helpful articles that discuss the implications of the changing demographic and economic profile of the nation's (and the world's) population, such as the impact of aging baby boomers on business and the composition of the U.S. workforce.

Other helpful resources merit mention as well. *Demographics USA* is a useful publication that provides market surveys on various U.S. demographic segments. It provides information on demographic groups' purchasing power, retail sales by type of merchandise, employment and payroll data, and forecasts of economic conditions at both the zip code and the county level. The buying power indices in *Demographics USA* indicate an area's purchasing potential for economy products, mid-priced products, and premium products. It also reports consumers' spending on particular types of products and services, such as apparel, entertainment, and appliances. Entrepreneurs can use *Demographics USA* to analyze the level of competition in a particular area, assess the sales potential of a particular location, compare consumers' buying power across a dozen categories, and more.

Lifestyle Market Analyst, a four-part annual publication, matches population demographics with lifestyle interests. Section 1 provides demographics and lifestyle information for 210 "Designated Market Areas" across the United States. Section 2 gives demographic and geographic profiles of 77 lifestyle interests that range from avid readers and dieters to wine aficionados and pet owners. Section 3 describes the dominant lifestyle interests for each of the 210 market areas. Section 4 provides comparisons of other activities that correspond with each lifestyle interest. Entrepreneurs can use *Lifestyle Market Analyst* to determine, for example, how likely members of a particular market segment are to own a dog, collect antiques, play golf, own a vacation home, engage in extreme sports, invest in stocks or bonds, or participate in a host of other activities.

Other sources of demographic data include the *Survey of Buying Power*, the *Editor and Publisher Market Guide*, *The American Marketplace: Demographics and Spending Patterns*, *Rand McNally's Commercial Atlas and Marketing Guide*, and *Site Selection* magazine. The *Survey of Buying Power*, having recently undergone the most extensive overhaul in its 80-year history, provides statistics, rankings, and projections for every county and media market in the United States, with demographic groups segmented by age, race, city, county, and state. This publication, now available only online (*www.surveyofbuyingpower.com*), also includes current information on retail spending and forecasts for each spending category. The data are divided into 323 metro markets, as defined by the Census Bureau, and 210 media markets, which are television or broadcast markets defined by Nielsen Media Research. The *Survey* also includes several unique statistics. Effective buying income (EBI) is a measure of disposable income, and the buying power index (BPI), for which the *Survey* is best known, is a unique measure of spending power that takes population, EBI, and retail sales into account to determine a market's ability to buy goods and services.

The *Editor and Publisher Market Guide* is similar to the *Survey of Buying Power* but provides additional information on markets. The *Editor and Publisher Market Guide* includes detailed economic and demographic information, ranging from population and income statistics to information on climate and transportation networks for all 3,096 counties in the United States and more than 1,600 key cities in both the United States and Canada.

The American Marketplace: Demographics and Spending Patterns provides useful demographic information in eight areas: education, health, income, labor force, living arrangements, population, race and ethnicity, and spending and wealth. Most of the tables in the text are derived from government statistics, but *The American Marketplace* also includes a discussion of the data in each table as well as a forecast of future trends. Many users say the primary advantage of *The American Marketplace* is its ease of use.

The *Commercial Atlas and Marketing Guide* provides data on more than 120,000 places in the United States, many of which are not available through Census reports. This guide, which includes two volumes, one an index and the other the actual guide, provides 11 economic indicators for every major geographic market; tables showing population trends, income, buying power, trade, and manufacturing activity; and large cross-reference maps. Its format makes it easy to collect large amounts of valuable data on any region in the country (and specific areas within a region).

Site Selection magazine (*www.siteselection.com*) is another useful resource that helps entrepreneurs determine the ideal location for their companies. Issues contain articles that summarize incentive programs offered by various states, profiles of each region of the country, and the benefits of locating in different states.

The task of analyzing various potential locations—gathering and synthesizing data on a wide variety of demographic and geographic variables—is one ideally suited for a computer. In fact, a growing number of entrepreneurs are relying on geographic information systems (GIS), powerful software programs that combine map drawing with databases, to pinpoint the ideal location for their businesses. GIS packages allow users to search through virtually any database and plot the results on a map of the country, an individual state, a specific city, or even a single city block. The visual display highlights what otherwise would be indiscernible business trends. For instance, entrepreneurs can use GIS software to plot their existing customer base on a map with colors representing the different population densities. Then they can zoom in on those areas with the greatest concentration of customers, mapping a detailed view of zip code borders or even city streets. GIS street files originate in the U.S. Census Department's TIGER (Topographically Integrated Geographic Encoding Referencing) file, which contains map information broken down for every square foot of each Metropolitan Statistical Area (MSA). TIGER files contain the name and location of every street in the country and detailed block statistics for the 345 largest urban areas. In essence, TIGER is a massive database of geographic features such as roads, railways, and political boundaries across the entire United States that, when linked with mapping programs and demographic databases, gives entrepreneurs incredible power to pinpoint existing and potential customers on easy-to-read digital maps. Many states and counties across the United States now provide GIS files online that allow entrepreneurs to identify sites that meet certain location criteria for their businesses.

The Small Business Administration's Small Business Development Center (SBDC) program also offers location analysis assistance to entrepreneurs. These centers, numbering more than 1,100 nationwide, provide training, counseling, research, and other specialized assistance to entrepreneurs and existing business owners on a wide variety of subjects—all at no charge! (To locate the SBDC nearest you, contact the SBA office in your state or go to the SBA's Small Business Development Center locator page at *www.sba.gov/aboutsba/sbaprograms/sbdc/sbdclocator/SBDC_LOCATOR.html.*)

For entrepreneurs interested in demographic and statistical profiles of international cities, Euromonitor International (*www.euromonitor.com*) and the Organization for Economic Development and Cooperation (OECD; *www.oecd.org*) are excellent resources.

Once an entrepreneur has identified the best region of the country, the next step is to evaluate the individual states in that region.

Selecting the State

Every state has an economic development office to recruit new businesses. Even though the publications produced by these offices will be biased in favor of locating in that state, they still are excellent sources of information and can help entrepreneurs assess the business climate in each state. Some of the key issues to explore include the laws, regulations, and taxes that govern businesses and incentives or investment credits the state may offer to businesses locating there. Table 1 shows the Small Business and Entrepreneurship Council's list of the most friendly and

TABLE 1 Most and Least Friendly States for Small Businesses

States Most Friendly to Small Businesses	States Least Friendly to Small Businesses
1. South Dakota	42. Hawaii
2. Nevada	43. Minnesota
3. Texas	44. Massachusetts
4. Wyoming	45. Rhode Island
5. Washington	46. Maine
6. Florida	47. Vermont
7. South Carolina	48. New York
8. Colorado	49. California
9. Alabama	50. New Jersey
10. Virginia	51. District of Columbia

Source: Raymond J. Keating, *Small Business Survival Index 2009: Ranking the Policy Environment for Entrepreneurship Across the Nation*, 14th Annual Edition, Small Business and Entrepreneurship Council, Oakton, Virginia, December 2009, p. 22.

least friendly states for small businesses, a ranking that evaluates 36 factors, including a variety of taxes, health care costs, regulatory costs, and others.

Other factors to consider when selecting a location include proximity to markets, proximity to raw materials, wage rates, quantity and quality of the labor supply, general business climate, and tax rates.

PROXIMITY TO MARKETS. Locating close to the markets they plan to serve is critical to manufacturers, especially when the cost of transporting finished goods is high relative to their value. Locations near customers offer a competitive advantage. Service firms often find that proximity to their clients is essential. If a business is involved in repairing equipment used in a specific industry, it should be located where that industry is concentrated. The more specialized a business, or the greater the relative cost of transporting the product to the customer, the more likely it is that proximity to the market will be of importance in the location decision.

ENTREPRENEURIAL
Profile

IKEA

IKEA, a Swedish maker of stylish, low-priced furniture with more than 300 stores in 35 countries (including 38 in the United States), recently opened its first U.S. manufacturing plant in Danville, Virginia, a location that gives the company convenient and inexpensive access to its distribution centers in Georgia, Maryland, and New Jersey and to its U.S. customers. Until IKEA opened the factory in Danville, the company had to ship goods to the United States from factories in Eastern Europe, which wiped out the cost advantages of operating factories in low-cost areas. "This kind of lightweight furniture is cheap to make, and transportation is a huge part of the overall cost," says one top manager.[6]

PROXIMITY TO NEEDED RAW MATERIALS. A business that requires raw materials that are difficult or expensive to transport may need a location near the source of those raw materials. For example, fish-process plants benefit from locating close to ports. Some companies locate close to the source of raw materials because of the cost of transporting heavy low-value materials over long distances. The Oil-Dri Corporation of America, founded by Nick Jaffe during the Great Depression, has two factories that make its Cat's Pride brand kitty litter located near major deposits of fuller's earth, the material from which the product is made.[7] For products in which bulk or weight is not a factor, locating close to suppliers can facilitate quick deliveries and reduce inventory-holding costs. The value of products and materials, their cost of transportation, and their unique functions interact to determine how close a business must be to its sources of supply.

WAGE RATES. Existing and anticipated wage rates provide another measure for comparison among states. Wages can sometimes vary from one state or region to another, significantly affecting a company's cost of doing business. For instance, according to the Bureau of Labor Statistics, the average hourly compensation for workers (including wages and benefits) ranges from a low of $24.72 in the South to a high of $32.13 in the Northeast.[8] Wage rate differentials within geographic regions can be even more drastic. When reviewing wage rates, entrepreneurs must be sure to measure the wage rates for jobs that relate to their particular industries or companies. In addition to surveys by the Bureau of Labor Statistics (*www.bls.gov*), local newspaper ads can give entrepreneurs an idea of the pay scale in an area. In addition, entrepreneurs can obtain the latest wage and salary surveys with an e-mail or telephone call to the local chambers of commerce for cities in the region under consideration. Entrepreneurs should study not only prevailing wage rates but also *trends* in rates. How does the rate of increase in wage rates compare to those in other states? Another factor influencing wage rates is the level of union activity in a state. How much union organizing activity has the state seen within the last 2 years? Is it increasing or decreasing? Which industries have unions targeted in the recent past?

LABOR SUPPLY. Business owners should know how many qualified people are available in the area to do the work required in the business. Some states attempt to attract industry with the promise of cheap labor. Unfortunately, businesses locating in those states may find unskilled, low-wage laborers who can be difficult to train. The size of an area's labor pool and the education, skills, and ability of its members determine a company's ability to fill jobs with qualified workers at reasonable wages. "The single biggest reason why anyone is moving companies is access to talent," says Tim Nitti, co-owner of location strategy company KLG.[9]

Knowing the exact nature of the labor needed and preparing job descriptions and job specifications in advance helps business owners determine whether there is a good match between their companies and the available labor pool. Checking educational statistics in the state to determine the number of graduates in relevant fields of study provides an idea of the local supply of qualified workers. This type of planning results in entrepreneurs finding locations with a steady source of quality workers.

ENTREPRENEURIAL
Profile

Tarran Pitschka: Wicked Quick

The idea for Tarran Pitschka's clothing line, Wicked Quick, came to him while he was standing between two funny cars at the starting line at the Pomona Speedway in California, but he chose to locate his company in Portland, Oregon. One of the principal reasons for Pitschka choosing Portland is the city's pool of talent. "This is one of the central spots in the world to draw on talent for the apparel business," he says. "There are so many creative people. I can get anything I want designed and made."[10]

Economists have long known that businesses thrive when they congregate in one place. "Companies that operate in clusters have greater access to talent," explains Jeffrey Grogan, partner at the Monitor Group, a Boston strategy consulting firm. They also serve as fertile ground for start-ups. For instance, North Carolina's Research Triangle, an area defined by the surrounding communities of Raleigh, Durham, and Chapel Hill, has become a Mecca for companies in high-tech industries, such as computer software, semiconductors, communications, pharmaceuticals, and biotech, because of the area's pool of highly skilled labor. Major colleges such as Duke University, the University of North Carolina, and North Carolina State University funnel talented graduates trained in fields such as virtual reality and market research into local companies. The resulting cluster of high-tech companies also leads to many business start-ups as employees leave to start their own companies, creating a hotbed of entrepreneurial activity.

BUSINESS CLIMATE. Assessing the business climate provides important information about the environment. What is the state's overall attitude toward this type of business? Has the state passed laws that impose restrictions on the way a company can operate? Does the state impose a corporate income tax? Is there an inventory tax? Does the state offer small business support programs or financial assistance to entrepreneurs? Some states have created environments that are "entrepreneur-friendly" based on these factors.

Profile

John and Tullaya Akins: Bangkok Cuisine Thai Restaurant

John and Tullaya Akins, owners of the Bangkok Cuisine Thai Restaurant in Sandpoint, Idaho, wanted to open a second Asian-themed restaurant. The copreneurs had selected a brick building in Sandpoint's downtown district that had housed a bicycle shop but changed their minds when they learned that the city would impose an impact fee (to tap into the city's water and sewer systems and to cover fire and police protection) of $26,000 to convert the building into a 45-seat restaurant. "That's make or break for us," says John. "We are shopping for a location in Ponderay (a nearby town with minimal impact fees) and the surrounding area that is more business friendly. It's too bad. We love this community."[11]

TAX RATES. Another important factor entrepreneurs must consider is the tax burden states impose on businesses and individuals. Income taxes may be the most obvious tax states impose on both business and individual residents, but entrepreneurs also must evaluate the impact of payroll taxes, sales taxes, property taxes, and specialized taxes on the cost of their operations. Currently, seven states impose no income tax on their residents, but state governments always impose taxes of some sort on businesses and individuals.[12] In some cases, states offer special tax rates or are willing to negotiate fees in lieu of taxes for companies that create jobs and stimulate the local economy.

Profile

LeBron James

Source: Johnny Louis/Newscom

When professional basketball player and entrepreneur LeBron James left the Cleveland Cavaliers to join the Miami Heat, many factors influenced the decision, including the states' tax rates. James owns several businesses, including LRMR Marketing, a sports marketing company, and King James Inc., the company that manages James' endorsements (which at $200 million to date outweigh his NBA earnings of $68 million). King James Inc. generates $28 million a year in endorsement revenue, and because Florida imposes no income tax James saves at least $1.8 million annually on his business income alone![13]

INTERNET ACCESS. Fast and reliable Internet access is another important factor in the location decision. Internet access through cable, DSL, or T1 lines is essential for high-tech companies and those engaging in e-commerce. Even those companies that may not do business over the Web use the Internet as a daily business tool for e-mail and information access. Companies that fall behind in high-tech communications soon find themselves at a severe competitive disadvantage.

TOTAL OPERATING COSTS. When scouting a state in which to locate a company, an entrepreneur must consider the total cost of operating a business there. For instance, a state may offer low utility rates, but its labor costs and tax rates may be among the highest in the nation. To select the ideal location, entrepreneurs must consider the impact of a state's total cost of operation on their business ventures. The state evaluation matrix in Table 2 provides a handy tool designed to help entrepreneurs determine which states best suit the most important location criteria for their companies. This same matrix can be adapted to analyze individual cities as well.

The next phase of the location selection process concentrates on selecting the best city.

TABLE 2 **State Evaluation Matrix**

Location Criterion	Weight 10 = High 1 = Low	Score 5 = High 1 = Low	State Weighted Score (Weight × Score)		
			Florida	Georgia	South Carolina
Quality of labor force		1 2 3 4 5			
Wage rates		1 2 3 4 5			
Union activity		1 2 3 4 5			
Energy costs		1 2 3 4 5			
Tax burden		1 2 3 4 5			
Educational/training assistance		1 2 3 4 5			
Start-up incentives		1 2 3 4 5			
Quality of life		1 2 3 4 5			
Availability of raw materials		1 2 3 4 5			
Other		1 2 3 4 5			
Other		1 2 3 4 5			
Total score					

*Assign to each location criterion a weight that reflects its relative importance (10 high to 1 low). Then score each state on a scale of 1 (low) to 5 (high). Calculate the weighted score (weight × score) for each state. Finally, add up the total weighted score for each state. The state with the highest total weighted score is the best location for your business.

IN THE ENTREPRENEURIAL
SPOTLIGHT A Total Transformation

The sound of diners' muffled conversations and clinking silverware and plates reverberate through the Mission Restaurant in Syracuse, New York, but the sounds that once occupied this space once were quite different. For more than a century, visitors to this building were more likely to hear choirs singing hymns and pastors preaching sermons. The building that houses Steve Morrison's restaurant, which specializes in fresh Pan-American cuisine, was home to the Syracuse Wesleyan Methodist Church, which was built in the 1840s and was an important stop on the Underground Railroad that helped slaves escape to freedom in the northern United States and Canada from 1831 to 1863. Today the bustling restaurant serves fresh, homemade Mexican, Southwestern, and South American specialty dishes to customers in a unique setting that sets it apart from its competition.

Like Steve Morrison, some small business owners are establishing their businesses in locations that once served other purposes. Transforming a church into a restaurant poses some unique engineering and design challenges, but there are benefits as well, including using the building's history as part of the restaurant's marketing strategy. In 2007, real estate developer Dick Friedman purchased the Charles Street Jail in Boston, which was built in 1851 as a model of modern jail reform. Built in the shape of a cross with four wings extending from a central, octagonal rotunda that stands 90 feet tall, the granite structure was hidden by brick walls and barbed wire for many years until it closed in 1990. After a $150 million renovation, the building is now home to the luxurious Liberty Hotel. It is conveniently situated in Boston's Beacon Hill neighborhood, providing guests with easy access to the amenities of downtown Boston, including shopping, entertainment, and dining. Transforming a prison into a luxury hotel "is not for the faint of heart," says Friedman, "but I think it was worth it."

The plush hotel is a unique combination of historic preservation and contemporary design even though guest rooms, with their floor-to-ceiling windows, flat-screen TVs, private bars, and luxurious beds, have almost nothing in common with the former cells that occupied the building. Yet the designers made sure to retain small touches of the building's "jailness." "We kept a variety of the jail's original cell doors and bars," says architect Gary Johnson. Designers also kept a portion of one of the original catwalks in the rotunda. In addition to 300 guest rooms, including 10 luxury suites with views of the Charles River, the hotel is home to meeting rooms, a grand ballroom, a restaurant, and a bar. The bar, Alibi, is located in the portion of the jail where intoxicated arrestees spent time sobering up and includes fully restored cell blocks with original iron-bar doors and a beautiful blue stone floor. In the restaurant, Clink, waitstaff wear uniforms adorned with hand-stenciled inmate numbers. Rather than use "Do not disturb" signs, guests hang signs that say "Solitary" on their doors. The hotel has become a popular spot for visitors to Boston and generates annual sales of $40 million.

Mary Liz Curtin and Stephen Scannell opened their furniture and gift shop, Leon and Lulu LLC (the business is named after the couple's cat, Leon Redbone Johnson, and their 120-pound Rottweiler, Lulu), in a building that once was a popular roller skating rink and Motown concert venue in Clawson, Michigan. They purchased the building for $750,000 in 2005 and spent $225,000 on renovation, keeping its original flooring, benches, trophy cases, scoreboard and signs. "We get letters from people who thank us for keeping the history alive," says Curtin. On weekends and during special events, employees skate through the store's aisles, offering drinks and cookies to shoppers. The store, with its eclectic collection of merchandise, generates sales of $2 million per year.

1. What are the advantages and the disadvantages of transforming historic buildings, such as the ones described here, into new business locations?
2. Work with several of your classmates to select a historic building in your area and outline a plan for transforming it into a space that is suitable for a business (or businesses). How would you incorporate the building's history into the business's marketing plan?

Sources: Based on Sarah E. Needleman, "Entrepreneurs Make Use of Odd Spaces," *Wall Street Journal*, May 4, 2010, p. B5; Ann Coppola, "Lockdown Luxury," *Corrections*, September 24, 2007, *www.corrections.com/articles/ 16699-lockdown-luxury;* "About Us," Mission Restaurant, *www.themission restaurant.com;* "Quick Facts," Liberty Hotel, *www.libertyhotel.com/quick_ facts/index.html;* "History," Leon and Lulu, *www.leonandlulu.com/history.*

The former Charles Street Jail is now the luxurious Liberty Hotel in downtown Boston.

Source: Michael Dwyer/Almay Images

The lobby of the Liberty Hotel retains some of the jail's original features and adds to the hotel's unique prison theme.

Source: CB2/ZOB/Newscom

Selecting the City

A company's location should match the market for its products or services, and assembling a demographic profile tells an entrepreneur how well a particular site measures up to his or her target market's profile. Entrepreneurs should consider a variety of factors when selecting a city.

Profile

Larry Reinstein:
Fresh City

Fresh City, a Needham, Massachusetts-based chain of 16 fast-casual restaurants that features a fresh, healthy menu, considers the population density and the education and income levels of an area when scouting potential locations. "We find that the better educated the consumer is, the more apt they are to be our kind of guest," says CEO Larry Reinstein. Fresh City has located its restaurants in communities with high concentrations of well-educated, high-income people in and around Boston and plans to open restaurants in Herndon, Virginia, just outside of Washington, D.C., which recently was named one of the healthiest cities in the United States.[14]

POPULATION TRENDS. Analyzing over time the lists of "best cities for business" compiled annually by many magazines reveals one consistent trend: Successful small companies in a city tend to track a city's population growth. In other words, more potential customers means that a small business has a better chance of success. Detroit, Michigan, once home to a thriving automotive industry, has seen its population shrink from a peak of 1.85 million in 1950 to just 800,000 people. Vacant commercial and residential properties account for 40 square miles of the city's total area of 139 square miles. Since 1999, median household income has declined 25 percent, creating a difficult environment for entrepreneurs.[15] Seattle, Washington, in contrast, is home to a large and growing population of highly educated young people; 43 percent of the city's population is between the ages of 20 and 44, the prime time for entrepreneurial activity. The city's diverse high-tech sector, convenient access to some of the most beautiful natural areas anywhere, availability of venture capital, and concentration of top medical centers, colleges, and universities make it a magnet for entrepreneurs. In 1975, two young entrepreneurs, Bill Gates and Paul Allen, launched a company called Microsoft in Seattle, which one location expert describes as "a high-tech and lifestyle Mecca."[16]

An entrepreneur should know more about a city and its various neighborhoods than do the people who live there. By analyzing population trends and other demographic data, an entrepreneur can examine a city in detail, and the location decision becomes more than "a shot in the dark." Studying the characteristics of a city's residents, including population sizes and density, growth trends, family size, age breakdowns, education, income levels, job categories, gender, religion, race, and nationality, gives entrepreneurs the facts they need to make an informed location decision. For example, with basic census data, entrepreneurs can determine the value of the homes in an area, how many rooms they contain, how many bedrooms they contain, what percentage of the population owns their homes, and the amount residents' monthly rental or mortgage payments are. Imagine how useful such information would be to someone about to launch a home accessories store!

POPULATION DENSITY. The number of people per square mile can be another important factor in determining the optimal business location. In many of the older cities in the eastern United States, people live or work in very high-density areas. Businesses that depend on high traffic volume benefit by locating in high-density areas.

Knowing the population density within a few miles of a potential location gives entrepreneurs a clear picture of whether a city can support their businesses. It can also help them develop the appropriate marketing strategies to draw customers. Fitness club owners have discovered that population density is one of the most important factors in selecting a suitable location. Experience has taught them that customers are willing to drive or walk only so far to visit a fitness club. Information on population density and other important demographic characteristics is available from the publications mentioned earlier in this chapter and from market research companies.

COMPETITION. For some retailers locating near competitors makes sense because similar businesses located near one another may serve to increase traffic flow to both. This location strategy works well for products for which customers are most likely to comparison shop. For instance, in many cities, auto dealers locate next to one another in a "motor mile," trying to create a shopping magnet for customers. The convenience of being able to shop for dozens of brands of cars all within a few hundred yards of one another draws customers from a sizable trading area. Locating near competitors is a common strategy for restaurants as well. Of course, this strategy has limits. Overcrowding of businesses of the same type in an area can create an undesirable impact on the profitability of all competing firms.

Studying the size of the market for a product or service and the number of existing competitors helps an entrepreneur determine whether he or she can capture a sufficiently large market share to earn a profit. Again, census reports can be a valuable source of information. *County Business Patterns* gives a breakdown of businesses in manufacturing, wholesale, retail, and service categories and estimates companies' annual payrolls and number of employees broken down by county. *Zip Code Business Patterns* provides the same data as *County Business Patterns*, except it organizes the data by zip code. The *Economic Census*, which is produced for years that end in "2" and "7," gives an overview of the businesses in an area—their sales (or other measure of output), employment, payroll, and form of organization. It covers eight industry categories, including retail, wholesale, service, manufacturing, construction, and others, and provides statistics not only at the national level, but also by state, MSA, county, places with 2,500 or more inhabitants, and zip code. The *Economic Census* is a useful tool for helping entrepreneurs determine whether the areas they are considering as a location are already saturated with competitors.

CLUSTERING. Some cities have characteristics that attract certain industries, and, as a result, companies tend to cluster there. **Clusters** are geographic concentrations of interconnected companies, specialized suppliers, distribution networks, and service providers that are present in a region.[17] According to Harvard professor Michael Porter, clusters are important because they allow companies in them to increase their productivity and to gain a competitive edge. For instance, with its highly trained, well-educated, and technologically literate workforce, Austin, Texas, has become a draw for high-tech companies. Home to Dell Inc. and HP, Austin offers many small technology companies exactly what they need to succeed.

When the concentration of companies in a city reaches the tipping point, other businesses in those industries tend to spring up there as well. Once a symbol of declining manufacturing in the Rust Belt, Cleveland, Ohio, is now home to a cluster of biomedical companies that have banded together to form an organization called BioEnterprise. Anchored by a network of superb medical institutions, including the Cleveland Clinic, Case Western University, University Hospitals, and Summa Health Systems, the biomedical cluster provides a world-class knowledge base and access to venture capital. BioEnterprise has created or recruited more than 100 biomedical companies and has helped them land nearly $1 billion in financing.

Profile
Jerry Silver: LucCell

Jerry Silver, president of LucCell, a small company that emerged from research at Case Western University, is counting on Cleveland's biomedical cluster to help it grow. LucCell is on the cutting edge of photogenetics, which uses light to change DNA, and already has raised $500,000 in start-up funding. The company's genetically engineered "bio-light switches" might someday trigger malfunctioning brain or spinal cord cells and revolutionize the treatment of disorders ranging from Parkinson's disease to paralysis.[18]

COMPATIBILITY WITH THE COMMUNITY. One of the intangibles that can be determined only by a visit to an area is the degree of compatibility a business has with the surrounding community. In other words, a small company's image must fit in with the character of a town and the needs and wants of its residents.

Profile
Joe Masher: Bow Tie Cinemas

Bow Tie Cinemas, a fourth-generation family-owned business, recently opened a 17-screen multiplex theater in Richmond, Virginia, the largest theater complex the company has ever opened. When selecting locations for its theaters, Bow Tie looks for communities that are consistent with its image, which involves bringing style and elegance back to the theater experience and providing patrons with superb movie presentations and service. Chief operating officer Joe Masher says that the chain looks for cities with active arts, medical, and educational communities. "Richmond was a perfect storm for all three," he says.[19]

LOCAL LAWS AND REGULATIONS. Before selecting a particular site within a city, small business owners must explore the local zoning laws to determine whether there are any ordinances that would place restrictions on business activity or that would prohibit establishing a business altogether. **Zoning** is a system that divides a city or county into small cells or districts to control the use of land, buildings, and sites. Its purpose is to contain similar activities in suitable locations. For instance, one section of a city may be zoned industrial to house manufacturing operations, whereas another section may be zoned commercial for retail businesses. An entrepreneur must explore the zoning regulations to make sure the site qualifies. In addition to limiting the activities that can take place at a site, zoning also may control the hours of operation, parking requirements, noise limitations, and size of the businesses located there. In some cases, an entrepreneur may appeal to the local zoning commission to rezone a site or to grant a **variance,** a special exception to a zoning ordinance. This tactic is risky, potentially time consuming, and could be devastating if the board disallows the variance.

TRANSPORTATION NETWORKS. Manufacturers and wholesalers in particular must investigate the quality of local transportation systems. If a company receives raw materials or ships finished goods by rail, is a location with rail access available in the city under consideration? What kind of highway access is available? Are there any plans in the future for major construction that might impact the desired location? Will transportation costs be reasonable? Does the transportation infrastructure allow for efficient distribution? The availability of loading and unloading zones may be an important feature for a product-based business location.

POLICE AND FIRE PROTECTION. Does the community in which you plan to locate offer adequate police and fire protection? An absence of adequate police and fire protection will result in higher insurance costs and increased risks for the owner.

COST OF UTILITIES AND PUBLIC SERVICES. Some entity that provides water and sewer services, trash collection, and other utilities should serve the location. Streets should be in good repair with adequate drainage. Not having these services in place translates into higher costs for a business over time.

INCENTIVES. Some cities and counties offer financial and other incentives to encourage businesses that will create jobs to locate within their borders. These incentives range from job training for workers and reduced tax rates to financial grants and loans.

ENTREPRENEURIAL
Profile

Mitch Butler and Steven White: Image Vision Labs

Mitch Butler and Steven White launched their software company, Image Vision Labs, from a corner table in a Starbucks in Plano, Texas. When they were looking for a permanent location for their company, however, the business partners selected the nearby small town of Anna, where they were lured by a $110,000 economic development grant from the town (its first) and a low-interest $100,000 loan from a revolving loan program that Anna funded with a grant from the U.S. Department of Agriculture. Image Vision Labs, which uses artificial intelligence and visual-recognition technology to help companies block objectionable content from being viewed on their networks, already has hired 10 people from Anna, a town of fewer than 2,000 residents, most of whom traditionally have had to commute to other areas for work.[20]

QUALITY OF LIFE. A final consideration when selecting a city is the quality of life it offers. Entrepreneurs have the freedom and the flexibility to locate their companies in cities that suit not only their business needs but also their personal preferences. When choosing locations for their companies, entrepreneurs often consider factors such as cultural events, outdoor activities, entertainment opportunities, safety, and the city's "personality." Cities that offer comfortable weather, cultural events, colleges and universities, museums, outdoor activities, concerts, unique restaurants, and an interesting nightlife have become magnets for entrepreneurs looking to start companies. Cities such as Austin, Boston, Seattle, San Francisco, Washington, Dallas, Minneapolis, Portland, Boulder, and others have become incubators for creativity and entrepreneurship as educated young people drawn by the cities' quality of life have moved in.

Joshua Onysko, founder of Pangea Organics, a company that markets a line of all-natural skin care products, had lived on the east coast and in Jackson Hole, Wyoming, but chose to locate his business in Boulder, Colorado. Personally, Onysko was attracted to the outdoor activities, including world-class ski slopes, available in Boulder. Professionally, he knew that the quality of life in Boulder and the nearby University of Colorado would allow him to attract the high-quality, skilled workforce that he needed to build his company. When he was ready to fill three new sales and marketing jobs, Onysko received more than 300 applications. Boulder also proved to be a business-friendly town with a strong entrepreneurial presence. Onysko credits his choice of location for playing a major role in Pangea's success; the company now generates annual sales of more than $7 million.[21]

Not only can a location in a city offering a high quality of life away from the workplace be attractive to an entrepreneur, but it also allows businesses to attract and retain a quality workforce. According to a study of the importance of location on recruiting employees conducted by the Human Capital Institute, the three most important factors in attracting talent are job opportunities, a clean and safe community, and an affordable cost of living.[22]

The Final Site Selection

Successful entrepreneurs develop a site evaluation system that is both detailed and methodical. Each type of business has different evaluation criteria, and experience has taught successful entrepreneurs to analyze the facts and figures behind each potential location in search of the best possible site. A manufacturer may need to consider access to customers, raw materials, suppliers, labor, and suitable transportation. Service firms need access to customers but can generally survive in lower-rent areas, whereas a retailer's prime consideration is customer traffic. The one element common to all three is the need to locate where customers want to do business.

The site location decision draws on the most precise information available on the makeup of the area. Using the sources of published statistics described earlier in this chapter, an entrepreneur can develop valuable insights regarding the characteristics of people and businesses in the immediate community. After narrowing the list of potential locations using statistics, entrepreneurs must visit each site for a firsthand view of its suitability. Many sites that look good "on paper" may be unsuitable because of other factors. On-site visits to potential locations are essential because they allow entrepreneurs to evaluate each site's intangible aspects.

Rental or lease rates are an important factor when choosing a site. The location with the lowest rental rate may not be the best deal, however. "Cheap" rental rates often indicate second-class locations (and the resulting poor revenues they generate). Of course, entrepreneurs must be sure that the rent or lease payments for a particular location fit comfortably into their companies' financial structure.

Gino's, an Italian restaurant that Gino Circiello opened on New York City's Lexington Avenue in 1945, proudly stuck to its mid-twentieth-century roots, much to the delight of its loyal customers. The restaurant, famous for its never-changing menu, moderate prices, and tomato-red wallpaper adorned with 314 leaping zebras, recently closed after the building's owner raised Gino's rent by $8,000 to more than $30,000 per month.[23]

Many businesses are downsizing their outlets to lower their start-up and operating costs and to allow for a greater number of location options that are not available to full-sized stores. Many quick-service restaurants are placing smaller, less expensive outlets in locations that cannot support a full-sized store and are finding that sales per square foot exceed those of traditional outlets.[24] Doughnut retailer Krispy Kreme is experimenting with its Neighborhood Shop and Kremery, small shops that are one-third the size of its regular "factory stores" that make and sell doughnuts on site. The smaller stores, which are located near factory stores that supply the doughnuts, allow the company to take its products to more customers by placing them in convenient locations that are not capable of housing a much larger traditional store. In a similar move,

Baskin-Robbins is using a similar concept called BR Express to set up shops in small spaces in airports and on college campuses.[25] Retailers and restaurateurs have discovered that these non-traditional locations can generate three to five times more traffic than locations in shopping centers and malls.

Finally, an entrepreneur must be careful to select a site that creates the right impression for a business in the customers' eyes. A company's location speaks volumes about a company's "personality."

IN THE ENTREPRENEURIAL
SPOTLIGHT   We'll Bring Our Location to You

Joshua Henderson, a chef who once cooked at the Avalon Hotel in Beverly Hills, is one of the few entrepreneurs who does not worry about whether his restaurant's location is suitable. If he finds business to be too slow in one locale, he simply moves to another one in just minutes. Henderson is one of a growing number of restaurateurs who operate food trucks that travel to different locations in a city, set up shop, serve hungry customers, and move on. Once shunned as nothing more than lowly lunch trucks slinging second-rate hash and bland sandwiches, these mobile eateries are a far cry from their forebears, offering gourmet cuisine equivalent to that offered in Michelin-starred restaurants, but at far lower prices. Henderson, owner of Skillet Street Food, operates two trucks that serve about 200 lunches each per day, generating sales of $400,000 per year.

Articles in popular food magazines and television shows such as the Food Network's *The Great Food Truck Race* are feeding the food-truck trend. A sluggish economy that led customers to look for less expensive dining options also has played a role in the trucks' popularity. New York's popular Rickshaw Dumpling Truck, whose dumpling recipes were created by Anita Lo, chef at Manhattan's upscale Annisa in Greenwich Village, sells six duck dumplings with sauce for just $6.50. In San Francisco, a skewer of escargot in puff pastry sells for $2 at the Spencer on the Go truck operated by Laurent Katgley, who owns Chez Spencer, an upscale French restaurant. At Hudson's on the Bend, a wild game restaurant in Austin, Texas, the average check is $75. However, when owner and chef Jeff Blank rolled out his food truck, The Mighty Cone, he priced his menu so that the average check is less than $10. Although a struggling economy caused sales at Hudson's on the Bend to decline by 25 percent, sales at The Mighty Cone, which specializes in fried chicken, shrimp, and avocado coated with a mixture of almonds, sesame seeds, corn-flakes, and chili flakes, filled the gap and allowed Blank to hire extra staff.

Start-up costs for a mobile restaurant range from $20,000 to $160,000 (or more, depending on the truck's setup), far below the cost of opening a full-service restaurant in a fixed location, especially in a large city. Kenny Lao, owner of the Rickshaw Dumpling Bar in New York's Chelsea district, was looking for a location in midtown Manhattan in which to open a second dumpling restaurant but was discouraged by the high rental rates of $200 to $300 per square foot. Restaurant owners know that high rental rates increase their fixed costs, which, in turn, increase their break-even points and make it more difficult to earn a profit. Lao was not willing to take that risk and instead chose to spend $150,000 to outfit the Rickshaw Dumpling Truck.

Many food truck operators find that their mobile restaurants give them a great deal of flexibility. In addition to their regular lunch runs, restaurateurs can dispatch them to street fairs, community festivals, or the campuses of large businesses or even rent them out for weddings and private events. Paul Shenkman, owner of Sam's Chowder House near San Francisco, recently launched Sam's ChowderMobile. "With Sam's ChowderMobile, we can bring a 'mobile seafood shack' with outstanding food right to companies at their locations," says Shenkman. "We can even hold lobster clambakes right on the beach or at your home or office."

To market their mobile restaurants, entrepreneurs often turn to social media, such as Facebook and Twitter, sending out tweets to their followers announcing the trucks' locations, and on their Web sites. Kogi, a popular Korean barbecue restaurant in Culver City, California, operates four Kogi trucks and uses Twitter to alert more than 70,000 loyal customers to the day's specials and the trucks' locations and routes.

Ordinances, regulations, and zoning laws that govern the licensing and operation of food trucks vary significantly from one city to another and sometimes pose significant barriers to mobile restaurateurs. In Seattle, food vendors can park their trucks only on private property, but many other cities sell permits that allow them to park in most public parking spots. In Los Angeles, food vendors must pay an annual licensing fee of $695 and buy a permit for

$340. In addition, trucks that stop in one spot for more than 2 hours must demonstrate that customers have access to a restroom that meets safety codes. Sacramento's city ordinances make operating a mobile food truck impractical. Mobile food vendors cannot stay in one commercial area for more than 30 minutes and cannot operate after 6 P.M. from November to March. Randall Selland, owner of gourmet restaurants The Kitchen and Ella Dining Room and Bar, was inspired by mobile vendors at a street food festival in San Francisco to launch his own food truck. However, Sacramento's restrictive regulations have put his plans on hold. Portland, Oregon, in contrast, welcomes mobile food vendors and counts more than 200 of them in operation. Bo Kwon, owner of Koi Fusion PDX, a food truck that sells Korean tacos, spent $90,000 outfitting his truck. Kwon has been so successful that he plans to put a second one on the road and, eventually, open a restaurant. "With this economy, [food trucks] have become an outlet for a lot of chefs," he says.

1. What advantages do food trucks have over stationary restaurants? Disadvantages?
2. Do you think that a mobile food truck would be successful in your community? If so, what kind of food truck? Explain your reasoning.

Sources: Based on Katy McLaughlin, "Food Truck Nation," *Wall Street Journal,* June 5, 2009, pp. W1, W4; Lisa Jennings, "Vendors Drive Traffic but Rev Up Operator Aggression," *Nation's Restaurant News,* June 8, 2009, *www.nrn.com/article/vendors-drive-traffic-rev-operator-aggression;* Lisa Jennings, "ChowderMobile Joins Growing Fleet of Food Trucks," *Nation's Restaurant News,* June 17, 2009, *www.nrn.com/article/chowdermobile-joins-growing-fleet-food-trucks;* Chris Macias, "Sacramento Says No to Hot New Food Trend," *Sacramento Bee,* August 23, 2010, *www.sacbee.com/2010/08/23/2975917/sacramento-says-no-to-hot-new.html.*

Location Criteria for Retail and Service Businesses

2. Describe the location criteria for retail and service businesses.

Few decisions are as important for retailers and service firms than the choice of a location. Because their success depends on a steady flow of customers, these businesses must locate their businesses with their target customers' convenience and preferences in mind. This section presents some of the important location criteria for retail and service businesses.

Trade Area Size

Every retail and service business should determine the extent of its **trading area,** the region from which a business can expect to draw customers over a reasonable time span. The primary variables that influence the scope of the trading area are the type and the size of the business. If a retail store specializes in a particular product line and offers a wide selection and knowledgeable salespeople, it may draw customers from a great distance. In contrast, a convenience store with a general line of merchandise has a small trading area because it is unlikely that customers will drive across town to purchase items that are available within blocks of their homes or businesses. As a rule, the larger the store, the greater its selection, and the better its service, the broader is its trading area. Businesses that offer a narrow selection of products and services tend to have smaller trading areas. For instance, the majority of a massage therapist's clients live within 3 to 5 miles of the location, with a secondary tier of clients who live within 5 to 10 miles. Clients who are willing to travel more than 15 minutes for a session are rare.[26]

The following environmental factors also influence trading area size.

RETAIL COMPATIBILITY. Shoppers tend to be drawn to clusters of related businesses. That is one reason shopping malls, lifestyle centers, and outlet shopping centers are popular destinations for shoppers and are attractive locations for retailers. The concentration of businesses pulls customers from a larger trading area than a single free-standing business does. Retail compatibility describes the benefits a company receives by locating near other businesses selling complementary products and services. Clever retailers choose their locations with an eye on the surrounding mix of businesses. For instance, grocery store operators prefer not to locate in shopping centers with movie theaters, offices, and fitness centers, all businesses whose customers occupy parking spaces for extended time periods. Drugstores, nail salons, and ice cream parlors have proved to be much better shopping center neighbors for grocers.

DEGREE OF COMPETITION. The size, location, and activity of competing businesses also influence the size of the trading area. If a business will be the first of its kind in a location, its trading area might be extensive. However, if the area already has multiple stores nearby that are direct competitors, its trading area is diminished significantly. Market saturation is a problem for businesses in many industries, ranging from fast-food restaurants to convenience stores.

TRANSPORTATION NETWORK. The transportation networks are the highways, roads, and public service routes that presently exist or are planned. An inconvenient location reduces the business's trading area. Entrepreneurs should check to see whether the transportation system works smoothly and is free of barriers that might prevent customers from reaching their store. Is it easy for customers traveling in the opposite direction to cross traffic? Do signs and lights allow traffic to flow smoothly?

PHYSICAL, CULTURAL, OR EMOTIONAL BARRIERS. Physical barriers may be parks, rivers, lakes, or any other obstruction that hinders customers' access to the area. Locating on one side of a large park may reduce the number of customers who will drive around it to get to the store. In urban areas, new immigrants tend to cluster together, sharing a common culture and language. These trading areas are defined by cultural barriers, where inhabitants patronize only the businesses in their neighborhoods. The Little Havana section of Miami or the Chinatown sections of San Francisco, New York, and Los Angeles are examples. One powerful emotional barrier is safety. If high-crime areas exist around a site, potential customers may not travel through the area to reach the business. The leaders of many large cities are focusing their efforts on reducing crime and eliminating barriers to potential shoppers.

POLITICAL BARRIERS AND CREATIONS OF LAW. Political barriers are creations of law. County, city, or state boundaries—and the laws within those boundaries—are examples. State tax laws sometimes create conditions in which customers cross to border states to save money. For instance, North Carolina imposes one of the lowest cigarette taxes in the country, and shops located near the state line do a brisk business in the product selling to customers from bordering states.

Entrepreneurs should evaluate the characteristics of a trading area thoroughly; the matrix in Table 3 is a helpful tool for conducting an analysis. Once entrepreneurs rank each factor in relative importance and assign a score on the 1 to 5 scale, they simply multiply the two values to get a score for each characteristic. Adding up the scores produces a total score. (Higher is better.)

TABLE 3 Retail Trading Area Analysis

Characteristics	Relative Importance 1 = Low, 10 = High	Trading Area Score 1 = Major Disadvantage, 5 = Major Advantage	Area A	Area B
	1 2 3 4 5 6 7 8 9 10	1 2 3 4 5		
Population size and density				
Per capita disposable income				
Total disposable income				
Educational levels of the population				
Age distribution				
Number and size of existing competitors				
Strength of existing competitors				
Level of market saturation				
Population growth projections				
Ease of access				
Other:				
Total score				

Customer Traffic

Perhaps the most important screening criterion for a potential retail and a service location is the number of potential customers passing by the site during business hours. To be successful, a business must be able to generate sufficient sales to surpass its break-even point, and doing that requires an ample volume of traffic. One of the key success factors for a convenience store, for instance, is a high-traffic location with easy accessibility. Entrepreneurs should know the traffic counts (pedestrian and auto) at the sites they are considering. Shoeshine stands and kiosks in airports are examples of service businesses that benefit from the high volume of potential customers who pass by.

Adequate Parking

If customers cannot find convenient and safe parking, they are not likely to stop in the area. Many downtown areas have lost customers because of inadequate parking. Although shopping malls typically average 5 parking spaces per 1,000 square feet of shopping space, many central business districts get by with 3.5 spaces per 1,000 square feet. Customers generally will not pay to park if parking is free at shopping centers or in front of competing stores. Even when a business provides free parking, some potential customers may not feel safe on the streets, especially after dark. Many large city business districts become virtual ghost towns at the end of the business day. A location where traffic vanishes after 6 P.M. may not be as valuable as mall and shopping center locations that mark the beginning of the prime sales at 6 P.M.

Expansion Potential

A location should be flexible enough to provide for expansion if success warrants it. Failure to consider this factor can force a successful business to open a second store when it would have been more advantageous to expand at its original location.

Visibility

No matter what a retailer sells or how well it serves customers' needs, it cannot survive without visibility. Highly visible locations simply make it easy for customers to make purchases. A site lacking visibility puts a company at a major disadvantage before it even opens its doors. In a competitive marketplace, customers seldom wish to search for a business when equally attractive alternatives are easy to locate.

Some service businesses, however, can select sites with less visibility if the majority of their customer contacts are by telephone, fax, or the Internet. For example, customers usually contact plumbers by telephone; so rather than locating close to their customer bases, plumbers have flexibility in choosing their locations. Similarly, businesses that work at their customers' homes, such as swimming pool services, can operate from their homes and service vans.

The Index of Retail Saturation

The **index of retail saturation (IRS)** is a measure of the potential sales per square foot of store space for a given product within a specific trading area. This measure combines the number of customers in a trading area, their purchasing power, and the level of competition. The index is the ratio of a trading area's sales potential for a particular product or service to its sales capacity:

$$IRS = \frac{C \times RE}{RF}$$

where:

C = Number of customers in the trading area

RE = Retail expenditures (the average dollar expenditure per person for the product in the trading area)

RF = Retail facilities (the total square feet of selling space allocated to the product in the trading area)

This computation is an important one for any retailer to make. Locating in an area already saturated with competitors results in dismal sales volume and often leads to failure.

To illustrate the IRS, suppose that an entrepreneur looking at two sites for a sports store finds that he needs sales of $175 per square foot to be profitable. Site 1 has a trading area with 25,875 potential customers, each of whom spends an average of $42 on sports gear annually; the only competitor in the trading area has 6,000 square feet of selling space. Site 2 has 27,750 potential customers spending an average of $43.50 on sports gear annually; two competitors occupy 8,400 square feet of space. The IRS of site 1 is:

$$IRS = \frac{25{,}875 \times 42}{6{,}000}$$

$$= \$181.12 \text{ sales potential per square foot}$$

The IRS of site 2 is:

$$IRS = \frac{27{,}750 \times 43.50}{8{,}400}$$

$$= \$143.71 \text{ sales potential per square foot}$$

Although site 2 appears to be more favorable on the surface, site 1 is the better location according to the index; site 2 fails to meet the minimum standard of $175 per square foot.

Reilly's Law of Retail Gravitation

Reilly's Law of Retail Gravitation, a classic work in market analysis published in 1931 by William J. Reilly, uses the analogy of gravity to estimate the attractiveness of a particular business to potential customers. The ability to draw customers is directly related to the extent to which customers see it as a "destination" and is inversely related to the distance customers must travel to reach the business. Reilly's model also provides a way to estimate the trade boundary between two market areas by calculating the "break point" between them. The break point between two primary market areas is the boundary between the two where customers become indifferent about shopping at one or the other. The key factor in determining this point of indifference is the size of the communities. If two nearby cities have the same population sizes, then the break point lies halfway between them. The following is the equation for Reilly's Law:[27]

$$BP = \frac{d}{1 + \sqrt{P_b/P_a}}$$

where:

BP = Distance in miles from location A to the break point

d = Distance in miles between locations A and B

P_a = Population surrounding location A

P_b = Population surrounding location B

For example, if city A and city B are 22 miles apart, and city A has a population of 22,500 and city B has a population of 42,900, the break point, according to Reilly's law is:

$$BP = \frac{22}{1 + \sqrt{42{,}900/22{,}500}} = 9.2 \text{ miles}$$

The outer edge of city A's trading area lies about 9 miles between city A and city B. Although only a rough estimate, this simple calculation using readily available data can be useful for screening potential locations.

Location Options for Retail and Service Businesses

3. Outline the basic location options for retail and service businesses.

Retail and service business owners can locate in seven basic areas: the central business district (CBD), neighborhoods, shopping centers and malls, near competitors, inside large retail stores, outlying areas, and at home. According to the International Council of Shopping Centers, the average cost to lease space in a shopping center is about $17 per square foot. At regional malls, lifestyle centers, and power centers, rental rates typically range from $20 to $25 per square foot. In central business locations, the average cost is between $35 and $45 per square foot (although rental rates can vary significantly in either direction of that average, depending upon the city).[28]

Central Business District

The **central business district (CBD)** is the traditional center of town—the downtown concentration of businesses established early in the development of most towns and cities. Entrepreneurs derive several advantages from a downtown location. Because businesses are centrally located, they attract customers from the entire trading area of the city. In addition, small businesses benefit from the traffic generated by other stores clustered in the downtown district. However, locating in a CBD does have certain disadvantages. Intense competition, high rental rates, traffic congestion, and inadequate parking facilities characterize some CBDs.

Beginning in the 1950s, many cities experienced difficulty in preventing the decay of their older downtown business districts as residents moved to the suburbs and began shopping at newer, more convenient shopping centers and malls. Today, however, many CBDs are experiencing rebirth as cities restore them to their former splendor and shoppers return. Many customers find irresistible the charming atmosphere that traditional downtown districts offer with their rich mix of stores, their unique architecture and streetscapes, and their historic character. Cities have begun to reverse the urban decay of their downtown business districts through proactive revitalization programs designed to attract visitors and residents alike to cultural events by locating major theaters and museums in the downtown area. In addition, many cities are providing economic incentives to real estate developers to build apartment and condominium complexes in the heart of the downtown area. Vitality is returning as residents live and shop in the once nearly abandoned downtown areas. The "ghost-town" image is being replaced by both younger and older residents who love the convenience and excitement of life at the center of the city.

Bill Cass and his wife Sam left their jobs designing shoes for Nike and moved to Langley, a small town on Washington's Whidbey Island, where they opened Nymbol's Secret Garden of Imagination in the scenic town's central business district. The Casses decided to open their unique shop, which sells an array of puppets, costumes, masks, jewelry, and other unique items, after visiting Langley, known as Washington's "Most Beautiful Waterfront Town," on a family vacation. Their shop benefits from its location near other interesting retail stores that together draw impressive numbers of customers, particularly during the busy tourist season.[29]

Neighborhood Locations

Small businesses that locate near residential areas rely heavily on the local trading areas for business. For example, many grocers and convenience stores located just outside residential subdivisions count on local clients for successful operation. One study of food stores found that the majority of the typical grocers' customers live within a 5-mile radius. The primary advantages of a neighborhood location include relatively low operating costs and rents and close contact with customers.

Shopping Centers and Malls

Until the early twentieth century, central business districts were the primary shopping venues in the United States. As cars and transportation networks became more popular in the 1920s, shopping centers began popping up outside cities' central business districts. Then, in October 1956, the nation's first shopping mall, Southdale, opened in the Minneapolis, Minnesota, suburb of Edina. Designed by Victor Gruen, the fully enclosed mall featured 72 shops anchored by 2 competing department stores (a radical concept at the time), a garden courtyard with a goldfish pond, an aviary, hanging plants, and artificial trees. With its multilevel layout and parking garage, Southdale was a huge success and forever changed the way Americans would shop.[30] Today, shopping centers and malls are a mainstay of the American landscape. Because many different types of stores operate under one roof, shopping malls give meaning to the term "one-stop shopping." In a typical month, nearly 191 million adults visit malls or shopping centers, which generate $2.25 trillion in annual sales.[31]

There are eight types of shopping centers (see Table 4).

NEIGHBORHOOD SHOPPING CENTERS. The typical neighborhood shopping center is relatively small, containing from 3 to 12 stores and serving a population of up to 40,000 people who live within a 10-minute drive. The anchor store in these centers is usually a supermarket or a drugstore. Neighborhood shopping centers typically are straight-line strip malls with parking available in front and primarily serve the daily shopping needs of customers in the surrounding area.

COMMUNITY SHOPPING CENTERS. A community shopping center contains from 12 to 50 stores and serves a population ranging from 40,000 to 150,000 people. The leading tenant often is a large department or variety store, a super drugstore, or a supermarket. Community shopping centers sell more clothing and other soft goods than do neighborhood shopping centers. Of the eight types of shopping centers, community shopping centers take on the greatest variety of shapes, designs, and tenants.

POWER CENTERS. A power center combines the drawing strength of a large regional mall with the convenience of a neighborhood shopping center. Anchored by several large specialty retailers, such as warehouse clubs, discount department stores, or large specialty stores, these centers target older, wealthier baby boomers, who want selection and convenience. Anchor stores usually account for 80 percent of power center space, compared with 50 percent in the typical community shopping center. Just as in a shopping mall, small businesses can benefit from the traffic generated by anchor stores, but they must choose their locations carefully so that they are not overshadowed by their larger neighbors.

THEME OR FESTIVAL CENTERS. Festival shopping centers employ a unifying theme that individual stores display in their décor and sometimes in the merchandise they sell. Entertainment is a common theme for these shopping centers, which often target tourists. Many festival shopping centers are located in urban areas and are housed in older, sometimes historic, buildings that have been renovated to serve as shopping centers.

OUTLET CENTERS. As their name suggests, outlet centers feature manufacturers' and retailers' outlet stores selling name-brand goods at a discount. Unlike most other types of shopping centers, outlet centers typically have no anchor stores; the discounted merchandise they offer draws sufficient traffic. Most outlet centers are open-air and are laid out in strips or in clusters, creating small "villages" of shops.

LIFESTYLE (OR TOWN) CENTERS. Typically located near affluent residential neighborhoods where their target customers live, lifestyle centers are designed to look less like shopping centers and malls and more like the busy streets in the central business districts that existed in towns and cities in their heyday. Occupied by many upscale national chain specialty stores such as Talbot's, Pier 1 Imports, Jos. A. Bank Clothiers, and others, these centers combine shopping convenience and entertainment ranging from movie theaters and open-air concerts to art galleries and people-watching. "Lifestyle centers create a shopping-leisure destination that's an extension of customers' personal lifestyles," says one industry expert.[32] The typical lifestyle center generates between $400 and $500 in sales per square foot compared to $381 in sales per square foot in traditional malls.[33] Lifestyle centers are among the most popular types of shopping centers being built today. The first lifestyle center, The Shops of Saddle Creek, opened in Germantown, Tennessee, in 1987. Today, more than 400 lifestyle centers operate across the United States.[34]

REGIONAL SHOPPING MALLS. The regional shopping mall serves a large trading area, usually from 5 to 15 miles or more in all directions. These enclosed malls contain from 50 to 100 stores and serve a population of 150,000 or more living within a 20- to 40-minute drive. The anchor is typically one or more major department stores, with smaller specialty stores occupying the spaces between the anchors. Clothing is one of the popular items sold in regional shopping malls.

SUPER-REGIONAL SHOPPING MALLS. A super-regional mall is similar to a regional mall but is bigger, containing more anchor stores and a greater variety of shops selling deeper lines of merchandise. Its trade area stretches up to 25 or more miles. Canada's West Edmonton Mall, the largest mall in North America, with more than 800 stores and 100 restaurants, is one of the most famous super-regional malls in the world. In addition to its abundance of retail shops, the mall contains an ice skating rink, a water park, an amusement park, miniature golf courses, and a 21-screen movie complex.

When evaluating a mall or shopping center location, an entrepreneur should consider the following questions:

- Is there a good fit with other products and brands sold in the mall or center?
- Who are the other tenants? Which stores are the anchors that will bring people into the mall or center?

TABLE 4 Types of Shopping Centers

Type of Shopping Center	Concept	Square Footage (including anchors)	Acreage	Typical Anchor		Anchor Ratio (%)[a]	Primary Trade Area (miles)[b]
				Number	Type		
Malls							
Regional center	General and fashion merchandise; mall (typically enclosed)	480,000–800,000	40–100	2 or more	Full-line department store; junior department store; mass merchant; discount department store; fashion apparel	50–70	5–15
Super-regional center	Similar to regional center but offers more variety	>800,000	60–120	3 or more	Full-line department store; junior department store; mass merchant; fashion apparel	50–70	5–25
Open-Air Centers							
Neighborhood center	Convenience	30,000–150,000	3–15	1 or more	Supermarket	30–50	3
Community center	General merchandise; convenience	100,000–350,000	10–40	2 or more	Discount department store; supermarket; drugstore; home improvement store; large specialty or discount apparel retailer	40–60	3–6
Lifestyle center	Upscale national chain specialty stores, dining, and entertainment in an outdoor setting	150,000–500,000, but can be larger or smaller	10–40	0–2	Not usually anchored in the traditional sense, but may include bookstore; large specialty retailers; multiplex cinema; small department store	0–50	8–12
Power center	Category-dominant anchors; few small business tenants	250,000–600,000	25–80	3 or more	Category killer; home improvement store; discount department store; warehouse club; off-price retailer	75–90	5–10
Theme/festival center	Leisure; tourist-oriented; retail and service	80,000–250,000	5–20	Unspecified	Restaurants; entertainment	N/A	25–75
Outlet center	Manufacturers' outlet stores	50,000–400,000	10–50	N/A	Manufacturers' outlet stores	N/A	25–75

[a] The share of a center's total square footage that is occupied by its anchors.
[b] The area from which 60 to 80 percent of the center's sales originate.
Source: International Council of Shopping Centers, New York.

▨ Demographically, is the center a good fit for your products or services? What are its customer demographics?

▨ How much foot traffic does the mall or center generate? How much traffic passes the specific site you are considering?

▨ How much vehicle traffic does the mall or center generate? Check its proximity to major population centers, the volume of tourists it draws, and the volume of drive-by freeway traffic. A mall or center that scores well on all three is more likely to be a winner.

▨ What is the mall's vacancy rate? What is the turnover rate of its tenants?

▨ How much is the rent and how is it calculated? Most mall tenants pay a base amount of rent plus a small percentage of their sales above a specified level.

▨ Is the mall or center successful? How many dollars in sales does it generate per square foot? Compare its record against industry averages. The International Council of Shopping Centers (*www.icsc.org*) is a good source of industry information.

A mall location is no guarantee of business success, however. Malls have been under pressure lately, and many weaker ones (known as "greyfields") have closed or have been redeveloped. The basic problem is an oversupply of mall space; there is 22.5 square feet of mall retail space for every person in the United States! Another problem is that many malls are showing their age; in fact, 85 percent of the malls in the United States are more than 20 years old.[35] In addition, the demographic makeup of an area's shoppers often changes over time, creating a new socioeconomic customer base that may or may not be compatible with a small company's target customer profile. As a result, many malls have undergone extensive renovations to emphasize "entertailing," adding entertainment features to their existing retail space in an attempt to generate more traffic. For instance, in addition to its 520 retail shops and 60 restaurants, Minneapolis's Mall of America, the second largest mall in the United States (located only a few miles from Southdale, the nation's first mall), includes a Nickelodeon Universe amusement park at its center, a 1.2 million gallon aquarium, a flight simulator, and a 14-screen movie complex in its 4.2 million square feet of space.[36]

Source: www.CartoonStock.com

Near Competitors

One of the most important factors in choosing a retail or service location is the compatibility of nearby stores with the retail or service customer. For example, stores selling high-priced goods such as cars or merchandise that requires comparisons, such as antiques, find it advantageous to locate near competitors to facilitate comparison shopping. Locating near competitors might be a key factor for success in businesses that sell goods that customers compare on price, quality, color, and other factors.

Although some business owners avoid locations near direct competitors, others see locating near rivals as an advantage. For instance, restaurateurs know that successful restaurants attract other restaurants, which, in turn, attract more customers. Many cities have at least one "restaurant row," where restaurants cluster together; each restaurant feeds customers to the others.

Locating near competitors has its limits, however. Clustering too many businesses of a single type into a small area ultimately will erode their sales once the market reaches the saturation point. As the number of gourmet coffee shops has exploded in recent years, many have struggled to remain profitable, often competing with three or four similar shops, all within easy walking distance of one another. When an area becomes saturated with competitors, the stores cannibalize sales from one another, making it difficult for all to survive.

Inside Large Retail Stores

Rather than compete against giant retailers, some small business owners are cooperating with them, locating their businesses inside the larger company's stores. These small companies offer products that the large retailers do not and benefit from the large volume of customer traffic the large stores attract. The world's largest retailer, Walmart, is host to several small businesses, including franchisees of fast-food chains Subway and McDonald's and medical clinics and banks. These stores within a store reap the benefits of the large volume of traffic from the more than 200 million people who shop at Walmart each year.

Outlying Areas

Generally, it is not advisable for a small business to locate in a remote area because accessibility and traffic flow are vital to retail and service success, but there are exceptions. Some companies have transformed their remote locations into part of their identities. Cabela's, a chain of 30 sporting goods stores founded in 1961 by brothers Dick and Jim Cabela, has had great success with stores in rather remote locations such as Kearny, Nebraska, and Mitchell, South Dakota. The extensive breadth and depth of Cabela's product line and its reputation for "entertailing" give potential customers a compelling reason to travel to the stores.

An entrepreneur should consider the cost of a location (its rental or lease expense) in light of its visibility to potential customers. If a less expensive location is difficult for customers to find and has a low traffic count, a business located there will have to spend a disproportionate amount of money on promotion. Consequently, a superior, highly visible location may offer lower total operating cost because of the traffic it generates. Many customers do not want to go exploring to find a business and, consequently, never bother to try.

Home-Based Businesses

For more than 15 million entrepreneurs, home is where the business is, and their numbers are swelling. One recent study from the SBA reports that 52 percent of all small companies are home-based and that more than 21 percent of home-based businesses generate more than $100,000 in annual revenue.[37] Many service businesses operate from entrepreneurs' homes. Because many service companies do not rely on customers to come to their places of business, incurring the expense of an office location is unnecessary. For instance, customers typically contact plumbers or exterminators by telephone, and the work is performed in customers' homes. Web-based and catalog retailers also operate from their homes.

When an economic downturn forced Billy Carmen to downsize his specialty tools company, Wizard Industries, he decided to eliminate the office-warehouse he had been renting in Los Angeles and run the business from his home. Carmen decided to move to Sebastopol, California, a town whose ordinances are friendly to home-based businesses, allowing him, for example, to put a business sign outside his home and have customers' packages picked up for delivery.[38]

Choosing a home location has disadvantages. It may affect family life, interruptions are more frequent, the refrigerator is all too handy, work is always just a few steps away, and isolation can be a problem. Another difficulty some home-based entrepreneurs face involves zoning laws. As their businesses grow and become more successful, entrepreneurs' neighbors often begin to complain about the increased traffic, noise, and disruptions from deliveries, employees, and customers who drive through their residential neighborhoods to conduct business. A judge recently ordered Jennifer Spiegel to close her business, Spiegel Farms, a wedding and event venue located on Spiegel's 62-acre farm in Campobello, South Carolina, after neighbors complained that operating the business violated the zoning regulations in their residential neighborhood. Spiegel had operated the business from her farm for nearly 9 years and had hosted more than 340 weddings.[39]

The Location Decision for Manufacturers

4. Explain the site selection process for manufacturers.

The criteria for the location decision for manufacturers are very different from those of retailers and service businesses; however, the decision can have just as much impact on the company's success. In some cases, a manufacturer has special needs that influence the choice of a location. When one manufacturer of photographic plates and film was searching for a location for a new plant, it had to limit its search to those sites with a large supply of available fresh water, a necessary part of its process. In other cases, zoning ordinances dictate a company's location decision. If a manufacturer's process creates offensive odors or excessive noise, it may be even further restricted in its choices.

The type of transportation facilities required dictates the location of a plant in some cases. Some manufacturers may need a location on a railroad siding, whereas others may need only access to interstate highways. Some companies ship bulk materials by ship or barge and consequently require a facility convenient to a navigable river or lake. The added cost of using multiple shipping methods (e.g., rail-to-truck or barge-to-truck) can significantly increase shipping costs and make a location unfeasible for a manufacturer. Because water is expensive to transport, companies that produce bottled water must choose their locations carefully. Ideally, a site is close to large markets but not so close that pollutants from major metropolitan areas diminish the quality of the water source. Companies must find springs that provide good-tasting water and enough space to build a bottling plant nearby.[40]

As fuel costs escalate, the cost of shipping finished products to customers also influences the location decision for many manufacturers, forcing them to open factories or warehouses in locations that are close to their primary markets to reduce transportation costs.

ENTREPRENEURIAL
Profile

Paul Beach:
Quallion LLC

Quallion LLC, a maker of lithium-ion batteries, recently built a $220 million factory near Los Angeles, California, because it offers easy, low-cost access to shipping ports that serve its customers, many of whom are located in the Far East. "One reason for our success is our close proximity to the ports of Los Angeles and Long Beach for shipping products in high volume," says Quallion president Paul Beach. "We have lower costs of transportation." Despite the burdens imposed by high operating costs and extensive government regulation, Southern California provides other critical inputs that Quallion requires, including a highly skilled pool of workers from which to draw and access to other high-tech firms.[41]

In some cases the perishability of the product dictates location. Vegetables and fruits must be canned in close proximity to the fields from which they are harvested. Companies that process and can fish must find locations at the water's edge. The ideal location is determined by quick and easy access to the perishable products.

Foreign Trade Zones

Created in 1934, foreign trade zones can be an attractive location for small manufacturers that engage in global trade and are looking to reduce or eliminate the tariffs, duties, and excise taxes they pay on the materials and parts they import and the goods they export. A **foreign trade zone** (see Figure 2) is a specially designated area in or near a U.S. customs port of entry that allows

FIGURE 2
**How a Foreign Trade
Zone (FTZ) Works**

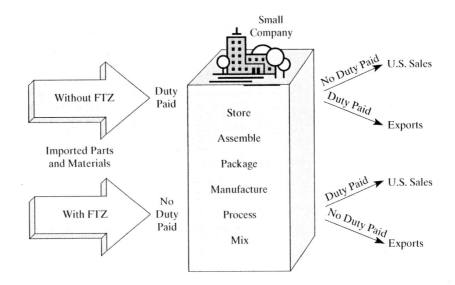

resident companies to import materials and components from foreign countries; assemble, process, manufacture, or package them; and then ship the finished product back out while either deferring, reducing, or eliminating tariffs and duties. As far as tariffs and duties are concerned, a company located in a foreign trade zone is treated as if it is located outside the United States. For instance, a maker of speakers can import components from around the world and assemble them at its plant located in a foreign trade zone. The company pays no duties on the components it imports or on the speakers it exports to other foreign markets. The only duties the manufacturer pays are on the speakers it sells in the United States. There are 256 foreign trade zones and 498 subzones, which are special foreign trade zones that are established for limited purposes, operating in the United States. The value of shipments into foreign trade zones has increased from $147 billion in 1998 to nearly $700 billion today.[42]

Empowerment Zones

5. Discuss the benefits of locating a start-up company in a business incubator.

Originally created to encourage companies to locate in economically blighted areas, **empowerment zones** offer businesses tax breaks on the investments they make within zone boundaries. Companies can get federal tax credits, grants, and loans for hiring workers living in empowerment zones and for investments they make in plant and equipment in the zones. Empowerment zones operate in both urban and rural areas, ranging from Los Angeles, California, to Sumter, South Carolina. Boston, Massachusetts has a technology-oriented business incubator located within a federal empowerment zone called TechSpace, which provides high-potential start-up businesses with a full-service facility featuring completely integrated information technology and business services.

Business Incubators

For many start-up companies, a business incubator may make the ideal initial location. A **business incubator** is an organization that combines low-cost, flexible rental space with a multitude of support services for its small business residents. The primary reason that communities establish incubators is to enhance economic development, create jobs, and diversify the local economy. The strategy works; 84 percent of the companies that graduate from incubators stay in the local community.[43]

**ENTREPRENEURIAL
Profile**

TechTown

TechTown, an incubator established by Wayne State University in 2000 in what once was a former GM building in Detroit, Michigan (engineers designed the original Chevrolet Corvette on the third floor), is home to more than 160 innovative start-up companies, most of which are high-tech companies concentrated in four industries: alternative energy, medical technology, logistics, and the Internet. Clean Emissions Fluids (CEF), one of TechTown's residents, has developed a computer-controlled fueling station that dispenses the appropriate mixture of biofuels and petroleum products to maximize a vehicle's efficiency. CEF, founded by former auto industry engineers Oliver Baer, Chris Channell, and Terri Teller, recently set up a small manufacturing operation in TechTown's newest building and has space to grow into as its sales increase. The incubator also has hosted more than 1,500 people with entrepreneurial dreams, many of them former auto industry employees, in a 10-week business start-up training program called FasTrac that is sponsored by the Kauffman Foundation.[44]

An incubator's goal is to nurture young companies during the volatile start-up period and to help them survive until they are strong enough to go out on their own. Most incubators (54 percent) are "mixed-use," hosting a variety of start-up companies, followed by incubators that focus on technology companies (see Figure 3).[45] The shared resources incubators typically provide their tenants include secretarial services, a telephone system, computers and software, fax machines, meeting space, and, sometimes, management consulting services and access to financing. Not only do these services save young companies money, but they also save them valuable time. Entrepreneurs can focus on getting their products and services to market rather than searching for the resources they need to build their companies. Many business incubators help their tenants gain access to capital; a survey by the National Business Incubation Association reports that 83 percent of incubators provide some kind of access to seed capital, ranging from help with obtaining federal grants to making connections with angel investors.[46]

The typical incubator has entry requirements that prospective residents must meet. Incubators also have criteria that establish the conditions a business must maintain to remain in the facility as well as the expectations for "graduation" into the business community. The typical start-up that lives in an incubator stays for an average of 3 years. More than 1,200 incubators operate across the United States, up from just 12 in 1980. Perhaps the greatest advantage of choosing to locate a start-up company in an incubator is a greater chance for success; according to the National Business Incubation Association, graduates from incubators have a success rate of 87 percent. Each year, business incubators help an estimated 27,000 start-up companies that provide full-time employment for more than 100,000 workers.[47]

Layout and Design Considerations

6. Describe the criteria used to analyze the layout and design considerations of a building, including the Americans with Disabilities Act.

Once an entrepreneur chooses the best location for his or her business, the next issue to address is designing the proper layout for the space to maximize sales (retail) or productivity (manufacturing or service). **Layout** is the logical arrangement of the physical facilities in a business that contributes to efficient operations, increased productivity, and higher sales. Planning for the most effective and efficient layout in a business environment can produce dramatic improvements in a company's operating effectiveness and efficiency. An attractive, effective layout can help a company's recruiting efforts, reduce absenteeism, and improve employee productivity and satisfaction. A recent U.S. Workplace Survey by global design firm Gensler reports that 90 percent of employees believe that better workplace design and layout improves their performance and productivity and the company's competitiveness, yet only 50 percent of workers say that their work environment encourages innovation.[48] The changing nature of work demands that workspace design also changes. Although many jobs require the ability to focus on "heads down," individual tasks, collaboration with coworkers is becoming a more significant component of work even when workers are scattered across the globe and "meet" virtually. An effective workspace

FIGURE 3
Business Incubators by Industry

Source: National Business Incubation Association, Athens, Ohio, 2010.

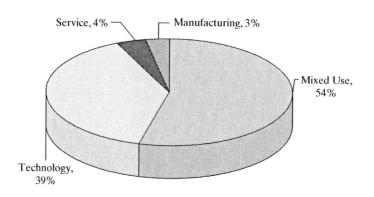

Service, 4%
Manufacturing, 3%
Mixed Use, 54%
Technology, 39%

must be flexible enough to accommodate and encourage both types of work. Increasingly, work is becoming more complex, team-based, technology dependent, and mobile; workspaces must change to accommodate these characteristics. The study by Gensler concludes that top performing companies have workspaces that are more effective than those of average companies, particularly for collaboration. Gensler also reports that employees at top performing companies spend 23 percent more time collaborating with their coworkers than do employees at average companies.[49]

When creating a layout, managers must consider its impact on space itself (comfort, flexibility, size, and ergonomics), the people who occupy it (type of work, special requirements, need for interaction, tasks performed), and the technology they use (communication, Internet access, and equipment).[50] The following factors have a significant impact on a space's layout and design.

Size and Adaptability

A building must offer adequate space and be adaptable to accommodate a business's daily operations. If space is restrictive at the outset of operations, efficiency will suffer. There must be room enough for customers' movement, inventory, displays, storage, work areas, offices, and restrooms. Haphazard layouts undermine employee productivity and can create organizational chaos. A business that launches in a location that is already overcrowded may find it limits its potential. The unfortunate result is that an owner may be required to make a premature and costly move to a new location.

As a business expands, a lack of adequate room or an inefficient configuration may limit future growth. Some businesses wait too long before moving into larger quarters, and they fail to plan their new space arrangements properly. To avoid this problem, experts recommend that new business owners plan their space requirements 1 to 2 years ahead and update the estimates every 6 months. When preparing the plan, entrepreneurs should include the expected growth in the number of employees, manufacturing, selling, or storage space requirements, and the number and location of branches to be opened.

ENTREPRENEURIAL
Profile

Gravity Tank

At Gravity Tank, a small design-strategy firm in Chicago, a layout that encourages collaboration is essential because employees often work together on project teams for several months. Designers came up with a flexible layout that includes work bays that can be reconfigured quickly and easily by moving lightweight dividers made from cardboard that hang from an overhead grid. Cork bulletin boards (which also serve as dividers) allow employees to share ideas easily, and the furnishings in each bay have built-in power outlets, Ethernet cables, and trays of office supplies, giving employees easy access to all of the tools they need to work. Employees have the flexibility they need in an office space, and Gravity Tank created the entire space for just $20,000.[51]

External Appearance

The physical appearance of a building determines the first impression that customers have of a business and contributes significantly to establishing its identity in customers' minds. Therefore, a building's appearance must be consistent with the entrepreneur's desired image for the business. Retailers, in particular, must recognize the importance of creating the proper image for their stores and how their shops' layout and physical facilities influence this image. In many ways, the building's appearance sets the tone for the customer's quality and service expectations. The appearance should reflect the "personality" of the business. Should the building project an exclusive image or an economical one? Is the atmosphere informal and relaxed, or it is formal and businesslike? Externally, the storefront, its architectural style and color, signs, entrances, and general appearance, give important clues to customers about a business's image. For example, a glass front enables a retail business to display merchandise easily and to attract potential customers' attention. Passersby can look in and see attractive merchandise displays or, in some cases, dedicated employees working.

Communicating the right signals through layout and physical facilities is an important step in attracting a steady stream of customers. Retail consultant Paco Underhill advises merchants to "seduce" passersby with their storefronts. "The seduction process should start a minimum of 10 paces away," he says. "A store's interior architecture is fundamental to the customer's experience— the stage upon which a retail company functions."[52]

ENTREPRENEURIAL
Profile

Williams-Sonoma

Williams-Sonoma, an upscale retailer of kitchenware, seduces passersby with window displays that look more like someone's kitchen than a retail shop. Stores in the chain change their eye-catching displays frequently to reflect the foods of the season. The goal is to sell and make customers feel welcome and to put them in a positive frame of mind. "If you have a positive feeling," says Julie Irwin, marketing professor at the University of Texas at Austin, "you're going to associate it with everything you see." Once inside a Williams-Sonoma store, an array of aromas rising from freshly-baked foods or hot beverages also lure customers and encourage them to stay, which increases the probability that they make a purchase.[53]

The following tips help entrepreneurs to create displays that sell:

- *Keep displays simple.* Simple, uncluttered arrangements of merchandise draw the most attention and have the greatest impact on potential customers.
- *Keep displays clean and up-to-date.* Dusty, dingy displays or designs that are outdated send the wrong message to customers.
- *Promote local events.* Small companies can show their support of the community by devoting part of the display window to promote local events.
- *Change displays frequently.* Customers don't want to see the same merchandise every time they visit a store. Experts recommend changing window displays at least quarterly. Businesses that sell fashionable items, however, should change their displays at least twice a month, if not weekly.
- *Get expert help, if necessary.* Some business owners have no aptitude for design! In that case, their best bet is to hire a professional to design window and in-store displays. If a company cannot afford a professional designer's fees, the entrepreneur should check with the design departments at local colleges and universities. There might be a faculty member or a talented student willing to work on a freelance basis.
- *Appeal to all of a customer's senses.* Effective displays engage more than one of a customer's senses. Who can pass up a bakery case of freshly baked, gooey cinnamon buns with their mouth-watering aroma wafting up to greet passersby?
- *Contact the companies whose products you sell to see whether they offer design props and assistance.* These vendors may offer additional insight and are aware of industry trends and competitor tactics.

Entrances

All entrances to a business should invite customers in. Wide entryways and attractive merchandise displays that are set back from the doorway can draw customers into a business. A store's entrance should catch passing customers' attention and draw them inside. "That's where you want somebody to slam on the brakes and realize they're going someplace new," says retail consultant Paco Underhill.[54] Retailers with heavy traffic flows such as supermarkets or drugstores often install automatic doors to ensure smooth traffic flow into and out of their stores. Retailers should remove any barriers that interfere with customers' easy access to the storefront. Broken sidewalks, sagging steps, mud puddles, and sticking or heavy doors not only create obstacles that might discourage potential customers, but they also create legal hazards for a business if they cause customers to be injured.

The Americans with Disabilities Act

The **Americans with Disabilities Act (ADA),** passed in July 1990, requires most businesses to make their facilities available to physically challenged customers and employees. In addition, the law requires businesses with 15 or more employees to accommodate physically challenged candidates in their hiring practices. Most states have similar laws, many of them more stringent than the ADA, that apply to smaller companies as well. The rules of the these state laws and the ADA's Title III are designed to ensure that mentally and physically challenged customers have equal access to a firm's goods or services. For instance, the act requires business owners to remove architectural and communication barriers when "readily achievable." The ADA allows flexibility in how a business achieves this equal access, however. For example, a restaurant either could provide menus in Braille or could offer to have a staff member read the menu to blind customers. A small dry cleaner might not be able to add a wheelchair ramp to its storefront without incurring significant expense, but the owner could comply with the ADA by offering curbside pickup and delivery services for disabled customers at no extra charge.

Although the law allows a good deal of flexibility in retrofitting existing structures, buildings that were occupied after January 25, 1993, must be designed to comply with all aspects of the law. For example, buildings with three stories or more must have elevators; anywhere the floor level changes by more than one-half inch, an access ramp must be in place. In retail stores, checkout aisles must be wide enough—at least 36 inches—to accommodate wheelchairs. Restaurants must have 5 percent of their tables accessible to wheelchair-bound patrons.

Complying with the ADA does not necessarily require businesses to spend large amounts of money. The Justice Department estimates that more than 20 percent of the cases customers have filed under Title III involved changes the business owners could have made at no cost, and another 60 percent would have cost less than $1,000![55] In addition, companies with $1 million or less in annual sales or with 30 or fewer full-time employees that invest in making their locations more accessible to all qualify for a tax credit. The credit is 50 percent of their expenses between $250 and $10,500. Businesses that remove physical, structural, and transportation barriers for disabled employees and customers also qualify for a tax deduction of up to $15,000.

The ADA also prohibits any kind of employment discrimination against anyone with a physical or mental disability. A physically challenged person is considered to be "qualified" if he or she can perform the essential functions of the job. The employer must make "reasonable accommodation" for a physically challenged candidate or employee without causing "undue hardship" to the business. Most businesses have found that making these reasonable accommodations for customers and employees has created a more pleasant environment and offer additional conveniences for all.

Signs

One of the lowest-cost and most effective methods of communicating with customers is a business sign. Signs communicate what a business does, where it is, and what it is selling. The United States is a very mobile society, and a well-designed, well-placed sign can be a powerful vehicle for reaching potential customers.

A sign should be large enough for passersby to read from a distance, taking into consideration the location and speed of surrounding traffic arteries. To be most effective, the message should be short, simple, and clear. A sign should be legible in both daylight and at night; proper illumination is a must. Contrasting colors and simple typefaces are best. The most common problems with business signs are that they are illegible, poorly designed, improperly located, poorly maintained, and have color schemes that are unattractive or hard to read.

Before investing in a sign, an entrepreneur should investigate the local community's sign ordinance. In some cities and towns, local regulations impose restrictions on the size, location, height, and construction materials used in business signs.

Interiors

Designing a functional, efficient interior layout demands research, planning, and attention to detail. Retailers in particular have known for a long time that their stores' layouts influence their customers' buying behavior. Retailers such as Cabela's, Barnes & Noble, and Starbucks use layouts that encourage customers to linger and spend time (and money). Others, such as Lowe's, Aldi, and Walmart, reinforce their discount images with layouts that communicate a warehouse environment, often complete with pallets, to shoppers. Luxury retailers such as Tiffany and Company, Coach, and Nordstrom create opulent layouts in which their upscale customers feel comfortable.

Technology has changed drastically the way employees, customers, and the environment interact with one another, but smart entrepreneurs realize that they can influence the effectiveness of those interactions with well-designed layouts. The result can be a boost to a company's sales and profits. For instance, as their customers' needs and expectations have changed, retailers have modified the layouts of their stores to meet those needs. Because shoppers are busier than ever and want an efficient shopping experience (particularly men), many retail stores have moved away from the traditional departments (e.g., shoes, cosmetics, men's suits) and are organizing their merchandise by "lifestyle categories," such as sports, women's contemporary, men's business casual, and others. These displays expose customers to merchandise that they otherwise might have missed and make it easier for them to, say, put together an entire outfit without having to roam from one department to another.

Designing an effective layout is an art and a science. **Ergonomics,** the science of adapting work and the work environment to complement employees' strengths and to suit customers' needs, is an integral part of a successful design. For example, chairs, desks, and table heights that allow people to work comfortably help employees perform their jobs faster and more easily. Design experts claim that improved lighting, better acoustics, and proper climate control benefit the company as well as employees. An ergonomically designed workplace can improve workers' productivity significantly and lower days lost due to injuries and accidents. A study for the Commission of Architecture and the Built Environment and the British Council for Offices reports that simple features such as proper lighting reduce absenteeism by 15 percent and increase productivity between 2.8 and 20 percent.[56]

Unfortunately, many businesses fail to incorporate ergonomic design principles into their layouts, and the result is costly. Every year, 1.8 million workers experience injuries related to repetitive motion or overexertion. The most frequent and most expensive workplace injuries are musculoskeletal disorders (MSDs), which cost U.S. businesses at least $15 billion in workers' compensation claims each year. According to the Occupational Safety and Health Administration (OSHA), MSDs account for 29.4 percent of all lost-workday injuries and illnesses and one-third of all workers compensation claims.[57] Workers who spend their days staring at computer monitors (a significant and growing proportion of the workforce) often are victims of MSDs.

The most common MSD is carpal tunnel syndrome (CTS), which occurs when repetitive motion causes swelling in the wrist that pinches the nerves in the arm and hand. Studies by the Bureau of Labor Statistics estimate that 3.7 percent of U.S. workers suffer from carpal tunnel syndrome and that the average worker with CTS loses 23 workdays, costing companies more than $2 billion per year.[58] The good news for employers, however, is that preventing injuries, accidents, and lost days does *not* require spending thousands of dollars on ergonomically correct solutions. Most of the solutions to MSDs are actually quite simple and inexpensive, ranging from installing equipment that eliminates workers' repetitive motions to introducing breaks during which workers engage in exercises designed by occupational therapists to combat MSDs.

When planning store, office, or plant layouts, business owners usually focus on minimizing costs. Although staying within a budget is important, minimizing injuries and enhancing employees' productivity with an effective layout should be the overriding issues. Many exhaustive studies have concluded that changes in office design have a direct impact on workers' performance, job satisfaction, and ease of communication. In a reversal of the trend toward open offices separated by nothing more than cubicles, businesses are once again creating private offices in their workspaces. Many businesses embraced open designs, hoping that they would lead to greater interaction among workers. Many companies, however, have discovered that most office workers need privacy and quiet surroundings to be productive. Rather than encourage teamwork, open offices leave workers distracted, frustrated, and less productive—just like the characters in the Dilbert cartoon strip. "Open offices do lead to more unstructured communication, but those same offices can lead to problems of [employee] concentration," says Babson College's Tom Davenport, whose research shows that workplace design has a direct impact on white-collar workers' performances and productivity.[59]

When evaluating an existing building's interior, an entrepreneur must be sure to determine the integrity of its structural components. Are the building's floors sufficiently strong to hold the business's equipment, inventories, and personnel? Strength is an especially critical factor for manufacturing firms that use heavy equipment. When multiple floors exist, are the upper floors anchored as solidly as the primary floor? Is the floor space adequate for safe and efficient movement of goods and people?

Floors and walls must be both functional and attractive. On the functional side, walls and ceilings should be fireproof and soundproof. Are the colors of walls and ceilings compatible, and do they create an attractive atmosphere for customers and employees? For instance, many high-tech companies use bright, bold colors in their designs because they appeal to their young employees. In contrast, more conservative companies, such as accounting firms and law offices, decorate with more subtle, subdued tones because they convey an image of trustworthiness and honesty. Upscale restaurants that want their patrons to linger over dinner use deep, luxurious tones and soft lighting to create the proper ambiance. Fast-food restaurants, in contrast, use strong, vibrant colors and bright lighting to encourage customers to get in and out quickly, ensuring the fast table turnover they require to be successful.

For many businesses, a drive-through window adds another dimension to the concept of customer convenience and is a relatively inexpensive way to increase sales. In the quick-service restaurant business, drive-through windows are an essential design component, accounting for 70 percent of sales, an increase from 60 percent in 2002.[60] Although drive-through windows are staples at fast-food restaurants and banks, they can add value for customers in other businesses as well, including drugstores, hardware stores, and even wedding chapels.

Lighting, Scent, and Sound

Retailers can increase sales by engaging all of customers' senses. Retail behavioral expert Paco Underhill, founder of Envirosell, a market research company, says that most of customers' unplanned purchases come after they touch, taste, smell, or hear something in a store. For example, stores that sell fresh food will see sales increase if they offer free samples to customers. "If somebody doesn't try 'em, they're not going to buy 'em," quips Underhill.[61] Lighting, scent, and sound are particularly important.

LIGHTING. Good lighting allows employees to work at maximum efficiency. Proper lighting is measured by the amount of light required to do a job properly with the greatest lighting efficiency. In a retail environment, proper lighting should highlight featured products and encourage customers to stop and look at them. "The lighting and the atmosphere created with the lighting really makes your store more spectacular," says the president of a design firm that specializes in restaurants and retail stores.[62] Efficiency also is essential because lighting consumes 24 percent of the total energy used in the typical commercial building.[63] Technological advances are increasing the popularity and lowering the cost of light-emitting diode (LED) lighting. LEDs use just 20 percent of the electricity of incandescent lights and 50 percent of compact fluorescent lights, and the best LED bulbs last 20 to 25 times longer than comparable incandescent bulbs.[64] LEDs also generate less heat, which reduces business's cooling costs.

Lighting provides a good return on investment given its overall impact on a business. Few people seek out businesses that are dimly lit because they convey an image of untrustworthiness. The use of natural light gives a business an open and cheerful look and can boost sales. A series of studies by energy research firm Heschong Mahone Group reports that stores using natural light experience sales that are 40 percent higher than those of similar stores using fluorescent lighting.[65] Similarly, a study by office furniture maker Haworth reports that employees who work in more natural environments (with natural light and external views) exhibit less job stress, more job satisfaction, and fewer ailments.[66]

SCENT. Research shows that scents can have a powerful effect in retail stores. The Sense of Smell Institute reports that the average human being can recognize 10,000 different aromas and can recall scents with 65 percent accuracy after 1 year, a much higher recall rate than visual stimuli produce. In one experiment, Eric Spangenberg of Washington State University diffused a subtle scent of vanilla into the women's department of a store and rose maroc into the men's department, he discovered that sales nearly doubled. He also discovered that if he switched the scents, sales in both departments fell well below their normal averages.[67]

Many companies—from casinos to retail stores—are beginning to understand the power of using scent as a marketing tool to evoke customers' emotions. Almost every bakery uses a fan to push the smell of fresh-baked breads and sweets into pedestrian traffic lanes, tempting them to sample some of their delectable goodies. "Smell has a greater impact on purchasing than everything else combined," says Alan Hirsch of the Smell & Taste Treatment & Research Foundation. "If something smells good, the product is perceived as good."[68] Thomas Pink, a company founded in 1984 by brothers James, Peter, and John Mullen in London that sells premium shirts, blouses, and ties, uses a signature "line-dried linen" scent in its 20 stores in the United States and others around the world.[69] Sony infuses its Style Stores with a blend of vanilla, orange, and cedar that is designed to make women shoppers feel more at ease.[70]

SOUND. Background music can be an effective merchandising tool if the type of music playing in a store matches the demographics of its target customers. Abercrombie & Fitch plays loud, upbeat music with a rhythmic beat that creates a nightclub-like atmosphere for its youthful customers, but Victoria's Secret uses classical music in its stores to reinforce an upscale image for its brand.[71] Research shows that music is a stimulant to sales because it reduces resistance; warps shoppers' sense of time, causing them to stay in the store longer; and helps to produce a positive mental association between the music and the store's intended image.[72] One rule seems clear for retail soundscapes: Slow is good. Because people's biorhythms often mirror the sounds around them, a gently meandering mix of classical music or soothing ambient noise encourages shoppers to slow down and relax. Classical music, in particular, makes shoppers feel affluent and boosts sales more than other types of music.[73] "If customers are moving less quickly," says shopping psychologist Tim Dennison, "they're more likely to engage with a product and make a purchase." The growing competition for the attention of time-pressed shoppers forces businesses to focus more on the total sensory experience they provide. "Retailers will have to make their stores more stimulating," says Dennison.[74]

Environmentally Friendly Design

Businesses are designing their buildings in more environmentally friendly ways not only because it is the right thing to do, but also because it saves money. In addition to saving energy (and the planet), companies that create well-planned, environmentally friendly designs see employee productivity increase by 3.5 to 10 percent.[75] Companies are using recycled materials; installing high-efficiency lighting, fixtures, and appliances; and incorporating LEED (Leadership in Energy and Environmental Design) principles into construction and renovation.

ENTREPRENEURIAL Profile

Joey Terrell: Denny's

Joey Terrell, a Denny's franchisee, recently built a new restaurant in Joliet, Illinois, that incorporates an environmentally friendly design. "It's one of the few LEED-certified restaurants in the country," says Terrell, who estimates that the restaurant saves $20,000 in utility costs alone per year. In addition to the operating savings it generates, the restaurant also cost $40,000 less to build than a traditional Denny's restaurant. Denny's is now incorporating many of the features in Terrell's restaurant into the design of its new outlets.[76]

▶ ENTREPRENEURSHIP IN ACTION ▶

Sneakerhead Heaven

For more than 30 years, Barry Pener has been managing Man of Fashion, a chain of 35 well-known stores that sell fashionable urban clothing and shoes founded by his grandfather in St. Louis, Missouri. In 2005, Pener noticed a new type of customer in his stores—sneakerheads, people (mostly men) who see sneakers as more than mere footwear and treat them as if they were works of art. Pener talked with his Nike sales representative, who confirmed the emerging trend. The sales representative told Pener about high-end sneaker stores in Los Angeles and New York City and suggested that he open a similar store in his Midwestern location. Pener flew to New York City to visit the stores, learn about their customers, and get ideas for opening his own high-end store in St. Louis. While there, he learned that sneakerheads tend to be

men between the ages of 18 and 34 who spend anywhere from $80 to $500 for a pair of upscale shoes from makers such as Nike, Puma, and Adidas. He also spotted a men's clothing store in New York City's funky SoHo district whose design caught his eye by creating a unique, exclusive look—the exact look that he wanted for his store aimed at sneakerheads.

Pener contacted the architectural firm that created the New York store's design and explained his plan to owner Carol Tobin. Several weeks later, Tobin pitched an unusual, counterintuitive idea for Pener's new store, which he had decided to name RSole. Rather than use a bold, in-your-face design, Tobin's idea was to create an "anonymous" storefront, one that would enhance its image of exclusivity. The theory is that an obscure storefront attracts elite shoppers. Pener loved the idea even though he knew that building a customer base would take more time. In the end, the wait would be worthwhile.

For his first RSole store, Pener secured a good location in St. Louis near the Washington University campus, and Tobin began transforming the space into something that looked more like an art gallery or a museum than a traditional shoe store. "They wanted to exhibit these sneakers they considered works of art in a way that would really emphasize the beauty, detail, and design of the sneakers," she says. The interior of the store is black, which makes the displays of colorful shoes "pop" and lends an air of sophistication and exclusivity to the store. Tobin also installed innovative lighting designs. "Black sucks up light," she says, "so we had to focus light intelligently. We installed fixtures at indirect angles in the walls and on the ceiling to add drama and draw attention to the shoes." Special, highly efficient LED lighting in the walls, some of which are recessed to create a "moving geometry," make displays of shoes look as though they are floating. The design also incorporates LED squares in the floor to define different selling areas and to create an entertaining, visually appealing element that guides customers through the store. The system, which borrows elements of theater lighting, allows employees to adjust the color and the intensity of the light the squares emit. "The LED squares direct people along certain paths, like emergency lighting," says Tobin.

Cash registers are located at the back of the store to create the image of a gallery, and Plexiglas panels "float" above the floor, creating displays and shelving that are unique and create a feeling of motion. "We wanted something exciting, something where the audio-visual component was alive so people weren't just seeing moving lights, but they were hearing music, maybe seeing a video of some music star doing something with the sneakers," Tobin explains. The panels along one wall are mounted on rods that allow them to rotate 360 degrees and lock at any position, giving employees the ability to vary the store layout. "We wanted [customers] to feel that there was movement and flexibility in the store," says Tobin.

The storefront uses an opaque film to coat the window glass that is interrupted by clear "peep holes" to pique customers' curiosity and encourage them to peer into the store from the street. "We opened, and I was really nervous," says Pener, because customer traffic was light. Three months later, however, customers had discovered the store. RSole was generating lots of buzz, particularly among its sneakerhead target customers, and foot traffic increased significantly. "Sneakerheads claim the store as their own and want to be associated with it," says Pener. RSole also received a marketing boost when celebrities such as Ted Ginn, Jr., of the Miami Dolphins and local hip-hop star Murphy Lee began shopping there. RSole sells more than 2,000 pairs of sneakers a month, and Pener recently opened a second location in Memphis, Tennessee. Pener credits his stores' unique layout and design with much of the success. "Without that, it would have been just another shoe store," he says.

1. What risks did Pener take by using a counterintuitive, gallery-like design in his RSole store? What was the payoff?
2. Use the Internet to conduct some basic research on sneakerheads. Is there a city in your state that you think would be a good location for an RSole store? Explain.
3. What role does the design of RSole's stores play in their success? Does RSole's unique interior design create the image for the store that Pener was seeking? Explain.

Sources: Based on Mina Kimes, "Secret Kicks," *FSB*, May 2009; Erin M. Loewe, "Shoe Envy," *All Business*, April 1, 2007, *www.allbusiness.com/ retail-trade/miscellaneous-retail/4165891-1.html.*

Layout: Maximizing Revenues, Increasing Efficiency, and Reducing Costs

7. Explain the principles of effective layouts for retailers, service businesses, and manufacturers.

The ideal layout depends on the type of business and on the entrepreneur's strategy for gaining a competitive edge. Retailers design their layouts with the goal of maximizing sales revenue; manufacturers design theirs to increase efficiency and productivity and to lower costs.

Layout for Retailers

Retail layout is the arrangement of merchandise in a store. A retailer's success depends, in part, on well-designed floor displays. Paco Underhill, retail consultant and author of *Why We Buy: The Science of Shopping*, calls a store's interior design "the stage on which a retail company functions."[77] Unfortunately, according to Underhill, most retailers do not consider what customers want to experience when designing their spaces.[78]

A retail layout should pull customers into the store and make it easy for them to locate merchandise; compare price, quality, and features; and ultimately make a purchase. In addition, a floor plan should take customers past displays of other items that they may buy on impulse. Research shows that 66 percent of all buying decisions are made once a customer enters a store, which means that the right layout can boost sales significantly. One study reports that 78 percent of general market shoppers make impulse purchases. Shoppers are heavily influenced by in-store displays, especially end-cap displays, those at the ends of aisles.[79]

Retailers have always recognized that some locations within a store are superior to others. Customer traffic patterns give the owner a clue to the best location for the highest gross margin items. Merchandise purchased on impulse and convenience goods should be located near the front of the store. Items people shop around for before buying and specialty goods attract their own customers and should not be placed in prime space. Prime selling space should be restricted to products that carry the highest markups.

Retail store layout evolves from a clear understanding of customers' buying habits. If customers come into the store for specific products and have a tendency to walk directly to those items, placing complementary products in their path increases sales. Observing customer behavior helps business owners to identify "hot spots," where merchandise sells briskly, and "cold spots," where it may sit indefinitely. By experimenting with factors such as traffic flow, lighting, aisle size, music type and audio levels, signs, and colors, an owner can discover the most productive store layout. For instance, one of the hot spots in a Barnes & Noble bookstore during the busy holiday season is the "Christmas table" at the front of the children's department. The table, which holds between 75 and 125 titles, draws consistent traffic and is the most desired spot for a book aimed at children.[80]

Business owners should display merchandise as attractively as their budgets allow. Customers' eyes focus on displays, which tell them the type of merchandise the business sells. It is easier for customers to relate to one display than to a rack or shelf of merchandise. Open displays of merchandise can surround the focal display, creating an attractive selling area. Retailers can boost sales by displaying together items that complement each other. For example, displaying ties near dress shirts or handbags next to shoes often leads to multiple sales.

Spacious displays provide shoppers an open view of merchandise and reduce the likelihood of shoplifting. An open, spacious image is preferable to a cluttered appearance. Display height is also important because customers won't buy what they cannot see or reach. When planning in-store displays, retailers should remember the following:

- **Make products easy to reach.** The average man is 68.8 inches tall, and the average woman is 63.6 inches tall. The average person's normal reach is 16 inches, and the extended reach is 24 inches. The average man's standing eye level is 62 inches from the floor, and the average woman's standing eye level is 57 inches from the floor.[81] Placing merchandise on very low or very high shelves discourages customers from making purchases. For example, putting hearing aid batteries on bottom shelves where the elderly have trouble getting to them or placing popular children's toys on top shelves where little ones cannot reach them hurts sales of these items. Walgreen's recently remodeled its store shelves to make products easier to reach.[82]
- **Shoppers prefer wide aisles.** One study found that shoppers, especially women, are reluctant to enter narrow aisles in a store. Narrow aisles force customers to jostle past one another, creating what experts call the "butt-brush factor." Open aisles allow customers to shop comfortably and encourage them to spend more time in a store.[83]
- **Placing shopping baskets in several areas around a store can increase sales.** Seventy-five percent of shoppers who pick up a basket buy something, compared to just 34 percent of customers who do not pick up a basket.[84] Smart retailers make shopping baskets available to customers throughout the store, not just at the entrance.
- **Make it easy to locate merchandise.** Making shoppers hunt for the items they want to buy lowers the probability that they will purchase an item and that they will return to a particular store. Easy-to-read signs, clearly marked aisles, and displays of popular items located near the entrance make it easy for shoppers to find their way around a store.

■ **Whenever possible, allow customers to touch the merchandise.** Customers are much more likely to buy items if they can pick them up. The probability that customers who are shopping for clothing will make purchases increases if they try on the garments. Therefore, having friendly sales representatives who offer to "start a dressing room" for customers who pick up articles of clothing pays off.[85]

Retailers should separate the selling and nonselling areas of a store and should never waste prime selling space with nonselling functions such as storage, receiving, office, and fitting areas. Although nonselling activities are necessary for a successful retail operation, they should not take precedence and occupy valuable selling and merchandising space. Many retailers place their nonselling departments in the rear of the building, recognizing the value of each foot of space in a retail store and locating their most profitable items in the best-selling areas. Entrepreneurs should use at least 80 percent of available retail space for selling and merchandising.

The various areas within a small store's interior space are not equal in generating sales revenue. Certain areas contribute more to revenue than others. The value of store space depends on floor location in a multistory building, location with respect to aisles and walkways, and proximity to entrances. Space values decrease as distance from the main entry-level floor increases. Selling areas on the main level contribute a greater portion to sales than do those on other floors because they offer greater exposure to customers than either basement or higher-level locations. Therefore, main-level locations carry a greater share of rent than other levels.

The layout of aisles in the store has a major impact on the customer exposure that merchandise receives. Items located on primary walkways should be assigned a higher share of rental costs and should contribute a greater portion to sales revenue than those displayed along secondary aisles. Space values also depend on the spaces' relative position to the store entrance, which serves as the "landing strip" for shoppers. A critical moment occurs when shoppers walk into a store as they slow down, try to orient themselves, and expand their peripheral vision to get a panoramic view of the retail spaces. An effective layout allows them to familiarize themselves with the retail landscape as quickly as possible.

ENTREPRENEURIAL
Profile

Old Navy

Clothing retailer Old Navy recently created a new layout for its stores using a "racetrack" layout in which the primary aisle starts at the store's entrance and loops through the entire store in a circular, square, or rectangular pattern. The goal of a racetrack layout is to expose customers to as much merchandise as possible and to encourage them to browse through other merchandise displayed on smaller "rabbit trails" that branch off of the main aisle. The new Old Navy layout also includes dressing rooms, a children's play area, and cash registers located in the center of the store and a "fundamentals" wall that displays low-priced items.[86]

Most American shoppers turn to the right when entering a store and will move around it counterclockwise.[87] That makes the front right-hand section of a retail store the "retail sweet spot." Retailers should put their best selling and highest profit margin items in this prime area. Only about one-fourth of a store's customers will go more than halfway into the store. Therefore, the farther away an area is from the entrance, the lower its value. Using these characteristics, Figure 4 illustrates space values for a typical small-store layout.

Understanding the value of store space ensures proper placement of merchandise. The items placed in the high-rent areas of the store should generate adequate sales and contribute enough profit to justify their high-value locations. The decline in value of store space from front to back of the shop is expressed in the 40-30-20-10 rule. This rule assigns 40 percent of a store's rental cost to the front quarter of the shop, 30 percent to the second quarter, 20 percent to the third quarter, and 10 percent to the final quarter. Each quarter of the store should contribute the same percentages of its sales revenue; if not, the business owner should reevaluate the store's layout.

FIGURE 4
The Space Value for a Small Store

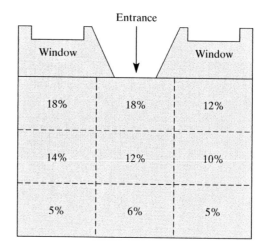

For example, suppose that the owner of a small retail store anticipates $520,000 in sales this year. Each quarter of the store should generate the following sales volume:

Front quarter	$520,000 × 0.40 = $208,000
Second quarter	$520,000 × 0.30 = $156,000
Third quarter	$520,000 × 0.20 = $104,000
Fourth quarter	$520,000 × 0.10 = $ 52,000
Total	**$520,000**

LESSONS FROM THE STREET-SMART ➤ entrepreneur

Creating a Layout and Design That Really Sells

Sephora, launched in 1993 as a French perfume chain, has stormed the makeup market in the United States, forcing other makeup retailers to change their tactics. For years, women shopping for makeup had two choices: drugstores that offered products in tightly sealed packages or department stores that required a hovering salesperson whose sales commission was tied to particular brands. Spotting an opportunity, managers at Sephora decided to break out of the traditional mold for marketing makeup, offering more than 13,000 products in one store and giving customers the freedom to explore and sample various types of makeup. Women can try lipsticks, eyeliners, blushes, and other products from more than 250 brands on their own, or they can ask for assistance from one of Sephora's highly trained sales associates.

The Street-Smart Entrepreneur offers business owners the following lessons learned by studying the factors behind Sephora's success.

Recognize that design and layout really are important, especially for retailers.

Customers look for visual cues to determine the character of a business. Your company's design and layout should reinforce the image you seek to create in your customers' minds. "The Sephora retail concept is rooted in aesthetics, presenting our clients with the most unique product assortment, store design, and client services," says Joey Manues, the company's store director. "Our locations became our advertising."

Make sure that your storefront offers a clean, inviting look that invites customers to enter.

Despite stocking more than 13,000 products, Sephora stores are always neat and orderly. The unspoken message Sephora sends to customers is clear: We offer a large selection of products, but they are always easy to find. Displays organize fragrances in alphabetical order and cosmetics by brand. Large storefront windows allow passersby to have a bird's-eye view of the store instantly and to see the breadth and depth of its product line.

Sephora's layout sends a clear signal to its customers: We offer an extensive selection of products, but they are easy to find.

Source: Wilfredo Lee/AP Wide World Photos

Create displays that "pop" to draw customers into your store.

Sephora stores showcase makeup and cosmetics in minimalist display cases that allow the vivid colors and appealing shapes of the products to draw customers in. The lipstick bar sparkles with more than 365 eye-popping colors, ranging from lavender and gold to blue and green, organized by hue. Strategically placed mirrors, cotton swabs, and makeup remover encourage customers to experiment—and buy.

Avoid pressuring customers.

Some businesses impose pushy salespeople on customers the moment they step into a store, a technique that turns off many customers and sends them bolting toward the exit. Sephora allows customers to browse at their own pace without pressure from a salesperson, which encourages them to linger. Some customers spend an hour or more trying out different products until they find those that are just right for them. Typically, the longer a customer stays, the more she buys.

Offer stellar customer service from well-trained employees.

Sephora does not abandon customers and leave them to fend for themselves. When a customer asks for assistance, sales associates are ready to bolt into action. Borrowing a page from Disney, Sephora calls its sales associates "cast members" and refers to the sales floor as "on stage." Cast members are highly trained, each one having completed a rigorous course of study on skin and hair care and general beauty that the company calls the Science of Sephora (S.O.S.) offered at Sephora University. Cast members offer customers free makeovers in scheduled appointments in specially designed staging areas.

Enhance your brand with visual cues.

All of Sephora's stores use the same color palette: black, white, and red. A red carpet welcomes customers at the entrance, and black-and-white floor tiles punctuate the stores' interior. The color theme also extends to the exterior, where bold black-and-white striped columns make storefronts stand out. Cast members dress in black designer tunics and slacks and wear no jewelry or makeup other than red lipstick and either red or clear nail polish—again reinforcing the brand with color. They also wear a single black glove, which serves as the ideal backdrop for displaying products (much like jewelers use black velvet backdrops to make their jewelry sparkle).

Make creative use of nonselling space to sell.

Sephora stores include beauty studios, where cast members offer customers a variety of 10-minute mini-classes on beauty tips and trends. Tutorials include topics such as

"Conceal and Reveal," "Day to Night," "Smoky Eye," and "A Clean Start." Beauty studios occupy space that Sephora could devote to product displays, but the way the company creatively uses this nonselling space actually generates sales that the company might not otherwise have made.

Sephora's success demonstrates the power of a store's layout and design. "Every aspect of the stores from their architectural layout and interior design to the background music to the customer experience is designed to reinforce a shopping experience that emphasizes freedom, exploration, discovery, and a personal definition of beauty," says CEO Daniel Richard.

Sources: Based on Leilani Salter, "Mississippi Just Got More Beautiful with Sephora Opening at Renaissance," *Mississippi Digital Daily*, May 10, 2010, www.msdigitaldaily.com/3/Lifestyles/CAT5/Mississippi%20just%20got%20more%20beautiful%20with%20Sephora%20opening%20at%20Renaissance/1805/default.aspx; "Sephora: Liberating Beauty Products," *Bloomberg Business Week*, January 25, 2006, www.businessweek.com/innovate/content/jan2006/id20060125_183621.htm.

Layout for Manufacturers

Manufacturing layout decisions take into consideration the arrangement of departments, workstations, machines, and stock-holding points within a production facility. The general objective is to arrange these elements to ensure a smooth workflow (in a production area) or a particular traffic pattern (in a service area).

Manufacturing facilities have come under increased scrutiny as firms attempt to improve quality, decrease inventories, and increase productivity through facilities that are integrated, flexible, and controlled. Facility layout has a dramatic effect on product mix, product processing, materials handling, storage, control, and production volume and quality. Some manufacturers are using 3-D simulation software (based on the same technology as the 3-D video games people play) to test the layout of their factory and its impact on employees and their productivity *before* they ever build them. The highly realistic simulations tell designers how well a particular combination of people, machinery, and environment interacts with one another. The software can identify potential problem areas, such as layouts that force workers into awkward positions that would cause injuries, equipment designs that cause workers to reach too far for materials, and layouts that unnecessarily add extra time to the manufacturing process by requiring extra materials handling or unneeded steps.[88]

FACTORS IN MANUFACTURING LAYOUT. The ideal layout for a manufacturing operation depends on several factors, including the following:

- *Type of product.* Product design and quality standards, whether the product is produced for inventory or for order, and physical properties, such as the size of materials and products' special handling requirements, susceptibility to damage, and perishability
- *Type of production process.* Technology used, types of materials handled, means of providing a service, and processing requirements in terms of number of operations involved and amount of interaction between departments and work centers
- *Ergonomic considerations.* To ensure worker safety, to avoid unnecessary injuries and accidents, and to increase productivity
- *Economic considerations.* Volume of production; costs of materials, machines, workstations, and labor; pattern and variability of demand; and length of permissible delays
- *Space availability within facility itself.* To ensure the space will adequately meet current and future manufacturing needs

TYPES OF MANUFACTURING LAYOUTS. Manufacturing layouts are categorized either by the work flow in a plant or by the production system's function. The three basic types of layouts that manufacturers can use separately or in combination are product, process, and fixed position. They differ in their applicability of different levels of manufacturing volume.

Product Layouts. In a **product (or line) layout,** a manufacturer arranges workers and equipment according to the sequence of operations performed on the product. Conceptually, the flow is an unbroken line from raw materials input to finished goods. This type of layout is applicable to rigid-flow, high-volume, continuous or mass-production operations or when the product is highly standardized. Automobile assembly plants, paper mills, and oil refineries are examples of product layouts. Product layouts offer the advantages of lower materials handling costs; simplified tasks that can be done with low-cost, lower-skilled labor; reduced amounts of work-in-process inventory; and relatively simplified production control activities. All units are routed along the same fixed path, and scheduling consists primarily of setting a production rate. Disadvantages of product layouts include their inflexibility, monotony of job tasks, high fixed investment in specialized equipment, and heavy interdependence of all operations. A breakdown in one machine or at one workstation can idle the entire line. Such a layout also requires the owner to duplicate many pieces of equipment in the manufacturing facility; duplication can be cost-prohibitive for a small firm.

Process Layouts. In a **process layout,** a manufacturer groups workers and equipment according to the general function they perform, without regard to any particular product. Process layouts are appropriate when production runs are short, when demand shows considerable variation and the costs of holding finished goods inventory are high, or when the product is customized. Process layouts have the advantages of being flexible for doing customer work and promoting job satisfaction by offering employees diverse and challenging tasks. Its disadvantages are the higher costs of materials handling, more skilled labor, lower productivity, and more complex production control. Because the workflow is intermittent, each job must be individually routed through the system and scheduled at the various work centers, and its status must be monitored individually.

Fixed-Position Layouts. In a **fixed-position layout,** the bulk of the final product is assembled in one spot; materials do not move down a line as in a product layout. Workers and equipment go to the materials rather than having the materials flow down a line to them. Aircraft assembly shops and shipyards typify this kind of layout.

DESIGNING LAYOUTS. The starting point in layout design is determining how and in what sequence product parts or service tasks flow together. One of the most effective techniques is to create an overall picture of the manufacturing process using assembly charts and process flowcharts. Given the tasks and their sequence and knowledge of the volume or products that can be produced, an entrepreneur can analyze space and equipment needs.

ANALYZING PRODUCTION LAYOUTS. Although there is no general procedure for analyzing the numerous interdependent factors that enter into layout design, specific layout problems lend themselves to detailed analysis. Two important criteria for selecting and designing a layout are worker effectiveness and materials handling costs.

Designing layouts ergonomically so that they maximize workers' strengths is especially important for manufacturers. Creating an environment that is comfortable and pleasant for workers will pay big benefits over time in the form of higher productivity, lower absenteeism and tardiness, and fewer injuries. Designers must be sure that they match the environment they create to workers' needs rather than trying to force workers to adapt to the environment.

Manufacturers can lower materials handling costs by using layouts designed to automate product flow whenever possible and to minimize flow distances and times. The extent of automation depends on the level of technology and amount of capital available, as well as behavioral considerations of employees. Flow distances and times are usually minimized by locating sequential processing activities or interrelated departments in adjacent areas. The following features are important to a good manufacturing layout:

1. Planned materials flow pattern
2. Straight-line layout where possible
3. Straight, clearly marked aisles
4. Backtracking kept to a minimum
5. Related operations close together
6. Minimum of in-process inventory
7. Easy adjustment to changing conditions
8. Minimum materials handling distances
9. Minimum of manual handling
10. No unnecessary rehandling of material
11. Minimum handling between operations
12. Materials delivered to production employees quickly
13. Use of gravity to move materials whenever possible
14. Materials efficiently removed from the work area

15. Materials handling done by indirect labor
16. Orderly materials handling and storage
17. Good housekeeping

Chapter Review

1. Explain the stages in the location decision.
   - The location decision is one of the most important decisions an entrepreneur will make, given its long-term effects on the company. An entrepreneur should look at the choice as a series of increasingly narrow decisions: Which region of the country? Which state? Which city? Which site?
   - Demographic statistics are available from a wide variety of sources, but government agencies such as the U.S. Census Bureau have a wealth of detailed data that can guide an entrepreneur in selecting the best location.
2. Describe the location criteria for retail and service businesses.
   - For retailers and many service businesses, the location decision is especially crucial. They must consider the size of the trade area, the volume of customer traffic, the number of parking spots, availability of room for expansion, and the visibility of a site.
3. Outline the basic location options for retail and service businesses.
   - Retail and service businesses have seven basic location options: central business districts (CBDs), neighborhoods, shopping centers and malls, near competitors, inside large retail stores, outlying areas, and at home.
4. Explain the site selection process for manufacturers.
   - A manufacturer's location decision is strongly influenced by local zoning ordinances. Some areas offer industrial parks designed specifically to attract manufacturers. Two crucial factors for most manufacturers are the accessibility to (and the cost of transporting) raw materials and the quality and quantity of available labor.
5. Discuss the benefits of locating a start-up company in a business incubator.
   - Business incubators are locations that offer flexible, low-cost rental space to their tenants as well as business and consulting services. Their goal is to nurture small companies until they are ready to "graduate" into the larger business community. Many government agencies and universities offer incubator locations.
6. Describe the criteria used to analyze the layout and design considerations of a building, including the Americans with Disabilities Act.
   - When evaluating the suitability of a particular building, an entrepreneur should consider several factors:
     - Size: Is the structure large enough to accommodate the business with some room for growth?
     - Construction and external appearance: Is the building structurally sound, and does it create the right impression for the business?
     - Entrances: Are they inviting?
     - Legal issues: Does the building comply with the Americans with Disabilities Act and, if not, how much will it cost to bring it up to standard?
     - Signs: Are they legible, well located, and easy to see?
     - Interior: Does the interior design contribute to your ability to make sales and is it ergonomically designed?
     - Lighting, scent, and sound: Is the lighting adequate to the tasks workers will be performing, and what is the estimated cost of lighting? Can the business use scents to stimulate sales? Is the background music the business use appropriate for its target audience?
7. Explain the principles of effective layout for retailers, service businesses, and manufacturers.
   - Layout for retail store and service businesses depends on the owner's understanding of customers' buying habits. Some areas of a retail store generate more sales per square foot and are, therefore, more valuable than others.
   - The goal of a manufacturer's layout is to create a smooth, efficient workflow. Three basic layout options exist: product, process, and fixed position. Two key considerations are worker productivity and materials handling costs.

Discussion Questions

1. How do most small business owners choose a location? Is this wise?
2. What factors should a manager consider when evaluating a region in which to locate a business? Where are such data available?
3. Outline the factors entrepreneurs should consider when selecting a state in which to locate a business.
4. What factors should a seafood-processing plant, a beauty shop, and an exclusive jewelry store consider in choosing a location?
5. What intangible factors might enter into the entrepreneur's location decision?
6. What are zoning laws? How do they affect the location decision?
7. What is the trade area? What determines a small retailer's trade area?
8. Why is it important to discover more than just the number of passersby in a traffic count?
9. What types of information can an entrepreneur collect from census data?
10. Why might a cheap location not be the best location?
11. What function does a small firm's sign serve? What are the characteristics of an effective business sign?
12. Explain the statement: "The portions of a small store's interior space are not of equal value in generating sales revenue." What areas are most valuable?
13. What are some of the major features that are important to a good manufacturing layout?

Business Plan Pro

For many businesses, analyzing the value of a potential business site is critical. Owners of retail- or service-based companies usually want high-traffic locations for optimal exposure. Owners of manufacturing, repair, or storage businesses must address issues regarding the location's suitability for their specific needs. Selecting the wrong location places a company at a disadvantage before it ever opens for business. This chapter emphasizes that selecting the right location is crucial to any business venture.

On the Web

The Web offers valuable information regarding location information. "Building a Guerrilla Marketing Plan" was the PRIZM information from Claritas, Inc. (*www.claritas.com/MyBestSegments/Default.jsp*). This information identifies the most common market segments in your zip code and may be a way to validate whether your location is in proximity to your target customers. PRIZM has categorized American consumer markets based on demographic and customer segmentation profiling research data by zip code. A restaurant or a retail business, for example, will find that locating close to its target customers is a key success factor. Additional information, such as traffic counts and other location attributes, are important factors to include in your business plan.

In the Software

Open your business plan and go to the "Your Company" section. Here is where you will describe your ideal, potential, or existing location. If the location you have chosen possesses many of the positive attributes mentioned in the chapter, identify your location as a strength. If your location has negative characteristics, recognize it as a weakness and develop a plan to address how you will overcome the challenges your location presents. If you determine that your location is a critical component for the success of the business, you should assess your location under the "Keys to Success" section. Remember to include the expense for your location—rent, lease, or mortgage payments—into the financial section of your plan.

Building Your Business Plan

Selecting your location is an important strategic business decision for most business ventures. Your business plan will help you profile, describe, and ultimately decide on the most attractive business location available. Once you have secured a location, your plan can leverage that location's strongest attributes to optimize customer exposure, sales, and profits.

Endnotes

1. Betty Joyce Nash, "West Virginia Glass Houses," *Region Focus*, Winter 2009, pp. 43–46.
2. Mark Henricks, "Hot Spots," *Entrepreneur*, October 2005, pp. 68–74.
3. Erick Schonfeld, "Forrester Forecast: Online Retail Sales Will Grow to $250 Billion by 2014," TechCrunch, March 8, 2010, *http://techcrunch. com/2010/03/08/forrester-forecast-online-retail-sales-will-grow-to-250-billion-by-2014/*.
4. Karen E. Klein, "Finding the Perfect Location," *BusinessWeek*, March 24, 2008, *www.businessweek.com/smallbiz/content/mar2008/ sb20080324_098559.htm?chan=smallbiz_smallbiz+index+page_top+ small+business+stories;* Nora Parker, "Johnny's Lunch Plans Franchise Expansion with LI," *Directions Magazine*, October 8, 2007, *www.directionsmag.com/article.php?article_id=2569&trv=1;* Chris Knape, "New Diner Downtown Is Johnny on the Spot," *Grand Rapids Press*, May 12, 2008, p. B4.
5. Jessica Bruder, "The Right Moves," *FSB*, April 2009, p. 16.
6. Daniel Brooks, "New IKEA Factory Hums," *Region Focus*, Fall 2009, p. 2.
7. "Oil-Dri Corporation of America," *Funding Universe*, *www. fundinguniverse.com/company-histories/OilDri-Corporation-of-America-Company-History.html*.
8. "Employer Costs for Employee Compensation for the Regions," Bureau of Labor Statistics, March 2010, *www.bls.gov/ro4/ro4ecec.htm*.
9. Jacquelyn Lynn, "Location Is Key," *Entrepreneur*, November 2008, p. 26.
10. Jason Daily, "Where to Be an Entrepreneur," *Entrepreneur*, August 2009, p. 51.
11. Ralph Bartholdt, "Couple: High Fees Preventing Dream of Sandpoint Restaurant," *Bonner County Daily Bee*, August 5, 2010, *http://bonnercountydailybee.com/articles/2010/08/05/news/ doc4c5a57423fa76606867788.txt*.
12. "State Individual Income Taxes 2007," Taxadmin.org, *www.taxadmin.org/FTA/rate/ind_inc.html*.
13. Michael McCann, "LeBron James and His Big Decision: Thoughts on the Role of Endorsement Income Potential and State Income Taxes," *Sports Law Blog*, July 8, 2010, *http://sports-law.blogspot.com/2010/07/ lebron-james-and-his-big-decision.html*.
14. David Farkas, "Site Selection: Where Good Food Means the Most," *Chain Leader*, September 1, 2009, pp. 14–17.
15. Alex P. Kellogg, "Black Flight Hits Detroit," *Wall Street Journal*, June 5–6, 2010, pp, A1, A12; Alex P. Kellogg, "Detroit's Smaller Reality," *Wall Street Journal*, February 27–28, 2010, p. A3.
16. Sue Shellenbarger, "The Next Youth-Magnet Cities," *Wall Street Journal*, September 30, 2009, p. D1; Garth Stein, "Seattle Grace," *Fast Company*, May 2009, pp. 92–96.
17. "Clusters and Cluster Development," Institute for Strategy and Competitiveness, Harvard Business School, *www.isc.hbs.edu/ econ-clusters.htm*.
18. Austin Carr, "Fast Cities 2010: Venture Capital Mindset," *Fast Company*, May 2010, p. 87; John Mangels, "Biotech Start-up Hopes Light-Activated Nerve Cells Will Make It a Northeast Ohio Star," Cleveland.com, September 1, 2009, *http://blog.cleveland.com/metro/ 2009/09/biotech_startup_hopes_lightact.html*.
19. David Van Den Berg, "Cinemas Prosper During Recession," *Region Focus*, Winter 2009, p. 2.
20. Sarah Kerner, "Anna Awards First Economic Development Grant," *Collin County Business Press*, August 2, 2010, *www.ccbizpress.com/ display.php?id=4175*.
21. Matt Woolsey, "America's Top 25 Towns to Live Well," *Forbes*, May 4, 2009, *www.forbes.com/2009/05/04/towns-cities-real-estate-lifestyle-real-estate-top-towns.html*.
22. "Worker Relocation Worries," *Inside Training Newsletter*, November 29, 2007, p. 1.
23. Gay Telese, "BASTA," *New Yorker*, May 31, 2010, *www.newyorker.com/talk/2010/05/31/100531ta_talk_talese*.
24. Ron Ruggless, "BK Debuts Whopper Bar Concept, Eyes On-site Arena in Plan to Beef Up Growth," *Nation's Restaurant News*, *www.nrn.com/landingPage.aspx?menu_id=1424&coll_id=676&id=364528;* "BK to Debut Whopper Bar Next Year," *Nation's Restaurant News*, October 7, 2008, *www.nrn.com/breakingNews.aspx?id=359160*.
25. Molly Gise, "Krispy Kreme Debuts Smaller 'Neighborhood Shop' Concept," *Nation's Restaurant News*, August 3, 2009, *www.nrn.com/ article/krispy-kreme-debuts-smaller-neighborhood-shop-concept*.
26. Shannon Perez, "6 Tips to Finding the Perfect Location for Your Practice," MassageTherapy.com, *www.massagetherapy.com/articles/ index.php/article_id/1377*.
27. Matt Rosenberg, "About Reilly's Law of Retail Gravitation," About.com, *http://geography.about.com/cs/citiesurbangeo/a/ aa041403a.htm;* G. I. Thrall and J. C. del Valle, "The Calculation of Retail Market Areas: The Reilly Model," *GeoInfoSystems*, Vol. 7, No. 4, 1997, pp. 46–49.
28. "U.S. Mall Vacancy Average Hits 9 Percent in Second Quarter, Report Says," International Council of Shopping Centers, July 7, 2010, *www.icsc.org/apps/news_item.php?id=2642*.
29. Carolyn Tamler, "Meet Nymbol, the Nicest Bogart in Langley, Washington," *Whidbey Island Life Examiner*, July 8, 2010, *www.examiner.com/life-in-seattle/meet-nymbol-the-nicest-bogart-langley-washington*.
30. Paul Lukas, "Our Malls, Ourselves," *Fortune*, October 18, 2004, pp. 243–256.
31. "Industry Fun Facts," International Council of Shopping Centers, *www.icsc.org/srch/about/impactofshoppingcenters/Did_You_Know.pdf*.
32. Parija Bhatnagar, "Not a Mall. It's a Lifestyle Center," *CNN/Money*, January 12, 2005, *http://money.cnn.com/2005/01/11/news/fortune500/ retail_lifestylecenter/*.
33. Kris Hudson and Vanessa O'Connell, "Recession Turns Malls into Ghost Towns," *Wall Street Journal*, May 22, 2009, pp. A1, A10.
34. Tony Tagliavia, "Ground Broken on New 'Lifestyle' Mall," *Wood Television*, October 6, 2009, *www.woodtv.com/dpp/news/local/kent_ county/knapp_crossing_groundbreaking*.
35. Paul Lukas, "Our Malls, Ourselves," *Fortune*, October 18, 2004.
36. "Industry Fun Facts," International Council of Shopping Centers; "About Mall of America," Mall of America, *www.mallofamerica.com/ about_moa_faqs.aspx*.
37. "Frequently Asked Questions," Small Business Administration, Office of Advocacy, September 2009, p.1; Ying Lowrey, *Start-up Business Characteristics and Dynamics: A Data Analysis of the Kauffman Firm Survey*, Small Business Administration Office of Advocacy, August 2009, p. 20.
38. Raymund Flandez, "Entrepreneurs Pack Up and Go Home," *Wall Street Journal*, June 2, 2009, pp. B1, B6.
39. Lynne P. Shackleford, "Injunction Forbids Weddings at Farm," *Spartanburg Herald-Journal*, June 28, 2009, p. A1; Jennifer Phillips, "Judge Orders Spiegel Farms to Close," *Fox Carolina*, July 30, 2009, *www.foxcarolina.com/news/20223898/detail.html*.
40. Deborah Ball, "Bottled Water Pits Nestle vs. Greens," *Wall Street Journal*, May 25, 2010, pp. A1, A16.
41. Ron Starner, "The Price of Success," *Site Selection*, September 2009, *www.siteselection.com/features/2009/sep/California/*.
42. Elizabeth Whiteman, Marc Chittum, and Michael Masserman, "Foreign Trade Zones Record Increase in Shipments," International Trade Administration, *http://trade.gov/press/publications/newsletters/ ita_0110/shorttakes_0110.asp*.
43. "Business Incubation FAQ," National Business Incubation Association, *www.nbia.org/resource_center/bus_inc_facts/index.php*.
44. Sarah E. Needleman, "Entrepreneurs Find New Way to Grow," *Wall Street Journal*, May 22, 1020, p. B5; Michael V. Copeland, "Making Detroit High Tech," *Fortune*, March 1, 2010, pp. 29–30; Nitasha Tiku and April Joyner, "Where Great Ideas Are Born," *Inc.*, May 2010, 44–47.
45. "Business Incubation FAQ," National Business Incubation Association.
46. "What Is Business Incubation?" National Business Incubation Association, March 31, 2006, *www.nbia.org/resource_center/ what_is/index.php*.
47. "Business Incubation FAQ," National Business Incubation Association.
48. *The Gensler Design + Performance Index: The U.S. Workplace Study*, Gensler Inc., October 22, 2008, p. 12.
49. "Workplace Design = Job Performance?" *Inside Training*, October 29, 2008, p. 1.
50. *The Integrated Workplace*, Office of Governmentwide Policy, Office of Real Property, Washington, DC: 2008, pp. 8–9.
51. Michal Lev-Ram, "How to Make Your Workspace Work Better," *Business 2.0*, November 2006, pp. 58–60.
52. Laura Tiffany, "The Rules of . . . Retailing," *Business Start-Ups*, December 1999, p. 106; Paul Keegan, "The Architect of Happy Customers," *Business 2.0*, August 2002, pp. 85–87.

53. Elizabeth Razzi, "Retailers' Siren Song," *Kiplinger's Personal Financial Magazine*, November 2000, pp. 130–134.
54. Tiffany, "The Rules of . . . Retailing," p. 106.
55. "Educational Kit," President's Committee on Employment of People with Disabilities, *www50.pcepd.gov/pcepd/archives/pubs/ek99/wholedoc.htm#decisions*.
56. Brian Amble, "Poor Workplace Design Damages Productivity," *Management-Issues*, May 23, 2006, *www.management-issues.com/2006/8/24/research/poor-workplace-design-damages-productivity.asp*.
57. "Injuries, Illnesses, and Fatalities," Bureau of Labor Statistics, U.S. Department of Labor, November 12, 2009, p. 1; "Proposal for an Ergonomics Program Standard," Occupational Health and Safety Administration, *www.osha-slc.gov/ergonomics-standard/ergo-faq.html*.
58. "Carpal Tunnel Syndrome," The National Women's Health Information Center, Department of Health and Human Services, *www.womenshealth.gov/faq/carpal-tunnel-syndrome.cfm*.
59. Linda Tischler, "Death to the Cubicle!" *Fast Company*, June 2005, pp. 29–30.
60. Mike Hughlett, "Drive-Throughs Done Right Ring up Returns," *Chicago Tribune*, November 28, 2008, *www.chicagotribune.com/business/chi-fri-drive-throughs-1128-nov28,0,4729183.story*.
61. "Paco Underhill: Shopping Scientist," *CBC News*, November 7, 2000, *www.cbc.ca/consumers/market/files/home/shopping/index.html*.
62. "The Five Guys Mistake," *QSR Magazine*, August 2010, *www.qsrmagazine.com/articles/second_location/144/fiveguys-1.phtml*.
63. Tiffany Meyers, "Waste Not," *Entrepreneur*, February 2008, p. 75.
64. Michael V. Copeland, "The Light Bulb Goes Digital," *Fortune*, February 8, 2010, pp. 33–38.
65. Jennifer Alsever, "Showing Products in a Better Light," *Business 2.0*, September 2005, p. 62.
66. Josh Gould, "Sustainable Workplace Design Creates Innovation Opportunities," *Buildings*, July 2009, *www.buildings.com/tabid/3413/ArticleID/8617/Default.aspx*.
67. *Dollars and Sense: The Impact of Multi-Sensory Marketing*, 4Imprint, 2009, p. 3, *http://info.4imprint.com/wp-content/uploads/blue-paper-sensory-marketing.pdf*.
68. Suzanne Hoppough, "What's That Smell?" *Forbes*, October 2, 2006, p. 76.
69. Ibid.
70. James Vlahos, "Scent and Sensibility," *New York Times*, September 9, 2007, *http://query.nytimes.com/gst/fullpage.html?res=9D07EFDC1E3AF93AA3575AC0A9619C8B63&sec=&spon=&pagewanted=2*.
71. *Dollars and Sense: The Impact of Multi-Sensory Marketing*, 4Imprint.
72. Colleen Bazdarich, "In the Buying Mood? It's the Muzak," *Business 2.0*, March 2002, p. 100.
73. Nadine Heintz, "Play Bach, Boost Sales," *Inc.*, January 2004, p. 23.
74. Theunis Bates, "Volume Control," Time.com, August 2, 2007, *www.time.com/time/printout/0,8816,1649304,00.html*.
75. Josh Gould, "Sustainable Workplace Design Creates Innovation Opportunities," *Buildings*, July 2009, *www.buildings.com/tabid/3413/ArticleID/8617/Default.aspx*.
76. Joey Terrell, "How I Turned My Denny's Green," *Entrepreneur*, January 2010, p. 100.
77. Paul Keegan, "The Architect of Happy Customers," *Business 2.0*, August 2002, pp. 85–87.
78. Russell Boniface, "I Spy a Shopper," *AIArchitect*, June 23, 2006, *www.aia.org/aiarchitect/thisweek06/0623/0623paco.cfm*.
79. "Survey: 43 Percent of Shoppers Rely on Lists," *Retail Shopping Experience*, August 19, 2010, *www.retailcustomerexperience.com/article/139799/Survey-43-percent-of-customers-rely-on-shopping-lists*.
80. Jeffrey A, Trachtenberg, "How a Children's Book Got a Christmas Break," *Wall Street Journal*, December 5, 2005, pp. B1, B5.
81. Tom Stevens, "Practice People," *IndustryWeek*, March 17, 1997, pp. 33–36.
82. Judy Sharpton, "I Love It When I'm Right," *Green Profit*, April 15, 2010, *www.ballpublishing.com/greenprofit/ViewArticle.aspx?articleid=17755*.
83. Zach Dundas, "The Butt-Brush Factor," *Willamette Weekly*, December 15, 2004, *http://wweek.com/story.php?story=5822*.
84. Paul Keegan, "The Architect of Happy Customers," *Business 2.0*, August 2002, pp. 85–87; Kenneth Labich, "This Man Is Watching You," *Fortune*, July 19, 1999, pp. 131–134.
85. Keegan, "The Architect of Happy Customers," pp. 85–87.
86. Rachel Tobin Ramos, "Old Navy Stores Go Under the Knife," *Atlanta Journal Constitution*, March 17, 2010, *www.ajc.com/business/old-navy-stores-go-378109.html*.
87. Boniface, "I Spy a Shopper."
88. "Release Me," *Entrepreneur*, January 1998, pp. 48–49.

Staffing and Leading a Growing Company

Learning Objectives

Upon completion of this chapter, you will be able to:

1. Explain the challenges involved in the entrepreneur's role as leader and what it takes to become a successful leader.
2. Describe the importance of hiring the right employees and how to avoid making hiring mistakes.
3. Explain how to build the kind of company culture and structure to support the company's mission and goals and to motivate employees to achieve them.
4. Understand the potential barriers to effective communication and describe how to overcome them.
5. Discuss the ways in which entrepreneurs can motivate their employees to achieve higher levels of performance.

The speed of the leader determines the rate of the pack.

—Anonymous

It doesn't make any difference whether the product is cars or
cosmetics. A company is only as good as the people it keeps.

—Mary Kay Ash

From Chapter 19 of *Effective Small Business Management: An Entrepreneurial Approach*, 10/e. Norman M. Scarborough.

The Entrepreneur's Role as Leader

1. Explain the challenges involved in the entrepreneur's role as leader and what it takes to be a successful leader.

To be successful, an entrepreneur must assume a wide range of roles, tasks, and responsibilities, but none is more important than the role of leader. Some entrepreneurs are uncomfortable assuming this role, but they must learn to be effective leaders if their companies are to grow and reach their potential. **Leadership** is the process of influencing and inspiring others to work to achieve a common goal and then giving them the power and the freedom to achieve it. Without leadership ability, entrepreneurs—and their companies—never rise above mediocrity. Entrepreneurs can learn to be effective leaders, but the task requires dedication, discipline, and hard work. In the past, business owners often relied on an autocratic management style, one built on command and control. Today's workforce is more knowledgeable, has more options, is more skilled, and, as a result, expects a different, more sophisticated style of leadership. Companies that fail to provide that leadership are at risk of losing their best employees. Leaders of small companies must gather information and make decisions with lightning-fast speed, and they must give workers the resources and the freedom to solve problems and exploit opportunities as they arise. Effective leaders empower employees to act in the best interest of the business.

Until recently, experts compared a leader's job to that of a symphony orchestra conductor. Like the symphony leader, an entrepreneur made sure that everyone in the company was playing the same score, coordinated individual efforts to produce a harmonious sound, and directed the orchestra members as they played. The conductor (entrepreneur) retained virtually all of the power and made all of the decisions about how the orchestra would play the music, without any input from the musicians themselves. Today's successful entrepreneur, however, is more like the leader of a jazz band, which is known for its improvisation, innovation, creativity, and free-wheeling style. "The success of a small [jazz band] rests on the ability to be agile and flexible, skills that are equally central to today's business world," says Michael Gold, founder of Jazz Impact, a company that teaches management skills through jazz.[1] Business leaders, like the leaders of jazz bands, should exhibit the following characteristics:

- *Innovative.* Leaders must step out of their own comfort zones to embrace new ideas; they avoid the comfort of complacency.
- *Passionate.* One of entrepreneurs' greatest strengths is their passion for their businesses. Members of their team feed off of that passion and draw inspiration from it.
- *Willing to take risks.* "[Taking] risk is not an option in jazz or for any company that wants to be solvent 10 years from now," says Gold.[2]
- *Adaptable.* Although leaders must stand on a bedrock of resolute values, like jazz band leaders, they must adapt their leadership styles to fit the situation and the people involved.

Management and leadership are not the same; yet, both are essential to a company's success. Leadership without management is unbridled; management without leadership is uninspired. Leadership gets a small business going; management keeps it going. In other words, leaders are the architects of small businesses; managers are the builders.

Some entrepreneurs are good managers yet are poor leaders; others are powerful leaders but are weak managers. The best bet for the latter is to hire people with solid management skills to help them to execute the vision they have for their companies. Stephen Covey, author of *Principle-Centered Leadership*, explains the difference between management and leadership in this way:

Leadership deals with people; management deals with things. You manage things; you lead people. Leadership deals with vision; management deals with logistics toward that vision. Leadership deals with doing the right things; management focuses on doing things right. Leadership deals with examining the paradigms on which you are operating; management operates within those paradigms. Leadership comes first, then management, but both are necessary.[3]

Leadership and management are intertwined; one without the other means that a small business is going nowhere. Leadership is especially important for companies in the growth phase, when entrepreneurs are hiring employees (often for the first time) and must keep the company and everyone in it focused on its mission as growth tests every seam in the fabric of the organizational structure. At this stage, selling everyone in the company on the mission, goals, and objectives for which the leader is aiming is crucial to a business's survival and success. "People don't want to be managed," says one CEO. "They want to be led."[4] Effective leaders exhibit certain behaviors. They:

- *Create a set of values and beliefs for employees and passionately pursue them.* Employees look to their leaders for guidance when making decisions. True leaders focus attention on the principles, values, and beliefs on which they founded their companies.
- *Establish a culture of ethics.* One of the most important tasks facing leaders is to mold a highly ethical culture for their companies. They also must demonstrate the character and the courage necessary to stick to the ethical standards that they create—especially in the face of difficulty.
- *Define and then constantly reinforce the vision they have for the company.* Effective leaders have a clear vision of where they want their companies to go, and they concentrate on communicating that vision to those around them. Unfortunately, this is one area in which employees say their leaders could do a better job. Clarity of purpose is essential to a successful organization because people want to be a part of something that is bigger than they are; however, the purpose must be more than merely achieving continuous quarterly profits.
- *Respect and support employees.* To gain the respect of their employees, leaders must first respect those who work for them.
- *Set the example for employees.* Leaders' words ring hollow if they fail to "practice what they preach." Few signals are transmitted to workers faster than the hypocrisy of leaders who sell employees on one set of values and principles and then act according to a different set.
- *Create a climate of trust in the organization.* Leaders who demonstrate integrity soon win the trust of their employees, an essential ingredient in the success of any organization. Honest, open communication and a consistent pattern of leaders doing what they say they will do serve to build trust in a business. Research suggests that building trust among employees is one of the most important tasks of leaders, wherever they may work. Building trust demands that leaders rely on three "Cs": competence (the leader is able to get the job done), consistency (the leader's actions are reliable, whatever the situation), and caring (the leader demonstrates compassion for those he or she leads).[5] Employees at small businesses are more likely to trust their leaders than employees at large companies.[6]
- *Build credibility with their employees.* To be effective, leaders must have credibility with their employees, a sometimes challenging task for entrepreneurs, especially as their companies grow and they become insulated from the daily activities of their businesses. To combat the problem of losing touch with the problems their employees face as they do their jobs, many managers periodically return to the front line to serve customers. For instance, at Southwest Airlines top managers spend 1 day each quarter loading baggage onto planes, checking passengers onto flights, serving as flight attendants, and performing other frontline jobs.[7] The idea is that top managers will make better decisions about policies and procedures if they see firsthand the impact of those decisions on customers and frontline employees.
- *Focus employees' efforts on challenging goals and keep them driving toward those goals.* Effective leaders have a clear vision of where they want their companies to go, and they are able to communicate their vision to those around them. Leaders must repeatedly reinforce the goals they set for their companies.
- *Provide the resources employees need to achieve their goals.* Effective leaders know that workers cannot do their jobs well unless they have the tools they need. They provide workers with not only the physical resources they need to excel, but also the necessary intangible resources, such as training, coaching, and mentoring.
- *Communicate with employees.* Leaders recognize that helping workers to see the company's overarching goal is just one part of effective communication; encouraging employee feedback and then listening is just as vital. In other words, they know that communication is a two-way street.
- *Value the diversity of workers.* Smart business leaders recognize the value of their workers' varied skills, abilities, backgrounds, and interests. When channeled in the right direction, diversity can be a powerful weapon in achieving innovation and maintaining a competitive edge.

- *Celebrate workers' successes.* Effective leaders recognize that workers want to be winners and do everything they can to encourage top performance among their people. The rewards they give are not always financial; in many cases, a reward may be as simple as a handwritten congratulatory note.
- *Value risk-taking.* Effective leaders recognize that in a rapidly changing competitive environment, they must make decisions with incomplete information and be willing to take risks to succeed.
- *Understand that leadership is multidimensional.* Smart leaders know that there is no single "best" style of leadership. The dimensions of leadership change depending on the people participating, the conditions and circumstances of the situation, and the desired outcome.
- *Value new ideas from employees.* Successful leaders know that because employees work every day on the front lines of the business, they see ways to improve quality, customer service, and business systems.
- *Understand that success really is a team effort.* Small companies typically depend more on their founding entrepreneurs than on anyone else. After all, someone has to take responsibility for the toughest decisions. However, effective leaders understand that their roles are only a small piece of the entire company puzzle.

*Larry McDonnell:
Waste Management*

Undercover Boss, a television series on CBS, features CEOs of companies ranging from Waste Management and Choice Hotels to White Castle and Hooters. The CEOs are disguised as new employees as they take on jobs on the front lines of their companies, where the "real work" is performed. In one episode, Larry McDonnell, CEO of Waste Management, cleans toilets and rides a garbage truck route. Along the way, he encounters hard-working people who do everything they can to help "the new guy" succeed and learns about the struggles workers face every day. In addition to seeing firsthand just how difficult many jobs can be, all of the CEOs had a superb refresher course in how important every worker's role is in the success of a company and how the policies that they and other senior managers create often make workers' jobs harder.

- *Encourage creativity among workers.* Rather than punish workers who take risks and fail, effective leaders are willing to accept failure as a natural part of innovation and creativity. They know that innovative behavior is the key to future success. They do everything they can to encourage creativity among workers.
- *Create an environment in which people have the motivation, the training, and the freedom to achieve the goals they have set.* Leaders know that *their* success depends on the success of their followers.
- *Become a catalyst for change.* With market and competitive climates changing so rapidly, entrepreneurs must reinvent their companies constantly. Although leaders must cling to the values and principles that form the bedrock of their companies, they must be willing to change, sometimes radically, the policies, procedures, and processes within their businesses. If a company is headed in the wrong direction, the leader's job is to recognize that and to get the company moving in the right direction. "No leader knows enough about the future to make the optimal decision every time, but it's better to set a clear course today and tackle problems that arise tomorrow," says Andy Grove, former CEO of Intel, the computer chip maker.[8]
- *Develop leadership talent.* Effective leaders look beyond themselves to spot tomorrow's leaders and take the time to help them grow into their leadership potential.
- *Maintain a sense of humor.* One of the most important tools a leader can have is a sense of humor. Without it, work can become dull and unexciting for everyone.
- *Behave with integrity at all times.* Real leaders know that they set the ethical tone in the organization. Even small lapses in a leader's ethical standards can have a significant impact on a company's ethical climate. Workers know they can trust leaders whose actions support their words. Similarly, they quickly learn not to trust leaders whose day-to-day dealings belie the principles they preach.
- *Keep an eye on the horizon.* Effective leaders are never satisfied with what they and their employees accomplished yesterday. They know that yesterday's successes are not enough to sustain their companies indefinitely. They see the importance of building and maintaining sufficient momentum to carry their companies to the next level.

Leading an organization, whatever its size, is one of the biggest challenges any entrepreneur faces. Yet, for an entrepreneur, leadership success is one of the key determinants of a company's success. Research suggests that there is no single "best" style of leadership; the style a leader uses depends, in part, on the situation at hand. Some situations are best suited for a participative leadership style, but in others an authoritarian style actually may be best. Research by Daniel Goleman and others suggests that today's workers tend to respond more to adaptive, humble leaders who are results-oriented and who take the time to cultivate other leaders in the organization.[9] The practice is known as **servant leadership**, a phrase coined by Robert Greenleaf in 1970. Servant leaders are servants *first* and leaders *second*, putting their employees and their employees' needs ahead of their own. They are more concerned about empowering others in the organization than they are at enhancing their own power bases. "Servant leadership is about getting people to a higher level by leading people at a higher level," says author Ken Blanchard.[10]

Entrepreneurs cannot bestow the mantle of "leader" on themselves. Managers may inherit their subordinates, but leaders have to *earn* their followers. An entrepreneur's employees determine whether he or she is worthy of leadership. *Without followers, there are no leaders.* Astute leaders know that their success depends on their employees' success. After all, the employees actually do the work, implement the strategies, and produce the results. Successful leaders establish an environment in which their followers can achieve success. Joe Tortorice, Jr., founder and CEO of Jason's Deli, a privately owned company with 219 restaurants in 28 states, says "People are looking for three things out of their leaders: direction, trust, and hope."[11]

To be effective, entrepreneurial leaders must perform four vital tasks:

- Hire the right employees and constantly improve their skills.
- Build an organizational culture and structure that allows both workers and the company to reach their potential.
- Communicate the vision and the values of the company effectively and create an environment of trust among workers.
- Motivate workers to higher levels of performance.

Hiring the Right Employees: The Company's Future Depends on It

2. Describe the importance of hiring the right employees and how to avoid making hiring mistakes.

The decision to hire a new employee is an important one for every business, but it is *especially* important for small businesses because the impact of a single hire on a small company is significant. "As an entrepreneur, every single hire is critical," says Stephen Fairley, CEO of the Rainmaker Institute, a business-coaching firm.[12] Every new employee a business owner hires determines the heights to which the company can climb—or the depths to which it will plunge. "Bad hires" can poison a small company's culture for years.

Hiring mistakes also are expensive. Although some employee turnover is healthy, high employee turnover rates cost companies billions of dollars annually. Employee turnover costs a company anywhere from one-half the value of an hourly worker's annual wages and benefits to 3 to 5 times the value of a manager's salary and benefits.[13] Consider a small business with 20 employees that has an employee turnover rate of 25 percent, the national average. Assuming that the employees earn wages that are consistent with the national average (about $39,200) and receive benefits that total 25 percent of their wages, the *minimum* turnover cost to the company is $122,500. The average turnover cost the company incurs is about $490,000!

Unfortunately, hiring mistakes in business are all too common. The culprit in most cases? The company's selection and hiring process. A recent survey by SurePayroll reports that 75 percent of business owners say that they have hired at least one employee they later wish they never had.[14] One study reported in the *Harvard Business Review* concludes that 80 percent of employee turnover is caused by bad hiring decisions.[15] Some small business owners invest more time and effort into deciding which copy machine to lease than which employee to hire for a key position.

The most common causes of a company's poor hiring decisions include:

- Managers who rely on candidates' descriptions of themselves rather than requiring candidates to demonstrate their abilities.
- Managers who fail to follow a consistent, evidence-based selection process. Forty-seven percent of managers admit that they make hiring decisions in 30 minutes or less,

and 44 percent of managers say that they rely on their intuition to make hiring decisions.

■ Managers who fail to provide candidates with sufficient information about what the jobs for which they are hiring actually entail.[16]

As crucial as finding good employees is to a small company's future, it is no easy task because entrepreneurs face a labor shortage, particularly among knowledge-based workers. The severity of this shortage will worsen as baby boomers retire in increasing numbers and the growth rate of the U.S. labor force slows.

How to Hire Winners

Even though the importance of hiring decisions is magnified in small companies, small businesses are most likely to make hiring mistakes because they lack the human resources experts and the disciplined hiring procedures large companies have. In many small businesses, the hiring process is informal, and the results often are unpredictable. The following guidelines can help entrepreneurs to hire winners and avoid making costly hiring mistakes as they build their team of employees.

COMMIT TO HIRING THE BEST TALENT. Smart entrepreneurs follow the old adage, "A players hire A players; B players hire C players." They are not threatened by hiring people who may be smarter and more talented than they are. In fact, they recognize that doing so is the best way to build a quality team.

ELEVATE RECRUITING TO A STRATEGIC POSITION IN THE COMPANY. Assembling a quality workforce begins with a sound recruiting effort. By investing time and money at this crucial phase of the staffing process, entrepreneurs can generate spectacular savings down the road by hiring the best talent. The recruiting process is the starting point for building quality into a company. Recruiting is so important that many entrepreneurs choose to become actively involved in the process themselves. Visionary entrepreneurs *never* stop recruiting because top quality talent is hard to find and is extremely valuable. Tom Bonney, founder of CMF Associates, a fast-growing financial consulting firm in Philadelphia, knows that finding superior talent is essential to the success of his service business. "I never stop recruiting," he says. "Even if I don't have a need, I am always looking."[17]

Attracting a pool of qualified job candidates requires not only constant attention but also creativity, especially among smaller companies that often find it difficult to match the more generous offers large companies make. With a sound recruiting strategy and a willingness to look in new places, however, smaller companies *can* hire and retain high-caliber employees. The following techniques will help.

Look inside the company first. One of the best sources for top prospects is right inside the company itself. A policy of promotion from within serves as an incentive for existing workers to upgrade their skills and to produce results. In addition, an entrepreneur already knows the employee's work habits, and the employee already understands the company's culture. At Advanced Technology Institute (ATI), a research and development management company in North Charleston, South Carolina, more than 60 percent of all jobs are filled from within the company.[18]

Encourage employee referrals. To cope with the shortage of available talent, many companies are offering their employees (and others) bonuses for referring candidates who come to work and prove to be valuable employees. Employees serve as reliable screens because they do not want to jeopardize their reputations with their employer. Employee referrals from social networks such as LinkedIn, Facebook, and Twitter allow employers to tap into their employees' network of contacts. At Dixon Schwabl, an advertising and public relations firm in Victor, New York, 90 percent of the company's new hires come from employee referrals. The system works well; employee turnover is less than 3 percent.[19]

Use multiple channels to recruit talent. Although newspaper ads still top employers' list of job postings, many businesses are successfully attracting candidates through other media, particularly the Internet. Posting job listings on career-oriented sites such as Monster.com, Hotjobs.com, and others not only expands a small company's reach far beyond an ad in a local newspaper, but also is very inexpensive. Employers also are connecting with potential employees (not all of whom are actively seeking new jobs) through their employees' networks of contacts; company blogs; career sites, such as LinkedIn; and social media sites, such as Facebook and Twitter. In fact, nearly 75 percent of companies use career and social networking sites to recruit employees, and 58 percent of managers say that they have hired an employee whom they found through these sites.[20]

ENTREPRENEURIAL

Profile

*Ronn Torossian:
5W Public Relations*

Ronn Torossian, founder of 5W Public Relations in New York City, has recruited several employees using Facebook and Twitter. The 75-person public relations firm has a LinkedIn profile, a company Facebook page, a blog, and a Twitter account that it uses to publicize job openings. "Social media absolutely does work to recruit new hires," he says.[21]

Recruit on campus. For many employers, college and university campuses remain an excellent source of workers, especially for entry-level positions. After screening résumés, a recruiter can interview a dozen or more high-potential students in just 1 day. Companies must be sure that the recruiters they send to campuses are professional, polished, and prepared to represent the company well because 42 percent of students say that their impression of a recruiter is the primary determinant of their perception of a company.[22]

Forge relationships with schools and other sources of workers. Some employers have found that forging long-term relationships with schools and other institutions can provide a valuable source of workers. As colleges and universities begin to offer students more internship opportunities, a small business can gain greatly by hosting one or more students for a semester or for the summer. The company has an opportunity to observe the student's work habits and, if positive, sell the student on a permanent position on his or her graduation.

ENTREPRENEURIAL

Profile

*Jeff Fissel and Wes
Cruver: KZO
Innovations*

Jeff Fissel launched his software company, KZO Innovations, during his senior year at George Mason University in Fairfax, Virginia, and wanted to tap into the vast pool of talent that surrounded him. Start-up capital was scarce, however, and Fissel and his cofounder Wes Cruver knew that they would have difficulty paying salaries even to part-time employees. With the help of a professor, the entrepreneurs approached the university's career services office with a proposal for internships at KZO Innovations in which students could earn college credit and gain practical work experience. "The interns are happy, and we are relieved to have a solid workforce," says Fissel. Several of the company's current 20 employees began their careers at KZO Innovations as student interns.[23]

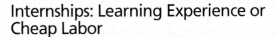

ENTREPRENEURSHIP IN ACTION

Internships: Learning Experience or Cheap Labor

David, a communications major at a large university in the Northeast, wanted to strengthen his résumé and accepted an unpaid internship at a small communications firm where he was guaranteed that he would "be fully involved in all of the work that the agency was doing." Eager to take on challenging assignments and learn new job-related skills, David reported for work. Unfortunately, he did he not receive any meaningful assignments (hello, photocopier!), and his supervisor rarely spoke to him. Regular employees left him out of staff meetings and sessions with clients, and the office was so unorganized that he never completed any real work.

Sarah, an intern at TOMS Shoes, a cross between a for-profit and nonprofit company founded by Blake Mycoskie that donates a pair of shoes to needy people for every pair it sells, has had an extremely positive and productive internship experience. A recent entry from her blog tells the story:

As the fifth week of our internship rolls around, the office is buzzing and the work is flowing steadily. We were promised on day 1 that we would be doing work that mattered at TOMS, not just typical intern grunt work—coffee runs and long hours at the copy machine. As the internship has continued to unfold, this promise has proved to be true. With several huge TOMS initiatives in the forefront, we have officially made the leap from "new interns" to marketers, graphic designers, event planners, online marketers, retail representatives, and more. What a rush!*

Like TOMS Shoes, small companies with their limited budgets can tap into a talented, highly motivated pool of workers at little or no cost through internship programs. "[Internships] were a natural fit," says Mycoskie. "College students were really drawn to what we were doing." Student interns benefit by gaining practical job experience and building a network of contacts, and many of them earn college credit for their internships. Some colleges require students to take on internships to qualify for graduation. Yet some people criticize unpaid internships, saying that companies are merely taking advantage of eager students who are willing to work for free just to gain work experience and industry connections. "[Internships] give companies an unfair business advantage," says Michael Tracy, an employment attorney. "It's the same as companies that pay people subminimum wage or that make people work unpaid overtime."

Shawn Graham, a successful author who worked an unpaid internship at a large financial services company while in college, is a proponent of requiring companies to pay their student interns, claiming that doing so makes interships much more practical for students. Graham says that he learned a great deal from his intership experience but it imposed a financial hardship.

> I had to buy suits to wear at the office (full disclosure—my mom helped finance the suits as I was a poor college student) and pay bus fare a few days a week. In the grand scheme of things, I don't think paying an intern at least minimum wage would be a huge hit to the bottom lines of most companies.

The U.S. Department of Labor has said very little about internships until April 2010, when it issued the following six guidelines based on the Fair Labor Standards Act of 1938:

1. The internship, even though it includes actual operation of the facilities of the employer, is similar to training that would be given in an educational environment.
2. The internship experience is for the benefit of the intern.
3. The intern does not displace regular employees, but works under close supervision of existing staff.

4. The employer that provides the training derives no immediate advantage from the activities of the intern, and on occasion its operations may actually be impeded.
5. The intern is not necessarily entitled to a job at the conclusion of the internship.
6. The employer and the intern understand that the intern is not entitled to wages for the time spent in the internship.

Companies that violate the rules on internships are subject to fines from the U.S. Department of Labor and state labor agencies.

When Ari Goldberg launched StyleCaster, a Web site that mixes fashion news, clothing recommendations, and social networking, he relied on a contingent of unpaid student interns from top universities to provide content and articles for the site. Michelle Halpern, a recent graduate from Syracuse University, saw an internship at StyleCaster as a way to launch a career as a journalist. She borrowed money for living expenses from her parents and moved to New York City to work more than 40 hours a week at no pay. Her hard work paid off. Not only did she have the opportunity to attend New York Fashion Week and mingle with designers and fashion moguls, but she also received an offer for a full-time (paid!) job at StyleCaster, making her the sixth intern to move into employee status. "An internship is an easier way to get a foot in the door and make contacts," says Halpern.

1. Which of the following viewpoints do you support? (1) Unpaid internships are an ideal way for students to gain experience and make contacts. (2) Unpaid internships are simply a way for companies to get free labor. Explain.
2. Should companies be required to pay student interns the minimum wage? What impact, if any, would this requirement have on employers', particularly small companies', willingness to offer internships?

Sources: Based on Shawn Graham, "Legal Debates Aside, Companies Should Pay Interns," *Fast Company*, May 4, 2010, *www.fastcompany.com/1637926/ legal-debates-aside-companies-should-pay-interns*; Laurie Pike, "The Full-Time Non-Employee," *Entrepreneur*, April 2010, pp. 81–87; Mark Grabowski, "Debate: Internship Reform Only Hurts Students," *AOL News*, June 21, 2010, *www.aolnews.com/opinion/article/debate-the-feds-internship-crackdown-only-hurts-students/19522287*; Angus Loten, "Why Interns Are Good for Business," *Inc.*, February 25, 2010, *www.inc.com/internships/2008/internship-horror-stories.html*; Seth Fiegerman, "11 Internship Horror Stories," *MainStreet*, February 23, 2010, *www.mainstreet.com/ slideshow/career/worst-internships-america.*

*Reprinted with permission from TOMS Shoes.

Recruit "retired" workers. By 2016, nearly 35 percent of workers in the United States will be 55 or older, and in 2019 the youngest members of the Baby Boom generation will turn 55.[24] According to the American Association of Retired Persons (AARP), 70 percent of these baby boomers plan to continue working after reaching retirement age to maintain their lifestyles.[25] To avoid labor shortages, small businesses must be ready to hire them, perhaps as part-time employees. Kevin McGillivray, owner of KEM Group, a financial services and tax preparation service in Danvers, Massachusetts, needed help during the busy tax season. He placed an ad on the Web site *www.retirementjobs.com*, and within a few days he had hired a former corporate controller and a retired H&R Block employee.[26] With a lifetime of work experience and time on their hands and a strong work ethic, retired workers can be the ideal solution to many entrepreneurs' labor problems. One survey by WorldatWork, an international association of human resource professionals, reports that just 49.4 percent of employers proactively pursue older workers in their recruiting efforts.[27] Older employees can be a valuable asset to small firms.

Consider using offbeat recruiting techniques. To attract the workers they need to support their growing businesses, some entrepreneurs have resorted to creative recruiting techniques, such as the following:

- Sending young recruiters to mingle with college students on spring break
- Sponsoring a "job shadowing" program that gives students and other prospects the opportunity to observe firsthand the nature of the work and the work environment
- Inviting college seniors to a company tailgating party at a sports event
- Posting "what it's like to work here" videos created by current employees on YouTube and other video sites
- Launching a monthly industry networking meeting for local workers at Internet companies
- Hosting or joining a local job fair
- Keeping a file of all of the workers mentioned in the "People on the Move" column in the business section of the local newspaper and then contacting them a year later to see whether they are happy in their jobs[28]

Offer what workers want. Adequate compensation and benefits are important considerations for job candidates, but other, less tangible factors also weigh heavily in a prospect's decision to accept a job. To recruit effectively, entrepreneurs must consider what a McKinsey and Company study calls the "employee value proposition," the factors that would make the ideal employee want to work for their businesses. Flexible work schedules and telecommuting that allow employees to balance the demands of work and life can attract quality workers to small companies. In fact, a study by staffing firm Robert Half International reports that after salary and benefits, flexible work schedules and telecommuting were the most important incentives in attracting employees.[29]

CREATE PRACTICAL JOB DESCRIPTIONS AND JOB SPECIFICATIONS. Business owners must recognize that what they do *before* they ever start interviewing candidates for a position determines to a great extent how successful they will be at hiring winners. The first step is to perform a **job analysis**, the process by which a firm determines the duties and nature of the jobs to be filled and the skills and experience required of the people who are to fill them. Without a proper job analysis, a hiring decision is, at best, a coin toss. The first step in conducting a job analysis is to develop a **job description**, a written statement of the duties, responsibilities, reporting relationships, working conditions, and methods and techniques, as well as materials and equipment, used in a job. A results-oriented job description explains what a job entails and the duties the person filling it is expected to perform. A detailed job description includes a job title, job summary, duties to be performed, nature of supervision, the job's relationship to others in the company, working conditions, and definitions of job-specific terms.

Preparing job descriptions may be one of the most important parts of the hiring process because it creates a blueprint for the job. Without this blueprint, managers tend to hire the person with experience whom they like the best. Useful sources of information for writing job descriptions include the manager's knowledge of the job, the workers currently holding the job, and the *Dictionary of Occupational Titles (DOT),* which is available at most libraries. The *Dictionary of Occupational Titles,* published by the Department of Labor, lists more than 20,000 job titles and descriptions and serves as a useful tool for getting an entrepreneur started when writing job descriptions. In addition to traditional approaches, Web-based technologies offer new ways to share these job descriptions through online job sites and podcasts.

The second objective of a job analysis is to create a **job specification**, a written statement of the qualifications and characteristics needed for a job stated in terms such as education, skills, and experience. A job specification shows the business owner what kind of person to recruit and establishes the standards an applicant must meet to do the job well. In essence, it is a written "success profile" of the ideal employee. Does the person have to be a good listener, empathetic, well-organized, decisive, a "self-starter?" Should he or she have experience in Java programming? An entrepreneur about to hire a new employee who will be telecommuting from home, for instance, would look for someone with excellent communication skills, problem-solving ability, a strong work ethic, and the ability to use technology comfortably. One of the best ways to develop this success profile is to study the top performers currently working for the company and to identify the characteristics that make them successful. Table 1 provides an example that links the tasks for a sales representative's job (drawn from job description) to the traits or characteristics an entrepreneur identified as necessary to succeed in that job. These traits become the foundation for writing the job specification.

SCREEN RÉSUMÉS. The starting point for screening prospective employees is reviewing candidates' résumés. A survey by CareerBuilder reports that 48 percent of human resource managers say that they receive 25 résumés for each job opening. In addition, 38 percent of the managers say that they spend less than 1 minute reviewing a résumé, and 18 percent spend less than 30 seconds![30] Table 2 describes some unusual items lifted from actual résumés.

CHECK REFERENCES. Entrepreneurs should take the time to check *every* applicant's references. Although many entrepreneurs see checking references as a formality and pay little attention to it, others realize the need to protect themselves (and their customers) from hiring unscrupulous workers. A reference check is necessary because more than half of job seekers lie in their résumés, often by inflating their job titles.[31] A recent study by OfficeTeam reports that employers drop 21 percent of job applicants after they conduct reference checks.[32] Rather than rely only on the references that candidates list on their résumés, wise employers call an applicant's previous employers and talk to their immediate supervisors to get a clear picture of the applicant's job performance, character, and work habits.

TABLE 1 Linking Tasks from the Job Description to the Traits Needed to Perform the Job

Job Task	Trait or Characteristic
Generate new leads and close new sales.	Outgoing, strong communication skills, persuasive, friendly
Make 15 "cold calls" per week.	A self-starter, determined, optimistic, independent, confident
Analyze customer needs and recommend proper equipment.	Good listener, intuitive, patient, empathetic
Counsel customers about options and features required.	Organized, polished speaker, "other" oriented
Prepare and explain financial records; negotiate finance contracts.	Honest, mathematically oriented, comfortable with numbers, understands basics of finance, computer literate
Retain existing customers.	Relationship builder, customer focused

TABLE 2 Résumé Bloopers

All of the following résumé bloopers are real. Would you hire someone who committed these blunders?

- A job candidate listed God as one of her references (but, strangely enough, did not list a telephone number).
- A woman listed "alligator watching" as one of her hobbies.
- A man included "Master of Time and the Universe" as part of his work experience.
- One candidate's résumé was 24 pages long, and she had been in the workforce only 5 years.
- A candidate wrote that he was "looking for a full-time position with minimal time commitment."
- Under "Accomplishments," one man listed that he "finished eighth in his class of 10."
- An applicant claimed that "You will want me to be Head Honcho in no time."
- A job seeker claimed that he spoke "English and Spinach."
- Under "Qualifications," one woman explained that her "twin sister has an accounting degree."
- A candidate listed as skills, "written communication = 3 years; verbal communication = 5 years."
- Under education, one young applicant said, "I have a bachelorette degree in computers."
- One job applicant claimed that he had 28 dog years of experience in sales (4 human years, we assume).
- A candidate included a video with his résumé. The purpose of the video: to hypnotize the manager and persuade him to hire the man.
- One job candidate claimed that he possessed "demonstrated ability at multi-tasting."
- Under "Education," one applicant claimed to have "repeated courses repeatedly."

Sources: Based on "Hiring Managers Share Most Memorable Resume Mistakes in New CareerBuilder Survey," *CareerBuilder*, September 15, 2010, *www.careerbuilder.com/share/aboutus/pressreleasesdetail.aspx?id= pr586&sd=9/15/2010&ed=9/15/2010*; "Funny Resume Bloopers, But Don't Let This Happen to You," Do It Yourself, *www.doityourself.com/stry/ara_funnyresumebloop*; "150 Funniest Resume Mistakes, Bloopers, and Blunders Ever," Job Mob, *http://jobmob.co.il/blog/funniest-resume-mistakes/*.

ENTREPRENEURIAL Profile

*Andy Levine:
Development
Counsellors
International*

Andy Levine, president of Development Counsellors International, now requires 12 references for the final stage of the interview process. "It can be pretty amusing when you ask for 12 references. Some candidates have an e-mail to us within an hour; some we never hear from again," says Levine. "When I call references, I start by trying to get them comfortable. I make it clear that what they say will not travel back to the person. Then I often ask, 'If you had to pick three words to describe this person, what are the first that come to mind?' It's very interesting, the picture that emerges after you've done eight or nine of these interviews."[33]

PLAN AN EFFECTIVE INTERVIEW. Once an entrepreneur knows what to look for in a job candidate, he or she can develop a plan for conducting an informative job interview. Too often, business owners go into an interview unprepared, and, as a result, they fail to get the information they need to judge the candidate's qualifications, qualities, and suitability for the job. A common symptom of failing to prepare for an interview is that the interviewer rather than the candidate does most of the talking. Effective interviewers spend about 25 percent of the interview talking and about 75 percent listening. Despite their popularity, interviews are less reliable in predicting job performance than samples of a candidate's work, job-knowledge tests, and peer ratings of past job performance.[34] The following tips improve the quality of the interview process:

- *Involve others in the interview process.* Solo interviews are prone to errors. A better process is to involve employees, particularly employees with whom the prospect would be working, in the interview process, either individually or as part of a panel.
- *Develop a series of core questions and ask them of every candidate.* Entrepreneurs will benefit if they rely on a set of relevant questions they ask in every interview. This will give the screening process consistency, and they can still customize each interview using impromptu questions based on an individual's responses.
- *Ask open-ended questions.* Open-ended questions demanding more than a "yes or no" response are most effective because they encourage candidates to talk about their work

experience in a way that will disclose the presence or the absence of the traits and characteristics entrepreneurs are seeking. Peter Bregman, CEO of Bregman Partners, a company that helps businesses implement change, says that one of the most revealing questions that an interviewer can ask candidates is "What do you do in your spare time?" To emphasize the importance of a candidate's hobbies, Bregman points to Captain C. B. "Sully" Sullenberger, the airline pilot who safely landed a disabled jet with 155 passengers on the Hudson River using skills that he learned from his hobby, flying gliders.[35]

- *Present hypothetical situations.* Building the interview around job-specific hypothetical situations gives the owner a preview of the candidate's actual work habits and attitudes. Rather than telling interviewers about what candidates might do, these scenarios give them insight into what candidates actually do (or have done) in job-related situations.

- *Probe for specific examples in the candidate's past work experience that demonstrate the necessary traits and characteristics.* A common mistake interviewers make is failing to get candidates to provide the detail they need to make an informed decision.

- *Inquire about recent successes and failures.* Smart interviewers look for candidates who describe them both with equal enthusiasm because they know that peak performers put as much into their failures as they do their successes and usually learn something valuable from their failures. Ask the candidates to provide examples of their successes and failures.

- *Create an informal setting.* Select a "non-interview" location that allows several employees to observe the candidate in an informal setting. Taking candidates on a plant tour or setting up a coffee break gives everyone a chance to judge a candidate's interpersonal skills and personality outside the formal interview process. These informal settings can be revealing. At Zappos, the online shoe store, recruiters often interview shuttle service drivers and administrative assistants to discover how job candidates treated them. "I want to know about that interaction," says recruiter Andrew Kovacs.[36]

Table 3 shows an example of some interview questions one manager uses to uncover the traits and characteristics he seeks in a top-performing sales representative.

Conducting the Interview

An effective interview contains three phases: breaking the ice, asking questions, and selling the candidate on the company.

BREAKING THE ICE. In the opening phase of the interview, the entrepreneur's primary goal is to create a relaxed environment. Icebreakers—questions about a hobby or special interest—get the

TABLE 3 Interview Questions for Candidates for a Sales Representative Position

Trait or Characteristic	Question
Outgoing, persuasive, friendly, a self-starter, determined, optimistic, independent, confident	How do you persuade reluctant prospects to buy? Can you give an example?
Good listener, patient, empathetic, organized, polished speaker, other-oriented	What would you say to a fellow salesperson who is getting more than her share of rejections and is having difficulty getting appointments?
Honest, customer-oriented, relationship builder	How do you feel when someone questions the truth of what you say? Can you give an example of how you handled this situation?

Other questions:

- If you owned a company, why would you hire yourself?
- If you were head of your department, what would you do differently? Why?
- How do you acknowledge the contributions of others in your department?

candidate to relax. These "icebreaker" questions also allow the interviewer an opportunity to gain valuable insight into the person. These questions generate little or no pressure and allow the interviewee to expound on something he or she knows a great deal about.

ASKING QUESTIONS. During the second phase of the interview, employers ask the questions from their question bank to determine the applicant's suitability for the job. Employers' primary job at this point is to *listen*. They also take notes during the interview to help them ask follow-up questions based on a candidate's comments and to evaluate a candidate after the interview is over. Experienced interviewers also pay close attention to a candidate's nonverbal clues, or body language, during the interview. They know that candidates may be able to say exactly what they want with their words but that the candidate's body language does not lie!

Some of the most valuable interview questions attempt to gain insight into the candidate's ability to reason, be logical, and be creative. In a **puzzle interview**, the goal is to determine how job candidates think by asking them offbeat, unexpected questions such as, "How would you weigh an airplane without scales?" "Why are manhole covers round?" or "How would you determine the height of a building using only a barometer?" At Zappos, interviewers ask candidates which superhero they would like to be and why.[37] Usually, the logic and creativity a candidate uses to derive an answer is much more important than the answer itself.

Another interview format is the **situational interview** in which the interviewer gives candidates a typical job-related situation (sometimes in the form of a role-playing exercise) and presents a series of open-ended questions to assess how the candidates might respond. One entrepreneur had a candidate deal with an "angry customer," who was played by a fellow interviewer. Studies show that situational interviews have a 54 percent accuracy rate in predicting future job performance, much higher than the 7 percent accuracy rate of the traditional interview.[38]

The **peer-to-peer interview** may provide a closer look at how prospective employees will get along with other staff. Applicants meet one-on-one with potential peers to ask questions about the job and the company. The employees share their assessment with the manager. This interview technique is becoming more common in companies, especially those in which work is team-based. "In a small organization, you're going to spend a lot of time together," says Michael Harris, an expert in peer-to-peer interviews. "It becomes even more important for the entrepreneur to share some of the [hiring] responsibility with employees."[39] Because employees are involved in the hiring process, they feel empowered and "buy into" the hiring process, which can be good for morale and productivity. Peer interviews also allow applicants to gain insight into an organization's culture.

ENTREPRENEURIAL
Profile

Rick Self: Advanced Technology Institute (ATI)

At Advanced Technology Institute (ATI), a research and development management company in North Charleston, South Carolina, managers conducted traditional 1- or 2-hour interviews. After making several bad hires, CEO Rick Self switched to peer-to-peer interviews that last at least half a day, involve several employees from all parts of the company, and include a lunch with employees from the department in which the applicant would work. The candidate's final interview is with the CEO. The goal is to judge how well applicants will fit into ATI's team-based work environment. "We're trying to find out what makes someone both good and happy to be here and then we bake that into a set of structured interviews," says Self.[40]

Managers should conduct training sessions with employees who will participate in the interviews to make certain that they know which questions are illegal and that keep their questions job-related.[41] The Equal Employment Opportunity Commission (EEOC) does not outlaw specific interview questions; rather, it recognizes that some questions can result in employment discrimination. If a candidate files charges of discrimination against a company, the burden of proof shifts to the employer to prove that all pre-employment questions were job related and non-discriminatory. Table 4 offers a quiz to help entrepreneurs understand the types of questions that are most likely to result in charges of discrimination.

TABLE 4 Is It Legal?

Legal	Illegal	Interview Question
❑	❑	1. Are you currently using illegal drugs?
❑	❑	2. Have you ever been arrested?
❑	❑	3. Do you have any children or do you plan to have children?
❑	❑	4. When and where were you born?
❑	❑	5. Is there any limit on your ability to work overtime or travel?
❑	❑	6. How tall are you? How much do you weigh?
❑	❑	7. Do you drink alcohol?
❑	❑	8. How much alcohol do you drink each week?
❑	❑	9. Would your religious beliefs interfere with your ability to do the job?
❑	❑	10. What contraceptive practices do you use?
❑	❑	11. Are you HIV positive?
❑	❑	12. Have you ever filed a lawsuit or worker's compensation claim against a former employer?
❑	❑	13. Do you have physical/mental disabilities that would interfere with doing your job?
❑	❑	14. Are you a U.S. citizen?

Answers: 1. Legal. 2. Illegal. Employers cannot ask about an applicant's arrest record, but they can ask if a candidate has ever been convicted of a crime. 3. Illegal. Employers cannot ask questions that could lead to discrimination against a particular group (e.g., women, physically challenged, etc.). 4. Illegal. The Civil Rights Act of 1964 bans discrimination on the basis of race, color, sex, religion, or national origin. 5. Legal. 6. Illegal. Unless a person's physical characteristics are necessary for job performance (e.g., lifting 100-pound sacks of mulch), employers cannot ask candidates such questions. 7. Legal. 8. Illegal. Notice the fine line between question 7 and question 8; this is what makes interviewing challenging. 9. Illegal. This question would violate the Civil Rights Act of 1964. 10. Illegal. What relevance would this have to an employee's job performance? 11. Illegal. Under the Americans with Disabilities Act, which prohibits discrimination against people with disabilities, people who are HIV positive or who have AIDS are considered "disabled." 12. Illegal. Workers who file such suits are protected from retribution by a variety of federal and state laws. 13. Illegal. This question also would violate the Americans with Disabilities Act. 14. Illegal. This question violates the Civil Rights Act of 1964.

The goal of the interview process is to find someone who is qualified to do the job well. By steering clear of questions about subjects that are peripheral to the job itself, employers are less likely to ask questions that will land them in court. Wise entrepreneurs ask their attorneys to review their bank of questions before using them in an interview. Table 5 describes a simple test for determining whether an interview question might be considered discriminatory.

SELLING THE CANDIDATE ON THE COMPANY. "A" players want to play for "A" teams. In the final phase of the interview, when employers have an attractive candidate, they should sell the benefits of working for the company. This phase begins by allowing the candidate to ask questions about the company, the job, or other issues. Experienced interviewers note the nature of these questions and the insights they give into the candidate's personality. This part of the interview offers employers a prime opportunity to explain to the candidate why the company is an attractive place to work. The best candidates will have other offers, and it is up to the entrepreneur to make sure they leave the interview wanting to work for the company. Finally, before closing the interview employers should thank the candidates and tell them what happens next. For example, "We will be contacting you about our decision within 2 weeks."

BACKGROUND CHECKS. Background checks are essential. In addition to turning up convictions for criminal activity, a background check can show whether a job candidate has been convicted of stealing from a previous employer. A check of a candidate's driving records will show convictions for DUI and other traffic violations. This information can save an entrepreneur thousands of dollars by avoiding a bad hire at a cost of $50 or less for a basic criminal records check. "A lot of times, employers argue that a background check is too expensive," says Zuni

TABLE 5   A Guide for Interview Questions

Small business owners can use the "OUCH" test as a guide for determining whether an interview question might be considered discriminatory:

- Does the question *Omit* references to race, religion, color, sex, or national origin?
- Does the question *Unfairly* screen out a particular class of people?
- Can you *Consistently* apply the question to every applicant?
- Does the question *Have* job-relatedness and business necessity?

Corkerton, president of Hilliard, Ohio-based RefCheck Information Services Inc. "But the litigation that comes as a result of not having done their due diligence and having been negligent in their hiring process can be far greater."[42]

A background check is a basic step in avoiding charges of negligent hiring, the failure to investigate the background of a prospective employee who proves to be dangerous to customers or other employees. For example, a Nebraska delivery driver for a pizza chain attacked a woman after delivering a pizza to her home. The employee had a previous sexual-assault conviction that a simple background check would have detected, preventing a tragedy, damage to the company's reputation, and the resulting litigation. A court ordered the pizza chain to pay the victim $175,000.[43]

Checking potential employees' social networking pages, such as those on Facebook and MySpace, also can provide a revealing look at the character of job candidates. A study by CareerBuilder reports that 22 percent of employers investigate job candidates' Facebook and MySpace pages and that one-third have discovered something there that caused them to reject a candidate.[44]

EMPLOYMENT TESTS. Although various state and federal laws have made using employment tests as screening devices more difficult in recent years, many companies find them quite useful. To avoid charges of discrimination, entrepreneurs must be able to prove that the employment tests they use are both valid and reliable. A **valid test** is one that measures what it is intended to measure: for example, aptitude for selling, creativity, integrity. A **reliable test** is one that measures consistently over time. Employers must also be sure that the tests they use measure aptitudes and factors that are job related. Many testing organizations offer ready-made tests that have been proved to be both valid and reliable. Entrepreneurs can use these tests safely. In today's environment, if a test has not been validated and proven to be reliable or is not job related, it is best not to use it.

ENTREPRENEURIAL
Profile

*Richard Linder:
PCA Skin Inc.*

PCA Skin Inc., a company based in Scottsdale, Arizona, that develops clinical skin care products, recently began using personality-based employment tests, and managers say that the tests, which take only 10 minutes to administer, have helped the company improve its hiring process. "We have had 65 candidates take the test," says CEO Richard Linder. The company has hired 17 new employees, and "so far, every hire we have made using the test has resulted in a successful placement."[45]

According to the U.S. Department of Labor, 75 percent of illegal drug users are employed, and those who are employed are most likely to work for small companies, which rely less on drug tests than large businesses.[46] In an attempt to avoid hiring illegal drug users, 84 percent of employers use pre-employment drug tests and 39 percent administer postemployment random drug tests.[47] Although administering drug tests adds expense to the hiring process, the cost is far less than that of the potential problems an employee with a drug habit causes. Employers who use drug tests should establish a policy and follow it consistently.

Experienced entrepreneurs do not rely on any one element in the employee-selection process. They look at the total picture painted by each part of a candidate's portfolio. They know that the hiring process provides them with one of the most valuable raw materials their companies count on for success—capable, hard-working people. They also recognize that hiring an employee is not a single event but the beginning of a long-term relationship.

IN THE ENTREPRENEURIAL
SPOTLIGHT — What a Great Place to Work!

New Belgium Brewing Company

"There's something wrong if making beer can't be fun," says Kim Jordan, CEO of New Belgium Brewing Company, the business she cofounded with her husband Jeff Lebesch in 1991. The idea for the company came to Lebesch while he was on a bicycle tour of Belgium, peddling his way through towns and villages that are famous for making superb, rich, boldly flavored craft beers. Inspired by his trip, Lebesch began brewing beer in his basement using dairy equipment that he modified for beer-making. Jordan became the tiny company's bottler, sales representative, distributor, marketing director, and financial manager.

Today, CEO Jordan works hard to make sure that her employees have fun while making New Belgium's unique line of craft beers, which includes Fat Tire (named after Lebesch's bicycle trip through Europe that inspired him to start the company), Skinny Dip (a seasonal beer for summer with a hint of lime), Mothership Wit Organic Wheat Beer (the company's first organic offering), and Blue Paddle (a Czech-inspired pilsner). She created an employee stock ownership plan in which every employee receives an ownership interest in the Fort Collins, Colorado-based company and a free custom bicycle after 1 year with the company. (New Belgium Brewing is an environmentally conscious company and encourages employees to follow its lead. The company has been using wind-powered electricity since 1999.) Employees now own one-third of the company. After 5 years with the company, every employee receives an all-expenses-paid trip to Belgium to learn about beer-making. Employees also receive two free six packs of beer each week. Jordan involves employees at all levels of the company when crafting New Belgium's strategic plan and budgets. "Operating a business in a way that is consistent with your values is particularly pleasing," says Jordan.

Daxko Inc.

One of David Gray's first goals when he became CEO of Daxko, a small company in Birmingham, Alabama, that provides software and technology services to nonprofits, was to reshape the company's culture. "I'm a big believer in corporate culture as a competitive advantage," Gray says. The transformation was successful; Daxko's culture more closely resembles those of companies in Silicon Valley than those in the traditional South. All new employees receive 15 paid vacation days, a free YMCA membership, and 6 weeks of paid parental leave. The company allocates $1,500 to each employee to spend on any kind of professional development activity they choose, and for every 7 years of service employees qualify for a 4-week paid sabbatical leave. To encourage interaction among employees and the creativity that it spawns, no one, including managers, has a private office. The company does have a work–play lounge that includes a 52-inch television and a Nintendo Wii. It is not uncommon to see employees on a break playing the latest video game or cheering on their "team" in a friendly Wii competition. "It's symbolic of a company that focuses on contributions instead of hours clocked," says one management consultant. Employees also connect with one another over the weekly free lunch, sometimes just to socialize and other times to discuss projects on which they are working. "It's pretty intense here," says product manager Saranda West. "Expectations for what I need to accomplish are clearly set, and if I can play Wii while doing it, that's even better."

1. Daxko's David Gray says, "I'm a big believer in corporate culture as a competitive advantage." Do you agree? Explain.
2. Why do company cultures like the ones at New Belgium Brewing Company and Daxko appeal to employees, particularly members of Generation X and Generation Y? Would you want to work for New Belgium Brewing or Daxko? Explain.

Sources: Based on Joseph V. Tirella, Malika Zouhali-Worrall, Alec Foege, David Koeppel, and Ian Mount, "Meet the New Boss," *FSB*, June 2009, pp. 63–68; "Our Story," New Belgium Brewing Company, *www.newbelgium .com/culture/our-story.aspx*; "About Daxko," Daxko, *http://daxko.com/ about-daxko/*.

Kim Jordan, CEO of New Belgium Brewing Company.

Source: New Belgium Brewing Company.

Building the Right Culture and Organizational Structure

3. Explain how to build the kind of company culture and structure to support the company's mission and goals and to motivate employees to achieve them.

Company culture is the distinctive, unwritten code of conduct that governs the behavior, attitudes, relationships, and style of an organization. It is the essence of "the way we do things around here." In many entrepreneurial companies, culture plays an important role in gaining a competitive edge. A company's culture has a powerful impact on the way people work together in a business, how they do their jobs, and how they treat their customers. Company culture manifests itself in many ways—from how workers dress and act to the language they use. At some companies, the unspoken dress code requires workers to wear suits and ties, but at many high-technology companies employees routinely show up in jeans, T-shirts, and flip-flops. In many companies, the culture creates its own language. At Disney theme parks, workers are not "employees"; they are "cast members." They do not merely go to work; their jobs are "parts in a performance." Customers are referred to as "guests." When a cast member treats someone to lunch, it's "on the mouse." Anything negative—such as a cigarette butt on a walkway—is "a bad Mickey," and anything positive is "a good Mickey."

An important ingredient in a company's culture is the performance objectives an entrepreneur sets and against which employees are measured. If entrepreneurs want integrity, respect, honesty, customer service, and other important values to be the foundation on which a positive culture can flourish, they must establish measures of success that reflect those core values. *Effective executives know that building a positive organizational culture has a direct, positive impact on the financial outcomes of an organization.* The intangible factors that comprise an organization's culture have an influence, either positive or negative, on the tangible outcomes of profitability, cash flow, return on equity, employee productivity, innovation and cost control. An entrepreneur's job is to establish a culture that creates a positive influence on the company's tangible outcomes. Companies that focus on creating a positive corporate culture have better financial performance than those that do not, according to the San Francisco-based Great Places to Work Institute.[48]

Sustaining a company's culture begins with the hiring process. Beyond the normal requirements of competitive pay and working conditions, the hiring process must focus on finding employees who share the values of the organization. "Companies are realizing that culture is as important as strategy and that they can't just look at the short term anymore," says Barbara Bilodeau, a manager at Boston-based Bain & Co.[49] Nurturing the right culture in a company can enhance a company's competitive position by improving its ability to attract and retain quality workers and by creating an environment in which workers can grow and develop. As a new generation of employees enters the workforce, companies are discovering that more relaxed, open cultures have an edge in attracting the best workers. These companies embrace nontraditional, fun cultures that incorporate concepts such as casual dress, team-based assignments, telecommuting, flexible work schedules, free meals, company outings, and many other unique options. Modern organizational culture relies on the following principles to create a productive, fun workplace:

- *Respect for the quality of work and a balance between work life and home life.* Modern companies recognize that their employees have lives away from work. These businesses offer flexible work schedules, part-time work, job sharing, telecommuting, sabbaticals, and conveniences such as on-site day care or concierge services that handle employees' errands. Work–life balance issues are becoming more important to employees, and companies that address them have an edge when it comes to recruiting and retaining a quality workforce. "Employers realize that by offering work–life programs, they are getting a lot in return in terms of productivity and commitment to the organization," says one consultant.[50]

ENTREPRENEURIAL
Profile

*Paul Graziani:
Analytical Graphics, Inc.*

Analytical Graphics, Inc. (AGI), a small company in Exton, Pennsylvania, that produces software for the space, defense, and intelligence industries, helps its employees balance the demands of work and life by providing three meals a day for employees and having a dry cleaning service make pickups and deliveries each week. AGI installed washers and dryers after younger workers said that they had trouble finding time to do laundry. CEO Paul Graziani says that increased workforce productivity more than offsets the costs of providing these perks.[51]

- *A sense of purpose.* These companies rely on a strong sense of purpose to connect employees to the company's mission. At motorcycle legend Harley-Davidson, employees are so in tune with the company's mission that some of them have tattoos of the company's name.

Achieving work-life balance: Paul Graziani, CEO of Analytical Graphics, Inc., says that increases in productivity more than offset the cost of installing washers and dryers for employees to use.

Source: AGI\Analytical Graphics, Inc.

- *Diversity.* The U.S. workforce is becoming more diverse; by 2039, the majority of the workforce will consist of minorities. Companies with appealing cultures embrace cultural diversity in their workforces, actively seeking out workers with different backgrounds. They recognize that a workforce with a rich mix of cultural diversity gives their companies more talent, skills, and abilities from which to draw. Because the entire world is now a potential market for many small companies, having a workforce that looks, acts, and thinks like their customers, with all of their ethnic, racial, religious, and behavioral variety, is a strength. Figure 1 shows the composition of the U.S. workforce in 1995, 2010, and 2050.
- *Integrity.* Employees want to work for a company that stands for honesty and integrity. They do not want to have to check their personal value systems at the door when they report to work. Indeed, many workers take pride in the fact they work for a company that is ethical and socially responsible.
- *Participative management.* Modern managers recognize that employees expect a participative management style to be part of a company's culture. Today's workforce does not respond well to the autocratic management styles of the past. To maximize productivity and encourage commitment to accomplishing the company's mission, entrepreneurs must trust and empower employees at all levels of the organization to make decisions and to take the actions they must to do their jobs well.
- *Learning environment.* Progressive companies encourage and support lifelong learning among their employees. They are willing to invest in their employees, improving their skills and helping them to reach their full potential. That attitude is a strong magnet for the best and brightest workers, who know that to stay at the top of their fields they must always be learning. Dealer.com, a small company in Burlington, Vermont, that provides online marketing services for the automotive industry, provides a multitude of training opportunities for its employees through uFuel, its online learning system. The company also offers its top performing employees a custom-designed MBA curriculum taught by professors at a local university.[52]
- *A sense of fun.* Children laugh an average of 400 times a day; however, by the time a person reaches age 35 he or she laughs on average just 15 times a day.[53] At many successful small companies, the lines between work and play are blurred, and laughter is common. The founders of these businesses see no reason for work and fun to be mutually exclusive. In fact, they believe that a workplace that creates a sense of fun makes it easier to recruit quality workers and encourages them to be more productive and more customer-oriented. "Healthy and sustainable organizations focus on the fundamentals: quality, service, fiscal responsibility, leadership—but they didn't forget to add fun to that

FIGURE 1
Racial and Ethnic Diversity of the U.S. Workforce: 1995, 2010, 2050

Sources: Bureau of the Census and the U.S. Equal Employment Opportunity Commission.

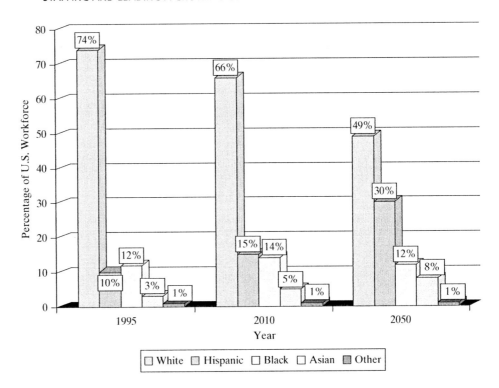

formula," says Leslie Yerkes, a consultant and author.[54] At Heinfeld, Meech, and Company, a CPA firm in Tucson, Arizona, the culture emphasizes excellence, honesty, teamwork, and respect in addition to fun. To relieve stress, employees participate in office "decathlons" that include events such as flying paper airplanes, playing paper football, and racing office chairs.[55]

■ *Engagement.* Employees who are fully engaged in their work take pride in making valuable contributions to the organization's success and derive personal satisfaction from doing so. Although engaged employees are a key ingredient in superior business performance, just 28 percent of employees in North America are fully engaged in their work, and 18 percent of them actually are disengaged.[56] What can managers do to improve employee engagement?

■ Constantly communicate the purpose and vision of the organization and why it matters.

■ Challenge employees to learn and advance in their careers and give them the resources and the incentives to do so.

■ Create a culture that encourages and rewards engagement.

Companies that build their cultures on these principles have an edge when it comes to attracting, retaining, and motivating workers. In other words, creating the right culture helps a small company compete more effectively.

No screening process is perfect, which is why small companies must make sure that every new hire is an appropriate fit with their culture. "Most [employee] turnover is from a lack of cultural match," says Julie Godshall Brown, president of Godshall and Godshall Personnel Consultants.[57]

Profile

Tony Hsieh: Zappos

At Zappos, the online shoe retailer, new hires go through an extensive 4-week orientation and training program in which they learn everything from the importance of customer service to the company's 10 core values. About 1 week into the program, the company offers its new hires $1,500 to quit. This might sound like a crazy idea, but only 10 percent of new employees accept the offer. Zappos uses the "bonus" to ensure that the employees it hires are engaged and committed to the company and are a good fit with its unique culture.[58]

MANAGING GROWTH AND A CHANGING CULTURE. As companies grow, they often experience dramatic changes in their culture. Procedures become more formal, operations grow more widespread, jobs take on more structure, communication becomes more difficult, and the company's personality often begins to change. As more workers come on board, employees find it more difficult to know everyone in the company and to understand how their jobs connect with others. This transition presents a new set of demands for the entrepreneur. Unless entrepreneurs work hard to maintain their companies' unique culture, they may wake up one day to find that they have sacrificed that culture—and the competitive edge that went with it—in the name of growth. Entrepreneurs must be aware of the challenges rapid growth brings with it; otherwise, they may find their companies crumbling around them as they reach warp speed. An entrepreneur's challenge is to walk a fine line between retaining the small company traits that are the seeds of the company's success and incorporating the elements of infrastructure that are essential to supporting and sustaining the company's growth.

Team-Based Management

As a company grows, its success may lie in the founder's willingness to shift from a top-down, single-leader structure to one that is team-based. Unlike the early days of a company when the founder handled much of the work alone, he or she must accept that the magnitude and the complexity of work requires delegating authority and empowering employees to make decisions. Leaders who build successful teams understand that each team member has a role to play and that every role plays a part in a bigger picture. Companies are relying more on team-based job designs as competition and complexity increase and business problems cross departmental and geographic boundaries. Even though converting from a traditional management style to a team approach requires a major change in management style, it is often easier to implement with a small number of workers.

A **self-directed work team** is a group of workers from different functional areas of a company who work together as a unit. The team operates largely without supervision, making decisions and performing tasks that once belonged only to managers. Some teams may be temporary, attacking and solving a specific problem, but many are permanent components of an organization's structure. As their name implies, these teams manage themselves, performing such functions as setting work schedules, ordering raw materials, evaluating and purchasing equipment, developing budgets, hiring and firing team members, and solving problems. Teams function best in environments in which the work is interdependent and people must interact to accomplish their goals. The goal is to get people working together to serve customers better. Johnsonville Sausage, a privately owned company founded in 1945 and based in Sheboygan Falls, Wisconsin, uses a team-based structure rather than traditional departments. The company hires "members" rather than employees, and supervisors have the title of "coaches," a not-so-subtle reminder of the role the company expects them to fill.[59]

Managers in companies using teams are just as involved as before, but the nature of their work changes dramatically. Before teams, managers were bosses who made most of the decisions affecting their subordinates alone. They often hoarded information and power for themselves. In a team environment, managers take on the role of coaches. They empower those around them to make decisions affecting their work and share information with their workers. As facilitators, their job is to support and to serve the teams functioning in the organization and to make sure the teams produce results.

Companies have strong, competitive reasons for using team-based management. Businesses that use teams effectively report significant gains in quality, reductions in cycle time, lower costs, increased customer satisfaction, and improved employee motivation and morale. A team-based approach is not appropriate for every organization, however. Although teams have saved some companies from extinction, for others, the team approach has failed. A team-based management system is *not* easy to start. Switching from a traditional organizational structure to a team-based one is filled with potential pitfalls. A common criticism of teams is groupthink, a concept identified by Yale psychology professor Irving Janis in his classic book, *Victims of Groupthink.* Janis observed that **groupthink** sometimes leads groups to build a false sense of confidence that leads to unsound decisions that team members would not have made individually.[60] Years later, Jerry Harvey described another danger of group decisions that he called the **Abilene Paradox**, a situation in which a group makes a decision that is precisely the *opposite* of what its individual members want to do. What makes the difference? What causes teams to fail? The following errors are common in team-oriented environments:

- Assigning a team an inappropriate task, one in which the team members may lack the necessary skills to be successful (lack of training and support).
- Creating work teams but failing to provide the team with meaningful performance targets.

■ Failing to deal with known underperformers and assuming that being part of a group will solve the problem; it doesn't.

■ Failing to compensate the members of the team equitably.

To ensure the success of the teams approach, entrepreneurs must do the following:

■ *Make sure that teams are appropriate for the company and the nature of the work.* A good starting point is to create a "map" of the company's work flow that shows how workers build a product or deliver a service. Is the work interdependent, complex, and interactive? If so, teamwork is likely to improve the company's performance.

■ *Form teams around the natural work flow and give them specific tasks to accomplish.* Teams can be effective only if managers challenge them to accomplish specific, measurable objectives. They need targets to shoot for.

■ *Provide adequate support and training for team members and leaders.* Team success requires a new set of skills. Workers must learn how to communicate, resolve conflict, support one another, and solve problems as a team. Smart managers see that team members get the training they need.

■ *Involve team members in determining how their performances will be measured, what will be measured, and when it will be measured.* Doing so gives team members a sense of ownership and pride about the tasks they are accomplishing.

■ *Make at least part of team members' pay dependent on team performance.* Companies that have used teams successfully still pay members individually, but they make successful teamwork a major part of an individual's performance review.

Figure 2 illustrates the four stages teams go through on their way to performing effectively and reaching set goals.

Communicating Effectively

Effective communication is the lifeblood of a successful company. It reinforces the organization's vision, connects employees to the business, fosters process improvement, facilitates change, and drives business results by changing employee behavior. An important and highly visible part of the entrepreneurs' role is to communicate the values, beliefs, and principles for which their

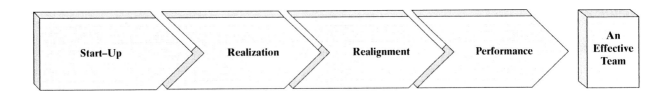

	Start–Up	Realization	Realignment	Performance	An Effective Team
Description	• High expectations • Unclear goals and roles • Anxiety and reliance on leader • Avoidance of tasks	• Recognition of time and effort required • Roadblocks • Frustration • Conflict	• Resetting of goals and roles • Development of trust and cooperation • Progress • Structure	• Involvement, openness, and teamwork • Commitment both to process and to task achievement	
Leadership Focus	• Help team focus on task • Provide goals and structure • Supervise and define accountability	• Emphasize task and process • Clarify expectations and roles • Encourage open discussions and address concerns • Ensure proper skills and resources	• Focus on process • Promote participation and team decision making • Encourage peer support • Provide feedback	• Focus on monitoring and feedback • Let team take responsibility for solving problems and making decisions	

FIGURE 2

The Stages of Team Development

4. Understand the potential barriers to effective communication and describe how to overcome them.

businesses stand. Entrepreneurs also must help employees to understand the importance of their roles and how they fit into the "big picture" of the company's success. Studies confirm that effective communication makes a difference in a company's performance. Management consulting firm Towers Watson reports that the return on investment over the last 5 years in companies with the most effective communications is 47 percent higher than the return for those with the least effective communications. The study also found a strong correlation between a company's communication effectiveness and its employee engagement level and retention rate.[61]

Improving Communication

A leader's foremost job is to communicate the company's vision to everyone in the company and to empower employees to accomplish the vision within the framework of the company's culture. Much of what leaders do involves communication; indeed, leaders spend about 80 percent of their time participating in some form of communication. To some managers, communicating means only one thing: sending messages to others. Although talking to people both inside and outside the organization is an important part of an entrepreneur's job, so is encouraging communication throughout the company at all levels and across all functional areas. "Communicators are evolving from crafting the content [of the message] to facilitating the discussion," says Sharon McIntosh, director of global communications at PepsiCo.[62]

ENTREPRENEURIAL
Profile
Analytical Graphics

At Analytical Graphics, the company that creates software for the aerospace and defense industries, managers implemented a system that encourages communication among employees. Every Friday, the company hosts a lunch meeting for all employees that includes "Storytime," during which employees from various departments describe the projects they are working on, how their work depends on the work of other departments, and how their work affects the company's clients. In addition to improving communication among workers, Storytime also enhances the sense of teamwork throughout the company.[63]

BARRIERS TO EFFECTIVE COMMUNICATION. One of the most frustrating experiences for entrepreneurs occurs when they ask an employee to do something and nothing happens. Although entrepreneurs are quick to perceive the failure to respond as the employee's lack of motivation or weak work ethic, often the culprit is improper communication. The primary reasons employees usually don't do what they are expected to do have little to do with their motivation and desire to work. Instead, workers often fail to do what they need to do because:

- They don't know what to do.
- They don't know how to do it.
- They don't have the authority to do it.
- They get no feedback on how well or how poorly they are doing it.
- They are either ignored or punished for doing it right.
- They realize that no one ever notices even if they *are* doing it right.

The common thread running through all of these causes is poor communication between the entrepreneur and employee. What barriers to effective communication must entrepreneurs overcome?

- *Managers and employees don't always feel free to say what they really mean.* CEOs and top managers in companies of any size seldom hear the truth about problems and negative results from employees. This less-than-honest feedback results from the hesitancy of subordinates to tell "the boss" bad news. Over time, this tendency paralyzes the upward communication in a company.
- *Ambiguity blocks real communication.* The same words can have different meanings to different people, especially in modern companies, where the workforce is likely to be highly diverse. For instance, an entrepreneur may tell an employee to "take care of this customer's problem as soon as you can." The owner may have meant "solve this problem by the end of the day" but the employee may think that fixing the problem by the end of the week will meet the owner's request.
- *Information overload causes the message to get lost.* With information from mail, telephone, faxes, e-mail, face-to-face communication, and other sources, employees in

modern organizations are bombarded with messages. With such a large volume of information washing over workers, it is easy for some messages to get lost.

- *Selective listening interferes with the communication process.* Sometimes people hear only what they want to hear, selectively tuning in and out on a speaker's message. The result is distorted communication.
- *Defense mechanisms block a message.* When people are confronted with information that upsets them or conflicts with their perceptions, they immediately put up defenses. Defense mechanisms range from verbally attacking the source of the message to twisting perceptions of reality to maintain self-esteem.
- *Conflicting verbal and nonverbal messages confuse listeners.* Nonverbal communication includes a speaker's mannerisms, gestures, posture, facial expressions, and other forms of body language. When a speaker sends conflicting verbal and nonverbal messages, research shows that listeners will believe the nonverbal message almost every time.

OVERCOMING COMMUNICATION BARRIERS. How can entrepreneurs overcome these barriers to become better communicators? The following tips will help:

- *Clarify your message before you attempt to communicate it.* Identify exactly what you want the receiver to think and do as a result of the message and focus on getting that point across clearly and concisely.
- *Use face-to-face communication whenever possible.* Although not always practical, face-to-face communication reduces the likelihood of misunderstandings because it allows for immediate feedback and nonverbal clues.
- *Be empathetic.* Put yourself in the place of those who will receive your message, and develop it accordingly.
- *Match your message to your audience.* An entrepreneur would be very unlikely to use the same words, techniques, and style to communicate his company's financial position to a group of industry analysts as he would to a group of workers on the factory floor.
- *Be organized.* Effective communicators organize their messages so that their audiences can understand them easily.
- *Encourage feedback.* Good leaders actively seek honest feedback from as many employees as possible. At computer chip maker Intel, managers routinely hold "skip-level meetings," in which managers meet with employees who are two levels down the organization. "It's a powerful tool for getting information," says Patricia Murray, the company's director of human resources.[64]
- *Get out of the office and talk to employees.* Some of the most meaningful conversations managers have take place when they leave their offices to "wander" through the workplace. Management author Tom Peters calls it "MBWA, management by wandering around."
- *Tell the truth.* The fastest way to destroy your credibility as a leader is to lie.
- *Don't be afraid to tell employees about the business, its performance, and the forces that affect it.* Too often, entrepreneurs assume that employees don't care about such details. Employees *are* interested in the business that employs them and want to understand where it is headed and how it plans to get there.

Listening

When one thinks about communication, listening typically does not come to mind, yet listening is an essential part of the communication process. Entrepreneurs must listen to what employees on the front line are learning about customers' needs and demands. "The key to success and growth is getting employees to tell you what's really going on," says Vineet Nayar, CEO of HCL Technologies and author of *Employees First, Customers Second.*[65] The employees who serve customers are the *real* experts in the company's day-to-day activities. They are in closer contact with potential problems and opportunities at the operating level than anyone else in the company, particularly managers. According to a survey by VitalSmarts, more than 90 percent of employees say that they know early on when projects are destined to fail, and 78 percent say they are currently working on a doomed project. More than three-fourths of employees compare their failing projects to a "slow motion train wreck."[66] Managers who take the time to listen to their frontline employees avoid many of these train wrecks. In addition, by encouraging employees to develop creative solutions to problems and innovative ideas for capitalizing on opportunities and then listening to and acting on them, entrepreneurs can make their companies more successful.

At Best Buy, the Minneapolis, Minnesota-based electronics retailer, managers focus on communicating with employees rather than at them and use a variety of social media tools to help them. The company uses its intranet to conduct weekly employee polls on a multitude of topics and has built wikis that allow employees with common interests to build a storehouse of valuable knowledge. "Wiki has been a great source for local store employees to learn details about their specific location's business goals, see what the competition is up to, find information on company strategy, and learn and share best practices," says Andy Hokenson, the company's senior specialist for dialogue and intranet. Senior managers participate in online "town hall meetings," in which employees ask questions about anything. Best Buy's IdeaX site encourages employees to submit and discuss ideas for improving the company's operations; so far, employees have submitted more than 6,500 ideas. The centerpiece of the company's communication system is the Watercooler, an online discussion forum that encourages employees to engage one another and managers in meaningful conversations. Managers recently proved how important the Watercooler is when they reduced the discount on employee purchases. Hundreds of employees expressed concern and explained how the discount encourages them to try out products that they then recommend to customers. Managers got the message and reinstated the full employee discount.[67]

Improvements such as these depend on entrepreneurs' ability to listen. To improve listening skills, entrepreneurs can use the PDCH formula: identify the speaker's *purpose*, recognize the *details* that support that purpose, see the *conclusions* they can draw from what the speaker is saying, and identify the *hidden* meanings communicated by body language and voice inflections.

The Informal Communication Network: The "Grapevine"

Despite all of the modern communication tools available, the grapevine, the informal lines of communication that exist in every company, remains an important link in a company's communication network. The grapevine carries vital information—and sometimes rumors—through every part of the organization with incredible speed. The grapevine kicks into overdrive when the information in a company's formal communication network is scarce. It is not unusual for employees to hear about important changes in an organization through the grapevine well before official communication channels transmit the news. Research shows that up to 70 percent of all organizational communication comes by way of the grapevine, yet many top managers are not aware of the efficiency with which this informal communication channel operates.[68] Text and instant messaging and e-mail increase the speed at which the grapevine transmits informal communications, all under the radar of management.

Knowing that employees are connected through the grapevine allows entrepreneurs to send out ideas to obtain reactions without making a formal announcement. When management is in the loop, the grapevine can be an excellent source of informal feedback. Smart managers recognize the grapevine's existence and use it as a communication tool to both send and receive meaningful information.

Kim Seymour, founder and owner of Cravings, a Raleigh, North Carolina, retail company that sells trendy maternity clothing and accessories, appreciates the value of listening to the employee grapevine for feedback. Seymour seeks advice from employees who teach her about merchandising, marketing, and customer relations. One employee brings 9 years of experience as a retail manager, experience Seymour did not have when she started the company. "There's no way someone is going to be an expert in every aspect of running a business," says Seymour.[69]

The Challenge of Motivating Workers

Motivation is the degree of effort an employee exerts to accomplish a task; it shows up as excitement about work. Motivating workers to higher levels of performance is one of the most difficult and challenging tasks facing a small business manager. Few things are more frustrating to an entrepreneur than an employee with a tremendous amount of talent who lacks the desire to use it. This section discusses four aspects of motivation: empowerment, job design, rewards and compensation, and feedback.

5. Discuss the ways in which entrepreneurs can motivate their employees to achieve higher levels of performance.

Empowerment

One motivating principle is empowerment. **Empowerment** involves giving workers at every level of the organization the authority, the freedom, and the responsibility to control their own work, to make decisions, and to take action to meet the company's objectives. Research indicates that employees experience increased initiative and motivation when they are empowered. Empowerment affects their self-confidence and the level of tenacity they display when faced with setbacks. Empowered employees take responsibility for making decisions and following them through to completion; they feel energized and excited by what they do and are more likely to achieve mutually agreed-upon goals.[70] Empowerment complements the team-based management style discussed earlier.

Empowerment builds on what real business leaders already know: that the people in their organizations bring with them to work an amazing array of talents, skills, knowledge, and abilities. Workers are willing—even anxious—to put these to use; unfortunately, in too many businesses suffocating management styles and poorly designed jobs quash workers' enthusiasm and motivation. Enlightened entrepreneurs recognize their workers' abilities, develop them, and then give workers the freedom and the power to use them. Entrepreneurs who share information, responsibility, authority, and power soon discover that their success (and their companies' success) is magnified many times over.

When implemented properly, empowerment can produce impressive results, not only for the business, but also for newly empowered employees. For the business, benefits typically include significant productivity gains, quality improvement, more satisfied customers, improved morale, and increased employee motivation. For workers, empowerment offers the chance to do a greater variety of work that is interesting and challenging. Empowerment challenges workers to make the most of their creativity, imagination, knowledge, and skills.

Not every worker *wants* to be empowered, however. Some will resist, wanting only to "put in their 8 hours and go home." Companies that move to an empowerment philosophy will lose about 5 percent of their workforce because some employees simply are unwilling or are unable to make the change. Another 75 percent of the typical workforce will accept empowerment and thrive under it, and the remaining 20 percent will pounce on it eagerly because they want to contribute their talents and their ideas.

Empowerment works best when entrepreneurs:

- *Are confident enough to give workers all the authority and responsibility they can handle.* Initially, this may involve giving workers the power to tackle relatively simple assignments. As their confidence and ability grow, most workers are eager to take on additional responsibility.
- *Play the role of coach and facilitator.* Smart owners empower their workers and then get out of the way so they can do their jobs.
- *Recognize that empowered employees will make mistakes.* The worst thing an owner can do when empowered employees make mistakes is to hunt them down and punish them. That teaches everyone in the company to avoid taking risks and to always play it safe—something no innovative small business can afford.
- *Hire people who can blossom in an empowered environment.* Empowerment is not for everyone. Owners quickly learn that as costly as hiring mistakes are, such errors are even more costly in an empowered environment. Ideal candidates are high-energy self-starters who enjoy the opportunity to grow and enhance their skills.
- *Train workers continuously to upgrade their skills.* Empowerment demands more of workers than traditional work methods. Managers are asking workers to solve problems and make decisions they have never made before. To handle these problems well, workers need training, especially in effective problem-solving techniques, communication, teamwork, and technical skills.
- *Trust workers to do their jobs.* Once workers are trained to do their jobs, owners must learn to trust them to assume responsibility for their jobs. After all, they are the real experts; they face the problems and challenges every day.
- *Listen to workers when they have ideas, solutions, or suggestions.* Because they are the experts on the job, employees often come up with incredibly insightful, innovative ideas for improving them—*if* entrepreneurs give them the chance. Surveying employees, for example, can become a critical part of companies' efforts to bolster employees' commitment

to their jobs, a concept called **employee engagement.** Engaged workers are more willing to help bosses and coworkers solve problems, take initiative, promote the company outside of work, and offer ideas for improving the company. Failing to acknowledge or act on employees' ideas sends them a clear message: Your ideas really don't count.

■ *Recognize workers' contributions.* One of the most important tasks an entrepreneur can perform is to recognize positive employee performance. In *The Carrot Principle*, authors Adrian Gostick and Chester Elton say that recognition must be frequent, specific and timely, and, of course, deserved.[71] Some businesses reward workers with monetary awards; others rely on recognition and praise; still others use a combination of money and praise. Whatever system an owner chooses, the key to keeping a steady flow of ideas, improvements, suggestions, and solutions is to recognize the people who supply them.

ENTREPRENEURIAL

Profile

Container Store and Build-A-Bear

At the Container Store, a chain of retail stores that sell a complete line of storage and organization products and is a frequent resident on *Fortune*'s "Best Companies to Work For" list, founder Kip Tindell encourages store managers to recognize employees who do outstanding work. Brian Edison, manager of a Container Store near Dallas, Texas, puts handwritten sticky notes of congratulations for jobs well done on employees' lockers. At Build-A-Bear, a chain of retail stores that allows kids (and adults) to build their own stuffed animals, managers hand out handwritten "Atta-bear" notes of recognition when employees excel at their jobs. These spontaneous, real-time rewards have special meaning to the employees who receive them.[72]

■ *Share information with workers.* For empowerment to succeed, entrepreneurs must make sure workers get adequate information, the raw material for good decision making. Some companies have gone beyond sharing information to embrace **open-book management,** in which employees have access to *all* of a company's records, including its financial statements. The goal of open-book management is to enable employees to understand why they need to raise productivity, improve quality, cut costs, and improve customer service. Under open-book management, employees:

■ Review and learn to understand the company's financial statements and other critical numbers in measuring its performance.
■ Learn that a significant part of their jobs is making sure those critical numbers move in the right direction.
■ Have a direct stake in the company's success through profit sharing, ESOPs, or performance-based bonuses.

ENTREPRENEURIAL

Profile

Anthony and Elizabeth Wilder: Anthony Wilder Design/Build

At Anthony Wilder Design/Build, a residential architecture and construction company in Cabin John, Maryland, copreneurs Anthony and Elizabeth Wilder practice open-book management with their 30 employees. The Wilders teach their employees how to read the company's financial and operating reports so that they can understand how their work and their department's work directly affects the firm's financial performance. The Wilders also changed the incentive system they use so that every quarter employees receive a portion of the company's net income rather than bonuses for their individual performances. Before, says Elizabeth, "they didn't have a stake in the outcome. Now they can feel it, see it, quantify it." Every month, employees meet for breakfast to discuss business and to brainstorm ways to improve the company's performance.[73]

Job Design

A recent survey by the Conference Board shows that only 45 percent of employees are satisfied with their jobs, a significant decrease from 61 percent in 1987. In addition, only 36 percent of workers under the age of 25 say they are satisfied. The survey also reports that 51 percent of workers find their jobs interesting, down from 70 percent in 1987.[74] Managers have learned that the job itself and the way it is designed can make it more interesting and can be a source of satisfaction and motivation for workers. During the industrial age, work was organized on the

At Anthony Wilder Design/Build, copreneurs Anthony and Elizabeth Wilder practice open-book management with their 30 employees.

Source: Anthony Wilder Design/ Build, Inc.

principle of **job simplification**, which involves breaking the work down into its simplest form and standardizing each task. Assembly line operations are based on job simplification. The scope of workers' jobs is extremely narrow, resulting in impersonal, monotonous, and boring work that creates little challenge or motivation for workers. The result is apathetic, unmotivated workers who care little about quality, customers, or costs.

To break this destructive cycle, some companies have redesigned workers' jobs. The following strategies are common: job enlargement, job rotation, job enrichment, flextime, job sharing, and flexplace.

Job enlargement (or **horizontal job loading**) adds more tasks to a job to broaden its scope. For instance, rather than an employee simply mounting four screws in computers coming down an assembly line, a worker might assemble, install, and test the entire motherboard (perhaps as part of a team). The idea is to make the job more varied and to allow employees to perform a more complete unit of work.

Job rotation involves cross-training employees so they can move from one job in the company to others, giving them a greater number and variety of tasks to perform. As employees learn other jobs within an organization, both their skills and their understanding of the company's purpose and processes rise. Cross-trained workers are more valuable because they give a company the flexibility to shift workers from low-demand jobs to those where they are most needed. As an incentive for workers to learn to perform other jobs within an operation, some companies offer skill-based pay, a system under which the more skills workers acquire, the more they earn.

Job enrichment (or **vertical job loading**) involves building motivators into a job by increasing the planning, decision making, organizing, and controlling functions—traditionally managerial tasks—workers perform. The idea is to make every employee a manager—at least a manager of his or her own job.

To enrich employees' jobs, a business owner must build five core characteristics into them:

- *Skill variety* is the degree to which a job requires a variety of different skills, talents, and activities from the worker. Does the job require the worker to perform a variety of tasks that demand a variety of skills and abilities, or does it force him to perform the same task repeatedly?
- *Task identity* is the degree to which a job allows the worker to complete a whole or identifiable piece of work. Does the employee build an entire piece of furniture (perhaps as part of a team), or does he merely attach four screws?
- *Task significance* is the degree to which a job substantially influences the lives or work of others—employees or final customers. Does the employee get to deal with customers, either internal or external? One effective way to establish task significance is to put employees in touch with customers so they can see how customers use the product or service they make.
- *Autonomy* is the degree to which a job gives a worker the freedom, independence, and discretion in planning and performing tasks. Does the employee make decisions affecting his work, or must he rely on someone else (e.g., the owner, a manager, or a supervisor) to "call the shots?"

■ *Feedback* is the degree to which a job gives the worker direct, timely information about the quality of his performance. Does the job give employees feedback about the quality of their work or does the product (and all information about it) simply disappear after it leaves the worker's station?

A study conducted by researchers at the University of New Hampshire and the Bureau of Labor Statistics concludes that employees of companies that use job enrichment principles are more satisfied than those who work in jobs designed using principles of simplification.[75]

Flextime is an arrangement under which employees work a normal number of hours but have flexibility about when they start and stop work. A recent study by the Families and Work Institute reports that 86 percent of employees say that a job that gives them the flexibility to balance work and family life is either very or extremely important.[76] Most flextime arrangements require employees to build their work schedules around a set of "core hours"—such as 10 A.M. to 2 P.M., but give them the freedom to set their schedules outside of those core hours. For instance, one worker might choose to come in at 7 A.M. and leave at 3 P.M. to attend her son's soccer game, and another may work from 11 A.M. to 7 P.M. Flextime not only raises worker morale, but it also makes it easier for companies to attract high-quality young workers who want rewarding careers without sacrificing their lifestyles. In addition, companies using flextime schedules experience higher levels of employee engagement and lower levels of tardiness, turnover, and absenteeism.

Blue Gecko, a Seattle-based company that provides database services and promises its customers a response to an emergency within 30 minutes no matter the time of day, uses technology to give its employees the flexibility to set their work schedules and locations. "Most of our work requires only an Internet connection and focus," says cofounder Sarah Novotny. Offering flextime helps her employees to keep their work and their lives in balance and to meet the company's 30-minute pledge to its customers. It also gives her company access to a larger pool of more qualified applicants.[77]

Flextime is becoming an increasingly popular job design strategy. A recent survey by Families and Work Institute found that 79 percent of the nation's workers have flexible schedules, up from 68 percent in 1998.[78] The number of companies using flextime is likely to continue to grow as companies find recruiting capable, qualified full-time workers more difficult and as technology makes working from a dedicated office space less important. Research shows that when considering job offers, candidates, particularly members of Generation Y, weigh heavily the flexibility of the work schedule companies offer.

Job sharing is a work arrangement in which two or more people share a single full-time job. For instance, two college students might share the same 40-hour-a-week job, one working mornings and the other working afternoons. Salary and benefits are prorated between the workers sharing a job. Because job sharing is a simple solution to the growing challenge of work–life balance, it is becoming more popular. Companies already using it are finding it easier to recruit and retain qualified workers. "Employers get the combined strengths of two people, but they only have to pay for one," says one hotel sales manager, herself a job sharer.[79]

Flexplace is a work arrangement in which employees work at a place other than the traditional office, such as a satellite branch closer to their homes or, in many cases, at home. Flexplace is an easy job design strategy for companies to use because of **telecommuting**. Using modern communication technologies such as iPads, smartphones, texting, e-mail, and laptop computers, employees have more flexibility in choosing where they work. Today, it is quite simple for workers to connect electronically to their workplaces (and to all of the people and the information there) from practically anywhere on the planet.

Employees at Barfield, Murphy, Shank, and Smith (BMSS), an accounting firm in Birmingham, Alabama, enjoy the benefits of flextime schedules, and many of them also telecommute. Jaclyn Collins, who has worked for the company since 2000, began telecommuting from her home office (which BMSS set up) in 2008 when her husband took a job in a community outside of Birmingham. During the hectic tax season, BMSS provides a valet, who runs errands for employees, and arranges for a laundry service to make pickups and deliveries twice a week. The result: an extremely low employee turnover rate of just 2 to 3 percent annually.[80]

According to a study by information technology provider CDW-G, 36 percent of private sector companies allow telecommuting, and 14 percent of private sector employees are telecommuters.[81] Telecommuting employees get the flexibility they seek and benefit from reduced commuting times and expenses, not to mention a less expensive wardrobe (bathrobes and bunny slippers compared to business suits and wingtips or high heels). Companies reap many benefits as well, including improved employee morale, less absenteeism, lower turnover, higher productivity, and more satisfied, more loyal employees. Studies show that telecommuting can reduce employee turnover by 20 percent and increase productivity between 15 and 20 percent.[82] Cisco Systems, a software provider, says that employees who telecommute show increased productivity, higher quality work, and more job satisfaction as a result of their ability to control their work–life balance.[83]

Before implementing telecommuting, entrepreneurs must address the following important issues:

- Does the nature of the work fit telecommuting? Obviously, some jobs are better suited for telecommuting than others.
- Have you selected the right employees for telecommuting? Telecommuting is not suitable for every job or for every worker. Experienced managers say that employees who handle it best are experienced workers who know their jobs well, are self-disciplined, and are good communicators.
- Can you monitor compliance with federal wage and hour laws for telecommuters? Generally, employers must keep the same employment records for telecommuters that they do for traditional office workers.
- Have you provided the necessary computer, communications, and ergonomically designed office equipment for employees to work offsite? Trying to "make do" with substandard equipment creates problems and frustration and undermines any telecommuting effort from the outset.
- Are you adequately insured? Employers should be sure that the telecommuting equipment that employees use in their homes is covered under their insurance policies.
- Can you keep in touch? Telecommuting works well as long as long-distance employees stay in touch with headquarters.
- Have you created an equitable telecommuting policy that defines under what conditions telecommuting is acceptable? One danger of telecommuting is that it can create resentment among employees who remain office-bound.

Rewards and Compensation

The rewards an employee receives from the job itself are intrinsic, but managers have a wide variety of extrinsic rewards to motivate workers at their disposal. The key to using rewards to motivate involves tailoring the reward system to the needs and characteristics of the workers. Effective reward systems tap into the values and issues that are important to people. Smart entrepreneurs take the time to learn what makes their employees "tick" and then build their reward system around those motivational factors. For instance, a technician making $30,000 a year may consider a chance to earn a $5,000 bonus to be a powerful motivator; an executive earning $200,000 a year may not.

Research by Globoforce, a Boston-based company that specializes in rewards and incentives, shows that small, frequent awards are more effective than periodic cash bonuses, which is good news for small companies that cannot always afford financial rewards. The study suggests that 80 to 90 percent of a company's employees should get some type of reward every year and that every week a company should be giving rewards to 5 percent of its employees (a concept known as continuous reinforcement). "Small awards all the time are a way to constantly touch people," he says. Jennifer Lepird, who works in the human resources department at software developer Intuit, recently spent several weeks and many long days integrating into Intuit's salary structure the employees at a company that Intuit had purchased. Her manager sent her a congratulatory e-mail thanking her for her quality work and a gift certificate worth $200. Lepird was thrilled. "The fact that somebody took the time to recognize the effort made the long hours just melt away," she says.[84]

One of the most popular rewards is money. Cash is an effective motivator—up to a point; its effects tend to be short-term. Many companies have moved to **pay-for-performance compensation systems**, in which employees' pay depends on how well they perform their jobs. In other words, extra productivity equals extra pay. By linking employees' compensation directly to the company's financial performance, an entrepreneur increases the likelihood that workers will achieve performance

Source: King Features Syndicate

targets that are in their best interest and in the company's best interest. A common application of the pay-for-performance concept is a **profit-sharing system**, in which a company shares a portion of its profit with the employees who work to produce it.

Heavy Construction Systems Specialists (HCSS), a company based in Sugarland, Texas, that develops software for the construction industry, has a profit-sharing system for its 106 employees as well as an employee stock purchase plan. In a recent year, CEO Mike Rydin says that HCSS employees received 22 percent of their base salaries through the profit-sharing system. All 106 employees also participate in the stock purchase plan, through which they own 30 percent of the company.[85]

Pay-for-performance systems work only when employees see a clear correlation between their performance and their pay. This offers an advantage for small companies when the employees can see a clearer impact their performance has on the company's profitability and ultimate success compared to their counterparts at large corporations. To be successful, however, pay-for-performance systems should meet the following criteria:

▓ *Performance-based.* Employees' incentive pay must be clearly and closely linked to their performances.
▓ *Relevant.* Entrepreneurs must set up the system so that employees see the connection between what they do every day on the job—selling to customers, producing a product, or anything else—and the rewards they receive under the system.
▓ *Simple.* The system must be simple enough so that employees understand and trust it. Complex systems that employees have difficulty understanding do not produce the desired results.
▓ *Equitable.* Employees must consider the system fair.
▓ *Inclusive.* The system should be inclusive. Entrepreneurs are finding creative ways to reward all employees, no matter what their jobs might be.

■ *Timely.* The company should make timely payouts to employees. A single annual payout is ineffective—employees have long since forgotten what they did to earn the incentive pay. The closer a reward payment is to the action that prompted it, the more effective it will be.

Money is not the only motivator entrepreneurs have at their disposal. Nonfinancial incentives can be more important sources of employee motivation. With a little creativity, small businesses can provide meaningful rewards that motivate employees without breaking the bank. Often the most meaningful motivating factors are the simplest—and least costly—ones, such as praise, recognition, respect, feedback, job security, and promotions. When an employee has done an exceptional job, an entrepreneur should be the first to recognize that accomplishment and to say "thank you." Praise is a simple and powerful motivational tool. "Praise is the most powerful driver of performance known to mankind," says Bob Nelson, a workplace consultant.[86] People enjoy getting praise and recognition; it is just human nature. As Mark Twain once said, "I can live for two months on a good compliment."

The Cheesecake Factory, the Calabasas, California-based restaurant chain, produces a newsletter, "Slice," that recognizes employees' exceptional performances by including stories on workers who go the extra mile to take care of their customers or other employees. A recent issue told the story of an employee who drove to Los Angeles International Airport to deliver a credit card to a customer who had left it in the restaurant. Claire Prager, the company's talent manager, says that the employees who are featured in the newsletter become celebrities in their locations and that the stories are an important part of the company's culture, often inspiring other employees to go the extra mile.[87]

One sure way to kill high performance is failing to recognize the performance and the employees responsible for it. Failing to praise good work eventually conveys the message that the owner either doesn't care about exceptional performance or cannot distinguish between good work and poor work. In either case, through inaction, the manager destroys employees' motivation to excel.

Rewards do *not* have to be expensive to be effective, but they should be creative and should have a direct link to employee performance. Consider how the following rewards for exceptional performance both recognize the employee's contribution and build a positive organizational culture:

■ At Nugget Market, a supermarket chain based in Woodland, California, top managers showed their appreciation for employees' hard work by washing associates' cars.[88]
■ The AAA Fair Credit Foundation in Salt Lake City, Utah, involves all of its employees in rewarding excellent performance. Employees recognize the extra efforts and special accomplishments of their coworkers by recommending them for "Dollar Days." When an employee earns eight Dollar Days, he or she cashes them in for a day off.[89]
■ At Adec Group, a Greenville, South Carolina-based company that manages communications across multiple channels for large companies, owner June Wilcox treats employees to company-paid movie outings and baseball games—during office hours—when they complete challenging assignments.

Whatever system of rewards they use, entrepreneurs will be most successful if they match rewards to employees' interests and tastes. For instance, the ideal reward for one employee might be tickets to a sports event; to another, it might be tickets to a theatrical performance. The better entrepreneurs know their employees' interests and tastes, the more effective they will be at matching rewards with performance.

In the future, entrepreneurs will rely more on nonmonetary rewards—praise, recognition, letters of commendation, and others—to create a work environment where employees take pride in their work. Under this system, employees enjoy what they do and find their work challenging, exciting, and rewarding. The benefit to the company is that these employees are more likely to act like owners of the business themselves. The goal of nonmonetary rewards is to let employees know that every person is important and that the company notices, appreciates, and recognizes excellent performance.

Performance Feedback

Entrepreneurs not only must motivate employees to excel in their jobs, but also focus employees' efforts on the right business targets. Providing feedback on progress toward those targets can be a

Creating a Winning Workplace

John Sullivan, a store director for Nugget Market, a family-owned grocery chain founded in 1926 and based in Woodland, California, is proud that his employer is on *Fortune*'s list of the "100 Best Companies to Work For." "We have a wonderful relationship in the store," says Sullivan. "We really are a family. I know [my coworkers'] kids, their husbands and wives, I know their dogs' and cats' names, what classes they are taking in school and whether they got a flat on the way to work. The nice thing about this company is that the associates are empowered to do what it takes to make their guests (customers) happy and meet their needs. I'm excited to come to work every day."

Entrepreneurs strive to create a work environment that nurtures a culture like the one at Nugget Market. Not all are successful, but the ones who are find that a winning workplace gives their companies a significant competitive advantage. What are these companies doing right? The following lessons from the Street-Smart Entrepreneur offer meaningful insight into creating a winning workplace:

- *Select the right employees.* Mike's Carwash, based in Indianapolis, Indiana, uses an intense screening process, hiring just 1 out of 100 applicants. Candidates take two tests, one that measures math aptitude and one that provides insight into their personalities. At least two employees interview every candidate and look for strong logical and social skills as well as an attitude of customer service.

- *Provide stable employment.* Winning workplaces do everything they can to avoid layoffs. Doing so creates an implied contract of trust with employees. Wegman's, rated as one of the best grocery chains in the country, has never had a layoff since its founding in 1916. Employees return the company's loyalty by sticking around. Eleven percent of the Rochester, New York-based company's employees have tenure of 15 or more years.

- *Give employees incentives to stay.* High employee turnover rates are costly and result in lost potential and "brain drain." To keep their employees, a growing number of small companies share their financial success with their workers through profit-sharing plans or employee stock ownership plans (ESOPs). Michael and Jack Kennedy, owners of Railroad Associates Corporation, a company in Hershey, Pennsylvania, that repairs railways, established an ESOP shortly after launching the company in 2000. Today, nonmanagerial employees own 40 percent of the company's stock and can qualify for bonuses of up to 50 percent of their regular pay for providing superior customer service, completing projects on time, and maintaining a good safety record. A recent study by the Cass Business School in London concludes that employee-owned businesses create jobs faster and typically outperform companies in which employees have no stake.

- *Offer training and advancement opportunities.* Winning workplaces invest in their employees. At Mike's Carwash, employees receive regular training on techniques for providing outstanding customer service. Every week, employees watch short videos that offer customer service tips and other job-related education and updates on company news and events. The company also offers tuition reimbursement of up to $2,500 annually for employees who want to continue their education.

- *Provide flexible work schedules.* Many employees face challenges as they attempt to balance the demands of work, family, and activities. Companies that provide flexible work schedules have an edge when it comes to attracting quality employees. At A Speaker for You, an event planning company in Louisville, Kentucky, employees set their own work and vacation schedules. "We have found that giving this kind of freedom to employees brings enhanced rewards to the company," says the company's president, Tim Green. "Employees have proven trustworthy over a long period of time. That is why we continue to grow."

- *Rely on innovative job design and participative management.* Many employees, especially young workers, want to join companies that offer a culture of participative management rather than a top-down, autocratic style. At Railroad Associates, owners Michael and Jack Kennedy have created a very flat organization structure with virtually no middle managers. They delegate the authority and the responsibility for making decisions and solving problems directly to their employees. The Kennedys also make sure that workers get plenty of training, in the classroom, online, and on the job, so that they are able to make good decisions.

Sources: Based on Kelly K. Spors, "Top Workplaces 2009," *Wall Street Journal*, September 28, 2009, pp. R4, R5; Ellen Galinsky, Shanny L. Peer, and Sheila Eby, *When Work Works: 2009 Guide to Bold New Ideas for*

Making Work Work, Families and Work Institute, 2009, pp. 37–38; "I Work for One of the 10 Best Companies," *Fortune*, 2010, *http://money.cnn.com/galleries/2010/fortune/1001/gallery.Bestcompanies_employees.fortune/5.html*; Sam Potter, "Employee Involvement Gets the Best," *Kipp Report*, September 7, 2010, *www.kippreport.com/2010/09/employee-involvement-gets-the-best/*.

powerful motivating force in a company. To strengthen the link between the entrepreneur's vision for the company and its operations, he or she must build a series of specific performance measures that serve as periodic monitoring points. For each critical element of the organization's performance—quality, financial performance, market position, productivity, employee development—he or she should develop specific measures that connect daily operational responsibilities with the company's overall strategic direction. These measures establish the benchmarks for measuring employees' performance and the company's progress. The adage "what gets measured and monitored gets done" is true in most organizations. An entrepreneur defines for everyone in the company what is most important by connecting the company's long-term strategy to its daily operations and measuring performance.

Providing feedback implies that entrepreneurs have established meaningful targets that serve as standards of performance for them, their employees, and the company as a whole. One characteristic successful people have in common is that they set goals and objectives—usually challenging ones—for themselves. Entrepreneurs are no different. Successful entrepreneurs usually set targets for performance that make them stretch to achieve, and then they encourage their employees to do the same. The result is that they keep their companies constantly moving forward.

For feedback to serve as a motivating force in a business requires entrepreneurs to follow the procedure illustrated in Figure 3, the feedback loop.

DECIDING WHAT TO MEASURE. The first step in the feedback loop is deciding what to measure. Every business has a set of numbers that are critical to its success, and these "critical numbers" are what entrepreneurs should focus on. Obvious critical numbers include sales, profits, profit margins, cash flow, and other standard financial measures. However, supporting these measurements is an additional set of critical numbers that are unique to a company's operations. In most cases, these are the numbers that actually drive profits, cash flow, and other financial measures—they are the company's *real* critical numbers.

DECIDING HOW TO MEASURE. Once an entrepreneur identifies his or her company's critical numbers, he or she must decide how to measure them. In some cases, identifying the critical

FIGURE 3
The Feedback Loop

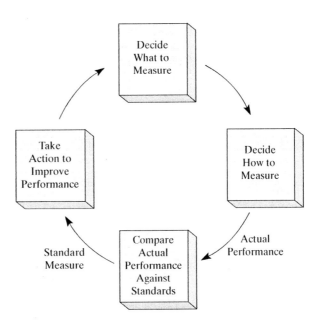

numbers defines the measurements owners must make, and measuring them simply becomes a matter of collecting and analyzing data. In other cases, the method of measurement is not as obvious—or as tangible. For instance, in some businesses social responsibility is a key factor, but how should managers measure their company's performance on such an intangible concept? One of the best ways to develop methods for measuring such factors is to use brainstorming sessions involving employees, customers, and even outsiders. For example, one company used this technique to develop a "fun index," which used the results of an employee survey to measure how much fun employees are having at work. The index is an indication of how satisfied they are with their work, the company, and their managers.

COMPARING ACTUAL PERFORMANCE AGAINST STANDARDS. In this stage of the feedback loop, the goal is to look for variances *in either direction* from company performance standards. In other words, opportunities to improve performance arise when there is a gap between "what should be" and "what is." The most serious deviations usually are those in which actual performance falls far below the standard. Entrepreneurs must focus their efforts on figuring out why actual performance is substandard. The goal is *not* to hunt down the guilty party (or parties) for punishment but to discover the cause of the poor performance and fix it. Managers should not ignore deviations in the other direction, however. If actual performance consistently exceeds the company's standards, it may be an indication that the standards are set too low.

TAKING ACTION TO IMPROVE PERFORMANCE. When managers or employees detect a performance gap, their next challenge is to decide on a course of action that will eliminate it. Typically, several suitable alternatives to solving a performance problem exist; the key is finding an acceptable solution that solves the problem quickly, efficiently, and effectively.

Performance Appraisal

One of the most common methods of providing feedback on employee performance is through **performance appraisal**, the process of evaluating an employee's actual performance against desired performance standards. Most performance appraisal programs strive to accomplish three goals:

1. To give employees feedback about how they are performing, which can be an important source of motivation
2. To provide entrepreneurs and employees the opportunity to create a plan for developing employee skills and abilities and for improving their performance
3. To establish a basis for determining promotions and salary increases

The primary purpose of performance appraisals is to encourage and to help employees improve their performance. Unfortunately, they can turn into uncomfortable confrontations that do nothing more than upset the employees, aggravate the entrepreneur, and destroy trust and morale. This may occur because the entrepreneur does not understand how to conduct an effective performance appraisal. Although U.S. businesses have been conducting performance appraisals for at least 75 years, most companies, their managers, and their employees are dissatisfied with the process. A survey by Salary.com shows that 60 percent of workers say that performance appraisals do not produce any useful feedback and fail to help them set meaningful objectives.[90] Common complaints include unclear standards and objectives, managers who lack information about employees' performances, managers who are unprepared or who lack honesty and sincerity, and managers who use general, ambiguous terms to describe employees' performances.

One complaint is that the performance appraisal happens only periodically: in most cases, just once a year. Employees do not have the opportunity to receive any ongoing feedback on a regular basis. All too often, managers save up all of the negative feedback to give employees and then dump it on them in the annual performance review. Doing so destroys employees' motivation and does *nothing* to improve their performance. What good does it do to tell an employee that 6 months earlier he or she botched an assignment and caused the company to lose a customer? Performance reviews that occur once or twice a year in an attempt to improve employees' performance are similar to working out once or twice a year in an attempt to get into top physical condition!

The lack of ongoing feedback is similar to asking employees to bowl in the dark. They can hear some pins falling, but they have no idea how many are down or which ones are left standing for the next frame. How motivated would you be to keep bowling? How do you know your score as you bowl? Managers should address problems when they occur rather than wait until the

► ENTREPRENEURSHIP IN ACTION ►

Spying or Protecting His Investment?

Ryan Elmore, owner of Pepper Jack's Neighborhood Grill, a neighborhood restaurant in Erie, Colorado, was confident that his employees were hard at work when he was away from the business. However, when Elmore installed a video surveillance system that allowed him to monitor the action in his restaurant online, he was shocked at what he saw. The restaurant manager who was on duty went home a few minutes after Elmore left, and cooks took shortcuts when they made the restaurant's signature fettuccine Alfredo. Employees took extended breaks, sat at tables and sent text messages, and doled out free dinners to their friends. "I couldn't believe it," says Elmore. "You may trust your employees, but you don't know what happens when you walk out the door."

Today, a networked video system is in place, and Elmore's 20 employees know that he is watching their performances even when he is away from the restaurant. Elmore can remotely view a customer's cash register receipt and call up the video of that transaction. He can determine whether employees are cleaning the restaurant when they are supposed to and whether they are smiling at customers and greeting them appropriately. He knows when meals arrive late at diners' tables and can detect employees who are eating unauthorized meals. Installation of the video system cost Elmore just $850 and a $160 monthly online subscription fee that gives him unlimited access to both live and archived video. The investment paid off quickly. While reviewing video, Elmore and his business partner, his wife Janel, noticed that the restaurant frequently was overstaffed. Adjusting employees' schedules to cover the busiest times alone saved the company $50,000 per year. The restaurant's food costs also declined 3 percent because servers stopped giving away free meals to their friends. Overall, Elmore was able to reduce the company's annual operating costs by $100,000. "The technology has more than paid for itself," he says.

Elmore admits that, initially, he felt guilty about "spying" on his employees, but the results have diminished that concern. "I want to know where every dollar is going," he says. "This is my life. Everything I have is riding on this." Remote monitoring of their business gives the Elmores the ability to have more free time away from the restaurant without surrendering control over it. Elmore credits the video system with helping him identify and reward one of his best workers. While watching videos, he noticed that one kitchen staff was cleaning more often than usual. When he investigated, Elmore discovered that the kitchen manager had created a contest to motivate her employees. Elmore was impressed and promoted her.

1. How would you feel about working for a business that uses a video system to monitor employees at work? Explain. Why do business owners use monitoring systems?
2. "Most employees do not like to be monitored, and it may cause some resentment," says one employment attorney. Do you agree? Explain.
3. Use the Web to research video monitoring of employees and prepare a list of at least five recommendations to help companies avoid legal problems.
4. Can you suggest other ways besides video monitoring that employers like Elmore can use to encourage employees to do their jobs well when the boss is away?

Source: Based on Jennifer Alsever, "Being Big Brother," *FSB*, October 2008, pp. 43–45.

performance appraisal session. Continuous feedback, both positive and negative, is a much more effective way to improve employees' performance and to increase their motivation than once-a-year feedback in a performance appraisal session.

Performance appraisals require planning and preparation on the entrepreneur's part. The following guidelines can help an entrepreneur create a performance appraisal system that actually works:

- *Link the employee performance criteria to the job description discussed earlier in this chapter.* To evaluate an employee's performance effectively, a manager must fully understand the responsibilities of the employee's position.
- *Establish meaningful, job-related, measurable, and results-oriented performance criteria.* The criteria should describe behaviors and actions, not traits and characteristics. What kind of behavior constitutes a solid performance in the job? Criteria that are quantifiable, such as customer satisfaction scores, the percentage of on-time shipments, and other specific measurements, rather than subjective criteria, such as leadership potential, initiative, and problem-solving ability, form the foundation of a meaningful performance evaluation.

- *Prepare for the appraisal session by outlining the key points you want to cover with employees.* Important points to include are employees' strengths and weaknesses and developing a plan for improving their performance.
- *Invite employees to provide an evaluation of their own job performance based on the performance criteria.* In one small company, workers rate themselves on a one-to-five scale in categories of job-related behavior and skills as part of the performance appraisal system. Then they meet with their supervisor to compare their evaluations with those of their supervisor and discuss them.
- *Be specific.* One of the most common complaints employees have about the appraisal process is that managers' comments are too general to be of any value. Offer the employees specific examples of their desirable or undesirable behavior.
- *Keep a record of employees' critical incidents—both positive and negative.* The most productive evaluations are those based on managers' direct observation of their employees' on-the-job performance. These records also can be vital in case legal problems arise.
- *Discuss employees' strengths and weaknesses.* An appraisal session is not the time to "unload" about everything employees have done wrong over the past year. Use it as an opportunity to design a plan for improvement and to recognize employees' strengths, efforts, and achievements.
- *Incorporate employees' goals into the appraisal.* Ideally, the standard against which to measure employees' performance is the goals they have played a role in setting. Workers are more likely to be motivated to achieve—and buy into—goals that they have helped establish.
- *Keep the evaluation constructive.* Avoid the tendency to belittle employees. Do not dwell on past failures. Instead, point out specific things they should do better and help them develop meaningful goals for the future and a strategy for getting there.
- *Praise good work.* Avoid focusing only on what employees do wrong. Take the time to express your appreciation for hard work and solid accomplishments.
- *Focus on behaviors, actions, and results.* Problems arise when managers move away from tangible results and actions and begin to critique employees' abilities and attitudes. Such criticism creates a negative tone for the appraisal session and undercuts its primary purpose.
- *Avoid surprises.* If entrepreneurs are doing their jobs well, performance appraisals should contain no surprises for employees or the owner. The ideal time to correct improper behavior or slumping performance is when it happens, not months later. Managers should provide employees with continuous feedback on their performance and use the appraisal session to keep employees on the right track.
- *Plan for the future.* Smart entrepreneurs use appraisal sessions as gateways to workers' future success. They spend only about 20 percent of the time discussing past performance; they use the remaining 80 percent of the time developing goals, objectives, and a plan for the future.

ENTREPRENEURIAL Profile

Brian Roth: Trufast

Brian Roth, CEO of Trufast, a small maker of fasteners located in Bryan, Ohio, realized that his company's performance appraisal process was ineffective. "The only thing the review did was cover the previous 2 weeks of performance," he says. "Basically, it was worthless." Roth revamped the entire process to focus on more frequent feedback and rewards. At the end of every quarter, all 80 of the company's employees meet with their supervisors, who assign up to 25 points in each of four areas: initiative, aptitude, flexibility, and attitude. Employees who score at least 70 points earn incentive pay; the higher their scores, the greater the bonus amount. More than 90 percent of Trufast's employees receive some bonus. Roth says that the program has reduced employee turnover and produces a return on investment of between 15 and 18 percent. "My employees keep asking me when the next review is and what they need to know to score well on it," says Roth. "That tells me all I need to know."[91]

Some companies allow employees to evaluate each other's performance in **peer reviews** or evaluate their boss's performance in **upward feedback**. These are aspects of a technique called **360-degree feedback**. Peer appraisals can be especially useful because an employee's coworkers see his or her on-the-job performance every day. As a result, peer evaluations tend to be more accurate and more valid than those of some managers. In addition, they may capture behavior that managers miss. Disadvantages of peer appraisals include the following: potential retaliation against coworkers who criticize, the possibility that appraisals will be reduced to "popularity contests," and the refusal of some workers to offer any criticism because they feel uncomfortable evaluating others. Some bosses using upward feedback report similar problems, including personal attacks and extreme evaluations by vengeful subordinates.

Regardless of the technique, employee feedback should be honest, clear, and respectful. Entrepreneurs will benefit from developing effective feedback skills as they grow the business and delegate additional responsibilities to employees.

Chapter Review

1. Explain the challenges involved in the entrepreneur's role as leader and what it takes to be a successful leader.
   - Leadership is the process of influencing and inspiring others to work to achieve a common goal and then giving them the power and the freedom to achieve it.
   - Management and leadership are not the same; yet both are essential to a small company's success. Leadership without management is unbridled; management without leadership is uninspired. Leadership gets a small business going; management keeps it going.

2. Describe the importance of hiring the right employees and how to avoid making hiring mistakes.
   - The decision to hire a new employee is an important one for every business, but its impact is magnified many times in a small company. Every "new hire" an entrepreneur makes determines the heights to which the company can climb or the depths to which it will plunge.
   - To avoid making hiring mistakes, entrepreneurs should develop meaningful job descriptions and job specifications, plan and conduct an effective interview, and check references before hiring any employee.

3. Explain how to build the kind of company culture and structure to support the company's mission and goals and to motivate employees to achieve them.
   - Company culture is the distinctive, unwritten code of conduct that governs the behavior, attitudes, relationships, and style of an organization. Culture arises from an entrepreneur's consistent and relentless pursuit of a set of core values that everyone in the company can believe in. Small companies' flexible structures can be a major competitive weapon.

4. Understand the potential barriers to effective communication and describe how to overcome them.
   - Research shows that managers spend about 80 percent of their time in some form of communication; yet their attempts at communicating sometimes go wrong. Several barriers to effective communication include: managers and employees don't always feel free to say what they really mean; ambiguity blocks real communication; information overload causes the message to get lost; selective listening interferes with the communication process; defense mechanisms block a message; and conflicting verbal and nonverbal messages confuse listeners.
   - To become more effective communicators, entrepreneurs should: clarify their messages before attempting to communicate them; use face-to-face communication whenever possible; be empathetic; match their messages to their audiences; be organized; encourage feedback; tell the truth; and not be afraid to tell employees about the business, its performance, and the forces that affect it.

5. Discuss the ways in which entrepreneurs can motivate their workers to higher levels of performance.
   - Motivation is the degree of effort an employee exerts to accomplish a task; it shows up as excitement about work. Four important tools of motivation are empowerment, job design, rewards and compensation, and feedback.
   - Empowerment involves giving workers at every level of the organization the power, the freedom, and the responsibility to control their own work, to make decisions, and to take action to meet the company's objectives.

- Job design techniques for enhancing employee motivation include job enlargement, job rotation, job enrichment, flextime, job sharing, and flexplace.
- Money is an important motivator for many workers, but not the only one. The key to using rewards such as recognition and praise to motivate involves tailoring them to the needs and characteristics of the workers.
- Giving employees timely, relevant feedback about their job performance through a performance appraisal system can also be a powerful motivator.

Discussion Questions

1. What is leadership? What is the difference between leadership and management?
2. What behaviors do effective leaders exhibit?
3. Why is it so important for small companies to hire the right employees? What can entrepreneurs do to avoid making hiring mistakes?
4. What is a job description? A job specification? What functions do they serve in the hiring process?
5. Outline the procedure for conducting an effective interview.
6. What are some alternative techniques to traditional interviews?
7. What is company culture? What role does it play in a small company's success? What threats does rapid growth pose for a company's culture?
8. What mistakes do companies make when switching to team-based management? What might companies do to avoid these mistakes? Explain the four stages teams typically experience.

9. What is empowerment? What benefits does it offer workers? The company? What must a small business manager do to make empowerment work in a company?
10. Explain the differences among job simplification, job enlargement, job rotation, and job enrichment. What impact do these different job designs have on workers?
11. Is money the "best" motivator? How do pay-for-performance compensation systems work? What other rewards are available to small business managers to use as motivators? How effective are they?
12. Suppose that a mail-order catalog company selling environmentally friendly products identifies its performance as a socially responsible company as a "critical number" in its success. Suggest some ways for the owner to measure this company's "social responsibility index."
13. What is a performance appraisal? What are the most common mistakes managers make in performance appraisals? What should small business managers do to avoid making those mistakes?

Business Plan Pro

This chapter discusses the importance of leadership, culture, organizational design, staffing, and managing the people who will work in your business. The "Management" section is where these issues are most often addressed within the business plan. This section of the plan captures the key information about your management team, including both its strengths and weaknesses. The management section of the business plan also addresses other personnel issues for your venture.

On the Web

Visit the Companion Web Site at *www.pearsonhighered.com/scarborough* and review the links associated. You will find resources that address leadership issues, interviewing techniques, employee motivation programs, culture, organizational structure,

and other topics that you may find helpful. These resources may offer additional insight for the human resource and managerial aspects of your business that you may want to incorporate into your business plan.

In the Software

Review the management section of your business plan and make certain that it addresses the important management and personnel issues for your venture. Check to see that your plan includes the relevant concepts. Think about the business culture that you plan to build. Assess the leadership abilities of the current management team. Are additional managers or other positions needed? Have you accounted for new hires and the anticipated expenses associated with adding these employees? Does your plan address factors that will allow you to retain existing employees? How do you plan to motivate employees to achieve high levels of performance?

Endnotes

1. Michael Gold, "Jazzin' CEO," *Manage Smarter*, January 9, 2008, p. 1.
2. Ibid.
3. Francis Huffman, "Taking the Lead," *Entrepreneur*, November 1993, p. 101.
4. Sam Allman, "Leadership vs. Management," *Successful Meetings*, October 2009, p. 12.
5. Matthew E. May, "The 3 C's of Trust," Open Forum, September 24, 2010, *www.openforum.com/idea-hub/topics/the-world/article/the-3-cs-of-trust-matthew-e-may*.
6. "Trust in Managers in Short Supply," Right Management, May 27, 2010, *www.right.com/news-and-events/press-releases/item8361.aspx*.
7. Ryan Underwood, "The CEO Next Door," *Fast Company*, September 2005, pp. 64–66; Jeffrey Pfeffer, "A Field Day for Executives," *Business 2.0*, December 2004, p. 88.
8. Jeffrey Pfeffer, "Executive-in-Chief," *Business 2.0*, March 1, 2005, *http://money.cnn.com/magazines/business2/business2_archive/2005/03/01/8253107/index.htm*.
9. Dave Zielinski, "New Ways to Look at Leadership," *Presentations*, June 2005, pp. 26–33.
10. "What Is Servant Leadership? Ken Blanchard," Greenleaf Center for Servant Leadership, *www.greenleaf.org/whatissl/KenBlanchard.html*.
11. Sam Oches, "It's the Customers, Stupid. Or Is It?" *QSR Magazine*, September 16, 2010, *www.qsrmagazine.com/articles/exclusives/0910/employees-1.phtml*.
12. Chris Penttila, "Hire Away," *Entrepreneur*, June 2007, p. 20.
13. "The Real Cost of Employee Turnover," Rainmaker Group, *www.therainmakergroupinc.com/add.asp?ID=94*.
14. "SurePayroll Main Street Insights: Small Business Owners Wasting Big Money on Hiring Decisions," SurePayroll, June 16, 2009, *www.surepayroll.com/spsite/press/releases/2009/release061609.asp*.
15. David Meyer, "Nine Recruiting and Selection Tips to Ensure Successful Hiring," About.com, *http://humanresources.about.com/od/selectemployees/a/staff_selection_p.htm*.
16. "Hiring Decisions Miss the Mark 50% of the Time," Corporate Executive Board, October 24, 2008, *http://ir.executiveboard.com/phoenix.zhtml?c=113226&p=irol-newsArticle&ID=1205091&highlight=;* "2 Out of 3 Managers Still Fear a Hiring Decision They'll Regret," DDI, March 16, 2009, *www.ddiworld.com/about/pr_releases_en.asp?id=211*.
17. Chris Pentilla, "Talent Scout," *Entrepreneur*, July 2008, p. 19.
18. Kelly K. Spors, "Top Workplaces 2009," *Wall Street Journal*, September 28, 2009, pp. R1, R4.
19. Jennifer Wang, "10 Companies Getting It Right," *Entrepreneur*, March 2010, p. 83.
20. "Most Businesses Use Social Nets for Hiring," *eMarketer*, July 13, 2010, *www.emarketer.com/Article.aspx?R=1007811*.
21. Chris Penttila, "Build a Social Media Hiring Strategy," *Entrepreneur*, July 1, 2009, *www.entrepreneur.com/hiringcenter/article202466.html*.
22. Jennifer J. Salopek, "Recruiters Look to Be Big Man on Campus," *Workforce Management*, September 2010, p. 12.
23. Joel Holland, "More Than What You Paid For," *Entrepreneur*, June 2010, p. 86.
24. Mitra Toossi, "Labor Force Projections to 2016: More Workers in Their Golden Years," *Monthly Labor Review*, November 2007, p. 33.
25. *Staying Ahead of the Curve 2007: The AARP Work and Career Study*, American Association of Retired Persons, September 2008, p. 8.
26. Gary M. Stern, "Hiring Older Workers," *Small Business Review*, February 11, 2007, *http://smallbusinessreview.com/human_resources/hiring_older_workers/index.html*.
27. *The Real Talent Debate: Will Aging Boomers Deplete the Workforce?* WorldatWork, Scottsdale, Arizona, 2007, p. 12.
28. "Innovating Human Resources," *BrainReactions*, January 16, 2007, *www.brainreactions.com/whitepapers/brainreactions_hr_innovation_paper.pdf*, pp. 11–14; Christopher Caggiano, "Recruiting Secrets," *Inc.*, October 1998, pp. 30–42.
29. Amy Barrett, "Making Telecommuting Work," *BusinessWeek*, October 17, 2008, *www.businessweek.com/magazine/content/08_70/s0810048750962.htm?chan=smallbiz_smallbiz+index+page_best+of+small+biz+magazine*.
30. "Survey: Up to 25 Applications Reviewed per Job," *Workforce Management*, September 16, 2010, *www.workforce.com/section/news/article/survey-up-25-applications-reviewed-per-job.php*.
31. "Smart Questions for Your Hiring Manager," *Inc.*, February 2007, p. 47.
32. "Survey: 21 Percent of Job Seekers Dropped After Reference Checks," *Workforce Management*, June 23, 2010, *www.workforce.com/section/news/article/survey-21-percent-job-seekers-dropped-after-reference.php*.
33. Andy Levine, "Dig We Must," *Inc.*, August 2006, p. 97.
34. Dan Heath and Chip Heath, "Hold the Interview," *Fast Company*, June 2009, pp. 51–52.
35. Peter Bregman, "The Interview Question You Should Always Ask," *Harvard Business Publishing*, January 27, 2009, *http://blogs.harvardbusiness.org/cs/2009/01/the_interview_question_you_sho.html*.
36. Ed Frauenheim, "Serious Hiring Keeps Zappos in a Fun Mood," *Workforce Management*, September 14, 2009, p. 20.
37. Ibid.
38. Chris Penttila, "Testing the Waters," *Entrepreneur*, January 2004, pp 72–73.
39. Chris Penttila, "Peering In," *Entrepreneur*, January 2005, pp. 70–71.
40. Spors, "Top Workplaces 2009."
41. Penttila, "Peering In," p. 71.
42. Richard Slawsky, "Reducing Risk: The Search for Reputable Employees," QSRWeb.com, August 9, 2007, *www.qsrweb.com/article.php?id=8390&na=1*.
43. Ibid.
44. Vasanth Sridharan, "22% of Employers Check Your Facebook Profile When They Are Looking to Hire You. That's It?" *Business Insider*, September 11, 2008, *www.businessinsider.com/2008/9/22-of-employers-check-your-facebook-profile-when-they-re-looking-to-hire-you-that-s-it-*.
45. Emily Maltby, "To Find Best Hires, Firms Become Creative," *Wall Street Journal*, November 17, 2009, *http://online.wsj.com/article/SB10001424052748704538404574539971535489470.html*.
46. "Drug Free Work Week," U.S. Department of Labor, *www.dol.gov/asp/programs/drugs/workingpartners/DFWW-Introduction.asp*.
47. McGuire Woods, "But I Have a Prescription! . . . Drug Testing in the Age of Medical Marijuana," *Society of Human Resource Managers*, July 1, 2010, *www.shrm.org/LegalIssues/StateandLocalResources/Pages/ButIHaveaPrescription.aspx*.
48. Jessica Marquez, "Kindness Pays . . . Or Does It?" *Workforce*, June 25, 2007, pp. 40–49.
49. Ibid.
50. Julia Chang, "Balancing Act," *Sales & Marketing Management*, February 2004, p. 16.
51. Spors, "Top Workplaces 2009."
52. "Top Small Company Workplaces," *Inc.*, 2010, *www.inc.com/top-workplaces/2010/profile/dealercom-mark-bonfigli.html*.
53. Jody Urquhart, "Creating a Fun Workplace . . . 13 Ways to Have Fun at Work," I Do Inspire, *www.idoinspire.com/?q=node/15*.
54. Nichole L. Torres, "Let the Good Times Roll," *Entrepreneur*, November 2004, p. 57.
55. Jennifer Wang, "10 Top Companies Getting It Right," *Entrepreneur*, March 2010, p. 83.
56. Jennifer Robison, "Despite the Downturn, Employees Remain Engaged," *Gallup Management Journal*, January 14, 2010, *http://gmj.gallup.com/content/125036/despite-downturn-employees-remain-engaged.aspx#3*.
57. Noelle Coyle, "Fish or Cut Bait?" *Black Box*, Quarter 1, 2010, p. 60.
58. Tony Hsieh, "How Zappos Infuses Culture Using Core Values," *Harvard Business Review*, May 24, 2010, *http://blogs.hbr.org/cs/2010/05/how_zappos_infuses_culture_using_core_values.html*; Sam Narisi, "You Hired Them—Now Pay Them to Quit?" *HR Recruiting Alert*, June 16, 2008, *www.hrrecruitingalert.com/new-onboarding-twist-bribing-hires-to-quit/*.
59. George A. Wolf, Jean A. Talaga, and Laurent Bernard, "A Matter of Transparency," *All Business*, June 1, 2009, *www.allbusiness.com/company-activities-management/management-benchmarking/12368521-1.html*.
60. David Freedman, "The Idiocy of Crowds," *Inc.*, September 2006, pp. 61–62.

61. *Capitalizing on Effective Communication: How Courage, Innovation, and Discipline Drive Business Results in Challenging Times, Communication ROI Study Report 2009/2010*, Towers Watson, November 2009, pp. 2–3; "How to Communicate with Employees," *Inc.*, May 1, 2010, *www.inc.com/magazine/20100501/guidebook-how-to-communicate-with-employees.html*, p. 1.

62. "Employee Engagement," *Motiv8*, May 26, 2010, *www.motiv8comm.com/IdeasandTrends/index_may26.html*.

63. Spors, "Top Workplaces 2009."

64. Mina Kimes, "How Can I Get Candid Feedback from My Employees?" *Fortune*, April 13, 2009, p. 24.

65. Kathy Gurchiek, "U.S. Rank-and-File Workers Feel Undervalued by Managers," *Society for Human Resource Managers*, July 16, 2010, *www.shrm.org/Publications/HRNews/Pages/WorkersFeelUndervalued.aspx*.

66. "Doomed!" *Inside Training*, February 22, 2007, p. 1.

67. "Employee Engagement," *Motiv8*; Robert B. Tucker, "Listening to Employees Is a Best Buy," *Blogging Innovation*, March 11, 2010, *www.business-strategy-innovation.com/2010/03/listening-to-employees-is-best-buy.html*.

68. "I Heard It Through the Grapevine," American Management Association, November 21, 2005, *www.amanet.org/training/articles/I-Heard-It-Through-the-Grapevine.aspx*.

69. Chris Penttila, "Live and Learn: You May Be the Boss, But That Doesn't Mean You Can't Let Your Employees Teach You a Thing or Two," *Entrepreneur*, June 2004, pp. 36–39.

70. "Empowering Your Employees," BNET, *www.bnet.com/2410-13059_23-95573.html*.

71. Daniel Akst, "The Rewards of Recognizing a Job Well Done," *Wall Street Journal*, January 31, 2007, p. D9.

72. Paul Keegan, "Maxine Clark and Kip Tindell," *Fortune*, February 8, 2010, pp. 68–72.

73. Spors, "Top Workplaces 2009."

74. Sarah E. Needleman, "Business Owners Try to Motivate Employees," *Wall Street Journal*, January 14, 2010, p. B5; "Americans' Job Satisfaction Falls to Record Low," *USA Today*, January 6, 2010, *www.usatoday.com/money/workplace/2010-01-05-job-satisfaction-use_N.htm*.

75. Robert D. Mohr and Cindy Zoghi, "Is Job Enrichment Really Enriching?" U.S. Department of Labor, U.S. Bureau of Labor Statistics, Office of Productivity and Technology, Washington, DC: January 2006, pp. 13–15.

76. Ellen Galinsky, Shanny L. Peer, and Sheila Eby, *When Work Works: 2009 Guide to Bold New Ideas for Making Work Work*, Families and Work Institute, 2009, p. 1.

77. Ibid., pp. 37–38.

78. Ellen Galinsky, James T. Bond, Kelly Sakai, Stacy S. Kim, and Nicole Giuntoli, *2008 National Study of Employers*, Families and Work Institute, New York: May 2008, p. 6.

79. Carol Kleiman, "Job Sharing Working Its Way into Mainstream," *Greenville News*, August 6, 2000, p. 3G.

80. Spors, "Top Workplaces 2009."

81. Gerry Blackwell, "Telecommuting Trend Taking Off for Small Biz," *Small Business Computing*, September 22, 2008, *www.smallbusinesscomputing.com/news/article.php/3773076*.

82. Meredith Levinson, "Survey: Telecommuting Improves Productivity, Lowers Cost," *CIO*, October 7, 2008, *www.cio.com/article/453289/Telecommuting_Improves_Productivity_Lowers_Costs_New_Survey_Finds*; Harriet Hagestad, "New Ways to Work: Telecommuting and Job Sharing," *CareerBuilder*, June 23, 2006, *www.careerbuilder.com/JobSeeker/careerbytes/CBArticle.aspx?articleID=369&cbRecursionCnt=1&cbsid=49944662f7b64dc38639d9a3ef87dd18-204624985-R5-4*.

83. "Cisco Study Finds Telecommuting Significantly Increases Employee Productivity, Work–Life Flexibility, and Job Satisfaction," Cisco, June 25, 2009, *http://newsroom.cisco.com/dlls/2009/prod_062609.html*.

84. Telis Demos, "Motivate Without Spending Millions," *Fortune*, April 12, 2010, pp. 37–38.

85. Spors, "Top Workplaces 2009."

86. Kevin Gray, "Can't Pay Your Employees What You'd Like? Praise Them Instead," BNET, January 19, 2010, *www.bnet.com/article/cant-pay-your-employees-what-youd-like-praise-them-instead/385221*.

87. Lisa Bertagnoli, "How to Motivate Restaurant Employees," *Restaurants and Institutions*, December 1, 2009, *www.rimag.com/article/ca6710028.html?rssid=272*.

88. Milton Moskowitz, Robert Levering, and Christopher Tkaczyk, "100 Best Companies to Work For," *Fortune*, February 8, 2010, p. 77.

89. Galinsky et al., *When Work Works*, pp. 20–21.

90. Scott Westcott, "Putting an End to End-of-Year Reviews," *Inc.*, December 2007, pp. 58–59.

91. Ibid.

Managing Inventory

Learning Objectives

Upon completion of this chapter, you will be able to:

1. Explain the various inventory control systems and the advantages and disadvantages of each.
2. Describe how just-in-time (JIT) and JIT II inventory control techniques work.
3. Describe methods for reducing losses from slow-moving inventory.
4. Discuss employee theft and shoplifting and how to prevent them.

If a product isn't selling, I want to get it out of there because it's taking up space that can be devoted to another part of my line that moves. Besides, having a product languish on the shelves doesn't do much for our image.

—Norman Melnick, chairman of Pentech International

Honesty pays, but it doesn't seem to pay enough to suit some people.

—F. M. Hubbard

Supply chain management and inventory control are closely linked. This chapter will discuss various inventory control methods, how to move "slow" inventory items, and how to protect inventory from theft. An entrepreneur's goal is to maximize the value of a company's inventory while reducing both the cost and the risks of owning inventory. The issue is significant; the largest expenditure for many small businesses is in inventory: raw materials, work-in-process, or finished goods.

Although many business owners understand the dangers of carrying excess inventory, they face a constant battle to avoid the problem. A study by the Aberdeen Group reports that 70 percent of businesses rate themselves "average" or "below average" on inventory management.[1] In addition, 91 percent report that they are making changes to their businesses, such as improving sales forecasting, enhancing replenishment strategies, and increasing the level of cooperation with vendors, to improve their ability to manage inventory more effectively.[2] For years, businesses maintained high levels of inventory so that the manufacturing or sales processes ran smoothly. Managers now realize that inventory simply masks other problems that a company may have, such as poor quality, sloppy supply chain management, improper pricing, inadequate marketing, inefficient layout, low productivity, and others. Reducing the amount of inventory a company carries exposes these otherwise hidden problems; only then can managers and employees solve them.

Another reason that business owners are lowering inventory levels is the high cost of carrying excess inventory. U.S. businesses incur $357 billion in carrying costs each year (19.3 percent of the total value of the inventory they hold), the majority of it in the form of taxes, depreciation, insurance, and obsolescence.[3] Holding inventory requires renting or purchasing additional warehouse space, increasing labor costs, boosting borrowing, and tying up a company's valuable cash unnecessarily. Companies with lean inventory levels lower their costs of operation, and those savings go straight to the bottom line. The potential payoff for managing inventory efficiently is huge; companies that switch to lean inventory systems can increase their profitability by 20 to 50 percent.

The information age has made techniques such as just-in-time (JIT) inventory systems available to even the smallest of businesses. Internet-based networks that connect a company seamlessly with its suppliers have dramatically reduced the time for needed parts or material to arrive and the need to hold inventory. At the other end of the pipeline, a company's customers expect to have what they need when they need it. In today's competitive market, few customers will wait beyond a reasonable time for items they want. Managing inventory properly requires business owners to master an intricate balancing act, keeping enough inventory on hand to meet customers' expectations but maintaining inventory levels low enough to avoid incurring excessive costs.

Managing inventory effectively requires an entrepreneur to implement the following seven interrelated steps:

1. *Develop an accurate sales forecast.* The proper inventory level for each item is directly related to the demand for that item. A business cannot sell merchandise that it does not have; conversely, an entrepreneur does not want to stock inventory that customers will not buy.

Profile

Dan Richardson: Northway Sports

Dan Richardson, owner of Northway Sports, a retailer in East Bethel, Minnesota, that sells Polaris all-terrain vehicles (ATVs), snowmobiles, and motorcycles, says that he lost several sales of Polaris' most popular ATV because the manufacturer had not been able to deliver the units he had ordered 5 months before. When a recession hit, Polaris, like most manufacturers, slashed production to keep its inventory lean and to avoid putting pressure on its dealers to purchase products that they could not sell. Polaris' forecasts showed sluggish sales. Several months later, however, surging demand for the company's products caught managers by surprise, and Polaris was unable to fill its dealers' orders.[4]

2. *Develop a plan to make inventory available when and where customers want it.* Inventory will not sell if customers have a difficult time finding it. If a company is constantly running out of items customers expect to find, its customer base will dwindle over time as shoppers look elsewhere for those items. An important component of superior customer service is making sure adequate quantities of items are available when customers want them. Two ways of measuring this aspect of customer service include calculating the percentage of customer

orders that a company ships on time and the percentage of the dollar volume of orders that it ships on time. Tracking these numbers over time gives business owners sound feedback on how well they are managing their inventory levels from the customer's perspective.

Polaris, the maker of all-terrain vehicles, snowmobiles, and motorcycles, once used a system that required dealers to place large orders of inventory twice a year. However, when sales slowed, the "stack 'em high, watch 'em fly" system caused problems with dealers and at Polaris. Today, Polaris has switched to a system that allows dealers to order smaller quantities of inventory more frequently, which allows them to maintain leaner inventories and match supply with customer demand more effectively.[5]

3. *Build relationships with your most critical suppliers to ensure that you can get the merchandise you need when you need it.* Business owners must keep suppliers and vendors aware of how their merchandise is selling and communicate their needs to them. Vendors and suppliers can be an entrepreneur's greatest allies in managing inventory. Increasingly, the word that describes the relationship between world-class companies and their suppliers is *partnership*.

4. *Set realistic inventory turnover objectives.* Keeping in touch with their customers' likes and dislikes and monitoring their inventory enable owners to estimate the most likely buying patterns for different types of merchandise. One of the factors having the greatest impact on a company's sales, cash flow, and ultimate success is its inventory turnover ratio.

5. *Compute the actual cost of carrying inventory.* Many business owners do not realize how expensive carrying inventory actually is. Without an accurate cost of carrying inventory, it is impossible to determine an optimal inventory level. Carrying costs include items such as interest on borrowed money, insurance expenses associated with the inventory, inventory-related personnel expenses, obsolescence, and others. When new product introductions make existing products obsolete, companies must hold inventory to an absolute minimum. For instance, in the computer industry the onrush of new technology causes the value of a personal computer held in inventory to decline 1 percent each week! This gives computer makers big incentives to keep their inventories as lean as possible.

George Falzon, owner of G. Falzon & Company, a small jewelry store in Holliston, Massachusetts, watched the cost of holding inventory, particularly engagement rings and wedding bands, increase as the prices of precious metals soared. A weak economy demanded that Falzon avoid overinvesting in inventory, which is a common cause of cash crises, but potential customers expect to see a wide selection of items when shopping. Falzon developed a clever solution: He began stocking replicas of jewelry pieces made from plated silver and cubic zirconium rather than platinum, silver, gold, and diamonds. Because most engagement and wedding pieces are special orders, customers do not mind looking at the replicas. Falzon says that stocking the replicas saves him about $75,000 in inventory, which allows him to display four times as many styles of engagement rings and wedding bands.[6]

6. *Use the most timely and accurate information system the business can afford to provide the facts and figures necessary to make critical inventory decisions.* Computers and modern point-of-sale terminals that are linked to a company's inventory records enable business owners to know exactly which items are selling and which ones are not. The owner of a chain of baby products stores uses a computer network to link all of his stores to the computer at central headquarters. Every night after the stores close, the point-of-sale terminals in each store download the day's sales to the central computer, which compiles an extensive sales and inventory report. When he walks into his office every morning, the owner reviews the report and can tell exactly which items are moving fastest, which are moving slowest, and which are not selling at all. He credits the system with the company's above-average inventory turnover ratio and much of his chain's success.

7. *Teach employees how inventory control systems work so that they can contribute to managing the firm's inventory on a daily basis.* All too often, the employees on the floor have no idea of how the various information systems and inventory control techniques operate or interact with one another. Consequently, the people closest to the inventory contribute little to

controlling it. Well-trained employees armed with information can be one of an entrepreneur's greatest weapons in the battle to control inventory. Fast changes in product demand require inventory control systems that are capable of responding quickly, allowing entrepreneurs and their employees to make adjustments to inventory levels on the fly.

The goal is to find and maintain the proper balance between the cost of holding inventory and the requirements to have merchandise on hand when customers demand it. Either extreme can be costly. If entrepreneurs focus solely on minimizing cost, they will undoubtedly incur stockouts, lost sales, and customer ill will because they cannot satisfy their customers' needs. For instance, researchers studying inventory control systems at Bulgari, a jewelry manufacturer headquartered in Rome, Italy, discovered that stockouts of just one popular item had lowered the company's profits by 5 percent of sales.[7] At the other extreme, entrepreneurs who attempt to hold enough inventory to meet every peak customer demand will find that high inventory costs diminish their chances of remaining profitable. "There's a fine line between not having racks of clearance [merchandise] from leftover inventory and cutting to the bone," says one retail expert.[8] Walking this inventory tightrope is never easy, but the following inventory control systems can help business owners strike a reasonable balance between the two extremes.

Inventory Control Systems

1. Explain the various inventory control systems and the advantages and disadvantages of each.

Regardless of the type of inventory control system business owners choose, they must recognize the importance of **Pareto's Law** (or the **80/20 Rule**), which holds that about 80 percent of the value of a company's sales revenue is generated by 20 percent of the items in its inventory. Sometimes a company's best-selling items are its highest-priced items, but more often they are low-priced items that sell in high volume. Because most sales are generated by a small percentage of items, entrepreneurs should focus the majority of their inventory control efforts on this 20 percent. Observing this simple principle ensures that entrepreneurs will spend time controlling only the most productive—and, therefore, most valuable—inventory items. With this technique in mind, we now examine three basic types of inventory control systems: perpetual, visual, and partial.

IN THE ENTREPRENEURIAL SPOTLIGHT

The Long Tail Theory: Is Pareto's Law Still Valid?

In 1896, Italian economist Vilfredo Pareto observed that 20 percent of people owned about 80 percent of wealth. Since then, Pareto's Law, or the 80/20 Rule, has been used to describe many aspects of business, including the idea that about 20 percent of a company's customers account for 80 percent of its sales. For instance, researchers in Japan analyzed nearly 100 million transactions and confirmed that 25 percent of convenience stores' customers account for 80 percent of their total sales. Pareto's Law also applies to a company's inventory: 80 percent of a company's sales come from only 20 percent of its products. The result is that managers focus their efforts on the "vital" 20 percent of items rather than the "trivial" remaining 80 percent.

Chris Anderson, editor of *Wired* magazine, claims that the Internet has the potential to limit the application

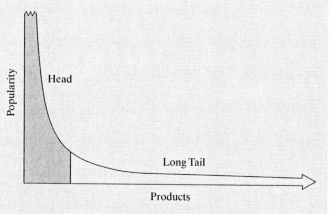

The New Marketplace

Source: Chris Anderson, "About Me," Long Tail, *www.longtail.com/ about.html.*

of Pareto's Law because it allows businesses to sell efficiently low-volume items that exactly match the unique needs, wants, and interests of small groups of customers in niche markets. Anderson called his theory the Long Tail Theory, because the Internet allows customers to migrate down the tail of the distribution curve (see accompanying figure). If the Long Tail Theory is true, it has significant implications for business owners and the way they manage their inventory. Anderson says that the 80 percent of a company's products that Pareto's Law considers "trivial" have the potential on the Internet to rival the sales volume of the 20 percent that the Law considers "vital."

Researchers at the Sloan School of Management at the Massachusetts Institute of Technology recently studied several years of data at a private-label women's clothing company that sold the same merchandise through its catalog and its Internet-based store. Their analysis showed that catalog sales conformed perfectly to the 80/20 Rule; 20 percent of the items in the catalog accounted for 80 percent of catalog sales. However, Internet customers purchased a greater variety of products even though the online store offered the exact same selection of items at the same prices. (After the company's managers saw the study's results, they adjusted their marketing strategy, sending fewer catalogs to their top online customers.) When Suunto began selling its Vector altimeter watch online, the company planned to offer only its most popular black and green model, which made up the top 20 percent of its product mix. However, the company quickly discovered that customers wanted offbeat colors as well, including unusual shades such as champagne and yellow. At Amazon.com, sales of obscure book titles that brick-and-mortar bookstores do not even carry account for almost 40 percent of book sales. Tyler Smith, cofounder of Niche Retail, a company that helps small companies develop online strategies for reaching niches, says that for many of his customers, "There's no historical top 20 percent, and the top sellers move quickly and change." The Long Tail Theory demands that business owners always be on the lookout for new, obscure products aimed at niche markets and for ways to market these "less popular" items online.

In 1999, when Tony Hsieh became CEO of Zappos, the largest online retailer of shoes (now owned by Amazon.com), he was unsure of which sales pattern to expect. "I thought the 80/20 Rule might apply," he says. Instead, many customers turned to Zappos, which stocks more than 1.5 million pairs of shoes across more than 1,000 brands, for unique, hard-to-find styles and sizes. At Zappos, whose fulfillment centers are bigger than 17 football fields, the top 20 percent of products account for 50 percent of the company's sales; the remaining 80 percent of its products make up the other half of its sales. "It varies from brick-and-mortar quite a bit," says Hsieh.

1. Use the Internet to research the Long Tail Theory and its applications. Does the theory appear to be valid? Explain your reasoning.
2. What implications does the Long Tail Theory have for small companies that do business online?

Sources: Based on Susan Greco, "A World Without Best Sellers: Creating a 'Long Tail' Product Mix," *Inc.*, September 2007, pp. 47–52; Takayuki Mizuno, Masahiro Toriyama, Takao Terano, and Misako Takayasu, "Pareto Law of Expenditure of a Person in Convenience Stores," *Physica A*, Vol. 387, 2008, pp. 3931–3935; "About Me," Long Tail, *www.longtail.com/about.html*; Erik Brynjolfssen, Yu (Jeffrey) Hu, and Duncan Simester, "Goodbye Pareto Principle, Hello Long Tail: The Effect of Search Costs on the Concentration of Product Sales," Sloan School of Management, Massachusetts Institute of Technology, November 2007, pp. 1–40; Erick Schonfeld, "Poking Holes in the Long Tail Theory," *Tech Crunch*, July 2, 2008, *http://techcrunch.com/2008/07/02/poking-holes-in-the-long-tail-theory/*.

Tony Hsieh, CEO of Zappos. At Zappos, the top 20 percent of products account for 50 percent of the company's sales.

Source: Brad Swonetz/Redux Pictures

Perpetual Inventory Systems

Perpetual inventory systems are designed to maintain a running count of the items in inventory. Although a number of different perpetual inventory systems exist, they all have a common element: They keep a continuous tally of each item added to or subtracted from the firm's stock of merchandise. A typical manual system uses a perpetual inventory sheet that includes fundamental product information such as the item's name, stock number, description, economic order quantity (EOQ), and reorder point.

These perpetual inventory sheets are usually placed next to the merchandise in the warehouse or storage facility. Whenever a shipment is received from a vendor, the quantity is entered in the receipt column and added to the total. When the item is sold and taken from inventory, it is simply deducted from the total. As long as this procedure is followed consistently, an entrepreneur can determine quickly the number of each product on hand. Bar-coding the inventory allows the process to be done by handheld scanners that are tied directly to a computerized inventory control system. Automating the perpetual inventory system makes it more accurate and reliable, and when inventory levels drop to the reorder trigger point the system generates purchase orders to replenish the supply.

Although consistent use of the system yields accurate inventory counts at any moment, sporadic use creates problems. If managers or employees take items out of stock or place them in inventory without recording them, the perpetual inventory sheet yields incorrect totals and can foul up the entire inventory control system. Another disadvantage of this system is the cost of maintaining it. If not computerized, keeping perpetual inventory records for a large number of items and ensuring the accuracy of the system can be unreasonable. Therefore, these systems are used most frequently and most successfully in controlling high-dollar-volume items that require strict monitoring. Management must watch these items closely and ensure that inventory records are accurate.

Advances in computerized cash registers have overcome many of the disadvantages of using the basic perpetual inventory system. Small businesses now can afford computerized **point of sale (POS) systems** that perform all of the functions of a traditional cash register and maintain an up-to-the minute inventory count. Although POS systems are not new (major retailers have been using them for more than 30 years), their affordable prices are. Not so long ago, most systems required large investments in hardware and software. Today, small business owners can set up POS systems on personal computers for less than $1,000.

Combining a POS system with Universal Product Code (bar code) labels and high-speed scanners gives a small business a state-of-the-art checkout system that feeds vital information into its inventory control system. These systems rely on an inventory database; as items are rung up on the register, product information is recorded and inventory balances are adjusted. Using the system, business owners can tell how quickly each item is selling and how many items are in stock at any time. In addition, their inventory records are more accurate and are always current. They also can generate instantly a variety of reports to aid in making purchasing decisions. The system can be programmed to alert owners when the supply of a particular item drops below a predetermined reorder point or even to print automatically a purchase order to the EOQ indicated. Finally, modern POS systems allow business owners to generate an array of inventory reports instantly. Entrepreneurs can slice and dice data in a multitude of ways, which allows them to determine which items are selling the fastest and which are moving the slowest. Timely reports such as these give entrepreneurs the ability to make sound decisions about scheduling advertising, running special promotions, offering discounts, and arranging store displays. Computerized POS systems also make it possible for entrepreneurs to use a basic perpetual inventory system for a large number of items, a task that, if performed manually, would be virtually impossible.

Visual Inventory Control Systems

The most common method of controlling inventory in a small business is the **visual control system**, in which managers simply conduct periodic visual inspections to determine the quantity of various items they should order. This system suits businesses that stock a large number of low-value items with low-dollar volume. Unfortunately, this method is also the least effective for ensuring accuracy and reliability. Oversights of key items often lead to stockouts and resulting lost sales. The biggest disadvantage of the visual control system is its inability to detect and to foresee shortages of inventory items.

In general, a visual inventory control system works best in firms in which daily sales are relatively consistent, the entrepreneur is closely involved with the inventory, the variety of merchandise is small, and items can be obtained quickly from vendors. For example, small firms dealing in perishable goods use visual control systems very successfully, and rarely, if ever, rely on analytical inventory control tools. For these firms, shortages are less likely to occur under a visual system; when they do occur, they are not likely to create major problems. Entrepreneurs who rely on visual systems must be alert to shifts in customer buying patterns that alter required inventory levels.

Partial Inventory Control Systems

For small business owners with limited time and money, the most viable option for inventory management is a partial inventory control system. These systems rely on the validity of Pareto's Law, or the 80/20 Rule. For example, if a small business carries 5,000 different items in stock, roughly 1,000 of them account for about 80 percent of the firm's sales volume. Experienced business owners focus their inventory control efforts on those 1,000 items. Unfortunately, many owners seek to maintain tight control over the remaining 4,000 items, a frustrating and wasteful practice. Entrepreneur John Payne says that Pareto's Law applied to the consumer electronics business that he ran for years; about 75 percent of his company's sales came from just 20 percent of the items he carried in inventory.[9] Smart entrepreneurs design their inventory control systems with this principle in mind. One of the most popular partial inventory control systems is the ABC system.

THE ABC METHOD OF INVENTORY CONTROL. The ABC method focuses control efforts on that small percentage of items that accounts for the majority of the firm's sales. The typical **ABC system** divides a firm's inventory into three major categories:

A items account for a high dollar usage volume.

B items account for a moderate dollar usage volume.

C items account for low dollar usage volume.

The **dollar usage volume** of an item measures the relative importance of that item in a company's inventory. Note that value is *not* necessarily synonymous with high unit cost. In some instances, a high-cost item that generates only a small dollar volume can be classified as an A item. More frequently, however, A items are those that are low to moderate in cost and high volume by nature.

The initial step in establishing an ABC classification system is to compute the annual dollar usage volume for each product (or product category). **Annual dollar usage volume** is simply the cost per unit of an item multiplied by the annual quantity used. For instance, Florentina, the owner of a speaker shop, may find that she sold 190 pairs of a popular brand of speakers during the previous year. If the speakers cost her $75 per unit, their annual dollar usage volume would be as follows:

$$190 \times \$75 = \$14,250$$

The next step is to arrange the products in descending order on the basis of the computed annual dollar usage volume. Once so arranged, they can be divided into appropriate classes by applying the following rule:

A items: roughly the top 15 percent of the items listed

B items: roughly the next 35 percent

C items: roughly the remaining 50 percent

For example, Florentina's small retail shop is interested in establishing an ABC inventory control system to lower losses from stockouts, theft, and other hazards. Florentina has computed the annual dollar usage volume for the store's merchandise inventory, as shown in Table 1. (For simplicity, we show only 12 inventory items.)

The ABC inventory control method divides the firm's inventory items into three classes, depending on the items' value. Figure 1 graphically portrays the segmentation of the items listed in Table 1.

The purpose of classifying items according to their annual dollar usage volume is to establish the proper degree of control over each item held in inventory. Clearly, it is wasteful and inefficient to exercise the same level of control over C items and A items. Items in the A classification should be controlled under a perpetual inventory system, with as much detail as necessary. Analytical tools and frequent counts may be required to ensure accuracy, but the extra cost of tight control for these valuable items is usually justified. Managers should not retain a large supply of reserve or safety stock because doing so ties up excessive amounts of money in inventory, but they must monitor the stock closely to avoid stockouts and the lost sales that result.

Control of B items should rely more on periodic control systems and basic analytical tools such as EOQ and reorder point analysis. Managers can maintain moderate levels of safety stock for these items to guard against shortages and can afford monthly, or even bimonthly, merchandise inspections. Because B items are not as valuable to the business as A items, less rigorous control systems are required.

C items typically constitute a minor proportion of the small firm's inventory value and, as a result, require the least effort and expense to control. These items are usually large in number and small in total value. The most practical way to control them is to use uncomplicated records and procedures. Large levels of safety stock for these items are acceptable because the cost of carrying them is usually minimal. Substantial order sizes often enable the business to take advantage of quantity discounts without having to place frequent orders. The cost involved in using detailed

TABLE 1 Calculating Annual Dollar Usage Volume and an ABC Inventory Analysis for Florentina's

Item	Annual Dollar Usage Volume	% of Annual Dollar Usage
Paragon	$374,100	42.00
Excelsior	294,805	33.10
Avery	68,580	7.70
Bardeen	54,330	6.10
Berkeley	27,610	3.10
Tara	24,940	2.80
Cattell	11,578	1.30
Faraday	9,797	1.10
Humboldt	8,016	0.90
Mandel	7,125	0.08
Sabot	5,344	0.06
Wister	4,453	0.05
Total	$890,678	100.00

Classification	Items	Annual Dollar Usage	% of Total
A	Paragon, Excelsior	$668,905	75.1
B	Avery, Bardeen, Berkeley, Tara	175,460	19.7
C	Cattell, Faraday Humboldt Mandel, Sabot, Wister	46,313	5.2
Total		$890,678	100.00

FIGURE 1
ABC Inventory Control

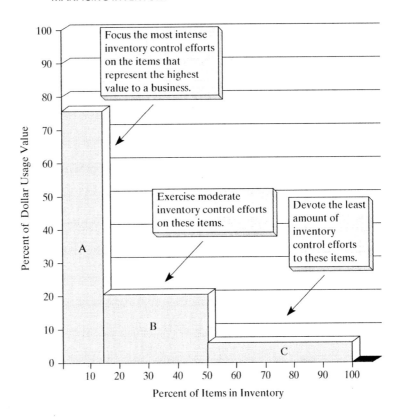

FIGURE 1
ABC Inventory Control

Focus the most intense inventory control efforts on the items that represent the highest value to a business.

Exercise moderate inventory control efforts on these items.

Devote the least amount of inventory control efforts to these items.

Percent of Dollar Usage Value

Percent of Items in Inventory

record keeping and inventory control procedures greatly outweighs the advantages gleaned from strict control of C items.

One practical technique for maintaining control over C items simply is the **two-bin system**, which keeps two separate bins full of material. The first bin is used to fill customer orders, and the second bin is filled with enough safety stock to meet customer demand during the lead time. When the first bin is empty, the owner places an order large enough to refill both bins with the vendor. During the lead time for the order, the manager uses the safety stock in the second bin to fill customer demand.

When storage space or the type of item makes a two-bin system impractical, an entrepreneur can use a **tag system**. Based on the same principles as the two-bin system, which is suitable for many manufacturers, the tag system applies to most retail, wholesale, and service firms. Instead of placing enough inventory to meet customer demand during lead time into a separate bin, the owner marks this inventory level with a brightly colored tag. When the supply is drawn down to the tagged level, the owner reorders the merchandise. Figure 2 illustrates the two-bin and tag systems of controlling C items.

In summary, business owners minimize total inventory costs when they spend time and effort controlling items that represent the greatest inventory value. Some inventory items require strict, detailed control techniques; other items simply do not justify the additional cost of tight controls. Because of its practicality, the ABC inventory system is commonly used in industry. In addition, the technique is easily computerized, speeding up the analysis and lowering its cost. Table 2 summarizes the use of the ABC control system.

Physical Inventory Count

Regardless of the type of inventory control system used, every small business owner must conduct a periodic physical inventory count. Even when a company uses a perpetual inventory system, the owner still must count the actual number of items on hand because errors inevitably occur. A physical inventory count allows owners to reconcile the actual amount of inventory in stock with the amount reported through the inventory control system. These

FIGURE 2
The Two-Bin and Tag Systems of Inventory Control

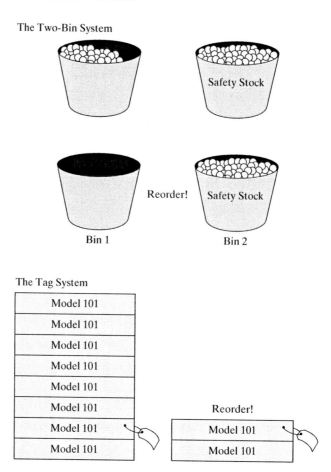

The Two-Bin System

Safety Stock

Reorder! Safety Stock

Bin 1   Bin 2

The Tag System

| Model 101 |
| Model 101 |
| Model 101 |
| Model 101 |
| Model 101 |
| Model 101 |
| Model 101 |
| Model 101 |

Reorder!

| Model 101 |
| Model 101 |

counts give managers a fresh start when determining the actual number of items on hand and enable them to evaluate the effectiveness and the accuracy of their inventory control systems.

The typical method of taking inventory involves two employees; one calls out the relevant information for each inventory item, and the other records the count on a tally sheet. There are two basic methods of conducting a physical inventory count. One alternative is to take inventory at regular intervals. Many businesses take inventory at the end of the year. In an attempt to minimize counting, many managers run special year-end inventory reduction sales. This **periodic count** generates the most accurate measurement of inventory. The other method of taking inventory, called **cycle counting**, involves counting a number of items on a continuous cycle. Instead of waiting until year-end to tally the entire inventory of items, an entrepreneur counts a

TABLE 2 ABC Inventory Control Features

Feature	A Items	B Items	C Items
Level of control	Monitor closely and maintain tight control.	Maintain moderate control.	Maintain loose control.
Reorder point	Based on forecasted requirements.	Based on EOQ calculations and past experience.	When level gets low, reorder.
Record keeping	Keep detailed records of receipts and disbursements.	Use periodic inspections and control procedures.	No records required.
Safety stock	Keep low levels of safety stock.	Keep moderate levels of safety stock.	Keep high levels of safety stock.
Inspection frequency	Monitor schedule changes frequently.	Check on changes in requirements periodically.	Make few checks on requirements.

few types of items each day or each week and checks the numbers against the inventory control system. Performing a series of "mini-counts" each day or each week allows for continuous correction of mistakes in inventory control systems and detects inventory problems faster than an annual count does.

Once again, technology can make the job of taking inventory much easier for small business owners. Electronic data interchange (EDI) and Web-based systems enable business owners to track their inventories and to place orders with vendors quickly and with few errors by linking them to their vendors electronically. These systems often rely on handheld computer terminals equipped with scanning devices. An employee runs the scanning device across a bar code label on the shelf that identifies the inventory item. Then the employee counts the items on the shelf and enters that number using the number pad on the terminal. By linking the handheld terminal to a computer, the employee then downloads the physical inventory count into the company's inventory control software in seconds.

In the past, suppliers simply manufactured a product, shipped it, and then sent the customer an invoice. To place an order, employees or managers periodically estimated how many units of a particular item they needed and when they needed them. Today, however, in many EDI or Web-based supply chain management systems, the vendor is tied directly into a company's POS system, monitoring it constantly. When the company's supply of a particular item drops to a preset level, the vendor automatically sends a shipment to replenish its stock to an established level. Information that once traveled by mail (or was never shared at all), such as shipping information, invoices, inventory balances, sales, even funds, now travel instantly between businesses and their suppliers. The result is a much more efficient system of purchasing, distribution, and inventory control.

ENTREPRENEURIAL
Profile

Michael Fidenza: Ideal Supply Company

When one of Ideal Supply Company's top customers asked the small supplier of industrial pipes and valves to set up an EDI system, general manager Michael Fidenza decided that doing so would give his company an edge over its rivals. "Our industry is old-fashioned," says Fidenza. "We tend to lag behind the times." Ideal Supply not only forged an even closer relationship with its big customer, but it also reaped benefits from its suppliers. Because Ideal Supply was one of the few companies in the industry with EDI capability, Fidenza was able to negotiate higher discounts from Ideal Supply's suppliers because of increased efficiencies in the purchasing process. "One of our vendors offered us an extra 5 percent in discounts," he says. "Another plugs in an extra $10,000 worth of product with every $50,000 purchase—just because we're EDI." Ideal Supply has earned an impressive return on its original investment of $5,000 for EDI hardware and software. Today, 80 percent of the company's purchases and 15 percent of its sales are processed through its EDI system.[10]

Radio Frequency Identification Tags (RFID)

Inventory control systems that use bar codes to track the movement of inventory through the supply chain have been around for years. Increasingly, businesses are replacing their bar code systems with more flexible systems based on **radio frequency identification (RFID)** tags that are attached to individual items or to shipments and transmit data to a company's inventory management system. Each tag, which is about the size of a grain of sand, contains a tiny microchip that stores a unique electronic product code (EPC) and a tiny antenna. Because the tags use short-range radio frequencies, they can transmit information under almost any condition, avoiding the line-of-sight restrictions bar code systems experience. Once activated, the tags perform like talking bar codes and enable business owners to identify, count, and track the inventory items to which they are attached, providing them with highly accurate, real-time information constantly. When a shipment arrives at a warehouse or retail store, the RFID tags signal an inventory system reader, an object about the size of a coin that records the identity, the quantity, and characteristics of each item now in stock. The reader relays the information to a central inventory control system so that business owners can have access to all of this information online. Some stores have installed "smart" shelves equipped with readers that detect the identity and quantity of the items placed on them. When a customer makes a purchase, the smart shelf sends a message to the inventory control system, telling it to reduce the number on hand by the number of items the customer buys. In essence, RFID technology allows business owners to locate and track an item at any point in the supply chain—from the raw material stage to the finished product.

Other retailers use RFID technology to make inventory counts a breeze. Employees simply walk the aisles of the store holding a special reader that scans the RFID tags of the items on store shelves. At some stores, fully integrated RFID systems allow cashiers to ring up customers' purchases by scanning the contents of an entire shopping cart in just seconds, minimizing the time that customers have to stand in checkout lines. The cost of RFID tags continues to fall, from $1 per tag in 2000 to about five cents today. As costs decline further and the reliability of the tags improve, more businesses will be adopting the technology to improve the degree of control they have over their inventory.

ENTREPRENEURIAL
Profile
Serge Blanco

Serge Blanco, a French company that manufactures upscale sportswear, uses RFID technology to track the movement of products from its factories to its 40 retail stores and the 320 independent retailers that sell its clothing across Europe and the Middle East. The factories place an RFID tag on every garment they produce, which allows the company to monitor the location of each item of clothing in its distribution center and to make sure that each one is shipped to the right store at the right time. Once the garments arrive at its stores, RFID readers continue tracking them. For instance, at the Serge Blanco store in Toulon, France, employees take inventory counts of the entire store every hour using handheld RFID readers! When a customer makes a purchase, a POS terminal records the individual item sold before an employee removes the RFID tag. The system transmits sales reports to headquarters and to factories so that managers know exactly which items are selling (and therefore must be reordered) and which ones are languishing on store shelves. RFID readers in the store's dressing rooms identify which items customers try on but do not buy. Another reader near the store exit alerts employees when a garment with a tag still attached passes by, which helps reduce losses to theft. Managers say that the system has increased sales, reduced stockouts, lowered costs, and increased efficiency.[11]

LESSONS FROM THE STREET-SMART entrepreneur

Best Practices in Inventory Management

Many entrepreneurs have discovered the dangers of excess inventory. Not only does it tie up a company's valuable cash unnecessarily, but it also hides a host of other operating problems that a company has and needs to address. When it comes to managing inventory, small business owners often face four problems:

1. They have too much of some products.
2. They have too little of other products.
3. They don't know what they have in stock.
4. They know what they have in stock but cannot find it.

Addressing these four problems requires business owners to create a system of inventory management based on best practices. "Effective inventory management allows a distributor to meet or to exceed customers' expectations of product availability by maintaining the amount of each item that will also maximize their company's net profit," says one expert. The following tips from the Street-Smart Entrepreneur about inventory management best practices help accomplish that goal:

- *Recognize the difference between your company's "stock" and its "stuff."* "Stock" is made up of the inventory that customers want and expect a company to have available. "Stuff" is everything else that is in the warehouse or stockroom and typically includes slow-moving items. The goal is to manage the stock in such a way that the company can meet customers' demand for items and make a profit and to get rid of everything else—the "stuff."
- *Set up an inventory management process that recognizes the value of your company's stock.* Remember that Pareto's Law, the 80/20 Rule, applies to many situations, particularly inventory control. About 20 percent of the items in a typical company's

inventory account for about 80 percent of its sales. The idea is to set up a system that exercises the greatest degree of control over the most valuable 20 percent of the company's items.

■ *Work with vendors and suppliers to keep the inventory of essential items as lean as possible.* Even companies that utilize just-in-time techniques find it necessary to carry inventory; however, they keep their levels of stock to a minimum. Look for suppliers that can meet your company's quality requirements and provide rapid deliveries on short notice. Sharing information with the members of your company's supply chain and connecting with them electronically are excellent ways to shorten the lead time on the items you order.

■ *Use computerized inventory control systems to monitor your company's stock.* Computerized inventory control systems that are linked to POS terminals allow entrepreneurs to know which items they have in stock at any time. The reports that these systems generate also help them to know which items are selling best and which items are not selling

Gary Peltz, second generation owner of Peltz Shoes, uses RFID labels to control inventory in his stores.

Source: Peltz Famous Brand Shoes

at all. This information leads to improved inventory decisions in the future and allows entrepreneurs to adjust their buying decisions on the fly. Gary Peltz, second-generation owner of Peltz Shoes, a family-run business with four locations in Florida, recently installed an RFID-based inventory control system. Each shoebox is tagged with a printed RFID label. To take inventory, employees simply push a mobile reader cart down the store's aisles. The cart captures the signals from every box on the sales floor and feeds the information to the store's computerized inventory management system. Because the system increased the company's ability to control its inventory, it paid for itself in just 1 year. The next step is to tie Peltz Shoes' POS terminals into the inventory control system to complete the sales loop.

■ *Track the inventory metrics that are most important to your company's success.* A business can improve only what it measures. Common metrics for inventory control include the inventory turnover rate (for the business as a whole and for individual products or product lines), gross profit margin, age of inventory, measures of overstock, customer order fill rate, number of backorders, and many others.

■ *Organize your warehouse or stockroom to make it easy to find the items you need.* Organizing a warehouse or stockroom based on the knowledge of which items are in highest demand and which ones are seldom needed allows businesses to minimize the cost of filling orders. Placing the fastest-moving items in the most accessible location, preferably nearest the packing and shipping area, minimizes the time that employees spend walking around the warehouse or stockroom. Once again, computerized inventory control systems can help by printing the warehouse "address" of the items that employees must "pick" to fill orders.

■ *Get rid of the "stuff."* Eliminating unwanted or unnecessary inventory frees up valuable cash and simplifies the inventory management process. Possible ideas include:
  ■ Reducing the price of the items to get rid of them.
  ■ Offer incentives to salespeople to sell slow-moving "stuff."
  ■ Offer the items for sale at an online auction house.

Sources: Adapted from Jon Schreibfeder, *The First Steps to Achieving Effective Inventory Control,* Microsoft Business Solutions, *http://download. microsoft.com/download/b/f/3/bf334d7f-ad07-458e-a716-fdf46a0cf63c/ eimwp1_invcontrol.pdf;* "Inventory Best Practices," *The Bottom Line,* Manufacturing Extension Partnership, June 2003, pp. 1–2.

As Serge Blanco's experience suggests, the impact of RFID technology, which actually dates back to World War II, on inventory control is enormous. "This is an innovative technology similar to the Internet," says Mark Roberti, editor of *RFID Journal.* "You can now make any object smart."[12] International consulting firm McKinsey and Company estimates that once in use, RFID technology has the ability to increase companies' revenues by as much as 6 percent by improving the availability of items that customers want to buy and reducing the time and energy that staff spend looking for merchandise.[13]

Just-In-Time Inventory Control Techniques

Just-in-Time Techniques

2. Describe how just-in-time (JIT) and JIT II inventory control techniques work.

Many U.S. businesses have turned to a popular inventory control technique called **just-in-time (JIT)** to reduce costly inventories and turn around their financial fortunes. Until recently, these companies had accepted the following long-standing principles of manufacturing: Long production runs of standard items are ideal; machines should be up and running as much as possible; machines must produce a large number of items to justify long setup times and high costs; similar processes should be consolidated into single departments; tasks should be highly specialized and simplified; and inventories (raw materials, work-in-process, and finished goods) should be large enough to avoid emergencies such as supply interruptions, strikes, and breakdowns.

The just-in-time philosophy, however, views excess inventory as a blanket that masks problems and as a source of unnecessary costs that inhibit a firm's competitive position. Under a JIT system, materials and inventory flow smoothly through the production process without stopping. They arrive at the appropriate location just in time instead of becoming part of a costly inventory stockpile. Just-in-time is a philosophy that seeks to improve a company's efficiency. One key measure of efficiency is the level of inventory on hand; the lower the level of inventory, the more efficient is the production system.

The heart of the JIT philosophy is eliminating waste in whatever form it may take—time wasted moving work in process from one part of a factory to another, money wasted when employees must scrap or rework an item because of poor quality, cash tied up unnecessarily in excess inventory because of a poorly designed process, and many others. Refer to Figure 3, which illustrates the seven wastes that just-in-time, TQM, Six Sigma, and other continuous improvement strategies are designed to eliminate.

Companies using JIT successfully embrace a broader philosophy of continuous improvement ("kaizen"). These companies encourage employees to find ways to improve processes by simplifying them, making them more efficient, and redesigning them to make them more flexible. A cornerstone of the JIT philosophy is making waste in a company visible. The idea is that hidden waste is easy to ignore; visible waste gives everyone an incentive to eliminate it. Managers at a small company that manufactures fabrics for use in the papermaking industry set off an area in the middle of the production floor and put all of the wasted fabrics there on display. The not-so-subtle message was "help us find ways to reduce this waste." Within a matter of months, with the help of suggestions from both individuals and teams of employees, the pile of waste shrank dramatically.

In the past, only large companies could reap the benefits of computerized JIT and inventory control software, but now a proliferation of inexpensive programs designed for PCs gives small companies that ability. The most effective businesses know that what is required is not simply the technology, but the critical strategic alliances with suppliers who are themselves technologically sophisticated enough to interact on a real-time basis to deliver what is needed, when it is needed. The ultimate goal is to drive excess inventory to as close to zero as possible.

ENTREPRENEURIAL Profile
Topshop

For British clothing retailer Topshop, now with three stores in the United States, a lean, just-in-time inventory control system is a key part of the company's strategy. Topshop has found a unique niche tucked between discount stores that sell cheap "fast fashion" and luxury retailers that sell pricey haute couture. Its most expensive items top out around $200, and its cutting-edge fashions have made its store popular with a broad demographic base, ranging from teens to women in their forties looking for the latest fashions. The company was struggling in the 1990s, when managers decided to stop competing on price and to "make a stand that we would become the fashion authority." To implement the new strategy of becoming a fashion destination, Topshop began working with its suppliers to speed deliveries of small batches of items to its stores, particularly its 90,000-square-foot flagship London store, which company buyers and designers see as a fashion laboratory. Three shipments of goods arrive each day at the London store, which means that merchandise turns over so quickly that many customers come back every week to see what is new. The London store allows managers to determine which items will sell best, and Topshop's supply chain is set up so that shipments arrive at its other outlets within 2 weeks, compared to 6 or 8 weeks at most clothing retailers. With Topshop's lean inventory, customers know that if they find an item that they like, they had better purchase it then. The result is that the flagship London store sees an average of 30,000 customers a day, half of whom make a purchase. Topshop says that it sells 30 pairs of panties ("knickers") per minute, 6,000 pairs of jeans per day, and 35,000 pairs of shoes per week. "It's mad," says a brand director. "The stock goes straight in and out the door."[14]

Advocates claim that when JIT is successfully implemented, companies experience five positive results:

1. Lower investment in inventory
2. Reduced inventory carrying and handling costs
3. Reduced cost from obsolescence of inventory
4. Lower investment in space for inventory and production
5. Reduced total manufacturing costs from the better coordination needed between departments to operate at lower inventory levels

Despite the many benefits JIT systems offer, they do carry risks. Any disruption in a company's supply chain, even for inexpensive, commonplace items, can cause the entire operation to come to a halt. Recently, nearly 70 percent of Japan's automobile production was paralyzed for several days after an earthquake damaged Riken Corporation, which supplies piston rings (which cost only $1.50 each) for all of the major Japanese automakers. Japanese carmakers rely heavily on the just-in-time philosophy, and they keep their inventories of parts extremely lean. Because piston rings are customized for each car model, automakers could not switch to alternate suppliers, and the interruption in the supply chain forced assembly plants to shut down temporarily.[15]

For JIT systems to be most productive, entrepreneurs must consider the human component of the equation as well. Two elements are essential:

1. *Mutual trust and teamwork.* Managers and employees view each other as equals, have a commitment to the organization and its long-term effectiveness, and are willing to work as a team to find and solve problems.
2. *Empowerment.* Effective organizations provide their employees with the authority to take action to solve problems. The objective is to have the problems dealt with at the lowest level and as quickly as possible.

JIT is most effective in repetitive manufacturing operations where companies traditionally have relied on holding significant levels of inventory, where production requirements can be forecasted accurately, and where suppliers and customers work together as partners throughout the supply chain. Experience shows that companies with the following characteristics have the greatest success with JIT:

- Reliable deliveries of all parts and supplies
- Short distance between customers and their vendors
- Consistently high quality of vendors' products
- Stable and predictable product demand that allows for accurate production schedules

Just-in-Time II Techniques

In the past, some companies that adopted JIT techniques discovered an unwanted side effect: increased hostility resulting from the increased pressure they put on their suppliers to meet tight and often challenging schedules. To resolve that conflict, many businesses have turned to an extension of JIT, just-in-time II (JIT II), which focuses on creating a close, harmonious relationship with a company's suppliers so that both parties benefit from increased efficiency. Lance Dixon, who created the JIT II concept when he was a manager at Bose Corporation, a manufacturer of audio equipment, sought to create a working environment that empowered the supplier within the customer's organization. To work successfully, JIT II requires suppliers and their customers to share what was once closely guarded information in an environment of trust and cooperation. Under JIT II, customers and suppliers work hand in hand, acting more like partners than mere buyers and sellers.

In many businesses practicing JIT II, suppliers' employees work onsite at the customer's plant, factory, or warehouse almost as if they were employees of the customer. These on-site workers are responsible for monitoring, controlling, and ordering inventory from their own companies. While at Bose, Dixon decided to try JIT II because it offered the potential to reduce significantly the company's inventory of materials and components, cut purchasing costs, and generate cost-cutting design and production tips from suppliers who understood Bose's process. This new alliance between suppliers and their customers formed a new supply chain that lowered costs at every one of its links. To protect against leakage of confidential information, Dixon had all of the employees from Bose's suppliers who worked in its plant sign confidentiality agreements. Dixon also put a ceiling on the amount each supplier's employee could order without previous authorization from Bose.[16]

Manufacturers are not the only companies benefiting from JIT II. In a retail environment, the concept is more commonly known as **efficient consumer response (ECR)**, but the principles are the same. Rather than build inventories of merchandise that might sit for months before selling (or worse, never sell at all), retailers that use ECR replenish their inventories constantly on an as-needed basis. Because vendors are linked electronically to the retailer's POS system, they can monitor the company's inventory and keep it stocked with the right merchandise mix in the right quantities. Both parties reduce the inventories they must carry and experience significant reductions in paperwork and ordering costs. JIT II and ECR techniques work best when two companies transact a significant amount of business that involves many different parts or products. Still, maintaining trust is the biggest barrier the companies must overcome.

IN THE ENTREPRENEURIAL SPOTLIGHT

Perry Ellis International: Integrated Inventory Control

Founded in 1969, Perry Ellis International, a Miami, Florida-based apparel company, has grown rapidly and now manages 27 different brands, including its namesake, Perry Ellis; Jantzen; Savane; Original Penguin; and others. The company manages a global supply network of more than 100 companies and distributes garments in 10 different clothing categories through 7 channels to a variety of regional, national, and international department stores and small independent specialty stores. Because Perry Ellis operates in the ever-changing fashion industry, the company must exercise tight control over its inventory to be successful. The company's inventory control system had evolved over time and was composed of a set of internally built components that were sagging under the company's fast growth. As a result, managers were not getting timely inventory reports, one key to success in the fashion apparel business.

Working with software provider Oracle, Perry Ellis created an integrated business system that links stores, warehouses, headquarters, and suppliers and gives everyone in the supply chain timely access to information about inventory levels. For instance, suppliers of fabric for Perry Ellis shirts can see which types of shirts are selling best and adjust their production schedules accordingly. "Retailers and their suppliers [are] partnering closer than they ever have before by sharing demand information in a bidirectional way," says one industry analyst. "Retailers are sharing more transaction and consumer information to help manufacturers with their sales and operations planning activities. Suppliers are sharing supply chain event and inventory information to help retailers better understand the status of products and how they're filling the channel." The new, integrated inventory control system gives managers a real-time picture of the company's diverse inventory, whether it is in warehouses, in transit, or in stores. "We have small stores, so there's not much room for inventory," says Luis Paez, chief information officer for Perry Ellis. "Having the right inventory in the right place at the right time becomes critical because we can't have a lot of [merchandise on hand]."

To make sure that happens, the new system relies on sales feedback from each store and automatic allocations that determine which items need to be replaced and ensure that each store is always fully stocked with items that customers are buying. The result is fewer stockouts and higher levels of customer satisfaction. The new system is working: It has increased the company's sales by 15 to 20 percent. Perry Ellis' retail stores are not the only beneficiaries of the new inventory control system; its department store customers also are gaining better control over their Perry Ellis–branded merchandise. Perry Ellis representatives share inventory reports with department store buyers and managers about which items are selling and where and are able to offer suggestions on price adjustments. In other words, the company has become a resource to its retail customers, helping them sell more merchandise at better prices. The new system slices and dices information down to the individual store level and

uses statistics and geographic information systems (GIS) data to generate reports that describe the groups of target customers that are driving sales of various products, allowing Perry Ellis and its retail customers to stock products with the greatest potential to sell in stores. "We work to have the right inventory at the right store at the right time for more than 12,000 stores," says Paez.

The new inventory control system at Perry Ellis enables the company and its department and specialty store customers to track ever-changing fashion trends and to respond to them quickly and efficiently—a must in the hotly competitive fashion world. "The ultimate goal of companies in the value chain is to become demand-driven," says an industry analyst. "Driven by a better understanding of what customers want and ultimately being able to translate that effectively into fulfilling the demand."

1. One key to the success of Perry Ellis' inventory control system is a supply chain that provides visibility of sales and inventory information for every business in the chain. Why are some companies hesitant to share sales and inventory data with their supply chain partners? What are the benefits of doing so?
2. What advantages does Perry Ellis reap by managing its inventory so carefully?

Source: Based on David A. Kelly, "Building a Seamless Retail System," *Profit*, August 2008, pp. 16–22.

Turning Slow-Moving Inventory into Cash

3. Describe methods for reducing losses from slow-moving inventory.

Managing inventory effectively requires a business owner to monitor the company's inventory turnover ratio and to compare it with that of other firms of similar size in the same industry. The inventory turnover ratio is calculated by dividing a company's cost of goods sold by its average inventory. This ratio expresses the number of times per year the business turns over its inventory. In most cases, the higher the inventory turnover ratio, the better the small firm's financial position will be. A very low inventory turnover ratio indicates that much of the inventory may be stale and obsolete or that the inventory investment is too large.

Because of the variability in demand and the cyclical nature of the market, auto dealers often struggle to maintain an adequate number of inventory turns and to keep the number of cars on their lots from ballooning, which drives up their operating costs. The longer a car sits on a dealer's lot, the greater is the cost of borrowing to pay for it. Auto companies consider 50 to 60 days' worth of cars to be an adequate inventory. When gasoline prices increase, however, dealers see large gas-guzzling SUVs languish on their lots, with inventories increasing to 100 days' worth. Inventories of fuel-efficient and hybrid models, however, fall to record lows. After one spike in gas prices, Toyota (which usually stocks 35 to 45 days' worth of inventory) reported that its Scion line, which it markets to young people, was down to 7.2 days' supply, and its hybrid Prius inventory stood at just 6 days' worth. Similarly, supply of its Fit was just 9 days.[17]

Slow-moving items carry a good chance of loss resulting from spoilage or obsolescence. Firms dealing in trendy fashion merchandise or highly seasonal items often experience losses as a result of being stuck with unsold inventory for long periods of time. Some small business owners are reluctant to sell these slow-moving items by cutting prices, but it is much more profitable to dispose of this merchandise quickly than it is to hold it in stock at regular prices.

Profile

Mickey Gee: Pants Store

Sales during the all-important holiday season at the Pants Store, a small chain of clothing stores near Birmingham, Alabama, were slower than owner Mickey Gee, whose father, Taylor, started the business in 1950, expected, leaving him with 20 percent more merchandise than normal. Gee used markdowns, some as much as 80 percent, to turn the slow-moving merchandise into cash. He also invested in an inventory control system that helps him identify which brands and which items are selling best (and which are not) in his four locations.[18]

A business owner who postpones marking down stale merchandise, fearing it will reduce profits and hoping that the goods will sell eventually at the regular price, is making a mistake. The longer the merchandise sits, the dimmer are the prospects of ever selling it, much less selling it at a profit. Pricing these items below regular price or even below cost is difficult, but it is much better than having valuable working capital tied up in unproductive assets.

The technique that Mickey Gee used, the markdown, is the most common technique for liquidating slow-moving merchandise. Not only is the markdown effective in eliminating slow-moving goods, but it also is a successful promotional tool. Advertising special prices on such merchandise helps a small business garner a larger clientele and contributes to establishing a favorable business image. Using special sales to promote slow-moving items helps create a functional program for turning over inventory more quickly. To get rid of a large supply of out-of-style neckties, one small business offered a "1-cent sale" to customers purchasing neckwear at the regular price. One retailer of stereos and sound equipment chooses an unusual holiday—President's Day—to sponsor an all-out blitz, including special sales, prices, and promotions to reduce its inventory. Other techniques that help eliminate slow-moving merchandise include the following:

- Creating middle-of-the-aisle display islands that attract customer attention
- Offering 1-day-only sales
- Giving quantity discounts for volume purchases
- Creating bargain tables with a variety of merchandise for customers to explore
- Using eye-catching lights and tickets marking sale merchandise
- Setting up an online store on eBay
- Using an inventory liquidation company to get rid of excess merchandise

As inventory control techniques become increasingly sophisticated and accurate, slow-moving inventory will never be "lost" in the supply chain. Aggressive methods of selling slower-moving inventory allow business owners to convert inventory into cash and to produce an acceptable inventory turnover ratio. The inventory management tools described in this chapter also play an important role in avoiding slow-moving merchandise. They highlight those items that are slow-moving, enabling business owners to avoid the mistake of ordering them again. In effect, this information on what *isn't* selling influences entrepreneurs' decisions about the merchandise they order in the future as much as information on those items that *are* selling well. The ability to avoid slow-moving items in the first place means that business owners can invest their working capital more effectively and produce faster inventory turnover ratios, lower costs, and higher profits.

Protecting Inventory from Theft

4. Discuss employee theft and shoplifting and how to prevent them.

Small companies are a big target for crime. Businesses lose nearly $92 million per day, about 5 percent of their total sales, to criminals, although the actual loss may be even greater because so many business crimes go unreported.[19] Whatever the actual loss is, its effect is staggering. If a company operates at a 5 percent net profit margin, it must generate an additional $20 in sales for every $1 lost to theft. Small companies are especially vulnerable because they often lack the sophistication to identify early on the illegal actions of employees or professional thieves and to implement controls to prevent theft and fraud. A study by the Association of Certified Fraud Examiners reports that small companies are the most frequent victims of theft and fraud and that the median loss for small companies is $155,000.[20] When a company has a small asset base, a loss from theft and fraud can be a crippling blow, threatening its very existence.

Many entrepreneurs believe that the primary sources of theft originate outside the business. In reality, most firms are victimized by their own employees.

Employee Theft

Ironically, the greatest criminal threat to small businesses comes from the inside. Employee theft accounts for the greatest proportion of the criminal losses businesses suffer and cost companies $39.5 million per day.[21] Because employees have access to the inner workings of a business, they can inflict more damage than shoplifters. One study reports that dishonest employees steal, on average, 6.6 times more per incident than shoplifters.[22] Unfortunately, employee theft is more prevalent than ever. Tim Dimoff, president of SACS Consulting & Investigative Services Inc., which is based in Mogadore, Ohio, gives one reason for the increased prevalence. "I call the attitude employees take in the workplace 'entitlement,'" he says. "They justify in their minds that they are entitled to take things because they work so hard." Dimoff adds that some businesses all but encourage employee theft. How? By failing to file criminal charges against employees caught stealing. Many business owners do not want the negative publicity that results from prosecuting employee thieves. Others worry about the cost to the company to prosecute, how the time away from management will affect the organization, and the impact that the incident will have on employee morale. Often it is easier just to ask the guilty employee to leave.[23]

The median length of time it takes employers to catch an employee who is stealing is 18 months, and managers usually discover the theft when another employee tips them off.[24] How can thefts go undetected for so long? Most thefts occur when employees take advantage of the opportunities to steal that small business owners unwittingly give them. Typically, small business owners are so busy building their companies that they rarely even consider the possibility of employee theft—until disaster strikes.

In addition, many small companies do not have adequate financial, audit, and security procedures in place. Fewer than 30 percent of small companies use internal audit teams as a loss prevention tool, compared to nearly 83 percent of large companies. Even though tips from employees are the most common way of discovering employee theft and fraud, only 15 percent of small companies have installed antifraud hotlines for employees to report suspicious activities.[25] Add to this mix of lax control procedures the high degree of trust that most small business owners place in their employees, and you have a perfect recipe for employee theft.

Profile

Berle Apparel Group

Berle Apparel Group, a family-owned manufacturer of men's trousers founded in 1946 in Charleston, South Carolina, recently discovered that a long-time employee had embezzled more than $600,000. The employee, who was the company's financial controller, diverted Berle's payroll tax payments to the Internal Revenue Service for more than 2 years by giving the IRS the impression that the company had gone out of business.[26]

What Causes Employee Theft?

Security experts estimate that 30 percent of workers pilfer small items from their employers and that 60 percent of employees will steal if given enough opportunity and motivation.[27] Employees steal from their companies for any number of reasons. Some may have a grudge against the company; others may have a drug, alcohol, or gambling addiction to support. Still others succumb to the temptation of an easy opportunity to steal because of a company's lack of proper controls. The Association of Certified Fraud Examiners reports that more than 85 percent of employees caught stealing have never been charged or convicted of a prior theft offense.[28]

Employees steal from the company for four reasons: need, greed, temptation, and opportunity. A business owner can control only temptation and opportunity. To minimize their losses to employee theft, business owners must understand how both the temptation and the opportunity to steal creep into their companies. The following are conditions that lead to major security gaps in small companies.

THE TRUSTED EMPLOYEE. The fact is that *any* employee can be a thief, although most are not. Slightly more than half of the workers who steal from their companies have been employed for less than 5 years, but long-time employees who steal cause more damage (median loss of $81,000 versus $260,000). Many entrepreneurs view their long-time employees almost as partners. This attitude, although not undesirable, can result in security breaches. Many owners refuse to believe that their most trusted employees present the greatest security threat, but these workers have the greatest accessibility to keys, cash registers, records, and even safe combinations. Because of their seniority, these employees hold key positions and are quite familiar with operations, and they know where weaknesses in control and security procedures lie.

Profile

Michael and John Koss: Koss Corporation

Michael and John Koss, second-generation owners of Koss Corporation, a Milwaukee, Wisconsin-based maker of stereo headphones, discovered that the company's vice president of finance had used her position to steal more than $31 million from the company over 6 years. She covered her theft for so long by inducing employees in the finance department to make fraudulent accounting entries that made her theft transactions appear to be legitimate. The employee, who had held her position at Koss for 18 years, used the money to finance purchases of cars, clothing, jewelry, home renovations, household furnishings, trips, and other personal expenditures.[29]

Business owners also should be wary of "workaholic" employees. Is this worker really dedicated to the company, or is he or she working so hard to cover up theft? Employee thieves are unwilling to take extended breaks from their jobs for fear of being detected. As long as a dishonest employee remains on the job, he or she can cover up theft. As a security precaution, business owners should require every employee to take vacations long enough so that someone else has to take over his or her responsibilities (at least 5 consecutive business days). Most schemes are relatively simple and require day-to-day maintenance to keep them going. Business failure records are filled with stories of firms in which the "ideal" employee turned out to be a thief. "In 90 percent of the cases in which people steal from their companies, the employer would probably have described this person, right up to the time the crime was discovered as a trusted employee," says one expert.[30]

DISGRUNTLED EMPLOYEES. Business owners also must monitor the performance of disgruntled employees. Employees are more likely to steal if they believe that their company treats them unfairly, and the probability of their stealing goes even higher if they believe that they themselves have been treated unfairly. Employees dissatisfied with their pay or their promotions may retaliate against an employer by stealing. Dishonest employees make up the difference between what they are paid and what they believe they are worth by stealing. Many believe pilfering is a well-deserved "perk."

ORGANIZATIONAL ATMOSPHERE. Many entrepreneurs unintentionally create an atmosphere that encourages employee dishonesty. Failing to establish formal controls and procedures invites theft. Nothing encourages dishonest employees to steal more than knowing they are unlikely to be caught. Four factors encourage employee theft:

1. The need or desire to steal (e.g., to support a habit or to cope with a sudden financial crisis)
2. A rationalization for the act (e.g., "They owe me this.")
3. The opportunity to steal (e.g., access to merchandise, complete control of financial functions)
4. The perception that there is a low probability of being caught (e.g., "Nobody will ever know.")

Owners must recognize that they set the example for security and honesty in the business. Employees place more emphasis on what owners *do* than on what they *say*. Entrepreneurs who install a complete system of inventory control and then ignore it are telling employees that security is unimportant. No one should remove merchandise, materials, or supplies from inventory without recording them properly. There should be no exceptions to the rules, even for bosses and their relatives. Managers should develop clear control procedures and establish penalties for violations. The single biggest deterrent (to employee theft) is a strong, top-down policy that is well communicated to all employees that theft will not be tolerated and that anyone caught stealing will be prosecuted—*no exceptions.*

Entrepreneurs must constantly emphasize the importance of security. Business owners must use every available opportunity to reduce employees' temptation to steal. One business owner relies on payroll inserts to emphasize to employees how theft reduces the funds available for growth, expansion, and higher wages. Another useful tool is a written code of ethics signed by every employee that spells out penalties for violations. Workers must understand that security is a team effort. Security rules and procedures must be reasonable, and owners must treat workers equitably. Unreasonable rules are no more effective—and may even be more harmful—than poorly enforced procedures. A work environment that fosters honesty at every turn serves as an effective deterrent to employee theft.

PHYSICAL BREAKDOWNS. Another major factor contributing to employee theft is weak physical security. The owner who pays little attention to the distribution of keys, safe combinations, and other entry devices is inviting theft. In addition, owners who fail to lock doors and windows or to install reliable alarm systems literally are leaving their businesses open to thieves both inside and outside the organization.

Open windows and unattended doors give dishonest employees a prime opportunity to slip stolen merchandise out of the plant or store. One security expert worked with a small manufacturing operation that was experiencing high levels of employee theft during the night shift. His investigation revealed that employees could exit the building through 14 different doors with little or no supervision. The company closed most of the exits, installed security cameras at those that remained open, and assigned managers to supervise the night shift. After implementing these simple changes, employee theft plummeted to nearly zero.[31]

Many businesses find that their profits go out with the trash, literally. When collecting trash, a dishonest employee may stash valuable merchandise in with the refuse and dump it in the receptacle. After the store closes, the thief returns to collect the loot. One drugstore owner lost more than $7,000 in merchandise in just 6 months through trash thefts.

IMPROPER CASH CONTROL. Many small business owners encourage employee theft by failing to implement proper cash control procedures. Without a system of logical, practical audit controls on cash, a firm will likely suffer internal theft. Dishonest employees quickly discover there is a low probability of detection and steal cash with impunity.

Cashiers clearly have the greatest accessibility to the firm's cash and, consequently, experience the greatest temptation to steal. The following scenario is all too common: A customer makes a purchase with the exact amount of cash and leaves quickly. The cashier fails to ring up the purchase and pockets the cash without anyone's knowledge. Some small business owners create a cash security problem by allowing too many employees to operate cash registers and handle customer payments. If a cash shortage develops, the owner is unable to trace responsibility.

A daily inspection of cash register transactions can point out potential employee theft problems. When transactions indicate an excessive number of voided transactions or no-sale transactions, the owner should investigate. A no-sale transaction could mean the register was opened to give a customer change or to steal cash. A large number of incorrect register transactions also are a sign of foul play. Clerks may be camouflaging thefts by voiding transactions, under-ringing sales amounts, or pretending to scan items at checkout without actually ringing them up (a problem known as "sweethearting").

To cut its losses from theft Famous Footwear, a chain of retail shoe stores, recently installed a cash register monitoring system in every store. The system records every cash register transaction and looks for suspicious patterns. Within a short time, the monitoring system cut the company's unexplained inventory losses in half. When she learned about the new system, one store manager, convinced that she would soon be caught, admitted to stealing more than $2,000 in cash.[32]

Cash shortages and overages are also clues that alert managers to possible theft. All small business owners are alarmed by cash shortages, but few are disturbed by cash overages. However, cash discrepancies in either direction are an indication of inept cashiering or of poor cash controls. The manager who investigates all cash discrepancies can greatly reduce the opportunity for cashiers to steal.

Preventing Employee Theft

Many incidents of employee theft go undetected, and of those employees who are caught stealing, only a small percentage is prosecuted. The burden of dealing with employee theft falls squarely on the owner's shoulders. Although business owners cannot eliminate employee theft, they can reduce its likelihood by using some relatively simple procedures and policies that are cost-effective to implement.

SCREEN EMPLOYEES CAREFULLY. Statistics show that, on average, 1 out of every 28 employees is caught committing employee theft.[33] Perhaps a business owner's greatest weapon against crime is a thorough pre-employment screening process. The best time to weed out prospective criminals is before hiring them! One security company conducted an analysis of more than 19,000 applicants for retail jobs and rated 19.3 percent of them as "high risk" candidates for employee theft.[34] Although state and federal regulations prohibit employers from invading job applicants' privacy and from using discriminatory devices in the selection process, employers have a legitimate right to determine job candidates' integrity and qualifications. A comprehensive selection process and reliable screening devices greatly reduce the chances that an entrepreneur will hire a thief. Smart entrepreneurs verify the information applicants provide on their résumés because they know that some of them will either exaggerate or misrepresent their qualifications. A thorough background check with references and previous employers also is essential. (One question that sheds light on a former employer's feelings toward a former employee is "Would you hire this person again?")

Some security experts recommend the use of **integrity tests**, paper-and-pencil tests that offer valuable insight into job applicants' level of honesty. Business owners can buy integrity tests for $20 or less that have already been validated (to avoid charges of discrimination) and that they can score on their own. Because drug addictions drive many employees to steal, employers also should administer drug tests consistently to all job applicants. The most reliable drug tests cost the company from $35 to $50 each, a small price to pay given the potential losses that can result from hiring an employee with a drug habit. In addition, business owners should conduct criminal background checks on every candidate they are considering hiring.

CREATE AN ENVIRONMENT OF HONESTY. Creating an environment of honesty and integrity starts at the top of an organization. This requires business owners to set an impeccable example for everyone else in the company. In addition to creating a standard of ethical behavior, business owners should strive to establish high morale among workers. A positive work environment in which employees see themselves as an important part of the team is an effective deterrent to employee theft. Establishing a written code of ethics and having employees sign "honesty clauses" offers tangible evidence of a company's commitment to honesty and integrity.

ESTABLISH A SYSTEM OF INTERNAL CONTROLS. The basis for maintaining internal security on the job is establishing a set of reasonable internal controls designed to prevent employee theft. An effective system of checks and balances goes a long way toward deterring internal crime; weak or inconsistently enforced controls are an open invitation for theft. The most basic rule is to separate among several employees related duties that might cause a security breach if assigned to a single worker. For instance, owners should avoid letting the employee who issues checks reconcile the company's bank statement. Similarly, the person who orders merchandise and supplies should not be the one who also approves those invoices for payment. Spreading these tasks among a number of employees makes organizing a theft more difficult. The owner of a small retail art shop learned this lesson the hard way. After conducting an inventory audit, he discovered that more than $25,000 worth of art supplies was missing. The owner finally traced the theft to the company bookkeeper, who was creating fictional invoices and then issuing checks to herself for the same amount.

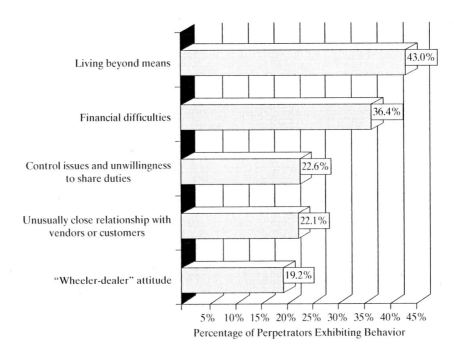

FIGURE 3

**Behaviors Exhibited by
Perpetrators of
Employee Theft**

*Source: 2010 Report to the Nations
on Occupational Fraud and Abuse,*
Association of Certified Fraud
Examiners, Austin, Texas, p. 70.

Living beyond means — 43.0%
Financial difficulties — 36.4%
Control issues and unwillingness to share duties — 22.6%
Unusually close relationship with vendors or customers — 22.1%
"Wheeler-dealer" attitude — 19.2%

5% 10% 15% 20% 25% 30% 35% 40% 45%
Percentage of Perpetrators Exhibiting Behavior

Business owners should insist that all company records be kept up-to-date. Sloppy record keeping makes theft difficult to detect. All internal documents—shipping, ordering, invoicing, and collecting—should be numbered. Missing numbers should arouse suspicion. One subtle way to test employees' honesty is to commit deliberate errors occasionally to see if employees detect them. If you send an extra case of merchandise to the loading dock for shipment, does the supervisor catch it, or does it disappear?

USE TECHNOLOGY TO REDUCE THEFT. Business owners can use a variety of technologies, often available at low cost, to minimize losses to employee theft and fraud. Kevin Donahue, owner of a Planet Beach franchise in McLean, Virginia, uses a security system that gives him access to his store's alarm system and security cameras from almost anywhere in the world over the Internet. "It gives me the ability to travel and manage my staff remotely," says Donahue, who paid $100 to install the system and pays a monthly fee of $39.[35]

WATCH FOR SIGNS OF EMPLOYEE THEFT. Research shows that employees who are stealing tend to exhibit certain behavior patterns (see Figure 3). Watch for them.

SET UP A HOTLINE. One of the most effective tools for preventing employee theft is to encourage employees to report suspicious activity. Perhaps the easiest way to encourage reporting it is to establish a hotline that allows employees to provide tips anonymously.

EMBRACE A ZERO TOLERANCE POLICY. Business owners should demonstrate zero tolerance for theft. They must adhere strictly to company policy when dealing with employees who violate the company's trust. When business owners catch an employee thief, the best course of action is to fire the perpetrator and to prosecute. Too often, owners take the attitude: "Resign, return the money, and we'll forget it." Letting thieves off, however, only encourages them to move on to other businesses where they will steal again. Prosecuting a former employee for theft is never easy, but it does send a clear signal about how the company views employee crime.

Notice in Figure 4 that although the primary cause of inventory shrinkage is employee theft, shoplifting also is a common problem.

FIGURE 4

Causes of Inventory Shrinkage

Source: 2010 National Retail Security Survey, National Retail Federation, Washington, D.C.

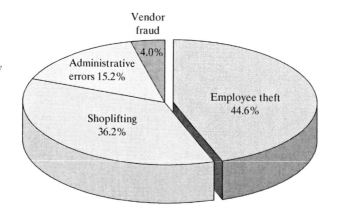

Vendor fraud 4.0%

Administrative errors 15.2%

Shoplifting 36.2%

Employee theft 44.6%

▶ E N T R E P R E N E U R S H I P IN ACTION ▶

FOUL PLAY

The Trusted Employee

Like many business owners, Karin Wilson saw sales slide at Page and Palette Inc., the bookstore in Fairhope, Alabama, that she co-owns with her husband, during the last recession. By the time the all-important holiday season arrived, the store was running low on its inventory of books. However, cash flow at Page and Palette was extremely tight, and Wilson was unable to convince her book suppliers to extend the store additional credit. One week before Christmas, Wilson happened to see the company's credit card bill, which indicated the Page and Palette was months behind on its payments and was racking up huge fees and interest expenses. She began investigating and soon discovered evidence that the company's bookkeeper, who had a personal account with the same bank, had been using money from the company's account to pay her personal credit card bill.

Wilson was shocked because the bookkeeper was one of her most trusted employees. She also discovered that the bookkeeper had used money intended to pay publishers for the store's book orders to write checks to herself. Wilson says that the former employee used the money that she embezzled from Page and Palette to pay for a membership in a local golf club and for private school tuition for her child. Wilson estimates that the former employee took about $150,000 over two-and-a-half years and covered the theft by forging reports that made it look as though she had paid the company's vendors and credit card bills. Because the theft left the store in a cash bind, Wilson was unable to order a sufficient inventory of books, which ultimately cost the business as much as 20 percent of its annual revenue in lost sales. "She realized quickly how trusting we were," says Wilson.

Since discovering that she was a victim of employee theft, Wilson has changed the way she operates her business. She destroyed the stamp bearing her signature that the former employee used on business checks. Employees no longer have access to the company's credit cards; Wilson now approves every credit card purchase. She also has the company's bank statements sent to her home rather than to the business.

The Desperate Employee

Brandon Ansel, owner of a Roly Poly sandwich and Biggby Coffee franchise in Jackson, Michigan, noticed that one of the restaurant's employees failed to deposit money from the cash register into the company's bank account daily. Instead, he would wait 3 or 4 days to deposit the cash. When Ansel questioned the employee, the man said that he was so busy that he could not get to the bank on time. Eventually, the employee began stretching the time between deposits to 9 days, and Ansel suspected that the man was skimming cash from each day's receipts. When Ansel confronted the man, he admitted that he was having severe financial problems and had taken the money with the intent of repaying it. A member of the man's family approached Ansel and paid him $9,000, the amount the former employee admitted that he had taken. Ansel decided not to press charges against his former employee. Ansel says that he, too, has changed some of his operating procedures and admits that as a small business owner he feels more susceptible to employee theft because he lacks the systems that larger companies have to alert managers to signs of theft.

1. What factors led to the thefts at Page and Palette and the Roly Poly–Biggby Coffee franchise?
2. Do you agree with Brandon Ansel's view that small businesses are more vulnerable to employee theft because they lack the systems to detect the signs of theft? Explain.
3. Do you agree with the approach that Brandon Ansel took with the employee who stole from his company? Explain.
4. List at least five steps business owners can take to prevent employee theft.

Source: Based on Simona Covel, "Small Businesses Face More Fraud in Downturn," *Wall Street Journal*, February 19, 2009, p. B5.

Shoplifting

The most frequent business crime is shoplifting. In fact, research shows that 1 of every 11 adults in the United States has shoplifted.[36] Retail businesses in the United States lose an estimated $11.7 billion annually to shoplifters each year, and small businesses suffer a significant share of those losses.[37] Shoplifting takes an especially heavy toll on small businesses because they usually have the weakest lines of defense against shoplifters. Shoplifting losses, which ultimately are passed on to the consumer, account for approximately 3 to 4 percent of the average price tag.

TYPES OF SHOPLIFTERS. Anyone who takes merchandise from a store without paying for it, no matter what the justification, is a shoplifter. Shoplifters look exactly like other customers. They can be young children in search of a new toy or elderly people who are short of money. *Anyone* can be a shoplifter, given the opportunity, the ability, and the desire to steal. Police have apprehended people from all walks of life—including wealthy socialites and famous celebrities—for shoplifting.

Fortunately for small business owners, most shoplifters are amateurs who steal because the opportunity presents itself. Many steal on impulse, and the theft is the first criminal act. Many of those caught have the money to pay for their "five-finger discounts." Observant business owners supported by trained store personnel can spot potential shoplifters and deter many shoplifting incidents; however, they must understand the shoplifter's profile. Experts identify five types of shoplifters.

Juveniles. Juveniles account for approximately one-half of all shoplifters. Many juveniles steal as a result of peer pressure. Most have little fear of prosecution, assuming they can hide behind their youth. When owners detect juvenile shoplifters, they must not let sympathy stand in the way of good judgment. Many hard-core criminals began their careers as shoplifters, and small business owners who fail to prosecute the youthful offender do nothing to discourage a life of crime. Juvenile offenders should be prosecuted through proper legal procedures just as any adult shoplifter would be.

Impulse Shoplifters. Impulse shoplifters steal on the spur of the moment when they succumb to temptation. These shoplifters do not plan their thefts, but when a prime opportunity to shoplift arises, they take advantage of it. For example, a salesperson may be showing a customer several pieces of jewelry. If the salesperson is called away, the customer might pocket an expensive ring and leave the store before the employee returns.

The most effective method of fighting impulse shoplifting is prevention. To minimize losses, the owner should remove the opportunity to steal by implementing proper security procedures and devices.

Shoplifters sometimes work in teams. Here a girl shoplifts computer software while a partner obstructs employees' view of the theft.

Source: PhotoEdit, Inc.

373

"The sign said buy one, get one free.
But I only needed one. The free one."

Shoplifters Supporting Other Criminal Behaviors. Shoplifters motivated to steal to support a drug or alcohol habit often are easy to detect because their behavior is usually unstable and erratic. One shoplifter recently apprehended was supporting a $100-a-day heroin habit by stealing small items from local retailers and then returning the merchandise for refunds. (The stores almost never asked for sales receipts.) Small business owners should exercise great caution in handling these shoplifters because they can easily become violent. Criminals deranged by drugs or alcohol might be armed and could endanger the lives of customers and employees if they are detained. It is best to let the police apprehend these shoplifters.

Kleptomaniacs. Kleptomaniacs have a compulsive need to steal even though they have little, if any, need for the items they shoplift. In many cases, these shoplifters could afford to purchase the merchandise they steal. Kleptomaniacs account for less than 5 percent of shoplifters, but their disease costs business owners a great deal. They need professional psychological counseling, and the owner only helps them by seeing that they are apprehended.

Professionals. A study by the National Retail Federation reports that 92 percent of businesses have been victims of professional shoplifters within the last year.[38] Professional shoplifters are individuals, groups, or gangs who steal merchandise in significant quantities as part of a criminal enterprise. These criminal operations rely on "boosters," people who are paid to steal merchandise from stores, and "fences," those who specialize in converting stolen goods into cash or drugs. Although professional shoplifters account for 32 percent of shoplifting incidents, the dollar impact of their thefts is disproportionately large. Losses to professional shoplifters are 54 times greater than the average shoplifting loss.[39] Police in Polk County, Florida, recently arrested 18 people who were part of a professional shoplifting ring that stole cosmetics, baby formula, over-the-counter drugs, and other items worth between $60 million and $100 million over a 5-year period. The thieves used specially made bags and purses with hidden compartments to conceal the stolen goods. "The thieves worked in pairs and in less than 3 minutes could walk out with as much as $4,000 in merchandise," says Sheriff Grady Judd. "They were so good that you could watch them steal and not be aware of what they were doing." The operation was so sophisticated that the thieves created schedules of the stores they would hit to avoid stealing from any one store too often and raising suspicion.[40]

Because professional shoplifters' business is theft, they are very difficult to detect and deter. Professional shoplifters tend to focus on expensive merchandise they can sell quickly to their fences, such as consumer electronics, appliances, guns, or jewelry. Usually the fences don't keep the stolen goods long, often selling them on online auction sites or at flea markets at a fraction of their value. Therefore, apprehending and prosecuting professional shoplifters is quite difficult. Police have apprehended professional shoplifters with detailed maps of a city's shopping districts, showing target stores and the best times to make a "hit." Furthermore, many professional shoplifters are affiliated with organized crime, and they are able to rely on their associates to avoid detection and prosecution. Table 4 provides some interesting facts about shoplifting.

DETECTING SHOPLIFTERS. Although shoplifters can be difficult to detect, business owners who know what to look for can spot them in action. Entrepreneurs must always be on the lookout for shoplifters, but they should be especially vigilant on Saturdays and around Christmas, when shoplifters can hide their thefts more easily in the frenzy of a busy shopping day.

Shoplifters can work alone or in groups. In general, impulse shoplifters prefer solitary thefts, whereas juveniles and professionals operate in groups. A common tactic for group shoplifters is for one member of the gang to create some type of distraction while other members steal the merchandise. Business owners should be wary of loud, disruptive groups that enter their stores.

TABLE 4 Shoplifting Facts

- Nearly $12 billion worth of goods are stolen from retailers each year. That's more than $1.3 million worth of merchandise per hour.
- There are approximately 27 million shoplifters (or 1 in 11 people) in the United States. More than 10 million people have been caught shoplifting in the last 5 years.
- Shoplifting affects more than the offender. It overburdens the police and the courts, adds to a store's security expenses, increases the cost of goods for legitimate shoppers, reduces sales tax dollars that go to communities, and hurts children and families.
- There is no such thing as a "typical" shoplifter. Anyone can be a shoplifter. Men and women shoplift about equally as often.
- Approximately 25 percent of shoplifters are kids. Fifty-five percent of adult shoplifters say they started shoplifting in their teens.
- Many shoplifters buy and steal merchandise in the same visit. Shoplifters commonly steal from $2 to $200 per incident, depending on the type of store and item(s) chosen.
- Shoplifting is often an impulse crime: 73 percent of adult and 72 percent of juvenile shoplifters don't plan to steal in advance.
- Eighty-six percent of kids say they know other kids who shoplift, and 66 percent say they hang out with those kids.
- Approximately 3 percent of shoplifters are "professionals" who steal solely for resale or profit as a business. These include drug addicts who steal to feed their habit, hardened professionals who steal as a lifestyle, and international shoplifting gangs who steal for profit as a business.
- Eighty-eight percent of retailers say that shoplifting losses from professional shoplifters has increased over the last 3 years.
- The majority of shoplifters are nonprofessionals who steal, not out of financial need or greed, but as a response to social and personal pressures in their lives.
- The excitement generated from "getting away with it" produces a chemical reaction that results in what shoplifters describe as an incredible "rush" or "high" feeling. Many shoplifters say that this high is their true reward rather than the merchandise itself.
- Drug addicts who have become addicted to shoplifting describe shoplifting as equally addicting as drugs.
- Even after getting caught, 57 percent of adults and 33 percent of juveniles say it is hard for them to stop shoplifting.
- Most nonprofessional shoplifters don't commit other types of crimes. They'll never steal an ashtray from your house and will return to you a $20 bill that you drop. Their criminal activity is restricted to shoplifting and, therefore, any rehabilitation program should be "offense specific" for this crime.
- The typical shoplifter steals an average of 1.6 times per week.

Sources: Information and statistics provided by the National Association for Shoplifting Prevention (NASP), *www.shopliftingprevention.org*; *2009 Organized Retail Crime Survey*, National Retail Federation, Washington, D.C., 2010, p. 5; Richard C. Hollinger and Amanda Adams, *2009 National Retail Security Survey*, University of Florida, pp. 9–10.

Solitary shoplifters are usually quite nervous. They avoid crowds and shy away from store personnel, preferring privacy to ply their trade. To make sure they avoid detection, they constantly scan the store for customers and employees. These shoplifters spend more time nervously looking around the store than examining merchandise. Also, they shop when the store is most likely to be understaffed, during early morning, lunch, or late evening hours. Shoplifters frequently linger in the same area for an extended time without purchasing anything. Customers who refuse the help of sales personnel or bring in large bags and packages (especially empty ones) also arouse suspicion.

Shoplifters have their own arsenal of tools to assist them in plying their trade. They often shop with booster boxes, shopping bags, umbrellas, bulky jackets, baby strollers, or containers disguised as gifts. These props often have hidden compartments that can be tripped easily, allowing the shoplifter to fill them with merchandise quickly.

Some shoplifters use specially designed coats with hidden pockets and compartments that can hold even large items. Small business owners should be suspicious of customers wearing out-of-season clothing (e.g., heavy coats in warm weather or rain gear on clear days) that could conceal stolen goods. Hooked belts also are used to enable the shoplifter to suspend items from hangers without being detected.

Another common tactic is "ticket switching," in which the shoplifter exchanges price tickets on items and pays a very low price for an expensive item. An inexperienced or unobservant cashier may charge $9.95 for a $30.00 item that the shoplifter remarked when no one was looking. A more elaborate scheme is one in which shoplifters create counterfeit bar codes that they paste over existing bar codes on packages so that when the item is scanned, it rings up at a much lower price. After 3 years, police finally nabbed a shoplifter who used this technique to steal more than $600,000 worth of toy LEGOs from dozens of stores in five western states. His phony bar codes caused $100 LEGO sets to ring up for just $19 at checkout counters. He then resold the LEGO sets at a markup on a Web site for toy collectors.[41]

One variation of traditional shoplifting techniques is the "grab-and-run" in which a shoplifter grabs an armload of merchandise located near an exit and then dashes out the door into a waiting getaway car. The element of surprise gives these thieves an advantage, and they are often gone before anyone in the store realizes what has happened.

DETERRING SHOPLIFTERS. The problem of shoplifting is worsening. Every year, business losses due to customer theft increase, and many companies are declaring war on shoplifting. Funds allocated for fighting shoplifting losses are best spent on *prevention*. By focusing on preventing shoplifting rather than on prosecuting violators after the fact, business owners take a strong stand in protecting their firms' merchandise. Of course, no prevention plan is perfect. When violations occur, owners must prosecute; otherwise the business becomes known as an easy target. Retailers say that when a store gets a reputation for being tough on shoplifters, thefts drop off.

Knowing what to look for dramatically improves a business owner's odds in combating shoplifting:

- *Watch the eyes.* Amateurs spend excessive time looking at the merchandise they're about to steal. Their eyes, however, are usually checking to see who (if anyone) is watching them.
- *Watch the hands.* Experienced shoplifters, like good magicians, rely on sleight of hand.
- *Watch the body.* Amateurs' body movements reflect their nervousness; they appear to be unnatural.
- *Watch the clothing.* Loose, bulky clothing is the uniform of the typical shoplifter.
- *Watch for devices.* Anything a customer carries is a potential concealing device.
- *Watch for loiterers.* Many amateurs must work up the nerve to steal.
- *Watch for switches.* Working in pairs, shoplifters will split duties; one will lift the merchandise, and, after a switch, the other will take it out of the store.

Store owners can take other steps to discourage shoplifting.

Train Employees to Spot Shoplifters. One of the best ways to prevent shoplifting is to train store personnel to be aware of shoplifters' habits and to be alert for possible theft. In fact, most security experts agree that alert employees are the best defense against shoplifters. Employees should look for nervous, unusual customers and monitor them closely. Shoplifters prefer to avoid sales personnel and other customers, and when employees approach them, shoplifters know they are being watched. Even when all salespeople are busy, an alert employee should approach the customer and say, "I'll be with you in a moment." Honest customers appreciate the clerk's politeness, and shoplifters are put off by the implied surveillance.

All employees should watch for suspicious people, especially those carrying the props of concealment. Employees in clothing stores must keep a tally of the items being taken into and out of dressing rooms. Some clothing retailers prevent unauthorized use of dressing rooms by locking them; customers who want to try on garments must check with a store employee first.

An alert cashier can be a tremendous boon to the store owner attempting to minimize shoplifting losses. A cashier who knows the store's general pricing policy and is familiar with the prices of many specific items is the best insurance against the ticket-switching shoplifter. A good cashier also should inspect all containers being sold; tool boxes, purses, briefcases, and other items can conceal stolen merchandise.

Employees should be trained to watch for group shoplifting tactics. A group of shoppers that enters the store and then disperses in all directions may be attempting to distract employees so that some gang members can steal merchandise. Sales personnel should watch closely the customer who lingers in one area for an extended time, especially one who examines a lot of merchandise but never purchases anything.

The sales staff should watch for customers who consistently shop during the hours when most employees are on breaks. Managers can help eliminate this cause of shoplifting by ensuring that their stores are well staffed at all times. Coordinating work schedules to ensure adequate coverage is a simple but effective method of discouraging shoplifting.

The cost of training employees to be alert to shoplifting "gimmicks" can be recouped many times over by preventing losses from retail theft. The local police department or chamber of commerce may be able to conduct training seminars for local small business owners and their employees, or security consulting firms might sponsor a training course on shoplifting techniques and protective methods. Refresher courses every few months can help keep employees sharp in spotting shoplifters.

Pay Attention to the Store Layout. A well-planned store layout also can be an effective obstacle in preventing shoplifting losses. Proper lighting throughout the store makes it easier for employees to monitor shoppers, whereas dimly lit areas give dishonest customers a prime opportunity to steal without detection. In addition, display cases should be kept low, no more than 3 or 4 feet high, so store personnel can have a clear view of the entire store. Display counters should have spaces between them; continuous displays create a barrier between customers and employees.

Business owners should keep small expensive items such as jewelry, silver, and accessories behind display counters or in locked cases with a sales clerk nearby. Valuable or breakable items also should be kept out of customer reach and should not be displayed near exits, where shoplifters can pick them up and quickly step outside. All merchandise displays should be neat and organized so that it will be noticeable if an item is missing.

Cash registers should be located so that cashiers have an unobstructed view of the entire store. Other protective measures include prominently posting signs describing the penalties involved for shoplifting and keeping unattended doors locked (within fire regulations). Exits that cannot be locked because of fire regulations should be equipped with noise alarms to detect any attempts at unauthorized exit.

Install Mechanical Devices. Another option business owners have in the attempt to reduce shoplifting losses is to install mechanical devices. A complete deterrence system can be expensive, but failure to implement one is usually more expensive. Tools such as two-way mirrors allow employees at one end of the store to monitor a customer at the other end, and one-way viewing windows enable employees to watch the entire store without being seen.

Other mechanical devices, such as closed-circuit TV cameras, convex wall mirrors, and peepholes, also help the owner protect the store from shoplifters. Not every small business can afford to install a closed-circuit camera system, but one clever entrepreneur got the benefit of such a system without the high cost. He installed one "live" camera and several "dummy" cameras that did not work. The cameras worked because potential shoplifters thought they were all live. Another high-tech weapon used against shoplifters is a mannequin named Anne Droid, which is equipped with a tiny camera behind one eye and a microphone in her nose!

An owner can deter ticket-switching shoplifters by using tamper-proof price tickets: perforated, gummed labels that tear away if a customer tries to remove them or price tags attached to merchandise by hard-to-break plastic strips. Some owners use multiple price tags concealed on items to deter ticket switchers. One of the most effective weapons for combating shoplifting is the electronic article surveillance (EAS) system, small tags that are equipped with electronic sensors that set off sound and light alarms if customers take them past a store exit. These tags are attached to the merchandise and can be removed only by employees with special shears. Owners using these electronic tags must make sure that all cashiers are consistent in removing them from items purchased legitimately; otherwise, they may be liable for false arrest or, at the very least, may cause customers embarrassment.

APPREHENDING SHOPLIFTERS. Despite all of the weapons business owners use to curtail shoplifting, the sad reality is that most of the time shoplifters are successful at plying their trade. Shoplifters say they are caught an average of only once in every 48 times they steal and that they are turned over to the police just 50 percent of the time. Of those shoplifters who do get caught, less than half are prosecuted. The chance that any shoplifter will actually go before a judge is about 1 in 100.[42] Building a strong case against a shoplifter is essential; therefore, small business owners must determine beforehand the procedures to follow once they detect a shoplifter. The store owner has to be certain that the shoplifter has taken or concealed the merchandise and has left the store with it. Although state laws vary, owners must do the following to make the charges stick:

1. *See* the person take or conceal the merchandise.
2. *Identify* the merchandise as belonging to the store.
3. *Testify* that it was taken with the intent to steal.
4. *Prove* that the merchandise was not paid for.

Most security experts agree that owners should never apprehend the shoplifter if they have lost sight of the suspect even for an instant. In that time, the person may have dumped the merchandise.

Another primary consideration in apprehending shoplifters is the safety of store employees. In general, employees should never directly accuse a customer of shoplifting and should never try to apprehend the suspect. The wisest course of action when a shoplifter is detected is to alert the police or store security personnel and let them apprehend the suspect. Apprehension *outside* the store is safest. This tactic strengthens the owner's case and eliminates unpleasant in-store scenes that upset other customers or that might be dangerous. Of course, if the stolen merchandise is very valuable, or if the criminal is likely to escape once outside, the owner may have no choice but to apprehend the shoplifter in the store.

Once business owners detect and apprehend a shoplifter, they must decide whether to prosecute. Many small business owners fail to prosecute because they fear legal entanglements or negative publicity. However, failure to prosecute encourages shoplifters to try again and gives the business the image of being an easy target. Of course, each case is an individual matter. For example, the owner may choose not to prosecute elderly or senile shoplifters or those who are mentally incompetent. But in most cases, prosecuting the shoplifter is the best option, especially for juveniles and first-time offenders. The business owner who prosecutes shoplifters consistently soon develops a reputation for toughness that most shoplifters hesitate to test. It is in the interest of every business owner to have that reputation.

Conclusion

Inventory control is one of those less-than-glamorous activities that business owners must perform if their businesses are to succeed. Although it doesn't offer the flash of marketing or the visibility of customer service, inventory control is no less important. In fact, business owners who invest the time and the resources to exercise the proper degree of control over their inventory soon discover that the payoff is huge!

Chapter Review

1. Explain the various inventory control systems and the advantages and disadvantages of each.
   - Inventory represents the largest investment for the typical small business. Unless properly managed, the cost of inventory will strain the firm's budget and cut into its profitability. The goal of inventory control is to balance the cost of holding and maintaining inventory with meeting customer demand.
   - Regardless of the inventory control system selected, business owners must recognize the relevance of the 80/20 Rule, which states that roughly 80 percent of the value of the firm's inventory is in about 20 percent of the items in stock. Because only a small percentage of items account for the majority of the value of the firm's inventory, managers should focus control on those items.
   - Three basic types of inventory control systems are available to the small business owner: perpetual, visual, and partial. Perpetual inventory control systems are designed to maintain a running count of the items in inventory. Although they can be expensive and cumbersome to operate by hand, affordable computerized point-of-sale (POS) terminals that deduct items sold from inventory on hand make perpetual systems feasible for small companies. The visual inventory system is the most common method of controlling merchandise in a small business. This system works best when shortages are not likely to cause major problems. Partial inventory control systems are most effective for small businesses with limited time and money. These systems operate on the basis of the 80/20 Rule.
   - The ABC system is a partial system that divides a firm's inventory into three categories depending on each item's dollar usage volume (cost per unit multiplied by quantity used per time period). The purpose of classifying items according to their value is to establish the proper degree of control over them. A items are most closely controlled by perpetual inventory control systems; B items use basic analytical tools; and C items are controlled by very simple techniques such as the two-bin system, the level control method, or the tag system.

2. Describe how just-in-time (JIT) and JIT II inventory control techniques work.
   - The just-in-time system of inventory control sees excess inventory as a blanket that masks production problems and adds unnecessary costs to the production operation. Under a JIT philosophy, the level of inventory maintained is the measure of efficiency. Materials and parts should not build up as costly inventory. They should flow through the production process without stopping, arriving at the appropriate location just in time.
   - JIT II techniques focus on creating a close, harmonious relationship with a company's suppliers so that both parties benefit from increased efficiency. To work successfully, JIT II requires suppliers and their customers to share what was once closely guarded information in an environment of trust and cooperation. Under JIT II, customers and suppliers work hand in hand, acting more like partners than mere buyers and sellers.

3. Describe methods for reducing losses from slow-moving inventory.
   - Managing inventory requires monitoring the company's inventory turnover ratio; slow-moving items result in losses from spoilage or obsolescence.
   - Slow-moving items can be liquidated by markdowns, eye-catching displays, or quantity discounts.

4. Discuss employee theft and shoplifting and how to prevent them.
   - Employee theft accounts for the majority of business losses due to theft. Most small business owners are so busy managing their companies' daily affairs that they fail to develop reliable security systems. Thus, they provide their employees with prime opportunities to steal.
   - The organizational atmosphere may encourage employee theft. The owner sets the organizational tone for security. A complete set of security controls, procedures, and penalties should be developed and enforced. Physical breakdowns in security invite employee theft. Open doors and windows, poor key control, and improper cash

controls are major contributors to the problem of employee theft. Employers can build security into their businesses by screening and selecting employees carefully. Orientation programs also help the employee to get started in the right direction. Internal controls, such as division of responsibility, spot checks, and audit procedures, are useful in preventing employee theft.

- Shoplifting is the most common business crime. Fortunately, most shoplifters are amateurs. Juveniles often steal to impress their friends, but prosecution can halt their criminal ways early on. Impulse shoplifters steal because the opportunity suddenly arises. Simple prevention is the best defense against these shoplifters. Alcoholics, vagrants, and drug addicts steal to supply some need and are usually easiest to detect. Kleptomaniacs have a compelling need to steal. Professionals are in the business of theft and can be very difficult to detect and quite dangerous.
- Three strategies are most useful in deterring shoplifters. First, employees should be trained to look for signs of shoplifting. Second, store layout should be designed with theft deterrence in mind. Finally, antitheft devices should be installed in the store.

Discussion Questions

1. Describe some of the incidental costs of carrying and maintaining inventory for the small business owner.
2. What is a perpetual inventory system? How does it operate? What are the advantages and disadvantages of using such a system?
3. What advantages and disadvantages does a visual inventory control system have over other methods?
4. For what type of business product line is a visual control system most effective?
5. What is the 80/20 Rule, and why is it important in controlling inventory?
6. Outline the ABC inventory control procedure. What is the purpose of classifying inventory items using this procedure?
7. Briefly describe the types of control techniques that should be used for A, B, and C items.
8. What is the basis for the JIT philosophy? Under what condition does a JIT system work best?
9. What is JIT II? What is its underlying philosophy? What risks does it present to businesses?
10. Outline the two methods of taking a physical inventory count. Why is it necessary for every small business manager to take inventory?

11. Why are slow-moving items dangerous to the small business? What can be done to liquidate them from inventory?
12. Why are small companies more susceptible to business crime than large companies?
13. Why is employee theft a problem for many small businesses? Briefly describe the reasons for employee theft.
14. Construct a profile of the employee most likely to steal goods or money from an employer. What four elements must be present for employee theft to occur?
15. Briefly outline a program that could help the typical small business owner minimize losses due to employee theft.
16. List and briefly describe the major types of shoplifters.
17. Outline the characteristics of a typical shoplifter that should arouse a small business manager's suspicions. What tools and tactics is a shoplifter likely to use?
18. Describe the major elements of a program designed to deter shoplifters.
19. How can proper planning of store layout reduce shoplifting losses?
20. What must an owner do to have a good case against a shoplifter? How should a suspected shoplifter be apprehended?

For many product-oriented businesses, inventory control represents a major investment. Unfortunately, many entrepreneurs fail to manage their inventory investments carefully, and this can lead to serious financial, managerial, and customer service problems. Fortunately, small companies can now afford to purchase inventory control systems that once were available only to large organizations.

Technological solutions supported by a sound inventory control system enable even the smallest companies to reap the benefits of maintaining proper inventory control systems.

On the Web

The Companion Web site at *www.pearsonhighered.com/ scarborough* offers a series of links that provide additional information regarding inventory control resources. Review these sites, specifically those that relate to your industry, and determine whether these sources may be useful to you as you build your plan.

In the Software

Review the "Products" section of your plan to make certain that you have included the inventory management issues discussed in this chapter. Does it describe how you plan to manage your inventory? What type of inventory control system will you use in your business? Is it perpetual, visual, or partial? Have you incorporated a description of that system into the plan?

Building Your Business Plan

Your business plan should describe your company's inventory control strategy. If inventory represents a significant investment for your business, you should invest the time required to develop this section of your plan and make sure that your financial forecasts capture this information as well. If you plan to purchase an inventory control system, be sure to include this as one of your expenses.

Endnotes

1. Sahir Anand and Chris Cunane, *Inventory Optimization: Retail Strategies for Eliminating Stockouts and Overstocks*, Aberdeen Group, May 2009, p. 4.
2. Nari Viswanathan, *Inventory Management: 3 Keys to Freeing Working Capital*, Aberdeen Group, May 2009, p. 4.
3. James A. Cooke, "Glimmers of Hope," State of Logistics Report, *Supply Chain Quarterly*, September 21, 2010, *www.supplychainquarterly.com/topics/State%20of%20Logistics%20Report/scq201005sol/*.
4. Joann S. Lublin, "Polaris, Maker of Sport Vehicles, Races to Catch Up with Business," *Wall Street Journal*, May 24, 2010, pp. B1–B2.
5. Ibid.
6. Simona Covel, "Looking for Cost Cuts in Lots of New Places," *Wall Street Journal*, October 16, 2008, p. B5.
7. "With Billions of Bytes of Customer Data, How Can Retailers Be 'Starved for Information?'" *Knowledge@Wharton*, August 2000, *http://pf.inc.com/articles/2000/08/20043.html*.
8. Pallavi Gogoi, "Retailers Pull Back, at a Cost," *Bloomberg Business Week*, August 7, 2008, *www.businessweek.com/bwdaily/dnflash/content/aug2008/db2008087_200562.htm?chan=top+news_top+news+index_news+++analysis*.
9. John Payne, "Pareto's Law—Your Formula for Success," *Ezine Articles*, January 25, 2005, *http://ezinearticles.com/?Paretos-Law—Your-Formula-For-Success&id=11091*.
10. Phaedra Hise, "Early Adoption Pays Off," *Inc.*, August 1996, p. 101.
11. Claire Swedburg, "Serge Blanco Store Takes Stock of RFID," *RFID Journal*, April 27, 2010, *www.rfidjournal.com/article/view/7561*.
12. Mark Henricks, "Tell and Show," *Entrepreneur*, April 2004, pp. 77–78.
13. Alex Niemeyer, Minsok H. Pak, and Sanjay Ramaswamy, "Smart Tags for Your Supply Chain," *McKinsey Quarterly*, No. 4, 2003, *www.mckinseyquarterly.com/article_page.aspx?ar=1347&L2=1&L3=26*.
14. Elizabeth Esfahani, "High Class, Low Price," *Business 2.0*, November 2006, pp. 74–76; Adam Smith, "How Topshop Changed Fashion," *Time*, May 24, 2007, *www.time.com/time/globalbusiness/article/0,9171,1625185,00.html*; "About Topshop," Topshop.com, *www.topshop.com/webapp/wcs/stores/servlet/StaticPageDisplay?storeId=12556&catalogId=19551&identifier=ts1%20about%20topshop*.
15. Amy Chozick, "A Key Strategy of Japan's Car Makers Backfires," *Wall Street Journal*, July 20, 2007, pp. B1, B5.
16. Mark Henricks, "On the Spot," *Entrepreneur*, May 1997, *www.entrepreneur.com/article/14178*.
17. Matthew Dolan, "Industry's Big Hope for Small Cars Fades," *Wall Street Journal*, March 23, 2009, p. B1; "Biggest by Default: Toyota May Be Number One, but It Still Faces Challenges," *Knowledge@Wharton*, February 4, 2009, *www.wharton.universia.net/index.cfm?fa=viewArticle&id=1666&language=english*; Neal E. Boudette, "Big Dealer to Detroit: Fix How You Make Cars," *Wall Street Journal*, February 9, 2007, pp. A1, A8; Sholnn Freeman, "Smaller Cars Enjoy New Chic," *Washington Post*, September 28, 2005, *www.washingtonpost.com/wp-dyn/content/article/2005/09/27/AR2005092701812.html*.
18. Dana Mattioli, "Little Shops Make Big Plays for the Holidays," *Wall Street Journal*, October 27, 2009, p. B5.
19. *2010 ACFE Report to the Nation on Occupational Fraud and Abuse*, Association of Certified Fraud Examiners, Austin, Texas, 2010, p. 4; Kathy Grannis, "Retail Fraud, Shoplifting Rates Decrease, According to National Retail Security Survey," National Retail Federation, June 15, 2010, *www.nrf.com/modules.php?name=News&op=viewlive&sp_id=945*.
20. *2010 ACFE Report to the Nation on Occupational Fraud and Abuse*, pp. 4–5, 29.
21. Grannis, "Retail Fraud, Shoplifting Rates Decrease, According to National Retail Security Survey."
22. "Theft Surveys," Jack L. Hayes International, Wesley Chapel, Florida, 2010, *www.hayesinternational.com/thft_srvys.html*.
23. Serri Pfeil, "Is There a Thief Among Us?" *Employment Review*, December 2000, pp. 37–38.
24. *2010 ACFE Report to the Nation on Occupational Fraud and Abuse*, pp. 14, 16.
25. *2010 ACFE Report to the Nation on Occupational Fraud and Abuse*, p. 39.
26. John P. McDermott, "Woman Charged in Fraud," *Charleston Post and Courier*, July 30, 2010, p. 7B; John P. McDermott, "Woman Pleads Guilty in Fraud," *Charleston Post and Courier*, September 17, 2010, *www.postandcourier.com/news/2010/sep/17/woman-pleads-guilty-in-fraud/*.
27. Nancy Germond, "Your Company Isn't Immune to Employee Theft," *All Business*, February 2, 2008, *www.allbusiness.com/crime-law-enforcement-corrections/crime-prevention/6623333-1.html*.
28. *2010 ACFE Report to the Nation on Occupational Fraud and Abuse*, p. 5.
29. "Koss Corp. Hires Chief Financial Officer," *Business Journal of Milwaukee*, January 18, 2010, *http://milwaukee.bizjournals.com/milwaukee/stories/2010/01/18/daily2.html*; Rich Kirchen, "Former Koss Exec Sachdeva Indicted on Six Counts," *Business Journal of Milwaukee*, January 20, 2010, *http://milwaukee.bizjournals.com/milwaukee/stories/2010/01/18/daily39.html*.
30. Robert T. Gray, "Clamping Down on Worker Crime," *Nation's Business*, April 1997, p. 44.
31. Scott Wescott, "Are Your Staffers Stealing?" *Inc.*, October 2006, pp. 33–35.
32. Calmetta Coleman, "Sticky Fingers," *Wall Street Journal*, September 8, 2000, pp. A1, A6.
33. "Theft Surveys," Jack L. Hayes International.
34. "Jack L. Hayes International Inc.'s 18th Annual Retail Theft Survey," 2006, *www.hayesinternational.com/thft_srvys.html*.
35. Raymund Flandez, "Stop That Thief," *Wall Street Journal*, June 12, 2008, *http://online.wsj.com/article/NA_WSJ_PUB:SB121322091260765769.html*.
36. Amanda C. Kooser, "Make the Cut?" *Entrepreneur*, February 2006, p. 26.
37. Grannis, "Retail Fraud, Shoplifting Rates Decrease, According to National Retail Security Survey."
38. *2009 Organized Retail Crime Survey*, National Retail Federation, Washington, D.C., 2010, p. 4.

39. Richard Hollinger and Lynn Langton, *2005 National Retail Security Survey Final Report*, University of Florida and the National Retail Federation, *www.crim.ufl.edu/research/srp/finalreport_2005.pdf*, pp. 27, 29.

40. *2009 Organized Retail Crime Survey*, National Retail Federation, pp. 3–4; "Operation 'Beauty Stop' Nabs 18 in $100 Million Theft Ring," WFTV, January 25, 2008, *www.wftv.com/news/15130764/detail.html*.

41. Ann Zimmerman, "As Shoplifters Use High-Tech Scams, Retail Losses Rise," *Wall Street Journal*, October 25, 2006, pp. A1, A12.

42. "Shoplifting Statistics," National Association for Shoplifting Prevention.

Management Succession and Risk Management Strategies in the Family Business

When it works right, nothing succeeds like a family firm. The roots run deep, embedded in family values. The flash of the fast buck is replaced with long-term plans. Tradition counts.

—Eric Calonius

Walk sober off before the sprightlier age comes titt'ring on and shoves you from the stage.

—Alexander Pope

From Chapter 20 of *Effective Small Business Management: An Entrepreneurial Approach*, 10/e. Norman M. Scarborough.

Family Businesses

1. Explain the factors necessary for a strong family business.

Nearly 90 percent of all companies in the United States, about 26.4 million businesses, are family owned. Yet family-owned businesses, those in which family members control ownership and/or decision making, are often overlooked by the media, which focus most of their attention on the larger companies in our economy. In reality, family businesses generate 64 percent of the U.S. gross domestic product, account for 62 percent of all employment and 78 percent of job creation, and pay 65 percent of all wages.[1] Despite common perceptions, not all family businesses are small. The average annual sales of family businesses in the United States are about $36.5 million, and 33 percent of *Fortune* 500 companies are family businesses.[2] Globally, family-owned businesses account for 70 to 90 percent of world GDP.[3] Some of the best-known companies in the world are family-owned, including Ford Motor Company, Samsung, Hyundai, Sainsbury, Mars, and Walmart. In fact, Sam Walton's heirs own 43 percent (1.7 billion shares) of the stock in the world's largest company, Walmart, and those shares are worth an estimated $92 billion, an amount that exceeds the GDP of 161 countries in the world.[4]

When a family business works right, it is a thing of beauty. Family members share deeply rooted values that guide the company and give it a sense of harmony. Family members understand and support one another as they work together to achieve the company's mission. That harmony can produce a significant financial payoff. A study by Jim Lee of Texas A&M University–Corpus Christi shows that family-owned businesses are more profitable and experience faster employment and revenue growth over time than nonfamily businesses.[5] Another study of companies in the Standard & Poor's 500 Index by Ronald Anderson, David Reeb, and Sattar Mansi found that family firms outperformed their nonfamily counterparts on a variety of financial measures.[6] Other research comparing the financial performances of similar sets of family and nonfamily businesses has concluded that "firms controlled by the founding family have greater value, are operated more efficiently, and carry less debt than other firms."[7]

Family businesses also have a dark side, and it stems from their lack of continuity. Sibling rivalries, fights over control of the business, and personality conflicts often lead to nasty battles that can tear families apart and destroy once thriving businesses. Long-standing feuds can make family relationships difficult, and, when mixed with business decisions and the wealth family businesses can create, the result can be explosive. When Dhirubhai Ambani, founder of Reliance Industries Ltd., one of India's most successful companies, died without a will, his sons, Mukesh and Anil, battled over how to run the extensive business empire they took over. After years of personal and legal battles, the brothers entered into an agreement brokered by their mother that split the company into pieces so that each could operate his share of the business independently of the other. "Since their father's death, the brothers have been trying to outdo and undercut each other," says one observer.[8]

The stumbling block for most family businesses is management succession; 70 percent of first-generation businesses fail to survive into the second generation, and, of those that do survive, only 12 percent make it to the third generation. Just 3 percent of family businesses survive to the fourth generation and beyond.[9] The leading causes of family business failures are inadequate estate planning, failure to create a management succession plan, and lack of funds to pay estate taxes.[10] Just when they are ready to make the transition from one generation of leaders to the next, family businesses are most vulnerable. As a result, the average life expectancy of a family business is 24 years, although some last *much* longer (see Table 1).[11]

Profile

Will Tuttle: Tuttle Farm

Will Tuttle, the 63-year-old patriarch of one of the oldest family businesses in the United States, Tuttle Farm in Dover, New Hampshire, recently announced that his generation will be the last to operate the farm. Founded in 1632 by John Tuttle with a land grant from England's King Charles II, Tuttle Farm has struggled with the encroachment of housing and commercial developments and the impact of a severe recession. Will Tuttle, who began helping his father on the farm at age 6, has listed the 134-acre farm for sale at $3.35 million. "This is a different business now," says Tuttle. "I don't see much opportunity for small farms to thrive."[12]

According to a study of family businesses across the globe by PriceWaterhouseCoopers, 27 percent of family business owners say that ownership of their companies will change hands within the next 5 years and 53 percent of the owners expect to pass their companies on to the next

TABLE 1 The World's Oldest Family Businesses.

William O'Hara, director of the Institute for Family Enterprise at Bryant College, and Peter Mandel have compiled a list of some of the world's oldest family businesses.

Company	Country	Nature of Business	Year Established
Hoshi Ryokan	Japan	Hotel	718
Château de Goulaine	France	Vineyard, museum, butterfly collection	1000
Fonderia Pontifica Marinelli	Italy	Bell foundry	1000
Barone Ricasoli	Italy	Wine and olive oil	1141
Barovier & Toso	Italy	Artistic glassmaking	1295
Hotel Pilgram Haus	Germany	Innkeeping	1304
Richard de Bas	France	High-quality paper maker	1326
Torrini Firenze	Italy	Goldsmiths	1369
Antinori	Italy	Wine	1385
Camuffo	Italy	Shipbuilding	1438
Baronnie de Coussergues	France	Wine	1495
Grazia Deruta	Italy	Ceramics	1500
Fabbrice D'Armi Beretta	Italy	Firearms production	1526
William Prym GmbH & Company	Germany	Copper, brass, haberdashery	1530
John Brooke & Sons	Great Britain	Textiles	1541
Codorniu	Spain	Wine	1551
Fonjallaz	Switzerland	Wine	1552

Source: William T. O'Hara and Peter Mandel, "The World's Oldest Family Companies," *Family Business,* *www.familybusinessmagazine.com/oldworld.html.*

generation of family members.[13] The best way to ensure the legacy of a family business and a successful transition from one generation of family owners to the next is to develop a succession plan for the company. Although business founders inevitably want their businesses to survive them and most intend to pass them on to their children, they do not always support their intentions by a plan to accomplish that goal. The study by PriceWaterhouseCoopers reports that 47 percent of family businesses have no succession plans in place (see Figure 1).[14] Another survey of family business owners by MassMutual Financial Group and Arthur Andersen reports that 19 percent had not engaged in any kind of estate planning other than creating a will.[15] For most family businesses, the greatest threat to survival comes from *within* the company rather than from outside it. Many entrepreneurs dream of their businesses continuing in the family but take no significant steps to make their dreams a reality.

David Bork, founder of the Aspen Family Business Conference, has identified several qualities that are essential to a successful family business: shared values, shared power, tradition, a willingness to learn, family behavior, and strong family ties.[16]

Shared Values

The first, and probably most overlooked, quality is a set of shared values. What family members value and believe about people, work, and money shapes their behavior toward the business. All members of a family business should talk openly to determine, in a nonjudgmental fashion, each one's values. Without shared values, it is difficult to create a sense of direction for a business.

To avoid the problems associated with conflicting values and goals, family business owners should consider taking the following actions:

- Make it clear to all family members that they are not required to join the business full-time. Family members' goals, ambitions, and talents should be foremost in their career decisions.
- Do not assume that a successor must come from within the family. Simply being born into a family does not guarantee that a person will make a good business leader.

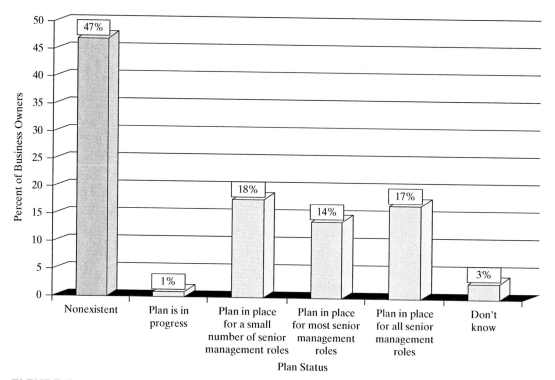

FIGURE 1

Status of Management Succession Plans in Small Businesses

Source: *Kin in the Game*, PriceWaterhouseCoopers Family Business Survey, 2010–2011, p. 22.

Profile

Pierre Bellon: Sodexho

When Pierre Bellon stepped down as CEO of Sodexho, the food management services business his grandfather started in 1895, he named as his successor Michael Landel, the first nonfamily member to lead the company. Landel, a 26-year veteran of Sodexho, had held a variety of positions in the family-controlled business, and Bellon was confident that Landel was the right person to lead the company. "You have to be completely in line with the culture of the family, share the same values, and have very strong respect for what they have done," says Landel.[17]

■ Give family members the opportunity to work outside the business initially to learn first-hand how others conduct business. Working for others allows family members to develop knowledge, confidence, and credibility before stepping back into the family business.

Shared Power

Shared power is not necessarily equal power. Rather, shared power is based on the idea that family members allow those people with the greatest expertise, ability, and knowledge in particular areas to handle decisions in those areas. Dividing responsibilities along the lines of expertise is an important way of acknowledging respect for each family member's talents and abilities.

Profile

Thad, Harold, and Ralph Garner: T.W. Garner Food Company

When Thad Garner invented a concoction of red peppers and vinegar called Texas Pete Hot Sauce during the Great Depression, he and his brothers, Harold and Ralph, built a business, T.W. Garner Food Company, around the product. Each assumed responsibilities in a different area of the company based on his talents and interests. Thad (known as "Mr. Texas Pete") took over the sales and marketing side of the business, while Harold managed its financial and operational aspects and Ralph handled production. Working together, the brothers built the company into a very successful business, selling millions of dollars' worth of Texas Pete a year.[18]

Tradition

Tradition is necessary for a family business because it serves to bond family members and to link one generation of business leaders to the next. However, founders must hold tradition in check when it becomes a barrier to change. The key is to select those traditions that provide a solid foundation for positive behavior while taking care not to restrict the future growth of the business. "The companies that are successful change their strategy after each generation," says Joachim Schwass, a professor of family business at Switzerland's IMD business school. "Bringing in the new generation and saying, 'Son, do as I did,' will not work."[19]

Maximilian Riedel, head of North American operations for Austrian glassmaker Riedel, which for 300 years has been famous for its feather-light fine crystal wine glasses, is next in line to take control of the family business. Like his father and grandfather did, Maximilian created a new line of wine glasses that has become one of the company's best selling products. The eleventh-generation glassmaker created a sensation among oenophiles with his revolutionary stemless "O" series of wine tumblers that are designed to convey the nuances of the aroma and the flavor of wine. (The wine glass is "the messenger of the wine," he says.) Every business decision that Maximilian makes is steeped in 250 years of family business history, but already he has shown that he is willing to take bold steps to innovate and keep the family business in tune with the demands of the twenty-first century.[20]

A Willingness to Learn

A willingness to learn and grow is the hallmark of any successful firm, and it is essential to a family business. The family business that remains open to new ideas and techniques is likely to reduce its risk of obsolescence. The current generation of leadership must set the stage for new ideas involving the next generation in today's decisions. In many cases, a formal family council serves as a mechanism through which family members can propose new ideas. Perhaps more important than a family council is fostering an environment in which family members trust one another enough to express their ideas, thoughts, and suggestions openly and honestly. Open discussion of the merits of new ideas is a tradition that has proved valuable for many family businesses' ability to sustain their competitive advantages.

Behaving Like Families

Families that play together operate family businesses that are more likely to stay together. Time spent together outside the business creates the foundation for the relationships family members have at work. Too often, life in a family business can degenerate into nothing but day after day of work and discussions of work at home. In some cases, work is the only way some parents interact with their children. When a family adds activities outside the scope of the business, however, new relationships develop in a different arena. A family should not force members to "play together" but instead should create an environment that welcomes every member into fun family activities. Planned activities should be broad enough in scope to involve all family members. In time, trust, respect, openness, and togetherness lead to behavior that communicates genuine caring and concern for the well-being of each family member, and that spills over into the working relationship as well.

A Strong Family Support Network

According to a global survey of family business owners, the most important advantage family businesses have is the strong support network from family members (see Figure 2). Strong family ties grow from one-on-one relationships. Shared time conveys the message that the family business is *more* than just a business; it is a group of people who care for one another working together for a common goal. The bond that a family business creates among relatives can be strong and enduring. "There's a love and a trust and a respect that can be very powerful when they are brought into a business environment," says Ross Nager, director of a center for family businesses.[21]

The same emotions that hold family businesses together can also rip them apart if they run counter to the company's and the family's best interest. Emotions run deep in family businesses, and the press is full of examples of once successful companies that have been ruined by family

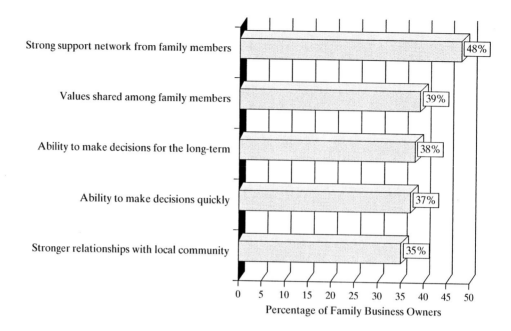

FIGURE 2

Advantages of the Family Business Model

Source: Thomas L. Kalaris, "Family Business: In Safe Hands?" *Barclays Wealth Insights*, 2009, p. 10.

feuds over who controls the company and how to run it. Conflict is a natural part of any business, but it can be especially powerful in family businesses because family relationships magnify the passions binding family members to the company (see Figure 3). Without a succession plan, those passions can explode into destructive behavior that can endanger the family business.

Exit Strategies

2. Understand the exit strategy options available to an entrepreneur.

Most family business founders want their companies to stay within their families, although in some cases maintaining family control is not practical. Sometimes no one in the next generation of family members has an interest in managing the company or has the necessary skills and experience to handle the job. Under these circumstances, the founder must look outside the family for leadership if the company is to survive. Whatever the case, entrepreneurs must confront their mortality and plan for the future of their companies. Having a solid management succession plan in place well before retirement is near is critical to success. Entrepreneurs should examine their options well before they decide to step down from the businesses they have founded. Three options are available to entrepreneurs who are planning to retire: sell to outsiders, sell to (nonfamily) insiders, or pass the business on to family members with the help of a management succession plan. We turn now to these three exit strategies.

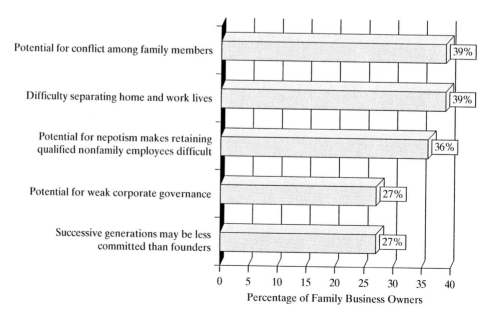

FIGURE 3

Disadvantages of the Family Business Model

Source: Thomas L. Kalaris, "Family Business: In Safe Hands?" *Barclays Wealth Insights*, 2009, p. 11.

IN THE ENTREPRENEURIAL
SPOTLIGHT Parent–Child Inc.

Thanks to the Great Recession, family businesses are taking on a slightly different look. When passed from one generation to the next, family businesses often have family members from two, sometimes three, generations working side-by-side. As many parents in their 40s and 50s are experiencing layoffs and their college-graduate children struggle to find even part-time jobs, a new type of family business is becoming more popular: companies cofounded by parents and children. At first blush, parents and children cofounding companies sounds like a recipe for feuding and fighting, but doing so offers many benefits. Parents bring experience, a network of contacts, business acumen, and money to the deal. Their children contribute enthusiasm, energy, and a working knowledge of technology skills, Internet savvy, and social media know-how. The combination can work together to create a dynamic business that has real staying power.

Arian Mahmoodi demonstrated entrepreneurial tendencies as a child, and his father, Farzad, was not surprised when at age 14 Arian launched a business buying and reselling Nintendo games on Amazon. Arian operated the business from his bedroom in his family's home in Hannawa Falls, New York, and counted on his parents to drive him to the post office to mail the games he sold to customers. "I'd wake up and package the orders in the morning before school," he says.

Arian had dreams of a bigger company and used the profits from his business to launch SellYourOldiPhone.com, a Web site through which he buys used and often broken iPhones, refurbishes them, and then resells them. After Arian sent out his first e-mail blast promoting his company, hundreds of orders poured in, and he turned to his father, a professor of supply chain management at Clarkson University in Pottsdam, New York, for help. Farzad helped his son organize his business, and together they assigned unique tracking numbers to customers and their orders.

SellYourOldiPhone.com was so successful that Arian replicated his business model a year later and launched SellYourOldMacBook.com. Arian, then 17 and preparing for college, and Farzad had grown into distinct and complementary roles in their small businesses. Arian, the chief executive officer, is the "face" of the companies and manages the Web sites and customer service. He also is responsible for the companies' advertising and pricing. Farzad handles the companies' accounting and legal matters and manages the supply chain (of course!). He also monitors the flow of iPhones and MacBooks to and from the technicians who refurbish them and determines which international markets the companies enter.

The father–son duo purchase and resell about 30 devices each week, generating about $230,000 in sales per year. Arian's focus is on growing the businesses, and he has reinvested all of the companies' earnings back into the businesses, using them to buy more phones and computers. Farzad enjoys using the companies as a laboratory where he can test various supply chain ideas. When Arian goes to college, they plan to hire an employee to take over most of the day-to-day operations.

So far, father and son have gotten along well as business partners. The respect that each has for the other is readily apparent, but both admit that they have had disagreements. While participating in a 3-week academic program at Cornell University, Arian discovered a bargain on accessories such as chargers and phone cases and placed a large order without telling his father. "I got a call from my Dad," he says with a smile. "'What is this? We have all these boxes.' He wasn't too happy because he couldn't park in the garage."

Perhaps the biggest issue between the two is how fast their companies should grow. Arian wants the companies on the fast track, but his father is pushing for a slower rate of growth so that his son can enjoy his college experience. For now, at least, Arian is willing to listen to his father's advice. "We're in agreement at this time to keep it as is," he says.

1. Work with a classmate to brainstorm the advantages and the disadvantages of starting a family business with a parent.
2. Would you be willing to go into business with a parent? Explain.
3. What recommendations can you make to someone who is about to launch a business with a parent?

Source: Based on Colleen Debaise, Emily Maltby, and Sarah E. Needleman, "Parent and Child Inc.," *Wall Street Journal*, November 15, 2010, http://online.wsj.com/article/SB10001424052748703794104575546553171806306.html.

Selling to Outsiders

Selling a business to an outsider is no simple task. Done properly, it takes time, patience, and preparation to locate a suitable buyer, strike a deal, and make the transition. Advance preparation, maintaining accurate financial records, and timing are the keys to a successful sale. Too often, however, business owners, like some famous athletes, stay with the game too long, until they and their businesses are well past their prime. They postpone selling until the last minute when they reach retirement age or when they face a business crisis. Such a "fire sale" approach rarely yields the maximum value for a business.

A straight sale may be best for those entrepreneurs who want to step down and turn the reins of the company over to someone else. However, selling a business outright is not an attractive exit strategy for those who want to stay on with the company or for those who want to surrender control of the company gradually rather than all at once.

Family-owned Snyder's of Hanover, founded in 1909 and now the world's largest maker of pretzels, recently agreed to merge with Lance Inc., a Charlotte, North Carolina-based manufacturer of snack crackers. Snyder's product line and extensive distribution network in grocery stores nationwide provide a solid strategic fit with Lance, which has strongholds in delis, convenience stores, and small retail stores. Lance issued 32.7 million shares of common stock to Snyder's shareholders, most of whom are members of the founding family.[22]

The financial terms of a sale also influence the selling price of the business and the number of potential bidders. Does the owner want "clean, cash only, 100 percent at closing" offers, or is he or she willing to finance a portion of the sale? A 100 percent, cash-only requirement dramatically reduces the number of potential buyers. However, the owner can exit the business "free and clear" and does not incur the risk that the buyer may fail to operate the business profitably and be unable to complete the financial transition.

Selling to Insiders

When entrepreneurs have no family members to whom they can transfer ownership or who want to assume the responsibilities of running a company, selling the business to employees is often the preferred option. In most situations, the options available to owners are (1) sale for cash plus a note, (2) a leveraged buyout, and (3) an employee stock ownership plan (ESOP).

A SALE FOR CASH PLUS A NOTE. Whether entrepreneurs sell their businesses to insiders, outsiders, or family members, they often finance a portion of the sales price. The buyer pays the seller a lump-sum amount of cash up front and the seller holds a promissory note for the remaining portion of the selling price, which the buyer pays off in installments. Because of its many creative financial options, this method of selling a business is popular with buyers. They can buy promising businesses without having to come up with the total purchase price all at one time. Sellers also appreciate the security and the tax implications of accepting payment over time. They receive a portion of the sale up front and have the assurance of receiving a steady stream of income in the future. In addition, they can stretch their tax liabilities from the capital gains on the sale over time rather than having to pay them in a single year. In many cases, sellers' risks are lower because they may even retain a seat on the board of directors to ensure that the new owners are keeping the business on track.

LEVERAGED BUYOUTS. In a **leveraged buyout (LBO)**, managers and/or employees borrow money from a financial institution and pay the owner the total agreed-upon price at closing; then they use the cash generated from the company's operations to pay off the debt. The drawback of this technique is that it creates a highly leveraged business. Because of the high levels of debt they take on, the new management team has very little room for error. Too many management mistakes or a slowing economy has led many highly leveraged businesses into bankruptcy.

If properly structured, LBOs can be attractive to both buyers and sellers. Because they get their money up front, sellers do not incur the risk of loss if the buyers cannot keep the business operating successfully. The managers and employees who buy the company have a strong incentive to make sure the business succeeds because they own a piece of the action and some of their capital is at risk in the business. The result can be a highly motivated workforce that works hard and makes sure that the company operates efficiently.

In one of the most successful LBOs in history, Jack Stack and a team of 12 other managers purchased an ailing subsidiary of International Harvester in an attempt to save their jobs and those of the 120 employees they managed. The new company, Springfield Remanufacturing Corporation (SRC), which specializes in engine remanufacturing for the automotive, trucking, agricultural, and construction industries, began with an astronomically high debt-to-equity ratio of 89:1, but the team of motivated managers and employees turned the company around. Today, SRC has more than 1,200 employees and 26 divisions that range from automotive engines to home furnishings.[23]

EMPLOYEE STOCK OWNERSHIP PLANS (ESOPs). Unlike LBOs, **employee stock ownership plans (ESOPs)** allow employees and/or managers (that is, the future owners) to purchase the business gradually, which frees up enough cash to finance the venture's growth. With an ESOP, employees contribute a portion of their earnings over time toward purchasing shares of the company's stock from the founder until they own the company outright. (Although in leveraged ESOPs, the ESOP borrows the money to buy the owner's stock up front. Then, using employees' contributions, the ESOP repays the loan over time. Another advantage of a leveraged ESOP is that the principal and the interest the ESOP borrows to buy the business are tax deductible, which can save thousands or even millions of dollars in taxes.) Transferring ownership to employees through an ESOP is a long-term exit strategy that benefits everyone involved. The owner sells the business to the people he or she can trust the most—his or her managers and employees. The managers and employees buy a business they already know how to run successfully. In addition, because they own the company, the managers and employees have a huge incentive to see that it operates effectively and efficiently. One study of ESOPs in privately held companies found that they increased sales, employment, and sales per employee by 2.4 percent a year.[24] Figure 4 shows the trend in the number of ESOPs and the number of employee owners.

The third exit strategy available to company founders is transferring ownership to the next generation of family members with the help of a comprehensive management succession plan.

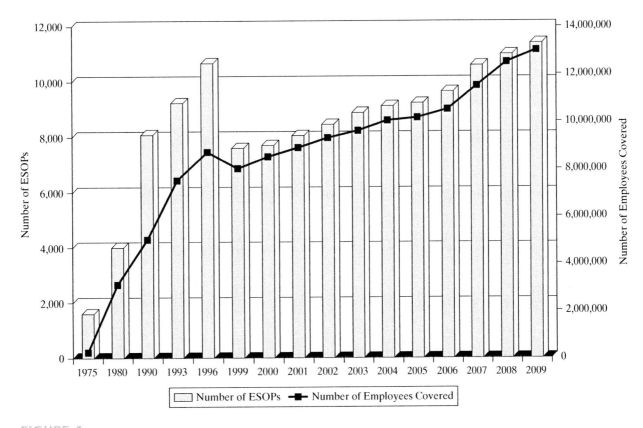

FIGURE 4

Employee Stock Ownership Plans

Source: "A Statistical Profile of Employee Ownership," National Center for Employee Ownership, 2010.

LESSONS FROM THE STREET-SMART ➤ entrepreneur

How to Set Up an ESOP

In 1978, long before people knew about the health benefits of whole-grain products, Bob Moore and his wife, Charlee, salvaged an abandoned 125-year-old flour mill and launched Bob's Red Mill Natural Foods, a company in Portland, Oregon, that produces a variety of products, from grain and flour to hot cereal and baking mixes. For Moore and his employees, the path was filled with challenges, including a fire that caused extensive damage to the old factory and the necessity of constantly investing in new equipment and technology. Moore expanded the company's reach to include customers in a handful of Western states, but the turning point came in 1993 when Moore brought in John Wagner as chief financial officer and co-owner. Together, Moore and Wagner focused on marketing the company's all-natural, whole-grain products at food and trade shows, where they garnered the attention of small health food stores, food distributors, and, eventually, grocery chains. "Now you can find our products in every province and state in North America and lots of places overseas," Moore says proudly.

Moore and Wagner launched a profit-sharing plan for their employees in 1995 and began sharing financial information with them weekly. They also conducted training sessions for employees on reading the company's financial statements. The training not only taught employees how to calculate their share of the company's profits but also enabled them to see exactly how the work they did every day affected the company's bottom line—and, therefore, their payouts.

As Moore passed the normal retirement age, employees began to wonder about their future, especially if Moore and Wagner decided to sell the company to a larger business. "Will we still have jobs?" they wondered. "Will the culture that we love so much change?"

Moore answered employees' lingering questions on his eighty-first birthday celebration. Moore and Wagner had decided not to sell Bob's Red Mill Natural Foods to a large company. Instead, they had created an employee stock ownership plan that would transfer ownership of the company to the 200 people whom they considered to be instrumental in its success. "It's been my dream all along to turn this company over to the employees, and to make that dream a reality is very, very special to me," says Moore. "This is the ultimate way to keep this business moving forward."

"The partners could have sold this company many times for a lot more money" says vice president of operations Dennis Vaughn, "but to them this company is about so much more than the money." After Moore announced the creation of the ESOP, he said modestly, "I thought some of them were going to kiss me. It went over very, very, very well." Roger Farnen, the company's quality assurance manager, says, "By creating the ESOP, Bob and the partners have fulfilled their ultimate quest for sharing success among all employees. Bob is passing the entrepreneurial torch on to his employees and is instilling in us that hard work provides rewards."

What steps should an entrepreneur who is interested in setting up an ESOP take? Consider the following advice from the Street-Smart Entrepreneur:

Step 1. Conduct a feasibility analysis to determine whether an ESOP is right for you and your company.

A company should be profitable and should have at least 20 employees to make an ESOP work. Creating the necessary plan documents and filing them with the proper government agencies costs about $10,000. A business valuation, which can range from $5,000 to $10,000 for a small company, is a necessity. Fixed costs of administering the ESOP run about $2,000 plus $20 to $30 per employee participant per year. A final consideration is whether the company will generate enough revenue to be able to repay the loan.

Step 2. Hire an attorney who specializes in ESOPs to help you develop a plan for creating and implementing an ESOP.

ESOPs can take many different forms, and an expert can help you determine the advantages and disadvantages of each one so that you can determine the one that is best for you and your company.

Step 3. Find the money to fund the ESOP.

About 75 percent of ESOPs are leveraged, which means that they borrow the money to purchase the owner's stock from the ESOP trust. Banks and other financial institutions usually find loans to ESOPs quite attractive.

Step 4. Establish a process to operate the ESOP.

Companies most often create an ESOP committee of managers and employees to provide guidance to the ESOP trust for managing the ESOP. The team also is responsible for communicating the details of the ESOP and the benefits of investing in it to company employees.

Barbara Gabel, who with her husband, Zach Zachowski, launched Zachary's Chicago Pizza in Oakland, California, in 1984, recently established an ESOP to transfer ownership of their business to their employees. "It's the ultimate exit strategy," says Gabel, referring to the benefits ESOPs provide both entrepreneurs and employees. Each year, employees at Zachary's receive an amount of stock that is equal to 25 percent of their salaries. General Manager J. P. LaRussa, who began working as a part-time dishwasher at Zachary's

the day it opened, says, "This breathes new life into the business in a very positive way."

Sources: Based on Karen E. Klein, "ESOPs on the Rise Among Small Businesses," *Bloomberg Business Week*, March 26, 2010, *www.businessweek.com/smallbiz/content/mar2010/sb20100325_591132.htm*; Theo Francis, "Inside Eileen Fisher's Employee Stock Plan," *Wall Street Journal*, January 22, 2007, pp. B1, B3; Alec Rosenberg, "Employees to Slice Up Zachary's Pizza," *Oakland Tribune*, June 27, 2003, *www.zacharys .com/news_oakland_tribune.html*; "ESOP Statistics," ESOP Association, *www.esopassociation.org/media/media_statistics.asp*; "How Small Is Too Small for an ESOP?" National Center for Employee Ownership, *www.nceo.org/library/howsmall.html*; "Steps to Setting up an ESOP," National Center for Employee Ownership, *www.nceo.org/library/steps.html*.

Management Succession

3. Discuss the stages of management succession.

Experts estimate that between 2001 and 2017, $12 trillion in wealth will be transferred from one generation to the next, representing the greatest transfer of wealth in history and much of it funneled through family businesses.[25] Most of the family businesses in existence today were started after World War II, and many of the founders who have not yet transferred ownership to the next generation now are at or past retirement age and are ready to pass the torch of leadership. A recent study by the Alliance of Merger and Acquisition Advisors reports that 70 percent of business owners plan to transfer ownership of their businesses by 2020 but that 90 percent of them do not have an adequate succession plan in place.[26]

For a smooth transition from one generation to the next, family businesses need a succession plan. Without a succession plan, family businesses face an increased risk of faltering or failing in the next generation. Those businesses with the greatest probability of surviving are the ones whose owners prepare a succession plan well before it is time to transfer control to the next generation. Succession planning also allows business owners to minimize the impact of taxes on their businesses, their estates, and their successors' wealth as well and to avoid saddling the next generation of ownership with burdensome debt.

Why, then, do so many entrepreneurs postpone succession planning until it is too late? Many business founders hesitate to let go of their businesses because their personal identities are so wrapped up in their companies. Over time, a founder's identity becomes so intertwined in the business that, in the entrepreneur's mind, there is no distinction between the two. The attitude is "I am the company, and the company is me."

Profile
Michael and Emily Powell: Powell's Books

When Michael Powell, who for 27 years had managed Powell's Books, the largest privately held chain of bookstores in the United States, reached age 66, he realized that it was time to begin transferring control of the company to his daughter, Emily, then 28, with the help of the 10-year transition plan he had created 7 years before. When Michael, who took over the family business from his father, talks about retiring from the company he built, however, he covers his face with his hands and his voice grows soft. "There are emotional issues in giving up control and ownership," he admits. "Half my brain says, 'Do it,' and the other half says, 'What are you doing?' This is business and family."[27]

Many entrepreneurs share Powell's feelings. According to a survey by the Monitor Group, less than 17 percent of business owners say that they expect to retire after leaving their businesses. (In fact, 45 percent say that they plan to start another company.)[28]

Another barrier to succession planning is that, in planning the future of the business, owners are forced to accept the painful reality of their own mortality. In addition, turning over the reins of a business they have sacrificed for, fretted over, and dedicated themselves to for so many years is extremely difficult to do—even if the successor is a son or daughter! Paul Snodgrass, son of the founder of Pella Products, a maker of apparel for work and outdoor activities, who accepted leadership of the company from his father, explains, "Dad loves you and wants you to take over the business, but he also put heart and soul into that business, and he's not going to let anybody screw it up—not even you."[29] Finally, many family business founders believe that controlling the business also gives them a degree of control over family members and family behavior.

Planning for management succession protects not only the founder's, successor's, and company's financial resources, but it also preserves what matters most in a successful business: its heritage and tradition. "Real succession planning involves developing a strategy for transferring the trust, respect, and goodwill built by one generation to the next," explains Andy Bluestone, who took over as president of the financial services company his father founded.[30] Management succession planning requires, first, an attitude of trusting others. It recognizes that other family members have a stake in the future of the business and want to participate in planning its future. Planning is an attitude that shows that decisions made with open discussion are more constructive than those without family input. Second, management succession is an evolutionary process and must reconcile an entrepreneur's inevitable anguish with the successors' desire for autonomy. Owners' emotional ties to their businesses usually are stronger than their financial ties. On the other side of the equation are the successors, who yearn to have the autonomy to run the business their way. These inherent conflicts can—and often do—result in skirmishes.

Succession planning reduces the tension and stress created by these conflicts by gradually "changing the guard." A well-developed succession plan is like the smooth, graceful exchange of a baton between runners in a relay race. The new runner still has maximum energy; the concluding runner has already spent his or her energy by running at maximum speed. The athletes never come to a stop to exchange the baton; instead, the handoff takes place on the move. The race is a skillful blend of the talents of all team members—an exchange of leadership so smooth and powerful that the business never falters, but accelerates, fueled by a new source of energy at each leg of the race.

Management succession involves a lengthy series of interconnected stages that begins very early in the life of the owner's children and extends to the point of final ownership transition (see Figure 5). If management succession is to be effective, it is necessary for the process to begin early in the successor's life (stage I). For instance, the owner of a catering business recalls putting his son to work in the family owned company at age 7. On weekends, the boy would arrive at dawn to baste turkeys and was paid in his favorite medium of exchange—doughnuts![31] In most cases, family business owners involve their children in their businesses while they are still in junior high or high school. In this phase, the tasks are routine, but the child is learning the basics of how the business operates. Young adults begin to appreciate the role the business plays in the life of the family. They learn firsthand about the values and responsibilities of running the company.

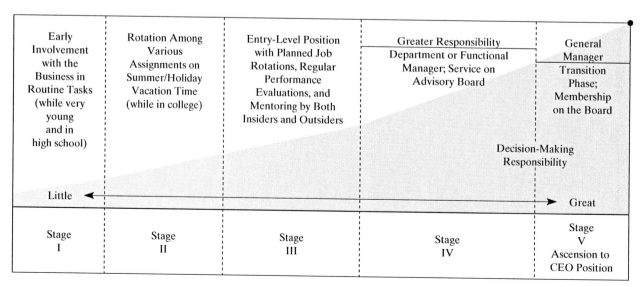

FIGURE 5
Stages in Management Succession

While in college, the successor moves to stage II of the continuum. During this stage, the individual rotates among a variety of job functions to both broaden his or her base of understanding of the business and to permit the parents to evaluate his or her skills. Upon graduation from college, the successor enters stage III. At this point, the successor becomes a full-time worker and ideally has already begun to earn the respect of coworkers through his behavior in the first two stages of the process. In some cases, the successor may work for a time outside of the family business to gain experience and to establish a reputation for competency that goes beyond "being the boss's kid." Stage III focuses on the successor's continuous development, often through a program designed to groom the successor using both family and nonfamily managers as mentors.

Profile

*The Joyner Family:
C. Dan Joyner Realtors*

From the time that Danny Joyner was a young boy "helping" his father in the real estate business that the elder Joyner was building, he knew that he wanted to join his father's company. "I've always known that this is what I would do," says Danny, who joined the company full time after graduating from college. Danny heads the successful company's commercial real estate division, and Dan's two daughters and a son-in-law also work in the family business. With a succession plan in place and all of his children in leadership positions in the company, founder Dan Joyner says that the company is positioned to make a smooth transition into the second generation of ownership.[32]

As the successor develops his or her skills and abilities, he or she moves to stage IV, in which real decision-making authority grows rapidly. Stage IV of the succession continuum is the period when the founder makes a final assessment of the successor's competence and ability to take full and complete control over the firm. The skills the successor needs include the following:

- *Financial abilities.* Understanding the financial aspect of a business, what its financial position is, and the managerial implications of that position are crucial to success.
- *Technical knowledge.* Every business has its own body of knowledge, ranging from how the distribution system works to the trends shaping the industry, that an executive must master.
- *Negotiating ability.* Much of business, whether buying supplies and inventory or selling to customers, boils down to negotiating, and a business owner must be adept at it.
- *Leadership qualities.* Leaders must be bold enough to stake out the company's future and then give employees the resources, the power, and the freedom to pursue it.
- *Communication skills.* Business leaders must communicate the vision they have for their businesses; good listening skills also are essential for success as a top manager.
- *Juggling skills.* Business owners must be able to handle multiple projects effectively. Like a juggler, they must maintain control over several important assignments simultaneously.
- *Integrity.* To be an effective leader of a family business, a successor must demonstrate honesty and integrity in business dealings.
- *Commitment to the business.* It helps if a successor has a genuine passion for the business. Leaders who have enthusiasm for what they do create a spark of excitement throughout the entire organization.[33]

The final stage in the management succession process involves the ultimate transition of organizational leadership. It is during this stage that the founder's role as mentor is most crucial.

Profile

*Laura Michaud: Beltone
Electronics Corporation*

Laura Michaud, who in 1980 became the third-generation owner of Beltone Electronics Corporation, a very successful maker of hearing aids that was founded in 1940, says that the training and mentoring that her father provided was key to her success to managing the family business. Her father insisted on an extensive training program that involved Michaud in all aspects of the company, including having her actually build a hearing aid. "You need to work in all areas of operations," says Michaud, who ran the company for 17 years before selling it to a larger company.[34]

Source: Wall Street Journal\Cartoon
Features Syndicate

"There has been a changing of the guard, Crampton."

In stage IV, the successor may become the organization's CEO, while the former CEO retains the title of chairman of the board. In other cases, the best solution is for the founder to step out of the business entirely and give the successor the chance to establish his or her own identity within the company. "Any leader's final legacy is building the next generation," says one business consultant.[35]

Developing a Management Succession Plan

4. Explain how to develop an effective management succession plan.

Families that are most committed to ensuring that their businesses survive from one generation to the next exhibit four characteristics: (1) They believe that owning the business helps achieve their families' missions. (2) They are proud of the values their businesses are built on and exemplify. (3) They believe that the business is contributing to society and makes it a better place to live. (4) They rely on management succession plans to assure the continuity of their companies.[36] Developing a management succession plan takes time and dedication, yet the benefits are well worth the cost. A sound succession plan enables a company to maintain its momentum and sense of purpose and direction.

It is important to start the planning process early, well before the founder's retirement. Succession planning is not the kind of activity an entrepreneur can do in a hurry, and the sooner an entrepreneur starts, the easier it will be. Unfortunately, too many entrepreneurs put it off until it is too late. "Very few privately owned businesses make it through several generations, and one reason is the failure of the senior generation to do any planning at all until it is too late in the game," says one expert.[37] Creating a succession plan involves the following steps.

Step 1: Select the Successor

The average tenure of the founder of a family business is 25 years.[38] Yet there comes a time for even the most dedicated founder to step down and hand the reins of the company to the next generation. Entrepreneurs should never assume that their children want to take control of the business, however. Above all, they should not be afraid to ask the question: "Do you really want to take over the family business?" Too often, children in this situation tell Mom and Dad what they want to hear out of loyalty, pressure, or guilt. It is critical to remember at this juncture in the life of a business that children do not necessarily inherit their parents' entrepreneurial skills and desires. By leveling with their children about the business and their options regarding a family succession, owners can know which heirs, if any, are willing to assume leadership of the business.

One of the worst mistakes entrepreneurs can make is to postpone naming a successor until just before they are ready to step down. One study by the Raymond Institute and MassMutual reports that 55 percent of family business owners age 61 or older have not yet designated a successor![39] The problem is especially acute when more than one family member works for the company and is interested in assuming leadership of it. Sometimes founders avoid naming successors because they don't want to hurt the family members who are not chosen to succeed them. However, both the business and the family will be better off if, after observing family members as they work in the business, the founder picks a successor based on skill and ability.

Profile

Rupert Murdoch: News Corporation

At age 79, Rupert Murdoch, CEO of News Corporation, had not yet named his successor even though two of his sons, Lachlan and James, have been involved in running the company. Lachlan resigned as the company's chief operating officer but remains on the board of directors; James has worked for News Corporation for 14 years in a variety of positions and is in charge of a division that accounts for 20 percent of the company's revenue. Although the elder Murdoch insists that he has no plans to retire, he says that he is confident that one of his children will emerge to succeed him as CEO. "Every parent likes to see that," he says.[40]

When naming a successor, merit is a better standard to use than gender or birth order. The key is to establish standards of performance, knowledge, education, and ability and then to identify the person who best meets those standards. As part of his company's succession plan, Joe De La Torre selected his daughter Gina to take over Juanita's Foods rather than his two sons because her financial skills and her ability to solve problems were what the company needed most.[41] Gina La Torre is part of a growing trend among family businesses; 34 percent of family business founders expect the next CEO to be a woman, quite a change from just a generation ago.[42]

Profile

Harry and Kirsten Vold: Harry Vold Rodeo Company

After 60 years, Harry Vold, founder of Harry Vold Rodeo Company, a business based in Pueblo West, Colorado, that supplies rodeos with bucking broncos and bulls, turned over the reins of the family business to the youngest of his six children, Kirsten, when she was just 25 years old. Although Harry expected one of his children to take over the business, he was a bit surprised that Kirsten was the one who showed the greatest potential and stepped forward. Kirsten, too, was somewhat surprised. "I was going to be a lawyer, drive a sports car, and live in L.A.," she says with a laugh. After graduating from the University of Southern Colorado, Kirsten took a job in sports marketing but soon felt the tug of the family business and returned home to take an active role in managing it. Kirsten worked hard to prove herself in an industry that men tend to dominate. "She's earned their respect," says her mother proudly. Transferring control from one generation to the next taxed the skills, patience, and ability of both Harry and Kirsten. "It was a struggle, a power struggle, along the way," she says. "For both of us, but it built character for both of us." Harry is pleased with the way things worked out. "I was a bit surprised to begin with, but I'm not now," he says. "I am totally confident that she makes the right decisions. As far as I'm concerned, she's all the cowgirl I need."[43]

Step 2: Create a Survival Kit for the Successor

Once he or she identifies a successor, an entrepreneur should prepare a survival kit and then brief the future leader on its contents, which should include all of the company's critical documents (wills, trusts, insurance policies, financial statements, bank accounts, key contracts, corporate bylaws, and so forth). The founder should be sure that the successor reads and understands all of the relevant documents in the kit. Other important steps the owner should take to prepare the successor to take over leadership of the business include:

- Create a strategic analysis for the future. Working with the successor, the entrepreneur should identify the primary opportunities and the challenges facing the company and the requirements for meeting them.
- On a regular basis, share with the successor his or her vision of the business's future direction, describing key factors that have led to its success and those that will bring future success.
- Be open and listen to the successor's views and concerns.

- Teach and learn at the same time.
- Identify the industry's key success factors.
- Tie the key success factors to the company's performance and profitability.
- Explain the company's overall strategy and how it creates a competitive advantage.
- Discuss the values and philosophy of the business and how they have inspired and influenced past actions.
- Discuss the people in the business and their strengths and weaknesses.
- Describe the philosophy underlying the firm's compensation policy and explain why employees are paid what they are.
- Make a list of the firm's most important customers and its key suppliers or vendors and review the history of all dealings with the parties on both lists.
- Discuss how to treat these key players to ensure the company's continued success and its smooth and error-free ownership transition.
- Develop a job analysis by taking an inventory of the activities involved in leading the company. This analysis can show successors those activities on which they should be spending most of their time.
- Document as much process knowledge—"how we do things"—as possible. After many years in their jobs, business owners are not even aware of their vast reservoirs of knowledge. For them, making decisions is a natural part of their business lives. They do it effortlessly because they have so much knowledge and experience. It is easy to forget that a successor will not have the benefit of those years of experience unless the founder communicates it.
- Include an ethical will, a document that explains to the next generation of leaders the ethical principles on which the company operates. An ethical will gives company founders the chance to bequeath to their heirs not only a business, but also the wisdom and ethical lessons learned over a lifetime.

ENTREPRENEURIAL
Profile

Paul Weber: Webers Hamburgers

In 1963, Paul Weber started Webers Hamburgers, a small restaurant that has become a landmark, in Ontario, Canada, known for its fresh, tasty burgers. Targeting vacationers and city dwellers looking for an escape, Weber selected a location near the small town of Orillia, about 2 hours north of Toronto. On a typical Saturday during the peak summer season, Webers serves about 800 hamburgers per hour, a pace that tests the restaurant's systems and employees. Managing the family business is second-generation owner Paul Weber, Jr., who grew up working in the restaurant and took over the family business in 1989. Paul Jr. credits much of the company's success to the systems that his father established, refined, and documented over more than a quarter of a century. In fact, Webers continues to document for future generations every part of their business, including the order processing procedure and the techniques they use to entertain guests when lines stretch across the parking lot.[44]

Hungry customers line up, waiting to get into Webers Hamburgers in Orillia, Ontario.

Source: Angelo Cavalli/SuperStock

Step 3: Groom the Successor

The process by which business founders transfer their knowledge to the next generation is gradual and often occurs informally as they spend time with their successors. Grooming the successor is the founder's greatest teaching and development responsibility, and it takes time, usually 5 to 10 years.

Profile

Brian Tuberman:
SCTR Systems

When the founder of SCTR Systems, a company created in 1967 that sells computerized retail systems to independent grocers, began looking for a successor (from outside the family, because none of his children were interested in taking over the family business) 12 years before he planned to retire, he recruited Brian Tuberman and immediately began grooming him to take over the company. Tuberman purchased the business from the founder in 2005 and credits the smooth transition of ownership to the lessons he learned from his mentor. "Everyone thought I was crazy to quit what I was doing to make plans for 12 years down the road," says Tuberman, "but the previous owner and I believed in each other and in the company and made it happen."[45]

To implement the succession plan, the founder must be:

- Patient, realizing that the transfer of power is gradual and evolutionary and that the successor should earn responsibility and authority one step at a time until the final transfer of power takes place.
- Willing to accept that the successor will make mistakes.
- Skillful at using the successor's mistakes as a teaching tool.
- An effective communicator and an especially tolerant listener.
- Capable of establishing reasonable expectations for the successor's performance.
- Able to articulate the keys to the successor's performance.

Teaching is the art of assisting discovery and requires letting go rather than controlling. When problems arise in the business, the founder should consider delegating some of them to the successor-in-training. The founder also must resist the tendency to wade in and fix the problem unless it is beyond the scope of the successor's ability. Most great teachers and leaders are remembered more for the success of their students than for their own success.

Step 4: Promote an Environment of Trust and Respect

Another priceless gift a founder can leave a successor is an environment of trust and respect. Trust and respect on the part of the founder and others fuel the successor's desire to learn and excel and build the successor's confidence in making decisions. Empowering the successor by gradually delegating responsibilities creates an environment in which all parties can objectively view the growth and development of the successor. Customers, creditors, suppliers, and staff members can gradually develop confidence in the successor. The final transfer of power is not a dramatic, wrenching change but a smooth, coordinated passage.

A problem for some founders at this phase is the meddling retiree syndrome, in which they continue to show up at the office after they have officially stepped down and get involved in business issues that no longer concern them. This tendency merely undermines the authority of the successor and confuses employees as to who really is in charge. Helen Dragas, who succeeded her father at the Dragas Company, a residential construction business, praises her father for handing the reins of the company over to her and then trusting her to handle them. "He gave me the authority and then he stepped back," she says of the successful transfer of leadership.[46]

Step 5: Cope with the Financial Realities of Estate and Gift Taxes

The final step in developing a workable management succession plan is structuring the transition to minimize the impact of estate, gift, and inheritance taxes on family members and the business. Entrepreneurs who fail to consider the impact of these taxes (which have been as high as 55 percent) may force their heirs to sell a successful business just to pay the estate's tax (commonly known as the "death tax") bill. Despite facing potentially large tax bills, 19 percent of senior generation owners have done no estate planning at all![47]

Just a few hours after Clayton Leverett's son, Whit, was born, the young father began to wonder whether Whit would be able to retain the family's 150-year-old Stillwater Ranch, a cattle ranch in Llano, Texas, now in its fifth generation of family ownership. Estate taxes have cut deeply into the Leverett family's land holdings and cattle operations twice before. The family was forced to sell thousands of acres of valuable land to pay estate taxes when Clayton's grandmother died in 2006. When Clayton's father died later that same year, the family faced the estate tax a second time, and once again had to sell acreage and lay off employees. Clayton also had to take on a second job to pay the estate tax. "We will only be able to sell only so much [land] before the ranch becomes unprofitable and we are forced to sell the entire operation," explains a frustrated Clayton.[48]

Although Congress eliminated the estate tax for 2010 (see Table 2), the tax has not evaporated forever. (When George Steinbrenner, owner of the New York Yankees, died in 2010, the year Congress repealed the estate tax, his heirs paid no estate taxes. Had Steinbrenner died in 2009, however, his heirs would have faced a stiff tax bill of $500 million![49]) More than two-thirds of adults believe that that estate tax should remain extinct, and research supports this view. A study by Antony Davies of Duquesne University reports that for every 4.5 percent increase in the estate tax (the average increase in the tax since 1993), 6,000 small businesses are liquidated or absorbed into large companies. Conversely, Davies' research suggests that repealing the tax would create 100,000 new businesses that would employ 2 million workers with a total payroll of $80 billion.[50]

Entrepreneurs who fail to engage in proper estate planning will subject their family members to a painful tax bite when they inherit the business. Entrepreneurs should be actively engaged in estate planning no later than age 45; those who start businesses early in their lives or whose businesses grow rapidly may need to begin as early as age 30. A variety of options exist that may prove to be helpful in reducing the estate tax liability. Each operates in a different fashion, but their objective remains the same: to remove a portion of business owners' assets out of their estates so that when they die those assets will not be subject to estate taxes. Many of these estate planning tools need time to work their magic, so the key is to put them in place early on in the life of the business.

TABLE 2 Changes in the Estate and Gift Taxes

After years of complaints from family business owners, Congress finally overhauled the often punishing structures of estate and gift taxes. The federal estate tax is actually interwoven with the gift tax, but under the modified law the impact of the two taxes began to differ in 2004. Congress repealed the estate tax in 2010, but resurrected it in 2011! The following table shows the trends in the exemptions and the minimum tax rates for the estate and gift taxes:

Year	Estate Tax Exemption	Gift Tax Exemption	Maximum Tax Rate
2001	$675,000	$675,000	55%
2002	$1 million	$1 million	50%
2003	$1 million	$1 million	49%
2004	$1.5 million	$1 million	48%
2005	$1.5 million	$1 million	47%
2006	$2 million	$1 million	46%
2007	$2 million	$1 million	45%
2008	$2 million	$1 million	45%
2009	$3.5 million	$1 million	45%
2010	Tax repealed	$1 million	35% (gifts only)
2011	$5 million	$5 million	35%
2012	?	?	?

No matter how the federal laws governing estate taxes may change over the next few years, entrepreneurs whose businesses have been successful must not neglect estate planning. Even though the federal estate tax burden has eased somewhat (at least for a while), many states have *increased* their estate tax rates.

BUY-SELL AGREEMENT. One of the most popular estate planning techniques is the buy-sell agreement. A **buy-sell agreement** is a contract that co-owners often rely on to ensure the continuity of a business. In a typical arrangement, the co-owners create a contract stating that each agrees to buy the others out in case of the death or disability of one. That way, the heirs of the deceased or disabled owner can "cash out" of the business while leaving control of the business in the hands of the remaining owners. The buy-sell agreement specifies a formula for determining the value of the business at the time the agreement is to be executed. One problem with buy-sell agreements is that the remaining co-owners may not have the cash available to buy out the disabled or deceased owner. To resolve this issue, many businesses buy life and disability insurance for each of the owners in amounts large enough to cover the purchase price of their respective shares of the business. Without the support of adequate insurance policies, a buy-sell agreement offers virtually no protection.

ENTREPRENEURIAL
Profile

*Junab Ali and Jay Uribe:
Mobius Partners*

Junab Ali and Jay Uribe, founders of Mobius Partners, a $25 million a year company that specializes in enterprise IT solutions, created a buy-sell agreement to protect themselves and their business in the event of the death or disability of a partner. Their agreement is supported by insurance policies on each partner, giving them the income security they need for their families and providing the remaining partner the financial resources to buy the shares of the missing partner.[51]

LIFETIME GIFTING. The owners of a successful business may transfer money to their children (or other recipients) from their estate throughout their lives. Current federal tax regulations allow individuals to make gifts of $13,000 per year, per parent, per recipient, that are exempt from federal gift taxes. Another benefit: Gift recipients do not have to pay taxes on the gift. For instance, husband-and-wife business owners could give $1.56 million worth of stock to their three children and their spouses over a period of 10 years without incurring any estate or gift taxes at all.

SETTING UP A TRUST. A **trust** is a contract between a grantor (the founder) and a trustee (generally a bank officer or an attorney) in which the grantor gives to the trustee legal title to assets (e.g., stock in the company), which the trustee agrees to hold for the beneficiaries (children). The beneficiaries can receive income from the trust, or they can receive the property in the trust, or both, at some specified time. Trusts can take a wide variety of forms, but two broad categories of trusts are available: revocable trusts and irrevocable trusts. A **revocable trust** is one that the grantor can change or revoke during his or her lifetime. Under present tax laws, however, the only trust that provides a tax benefit is an **irrevocable trust**, in which the grantor cannot require the trustee to return the assets held in trust. The value of the grantor's estate is lowered because the assets in an irrevocable trust are excluded from the value of that estate. However, an irrevocable trust places severe restrictions on the grantor's control of the property placed in the trust. Business owners use several types of irrevocable trusts to lower their estate tax liabilities:

Bypass Trust. The most basic type of trust is the bypass trust, which allows a business owner to put up to $3 million into trust naming his or her spouse as the beneficiary upon the owner's death. The spouse receives the income from the trust throughout his or her life, but the principal in the trust bypasses the surviving spouse's estate and goes to the couple's heirs free of estate taxes upon the spouse's death. A bypass trust is particularly useful for couples who plan their estates together. By leaving assets to one another in bypass trusts, they can make sure that their assets are taxed only once between them. However, entrepreneurs should work with experienced attorneys to create bypass trusts because the IRS requires that they contain certain precise language to be valid.

Irrevocable Life Insurance Trust (ILIT). This type of trust allows a business owner to keep the proceeds of a life insurance policy out of his or her estate and away from estate taxes, freeing up that money to pay the taxes on the remainder of the estate. To get the tax benefit, business owners must be sure that the business or the trust (rather than themselves) owns the insurance policy. The primary disadvantage of an irrevocable life insurance trust is that if the owner dies within 3 years of establishing it, the insurance proceeds *do* become part of the estate and *are* subject to estate taxes. Because the trust is irrevocable, it cannot be amended or rescinded once it is established. Like most trusts, ILITs must meet stringent requirements to be valid, and entrepreneurs should use experienced attorneys to create them.

Irrevocable Asset Trust. An irrevocable asset trust is similar to a life insurance trust except that it is designed to pass the assets in the parents' estate on to their children. The children do not have control of the assets while the parents are still living, but they do receive the income from those assets. Upon the parents' death, the assets in the trust go to the children without being subjected to the estate tax.

Grantor Retained Annuity Trust (GRAT). A grantor retained annuity trust (GRAT) is a special type of irrevocable trust and has become one of the most popular tools for entrepreneurs to transfer ownership of a business while maintaining control over it and minimizing estate taxes. Under a GRAT, an owner can put property in an irrevocable trust for a maximum of 10 years. While the trust is in effect, the grantor (owner) retains the voting power and receives the interest income from the property in the trust. At the end of the trust (not to exceed 10 years), the property passes to the beneficiaries (heirs). The beneficiaries are required to pay the gift tax on the value of the assets placed in the GRAT but pay no estate tax on them. However, the IRS taxes GRAT gifts according to their discounted present value because the heirs did not receive use of the property while it was in trust. The primary disadvantage of using a GRAT in estate planning is that if the grantor dies during the life of the GRAT, its assets pass back into the grantor's estate. These assets then become subject to the full estate tax.

Establishing a trust requires meeting many specific legal requirements and is not something business owners should do on their own. It is much better to hire experienced attorneys, accountants, and financial advisors to assist in creating them. Although the cost of establishing a trust can be high, the tax savings they generate are well worth the expense.

ESTATE FREEZE. An **estate freeze** attempts to minimize estate taxes by having family members create two classes of stock for the business: (1) preferred voting stock for the parents and (2) nonvoting common stock for the children. The value of the preferred stock is frozen, whereas the common stock reflects the anticipated increased market value of the business. Any appreciation in the value of the business after the transfer is not subject to estate taxes. However, the parent must pay gift tax on the value of the common stock given to the children. The value of the common stock is the total value of the business less the value of the voting preferred stock retained by the parent. The parents also must accept taxable dividends at the market rate on the preferred stock they own.

FAMILY LIMITED PARTNERSHIP. Creating a **family limited partnership (FLP)** allows business-owning parents to transfer their company to their children (thus lowering their estate taxes) while still retaining control over it for themselves. To create an FLP, the parents (or parent) set up a partnership among themselves and their children. The parents retain the general partnership interest, which can be as low as 1 percent, and the children become the limited partners. As general partners, the parents control both the limited partnership and the family business. In other words, nothing in the way the company operates has to change. Over time, the parents can transfer company stock into the limited partnership, ultimately passing ownership of the company to their children.

One of the principal tax benefits of an FLP is that it allows discounts on the value of the shares of company stock the parents transfer into the limited partnership. Because a family business is closely held, shares of ownership in it, especially minority shares, are not as marketable as those of a publicly held company. As a result, company shares transferred into the limited partnership are discounted at 20 to 50 percent of their full market value, producing a large tax savings for everyone involved. The average discount is 40 percent, but that amount varies based on the industry and the individual company involved. A business owner should consider an FLP as part of a succession plan "when there has been a buildup of substantial value in the business and the older generation has a substantial amount of liquidity," says one expert.[52]

Because of their ability to reduce estate and gift taxes, FLPs have become one of the most popular estate planning tools in recent years. However, a Tax Court ruling against a Texas entrepreneur who, 2 months before he died, established an FLP that contained both business and personal assets, cast a pall over the use of FLPs as estate planning tools. Another case, however, calmed estate planners' fears and reestablished the use of FLPs as legitimate estate planning tools as long as entrepreneurs create them properly. The following tips will help entrepreneurs establish an FLP that will withstand legal challenges:

- Establish a legitimate business reason other than avoiding estate taxes, such as transferring a business over time to the next generation of family members, for creating the FLP and document it on paper.
- Make sure all members of the FLP make contributions and take distributions according to a predetermined schedule. "Don't allow partners to use partnership funds to pay for personal expenses and do not time partnership distributions with personal needs for cash," says one attorney.[53]
- Do not allow members to put all of their personal assets (such as a house, automobiles, or personal property) into the FLP. Commingling personal and business assets in an FLP raises a red flag to the IRS.
- Maintain proper records for establishing and operating the FLP.
- Expect an audit of the FLP. The IRS tends to scrutinize FLPs; be prepared for a thorough audit.[54]

Gordon Van Tuinen founded West Michigan Uniform (WMU) in Holland, Michigan, in 1963 and managed it until he retired in 1983, when his son Ken took over as CEO. To transfer the family business to Ken and his four other children, Gordon relied on a variety of estate planning tools, including lifetime gifting and an estate freeze. Ken, who owns the majority of shares in WMU, is now engaged in planning to give control of the company to the third generation of family members with the goal of minimizing the impact of estate taxes. In addition to using lifetime gifting to transfer shares of the company to his three children, one of whom works in the business, Ken created three family limited partnerships that will allow the children to assume ownership of the company over time without incurring oppressive tax bills.[55]

Developing a succession plan and preparing a successor requires a wide variety of knowledge and skills, some of which the business founder will not have. That's why it is important to bring experts into the process when necessary. Entrepreneurs often call on their attorneys, accountants, insurance agents, and financial planners to help them build a succession plan that works best for their particular situations. Because the issues involved can be highly complex and charged with emotion, bringing in trusted advisors to help improves the quality of the process and provides an objective perspective.

Risk Management Strategies

5. Understand the four risk management strategies.

Insurance is an important part of creating a management succession plan because it can help business owners minimize the taxes on the estates they pass on to their heirs and can provide much needed cash to pay the taxes the estate does incur. However, insurance plays an important role in many other aspects of a successful business—from covering employee injuries to protecting against natural disasters that might shut a business down temporarily. When most small business owners think of risks such as these, they automatically think of insurance. However, insurance companies are the first to point out that insurance does not solve all risk problems. A more comprehensive strategy is risk management, which takes a proactive approach to dealing with the risks that businesses face daily. A survey by the National Federation of Independent Businesses shows that just 38 percent of small companies have an emergency preparedness plan for dealing with either a natural or manmade disaster.[56] At least 25 percent of small businesses that are forced to close after a major disaster never reopen; among small businesses that have no disaster plan, the percentage that never reopen jumps to 50 percent.[57] "Small companies often spend more time planning the company picnic than planning for an event that could put them out of business," says one insurance expert.[58] Dealing with risk successfully requires a combination of four risk management strategies: avoiding, reducing, anticipating, and transferring risk.

Avoiding risk requires a business to take actions to shun risky situations. For instance, conducting credit checks of customers decreases losses from bad debts. Wise managers know that they can avoid some risks simply by taking proactive management actions. Workplace safety improves when business owners implement programs designed to make all employees aware of the hazards of their jobs and how to avoid being hurt. Business owners who have active risk identification and prevention programs can reduce their potential insurance costs as well as create a safer, more attractive work environment for their employees. Because avoiding risk altogether usually is not practical, however, a strategy of reducing risk becomes necessary.

A risk-reducing strategy requires a company to take steps to lower the level of risk associated with a situation. Risk reduction strategies do not eliminate risk, but they lessen its impact. Even with avoidance and reduction strategies, the risk is still present; thus, losses can occur.

Profile

George Pauli: Great Embroidery LLC

George Pauli, owner of Great Embroidery LLC in Mesa, Arizona, recently installed back-up generators for the two machines that he uses to stitch logos on 12 garments at a time. Pauli's business experiences power interruptions about six times a year, and before he installed the generators each incident cost him at least $120 in lost merchandise because the machines' needles could not resume exactly where they had left off when the power shut off.[59]

Risk anticipation strategies promote self-insurance. Knowing that some element of risk still exists, a business owner puts aside money each month to cover potential losses. Sometimes a self-insurance fund may not be large enough to cover the losses from a particular situation. When this happens, a business stands to lose despite the best efforts to anticipate risk, especially in the first few years before the fund is fully funded and able to cover large claims. Most businesses, therefore, include in their risk strategies some form of insurance to transfer risk.

Profile

Racine Federated

Managers at Racine Federated, a small company in Racine, Wisconsin, that sells industrial instruments, machinery, and tools, grew tired of watching the cost of health care coverage for their 110 employees climb every year and decided to establish a self-insurance fund to cover employees' health care benefits. If employees' claims were low in a given year, Racine would save money over what it would have paid in insurance premiums. If several workers suffered catastrophic injuries or illnesses at once, however, the company could face a cash crisis. Recognizing that a self-insurance strategy alone could be risky, Racine purchased a "stop-loss" policy, which takes over payment if any individual employee's health care costs exceed $55,000 a year. Racine also hired a company to handle all of the insurance paperwork. In the 7 years since switching to self-insurance, Racine has saved $300,000 over the cost of the company's old insurance plan without reducing its coverage.[60]

George Pauli, owner of Great Embroidery LLC, installed back-up generators for his company as part of a risk reduction strategy.

Source: Andy DeLisle/Wonderful Machine

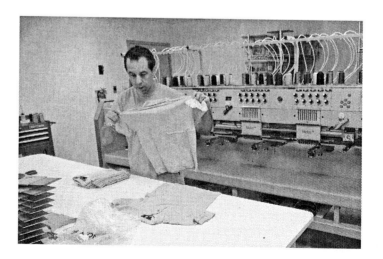

Self-insurance is not for every business owner, however. For businesses with fewer than 50 employees, self-insurance is usually not a wise choice because there is so much variation in the number and size of annual claims. Self-insuring also is time-consuming, requiring business owners to take a more active role in managing their companies' insurance needs. Companies using self-insurance should be financially secure with a relatively stable workforce and should see it as a long-term strategy for savings.

Risk transfer strategies depend on using insurance. Insurance is a risk transfer strategy because an individual or a business transfers some of the costs of a particular risk to an insurance company, which is set up to spread out the financial burdens of risk. During a specific time period, the insured business pays money (a premium) to an insurance carrier (either a private company or a government agency). In return, the carrier promises to pay the insured a certain amount of money in the event of a loss. Small companies across the United States are feeling the pinch of rapidly escalating insurance costs and are devising creative ways to control their insurance costs.

Captive insurance, which is a hybrid of self-insurance and risk transfer strategies, is a technique that large businesses have used for years that is gaining popularity among small businesses. To implement a captive insurance strategy, small companies band together to create their own insurance company and contribute enough capital to cover a defined level of risk. The group outsources the daily management of the insurance company to a business that specializes in that area and then purchases reinsurance to cover losses above the amount that they have contributed. Over time, if the group experiences no large losses, the excess capital paid into the insurance company goes back to the businesses as dividends. Currently, 27 states and the District of Columbia have passed legislation authorizing insurance captives.

Profile

Dudley Miles:
J.D. Miles & Sons

Dudley Miles, CEO of J.D. Miles & Sons, a roofing contractor founded by his grandfather in 1910, was plagued by escalating insurance premiums that threatened his company's profitability. Working through Roof Connect, an industry association, Miles convinced 25 other roofing contractors to band together to create a captive insurance company. The small businesses agreed to self-insure losses up to $500,000 and purchased reinsurance to cover larger losses. They also adopted several risk reduction strategies such as quarterly safety inspections and random drug tests for employees. The result has been a reduction in the number of claims, improved safety records, and lower premiums than the members of the plan were paying before.[61]

The Basics of Insurance

6. Discuss the basics of insurance for small businesses.

Insurance is the transfer of risk from one entity (an individual, a group, or a business) to an insurance company. Without insurance, many of the products and services that businesses provide would be impossible because the risk of overwhelming financial loss would be too great given the litigious society in which we live. Yet many small business owners ignore their companies' insurance needs or buy insurance coverage for their companies but not enough to protect them from the most basic risks such as property damage, fire, theft, and liability. Home-based business owners, in particular, put their companies at risk. According to the Independent Insurance Agents & Brokers of America, 58 percent of home-based business owners lack adequate insurance to protect them against liability, property damage, or loss.[62]

To be insurable, a situation or hazard must meet the following requirements:

1. It must be possible to calculate the actual loss being insured. For example, it would probably not be possible to insure an entire city against fire because too many variables are involved. It is possible, however, to insure a specific building.
2. It must be possible to select the risk being insured. No business owner can insure against every potential hazard, but insurance companies offer a wide variety of policies. One company even offers an alien abduction policy ($150 a year for $150 million of coverage) and has actually paid one claim! Another offers werewolf insurance, but the policy pays only if the insured turns into a werewolf.[63] Famous insurer Lloyd's of London has insured

Entrepreneurs can buy insurance to protect themselves and their companies from almost any calamity. One insurance company actually offers werewolf insurance!

Source: Lon Chaney\Alamy

coffee taster Gennarro Pelliccia's tongue and taste buds for £10 million. Pelliccia, who samples coffees for Costa Coffee, says, "In my profession, my taste buds and sensory skills are crucial. My taste buds allow me to distinguish any defects, which enables me to protect and guarantee Costa's unique Mocha Italia blend." Lloyd's also once wrote a policy to insure the smile of actress America Ferrera, star of the television show *Ugly Betty*, for $10 million.[64]

3. There must be enough potential policyholders to assume the risk. A tightrope walker who specializes in walking between tall downtown buildings would have difficulty purchasing insurance because there are not enough people engaging in that activity to spread the risk sufficiently.

Perhaps the biggest barrier facing entrepreneurs is the difficulty of understanding the nature of the risks that they and their businesses face. The risk management pyramid (see Figure 6) helps entrepreneurs decide how they should allocate their risk management dollars. Begin by identifying the primary risks your company faces: for example, a fire in a manufacturing plant, a lawsuit from a customer injured by your company's product, a computer system meltdown, an earthquake, and so on. Then rate each event on three factors:

1. *Severity.* How much would the event affect your company's ability to operate?
2. *Probability.* How likely is the event to occur?
3. *Cost.* How much would it cost your company if the event occurred?

Rate the event on each of these three factors using a simple scale: A (high) to D (low). For instance, a small technology company might rate a fire in its offices as BDA. On the other hand, that same company might rank a computer system crash as ABA. Using the risk management pyramid, a business owner sees that the event rated ABA is higher on the risk scale than the event rated BDA. Therefore, this company would focus more of its risk management dollars on preventing a computer system crash than on protecting against an office fire.

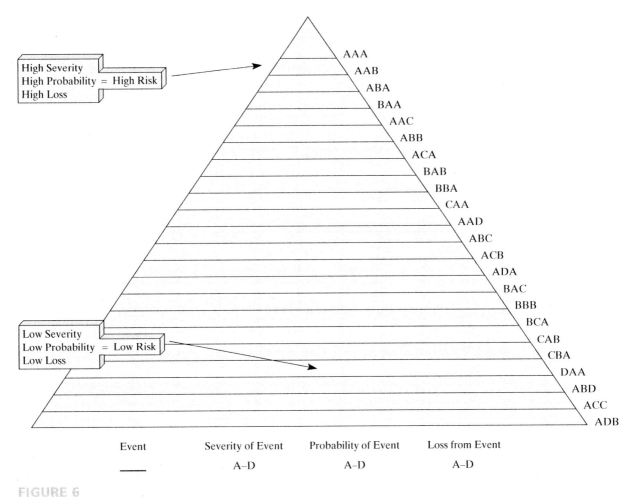

FIGURE 6
The Risk Management Pyramid

Types of Insurance

No longer is the cost of insurance an inconsequential part of doing business. Now the ability to get adequate coverage and to pay the premiums is a significant factor in starting and running a small business. Sometimes just *finding* coverage for their businesses is a challenge for entrepreneurs.

ENTREPRENEURIAL

Profile

Jane Reifert:
Incredible Adventures

For Incredible Adventures, a small Sarasota, Florida-based company that offers customers the opportunity to fly in a Russian MiG jet fighter; experience weightlessness; go to the edge of space; swim with sharks; or make a high-altitude, low-opening (HALO) sky dive; in addition to many other exciting adventures, purchasing insurance is a challenge. President Jane Reifert says that she spends as much time with lawyers and insurance agents as she does with customers. "You can insure people swimming in shark-infested waters, but you can't insure people inside shark cages," she says incredulously.[65]

A wide range of business, individual, and group insurance is available to small business owners, and deciding which ones are necessary can be difficult. Some types of insurance are essential to providing a secure future for the company; others may provide additional employee benefits. The four major categories of insurance are property and casualty insurance, life and disability insurance, health insurance and workers' compensation coverage, and liability insurance. Each category is divided into many specific types, each of which has many variations offered by insurance companies. Business owners should begin by purchasing a basic **business owner's policy (BOP)**, which typically includes basic property and casualty insurance and liability insurance coverage. BOPs alone are not sufficient to meet most small business owners' insurance needs, however. Entrepreneurs should start with BOPs and then customize their insurance coverage to suit their companies' special needs by purchasing additional types of coverage.

PROPERTY AND CASUALTY INSURANCE. Property and casualty insurance covers a company's tangible assets, such as buildings, equipment, inventory, machinery, signs, and others that might be damaged, destroyed, or stolen. Business owners should be sure that their policies cover the replacement cost of their property, not just its value at the time of the loss, even if this coverage costs extra. One business owner whose policy covered the replacement cost of his company's building was glad he had purchased the extra coverage when he suffered a devastating fire loss. When he began rebuilding, he discovered that the cost to comply with current building code regulations was much higher than merely replacing the previous structure.

Specific types of property and casualty insurance include property, surety, marine and inland marine, crime, liability, business interruption, motor vehicle, and professional liability insurance.

Property insurance protects a company's assets against loss from damage, theft, or destruction. It applies to automobiles, boats, homes, office buildings, stores, factories, and other items of property. Some property insurance policies are broadly written to include all of an individual's property up to some maximum amount of loss, whereas other policies are written to cover only one building or one specific piece of property, such as a company car. Many natural disasters, such as floods and earthquakes, are not covered under standard property insurance; business owners must buy separate insurance policies for those particular events.

Within the last decade, business owners across the United States have suffered billions of dollars in losses from natural disasters ranging from tornadoes and hurricanes to snow and ice storms. Many of the businesses that lacked proper insurance coverage were forced to close for good, and others are still struggling to recover.

Profile

*The Brennan Family:
Ralph Brennan
Restaurant Group*

Even with adequate insurance, it took the Brennans, New Orleans' famous family of restaurateurs, more than a year to reopen the celebrated Commander's Palace after Hurricane Katrina severely damaged the historic Garden District building that housed it. Almost all of the interior of the building, which was constructed in 1880, had to be rebuilt because of water damage, and more than 80 percent of the kitchen equipment had to be replaced. Charlie Williamson, vice president of the Ralph Brennan Restaurant Group, says that the company's disaster preparation plan has grown from 2 pages before the hurricane to a 68-page booklet that covers not only operating plans but also technology and communications plans.[66]

A company's BOP may insure the buildings and contents of a factory for loss from fire or natural disaster, but the owner may also buy insurance, called extra expense coverage, to cover expenses that occur while the destroyed factory is being rebuilt. **Extra expense coverage** pays for the costs of temporarily relocating workers and machinery so that a business can continue to

After suffering damage from Hurricane Katrina, New Orleans' famous Commander's Palace restaurant is now fully restored. Even with adequate insurance coverage, the restoration took more than a year.

Source: © Angelo Cavalli/SuperStock

operate while it rebuilds or repairs its factory. A similar type of insurance, called **business interruption insurance**, covers business owners' lost income and ongoing expenses in case their companies cannot operate for an extended period of time. As devastating as interruptions can be to a small company, studies show that 55 percent of small business owners do not purchase business interruption coverage and that 63 percent of them do not know how the coverage works.[67] Even more alarming is the fact that 25 percent of businesses whose operations are interrupted by a disaster never reopen.[68]

Wendy Stevens, who owns Alloy Design, a business in Boyertown, Pennsylvania, that manufactures accessories and home decorations out of stainless steel, watched helplessly as more than 100 firefighters battled a blaze that ultimately claimed the building that housed her company. "I remember feeling huge waves of nausea and thinking, 'My business is gone,'" she says. "Everything was destroyed—equipment, inventory, paperwork. All that remained were two stone walls, a floor, and 20 years of designing, building, and selling my product." Fortunately, Stevens had good insurance coverage, including property and inventory insurance as well as business interruption insurance. One year after the fire, Stevens was back in business. "After losing everything, I've managed to bounce back with even better products and to expand into new markets. I'm now selling in four different countries."[69]

Machinery and equipment insurance is a common addition for many businesses and covers a wide range of problems with equipment such as production machinery, electrical systems, HVAC systems, and others. For instance, a restaurant that loses thousands of dollars' worth of food when a freezer breaks down would be covered for its loss under machinery and equipment insurance.

Auto insurance policies offer liability coverage that protects against losses resulting from injuries, damage, or theft involving the use of company vehicles. A typical BOP does not include liability coverage for automobiles; business owners must purchase a separate policy for auto insurance. The automobiles a business owns must be covered by a commercial policy, not a personal one.

Electronic data processing (EDP) insurance covers losses from the theft or loss of computers and data, the impact of computer viruses and computer system failures, intrusion by hackers, and invasion of customer information stored in company databases. EDP insurance has become more important as businesses have moved their operations online and engage in increasing volumes of e-commerce. Thomas Shipley, whose company sells business accessories, generates 30 percent of his sales from the company's Web site. Shipley purchased an EDP policy that protects his business from, among other things, hackers and viruses. The policy costs $14,000 a year, but Shipley says it is well worth the price to protect his company that now brings in more than $10 million in sales a year.[70]

A business may also purchase **surety insurance**, which protects against losses to customers that occur when a company fails to complete a contract on time or completes it incorrectly. Surety protection guarantees customers that they will get either the products or services they purchased or the money to cover losses from contractual failures.

Businesses also buy insurance to protect themselves from losses that occur when either finished goods or raw materials are lost or destroyed while being shipped. **Marine insurance** is designed to cover the risk associated with goods in transit. The name of this insurance goes back to the days when a ship's cargo was insured against high risks associated with ocean navigation.

Crime insurance does not deter crime, but it can reimburse the small business owner for losses from the "three Ds": dishonesty, disappearance, and destruction. Business owners should ask their insurance brokers or agents exactly what their crime insurance policies cover; after-the-fact insurance coverage surprises are seldom pleasant. Premiums for crime policies vary depending on the type of business, store location, number of employees, quality of the business's security system, and the business's history of losses. Coverage may include fidelity bonds, which are designed to reimburse business owners for losses from embezzlement and employee theft. Forgery bonds reimburse owners for losses sustained from the forgery of business checks.

LIFE AND DISABILITY INSURANCE. Unlike most forms of insurance, life insurance does not pertain to avoiding risk because death is a certainty for everyone. Rather, **life insurance** protects families and businesses against loss of income, security, or personal services that results from an individual's untimely death. Life insurance policies are usually issued with a face amount payable to a beneficiary upon the death of the insured. Life insurance for business protection, although not as common as life insurance for family protection, is becoming more popular. As you learned in the section on management succession, life insurance policies are an important part of many estate planning tools. In addition, many businesses insure the lives of key executives to offset the costs of having to make a hurried and often unplanned replacement of important managers.

When it comes to assets that are expensive to replace, few are more costly than the key people in a business, including the owner. What would it take to replace a company's top sales representative? Its production supervisor? Clearly, money alone cannot solve the problem, but it does allow a business to find and train their replacements and to cover the profits lost because of their untimely deaths or disabilities. That is the idea behind **key-person insurance**, which provides valuable working capital to keep a business on track while it reorganizes and searches for the right person to replace the loss of someone in a key position in the company.

Disability insurance protects an individual in the event of unexpected and often very expensive disabilities. Because a sudden disability limits a person's ability to earn a living, the insurance proceeds are designed to help make up the difference between what that person could have expected to earn if the accident had not occurred. Sometimes called income insurance, these policies usually guarantee a stated percentage of an individual's income—usually around 60 percent—while he or she is recovering and is unable to run a business. Short-term disability policies cover the 90-day gap between the time a person is injured and when workers' compensation payments begin. Long-term disability policies pay for lost income after 90 days or longer. In addition to the portion of income a policy will replace, another important factor to consider when purchasing disability insurance is the waiting period, the time gap between when the disability occurs and the disability payments begin. Although many business owners understand the importance of maintaining adequate life insurance coverage, fewer see the relevance of maintaining proper coverage for disabilities. For most people, the likelihood of a disability is three to five times greater than the risk of death; nearly 30 percent of workers between the ages of 35 and 65 will be unable to work for 90 days or longer due to a disability.[71]

Business owners can supplement traditional disability policies with **business overhead expense (BOE) insurance**. Designed primarily for companies with fewer than 15 employees, a BOE policy will replace 100 percent of a small company's monthly overhead expenses such as rent, utilities, insurance, taxes, and others if the owner is incapacitated. Payments typically begin 30 days after the owner is incapacitated and continue for up to 2 years.

HEALTH INSURANCE AND WORKERS' COMPENSATION. According to the National Federation of Independent Businesses (NFIB), small business owners' greatest concern for the last 25 years has been the skyrocketing cost of health insurance.[72] Currently, health care spending in the United States accounts for 17.3 percent of GDP, an amount that will increase to 20 percent by 2017.[73] The average small company spends on average $5,046 per year on health care insurance premiums for an employee. Because of the high cost of providing health care coverage for employees, only 68 percent of small businesses offer health insurance to their employees, compared to 99 percent of large companies (see Figure 7).[74] As health care costs steadily climb and the average age of the workforce continues to increase, small companies are having more difficulty providing coverage for their employees (see Figure 8). The primary reason cited by small business owners who do not offer health insurance is the high cost.[75] Small businesses actually pay 18 percent more than large companies for the same health insurance because of higher broker fees and costs of administering health care plans for a smaller number of employees.[76] "The corporate world really spoiled me," says Sandy Dixon, who left a large company to start Interior Arrangements, an interior redesign company in Evergreen, Colorado. "[When I started my business,] I was

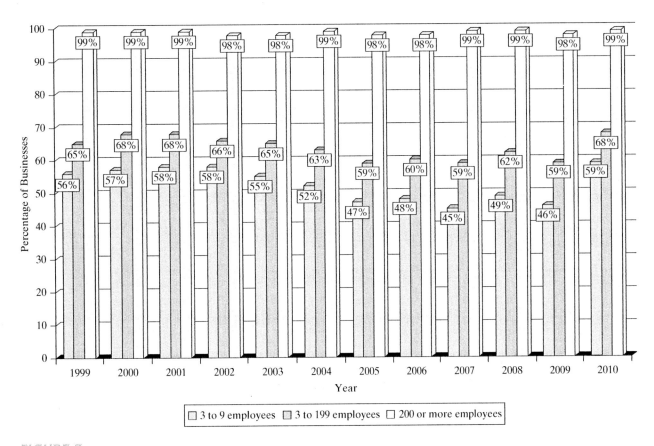

FIGURE 7
Percentage of Companies Offering Health Benefits by Company Size

Source: Employer Health Benefits: 2010 Summary of Findings, Kaiser Family Foundation and Health Research and Education Trust, p. 5.

really surprised by the high cost of health insurance and suddenly had a new appreciation for this corporate perk."[77]

Health insurance has become an extremely important benefit to most workers. Small companies that offer thorough health care coverage often find that it gives them an edge in attracting and retaining a quality workforce. In fact, 86 percent of business owners cite health care as the most important benefit to attracting and retaining quality workers.[78]

FIGURE 8
Average Annual Health Insurance Premiums for Family Coverage

Source: Employer Health Benefits: 2010 Summary of Findings, Kaiser Family Foundation and Health Research and Education Trust, p. 1.

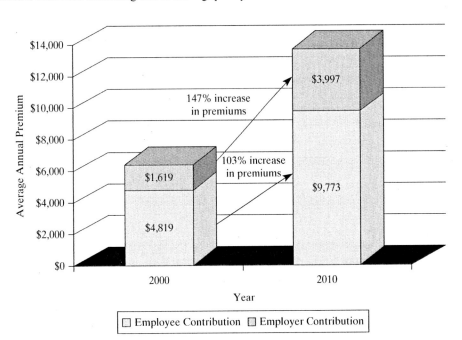

Jeff Harvey, CEO of Burgerville, a regional chain of 39 burger restaurants founded in Vancouver, Washington, in 1961 by George Propstra, recently began paying at least 90 percent of health insurance premiums for part-time employees who work at least 20 hours per week, a benefit that most food-service companies do not offer part-time employees. Even though the added benefit nearly doubled the 1,500-employee company's health care costs from $2.1 million annually to $4.1 million, Harvey says that the move actually has saved the company money by lowering its employee turnover rate and increasing employee productivity. Burgerville's employee turnover rate is less than half the industry average, a significant savings when replacing and training a restaurant worker costs on average $1,700. Harvey says the company is considering launching a wellness program to help employees lead healthier lifestyles and to lower health insurance claims.[79]

A key to providing proper health care coverage while keeping costs in check is to offer the benefits that are most important to your employees and to avoid spending money unnecessarily on coverage that does not apply to them. Although the Affordable Care Act, a bill passed in 2010 that is designed to provide health care coverage for a greater number of people, stands to change the mechanics of health care in the United States, employers face four basic health care options: traditional indemnity plans, managed care plans, health savings accounts, and self-insurance.

Traditional Indemnity Plans. Under these plans, employees choose their own health care providers, and the insurance company either pays the provider directly or reimburses employees for the covered amounts.

Managed Care Plans. As part of employers' attempts to put a lid on escalating health care costs, these plans have become increasingly popular. Three variations—the health maintenance organization (HMO), the preferred provider organization (PPO), and the point of service (POS)—are most common. An HMO is a prepaid health care arrangement under which employees must use health care providers who are employed by or are under contract with the HMO their company uses. Although they lower health care costs, employees have less freedom in selecting physicians under an HMO. Under a PPO, an insurance company negotiates discounts for health care with certain physicians and hospitals. If employees choose a health care provider from the approved list, they pay only a small fee for each office visit (often just $10 to $25). The insurance company pays the remainder. Employees may select a provider outside the PPO, but they pay more for the service. A POS is a hybrid of an HMO and a PPO that gives employees the freedom to select their health care providers (as with a PPO) and lowers costs (as with an HMO). As long as employees choose a primary care physician within the approved network, the POS will pay for that care and for care by specialists, even those outside the network, as long as the primary care physician makes the referral. PPOs are the most common managed care plans (53 percent of employers who offer health benefits use them), followed by POSs (25 percent) and HMOs (24 percent).[80]

Health Savings Accounts (HSAs). Created as part of a major Medicare overhaul in 2003, health savings accounts (HSAs) are similar to IRAs except employees' contributions are used for medical expenses rather than for retirement. An HSA is a special savings account coupled with a high-deductible (typically $1,000 to $5,000 for an individual) insurance policy that covers major medical expenses. Employees or employers contribute pre-tax dollars (up to a defined ceiling) from their paychecks into the fund and use them as they need to. Withdrawals from an HSA are not taxed as long as the money is used for approved medical expenses. Unused funds can accumulate indefinitely and earn tax-free interest. HSAs offer employees incentives to contain their health care costs, but the employer must choose both an insurance carrier to provide coverage and a custodial firm to manage employees' accounts. Although critics contend that consumer-driven plans push a greater portion of health care expenses onto employees, these plans continue to grow in popularity among small businesses because of their potential to rein in escalating costs. The average annual premium for an HSA for a small company is $4,454, which is 13.1 percent lower than the cost of traditional managed care plans.[81] Although self-employed individuals find HSAs attractive, employers are adding them to their menu of health care options for employees. More than 8 million employees are covered by HSAs, a significant increase from 1 million in 2005.[82]

Andrew Field, owner of PrintingforLess.com, a Web-based printing company, had seen health care costs for his company's 130 employees increase by double-digit rates year after year and decided to switch from a traditional plan to an HSA plan. The change allowed him to provide his employees with better, more flexible coverage and the freedom to decide how to spend their health care dollars without any increase in cost. Although PrintingforLess.com did encounter a few problems in making the switch, Field and his employees are pleased with the HSA. "We were worried that it might have some bad side effects," he says. "but it's better than we thought."[83]

Self-Insurance. As you learned earlier in this chapter, some business owners choose to insure themselves for health coverage rather than to incur the costs of fully insured plans offered by outsiders. The benefits of self-insurance include greater control over the plan's design and the coverage it offers, fewer paperwork and reporting requirements, and, in some cases, lower costs. The primary disadvantage, of course, is the possibility of having to pay large amounts to cover treatments for several employees' major illnesses at the same time, which can strain a small company's cash flow. Many self-insured businesses limit their exposure to such losses by purchasing stop-loss insurance, under which the business owner pays for health care expenses up to a predetermined point; beyond that point, the stop-loss policy takes over the expenses.

Another type of health-related coverage is **workers' compensation**, which is designed to cover employees who are injured on the job or who become sick as a result of a work environment. Worker's compensation is a mandatory insurance program; companies that fail to offer workers' compensation must pay out-of-pocket for workers' claims and face penalties from the state. Before passage of workers' compensation legislation in 1911, an employee injured on the job had to bring a lawsuit to prove the employer was liable for the worker's injury. Because of the red tape and expenses involved in these lawsuits, many employees never received compensation for job-related accidents and injuries. Although the details of coverage vary from state to state, workers' compensation laws require employers to purchase insurance that provides benefits and medical and rehabilitation costs for employees injured on the job. The amount of compensation an injured employee receives depends on a fixed schedule of payment benefits based on three factors: the wages or salary that the employee was earning at the time of the accident or injury, the seriousness of the injury, and the extent of the disability to the employee.

Only two states, New Jersey and Texas, do not require companies to purchase workers' compensation coverage once they reach a certain size (usually three or more employees). Usually, the state sets the rates businesses pay for workers' compensation coverage, and business owners purchase their coverage from private insurance companies. Rapidly escalating workers' compensation rates, driven in large part by rising medical expenses, have become a major concern for small businesses across the nation. Companies in Alaska face the highest workers' compensation costs in the nation.[84] McGraw's Custom Construction in Sitka, Alaska, saw its workers' compensation costs go from \$146,950 to \$315,110 in just 2 years![85] Rates vary by industry, business size, and the number of claims a company's workers make. For instance, workers' compensation premiums are higher for a timber cutting business than for a retail gift store. Table 3 shows the 10 occupations with the greatest number of injuries and illnesses. Whatever industry they are in, business owners can reduce their workers' compensation costs by improving their employees' safety records.

Core Systems, a plastic injection molding company based in Painesville, Ohio, was growing so fast that its accidents began to spiral out of control. Not only were employees being injured, but morale was down and workers' compensation costs were way up. In an effort to contain the rapidly rising costs, human resources director Maggine Fuentes, launched a safety system that combed through company records looking for accident and injury patterns and then focused on training and soliciting employee suggestions for improvement. The system made safety a priority at Core Systems and reduced both the number and the severity of accidents in the plant, which has lowered the company's workers' compensation cost by \$277,000 so far.[86]

TABLE 3 Ten Most Dangerous Occupations

Rank	Occupation	Percentage of Total Injuries and Illnesses
1	Nonconstruction laborers	7.4%
2	Truck drivers (heavy)	5.4%
3	Nursing aides and orderlies	4.1%
4	Construction workers	2.9%
5	Retail salespeople	2.7%
6	Janitors and cleaners	2.6%
7	Truck drivers (light)	2.6%
8	Maintenance and repair workers	1.9%
9	Registered nurses	1.8%
10	Maids and housekeeping cleaners	1.7%

Source: "Workplace Safety/Workers Comp," Insurance Information Institute, *www.iii.org/facts_statistics/workplace-safety-workers-comp.html.*

▶ ENTREPRENEURSHIP IN ACTION ▶

What Can We Do to Help You Stay Healthy?

In 1997, when Jason Crawforth started Treetop Tech, a software development company in Boise, Idaho, he did not offer company-sponsored health insurance because he believed that his small company could not afford the cost. He soon realized, however, that he could not afford *not* to offer health insurance. "We started losing potential employees because of that," he says. In 2000, Crawforth added health insurance coverage to his employees' benefits package, just in time to watch premiums skyrocket over the next decade.

Crawforth, like many small business owners, is struggling to cope with health insurance premiums that have increased by 114 percent since 2000, compared to an increase of just 27 percent in the consumer price index over the same period. According to a survey by Aflac Inc. and Accelerant Research, 62 percent of small business owners say it is more difficult to offer a strong benefits package than 1 year before, and 52 percent say they have reduced their health insurance coverage. Donna Partin, who owns three Merry Maids franchises, two in Pennsylvania and one in Florida, that employ a total of 50 workers, says that her company's health insurance premiums have tripled since 2000. "I'm paying more for less and less [coverage] every year," she says. Partin pays $5,000 per month to insure her employees in Pennsylvania, where only one-third of her workforce has opted for coverage. The others cannot afford their portion of the health insurance premium. Partin says that she cannot afford coverage for her employees

in Florida, something that causes her concern because her business requires trustworthy workers to go into clients' homes to clean. As health care insurance costs continue to escalate, Partin, like many small business owners, worries that she will be at a disadvantage in attracting and retaining quality workers if she has to pare back or even eliminate coverage.

Thomas Johnson, owner of Thomas A. Johnson Furniture, a company that builds custom, handmade furniture in Lynchburg, Virginia, emigrated from Ghana, West Africa, to the United States with just $20, a willingness to work hard, and a desire to own a business. Today, the master craftsman has eight employee apprentices who work beside him, learning to make fine furniture. Unable to afford the premiums for a group health insurance plan, Johnson pays out-of-pocket for his employees' medical expenses. Skilled woodworkers are difficult to find, and Johnson cannot afford to lose any of his employees, in whom he has invested thousands of hours of training. "My workers are part of my business and part of my family," he says. To him, paying their medical expenses is a matter of honor—and practicality—but it also is risky. By paying for his workers' medical expenses, Johnson may have set a precedent that could obligate him to pay for all of his employees' expenses—even in the case of a catastrophic illness that might cost hundreds of thousands of dollars to treat.

About 70 percent of health care costs arise from *preventable* chronic diseases, a fact that has led many businesses to implement wellness programs that are designed to put the brakes on cost increases by giving employees incentives to get and stay healthy by quitting smoking, maintaining an ideal weight, reducing stress, and exercising regularly. Employers typically pay between $100 and $300 per person per year in incentives, a small price to pay compared to the additional $16,000 lifetime health care costs associated with an employee who smokes. The same holds true for overweight employees; health care costs are $1,400 more per year for obese workers than those who maintain a healthy weight. One-third of small companies offer wellness programs that include onsite fitness centers or memberships for offsite fitness centers, smoking cessation programs, online tracking tools, onsite health checks, and other features. Not only do wellness programs improve employees' health, but they also produce an impressive return on investment—up to $6 on average for every $1 invested. Mike Faith, founder of Headsets.com in San Francisco, California, stocks the break room with healthy snacks and fresh fruit for his 52 employees. He also offers them subsidized gym memberships and help with smoking cessation, including free nicotine patches.

"You don't need to spend a lot of money on these programs," says Dan Dauphinee, operations manager at Northeastern Log Homes, a small business in Kenduskeag, Maine. Northeastern Log Homes recently created a walking trail for its 100 employees, who are encouraged to exercise during their breaks. The company also offers fruits and vegetables in its snack room at subsidized prices. Northeastern Log Homes gives employees who engage in its wellness program discounts on their portion of health insurance premiums. Components of the wellness program range from nutrition lectures to walking challenges. "When you look at a culture that has healthy, happy employees and your health insurance costs are not going up, that's the justification," says Dauphinee.

1. Is it ethical for companies to reduce their health care costs by offering employees incentives to get and stay healthy? Explain.
2. How much control should companies have over employees' lifestyles away from the workplace?

Sources: Based on Patricia B. Gray, "HealthCure," *FSB*, February 2009, pp. 57–65; Robert Langreth, "Healthy Bribes," *Forbes*, August 24, 2009, p. 72; Mark Henricks, "An Apple a Day . . ." *Entrepreneur*, March 2008, pp. 19–20; E. B. Solomont, "Companies Find Inexpensive Ways to Promote Wellness," *Workforce Management*, March 2009, *www.workforce.com/section/ benefits-compensation/feature/companies-find-inexpensive-ways-promote- wellness/index.html*; John Cummings, "Finding the ROI in Wellness Incentives," *Business Finance*, August 11, 2008, *http://businessfinancemag.com/article/ finding-roi-wellness-incentives-0811;* Simone Richards, "Small Businesses Struggle to Offer Healthcare," *Black Enterprise*, July 15, 2009, *www. blackenterprise.com/business/business-news/2009/07/15/small-businesses- struggle-to-offer-healthcare/.*

LIABILITY INSURANCE. One of the most common types of insurance coverage is liability insurance, which protects a business against losses resulting from accidents or injuries people suffer on the company's property, from its products or services, and damage the company causes to others' property. Most BOPs include basic liability coverage; however, the limits on the typical policy are not high enough to cover the potential losses many small business owners face. For example, one "slip-and-fall" case involving a customer who is injured by slipping and falling on a wet floor could easily exceed the standard limits on a basic BOP. Claims from customers injured by a company's product or service also are covered by its liability policy. Although most product liability lawsuits are settled out of court, the median award for those that go to court is nearly $2 million.[87]

Even though courts have dismissed them, some small companies have been targets of frivolous lawsuits because they are seen as easy targets. Frivolous lawsuits can cost a small company thousands of dollars to defend, however. Jin and Soo Chung, owners of Custom Cleaners in Washington, D.C., recently were hit with a $54 million lawsuit by a customer after the dry cleaner lost a pair of the customer's pants! The trial court ruled for Custom Cleaners, but plaintiff Roy Pearson filed an appeal, extending the legal nightmare for the small business owners, who incurred $83,000 in legal fees to defend themselves.[88] With jury awards in product liability cases often reaching into the millions of dollars, entrepreneurs who fail to purchase sufficient liability coverage may end up losing their businesses. Most insurance experts recommend purchasing a commercial general liability policy that provides coverage of at least $2 million to $3 million for the typical small business. As a result, many business owners find it necessary to purchase additional liability coverage for their companies.

Another important type of liability insurance for many small businesses is **professional liability insurance**, or **"errors and omissions" coverage**. This insurance protects against damage a business causes to customers or clients as a result of an error an employee makes or an employees' failure to take proper care and precautions. For instance, a land surveyor may miscalculate the location of a customer's property line. If the landowner relies on that

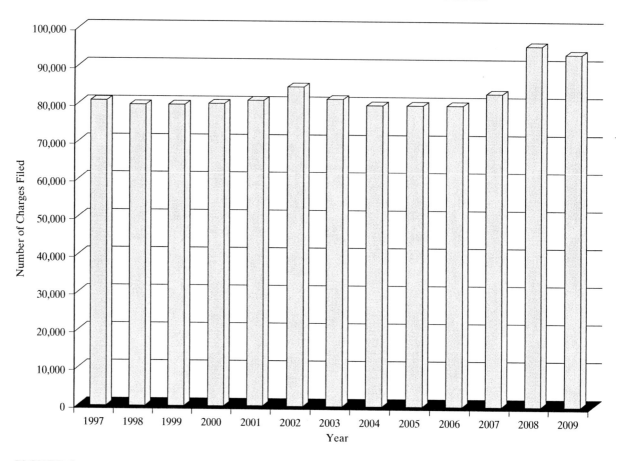

FIGURE 9
Number of Employment Charges Filed with EEOC

Source: Based on data from the Equal Employment Opportunity Commission, *www.eeoc.gov/eeoc/statistics/enforcement/all.cfm.*

property line to build a structure on what he thinks is his land and it turns out to be on his neighbor's land, the surveyor is liable for damages. Doctors, dentists, attorneys, and other professionals protect themselves through a similar kind of insurance, malpractice insurance, which protects them against the risk of lawsuits arising from errors in professional practice or judgment.

Employment practices liability (EPL) insurance provides protection against claims arising from charges of employment discrimination, improper discipline, wrongful termination, sexual harassment, and violations of the Americans with Disabilities Act, the Family and Medical Leave Act, and other employment legislation (see Figure 9). Although two-thirds of small business owners express concern that an employee will bring an EPL suit against them, only 1.2 percent carry EPL insurance.[89] Although most violations of these employment laws are not intentional but are the result of either carelessness or lack of knowledge, the company that violates them is still liable. Losing an employment practices liability case (employees win 58 percent of EPL cases) can be very expensive; the median jury award in EPL cases is $253,000.[90] Because they often lack full-time human resources professionals, small companies are especially vulnerable to charges of improper employment practices, making this type of insurance coverage all the more important to them. Seven employees at a franchised restaurant claimed that their supervisor had sexually harassed them by touching them inappropriately and making lewd comments and demands for sex. The young women complained about the harassment to the restaurant's general manager, who failed to investigate or act on their complaints. The restaurant owner negotiated an out-of-court settlement with the plaintiffs for $400,000, an amount that could force many small companies to close.[91]

Every business's insurance needs are somewhat unique, requiring owners to customize the insurance coverage they purchase. Entrepreneurs also must keep their insurance coverage updated as their companies grow; when companies expand, so do their insurance needs.

Controlling Insurance Costs

Small business owners face constantly rising insurance premiums. Entrepreneurs can take steps to lower insurance costs, however. To control the cost of insurance, owners should take the following steps:

1. *Pursue a loss-control program by making risk reduction a natural part of all employees' daily routine.* As discussed earlier in this chapter, risk reduction minimizes claims and eventually lowers premiums. Establishing a loss-control program means taking steps such as installing modern fire alarms, sprinkler systems, safety programs, and sophisticated security systems.

2. *Increase their policies' deductibles.* If a business can afford to handle minor losses, the owner can save money by raising the deductible to a level that protects the business against catastrophic events but, in effect, self-insures against minor losses. Business owners must determine the amount of financial exposure they can reasonably accept.

3. *Work with qualified professional insurance brokers or agents.* Business owners should do their homework before choosing insurance brokers or agents. This includes checking their reputation, credentials, and background by asking them to supply references.

4. *Work actively with brokers to make sure they understand business owners' particular needs.* Brokers need to know about entrepreneurs' businesses and objectives for insurance coverage. They can help only if they know their clients' needs and the degree of risk they are willing to take.

5. *Work with brokers to find competitive companies that want small companies' insurance business and have the resources to cover losses when they arise.* The price of the premium should never be an entrepreneur's sole criterion for selecting insurance. The rating of the insurance company should always be a primary consideration. What good is it to have paid low premiums if, after a loss, a business owner finds that the insurance company is unable to pay? Many small business owners learned costly lessons when their insurance companies, unable to meet their obligations, filed for bankruptcy protection.

6. *Utilize the resources of your insurance company.* Many insurers provide risk management inspections designed to help business owners assess the level of risk in their companies either for free or for a minimal fee. Smart entrepreneurs view their insurance companies as partners in their risk management efforts.

7. *Conduct a periodic insurance audit.* Reviewing your company's coverage annually can ensure that insurance coverage is adequate and can lead to big cost savings as well.

Profile

Keith Alper: Creative Products Group

Keith Alper, owner of Creative Products Group (CPG), a business that produces videos for *Fortune* 500 companies, was surprised to discover that CPG was wasting thousands of dollars on policies it did not need. Many employees were classified incorrectly for workers' compensation coverage, several policies duplicated the coverage of others, and the company was paying for auto insurance on four cars when it had only three! In all, Alper was able to shave more than $10,000 off of the company's $75,000 annual insurance bill.[92]

8. *Compile discrimination, harassment, hiring, and other employment polices into an employee handbook and train employees to use them.* Companies that take an active approach to avoiding illegal employment practices have less exposure to lawsuits and, therefore, may be able to negotiate lower premiums.

Since World War II, businesses have been and continue to be the principal suppliers of health insurance in our society. To control the cost of health insurance, small business owners should consider the following steps:

1. *Increase the dollar amount of employee contributions and the amount of the employee deductibles.* Neither option is desirable, but rising medical costs have resulted in individuals becoming more responsible for their own health insurance and self-insuring to cover high deductibles.

2. *Switch to PPOs, POS plans, or HMOs.* Higher premium costs have encouraged some small business owners to reevaluate PPOs, POS plans, and HMOs as alternatives to traditional

health insurance policies. Although some employees resent limitations on their choice of providers, PPOs, HMOs, and POS plans have become the primary vehicles for companies to provide health care coverage to their employees.

3. *Consider joining an insurance pool.* Small businesses can lower their insurance premiums by banding together to purchase coverage. In many states, chambers of commerce, trade associations, and other groups form insurance pools that small businesses can join, spreading risk over a larger number of employees. In Cleveland, Ohio, for example, about 14,000 small companies purchase health insurance for their employees through the Council of Smaller Enterprises, a division of the chamber of commerce, at rates that are 8 percent below those that the owners could negotiate individually.[93]

4. *Keep employees informed.* By giving employees information about the costs and the benefits of various treatment alternatives and medications, employers empower their workers to make informed decisions that can lower health care costs.

5. *Conduct a yearly utilization review.* A review may reveal that your employees' use of their policies is statistically lower, which may provide you leverage to negotiate lower premiums or to switch to an insurer that wants a business with your track record and offers lower premiums.

6. *Make sure your company's health plan fits your employees' needs.* One of best ways to keep health care costs in check is to offer only those benefits that employees actually need. Getting employee input is essential to the process.

7. *Create a wellness program for all employees.* We have all heard the old adage that an ounce of prevention is worth a pound of cure, but when it comes to the high cost of medical expenses, this is especially true! Companies that have created wellness programs report cost savings of up to $6 for every $1 they invest. Employees involved in wellness programs not only incur lower health care expenses, but they also tend to be more productive as well. "Companies are reforming their own health care costs by recognizing that healthy workers cost less, are more productive, and are better for the company as a whole," says the president of a nonprofit health and productivity company.[94] Providing a wellness program does not mean building an expensive gym, however. Instead, it may be as simple as providing routine checkups from a nurse, incentives for quitting smoking, weight-loss counseling, or after-work athletic games that involve as many employees as possible. One recent study reports that 71 percent of companies offer their employees financial incentives to participate in wellness programs.[95]

Jon Wheeler, CEO of Wheeler Interests, a real estate management company based in Virginia Beach, Virginia, incorporated an employee wellness program into his business from the outset. He transformed empty office space into a small gym, brought in a personal trainer, and offered smoking cessation and other wellness programs for his employees. Wheeler also gives employees a mid-day kayaking break and allows them to set their own vacation times as long as they get their work done.[96]

8. *Conduct a safety audit.* Reviewing the workplace with a safety professional to look for ways to improve its safety has the potential for saving some businesses thousands of dollars a year in medical expenses and workers' compensation claims. The National Safety Council offers helpful information on creating a safe work environment.

9. *Create a safety manual and use it.* Incorporating the suggestions for improving safety into a policy manual and then using it will reduce the number of on-the-job accidents. Training employees, even experienced ones, in proper safety procedures is also effective.

10. *Create a safety team.* Assigning the responsibility for workplace safety to workers themselves can produce amazing results. When one small manufacturer turned its safety team over to employees, the plant's lost time due to accidents plummeted to zero for 3 years straight! The number of accidents is well below what it was when managers ran the safety team, and managers say that's because employees now "own" safety in the plant.

The key to controlling insurance costs is aggressive prevention. Entrepreneurs who actively manage the risks to which their companies are exposed find that they can provide the insurance coverage their businesses need at a reasonable cost. Finding the right insurance coverage to protect their businesses is no easy matter for business owners. The key is to identify the risks that represent the greatest threat to a company and then to develop a plan for minimizing their risk of occurrence and insuring against them if they do.

Chapter Review

1. Explain the factors necessary for a strong family business.
   - Nearly 90 percent of all companies in the United States are family owned. Family businesses generate 64 percent of the U.S. gross domestic product, account for 62 percent of employment, and pay 65 percent of all wages. Several factors are important to maintaining a strong family business, including shared values, shared power, tradition, a willingness to learn, behaving like families, and strong family ties.

2. Understand the exit strategy options available to an entrepreneur.
   - Family business owners wanting to step down from their companies can sell to outsiders, sell to insiders, or transfer ownership to the next generation of family members. Common tools for selling to insiders (employees or managers) include sale for cash plus a note, leveraged buyouts (LBOs), and employee stock ownership plans (ESOPs).
   - Transferring ownership to the next generation of family members requires a business owner to develop a sound management succession plan.

3. Discuss the stages of management succession.
   - Unfortunately, 70 percent of first-generation businesses fail to survive into the second generation, and, of those that do survive, only 12 percent make it to the third generation. One of the primary reasons for this lack of continuity is poor succession planning. Planning for management succession protects not only the founder's, successor's, and company's financial resources, but it also preserves what matters most in a successful business: its heritage and tradition. Management succession planning can ensure a smooth transition only if the founder begins the process early on.

4. Explain how to develop an effective management succession plan.
   - A succession plan is a crucial element in transferring a company to the next generation. Preparing a succession plan involves five steps: (1) Select the successor. (2) Create a survival kit for the successor. (3) Groom the successor. (4) Promote an environment of trust and respect. (5) Cope with the financial realities of estate taxes.
   - Entrepreneurs can rely on several tools in their estate planning, including buy-sell agreements, lifetime gifting, trusts, estate freezes, and family limited partnerships.

5. Understand the four risk management strategies.
   - Four risk strategies are available to the small business: avoiding, reducing, anticipating, and transferring risk.

6. Discuss the basics of insurance for small businesses.
   - Insurance is a risk transfer strategy. Not every potential loss can be insured. Insurability requires that it be possible to estimate the amount of actual loss being insured against and identify the specific risk and that there be enough policyholders to spread out the risk.
   - The four major types of insurance small businesses need are property and casualty insurance, life and disability insurance, health insurance and workers' compensation coverage, and liability insurance.
   - Property and casualty insurance covers a company's tangible assets, such as buildings, equipment, inventory, machinery, signs, and others that have been damaged, destroyed, or stolen. Specific types of property and casualty insurance include extra expense coverage, business interruption insurance, surety insurance, marine insurance, crime insurance, fidelity insurance, and forgery insurance.
   - Life and disability insurance also comes in various forms. Life insurance protects a family and a business against the loss of income and security in the event of the owner's death. Disability insurance, like life insurance, protects an individual in the event of unexpected and often very expensive disabilities.
   - Health insurance is designed to provide adequate health care for business owners and their employees. The most common managed health plans are preferred provider organizations (PPOs), point of service (POS) operations, and health maintenance

organizations (HMOs). Workers' compensation is designed to cover employees who are injured on the job or who become sick as a result of a work environment.

- Liability insurance protects a business against losses resulting from accidents or injuries people suffer on the company's property, from its products or services, and damage the company causes to others' property. Typical liability coverage includes professional liability insurance or "errors and omissions" coverage, which protects against damage a business causes to customers or clients as a result of an error an employee makes or an employee's failure to take proper care and precautions. Doctors, dentists, attorneys, and other professionals protect themselves through a similar kind of insurance, malpractice insurance, which protects them against the risk of lawsuits arising from errors in professional practice or judgment. Employment practices liability insurance provides protection against claims arising from charges of employment discrimination, sexual harassment, and violations of the Americans with Disabilities Act, the Family and Medical Leave Act, and other employment legislation.

Discussion Questions

1. What factors must be present for a strong family business?
2. Discuss the stages of management succession in a family business.
3. What steps are involved in building a successful management succession plan?
4. What exit strategies are available to entrepreneurs wanting to step down from their businesses?
5. What strategies can business owners employ to reduce estate and gift taxes?
6. Can insurance eliminate risk? Why or why not?
7. Outline the four basic risk management strategies and give an example of each.
8. What problems occur most frequently with a risk anticipation strategy?
9. What is insurance? How can insurance companies bear such a large risk burden and still be profitable?
10. Describe the requirements for insurability.
11. Briefly describe the various types of insurance coverage available to small business owners.
12. What kinds of insurance coverage would you recommend for the following businesses?
    a. A manufacturer of steel beams
    b. A retail gift shop
    c. A small accounting firm
    d. A limited liability partnership involving three dentists
13. What can business owners do to keep their insurance costs under control?

Business Plan Pro

Family-owned businesses dominate the landscape of U.S. companies, but they face a dangerous threat from within: management succession. Most family businesses fail to survive into the second generation and beyond. The problem usually is the result of a lack of planning for a smooth transition from one generation of management to the next. The business plan can assist in this process.

On the Web

Under the tab on the Companion Web site at *www. pearsonhigh-ered.com/scarborough* is a list of online resources that deal with succession planning and risk management. You will find resources that address issues related to managing a family business, planning for management succession, and managing business risk.

In the Software

If the business has issues regarding succession planning, capture those thoughts in your plan. This is also an opportunity to discuss risk management and exit strategies. What types of insurance coverage does your company require? Be sure to incorporate the cost of insurance coverage in your financial forecasts. Remember: You can add or modify outline topics within Business Plan Pro by right-clicking the outline in the left-hand navigation of the software.

Building Your Business Plan

One of the best ways to prevent a family-owned business from becoming just another management succession failure statistic is to develop a management succession plan early on in the life of the company. The business plan can be a vehicle to help with this discussion and document the plan to make this transition. The plan can also enable an entrepreneur to document ideas and plans regarding risk management and potential exit strategies.

Endnotes

1. "Facts About Family Business," S. Dale High Center for Family Business at Elizabethtown College, *www.centerforfamilybusiness.org/facts.asp;* MassMutual Family Business Network, *www.massmutual.com/fbn/index.htm;* "Family Business Facts," Family Business Institute, *www.ffi.org/looking/fbfacts_us.pdf.*
2. James Lea, "Five Ways Family Firms Can Thrive," Family Business Bizjournals.com, February 2, 2004, *www.bizjournals.com/extraedge/consultants/family_business/2004/02/02/column180.html.*
3. Thomas L. Kalaris, "Family Business: In Safe Hands?" *Barclays Wealth Insights,* 2009, p. 3.
4. "Country Comparison: GDP," *World Fact Book,* Central Intelligence Agency, *www.cia.gov/library/publications/the-world-factbook/rankorder/2001rank.html;* "A $238 Million Morning for the Walton Family," Wal-Mart Watch, March 5, 2009, *http://walmartwatch.com/blog/archives/a_238_million_dollar_morning_for_the_walton_family/;* "Wal-Mart Stores Inc," *CNNMoney,* November 10, 2010, *http://money.cnn.com/quote/quote.html?symb=WMT.*
5. Tony Taylor, "Small Businesses Show Relative Strength," *GSA Business,* September 4, 2006, p. 22; Jim Lee, "Family Firm Performance: Further Evidence," *Family Business Review,* June 2006, Vol. 19, No. 2, pp. 103–114.
6. "Research Reveals: Family Firms Perform Better," *Family Business Advisor,* March 2003, Vol. 12, No. 3, p. 1.
7. Nicholas Stein, "The Age of the Scion," *Fortune,* April 2, 2001, pp. 121–128.
8. Amol Sharma, "Reliance Rivals Vow to Play Nice," *Wall Street Journal,* May 24, 2010, *http://online.wsj.com/article/SB10001424052748704226004575262281639883648.html.*
9. "Facts and Perspectives on Family Business Around the World: United States," Family Business Institute, *www.ffi.org/looking/fbfacts_us.pdf.*
10. Ibid.
11. Ibid.
12. Peter Schworm, "End of a 378-Year Era," *Boston.com,* July 27, 2010, *www.boston.com/news/local/new_hampshire/articles/2010/07/27/nations_oldest_running_family_farm_put_on_market_in_nh/.*
13. *Kin in the Game,* PriceWaterhouseCoopers Family Business Survey, 2010–2011, p. 21.
14. Ibid.
15. "Facts and Perspectives on Family Business Around the World: United States," Family Business Institute, *www.ffi.org/looking/fbfacts_us.pdf.*
16. Sharon Nelton, "Ten Keys to Success in Family Business," *Nation's Business,* April 1991, pp. 44–45.
17. Toddi Gunter, "Moving Up to the Top of a Family Empire," *Wall Street Journal,* June 22, 2010, p. D4.
18. "Family Members Fight over Control of Texas Pete Hot Sauce Empire," *Greenville News,* May 17, 1997, p. 11D.
19. Stein, "The Age of the Scion," p. 124.
20. Eugenia Levenson, "Road Warrior," *Fortune,* November 27, 2006, p. 276; Hsiao-Ching Chao, "Maximilian Riedel Has the Stemware Industry in the Palm of His Hand," *Seattle Post-Intelligencer,* April 13, 2005, *http://seattlepi.nwsource.com/food/219827_riedel13.html;* Anthony Giglio, "Glass Menagerie," *Boston Magazine,* April 2006, *www.bostonmagazine.com/dining_food_wine/articles/boston_magazine_liquids_specialty_wineglasses/.*
21. Stein, "The Age of the Scion," p. 124.
22. Mike Armstrong, "PhillyInc: There's a Twist in the Pennsylvania Pretzel-Merger Saga," *Philly.com,* July 23, 2010, *www.philly.com/philly/business/homepage/20100723_PhillyInc__There_s_a_twist_in_the_Pennsylvania_pretzel-merger_saga.html.*
23. Bo Burlingham, "Why a CEO Needs to Have a Plan B," *Inc.,* May 2009, *www.inc.com/magazine/20090501/why-a-ceo-needs-to-have-a-plan-b.html.*
24. "Employee Ownership and Corporate Performance," National Center for Employee Ownership, *www.nceo.org/library/esop_perf.html.*
25. Paul J. Lim, "Putting Your House in Order," *U.S. News & World Report,* December 10, 2001, p. 38.
26. Lydia Dishman, "Keys to the Kingdom," *Black Box,* Quarter 1, 2010, pp. 67–71.
27. Claire Cain Miller, "Chapter Two," *Forbes,* December 25, 2006, p. 72.
28. Carol Tice, "Lost in Transition," *Entrepreneur,* November 2006, p. 102.
29. TCPN Quotations Center, *www.cyber-nation.com/victory/quotations/subject/quotes_subjects_f_to_h.html#f.*
30. Andy Bluestone, "Succession Planning Isn't Just About Money," *Nation's Business,* November 1996, p. 6.
31. Shelly Branch, "Mom Always Liked You Best," *Your Company,* April/May 1998, pp. 26–38.
32. Taylor, "Small Businesses Show Relative Strength," pp. 22, 24.
33. Patricia Schiff Estess, "Heir Raising," *Entrepreneur,* May 1996, pp. 80–82.
34. Tice, "Lost in Transition," pp. 101–103.
35. Jacquelyn Lynn, "What Price Successor?" *Entrepreneur,* November 1999, p. 146.
36. Craig E. Aronoff and John L. Ward, "Why Continue Your Family Business," *Nation's Business,* March 1998, pp. 72–74.
37. Jeremy Quittner, "Creating a Legacy," *BusinessWeek,* June 25, 2007, *www.businessweek.com/magazine/content/07_26/b4040443.htm?chan=search.*
38. Lee Smith, "The Next Generation," *Your Company,* October 1999, pp. 36–46.
39. "New Nationwide Survey Points to Bright Spot in American Economy—Family-Owned Businesses," MassMutual Financial Group, *www.massmutual.com/mmfg/about/pr_2003/01_22_03.html.*
40. Brett Pulley, "Murdoch Son Also Rises as Shareholders Study CEO Succession," *Bloomberg,* October 22, 2010, *www.bloomberg.com/news/2010-10-22/murdoch-son-also-rising-as-shareholders-focus-on-news-corp-ceo-succession.html.*
41. Annetta Miller, "You Can't Take It with You," *Your Company,* April 1999, pp. 28–34.
42. "Family Business Facts," Family Business Institute.
43. Frank Silverstein, "Daddy's Cowgirl Takes Over the Rodeo Business," MSNBC, August 30, 2009, *www.msnbc.msn.com/id/32573940/ns/business-small_business;* Courtney Elam, "Kirsten Vold," Harry Vold Rodeo Company, *www.harryvoldrodeo.com/staff.html.*
44. John Warrillow, "Leave the Business to the Kids? Maybe Not," *Wall Street Journal,* June 10, 2010, *http://online.wsj.com/article/SB10001424052748704575304575296523166009344.html.*
45. Karen E. Klein, "Succession Planning Without an Heir," *BusinessWeek,* June 20, 2007, *www.businessweek.com/smallbiz/content/jun2007/sb20070620_135303.htm?chan=search.*
46. Sharon Nelton, "Why Women Are Chosen to Lead," *Nation's Business,* April 1999, p. 51.
47. "New Nationwide Survey Points to Bright Spot in American Economy—Family-Owned Businesses," MassMutual Financial Group.
48. Dick Patten, "The Death Tax Is Kiiling Family Businesses," *Daily Caller,* October 8, 2010, *http://dailycaller.com/2010/10/08/the-death-tax-is-killing-family-businesses/;* Amanda Hill, "Estate Taxes Could Mean 'Death' of Family Farms and Ranches," *Texas Agriculture News,* September 27, 2010, *www.nodeathtax.org/news/estate-tax-could-mean-death-of-family-farms-and-ranches.*
49. Brad Hamilton and Jeane MacIntosh, "Death'$ Perfect Timing," *New York Post,* July 14, 2010, *www.nypost.com/p/news/local/death_perfect_timing_NusLyGlMu8cn8kyepprVJP?CMP=OTC-rss&FEEDNAME=.*
50. Patten, "The Death Tax Is Killing Family Businesses."
51. Quittner, "Creating a Legacy."
52. Joan Szabo, "Spreading the Wealth," *Entrepreneur,* July 1997, pp. 62–64.
53. Gay Jervey, "Family Ties," *FSB,* March 2006, p. 60.
54. Ibid.; Tom Herman, "Court Ruling Bolsters Estate Planning Tool," *Wall Street Journal,* May 27, 2004, p. D1.
55. Quittner, "Creating a Legacy."
56. William J. Dennis, "National Small Business Poll: Disasters," *National Federation of Independent Businesses,* 2004, Vol. 4, No. 5, pp. 5–6.
57. Joseph King, "Disasters Highlight Need for Business Continuity Planning," Institute for Business & Home Safety, September 7, 2010, *www.disastersafety.org/newsroom/view.asp?id=13291&Mode=List;* Emily Maltby, "Readying for the Worst," *Wall Street Journal,* September 9, 2009, *http://online.wsj.com/article/SB125250249415695553.html.*
58. Daniel Tynan, "In Case of Emergency," *Entrepreneur,* April 2003, p. 60.
59. Sarah E. Needleman, "Lights Out Means Lost Sales," *Wall Street Journal,* July 22, 2010, p. B6.
60. Elizabeth Hockerman, "When to Self-Insure?" *Small Business Times,* May 12, 2006, *www.biztimes.com/news/2006/5/12/when-to-self-insure.*
61. Jeanne Lee and Brandi Stewart, "Build Your Own Insurance Company," *FSB,* September 2007, pp. 28–31.
62. Tiana Velez, "A Home Business Needs Insurance," *Arizona Daily Star,* June 5, 2006, *www.azstarnet.com/allheadlines/132077.*

63. Kimberly Lankford, "Weird Insurance," *Kiplinger's Personal Finance Magazine*, October 1998, pp. 113–116.

64. "Costa Coffee Taster: One of the 10 Weirdest Insurance Policies," *The Telegraph*, March 9, 2009, *www.telegraph.co.uk/finance/personalfinance/insurance/specialrisks/4962817/Costa-Coffee-taster-Ten-of-the-weirdest-insurance-policies.html;* "Costa's Coffee Taster Has Tongue Insured for £10 Million," *The Telegraph*, March 9, 2009, *www.telegraph.co.uk/foodanddrink/foodanddrinknews/4957333/Costa-Coffees-taster-has-tongue-insured-for-10-million.html.*

65. John Fried, "Having Fun Yet?" *Inc.*, March 2006, pp. 75–77; "Incredible Adventures: Our Story," Incredible Adventures, *www.incredible-adventures.com/about_us.html;* Esther Dyson, "I Live and Die by Waivers," Esther Dyson's Flight School, May 11, 2007, *www.edventure.com/flightschool/blog/?p=4.*

66. Joyce M. Rosenberg, "Preparing a Disaster Plan Gets Serious," *Los Angeles Times,* August 16, 2007, *www.latimes.com/business/la-fi-smalldisaster16aug16,1,4272739.story?coll=la-headlines-business&ctrack=1&cset=true;* "Famed Restaurant Reopens Today," *Greenville News*, October 1, 2006, p. 4B.

67. Larry Kanter, "Smart Questions for Your Insurance Agent," *Inc.*, August 2006, p. 40; Michele Marchetti, "Thrown Off Track," *FSB*, February 2004, pp. 66–69.

68. Heidi Ernst, "The Best Line of Defense," Advertising Insert, *FSB*, July/August 2007, p. 80.

69. Jan Norman, "Business Disaster Can Strike at Any Time," *Greenville News*, April 4, 2004, p. E1.

70. Ilan Mochari, "A Security Blanket for Your Web Site," *Inc.*, December 2000, pp. 133–134.

71. Andrew Smyth, "Council for Disability Awareness Launches Consumer Website," *The Insurance Policy*, November 3, 2006, *www.theinsurancepolicy.com/new_insurance_agents/disability_insurance/.*

72. "Issues: Health Care Reform," National Federation of Independent Businesses, *www.nfib.com/issues-elections/healthcare.*

73. Kate Pickert, "The Unsustainable U.S. Healthcare System," *Time,* February 4, 2010, *http://swampland.blogs.time.com/2010/02/04/the-unsustainable-u-s-health-care-system/;* "Health Care Insurance Costs," National Coalition on Health Care, *www.nchc.org/facts/cost.shtml.*

74. *Employer Health Benefits 2010 Summary of Findings*, Kaiser Family Foundation and Health Research and Educational Trust, p. 5.

75. Ibid., p. 40.

76. Daniel Wityk, "Small Business Health Insurance," National Center for Policy Analysis, February 11, 2009, p. 1.

77. Eileen Figure Sandlin, "Finding Health Insurance as a Start-up," *Entrepreneur*, October 2006, *www.entrepreneur.com/management/insurance/typesofinsurance/article168504.html.*

78. *Intuit Payroll Survey 2009*, Intuit, *http://quickbooks.blogs.com/Intuit%20Payroll%20Survey%20-%20One%20Sheet.pdf*, p. 3.

79. Sarah E. Needleman, "Burger Chain's Health Care Recipe," *Wall Street Journal*, August 31, 2009, *http://online.wsj.com/article/SB125149100886467705.html.*

80. *Employer Health Benefits 2010 Survey*, Kaiser Family Foundation and Health Research and Educational Trust, p. 62.

81. Ibid., p. 15.

82. "Census Shows 8 Million People Covered by HSA/High-Deductible Health Plans," America's Health Insurance Plans, Center for Policy Research, January 2009, p. 4; *Behind the Numbers: Medical Cost Trends for 2010*, PriceWaterhouseCoopers, Health Research Institute, 2010, p. 7.

83. Colleen DeBaise, "Small Business Owners Try HSAs to Trim Health Costs," *Smart Money*, July 6, 2007, *www.smartmoney.com/smallbiz/index.cfm?story=20060511.*

84. "Workers' Compensation Insurance: The Role of State Funds, Market Trends, and Economic Influences," Insurance Information Institute, October 12, 2010, p. 16.

85. Greg O'Claray, "Alaska Needs Workers' Compensation Reform Now," National Federation of Independent Businesses, March 14, 2005, *www.nfib.com/object/IO_20952.html.*

86. Aaron Dalton, "Best Practices: Rapid Recovery," *IndustryWeek*, March 1, 2005, *www.industryweek.com/ReadArticle.aspx?ArticleId=10001.*

87. "Litigiousness," Insurance Information Institute, 2010, *www.iii.org/facts_statistics/litigiousness.html.*

88. Marc Fisher, "Judge Who Seeks Millions for Lost Pants Has His (Emotional) Day in Court," *Washington Post*, June 13, 2007, *www.washingtonpost.com/wp-dyn/content/article/2007/06/12/AR2007061201667.html;* "Dry Cleaner Raises Enough Cash to Pay Legal Fees," *WUSA9.com*, August 13, 2007, *www.wusa9.com/news/news_article.aspx?storyid=61690.*

89. "Employment Practices Liability Awareness Lacking for Some Small Business Owners," InsuranceNewsNet, February 3, 2010, *http://insurancenewsnet.com/article.aspx?id=157763.*

90. "Employment Law: Jury Awards, Trends, and Statistics," Thomas Fenner Woods Agency, November 2010, *www.tfwinsurance.com/news/11_2010/nl_employeem_9.php.*

91. "Employment Practices Liability Insurance for Restaurants," Restaurant Association of Maryland, October 2009, *www.marylandrestaurants.com/membership/foodserv_benefits/documents/09-199RAMEPLforRestaurants.pdf.*

92. Ilan Mochari, "Bug Your Broker," *Inc.*, August 2000, pp. 127–128.

93. Patricia B. Gray, "Health Care," *FSB*, February 2009, pp. 57–65.

94. Susan Caminiti, "Keeping America Fit," *Fortune*, May 3, 2010, p. S1.

95. Patricia F. Weisberg, "Wellness Programs: Legal Requirements and Risks," *Workforce Management*, March 2010, *www.workforce.com/section/legal/feature/wellness-programs-legal-requirements-risks/.*

96. Karene Spaeder, "Shape Up," *Entrepreneur*, September 2008, p. 26.

The Legal Environment: Business Law and Government Regulation

The welfare of the people is the ultimate law.

—Cicero

A wise and frugal government, which shall leave men free to regulate their own pursuits of industry and improvement, and shall not take from the mouth of labor the bread it has earned—this is the sum of good government.

—Thomas Jefferson

Learning Objectives

Upon completion of this chapter, you will be able to:

1 Explain the basic elements required to create a valid, enforceable contract.

2 Outline the major components of the Uniform Commercial Code governing sales contracts.

3 Discuss the protection of intellectual property rights using patents, trademarks, and copyrights.

4 Explain the basics of the law of agency.

5 Explain the basics of bankruptcy law.

6 Explain some of the government regulations affecting small businesses, including those governing trade practices, consumer protection, consumer credit, and the environment.

From Chapter 22 of *Effective Small Business Management: An Entrepreneurial Approach*, 10/e. Norman M. Scarborough.

The legal environment in which small businesses operate is becoming more complex, and entrepreneurs must understand the basics of business law if they are to avoid legal entanglements. Situations that present potential legal problems arise every day in most small businesses, although the majority of small business owners never recognize them. Routine transactions with customers, suppliers, employees, government agencies, and others have the potential to develop into costly legal problems. For example, a manufacturer of lawnmowers might face a lawsuit if a customer injures himself while using the product, or a customer who slips on a wet floor while shopping could sue the retailer for negligence. A small manufacturer who reneges on a contract for a needed raw material when she finds a better price elsewhere may be open to a breach of contract suit. Even when they win a lawsuit, small businesses often lose because the costs of defending themselves can run quickly into thousands of dollars, depleting their already scarce resources.

ENTREPRENEURIAL
Profile

Tami Cromar: My Dough Girl/RubySnap

General Mills, the giant food company that owns Pillsbury and its iconic Dough Boy character, forced Tami Cromar, owner of a tiny cookie bakery, My Dough Girl, to find a new name for her retro-themed business, which is located in Salt Lake City, Utah. General Mills, with annual sales of more than $16 billion, sent Cromar a cease-and-desist letter that threatened legal action because her company's name infringed on Pillsbury's trademark and diminished its value. Cromar, whose cookie company generates annual sales of $100,000, lacked the resources for a legal battle. She complied and changed the name of her company to RubySnap. "Life isn't fair, and sometimes you just have to figure out a solution and move on," she says. Cromar says that she never considered the Pillsbury Doughboy when she selected the original name for her business; instead, she drew her inspiration from a comment by her husband, who referred to her as "my dough girl." Cromar thought the name fit well with the cookie company's retro theme, which uses World War II era pinup girls reminiscent of those that adorned the noses of U.S. airplanes in World War II. Explaining General Mills' action, a spokesman says, "We needed to protect our trademarks—and we did."[1]

Even if small companies have the resources to endure a legal battle, lawsuits are bothersome distractions that prevent entrepreneurs from focusing their energy on running their businesses. In addition, one big judgment against a small company in a legal case could force it out of business. Judgments, the financial penalties that a company must pay if it loses a lawsuit, take three forms: compensatory, consequential, and punitive damages. As their name implies, **compensatory damages** are the monetary damages that are designed to place the plaintiff in the same position he or she would have been in had the contract been performed. In other words, compensatory damages require the defendant to pay the actual amount of loss the plaintiff incurred because of the defendant's actions. Suppose that a small manufacturer creates a contract to deliver 1,000 plastic barrels for $80 per unit by a particular date. If it fails to do so and the customer must purchase the barrels from another supplier for $88 per unit and pay an additional $500 for rush delivery, the customer's compensatory damages are $8,500 (1,000 barrels × $8 price difference, plus $500 rush delivery charges). **Consequential damages** are awarded to offset the losses suffered by the plaintiff that go beyond simple compensatory damages because of lasting effects of the damage. If the customer in the previous example lost $15,000 in sales because it did not receive the barrels on time, it could request consequential damages in that amount. For a party to recover consequential damages, the breaching party must have known the consequences of the breach. Courts typically award **punitive damages** in cases in which the defendant engages in intentionally wrongful behavior or behavior that is so negligent or reckless that it is considered intentional. As the name suggests, punitive damages are intended to punish the wrongdoer. The due process clause of the fourteenth amendment to the U.S. Constitution prohibits grossly excessive punitive awards, and many states impose limits on punitive damages in court cases.

Profile

*Mark Volper and Boris
and Marina Smordinsky:
Amerigraphics*

Mark Volper and Boris and Marina Smordinsky owned Amerigraphics, a printing and graphic design company in Sherman Oaks, California, where they leased first-floor space from a landlord. The entrepreneurs had property insurance and business interruption insurance with the Mercury Casualty Company when a broken hot water heater on the second floor flooded their business, destroying almost all of the company's equipment and materials. Volper filed a preliminary claim with Mercury for $43,000, but Mercury paid Amerigraphics only $10,000 toward the loss. After completing a valuation of the damage, Volper filed a claim for $73,000 under the property insurance policy and $59,467 of business expenses under the business interruption policy. Two years later, Mercury sent Amerigraphics a check for $23,000 as "payment in full" for its losses. Amerigraphics sued Mercury for breach of contract and of good faith and fair dealing. A jury ruled in Amerigraphic's favor and awarded the small company compensatory damages of $130,000 and punitive damages of $3 million. A judge later reduced the punitive damages to $1.7 million, 10 times the amount of compensatory damages. A court of appeals later reduced the punitive damages further, to $500,000, 3.8 times the amount of compensatory damages.[2]

Small business owners should know the basics of the laws that govern business practices to minimize the chances that their decisions and actions lead to costly lawsuits. This chapter is not designed to make you an expert in business law or the regulations that govern businesses, but rather to make you aware of the fundamental legal issues that every business owner should know. Entrepreneurs should consult their attorneys for advice on legal questions involving specific situations.

The Law of Contracts

1. Explain the elements required to create a valid, enforceable contract.

Contract law governs the rights and obligations among the parties to an agreement (contract). It is a body of laws that affects virtually every business relationship. A **contract** is simply a legally binding agreement. It is a promise or a set of promises for the breach of which the law gives a remedy, or the performance of which the law enforces. A contract arises from an agreement, and it creates an obligation among the parties involved. Although almost everyone has the capacity to enter into a contractual agreement (freedom of contract), not every contract is valid and enforceable. A **valid contract** has four elements:

1. *Agreement.* An agreement is composed of a valid offer from one party that is accepted by the other.
2. *Consideration.* Consideration is something of legal (not necessarily economic) value that the parties exchange as part of their bargain.
3. *Contractual capacity.* The parties must be adults capable of understanding the consequences of their agreement.
4. *Legality.* The parties' contract must be for a legal purpose.

In addition, to be enforceable, a contract must meet two supplemental requirements: genuineness of assent and form. *Genuineness of assent* is a test to make sure that the parties' agreement is genuine and not subject to problems such as fraud, misrepresentation, or mistakes. *Form* involves the writing requirement for certain types of contracts. Although not every contract must be in writing to be enforceable, the law does require some contracts to be evidenced by a writing.

Agreement

Agreement requires a "meeting of the minds" and is created by an offer and an acceptance. One party must make an offer to another, who must accept that offer. Agreement is governed by the **objective theory of contracts**, which states that a party's intention to create a contract is measured by outward facts—words, conduct, and circumstances—rather than by subjective, personal intentions. When settling contract disputes, courts interpret the objective facts surrounding the contract from the perspective of an imaginary reasonable person. Agreement requires that one of the parties to a contract make an offer and the other an acceptance.

Klick-Lewis, a car dealership, offered a new Chevrolet Beretta as a prize to any person who hit a hole-in-one on the ninth hole of a golf tournament. It displayed the car at the tee box of the ninth hole with a sign saying, "HOLE-IN-ONE Wins this 1988 Chevrolet Beretta GI Courtesy of Klick-Lewis Buick-Chevrolet-Pontiac $49.00 OVER FACTORY INVOICE in Palmyra." Amos Carbaugh was playing in the East End Open Golf Tournament and scored a hole-in-one on the ninth hole, but when he attempted to claim the prize, Klick-Lewis refused to sell him the car at $49.00 over invoice. The dealer said that it had offered the car as a prize in another golf tournament that had taken place 2 days earlier and that it had simply neglected to remove the car and the sign before the tournament in which Carbaugh was playing. Carbaugh filed a lawsuit against Klick-Lewis and won the right to buy the car at $49.00 over invoice. The court said that based on the objective theory of contracts, an imaginary reasonable person in Carbaugh's position would have believed that the dealership was making an offer, citing the presence of the sign, the car, and no mention of a specific golf tournament. Klick-Lewis's subjective intent was irrelevant.[3]

OFFER. An **offer** is a promise or commitment to do or refrain from doing some specified thing in the future. For an offer to stand there must be an intention to be bound by it. The terms of the offer must be defined and reasonably certain, and the offeror (the party making the offer) must communicate the offer to the offeree (the party to whom the offer is made). The offeror must genuinely intend to make an offer, and the offer's terms must be definite, not vague. The following terms must either be expressed or be capable of being implied in an offer: the parties involved, the identity of the subject matter (which goods or services), and the quantity. Other terms of the offer should specify price, delivery terms, payment terms, timing, and shipping terms. Although these elements are not required, the more terms a party specifies, the more likely it is that an offer exists.

Courts often supply missing terms in a contract for the sale of goods when there is a reliable basis for doing so. For instance, the court usually supplies a time term that is reasonable for the circumstances. It supplies a price term (a reasonable price at the time of delivery) if a readily ascertainable market price exists; otherwise, a missing price term defeats the contract. On rare occasions, courts supply a quantity term, but a missing quantity term usually defeats a contract. For example, a small retailer who mails an advertising circular to a large number of customers is not making an offer because one major term—quantity—is missing. Most ads are not offers but are invitations for an offer. Similarly, price lists and catalogs sent to potential customers are not offers.

In general, an offeror can revoke an offer at any time prior to acceptance, but two exceptions to this rule exist: an option contract and a merchant's firm offer. In an **option contract**, the parties create a separate contract to keep an offer open for a particular time period. Option contracts are common in real estate transactions. For instance, the owner of a fast-food franchise created an option contract with the owner of a piece of land that the franchisee was considering purchasing. The landowner made an offer to sell the property to the franchisee, who wanted time to study the demographics, traffic count, and other data at the potential location but did not want to lose a promising piece of real estate by having the owner sell it to someone else. The franchisee and the landowner created an option contract; the franchisee paid the landowner $5,000 for a 6-month option on the land, which meant that the landowner could not revoke his offer to sell the property during the 6-month option.

The other exception to the revocation-before-acceptance rule is a **merchant's firm offer**. If a merchant seller (a merchant is defined later in this chapter in the section on the Uniform Commercial Code) makes a promise or assurance to hold an offer open in a signed writing, the offer is irrevocable for the stated time period or, if no time is stated, for a reasonable time period. Neither time period can exceed 90 days, however.

An offeror must communicate the offer to the other party because one cannot agree to a contract unless he or she knows it exists. The offeror may communicate an offer verbally, in writing, or by action.

Offers do not last forever. Several actions by either the offeror or the offeree can cause an offer to terminate. In addition, the law itself can cause an offer to cease to exist. As you have learned, an offeror can revoke an offer as long as he or she does so before the offeree accepts it. The offeree can cause an offer to terminate by rejecting the offer (e.g., saying "no" to it) or by making a counteroffer. For instance, suppose that an entrepreneur offers to purchase a piece of land for $175,000. The landowner responds, "Your price is too low, but I'll sell it to you for $190,000." When the landowner made the counteroffer, the entrepreneur's original offer terminated. An offer terminates by operation of the law if the time specified in the offer has elapsed (e.g., "This offer is good until noon on October 7") if the subject matter of the offer is destroyed before the offeree accepts, or if either the offeror or the offeree dies or becomes incapacitated before the offeree accepts the offer.

ACCEPTANCE. Only the person to whom the offer is made (the offeree) can accept an offer and create a contract. The offeree must accept voluntarily, agreeing to the terms exactly as the offeror presents them. When an offeree suggests alternative terms or conditions to those in the original offer, he or she is implicitly rejecting the original offer and making a counteroffer. Common law requires that the offeree's acceptance exactly match the original offer. This is called the **mirror image rule**, which says that an offeree's acceptance must be the mirror image of the offeror's offer.

Generally, silence by the offeree cannot constitute acceptance, even if the offer contains statements to the contrary. For instance, when an offeror claims, "If you do not respond to this offer by Friday at noon, I conclude your silence to be your acceptance," no acceptance exists even if the offeree does remain silent. The law requires an offeree to act affirmatively to accept an offer in most cases.

An offeree must accept an offer by the means of communication authorized by and within the time limits specified by the offeror. Generally, offers accepted by alternative media or after specified deadlines are ineffective. If the offeror specifies no means of communication, the offeree must use the same medium used to extend the offer (or a faster method). According to the **mailbox rule**, if an offeree accepts by mail, the acceptance is effective when the offeree drops the letter in the mailbox, even if it never reaches the offeror. In addition, all offers must be properly dispatched; that is, they must be properly addressed, noted, and stamped.

Consideration

Contracts are based on promises, and because it is often difficult to distinguish between promises that are serious and those that are not, courts require that consideration be present in virtually every contract. **Consideration** is something of *legal* value (*not* necessarily economic value) that the parties to a contract bargain for and exchange as the "price" for the promise given. Consideration can be money, but parties most often swap promises for promises. For example, when a buyer promises to buy an item and a seller promises to sell it, the parties have exchanged valuable consideration. The buyer's promise to buy and the seller's promise to sell constitute the consideration for their contract. To comprise valuable consideration, a promise must impose a liability or create a duty.

For a contract to be binding, the two parties involved must exchange valuable consideration. The absence of consideration makes a promise unenforceable. A promise to perform something one is already legally obligated to do is not valuable consideration. Because consideration is something that a promisor requires in exchange for his promise, past consideration is not valid. In addition, under common law new promises require new consideration. For instance, if two businesspeople have an existing contract for performance of a service, any modifications to that contract must be supported by new consideration. In many states, promises made in exchange for "love and affection" are not enforceable because the contract lacks valuable consideration.

One important exception to the requirement for valuable consideration is **promissory estoppels**. Under this rule, a promise that induces another party to act can be enforceable without consideration if the promisee substantially and justifiably relies on the promise. Thus, promissory estoppel is a substitute for consideration.

Joseph Hoffman owned a bakery in Wautoma, Wisconsin, but wanted to open a Red Owl grocery store. He approached Edward Lukowitz, a division manager for Red Owl, and told him that he had $18,000 to invest in a Red Owl franchise. Lukowitz assured Hoffman that $18,000 was sufficient to set up as a Red Owl franchisee. Lukowitz suggested that Hoffman needed experience running a grocery store before he became a Red Owl franchisee, and Hoffman purchased a small grocery store in Wautoma. After several months, Red Owl confirmed that Hoffman was operating the store at a profit. Lukowitz then told Hoffman that he would have to sell the grocery store to purchase a Red Owl franchise, and Hoffman sold the store to one of his employees. In a meeting, Lukowitz assured Hoffman that "everything is ready to go. Get your money together and we are set." Shortly after this meeting Lukowitz told Hoffman that he would have to sell the bakery business and building, and that this was the only "hitch" that remained. Hoffman sold the bakery and the building and moved to Chilton, Wisconsin, where Red Owl had found a potential site for a store. During this time, however, Red Owl Stores raised the price of the franchise from $18,000 to $24,100, and later to $26,100. Hoffman ended negotiations with Red Owl and filed a lawsuit, claiming that although Hoffman had not given any consideration, he had justifiably relied on Red Owl's promises to his detriment. The court applied the doctrine of promissory estoppel and ruled in favor of Hoffman.[4]

In most cases, courts do not evaluate the adequacy of consideration given for a promise. In other words, there is no legal requirement that the consideration the parties exchange be of approximately equal value. Even if the value of the consideration one party gives is small compared to the value of the bargain to the other party, the bargain stands. Why? The law recognizes that people have the freedom to contract and that they are just as free to enter into "bad" bargains as they are to enter into "good" ones. Only in extreme cases (e.g., cases affected by mistakes, misrepresentation, fraud, duress, and undue influence) will the court examine the value of the consideration provided in a trade.

Contractual Capacity

The third element of a valid contract requires that the parties involved in it must have contractual capacity for it to be enforceable. Not every person who attempts to enter into a contract has the capacity to do so. Under common law, minors, intoxicated people, and mentally incapacitated people lack or have limited contractual capacity. As a result, contracts these people attempt to enter are *voidable*; that is, the party can annul or disaffirm the contract at his or her option.

MINORS. Minors constitute the largest group of individuals without contractual capacity. In most states, anyone under age 18 is a minor. With a few exceptions, any contract made by a minor is voidable at the minor's option. In addition, a minor can disaffirm a contract during minority and for "a reasonable time" afterwards. The adult involved in the contract cannot disaffirm it simply because he or she is dealing with a minor.

In most states, if a minor receives the benefit of a completed contract and then disaffirms that contract, he or she must fulfill the **duty of restoration** by returning the benefit. In other words, the minor must return any consideration he or she has received under the contract to the adult and is entitled to receive any consideration he or she gave the adult under the contract. The minor must return the benefit of the contract no matter what its condition is. For instance, suppose that Brighton, a 16-year-old minor, purchases a mountain bike for $415 from Cycle Time, a small bicycle shop. After riding the bike for a little more than a year, Brighton decides to disaffirm the contract. Under the law, all he must do is return the mountain bike to Cycle Time, whatever condition it is in (pristine, used, wrecked, or rubble), and he is entitled to get all of his money back. In most states, he does not have to pay Cycle Time for the use of the bike or the damage done to it. A few states impose an additional duty on minors. The **duty of restitution** requires that minors who disaffirm contracts return any consideration they received to the adult and pay a "reasonable value" for the depreciation of or damage to the item (which is usually less than the actual value of the depreciation of or damage to the item). Adults enter into contracts with minors at their own risk.

Parents are usually not liable for any contracts made by their children, although a cosigner is bound equally with a minor. Entrepreneurs can protect themselves when dealing with minors by requiring an adult to cosign. If the minor disaffirms the contract, the adult cosigner remains bound by it.

INTOXICATED PEOPLE. A contract entered into by an intoxicated person can be either voidable or valid, depending on the person's condition when entering into the contract. If a person's reason and judgment are impaired so that he or she does not realize that he or she is making a contract, the contract is voidable (even if the intoxication was voluntary) and the intoxicated person must return the benefit. However, if the intoxicated person understands that he or she is forming a contract, although it may be foolish, the contract is valid and enforceable.

PEOPLE WITH MENTAL INCAPACITIES. A contract entered into by a person with a mental incapacity can be void, voidable, or valid, depending on the person's mental state. Those people who have been judged to be so mentally incompetent that a guardian is appointed for them cannot enter into a valid contract. If such a person does make a contract, it is *void* (i.e., it does not exist). A mentally incompetent person who has not been legally declared insane nor appointed a guardian (e.g., someone suffering from Alzheimer's disease) is bound by a contract if he or she was lucid enough at the time of the contract to comprehend its consequences. However, if at the time of entering the contract that person was so mentally incompetent that he or she could not realize what was happening or could not understand the terms of the agreement, the contract is voidable. Just as with minors, he or she must return any benefit received under the contract.

Legality

The final element required for a valid contract is legality. The purpose of the parties' contract must be legal. Because society imposes certain standards of conduct on its members, contracts that are illegal (criminal or tortuous) or against public policy are void. Examples of these situations include contracts in which the stated interest rate exceeds the rate allowed by a state's usury laws; gambling that is conducted in states where that type of gambling is illegal (e.g., casino games via the Internet); business transactions that violate a state's blue laws (creating certain types of contracts on Sunday); activities that require a practitioner to have a license (e.g., attorneys, real estate brokers, contractors, and others); and free-standing contracts that restrain competition and trade.

If a contract contains both legal and illegal elements, courts will enforce the legal parts as long as they can separate the legal portion from the illegal portion. However, in some contracts certain clauses are so unconscionable that the courts will not enforce them. Usually, the courts do not concern themselves with the fairness of a contract between parties because of the parties' freedom to contract. However, in the case of unconscionable contracts the terms are so harsh and oppressive to one party that the courts often rule the clause to be void. These clauses, called **exculpatory clauses**, frequently attempt to free one party of all responsibility and liability for an injury or damage that might occur. For instance, suppose that Miguel Ferras signs an exculpatory clause when he leaves his new BMW with an attendant at a parking garage. The clause states that the garage is "not responsible for theft, loss, or damage to cars or articles left in cars due to fire, theft, or other causes." The attendant leaves Miguel's car unattended with the keys in the ignition, and a thief steals the car. A court would declare the exculpatory clause void because the garage owes a duty to its customers to exercise reasonable care to protect their property, a duty it breached because of gross negligence.

Genuineness of Assent and the Form of Contracts

A contract that contains the four elements just discussed—agreement, consideration, capacity, and legality—is *valid*, but a valid contract may be unenforceable because of two possible defenses against it: genuineness of assent and form. **Genuineness of assent** serves as a check on the parties' agreement, verifying that it is genuine and not subject to mistakes, misrepresentation, fraud, duress, or undue influence. The existence of a contract can be affected by mistakes that one or both parties to the contract make. Different types of mistakes exist, but only mistakes of *fact*

Only six types of contracts must be in writing under the Statute of Frauds. However, smart entrepreneurs know that putting their contracts in writing offers the greatest protection if a dispute arises.

Source: © Cusp/SuperStock

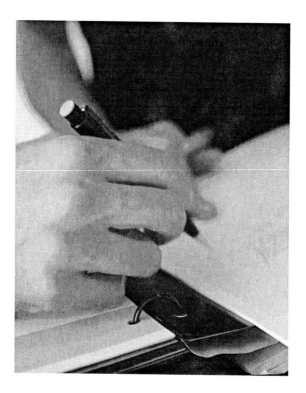

permit a party to disaffirm a contract. Suppose that a small contractor submits a bid on the construction of a bridge, but the bidder mistakenly omits the cost of some materials. The client accepts the contractor's bid because it is $32,000 below all others. If the client knew or should have known of the mistake, the contractor can disaffirm the contract; otherwise, he must build the bridge at the bid price.

Fraud also makes a contract voidable because no genuineness of assent exists. **Fraud** is the intentional misrepresentation of a material fact, justifiably relied on, that results in injury to the innocent party. The misrepresentation with the intent to deceive can result from words, silence, or conduct. Suppose a small retailer purchases a new security system from a dealer who promises it will provide 20 years of reliable service and lower the cost of operation by 40 percent. The dealer then knowingly installs a used, unreliable system. In this case, the dealer has committed fraud, and the retailer can either rescind the contract with his original position restored or enforce it and seek damages for injuries.

Duress, forcing an individual into a contract by fear or threat, eliminates genuineness of assent. The innocent party can choose to carry out the contract or to disaffirm it. For example, if a supplier forces the owner of a small video arcade to enter a contract to lease his machines by threat of personal injury, the supplier is guilty of duress. Blackmail and extortion used to induce another party to enter a contract also constitute duress.

Generally, the law does not require contracts to follow a prescribed form; a contract is valid whether it is written or oral. Most contracts do *not* have to be in writing to be enforceable, but for convenience and protection a small business owner should insist that every contract be in writing. If a contract is oral, the party attempting to enforce it must first prove its existence and then establish its actual terms. Although each state has its own rules, the common law's Statute of Frauds generally requires the following contracts to be in writing:

- Contracts for the sale of land
- Contracts involving lesser interests in land (e.g., rights-of-way or leases that last more than 1 year)
- Contracts that cannot, by their terms, be performed within 1 year
- Collateral contracts, such as promises to answer for the debt or duty of another
- Promises by the administrator or executor of an estate to pay a debt of the estate personally
- Contracts for the sale of goods (as opposed to services) priced at $500 or more

Breach of Contract

The majority of contracts are discharged by both parties fully performing the terms of their agreement. Occasionally, however, one party fails to perform as agreed. This failure is called *breach of contract*, and the injured party has certain remedies available. A breach of contract can be either a minor breach, in which substantial, but not complete, performance occurs, or a material breach of contract associated with nonperformance or inferior performance. In cases where there exists a minor breach of contract, the party "in breach" may agree to complete the specific terms of the contract or compensate the other party for the unperformed component of the contract. If these two remedies are not accepted, the next step is legal action to recover the cost to repair the defect.

In contrast, a *material breach* occurs when a party renders inferior performance that impairs or destroys the essence of the contract. The nonbreaching party may either rescind the contract and recover restitution or affirm the contract and recover damages. Of course, the injured party must make a reasonable effort to minimize the damages incurred by the breach.

Profile

Leroy Greer v. 1-800-FLOWERS

Leroy Greer, a married man who was going through a divorce, filed a $1 million lawsuit for breach of contract against 1-800-FLOWERS for revealing to his wife that he was having an affair with another woman. When Greer ordered a cuddly stuffed animal and a dozen long-stem red roses for his girlfriend, he asked that the company keep his purchase private and was referred to 1-800-FLOWERS' privacy policy, which states that customers can ask the company not to share personal information with "third parties." Greer says that 1-800-FLOWERS violated its privacy policy by sending a thank you note for his order to his home, where his wife saw it. When she called the company, a customer service representative faxed a copy of the receipt from her husband's clandestine purchase. After Greer's wife learned about her husband's affair, she asked for a much larger divorce settlement, $300,000, in addition to child support, and Greer sued 1-800-FLOWERS. A U.S. district court in Texas later dismissed Greer's case.[5]

In some cases, monetary damages are inadequate to compensate an injured party for a defendant's breach of contract. The only remedy that would compensate the nonbreaching party might be specific performance of the act promised in the contract. **Specific performance** is usually the remedy for breached contracts dealing with unique items (e.g., antiques, land, and animals). For example, if an antique auto dealer enters a contract to purchase a rare Corvette and the other party breaches the contract, the dealer may sue for specific performance; that is, the dealer may ask the court to order the breaching party to sell the antique car. Courts rarely invoke the remedy of specific performance. Generally, contracts for performance of personal services are not subject to specific performance.

▶ E N T R E P R E N E U R S H I P IN ACTION ▶

What a Bargain!

Managers at Best Buy, a retailer of consumer electronics, were embarrassed when the company's Web site, *www.bestbuy.com*, listed a 52-inch Samsung high-definition television for just $9.99. The listing was a mistake; the price Best Buy intended to post for the TV was $1,699.99 with a flat $70 shipping charge. By the time the company realized the error and corrected it, several customers had placed orders, some for as many as 10 TVs.

"There was an online pricing error on a 52-inch Samsung television this morning," said a Best Buy spokeswoman. "We have corrected the issue and apologize for any confusion this may have caused. We will not be honoring the incorrect price and, again, apologize for the mistake. All current and previous orders made for the TV at this price on BestBuy.com will be cancelled, and customers will be refunded in full for the purchase."

The company's Web site says that Best Buy reserves the right to "revoke offers or correct errors" even if the company has charged customers' credit cards. Some customers were upset after learning that they would not be getting the good deal that they thought they would get, but others took the news in stride. Debra Green, whose daughter found out about the deal on Facebook, ordered a television at the $9.99 price and received an order confirmation e-mail and an estimated delivery date. "I thought it was too good a deal to pass up," she says.

1. Was Best Buy's advertisement on its Web site a valid offer? Explain.
2. Should Best Buy be held to the $9.99 price that it advertised for this television? Explain.
3. Evaluate the manner in which Best Buy handled the mistake. Can you offer other suggestions for ways to deal with the mistake that might have been more effective or even good for the company?

Sources: Based on "I Don't Care What You Think. I Call a Do-over," *Get to the Point*, October 1, 2009, p. 1; Nathalie Tadena, "Best Buy's $9.99 Flat Screen TV Sale a Pricing Mistake," ABC News, August 12, 2009, *http://abcnews.go.com/Business/story?id=8311580&page=1*; Abbi Tatton, "Best Buy Will Not Honor $9.99 Big-Screen TV Deal," CNN, August 13, 2009, *http://articles.cnn.com/2009-08-13/us/bestbuy.mistake_1_multiple-orders-pricing-error-customers?_s=PM:US*.

The Uniform Commercial Code (UCC)

2. Outline the major components of the Uniform Commercial Code governing sales contracts.

For many years, sales contracts relating to the exchange of goods were governed by a loosely defined system of rules and customs called the *Lex Mercatoria* (Merchant Law). Many of these principles were assimilated into U.S. common law through court opinions, but they varied widely from state to state, making interstate commerce difficult and confusing for businesses. In 1952, the commission on Uniform State Laws created the **Uniform Commercial Code** (or the **UCC** or the **Code**) to replace the hodge-podge collection of confusing, often conflicting, state laws that governed basic commercial transactions with a document designed to provide uniformity and consistency. The UCC replaced numerous statutes governing trade when each of the states, the District of Columbia, and the Virgin Islands adopted it. (Louisiana has adopted only articles 1, 3, 4, and 5.) The Code does not alter the basic tenets of business law established by common law; instead, it unites and modernizes them into a single body of law. In some cases, however, the Code changes some of the specific rules under common law. The Code consists of 10 articles, but we will discuss the general principles relating to one of its most common sections, Article 2, which governs the sale of goods. The UCC creates a "caste system" of merchants and nonmerchants and requires merchants to have a higher degree of knowledge and understanding of the Code.

Sales and Sales Contracts

Every sales contract is subject to the basic principles of law that govern all contracts—agreement, consideration, capacity, and legality. However, when a contract involves the sale of goods, the UCC imposes rules that may vary slightly or substantially from basic contract law. Article 2 governs *only* contracts for the *sale of goods*, but it pertains to *every* sale of goods, whether the good involved is a 79-cent pen or a billion-dollar battleship. To be considered a good, an item must be personal property that is tangible and moveable (e.g., not real estate or services), and a "sale" is "the passing of title from the seller to the buyer for a price" (UCC Sec. 2-106[1]). The UCC does *not* cover the sale of services, although certain "mixed transactions," such as the sale by a garage of car parts (goods) and repairs (a service) will fall under the Code's jurisdiction if the goods are the dominant element of the contract.

In addition to the rules it applies to the sale of goods in general, the Code imposes special standards of conduct in certain instances when merchants sell goods to one another. Usually, a person is considered a professional **merchant** if he "deals in goods of the kind" involved in the contract, has special knowledge of the business or of the goods, employs a merchant agent to conduct a transaction for him, or holds himself out to be a merchant.

Although the UCC requires that the same elements outlined in common law be present in forming a sales contract, it relaxes many of the specific restrictions. For example, the UCC states that a contract exists even if the parties omit one or more terms (price, delivery date, place of delivery, quantity), as long as they intended to make a contract and there is a reasonably certain method for the court to supply the missing terms. Suppose a manufacturer orders a shipment of needed raw materials from her usual supplier without asking the price. When the order arrives, the price is substantially higher than she expected, and she attempts to disaffirm the contract. The Code verifies the existence of a contract and assigns to the shipment a price that is reasonable at the time of delivery.

Common law requires that acceptance of an offer to be exactly the same as the offer; an acceptance that adds some slight modification is no acceptance at all, and no contract exists. Any modification constitutes a counteroffer. However, the UCC states that as long as an offeree's response (words, writing, or actions) indicates a sincere willingness to accept the offer, it is a legitimate acceptance, even if the offeree adds terms. This section of the UCC is known as "the battle of the forms." In dealings between nonmerchant buyers and sellers, these added terms become "proposals for addition." In other words, a contract is formed on the offeror's original terms. Between merchants, however, these additional proposals *automatically* become part of the contract unless they materially alter the original contract, the offer expressly states that no terms other than those in the offer will be accepted, or the offeror objects to the particular terms within a reasonable time. In other words, the contract is formed on the offeree's modified terms. For example, suppose that an appliance wholesaler offers to sell a retailer a shipment of appliances for $5,000 plus freight. The retailer responds, "I accept," but includes an additional term by stating, "Delivery within 3 days." A contract exists, and the addition will become part of the contract unless the wholesaler objects within a reasonable time.

When the offeree includes a term in the acceptance that *contradicts* a term in the offeror's original offer, the UCC says that the two terms cancel out each other. What, then, are the terms of the resulting contract? The UCC turns to its gap-filling rules, which establish reasonable terms for prices, delivery dates, warranties, payment times, and other topics, to supply the disputed term.

ENTREPRENEURIAL Profile

Superior Boiler Works v. R.J. Sanders Company

The R.J. Sanders Company won a contract to install the heating system at a federal prison and negotiated a contract with Superior Boiler Works to purchase three large commercial boilers for the project. On March 27, Superior sent an offer to Sanders in which it offered to sell three boilers for $156,000 with an estimated delivery time of 4 weeks. After several discussions, Sanders sent a purchase order to Superior on July 20 for three boilers, agreeing to pay $145,827 and stating a delivery date of 4 weeks (August 20). Superior responded by sending Sanders a sales order in which it agreed to the price but stated a shipping date of October 1. Superior shipped the boilers on October 1, just as it had promised, and they arrived at Sanders on October 5. This delivery date forced Sanders to rent temporary boilers at a cost of $45,315, and Sanders sent Superior a check for $100,000 with a note explaining that the deduction was to offset the cost of the rented boilers. Superior sued Sanders for the $45,000 difference, claiming that the October 1 shipping date was reasonable. The Supreme Court of Rhode Island ruled that the parties' conflicting delivery terms canceled out each other. The court then applied the UCC's gap-filling rules (boilers are goods), which state that the time for delivery of the goods must be "a reasonable time." The court ruled in favor of Superior, stating that the October 1 shipping date was within a reasonable time.[6]

The UCC significantly changes the common law requirement that a contract modification requires new consideration. ("New promises require new consideration.") Under the Code, modifications to contract terms are binding *without* new consideration if they are made in good faith. ("New promises do *not* require new consideration.") For example, suppose that a small building contractor forms a contract to purchase a shipment of lumber for $1,200. After the agreement but before the lumber is delivered, a hurricane causes the price of the lumber to double, and the supplier notifies the contractor that the price of the lumber shipment has increased to $2,400. The contractor reluctantly agrees to the additional cost but later refuses to pay. According to UCC, the contractor must pay the higher price because the contract modification requires no new consideration.

The Code also has its own Statute of Frauds provision relating to the form of contracts for the sale of goods. If the price of the goods is $500 or more, the contract must be in writing to be enforceable. Of course, the parties can agree orally and then follow up with a written memorandum. The Code does not require both parties to sign the written agreement, but it must be signed by the party against whom enforcement is sought (which is impossible to tell before a dispute arises, so it is a good idea for *both* parties to sign the agreement at the outset).

The UCC includes a special provision involving the writing requirement for contracts between merchants. If merchants form a verbal contract for the sale of goods priced at $500 or more and one of them sends a written confirmation of the deal to the other, the merchant receiving the confirmation must object to it *in writing* within 10 days. Otherwise, the contract is enforceable against *both* merchants, even though the merchant receiving the confirmation has not actually signed anything.

Once the parties create a sales contract, they are bound to perform according to its terms. Both the buyer and the seller have certain duties and obligations under the contract. Generally, the Code assigns the obligations of "good faith" (defined as "honesty in fact in the conduct or transaction concerned") and "commercial reasonableness" (commercial standards of fair dealing) to both parties.

The seller must make delivery of the items involved in the contract, but "delivery" is not necessarily physical delivery. The seller simply must make the goods available to the buyer. The contract normally outlines the specific details of the delivery, but occasionally the parties omit this provision. In this instance, the place of delivery will be the seller's place of business, if one exists; otherwise, it is the seller's residence. If both parties know the usual location of the identified goods, that location is the place of delivery (e.g., a warehouse). In addition, the seller must make the goods available to the buyer at a reasonable time and in a reasonable manner. All goods covered by the contract are to be delivered in one shipment unless the parties' agreement states otherwise.

A buyer must accept the delivery of conforming goods from the seller. Of course, the buyer has the right to inspect the goods in a reasonable manner and at any reasonable time or place to ensure that they are conforming goods before making payment. However, C.O.D. terms prohibit the right to advance inspection unless the contract specifies otherwise. The UCC also says that if goods or tender of delivery fail, in any respect, to conform to the contract, the buyer is not required to accept them.

A buyer can indicate his acceptance of the goods in several ways. Usually the buyer indicates acceptance by an express statement that the goods are suitable. This expression can be by words or by conduct. Suppose that a small electrical contractor orders a truck to use in her business. When she receives it, she equips it to suit her business, including a company decal on each door. Later the contractor attempts to reject the truck and return it. By customizing the truck, the buyer has indicated her acceptance of the truck. In addition, the Code assumes acceptance if the buyer has a reasonable opportunity to inspect the goods and has failed to reject them within a reasonable time.

A buyer has the duty to pay for the goods on the terms stated in the contract when they are received. A seller cannot require payment before the buyer receives the goods. Unless otherwise stated in the contract, payment must be in cash.

Breach of Sales Contracts

As we have seen, when a party to a sales contract fails to perform according to its terms, that party has breached the contract. The law provides the innocent (nonbreaching) party numerous remedies, including damage awards and the right to retain possession of the goods. The object of these remedies is to place the innocent party in the same position as if the contract had been completed. The parties to the contract may specify their own damages in case of breach. These provisions, called **liquidated damages**, must be reasonable and cannot be in the nature of a penalty. For example, suppose that Alana Mitchell contracts with a local carpenter to build a booth from which she plans to sell crafts. The parties agree that if the carpenter does not complete the booth by September 1 Mitchell will receive $500. If the liquidated damages had been $50,000, they would be unenforceable because such a large amount of money is clearly a penalty.

An unpaid seller has certain remedies available under the terms of the Code. Under a seller's lien, every seller has the right to maintain possession of the goods until the buyer pays for them. In addition, if the buyer uses a fraudulent payment to obtain the goods, the seller has the right to recover them. If the seller discovers that the buyer is insolvent, the seller can withhold delivery of the goods until the buyer pays in cash. If a seller ships goods to an insolvent buyer, the seller can require their return within 10 days after receipt. In some cases, the buyer breaches a contract while the goods are still unfinished in the production process. When this occurs, the seller must use "reasonable commercial judgment" to decide whether to sell them for scrap or complete them and resell them elsewhere. In either case, the buyer is liable for any loss the seller incurs. Of course, the seller has the right to withhold performance when the buyer breaches the sales contract.

When the seller breaches a contract, the buyer also has specific remedies available. For instance, if the goods do not conform to the contract's terms, the buyer has the right to reject them. If the seller fails to deliver the goods, the buyer can sue for the difference between the contract price and the market price at the time that the buyer discovers the breach. When the buyer accepts goods and then discovers that they are defective or nonconforming, he or she must notify the seller of the breach. In this instance, damages amount to the difference between the value of the goods delivered and their value if they had been delivered as promised. If a buyer pays for goods that the seller retains, the buyer can take possession of the goods if the seller becomes insolvent within 10 days after receiving the first payment. If the seller unlawfully withholds the goods from the buyer, the buyer can recover them. Under certain circumstances, a buyer can obtain specific performance of a sales contract; that is, the court orders the seller to perform according to the contract's terms. As mentioned earlier, specific performance is a remedy when the goods involved are unique or unavailable on the market. Finally, if the seller breaches the contract, the buyer has the right to rescind the contract; if the buyer has paid any part of the purchase price, the seller must refund it.

Whenever a party breaches a sales contract, the innocent party must bring suit within a specified period of time. The Code sets the statute of limitations at 4 years. In other words, any action for a breach of a sales contract must begin within 4 years after the breach occurred.

Sales Warranties and Product Liability

The U.S. economy once emphasized the philosophy of *caveat emptor*, "let the buyer beware," but today the marketplace enforces a policy of *caveat venditor*, "let the seller beware." **Tort law** deals with cases in which one party commits a wrong against another party and causes injury or damage to the person and/or his or her property. Tort law covers a wide range of topics, including defamation of character, false imprisonment (e.g., wrongly detaining a suspected shoplifter), fraud, wrongful interference with a contractual relationship, and others. Tort liability represents a significant risk for small companies. A study by the U.S. Chamber Institute for Legal Reform reports that small companies bear 81 percent of total tort liability costs for a total of $152 billion per year. Tort liability costs businesses with less than $10 million in annual sales $14.59 for every $1,000 of revenue; in other words, a small company with $5 million in revenue incurs, on average, $72,960 in tort-related costs each year.[7] Entrepreneurs must be aware of two general categories related to torts that involve the quality and reliability of the products they sell: sales warranties and product liability.

SALES WARRANTIES. Simply stated, a **sales warranty** is a promise or a statement of fact by the seller that a product will meet certain standards. Because a breach of warranty is a breach of promise, the buyer has the right to recover damages from the seller. Several different types of warranties can arise in a sale. A seller creates an **express warranty** by making statements about the condition, quality, and performance of the good that the buyer substantially relies on. Sellers create express warranties by words or actions. For example, a manufacturer selling a shipment of cloth to a customer with the promise that "it will not shrink" is creating an express warranty. Similarly, the jeweler who displays a watch in a glass of water for promotional purposes creates an express warranty that "this watch is waterproof" even though no such promise is ever spoken. Generally, an express warranty arises if the seller indicates that the goods conform to any promises of fact the seller makes, to any description of them (e.g., printed on the package or statements of fact made by salespersons), or to any display model or sample (e.g., a floor model used as a demonstrator).

Whenever someone sells goods, the UCC automatically implies certain types of warranties unless the seller specifically excludes them. These **implied warranties** take several forms. Sellers, simply by offering goods for sale, imply a **warranty of title**, which promises that their title to the goods is valid (i.e., no liens or claims exist) and that transfer of title is legitimate. A seller can disclaim a warranty of title only by using very specific language in a sales contract.

An implied **warranty of merchantability** applies to every merchant seller, and the only way to disclaim it is by mentioning the term "warranty of merchantability" in a conspicuous manner.

An implied warranty of merchantability assures the buyer that the product will be of average quality—not the best and not the worst. In other words, merchantable goods are "fit for the ordinary purposes for which such goods are used."[8] For example, a commercial refrigeration unit that a food store purchases should keep food cold.

Profile

Webster v. Blue Ship Tea Room

Priscilla Webster, a longtime New England resident, ordered a bowl of fish chowder at the Blue Ship Tea Room, a Boston restaurant that overlooked the ocean. After eating three or four spoonfuls, Webster felt something caught in her throat. It turned out to be a fish bone that was in the bowl of chowder she had ordered. Webster had to undergo two surgical procedures to remove the bone from her throat, and she filed a lawsuit against the restaurant, claiming that it had breached the implied warranty of merchantability. The Supreme Court of Massachusetts ruled in favor of the Blue Ship Tea Room, stating that "the occasional presence of [fish bones] in chowders is . . . to be anticipated and . . . [does] not impair their fitness or merchantability." Because the fish bone in the fish chowder was not a foreign object, but one that a person could reasonably expect to find in chowders on occasion, the court decided that the restaurant had not breached a warranty of merchantability.[9]

An implied **warranty of fitness for a particular purpose** arises when a seller knows the particular reason for which a buyer is purchasing a product and knows that the buyer is depending on the seller's judgment to select the proper item. For example, suppose a contractor asks the owner of a paint store for a paint that adheres to metal roofs. The store owner sells the contractor paint that he says will do the job, but 2 months later, the paint is peeling off. The owner has violated the warranty of fitness for a particular purpose.

The Code also states that the only way a merchant can disclaim an implied warranty is to include the words "sold as is" or "with all faults," stating that the buyer purchases the product as it is, without any guarantees. The following statement is usually sufficient to disclaim most warranties, both express and implied: "Seller hereby disclaims all warranties, express and implied, including all warranties of merchantability and all warranties of fitness for a particular purpose." To protect a business, the statement must be printed in bold letters and placed in a conspicuous place on the product or its package.

PRODUCT LIABILITY. At one time only the parties directly involved in the execution of a contract were bound by the law of sales warranties. Today, the UCC and the states have expanded the scope of warranties to include any person (including bystanders) incurring personal or property damages caused by a faulty product. In addition, most states allow an injured party to sue *any* seller in the chain of distribution for breach of warranty (a concept known as *joint and several liability*). Product liability is built on the principle that a person who introduces a product into the stream of commerce owes a duty of care, not only to the person who first purchases the product, but also to anyone else who might foreseeably come into contact with it. A company that may be responsible for only a small percentage of the responsibility for a person's injury may end up bearing the majority of the damage award in the case. If a small company is hit with a product liability lawsuit, the results can be devastating. Figure 1 shows the number of product liability lawsuits filed in recent years.

Many customers who ultimately file suit under product liability laws base their claims on **negligence**, when a manufacturer or distributor fails to do something that a "reasonable" person would do. Typically, negligence claims arise from one or more of the following charges:

- *Negligent design.* In claims based on negligent design, a buyer claims that an injury occurred because the manufacturer designed the product improperly. To avoid liability charges, a company does not have to design products that are 100 percent safe, but it must design products that are free of "unreasonable" risks.
- *Negligent manufacturing.* In cases claiming negligent manufacturing, a buyer claims that a company's failure to follow proper manufacturing, assembly, or inspection procedures allowed a defective product to get into the customer's hands and cause injury. A company must exercise "due care" (including design, assembly, and inspection) to make its products safe when they are used for their intended purpose.

FIGURE 1

Number of Product Liability Lawsuits

Source: "Product Liability Cases Commenced," Judicial Business of the United States Courts 2009. *www.uscourts.gov/Statistics/Judicial Business/JudicialBusiness2009.aspx.*

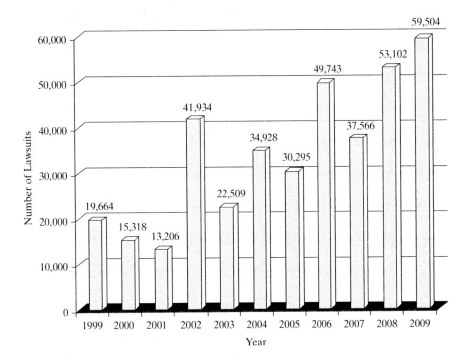

■ *Failure to warn.* Although manufacturers do not have to warn customers about obvious dangers of using their products, they must warn them about the dangers of normal use and of foreseeable misuse of the product. (Have you ever read the warning label on a stepladder?) Many businesses hire attorneys to write the warning labels they attach to their products and include in their instructions.[10]

Another common basis for product liability claims against businesses is **strict liability**, which states that a manufacturer is liable for its actions no matter what its intentions or the extent of its negligence. Unlike negligence, a claim of strict liability does not require the injured party to prove that the company's actions were unreasonable. The injured person must prove only that the company manufactured or sold a product that was defective and that it caused the injury when used in a way that was foreseeable. Whereas negligence charges focus on a party's *conduct*, strict liability focuses on the *product*. For instance, the head of an axe flies off its handle, injuring the user. To sue the manufacturer under strict liability, the customer must prove that the defendant sold the axe, the axe was unreasonably dangerous to the customer because it was defective, the customer incurred physical harm to person or to property, and the defective axe was the proximate cause of the injury or damage. If these allegations are true, the axe manufacturer's liability is virtually unlimited.

Protection of Intellectual Property Rights

3. Discuss the protection of intellectual property rights using patents, trademarks, and copyrights.

Entrepreneurs excel at coming up with innovative ideas for creative products and services. Many entrepreneurs build businesses around intellectual property, products and services that are the result of the creative process and have commercial value. New methods that are capable of teaching foreign languages at an accelerated pace, hit songs with which we can sing along, books that bring a smile, and new drugs that fight diseases are just some of the ways intellectual property makes our lives better or more enjoyable.

Unfortunately, thieves are escalating their efforts to steal intellectual property by selling counterfeit merchandise. Sales of counterfeit goods cost U.S. businesses between $500 and $600 billion per year, an amount that represents 5 to 7 percent of the value of world trade![11] The problem extends far beyond pirated software, fake shoes and handbags, and knockoffs of expensive watches or the latest styles of designer clothing. Authorities have discovered pirates selling counterfeit helicopter, airplane, and auto parts; prescription medications (including blood pressure medication and birth control pills); and many other products. A tidal wave of counterfeit products, mostly originating in China (which accounts for about 80 percent of the counterfeit items that authorities confiscate), Hong Kong, India, and Taiwan, is flooding the world.[12] The U.S. Justice Department recently seized 82 Web sites, 70 of them located in China, for selling counterfeit goods supposedly from companies such as Coach, Disney, Oakley, Louis Vuitton,

TABLE 1 Top 10 Products Seized by U.S. Customs Agents

In a typical year, U.S. customs agents make about 15,000 seizures of counterfeit goods coming into the United States. These seizures represent only a portion of the total traffic in pirated goods. Which items are most often pirated?

Rank	Product	Percentage of Counterfeit Goods Seized
1	Footwear	38.2%
2	Consumer electronics	12.2%
3	Handbags, wallets, and backpacks	8.2%
4	Apparel	8.2%
5	Watches and parts	6.0%
6	Computers and hardware	4.8%
7	Media	4.2%
8	Pharmaceuticals	4.2%
9	Jewelry	4.0%
10	Toys and electronic games	2.1%

Source: Intellectual Property: Observations on Efforts to Quantify the Economic Effects of Counterfeit and Pirated Goods, U.S. Government Accountability Office, April 2010, p. 7.

Nike, and others to unsuspecting consumers.[13] Table 1 shows the 10 counterfeit products that U.S. Customs agents most commonly seize.

Entrepreneurs can protect their intellectual property from unauthorized use with the help of three important tools: patents, trademarks, and copyrights.

Patents

A **patent** is a grant from the federal government's Patent and Trademark Office (PTO) to the inventor of a product, giving the exclusive right to make, use, or sell the invention in this country for 20 years from the date of filing the patent application. The purpose of giving an inventor a 20-year monopoly over a product is to stimulate creativity and innovation. After 20 years, the patent expires and cannot be renewed. Most patents are granted for new product inventions, but **design patents**, issued for 3.5, 7, or 14 years beyond the date the patent is issued, are given to inventors who make new, original, and ornamental changes in the design of existing products that enhance their sales. Inventors who develop a new plant can obtain a **plant patent** (issued for 7 years), provided they can reproduce the plant asexually (e.g., by grafting or cross-breeding rather than planting seeds). To be patented, a device must be new (but not necessarily better; see Figure 2), not obvious to a person of ordinary skill or knowledge in the related field, and useful. An inventor cannot patent a device if it has been publicized in print anywhere in the world or if it has been used or offered for sale in this country prior to the date of the patent application. A U.S. patent is granted only to the true inventor, not to a person who discovers another's invention. No one can copy or sell a patented invention without getting a license from its creator. A patent does not give one the right to make, use, or sell an invention, but rather the right to exclude others from making, using, or selling it.

In recent years, the PTO has awarded companies, primarily Web-based businesses, patents on their business methods. Rather than giving them the exclusive rights to a product or an invention, a business method patent protects the way a company conducts business. For instance, Amazon.com earned a patent on its "1-Click" Web-based checkout process, precluding other e-tailers from using it. Priceline.com has a patent on its business model of "buyer-driven commerce," in which customers name the prices they are willing to pay for airline tickets, hotel rooms, and other items.

Although inventors have no guarantee of getting a patent, they can enhance their chances considerably by following the basic steps suggested by the PTO. Before beginning the lengthy and involved procedure, inventors should obtain professional assistance from a patent practitioner—a patent attorney or a patent agent—who is registered with the PTO. Only attorneys and agents who are officially registered may represent an inventor seeking a patent. Approximately 98 percent of all inventors rely on these patent experts to steer them through the convoluted process.[14] One experienced patent attorney says that the cost to obtain a patent ranges from $4,000 for a simple invention to $25,000 or more for a highly complex one.[15]

US007484328B1

(12) United States Patent
Daugherty

(10) **Patent No.:** US 7,484,328 B1
(45) **Date of Patent:** Feb. 3, 2009

(54) **FINGER MOUNTED INSECT DISSUASION DEVICE AND METHOD OF USE**

(76) Inventor: **John Richard Daugherty**, 1647 N. Woodhollow Way, Flagstaff, AZ (US) 86004

(*) Notice: Subject to any disclaimer, the term of this patent is extended or adjusted under 35 U.S.C. 154(b) by 122 days.

(21) Appl. No.: **11/080,023**

(22) Filed: **Mar. 15, 2005**

Related U.S. Application Data

(63) Continuation-in-part of application No. 10/839,590, filed on May 5, 2004, now abandoned.

(51) **Int. Cl.**
A01M 3/02 (2006.01)
A01M 3/00 (2006.01)

(52) **U.S. Cl.** 43/137; 43/134

(58) **Field of Classification Search** 43/137, 43/134
See application file for complete search history.

(56) **References Cited**

U.S. PATENT DOCUMENTS

36,652	A	10/1862	Jacobs	
97,161	A	* 11/1869	Buttles	43/134
160,606	A	* 3/1875	Marsh	43/134
542,464	A	* 7/1895	Chase	43/137
599,404	A	* 2/1898	Robertson	43/134
609,160	A	* 8/1898	McWithey	43/134
648,336	A	* 4/1900	Bellamy	273/317.2
974,887	A	11/1910	Huddle	
1,099,342	A	* 6/1914	Copenhaver	43/137
1,206,976	A	12/1916	Barth	
1,354,775	A	* 10/1920	Moore	43/137
1,412,312	A	* 4/1922	Little	43/137
1,479,046	A	* 1/1924	Herbert	43/137
1,500,442	A	* 7/1924	Cooper	43/137
1,639,559	A	* 8/1927	Gatch	43/137
1,650,548	A	* 11/1927	Sullivan	43/137
1,656,969	A	* 1/1928	Adolph	43/137
1,660,011	A	* 2/1928	Linding	43/137
1,662,264	A	* 3/1928	Henderson	43/137
1,763,205	A	* 6/1930	Winbigler	273/317.2
1,820,360	A	* 8/1931	Meggitt	43/137
1,861,688	A	* 6/1932	Crawford	43/137
1,942,252	A	* 1/1934	Martin	43/137
1,967,384	A	* 7/1934	Urbanek	43/137

(Continued)

FOREIGN PATENT DOCUMENTS

DE   29712704 U1 * 11/1997

(Continued)

Primary Examiner—Darren W Ark
(74) *Attorney, Agent, or Firm*—John R. Daugherty

(57) **ABSTRACT**

An insect dissuasion method that incorporates a miniature fly swatter adapted to be fixed onto an end of a human finger. An insect can be discouraged by simply flexing, slowly encroaching upon and then "flicking" the finger with the attached device to strike the insect. Devices of the present invention are designed to be removably attached to a finger by a ring-like structure. The ring-like structure is tailored to slip onto and engage a finger in various positions and remain attached to the finger when the finger is flicked. Joined to the ring-like structure is an extension shaft that terminates in an insect engagement head. The length and/or cross-sectional profile of the extension shaft can be altered as well as the shape of the head portion or ring-like structure.

3 Claims, 13 Drawing Sheets

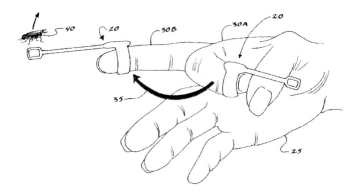

FIGURE 2
Design Patent 7,484,328, Finger-Mounted Insect Dissuasion Device

THE PATENT PROCESS. Since George Washington signed the first patent law in 1790, the U.S. Patent and Trademark Office has issued patents on everything imaginable (and some unimaginable items, too), including mouse traps, animals (genetically engineered mice), games, and various fishing devices. To date, the PTO has issued more than 7 million patents, and it receives more than 400,000 new applications each year. The first patent was issued to Samuel Hopkins on July 31, 1790, for an improved method for making potash, an ingredient in fertilizer and other products.[16] Patent number 7 million went to DuPont senior researcher John P. O'Brien for polysaccharide fibers (which have cotton-like properties, are biodegradable, and are useful in textile applications) and a process for producing them. Figure 3 shows the trend in the number of patent applications and number of patents actually granted in recent years.

To receive a patent, an inventor must follow these steps:

- *Establish the invention's novelty.* An invention is not patentable if it is known or has been used in the United States or has been described in a printed publication in the United States or a foreign country.
- *Document the device.* To protect a patent claim, inventors should be able to verify the date on which they first conceived the idea for their invention. Inventors can document a device by keeping dated records (including drawings) of their progress on the invention and by having knowledgeable friends witness these records. Inventors also can file a disclosure document with the PTO—a process that includes writing a letter describing the invention and sending a check for $10 to the PTO. A disclosure document is *not* a patent application, but it does provide evidence of the date an inventor conceived an invention.
- *Search existing patents.* To verify that the invention truly is new, nonobvious, and useful, inventors must conduct a search of existing patents on similar products. The purpose of the search is to determine whether the inventor has a chance of getting a patent. Most inventors hire professionals trained in conducting patent searches to perform the research. Inventors themselves can conduct an online search of all patents granted by the PTO since 1976 from the office's Web site. An online search of these patents does not include sketches; however, subscribers to Delphion's Research Intellectual Property Network can access patents, including sketches, as far back as 1971 at *www.delphion.com.*
- *Study search results.* Once the patent search is finished, inventors must study the results of the search to determine their chances of getting a patent. To be patentable, a device must be sufficiently different from what has been used or described before and must not be obvious to a person having ordinary skill in the area of technology related to the invention.

FIGURE 3

Number of Patent Applications and Number of Patents Granted, 1980–2009

Source: U.S. Patent and Trademark Office.

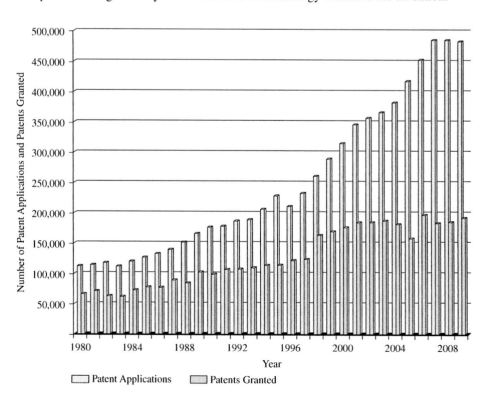

- ▦ *Submit the patent application.* An inventor must file an application describing the invention with the PTO. This description, called the patent's claims, should be broad enough so that others cannot easily engineer around the patent, rendering it useless. However, they cannot be so narrow as to infringe on patents that other inventors already hold. The typical patent application runs 20 to 40 pages, although some, especially those for biotech or high-tech products, are tens of thousands of pages long.
- ▦ *Prosecute the patent application.* Before the PTO will issue a patent, one of its examiners studies the application to determine whether the invention warrants a patent. If the PTO rejects the application, the inventor can amend the application and resubmit it to the PTO. The average time for a patent to be issued is 35 months, and the head of the PTO says that as the backlog of patent applications grows ever larger the average time will double within 5 years.[17]

Defending a patent against "copycat producers" can be expensive and time-consuming, but it often is necessary to protect an entrepreneur's idea. Patent lawsuits are on the rise; the number filed annually has more than tripled since the early 1980s.[18] Unfortunately, the cost of defending a patent has increased as well; the average cost of a patent infringement case is about $2 million for each side.[19] However, the odds of winning are in the patent holder's favor; more than 60 percent of those holding patents win their infringement suits.[20]

Trademarks

A **trademark** is any distinctive word, phrase, symbol, design, name, logo, slogan, or trade dress that a company uses to identify the origin of a product or to distinguish it from other goods on the market. (A **service mark** is the same as a trademark except that it identifies and distinguishes the source of a service rather than a product.) A trademark serves as a company's "signature" in the marketplace. A trademark can be more than just a company's logo, slogan, or brand name; it can also include symbols, shapes, colors, smells, or sounds. For instance, Coca-Cola holds a trademark on the shape of its bottle, and NBC owns a trademark on its three-toned chime. Components of a product's identity such as these are part of its **trade dress**, the unique combination of elements that a company uses to create a product's image and to promote it. For instance, a Mexican restaurant chain's particular décor, color schemes, design, and overall "look and feel" comprise its trade dress. To be eligible for trademark protection, trade dress must be inherently unique and distinctive to a company, and another company's use of that trade dress must be likely to confuse customers.

In-N-Out Burger has successfully defended its trademark and trade dress against infringers over the years.

Source: David Touchtone/Alamy Images

In-N-Out Burger, a popular chain of hamburger restaurants based in Irvine, California, with 232 locations in four western states, has successfully defended its trademark against a number of infringers over the years. In one case, a judge forced Chadder's, a Utah-based hamburger chain, to stop using product names that In-N-Out had trademarked, such as "Double, Double" and "Protein Burger," on its menu. Recently, In-N-Out filed a trademark infringement lawsuit against Nicky's In-N-Out, a hamburger restaurant in Bronzeville, Illinois. At issue was the similarity of Nicky's name and use of a yellow arrow in its logo and on its sign positioned at an angle that was almost identical to the one that In-N-Out uses. "Consumers have come to associate our In-N-Out name and arrow with the highest in food quality and freshness," says the company's attorney. "We will vigorously defend our trademarks and trade dress against any and all infringers." The companies settled the lawsuit after Nicky's agreed to stop using trademarked items that might confuse customers.[21]

There are 1.5 million trademarks registered in the United States, 900,000 of which are in actual use. Federal law permits a manufacturer to register a trademark, which prevents other companies from employing a similar mark to identify their goods. Before 1989, a business could not reserve a trademark in advance of use. Today, the first party that either uses a trademark in commerce or files an application with the PTO has the ultimate right to register that trademark. The PTO takes approximately 11 months to process a trademark application.[22] Unlike patents and copyrights, which are issued for limited amounts of time, trademarks last indefinitely as long as the holder continues to use it. However, a trademark cannot keep competitors from producing the same product and selling it under a different name. It merely prevents others from using the same or confusingly similar trademark for the same or similar products.

Many business owners are confused by the use of the symbols ™ and ®. Anyone who claims the right to a particular trademark (or servicemark) can use the ™ (or ᔆᴹ) symbols without having to register the mark with the PTO. The claim to that trademark or servicemark may or may not be valid, however. Only those businesses that have registered their marks with the PTO can use the ® symbol. Entrepreneurs do not have to register trademarks or service-marks to establish their rights to those marks; however, registering a mark with the PTO does give entrepreneurs greater power to protect their marks. Filing an application to register a trademark or servicemark is relatively easy, but it does require a search of existing names. Entrepreneurs can use the Trademark Electronic Search System (TESS) at the U.S. Patent and Trademark Office's Web site (*www.uspto.gov*) to determine whether a business or product name is already trademarked.

ENTREPRENEURIAL Profile

Barbara Allen: Mrs. Allen's SHED-STOP

When Barbara Allen launched a business selling an old family recipe of oils and vitamins that prevents pets from shedding, she named her product Mrs. Allen's SHED-STOP. Rather than applying for a patent for her product, however, Allen chose to register its name as a trademark. "If we went the patent route," she explains, "we'd have to divulge the formula. So we decided on the 'Coca-Cola' approach—trademark the name and keep the formula secret."[23]

An entrepreneur may lose the exclusive right to a trademark if it loses its unique character and becomes a generic name or if the company abandons its trademark by failing to market the brand adequately. *Aspirin, escalator, thermos, brassiere, superglue, yo-yo,* and *cellophane* all were once enforceable trademarks that have become common words in the English language. These generic terms can no longer be licensed as a company's trademark.

"There's a Mr. Egg McMuffin here who says we've been using his name without permission."

Copyrights

A **copyright** is an exclusive right that protects the creators of original works of authorship, such as literary, dramatic, musical, and artistic works (e.g., art, sculptures, literature, software, music, videos, video games, choreography, motion pictures, recordings, and others). The internationally recognized symbol © denotes a copyrighted work. A copyright protects only the form in which an idea is expressed, not the idea itself. A copyright on a creative work comes into existence the moment its creator puts that work into a tangible form. Just as with a trademark, obtaining basic copyright protection does not require registering the creative work with the U.S. Copyright Office; doing so, however, gives creators greater protection over their work. When author J. K. Rowling wrote the manuscripts for the immensely popular *Harry Potter* series, she automatically had a copyright on her creation. To secure her works against infringement, however, Rowling registered the copyright with the U.S. Copyright Office. Copyright applications must be filed with the Copyright Office in the Library of Congress for a fee of $35 per application. A valid copyright on a work lasts for the life of the creator plus 70 years after his or her death. (A copyright lasts 75 to 100 years if the copyright holder is a business.) When a copyright expires, the work becomes public property and can be used by anyone free of charge.

Because they are easy to duplicate, computer software, CDs, and DVDs are among the most-often-pirated items by copyright infringers. Copyright piracy costs U.S. companies an estimated $58 billion a year in lost sales.[24] The software and music industries alone lose $15.4 billion annually to pirates.[25]

Protecting Intellectual Property

Acquiring the protection of patents, trademarks, and copyrights is useless unless an entrepreneur takes action to protect those rights in the marketplace. Unfortunately, some businesspeople do not respect others' rights of ownership to products, processes, names, and works and infringe on those rights with impunity. In other cases, the infringing behavior simply is the result of a lack of knowledge about others' rights of ownership. After acquiring the proper legal protection through patents, copyrights, or trademarks, entrepreneurs must monitor the market (and the Internet in particular) for unauthorized copycat users. If an entrepreneur has a valid patent, trademark, or copyright, stopping an infringer usually requires nothing more than a stern "cease and desist" letter from an attorney. Offenders usually want to avoid expensive legal battles and agree to stop their illegal behavior. If that tactic fails, the entrepreneur may have no choice but to bring an infringement lawsuit, many of which end up being settled out of court.

The primary weapon an entrepreneur has to protect patents, trademarks, and copyrights is the legal system. The major problem with relying on the legal system to enforce ownership rights is the cost of infringement lawsuits, which can quickly exceed the budget of most small business. Legal battles usually are expensive. Before bringing a lawsuit, an entrepreneur must consider the following issues:

- Can the opponent afford to pay if you win?
- Do you expect to get enough from the suit to cover the costs of hiring an attorney and preparing a case?
- Can you afford the loss of time, money, and privacy from the ensuing lawsuit?

The Law of Agency

4. Explain the basics of the law of agency.

An **agent** is one who stands in the place of and represents another in business dealings. Although he has the power to act for the principal, an agent remains subject to the principal's control. Many entrepreneurs do not realize that their employees are agents while performing job-related tasks. Employers are liable only for those acts that employees perform within the scope of employment. For example, if an employee loses control of a flower shop's delivery van while making a delivery and crashes into several parked cars, the owner of the flower shop (the principal) and the employee (the agent) are liable for any damages caused by the crash. Even if the accident occurred while the employee was on a small detour of his own (e.g., to stop by his house), the owner is still liable for damages as long as the employee is working "within the scope of his employment." Normally, an employee is considered to be within the scope of his or her employment if the employee is motivated in part by the principal's action and if the place and time for performing the act is not significantly different from what is authorized.

Any person, even those lacking contractual capacity, can serve as an agent, but a principal must have the legal capacity to create contracts. Both the principal and the agent are bound by the requirements of a fiduciary relationship, one characterized by trust and good faith. In addition, each party has specific duties to the other. An agent's duties include the following:

- *Loyalty*. Every agent must be faithful to the principal in all business dealings.
- *Performance*. An agent must perform his or her duties according to the principal's instructions.
- *Notification*. The agent must notify the principal of all facts and information concerning the subject matter of the agency.
- *Duty of care*. An agent must act with reasonable care when performing duties for the principal.
- *Accounting*. An agent is responsible for accounting for all profits and property received or distributed on the principal's behalf.

A principal's duties include the following:

- *Compensation*. Unless a free agency is created, the principal must pay the agent for his or her services.
- *Reimbursement*. The principal must reimburse the agent for all payments made for the principal or any expenses incurred in the administration of the agency.
- *Cooperation*. Every principal has the duty to indemnify the agent for any authorized payments or any loss or damages incurred by the agent, unless the liability is the result of the agent's mistake.
- *Safe working conditions*. The law requires a principal to provide a safe working environment for all agents. Workers' compensation laws cover an employer's liability for injuries agents receive on the job.

As agents, employees can bind a company to agreements, even if the owner did not intend for them to do so. An employee can create a binding obligation, for instance, if the business owner represents him or her as authorized to perform such transactions. For example, the owner of a flower shop who routinely permits a clerk to place orders with a supplier has given that employee *apparent authority* for purchasing. Similarly, employees have *implied authority* to create agreements when performing the normal duties of their jobs. For example, the chief financial officer of a company has the authority to create binding agreements when dealing with the company's bank.

One issue related to agency that many businesses confront is whether their workers are employees who are directly under their control or independent contractors who are hired temporarily by contract to perform a job. Because employers do not have to incur payroll taxes or provide health care or other benefits to independent contractors, paying an independent contractor is less expensive than hiring an employee to do the same job. In addition, an employer is liable for negligent acts by an employer but is not liable for the negligent acts of an independent contractor. Some businesses have experienced disputes with the IRS over the status of workers that they claim are independent contractors and the IRS considers employees. The difference boils down to the right of control. The more control that an employer exercises over a worker, the more likely it is that he or she is an employee. If, however, the employer controls only the final result of the work, the worker is most likely an independent contractor. The IRS provides guidelines for determining the difference between employees and independent contractors on its Web site at *www.irs.gov*.

Bankruptcy

5. Explain the basics of bankruptcy law.

Bankruptcy occurs when a business is unable to pay its debts as they come due. Although filing for bankruptcy traditionally has had a social stigma attached to it, today it has become an accepted business strategy for troubled companies (see Figure 4). Companies such as General Motors, Six Flags (theme park operator), the Greenbrier (a historic Virginia hotel), Circuit City (electronics retailer), Linens and Things (home accessories retailer), Interstate Bakeries (maker of Twinkies and Wonder Bread), and many others have filed for bankruptcy recently. Some of these companies have vanished, but others have emerged from bankruptcy and continue to operate.

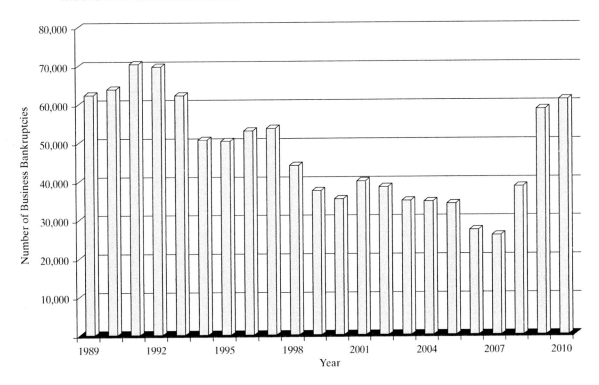

FIGURE 4
Number of Business Bankruptcies

Source: American Bankruptcy Institute, 2010, *www.abiworld.org/ContentManagement/ContentDisplay.cfm?ContentID=8149.*

Forms of Bankruptcy

Many people who file for bankruptcy are small business owners seeking protection from creditors created by the Bankruptcy Reform Act of 1978, which was amended in 2005. The Bankruptcy Reform Act of 2005 requires debtors to pay as many of their debts as possible rather than having them discharged by bankruptcy. The majority of bankruptcies related to small businesses. Usually, small business owners in danger of failing choose from two types of bankruptcies: **liquidation** and **reorganization**.

LIQUIDATIONS. The business simply declares all of its debts and turns over all of its assets to a trustee, who is elected by the creditors or appointed by a court. The trustee sells the assets and distributes all proceeds first to secured creditors and then to unsecured creditors (which include stockholders). Depending on the outcome of the asset sale, creditors can receive anywhere between 0 and 100 percent of their claims against the bankrupt company. Once the bankruptcy proceeding is complete, any remaining debts are discharged, and the company disappears.

ENTREPRENEURIAL
Profile

The LeRoy Family: Tavern on the Green

The LeRoy family, owners of Tavern on the Green, one of New York City's most famous restaurants, after the city refused to renew its contract with them. The LeRoys had operated the restaurant, which was located in Central Park, since 1976. An auction of the historic restaurant's assets, which included Tiffany lamps, Baccarat crystal, and hand-painted murals, failed to generate enough money to pay off the restaurant's debts.[26]

Straight bankruptcy proceedings can be started by filing either a voluntary or an involuntary petition. A voluntary case starts when the debtor files a petition with a bankruptcy court, stating the names and addresses of all creditors, the debtor's financial position, and all property the debtor owns. In contrast, creditors start an involuntary petition by filing with the bankruptcy court. If there are 12 or more creditors, at least 3 of them with unsecured claims totaling $14,425 or more must file the involuntary petition. If a debtor has fewer than 12 creditors, only 1 of them having a claim of $14,425 or more is required to file. As soon as a petition (voluntary or involuntary) is filed in a bankruptcy court, all creditors' claims against the debtor are suspended. Called an **automatic stay**, this provision prevents creditors from collecting any of the debts the debtor owed them before filing the petition. In other words, no creditor can begin or continue to pursue debt collection once the petition is filed.

Not every asset an individual bankrupt debtor owns is subject to court attachment; certain assets are exempt, although each state establishes its own exemptions. Most states make an allowance for equity in a home, interest in an automobile, and interest in a large number of personal items and other personal assets. Federal law allows a $21,625 exemption for a home, an $11,525 exemption for household items and clothing, a $3,450 exemption for equity in a car, and several other exemptions.

The law does not allow a debtor to transfer the ownership of property to others to avoid its seizure in a bankruptcy. If a debtor transfers property within 1 year of the filing of a bankruptcy petition, the trustee can ignore the transfer and claim the assets. In addition, a court will overturn any transfer of property made for the express purpose of avoiding repayment of debts (called **fraudulent conveyance**). The new law also enables a judge to petition if it is a "substantial abuse" of the bankruptcy code.

REORGANIZATION. For a small business weakened by a faltering economy, excessive debt load, or management mistakes. The philosophy behind this form of bankruptcy is that ailing companies can prosper again if given a fresh start with less debt. Bankruptcy filing protects a company's assets from creditors' legal actions while it formulates a plan for reorganization and repaying or settling its debts or for selling the business. In most cases, a small business and its creditors negotiate a settlement in which the company repays a percentage of its debts, with the remainder of them dismissed. The business continues to operate under the court's direction, but creditors cannot foreclose on it, nor can they collect any prebankruptcy debts the company owes.

The average duration of bankruptcies is declining as companies realize the benefits of exiting bankruptcy as quickly as possible. Unlike a typical bankruptcy, which may take 2 or more years to complete, Section 363 bankruptcy allows a bankrupt company to sell assets quickly, free and clear of all liens, and emerge from bankruptcy in as little as 30 to 60 days. Because of Section 363, automaker Chrysler completed its bankruptcy in just 42 days. Another exemption allows a fast-track version of bankruptcy for small businesses with liabilities that do not exceed $2 million that streamlines the process and is less expensive.

A bankruptcy filing can be either voluntary or involuntary. Once the petition is filed, an automatic stay goes into effect and the debtor has 120 days to file a reorganization plan with the court. Usually, the court does not replace management with an appointed trustee; instead, the bankrupt party, called the *debtor in possession,* serves as trustee. If the debtor fails to file a plan within the 120-day limit, any party involved in the bankruptcy, including creditors, may propose a plan. The plan must identify the various classes of creditors and their claims, outline how each class will be treated, and establish a method to implement the plan. It also must spell out the debts that the company cannot pay, those that it can pay, and the methods the debtor will use to pay them.

Once the plan is filed, the court must decide whether to approve it. A court will approve a plan if a majority of each of the three classes of creditors—secured, priority, and unsecured—votes in favor of it. The court will confirm a plan if it has a reasonable chance of success, is submitted in good faith, and is "in the best interest of the creditors." If the court rejects the plan, the creditors must submit a new one for court approval.

The greatest of which is a chance to survive. In addition, employees keep their jobs, and customers get an uninterrupted supply of goods and services. However, there are costs involved in bankruptcy proceedings. Customers, suppliers, creditors, and often employees lose confidence in a company's ability to succeed.

Profile

*Eva Christian: Café
Boulevard*

Eva Christian, owner of several restaurants in Dayton, Ohio, filed for bankruptcy protection for Café Boulevard, a restaurant located in the city's Oregon Historic District. Christian operated Café Boulevard for 12 years, but a weak economy, rising food prices and operating costs, and a 12 percent decline in sales decimated the company's ability to pay its debts. When Christian filed for bankruptcy, the restaurant had $56,000 in assets and $362,000 in liabilities, including outstanding debts for bank loans; federal, state, and city taxes; and others. "When I decided to file for bankruptcy, I was crushed," says Christian, "but it gives people the opportunity to bounce back." Christian did bounce back; she continues to operate the restaurant but decided to transform it into Boulevard Haus, a modern, casual German restaurant and bar.[27]

IN THE ENTREPRENEURIAL
SPOTLIGHT   A Second Chance at Success

In 1988, Theodore Delgaizo and two partners started their own engineering company in Exton, Pennsylvania, with a little of their own capital and a $60,000 bank loan secured by each of their homes. They built a successful business that specialized in designing gas plants for energy companies, and by 2000 Main Line Engineering Associates (MLEA) had 20 employees, sales of $1.5 million, and solid profits. Delgaizo, now the sole owner of MLEA, landed a big job to manage the construction of a liquid nitrogen plant in Nova Scotia for a rubber recycler. It was the company's first foray into full-fledged construction management, which required MLEA to hire contractors and manage the entire project, including ordering the materials and equipment required to complete the job.

Delgaizo purchased $1.5 million worth of equipment for the factory from suppliers on credit, but problems soon started. The conglomerate that owned the rubber recycling business sold it to another company, and that company decided to scrap the liquid nitrogen project. MLEA had collected $100,000 for the original design work it had done for the factory but was on the hook for the $1.5 million of equipment and materials it had purchased—the equivalent of the company's entire annual revenue. "We were too small a business to finance that type of deal," says Delgaizo.

MLEA sued the client for breach of contract and won a verdict; however, the client made no payments. MLEA ended up settling the case for pennies on the dollar a few years later. In the meantime, the company's creditors, who were expecting payment in 120 days, were demanding

cash. The company's cash flow was decimated after it lost two significant bids that it had expected to win. By then, 3 of MLEA's 12 suppliers had filed suit against it. Smothering under a $2 million debt load, Delgaizo saw only one viable option: Delgaizo had always viewed bankruptcy negatively but soon realized that it can be the only lifeline for a good company that has been hammered by a series of management mistakes and unfortunate events—a company like his.

Delgaizo put together a detailed reorganization plan for the court, which appointed a trustee to oversee the company. Included in his plan was a repayment schedule on which all of MLEA's creditors would vote. Delgaizo had to review every debt the company owed, classifying it as either "assumed" (those the company would pay in full, such as utility bills) and "rejected" (those on which the company would pay only a fraction of the total debt, such as the purchases for the liquid nitrogen plant). "I told the judge that we would never take on another turnkey project again," says Delgaizo. "For us, getting out of trouble meant getting back to basics." In the end, a majority of creditors approved the reorganization plan, which called for full payment to an asset-based lender that had extended the company a line of credit to keep it afloat and 15 cents on the dollar to the nitrogen project's vendors. The move erased $1 million from MLEA's balance sheet and gave it the chance for a fresh start. Delgaizo had to file monthly progress reports with the court-appointed trustee and laid off half of the company's employees. Still, cash flow was tight. "The remaining staffers went several months with no pay," admits Delgaizo. Although 70 percent of companies that file for bankruptcy ultimately are liquidated, MLEA is an exception. After emerging from bankruptcy, MLEA has recovered, rehiring three former employees and one new one. Delgaizo has secured a $300,000 line of credit to cover operating expenses when normal swings in receipts cause its cash balance to dip. MLEA is on track to generate $2 million in annual sales and expects to repay its remaining $178,000 debt within 2 years. Now a much wiser business owner, Delgaizo is thankful that bankruptcy gave him and his company a second chance at success, and he intends to make the most of it.

1. What advantages does bankruptcy offer troubled companies? What disadvantages do companies that file for bankruptcy incur?
2. Use the Web to research other companies that have declared bankruptcy. Select one company that is of interest to you and prepare a one-page report that describes the sequence of events that led to the bankruptcy, the company's plan for reorganizing, and the outcome for the company.

Source: Based on Melanie Lindner, "A Debtor's Tale," *Forbes*, May 25, 2009, pp. 50–52.

Government Regulation

6. Explain some of the government regulations affecting small businesses, including those governing trade practices, consumer protection, consumer credit, and the environment.

Although most entrepreneurs recognize the need for some government regulation of business, most believe the process is overwhelming and out of control. Government regulation of business is far from new; in fact, Congress created the first regulatory agency, the Interstate Commerce Commission, in 1887. The Great Depression of the 1930s triggered a great deal of regulation of business. From the 1930s on, laws regulating business practices and the creation of government agencies to enforce the regulations have expanded continuously. Not to be outdone by the federal regulators, most states have created their own regulatory agencies to create and enforce a separate set of rules and regulations. Small business owners often feel overwhelmed by the paperwork required to respond to all of the government agencies trying to regulate them. For instance, an entrepreneur who wants to start an auto repair shop must contend with 38 sets of regulations from 18 federal, state, and local agencies.[28]

The major complaint that small business owners have concerning government regulation concerns the cost of compliance. The Small Business Administration's Office of Advocacy estimates that complying with government regulation costs businesses $1.75 trillion per year.[29] Because many of the costs of complying with regulations are fixed, the impact of the regulatory burden is greater on small businesses than on big businesses. Large companies can spread the cost of compliance over a larger number of employees and, consequently, have a lower regulatory cost per employee. A Small Business Administration study shows that the cost of compliance per employee for small companies with 1 to 20 workers is $10,585, which is 36 percent higher than the $7,755 cost per employee at companies with more than 500 workers.[30] Figure 5 shows the cost of complying with federal regulations by company size.

In a competitive market, small companies cannot simply pass these additional costs on to their customers, and, consequently, they experience a squeeze on their profit margins. The Small Business Regulatory Enforcement and Fairness Act (SBREFA) offers business owners some hope. SBREFA amended the Regulatory Flexibility Act of 1980, which Congress passed in response to small business owners' frustration at an ever-increasing burden of federal regulation. SBREFA's purpose is to require government agencies to consider the impact of their regulations on small companies and gives business owners more input into the regulatory process.

Most business owners agree that some government regulation is necessary. There must be laws governing working safety, environmental protection, package labeling, consumer credit, and other relevant issues because some dishonest, unscrupulous managers will abuse the opportunity to serve the public's interest. It is not the regulations that protect workers and consumers and achieve social objectives to which business owners object, but those that produce only marginal benefits relative to their costs. Owners of small companies, especially, seek relief from wasteful and meaningless government regulations, charging that the cost of compliance exceeds the benefits gained.

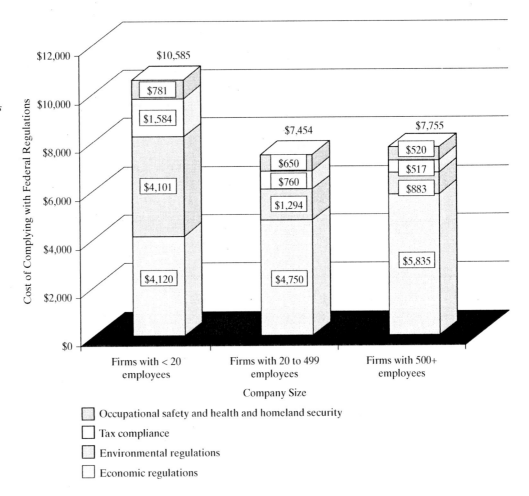

Federal Regulatory Compliance Cost by Company Size

Source: Nicole V. Crain and Mark Crain, *The Impact of Regulatory Costs on Small Firms*, Small Business Administration Office of Advocacy, September 2010, p. 7.

ENTREPRENEURIAL

Profile

Dale and Spencer Bell: San Tan Flat Saloon & Grill

Dale Bell, co-owner with his son, Spencer, of San Tan Flat Saloon & Grill in Queen Creek, Arizona, spent 3 years in a legal battle after officials in Pinal County ruled that Bell's restaurant violated an ordinance passed in 1962 that banned outdoor dance halls. The county threatened to fine the Bells more than $700,000 ($700 for each day they allowed dancing on the outdoor patio and courtyard at the restaurant they own), citing the ordinance that requires dance halls to be "within a completely closed structure." In the case, the Bells pointed out that they do not charge customers to dance and that 99 percent of their revenue comes from food and beverage sales, with the remainder generated by T-shirt sales and billiards. They argued that allowing customers to dance does not transform their restaurant, which serves 3,000 to 5,000 customers per week, into a dance hall. A state judge ruled in favor of the Bells, but Dale says that during the legal dispute their customer base declined by 30 percent because of the perception that customers themselves would be fined if they were caught dancing outside.[31]

Trade Practices

SHERMAN ANTITRUST ACT. Contemporary society places great value on free competition in the marketplace, and antitrust laws reflect this. The notion of *laissez-faire*—that the government should not interfere with the operation of the economy—that once dominated U.S. markets no longer prevails. One of the earliest trade laws was the Sherman Antitrust Act, which was passed in 1890 to promote competition in the U.S. economy. This act is the foundation on which antitrust policy in the United States is built and was aimed at breaking up the most powerful monopolies of the late nineteenth century. The Sherman Antitrust Act contains two primary provisions affecting growth and trade among businesses.

Section I forbids "every contract, combination in the form of trust or otherwise, or conspiracy, in restraint of trade or commerce among the several states, or with foreign nations." This section outlaws any agreement among sellers that might create an unreasonable restraint on free trade in the marketplace. For example, a group of small and medium-size regional supermarkets formed a cooperative association to purchase products to resell under private labels only in restricted geographic regions. The U.S. Supreme Court ruled that their action was an attempt to restrict competition by allocating territories and had "no purpose except stifling of competition."[32]

Section II of the Sherman Antitrust Act makes it illegal for any person to "monopolize or attempt to monopolize any part of the trade or commerce among the several states, or with foreign nations." The primary focus of Section II is on preventing the undesirable effects of monopoly power in the marketplace.

CLAYTON ACT. Congress passed the Clayton Act in 1914 to strengthen federal antitrust laws by spelling out specific monopolistic activities. The major provisions of the Clayton Act forbid the following activities:

- *Price discrimination.* A firm cannot charge different customers different prices for the same product, unless the price discrimination is based on an actual cost savings, is made to meet a lower price from competitors, or is justified by a difference in grade, quality, or quantity sold.
- *Exclusive dealing and tying contracts.* A seller cannot require a buyer to purchase only his or her product to the exclusion of other competitive sellers' products (an exclusive dealing agreement). In addition, the act forbids sellers to sell a product on the condition that the buyer agrees to purchase another product the seller offers (a tying agreement). For example, a computer manufacturer could not sell a computer to a business and, as a condition of the sale, require the firm to purchase software as well.
- *Purchasing stock in competing corporations.* A business cannot purchase the stock or assets of another business when the effect may be to substantially lessen competition. This does not mean that a corporation cannot hold stock in a competing company; the rule is designed to prevent horizontal mergers that reduce competition. The Federal Trade Commission and the Antitrust Division of the Justice Department enforce this section, evaluating the market shares of the companies involved and the potential effects of a horizontal merger before ruling on its legality.
- *Interlocking directorates.* The act forbids interlocking directorates—a person serving on the board of directors of two or more competing companies.

► ENTREPRENEURSHIP IN ACTION ►

Is the NFL Subject to the Sherman Antitrust Act?

For years, the National Football League (NFL) sold non-exclusive rights to manufacture the insignia caps for its 32 teams to several companies, including American Needle Inc., a small manufacturer founded in 1918 in Buffalo Grove, Illinois. In 2000, the NFL sold a 10-year exclusive license to manufacture NFL caps to Reebok, a division of Germany's Adidas AG, a move that ended American Needle's right to manufacture and market the highly profitable caps. American Needle filed a lawsuit against the NFL, claiming that the agreement among the NFL, its 32 teams, and Reebok violated the Sherman Antitrust Act of 1890, which prohibits "every contract . . . in restraint of trade." American Needle, which makes caps for major league baseball teams, contends that the exclusive licensing deal amounts to collusion that limits competition by authorizing only one manufacturer of NFL caps. In other

words, the contract that binds the NFL, its 32 teams, and Reebok constitutes an agreement among competitors that is illegal because it restrains trade.

The NFL claims that because it operates as a single entity, there could be no collusion among its 32 teams, which, in turn, precludes any violations of the Sherman Antitrust Act. Even though NFL teams compete against one another on the field and when drafting players, they must cooperate with one another concerning the rules of the game and the structure of the draft. It is this unique interaction between competition and cooperation that lies at the heart of the case, which ended up on the docket of the United States Supreme Court.

Writing the opinion in a unanimous 9-0 ruling, Justice John Paul Stevens (now retired) reversed the decision by the Court of Appeals for the Seventh Circuit in favor of the NFL. Stevens wrote that the lower court erred by classifying "NFL football" as a single entity that competes against other forms of entertainment and discounting the fact that NFL teams

A recent ruling by the U.S. Supreme Court means that the NFL, which controls the licensing for the insignia caps for its 32 teams, is subject to the Sherman Antitrust Act.

Source: Kevin Terrell/AP Wide World Photos

compete against one another not only on the field but also in the marketplace. NFL teams compete for players, fans, and ticket sales and "for intellectual property," he wrote. "To a firm making hats, the Saints and the Colts are two potentially competing suppliers of valuable trademarks." Stevens went on to compare an NFL team to a maker of nuts and bolts. "A nut and bolt can only operate together, but an agreement between nut and bolt manufacturers is still subject" to the Sherman Antitrust Act. The Supreme Court ruled that agreements are not exempt from the Sherman Antitrust Act if those agreements "bring together independent centers of decision making." The Court's ruling means that the essence of the Sherman Antitrust Act—that competitors cannot conspire in ways that limit competition or harm consumers—applies to the NFL. "The fact that NFL teams share an interest in making the league successful and profitable, and that they must cooperate in the production and scheduling of games, provides a perfectly sensible justification for making a host of collective decisions," said Stevens. "But the conduct at the issue of this case is still concerted activity under the Sherman Act."

Experts say that a ruling in favor of the NFL could have given NFL teams extraordinary power to set prices of everything from players' salaries and tickets to team caps

and hot dogs sold in their stadiums. It is too early to tell what impact—if any—the Court's decision in this case will have on the collective bargaining process in which the players' union negotiates an employment agreement with the NFL. The decision does, however, give small companies such as American Needle the opportunity to compete for contracts to manufacture and sell items bearing the logos of NFL teams.

1. Develop an argument for the Supreme Court that supports American Needle's case.
2. Develop an argument for the Supreme Court that supports the NFL's case.
3. Which of the two arguments to you find more compelling? In other words, do you agree with the Supreme Court's decision in this case? Explain.

Sources: Based on Jess Bravin and Matthew Futterman, "Court Makes NFL Play Defense," *Wall Street Journal*, May 25, 2010, p. A4; Michael McCann, "Why American Needle–NFL Is the Most Important Case in Sports History," *Sports Illustrated*, January 12, 2010, *http://sportsillustrated.cnn.com/2010/writers/michael_mccann/01/12/americanneedlev.nfl/index.html*; K. Craig Wildfang and Ryan Marth, "*American Needle v. NFL*: The Supreme Court Stops NFL's Drive for Antitrust Immunity," Robbins, Kaplan, Miller, and Ciresi, May 24, 2001, *www.rkmc.com/American-Needle-v-NFL-The-Supreme-Court-Stops-NFL%27s-Drive-for-Antitrust-Immunity.htm*; American Needle Inc. v. NFL, U.S. Supreme Court, 08-661, October 2010.

FEDERAL TRADE COMMISSION ACT. To supplement the Clayton Act, Congress passed the Federal Trade Commission Act in 1914, which created the Federal Trade Commission (FTC) and gave it a broad range of powers. Section 5 gives the FTC the power to prevent "unfair methods of competition in commerce and unfair or deceptive acts or practices in commerce." To be considered deceptive, a company's activity must involve a material misrepresentation that is likely to mislead a consumer who is acting in a reasonable manner.

Recent amendments have expanded the FTC's powers. The FTC's primary targets are those businesses that engage in unfair trade practices, often brought to the surface by consumer complaints. In addition, the agency has issued a number of trade regulation rules defining acceptable and unacceptable trade practices in various industries. Its major weapon is a "cease and desist order," commanding the violator to stop its unfair trade practices.

The FTC Act and the Lanham Trademark Act of 1988 (plus state laws) govern the illegal practice of deceptive advertising. In general, the FTC can review any advertisement that might mislead people into buying a product or service they would not buy if they knew the truth. For instance, if a small business advertised a "huge year-end inventory reduction sale" but kept its prices the same as its regular prices, it is violating the law.

ROBINSON-PATMAN ACT. Although the Clayton Act addressed price discrimination and the FTC forbade the practice, Congress found the need to strengthen the law because many businesses circumvented the original rules. In 1936, Congress passed the Robinson-Patman Act, which further restricted price discrimination in the marketplace. The act forbids any seller "to discriminate in price between different purchases of commodities of like grade and quality" unless there are differences in the cost of manufacture, sale, or delivery of the goods. Even if a price-discriminating firm escaped guilt under the Clayton Act, it violated the Robinson-Patman Act. Traditionally, the FTC has had the primary responsibility of enforcing the Robinson-Patman Act.

Consumer Protection

Since the early 1960s, legislators have created many laws aimed at protecting consumers from unscrupulous sellers, unreasonable credit terms, and mislabeled or unsafe products. Early laws focused on ensuring that food and drugs sold in the marketplace were safe and of proper quality. The first law, the Pure Food and Drug Act, passed in 1906, regulated the labeling of various food and drug products. Later amendments empowered government agencies to establish safe levels of food additives and to outlaw carcinogenic (cancer-causing) additives. In 1938, Congress passed the Food, Drug, and Cosmetics Act, which created the Food and Drug Administration (FDA). The FDA is responsible for establishing standards of safe over-the-counter drugs; inspecting food and drug manufacturing operations; performing research on food, additives, and drugs; regulating drug labeling; and other related tasks.

Congress has also created a number of laws to establish standards pertaining to product labeling for consumer protection. Since 1976, manufacturers have been required to print accurate information about the quantity and content of their products in a conspicuous place on the package. Generally, labels must identify the raw materials used in the product, the manufacturer, the distributor (and its place of business), the net quantity of the contents, and the quantity of each serving if the package states the number of servings. The law also requires labels to be truthful. For example, a candy bar labeled "new, bigger size" must actually be bigger. These requirements, created by the Fair Packaging and Labeling Act of 1976, were designed to improve the customers' ability to comparison shop. A 1970 amendment to the Fair Packaging and Labeling Act, the Poison Prevention Packaging Act, required manufacturers to install childproof caps on all products that are toxic.

With the passage of the Consumer Products Safety Act in 1972, Congress created the Consumer Product Safety Commission (CPSC) to control potentially dangerous products sold to consumers, and it has broad powers to regulate manufacturers and sellers of consumer products. For instance, the CPSC can set safety requirements for consumer products, and it has the power to ban the production of any product it considers hazardous to consumers. It can also order vendors to remove unsafe products from their shelves. In addition to enforcing the Consumer Product Safety Act, the CPSC is also charged with enforcing the Refrigerator Safety Act, the Federal Hazardous Substance Act, the Child Protection and Toy Safety Act, the Poison Prevention Package Act, and the Flammable Fabrics Act.

The Magnuson-Moss Warranty Act, passed in 1975, regulates written warranties that companies offer on the consumer goods they sell. The act does not require companies to offer warranties; it only regulates the warranties companies choose to offer. It also requires businesses to state warranties in easy-to-understand language and defines the conditions warranties must meet before they can be designated as "full warranties."

Are Your Ads Setting You Up for Trouble?

When a Florida auto dealer offered a "free 4-day, 3-night vacation to Acapulco" for any customer purchasing a new car or van, he had no idea of the legal problems his advertisement would create. A customer who bought a van from the dealer felt cheated when he discovered that the "free vacation" was actually a sales promotion for a time-share condominium and was overrun with restrictions, conditions, and qualifications. Believing the ad was deceptive, the customer filed a lawsuit against the dealer. The jury ruled against the car dealer and awarded the customer $1,768 in compensatory damages and $667,000 in punitive damages.

Entrepreneurs sometimes run afoul of the laws concerning advertising because they do not know how to comply with legal requirements. The FTC is the federal agency that regulates advertising and deals with problems created by deceptive ads. Under federal and state laws, an advertisement is unlawful if it misleads or deceives a reasonable customer, even if the business owner responsible for it had no intention to deceive. Any ad containing a false statement is in violation of the law, although the entrepreneur may not know that the statement is false. The FTC judges an ad by the overall impression it creates, not by the technical truthfulness of its individual parts.

What can entrepreneurs do to avoid charges of deceptive advertising? The following tips from the Street-Smart Entrepreneur will help:

- *Make sure that your ads are accurate.* Avoid creating ads that promise more than a product or service can deliver. Take the time to verify the accuracy of every claim or statement in your ads. If a motor oil protects an engine from damage, don't claim that it will repair damage that already exists in an engine—unless you can prove that it actually does.
- *Understand the difference between sales "puffery" and false advertising.* The distinction is not always clear. Sales puffery involves claims that are so general or so exaggerated that they would not confuse customers. (How many times have you seen a small restaurant advertising that it has "the best hot dog in town"?) The more specific and fact-based the claims in an ad are, the more likely they are to pose problems for a company if they are false or if the company has no factual basis for making them. When Pizza Hut ("Best Pizza Under One Roof") filed

a false advertising claim against Papa John's Pizza over a Papa John's ad that claimed "Better Ingredients, Better Pizza," a federal court of appeals ruled that Papa John's claim was puffery and that the company could continue to use it *if* it stopped making specific fact-based claims in the same ad that its tomato paste and dough were superior. For instance, the ad for Papa John's claimed that its sauce, which was made from "vine-ripened tomatoes," was superior to Pizza Hut's "remanufactured tomato sauce." Because Papa John's had no facts to prove this claim, the court ruled that this was false advertising.

- *Get permission to use quotations, pictures, and endorsements.* Never use material in an ad from an outside source unless you get written permission to do so. One business owner got into trouble when he inserted a photograph of a famous athlete without his permission into an ad for his company's service.
- *Be careful when you compare competitor's products or services to your own.* False statements that harm the reputation of a competitor's business, products, or services not only may result in charges of false advertising but also in claims of trade libel. Make sure that any claims in your ads comparing your products to competitors' are fair and accurate. You can use a competitor's trademark in your advertising (for purposes of comparison, for example) as long as it does not cause confusion among customers concerning the origin of the product or its affiliation with the competitor.
- *Stock sufficient quantities of advertised items.* Businesses that advertise items for sale must be sure to have enough units on hand to meet anticipated demand. If you suspect that demand may outstrip your supply, state in the ad that quantities are limited.
- *Avoid "bait and switch" advertising.* This illegal technique involves advertising an item for sale at an attractive price when a business has no real intention of selling that product at that price. Companies using this technique often claim to have sold out of the advertised special. Their goal is to lure customers in with the low price and then switch them over to a similar product at a higher price.
- *Use the word "free" carefully and accurately.* Every advertiser knows that one of the most powerful

words in advertising is "free." However, anything you advertise as being free must actually be free. For instance, suppose a business advertises a free paintbrush to anyone who buys a gallon of a particular type of paint for $11.95. If the company's regular price for this is less than $11.95, the ad is deceptive because the paintbrush is not really free.

- *Be careful of what your ad does not say.* Omitting information from an ad that leaves customers with a false impression about a product or service and its performance is also a violation of the law.
- *Describe sale prices and "savings" carefully.* Business owners sometimes get into trouble with false advertising when they advertise items at prices that offer huge "savings" over their "regular" prices.

One jeweler violated the law by advertising a bracelet for $299, a savings of $200 from the item's regular $499 price. In reality, the jeweler had never sold the item at its $499 "regular" price; the item's normal price was the $299 he advertised as the "sale" price.

Sources: Adapted from *Guides Against Bait Advertising,* Federal Trade Commission, *www.gov/bcp/guides/baitads-gd.htm; Frequently Asked Questions: A Guide for Small Business,* Federal Trade Commission, *www.ftc.gov/bcp/conline/pubs/buspubs/ad-faqs.htm;* Carlotta Roberts, "The Customer's Always Right," *Entrepreneur,* November 20, 2002, *www.entrepreneur.com/article/0,4621.284044.00.html;* James Astrachan, "False Advertising Primer," Astrachan, Gunst, Thomas, PLC, 2006, *www.aboutfalseadvertising.com/index1_files/False%20Advertising%20Primer.pdf,* p. 14; "Seven Rules for Legal Advertising," *Inc.* (n.d.), *www.inc.com/search/20153.html;* "Consumer Protection Laws," *Inc.* (n.d.), *www.inc.com/search/19691.html.*

The Telemarketing and Consumer Fraud and Abuse Protection Act of 1994 put in place the following restrictions on telemarketers:

- Calling a person's residence outside the hours of 8:00 A.M. to 8:00 P.M.
- Claiming an affiliation with a government agency where such an affiliation does not exist.
- Claiming an ability to improve a customer's credit record or obtain a loan for a person regardless of that person's credit history.
- Not telling the receiver of the call that it is a sales call.
- Claiming an ability to recover goods or money lost by a consumer.

Consumer Credit

Another area subject to intense government regulation is consumer credit. This section of the law has grown in importance as credit has become a major part of many consumer purchases. The primary law regulating consumer credit is the Truth in Lending Act of 1969. This law requires sellers who extend credit and lenders to fully disclose the terms and conditions of credit arrangements. The FTC is responsible for enforcing the Truth in Lending Act. The law outlines specific requirements that any firm that offers, arranges, or extends credit to customers must meet. The two most important terms of the credit arrangement that lenders must disclose are the finance charge and the annual percentage rate. The finance charge represents the total cost—direct and indirect—of the credit, and the annual percentage rate (APR) is the relative cost of credit stated in annual percentage terms.

The Truth in Lending Act applies to any consumer loan for less than $25,000 (or loans of any amount secured by mortgages on real estate) that includes more than four installments. Merchants extending credit to customers must state clearly the following information, using specific terminology:

- The price of the product
- The down payment and any trade-in allowance made
- The unpaid balance owed after the down payment
- The total dollar amount of the finance charge
- Any prepaid finance charges or required deposit balances, such as points, service charges, or lenders' fees
- Any other charges not include in the finance charge
- The total amount to be financed
- The unpaid balance
- The deferred payment price, including the total cash price and finance and incidental charges

- The date on which the finance charge begins to accrue
- The annual percentage rate of the finance charge
- The number, amount, and due dates of payments
- The penalties imposed in case of delinquent payments
- A description of any security interest the creditor holds
- A description of any penalties imposed for early repayment of principal

Another provision of the Truth in Lending Act limits a credit card holder's liability in case the holder's card is lost or stolen. As long as the holder notifies the company of the missing card, the holder is liable for only $50 of any amount that an unauthorized user might charge on the card (or zero if the holder notifies the company before any unauthorized use of the card).

In 1974, Congress passed the Fair Credit Billing Act, an amendment to the Truth in Lending Act. Under this law, a credit card holder may withhold payment on a faulty product, providing he or she has made a good faith effort to settle the dispute first. A credit card holder can also withhold payment to the issuing company if he or she believes the bill is in error. The cardholder must notify the issuer within 60 days but is not required to pay the bill until the dispute is settled. The creditor cannot collect any finance charge during this period unless there was no error.

Another credit law designed to protect consumers is the Equal Credit Opportunity Act of 1974, which prohibits discrimination in granting credit based on race, religion, national origin, color, gender, marital status, or whether the individual receives public assistance payments.

In 1970, Congress created the Fair Credit Reporting Act to protect consumers against the circulation of inaccurate or obsolete information pertaining to credit applications. Under this act, the consumer can request the nature of any credit investigation, the type of information assembled, and the identity of those persons receiving the report. The law requires that any obsolete or misleading information contained in the file be updated, deleted, or corrected.

Congress enacted the Fair Debt Collection Practices Act in 1977 to protect consumers from abusive debt collection practices. The law does not apply to business owners collecting their own debts, but only to debt collectors working for other businesses. The act prevents debt collectors from doing the following:

- Contacting the debtor at his or her workplace if the employer objects
- Using intimidation, harassment, or abusive language to pester the debtor
- Calling on the debtor at inconvenient times (before 8 A.M. or after 9 P.M.)
- Contacting third parties (except parents, spouses, and financial advisers) about the debt
- Contacting the consumer after receiving notice of refusal to pay the debt (except to inform the debtor of the involvement of a collection agency)
- Making false threats against the debtor

The Consumer Leasing Act of 1976 amended the Truth in Lending Act for the purpose of providing meaningful disclosure to consumers who lease goods. The lease period must be more than 4 months, and the dollar value of the lease obligation cannot exceed $25,000.

In 2003, Congress passed the Fair and Accurate Transactions Act (the FACT Act) to address the fastest growing crime in the United States: identity theft. Experts estimate that 11 million people in the United States are victims of identity theft each year, most often in the form of credit card fraud. The total amount of fraud exceeds $50 billion per year.[33] The FACT Act allows victims of identity theft to file theft reports with credit reporting agencies and requires those agencies to include "fraud alerts" in their credit reports.

Environmental Law

In 1970, Congress created the Environmental Protection Agency (EPA) and gave it the authority to create laws that would protect the environment from pollution and contamination. Although the EPA administers a number of federal environmental statutes, four in particular stand out: the Clean Air Act, the Clean Water Act, the Resource Conservation and Recovery Act, and the Pollution Prevention Act.

THE CLEAN AIR ACT. To reduce the problems associated with global warming, acid rain, and airborne pollution, Congress passed the Clean Air Act in 1970 (and several amendments since then). The act targets everything from coal-burning power plants to automobiles. The Clean Air Act assigned the EPA the task of developing national air quality standards for carbon monoxide, hydrocarbons, sulfur oxide, ozone, lead, and other harmful substances. The agency works with state and local governments to enforce compliance with these standards.

THE CLEAN WATER ACT. The Clean Water Act, passed in 1972, set out to make all navigable waters in the United States suitable for fishing and swimming by 1983 and to eliminate the discharge of pollutants into those waters by 1985. Although the EPA has made progress in cleaning up many bodies of water, it has yet to achieve these goals. The Clean Water Act requires each state to establish water quality standards and to develop plans to reach them. The act also prohibits the draining, dredging, or filling wetlands without a permit. The Clean Water Act also addresses the issues of providing safe drinking water and cleaning up oil spills in navigable waters.

THE RESOURCE CONSERVATION AND RECOVERY ACT. Congress passed the Resource Conservation and Recovery Act (RCRA) in 1976 to deal with solid waste disposal. The RCRA, which was amended in 1984, sets guidelines by which solid waste landfills must operate, and it establishes rules governing the disposal of hazardous wastes. The RCRA's goal is to prevent solid waste from contaminating the environment. What about those waste disposal sites that are already contaminating the environment? In 1980, Congress passed the Comprehensive Environmental Response, Compensation, and Liability Act (CERCLA) to deal with those sites. The act created the Superfund, a special federal fund set up to finance and to regulate the cleanup of solid-waste disposal sites that are polluting the environment.

THE POLLUTION PREVENTION ACT OF 1990. The Pollution Prevention Act of 1990 set forth a public policy statement that offered rewards to firms that reduced the creation of pollution. The federal government provides matching funds to states for programs that promote the use of "source reduction techniques" dealing with pollution problems. This is a milestone piece of legislation because it replaces the regulatory "stick" approach resented by business with a "carrot" approach that rewards businesses for positive actions that reduce pollution.

Chapter Review

1. Explain the basic elements required to create a valid, enforceable contract.
   - A valid contract must contain these elements: agreement (offer and acceptance), consideration, capacity, and legality. A contract can be valid and yet unenforceable because it fails to meet two other conditions: genuineness of assent and proper form.
   - Most contracts are fulfilled by both parties performing their promised actions; occasionally, however, one party fails to perform as agreed, thereby breaching the contract. Usually, the nonbreaching party is allowed to sue for monetary damages that would place the party in the same position he or she would have been in had the contract been performed. In cases where money is an insufficient remedy, the injured party may sue for specific performance of the contract's terms.
2. Outline the major components of the Uniform Commercial Code governing sales contracts.
   - The Uniform Commercial Code (UCC) was an attempt to create a unified body of law governing routine business transactions. Of the 10 articles in the UCC, Article 2 on the sale of goods affects many business transactions.
   - Contracts for the sale of goods must contain the same four elements of a valid contract, but the UCC relaxes many of the specific restrictions that common law imposes on contracts. Under the UCC, once the parties create a contract, they must perform their duties in good faith.
   - The UCC also covers sales warranties. A seller creates an express warranty when he makes a statement about the performance of a product or indicates by example certain characteristics of the product. Sellers automatically create other warranties— warranties of title, implied warranties of merchantability, and, in certain cases, implied warranties of fitness for a particular purpose—when they sell a product.

3. Discuss the protection of intellectual property rights using patents, trademarks, and copyrights.
   - A patent is a grant from the federal government that gives an inventor exclusive rights to an invention for 20 years. To submit a patent, an inventor must establish novelty, document the device, search existing patents, study the search results, submit a patent application to the U.S. Patent and Trademark Office, and prosecute the application.
   - A trademark is any distinctive word, symbol, or trade dress that a company uses to identify its product or to distinguish it from other goods. It serves as the company's "signature" in the marketplace.
   - A copyright protects original works of authorship. It covers only the form in which an idea is expressed and not the idea itself and lasts for 70 years beyond the creator's death.

4. Explain the basic workings of the law of agency.
   - In an agency relationship, one party (the agent) agrees to represent another (the principal). The agent has the power to act for the principal but remains subject to the principal's control. While performing job-related tasks, employees play an agent's role.
   - An agent has the following duties to a principal: loyalty, performance, notification, duty of care, and accounting. The principal has certain duties to the agent: compensation, reimbursement, cooperation, indemnification, and safe working conditions.

5. Explain the basics of bankruptcy law.
   - Entrepreneurs whose businesses fail often have no other choice but to declare bankruptcy. Liquidations, the business sells its assets, pays what debts it can, and disappears; Reorganizations, the business asks that its debts be forgiven or restructured and then re-emerges.

6. Explain some of the government regulations affecting small businesses, including those governing trade practices, consumer protection, consumer credit, and the environment.
   - Businesses operate under a multitude of government regulations governing many areas, including trade practices, where laws forbid restraint of trade; price discrimination; exclusive dealing and tying contracts; purchasing controlling interests in competitors; and interlocking directorates.
   - Other areas subject to government regulations include consumer protection (the Food, Drug, and Cosmetics Act and the Consumer Product Safety Act) and consumer credit [the Consumer Credit Protection Act (CCPA), the Fair Debt Collection Practices Act, and the Fair Credit Reporting Act], and the environment [the Clean Air Act, the Clean Water Act, the Resource Conservation and Recovery Act (RCRA), and the Pollution Prevention Act].

Discussion Questions

1. What is a contract? List and describe the four elements required for a valid contract. Must a contract be in writing to be valid?
2. What constitutes an agreement?
3. What groups of people lack contractual capacity? How do the courts view contracts that minors create? Intoxicated people? Insane people?
4. What circumstances eliminate genuineness of assent in the parties' agreement?
5. What is breach of contract? What remedies are available to a party injured by a breach?

6. What is the Uniform Commercial Code? To which kinds of contracts does the UCC apply? How does it alter the requirements for a sale contract?
7. Under the UCC, what remedies does a seller have when a buyer breaches a sales contract? What remedies does a buyer have when a seller breaches a contract?
8. What is a sales warranty? Explain the different kinds of warranties sellers offer.
9. Explain the different kinds of implied warranties the UCC imposes on sellers of goods. Can sellers disclaim these implied warranties? If so, how?

10. What is product liability? Explain the charges that most often form the basis for product liability claims. What must a customer prove under these charges?

11. What is intellectual property? What tools do entrepreneurs have to protect their intellectual property?

12. Explain the differences among patents, trademarks, and copyrights. What does each protect? How long does each last?

13. What must an inventor prove to receive a patent?

14. Briefly explain the patent application process.

15. What is an agent? What duties does an agent have to a principal? What duties does a principal have to an agent?

16. Explain the following statement: "For each benefit gained by regulation, there is a cost."

Business Plan Pro

Navigating the increasingly complex waters of the legal and regulatory environment is no easy task for entrepreneurs. Today's entrepreneurs must understand the basics of business law and government regulations if they are to operate successful businesses. Having access to a qualified attorney to serve as a business advisor is wise, but having a fundamental understanding of how to avoid potential legal entanglements is also important. Some entrepreneurs learn the importance of understanding business law and government regulation only after they face an expensive legal battle or are required to pay a costly fine. Solid planning can avoid this and the business plan can be a tool for the entrepreneur to accomplish this important task.

On the Web

If you have existing or future concerns regarding potential legal issues facing your company, begin by conducting additional research on the Web. The Companion Web site at *www.pearson highered.com/scarborough* offers some general information that you may find useful. Industry associations also may provide resources that address more common issues. Does your company face special legal issues? Is your business subject to regulation by one or more government agencies? If so, be sure that your plan addresses these matters. The more you know—and plan for now—the better. Incorporate any insights you gain from these resources into your business plan.

In the Software

At this point, the only section remaining in your business plan is the executive summary. Even though it is the first section in the plan, it is the last section completed. Because many potential lenders and investors read the executive summary first, your plan may be judged on its value and impact alone. An executive summary is a brief overview of your entire plan. Its purpose is to concisely highlight the key points of the business plan, saving readers time and preparing them for the upcoming content. The executive summary must be clear and concise. It should allow readers to grasp the essence of the business plan very quickly. An executive summary should also entice the reader to read the entire plan. It should be compelling, enabling the reader to see your vision for the venture, and motivating them to read on. For these reasons, the executive summary is the most important section of the business plan. If it fails to accomplish its tasks, the business plan may not be read.

Review the executive summary from a sample plan that you have found beneficial. To get an idea of how an executive summary should flow, you may also want to review these plans: Pegasus Sports, Hand's On Children's Museum, Salvador's Inc., and The Daily Perc. Identify attributes within other executive summaries that you find engaging and incorporate those elements into your plan's executive summary.

Write your executive summary in Business Plan Pro. Remember, this section incorporates key highlights of information in the plan ahead. Keep it brief—ideally two pages or less—and to the point.

Building Your Business Plan

The chapter in this text have guided you through all of the key aspects of creating a business plan. The final task you will complete, and one that many consider to be the single most important section, is the executive summary. Once this section is completed, your business plan is ready. Share your business plan with others whom you trust and respect. Test its effectiveness in describing your business venture. Ask for feedback. Modify sections that are unclear or fail to effectively communicate your business's message to others.

And then . . . when you are ready and the plan feels solid, the ultimate test is the answer to this question: "Would *you* invest in the venture?"

Endnotes

1. Steve Karnowski, "Tiny Bakery Feels Wrath of Doughboy," *Minnesota Public Radio*, August 10, 2010, *http://minnesota.publicradio.org/display/web/2010/08/10/doughboy-vs-doughgirl/*; "Dough Girl's New Name Is a 'Snap,'" *Salt Lake City Tribune*, December 2, 2010, *www.sltrib.com/sltrib/blogsvulture/50784083-56/dough-girl-company-cromar.html.csp*.

2. Rebecca Aherne, "Punitive Damages Award Reduced from $1.7 Million to $500,000," Kelly, Hockel, and Slein, PLC, March 23, 2010, *www.khklaw.com/articles/punitive-damage-award-against-insurer-which-mishandled-claim-for-business-interruption-coverage-reduced-from-1-7-million-to-500000/*.

3. *Carbaugh v. Klick-Lewis*, 561 A.sd 1248 (Pa 1989).

4. *Hoffman v. Red Owl Stores, Inc.*, 133 N.W. 2ed 267 (1965) 26 Wis. 2ed 683.

5. Scott Michels, "Man Sues for Revealing Affair," ABC News, August 10, 2007, *http://news.aol.com/story/ar/_a/man-sues-florist-for-revealing-affair/20070810160709990001*; Noah Oppenheim, "Man Sues Florist for Revealing Affair," MSNBC, August 13, 2007, *http://allday.msnbc.msn.com/archive/2007/08/13/314223.aspx?p=1*; Leroy Greer v. 1-800-FLOWERS, 2007, U.S. Dist. Lexis 73961.

6. *Superior Boiler Works v. R.J. Sanders, Inc.*, 1998 R.I. Lexis 153, Supreme Court of Rhode Island, 1998.

7. *Tort Liability Costs for Small Businesses*, U.S. Chamber Institute for Legal Reform, July 2010, pp. 2, 10.

8. UCC Section 2-314[1-C].

9. *Webster v. Blue Ship Tea Room*, 198 N.E. 2d 309 (Mass. 1964); 347 Mass. 421.

10. "Product Liability Basics," *Inc.*, February 2000, *www.inc.com/articles/2000/02/17249.html*.

11. "U.S. Firms Paying High Price for Global IP Theft," A. E. Feldman, August 4, 2009, *http://blog.aefeldman.com/2009/08/04/us-firms-paying-high-price-for-global-ip-theft/*.

12. Doug Palmer, "U.S. Seizes Web Sites in Fake Goods Crackdown," *Reuters*, November 29, 2010, *www.reuters.com/article/idUSTRE6AS4PW20101129*; *Intellectual Property: Observations on Efforts to Quantify the Economic Effects of Counterfeit and Pirated Goods*, U.S. Government Accountability Office, April 2010, p. 8.

13. Jeff Bliss and Sara Folden, "U.S. Seizes 82 Web Sites on Allegations They Sold Fake Goods, Holder Says," *Bloomberg*, November 29, 2010, *www.bloomberg.com/news/2010-11-29/u-s-seizes-82-websites-on-allegations-they-sold-fake-goods-holder-says.html*.

14. Anne Field, "How to Knock out Knock Offs," *BusinessWeek*, March 14, 2005, *www.businessweek.com/@@7oPzcIQQnIwLqxsA/magazine/content/05_11/b3924446.htm*.

15. Eugene R. Quinn, "Cost of Obtaining a Patent," IP Watchdog, August 15, 2007, *www.ipwatchdog.com/patent_cost.html*.

16. "U.S. Patent History," The Great Idea Finder, *www.ideafinder.com/history/inventions/uspatent.htm*; "U.S. Patent and Trademark Office Issues Seven Millionth Patent," U.S. Patent and Trademark Office, February 14, 2006, *www.uspto.gov/web/offices/com/speeches/06-09.htm*.

17. Jim Singer, "How Long Does Patent and Trademark Prosecution Take?" *IP Spotlight*, November 23, 2010, *http://ipspotlight.com/2010/11/23/how-long-does-patent-and-trademark-prosecution-take-2010-update/*; "Patent Performance," U.S. Patent and Trademark Office, *www1.uspto.gov/web/offices/com/annual/2005/040201_patentperform.html*.

18. James Bessen and Michael Meurer, "The Patent Litigation Explosion," Technological Innovation and Intellectual Property, October 24, 2005, *www.researchoninnovation.org/WordPress/?p=59*.

19. David Whitford, "Vision Quest," *FSB*, April 2006, pp. 45–46.

20. Kris Frieswick, "License to Steal?" *CFO*, September 2001, pp. 89–91; Megan Barnett, "Patents Pending," *U.S. News & World Report*, June 10, 2002, pp. 33–34; Tomima Edmark, "On Guard," *Entrepreneur*, August 1997, pp. 92–94; Tomima Edmark, "On Guard," *Entrepreneur*, February 1997, pp. 109–111.

21. Lorene Yue, "In-N-Out Burger, Sues Over S. Side Shop's Logo, Name," *Chicago Business*, July 1, 2009, *www.chicagobusiness.com/article/20090701/NEWS07/200034610/in-n-out-burger-sues-over-s-side-shops-logo-name*; Nancy Luna, "In-N-Out Settles Suit Against Chicago-area Copycat," *Orange County Register*, August 5, 2009, *http://fastfood.ocregister.com/2009/08/05/in-n-out-settles-copycat-lawsuit/30195/?replytocom=39933*; "Love It, but Don't Copy It: In-N-Out's Lesson to Wannabes," *Wall Street Journal*, August 10, 2010, *http://blogs.wsj.com/law/2009/08/10/love-it-but-dont-copy-it-in-n-outs-lesson-to-wannabes/*.

22. *Summary of Financial and Performance Highlights*, USPTO 2009, *www.uspto.gov/web/offices/com/annual/2009/par_01.html*.

23. Lance Frazer, "A Small Biz Guide to Trademarks, Patents, and Copyrights," *E-Merging Business*, Fall/Winter 2000, pp. 112–115.

24. Andrew Pincus, "Protecting the Internet from Online Pirates," *The Hill*, November 17, 2010, *http://thehill.com/blogs/congress-blog/technology/129645-protecting-the-internet-from-online-pirates*.

25. "2009 Estimated Trade Losses Due to Copyright Piracy," International Intellectual Property Alliance, June 11, 2010, *www.iipa.com/pdf/IIPA2010USTRDecisionsSpecial301TableofEstimatedTradeLossesandPiracyLevels061110.pdf*.

26. Elissa Elan, "Tavern on the Green Prepares for Auction," *Nation's Restaurant News*, December 16, 2009, *www.nrn.com/article/tavern-green-prepares-auction*; Elissa Elan, "NYC Wins Tavern on the Green Name," *Nation's Restaurant News*, March 10, 2010, *www.nrn.com/article/nyc-wins-tavern-green-name*; Elissa Elan, "Tavern on the Green Goes Out with a Bang," *Nation's Restaurant News*, January 4, 2009, *www.nrn.com/article/tavern-green-goes-out-bang*.

27. "Business Bankruptcies Are Climbing," *APP*, July 21, 2009, *www.app.com/apps/pbcs.dll/article?AID=/20090721/BUSINESS*; Mark Fisher, "Café Boulevard files for Bankruptcy Reorganization, Will Continue to Operate," *Dayton Daily News*, April 22, 2009, *www.daytondailynews.com/blogs/content/shared-gen/blogs/dayton/taste/entries/2009/04/22/cafe_boulevard_seeks_bankruptc.html*; Mark Fisher, "Café Bulevard Morphs into German Restaurant," *Dayton Daily News*, October 1, 2009, *www.daytondailynews.com/o/content/shared-gen/blogs/dayton/taste/entries/2009/10/01/cafe_boulevard_to_morph_into_g.html*.

28. Andrea James, "Small Business Owners Vent Their Regulation Frustrations," *Seattle Post-Intelligencer*, August 20, 2007, *www.sba.gov/advo/research/rs264.pdf*.

29. Nicole V. Crain and Mark Crain, *The Impact of Regulatory Costs on Small Firms*, Small Business Administration Office of Advocacy, September 2010, p. iv.

30. Ibid., p. 6.

31. Brandi Stewart, "The Last Dance," *FSB*, October 2008, p. 21; Brandi Stewart, "Arizona Saloon Owner Takes Down Antiquated Dance Ban," *Happy News*, October 2, 2008, *www.happynews.com/news/1022008/arizona-saloon-owner-takes-down-antiquated-dance-ban.htm*.

32. *United States v. Topco Associates Inc.*, 405 U.S. 596 (1972).

33. "Javelin Study Finds Identity Fraud Reached New High in 2009, but Consumers Are Fighting Back," *PR Newswire*, February 10, 2010, *www.prnewswire.com/news-releases/javelin-study-finds-identity-fraud-reached-new-high-in-2009-but-consumers-are-fighting-back-83987287.html*.

Ethics and Social Responsibility: Doing the Right Thing

Relativity applies to physics, not ethics.

—Albert Einstein

The high caliber organization is merely a reflection of its people.

—Price Pritchett

Learning Objectives

Upon completion of this chapter, you will be able to:

1 Define business ethics and describe the three levels of ethical standards.
2 Determine who is responsible for ethical behavior and why ethical lapses occur.
3 Explain how to establish and maintain high ethical standards.
4 Define social responsibility.
5 Understand the nature of business's responsibility to the environment.
6 Describe business's responsibility to employees.
7 Explain business's responsibility to customers.
8 Discuss business's responsibility to investors.
9 Describe business's responsibility to the community.

Business ethics involves the moral values and behavioral standards that businesspeople draw on as they make decisions and solve problems. It originates in a commitment to do what is right. Ethical behavior—doing what is "right" as opposed to what is "wrong"—starts at the top of an organization with the entrepreneur. Entrepreneurs' personal values and beliefs influence the way they lead their companies and are apparent in every decision they make, every policy they write, and every action they take. Entrepreneurs who succeed in the long term have a solid base of personal values and beliefs that they articulate to their employees and put into practice in ways that others can observe. Values-based leaders do more than merely follow rules and regulations; their consciences dictate that they do what is right.

In some cases, ethical dilemmas are apparent. Entrepreneurs are keenly aware of the ethical entrapments awaiting them and know that society will hold them accountable for their actions. More often, however, ethical issues are less obvious, cloaked in the garb of mundane decisions and everyday routine. Because they can easily catch entrepreneurs off guard and unprepared, these ethical "sleepers" are most likely to ensnare business owners, soiling their reputations and those of their companies. To make proper ethical choices, entrepreneurs must first be aware that a situation with ethical implications exists.

Complicating the issue even more is that, in some ethical dilemmas, no clear-cut, right or wrong answers exist. There is no direct conflict between good and evil, right and wrong, or truth and falsehood. Instead, there is only the issue of conflicting interests among a company's **stakeholders**, the various groups and individuals who affect and are affected by a business. These conflicts force entrepreneurs to identify their stakeholders and to consider the ways in which they will deal with them (see Figure 1). For instance, when the founders of a small producer of frozen foods make business decisions, they must consider the impact of those decisions on many stakeholders, including the team of employees who own work there, the farmers and companies that supply the business with raw materials, the union that represents employees in collective bargaining, the government agencies that regulate a multitude of activities, the banks that provide the business with financing, the stockholders who own shares of the company's stock, the general public the business serves, the community in which the company operates, and the customers who buy the company's products. When making decisions, entrepreneurs often must balance the needs and demands of a company's stakeholders, knowing that whatever the final decision is, not every group will be satisfied. Figure 2 shows the results of a survey by McKinsey & Company of global CEOs about the stakeholders that will have the greatest effect on their businesses in the next 3 to 5 years.

Ethical leaders approach their organizational responsibilities with added dimensions of thought and action. They link ethical behaviors to organizational outcomes and incorporate social responsibility into daily decisions. They establish ethical behavior and concern for the environment as an integral part of organizational training and eventually as part of company culture. What does this mean from a practical standpoint? How does a commitment to "doing the right thing" apply to employees, customers, and other stakeholders, and how does it affect an

FIGURE 1
Key Stakeholders

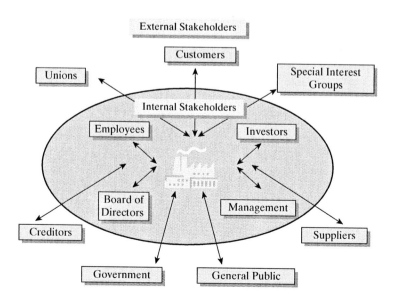

Which Stakeholders Will Have the Greatest Effect on Your Company's Economic Value in the Next 3 to 5 Years?

Source: McKinsey and Company, 2010.

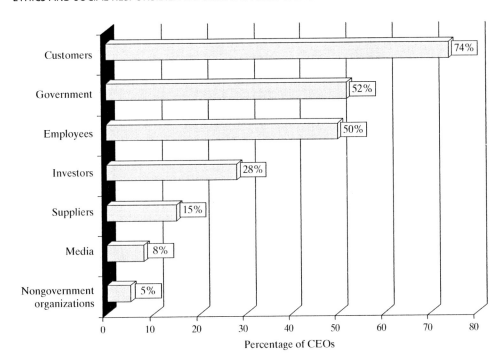

entrepreneur's daily decision making? For example, makers of PCs and laptops faced an ethical dilemma when China's Ministry of Industry and Information Technology issued a mandate that required every PC and laptop sold in China to be preloaded with Web-filtering software that blocks access to particular Web sites. Government officials say that the software, Green Dam Youth Escort, prevents Chinese citizens from accessing pornographic Web sites. Critics contend that because the software also blocks access to Web sites with political content of which the Chinese government disapproves, it gives the government greater censorship power over Internet users inside China. If the managers of the computer makers decide not to sell their products in China (their largest market after the United States), they sacrifice hundreds of millions of dollars in sales and profits. If they fail to comply with the government mandate, they put at risk the investments that they have made in factories and research centers in China. Complying with the government's requirement, however, opens PC makers to a backlash from charges of supporting censorship and limits on basic human rights.[1] Balancing the demands of various stakeholders to make ethical decisions is no easy task.

Business operates as an institution in our often complex and ever-evolving society. As such, every entrepreneur is expected to behave in ways that are compatible with the value system of society. It is society that imposes the rules of conduct for all business owners in the form of ethical standards of behavior and responsibilities to act in ways that benefit the long-term interest of all. Society expects business owners to strive to earn a profit on their investments. Ethics and social responsibility simply set behavioral boundaries for decision makers. Ethics is a branch of philosophy that studies and creates theories about the basic nature of right and wrong, duty, obligation, and virtue. Social responsibility involves how an organization responds to the needs of the many elements in society, including shareholders, lenders, employees, consumers, governmental agencies, and the environment. Because business is allowed to operate in society, it has an obligation to behave in ways that benefit all of society.

An Ethical Perspective

1. Define business ethics and describe three levels of ethical standards.

Business ethics consist of the fundamental moral values and behavioral standards that form the foundation for the people of an organization as they make decisions and interact with stakeholders. Business ethics is a sensitive and highly complex issue, but it is not a new one. In 560 B.C., the Greek philosopher Chilon claimed that a merchant does better to take a loss than to make a dishonest profit.[2] Maintaining an ethical perspective is essential to creating and protecting a company's reputation, but it is no easy task. Ethical dilemmas lurk in the decisions—even the most mundane ones—that entrepreneurs make every day. Succumbing to unethical temptations ultimately can destroy a company's reputation, one of the most precious and most fragile possessions of any business.

Building a reputation for ethical behavior typically takes a long time; unfortunately, destroying that reputation requires practically no time at all, and the effects linger for some time. One top manager compares a bad reputation to a hangover. "It takes a while to get rid of, and it makes everything else hurt," he says.[3] Many businesses flounder or even fail after their owners or managers are caught acting unethically.

Steve Warshak, founder of Berkeley Premium Nutraceuticals (BPN), a Cincinnati, Ohio-based company that sold a variety of health supplements, including its blockbuster product Enzyte, was convicted on 93 counts of mail fraud, credit card fraud, bank fraud, money laundering, and obstruction of justice. Federal prosecutors claimed that Warshak created "a cycle of fraud upon fraud," bilking his customers out of more than $100 million by "giving" them a free sample of the "all natural male enhancement product" and then charging their credit cards for repeat orders that they never placed. At its peak, BPN employed 1,400 people and fielded 65,000 customer calls per day. After a judge sentenced Warshak to 25 years in prison, BPN fell into bankruptcy and was bought by a Cincinnati businessman, who renamed the company Vianda.[4]

Three Levels of Ethical Standards

There are three levels of ethical standards:

1. *The law*, which defines for society as a whole those actions that are permissible and those that are not. The law merely establishes the minimum standard of behavior. Actions that are legal, however, may not be ethical. Simply obeying the law is insufficient as a guide for ethical behavior; ethical behavior requires more. Few ethical issues are so simple and one dimensional that the law can serve as the acid test for making a decision.
2. *Organizational policies and procedures*, which serve as specific guidelines for people as they make daily decisions. Many colleges and universities have created honor codes, and companies rely on policies covering everything from sexual harassment and gift giving to hiring and whistle-blowing.
3. The *moral stance* that employees take when they encounter a situation that is not governed by levels one and two. The values people learn early in life at home, in the church or synagogue, in school, and at work are key ingredients at this level. Another determinant of ethical behavior is *training*. As Aristotle said thousands of years ago, you get a good adult by teaching a child to do the right thing. A company's culture can serve either to support or undermine its employees' concept of what constitutes ethical behavior.

Ethics is something that every businessperson faces daily; most decisions involve some degree of ethical judgment. Over the course of a career, entrepreneurs can be confident that they will face some tough ethical choices. But that is not necessarily bad! Situations such as these give entrepreneurs the opportunity to flex their ethical muscles and do what is right. Entrepreneurs set the ethical tone for their companies. The ethical stance employees take when faced with a difficult decision often reflects the entrepreneur's values.

Establishing an Ethical Framework

To cope successfully with the many ethical decisions they face, entrepreneurs must develop a workable ethical framework to guide themselves and the organization. Although many frameworks exist, the following four-step process works quite well.

Step 1. Recognize the ethical dimensions involved in the dilemma or decision. Before entrepreneurs can make informed ethical decisions, they must recognize that an ethical situation exists. Only then is it possible to define the specific ethical issues involved. Too often business owners fail to take into account the ethical impact of a particular course of action until it is too late. To avoid ethical quagmires, entrepreneurs must consider the ethical forces at work in a situation—honesty, fairness, respect for the community, concern for the environment, trust, and others—to have a complete view of the decision.

Step 2. Identify the key stakeholders involved and determine how the decision will affect them. Every business influences, and is influenced by, a multitude of stakeholders. Frequently, the demands of these stakeholders conflict with one another, putting a business in the position of having to choose which groups to satisfy and which to alienate. Before making a decision, managers must sort out the conflicting interests of the various stakeholders by determining which ones have important stakes in the situation. Although this analysis may not resolve the conflict, it will prevent the company from inadvertently causing harm to people it may have failed to consider. More companies are measuring their performance using a **triple bottom line (3BL)** that, in addition to the traditional measure of profitability, includes the commitment to ethics and social responsibility and the impact on the environment ("profit, people, and planet").

ENTREPRENEURIAL
Profile

*King Arthur Flour
Company*

King Arthur Flour Company, founded in Boston, Massachusetts, in 1790, uses the 3BL to measure its performance. The company is profitable, with annual sales of more than $61 million, and it is now 100 percent owned by its 160 employees, each of whom receives up to 40 hours of paid time each year to work for a nonprofit organization of their choice. King Arthur Flour has a reputation as a good corporate citizen, donating 5 percent of its profits to charitable organizations and schools. The company also is an advocate of environmental sustainability, focusing on energy efficiency, recycling, preservation of natural resources, and other efforts.[5]

Step 3. Generate alternative choices and distinguish between ethical and unethical responses. When entrepreneurs are generating alternative courses of action and evaluating the consequences of each one, they can use the questions in Table 1 to guide them. Asking and answering questions such as these ensure that everyone involved is aware of the ethical dimensions of the issue.

Step 4. Choose the "best" ethical response and implement it. At this point, there likely will be several ethical choices from which managers can pick. Comparing these choices with the "ideal" ethical outcome may help managers make the final decision. The final choice must be consistent with the company's goals, culture, and value system as well as those of the individual decision makers.

TABLE 1 Questions to Help Identify the Ethical Dimension of a Situation

Principles and Codes of Conduct

- Does this decision or action meet my standards for how people should interact?
- Does this decision or action agree with my religious teachings or beliefs (or with my personal principles and sense of responsibility)?
- How will I feel about myself if I do this?
- Do we (or I) have a rule or policy for cases like this?
- Would I want everyone to make the same decision and take the same action if faced with these circumstances?
- What are my true motives for considering this action?

Moral Rights

- Would this action allow others freedom of choice in this matter?
- Would this action involve deceiving others in any way?

Justice

- Would I feel this action was just (right) if I were on the other side of the decision?
- How would I feel if this action were done to me or someone close to me?
- Would this action or decision distribute benefits justly?
- Would it distribute hardships or burdens justly?

Consequences and Outcomes

- What will be the short- and long-term consequences of this action?
- Who will benefit from this course of action?
- Who will be hurt?
- How will this action create good and prevent harm?

(continued)

TABLE 1 Continued

Public Justification

- How would I feel (or how will I feel) if (or when) this action becomes public knowledge?
- Will I be able to explain adequately to others why I have taken the action?
- Would others feel that my action or decision is ethical or moral?

Intuition and Insight

- Have I searched for all alternatives? Are there other ways I could look at this situation? Have I considered all points of view?
- Even if there is sound rationality for this decision or action, and even if I could defend it publicly, does my inner sense tell me it is right?
- What does my intuition tell me is the ethical thing to do in this situation? Have I listened to my inner voice?

Source: Sherry Baker, "Ethical Judgment," *Executive Excellence,* March 1992, pp. 7–8. Reprinted with permission by Leadership Excellence.

Who Is Responsible for Ethical Behavior?

2. Determine who is responsible for ethical behavior and why ethical lapses occur.

Although companies may set ethical standards and offer guidelines for employees, the ultimate decision on whether to abide by ethical principles rests with the *individual.* In other words, companies really are not ethical or unethical; individuals are. Managers, however, can greatly influence individual behavior within the company. That influence must start at the *top* of the organization. A founder or chief executive officer who practices ethical behavior establishes the moral tone for the entire organization. Table 2 summarizes the characteristics of the three ethical styles of management: immoral, amoral, and moral management:

- *Immoral management.* Immoral managers are motivated by selfish reasons such as their own gains or those of the company. The driving force behind immoral management is *greed*: achieving personal or organizational success at any cost. Immoral management is the polar opposite of ethical management; immoral managers do what they can to

TABLE 2 Approaches to Business Ethics

Organizational Characteristics	Immoral Management	Amoral Management	Moral Management
Ethical norms	Management decisions, actions, and behavior imply a positive and active opposition to what is moral (ethical). Decisions are discordant with accepted ethical principles. An active negation of what is moral is implicit.	Management is neither moral nor immoral; decisions are not based on moral judgments. Management activity is not related to any moral code. A lack of ethical perception and moral awareness may be implicit.	Management activity conforms to a standard of ethical, or right, behavior. Management activity conforms to accepted professional standards of conduct. Ethical leadership is commonplace.
Motives	Selfish. Management cares only about its or its company's gains.	Well intentioned but selfish in the sense that impact on others is not considered.	Good. Management wants to succeed but only within the confines of sound ethical precepts such as fairness, justice, and due process.
Goals	Profitability and organizational success at any price.	Profitability. Other goals are not considered.	Profitability within the confines of legal obedience and ethical standards.
Orientation toward law	Legal standards are barriers that management must overcome to accomplish what it wants.	Law is the ethical guide, preferably the letter of the law. The central question is, what can we do legally?	Obedience toward letter and spirit of the law. Law is a minimal ethical behavior. Prefer to operate well above what law mandates.
Strategy	Exploit opportunities for corporate gain. Cut corners when it appears useful.	Give managers free rein. Personal ethics may apply, but only if managers choose. Respond to legal mandates if caught and required to do so.	Live by sound ethical standards. Assume leadership position when ethical dilemmas arise. Enlightened self-interest.

Source: Archie B. Carroll, "In Search of the Moral Manager," *Business Horizons,* March–April, 1987, pp. 7–15.

circumvent laws and moral standards and are not concerned about the impact that their actions have on others.

- *Amoral management.* The principal goal of amoral managers is to earn a profit, but their actions differ from those of immoral managers in one key way: They do not purposely violate laws or ethical standards. Instead, amoral managers neglect to consider the impact their decisions have on others; they use free-rein decision making without reference to ethical standards. Amoral management is not an option for socially responsible businesses.
- *Moral management.* Moral managers also strive for success but only within the boundaries of legal and ethical standards. Moral managers are not willing to sacrifice their values and violate ethical standards just to make a profit. Managers who operate with this philosophy see the law as a minimum standard for ethical behavior.

The Benefits of Moral Management

One of the most common misconceptions about business is that there is a contradiction between earning a profit and maintaining high ethical standards. In reality, companies have learned that these two goals are consistent with one another. Tom Chappell, founder of Tom's of Maine and Rambler's Way Farm, companies known almost as well for their ethical and socially responsible behavior as for their natural personal care products and environmentally friendly clothing, says, "You can make money and do good at the same time. They are not separate acts."[6] Many entrepreneurs launch businesses with the idea of making a difference in society. They quickly learn that to "do good" their companies must first "do well." Fran Rathke, CFO of Vermont-based Green Mountain Coffee Roasters, a small company known for its commitment to social responsibility, says, "We are motivated to achieve success because the more profitable we are, the more good we can do in the world."[7] According to a survey by the public relations firm Edelman, 83 percent of U.S. consumers say that transparent and honest practices and operating as a business that one can trust are the most important factors in a company's reputation.[8]

Profile

Larry O'Toole: Gentle Giant Moving Company

Larry O'Toole, who founded Gentle Giant Moving Company, a Boston, Massachusetts-based moving company, with $17 and a borrowed truck, understands the importance of moral management in building trust and a solid reputation for his business in the communities that it serves. "We want to give back," says O'Toole. "That's part of our culture." After a devastating earthquake struck Haiti, Gentle Giant used its moving trucks to collect medical supplies from local businesses and residents and donated them to the nonprofit group Partners in Health. The company also operates a charitable foundation that focuses on developing character in young people and preventing homelessness.[9]

Although behaving ethically has value in itself, there are many other benefits to companies that adhere to high ethical standards. First, companies avoid the damaging fallout from unethical behavior on their reputations. Unethical businesses usually gain only short-term advantages; over the long run, unethical decisions don't pay. It's simply not good business.

Second, a solid ethical framework guides managers as they cope with an increasingly complex network of influence from external stakeholders. Dealing with stakeholders is much easier if a company has a solid ethical foundation on which to build.

Third, businesses with solid reputations as ethical companies find it easier to attract and retain quality workers. Explaining why she came to work for Timberland, a socially responsible maker of shoes, Helen Kellogg, a senior manager, says, "I was looking for a company that had a conscience." Timberland gives every employee 40 hours of paid leave every year to work on volunteer projects. Bonnie Monahan, a Timberland vice president who organized a bike-a-thon that raised $50,000 for a local charity, says that she has turned down "several lucrative job offers" from larger companies to stay with Timberland, where "you don't have to leave your values at the door." Every year, Timberland sponsors Serv-a-palooza, a 1-day blitz of community service that involves 170 projects in 27 countries.[10]

Fourth, ethical behavior has a positive impact on a company's bottom line. Research by Dov Seidman, a management consultant, shows that companies that outperform their competitors ethically also outperform them financially.[11]

Finally, a company's ethical philosophy has an impact on its ability to provide value for its customers. The "ethics factor" is difficult to quantify, yet it is something that customers consider when deciding where to shop and which company's products to buy. "Do I want people buying Timberland boots as a result of the firm's volunteer efforts?" asks CEO Jeffrey Swartz. "You bet."[12] Timberland's commitment to "doing good" in addition to "doing well" is expressed in its slogan, "Boots, Brand, Belief." Like other social entrepreneurs, Swartz's goal is to manage the company successfully so that he can use its resources to combat social problems.

Entrepreneurs must recognize that ethical behavior is an investment in the company's future rather than merely a cost of doing business. Table 3 shows the results of a comprehensive study that was conducted by the American Management Association of global human resources directors, who were asked about the reasons for their companies' engaging in ethical behavior and the factors that drive business ethics today.

Why Ethical Lapses Occur

Even though most small business owners run their companies ethically, business scandals involving Enron, WorldCom, Tyco, and other high-profile companies have sullied the reputations of businesses of all sizes. The best way for business owners to combat these negative public perceptions is to run their business ethically. When faced with an ethical dilemma, however, not every entrepreneur or employee will make the right decision. According to KPMG's Integrity Survey, 74 percent of workers say that they have observed ethical lapses in their companies within the last year.[13] (Forty-six percent of employees say that misconduct they observed would cause "a significant loss of public trust if discovered.") Many unethical acts are committed by normally decent people who believe in moral values. Figure 3 shows the results of an integrity survey that identifies the primary causes of misconduct in businesses.

Let's explore some of these causes of ethical lapses in more detail.

AN UNETHICAL EMPLOYEE. Ethical decisions are individual decisions, and some people are corrupt. Try as they might to avoid them, small businesses occasionally find that they have hired a "bad apple." Eliminating unethical behavior requires eliminating these bad apples.

AN UNETHICAL ORGANIZATIONAL CULTURE. In some cases, a company's culture has been poisoned with an unethical overtone; in other words, the problem is not the "bad apple" but the "bad barrel." Pressure to prosper produces an environment that creates conditions that reward unethical behavior, and employees act accordingly. Studies show that companies with strong ethical cultures experience fewer ethical violations than those with weak ethical cultures.[14] To create an environment that encourages ethical behavior, entrepreneurs should:

■ *Set the tone.* "The character of the leader casts a long shadow over the organization and can determine the character of the organization itself," says one business executive.[15] What you do, how you do it, and what you say set the tone for your employees. The values you profess must be aligned with the behaviors you demonstrate.

TABLE 3 **Reasons to Run a Business Ethically and the Factors That Drive Business Ethics**

Top Five Reasons to Run a Business Ethically

1. Protect brand and company reputation
2. It is the right thing to do
3. Maintain customers' trust and loyalty
4. Maintain investors' confidence
5. Earn public acceptance and recognition

Top Five Factors That Drive Business Ethics

1. Corporate scandals
2. Marketplace competition
3. Demands by investors
4. Pressure from customers
5. Globalization

Source: The Ethical Enterprise: A Global Study of Business Ethics 2005–2015, American Management Association/Human Resource Institute, 2006, p. 2.

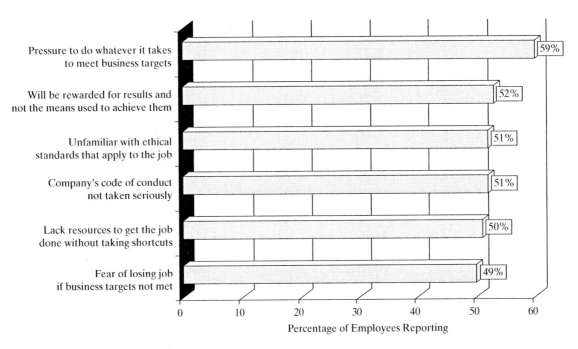

FIGURE 3
Causes of Ethical Lapses

Source: KPMG Integrity Survey, 2008–2009, KPMG LLC, 2009, p. 6.

- *Establish and enforce policies.* Set appropriate policies for your organization. Communicate them on a regular basis and adhere to them yourself so that others can see. Show zero tolerance for ethical violations and realize that the adage "Don't do as I do; do as I say" does *not* work. Without a demonstration of real consequences and personal accountability from the CEO, organizational policies are meaningless.
- *Educate and recruit.* Consider using a formal education program to enhance the understanding of and commitment to ethical behavior. Find colleges and universities that incorporate business ethics into courses and make them prime recruiting sources. Tina Byles Williams, owner of FIS Group, an investment advising and management firm, understands how important it is to hire honest employees with a strong sense of ethics. Although Williams knows that there is no foolproof hiring method, she has redesigned her company's selection process with an emphasis on screening for integrity.[16]
- *Separate related job duties.* This is a basic organizational concept. Not allowing the employee who writes checks to reconcile the company bank statement is one example.
- *Reward ethical conduct.* The reward system is a large window into the values of an organization. If you reward a behavior, people have a tendency to repeat the behavior.
- *Eliminate "undiscussables."* One of the most important things entrepreneurs can do to promote ethical behavior is to instill the belief that it is acceptable for employees to question what happens above them. Doing away with undiscussables makes issues transparent and promotes trust both inside and outside the company.[17]

MORAL BLINDNESS. Sometimes fundamentally ethical people commit unethical blunders because they are blind to the implications of their conduct. Moral blindness may be the result of failing to realize that an ethical dilemma exists, or it may arise from a variety of mental defense mechanisms. One of the most common mechanisms is rationalization:

"Everybody does it."

"If they were in my place, they'd do it too."

"Being ethical is a luxury I cannot afford right now."

"The impact of my decision/action on (whomever or whatever) is not my concern."

"I don't get paid to be ethical; I get paid to produce results."

TABLE 4 **Ethics Research Reveals Features of Ethical Cultures**

1. Leaders support and model ethical behavior.
2. Consistent communications come from all company leaders.
3. Ethics is integrated into the organization's goals, business processes, and strategies.
4. Ethics is part of the performance management system.
5. Ethics is part of the company's selection criteria and its selection process.

Source: The Ethical Enterprise: A Global Study of Business Ethics 2005–2015, American Management Association/Human Resource Institute, 2006, pp. 5, 6, 10.

Conducting ethics training and creating a culture that encourages employees to consider the ethical impact of their decisions reduces the likelihood of moral blindness. Instilling a sense of individual responsibility and encouraging people at all levels of an organization to speak up when they see questionable actions create a company-wide ethical conscience.

COMPETITIVE PRESSURES. If competition is so intense that a company's survival is threatened, managers may begin to view what were once unacceptable options as acceptable. Managers and employees are under such pressure to produce that they may sacrifice their ethical standards to reduce the fear of failure or the fear of losing their jobs. Without a positive organizational culture that stresses ethical behavior regardless of the consequences, employees respond to feelings of pressure and compromise their personal ethical standards to ensure that the job gets done.

OPPORTUNITY PRESSURES. When the opportunity to "get ahead" by taking some unethical action presents itself, some people cannot resist the temptation. The greater the reward or the smaller the penalty for unethical acts, the greater is the probability that such behavior will occur. If managers, for example, condone or even encourage unethical behavior, they can be sure it will occur. Those who succumb to opportunity pressures often make one of two mistakes: They overestimate the cost of doing the right thing, or they underestimate the cost of doing the wrong thing. Either error can lead to disaster.

GLOBALIZATION OF BUSINESS. The globalization of business has intertwined what once were distinct cultures. This cultural cross-pollination has brought about many positive aspects, but it has created problems as well. Companies have discovered that there is no single standard of ethical behavior that applies to all business decisions in the international arena. Practices that are illegal in one country may be perfectly acceptable, even expected, in another. Actions that would send a businessperson to jail in Western nations are common ways of working around the system in others.

Table 4 provides a summary of important ethics research concerning the characteristics that are most important to establishing an ethical culture.

Establishing Ethical Standards

3. Explain how to establish and maintain high ethical standards.

A study by the Southern Institute for Business and Professional Ethics found that small companies are less likely than large ones to have ethics programs.[18] Although they may not have formal ethics programs, entrepreneurs can encourage employees to become familiar with the following ethical tests for judging behavior:

- *The utilitarian principle.* Choose the option that offers the greatest good for the greatest number of people.
- *Kant's categorical imperative.* Act in such a way that the action taken under the circumstances could be a universal law or rule of behavior.
- *The professional ethic.* Take only those actions that a disinterested panel of professional colleagues would view as proper.
- *The Golden Rule.* Treat other people the way you would like them to treat you.
- *The television test.* Would you and your colleagues feel comfortable explaining your actions to a national television audience?
- *The family test.* Would you be comfortable explaining to your children, your spouse, and your parents why you took this action?[19]

Although these tests do not offer universal solutions to ethical dilemmas, they do help employees identify the moral implications of the decisions they face. People must be able to understand the ethical impact of their actions before they can make responsible decisions. Table 5 describes 10 ethical principles that differentiate between right and wrong, thereby offering a guideline for ethical behavior.

Maintaining Ethical Standards

Establishing ethical standards is only the first step in an ethics-enhancing program; implementing and maintaining those standards is the real challenge facing management. What can entrepreneurs do to integrate ethical principles into their companies?

CREATE A COMPANY CREDO. A **company credo** defines the values underlying the entire company and its ethical responsibilities to its stakeholders. It offers general guidance in ethical issues. The most effective credos capture the elusive essence of a company—what it stands for and why it's important—and they can be a key ingredient in a company's competitive edge. A company credo is especially important for a small company, where the entrepreneur's values become the values driving the business. A credo is an excellent way to transform those values into guidelines for employees' ethical behavior.

TABLE 5 Ten Ethical Principles to Guide Behavior

The study of history, philosophy, and religion reveals a strong consensus about certain universal and timeless values that are central to leading an ethical life.

1. *Honesty.* Be truthful, sincere, forthright, straightforward, frank, and candid; do not cheat, lie, steal, deceive, or act deviously.
2. *Integrity.* Be principled, honorable, upright, and courageous and act on convictions; do not be two-faced or unscrupulous or adopt an ends-justifies-the-means philosophy that ignores principle.
3. *Promise-keeping.* Be worthy of trust, keep promises, fulfill commitments, and abide by the spirit as well as the letter of an agreement; do not interpret agreements in a technical or legalistic manner in order to rationalize noncompliance or to create excuses for breaking commitments.
4. *Fidelity.* Be faithful and loyal to family, friends, employers, and country; do not use or disclose information earned in confidence; in a professional context, safeguard the ability to make independent professional judgments by scrupulously avoiding undue influences and conflicts of interest.
5. *Fairness.* Be fair and open-minded, be willing to admit error, and, when appropriate, change positions and beliefs and demonstrate a commitment to justice, the equal treatment of individuals, and tolerance for diversity; do not overreach or take undue advantage of another's mistakes or adversities.
6. *Caring for others.* Be caring, kind, and compassionate; share, be giving, serve others; help those in need and avoid harming others.
7. *Respect for others.* Demonstrate respect for human dignity, privacy, and the right to self-determination for all people; be courteous, prompt, and decent; provide others with the information they need to make informed decisions about their own lives; do not patronize, embarrass, or demean.
8. *Responsible citizenship.* Obey just laws [if a law is unjust, openly protest it]; exercise all democratic rights and privileges responsibly by participation [voting and expressing informed views], social consciousness, and public service; when in a position of leadership or authority, openly respect and honor democratic processes of decision making, avoid secrecy or concealment of information, and ensure others have the information needed to make intelligent choices and exercise their rights.
9. *Pursuit of excellence.* Pursue excellence in all matters; in meeting personal and professional responsibilities, be diligent, reliable, industrious, and committed; perform all tasks to the best of your ability, develop and maintain a high degree of competence, and be well informed and well prepared; do not be content with mediocrity, but do not seek to win "at any cost."
10. *Accountability.* Be accountable; accept responsibility for decisions, for the foreseeable consequences of actions and inactions, and for setting an example for others. Parents, teachers, employers, many professionals, and public officials have a special obligation to lead by example and to safeguard and advance the integrity and reputation of their families, companies, professions, and the government; avoid even the appearance of impropriety and take whatever actions are necessary to correct or prevent inappropriate conduct by others.

Source: Michael Josephson, "Teaching Ethical Decision Making and Principled Reasoning," *Ethics: Easier Said Than Done,* Winter 1988, pp. 28–29. *www.JosephsonInstitute.org.*

DEVELOP A CODE OF ETHICS. A **code of ethics** is a written statement of the standards of behavior and ethical principles a company expects from its employees. A code of ethics spells out what kind of behavior is expected (and what kind will not be tolerated) and offers everyone in the company concrete guidelines for dealing with ethics every day on the job. Although creating a code of ethics does not guarantee 100 percent compliance with ethical standards, it does tend to foster an ethical atmosphere in a company. Workers who will be directly affected by the code should have a hand in developing it.

ENFORCE THE CODE FAIRLY AND CONSISTENTLY. Managers must take action whenever they discover ethical violations. If employees learn that ethical breaches go unpunished, the code of ethics becomes meaningless. Enforcement of the code of ethics demonstrates to everyone that you believe that ethical behavior is mandatory.

CONDUCT ETHICS TRAINING. Instilling ethics in an organization's culture requires more than creating a code of ethics and enforcing it. Managers must show employees that the organization truly is committed to practicing ethical behavior. One of the most effective ways to display that commitment is through ethical training designed to raise employees' consciousness of potential ethical dilemmas. Ethics training programs not only raise employees' awareness of ethical issues, but they also communicate to employees the core of the company's value system.

HIRE AND PROMOTE THE RIGHT PEOPLE. Ultimately, the decision in any ethical situation belongs to the individual. Hiring people with strong moral principles and values is the best insurance against ethical violations. To make ethical decisions, people must have: (1) *ethical commitment*—the personal resolve to act ethically and do the right thing; (2) *ethical consciousness*—the ability to perceive the ethical implications of a situation; and (3) *ethical competency*—the ability to engage in sound moral reasoning and develop practical problem-solving strategies.[20]

PERFORM PERIODIC ETHICS AUDITS. One of the best ways to evaluate the effectiveness of an ethics system is to perform periodic audits. These reviews send a signal to employees that ethics is not just a passing fad.

ESTABLISH HIGH STANDARDS OF BEHAVIOR, NOT JUST RULES. No one can legislate ethics and morality, but managers can let people know the level of performance they expect. It is essential to emphasize to *everyone* in the organization the importance of ethics. All employees must understand that ethics is *not* negotiable. The role that an entrepreneur plays in establishing high ethical standards is critical; no one has more influence over the ethical character of a company than its founder. One experienced entrepreneur offers this advice to business owners: "Stick to your principles. Hire people who want to live by them, teach them thoroughly, and insist on total commitment."[21]

SET AN IMPECCABLE ETHICAL EXAMPLE AT ALL TIMES. Remember that ethics starts at the top. Far more important than credos and codes is the example the company's leaders set. If managers talk about the importance of ethics and then act in an unethical manner, they send mixed signals to employees. Workers believe managers' *actions* more than their words.

CREATE A CULTURE THAT EMPHASIZES TWO-WAY COMMUNICATION. A thriving ethical environment requires two-way communication. Employees must have the opportunity to report any ethical violations they observe. A reliable, confidential reporting system is essential to a whistle-blowing program, in which employees anonymously report breaches of ethical behavior through proper channels.

INVOLVE EMPLOYEES IN ESTABLISHING ETHICAL STANDARDS. Encourage employees to offer feedback on how to establish standards. Involving employees improves the quality of a company's ethical standards and increases the likelihood of employee compliance.

Social Responsibility and Social Entrepreneurship

4. Define social responsibility.

The concept of social responsibility has evolved from that of a nebulous "do-gooder" to one of "social steward," with the expectation that businesses will produce benefits not only for themselves but also for society as a whole. Society is constantly redefining its expectations of business and now holds companies of all sizes to high standards of ethics and social responsibility. Companies must

► ENTREPRENEURSHIP IN ACTION ►

Is That Ethical?

Online Reviews

Buying online offers shoppers convenience, but making online purchases can be risky because of the potential for fraud. Another challenge that online retailers must overcome is shoppers' inability to examine merchandise firsthand, which explains the popularity of online reviews. A recent study by Nielsen reports that 70 percent of global online shoppers trust user reviews of products and services. Unfortunately, shoppers' trust in online reviews has led to some companies posting fake user reviews. Lifestyle Lift, a cosmetic surgery company that sells laser skin treatments that tighten and tone aging skin, was charged with posting fake user reviews of its procedures on several Web sites where customers rate and review products and services. The "patients" were not real patients after all; they turned out to be employees whom the company had paid to post positive reviews of its services. One critic says, "I know of other companies that do the same thing (post fake reviews), and they suffer from an underlying insecurity about the true value of their products and services and their business practices." Other companies, such as Overstock.com, post genuine customer reviews, even bad ones, so that customers can make more informed purchase decisions.

Advertising Buns

KFC, the world's most popular chicken fast-food chain, recently paid women on college campuses $500 to wear tight-fitting sweatpants with the words "Double Down" printed in large letters across the seat as they handed out discount coupons. The unusual advertising medium promoted the company's new line of bunless Double Down sandwiches. The campaign is aimed at the Double Down target market: young men between the ages of 18 and 25. KFC managers decided to take a different approach to reach its target customers after a survey of people aged 18 and 25 indicated that many young adults could not identify the company's signature character, Colonel Sanders, in its ads.

The ads caused some controversy on college campuses. "It's obnoxious to use women's bodies to sell fundamentally unhealthy products," says Terry O'Neill, president of the National Organization for Women. A marketing professor at one of the colleges included in the promotion says, "It'll get attention, but it probably will be a waste of money. I don't see how it helps." KFC's marketing vice president, however, believes the promotion is an effective way to reach target customers. "We've taken a page out of the book of some apparel companies and sororities that have promoted this way for years," he says.

1. Is it ethical for a company to post fake online reviews promoting its products and services? Does doing so cause harm? Explain.
2. Is KFC's advertising campaign ethical? Explain.

Sources: Based on Claire Cain Miller, "Company Settles Case of Reviews It Faked," *New York Times,* July 14, 2009, *www.nytimes.com/2009/07/15/technology/internet/15lift.html;* Bryan Stapp, "Fake User Reviews Are a No-No," *Loud Amplifier Marketing,* July 16, 2009, *www.loudamplifiermarketing.com/fake-user-reviews-are-a-no-no/;* Bruce Horovitz, "KFC Pays College Women for Ad Space on Buns," *USA Today,* September 22, 2010, *www.usatoday.com/money/industries/food/2010-09-22-kfc22_ST_N.htm;* Trang Do, "KFC Advertising Bun-less Sandwiches on Buns of College Students," WAFF 48 News, October 23, 2010, *www.waff.com/Global/story.asp?S=13208785.*

Source: © Scott Adams/Dist. by United Feature Syndicate, Inc.

go beyond "doing well"—simply earning a profit—to "doing good"—living up to their social responsibility. They also must recognize the interdependence of business and society. Each influences the other, and both must remain healthy to sustain each other over time.

Companies that are most successful in meeting their social responsibility select causes that are consistent with their core values and their employees' interests and skill sets. In fact, some entrepreneurs allow employees to provide input into the decision concerning which causes to support. A common strategy is to allow employees to provide pro bono work for the charitable organizations they support. Employees at Gumas Advertising, an advertising agency in San Francisco, founded by John Gumas, create marketing campaigns and perform other services for the San Francisco Giants Community Fund, a nonprofit organization that helps underprivileged youth to lead quality lives. Employees at the agency also benefit from their support of the cause. "It gives us a rallying point," says Gumas. [22]

A recent survey by SurePayroll reports that 55 percent of small business's mission statements include a reference to achieving some type of social goal.[23] Indeed, entrepreneurs are using their resources and sphere of influence not only to generate a profit but also to tackle challenging problems confronting the global economy, including pollution, habitat destruction, human rights, AIDS, hunger, poverty, and others. These **social entrepreneurs**, people who start businesses so that they can create innovative solutions to society's most vexing problems, see themselves as change agents for society. Social entrepreneurs use their creativity to develop solutions to social problems that range from cleaning up the environment to improving working conditions for workers around the world; their goal is to use their businesses to make money *and* to make the world a better place to live. The Global Entrepreneurship Monitor survey of entrepreneurial activity in 54 countries reports that 36 percent of entrepreneurs launch for-profit companies that also include a social responsibility focus.[24] Bill Drayton, founder of Ashoka, an organization that promotes social entrepreneurship, says, "Social entrepreneurs are not content just to give a fish or teach [someone] how to fish. They will not rest until they have revolutionized the fishing industry."[25]

June Wilcox, Tim Mesaric, and John Hampson already were successful entrepreneurs when they decided to launch TimesTwo, a company based in Greenville, South Carolina, that donates a product to a charitable organization for every one that is sells. The three entrepreneurs operate Adec Group, a successful small company that manages Web content for large businesses, but were inspired by TOMS Shoes' business model to create a company with a focus on social responsibility. "Everyone in our company (Adec Group) has a servant heart," says Wilcox. "Each quarter we take turns choosing a service project we all do together. Those days, we're happiest and most satisfied. Then I saw an interview with TOMS Shoes founder Blake Mycoskie. He was sharing his story in hope that other businesses would copy his model of a business built to do good. I took the idea to my colleagues, and TimesTwo was born." TimesTwo's initial product offerings, all of which are adorned with the company's catchy "Buy. Give." logo, included a variety of baby products (e.g., blankets, towels, bibs, and snap shirts) but has expanded to include personal care items and school supplies.[26]

In a free enterprise system, companies that fail to respond to their customers' needs and demands soon go out of business. Today, customers are increasingly demanding the companies they buy goods and services from to be socially responsible. When customers shop for "value," they no longer consider only the price–performance relationship of the product or service; they also consider the company's stance on social responsibility. Whether a company supports a social or environmental cause has a significant effect on shoppers' behavior. A study by Cone LLC reports that 80 percent of U.S. consumers are likely to switch to a brand that they perceive is similar in price and quality if the company supports a cause. The study also concludes that 75 percent of consumers say that a company supporting a worthy cause affects where they shop and what they buy, and 76 percent say it affects the products and services they recommend to other people.[27] Other studies report that when price, service, and quality are equal among competitors customers buy from the company that has the best reputation for social responsibility.

Other studies show a connection between social responsibility and profitability. One team of researchers evaluated 52 studies on corporate social responsibility that were conducted over 30 years and concluded that a positive correlation existed between a company's profitability and its reputation for ethical, socially responsible behavior. The relationship also was self-reinforcing.

"It's a virtuous cycle," says Sara Rynes, one of the researchers. "As a company becomes more socially responsible, its reputation and financial performance go up, which causes them to become even more socially responsible."[28] The message is clear: Companies that incorporate social responsibility into their competitive strategies outperform those that fail to do so. Today's socially wired, transparent economy makes ethical and socially responsible behavior highly visible and, conversely, improper behavior more difficult to hide.

Putting Social Responsibility into Practice

One problem businesses face is defining just what socially responsible behavior is. Is it manufacturing environmentally friendly products? Is it donating a portion of profits to charitable organizations? Is it creating jobs in inner cities plagued by high unemployment levels? The nature of a company's social responsibility efforts depends on how its owners, employees, and other stakeholders define what it means to be socially responsible. Typically, businesses have responsibilities to several key stakeholders, including the environment, employees, customers, investors, and the community.

IN THE ENTREPRENEURIAL SPOTLIGHT   Making a Profit and Making a Difference

Entrepreneurs have learned that one of the most effective ways to connect with their customers is to support a cause about which their customers care. According to the Cone Cause Evolution Study, 85 percent of consumers say that they have a more positive image of a company when it supports a cause that is important to them. By forging partnerships with nonprofit and social causes, small businesses not only can make a difference in the world but also can improve their visibility in the marketplace and increase sales.

iContact

When Ryan Allis and Aaron Houghton met at the University of North Carolina at Chapel Hill, each of them owned companies that provided Web design and marketing services. The two joined forces to launch iContact Corporation, a business based in Morrisville, North Carolina, that provides a Web-based e-mail list management tool.

Just 2 years after launch, iContact became profitable, which allowed Allis and Houghton to do something that they had planned to do all along: implement the "4-1's Corporate Responsibility Program." Through the 4-1's, iContact would donate to charitable organizations 1 percent of its employees' time, 1 percent of its e-mail marketing products, 1 percent of its payroll (in addition to matching up to $300 of each employee's individual donations), and 1 percent of its equity to the iContact Foundation, which is designed to support a variety of worthy causes.

Houghton and Allis believe that the best way to make the world a better place to live is through social entrepreneurship. "My advice for college students who are considering starting a nonprofit is to consider doing it with a for-profit model," says Allis. The young entrepreneurs believe that for-profit companies produce better results by generating profits that they can funnel into important causes and charitable organizations than nonprofit entities whose leaders are distracted by having to chase donations constantly.

In just 5 years, iContact's revenue increased from $300,000 to $26.4 million, and the company now has more than 200 employees and an annual payroll of $11 million. In one recent year, iContact made $109,000 in cash donations, provided nearly 700 nonprofit organizations free use of its e-mail marketing management software, and gave its employees 500 paid days off to perform volunteer work for 63 different organizations. As their company grows, Allis and Houghton say that iContact's giving will grow in step. "Therein lies the power of social entrepreneurship," says Allis.

1. Do you agree with Ryan Allis' advice that the best way to support a cause is to create a for-profit business? Explain.
2. What benefits does iContact realize by dedicating a portion of their sales and business resources to charitable causes?
3. Select a local small business and work with a team of your classmates to brainstorm ideas for a social responsibility strategy that helps a charitable organization or social cause and produces benefits for the small company. What advice can you offer a small business that is considering supporting a nonprofit organization or social cause?

Sources: Based on 2010 Cone Cause Evolution Study, Cone LLC, p. 5; Joel Holland, "Save the World, Make a Million," *Entrepreneur*, April 2010, p. 76.

Business's Responsibility to the Environment

5. Understand the nature of business's responsibility to the environment.

Driven by their customers' interest in protecting the environment, companies have become more sensitive to the impact their products, processes, and packaging have on the planet. Environmentalism has become, and will continue to be, one of the dominant issues for companies worldwide because consumers have added another item to their list of buying criteria: environmental friendliness and safety. Companies have discovered that sound environmental practices make for good business. In addition to lowering their operating costs, environmentally safe products attract environmentally conscious customers and can give a company a competitive edge in the marketplace. Socially responsible business owners focus on the three Rs: reduce, reuse, and recycle:

- *Reduce* the amount of energy and materials used in your company, from the factory floor to the copier room.
- *Reuse* whatever you can.
- *Recycle* the materials that you must dispose of.

ENTREPRENEURIAL
Profile

Jonathan, Yair, and Helen Marcoschamer: Ecoist

Jonathan Marcoschamer and his mother, Helen Marcoschamer, displaying handbags that their company, Ecoist, makes from recycled candy wrappers, food packages, and soft drink labels.

Source: C.W. Griffin/Miami Herald/MCT/Newscom

After a family trip to Mexico, Jonathan, Yair, and Helen Marcoschamer were inspired by the handbags they saw in a street market that local artisans made from potato chip bags and candy wrappers. When they returned to their Miami, Florida, home, the three started Ecoist, a small company that makes a variety of stylish totes, bags, clutches, and bracelets from misprinted or discarded product packages. Ecoist has partnered with Coca-Cola, Disney, Frito-Lay, Mars, Cliff Bar, Aveda, and other companies to sponsor product lines using their products' packaging. To date, Ecoist has prevented more than 40 million wrappers from going into landfills and used them to create fashionable consumer products. "You can help save the planet and look good doing it," say the Marcoshamers. The company also partners with Trees for the Future to plant a tree for every bag it sells. Ecoist has planted more than 100,000 trees in Haiti, Uganda, India, and other countries.[29]

Many progressive small companies are taking their environmental policies a step further, creating redesigned, "clean" manufacturing systems that focus on *avoiding* waste and pollution and using resources efficiently. Such efforts require a different manufacturing philosophy. These companies design their products, packaging, and processes from the start with the environment in mind, working to eliminate hazardous materials and by-products and looking for ways to turn what had been scrap into salable products. This approach requires an ecological evaluation of every part of the process, from the raw materials that go into a product to the disposal or reuse of the packaging that contains it.

ENTREPRENEURIAL
Profile

Joshua Onysko and Pangea Organics

Joshua Onysko, founder of Pangea Organics, incorporates clean manufacturing principles into his business, which uses organic, all-natural ingredients such as beeswax, almond oil, and sweet basil to produce the company's line of soaps and body lotions. Pangea's packaging is made from 100 percent recycled paper using a "zero waste" process. The packages even include the seeds of herbs such as basil and amaranth. Once customers remove the product, they simply soak the package in water for 1 minute, plant it, and wait for the seeds to sprout! Pangea's 10,000-square-foot factory in Denver, Colorado, is powered completely by wind, and a 2,500-square-foot garden provides lunch for the company's 22 employees 7 months out of the year. Onysko says that Pangea is gearing up for an audit of its environmental impact so that the company can be even more environmentally sensitive.[30]

TABLE 6 Environmentally Responsible Questions

What can companies do to be more environmentally friendly? The following questions can help entrepreneurs evaluate their companies' impact on the environment.

- Are we trying to reduce the volume of our packaging?
- How do we deal with disposal?
- Are we recycling in the office?
- Can we get beyond the concept of volume sales to build products that last?
- Are we reducing waste and substituting toxic substances with nontoxic ones?
- Are we reformulating waste for resale?
- Do we have a formal environmental policy?
- Do we go beyond compliance?
- Are we uniformly stringent environmentally in operations outside, as well as inside, the United States?
- Do we educate employees about the hazards of working with toxic materials?
- Do we encourage employees to submit proposals on how to reduce waste?
- Do we conserve energy?
- Are we avoiding paying taxes, when those tax dollars might go to support environmental programs?
- How do our operations affect the communities they're in, including indigenous people in other countries?

Source: From Therese R. Welter, "A Farewell to Arms," *Industry Week*, August 20, 1990, p. 42. Reprinted with permission of Penton Media.

Table 6 offers a list of questions that environmentally responsible entrepreneurs should ask themselves.

Business's Responsibility to Employees

6. Describe business's responsibility to employees.

Few stakeholders are as important to a business as its employees. It is common for managers to *say* that their employees are their most valuable resource, but the truly excellent ones actually *treat* them that way. Employees are at the heart of increases in productivity, and they add the personal touch that puts passion in customer service. In short, employees produce the winning competitive advantage for an entrepreneur. Entrepreneurs who understand the value of their employees follow a few simple procedures by:

- Listening to employees and respecting their opinions.
- Asking for their input; involving them in the decision-making process.
- Providing regular feedback—positive and negative—to employees.
- Telling them the truth—always.
- Letting them know exactly what's expected of them.
- Rewarding employees for performing their jobs well.
- Trusting them; creating an environment of respect and teamwork.

ENTREPRENEURIAL Profile

Tom, Kevin, and Larry Walter: Tasty Catering

Because of its employee-centered culture, Tasty Catering recently was named the Top Small Company Workplace in the United States.

Source: Tasty Catering

In 1984, brothers Tom, Kevin, and Larry Walter were operating Tasty Dawg, a hot dog stand in Elk Grove Village, Illinois, and received so many requests for catering jobs that they launched Tasty Catering. Today, the family-owned business, which caters an average of 30 events each day, has 58 full-time employees and annual sales of $6.1 million and was recently named Caterer of the Year and the Top Small Company Workplace in the United States. In 2007, Director of Communications Jamie Pritscher arranged for an outside provider to conduct a 65-question employee survey that included asking "What changes would you make if you owned Tasty Catering?" The survey led managers to launch a weekly bilingual employee newsletter that shows the company's financial status and includes articles featuring news and accomplishments in each department. Tasty Catering promotes from within, a strategy that increases employee loyalty; the average tenure of its employees is 7.5 years. "We have always tried to manage Tasty Catering on the philosophy that if we take care of our employees and our customers, we will be successful," says Kevin. The company also lives up to its social responsibility as a good corporate citizen, supporting programs at local schools and hosting an annual holiday party with food and gifts for families in need. Tasty Catering is working to make its operations more energy efficient and environmentally friendly. The plates it uses at picnics are made from recycled fiber, and the cups and cutlery are made from corn and potato starch. Tasty Catering recycles tons of material and has renovated its building to be as energy efficient as possible. Complimentary daily meals encourage employees to get together, learn from one another, and communicate more effectively.[31]

Entrepreneurs who are trying to meet their social responsibility to their employees face several important issues, including cultural diversity, drug testing, AIDs, sexual harassment, and privacy.

CULTURAL DIVERSITY IN THE WORKPLACE. The United States has always been a nation of astonishing cultural diversity (see Figure 4), a trait that has imbued it with an incredible richness of ideas and creativity. Indeed, this diversity is one of the driving forces behind the greatest entrepreneurial effort in the world, and it continues to grow. The United States, in short, is moving toward a "minority majority," and significant demographic shifts will affect virtually every aspect of business. Nowhere will this be more visible than in the makeup of the nation's workforce (see Figure 5). In 2020, members of five different generations will be working side-by-side in the United States.[32] By 2039, the *majority* of the workforce in the United States will be members of a minority.[33] The Hispanic population is the fastest growing sector in the United States, and Hispanics now comprise the largest minority population in the nation.

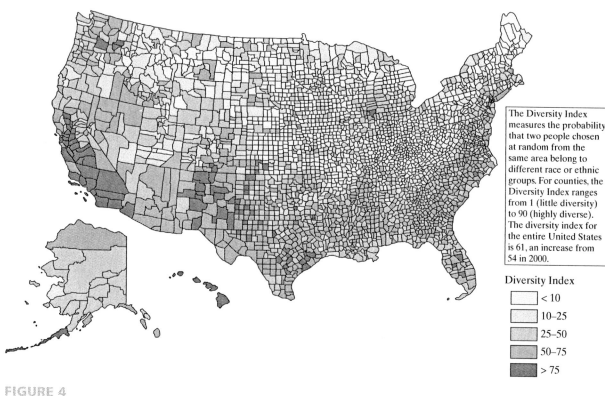

2010 Diversity Index by Country

The Diversity Index measures the probability that two people chosen at random from the same area belong to different race or ethnic groups. For counties, the Diversity Index ranges from 1 (little diversity) to 90 (highly diverse). The diversity index for the entire United States is 61, an increase from 54 in 2000.

Diversity Index
< 10
10–25
25–50
50–75
> 75

FIGURE 4
2010 Diversity Index by County

FIGURE 5

Composition of the U.S. Workforce

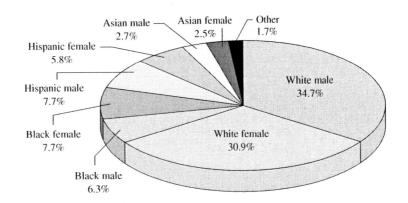

FIGURE 5

Composition of the U.S. Workforce

This rich mix of generations, cultures, and backgrounds within the workforce presents both opportunities and challenges to employers. One of the chief benefits of a diverse workforce is the unique blend of perspectives, skills, talents, and ideas employees have to offer. Also, the changing composition of the nation's population will change the customer base. What better way is there for an entrepreneur to deal with culturally diverse customers than to have a culturally diverse workforce? "No matter who you are, you're going to have to work with people who are different from you," says Ted Childs, vice president of global workforce diversity for IBM. "You're going to have to sell to people who are different from you, buy from people who are different from you, and manage people who are different from you."[34]

Managing a culturally diverse workforce presents a real challenge for employers, however. Molding workers with highly varied beliefs, backgrounds, and biases into a unified team takes time and commitment. Stereotypes, biases, and prejudices present barriers that workers and managers must constantly overcome. Communication may require more effort because of language differences. In many cases, dealing with diversity causes a degree of discomfort for entrepreneurs because of the natural tendency to associate with people who are similar to ourselves. These reasons and others cause some entrepreneurs to resist the move to a more diverse workforce, a move that threatens their ability to create a competitive edge.

How can entrepreneurs achieve unity through diversity? The only way is by *managing* diversity in the workforce. In *Best Practices of Private Sector Employers*, an Equal Employment Opportunity Commission task force suggests following a "SPLENDID" approach to diversity:

- *Study.* Business owners cannot solve problems they don't know exist. Entrepreneurs must familiarize themselves with issues related to diversity, including relevant laws.
- *Plan.* Recognizing the makeup of the local population, entrepreneurs must set targets for diversity hiring and develop a plan for achieving them.
- *Lead.* A diversity effort starts at the top of the organization with managers communicating their vision and goals to everyone in the company.
- *Encourage.* Company leaders must encourage employees at all levels of an organization to embrace the diversity plan.
- *Notice.* Entrepreneurs must monitor their companies' progress toward achieving diversity goals.
- *Discussion.* Managers must keep diversity on the company's radar screen by communicating the message that diversity is vital to business success.
- *Inclusion.* Involving employees in the push to achieve diversity helps break down barriers that may arise.
- *Dedication.* Achieving diversity in a business does not happen overnight, but entrepreneurs must be persistent in implementing their plans.[35]

The goal of diversity efforts is to create an environment in which all types of workers—men, women, Hispanic, African American, white, disabled, homosexual, elderly, and others—can flourish and can give top performances to their companies. In fact, researchers at Harvard University report that companies that embrace diversity are more productive than those that shun it. A distinguishing factor that companies supporting diversity share is the willingness of people to learn from their coworkers' different backgrounds and life experiences.[36]

Managing a culturally diverse workforce requires a different way of thinking, however, and that requires training. In essence, diversity training helps make everyone aware of the dangers of bias, prejudice, and discrimination, however subtle or unintentional they may be. Managing a culturally diverse workforce successfully requires a business owner to:

- *Assess your company's diversity needs.* The starting point for an effective diversity management program is assessing a company's needs. Surveys, interviews, and informal conversations with employees can be valuable tools. Several organizations offer more formal assessment tools—cultural audits, questionnaires, and diagnostic forms—that also are useful.

- *Learn to recognize and correct your own biases and stereotypes.* One of the best ways to identify your own cultural biases is to get exposure to people who are not like you. By spending time with those who are different from you, you will learn quickly that stereotypes simply don't hold up. Giving employees the opportunity to spend time with one another is an excellent way to eliminate stereotypes. The owner of one small company with a culturally diverse staff provides lunch for his workers every month with a seating arrangement that encourages employees to mix with one another.

- *Avoid making invalid assumptions.* Decisions that are based on faulty assumptions are bound to be flawed. False assumptions built on inaccurate perceptions or personal bias have kept many qualified minority workers from getting jobs and promotions. Make sure that it does not happen in your company.

- *Push for diversity in your management team.* To get maximum benefit from a culturally diverse workforce, a company must promote nontraditional workers into top management. A culturally diverse top management team that can serve as mentors and role models provides visible evidence that nontraditional workers can succeed.

- *Concentrate on communication.* Any organization, especially a culturally diverse one, will stumble if lines of communication break down. Frequent training sessions and regular opportunities for employees to talk with one another in a nonthreatening environment can be extremely helpful.

- *Make diversity a core value in the organization.* For a cultural diversity program to work, top managers must "champion" the program and take active steps to integrate diversity throughout the entire organization.

- *Continue to adjust your company to your workers.* Rather than pressure workers to conform to the company, those entrepreneurs with the most successful cultural diversity programs are constantly looking for ways to adjust their businesses to their workers. Flexibility is the key.

As business leaders look to the future, an increasingly diverse workforce stares back. People with varying cultural, racial, gender, and lifestyle perspectives seek opportunity and acceptance from coworkers, managers, and business owners. Currently, women make up nearly 48 percent of the U.S. workforce, and minority workers comprise more than 34 percent of the labor force.[37] Businesses that value the diversity of their workers and the perspectives they bring to work enjoy the benefits of higher employee satisfaction, commitment, retention, creativity, and productivity than those companies that ignore the cultural diversity of their workers. In addition, they deepen the loyalty of their existing customers and expand their market share by attracting new customers. In short, diversity is a winning proposition from every angle!

DRUG TESTING. One of the realities of our society is substance abuse. The second reality, which entrepreneurs now must face head on, is that substance abuse has infiltrated the workplace. In addition to the lives it ruins, substance abuse takes a heavy toll on business and society. Drug and alcohol abuse by employees results in reduced productivity (an estimated $81 billion per year), increased medical costs, higher accident rates, and higher levels of absenteeism. Alarmingly, 77 percent of all substance abusers are employed.[38] Small companies bear a disproportionate share of the burden because they are less likely to have drug-testing programs than large companies, and thus are more likely to hire people with substance abuse problems. Abusers who know that they cannot pass a drug test simply apply for work at companies that do not use drug tests. In addition, because the practice of drug testing remains a controversial issue, its random use can lead to a variety of legal woes for employers, including invasion of privacy, discrimination, slander, or defamation of character.

An effective, proactive drug program should include the following five elements:

1. *A written substance abuse policy.* The first step is to create a written policy that spells out the company's position on drugs. The policy should state its purpose, prohibit the use of

drugs on the job (or off the job if it affects job performance), specify the consequences of violating the policy, explain the drug testing procedures the company will use, and describe the resources available to help troubled employees.

2. *Training for supervisors to detect substance-abusing workers.* Supervisors are in the best position to identify employees with alcohol or drug problems and to encourage them to get help. The supervisor's job, however, is not to play "cop" or "therapist." The supervisor should identify problem employees early and encourage them to seek help. The focal point of the supervisor's role is to track employees' performances against their objectives to identify employees with performance problems. Vigilant managers look for the following signs:

- Frequent tardiness or absences accompanied by questionable excuses
- Long lunch, coffee, or bathroom breaks
- Frequently missed deadlines
- Withdrawal from or frequent arguments with fellow employees
- Overly sensitive to criticism
- Declining or inconsistent productivity
- Inability to concentrate on work
- Disregard for personal safety or the safety of others
- Deterioration of personal appearance

3. *An employee education program.* Business owners should take time to explain the company's substance abuse policy, the reasons behind it, and the help that is available to employees who have substance abuse problems. Every employee should participate in training sessions, and managers should remind employees periodically of the policy, the problem, and the help that is available. Some companies have used inserts in pay envelopes, home mailings, lunch speakers, and short seminars as part of their ongoing educational efforts.

4. *A drug testing program, when necessary.* Experts recommend that business owners seek the advice of an experienced attorney before establishing a drug testing program. Pre-employment testing of job applicants generally is a safe strategy to follow, as long as it is followed consistently. Testing current employees is a more complex issue, but, again, consistency is the key.

5. *An employee assistance program (EAP).* No drug-battling program is complete without a way to help addicted employees. An **employee assistance program (EAP)** is a company-provided benefit designed to help reduce workplace problems such as alcoholism, drug addiction, a gambling habit, and other conflicts and to deal with them when they arise. Although some troubled employees may balk at enrolling in an EAP, the company controls the most powerful weapon in motivating them to seek and accept help: *their jobs.* The greatest fear that substance-abusing employees have is losing their jobs, and the company can use that fear to help workers recover. EAPs, which cost between $18 and $30 per employee each year to operate, are an effective weapon in the battle against workplace substance abuse. Research shows that EAPs can pay for themselves quickly by reducing absenteeism and tardiness by 25 percent and increasing productivity by 25 percent.[39]

ENTREPRENEURIAL Profile

Eastern Industries

Eastern Industries, a Pennsylvania-based company that produces building supplies, concrete, asphalt, and stone, operates in an industry that traditionally has been plagued by substance abuse problems. (A recent study shows that 15.1 percent of workers in the construction industry had substance abuse problems, second only to the food service industry.) Initially, Eastern's substance abuse policy was simple: We test for drugs, and if you fail the test you are fired. The all-or-nothing policy affected the company's ability to keep and retain skilled workers, and company managers decided to change it to a policy that includes prevention, testing, and rehabilitation. Eastern includes educational sessions on substance abuse in its employee orientation program and ongoing programs for all workers. If an employee fails a drug test, he or she can enroll in an employee assistance program that includes rehabilitation that, once successfully completed, allows the worker to return to his or her job. Managers at Eastern say the program has been a tremendous success, allowing them to keep good workers they would have lost under the old policy and giving employees the opportunity to correct bad decisions and keep their jobs.[40]

HIV/AIDS. One of the most serious health problems to strike the world is HIV/AIDS (acquired immune deficiency syndrome). Health care experts estimate that more than 1.5 million people in the United States have HIV/AIDS, and 56,000 new cases are diagnosed each year. HIV/AIDS claims the lives of about 18,000 people annually.[41] This deadly disease, for which no cure yet exists, poses an array of ethical dilemmas for business, ranging from privacy to discrimination. AIDS has had an impact on our economy in the form of billions of dollars in lost productivity and increased health care costs. For most business owners, the issue is not one of *whether* one of their employees will contract AIDS but *when*.

Coping with AIDS in the workplace is not like managing normal health care issues because of the fear and misunderstanding the disease creates among coworkers. When confronted by the disease, many employers and employees operate out of misconceptions and fear, resulting in "knee-jerk" reactions that are illegal, including firing the worker and telling other employees. Too many entrepreneurs know very little about their legal obligation to employees with AIDS. In fact, AIDS is considered a disability and is covered by the Americans with Disabilities Act (ADA). This legislation prohibits discrimination against any person with a disability, including AIDS, in hiring, promoting, discharging, or compensation. In addition, employers are required to make "reasonable accommodations" that will allow an AIDS-stricken employee to continue working. Some examples of these accommodations include job sharing, flexible work schedules, job reassignment, sick leave, and part-time work.

Coping with AIDS in a socially responsible manner requires a written policy and an educational program, ideally implemented *before* the need arises. When dealing with AIDS, entrepreneurs must base their decisions on facts rather than on emotions, so they must be well informed. As with drug testing, it is important to ensure that a company's AIDS policies are legal. In general, a company's AIDS policy should include the following:

- *Employment.* Companies must allow employees with AIDS to continue working as long as they can perform the job.
- *Discrimination.* Because AIDS is a disability, employers cannot discriminate against qualified people with the disease who can meet job requirements.
- *Employee benefits.* Employees with AIDS have the right to the same benefits as those with any other life-threatening illness.
- *Confidentiality.* Employers must keep employees' medical records strictly confidential.
- *Education.* An AIDS education program should be a part of every company's AIDS policy. The time to create and implement one is before the problem arises. As part of its AIDS program, one small company conducted informational seminars, distributed brochures and booklets, established a print and video library, and even set up individual counseling for employees.
- *Reasonable accommodations.* Under the ADA, employers must make "reasonable accommodations" for employees with AIDS. These may include extended leaves of absence, flexible work schedules, restructuring a job to require less-strenuous duties, purchasing special equipment to assist affected workers, and other modifications.

SEXUAL HARASSMENT. Sexual harassment is a problem in the workplace, and thousands of workers file sexual harassment charges with the Equal Employment Opportunity Commission against their employers every year (see Figure 6). A survey by Reuters-Ipsos reports that 10 percent of workers in 24 countries say that they have been physically or sexually harassed. Employees in India were most likely to report sexual harassment (26 percent), and those in France and Sweden were least likely (3 percent). The incidence of sexual harassment in the United States is slightly below the global average at 9 percent.[42] Sexual harassment is a violation of Title VII of the Civil Rights Act of 1964 and is considered to be a form of sex discrimination. Studies show that sexual harassment occurs in businesses of all sizes, but small businesses are especially vulnerable because they typically lack the policies, procedures, and training to prevent it. Even cartoon strip characters are not immune to sexual harassment charges. In Mort Walker's long-running "Beetle Bailey" comic strip, Miss Buxley once filed charges against General Halftrack because of his leering stares and sexual and untoward comments.[43]

Sexual harassment is any unwelcome sexual advance, request for sexual favors, and other verbal or physical sexual conduct made explicitly or implicitly as a condition of employment. Women bring about 84 percent of all sexual harassment charges.[44] Jury verdicts reaching into the millions of dollars are not uncommon. Retaliation such as demotions and assignments to less attractive work against employees who file complaints of sexual harassment occurs too often. The

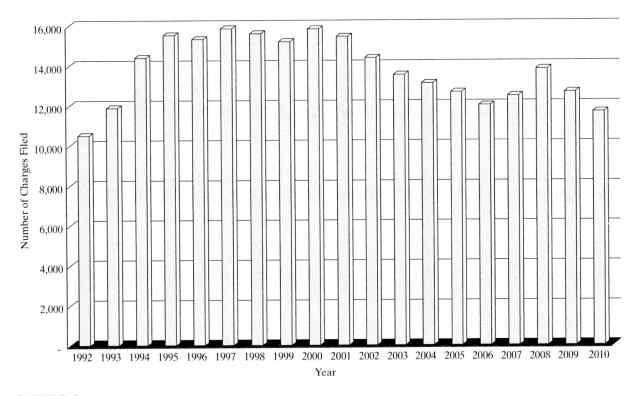

FIGURE 6

Number of Sexual Harassment Charges Filed

Source: Equal Employment Opportunity Commission, 2010.

most common form of employer retaliation is termination. Several types of behavior may result in sexual harassment charges.

Quid Pro Quo Harassment. The most blatant, and most potentially damaging, form of sexual harassment is *quid pro quo* ("something for something"), in which a superior conditions the granting of a benefit (promotion, raise, etc.) upon the receipt of sexual favors from a subordinate. Only managers and supervisors, not coworkers, can engage in *quid pro quo* harassment.

Only managers can engage in *quid pro quo* sexual harassment.

Source: RubberBall/SuperStock, Inc.

Hostile Environment. Behavior that creates an abusive, intimidating, offensive, or hostile work environment also constitutes sexual harassment. A hostile environment usually requires a *pattern* of offensive sexual behavior rather than a single, isolated remark or display. When judging whether a hostile environment exists, courts base their decisions on how a "reasonable woman" would perceive the situation. (The previous standard was that of a "reasonable person.") Although not easily defined, a hostile work environment is one in which continuing unwelcome sexual conduct in the workplace interferes with an employee's work performance. Most sexual harassment charges arise from claims of a hostile environment.

Harassment by Nonemployees. An employer can be held liable for third parties (customers, sales representatives, and others) who engage in sexual harassment if the employer has the ability to stop the improper behavior. For example, one company required a female employee to wear an extremely skimpy, revealing uniform. She complained to her boss that the uniform encouraged members of the public to direct offensive comments and physical contact toward her. The manager ignored her complaints, and later she refused to wear the uniform, which resulted in her dismissal. When she filed a sexual harassment claim, the court held the company accountable for the employee's sexual harassment by nonemployees because it required her to wear the uniform after she complained of the harassment.[45]

No business wants to incur the cost of defending itself against charges of sexual harassment, but those costs can be devastating for a small business. Multimillion-dollar jury awards in harassment cases are becoming increasingly common because the Civil Rights Act of 1991 allows victims to collect punitive damages and emotional distress awards. A jury awarded Shannen De La Cruz $2.16 million in damages after she won a lawsuit in which she claimed that her supervisor at the casino where she worked as a card dealer made inappropriate comments and sexual innuendo towards her. After De La Cruz reported the behavior to the company's human resource manager, a woman who also had filed (and settled) a sexual harassment suit against the company, the supervisor began disciplining her for minor and fabricated violations. Managers at the company did nothing to stop the supervisor's actions. The supervisor fired De La Cruz after he discovered that she was exploring legal action against the company over the harassment. On appeal, a judge affirmed the lower court's ruling but reduced the award to $1.26 million.[46]

The U.S. Supreme Court has expanded the nature of an employer's liability for sexual harassment, rejecting the previous standard that the employer had to be negligent to be liable for a supervisor's improper behavior toward employees. In *Burlington Industries v. Ellerth,* the Court ruled that an employer can be held liable *automatically* if a supervisor takes a "tangible employment action," such as failing to promote or firing an employee whom he has been sexually harassing. The employer is liable even if he was not aware of the supervisor's conduct. If a supervisor takes no tangible employment action against an employee but engages in sexually harassing behavior, such as offensive remarks, inappropriate touching, or sexual advances, the employer is not *automatically* liable for the supervisor's conduct. However, an employer would be liable for such conduct if, for example, he knew (or should have known) about the supervisor's behavior and failed to stop it.[47]

A company's best weapons against sexual harassment are education, policy, and procedures.

Education. Preventing sexual harassment is the best solution, and the key to prevention is educating employees about what constitutes sexual harassment. Training programs are designed to raise employees' awareness of what might be offensive to other workers and how to avoid sexual harassment altogether.

Policy. Another essential ingredient is a meaningful policy against sexual harassment that management can enforce. The policy should:

- Clearly define what behaviors constitute sexual harassment.
- State in clear language that harassment will not be tolerated in the workplace.
- Identify the responsibilities of supervisors and employees in preventing harassment.
- Define the sanctions and penalties for engaging in harassment.
- Spell out the steps to take in reporting an incident of sexual harassment.

In another case, the Supreme Court ruled that an employer was liable for a supervisor's sexually harassing behavior even though the employee never reported it. The company's liability stemmed from its failure to communicate its sexual harassment policy throughout the organization.

This ruling makes employers' policies and procedures on sexual harassment the focal point of their defense.

Procedure. Socially responsible companies provide a channel for all employees to express their complaints. Choosing a person inside the company (perhaps someone in the human resources area) and one outside the company (a close advisor or attorney) is a good strategy because it gives employees a choice about how to file a complaint. At least one of these people should be a woman. When a complaint arises, managers should:

- Listen to the complaint carefully without judging. Taking notes is a good idea. Tell the complainant what the process involves. Never treat the complaint as a joke.
- Investigate the complaint *promptly*, preferably within 24 hours. Failure to act quickly is irresponsible and illegal. Table 7 offers suggestions for conducting a sexual harassment investigation.
- Interview the accused party and any witnesses who may be aware of a pattern of harassing behavior *privately* and separately.
- Keep findings confidential.
- Decide what action to take, relying on company policy as a guideline.
- Inform both the complaining person and the alleged harasser of the action taken.
- Document the entire investigation.[48]

The accompanying "Lessons from the Street-Smart Entrepreneur" feature includes a quiz on sexual harassment for both employees and managers.

PRIVACY. Modern technology has given business owners the ability to monitor workers' performances as they never could before, but where is the line between monitoring productivity and invasion of privacy? With a few mouse clicks, it is possible for managers to view e-mail messages employees send to one another, listen to voice-mail or telephone conversations, and actually see what is on their monitors while they are sitting at their computer terminals. Managers use electronic monitoring to track customer service representatives, word processing clerks, data entry technicians, and other workers for speed, accuracy, and productivity. Even truck drivers, the lone rangers of the road, are not immune to electronic tracking. Most major trucking companies

TABLE 7 What to Do When an Employee Files a Sexual Harassment Complaint

When an employee files a sexual harassment complaint, the Equal Employment Opportunity Commission (EEOC) recommends that employers (1) question both parties in detail and (2) probe for corroborative evidence. Here is a checklist to help when following these EEOC recommendations:

- Analyze the victim's story for sufficient detail, internal consistency, and believability.
- Do not attach much significance to a general denial by the accused harasser.
- Search completely and thoroughly for evidence that corroborates either person's story.
- You can do this by:
  - interviewing coworkers, supervisors, and managers;
  - obtaining testimony from individuals who observed the accuser's demeanor immediately after the alleged incident of harassment; and
  - talking to people with whom the alleged victim discussed the incident (e.g., coworkers, a doctor, or a counselor).
- Ask other employees whether they noticed changes in the accusing individual's behavior at work or in the alleged harasser's treatment of him or her.
- Look for evidence of other complaints, either by the victim or other employees.
- Follow up on evidence that other employees were sexually harassed by the same person.

To make a fair and legal decision on a sexual harassment complaint, you must find out as much information as you can, not only on the incident itself, but also on the victim's and accuser's personalities, surroundings, and relationships. To accomplish this task, you need to ask many questions not only of the victim and the accuser but also of any witnesses to the incident.

Source: "Questions for Investigations," Women's Studies Database at the University of Maryland, *www.mith2.umd.edu/WomensStudies/GenderIssues/SexualHarassment/questions-for-investigations.*

LESSONS FROM THE STREET-SMART entrepreneur

How to Avoid Sexual Harassment Charges

The Equal Employment Opportunity Commission (EEOC) handles about 13,000 charges of sexual harassment each year from both women and men. Not surprisingly, women file 84 percent of the charges. Experts say that many other employees are sexually harassed but never file charges because of the stigma associated with doing so. What can you do to ensure you provide your employees a safe work environment that is free of sexual harassment? Consider the following case and then take the quizzes that follow on sexual harassment.

Theresa Waldo was the only woman working in the transmission lines department, a traditionally male-dominated job in which workers maintain and repair high-voltage power lines, sometimes at heights up to 250 feet, for Consumers Energy (CE). Her supervisor told her that the company did not "have women in this department," had never had them there, and that "they are not strong enough" to do the job. Despite resistance from her supervisor and her coworkers, Waldo, who started her career with CE as a meter reader, was participating in a 4-year Line Apprentice Training Program that would entitle her to a higher paying job. On several occasions, Waldo's supervisor told her that he would "wash her out" of the apprenticeship program.

During her time in the apprenticeship program, Waldo alleges that she faced an "abusive and dysfunctional environment" in which she was constantly "bombarded with sexually abusive and derogatory language and conduct." Male coworkers subjected her to magazines, calendars, playing cards, and other items that contained photographs of nude women. They also referred to Waldo using derogatory, sexually offensive names and on one 90-degree day intentionally locked her in a port-a-potty for 20 minutes. On another occasion, her supervisor ordered her to clean up the tobacco spit of the male workers; when she refused, her coworkers locked her in a trailer. Waldo complained to the company's management about the sexual harassment on several occasions, but managers failed to take any meaningful action to stop the behavior.

After Waldo had successfully completed 3 years of the apprenticeship program, CE removed her from it and transferred her to the Sub Metro Department, where her pay was $4 less per hour. She filed a sexual harassment charge, alleging that the company had created a hostile work environment, committed sexual harassment, and engaged in gender discrimination and retaliation.

Does Waldo have a legitimate sexual harassment complaint? Explain.

Yes. Although the jury in the trial ruled in favor of the *employer* on all claims, the judge granted Waldo's motion for a new trial, acknowledging that the jury's verdict on the hostile work environment and sexual harassment should be set aside because of the "clear evidence presented" in the case. The court ruled that the evidence "demonstrated egregious actions and sexually offensive and demeaning language" directed at Waldo. The court concluded that the harassment created "an intimidating, hostile, and offensive work environment" and that CE "knew of the harassment and failed to implement proper and appropriate corrective action." At the second trial, a jury ruled in Waldo's favor and granted her $400,000 in compensatory damages and $7.5 million in punitive damages.

One of the primary causes of sexual harassment in the workplace is the lack of education concerning what constitutes harassment. The following quizzes ask you to assume the roles of an employee and of a manager when answering the questions. Learning from these quizzes can help your company avoid problems with sexual harassment.

Test for Employees

Answer the following true/false questions:

1. If I just ignore unwanted sexual attention, it will usually stop.
2. If I don't mean to sexually harass another employee, he or she cannot perceive my behavior as sexually harassing.
3. Some employees don't complain about unwanted sexual attention from another worker because they don't want to get that person in trouble.
4. If I make sexual comments to someone and that person doesn't ask me to stop, I can assume that my behavior is welcome.
5. To avoid sexually harassing a woman who comes to work in a traditionally male workplace, men simply should not haze her.
6. A sexual harasser may be told by a court to pay part of a judgment to the employee he or she harassed.
7. A sexually harassed man does not have the same legal rights as a woman who is sexually harassed.
8. About 84 percent of all sexual harassment in today's workplace is done by males to females.
9. Sexually suggestive pictures or objects in a workplace don't create a liability unless someone complains.

10. Displaying nude pictures can constitute a hostile work environment even though most employees in the workplace think they are harmless.

11. Telling someone to stop his or her unwanted sexual behavior usually doesn't do any good.

Answers: (1) False, (2) False, (3) True, (4) False, (5) False, (6) True, (7) False, (8) True, (9) False, (10) True, (11) False.

Test for Managers

Answer the following true/false questions:

1. Men in male-dominated workplaces usually have to change their behavior when a woman begins working there.

2. Employers are not liable for the sexual harassment of one of their employees unless that employee loses specific job benefits or is fired.

3. Supervisors can be liable for sexual harassment committed by one of their employees against another.

4. Employers can be liable for the sexually harassing behavior of management personnel even if they are unaware of that behavior and have a policy forbidding it.

5. It is appropriate for a supervisor, when initially receiving a sexual harassment complaint, to determine whether the alleged recipient overreacted or misunderstood the alleged harasser.

6. When a supervisor tells an employee that an allegation of sexual harassment has been made against the employee, it is best to ease into the allegation instead of being direct.

7. Sexually suggestive visuals or objects in a workplace don't create a liability unless an employee complains about them and management allows them to remain.

8. The lack of sexual harassment complaints is a good indication that sexual harassment is not occurring.

9. It is appropriate for supervisors to tell an employee to handle unwelcome sexual behavior if they think that the employee is misunderstanding the behavior.

10. The *intent* behind employee A's sexual behavior is more important than the *impact* of that behavior on employee B when determining whether sexual harassment has occurred.

11. If a sexual harassment problem is common knowledge in a workplace, courts assume that the employer has knowledge of it.

Answers: (1) False, (2) False, (3) True, (4) True, (5) False, (6) False, (7) False, (8) False, (9) False, (10) False, (11) True.

Sources: Reprinted with permission from *IndustryWeek*, November 18, 1991, p. 40. Copyright Penton Publishing, Cleveland, Ohio; *Sexual Harassment Manual for Managers and Supervisors* (Chicago: Commerce Clearing House), 1992, p. 22; Andrea P. Brandon and David R. Eyler, *Working Together* (New York: McGraw-Hill), 1994; *Theresa Waldo v. Consumers Energy Company*, 2010 U.S. District Lexus 55068; 109 Fair Employment Practices Case (BNA) 11348, June 4, 2010; John Agar, "Consumers Energy Ordered to Pay $8 Million in Sexual Harassment Lawsuit Verdict," *Mlive*, October 8, 2010, *www.mlive.com/news/grand-rapids/index.ssf/2010/10/consumers_energy_ordered_to_pa.html*.

outfit their trucks with GPS devices that they use to monitor drivers' exact locations at all times, regulate their speed, make sure they stop only at approved fueling points, and ensure that they take the legally required hours of rest. Although many drivers support the use of these devices, others worry about their tendency to create George Orwell's "Big Brother" syndrome.

E-mail also poses an ethical problem for employers. Internet users send more than 247 billion e-mails each day.[49] Although most e-mails are unwanted spam, e-mail messages are a common way for employees to communicate with one another. Most workers do not realize that, in most states, employers legally can monitor their e-mail and voice-mail messages without notification. Only two states (Connecticut and Delaware) require companies to notify employees that they are monitoring e-mail. According to the Electronic Monitoring & Surveillance Survey, 43 percent of businesses monitor employees' e-mail and 28 percent have fired employees for misusing e-mail.[50] To avoid ethical (and legal) problems, business owners should follow these guidelines:

■ *Establish a clear policy for monitoring employees' communications.* Employees should know that the company is monitoring their e-mails and other forms of communication, and the best way to make sure they do is to create an unambiguous policy. Once you create a policy, be sure to follow it. Some managers ask employees to sign a consent form acknowledging that they have read and understand the company's monitoring policy.

■ *Create guidelines for the proper use of the company's communication technology and communicate them to everyone.* A company's policies and guidelines should be reasonable and should reflect employees' reasonable expectations of privacy.

■ *Monitor in moderation.* Employees resent monitoring that is unnecessarily invasive. In addition, excessively draconian monitoring may land a company in a legal battle.

► ENTREPRENEURSHIP IN ACTION ►

Think Before You Send That E-mail

Bonita Bourke and Rhonda Hall worked as customer service representatives for Nissan Motor Corporation, where they helped managers and employees at dealerships resolve problems with a new computer system that the company had implemented to help run dealerships more efficiently. During a training session on the system, one of Bonita Bourke's coworkers, Lori Eaton, was demonstrating how dealerships could use the system's e-mail feature as a management tool. As part of the demonstration, she randomly selected an e-mail that Bourke had sent to an employee at a Nissan dealership. Unfortunately, the e-mail was a personal one rather than one with a business purpose and contained sexual comments.

Eaton reported the incident to her supervisor, who reviewed the e-mails of all of the employees in Bourke's work group. He found a substantial number of e-mails from Bourke and Hall with similar content, much of it sexual and inappropriate in a business setting. The supervisor issued written warnings to both Bourke and Hall for violating the company's policy that prohibits the use of Nissan's e-mail system for personal purposes.

According to previous job evaluations, Bourke's job performance was substandard, and after the e-mail incident her performance declined. Eleven months after the e-mail incident, Bourke's job evaluation was rated "needs improvement," the second lowest category. Hall also received negative performance reviews during this time. Her supervisor wrote that she spent too much time on personal business and that she needed to demonstrate more initiative to learn the new computer system. She received the lowest performance rating, which was "unsatisfactory." Two months later, Bourke and Hall filed complaints with the human resources department, claiming that the company had invaded their privacy by reading their e-mail messages.

Two weeks later, Bourke's supervisor told her that if her performance did not improve over the next 3 months, she would be fired. She resigned the next day, the same day that Nissan fired Hall. Bourke and Hall filed a lawsuit against Nissan, alleging invasion of privacy, wrongful termination, and violation of the right to privacy under the U.S. Constitution. They argued that because the company gave them passwords to access the computer system and told them to safeguard their passwords, they believed that their e-mail messages would remain private. In its answer

to the lawsuit, Nissan argued that employees had no reasonable expectation of privacy in their e-mail communications. The company pointed to a statement of company policy that the plaintiffs had signed: It is "company policy that employees restrict their use of company-owned computer hardware and software to company business." Furthermore, both employees knew that managers sometimes reviewed the e-mail messages that employees sent. Nissan argued that given these facts, employees could not reasonably expect that their e-mail communications were private.

Many e-mail privacy cases, including *Bourke v. Nissan Motor Corporation,* have landed in the courts in recent years. E-mail monitoring is a common practice among companies; 43 percent of companies say they monitor employees' e-mail. The best way for companies to avoid legal problems over e-mail privacy is to create a policy that states that employees have no expectation that their e-mails are private and that the company reserves the right to monitor e-mail activity. The policy also should address the appropriate use of the company's e-mail system. Employees should sign the policy as well.

Many workers are blissfully unaware that their e-mail activity is anything but private. "If your e-mails are being monitored and you send a message that violates your company's policy and you are terminated for that message, you will have a hard time making a claim of invasion of privacy stick," says one expert. However, courts in some states have upheld employees' right to e-mail privacy because they require "all party consent" for an employer to monitor e-mail communications. In other words, both the sender and the receiver of the e-mail message must be aware that the company is monitoring their communications.

1. If you were the judge in the *Bourke v. Nissan Motor Corporation* case, how would you rule? Explain your reasoning.
2. What steps can companies that monitor employees' e-mail take to protect themselves against invasion of privacy lawsuits?

Sources: Adapted from 2005 Electronic Monitoring & Surveillance Survey, "Many Companies Monitoring, Recording, Videotaping—and Firing—Employees," American Management Association, *www.amanet.org/ press/amanews/ems05.htm*; Andrea Coombes, "Privacy at Work: Don't Count on It: Employers Are Tracking E-mail," *CareerJournal.com,* July 1, 2005, *www.careerjournal.com/myc/killers/20050701-coombes.html*; *Bourke v. Nissan Motor Corporation,* No. B068705 (Cal. Ct. App. July 26, 1993).

Business's Responsibility to Customers

7. Explain business's responsibility to customers.

One of the most important groups of stakeholders that a business must satisfy is its *customers*. Building and maintaining a base of loyal customers is no easy task; it requires more than just selling a product or a service. The key is to build relationships with customers. Socially responsible companies recognize their duty to abide by the Consumer Bill of Rights, first put forth by President John Kennedy. This document gives consumers the following rights.

RIGHT TO SAFETY. The right to safety is the most basic consumer right. Companies have the responsibility to provide their customers with safe, quality products and services. The greatest breach of trust occurs when businesses produce products that, when properly used, injure customers. Product liability cases can be controversial, such as the McDonald's coffee lawsuit, in which a jury found that the fast-food giant's coffee was too hot when served and caused a serious injury when a customer at a drive-through window spilled coffee in her lap. In other situations, the evidence is clear that a product suffers from fundamental flaws in either design or construction and caused an injury to its user when used properly.

Many companies have responded by placing detailed warning labels on their products that sometimes insult customers' intelligence. Consider the following actual examples from product warning labels:

- "Do not eat toner" on a toner cartridge for a laser printer
- "Never operate your speakerphone while driving," a warning attached to a "Drive 'N' Talk" speakerphone for use with cell phones
- "Do not use orally" on a toilet bowl cleaning brush
- "Do not try to dry your phone in a microwave oven" in the instructions for a cellular phone
- "Caution: Remove infant before folding for storage" on a baby stroller[51]

RIGHT TO KNOW. Consumers have the right to honest communication about the products and services they buy and the companies that sell them. In a free market economy, information is one of the most valuable commodities available. Customers often depend on companies for the information they need to make decisions about price, quality, features, and other factors. As a result, companies have a responsibility to customers to be truthful in their advertising.

Unfortunately, not every business recognizes its social responsibility to be truthful in advertising. The Federal Trade Commission (FTC) filed a false advertising lawsuit against a small company that was selling an exercise device that the company claimed would allow users "to lose from 4 to 14 inches guaranteed in just 7 days" by "supercharging their blood with fat-burning oxygen." The infomercial that promoted the $54.85 device (including shipping and handling) ran more than 2,000 times on cable channels across the nation. As a result of the FTC's action, the company agreed to refund to customers $2.6 million and to stop their false advertising campaign.[52] Businesses that rely on unscrupulous tactics may profit in the short-term, but they will not last in the long-run.

Right to Be Heard

The right to be heard suggests that the channels of communication between companies and their customers run in both directions. Socially responsible businesses provide customers with a mechanism for resolving complaints about products and services. Some companies have established a consumer ombudsman to address customer questions and complaints. Others have created customer hotlines, toll-free numbers designed to serve customers more effectively.

Another effective technique for encouraging two-way communication between customers and companies is the customer report card. The Granite Rock Company, a business that supplies a variety of building materials to construction companies, relies on an annual report card from its customers to learn how to serve them better. Although the knowledge a small business owner gets from customer feedback is immeasurable for making improvements, only 1 in 12 small companies regularly schedules customer satisfaction surveys like Granite Rock's.

RIGHT TO EDUCATION. Socially responsible companies give customers access to educational programs about their products and services and how to use them properly. The goal is to give customers enough information to make informed purchase decisions. A product that is the wrong solution to the customer's needs results in a disappointed customer who is likely to blame the manufacturer or retailer for the mistake. Consumer education is an inexpensive investment in customer satisfaction and the increased probability that a satisfied customer is a repeat buyer.

RIGHT TO CHOICE. Inherent in the free enterprise system is the consumer's right to choose among competing products and services. Socially responsible companies do not restrict competition, and they abide by the United States' antitrust policy, which promotes free trade and competition in the market. The foundation of this policy is the Sherman Antitrust Act of 1890, which forbids agreements among sellers that restrain trade or commerce and outlaws any attempts to monopolize a market.

Business's Responsibility to Investors

8. Discuss business's responsibility to investors.

Companies have the responsibility to provide investors with an attractive return on their investment. Although earning a profit may be a company's *first* responsibility, it is not its *only* responsibility; meeting its ethical and social responsibility goals is also a key to success. Investors today want to know that entrepreneurs are making ethical decisions and acting in a socially responsible manner. In a survey by Opinion Research Corporation, 76 percent of investors say that they would move their investments from companies that engage in unethical but legal behavior, even if the company's action produced a high return on their investment.[53] Another study shows that a company's financial returns are the *least* important factor that influences public perception of its reputation.[54] Maintaining high standards of ethics and social responsibility translates into a business culture that sets the stage for a profitable business operation.

Companies also have the responsibility to report their financial performances in an accurate and timely fashion to their investors. Businesses that misrepresent or falsify their financial and operating records are guilty of violating the fiduciary relationship with their investors.

ENTREPRENEURIAL Profile

Richard Priddy and Charles Sample: TVI Corporation

Richard Priddy, CEO of TVI Corporation, and Charles Sample, the company's CFO, were sentenced to prison and ordered to pay $595,000 in restitution for defrauding the company of more than $1.4 million. Priddy and Sample learned that they could purchase from a company in Seattle at significantly lower prices the same parts that TVI had been buying from another vendor. Rather than allow TVI to switch to the lower cost supplier, they formed a separate company, Containment & Transfer Systems, LLC (CATS), to purchase the parts from the Seattle company and resell them to TVI. Over the next 5 years, Priddy and Sample hid the fact that they owned CATS from the TVI board and investors and defrauded TVI of more than $1.4 million before board members discovered the executives' illicit actions.[55]

Business's Responsibility to the Community

9. Discuss business's responsibility to the community.

As corporate citizens, businesses have a responsibility to the communities in which they operate. In addition to providing jobs and creating wealth, companies contribute to the local community in many different ways. Socially responsible businesses are aware of their duty to put back into the community some of what they take out as they generate profits; their goal is to become a neighbor of choice.

Experts estimate that 80 percent of companies worldwide engage in some type of socially responsible activity.[56] The following are just a few examples of ways small businesses have found to give back to their communities:

- Act as volunteers for community groups such as the American Red Cross, United Way, literacy programs, and a community food bank.
- Participate in projects that aid the elderly or economically disadvantaged.
- Adopt a highway near the business to promote a clean community.

In a recent survey, 75 percent of consumers say that companies living up to their social responsibility is important even during economic recessions.[57] Even small companies that may be short on funding can support causes by choosing them strategically and discovering creative ways to help them. The key to choosing the "right" cause is finding one that makes an impact and whose purpose resonates with customers, employees, and owners. Small companies can commit their employees' talent and know-how, not just dollars, to carefully chosen social causes and then tell the world about their cause and their dedication to serving it. By forging meaningful partnerships, both the businesses and the causes benefit in unique ways. Over the years, companies have helped social causes enjoy financial rewards and unprecedented support. In addition to doing good, companies have been able to enhance their reputations, deepen employee loyalty, strengthen ties with business partners, and sell more products or services.

Bomb-sniffing dogs in the Middle East wearing body-cooling vests donated by Glacier Tek, the small company that created the special vests.

Source: Glacier Tek

Ray Booska, founder of Glacier Tek, a West Melbourne, Florida-based company that makes body-cooling vests for a variety of applications, learned about the challenges that the intense heat in the Middle East creates for bomb-sniffing dogs stationed there on military duty and decided that his company could help. Booska and his team of designers tested several prototypes on Booska's retired police dog, Fritz, before finding one that worked to their satisfaction. The vest is made of a nontoxic coolant that works like gel ice packs and can be recharged in just 15 minutes. Glacier Tek added the canine vest to its product line but has donated more than 500 of them to dogs in military zones in the Middle East. "These dogs save the lives of our sons and daughters," says Booska, "and we're going to do everything we can to help them."[58]

Entrepreneurs such as Booska who demonstrate their sense of social responsibility not only make their communities better places to live and work but also stand out from their competitors. Their efforts to operate ethical, socially responsible businesses create a strong sense of loyalty among their customers and their employees.

Conclusion

Businesses must do more than merely earn profits; they must act ethically and in a socially responsible manner. Establishing and maintaining high ethical and socially responsible standards must be a top concern of every business owner. Managing in an ethical and socially responsible manner presents a tremendous challenge, however. There is no universal definition of ethical behavior, and what is considered ethical may change over time and may be different in other cultures.

Finally, business owners and managers must recognize the key role they play in influencing their employees' ethical and socially responsible behavior. What owners and managers *say* is important, but what they *do* is even more important! Employees in a small company look to the owner and managers as models; therefore, these owners and managers must commit themselves to following the highest ethical standards if they expect their employees to do so.

Chapter Review

1. Define business ethics and describe the three levels of ethical standards.
   - Business ethics involves the fundamental moral values and behavioral standards that form the foundation for the people of an organization as they make decisions and interact with the organization's stakeholders. Small business managers must consider the ethical and social as well as the economic implications of their decisions.
   - The three levels of ethical standards are (1) the law, (2) the policies and procedures of the company, and (3) the moral stance of the individual.

2. Determine who is responsible for ethical behavior and why ethical lapses occur.
- Managers set the moral tone of the organization. There are three ethical styles of management: immoral, amoral, and moral. Although moral management has value in itself, companies that operate with this philosophy discover other benefits, including a positive reputation among customers and employees.
- Ethical lapses occur for a variety of reasons:
  Some people are corrupt ("the bad apple").
  The company culture has been poisoned ("the bad barrel").
  Competitive pressures push managers to compromise.
  Managers are tempted by an opportunity to "get ahead."
  Managers in different cultures have different views of what is ethical.

3. Explain how to establish and maintain high ethical standards.
- Philosophers throughout history have developed various tests of ethical behavior: the utilitarian principle, Kant's categorical imperative, the professional ethic, the Golden Rule, the television test, and the family test.
- A small business manager can maintain high ethical standards in the following ways:
  Create a company credo.
  Develop a code of ethics.
  Enforce the code fairly and consistently.
  Hire the right people.
  Conduct ethical training.
  Perform periodic ethical audits.
  Establish high standards of behavior, not just rules.
  Set an impeccable ethical example at all times.
  Create a culture emphasizing two-way communication.
  Involve employees in establishing ethical standards.

4. Define social responsibility.
- Social responsibility is the awareness of a company's managers of the social, environmental, political, human, and financial consequences of their actions.

5. Understand the nature of business's responsibility to the environment.
- Environmentally responsible business owners focus on the three Rs: reduce, reuse, recycle: *reduce* the amount of materials used in the company from the factory floor to the copier room; *reuse* whatever you can; and *recycle* the materials that you must dispose of.

6. Describe business's responsibility to employees.
- Companies have a duty to act responsibly toward one of their most important stakeholders: their employees. Businesses must recognize and manage the cultural diversity that exists in the workplace; establish a responsible strategy for combating substance abuse in the workplace (including drug testing) and dealing with AIDS; prevent sexual harassment; and respect employees' right to privacy.

7. Explain business's responsibility to customers.
- Every company's customers have a right to safe products and services; to honest, accurate information; to be heard; to education about products and services; and to choices in the marketplace.

8. Discuss business's responsibility to investors.
- Companies have the responsibility to provide investors with an attractive return on their investments and to report their financial performances in an accurate and timely fashion to their investors.

9. Describe business's responsibility to the community.
- Increasingly, companies are seeing a need to go beyond "doing well" to "doing good"—being socially responsible community citizens. In addition to providing jobs and creating wealth, companies contribute to the local community in many different ways.

Discussion Questions

1. What is ethics? Discuss the three levels of ethical standards.
2. In any organization, who determines ethical behavior? Briefly describe the three ethical styles of management. What are the benefits of moral management?
3. Why do ethical lapses occur in businesses?
4. Describe the various methods for establishing ethical standards. Which is most meaningful to you? Explain.
5. What can business owners do to maintain high ethical standards in their companies?
6. What is social responsibility?
7. Describe business's social responsibility to each of the following areas:
   - The environment
   - Employees
   - Customers
   - Investors
   - The community
8. What can businesses do to improve the quality of our environment?
9. Should companies be allowed to test employees for drugs? Explain. How should a socially responsible drug testing program operate?
10. Many owners of trucking companies use electronic communications equipment to monitor their drivers on the road. They say that the devices allow them to remain competitive and to serve their customers better by delivering shipments of vital materials exactly when their customers need them. They also point out that the equipment can improve road safety by ensuring that drivers get the hours of rest the law requires. Opponents argue that the surveillance devices work against safety. "The drivers know they're being watched," says one trucker. "There's an obvious temptation to push." What do you think? What ethical issues does the use of such equipment create? How should a small trucking company considering the use of such equipment handle these issues?
11. What rights do customers have under the Consumer Bill of Rights? How can businesses ensure those rights?

Business Plan Pro

Businesses have a responsibility to both "do well"—earn a profit, remain financially sound, and stay in business—and "do good"—operate ethically and meet their responsibility to society. It is critical for business owners to recognize their obligation to operate their businesses in an ethical and socially responsible manner. They must consider these issues as essential elements of a successful and sustainable business. They must create a culture that encourages employees to recognize ethical dilemmas and to do what is right when faced with ethical dilemmas. Values-based leaders integrate the ethical dimensions of their actions and decisions as well as those of their employees into the fabric of their companies' culture. They establish ethical guidelines, conduct training sessions in ethics, and, most important, set an example for ethical behavior in the organization. These leaders understand that ethical behavior does not simply happen in an organization; it is the result of a conscious effort that involves everyone. They also recognize that their companies have a responsibility to society that extends far beyond merely earning a profit. The business plan must capture this broader sense of ethical and social responsibility to all stakeholders.

On the Web

The Internet offers a wealth of information regarding business ethics and a company's responsibility to investors, employees, customers, the community, and the environment. You will find some of these resources on the Companion Web Site at *www.pearsonhighered.com/scarborough*. These links may help you to integrate ethical standards into the fabric of your business plan.

In the Software

Review all divisions of your plan. Attempt to take an objective look to determine whether your plan communicates a values-based leadership approach. Consider these questions:

- How does your plan describe the company's responsibility to its employees?
- How does the plan describe its responsibility to investors?
- How does your plan describe its responsibility to customers?
- What does the business plan communicate about the company's responsibility to the community?
- Does the plan explain how the business operates in an environmentally responsible manner?
- Does the plan describe a business that offers long-term sustainability?

Building Your Business Plan

The business plan will help you to identify the key stakeholders in your company, verbalize your philosophy of business ethics, identify the best way to establish high ethical standards, and explain the level of your company's commitment to socially responsible actions. Consider including the description of your philosophy of ethics and social responsibility in the plan's "Strategy and Implementation" section. Your analysis of these important issues also may lead you to modify your company's mission statement.

Endnotes

1. Michael Barkoviak, "PC Makers Still Not Pleased with Chinese Censorship Software," *Daily Tech*, June 30, 2009, *www.dailytech.com/ PC+Makers+Still+Not+Pleased+With+Chinese+Censorship+Software/ article15560.htm*; Rex Crum, "PC Makers Assess How to Deal with China's Green Dam," *Market Watch*, June 23, 2009, *www.marketwatch.com/ story/green-dam-issue-grows-between-pc-makers-and-china*; Loretta Chao, "China Squeezes PC Makers," *Wall Street Journal*, June 8, 2009, pp. A1, A10.

2. Vernon R. Loucks, Jr., "A CEO Looks at Ethics," *Business Horizons*, March–April 1987, p. 2.

3. Susan Caminiti, "The Payoff from a Good Reputation," *Fortune*, February 10, 1992, p. 74.

4. Amy Wallace, "The Rise and Fall of the Cincinnati Boner King," *GQ*, September 2009, *www.gq.com/news-politics/mens-lives/200909/ smilin-bob-enzyte-steve-warshak-male-enhancement*.

5. "Top Small Workplaces—2008 Winner: King Arthur Flour Company," *Winning Workplaces*, *www.winningworkplaces.org/topsmallbiz/ 2008winners/tsw2008_kingarthurflour.php*; "Good Works," King Arthur Flour Company, *www.kingarthurflour.com/about/ goodworks.html*.

6. Richard C. Morais, "A River Runs Through It," *Forbes*, March 16, 2009, p. 90.

7. Kate O'Sullivan, "Virtue Rewarded," *CFO*, October 2006, p. 51.

8. *2010 Edelman Trust Barometer*, Edelman Financial Services, 2010, p. 6.

9. Jim Witkin, "Despite Struggles, Entrepreneurs Find Ways to Give Back," *New York Times*, September 15, 2010, *www.nytimes.com/ 2010/09/16/business/smallbusiness/16sbiz.html*.

10. O'Sullivan, "Virtue Rewarded"; Jennifer Reingold, "Walking the Walk," *Fast Company*, November 2005, pp. 81–85; Joseph Pereira, "Doing Good and Doing Well at Timberland," *Wall Street Journal*, September 9, 2003, pp. B1–B10.

11. Richard McGill Murphy, "Why Doing Good Is Good for Business," *Fortune*, February 8, 2010, pp. 91–95.

12. Pereira, "Doing Good and Doing Well at Timberland."

13. *Integrity Survey 2008–2009*, KPMG LLC, 2009, p. iii.

14. *The Importance of Ethical Culture: Increasing Trust and Driving Down Risks*, Ethics Resource Center, Arlington, Virginia, 2010, p. 5.

15. Patricia Wallington, "Honestly?!" *CIO*, March 15, 2003, p. 42.

16. Mark Henricks, "Well, Honestly!" *Entrepreneur*, December 2006, p. 103.

17. Patricia Wallington, "Total Leadership—Ethical Behavior Is Essential," *CIO*, March 15, 2003, *www.cio.com/article/31779/Total_ Leadership_Ethical_Behaviour_Is_Essential*.

18. Joshua Kurlantzick, "Liar, Liar," *Entrepreneur*, October 2003, pp. 68–71.

19. Gene Laczniak, "Business Ethics: A Manager's Primer," *Business*, January–March 1983, pp. 23–29.

20. Michael Josephson, "Teaching Ethical Decision Making and Its Principled Reasoning," *Ethics: Easier Said Than Done*, Winter 1988, p. 28.

21. John Rutledge, "The Portrait on My Wall," *Forbes*, December 30, 1996, p. 78.

22. Jim Witkin, "Despite Struggles, Entrepreneurs Find Ways to Give Back," *New York Times*, September 15, 2010, *www.nytimes.com/ 2010/09/16/business/smallbusiness/16sbiz.html*.

23. SurePayroll Insights Survey: Economy Woes Squeeze Small Business Charity, SurePayroll, May 28, 2008, *www.surepayroll.com/spsite/press/ releases/2008/release052808.asp*.

24. Niels Bosma and Jonathan Levie, *Global Entrepreneurship Monitor 2009 Global Report*, 2009, *www.gemconsortium.org*, p. 49.

25. "What Is a Social Entrepreneur?" Ashoka, *www.ashoka.org/ social_entrepreneur*.

26. Katrina Daniel, "Customers Buy, Company Gives," *Womenetics*, November 23, 2010, *www.womenetics.com/philanthropy/733- customers-buy-company-gives*.

27. *2010 Cone Cause Evolution Study*, Cone LLC, Boston, Massachusetts: 2010, pp. 6, 8.

28. Edward Iwata, "Businesses Grow More Socially Conscious," *USA Today*, February 14, 2007, *www.usatoday.com/money/companies/ 2007-02-14-high-purpose-usat_x.htm*.

29. "About Ecoist," Ecoist, *www.ecoist.com/pc/about/intro.asp*.

30. Chris Penttila, "Shades of Green," *Entrepreneur*, August 2007, pp. 19–20; "Nature Meet Nurture," Pangea Organics, *www.pangeaorganics.com/home.html*.

31. "Top Small Company Workplaces 2010 Winner," Winning Workplaces, *www.winningworkplaces.org/topsmallbiz/2010winners/tsw2010_ tastycatering.php*; Bruce Christian, "Caterer of the Year," *Catering Magazine*, May 2008, pp. 28–30.

32. Jennifer J. Salopek, "The 2020 Workplace," *Workforce Management*, June 2010, pp. 36–40.

33. Juan Rodriguez, "U.S. Workforce Will Be Smaller, More Diverse in 2050," *Diversity Jobs*, August 14, 2008, *http://diversityjobs.com/ news/us-workforce-will-be-smaller-more-diverse-in-2050/*.

34. Keith H. Hammonds, "Difference Is Power," *Fast Company*, July 2000, p. 58.

35. Best Practices of Private Sector Employers, Equal Employment Opportunity Commission (Washington, DC, 2003), *www.eeoc.gov/ abouteeoc/task_reports/prac2.html*.

36. Martha Lagace, "Racial Diversity Pays Off," Harvard Business School: *Working Knowledge*, June 21, 2004, *http://hbsworkingknowledge.hbs.edu/ item.jhtml?id=4207&t=organizations*.

37. Fay Hanson, "Diversity of a Different Color," *Workforce Management*, June 2010, pp. 23–26.

38. Amy Preiss, "Substance Abuse in the Workplace," University of Phoenix, June 29, 2009, *www.phoenix.edu/profiles/faculty/amy-preiss/ articles/abuse-in-the-workplace.html*.

39. Gina Ruiz, "Expanded EAPs Lend a Hand to Employer's Bottom Line," *Workforce Management*, January 16, 2006, pp. 46–47.

40. *The President's National Drug Control Strategy*, February 2007, *www.whitehousedrugpolicy.gov/publications/policy/ndcs07/*, pp. 14–15; "Nationwide Survey Shows Most Illicit Drug Users and Heavy Alcohol Users Are in the Workplace and May Pose Special Problems," Substance Abuse and Mental Health Services Administration, U.S. Department of Health and Human Services, July 17, 2007, *http://oas.samhsa.gov/work2k7/press.htm*.

41. *The National Survey on Drug Abuse and Health Report*, Substance Abuse and Mental Health Services Administration, U.S. Department of Health and Human Services, December 2010, p. 1.

42. Belinda Goldsmith, "Indians Most Likely to Report Sexual Harassment at Work—Poll," *Reuters*, August 12, 2010, *http://in.reuters.com/ article/idINIndia-50803120100812*.

43. Amy Wilson, "Inappropriate Behavior Lands Beetle Bailey's General in Hot Water," *Greenville News*, November 22, 1992, p. 20D.

44. "Sexual Harassment Charges," Equal Employment Opportunity Commission, 2010, *www.eeoc.gov/eeoc/statistics/enforcement/ sexual_harassment.cfm*.

45. *Sexual Harassment Manual for Managers and Supervisors* (Chicago: Commerce Clearing House, 1992), pp. 25–26.

46. Lori A. Carter, "$2 Million Harassment Verdict Against Petaluma Card Room," *Press Democrat*, August 5, 2010, *www.petaluma360.com/ article/20100805/COMMUNITY/100809800?p=3&tc=pg&tc=ar*; Lori A. Carter, "Judge Reduces Jury Award in Petaluma Card Room Sexual Harassment Case," *Press Democrat*, October 8, 2010, *www.pressdemocrat.com/article/20101008/ARTICLES/101009447*.

47. *Burlington Industries v. Ellerth* (97-569) 123 F.3d 490; "Employer Liability for Harassment," Equal Employment Opportunity Commission, *www.eeoc.gov/types/harassment.html*.

48. Nicole P. Cantey, "High Court Rules Same Sex Harassment Is Against the Law," *South Carolina Business Journal*, August 1998, p. 3; Jack Corcoran, "Of Nice and Men," *Success*, June 1998, pp. 64–67.

49. "Internet 2009 in Numbers," Royal Pingdom, January 22, 2010, *http://royal.pingdom.com/2010/01/22/internet-2009-in-numbers/*.

50. *2007 Electronic Monitoring and Surveillance Survey*, American Management Association, February 28, 2008, *http://press.amanet.org/ press-releases/177/2007-electronic-monitoring-surveillance-survey/*.

51. "13th Annual Wacky Warning Labels Contest Winners Selected on National Television," Wacky Warning Labels, July 12, 2010, *www .wackywarninglabelstv.com/press-releases/2010/7/12/13th-annual- wacky-warning-labels-contest-winners-selected-on.html*; "M-Law's Tenth Annual Wacky Warning Label Contest," Wacky Warning Labels, January 4, 2007, *www.wackywarnings.com*; "Things People Said: Warning Labels," Rinkworks, *www.rinkworks.com/said/ warnings.shtml*.

52. "FTC Charges BodyFlex with False Advertising," ConsumerAffairs.com, November 10, 2003, *http://consumeraffairs.com/ news03/bodyflex.html*; "BodyFlex to Offer $2.6 Million in Refunds," ConsumerAffairs.com, September 1, 2004, *www.consumeraffairs.com/news04/bodyflex.html*.

53. Thomas Kostigen, "Ethics Trumps Returns," Market Watch, July 13, 2007, *www.marketwatch.com/news/story/story.aspx?guid= %7BC3CA306A-4BD5-4250-85C2-98D60F699CAB%7D&siteid=rss*.

54. *2010 Edelman Trust Barometer*, Edelman Financial Services, 2010, p. 6.

55. "Examples of Corporate Fraud Investigations 2010: Corporate CEO, Vice President and Accountant Sentenced for Defrauding Maryland Company of Over $1.4 Million," Internal Revenue Service, *www.irs.gov/compliance/enforcement/article/0,,id=213768,00.html*.

56. Ruben Hernandez-Murillo and Christopher J. Martinek, "Corporate Social Responsibility Can Be Profitable," *Regional Economist*, April 2009, pp. 4–5.

57. Corporate Social Responsibility Branding Survey, Penn, Schoen, Berland and Burson-Marseller, 2010, *www.psbresearch.com/ files/CSR%20 Branding%20Survey%202010%20EXTERNAL% 20FINAL.pdf*, p. 1.

58. Elise Reinemann, "Chilly Dogs," *FSB*, September 2008, pp. 18–19.

Management Succession and Risk Management Strategies in the Family Business

Learning Objectives

Upon completion of this chapter, you will be able to:

1 Explain the factors necessary for a strong family business.
2 Understand the exit strategy options available to an entrepreneur.
3 Discuss the stages of management succession.
4 Explain how to develop an effective management succession plan.
5 Understand the four risk management strategies.
6 Discuss the basics of insurance for small businesses.

When it works right, nothing succeeds like a family firm. The roots run deep, embedded in family values. The flash of the fast buck is replaced with long-term plans. Tradition counts.

—Eric Calonius

Walk sober off before the sprightlier age comes titt'ring on and shoves you from the stage.

—Alexander Pope

Family Businesses

1. Explain the factors necessary for a strong family business.

Nearly 90 percent of all companies in the United States, about 26.4 million businesses, are family owned. Yet family-owned businesses, those in which family members control ownership and/or decision making, are often overlooked by the media, which focus most of their attention on the larger companies in our economy. In reality, family businesses generate 64 percent of the U.S. gross domestic product, account for 62 percent of all employment and 78 percent of job creation, and pay 65 percent of all wages.[1] Despite common perceptions, not all family businesses are small. The average annual sales of family businesses in the United States are about $36.5 million, and 33 percent of *Fortune* 500 companies are family businesses.[2] Globally, family-owned businesses account for 70 to 90 percent of world GDP.[3] Some of the best-known companies in the world are family-owned, including Ford Motor Company, Samsung, Hyundai, Sainsbury, Mars, and Walmart. In fact, Sam Walton's heirs own 43 percent (1.7 billion shares) of the stock in the world's largest company, Walmart, and those shares are worth an estimated $92 billion, an amount that exceeds the GDP of 161 countries in the world.[4]

When a family business works right, it is a thing of beauty. Family members share deeply rooted values that guide the company and give it a sense of harmony. Family members understand and support one another as they work together to achieve the company's mission. That harmony can produce a significant financial payoff. A study by Jim Lee of Texas A&M University–Corpus Christi shows that family-owned businesses are more profitable and experience faster employment and revenue growth over time than nonfamily businesses.[5] Another study of companies in the Standard & Poor's 500 Index by Ronald Anderson, David Reeb, and Sattar Mansi found that family firms outperformed their nonfamily counterparts on a variety of financial measures.[6] Other research comparing the financial performances of similar sets of family and nonfamily businesses has concluded that "firms controlled by the founding family have greater value, are operated more efficiently, and carry less debt than other firms."[7]

Family businesses also have a dark side, and it stems from their lack of continuity. Sibling rivalries, fights over control of the business, and personality conflicts often lead to nasty battles that can tear families apart and destroy once thriving businesses. Long-standing feuds can make family relationships difficult, and, when mixed with business decisions and the wealth family businesses can create, the result can be explosive. When Dhirubhai Ambani, founder of Reliance Industries Ltd., one of India's most successful companies, died without a will, his sons, Mukesh and Anil, battled over how to run the extensive business empire they took over. After years of personal and legal battles, the brothers entered into an agreement brokered by their mother that split the company into pieces so that each could operate his share of the business independently of the other. "Since their father's death, the brothers have been trying to outdo and undercut each other," says one observer.[8]

The stumbling block for most family businesses is management succession; 70 percent of first-generation businesses fail to survive into the second generation, and, of those that do survive, only 12 percent make it to the third generation. Just 3 percent of family businesses survive to the fourth generation and beyond.[9] The leading causes of family business failures are inadequate estate planning, failure to create a management succession plan, and lack of funds to pay estate taxes.[10] Just when they are ready to make the transition from one generation of leaders to the next, family businesses are most vulnerable. As a result, the average life expectancy of a family business is 24 years, although some last *much* longer (see Table 1).[11]

ENTREPRENEURIAL Profile

Will Tuttle: Tuttle Farm

Will Tuttle, the 63-year-old patriarch of one of the oldest family businesses in the United States, Tuttle Farm in Dover, New Hampshire, recently announced that his generation will be the last to operate the farm. Founded in 1632 by John Tuttle with a land grant from England's King Charles II, Tuttle Farm has struggled with the encroachment of housing and commercial developments and the impact of a severe recession. Will Tuttle, who began helping his father on the farm at age 6, has listed the 134-acre farm for sale at $3.35 million. "This is a different business now," says Tuttle. "I don't see much opportunity for small farms to thrive."[12]

According to a study of family businesses across the globe by PriceWaterhouseCoopers, 27 percent of family business owners say that ownership of their companies will change hands within the next 5 years and 53 percent of the owners expect to pass their companies on to the next

TABLE 1 **The World's Oldest Family Businesses.**

William O'Hara, director of the Institute for Family Enterprise at Bryant College, and Peter Mandel have compiled a list of some of the world's oldest family businesses.

Company	Country	Nature of Business	Year Established
Hoshi Ryokan	Japan	Hotel	718
Château de Goulaine	France	Vineyard, museum, butterfly collection	1000
Fonderia Pontifica Marinelli	Italy	Bell foundry	1000
Barone Ricasoli	Italy	Wine and olive oil	1141
Barovier & Toso	Italy	Artistic glassmaking	1295
Hotel Pilgram Haus	Germany	Innkeeping	1304
Richard de Bas	France	High-quality paper maker	1326
Torrini Firenze	Italy	Goldsmiths	1369
Antinori	Italy	Wine	1385
Camuffo	Italy	Shipbuilding	1438
Baronnie de Coussergues	France	Wine	1495
Grazia Deruta	Italy	Ceramics	1500
Fabbrice D'Armi Beretta	Italy	Firearms production	1526
William Prym GmbH & Company	Germany	Copper, brass, haberdashery	1530
John Brooke & Sons	Great Britain	Textiles	1541
Codorniu	Spain	Wine	1551
Fonjallaz	Switzerland	Wine	1552

Source: William T. O'Hara and Peter Mandel, "The World's Oldest Family Companies," *Family Business,* *www.familybusinessmagazine.com/oldworld.html.*

generation of family members.[13] The best way to ensure the legacy of a family business and a successful transition from one generation of family owners to the next is to develop a succession plan for the company. Although business founders inevitably want their businesses to survive them and most intend to pass them on to their children, they do not always support their intentions by a plan to accomplish that goal. The study by PriceWaterhouseCoopers reports that 47 percent of family businesses have no succession plans in place (see Figure 1).[14] Another survey of family business owners by MassMutual Financial Group and Arthur Andersen reports that 19 percent had not engaged in any kind of estate planning other than creating a will.[15] For most family businesses, the greatest threat to survival comes from *within* the company rather than from outside it. Many entrepreneurs dream of their businesses continuing in the family but take no significant steps to make their dreams a reality.

David Bork, founder of the Aspen Family Business Conference, has identified several qualities that are essential to a successful family business: shared values, shared power, tradition, a willingness to learn, family behavior, and strong family ties.[16]

Shared Values

The first, and probably most overlooked, quality is a set of shared values. What family members value and believe about people, work, and money shapes their behavior toward the business. All members of a family business should talk openly to determine, in a nonjudgmental fashion, each one's values. Without shared values, it is difficult to create a sense of direction for a business.

To avoid the problems associated with conflicting values and goals, family business owners should consider taking the following actions:

- Make it clear to all family members that they are not required to join the business full-time. Family members' goals, ambitions, and talents should be foremost in their career decisions.
- Do not assume that a successor must come from within the family. Simply being born into a family does not guarantee that a person will make a good business leader.

499

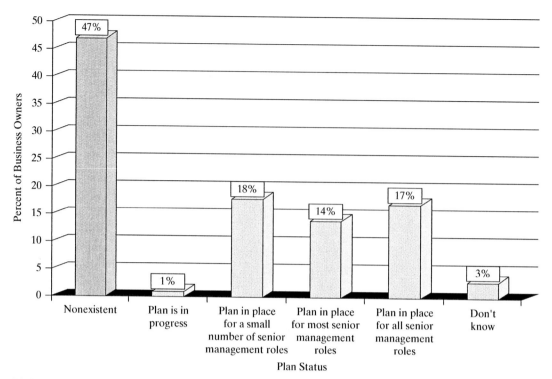

FIGURE 1

Status of Management Succession Plans in Small Businesses

Source: Kin in the Game, PriceWaterhouseCoopers Family Business Survey, 2010–2011, p. 22.

Profile

Pierre Bellon: Sodexho

When Pierre Bellon stepped down as CEO of Sodexho, the food management services business his grandfather started in 1895, he named as his successor Michael Landel, the first nonfamily member to lead the company. Landel, a 26-year veteran of Sodexho, had held a variety of positions in the family-controlled business, and Bellon was confident that Landel was the right person to lead the company. "You have to be completely in line with the culture of the family, share the same values, and have very strong respect for what they have done," says Landel.[17]

▓ Give family members the opportunity to work outside the business initially to learn first-hand how others conduct business. Working for others allows family members to develop knowledge, confidence, and credibility before stepping back into the family business.

Shared Power

Shared power is not necessarily equal power. Rather, shared power is based on the idea that family members allow those people with the greatest expertise, ability, and knowledge in particular areas to handle decisions in those areas. Dividing responsibilities along the lines of expertise is an important way of acknowledging respect for each family member's talents and abilities.

Profile

Thad, Harold, and Ralph Garner: T.W. Garner Food Company

When Thad Garner invented a concoction of red peppers and vinegar called Texas Pete Hot Sauce during the Great Depression, he and his brothers, Harold and Ralph, built a business, T.W. Garner Food Company, around the product. Each assumed responsibilities in a different area of the company based on his talents and interests. Thad (known as "Mr. Texas Pete") took over the sales and marketing side of the business, while Harold managed its financial and operational aspects and Ralph handled production. Working together, the brothers built the company into a very successful business, selling millions of dollars' worth of Texas Pete a year.[18]

Tradition

Tradition is necessary for a family business because it serves to bond family members and to link one generation of business leaders to the next. However, founders must hold tradition in check when it becomes a barrier to change. The key is to select those traditions that provide a solid foundation for positive behavior while taking care not to restrict the future growth of the business. "The companies that are successful change their strategy after each generation," says Joachim Schwass, a professor of family business at Switzerland's IMD business school. "Bringing in the new generation and saying, 'Son, do as I did,' will not work."[19]

Profile

*Maximilian Riedel:
Riedel Glas Austria*

Maximilian Riedel, head of North American operations for Austrian glassmaker Riedel, which for 300 years has been famous for its feather-light fine crystal wine glasses, is next in line to take control of the family business. Like his father and grandfather did, Maximilian created a new line of wine glasses that has become one of the company's best selling products. The eleventh-generation glassmaker created a sensation among oenophiles with his revolutionary stemless "O" series of wine tumblers that are designed to convey the nuances of the aroma and the flavor of wine. (The wine glass is "the messenger of the wine," he says.) Every business decision that Maximilian makes is steeped in 250 years of family business history, but already he has shown that he is willing to take bold steps to innovate and keep the family business in tune with the demands of the twenty-first century.[20]

A Willingness to Learn

A willingness to learn and grow is the hallmark of any successful firm, and it is essential to a family business. The family business that remains open to new ideas and techniques is likely to reduce its risk of obsolescence. The current generation of leadership must set the stage for new ideas involving the next generation in today's decisions. In many cases, a formal family council serves as a mechanism through which family members can propose new ideas. Perhaps more important than a family council is fostering an environment in which family members trust one another enough to express their ideas, thoughts, and suggestions openly and honestly. Open discussion of the merits of new ideas is a tradition that has proved valuable for many family businesses' ability to sustain their competitive advantages.

Behaving Like Families

Families that play together operate family businesses that are more likely to stay together. Time spent together outside the business creates the foundation for the relationships family members have at work. Too often, life in a family business can degenerate into nothing but day after day of work and discussions of work at home. In some cases, work is the only way some parents interact with their children. When a family adds activities outside the scope of the business, however, new relationships develop in a different arena. A family should not force members to "play together" but instead should create an environment that welcomes every member into fun family activities. Planned activities should be broad enough in scope to involve all family members. In time, trust, respect, openness, and togetherness lead to behavior that communicates genuine caring and concern for the well-being of each family member, and that spills over into the working relationship as well.

A Strong Family Support Network

According to a global survey of family business owners, the most important advantage family businesses have is the strong support network from family members (see Figure 2). Strong family ties grow from one-on-one relationships. Shared time conveys the message that the family business is *more* than just a business; it is a group of people who care for one another working together for a common goal. The bond that a family business creates among relatives can be strong and enduring. "There's a love and a trust and a respect that can be very powerful when they are brought into a business environment," says Ross Nager, director of a center for family businesses.[21]

The same emotions that hold family businesses together can also rip them apart if they run counter to the company's and the family's best interest. Emotions run deep in family businesses, and the press is full of examples of once successful companies that have been ruined by family

FIGURE 2
**Advantages of the
Family Business Model**

Source: Thomas L. Kalaris, "Family
Business: In Safe Hands?" *Barclays
Wealth Insights*, 2009, p. 10.

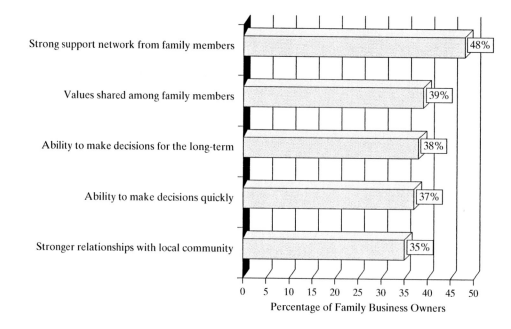

feuds over who controls the company and how to run it. Conflict is a natural part of any business, but it can be especially powerful in family businesses because family relationships magnify the passions binding family members to the company (see Figure 3). Without a succession plan, those passions can explode into destructive behavior that can endanger the family business.

Exit Strategies

2. Understand the exit strategy
options available to an
entrepreneur.

Most family business founders want their companies to stay within their families, although in some cases maintaining family control is not practical. Sometimes no one in the next generation of family members has an interest in managing the company or has the necessary skills and experience to handle the job. Under these circumstances, the founder must look outside the family for leadership if the company is to survive. Whatever the case, entrepreneurs must confront their mortality and plan for the future of their companies. Having a solid management succession plan in place well before retirement is near is critical to success. Entrepreneurs should examine their options well before they decide to step down from the businesses they have founded. Three options are available to entrepreneurs who are planning to retire: sell to outsiders, sell to (nonfamily) insiders, or pass the business on to family members with the help of a management succession plan. We turn now to these three exit strategies.

FIGURE 3
**Disadvantages of the
Family Business Model**

Source: Thomas L. Kalaris, "Family
Business: In Safe Hands?" *Barclays
Wealth Insights*, 2009, p. 11.

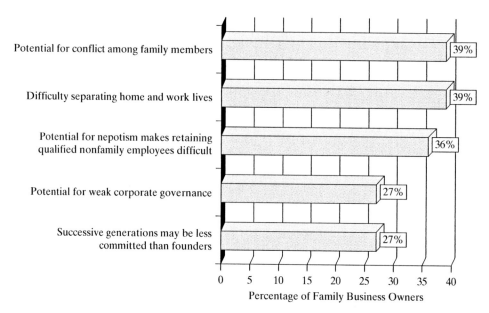

IN THE ENTREPRENEURIAL
SPOTLIGHT Parent–Child Inc.

Thanks to the Great Recession, family businesses are taking on a slightly different look. When passed from one generation to the next, family businesses often have family members from two, sometimes three, generations working side-by-side. As many parents in their 40s and 50s are experiencing layoffs and their college-graduate children struggle to find even part-time jobs, a new type of family business is becoming more popular: companies cofounded by parents and children. At first blush, parents and children cofounding companies sounds like a recipe for feuding and fighting, but doing so offers many benefits. Parents bring experience, a network of contacts, business acumen, and money to the deal. Their children contribute enthusiasm, energy, and a working knowledge of technology skills, Internet savvy, and social media know-how. The combination can work together to create a dynamic business that has real staying power.

Arian Mahmoodi demonstrated entrepreneurial tendencies as a child, and his father, Farzad, was not surprised when at age 14 Arian launched a business buying and reselling Nintendo games on Amazon. Arian operated the business from his bedroom in his family's home in Hannawa Falls, New York, and counted on his parents to drive him to the post office to mail the games he sold to customers. "I'd wake up and package the orders in the morning before school," he says.

Arian had dreams of a bigger company and used the profits from his business to launch SellYourOldiPhone.com, a Web site through which he buys used and often broken iPhones, refurbishes them, and then resells them. After Arian sent out his first e-mail blast promoting his company, hundreds of orders poured in, and he turned to his father, a professor of supply chain management at Clarkson University in Pottsdam, New York, for help. Farzad helped his son organize his business, and together they assigned unique tracking numbers to customers and their orders.

SellYourOldiPhone.com was so successful that Arian replicated his business model a year later and launched SellYourOldMacBook.com. Arian, then 17 and preparing for college, and Farzad had grown into distinct and complementary roles in their small businesses. Arian, the chief executive officer, is the "face" of the companies and manages the Web sites and customer service. He also is responsible for the companies' advertising and pricing. Farzad handles the companies' accounting and legal matters and manages the supply chain (of course!). He also monitors the flow of iPhones and MacBooks to and from the technicians who refurbish them and determines which international markets the companies enter.

The father–son duo purchase and resell about 30 devices each week, generating about $230,000 in sales per year. Arian's focus is on growing the businesses, and he has reinvested all of the companies' earnings back into the businesses, using them to buy more phones and computers. Farzad enjoys using the companies as a laboratory where he can test various supply chain ideas. When Arian goes to college, they plan to hire an employee to take over most of the day-to-day operations.

So far, father and son have gotten along well as business partners. The respect that each has for the other is readily apparent, but both admit that they have had disagreements. While participating in a 3-week academic program at Cornell University, Arian discovered a bargain on accessories such as chargers and phone cases and placed a large order without telling his father. "I got a call from my Dad," he says with a smile. "'What is this? We have all these boxes.' He wasn't too happy because he couldn't park in the garage."

Perhaps the biggest issue between the two is how fast their companies should grow. Arian wants the companies on the fast track, but his father is pushing for a slower rate of growth so that his son can enjoy his college experience. For now, at least, Arian is willing to listen to his father's advice. "We're in agreement at this time to keep it as is," he says.

1. Work with a classmate to brainstorm the advantages and the disadvantages of starting a family business with a parent.
2. Would you be willing to go into business with a parent? Explain.
3. What recommendations can you make to someone who is about to launch a business with a parent?

Source: Based on Colleen Debaise, Emily Maltby, and Sarah E. Needleman, "Parent and Child Inc.," *Wall Street Journal,* November 15, 2010, *http:// online.wsj.com/article/SB10001424052748703794104575546553171806306. html.*

Selling to Outsiders

Selling a business to an outsider is no simple task. Done properly, it takes time, patience, and preparation to locate a suitable buyer, strike a deal, and make the transition. Advance preparation, maintaining accurate financial records, and timing are the keys to a successful sale. Too often, however, business owners, like some famous athletes, stay with the game too long, until they and their businesses are well past their prime. They postpone selling until the last minute when they reach retirement age or when they face a business crisis. Such a "fire sale" approach rarely yields the maximum value for a business.

A straight sale may be best for those entrepreneurs who want to step down and turn the reins of the company over to someone else. However, selling a business outright is not an attractive exit strategy for those who want to stay on with the company or for those who want to surrender control of the company gradually rather than all at once.

Family-owned Snyder's of Hanover, founded in 1909 and now the world's largest maker of pretzels, recently agreed to merge with Lance Inc., a Charlotte, North Carolina-based manufacturer of snack crackers. Snyder's product line and extensive distribution network in grocery stores nationwide provide a solid strategic fit with Lance, which has strongholds in delis, convenience stores, and small retail stores. Lance issued 32.7 million shares of common stock to Snyder's shareholders, most of whom are members of the founding family.[22]

The financial terms of a sale also influence the selling price of the business and the number of potential bidders. Does the owner want "clean, cash only, 100 percent at closing" offers, or is he or she willing to finance a portion of the sale? A 100 percent, cash-only requirement dramatically reduces the number of potential buyers. However, the owner can exit the business "free and clear" and does not incur the risk that the buyer may fail to operate the business profitably and be unable to complete the financial transition.

Selling to Insiders

When entrepreneurs have no family members to whom they can transfer ownership or who want to assume the responsibilities of running a company, selling the business to employees is often the preferred option. In most situations, the options available to owners are (1) sale for cash plus a note, (2) a leveraged buyout, and (3) an employee stock ownership plan (ESOP).

A SALE FOR CASH PLUS A NOTE. Whether entrepreneurs sell their businesses to insiders, outsiders, or family members, they often finance a portion of the sales price. The buyer pays the seller a lump-sum amount of cash up front and the seller holds a promissory note for the remaining portion of the selling price, which the buyer pays off in installments. Because of its many creative financial options, this method of selling a business is popular with buyers. They can buy promising businesses without having to come up with the total purchase price all at one time. Sellers also appreciate the security and the tax implications of accepting payment over time. They receive a portion of the sale up front and have the assurance of receiving a steady stream of income in the future. In addition, they can stretch their tax liabilities from the capital gains on the sale over time rather than having to pay them in a single year. In many cases, sellers' risks are lower because they may even retain a seat on the board of directors to ensure that the new owners are keeping the business on track.

LEVERAGED BUYOUTS. In a **leveraged buyout (LBO)**, managers and/or employees borrow money from a financial institution and pay the owner the total agreed-upon price at closing; then they use the cash generated from the company's operations to pay off the debt. The drawback of this technique is that it creates a highly leveraged business. Because of the high levels of debt they take on, the new management team has very little room for error. Too many management mistakes or a slowing economy has led many highly leveraged businesses into bankruptcy.

If properly structured, LBOs can be attractive to both buyers and sellers. Because they get their money up front, sellers do not incur the risk of loss if the buyers cannot keep the business operating successfully. The managers and employees who buy the company have a strong incentive to make sure the business succeeds because they own a piece of the action and some of their capital is at risk in the business. The result can be a highly motivated workforce that works hard and makes sure that the company operates efficiently.

Profile

Jack Stack: Springfield Remanufacturing Corporation

In one of the most successful LBOs in history, Jack Stack and a team of 12 other managers purchased an ailing subsidiary of International Harvester in an attempt to save their jobs and those of the 120 employees they managed. The new company, Springfield Remanufacturing Corporation (SRC), which specializes in engine remanufacturing for the automotive, trucking, agricultural, and construction industries, began with an astronomically high debt-to-equity ratio of 89:1, but the team of motivated managers and employees turned the company around. Today, SRC has more than 1,200 employees and 26 divisions that range from automotive engines to home furnishings.[23]

EMPLOYEE STOCK OWNERSHIP PLANS (ESOPs). Unlike LBOs, **employee stock ownership plans (ESOPs)** allow employees and/or managers (that is, the future owners) to purchase the business gradually, which frees up enough cash to finance the venture's growth. With an ESOP, employees contribute a portion of their earnings over time toward purchasing shares of the company's stock from the founder until they own the company outright. (Although in leveraged ESOPs, the ESOP borrows the money to buy the owner's stock up front. Then, using employees' contributions, the ESOP repays the loan over time. Another advantage of a leveraged ESOP is that the principal and the interest the ESOP borrows to buy the business are tax deductible, which can save thousands or even millions of dollars in taxes.) Transferring ownership to employees through an ESOP is a long-term exit strategy that benefits everyone involved. The owner sells the business to the people he or she can trust the most—his or her managers and employees. The managers and employees buy a business they already know how to run successfully. In addition, because they own the company, the managers and employees have a huge incentive to see that it operates effectively and efficiently. One study of ESOPs in privately held companies found that they increased sales, employment, and sales per employee by 2.4 percent a year.[24] Figure 4 shows the trend in the number of ESOPs and the number of employee owners.

The third exit strategy available to company founders is transferring ownership to the next generation of family members with the help of a comprehensive management succession plan.

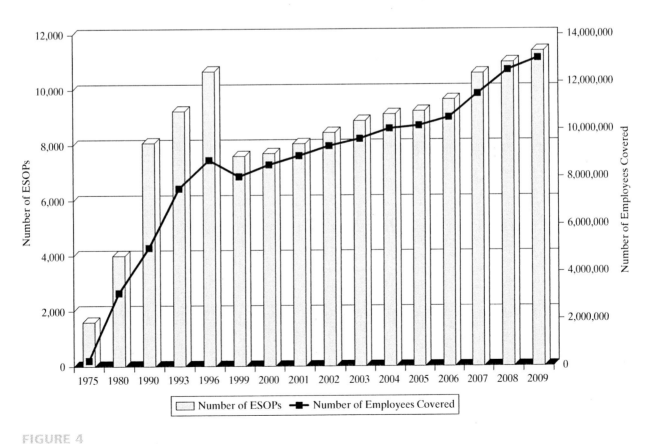

FIGURE 4

Employee Stock Ownership Plans

Source: "A Statistical Profile of Employee Ownership," National Center for Employee Ownership, 2010.

How to Set Up an ESOP

In 1978, long before people knew about the health benefits of whole-grain products, Bob Moore and his wife, Charlee, salvaged an abandoned 125-year-old flour mill and launched Bob's Red Mill Natural Foods, a company in Portland, Oregon, that produces a variety of products, from grain and flour to hot cereal and baking mixes. For Moore and his employees, the path was filled with challenges, including a fire that caused extensive damage to the old factory and the necessity of constantly investing in new equipment and technology. Moore expanded the company's reach to include customers in a handful of Western states, but the turning point came in 1993 when Moore brought in John Wagner as chief financial officer and co-owner. Together, Moore and Wagner focused on marketing the company's all-natural, whole-grain products at food and trade shows, where they garnered the attention of small health food stores, food distributors, and, eventually, grocery chains. "Now you can find our products in every province and state in North America and lots of places overseas," Moore says proudly.

Moore and Wagner launched a profit-sharing plan for their employees in 1995 and began sharing financial information with them weekly. They also conducted training sessions for employees on reading the company's financial statements. The training not only taught employees how to calculate their share of the company's profits but also enabled them to see exactly how the work they did every day affected the company's bottom line—and, therefore, their payouts.

As Moore passed the normal retirement age, employees began to wonder about their future, especially if Moore and Wagner decided to sell the company to a larger business. "Will we still have jobs?" they wondered. "Will the culture that we love so much change?"

Moore answered employees' lingering questions on his eighty-first birthday celebration. Moore and Wagner had decided not to sell Bob's Red Mill Natural Foods to a large company. Instead, they had created an employee stock ownership plan that would transfer ownership of the company to the 200 people whom they considered to be instrumental in its success. "It's been my dream all along to turn this company over to the employees, and to make that dream a reality is very, very special to me," says Moore. "This is the ultimate way to keep this business moving forward."

"The partners could have sold this company many times for a lot more money" says vice president of operations Dennis Vaughn, "but to them this company is about so much more than the money." After Moore announced the creation of the ESOP, he said modestly, "I thought some of them were going to kiss me. It went over very, very, very well." Roger Farnen, the company's quality assurance manager, says, "By creating the ESOP, Bob and the partners have fulfilled their ultimate quest for sharing success among all employees. Bob is passing the entrepreneurial torch on to his employees and is instilling in us that hard work provides rewards."

What steps should an entrepreneur who is interested in setting up an ESOP take? Consider the following advice from the Street-Smart Entrepreneur:

Step 1. Conduct a feasibility analysis to determine whether an ESOP is right for you and your company.

A company should be profitable and should have at least 20 employees to make an ESOP work. Creating the necessary plan documents and filing them with the proper government agencies costs about $10,000. A business valuation, which can range from $5,000 to $10,000 for a small company, is a necessity. Fixed costs of administering the ESOP run about $2,000 plus $20 to $30 per employee participant per year. A final consideration is whether the company will generate enough revenue to be able to repay the loan.

Step 2. Hire an attorney who specializes in ESOPs to help you develop a plan for creating and implementing an ESOP.

ESOPs can take many different forms, and an expert can help you determine the advantages and disadvantages of each one so that you can determine the one that is best for you and your company.

Step 3. Find the money to fund the ESOP.

About 75 percent of ESOPs are leveraged, which means that they borrow the money to purchase the owner's stock from the ESOP trust. Banks and other financial institutions usually find loans to ESOPs quite attractive.

Step 4. Establish a process to operate the ESOP.

Companies most often create an ESOP committee of managers and employees to provide guidance to the ESOP trust for managing the ESOP. The team also is responsible for communicating the details of the ESOP and the benefits of investing in it to company employees.

Barbara Gabel, who with her husband, Zach Zachowski, launched Zachary's Chicago Pizza in Oakland, California, in 1984, recently established an ESOP to transfer ownership of their business to their employees. "It's the ultimate exit strategy," says Gabel, referring to the benefits ESOPs provide both entrepreneurs and employees. Each year, employees at Zachary's receive an amount of stock that is equal to 25 percent of their salaries. General Manager J. P. LaRussa, who began working as a part-time dishwasher at Zachary's

the day it opened, says, "This breathes new life into the business in a very positive way."

Sources: Based on Karen E. Klein, "ESOPs on the Rise Among Small Businesses," *Bloomberg Business Week*, March 26, 2010, *www.businessweek.com/smallbiz/content/mar2010/sb20100325_591132.htm*; Theo Francis, "Inside Eileen Fisher's Employee Stock Plan," *Wall Street Journal*, January 22, 2007, pp. B1, B3; Alec Rosenberg, "Employees to Slice Up Zachary's Pizza," *Oakland Tribune*, June 27, 2003, *www.zacharys.com/news_oakland_tribune.html*; "ESOP Statistics," ESOP Association, *www.esopassociation.org/media/media_statistics.asp*; "How Small Is Too Small for an ESOP?" National Center for Employee Ownership, *www.nceo.org/library/howsmall.html*; "Steps to Setting up an ESOP," National Center for Employee Ownership, *www.nceo.org/library/steps.html*.

Management Succession

3. Discuss the stages of management succession.

Experts estimate that between 2001 and 2017, $12 trillion in wealth will be transferred from one generation to the next, representing the greatest transfer of wealth in history and much of it funneled through family businesses.[25] Most of the family businesses in existence today were started after World War II, and many of the founders who have not yet transferred ownership to the next generation now are at or past retirement age and are ready to pass the torch of leadership. A recent study by the Alliance of Merger and Acquisition Advisors reports that 70 percent of business owners plan to transfer ownership of their businesses by 2020 but that 90 percent of them do not have an adequate succession plan in place.[26]

For a smooth transition from one generation to the next, family businesses need a succession plan. Without a succession plan, family businesses face an increased risk of faltering or failing in the next generation. Those businesses with the greatest probability of surviving are the ones whose owners prepare a succession plan well before it is time to transfer control to the next generation. Succession planning also allows business owners to minimize the impact of taxes on their businesses, their estates, and their successors' wealth as well and to avoid saddling the next generation of ownership with burdensome debt.

Why, then, do so many entrepreneurs postpone succession planning until it is too late? Many business founders hesitate to let go of their businesses because their personal identities are so wrapped up in their companies. Over time, a founder's identity becomes so intertwined in the business that, in the entrepreneur's mind, there is no distinction between the two. The attitude is "I am the company, and the company is me."

ENTREPRENEURIAL
Profile

Michael and Emily Powell: Powell's Books

When Michael Powell, who for 27 years had managed Powell's Books, the largest privately held chain of bookstores in the United States, reached age 66, he realized that it was time to begin transferring control of the company to his daughter, Emily, then 28, with the help of the 10-year transition plan he had created 7 years before. When Michael, who took over the family business from his father, talks about retiring from the company he built, however, he covers his face with his hands and his voice grows soft. "There are emotional issues in giving up control and ownership," he admits. "Half my brain says, 'Do it,' and the other half says, 'What are you doing?' This is business and family."[27]

Many entrepreneurs share Powell's feelings. According to a survey by the Monitor Group, less than 17 percent of business owners say that they expect to retire after leaving their businesses. (In fact, 45 percent say that they plan to start another company.)[28]

Another barrier to succession planning is that, in planning the future of the business, owners are forced to accept the painful reality of their own mortality. In addition, turning over the reins of a business they have sacrificed for, fretted over, and dedicated themselves to for so many years is extremely difficult to do—even if the successor is a son or daughter! Paul Snodgrass, son of the founder of Pella Products, a maker of apparel for work and outdoor activities, who accepted leadership of the company from his father, explains, "Dad loves you and wants you to take over the business, but he also put heart and soul into that business, and he's not going to let anybody screw it up— not even you."[29] Finally, many family business founders believe that controlling the business also gives them a degree of control over family members and family behavior.

Planning for management succession protects not only the founder's, successor's, and company's financial resources, but it also preserves what matters most in a successful business: its heritage and tradition. "Real succession planning involves developing a strategy for transferring the trust, respect, and goodwill built by one generation to the next," explains Andy Bluestone, who took over as president of the financial services company his father founded.[30] Management succession planning requires, first, an attitude of trusting others. It recognizes that other family members have a stake in the future of the business and want to participate in planning its future. Planning is an attitude that shows that decisions made with open discussion are more constructive than those without family input. Second, management succession is an evolutionary process and must reconcile an entrepreneur's inevitable anguish with the successors' desire for autonomy. Owners' emotional ties to their businesses usually are stronger than their financial ties. On the other side of the equation are the successors, who yearn to have the autonomy to run the business their way. These inherent conflicts can—and often do—result in skirmishes.

Succession planning reduces the tension and stress created by these conflicts by gradually "changing the guard." A well-developed succession plan is like the smooth, graceful exchange of a baton between runners in a relay race. The new runner still has maximum energy; the concluding runner has already spent his or her energy by running at maximum speed. The athletes never come to a stop to exchange the baton; instead, the handoff takes place on the move. The race is a skillful blend of the talents of all team members—an exchange of leadership so smooth and powerful that the business never falters, but accelerates, fueled by a new source of energy at each leg of the race.

Management succession involves a lengthy series of interconnected stages that begins very early in the life of the owner's children and extends to the point of final ownership transition (see Figure 5). If management succession is to be effective, it is necessary for the process to begin early in the successor's life (stage I). For instance, the owner of a catering business recalls putting his son to work in the family owned company at age 7. On weekends, the boy would arrive at dawn to baste turkeys and was paid in his favorite medium of exchange— doughnuts![31] In most cases, family business owners involve their children in their businesses while they are still in junior high or high school. In this phase, the tasks are routine, but the child is learning the basics of how the business operates. Young adults begin to appreciate the role the business plays in the life of the family. They learn firsthand about the values and responsibilities of running the company.

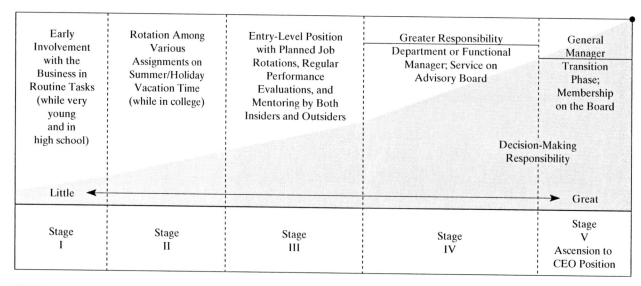

FIGURE 5
Stages in Management Succession

While in college, the successor moves to stage II of the continuum. During this stage, the individual rotates among a variety of job functions to both broaden his or her base of understanding of the business and to permit the parents to evaluate his or her skills. Upon graduation from college, the successor enters stage III. At this point, the successor becomes a full-time worker and ideally has already begun to earn the respect of coworkers through his behavior in the first two stages of the process. In some cases, the successor may work for a time outside of the family business to gain experience and to establish a reputation for competency that goes beyond "being the boss's kid." Stage III focuses on the successor's continuous development, often through a program designed to groom the successor using both family and nonfamily managers as mentors.

Profile

The Joyner Family:
C. Dan Joyner Realtors

From the time that Danny Joyner was a young boy "helping" his father in the real estate business that the elder Joyner was building, he knew that he wanted to join his father's company. "I've always known that this is what I would do," says Danny, who joined the company full time after graduating from college. Danny heads the successful company's commercial real estate division, and Dan's two daughters and a son-in-law also work in the family business. With a succession plan in place and all of his children in leadership positions in the company, founder Dan Joyner says that the company is positioned to make a smooth transition into the second generation of ownership.[32]

As the successor develops his or her skills and abilities, he or she moves to stage IV, in which real decision-making authority grows rapidly. Stage IV of the succession continuum is the period when the founder makes a final assessment of the successor's competence and ability to take full and complete control over the firm. The skills the successor needs include the following:

- *Financial abilities.* Understanding the financial aspect of a business, what its financial position is, and the managerial implications of that position are crucial to success.
- *Technical knowledge.* Every business has its own body of knowledge, ranging from how the distribution system works to the trends shaping the industry, that an executive must master.
- *Negotiating ability.* Much of business, whether buying supplies and inventory or selling to customers, boils down to negotiating, and a business owner must be adept at it.
- *Leadership qualities.* Leaders must be bold enough to stake out the company's future and then give employees the resources, the power, and the freedom to pursue it.
- *Communication skills.* Business leaders must communicate the vision they have for their businesses; good listening skills also are essential for success as a top manager.
- *Juggling skills.* Business owners must be able to handle multiple projects effectively. Like a juggler, they must maintain control over several important assignments simultaneously.
- *Integrity.* To be an effective leader of a family business, a successor must demonstrate honesty and integrity in business dealings.
- *Commitment to the business.* It helps if a successor has a genuine passion for the business. Leaders who have enthusiasm for what they do create a spark of excitement throughout the entire organization.[33]

The final stage in the management succession process involves the ultimate transition of organizational leadership. It is during this stage that the founder's role as mentor is most crucial.

Profile

Laura Michaud: Beltone
Electronics Corporation

Laura Michaud, who in 1980 became the third-generation owner of Beltone Electronics Corporation, a very successful maker of hearing aids that was founded in 1940, says that the training and mentoring that her father provided was key to her success to managing the family business. Her father insisted on an extensive training program that involved Michaud in all aspects of the company, including having her actually build a hearing aid. "You need to work in all areas of operations," says Michaud, who ran the company for 17 years before selling it to a larger company.[34]

Source: Wall Street Journal\Cartoon
Features Syndicate

"There has been a changing of the guard, Crampton."

In stage IV, the successor may become the organization's CEO, while the former CEO retains the title of chairman of the board. In other cases, the best solution is for the founder to step out of the business entirely and give the successor the chance to establish his or her own identity within the company. "Any leader's final legacy is building the next generation," says one business consultant.[35]

Developing a Management Succession Plan

4. Explain how to develop an effective management succession plan.

Families that are most committed to ensuring that their businesses survive from one generation to the next exhibit four characteristics: (1) They believe that owning the business helps achieve their families' missions. (2) They are proud of the values their businesses are built on and exemplify. (3) They believe that the business is contributing to society and makes it a better place to live. (4) They rely on management succession plans to assure the continuity of their companies.[36] Developing a management succession plan takes time and dedication, yet the benefits are well worth the cost. A sound succession plan enables a company to maintain its momentum and sense of purpose and direction.

It is important to start the planning process early, well before the founder's retirement. Succession planning is not the kind of activity an entrepreneur can do in a hurry, and the sooner an entrepreneur starts, the easier it will be. Unfortunately, too many entrepreneurs put it off until it is too late. "Very few privately owned businesses make it through several generations, and one reason is the failure of the senior generation to do any planning at all until it is too late in the game," says one expert.[37] Creating a succession plan involves the following steps.

Step 1: Select the Successor

The average tenure of the founder of a family business is 25 years.[38] Yet there comes a time for even the most dedicated founder to step down and hand the reins of the company to the next generation. Entrepreneurs should never assume that their children want to take control of the business, however. Above all, they should not be afraid to ask the question: "Do you really want to take over the family business?" Too often, children in this situation tell Mom and Dad what they want to hear out of loyalty, pressure, or guilt. It is critical to remember at this juncture in the life of a business that children do not necessarily inherit their parents' entrepreneurial skills and desires. By leveling with their children about the business and their options regarding a family succession, owners can know which heirs, if any, are willing to assume leadership of the business.

One of the worst mistakes entrepreneurs can make is to postpone naming a successor until just before they are ready to step down. One study by the Raymond Institute and MassMutual reports that 55 percent of family business owners age 61 or older have not yet designated a successor![39] The problem is especially acute when more than one family member works for the company and is interested in assuming leadership of it. Sometimes founders avoid naming successors because they don't want to hurt the family members who are not chosen to succeed them. However, both the business and the family will be better off if, after observing family members as they work in the business, the founder picks a successor based on skill and ability.

Profile

Rupert Murdoch: News Corporation

At age 79, Rupert Murdoch, CEO of News Corporation, had not yet named his successor even though two of his sons, Lachlan and James, have been involved in running the company. Lachlan resigned as the company's chief operating officer but remains on the board of directors; James has worked for News Corporation for 14 years in a variety of positions and is in charge of a division that accounts for 20 percent of the company's revenue. Although the elder Murdoch insists that he has no plans to retire, he says that he is confident that one of his children will emerge to succeed him as CEO. "Every parent likes to see that," he says.[40]

When naming a successor, merit is a better standard to use than gender or birth order. The key is to establish standards of performance, knowledge, education, and ability and then to identify the person who best meets those standards. As part of his company's succession plan, Joe De La Torre selected his daughter Gina to take over Juanita's Foods rather than his two sons because her financial skills and her ability to solve problems were what the company needed most.[41] Gina La Torre is part of a growing trend among family businesses; 34 percent of family business founders expect the next CEO to be a woman, quite a change from just a generation ago.[42]

Profile

Harry and Kirsten Vold: Harry Vold Rodeo Company

After 60 years, Harry Vold, founder of Harry Vold Rodeo Company, a business based in Pueblo West, Colorado, that supplies rodeos with bucking broncos and bulls, turned over the reins of the family business to the youngest of his six children, Kirsten, when she was just 25 years old. Although Harry expected one of his children to take over the business, he was a bit surprised that Kirsten was the one who showed the greatest potential and stepped forward. Kirsten, too, was somewhat surprised. "I was going to be a lawyer, drive a sports car, and live in L.A.," she says with a laugh. After graduating from the University of Southern Colorado, Kirsten took a job in sports marketing but soon felt the tug of the family business and returned home to take an active role in managing it. Kirsten worked hard to prove herself in an industry that men tend to dominate. "She's earned their respect," says her mother proudly. Transferring control from one generation to the next taxed the skills, patience, and ability of both Harry and Kirsten. "It was a struggle, a power struggle, along the way," she says. "For both of us, but it built character for both of us." Harry is pleased with the way things worked out. "I was a bit surprised to begin with, but I'm not now," he says. "I am totally confident that she makes the right decisions. As far as I'm concerned, she's all the cowgirl I need."[43]

Step 2: Create a Survival Kit for the Successor

Once he or she identifies a successor, an entrepreneur should prepare a survival kit and then brief the future leader on its contents, which should include all of the company's critical documents (wills, trusts, insurance policies, financial statements, bank accounts, key contracts, corporate bylaws, and so forth). The founder should be sure that the successor reads and understands all of the relevant documents in the kit. Other important steps the owner should take to prepare the successor to take over leadership of the business include:

- Create a strategic analysis for the future. Working with the successor, the entrepreneur should identify the primary opportunities and the challenges facing the company and the requirements for meeting them.
- On a regular basis, share with the successor his or her vision of the business's future direction, describing key factors that have led to its success and those that will bring future success.
- Be open and listen to the successor's views and concerns.

■ Teach and learn at the same time.

■ Identify the industry's key success factors.

■ Tie the key success factors to the company's performance and profitability.

■ Explain the company's overall strategy and how it creates a competitive advantage.

■ Discuss the values and philosophy of the business and how they have inspired and influenced past actions.

■ Discuss the people in the business and their strengths and weaknesses.

■ Describe the philosophy underlying the firm's compensation policy and explain why employees are paid what they are.

■ Make a list of the firm's most important customers and its key suppliers or vendors and review the history of all dealings with the parties on both lists.

■ Discuss how to treat these key players to ensure the company's continued success and its smooth and error-free ownership transition.

■ Develop a job analysis by taking an inventory of the activities involved in leading the company. This analysis can show successors those activities on which they should be spending most of their time.

■ Document as much process knowledge—"how we do things"—as possible. After many years in their jobs, business owners are not even aware of their vast reservoirs of knowledge. For them, making decisions is a natural part of their business lives. They do it effortlessly because they have so much knowledge and experience. It is easy to forget that a successor will not have the benefit of those years of experience unless the founder communicates it.

■ Include an ethical will, a document that explains to the next generation of leaders the ethical principles on which the company operates. An ethical will gives company founders the chance to bequeath to their heirs not only a business, but also the wisdom and ethical lessons learned over a lifetime.

ENTREPRENEURIAL

Profile

Paul Weber: Webers Hamburgers

In 1963, Paul Weber started Webers Hamburgers, a small restaurant that has become a landmark, in Ontario, Canada, known for its fresh, tasty burgers. Targeting vacationers and city dwellers looking for an escape, Weber selected a location near the small town of Orillia, about 2 hours north of Toronto. On a typical Saturday during the peak summer season, Webers serves about 800 hamburgers per hour, a pace that tests the restaurant's systems and employees. Managing the family business is second-generation owner Paul Weber, Jr., who grew up working in the restaurant and took over the family business in 1989. Paul Jr. credits much of the company's success to the systems that his father established, refined, and documented over more than a quarter of a century. In fact, Webers continues to document for future generations every part of their business, including the order processing procedure and the techniques they use to entertain guests when lines stretch across the parking lot.[44]

Hungry customers line up, waiting to get into Webers Hamburgers in Orillia, Ontario.

Source: Angelo Cavalli/SuperStock

Step 3: Groom the Successor

The process by which business founders transfer their knowledge to the next generation is gradual and often occurs informally as they spend time with their successors. Grooming the successor is the founder's greatest teaching and development responsibility, and it takes time, usually 5 to 10 years.

Profile

Brian Tuberman:
SCTR Systems

When the founder of SCTR Systems, a company created in 1967 that sells computerized retail systems to independent grocers, began looking for a successor (from outside the family, because none of his children were interested in taking over the family business) 12 years before he planned to retire, he recruited Brian Tuberman and immediately began grooming him to take over the company. Tuberman purchased the business from the founder in 2005 and credits the smooth transition of ownership to the lessons he learned from his mentor. "Everyone thought I was crazy to quit what I was doing to make plans for 12 years down the road," says Tuberman, "but the previous owner and I believed in each other and in the company and made it happen."[45]

To implement the succession plan, the founder must be:

■ Patient, realizing that the transfer of power is gradual and evolutionary and that the successor should earn responsibility and authority one step at a time until the final transfer of power takes place.
■ Willing to accept that the successor will make mistakes.
■ Skillful at using the successor's mistakes as a teaching tool.
■ An effective communicator and an especially tolerant listener.
■ Capable of establishing reasonable expectations for the successor's performance.
■ Able to articulate the keys to the successor's performance.

Teaching is the art of assisting discovery and requires letting go rather than controlling. When problems arise in the business, the founder should consider delegating some of them to the successor-in-training. The founder also must resist the tendency to wade in and fix the problem unless it is beyond the scope of the successor's ability. Most great teachers and leaders are remembered more for the success of their students than for their own success.

Step 4: Promote an Environment of Trust and Respect

Another priceless gift a founder can leave a successor is an environment of trust and respect. Trust and respect on the part of the founder and others fuel the successor's desire to learn and excel and build the successor's confidence in making decisions. Empowering the successor by gradually delegating responsibilities creates an environment in which all parties can objectively view the growth and development of the successor. Customers, creditors, suppliers, and staff members can gradually develop confidence in the successor. The final transfer of power is not a dramatic, wrenching change but a smooth, coordinated passage.

A problem for some founders at this phase is the meddling retiree syndrome, in which they continue to show up at the office after they have officially stepped down and get involved in business issues that no longer concern them. This tendency merely undermines the authority of the successor and confuses employees as to who really is in charge. Helen Dragas, who succeeded her father at the Dragas Company, a residential construction business, praises her father for handing the reins of the company over to her and then trusting her to handle them. "He gave me the authority and then he stepped back," she says of the successful transfer of leadership.[46]

Step 5: Cope with the Financial Realities of Estate and Gift Taxes

The final step in developing a workable management succession plan is structuring the transition to minimize the impact of estate, gift, and inheritance taxes on family members and the business. Entrepreneurs who fail to consider the impact of these taxes (which have been as high as 55 percent) may force their heirs to sell a successful business just to pay the estate's tax (commonly known as the "death tax") bill. Despite facing potentially large tax bills, 19 percent of senior generation owners have done no estate planning at all![47]

Profile

*Clayton Leverett:
Stillwater Farm*

Just a few hours after Clayton Leverett's son, Whit, was born, the young father began to wonder whether Whit would be able to retain the family's 150-year-old Stillwater Ranch, a cattle ranch in Llano, Texas, now in its fifth generation of family ownership. Estate taxes have cut deeply into the Leverett family's land holdings and cattle operations twice before. The family was forced to sell thousands of acres of valuable land to pay estate taxes when Clayton's grandmother died in 2006. When Clayton's father died later that same year, the family faced the estate tax a second time, and once again had to sell acreage and lay off employees. Clayton also had to take on a second job to pay the estate tax. "We will only be able to sell only so much [land] before the ranch becomes unprofitable and we are forced to sell the entire operation," explains a frustrated Clayton.[48]

Although Congress eliminated the estate tax for 2010 (see Table 2), the tax has not evaporated forever. (When George Steinbrenner, owner of the New York Yankees, died in 2010, the year Congress repealed the estate tax, his heirs paid no estate taxes. Had Steinbrenner died in 2009, however, his heirs would have faced a stiff tax bill of $500 million![49]) More than two-thirds of adults believe that that estate tax should remain extinct, and research supports this view. A study by Antony Davies of Duquesne University reports that for every 4.5 percent increase in the estate tax (the average increase in the tax since 1993), 6,000 small businesses are liquidated or absorbed into large companies. Conversely, Davies' research suggests that repealing the tax would create 100,000 new businesses that would employ 2 million workers with a total payroll of $80 billion.[50]

Entrepreneurs who fail to engage in proper estate planning will subject their family members to a painful tax bite when they inherit the business. Entrepreneurs should be actively engaged in estate planning no later than age 45; those who start businesses early in their lives or whose businesses grow rapidly may need to begin as early as age 30. A variety of options exist that may prove to be helpful in reducing the estate tax liability. Each operates in a different fashion, but their objective remains the same: to remove a portion of business owners' assets out of their estates so that when they die those assets will not be subject to estate taxes. Many of these estate planning tools need time to work their magic, so the key is to put them in place early on in the life of the business.

TABLE 2 Changes in the Estate and Gift Taxes

After years of complaints from family business owners, Congress finally overhauled the often punishing structures of estate and gift taxes. The federal estate tax is actually interwoven with the gift tax, but under the modified law the impact of the two taxes began to differ in 2004. Congress repealed the estate tax in 2010, but resurrected it in 2011! The following table shows the trends in the exemptions and the minimum tax rates for the estate and gift taxes:

Year	Estate Tax Exemption	Gift Tax Exemption	Maximum Tax Rate
2001	$675,000	$675,000	55%
2002	$1 million	$1 million	50%
2003	$1 million	$1 million	49%
2004	$1.5 million	$1 million	48%
2005	$1.5 million	$1 million	47%
2006	$2 million	$1 million	46%
2007	$2 million	$1 million	45%
2008	$2 million	$1 million	45%
2009	$3.5 million	$1 million	45%
2010	Tax repealed	$1 million	35% (gifts only)
2011	$5 million	$5 million	35%
2012	?	?	?

No matter how the federal laws governing estate taxes may change over the next few years, entrepreneurs whose businesses have been successful must not neglect estate planning. Even though the federal estate tax burden has eased somewhat (at least for a while), many states have *increased* their estate tax rates.

BUY-SELL AGREEMENT. One of the most popular estate planning techniques is the buy-sell agreement. A **buy-sell agreement** is a contract that co-owners often rely on to ensure the continuity of a business. In a typical arrangement, the co-owners create a contract stating that each agrees to buy the others out in case of the death or disability of one. That way, the heirs of the deceased or disabled owner can "cash out" of the business while leaving control of the business in the hands of the remaining owners. The buy-sell agreement specifies a formula for determining the value of the business at the time the agreement is to be executed. One problem with buy-sell agreements is that the remaining co-owners may not have the cash available to buy out the disabled or deceased owner. To resolve this issue, many businesses buy life and disability insurance for each of the owners in amounts large enough to cover the purchase price of their respective shares of the business. Without the support of adequate insurance policies, a buy-sell agreement offers virtually no protection.

ENTREPRENEURIAL

Profile

Junab Ali and Jay Uribe:
Mobius Partners

Junab Ali and Jay Uribe, founders of Mobius Partners, a $25 million a year company that specializes in enterprise IT solutions, created a buy-sell agreement to protect themselves and their business in the event of the death or disability of a partner. Their agreement is supported by insurance policies on each partner, giving them the income security they need for their families and providing the remaining partner the financial resources to buy the shares of the missing partner.[51]

LIFETIME GIFTING. The owners of a successful business may transfer money to their children (or other recipients) from their estate throughout their lives. Current federal tax regulations allow individuals to make gifts of $13,000 per year, per parent, per recipient, that are exempt from federal gift taxes. Another benefit: Gift recipients do not have to pay taxes on the gift. For instance, husband-and-wife business owners could give $1.56 million worth of stock to their three children and their spouses over a period of 10 years without incurring any estate or gift taxes at all.

SETTING UP A TRUST. A **trust** is a contract between a grantor (the founder) and a trustee (generally a bank officer or an attorney) in which the grantor gives to the trustee legal title to assets (e.g., stock in the company), which the trustee agrees to hold for the beneficiaries (children). The beneficiaries can receive income from the trust, or they can receive the property in the trust, or both, at some specified time. Trusts can take a wide variety of forms, but two broad categories of trusts are available: revocable trusts and irrevocable trusts. A **revocable trust** is one that the grantor can change or revoke during his or her lifetime. Under present tax laws, however, the only trust that provides a tax benefit is an **irrevocable trust**, in which the grantor cannot require the trustee to return the assets held in trust. The value of the grantor's estate is lowered because the assets in an irrevocable trust are excluded from the value of that estate. However, an irrevocable trust places severe restrictions on the grantor's control of the property placed in the trust. Business owners use several types of irrevocable trusts to lower their estate tax liabilities:

Bypass Trust. The most basic type of trust is the bypass trust, which allows a business owner to put up to $3 million into trust naming his or her spouse as the beneficiary upon the owner's death. The spouse receives the income from the trust throughout his or her life, but the principal in the trust bypasses the surviving spouse's estate and goes to the couple's heirs free of estate taxes upon the spouse's death. A bypass trust is particularly useful for couples who plan their estates together. By leaving assets to one another in bypass trusts, they can make sure that their assets are taxed only once between them. However, entrepreneurs should work with experienced attorneys to create bypass trusts because the IRS requires that they contain certain precise language to be valid.

Irrevocable Life Insurance Trust (ILIT). This type of trust allows a business owner to keep the proceeds of a life insurance policy out of his or her estate and away from estate taxes, freeing up that money to pay the taxes on the remainder of the estate. To get the tax benefit, business owners must be sure that the business or the trust (rather than themselves) owns the insurance policy. The primary disadvantage of an irrevocable life insurance trust is that if the owner dies within 3 years of establishing it, the insurance proceeds *do* become part of the estate and *are* subject to estate taxes. Because the trust is irrevocable, it cannot be amended or rescinded once it is established. Like most trusts, ILITs must meet stringent requirements to be valid, and entrepreneurs should use experienced attorneys to create them.

Irrevocable Asset Trust. An irrevocable asset trust is similar to a life insurance trust except that it is designed to pass the assets in the parents' estate on to their children. The children do not have control of the assets while the parents are still living, but they do receive the income from those assets. Upon the parents' death, the assets in the trust go to the children without being subjected to the estate tax.

Grantor Retained Annuity Trust (GRAT). A grantor retained annuity trust (GRAT) is a special type of irrevocable trust and has become one of the most popular tools for entrepreneurs to transfer ownership of a business while maintaining control over it and minimizing estate taxes. Under a GRAT, an owner can put property in an irrevocable trust for a maximum of 10 years. While the trust is in effect, the grantor (owner) retains the voting power and receives the interest income from the property in the trust. At the end of the trust (not to exceed 10 years), the property passes to the beneficiaries (heirs). The beneficiaries are required to pay the gift tax on the value of the assets placed in the GRAT but pay no estate tax on them. However, the IRS taxes GRAT gifts according to their discounted present value because the heirs did not receive use of the property while it was in trust. The primary disadvantage of using a GRAT in estate planning is that if the grantor dies during the life of the GRAT, its assets pass back into the grantor's estate. These assets then become subject to the full estate tax.

Establishing a trust requires meeting many specific legal requirements and is not something business owners should do on their own. It is much better to hire experienced attorneys, accountants, and financial advisors to assist in creating them. Although the cost of establishing a trust can be high, the tax savings they generate are well worth the expense.

ESTATE FREEZE. An **estate freeze** attempts to minimize estate taxes by having family members create two classes of stock for the business: (1) preferred voting stock for the parents and (2) nonvoting common stock for the children. The value of the preferred stock is frozen, whereas the common stock reflects the anticipated increased market value of the business. Any appreciation in the value of the business after the transfer is not subject to estate taxes. However, the parent must pay gift tax on the value of the common stock given to the children. The value of the common stock is the total value of the business less the value of the voting preferred stock retained by the parent. The parents also must accept taxable dividends at the market rate on the preferred stock they own.

FAMILY LIMITED PARTNERSHIP. Creating a **family limited partnership (FLP)** allows business-owning parents to transfer their company to their children (thus lowering their estate taxes) while still retaining control over it for themselves. To create an FLP, the parents (or parent) set up a partnership among themselves and their children. The parents retain the general partnership interest, which can be as low as 1 percent, and the children become the limited partners. As general partners, the parents control both the limited partnership and the family business. In other words, nothing in the way the company operates has to change. Over time, the parents can transfer company stock into the limited partnership, ultimately passing ownership of the company to their children.

One of the principal tax benefits of an FLP is that it allows discounts on the value of the shares of company stock the parents transfer into the limited partnership. Because a family business is closely held, shares of ownership in it, especially minority shares, are not as marketable as those of a publicly held company. As a result, company shares transferred into the limited partnership are discounted at 20 to 50 percent of their full market value, producing a large tax savings for everyone involved. The average discount is 40 percent, but that amount varies based on the industry and the individual company involved. A business owner should consider an FLP as part of a succession plan "when there has been a buildup of substantial value in the business and the older generation has a substantial amount of liquidity," says one expert.[52]

Because of their ability to reduce estate and gift taxes, FLPs have become one of the most popular estate planning tools in recent years. However, a Tax Court ruling against a Texas entrepreneur who, 2 months before he died, established an FLP that contained both business and personal assets, cast a pall over the use of FLPs as estate planning tools. Another case, however, calmed estate planners' fears and reestablished the use of FLPs as legitimate estate planning tools as long as entrepreneurs create them properly. The following tips will help entrepreneurs establish an FLP that will withstand legal challenges:

- Establish a legitimate business reason other than avoiding estate taxes, such as transferring a business over time to the next generation of family members, for creating the FLP and document it on paper.
- Make sure all members of the FLP make contributions and take distributions according to a predetermined schedule. "Don't allow partners to use partnership funds to pay for personal expenses and do not time partnership distributions with personal needs for cash," says one attorney.[53]
- Do not allow members to put all of their personal assets (such as a house, automobiles, or personal property) into the FLP. Commingling personal and business assets in an FLP raises a red flag to the IRS.
- Maintain proper records for establishing and operating the FLP.
- Expect an audit of the FLP. The IRS tends to scrutinize FLPs; be prepared for a thorough audit.[54]

Profile

Gordon and Ken Van Tuinen: West Michigan Uniform

Gordon Van Tuinen founded West Michigan Uniform (WMU) in Holland, Michigan, in 1963 and managed it until he retired in 1983, when his son Ken took over as CEO. To transfer the family business to Ken and his four other children, Gordon relied on a variety of estate planning tools, including lifetime gifting and an estate freeze. Ken, who owns the majority of shares in WMU, is now engaged in planning to give control of the company to the third generation of family members with the goal of minimizing the impact of estate taxes. In addition to using lifetime gifting to transfer shares of the company to his three children, one of whom works in the business, Ken created three family limited partnerships that will allow the children to assume ownership of the company over time without incurring oppressive tax bills.[55]

Developing a succession plan and preparing a successor requires a wide variety of knowledge and skills, some of which the business founder will not have. That's why it is important to bring experts into the process when necessary. Entrepreneurs often call on their attorneys, accountants, insurance agents, and financial planners to help them build a succession plan that works best for their particular situations. Because the issues involved can be highly complex and charged with emotion, bringing in trusted advisors to help improves the quality of the process and provides an objective perspective.

Risk Management Strategies

5. Understand the four risk management strategies.

Insurance is an important part of creating a management succession plan because it can help business owners minimize the taxes on the estates they pass on to their heirs and can provide much needed cash to pay the taxes the estate does incur. However, insurance plays an important role in many other aspects of a successful business—from covering employee injuries to protecting against natural disasters that might shut a business down temporarily. When most small business owners think of risks such as these, they automatically think of insurance. However, insurance companies are the first to point out that insurance does not solve all risk problems. A more comprehensive strategy is risk management, which takes a proactive approach to dealing with the risks that businesses face daily. A survey by the National Federation of Independent Businesses shows that just 38 percent of small companies have an emergency preparedness plan for dealing with either a natural or manmade disaster.[56] At least 25 percent of small businesses that are forced to close after a major disaster never reopen; among small businesses that have no disaster plan, the percentage that never reopen jumps to 50 percent.[57] "Small companies often spend more time planning the company picnic than planning for an event that could put them out of business," says one insurance expert.[58] Dealing with risk successfully requires a combination of four risk management strategies: avoiding, reducing, anticipating, and transferring risk.

Avoiding risk requires a business to take actions to shun risky situations. For instance, conducting credit checks of customers decreases losses from bad debts. Wise managers know that they can avoid some risks simply by taking proactive management actions. Workplace safety improves when business owners implement programs designed to make all employees aware of the hazards of their jobs and how to avoid being hurt. Business owners who have active risk identification and prevention programs can reduce their potential insurance costs as well as create a safer, more attractive work environment for their employees. Because avoiding risk altogether usually is not practical, however, a strategy of reducing risk becomes necessary.

A risk-reducing strategy requires a company to take steps to lower the level of risk associated with a situation. Risk reduction strategies do not eliminate risk, but they lessen its impact. Even with avoidance and reduction strategies, the risk is still present; thus, losses can occur.

George Pauli, owner of Great Embroidery LLC in Mesa, Arizona, recently installed back-up generators for the two machines that he uses to stitch logos on 12 garments at a time. Pauli's business experiences power interruptions about six times a year, and before he installed the generators each incident cost him at least $120 in lost merchandise because the machines' needles could not resume exactly where they had left off when the power shut off.[59]

Risk anticipation strategies promote self-insurance. Knowing that some element of risk still exists, a business owner puts aside money each month to cover potential losses. Sometimes a self-insurance fund may not be large enough to cover the losses from a particular situation. When this happens, a business stands to lose despite the best efforts to anticipate risk, especially in the first few years before the fund is fully funded and able to cover large claims. Most businesses, therefore, include in their risk strategies some form of insurance to transfer risk.

Managers at Racine Federated, a small company in Racine, Wisconsin, that sells industrial instruments, machinery, and tools, grew tired of watching the cost of health care coverage for their 110 employees climb every year and decided to establish a self-insurance fund to cover employees' health care benefits. If employees' claims were low in a given year, Racine would save money over what it would have paid in insurance premiums. If several workers suffered catastrophic injuries or illnesses at once, however, the company could face a cash crisis. Recognizing that a self-insurance strategy alone could be risky, Racine purchased a "stop-loss" policy, which takes over payment if any individual employee's health care costs exceed $55,000 a year. Racine also hired a company to handle all of the insurance paperwork. In the 7 years since switching to self-insurance, Racine has saved $300,000 over the cost of the company's old insurance plan without reducing its coverage.[60]

George Pauli, owner of Great Embroidery LLC, installed back-up generators for his company as part of a risk reduction strategy.

Source: Andy DeLisle/Wonderful Machine

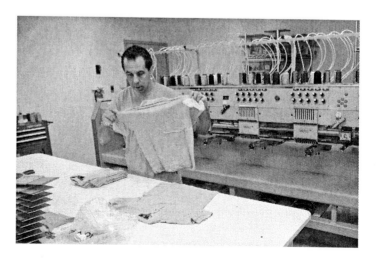

Self-insurance is not for every business owner, however. For businesses with fewer than 50 employees, self-insurance is usually not a wise choice because there is so much variation in the number and size of annual claims. Self-insuring also is time-consuming, requiring business owners to take a more active role in managing their companies' insurance needs. Companies using self-insurance should be financially secure with a relatively stable workforce and should see it as a long-term strategy for savings.

Risk transfer strategies depend on using insurance. Insurance is a risk transfer strategy because an individual or a business transfers some of the costs of a particular risk to an insurance company, which is set up to spread out the financial burdens of risk. During a specific time period, the insured business pays money (a premium) to an insurance carrier (either a private company or a government agency). In return, the carrier promises to pay the insured a certain amount of money in the event of a loss. Small companies across the United States are feeling the pinch of rapidly escalating insurance costs and are devising creative ways to control their insurance costs.

Captive insurance, which is a hybrid of self-insurance and risk transfer strategies, is a technique that large businesses have used for years that is gaining popularity among small businesses. To implement a captive insurance strategy, small companies band together to create their own insurance company and contribute enough capital to cover a defined level of risk. The group outsources the daily management of the insurance company to a business that specializes in that area and then purchases reinsurance to cover losses above the amount that they have contributed. Over time, if the group experiences no large losses, the excess capital paid into the insurance company goes back to the businesses as dividends. Currently, 27 states and the District of Columbia have passed legislation authorizing insurance captives.

Profile

*Dudley Miles:
J.D. Miles & Sons*

Dudley Miles, CEO of J.D. Miles & Sons, a roofing contractor founded by his grandfather in 1910, was plagued by escalating insurance premiums that threatened his company's profitability. Working through Roof Connect, an industry association, Miles convinced 25 other roofing contractors to band together to create a captive insurance company. The small businesses agreed to self-insure losses up to $500,000 and purchased reinsurance to cover larger losses. They also adopted several risk reduction strategies such as quarterly safety inspections and random drug tests for employees. The result has been a reduction in the number of claims, improved safety records, and lower premiums than the members of the plan were paying before.[61]

The Basics of Insurance

6. Discuss the basics of insurance for small businesses.

Insurance is the transfer of risk from one entity (an individual, a group, or a business) to an insurance company. Without insurance, many of the products and services that businesses provide would be impossible because the risk of overwhelming financial loss would be too great given the litigious society in which we live. Yet many small business owners ignore their companies' insurance needs or buy insurance coverage for their companies but not enough to protect them from the most basic risks such as property damage, fire, theft, and liability. Home-based business owners, in particular, put their companies at risk. According to the Independent Insurance Agents & Brokers of America, 58 percent of home-based business owners lack adequate insurance to protect them against liability, property damage, or loss.[62]

To be insurable, a situation or hazard must meet the following requirements:

1. It must be possible to calculate the actual loss being insured. For example, it would probably not be possible to insure an entire city against fire because too many variables are involved. It is possible, however, to insure a specific building.
2. It must be possible to select the risk being insured. No business owner can insure against every potential hazard, but insurance companies offer a wide variety of policies. One company even offers an alien abduction policy ($150 a year for $150 million of coverage) and has actually paid one claim! Another offers werewolf insurance, but the policy pays only if the insured turns into a werewolf.[63] Famous insurer Lloyd's of London has insured

Entrepreneurs can buy insurance to protect themselves and their companies from almost any calamity. One insurance company actually offers werewolf insurance!

Source: Lon Chaney\Alamy

coffee taster Gennarro Pelliccia's tongue and taste buds for £10 million. Pelliccia, who samples coffees for Costa Coffee, says, "In my profession, my taste buds and sensory skills are crucial. My taste buds allow me to distinguish any defects, which enables me to protect and guarantee Costa's unique Mocha Italia blend." Lloyd's also once wrote a policy to insure the smile of actress America Ferrera, star of the television show *Ugly Betty*, for $10 million.[64]

3. There must be enough potential policyholders to assume the risk. A tightrope walker who specializes in walking between tall downtown buildings would have difficulty purchasing insurance because there are not enough people engaging in that activity to spread the risk sufficiently.

Perhaps the biggest barrier facing entrepreneurs is the difficulty of understanding the nature of the risks that they and their businesses face. The risk management pyramid (see Figure 6) helps entrepreneurs decide how they should allocate their risk management dollars. Begin by identifying the primary risks your company faces: for example, a fire in a manufacturing plant, a lawsuit from a customer injured by your company's product, a computer system meltdown, an earthquake, and so on. Then rate each event on three factors:

1. *Severity.* How much would the event affect your company's ability to operate?
2. *Probability.* How likely is the event to occur?
3. *Cost.* How much would it cost your company if the event occurred?

Rate the event on each of these three factors using a simple scale: A (high) to D (low). For instance, a small technology company might rate a fire in its offices as BDA. On the other hand, that same company might rank a computer system crash as ABA. Using the risk management pyramid, a business owner sees that the event rated ABA is higher on the risk scale than the event rated BDA. Therefore, this company would focus more of its risk management dollars on preventing a computer system crash than on protecting against an office fire.

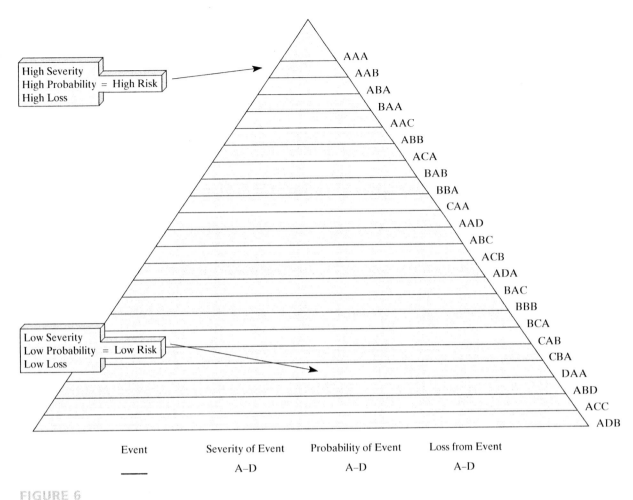

FIGURE 6
The Risk Management Pyramid

Types of Insurance

No longer is the cost of insurance an inconsequential part of doing business. Now the ability to get adequate coverage and to pay the premiums is a significant factor in starting and running a small business. Sometimes just *finding* coverage for their businesses is a challenge for entrepreneurs.

Profile

Jane Reifert:
Incredible Adventures

For Incredible Adventures, a small Sarasota, Florida-based company that offers customers the opportunity to fly in a Russian MiG jet fighter; experience weightlessness; go to the edge of space; swim with sharks; or make a high-altitude, low-opening (HALO) sky dive; in addition to many other exciting adventures, purchasing insurance is a challenge. President Jane Reifert says that she spends as much time with lawyers and insurance agents as she does with customers. "You can insure people swimming in shark-infested waters, but you can't insure people inside shark cages," she says incredulously.[65]

A wide range of business, individual, and group insurance is available to small business owners, and deciding which ones are necessary can be difficult. Some types of insurance are essential to providing a secure future for the company; others may provide additional employee benefits. The four major categories of insurance are property and casualty insurance, life and disability insurance, health insurance and workers' compensation coverage, and liability insurance. Each category is divided into many specific types, each of which has many variations offered by insurance companies. Business owners should begin by purchasing a basic **business owner's policy (BOP)**, which typically includes basic property and casualty insurance and liability insurance coverage. BOPs alone are not sufficient to meet most small business owners' insurance needs, however. Entrepreneurs should start with BOPs and then customize their insurance coverage to suit their companies' special needs by purchasing additional types of coverage.

PROPERTY AND CASUALTY INSURANCE. Property and casualty insurance covers a company's tangible assets, such as buildings, equipment, inventory, machinery, signs, and others that might be damaged, destroyed, or stolen. Business owners should be sure that their policies cover the replacement cost of their property, not just its value at the time of the loss, even if this coverage costs extra. One business owner whose policy covered the replacement cost of his company's building was glad he had purchased the extra coverage when he suffered a devastating fire loss. When he began rebuilding, he discovered that the cost to comply with current building code regulations was much higher than merely replacing the previous structure.

Specific types of property and casualty insurance include property, surety, marine and inland marine, crime, liability, business interruption, motor vehicle, and professional liability insurance.

Property insurance protects a company's assets against loss from damage, theft, or destruction. It applies to automobiles, boats, homes, office buildings, stores, factories, and other items of property. Some property insurance policies are broadly written to include all of an individual's property up to some maximum amount of loss, whereas other policies are written to cover only one building or one specific piece of property, such as a company car. Many natural disasters, such as floods and earthquakes, are not covered under standard property insurance; business owners must buy separate insurance policies for those particular events.

Within the last decade, business owners across the United States have suffered billions of dollars in losses from natural disasters ranging from tornadoes and hurricanes to snow and ice storms. Many of the businesses that lacked proper insurance coverage were forced to close for good, and others are still struggling to recover.

ENTREPRENEURIAL
Profile

*The Brennan Family:
Ralph Brennan
Restaurant Group*

Even with adequate insurance, it took the Brennans, New Orleans' famous family of restaurateurs, more than a year to reopen the celebrated Commander's Palace after Hurricane Katrina severely damaged the historic Garden District building that housed it. Almost all of the interior of the building, which was constructed in 1880, had to be rebuilt because of water damage, and more than 80 percent of the kitchen equipment had to be replaced. Charlie Williamson, vice president of the Ralph Brennan Restaurant Group, says that the company's disaster preparation plan has grown from 2 pages before the hurricane to a 68-page booklet that covers not only operating plans but also technology and communications plans.[66]

A company's BOP may insure the buildings and contents of a factory for loss from fire or natural disaster, but the owner may also buy insurance, called extra expense coverage, to cover expenses that occur while the destroyed factory is being rebuilt. **Extra expense coverage** pays for the costs of temporarily relocating workers and machinery so that a business can continue to

After suffering damage from Hurricane Katrina, New Orleans' famous Commander's Palace restaurant is now fully restored. Even with adequate insurance coverage, the restoration took more than a year.

Source: © Angelo Cavalli/SuperStock

operate while it rebuilds or repairs its factory. A similar type of insurance, called **business interruption insurance**, covers business owners' lost income and ongoing expenses in case their companies cannot operate for an extended period of time. As devastating as interruptions can be to a small company, studies show that 55 percent of small business owners do not purchase business interruption coverage and that 63 percent of them do not know how the coverage works.[67] Even more alarming is the fact that 25 percent of businesses whose operations are interrupted by a disaster never reopen.[68]

Wendy Stevens, who owns Alloy Design, a business in Boyertown, Pennsylvania, that manufactures accessories and home decorations out of stainless steel, watched helplessly as more than 100 firefighters battled a blaze that ultimately claimed the building that housed her company. "I remember feeling huge waves of nausea and thinking, 'My business is gone,'" she says. "Everything was destroyed—equipment, inventory, paperwork. All that remained were two stone walls, a floor, and 20 years of designing, building, and selling my product." Fortunately, Stevens had good insurance coverage, including property and inventory insurance as well as business interruption insurance. One year after the fire, Stevens was back in business. "After losing everything, I've managed to bounce back with even better products and to expand into new markets. I'm now selling in four different countries."[69]

Machinery and equipment insurance is a common addition for many businesses and covers a wide range of problems with equipment such as production machinery, electrical systems, HVAC systems, and others. For instance, a restaurant that loses thousands of dollars' worth of food when a freezer breaks down would be covered for its loss under machinery and equipment insurance.

Auto insurance policies offer liability coverage that protects against losses resulting from injuries, damage, or theft involving the use of company vehicles. A typical BOP does not include liability coverage for automobiles; business owners must purchase a separate policy for auto insurance. The automobiles a business owns must be covered by a commercial policy, not a personal one.

Electronic data processing (EDP) insurance covers losses from the theft or loss of computers and data, the impact of computer viruses and computer system failures, intrusion by hackers, and invasion of customer information stored in company databases. EDP insurance has become more important as businesses have moved their operations online and engage in increasing volumes of e-commerce. Thomas Shipley, whose company sells business accessories, generates 30 percent of his sales from the company's Web site. Shipley purchased an EDP policy that protects his business from, among other things, hackers and viruses. The policy costs $14,000 a year, but Shipley says it is well worth the price to protect his company that now brings in more than $10 million in sales a year.[70]

A business may also purchase **surety insurance**, which protects against losses to customers that occur when a company fails to complete a contract on time or completes it incorrectly. Surety protection guarantees customers that they will get either the products or services they purchased or the money to cover losses from contractual failures.

Businesses also buy insurance to protect themselves from losses that occur when either finished goods or raw materials are lost or destroyed while being shipped. **Marine insurance** is designed to cover the risk associated with goods in transit. The name of this insurance goes back to the days when a ship's cargo was insured against high risks associated with ocean navigation.

Crime insurance does not deter crime, but it can reimburse the small business owner for losses from the "three Ds": dishonesty, disappearance, and destruction. Business owners should ask their insurance brokers or agents exactly what their crime insurance policies cover; after-the-fact insurance coverage surprises are seldom pleasant. Premiums for crime policies vary depending on the type of business, store location, number of employees, quality of the business's security system, and the business's history of losses. Coverage may include fidelity bonds, which are designed to reimburse business owners for losses from embezzlement and employee theft. Forgery bonds reimburse owners for losses sustained from the forgery of business checks.

LIFE AND DISABILITY INSURANCE. Unlike most forms of insurance, life insurance does not pertain to avoiding risk because death is a certainty for everyone. Rather, **life insurance** protects families and businesses against loss of income, security, or personal services that results from an individual's untimely death. Life insurance policies are usually issued with a face amount payable to a beneficiary upon the death of the insured. Life insurance for business protection, although not as common as life insurance for family protection, is becoming more popular. As you learned in the section on management succession, life insurance policies are an important part of many estate planning tools. In addition, many businesses insure the lives of key executives to offset the costs of having to make a hurried and often unplanned replacement of important managers.

When it comes to assets that are expensive to replace, few are more costly than the key people in a business, including the owner. What would it take to replace a company's top sales representative? Its production supervisor? Clearly, money alone cannot solve the problem, but it does allow a business to find and train their replacements and to cover the profits lost because of their untimely deaths or disabilities. That is the idea behind **key-person insurance**, which provides valuable working capital to keep a business on track while it reorganizes and searches for the right person to replace the loss of someone in a key position in the company.

Disability insurance protects an individual in the event of unexpected and often very expensive disabilities. Because a sudden disability limits a person's ability to earn a living, the insurance proceeds are designed to help make up the difference between what that person could have expected to earn if the accident had not occurred. Sometimes called income insurance, these policies usually guarantee a stated percentage of an individual's income—usually around 60 percent—while he or she is recovering and is unable to run a business. Short-term disability policies cover the 90-day gap between the time a person is injured and when workers' compensation payments begin. Long-term disability policies pay for lost income after 90 days or longer. In addition to the portion of income a policy will replace, another important factor to consider when purchasing disability insurance is the waiting period, the time gap between when the disability occurs and the disability payments begin. Although many business owners understand the importance of maintaining adequate life insurance coverage, fewer see the relevance of maintaining proper coverage for disabilities. For most people, the likelihood of a disability is three to five times greater than the risk of death; nearly 30 percent of workers between the ages of 35 and 65 will be unable to work for 90 days or longer due to a disability.[71]

Business owners can supplement traditional disability policies with **business overhead expense (BOE) insurance**. Designed primarily for companies with fewer than 15 employees, a BOE policy will replace 100 percent of a small company's monthly overhead expenses such as rent, utilities, insurance, taxes, and others if the owner is incapacitated. Payments typically begin 30 days after the owner is incapacitated and continue for up to 2 years.

HEALTH INSURANCE AND WORKERS' COMPENSATION. According to the National Federation of Independent Businesses (NFIB), small business owners' greatest concern for the last 25 years has been the skyrocketing cost of health insurance.[72] Currently, health care spending in the United States accounts for 17.3 percent of GDP, an amount that will increase to 20 percent by 2017.[73] The average small company spends on average $5,046 per year on health care insurance premiums for an employee. Because of the high cost of providing health care coverage for employees, only 68 percent of small businesses offer health insurance to their employees, compared to 99 percent of large companies (see Figure 7).[74] As health care costs steadily climb and the average age of the workforce continues to increase, small companies are having more difficulty providing coverage for their employees (see Figure 8). The primary reason cited by small business owners who do not offer health insurance is the high cost.[75] Small businesses actually pay 18 percent more than large companies for the same health insurance because of higher broker fees and costs of administering health care plans for a smaller number of employees.[76] "The corporate world really spoiled me," says Sandy Dixon, who left a large company to start Interior Arrangements, an interior redesign company in Evergreen, Colorado. "[When I started my business,] I was

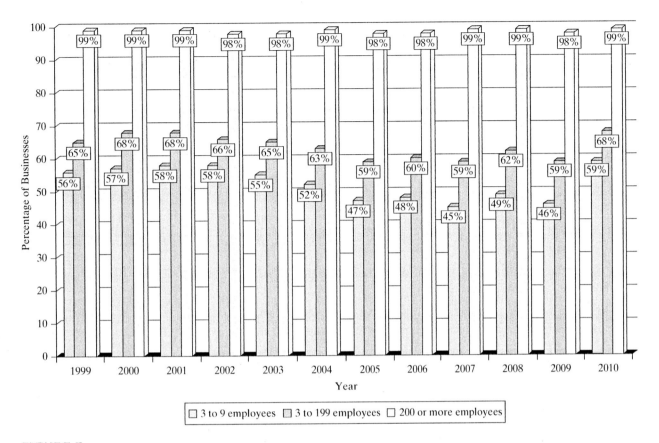

Percentage of Companies Offering Health Benefits by Company Size

Source: Employer Health Benefits: 2010 Summary of Findings, Kaiser Family Foundation and Health Research and Education Trust, p. 5.

really surprised by the high cost of health insurance and suddenly had a new appreciation for this corporate perk."[77]

Health insurance has become an extremely important benefit to most workers. Small companies that offer thorough health care coverage often find that it gives them an edge in attracting and retaining a quality workforce. In fact, 86 percent of business owners cite health care as the most important benefit to attracting and retaining quality workers.[78]

**Average Annual Health
Insurance Premiums
for Family Coverage**

*Source: Employer Health Benefits:
2010 Summary of Findings*, Kaiser
Family Foundation and Health
Research and Education Trust, p. 1.

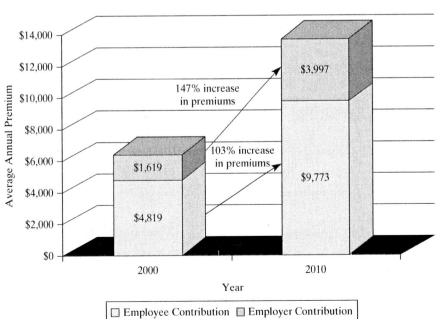

Jeff Harvey, CEO of Burgerville, a regional chain of 39 burger restaurants founded in Vancouver, Washington, in 1961 by George Propstra, recently began paying at least 90 percent of health insurance premiums for part-time employees who work at least 20 hours per week, a benefit that most food-service companies do not offer part-time employees. Even though the added benefit nearly doubled the 1,500-employee company's health care costs from $2.1 million annually to $4.1 million, Harvey says that the move actually has saved the company money by lowering its employee turnover rate and increasing employee productivity. Burgerville's employee turnover rate is less than half the industry average, a significant savings when replacing and training a restaurant worker costs on average $1,700. Harvey says the company is considering launching a wellness program to help employees lead healthier lifestyles and to lower health insurance claims.[79]

A key to providing proper health care coverage while keeping costs in check is to offer the benefits that are most important to your employees and to avoid spending money unnecessarily on coverage that does not apply to them. Although the Affordable Care Act, a bill passed in 2010 that is designed to provide health care coverage for a greater number of people, stands to change the mechanics of health care in the United States, employers face four basic health care options: traditional indemnity plans, managed care plans, health savings accounts, and self-insurance.

Traditional Indemnity Plans. Under these plans, employees choose their own health care providers, and the insurance company either pays the provider directly or reimburses employees for the covered amounts.

Managed Care Plans. As part of employers' attempts to put a lid on escalating health care costs, these plans have become increasingly popular. Three variations—the health maintenance organization (HMO), the preferred provider organization (PPO), and the point of service (POS)—are most common. An HMO is a prepaid health care arrangement under which employees must use health care providers who are employed by or are under contract with the HMO their company uses. Although they lower health care costs, employees have less freedom in selecting physicians under an HMO. Under a PPO, an insurance company negotiates discounts for health care with certain physicians and hospitals. If employees choose a health care provider from the approved list, they pay only a small fee for each office visit (often just $10 to $25). The insurance company pays the remainder. Employees may select a provider outside the PPO, but they pay more for the service. A POS is a hybrid of an HMO and a PPO that gives employees the freedom to select their health care providers (as with a PPO) and lowers costs (as with an HMO). As long as employees choose a primary care physician within the approved network, the POS will pay for that care and for care by specialists, even those outside the network, as long as the primary care physician makes the referral. PPOs are the most common managed care plans (53 percent of employers who offer health benefits use them), followed by POSs (25 percent) and HMOs (24 percent).[80]

Health Savings Accounts (HSAs). Created as part of a major Medicare overhaul in 2003, health savings accounts (HSAs) are similar to IRAs except employees' contributions are used for medical expenses rather than for retirement. An HSA is a special savings account coupled with a high-deductible (typically $1,000 to $5,000 for an individual) insurance policy that covers major medical expenses. Employees or employers contribute pre-tax dollars (up to a defined ceiling) from their paychecks into the fund and use them as they need to. Withdrawals from an HSA are not taxed as long as the money is used for approved medical expenses. Unused funds can accumulate indefinitely and earn tax-free interest. HSAs offer employees incentives to contain their health care costs, but the employer must choose both an insurance carrier to provide coverage and a custodial firm to manage employees' accounts. Although critics contend that consumer-driven plans push a greater portion of health care expenses onto employees, these plans continue to grow in popularity among small businesses because of their potential to rein in escalating costs. The average annual premium for an HSA for a small company is $4,454, which is 13.1 percent lower than the cost of traditional managed care plans.[81] Although self-employed individuals find HSAs attractive, employers are adding them to their menu of health care options for employees. More than 8 million employees are covered by HSAs, a significant increase from 1 million in 2005.[82]

Profile

Andrew Field and PrintingforLess.com

Andrew Field, owner of PrintingforLess.com, a Web-based printing company, had seen health care costs for his company's 130 employees increase by double-digit rates year after year and decided to switch from a traditional plan to an HSA plan. The change allowed him to provide his employees with better, more flexible coverage and the freedom to decide how to spend their health care dollars without any increase in cost. Although PrintingforLess.com did encounter a few problems in making the switch, Field and his employees are pleased with the HSA. "We were worried that it might have some bad side effects," he says. "but it's better than we thought."[83]

Self-Insurance. As you learned earlier in this chapter, some business owners choose to insure themselves for health coverage rather than to incur the costs of fully insured plans offered by outsiders. The benefits of self-insurance include greater control over the plan's design and the coverage it offers, fewer paperwork and reporting requirements, and, in some cases, lower costs. The primary disadvantage, of course, is the possibility of having to pay large amounts to cover treatments for several employees' major illnesses at the same time, which can strain a small company's cash flow. Many self-insured businesses limit their exposure to such losses by purchasing stop-loss insurance, under which the business owner pays for health care expenses up to a predetermined point; beyond that point, the stop-loss policy takes over the expenses.

Another type of health-related coverage is **workers' compensation**, which is designed to cover employees who are injured on the job or who become sick as a result of a work environment. Worker's compensation is a mandatory insurance program; companies that fail to offer workers' compensation must pay out-of-pocket for workers' claims and face penalties from the state. Before passage of workers' compensation legislation in 1911, an employee injured on the job had to bring a lawsuit to prove the employer was liable for the worker's injury. Because of the red tape and expenses involved in these lawsuits, many employees never received compensation for job-related accidents and injuries. Although the details of coverage vary from state to state, workers' compensation laws require employers to purchase insurance that provides benefits and medical and rehabilitation costs for employees injured on the job. The amount of compensation an injured employee receives depends on a fixed schedule of payment benefits based on three factors: the wages or salary that the employee was earning at the time of the accident or injury, the seriousness of the injury, and the extent of the disability to the employee.

Only two states, New Jersey and Texas, do not require companies to purchase workers' compensation coverage once they reach a certain size (usually three or more employees). Usually, the state sets the rates businesses pay for workers' compensation coverage, and business owners purchase their coverage from private insurance companies. Rapidly escalating workers' compensation rates, driven in large part by rising medical expenses, have become a major concern for small businesses across the nation. Companies in Alaska face the highest workers' compensation costs in the nation.[84] McGraw's Custom Construction in Sitka, Alaska, saw its workers' compensation costs go from $146,950 to $315,110 in just 2 years![85] Rates vary by industry, business size, and the number of claims a company's workers make. For instance, workers' compensation premiums are higher for a timber cutting business than for a retail gift store. Table 3 shows the 10 occupations with the greatest number of injuries and illnesses. Whatever industry they are in, business owners can reduce their workers' compensation costs by improving their employees' safety records.

Profile

Core Systems

Core Systems, a plastic injection molding company based in Painesville, Ohio, was growing so fast that its accidents began to spiral out of control. Not only were employees being injured, but morale was down and workers' compensation costs were way up. In an effort to contain the rapidly rising costs, human resources director Maggine Fuentes, launched a safety system that combed through company records looking for accident and injury patterns and then focused on training and soliciting employee suggestions for improvement. The system made safety a priority at Core Systems and reduced both the number and the severity of accidents in the plant, which has lowered the company's workers' compensation cost by $277,000 so far.[86]

TABLE 3 Ten Most Dangerous Occupations

Rank	Occupation	Percentage of Total Injuries and Illnesses
1	Nonconstruction laborers	7.4%
2	Truck drivers (heavy)	5.4%
3	Nursing aides and orderlies	4.1%
4	Construction workers	2.9%
5	Retail salespeople	2.7%
6	Janitors and cleaners	2.6%
7	Truck drivers (light)	2.6%
8	Maintenance and repair workers	1.9%
9	Registered nurses	1.8%
10	Maids and housekeeping cleaners	1.7%

Source: "Workplace Safety/Workers Comp," Insurance Information Institute, *www.iii.org/facts_statistics/workplace-safety-workers-comp.html.*

▶ ENTREPRENEURSHIP IN ACTION ▶

What Can We Do to Help You Stay Healthy?

In 1997, when Jason Crawforth started Treetop Tech, a software development company in Boise, Idaho, he did not offer company-sponsored health insurance because he believed that his small company could not afford the cost. He soon realized, however, that he could not afford *not* to offer health insurance. "We started losing potential employees because of that," he says. In 2000, Crawforth added health insurance coverage to his employees' benefits package, just in time to watch premiums skyrocket over the next decade.

Crawforth, like many small business owners, is struggling to cope with health insurance premiums that have increased by 114 percent since 2000, compared to an increase of just 27 percent in the consumer price index over the same period. According to a survey by Aflac Inc. and Accelerant Research, 62 percent of small business owners say it is more difficult to offer a strong benefits package than 1 year before, and 52 percent say they have reduced their health insurance coverage. Donna Partin, who owns three Merry Maids franchises, two in Pennsylvania and one in Florida, that employ a total of 50 workers, says that her company's health insurance premiums have tripled since 2000. "I'm paying more for less and less [coverage] every year," she says. Partin pays $5,000 per month to insure her employees in Pennsylvania, where only one-third of her workforce has opted for coverage. The others cannot afford their portion of the health insurance premium. Partin says that she cannot afford coverage for her employees

in Florida, something that causes her concern because her business requires trustworthy workers to go into clients' homes to clean. As health care insurance costs continue to escalate, Partin, like many small business owners, worries that she will be at a disadvantage in attracting and retaining quality workers if she has to pare back or even eliminate coverage.

Thomas Johnson, owner of Thomas A. Johnson Furniture, a company that builds custom, handmade furniture in Lynchburg, Virginia, emigrated from Ghana, West Africa, to the United States with just $20, a willingness to work hard, and a desire to own a business. Today, the master craftsman has eight employee apprentices who work beside him, learning to make fine furniture. Unable to afford the premiums for a group health insurance plan, Johnson pays out-of-pocket for his employees' medical expenses. Skilled woodworkers are difficult to find, and Johnson cannot afford to lose any of his employees, in whom he has invested thousands of hours of training. "My workers are part of my business and part of my family," he says. To him, paying their medical expenses is a matter of honor—and practicality—but it also is risky. By paying for his workers' medical expenses, Johnson may have set a precedent that could obligate him to pay for all of his employees' expenses—even in the case of a catastrophic illness that might cost hundreds of thousands of dollars to treat.

About 70 percent of health care costs arise from *preventable* chronic diseases, a fact that has led many businesses to implement wellness programs that are designed to put the brakes on cost increases by giving employees incentives to get and stay healthy by quitting smoking, maintaining an ideal weight, reducing stress, and exercising regularly. Employers typically pay between $100 and $300 per person per year in incentives, a small price to pay compared to the additional $16,000 lifetime health care costs associated with an employee who smokes. The same holds true for overweight employees; health care costs are $1,400 more per year for obese workers than those who maintain a healthy weight. One-third of small companies offer wellness programs that include onsite fitness centers or memberships for offsite fitness centers, smoking cessation programs, online tracking tools, onsite health checks, and other features. Not only do wellness programs improve employees' health, but they also produce an impressive return on investment—up to $6 on average for every $1 invested. Mike Faith, founder of Headsets.com in San Francisco, California, stocks the break room with healthy snacks and fresh fruit for his 52 employees. He also offers them subsidized gym memberships and help with smoking cessation, including free nicotine patches.

"You don't need to spend a lot of money on these programs," says Dan Dauphinee, operations manager at Northeastern Log Homes, a small business in Kenduskeag, Maine. Northeastern Log Homes recently created a walking trail for its 100 employees, who are encouraged to exercise during their breaks. The company also offers fruits and vegetables in its snack room at subsidized prices. Northeastern Log Homes gives employees who engage in its wellness program discounts on their portion of health insurance premiums. Components of the wellness program range from nutrition lectures to walking challenges. "When you look at a culture that has healthy, happy employees and your health insurance costs are not going up, that's the justification," says Dauphinee.

1. Is it ethical for companies to reduce their health care costs by offering employees incentives to get and stay healthy? Explain.
2. How much control should companies have over employees' lifestyles away from the workplace?

Sources: Based on Patricia B. Gray, "HealthCure," *FSB*, February 2009, pp. 57–65; Robert Langreth, "Healthy Bribes," *Forbes*, August 24, 2009, p. 72; Mark Henricks, "An Apple a Day . . ." *Entrepreneur*, March 2008, pp. 19–20; E. B. Solomont, "Companies Find Inexpensive Ways to Promote Wellness," *Workforce Management*, March 2009, *www.workforce.com/section/ benefits-compensation/feature/companies-find-inexpensive-ways-promote- wellness/index.html*; John Cummings, "Finding the ROI in Wellness Incentives," *Business Finance*, August 11, 2008, *http://businessfinancemag.com/article/ finding-roi-wellness-incentives-0811*; Simone Richards, "Small Businesses Struggle to Offer Healthcare," *Black Enterprise*, July 15, 2009, *www. blackenterprise.com/business/business-news/2009/07/15/small-businesses- struggle-to-offer-healthcare/*.

LIABILITY INSURANCE. One of the most common types of insurance coverage is liability insurance, which protects a business against losses resulting from accidents or injuries people suffer on the company's property, from its products or services, and damage the company causes to others' property. Most BOPs include basic liability coverage; however, the limits on the typical policy are not high enough to cover the potential losses many small business owners face. For example, one "slip-and-fall" case involving a customer who is injured by slipping and falling on a wet floor could easily exceed the standard limits on a basic BOP. Claims from customers injured by a company's product or service also are covered by its liability policy. Although most product liability lawsuits are settled out of court, the median award for those that go to court is nearly $2 million.[87]

Even though courts have dismissed them, some small companies have been targets of frivolous lawsuits because they are seen as easy targets. Frivolous lawsuits can cost a small company thousands of dollars to defend, however. Jin and Soo Chung, owners of Custom Cleaners in Washington, D.C., recently were hit with a $54 million lawsuit by a customer after the dry cleaner lost a pair of the customer's pants! The trial court ruled for Custom Cleaners, but plaintiff Roy Pearson filed an appeal, extending the legal nightmare for the small business owners, who incurred $83,000 in legal fees to defend themselves.[88] With jury awards in product liability cases often reaching into the millions of dollars, entrepreneurs who fail to purchase sufficient liability coverage may end up losing their businesses. Most insurance experts recommend purchasing a commercial general liability policy that provides coverage of at least $2 million to $3 million for the typical small business. As a result, many business owners find it necessary to purchase additional liability coverage for their companies.

Another important type of liability insurance for many small businesses is **professional liability insurance**, or **"errors and omissions" coverage**. This insurance protects against damage a business causes to customers or clients as a result of an error an employee makes or an employees' failure to take proper care and precautions. For instance, a land surveyor may miscalculate the location of a customer's property line. If the landowner relies on that

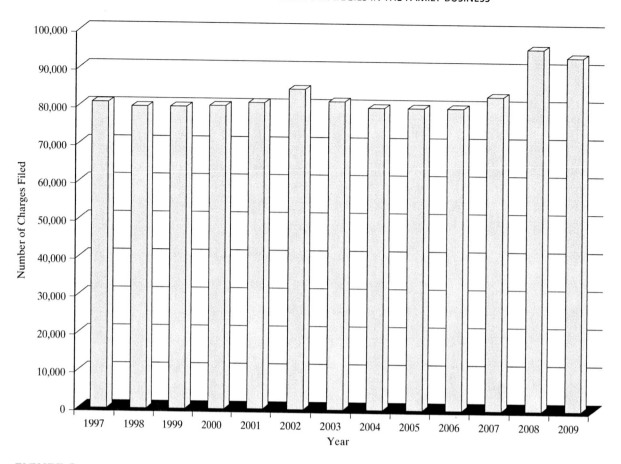

FIGURE 9

Number of Employment Charges Filed with EEOC

Source: Based on data from the Equal Employment Opportunity Commission, *www.eeoc.gov/eeoc/statistics/enforcement/all.cfm.*

property line to build a structure on what he thinks is his land and it turns out to be on his neighbor's land, the surveyor is liable for damages. Doctors, dentists, attorneys, and other professionals protect themselves through a similar kind of insurance, malpractice insurance, which protects them against the risk of lawsuits arising from errors in professional practice or judgment.

Employment practices liability (EPL) insurance provides protection against claims arising from charges of employment discrimination, improper discipline, wrongful termination, sexual harassment, and violations of the Americans with Disabilities Act, the Family and Medical Leave Act, and other employment legislation (see Figure 9). Although two-thirds of small business owners express concern that an employee will bring an EPL suit against them, only 1.2 percent carry EPL insurance.[89] Although most violations of these employment laws are not intentional but are the result of either carelessness or lack of knowledge, the company that violates them is still liable. Losing an employment practices liability case (employees win 58 percent of EPL cases) can be very expensive; the median jury award in EPL cases is $253,000.[90] Because they often lack full-time human resources professionals, small companies are especially vulnerable to charges of improper employment practices, making this type of insurance coverage all the more important to them. Seven employees at a franchised restaurant claimed that their supervisor had sexually harassed them by touching them inappropriately and making lewd comments and demands for sex. The young women complained about the harassment to the restaurant's general manager, who failed to investigate or act on their complaints. The restaurant owner negotiated an out-of-court settlement with the plaintiffs for $400,000, an amount that could force many small companies to close.[91]

Every business's insurance needs are somewhat unique, requiring owners to customize the insurance coverage they purchase. Entrepreneurs also must keep their insurance coverage updated as their companies grow; when companies expand, so do their insurance needs.

Controlling Insurance Costs

Small business owners face constantly rising insurance premiums. Entrepreneurs can take steps to lower insurance costs, however. To control the cost of insurance, owners should take the following steps:

1. *Pursue a loss-control program by making risk reduction a natural part of all employees' daily routine.* As discussed earlier in this chapter, risk reduction minimizes claims and eventually lowers premiums. Establishing a loss-control program means taking steps such as installing modern fire alarms, sprinkler systems, safety programs, and sophisticated security systems.

2. *Increase their policies' deductibles.* If a business can afford to handle minor losses, the owner can save money by raising the deductible to a level that protects the business against catastrophic events but, in effect, self-insures against minor losses. Business owners must determine the amount of financial exposure they can reasonably accept.

3. *Work with qualified professional insurance brokers or agents.* Business owners should do their homework before choosing insurance brokers or agents. This includes checking their reputation, credentials, and background by asking them to supply references.

4. *Work actively with brokers to make sure they understand business owners' particular needs.* Brokers need to know about entrepreneurs' businesses and objectives for insurance coverage. They can help only if they know their clients' needs and the degree of risk they are willing to take.

5. *Work with brokers to find competitive companies that want small companies' insurance business and have the resources to cover losses when they arise.* The price of the premium should never be an entrepreneur's sole criterion for selecting insurance. The rating of the insurance company should always be a primary consideration. What good is it to have paid low premiums if, after a loss, a business owner finds that the insurance company is unable to pay? Many small business owners learned costly lessons when their insurance companies, unable to meet their obligations, filed for bankruptcy protection.

6. *Utilize the resources of your insurance company.* Many insurers provide risk management inspections designed to help business owners assess the level of risk in their companies either for free or for a minimal fee. Smart entrepreneurs view their insurance companies as partners in their risk management efforts.

7. *Conduct a periodic insurance audit.* Reviewing your company's coverage annually can ensure that insurance coverage is adequate and can lead to big cost savings as well.

ENTREPRENEURIAL

Profile

Keith Alper: Creative Products Group

Keith Alper, owner of Creative Products Group (CPG), a business that produces videos for *Fortune* 500 companies, was surprised to discover that CPG was wasting thousands of dollars on policies it did not need. Many employees were classified incorrectly for workers' compensation coverage, several policies duplicated the coverage of others, and the company was paying for auto insurance on four cars when it had only three! In all, Alper was able to shave more than $10,000 off of the company's $75,000 annual insurance bill.[92]

8. *Compile discrimination, harassment, hiring, and other employment polices into an employee handbook and train employees to use them.* Companies that take an active approach to avoiding illegal employment practices have less exposure to lawsuits and, therefore, may be able to negotiate lower premiums.

Since World War II, businesses have been and continue to be the principal suppliers of health insurance in our society. To control the cost of health insurance, small business owners should consider the following steps:

1. *Increase the dollar amount of employee contributions and the amount of the employee deductibles.* Neither option is desirable, but rising medical costs have resulted in individuals becoming more responsible for their own health insurance and self-insuring to cover high deductibles.

2. *Switch to PPOs, POS plans, or HMOs.* Higher premium costs have encouraged some small business owners to reevaluate PPOs, POS plans, and HMOs as alternatives to traditional

health insurance policies. Although some employees resent limitations on their choice of providers, PPOs, HMOs, and POS plans have become the primary vehicles for companies to provide health care coverage to their employees.

3. *Consider joining an insurance pool.* Small businesses can lower their insurance premiums by banding together to purchase coverage. In many states, chambers of commerce, trade associations, and other groups form insurance pools that small businesses can join, spreading risk over a larger number of employees. In Cleveland, Ohio, for example, about 14,000 small companies purchase health insurance for their employees through the Council of Smaller Enterprises, a division of the chamber of commerce, at rates that are 8 percent below those that the owners could negotiate individually.[93]

4. *Keep employees informed.* By giving employees information about the costs and the benefits of various treatment alternatives and medications, employers empower their workers to make informed decisions that can lower health care costs.

5. *Conduct a yearly utilization review.* A review may reveal that your employees' use of their policies is statistically lower, which may provide you leverage to negotiate lower premiums or to switch to an insurer that wants a business with your track record and offers lower premiums.

6. *Make sure your company's health plan fits your employees' needs.* One of best ways to keep health care costs in check is to offer only those benefits that employees actually need. Getting employee input is essential to the process.

7. *Create a wellness program for all employees.* We have all heard the old adage that an ounce of prevention is worth a pound of cure, but when it comes to the high cost of medical expenses, this is especially true! Companies that have created wellness programs report cost savings of up to $6 for every $1 they invest. Employees involved in wellness programs not only incur lower health care expenses, but they also tend to be more productive as well. "Companies are reforming their own health care costs by recognizing that healthy workers cost less, are more productive, and are better for the company as a whole," says the president of a nonprofit health and productivity company.[94] Providing a wellness program does not mean building an expensive gym, however. Instead, it may be as simple as providing routine checkups from a nurse, incentives for quitting smoking, weight-loss counseling, or after-work athletic games that involve as many employees as possible. One recent study reports that 71 percent of companies offer their employees financial incentives to participate in wellness programs.[95]

Jon Wheeler, CEO of Wheeler Interests, a real estate management company based in Virginia Beach, Virginia, incorporated an employee wellness program into his business from the outset. He transformed empty office space into a small gym, brought in a personal trainer, and offered smoking cessation and other wellness programs for his employees. Wheeler also gives employees a mid-day kayaking break and allows them to set their own vacation times as long as they get their work done.[96]

8. *Conduct a safety audit.* Reviewing the workplace with a safety professional to look for ways to improve its safety has the potential for saving some businesses thousands of dollars a year in medical expenses and workers' compensation claims. The National Safety Council offers helpful information on creating a safe work environment.

9. *Create a safety manual and use it.* Incorporating the suggestions for improving safety into a policy manual and then using it will reduce the number of on-the-job accidents. Training employees, even experienced ones, in proper safety procedures is also effective.

10. *Create a safety team.* Assigning the responsibility for workplace safety to workers themselves can produce amazing results. When one small manufacturer turned its safety team over to employees, the plant's lost time due to accidents plummeted to zero for 3 years straight! The number of accidents is well below what it was when managers ran the safety team, and managers say that's because employees now "own" safety in the plant.

The key to controlling insurance costs is aggressive prevention. Entrepreneurs who actively manage the risks to which their companies are exposed find that they can provide the insurance coverage their businesses need at a reasonable cost. Finding the right insurance coverage to protect their businesses is no easy matter for business owners. The key is to identify the risks that represent the greatest threat to a company and then to develop a plan for minimizing their risk of occurrence and insuring against them if they do.

Chapter Review

1. Explain the factors necessary for a strong family business.
   - Nearly 90 percent of all companies in the United States are family owned. Family businesses generate 64 percent of the U.S. gross domestic product, account for 62 percent of employment, and pay 65 percent of all wages. Several factors are important to maintaining a strong family business, including shared values, shared power, tradition, a willingness to learn, behaving like families, and strong family ties.
2. Understand the exit strategy options available to an entrepreneur.
   - Family business owners wanting to step down from their companies can sell to outsiders, sell to insiders, or transfer ownership to the next generation of family members. Common tools for selling to insiders (employees or managers) include sale for cash plus a note, leveraged buyouts (LBOs), and employee stock ownership plans (ESOPs).
   - Transferring ownership to the next generation of family members requires a business owner to develop a sound management succession plan.
3. Discuss the stages of management succession.
   - Unfortunately, 70 percent of first-generation businesses fail to survive into the second generation, and, of those that do survive, only 12 percent make it to the third generation. One of the primary reasons for this lack of continuity is poor succession planning. Planning for management succession protects not only the founder's, successor's, and company's financial resources, but it also preserves what matters most in a successful business: its heritage and tradition. Management succession planning can ensure a smooth transition only if the founder begins the process early on.
4. Explain how to develop an effective management succession plan.
   - A succession plan is a crucial element in transferring a company to the next generation. Preparing a succession plan involves five steps: (1) Select the successor. (2) Create a survival kit for the successor. (3) Groom the successor. (4) Promote an environment of trust and respect. (5) Cope with the financial realities of estate taxes.
   - Entrepreneurs can rely on several tools in their estate planning, including buy-sell agreements, lifetime gifting, trusts, estate freezes, and family limited partnerships.
5. Understand the four risk management strategies.
   - Four risk strategies are available to the small business: avoiding, reducing, anticipating, and transferring risk.
6. Discuss the basics of insurance for small businesses.
   - Insurance is a risk transfer strategy. Not every potential loss can be insured. Insurability requires that it be possible to estimate the amount of actual loss being insured against and identify the specific risk and that there be enough policyholders to spread out the risk.
   - The four major types of insurance small businesses need are property and casualty insurance, life and disability insurance, health insurance and workers' compensation coverage, and liability insurance.
   - Property and casualty insurance covers a company's tangible assets, such as buildings, equipment, inventory, machinery, signs, and others that have been damaged, destroyed, or stolen. Specific types of property and casualty insurance include extra expense coverage, business interruption insurance, surety insurance, marine insurance, crime insurance, fidelity insurance, and forgery insurance.
   - Life and disability insurance also comes in various forms. Life insurance protects a family and a business against the loss of income and security in the event of the owner's death. Disability insurance, like life insurance, protects an individual in the event of unexpected and often very expensive disabilities.
   - Health insurance is designed to provide adequate health care for business owners and their employees. The most common managed health plans are preferred provider organizations (PPOs), point of service (POS) operations, and health maintenance

organizations (HMOs). Workers' compensation is designed to cover employees who are injured on the job or who become sick as a result of a work environment.

- Liability insurance protects a business against losses resulting from accidents or injuries people suffer on the company's property, from its products or services, and damage the company causes to others' property. Typical liability coverage includes professional liability insurance or "errors and omissions" coverage, which protects against damage a business causes to customers or clients as a result of an error an employee makes or an employee's failure to take proper care and precautions. Doctors, dentists, attorneys, and other professionals protect themselves through a similar kind of insurance, malpractice insurance, which protects them against the risk of lawsuits arising from errors in professional practice or judgment. Employment practices liability insurance provides protection against claims arising from charges of employment discrimination, sexual harassment, and violations of the Americans with Disabilities Act, the Family and Medical Leave Act, and other employment legislation.

Discussion Questions

1. What factors must be present for a strong family business?
2. Discuss the stages of management succession in a family business.
3. What steps are involved in building a successful management succession plan?
4. What exit strategies are available to entrepreneurs wanting to step down from their businesses?
5. What strategies can business owners employ to reduce estate and gift taxes?
6. Can insurance eliminate risk? Why or why not?
7. Outline the four basic risk management strategies and give an example of each.
8. What problems occur most frequently with a risk anticipation strategy?
9. What is insurance? How can insurance companies bear such a large risk burden and still be profitable?
10. Describe the requirements for insurability.
11. Briefly describe the various types of insurance coverage available to small business owners.
12. What kinds of insurance coverage would you recommend for the following businesses?
    a. A manufacturer of steel beams
    b. A retail gift shop
    c. A small accounting firm
    d. A limited liability partnership involving three dentists
13. What can business owners do to keep their insurance costs under control?

Business Plan Pro

Family-owned businesses dominate the landscape of U.S. companies, but they face a dangerous threat from within: management succession. Most family businesses fail to survive into the second generation and beyond. The problem usually is the result of a lack of planning for a smooth transition from one generation of management to the next. The business plan can assist in this process.

On the Web

Under the tab on the Companion Web site at *www. pearsonhigh-ered.com/scarborough* is a list of online resources that deal with succession planning and risk management. You will find resources that address issues related to managing a family business, planning for management succession, and managing business risk.

In the Software

If the business has issues regarding succession planning, capture those thoughts in your plan. This is also an opportunity to discuss risk management and exit strategies. What types of insurance coverage does your company require? Be sure to incorporate the cost of insurance coverage in your financial forecasts. Remember: You can add or modify outline topics within Business Plan Pro by right-clicking the outline in the left-hand navigation of the software.

Building Your Business Plan

One of the best ways to prevent a family-owned business from becoming just another management succession failure statistic is to develop a management succession plan early on in the life of the company. The business plan can be a vehicle to help with this discussion and document the plan to make this transition. The plan can also enable an entrepreneur to document ideas and plans regarding risk management and potential exit strategies.

Endnotes

1. "Facts About Family Business," S. Dale High Center for Family Business at Elizabethtown College, *www.centerforfamilybusiness.org/facts.asp;* MassMutual Family Business Network, *www.massmutual.com/fbn/index.htm;* "Family Business Facts," Family Business Institute, *www.ffi.org/looking/fbfacts_us.pdf.*

2. James Lea, "Five Ways Family Firms Can Thrive," Family Business Bizjournals.com, February 2, 2004, *www.bizjournals.com/extraedge/consultants/family_business/2004/02/02/column180.html.*

3. Thomas L. Kalaris, "Family Business: In Safe Hands?" *Barclays Wealth Insights,* 2009, p. 3.

4. "Country Comparison: GDP," *World Fact Book,* Central Intelligence Agency, *www.cia.gov/library/publications/the-world-factbook/rankorder/2001rank.html;* "A $238 Million Morning for the Walton Family," Wal-Mart Watch, March 5, 2009, *http://walmartwatch.com/blog/archives/a_238_million_dollar_morning_for_the_walton_family/;* "Wal-Mart Stores Inc," *CNNMoney,* November 10, 2010, *http://money.cnn.com/quote/quote.html?symb=WMT.*

5. Tony Taylor, "Small Businesses Show Relative Strength," *GSA Business,* September 4, 2006, p. 22; Jim Lee, "Family Firm Performance: Further Evidence," *Family Business Review,* June 2006, Vol. 19, No. 2, pp. 103–114.

6. "Research Reveals: Family Firms Perform Better," *Family Business Advisor,* March 2003, Vol. 12, No. 3, p. 1.

7. Nicholas Stein, "The Age of the Scion," *Fortune,* April 2, 2001, pp. 121–128.

8. Amol Sharma, "Reliance Rivals Vow to Play Nice," *Wall Street Journal,* May 24, 2010, *http://online.wsj.com/article/SB10001424052748704226004575262281639883648.html.*

9. "Facts and Perspectives on Family Business Around the World: United States," Family Business Institute, *www.ffi.org/looking/fbfacts_us.pdf.*

10. Ibid.

11. Ibid.

12. Peter Schworm, "End of a 378-Year Era," *Boston.com,* July 27, 2010, *www.boston.com/news/local/new_hampshire/articles/2010/07/27/nations_oldest_running_family_farm_put_on_market_in_nh/.*

13. *Kin in the Game,* PriceWaterhouseCoopers Family Business Survey, 2010–2011, p. 21.

14. Ibid.

15. "Facts and Perspectives on Family Business Around the World: United States," Family Business Institute, *www.ffi.org/looking/fbfacts_us.pdf.*

16. Sharon Nelton, "Ten Keys to Success in Family Business," *Nation's Business,* April 1991, pp. 44–45.

17. Toddi Gunter, "Moving Up to the Top of a Family Empire," *Wall Street Journal,* June 22, 2010, p. D4.

18. "Family Members Fight over Control of Texas Pete Hot Sauce Empire," *Greenville News,* May 17, 1997, p. 11D.

19. Stein, "The Age of the Scion," p. 124.

20. Eugenia Levenson, "Road Warrior," *Fortune,* November 27, 2006, p. 276; Hsiao-Ching Chao, "Maximilian Riedel Has the Stemware Industry in the Palm of His Hand," *Seattle Post-Intelligencer,* April 13, 2005, *http://seattlepi.nwsource.com/food/219827_riedel13.html;* Anthony Giglio, "Glass Menagerie," *Boston Magazine,* April 2006, *www.bostonmagazine.com/dining_food_wine/articles/boston_magazine_liquids_specialty_wineglasses/.*

21. Stein, "The Age of the Scion," p. 124.

22. Mike Armstrong, "PhillyInc: There's a Twist in the Pennsylvania Pretzel-Merger Saga," *Philly.com,* July 23, 2010, *www.philly.com/philly/business/homepage/20100723_PhillyInc__There_s_a_twist_in_the_Pennsylvania_pretzel-merger_saga.html.*

23. Bo Burlingham, "Why a CEO Needs to Have a Plan B," *Inc.,* May 2009, *www.inc.com/magazine/20090501/why-a-ceo-needs-to-have-a-plan-b.html.*

24. "Employee Ownership and Corporate Performance," National Center for Employee Ownership, *www.nceo.org/library/esop_perf.html.*

25. Paul J. Lim, "Putting Your House in Order," *U.S. News & World Report,* December 10, 2001, p. 38.

26. Lydia Dishman, "Keys to the Kingdom," *Black Box,* Quarter 1, 2010, pp. 67–71.

27. Claire Cain Miller, "Chapter Two," *Forbes,* December 25, 2006, p. 72.

28. Carol Tice, "Lost in Transition," *Entrepreneur,* November 2006, p. 102.

29. TCPN Quotations Center, *www.cyber-nation.com/victory/quotations/subject/quotes_subjects_f_to_h.html#f.*

30. Andy Bluestone, "Succession Planning Isn't Just About Money," *Nation's Business,* November 1996, p. 6.

31. Shelly Branch, "Mom Always Liked You Best," *Your Company,* April/May 1998, pp. 26–38.

32. Taylor, "Small Businesses Show Relative Strength," pp. 22, 24.

33. Patricia Schiff Estess, "Heir Raising," *Entrepreneur,* May 1996, pp. 80–82.

34. Tice, "Lost in Transition," pp. 101–103.

35. Jacquelyn Lynn, "What Price Successor?" *Entrepreneur,* November 1999, p. 146.

36. Craig E. Aronoff and John L. Ward, "Why Continue Your Family Business," *Nation's Business,* March 1998, pp. 72–74.

37. Jeremy Quittner, "Creating a Legacy," *BusinessWeek,* June 25, 2007, *www.businessweek.com/magazine/content/07_26/b4040443.htm?chan=search.*

38. Lee Smith, "The Next Generation," *Your Company,* October 1999, pp. 36–46.

39. "New Nationwide Survey Points to Bright Spot in American Economy—Family-Owned Businesses," MassMutual Financial Group, *www.massmutual.com/mmfg/about/pr_2003/01_22_03.html.*

40. Brett Pulley, "Murdoch Son Also Rises as Shareholders Study CEO Succession," *Bloomberg,* October 22, 2010, *www.bloomberg.com/news/2010-10-22/murdoch-son-also-rising-as-shareholders-focus-on-news-corp-ceo-succession.html.*

41. Annetta Miller, "You Can't Take It with You," *Your Company,* April 1999, pp. 28–34.

42. "Family Business Facts," Family Business Institute.

43. Frank Silverstein, "Daddy's Cowgirl Takes Over the Rodeo Business," MSNBC, August 30, 2009, *www.msnbc.msn.com/id/32573940/ns/business-small_business;* Courtney Elam, "Kirsten Vold," Harry Vold Rodeo Company, *www.harryvoldrodeo.com/staff.html.*

44. John Warrillow, "Leave the Business to the Kids? Maybe Not," *Wall Street Journal,* June 10, 2010, *http://online.wsj.com/article/SB10001424052748704575304575296523166009344.html.*

45. Karen E. Klein, "Succession Planning Without an Heir," *BusinessWeek,* June 20, 2007, *www.businessweek.com/smallbiz/content/jun2007/sb20070620_135303.htm?chan=search.*

46. Sharon Nelton, "Why Women Are Chosen to Lead," *Nation's Business,* April 1999, p. 51.

47. "New Nationwide Survey Points to Bright Spot in American Economy—Family-Owned Businesses," MassMutual Financial Group.

48. Dick Patten, "The Death Tax Is Killing Family Businesses," *Daily Caller,* October 8, 2010, *http://dailycaller.com/2010/10/08/the-death-tax-is-killing-family-businesses/;* Amanda Hill, "Estate Taxes Could Mean 'Death' of Family Farms and Ranches," *Texas Agriculture News,* September 27, 2010, *www.nodeathtax.org/news/estate-tax-could-mean-death-of-family-farms-and-ranches.*

49. Brad Hamilton and Jeane MacIntosh, "Death'$ Perfect Timing," *New York Post,* July 14, 2010, *www.nypost.com/p/news/local/death_perfect_timing_NusLyGlMu8cn8kyepprVJP?CMP=OTC-rss&FEEDNAME=.*

50. Patten, "The Death Tax Is Killing Family Businesses."

51. Quittner, "Creating a Legacy."

52. Joan Szabo, "Spreading the Wealth," *Entrepreneur,* July 1997, pp. 62–64.

53. Gay Jervey, "Family Ties," *FSB,* March 2006, p. 60.

54. Ibid.; Tom Herman, "Court Ruling Bolsters Estate Planning Tool," *Wall Street Journal,* May 27, 2004, p. D1.

55. Quittner, "Creating a Legacy."

56. William J. Dennis, "National Small Business Poll: Disasters," *National Federation of Independent Businesses,* 2004, Vol. 4, No. 5, pp. 5–6.

57. Joseph King, "Disasters Highlight Need for Business Continuity Planning," Institute for Business & Home Safety, September 7, 2010, *www.disastersafety.org/newsroom/view.asp?id=13291&Mode=List;* Emily Maltby, "Readying for the Worst," *Wall Street Journal,* September 9, 2009, *http://online.wsj.com/article/SB125250249415695553.html.*

58. Daniel Tynan, "In Case of Emergency," *Entrepreneur,* April 2003, p. 60.

59. Sarah E. Needleman, "Lights Out Means Lost Sales," *Wall Street Journal,* July 22, 2010, p. B6.

60. Elizabeth Hockerman, "When to Self-Insure?" *Small Business Times,* May 12, 2006, *www.biztimes.com/news/2006/5/12/when-to-self-insure.*

61. Jeanne Lee and Brandi Stewart, "Build Your Own Insurance Company," *FSB,* September 2007, pp. 28–31.

62. Tiana Velez, "A Home Business Needs Insurance," *Arizona Daily Star,* June 5, 2006, *www.azstarnet.com/allheadlines/132077.*

63. Kimberly Lankford, "Weird Insurance," *Kiplinger's Personal Finance Magazine*, October 1998, pp. 113–116.
64. "Costa Coffee Taster: One of the 10 Weirdest Insurance Policies," *The Telegraph*, March 9, 2009, *www.telegraph.co.uk/finance/personalfinance/insurance/specialrisks/4962817/Costa-Coffee-taster-Ten-of-the-weirdest-insurance-policies.html;* "Costa's Coffee Taster Has Tongue Insured for £10 Million," *The Telegraph*, March 9, 2009, *www.telegraph.co.uk/foodanddrink/foodanddrinknews/4957333/Costa-Coffees-taster-has-tongue-insured-for-10-million.html.*
65. John Fried, "Having Fun Yet?" *Inc.*, March 2006, pp. 75–77; "Incredible Adventures: Our Story," Incredible Adventures, *www.incredible-adventures.com/about_us.html;* Esther Dyson, "I Live and Die by Waivers," Esther Dyson's Flight School, May 11, 2007, *www.edventure.com/flightschool/blog/?p=4.*
66. Joyce M. Rosenberg, "Preparing a Disaster Plan Gets Serious," *Los Angeles Times,* August 16, 2007, *www.latimes.com/business/la-fi-smalldisaster16aug16,1,4272739.story?coll=la-headlines-business&ctrack=1&cset=true;* "Famed Restaurant Reopens Today," *Greenville News*, October 1, 2006, p. 4B.
67. Larry Kanter, "Smart Questions for Your Insurance Agent," *Inc.*, August 2006, p. 40; Michele Marchetti, "Thrown Off Track," *FSB*, February 2004, pp. 66–69.
68. Heidi Ernst, "The Best Line of Defense," Advertising Insert, *FSB*, July/August 2007, p. 80.
69. Jan Norman, "Business Disaster Can Strike at Any Time," *Greenville News*, April 4, 2004, p. E1.
70. Ilan Mochari, "A Security Blanket for Your Web Site," *Inc.*, December 2000, pp. 133–134.
71. Andrew Smyth, "Council for Disability Awareness Launches Consumer Website," *The Insurance Policy*, November 3, 2006, *www.theinsurancepolicy.com/new_insurance_agents/disability_insurance/.*
72. "Issues: Health Care Reform," National Federation of Independent Businesses, *www.nfib.com/issues-elections/healthcare.*
73. Kate Pickert, "The Unsustainable U.S. Healthcare System," *Time,* February 4, 2010, *http://swampland.blogs.time.com/2010/02/04/the-unsustainable-u-s-health-care-system/;* "Health Care Insurance Costs," National Coalition on Health Care, *www.nchc.org/facts/cost.shtml.*
74. *Employer Health Benefits 2010 Summary of Findings*, Kaiser Family Foundation and Health Research and Educational Trust, p. 5.
75. Ibid., p. 40.
76. Daniel Wityk, "Small Business Health Insurance," National Center for Policy Analysis, February 11, 2009, p. 1.
77. Eileen Figure Sandlin, "Finding Health Insurance as a Start-up," *Entrepreneur*, October 2006, *www.entrepreneur.com/management/insurance/typesofinsurance/article168504.html.*
78. *Intuit Payroll Survey 2009*, Intuit, *http://quickbooks.blogs.com/Intuit%20Payroll%20Survey%20-%20One%20Sheet.pdf*, p. 3.
79. Sarah E. Needleman, "Burger Chain's Health Care Recipe," *Wall Street Journal*, August 31, 2009, *http://online.wsj.com/article/SB125149100886467705.html.*
80. *Employer Health Benefits 2010 Survey*, Kaiser Family Foundation and Health Research and Educational Trust, p. 62.
81. Ibid., p. 15.
82. "Census Shows 8 Million People Covered by HSA/High-Deductible Health Plans," America's Health Insurance Plans, Center for Policy Research, January 2009, p. 4; *Behind the Numbers: Medical Cost Trends for 2010*, PriceWaterhouseCoopers, Health Research Institute, 2010, p. 7.
83. Colleen DeBaise, "Small Business Owners Try HSAs to Trim Health Costs," *Smart Money*, July 6, 2007, *www.smartmoney.com/smallbiz/index.cfm?story=20060511.*
84. "Workers' Compensation Insurance: The Role of State Funds, Market Trends, and Economic Influences," Insurance Information Institute, October 12, 2010, p. 16.
85. Greg O'Claray, "Alaska Needs Workers' Compensation Reform Now," National Federation of Independent Businesses, March 14, 2005, *www.nfib.com/object/IO_20952.html.*
86. Aaron Dalton, "Best Practices: Rapid Recovery," *IndustryWeek*, March 1, 2005, *www.industryweek.com/ReadArticle.aspx?ArticleId=10001.*
87. "Litigiousness," Insurance Information Institute, 2010, *www.iii.org/facts_statistics/litigiousness.html.*
88. Marc Fisher, "Judge Who Seeks Millions for Lost Pants Has His (Emotional) Day in Court," *Washington Post*, June 13, 2007, *www.washingtonpost.com/wp-dyn/content/article/2007/06/12/AR2007061201667.html;* "Dry Cleaner Raises Enough Cash to Pay Legal Fees," *WUSA9.com*, August 13, 2007, *www.wusa9.com/news/news_article.aspx?storyid=61690.*
89. "Employment Practices Liability Awareness Lacking for Some Small Business Owners," InsuranceNewsNet, February 3, 2010, *http://insurancenewsnet.com/article.aspx?id=157763.*
90. "Employment Law: Jury Awards, Trends, and Statistics," Thomas Fenner Woods Agency, November 2010, *www.tfwinsurance.com/news/11_2010/nl_employeem_9.php.*
91. "Employment Practices Liability Insurance for Restaurants," Restaurant Association of Maryland, October 2009, *www.marylandrestaurants.com/membership/foodserv_benefits/documents/09-199RAMEPLforRestaurants.pdf.*
92. Ilan Mochari, "Bug Your Broker," *Inc.*, August 2000, pp. 127–128.
93. Patricia B. Gray, "Health Care," *FSB*, February 2009, pp. 57–65.
94. Susan Caminiti, "Keeping America Fit," *Fortune*, May 3, 2010, p. S1.
95. Patricia F. Weisberg, "Wellness Programs: Legal Requirements and Risks," *Workforce Management*, March 2010, *www.workforce.com/section/legal/feature/wellness-programs-legal-requirements-risks/.*
96. Karene Spaeder, "Shape Up," *Entrepreneur*, September 2008, p. 26.

ge references followed by "f" indicate illustrated
ures or photographs; followed by "t" indicates a
le.

Children's Online Privacy Protection Act (COPPA)
  legislation, 127, 456, 482, 530
  social networking, 13, 187, 315-316

300-FLOWERS, 431

20
  competitive advantage, 477
  Web, 55-56, 144, 493

, 348

A) loan guaranty program, 134

11
  freedom and, 276
  tourism, 76

Basic Guide to Exporting, 60
AA, 339, 521
ARON, 166-167, 221, 262, 475, 536
ARP, 317
andonment rate, 191-192
3C News, 81, 432
3C system, 355
bercrombie, 296
bstract, 111, 266
usive language, 455
ccelerated depreciation
  effects of, 438
cceptable sample error
  determining, 9, 86, 342, 465
cceptance
  mailbox rule, 427
  mirror image rule, 427
  time of, 48, 426
ccess to raw materials
  differential, 124
ccident prevention
  safety audit, 532
ccidents
  examples of, 302
  preventing, 294
  reducing, 529
  workers' compensation costs, 527
CCION International, 137
ccountability
  of employees, 468-469
  team, 169, 328-329
ccounting
  balance of payments, 47
  control and, 169, 368
  corporate governance, 502
  future of, 502
  multinational, 46
  standards for, 456
ccounting information
  consistency, 19, 311, 432, 485
  relevance, 322, 379, 524
ccounting measures
  adjusted, 354
  limitations, 9
ccounting performance

ratios, 120
Accounting principles
  controller, 367
  cost of goods sold, 102, 225, 365
  depreciation, 100-101, 235
  financial statements, 101, 511
  fixed assets, 139
  inventory turnover ratio, 365
  leverage, 39, 305
  liabilities, 504
  merchandise inventory, 356
  operating expenses, 100
  retained earnings, 140
  return on equity, 325
  selling expenses, 102
  working capital, 139, 168, 234
Accounting system
  mechanics of, 46
Accounts
  Merchandise Inventory, 356
Accounts receivable
  credit policies, 141
  discounting, 111, 123
  extending credit, 65
  factoring, 140-141
  turnover ratio, 119, 379
  uncollectible, 123
accounts receivable (A/R)
  as collateral, 108, 120
  pledging, 118
Accounts-receivable management
  terms of sale, 256
Accredited investors, 174
Ace, 134
Ace Hardware, 134
Acquisitions
  unfriendly, 169
ACS, 40, 266
Activity times
  variability in, 365
Ad copy, 25
Adams, Scott, 473
AddMenu action
  changes to, 80
Address Verification System (AVS), 108
Adec Group, 339, 474
Adidas, 296, 450
Adjusted R-square
  Equation, 282, 363
Adler, Carlye, 122
Administrative agencies
  hybrid, 128
  local, 16, 52, 113-114, 189-190, 304, 317, 372, 448
Administrative costs
  allocating, 450
Administrative issues under collective bargaining
  seniority, 231, 368
Administrator, 146, 430
Admiral, 164
Advance rate, 122-123
Advance rates, 123
Advent, 51
adverse selection and market for "lemons"
  financial markets, 114, 158
Adverse supply shock
  temporary, 86, 433
advertisement
  headline, 32
  proof, 32
Advertising
  advertising campaign, 9-10, 473
  banner, 22, 184
  Blog, 14, 185, 315, 535
  campaign, 2, 473
  clutter, 2-3, 210
  contextual, 22-23
  co-op, 262

cooperative, 22, 262
  costs of, 15, 54, 94, 173, 184
  creep, 367
  disadvantages, 1, 163, 354, 502-503
  display ads, 22-23
  efficiency of, 80, 184
  ethics in, 472
  global markets, 54-55, 184
  green, 8, 210, 301, 353
  history of, 175
  informational, 24
  interactive display, 34
advertising
  Internet-based, 262, 353
  legal environment, 425-427
Advertising
  nature of, 9, 175, 365, 455, 475
  Outdoor, 5
  privacy and, 107, 181
  Product placement, 5
  profitability and, 474
  regulations and, 29
  reminder, 26
  reminder ads, 26
  rule of thumb for, 36
  self-esteem, 2
  socially responsible, 175, 187, 474-475
  specialty, 9, 365, 535
  strengths of, 182
  Super Bowl, 15-16, 182
  target audience, 3
  transit, 27, 365
  unwanted, 189
  Viral, 14
Advertising appeals
  fear, 10, 186
  humor, 188
  music, 13, 211
  sex, 494
Advertising budget methods
  objective and task, 35
Advertising campaign management
  advertising budget, 1
Advertising campaigns, 2
advertising expenditures, 9-10
Advertising management
  advertising agencies, 17, 164
Advertising media
  outdoor advertising, 28-29
  point-of-purchase ads, 27
  specialty advertising, 26-27
  transit advertising, 30
Advertising media selection
  international markets, 54, 503
  outdoor, 5, 276-277, 508
advertising medium, 10-11, 182, 473
Advertising objectives
  continuity, 10, 498
  cost per thousand (CPM), 11
Advertising, online
  affiliate marketing, 199
  banners, 22
  chat rooms, 196
  video ads, 21
  viral marketing, 14
Advertising plan, 9
Advisory board, 150, 508
Advocate, 465
Advocates, 363
Aesthetics
  visual, 300-301
Affiliate marketing, 199
Affordable method, 35
Afghanistan, 52
Aflac, 528
AFLAC Inc., 528
AFL-CIO

negotiations, 74-76
Africa
  Egypt, 66
  Nigeria, 65
  South, 46
  South Africa, 66
  Zimbabwe, 44
After-tax earnings, 128
Age, consumer identity
  baby boomers, 94
Age discrimination
  damages, 453, 486, 530
  E.E.O.C., 321, 485-486, 530
  justification, 451, 529
agencies
  for small business, 454
  regulatory, 448-449
Agency
  apparent, 444
  independent contractors, 444
  theory, 44
Agency costs
  of debt, 115-117
  options and, 178-179
agency funds
  accounting for, 72, 139, 444
  financial statements for, 175
  simpler, 159
agents
  exporting, 53-54
  limitations on, 56, 532
  property and casualty insurance, 521-522
  registered, 438
  report, 474, 535
  special, 66, 521
Aggregate demand
  fluctuations in, 62, 151
  inflation, 47, 91
Aggregate demand curve
  interest rates and, 138
Aggregate expenditure
  equation for, 282
Aggregate functions
  Count, 15
Aggregate money demand
  interest rate and, 137
Aggregate planning
  discussion questions, 144, 218, 380, 457, 534
aggregate supply
  curve , 353
aggression, 279
Agile, 249-250, 310
aging, 94, 267, 347, 473
Agreements
  bilateral, 47
Agreement(s)
  consensus, 75
Agreements
  franchise, 80
  GATS, 76
  GATT, 76
  licensing, 78, 450-451
  limited partnerships, 533
Agricultural products
  in world trade, 53
AIDS Discrimination
  company policy, 371, 485
  defamation, 480
  disclosure, 455
  educational program, 482
  invasion of privacy, 480
AIDS in the workplace, 482
Air pollutants
  carbon monoxide, 456
  ozone, 456
air pollution
  toxic, 477
airline pilots, 135
AIS access-based strategic position
  cookie, 76, 424
  threats, 45, 346, 455
Akamai, 194
Alabama International Trade Center, 146
Alar and the apple industry
  public perception of, 490
Alaska, 22, 527
Alba, Jessica, 243
Albania, 225
Alcohol abuse, 480

Alcoholism, 481
Aldi, 293
Alexander, Jan, 10, 81
Algorithm, 202
Ali, Junab, 515
Alien, 16, 45, 519
Allen, Barbara, 442
Allen, Paul, 274
Alliance of Merger and Acquisition Advisors, 507
Almay, 57, 273
Alper, Keith, 531
Alsever, Jennifer, 307, 343
Altany, David, 75
Alternative courses of action, 465
Alternatives
  brainstorming, 342
Alzheimer's disease, 429
Amazon
  business model, 190, 438, 502-503
  competition, 2-3, 88-89, 190
  patents, 437-438
Amazon.com
  benchmarking, 231
  domain names, 207-208
  fiscal year, 145-146
  market leader, 94
  net profit, 119, 360
Amazon.com annual report, notes
  long-term debt, 128
America Online (AOL)
  pricing strategy, 95-96
American Apparel, 204
American Association for the Advancement of Science
  global warming, 455
American Association of Retired Persons (AARP), 317
American Chemistry Council (ACC)
  evaluation of, 251
  target audiences, 15
American Community Survey, 266
American depositary receipts (ADRs)
  advantages and disadvantages, 251
  sponsored, 58
American Life Project, 200
American Marketplace: Demographics and Spending
    Patterns, 267-268
American Pearl, 209
American Red Cross, 490
Americans with Disabilities Act
  reasonable accommodations, 293
Americans with Disabilities Act (ADA)
  drug testing, 478
  employee compensation, 306
  essential functions, 293
  mental disabilities, 322
AMEX Products, Inc
  bank statement, 469
Amherst, 4
Amoral management, 466-467
Amortization schedule, 120
Analysis
  break-even, 102, 144, 178, 281
  external, 202, 232, 304
  gap, 260
  process capability, 232
  process for, 304
  profitability, 226, 465-466, 512
  SWOT, 79
Analysis of variance
  Assumptions, 144, 178
Analysis of variance (ANOVA)
  assumptions, 144, 178
  Excel and, 513
Analysis, SWOT, 79
Analyzing
  transactions, 107
Anchors, 284-285
Anderson, Chris, 352
Anderson, Mae, 146
Anderson, Ronald, 498
Angel Capital Association, 179
Angel financing, 154
Angel investor, 154
angel investors, 150, 290
angel networks, 157
Angels, 147
Annual cost, 235
Annual dollar usage volume, 355-356
Annual interest, 123, 242
Annual report, 40, 145, 489

Anonymity, 156, 199
Antidumping Act, 71
Antidumping laws, 71
Antinori, 499
Antitrust Division of the Justice Department
  trade practices, 448-449
Antitrust law
  The Clayton Act, 450-452
Antitrust laws
  enforcement of, 472
  exemptions from, 173
  price discrimination and, 452
  Sherman Act, 451
antitrust laws, U.S.
  Sherman Antitrust Act, 449-450, 490
Appearance Plus, 5
Appel, Timothy, 105
Apple
  iTunes, 96
  penetration pricing, 94
Applicants
  attracting, 317, 480
Applications and infrastructure of e-commerce
  tools for, 74, 196, 227, 516
Applied regression analysis
  documentation, 131-132
Appraisal methods, problems with
  unclear standards, 342
Appraisal system, 343-344
Appreciation
  rate of, 186
apprenticeship, 486
Arbitron, 40
Arc elasticity
  revenue and, 108
archive, 347, 459
Archives, 40, 145, 307, 535
Area development, 59
Aristotle, 80, 464
Arizona, 13, 51, 89, 116, 150, 323, 449, 518
ARM, 294
Arrangements
  surety, 523
Arrivals, 24
Arsenal, 376
Article 2 (Sales), of UCC
  Statute of Frauds, 433
Artisans, 85, 476
artwork, 114
Ashoka, 474
Asia
  Japan, 75
  South Korea, 75
Asia-Pacific, 75
Aspen Family Business Conference, 499
Assault, 323
Assent
  genuineness of, 425
  voluntary, 429
Asset management rms
  pension funds, 128
Asset market approach
  difficulties, 371
Asset-backed securities (ABS)
  credit risks, 139
Asset/liability management
  financial institutions, 128, 506
Assets
  acquisitions of, 128
  alternative, 139, 177
  bank, 117, 515
  capital, 57, 117-118, 150-152, 366, 447, 524
  cost of, 45-46, 124, 176-177, 365, 448-449, 516
  disposal of, 456
  financing, 56, 117-128, 150-152
  investment, 57, 117, 177-178, 365
  liquid, 123, 447
  liquidating, 366
  long-term, 56, 120, 152, 524
  loss of, 57, 177, 367, 523-524
  net, 119, 150, 366
  operating, 46, 117, 365, 447-448, 517
  quick, 137
  replacing, 45, 522
  risk of, 140, 152, 524
  risky, 45, 117, 518
  savings and loan associations, 126
Asset(s)
  turnover, 365-366

sets (A)
missing, 515
sets, banking
commercial banks, 117
sociation of Certified Fraud Examiners, 366-367
sociation of Retired Persons (AARP), 317
sortment
depth of, 300
merchandise, 299
surance of Learning Exercises
Chapter 11, 83
Chapter 2, 497
ymmetric information
markets with, 55-56
mosphere
retail stores, 282-283
mospherics, 41
&T Small Business Lending, 125
ackers, 215
ctions, online
price transparency, 189
dience
Active, 15
Brand equity, 2
Consumers, 2, 183-184
Development, 10, 143-145
Expectations, 182
dience
expectations of, 182
dience
Identity, 184
Involvement, 17
Mass, 10
Measured, 2
dience
offending, 199
dience
Participants, 34
Participation, 15, 471
Passive, 29
Segmentation, 19, 305
dience
skeptical, 2
ditor's opinions
qualified, 64
thority
functional, 328, 508
on the job, 231, 333, 444, 472
scope of, 443, 513
thorization
of sales, 365
to insurance
deductible, 536
fraud, 107, 142, 366, 425, 473
low-cost, 288-289
to insurance policies, 523
tocratic, 310
tomobile industry
franchising, 49, 264
tomobile production
redesign, 229, 524
vailability of capital, 148
veda, 476
verage annual returns
of securities, 169
verage collection period, 119
verage expenditure
curve, 237, 353
verage inventory, 119, 235-236, 351
verage life, 498
verage inventory turnover ratio, 119, 351
verage payable period ratio, 119
verage products
production process and, 104
very, 356
xe, 437

2B (Business-to-Business) e-commerce
business models, 189
supply chain management and, 350
AA, 521
accarat, 445
ack office, 72, 194
ackground checks
effectiveness of, 29-30
improving, 232, 532
methods of, 107, 143, 358
ag Borrow or Steal, 5

Bag, Borrow Or Steal, 5
Bail, 194
Bain & Co., 325
Baker, Sherry, 466
Bakery, 4, 126, 185, 292, 424
Bakhash, Eddie, 209
Balance of payment accounts
international trade and, 79
balance of payments
capital account, 118
Balance of payments (BOP)
basics of, 318, 443-444
Balance sheets
pro forma, 144
Baldrige Award, 261
Baldrige, Malcolm, 261
Balk, 48, 481
Balking, 132
Ball, Deborah, 306
Bamboo Lingerie, 37
Band of Angels, 157
Banding, 532
bands, 310, 351
Bank confirmation
receipt, 66
Bank draft, 66
Bank failures
in Japan, 46
Bank financing, 124
Bank for International Settlements (BIS)
structure of, 159, 450
bank loans
lines of credit, 117-118
Bank loans
money and, 5, 116, 149
Bank statement, 370, 469
Bank statements, 372
Bankers Association for Foreign Trade, 65
Banking
crises, 114
Banking, and stock markets
branches, 78, 291
equity capital, 124, 147
loan portfolios, 125
nontraditional, 144, 178, 278, 325, 480
banking crisis, 114
Bankruptcy
bankruptcy code, 446
exemptions, 446
bankruptcy
involuntary, 446
small business, 154, 423, 530-531
Banks
loans from, 114
loans of, 114
private, 65-66, 115-116, 148-149, 294
run, 107, 131, 169, 287, 505-506
savings, 116, 147, 296
statements, 121-122, 170, 506
banner ads
ineffective, 10, 427
Bar codes, 359
Barclays, 502
Bargaining process
later stages, 164
Barlow, Stephanie, 75, 122
Barnes & Noble, 89, 255, 293
Barneys, 94, 204
Barneys New York, 94
Barone Ricasoli, 499
Barovier & Toso, 499
Barrett, Amy, 347
Barriers
international trade, 43-44
to exporting, 60-63
Barriers created by government
licenses, 54
patents and copyrights, 442
barriers to entry
economies of scale, 94
Barriers to trade
elimination of, 76
Bartholomew, Doug, 262
Bartley, Christian, 64
Base pay
purchasing power, 241, 281
Baseball
Major League Baseball, 450
baseball players

salaries, 315, 451
Basel II
collateral, 133
Baseline project plan (BPP), developing
management issues, 261, 381
Basic assumptions, 73
Basic seven (B7) tools of quality
control charts, 232-233
Pareto charts, 232
Baskin-Robbins, 278
Bass, 251
BATNA (Best Alternative to a Negotiated Agreement)
reality and, 270
Battery, 52
Battle of the forms, 433
Bay, 53, 291
Bayesian analysis
advantages and disadvantages of, 144, 251, 352, 506
BBBOnLine, 189
BBC, 262
BBC News, 262
Beacon, 272
Beauty, 16, 73, 111, 127, 297, 498
behavior modification
punishment, 342
behavioral biases
investors, 461-463
believability, 485
Bell, David, 192
Bell Telephone, 154
Beltone Electronics Corporation, 509
Beneficiaries
income, 515-516
remainder, 515
trusts, 515-516
Benefit and safety programs
safety programs, 531
Benefits
contingent, 316
cuts in, 381
extended, 72, 126, 279, 447, 482
for small businesses, 52-54, 124, 184, 269, 313, 379, 446, 519
holidays, 208, 381
sick leave, 482
survivor, 220
Benefits (indirect financial compensation)
autonomy, 335, 508
flextime, 335-336
job sharing, 325, 482
part-time work, 325, 482
preferred provider organization (PPO), 526
relocation, 306
sabbaticals, 325
skill variety, 335
task identity, 335
task significance, 335
telecommuting, 317-318
workers' compensation, 294, 444, 521
Benefits (of strategic management)
Of a diverse workforce, 479
Benefits program
employee input, 532
employment laws, 530
legally required, 487
Benioff, Mark, 128
Bennett Infiniti Inc., 40
Bennett, Jamey, 255
Bennett, Rob, 27
Bertagnoli, Lisa, 348
Best efforts, 172, 518
Best efforts agreement, 172
Best practices, 193, 231, 332, 360-361, 479
Best Practices of Private Sector Employers, 479
Beta distribution
variance, 276
Better Business Bureau (BBB)
learning from, 221, 486
BetterWeb, 214
Bezos, Jackie, 154
Bhatnagar, Parija, 306
Bicycles, 48-49
Bid, 23, 203, 430
bid price, 203, 430
Bids, 203, 447
Big Brother, 343
Big City Mountaineers, 5
"Big Mac index"

Bloomberg, 111, 302, 381, 535
International Monetary Fund, 44
OECD, 268
SmartMoney, 536
World Bank, 67
Bike, 48, 428, 467
Bill of lading, 66
Billboard, 28, 200
Billing, 108, 140, 194, 228, 455
bills of exchange
checks, 372, 518
parties to, 425
Bills of lading
clean, 66
order, 32, 66, 372, 512
straight, 446
Bing, 23, 203
Binomial distribution
Characteristics, 49, 253, 274-275, 359, 510
Standard deviation, 245
standard deviation of, 245
biotechnology, 162
Bird, 85
Birth control, 71, 437
Biz, 122, 155, 208, 347-348, 459
Black Enterprise, 529
Black-Scholes
formula, 327
Blanepain, 88
Bloch, Michael, 111
Blockbuster, 464
Blocked funds
moving, 96, 360
Blogger, 220
blogging
tips for, 221
Blogs
advertising on, 17
Blogs
building, 187, 314, 458
educational, 15, 316, 536
blogs
Focus on, 16, 180, 189-190
blogs/blogging
search engines for, 203
tone of, 187
Bloom, 180
Blue Cross and Blue Shield
HMOs, 526
PPOs, 526
Blue Gecko, 336
Blue Jeans Cable, 193
Blue laws, 429
Blue Nile, 199
Blue Ship Tea Room, 436
Bluestone, Andy, 508
board of directors
insiders, 172, 504
outsiders, 504
Boards of directors
function of, 203
body
of messages, 25
Body of knowledge, 509
Boeing Company
break-even point, 110, 144, 281
Bond
option, 126-127
Bond markets
differences among, 11, 147
emerging markets, 44
Bonds
conversion, 127
fidelity, 523
issuing, 127-128
maturity of, 128
mortgage, 126-127, 266
payment, 125
revenue bonds, 128
risks associated with, 523
Bones, 436
Boniface, Russell, 307
Bonney, Tom, 314
Bono, 106, 474
bonuses
annual, 167, 187, 313
Book value
per share, 171
Bootstrapping, 153

Bork, David, 499
Bose, 364
Bose Corporation, 364
Boundaries, 49, 138, 268, 328, 463
Bounds, Gwendolyn, 146
BP, 146, 282
BP Oil, 146
Brainstorming
alternatives, 342
Branch, Shelly, 535
Brand
characters, 25
crisis, 176
dilution, 177
equity, 2, 136, 148-150, 475
promise, 270
slogans, 25
brand loyalty, 2, 94
Brand manager, 135
Brand names
defending, 441
Brand recognition, 185
Branding
Cities, 40
Interactive, 40
On the web, 39
strategy, 37-39, 494
Brands
Destination, 284, 363
Brand(s)
life cycle, 94-95
Brands
private-label, 353
Brand(s)
sponsorship, 15
undifferentiated, 92
Brands/branding
exclusive, 98
Bravo, 251-252
Brazil
exchange rates, 61
Breach
material, 424
of contract, 424
of sales contracts, 434
of warranty, 435-436
Breach of sales contracts, 434
Break-even analysis
fixed costs, 46, 101-103, 278, 506
variable costs, 101-103
Break-even point
calculation of, 306
in units, 110
Bredin, James, 75
Bregman Partners, 320
Bregman, Peter, 320
Brennan family, 522
Brick-and-mortar retailers, 183
Bricks-and-mortar
advertising and promotion, 1, 93
Briggs, John, 190
Brigham Young University, 161
Brin, Sergey, 149
British Petroleum (BP)
trademark, 46
Broadband
in the United States, 160
Broadcast media
product placement, 5
Brokerages, online
top online, 353
Brokers
commission, 530
securities, 126
Brown, Lieca, 231
Budget deficit
debt and, 128-129
budget deficits
of government, 129
Budgets
flexible, 317
static, 16
Budget(s) advertising
affordable, 5, 93, 264, 354
objective-and-task, 36
percentage-of-sales, 36
Budgets/budgeting
marketing communications, 36
top-down, 328

Buick, 426
Build-A-Bear Workshop, 128
Bulgari, 88, 204, 352
Bulk materials, 288
BULL, 148
Bulletin boards, 201-202, 291
Bunch, John, 87
Burden of proof, 321
Bureau of Labor Statistics (BLS)
Consumer Price Index, 528
Bureau of National Affairs, 55
Bureau of the Census, 40, 80, 266-267, 327
Bureaucrats, 67
Burlington Industries, 484
business
market segmentation, 19
Business
regulation, 152, 288, 424
Business and industry public relations
corporate social responsibility, 474
Business buyer behavior
e-procurement, 249
Business cycle(s)
forecasts of, 267
severity of, 215, 314, 521
Business environment
data in, 268, 354
driving forces, 478
Business environment boundaries, redefining
corporate
core competencies, 189
business ethics
government regulation, 71, 288, 424-425
Business failures, 498
Business financing, 115, 154
business forms
business trust, 196
Business growth
challenges of, 167, 240
business incubators, 289-290
Business Insurance
business interruption insurance, 425, 523
Business intelligence (BI)
clustering, 275
Business, Internet use by, 162, 221
Business Loan Express, 135
Business loans, 114, 154
business model
diversity of, 72, 480
business models
social networks, 314
Business necessity, 323
Business overhead expense (BOE) insurance, 524
Business ownership
and venture capital, 143, 150
IPOs, 167-170
joint ventures, 54
start-up costs, 116, 159, 187, 278
succession plans, 499
Business ownership forms
joint venture, 54-55, 160
S corporations, 118
Business plan
financial plan, 80, 99-100
marketing plan, 93, 158
Business plan development
feasibility analysis, 506
Business plan elements
executive summary, 40, 80, 458
business plans
financial projections, 125, 176
lenders and investors, 148, 458
market analysis, 63, 282
business press, 306
Business process modeling notation (BPMN)
standard for, 467
symbols, 5, 441-442
Business processes
cycle time, 229, 328, 428
documenting, 65
business record retention
filtering software, 463
for marketing, 36, 123, 150
Business scandals, 468
Business valuation
net worth, 128, 168
of accounts receivable, 122
Business Week, 111, 151, 290, 381, 507
Businesses

failure of, 224, 510
sinesses
  labor-intensive, 79
  reputation of, 453, 471
sinesses
  restructuring, 135, 482
siness-to-business (B2B) e-commerce
  dynamic pricing, 96
  social networking and, 221
siness-to-business (B2B) electronic commerce
  Electronic Data Interchange (EDI), 359
siness-to-business buying decision
  vendor selection, 225
siness-to-consumer (B2C) electronic commerce
  search engine marketing, 16, 201-202
ttons
  Create, 26, 204-208
yer preferences, 249
yers
  knowledgeable, 34
  remedies, 23, 434
  taxes, 505
ying
  impulse, 298
yout, 158, 504
y-sell agreement, 515
y-sell agreements, 533
zz marketing
  company employees, 507
laws, 511
product pricing, 98
-product pricing, 98
-products, 98, 476
tes, 381

bela's, 287
dbury, 58
fé in the Park, 253
AFTA, 75-76
ahners Research, 7
alamunci, John, 264
alculating data
  gross profit, 102
  net sales, 100
alifornia
  oil spill, 138
ll to action, 25
meras
  smart, 370
ampaign plan
  targeting, 3, 93, 203
amuffo, 499
anada
  NAFTA, 75-76
andidates for employment
  minorities, 137, 326
  older workers, 317
  succession planning and, 534
  telecommuters, 337
annibalize, 287
AN-SPAM Act, 25, 198
ap, 134, 298
apabilities
  complementary, 22
apacity
  flexibility, 17, 182, 253, 281
  safety, 280, 457
apital
  accounts, 65, 119, 153, 243, 367, 524
  availability of, 48, 114, 148, 190, 265
  borrowing, 114-115, 153, 365
  debt financing, 114, 168
  demand for, 61, 139, 172, 235
  equity financing, 114, 147-153
  excess, 62, 136, 366, 519
  fixed capital, 151-152
  flight, 306
  gains, 57, 175, 233, 504
  human, 177, 277, 314
  increase in, 141, 203, 306, 525
  investment and, 59, 233
  market for, 58, 169, 259, 274-275
  physical, 47, 121, 188, 266-267, 380
  quantities of, 176, 260
apital
  raising, 130, 148
  start-up, 115-118, 148, 204, 275, 315
apital

supply of, 234, 365-366, 446
venture, 47, 117, 147, 195, 266
Capital Access Programs (CAPs), 138
Capital allocation
  limits on, 120
Capital asset pricing model (CAPM)
  intuition, 314
  recipe for, 56, 99, 146, 367, 503
Capital budgeting
  cash flows, 117, 151, 234
  guidelines for, 195
  internal rate of return, 158
  risk and, 278
  risk in, 125, 504
Capital, invested, 128, 160-161, 266
capital investments, 114, 160
Capital market
  assumptions about, 178
Capital markets
  Western Europe, 68, 137
Capital mobility
  increases, 57, 127, 149, 233
capital projects fund (CPF)
  completion of, 43, 113, 147
Capital Projects Funds (CPFs)
  entries, 368
Capital punishment
  economics of, 176
Capital requirements
  small banks, 118
Capital stock
  audit of, 517
capital structure
  optimal, 274, 312
CAPLine program, 135
CAPS, 16, 138, 450-452
Captive-product pricing, 97
Carbaugh, Amos, 426
Carbon monoxide, 456
CARE
  duty of, 428
Career development
  performance appraisal system, 346
Career sites, 315
Careers in retailing
  E-commerce, 181-183
  public relations, 314-315
  researching, 266
Caribbean, 50, 137
Carlton, Brian, 149
Carnegie Mellon University, 214
Carolina Classic Boats, 51
carpal tunnel syndrome, 294
carpal tunnel syndrome (CTS), 294
Carrying costs
  of inventory, 223, 350-352
Cartier, 88
Case studies
  global strategy, 46
  in international business, 46, 199
  job performance, 321-322, 481
  location strategy, 274
Case study, industry/competition, forces bargaining
    power of buyers
  substitute products, 84, 225
Case Western University, 275
Cases
  Six Sigma, 260
Cash
  controlling, 163, 233, 352, 532
  profits and, 366
  requirements for, 534
  stock of, 354
Cash disbursements
  subsequent, 166, 241
Cash flow
  adjusting, 343
  challenges, 58, 107, 121, 155, 240, 328, 506
  discounted, 140, 242, 516
  employee theft, 235, 349
  net operating, 105-106
  parent, 149, 515
  terminal, 359-360
Cash flow cycle, 119
Cash flows
  relevant, 110, 144, 174, 250, 448
  uniform, 517
cash flows (C)
  stream of, 291, 504

Cash flows statements
  layout, 291-292, 350
Cash in advance, 65
Cash inflows
  variability of, 240
cash management
  business plans and, 162
  inventory and, 118-119, 194, 240, 352
Cash flows
  conservative, 117
Casualty insurance, 521-522
Catalyst, 136, 312
Catastrophic loss
  health insurance coverage, 528
Category
  extension, 284
Category killer, 285
Caterpillar Inc., 254
Caulfield, Brian, 262
Cause marketing, 5
caveat emptor, 435
caveat venditor, 435
CBS, 155, 312
CBS News, 40
C-commerce
  barriers to, 60
CDW, 337
CEIG, 149
Celebrities
  spokespersons, 4
Celebrity
  Global, 179-180
  Industry, 16, 179
Cell(s)
  range of, 30
Censorship, 463
Census, 40, 80, 266-268, 327
census data, 266
Census of Population
  drawbacks, 59
Center for Entrepreneurship, 176
Center for Systems Management, 256
Center for Venture Financing, 156
Central America
  Costa Rica, 65
  Mexico, 46
Central America Free Trade Agreement, 76
Central business district (CBD), 282-283
Central business districts, 281
CEOs (chief executive officers)
  blogs, 179-180, 347, 459
Certainty, 524
Certificates of deposits (CDs)
  small, 268-270, 373, 443
Certified development company (CDC), 136
CFM, 40-41, 111, 145-146, 180, 229, 307, 381, 445,
    494, 530
CFO, 99, 145, 254, 459, 467
CFR, 66
Chafkin, Max, 41, 213
Chamber of Commerce, 170, 252, 377, 532
Chanel, 5
Change program
  momentum, 232, 312, 510
Channel One, 17
Channel strategy
  members , 501
  movies, 16, 71
Channels
  arrangements, 159
  coordination, 363
Channels of distribution, 63, 94, 186
Chantecaille, 94
Chaplin, Heather, 155
Chappell, Tom, 467
Chapter 11 reorganization
  financial reporting, 169
Chapter 11 reorganization bankruptcy
  automatic stay, 446
  proceedings, 446-447
Chapter 13 adjustment of debts bankruptcy
  filing for, 444
Chapter 7 liquidation bankruptcy
  discharge, 456
Character loans, 121
Chargebacks, 216
Charismatic leadership
  consequences of, 465
  positive and negative, 343-344

Charitable organizations, 465
Charities, 187
Charts
    Line, 234
Chat, 188
Chat rooms, 196
checks
    certified, 371
    forged, 359
Checks and balances, 370
Cheesecake, 339
Cheesecake Factory, 339
Chelsea, 278
Chen, Steve, 169
Chevrolet, 289, 426
Chevron, 160
Chief executive officers (CEOs)
    tenure of, 478, 510
    vision of, 311, 511
Child Protection and Toy Safety Act, 452
Child support, 431
Children
    outsourcing, 68-69
Childs, Ted, 479
Chile, 44
Chilon, 463
China
    brokers, 58
    counterfeit products, 71, 437-438
    economic growth, 44
    exports, 44
    GDP, 45
    government regulations, 65
    hiring, 46, 464
    labor costs, 67-68
    piracy, 71, 246
    political environment, 47
    population, 44
    production in, 257
    tariffs on, 70
    trade agreements, 43
    trade and, 43-44
    trade with, 71
China's Ministry of Industry, 463
choice
    freedom of, 465
Chozick, Amy, 381
Chrysler Corporation
    job security, 339
    profit-sharing plans, 340
Château de Goulaine, 499
Chung, Soo, 529
Cigarette taxes, 280
Circuit City, 444
Cities
    competition in, 267
Civil Rights
    Act of 1964, 322, 482
    Act of 1991, 484
    business necessity, 323
    compensatory damages, 424-425, 486
    composition, 479
    discrimination, 321-323, 450, 482
    employer, 321, 444, 483-484
    punitive damages, 424-425, 484
    quantity, 223, 450
    Title VII, 482
Civil Rights Act
    of 1964, 322, 482
    of 1991, 484
Civil Rights Act of 1991 (CRA 1991)
    burden of proof, 321
Claims
    fraudulent, 434
    proof of, 7
    settlement, 446, 530
Claritas, 305
Clark, Elizabeth, 62
Clarke, Ted, 135
Clauses
    exculpatory, 429
Clayton Act
    Section 2, 96
Clayton Act (1914)
    Section 2 of, 96
Clayton, Sue, 10
Clean bill of lading, 66
Clearing, 10, 111, 487
Clearwire, 160-161

Cleveland Clinic, 275
Cleveland's, 275
click fraud, 23, 203
click through, 22
Click-through
    ratio, 144, 281, 365
Click-through rate, 22-23, 197-198
click-through rate (CTR), 213
Click-through rates, 40, 184
ClickZ, 193
Clifford, Stephanie, 146
Climate
    and customs, 46
Close substitute, 17
CMF Associates, 314
CNN
    video, 145
coaching
    active, 164
coal-burning power plants, 456
Coastal waters
    contamination, 455
Coats for Kids, 5
Coca-Cola Company
    trade barriers, 79
Codetermination, 46
Coding
    sheets, 354
Codorniu, 499
coffee shop example, monopolistically competitive firm
    demand curve, 109
Coleman, 381
Colera, Johnny, 264
collaboration
    web-based, 155-156
collateral
    personal guarantees, 118
    small businesses, 107-108, 115
Collection period, 119
collective bargaining
    items, 451
College recruiting for employment candidates
    internships, 315
college students
    credit cards and, 146
Colleges and universities, accounting for
    loan funds, 130
Color
    trade dress, 441
Column charts
    two-dimensional, 21
Colvin, Geoff, 93
Combo Box
    Wizard, 110
Comcast, 160
"comfort zone"
    constant, 52
    leaders, 311
comics, 21
Commerce Clearing House, 487
Commerce Department, 55, 129
Commerce metrics, 213
Commercial applications, 131
Commercial Atlas and Marketing Guide, 267-268
Commercial banks,, 117
Commercial Finance Association, 124
Commercial liability insurance (Continued)
    professional liability insurance, 522
Commercial loans, 118
Commercial mortgages, 120
Commercial Service International Contacts (CSIC)
    List, 55
commercial transactions
    credit card fraud, 107-108, 455
commercialization, 131
Commission of Architecture and the Built Environment, 294
Common market, 305
Common resources
    property rights and, 158
Common size financial statements
    income statement, 102
common stock
    limited liability, 122, 534
    nonvoting, 516
Common stock market
    stock exchanges, 169
Common thread, 330
Common-law doctrine

consideration in, 378
Communication
    and leadership, 310
    ethics and, 471-473
    flow of, 21, 227, 334
communication
    unified, 479
Communication
    word-of-mouth, 38
Communication channels
    nonpersonal, 38
Communication planning
    word of mouth, 13
Communication strategy
    Dubai, 57
Communication, supportive
    obstacles to, 70
Communication system, 332
Communications
    retailing, 182
Community Development Block Grants
    Community Development Block Grants (CDBGs), 130
Community development financial institutions (CDFIs), 138
Community property
    real property, 126, 306
Community shopping center, 284
Community shopping centers, 284
CommunityExpress, 134
Comp Benefits, 170
companies
    sustainable, 176, 224, 326, 493
COMPANY
    pricing policies, 89
Company pension plans
    disability and, 482
    retirement age, 317, 504
Company pricing policies, 109
Comparative accounting/Europe
    Germany, 46
comparative advantage
    in international trade, 52
Comparative global industrial relations
    Far East, 288
Compensation
    employees' goals, 344
    performance-based, 338
    reward systems, 337
    senior managers, 332
    team-based, 231-232, 321
    training and, 527
Compensation and benefits, 317
Compensation for employees
    geography, 181, 306
    job evaluation, 488
    minimum wage, 316
Compensation laws
    Fair Labor Standards Act, 316
Compensation surveys
    considerations, 317
Competence
    distinctive, 165
Competency, 509
competition
    efficiency and, 297
    for retail and service businesses, 279
    global entrepreneurship, 163
    importing and, 68
    market and, 39, 94, 136
    monopolistic, 450
    nonprice, 89
Competition
    pure, 84, 452
    reduced, 87, 228-229, 332
Competition, online, 190
Competitive advantage
    employees as, 227, 312, 513
    in small companies, 156, 367
    intellectual property rights and, 158
    layers of, 224
    speed as, 46
    talent and, 164, 491
Competitive strategy
    decisions about, 77, 310-311, 354, 471
    incentive pay, 339
Competitors
    ability to manage, 170
Complementary products, 22, 110, 188, 279

mpliance
  target, 473
mposition, 267, 326, 479
mprehensive Annual Financial Report (CAFR)
  financial section, 179, 305
  infrastructure, 56, 136, 187, 266, 328
mpuPay, 169
mputer budget
  printers, 30
mputer Central, 351
mputer fraud adware (advertiser supported
       software)
  malware, 215
  phishing, 220
  posing, 215
  skimming, 109, 372
  spyware, 215
  virus, 215
mputer industry
  mission statements, 474
omputer security, 215-216
omputer Security Institute, 216
mputer systems
  security of, 107, 181
omputerized databases, of secondary data
  directories of, 55
  offline, 220
omputer-supported collaboration tools
  wikis, 201, 332
mScore, 189
on artists, 142-143
oncealment, 377, 471
oncept generation
  creative process, 437
onditional Formatting
  rule, 211
onditions
  precedent, 93
ondominium, 283, 453
one, 278, 474-475
onference Board, 334
onfidence interval
  proportion, 214
onfidence, level of
  most commonly used, 101
onfirmatory factor analysis (CFA)
  modifying, 63, 249
onfirming bank, 67
onflict
  channel, 365
ongestion, 30, 283
onjoint methodologies, alternative
  choosing, 177, 202, 288
onnectivity, 264
onscientiousness, 3
onsensus
  agreements, 75-76, 471
onsent, 487
onsequential damages, 424
onsideration
  adequacy of, 428
  illegal, 429, 531
onsignee, 259
onsignor, 259
onsolidation working papers
  sequence of, 448
onspiracy, 449
onstant Contact, 24-25, 69, 220
onstant terms
  estimates, 31, 70, 100, 114, 188, 244
Constitution of the United States
  bankruptcy law, 423
  Due Process Clause, 424
  Fourteenth Amendment, 424
  interstate commerce, 432
Constraint management
  at Southwest Airlines, 311
Consumer
  publications, 53, 274, 535
Consumer behavior, online
  advertising methods, 31
  in e-commerce, 189-190
Consumer buyer behaviors
  purchasing process, 249
onsumer choices
  price discrimination, 450
Consumer concerns (e-commerce)
  security issues, 198
Consumer credit, 111, 423

Consumer Credit Protection Act, 457
Consumer decision making
  crossing, 74
consumer market
  lifestyle, 267, 375, 480
Consumer marketing
  blunders, 51
  demographics, 5, 47, 267-268
Consumer Price Index (CPI)
  biased, 10, 198, 268
Consumer Product Safety Act, 452
Consumer Product Safety Commission, 452
Consumer Products Safety Act, 452
Consumer protection
  Federal Trade Commission (FTC), 451
  Food and Drug Administration (FDA), 452
Consumer relations
  consumer complaints, 452
Consumer(s)
  as partners, 363
consumers
  disadvantaged, 490
Consumer(s)
  ECR, 364
  lifestyles, 526
  mature, 94
Consumers
  protection of, 437
  theft, 455
  with disabilities, 307
Consumer-to-consumer (C2C)
  personal services, 431
Consumption expenditures
  disposable income and, 47
Contact points, 60
Container Store, 334
Containment, 490
Contemporary environment
  battle of the forms, 433
  entrepreneurship, 179, 186-188, 268, 472
  right to recover, 434-435
  shipping terms, 426
Content
  Experiential, 111
content, online
  book industry, 89
Content reports, 213
Content reports, Web analytics, 199, 474
Contextual ads, 22-23
contingency plans, 249
Contingent workers
  employee benefits, 72, 521
  part-time employees, 315
continuous improvement, 213, 226-227, 362
Continuous probability distributions
  Normal distribution, 244
Continuous review (Q) system
  two-bin system, 357-358
Contract disputes, 425
Contract price, 435
contracts
  agent's, 444
Contract(s)
  breach of, 424-425
contracts
  capacity to enter into, 425
  disaffirm, 428
  duress, 428-430
  exculpatory clauses, 429
Contract(s)
  executed, 515
contracts
  form, 22, 64, 143, 173, 425
Contract(s)
  in restraint of trade, 449
  installment, 108-109
  interference with, 435
Contracts:
  letter of credit, 65
Contract(s)
  objective theory of, 425-426
  requirement, 425
contracts
  sale of goods, 426
  tying, 450
Contract(s)
  unenforceable, 434
  voidable, 428
Contracts, financial contracting

mortgages, 120, 454
  rights and obligations, 76, 425
Contractual, 136, 425, 523
Contractual entry strategies
  leasing, 115, 200
Contrived deterrence
  success, 381
Control
  accounting and, 236, 503
  markdown, 366
  risk management and, 534
control charts
  procedure for, 261, 303, 346
control concepts
  internal control, 169
Control methods, 350
Controlling process
  measuring performance, 341
Controlling share, 163
Controls Group
  Labels, 378, 450
Convenience goods, 298
Convenience store, 250, 279
Conversion rate, 16, 191
Convertible currency, 59
Conveyance, 446
Cook, Catherine, 154
Cook, Dave, 154
Coombes, Andrea, 155, 488
Cooperation
  argument for, 451
cooperative advertising, 37-38
Cooperatives, 53, 127, 208, 241
Copernicus, 44
Copreneurs, 131, 193, 271, 334-335
copyright protection, 57, 443
copyrights
  infringement, 441
Copyright(s)
  obtaining, 459
copyrights
  original works, 443
Core
  competencies, 206
Core business processes, 230
Core hours, 336
Core Systems, 527
Core values
  freedom, 300, 310, 465, 509
  progress, 329, 479, 500
Corn, 58, 225, 478
Cornell University, 160, 503
corporate bonds
  defaults, 123
  rates and, 266
Corporate culture
  management style, 310
corporate debt
  private debt, 128
Corporate Executive Board, 347
Corporate finance, 172
Corporate fraud, 495
Corporate governance
  key players, 512
  reform, 81, 316, 536
  trade-off of, 68
Corporate income taxes
  disclosures, 173
Corporate performance, 535
corporate responsibility
  motivations for, 178
Corporate senior instruments
  bank loans, 115
Corporate venture capital, 152
Corporatewide pay-for-performance plans
  successful implementation, 233
Corporations
  alien, 45
  management team, 158
  officers, 119
  publicly held, 167
Corum, 88
Corvette, 289, 431
Cost
  of common stock, 174
  of equity, 114, 147-148
  of goods sold, 89
  of magazines, 21
  of obsolescence, 235

of television advertising, 17
Cost allocation
  contracts and, 21
Cost and Freight, 96
Cost control
  performance reviews, 342
Cost curves
  total variable, 105
Cost effect
  of productivity, 325
Cost issues
  of production, 236
Cost of compliance, 448
cost of debt
  calculation, 144, 239
cost of goods sold
  of capital, 64, 114, 147-148, 303
Cost of living, 277
Cost per acquisition (CPA), 213
cost per click, 203
Cost per unit, 235, 355
Cost reduction
  China and, 58
  labor and, 105, 135, 316
Costa Coffee, 520
Cost-based (cost-plus) pricing
  alternative methods, 92
Cost-benefit analysis
  techniques used in, 98
Cost-cutting, 364
Costing
  absorption, 101-102
  job, 106, 293-295
  long run, 103
  short run, 103
  standard, 104
Cost-plus pricing method, 101
Costs
  adjustment, 303
  and market share, 162
Cost(s)
  carrying, 224, 350
  classifications, 19
Costs
  contracts for, 87
Cost(s)
  crash, 520
  cutting, 86, 249, 364, 527
  discretionary, 92, 175
Costs
  e-commerce and, 107, 183-195
  entry, 48, 93, 288, 485
  historical, 353
  implicit, 242
Cost(s)
  joint, 54-56, 436
Costs
  labor and materials, 105, 135
  learning curve, 95
  low labor costs, 68
  magazine advertising, 26
  of distribution, 53, 94, 186, 240, 436
  of inflation, 87
  of insurance, 126, 517-519
Costs:
  of labor, 72, 270, 336, 423
  of transportation, 269
Cost(s)
  opportunity costs, 240
Costs
  out-of-pocket, 527-528
  product lines, 61-62, 175, 252, 361, 476
  profit and, 48, 170, 360
  raw material, 86, 169, 251-252, 334, 360, 424
  replacement, 522
Cost(s)
  setup, 235-236, 362
Costs
  stockouts, 100, 234, 352
  supply and, 84, 262
  supply chain management, 224-230, 350
  surveys, 33, 140, 267, 381, 480
  television advertising, 16-17
  total fixed, 105
Cost(s)
  treasury, 114
Costs
  uncertainty, 110
Cost(s)

unit, 84, 235-237, 355, 436
Costs of broadcast media
  e-mail advertising, 23-24
cotton, 88, 140, 164, 301, 440
Counseling
  credit, 110-111
Counseling firms
  retaining, 168
Counterfeit, 71, 376, 437-438
Counterfeit goods, 437-438
Counterfeit products, 71, 437-438
Counters, 125, 376-377
Countertrade
  offset, 59
Countertrading, 49
Counties USA, 266
Country of origin
  labeling of, 452
  status and, 477
  tariffs and, 76
Country risk:
  terrorism, 71
Country's culture, 199
County and City Data Book, 266
County Business Patterns, 275
courts
  jurisdiction, 432
Cox, David, 194
Cp, 262
CPT, 66
cracker, 212
Cracker Jacks, 212
Crackers, 504
cracking, 69
Craftsman, 528
Cravings, 332
Crawl, 202
creating the message
  communication tools, 332
Creative Bakers, 61
Creative process
  illumination, 29
  incubation, 290
  transformation, 233, 272, 324
Creative Products Group, 531
Creativity
  and entrepreneurship, 194-196, 276
  ideas and, 76, 228, 478
  in advertising, 16
  threats to, 31
Credit
  collateral for, 123
  letters of, 66-67, 339
  pricing strategies and, 93
  secured, 117, 447-448
  selling on, 206
  unsecured, 118-120
credit card processing, 205
Credit cards
  MasterCard, 107
  online transactions, 107, 211
  online transactions for, 107
  Visa, 107
Credit default swap
  spread, 141, 448, 519
Credit default swap (CDS)
  index, 111, 132, 151, 219, 306-307, 381, 451
credit history, 115, 454
Credit insurance, 65-66
Credit period, 242-243
Credit ratings, 125, 253
Credit record, 454
Credit Suisse, 170
Credit union, 127
Creditor, 115, 455
creditors, 123, 445-447, 462, 513
creditworthiness, 66, 121
Crime
  common, 129, 280, 321, 367, 456, 523-524
  intent, 372
criminal background checks, 370
Criminal law
  types of crimes, 375
Criminal procedure
  arrest, 322, 378
crisis management
  Hurricane Katrina, 87, 522
Critical chain method (CCM)
  manual, 228, 494

Critical mass, 179
Critical path method (CPM)
  origin of, 441
Cross-marketing, 188
Cross-promotions, 200
Cuba
  embargo on, 71
Cultural considerations
  importing, 49
Cultural customs, 73
cultural differences
  business ethics and, 491
  reports and, 63
Cultural environments
  ethical behavior and, 492
Cultural stabilization
  religion, 471
Culture
  and teamwork, 231, 329, 477
  clusters, 279
  colors and, 199
  language and, 51
Curiosity, 13, 297
Currencies
  of countries, 77
Currency
  drain, 59
  vehicle, 149
Current asset management
  inventory management, 350
Current situation analysis
  SWOT Analysis, 79
Custom Cleaners, 529
Customer astonishment, 232
customer databases
  direct marketing and, 30
Customer relationship management (CRM)
  metrics for, 361
Customer relationships, building
  at Zappos, 320-321
customer satisfaction
  scales, 321
Customer satisfaction surveys, 489
Customer service
  terminating, 259
Customer traffic, 264
Customer value
  marketing strategy and, 79
Customers
  competitors and, 84
  effective layouts, 263
  exporting and, 61
  fiscal years, 175
  perspective of, 77, 425
  product design and, 302
  unprofitable, 122, 514
  Web site design, 124, 189
Customs
  climate and, 47
Customs agents, 438
Customs brokers, 65
Cyber crimes
  state laws, 173
Cybercrime
  hackers, 215
Cycle counting, 358
Cycle service level (CSL)
  seasonal items, 365
cycles and "rolling planning"
  regulatory compliance, 449

D
Dahl, Darren, 180
Dahl, Howard, 59
Daily News, 40, 459
Daimler, 149
Dairy Queen, 97
Damage
  property, 137-139, 435-438, 519
  spoilage, 235
Damages
  compensatory, 424-425, 486
  for breach of contract, 425
  general, 424, 485, 529-530
  goods, 426
  increasing, 215
  liquidated, 434
  monetary, 424
  punitive, 424-425, 484

ngerous products, 452
rren, Dahl, 180
rtmouth Pharmaceuticals, 31
shes, 376
ta
  Classification, 355
  cleaning, 343
  coding, 354
ta
  flow, 106, 144, 253, 274, 341
  interdependence of, 303
  linking, 106, 249, 359
  Ratio, 144, 281, 365
  safeguards, 215
  sorting, 229
  validity, 355
  warehouse, 354
  warehouses, 364-365
ta flow diagram (DFD)
  mechanics, 526
ta management
  large volume, 331
ta Tables
  profit and loss, 144
ta warehousing
  real-time, 194, 249-250, 359
tabase design
  common problems, 56
ta-base management
  by vendor, 251
tabases
  administering, 524
avenport, Tom, 294
avis, Brian, 146
vis, Brian, 146
y care, 325
AY function
  DATE and, 215
ayton, 447
32, 381
BMS (Database Management System)
  capabilities of, 231
DP, 66
DU, 66
eadweight loss
  gift giving, 464
bit, 107, 126, 215
bit cards, 107
bt
  credit card, 111, 114
  credit score and, 139
bt capital
  asset-based lenders, 122-123
  commercial loans, 118
  equipment suppliers, 125
  floor planning, 119
  inventory financing, 123
  long-term loans, 120
  private placements, 128, 152
  savings and loan associations (S&Ls), 126
  short-term loans, 118
  Small Business Lending Companies (SBLCs), 129
  stock brokerage houses, 126
  traditional bank loans, 118
bt (D)
  growth and, 113, 152
bt financing
  intermediate and long-term loans, 120
  internal methods, 140
  other sources of, 64, 116, 155
  SBA guaranteed loans, 135
  Small Business Administration, 55-56, 113
  small business lending companies, 129
  state and local loan development programs, 138
  trade credit, 108-110, 124-125
bt Service Funds (DSFs)
  sources of financing, 132, 148
bt to equity, 125
bt-to-equity ratio, 505
ecay, 283
eceptive advertising, 452-453
ecision making
  acceptance and, 468
  and risk management, 497
  biases, 479-480
  branding, 495
  by managers, 348
  children and, 68, 508
Dedication, 233, 310, 479, 510
Deductibles, 531

intuitive, 165, 192, 318
problem solvers, 7
weights, 89, 251
Decision models
  for outsourcing, 68
Decision variables, choosing
  objectivity, 250
Decisions
  programmed, 354
  to advertise, 10-11
Deductible, 505
Deduction, 293, 433
Defamation of character, 435, 480
Default, 81, 118, 154, 302, 381
Defects, 226-228, 520
Defense mechanisms, 331, 469
deferred payment, 454
Defined-contribution plans
  profit-sharing, 338, 506
  SEP, 306
Delaney, Kevin, 180
Delaney, Laurel, 78
delay options
  investment opportunity, 178
Delivery
  place of, 66, 258, 432
  tender of, 434
Delivery time, 433
Dell Inc., 188, 275
Deloitte, 180
DeLozier, M. Wayne, 265
Delphion, 440
Demand
  during lead time, 245, 357
  fluctuating, 90
  for capital, 140, 148
  for employees, 336
  linear, 244
  stockouts and, 356
  tastes and preferences, 61
demand curve
  import, 243
  individual's, 92
Demand for labor
  population and, 44, 266-267
Demand for money
  factors affecting, 63
  stability of, 47, 144
Demand for products
  potential markets and, 77
Deming, W. Edwards
  Cycle, 227
  teamwork, 230-231
  Variation, 230
Deming's 14 points, 233
Demographic characteristics, 274
Demographic data
  for cities, 266
  location information, 266
Demographic forces
  Variables, 267
Demographic information, 175, 266-268
Demographic segmentation
  by age, 267
demographic shifts, 478
demographics
  ethnicity, 268
Demographics USA, 267
Demos, Telis, 348
Denial-of-service (DoS) attack
  stopping, 221, 379
Dennison, Tim, 296
Denny's, 296
Density, 47, 274
Dentists, 117, 530
Department of Agriculture
  livestock, 132
Department of Commerce, 55, 129
Department of Commerce, U.S., 55, 129
Department of Defense, 117
Department of Health and Human Services, 307, 494
Department of Housing and Urban Development
  Department of Housing and Urban Development (HUD), 130
Department of Justice
  Antitrust Division, 450
Department of Justice (DOJ)
  Antitrust Division of, 450
Department of Labor (DOL)

Dictionary of Occupational Titles, 318
Departmental accounting
  contribution margin, 102
  net income, 100, 225
Depletion, 244
Design
  environmentally friendly, 346, 475
Design firms, 17
Design of e-commerce Web site
  domain name, 208
  navigation, 39, 189, 523
  shipping charges, 66, 207
Design props and assistance, 292
Desktop publishing, 4
desktop publishing software, 4
Destination
  Clubs, 284
  Malls, 283-285
Destination contract, 258
Detailed analysis, 303
Developing countries
  per capita income, 47
Development assistance, 56
Development costs, 95
Development Counsellors International, 319
Development of accounting
  educational level, 47
  taxation, 48
Dial, 19, 182
Dictionary, 162, 318
Dictionary of Occupational Titles (DOT), 318
Digg, 157
Digital billboards, 29
digital cameras, 257
digital marketing, 198
Digital media, 12
Digital River, 220
Digital world
  Internet access, and, 264
Dilution
  of shares, 169
Dimoff, Tim, 367
Direct competitors, 110, 280
Direct expenses, 171
Direct financial compensation
  luck, 150
  skill-based pay, 335
Direct franchising, 59
Direct investment
  mail marketing, 24-25, 220
Direct labor, 101-103, 135
Direct Mail Association, 31
direct marketing
  direct-response television, 17
  investment for, 379
Direct Marketing Association, 24
Direct materials, 101
Direct public offerings (DPOs), 174
Direct stock offerings, 174-175
Direct-cost income statement, 102
direct-mail advertising
  other techniques, 188, 366
Direct-response marketing
  radio and, 183
  television and, 4, 324
disabilities
  employees with, 481-482
Disability Discrimination
  accommodations, 293
  harassment, 455, 482-483, 530-531
Disability payments, 524
Disaster loans, 137-138
Discipline of employees
  rules and regulations, 448, 462
Disclosure
  prospective, 175
Disclosure Document, 174, 440
Discount coupons, 24, 97, 473
Discount loans (advances)
  three types of, 109, 147, 223
discount rates
  loans and, 65, 125-126
  venture capital, 128, 166-167, 266
discount stores, 362
Discriminant model, estimation and assessing overall fit
  rule of thumb, 25, 155, 211
Discrimination
  civil rights, 322, 482

color, 293, 322-323, 455
disability, 293, 482, 533
intentional, 530
national origin, 322-323, 455
race, 322-323, 455
racial, 480
religious, 322
retaliation, 482-483
sexual harassment, 482-483, 530
Discriminatory employment practices
misleading information, 455
Disgruntled employees, 368
disinterested, 470
Displays
assortment, 300
rack, 298
Disposal of products
donating, 4-5, 77, 475
disruption, 180, 247, 363
Dissatisfied customers, 13
Distributing products
distribution centers, 250, 269
distribution channel, 51, 254
materials handling, 302-304
physical distribution, 47
Distribution
in global markets, 54
distribution channels
inadequate, 281
push, 227, 361
Distribution strategy, 63-64
District court, 431
District of Columbia, 269, 432, 519
Diversity
diversity training, 479
Diversity management program, 480
Dividends
tax on, 516
Divisional performance
ambiguity, 330
Dixon, Lance, 364
Dixon, Sandy, 524
DMAIC, 230
DMAIC process, 230
DNA, 275
Do Not Track list, 184
documentation
adequate, 47
Dodes, Rachel, 111
Dogs, 14, 188, 264, 451, 491
Dollar (U.S.)
falling, 194, 342
Domain, 207-208
domain name
top-level domain, 208
Domain names
trademarks and, 208, 441
Domenik, Steve, 165
Domestic barriers to international trade, 79
Domestic companies, 51-54
Domestic market, 45-46
Dominant strategy
incentives, 32, 63, 95, 268, 337, 361, 532
Dominican Republic, 75-76
Dominican Republic-Central America Free Trade
Agreement (CAFTA-DR), 76
Domino, 35
Domino's, 58, 182
Domino's Pizza, 58
Donnelly, 256
Donnelly, Harriet, 256
downloads, 96, 179, 359
drafts
sight, 67
Dragas Company, 513
Dragas, Helen, 513
Drayton, Bill, 474
Dress code, 325
drinking water
protection, 271, 454-455, 523
Drug tests, 323, 370, 480, 519
Drugstores, 89, 279
DSL, 271
Dual, 184
Dual-career couples, 184
DUB, 37
Due diligence, 163, 323
Due diligence, existing businesses
financial condition, 170

legal considerations, 48
questions to ask, 253
due process, 424, 466
Due process clause, 424
Duke University, 270
Dunkel, Tom, 75
Duty of restitution, 428
Duty of restoration, 428
Duty to indemnify, 444
Duty to pay, 434
Dvorak, Phred, 257
Dynamic trading in e-auctions
exchanges, 169, 264

E

E-active marketing
search engine optimization, 52, 197
Early stage capital, 131
Earnings
forecasts, 56
retained, 115, 152
test, 503
East India Company, 53
Easter, Pat, 135
Eastern Europe, 255, 269
Eastern Industries, 481
"Eat your own DNA"
eBay, 14, 51, 145, 189
Eaton, 488
Eaton, Lori, 488
E-business
e-marketing and, 220
E-commerce
factors to consider, 185, 269
global reach, 199
E-commerce
growth in, 12, 130
myths of, 181
privacy and security, 181
shopping carts, 189
statutes, 432
tracking results, 218
e-commerce
Web analytics, 108, 184
Web privacy and security, 214
websites, 220
E-commerce components
method of payment, 67, 107
shopping cart, 193
E-commerce (EC)
resources for, 55-56
E-commerce strategies
community development, 130
search engine optimization (SEO) strategy, 201
Economic activity
prohibited, 127
Economic analysis
costs and, 84, 226-228, 276-277
Economic Census, 275
Economic development
in India, 46, 154
Economic Development Administration, 129
Economic Development Administration (EDA), 129
Economic environment
gross domestic product (GDP), 45
recession, 92, 139
retailers and, 288
Economic freedom
around the world, 45-46, 150, 289, 535
Economic growth
comparisons of, 267
health and, 307, 449
rates of, 123
economic incentives, 283
economic order quantity (EOQ)
carrying costs, 236-237
lead time, 244-245, 357
reorder point, 223, 354
economic systems
market economies, 45
market economy, 489
physical resources, 311
Economic value
collusion, 450
Economics
network, 47
economies of scale
quantity discounts, 240-241
Economies of scope

existence, 443
rare, 279
valuable, 59-60, 95, 252-253, 335, 501
Economist, 61, 111, 220-221, 352, 495
Economist Intelligence Unit, 61
Economy
stimulating, 130
underground, 272
EDI, 359
Editor and Publisher Market Guide, 267
Edmunds, Gladys, 111
Education
entrepreneurial, 1, 43-44, 83-84, 113-114, 147-148,
181, 223, 263-264, 309, 349-350,
423-424, 461, 497-498
Education and training
by small businesses, 12, 114
Education level, 17, 266
Educational levels, 17, 280
EEO enforcement/compliance of laws
regulatory agencies, 448
Efficiency gains in comparative advantage
of standardization, 29
Effective communications
electronic communications, 493
employee handbook, 531
Effective layouts, 263
Effectiveness
of advertising, 8-9
of promotion, 38
Efficiency
in production, 249
of output, 230
wages, 151
Efficiency, OM and
capacity and, 34
Efficient consumer response, 364
Efficient consumer response (ECR), 364
Eisenberg, Bryan, 193
El Salvador, 76
Electric cars, 149
Electronic article surveillance, 378
Electronic business, 191
Electronic checks, 107
Electronic communications, 493
Electronic data processing (EDP) insurance, 523
Electronic monitoring, 485
Electronic Monitoring & Surveillance Survey, 487-488
Electronic Product Code (EPC), 359
Elliott, Stuart, 6
Ellis, Perry, 364-365
Elton, Chester, 334
E-mail
advertising , 21
unsolicited, 13, 142, 197
usage, 26, 195
E-mail monitoring, 488
EMarketer, 22, 347
E-marketing
Web and, 150, 186-187
embargoes, 71
Embezzlement, 523
EMC, 52
Employee assistance program (EAP), 481
Employee engagement, 327
Employee health and safety
abroad, 45-46
job stress, 295
Employee involvement, 231
Employee orientation, 481
Employee relations, developing
communication channels, 332
Employee rights
Title VII of the Civil Rights Act of 1964, 482
Employee rights, challenges in
electronic monitoring, 485
smoking, 529
whistle-blowing, 464
Employee safeguards
termination, 483, 530
Employee satisfaction, 480
Employee selection
screening and, 380
Employee stock ownership plan (ESOP), 504
Employee stock ownership plans (ESOPs), 168, 340,
505
Employees
discharging, 482
exempt, 515

loyees
  iring the right, 309
  aid off, 162, 447
  oyalty of, 480
loyees
  nentoring, 311, 508-509
loyees
  overtime and, 229
loyees
  art-time, 64, 193, 315, 482, 503
loyees
  erformance appraisals, 343-344
loyees
  rivacy of, 198
loyees
  etired, 317, 450
  afety and, 294, 449
loyees
  afety of, 225, 378, 481
loyees
  iolent, 71, 374
  vorker productivity, 226, 304
ployer payroll taxes
  aying, 65, 257, 444, 477
ployment
  oreach, 370
  amily and, 498
  good faith, 444
  nisrepresentation, 451
ployment interview(s)
  nterpersonal skills, 320
  ack of training, 328
  instructured, 294
ployment law
  amily and medical leave, 530
ployment laws
  disabilities, 290, 322, 482, 530
Equal Employment Opportunity Commission
  (EEOC), 321, 485-486
ployment practices liability, 530
ployment process
  performance management, 220
ployment tests
  ob-knowledge, 319
powerment zones, 289
oding, 268
orsement of bills and notes
  restrictive, 173, 279
ergy derivatives
  electricity, 295
ancements, 93
on
code of conduct, 469
erprise
  measures, 498
search, 200-201, 373
erprise system, 474
erprise systems
  modules, 381
ertainment
  Branded, 124
  Educational, 272
ertainment industry, online
  Hollywood, 5
ertainment, online
  in social networking, 200
ity, 128, 241, 276, 450, 519
ity-relationship data modeling
  variations, 93
ity-relationship (E-R) data model
  entities, 475
repreneurial firms, HRM in
  differences in, 47
trepreneurs
  celebrity, 17-18, 179
  characteristics of successful, 165
  diversity, 72, 311, 478-480
  family-run, 87
  female, 3, 94, 479
  home-based business, 193, 519
  solo, 319
  tenacity, 333
  women as, 5
trepreneur's Toolkit sections
  export financing, 127
trepreneurship
  entrepreneurs, 136-137, 152-154, 181-182, 267,
    471
  success in, 136, 181

Entry
  deterring, 370
Entry modes, selection and management of
  contractual, 136, 428, 523
Environment and development
  And population, 266
  And urban development, 130
Environment (natural)
  ethics and social responsibility, 461-469
Environmental challenges
  workforce diversity, 479
Environmental impact statement (EIS)
  contents, 193, 250, 522
Environmental law, 455
Environmental policy
  1970s, 131
  market forces, 84
  Pollution Prevention Act, 455-457
Environmental quality
  pollution and, 455
Envirosell, 295
Epinions, 219
Equal Credit Opportunity Act, 455
Equal Credit Opportunity Act of 1974, 455
Equal Employment Opportunity (EEO)
  complying with, 177, 293, 448-449, 463
  job analysis, 317-318
  noncompliance, 471
Equal employment opportunity (EEO) laws
  diversity management, 480
Equipment
  debt capital, 113-115
  idle, 122, 257, 303
  suppliers of, 136, 251, 364
Equipment suppliers, 125
Equity
  assets and, 445
Equity capital
  corporate venture capital, 152
  personal savings, 147
equity capital, raising
  for private companies, 161
  ownership and, 535
equity (E)
  market value of, 126
equity financing
  angels, 147
  foreign stock markets, 175
  friends and family members, 153-154
  public stock sale, 167
  simplified registrations and exemptions, 173-174
  venture capital companies, 149
Equity Funding
  initial public offering, 149
Equity markets
  concentration, 268, 353
Equity financing sources
  partners as, 177
Equity, sourcing globally
  visibility and, 3
Equity/equities
  stockholders, 169, 445
Erickson, 12
Ericsson, 165
"Errors and omissions" coverage, 529
Esfahani, Elizabeth, 381
ESOP, 340, 504
ESOP Association, 507
ESOPs, 168, 334, 505-506
ESRI, 478
Essential functions, 293
Established products and services, 95
Estate
  dominant, 432
Estate freeze, 516-517
Estate tax, 514
Estates
  heirs, 513-517
Estoppel, 427-428
E.T., 348
Ethical behavior
  moral awareness, 466
ethical choices, 462
Ethical culture, 311, 470
Ethical decision making
  governments and, 53
Ethical judgment, 464
ethical principles, 466, 512
Ethical responsibilities, 471

ethical, social, and political issues
  intellectual property rights, 158, 423
Ethics
  counseling, 482
  environment and, 486
  essential elements of, 493
  morality, 472
  perspectives, 479-480
  social responsibility and, 465
  teaching, 4, 464
  visuals, 487
  Web-based, 475
Ethics and social responsibility
  unsafe products, 452
Ethnic groups, 478
Ethnicity, 268
Eureka, 201
Euromonitor, 268
Euromonitor International, 268
Europe
  in Africa, 46
European Community, 72
Event
  Independent, 119, 318, 364, 524
Event marketing
  cross-promotions, 200
Event(s)
  experiences, 518
Evolutionary products, 93
Exception rate
  estimated, 172
Excess capital, 519
Exchange rate dynamics
  simple model, 244
Exchange rate forecasts
  causes, 5, 294, 330, 351, 429, 534
exchange rate risk
  exposure to, 30, 48
Exchange rates
  indices, 267
Exchange rate(s)
  spot, 21, 121
Exchange rates
  stability, 47, 178-179
excise taxes, 288
Excite, 175
Exclusive licensing, 450
Exclusives, 347
Exculpatory clause, 429
Exculpatory clauses, 429
executive compensation
  other benefits, 444, 467
Executive summary, 40, 80, 458
Exempt, 127, 451, 515
Exemptions, 147, 446, 514
exercise equipment, 89
Exhibits, 33
Existing business acquisition
  business valuation, 506
Existing business(es)
  due diligence, 163, 323
  financing options, 150
Existing businesses, seller's view
  employee stock ownership plan (ESOP), 504
  exit strategies, 149, 502
exit strategies
  employee stock ownership plan, 504
  family limited partnership, 516
Expansion capital, 137
Expansion potential, 281
Expatriate training and development
  for managers, 485
Expectancy, 498
Expenditure accounting (governmental funds)
  controls and procedures, 368
Expenditures
  planned, 33, 280
Expenses
  research and development, 143
Experian, 191
Experian CheetahMail, 191
Exploitive targeting
  children, 511
exploits, 186
Exponential smoothing
  double, 220
export credit insurance, 65-66
Export goods and services, 60
Export license, 66

export management companies, 52-53
Export management companies (EMCs), 52
Export merchants, 53
Export Programs Guide, 60
Export promotion, 55
Export regulations, 65
Export strategy
    export process, 76
export trading companies, 53
Export trading companies (ETCs), 53
Export-Import Bank, 65-66, 127
Exporting
    payment methods, 65
    potential for, 47
    trade missions, 64
exports
    from China, 70-71
    movie, 81
Exports/exporting
    pitfalls, 56
eXtensible Markup Language (XML)
    tags, 381
External customers, 232
External recruiting sources
    career sites, 315
    employee referrals, 314
External recruitment methods (traditional)
    recruiters, 317
External stakeholders, 186, 462
Extinction, 328
Extortion, 430
Extra expense coverage, 522
Extreme sports, 267
extrinsic rewards, 337
Eye on the Global Economy
    Yuan in, 56
Eye on the U.S. economy
    taxes in, 280

F

Fabbrice D'Armi Beretta, 499
Face value
    life insurance policy, 515
Facebook
    privacy policy, 186, 431
Fact finder, 40
Fact sheets, 266
Factor analysis
    processes of, 231
Factor(s)
    trade in, 47
factors of production
    capital in, 141, 234
    market system, 169
Factory overhead, 101-103
Factory overhead costs, 101
Fad, 472
Fahmy, Dalia, 179-180
Failure
    to warn, 437
Failure rate
    for businesses, 45, 280, 432
Failure to warn, 437
Fair Credit Billing Act, 455
Fair Credit Reporting Act, 455
Fair Debt Collection Practices Act, 455
Fair employment, 487
Fair Packaging and Labeling Act, 452
Fairley, Stephen, 313
Fajita Grill, 24
false advertising, 453, 489
False imprisonment, 435
Families and Work Institute, 336
Family
    financial officer, 444, 506
Family and Medical Leave Act, 530
Family businesses
    insurance costs, 276, 518-519
    management succession, 497-498
    management succession plans, 500
    oldest, 22, 104, 228, 498-499
    risk management strategies, 497
Family coverage, 525
Family Leave
    vacation time, 508
Family limited partnership (FLP), 516
Family limited partnerships, 517
Family test, 470
Family-owned businesses, 498

Fan(s)
    Television, 26
Fantasy, 157
FAQs, 306, 454
Farkas, David, 306
Fashion trends, 365
FDA, 225, 452
Feasibility
    study, 505
Federal budget
    in 2007, 16, 54
Federal estate tax, 514
Federal government accounting
    Department of the Treasury, 114
    environment of, 370, 513
    execution, 436
    federal agencies, 55, 131-132
Federal Hazardous Substance Act, 452
Federal income tax
    tax credits, 289
Federal loan programs, 143
Federal Register
    website, 220
Federal regulation, 448
Federal revenues, 70
Federal Trade Commission Act (FTC Act)
    Section 5, 136, 451
Federal Trade Commission (FTC)
    investigations, 485
Federation of International Trade Associations, 53
Federation of International Trade Associations (FITA), 53
FedEx Corporation, plant assets
    depreciating, 141
Feedback loop, 341-342
Fees
    investment company, 128
    unpaid, 454
Fendi, 5
Fenway Park, 130
Fertman, Don, 56
Festival shopping centers, 284
Fiat, 132
Fidelity, 471, 523
Fidelity bonds, 523
Fidenza, Michael, 359
Fiduciary, 444, 490
Fiduciary relationship, 444, 490
Field, Andrew, 527
Fifth Amendment
    Due Process Clause of, 424
file service
    for programs, 456
Filing expenses, 170
Final price, 85-86, 172, 256
finance companies, 122
finance department, 368
Financial and risk management
    risk transfer, 519
Financial capital markets
    workings of, 367
Financial crises, international
    S&Ls, 126
financial crisis
    banks in, 125
    investments and, 154
financial distress
    who pays, 369
financial institutions
    investment banks, 170
Financial institutions
    stock markets, 175
financial markets
    globalization of, 49, 224
    primary markets, 288
Financial markets, international
    firms and, 140, 157
Financial markets/institutions
    stockbrokers, 126, 157
Financial measures
    of supply chains, 261
financial options
    exercising, 105
Financial plans
    critical numbers, 334
    financial reports, 119
Financial ratio analysis
    gross profit margin, 99, 361
    inventory turnover, 119, 260, 351

Financial regulation
    consumer protection, 423
Financial reporting statements
    proprietary, 57
Financial reports, 119
financial risk management
    benchmarks, 220, 341
Financial statements
    cycles of, 87
    pro forma statements, 144
financial structures, of foreign subsidiaries
    financing in, 129, 154
financing
    insufficient, 139
Financing
    internal methods of, 140
    low-interest, 149, 276
financing
    of small businesses, 115
    projects, 129-130, 168
financing
    securing, 57, 119, 177
    wholesalers, 53, 122, 276
Financing sources
    federal loan programs, 143
    planning for capital needs, 151
    Small Business Administration (SBA), 114
Financing/funding
    bootstrapping, 153
    friends and family, 153-154
    grants, 118, 276
Fines, 316
Finished goods, 57, 101, 123, 269, 350, 523
Finished goods inventory, 303
Finland, 44
Fiore, Scott, 9
Fire protection, 276
firewalls, 215
Firm commitment, 172
Firm commitment agreement, 172
Firms
    inefficiency, 249
firms
    shutting down, 138
Firms
    visionary, 8
firm-specific political risks
    Overseas Private Investment Corporation, 65
FIS Group, 469
Fiscal policy
    decreases, 518
    in 2008, 336
    since 1993, 514
Fiscal years, 175
Fischer, Scott, 256
Fitch, 296
Fitzgerald, Michael, 262
fixed assets
    gross, 45, 99, 533
Fixed capital, 151-152
Fixed expenses, 101-102
Fixed interest rates, 128
Fixed investment, 303
Fixed overhead costs
    variances, 342
Fixed price, 127
Fixed-position layout, 303
Fixed-position layouts, 303
Flammable Fabrics Act, 452
Flash, 17, 109, 378, 497
Flash memory, 27
Flat organization structure, 340
Fleishman-Hillard, 219
Flexibility
    transportation networks, 276
Flexplace, 335-336
Flextime, 335-336
Flip-flops, 325
flipping, 154
Floating exchange rate regime
    managed, 104
Floating exchange rates
    case against, 380
Floor planning, 119
F.O.B. buyer, 261
F.O.B. seller, 261
Focus strategy, 196
Follow-the-leader pricing, 98
Fonjallaz, 499

od & Wine, 4
od additives, 452
od and Drug Act, 452
od and Drug Administration, 452
od Company, 424, 500
od prices, 447
od-oriented retailers
    convenience store, 250, 279
otprint, 129
rcing, 45, 118, 288, 430
recast error
    percentage, 144, 231-232, 454-455, 469, 528
recasting methods
    counting, 358
reign currency translation
    adjustments, 58, 187
    elsewhere, 211, 435
reign direct investment (FDI)
    economic effects of, 81, 438
    management issues in, 62
eign direct investments (FDI)
    to China, 64, 225
reign distributors, 54-55
eign exchange market
    in London, 73, 187, 340
reign investment
    geographic limitations, 130
reign licensing, 49
eign markets
    exporting to, 63
    international franchising, 49
reign stock markets, 175
reign trade zone (FTZ), 289
reign trade zones, 288-289
reign-exchange market
    currencies, 44
reign-exchange markets
    players on, 195
mal communication network, 332
rmal organizational communication
    encouraging, 229, 311, 470
rms
    standardized, 37
rrester Research, 183
rtunato, Laura, 75
rtune 500 companies, 177, 498
rum, 32, 332
rward prices
    of commodities, 452
rward vertical integration
    threat, 17
unding team, 164
OX, 80, 179
OX News, 80
anchise, 57, 133, 264, 371-372, 428
anchising
    growth strategy, 57
    master franchising, 59
ancis, Theo, 507
aud
    suspected, 372, 435
aud computer fraud
    perpetrators of, 371
azee, Valerie, 75
ree agency, 444
ree cash flow (FCF)
    adjustments to, 58, 213, 352
ree enterprise, 474
ree lunch, 324
ree market, 489
ree trade zone, 76
ee zones
    subzones, 289
reedom of contract, 425
eeman, Sholnn, 381
eelancers, 4
reight charges, 66, 96
reight forwarders, 65
requency distribution
    Joint, 49, 160, 436
    Tables, 268
riendships, 154-155
ieswick, Kris, 459
rivolous lawsuits, 529
ront fee, 138
ront office, 229
rontline, 311
rozen foods, 462
ryer, Bronwyn, 220

FSB, 35, 111, 122, 179-180, 221, 297, 324, 459, 495, 529
Fuentes, Maggine, 527
Full price, 97-98, 205
Full-absorption income statement, 102
Full-time workers, 336
Fully insured, 527
Fun, 24, 306, 324-327, 501
Functional manager, 508
Functional strategies
    and people, 24, 294, 328
Function(s)
    LEFT, 74, 92, 257
    MODE, 145
Functions of management
    Staffing, 309-315
Fund net assets
    restricted, 127, 450
Funding, 127-128, 148-152, 187, 275, 490
Fund-raising, 175
Fuse, 204
Futterman, Matthew, 451
Future considerations
    capital requirements, 127, 151-153
future of IT
    internal controls, 370
    staffing, 311-315

G
Gabel, Barbara, 507
gadgets, 201, 257
Gallup, 347
Garner, Ralph, 500
Garner, Thad, 500
Gas prices, 365
Gateway, 56, 184
gateways, 344
GE Capital, 123
GE Capital Solutions, 125
Gearing, 31, 476
Gen X, 206
Gen Y employees
    engaging, 51, 137, 200, 271, 458, 468, 520
    perks, 325
Gender differences
    in performance appraisals, 346
Genentech, 158
Genentech Inc., 158
General Agreement on Tariffs and Trade (GATT 1947)
    Uruguay Round, 76
General Agreement on Tariffs and Trade (GATT 1994)
    contents of, 219, 250, 360, 522
General capital assets (GCA)
    estimated cost, 304
    indicators of, 48
    transfers, 446, 519
General Fund and Special Revenue Fund
    year-end, 358, 452
General merchandise retailers
    specialty store, 365
    variety store, 284
General Motors
    JIT philosophy, 379
General Motors (GM)
    health benefits, 506
generation X, 206, 324
Generations, 478-479, 502-503
Genetic engineering, 158
Gensler, 290-291
Genuineness of assent, 425
Geographic coverage, 20
Geographic information system (GIS)
    TIGER, 268
geographic information systems, 268, 365
geographic information systems (GIS), 268, 365
Geographic market, 268
Geographic pricing, 96
Geographic regions, 96, 270, 450
Gersh, Lewis, 156
Ghana, 528
Giant, 29, 44, 89-90, 168, 182, 265, 424, 467
Giant Food, 424
Giant retailers, 90, 287
Gibson, 111, 202
Gibson, Richard, 111
Gilbert, Susan, 253
Gillette, 97
Gillette, King, 97
Gillette razors, 97

Global
    Campaign, 47, 256, 473
    citizens, 463
Global advertising
    copy and, 29
Global asset allocation
    optimization, 52, 221
Global benchmarks
    scope, 501
global business global supply chains
    localization, 199
Global company profiles
    McDonald's, 58, 111, 265, 489
Global e-marketing
    Internet users, worldwide, 50, 182
Global entrepreneurship
    countertrading, 49
    establishing international locations, 49
    foreign licensing, 49
    international trade agreements, 55
    trade intermediaries, 49
    Web presence, 49, 185-186
Global Entrepreneurship Monitor, 153, 474
Global Entrepreneurship Monitor (GEM), 153
Global HRM
    codetermination, 46
Global industry analysis
    competitive strategies, 226, 475
Global managers, environment
    contract law, 425
Global market segmentation
    psychographic, 264
Global marketing
    cultural environment, 47
    economic environment, 47
    McDonald's and, 58, 287
Global markets
    trade restrictions, 47
Global networks, 54
Global One, 77
Global purchasing, 224
Global retailing
    department stores and, 364
global warming, reducing
    politics, 494
Global/International Issues (Chapter 11)
    Weak economy, 351, 447
Globalization
    and trade, 59
Globalizing, 45
Globus, 55
Glover, M. Katherine, 75
GNP, 47
Go Daddy, 208
Goals
    SMART, 115, 192, 311-312
    substitute, 190
going public, 167-169
"going public", 167
Gold Key Program, 58
Gold Key Service, 55
Gold, Michael, 310
Gold rush, 195
Goldsmiths, 499
Good Housekeeping, 198, 304
Good Housekeeping Seal, 198
Good Housekeeping seal of approval, 198
Goodman, Gail, 25
Goods
    bundling, 97
    defense, 52, 373, 451
    durable, 29
    imports of, 71
    inferior, 84, 431
    intermediate, 125
    unfinished, 434
Goodyear, 122
Google
    News, 40, 155, 200
Google's AdWords, 202
Goulson, George, 264
Government agencies
    for information, 60, 189
Government bonds, market quotations
    marketability of, 169
Government debt
    burden of, 177, 448
Government intervention
    dealing with, 59, 428-429, 472, 518

Government purchases
reductions in, 129
Government regulation
of pricing, 172
government regulations
antitrust policy, 449
Government securities, 126
GPS, 487
GQ, 494
Graduate school, 176
Granite Rock Company, 489
Grant Thornton, 44, 170
Grantor retained annuity trust (GRAT), 516
grapevine, 332
Gravity Tank, 291
Grazia Deruta, 499
Great Lakes, 146
Great Places to Work Institute, 325
Greco, Michael, 31
Green, Anthony, 24
Green, Gloria, 32
Green Mountain Coffee, 467
Green Mountain Coffee Roasters, 467
Greenleaf, Robert, 313
Greer, 225, 459
Greer, Leroy, 431
Grensing-Pophal, Lin, 39
Grooming, 513
Gross domestic product (GDP)
country-specific, 44, 199
of the world, 45, 199
per capita, 47, 280
gross domestic products (GDP)
of world, 44, 437, 498
gross margin, 298
Gross private domestic investment
inventory investment, 235, 365
Group insurance
dental, 171
major medical, 526
term life, 126
underwriting, 170-171
Group/organizational incentives
ownership plans, 340, 533
stock ownership plans, 340, 533
Groups
leaders in, 98
treatment, 532
work teams, 328
Grove, Andy, 312
Growth, economic
And the environment, 187, 448, 463
Growth stage, 156
Growth strategies
market penetration, 94
Growth strategy, 57
Gruen, Victor, 283
Gruner, Stephanie, 175
Guarantee of payment, 67
Guaranteed loans, 116
Guaranty fee, 135
Guatemala, 76
Gucci, 5
Guerilla marketing strategies
uniqueness, 15, 77, 88
Gurchiek, Kathy, 348

H

Hacker, 51
Hackers, 211, 523
Haiti, 467
Hall, Jody, 4
Hall, Rhonda, 488
Halo, 521
Hamilton, Alexander, 70
Handling charges, 191
Handling costs, 303-304, 363
Hansen Wholesale, 242
Hanson, Fay, 494
Hard currency, 78
Hard drive, 215
Hardware
storage, 354
Harmonized Tariff Schedule, 70
Harper, Betsy, 25
Harris Interactive, 183
Harris, Michael, 321
Harvard University, 479
Harvesting, 249

Hash, 278
Hawaii, 269
Haworth, 295
Hazardous materials, 476
Hazardous waste
recycled, 476
HCL, 331
HCL Technologies, 331
Headden, Susan, 32
headers, 210
Headline, 32, 180
Headlines, 21, 202
Health
drug abuse, 494
employee assistance program, 481
Occupational Safety and Health Administration
(OSHA), 294
wellness programs, 532
Health and wellness programs
health care plans, 524
Health care costs, 269, 482, 518
Health care insurance
types of coverage, 521
Health care organizations, accounting for
donations, 475
Health care plans
health savings accounts, 526
managed care plans, 526
preferred provider organizations, 533
health insurance
accident and, 527
catastrophic, 518
exchange for, 127
health maintenance organization, 526
high-deductible, 536
preferred provider organization, 526
traditional indemnity plans, 526
Health of employees
alcohol abuse, 480
substance abuse, 480-481
Health problems, 482
Health savings accounts, 526
Health-care problems, in U.S
waste and inefficiency, 227
Heath, Chip, 347
Heirs, 498
Help
usable, 120, 251
Henricks, Mark, 81, 179, 306, 381, 494, 529
Herbal Remedy, 9
Herhold, Scott, 162
Heritage, 508
Herman, Tom, 535
Hershey, 340
Heschong Mahone Group, 295
High prices, 87
High-speed Internet access, 264
High-tech products, 441
hiring
negligent, 323, 444
hiring practices, 292
hiring process, 313-314
Hirsch, Alan, 295
hits, 115, 195, 306
HIV/AIDS, 482
Hoffman, Joseph, 428
Holding cost, 235-236
Holding costs, 235, 269
Holland, 85, 347, 475, 517
Home shopping, 17
Home-based business, 193, 519
Home-based businesses
statistics for, 145, 268
Homeland security, 449
Homelessness, 467
Homeowner's insurance
earthquakes, 137, 522
floods, 137, 522
Home/work
boundaries, 49, 138, 268, 463
Honduras, 76
Honesty testing
paper-and-pencil, 370
Hoover's, 180
Hopkins, Samuel, 440
Horizontal job loading, 335
horizontal merger, 450
horizontal mergers, 450
Horovitz, Bruce, 473

Hoshi Ryokan, 499
Hostile environment, 484
Hostile work environment, 484
Hostility, 364
Hotel Pilgram Haus, 499
HotJobs, 314
Hotlines, 367, 489
Hotspots, 131
Hourly compensation, 270
Households
White, 21
Housing and Urban Development (HUD), 130
housing market
shortages, 248
Housing prices
in California, 108
Howl-O-Ween, 188
H&R Block, 317
HRM and business periodicals
general business, 269
HSAs, 526
Hsieh, Tony, 190-191, 327, 353
HSN, 18
Hsu, Paul, 60
Hudson, Jennifer, 5
Hudson, Kris, 306
Hudson, Marianne, 157
Hudson River, 320
Hudson's Bay Company, 53
Hue, 29, 301
Hughes, Paul, 32
Hughlett, Mike, 307
Human Resource Certification Institute (HRCI)
compensation and benefits, 317
Human resource information system (HRIS)
applications for, 137, 149
security and privacy, 107
Human resource, job design, work management and
competitive advantage for, 255, 477
labor standards, 316
Human Resource Management
equal employment opportunity, 321, 479, 530
wages and salaries, 151
Human resource management (HRM)
evidence-based, 313
in small businesses, 128, 230, 500
Human resource managers, 318
human resources management (HRM)/payroll cycle
daily activities, 311
human rights
of workers, 315-317, 444, 468
human safeguards
nonemployees, 484
Hurly, Chad, 169
Hurricane(s)
Katrina, 87, 522
Hwang, Shelly, 13
Hyatt, 111
Hyperinflation, 46
Hyperlinks, 209
Hypertext markup language (HTML)
validation, 160

I

Iceland, 58, 225
ICRC (International Committee of the Red Cross)
funding, 131, 161, 187, 490
I.D., 40, 81, 111, 495, 535-536
Id, 40, 81, 111, 495, 535-536
Identification
recognizing, 518
Identifier, 381
IKEA, 269
Ill will, 234, 352
Illumination, 29, 293
IMC campaign
Travel, 15, 204
Immediacy, 20
Immoral management, 466
Imperfect competition
nonprice competition, 89
Implied authority, 444
implied contract, 340
Implied warranties
of fitness for a particular purpose, 436
of merchantability, 436
Implied warranty, 435-436
Importers, 52
Imports

of sugar, 71
restrictions on, 136
pression management
excuses, 471
tactics of, 98
provisation, 310
pulse purchases, 298
entive pay plans
performance criteria, 343-344
time horizon, 108
entive plans
employee stock ownership, 168, 340, 504-506
entives
employee stock ownership plans (ESOPs), 340, 533
nonfinancial incentives, 339
idence, 482
idents, 370
lusion, 479
come
disposable, 39, 47, 266-267
farm, 514
protecting, 517
race and, 268
rental, 274
wage, 272
come distribution changes in top end of
recent changes in, 127
come elasticity of demand
globally, 46
come levels, 274
come redistribution
scale of, 47, 272
come statement
time periods, 279
come statements
direct-cost, 105
full-absorption, 101-102
come tax
effect, 131, 366, 516
come tax planning
state and local, 143
complete information, 312
credible Adventures, 521
cubation, 290
cubator, 263
cubators, 276
demnity plans, 526
dependent demand, inventory models and
minimizing costs, 294
reorder points, 243
dependent Insurance Agents & Brokers of America, 519
dex numbers
Consumer price, 528
dex of retail saturation, 281
dex of retail saturation (IRS), 281
ditex, 255
dividual demand
price changes and, 84
dividual differences, measuring and interpreting
internal consistency, 485
dividual income tax
complications, 88
dividual retirement plans
IRAs, 526
dividual-based pay plans
advantages to, 20, 212
duction, 138
dustrial property
inventions, 438
dustries
attractiveness, 178
concentrations of, 266
declining, 98, 266, 481
dustry
growth rate of, 183
trade associations, 53, 189, 252
dustry trade associations, 53, 189, 252
dustry Week, 477
ferior performance, 431
flation
hyperinflation, 46
in Germany, 46
flation base period
inflation rate, 47
flation targeting
in Canada, 44
fluence tactics

combinations of, 19
Influences on channel strategy
availability of intermediaries, 48
environmental factors, 63
Infomercial, 17-18, 489
infomercials, 17-18
informal communication network, 332
Informal communications, 332
Information access, 271
Information appropriateness
timeliness, 19-20
information delivery
best practices, 193, 231, 332, 360-361, 494
Information flows, 249
Information gathering/processing
consumers in, 107
Information management systems
communication system, 332
enterprise system, 474
information security access control list (ACL)
Internet protocol (IP), 108
Information Security Magazine, 216
Information seeking, 206
Information system (IS)
responsibilities in, 500
Information systems
computer network, 351
Secure Sockets Layer (SSL), 216
information systems hardware
motherboard, 335
scanners, 354
information systems (IS)
literacy, 47, 490
Information systems security
security breaches, 367
viruses, 215, 523
information technology (IT)
budgets, 23, 67, 96, 166, 201, 316
InformationWeek, 110, 262
Infrastructure
investments in, 195
Inheritance, 150, 513
Initial markup, 100
Injections, 142, 160
Injury to the innocent party, 430
In-N-Out Burger, 441
Innovation process
integrating, 184, 233
In-process inventory, 229, 303
Input(s)
shared, 533
Inserts, 368, 481
Insiders, 172, 502
Inspections, 232, 354, 519
Installment loans, 108, 120
instant messaging about
security threats, 215
Instrument(s), financial market
capital market, 156
Insurable interest
coverage of, 16
Insurance
deposit, 142
export credit, 65-66
health maintenance organization (HMO), 526
private insurers, 66
score, 139
stop-loss, 527
workers' compensation coverage, 521
Insurance benefits
cost control, 93
preferred provider organizations (PPOs), 533
Insurance brokers, 523
insurance companies
investment strategies, 163
Insurance companies, and pension funds
property and casualty, 521-522
Insurance costs, 276, 518-519
Intangible resources, 311
Integrated human resource information systems (HRIS)
performance management system, 470
integrated marketing
sports teams, 157
Intel
Celeron, 91
Intel Capital, 160
Pentium, 91
Intellectual property (IP) protection

patent applications, 440-441
patents and, 48, 442
Intensive strategies
Market penetration, 94
Intent to deceive, 430
Intentional fieldworker errors
control of, 194, 356-357, 535
Intentional misrepresentation, 430
Intentions, 425, 499
Interaction
Explained, 319
Interactive experience, 184
Interactive Magic, 73
interactivity, 188
intercompany sales
of inventory items, 355
intercultural communication
on the web, 178, 186-187, 317
interest
insurable, 260
Interest expense, 120, 168
Interest income, 108, 516
Interest rate risk
credit and, 65-66, 107, 119, 454
Interest rates
prime rate, 114
savings accounts, 526
Interest-rate risk
nonexistent, 67, 142, 500
Interface and dialogue design
feedback in, 343
interim financial reports
advertising costs, 11
Interior Arrangements, 524
Interlocking directorates, 457
Internal audit, 367
Internal controls, 370
internal environment
hiring procedures, 314
Internal funding
Toyota, 381
Internal service funds
physical inventory, 357-359
self-insurance fund, 518
Internal stakeholders, 462
International advertising
cultural considerations, 47
going global, 44-47, 137
International Association of Business Communicators (IABC)
Research Foundation, 295
International bonds
dealing in, 252, 365
international business
environment for, 165, 269, 444, 518
exporters, 52, 137
General Agreement on Tariffs and Trade, 76
importers, 52
licensing arrangements, 49
North American Free Trade Agreement, 75-76
International business
World Trade Organization (WTO), 75-76
International Council of Shopping Centers, 282
International experience, 160
International Franchise Association, 57-58
International franchising, 49
International freight forwarders, 65
International Harvester, 505
International implications
performance feedback, 339
repatriation, 48
International industries
global opportunities, 47
International Jensen Inc., 77
International Labor Organization (ILO)
Governing Body, 79
International law
letters of credit, 66-67
sales contracts, 64, 432
International law(s)
key issues, 61, 268
international logistics
international freight forwarders, 65
nontariff barriers, 47-48
International market, 55
International operations
raw materials and, 45, 304
international portfolios
investors in, 173-174

International relations
    Middle East, 50
international strategy
    distinctive competence, 165
international trade
    cash in advance, 65
    changes over time, 286
    foreign trade zones, 288-289
    Free trade, 69-70, 449, 490
    lending and, 140
    losses, 65, 107-108, 125, 235, 349, 531
International Trade Administration, 55-56, 306
International Trade Commission, 70-71
International Trade Commission (ITC), 79
International Trade Library, 55
International Trade Program, 137
Internet
    and public relations, 314
    customer service on, 191
    electronic data interchange, 249
    for research, 220
    layers, 215
    malls, 281-282
    personalization, 205
    podcasts, 188, 318
    product reviews, 13, 200
    publicity, 16
    RSS feeds, 200
    salary surveys, 270
    social networking sites, 187, 315
    Social networks, 314
    texting, 336
Internet access
    time online, 183
Internet advertising, 21
Internet law
    Internet service providers, 216
Internet Merchant Account, 216
Internet privacy, 214
Internet Protocol (IP)
    masks, 350
Internship, 315
Internships, 315
Interstate Bakeries, 444
Interstate Commerce Commission, 448
Interstitial ads, 22
Intertemporal trade
    extent of, 279
Interviewing
    asking questions, 321
    background check, 322-323
Interviews
    puzzle, 321
    situational, 321
Interviews, in data-gathering
    open-ended questions, 319
Intoxication, 429
Intrastate offerings, 152
Intrastate offerings (Rule 147), 152
Intruders, 215
Intrusion, 23, 215, 523
Intrusion detection, 215
Intrusion detection software, 215
Intrusion detection systems (IDS)
    log files, 108
Intuit, 167, 337, 536
Invasion of privacy, 480
Invention, 438
Inventor, 146, 149, 441
Inventories
    work-in-process, 303, 350
Inventory
    anticipation, 534
    finished goods, 123, 269, 350, 523
    in transit, 258, 365, 523
    just-in-time, 123, 243, 349-350
    obsolescence, 235, 350-351
    ordering costs, 236-237, 364
    perpetual, 118, 352
    perpetual inventory system, 354
    placement, 5, 115, 203
    purchase discounts, 223
    raw materials, 123, 225, 269, 350, 452, 523
    safety stock, 244-245, 356-358
    sales taxes, 271
    shipping costs, 190, 240
    shrinkage, 371-372
inventory control
    point-of-sale, 250, 351

    safety stock in, 357
Inventory costs, 184, 234-235, 352
Inventory data, 365
Inventory decisions, 244, 351
Inventory financing, 123
Inventory investment, 235, 365
inventory level, 244-245, 350-351
Inventory loans, 125
inventory management
    control systems, 349
    costs of holding inventory, 235
    economic order quantity, 223, 354
    inventory analysis, 356
    inventory carrying costs, 236
    inventory control systems, 349
    inventory shrinkage, 371-372
    just-in-time inventory control techniques, 362
    just-in-time (JIT), 349-350
    Kanban, 228
    slow-moving inventory, 365-366
    techniques for, 37, 95, 340
inventory management system, 359
Inventory shrinkage, 371-372
Inventory tax, 270
Inventory turnover, 119, 260, 351
Inventory turnover objectives, 351
Inventory turnover rate, 361
Inventory turns, 365
Inverted pyramid, 265
Investigating, 372
investment proposals, 157
Investors
    accredited, 174
investors
    angel, 150, 290
Investors
    dividends and, 158
    nonaccredited, 174
Invitation, 123, 192, 370
IOUs, 127
IP addresses, 203
iPods, 13
iProspect, 202
IPsec (IP security)
    gateway, 193
IPSOS, 482
Iraq, 71-72
Irrevocable asset trust, 516
Irrevocable life insurance trust, 515-516
Irrevocable life insurance trust (ILIT), 515
Irrevocable trust, 516
Irrevocable trusts, 515
IRS forms
    Return, 24, 53, 210, 330, 434, 515
Irving, Janis, 328
Israel, 54
issuance costs
    of IPOs, 169
Issues
    compatible, 57, 294, 463
Issuing bank, 107
Iwata, Edward, 494

J
Jackson, Greg, 51
Jacobs, Marc, 204
James, LeBron, 271
Janis, Irving, 328
Jantzen, 364
Japan
    acquired advantage and
    export assistance, 53-55
    trading companies, 53
Japan aging population
    beauty, 16, 111, 498
Jazz Impact, 310
Jen-Mor Florists, 87
Jennings, Lisa, 279
Jeremy, 80-81, 104, 535
Jet Stream Car Wash, 135
Jimmy Choo, 5
Jin, 81, 529
JIT II, 349
JIT system, 362
J&N Enterprises, 61
job applicants
    testing of, 481
Job description
    job specification, 318
    job summary, 317

job descriptions
    honesty in, 368
    standards of performance, 341
Job design
    empowerment and, 333
    enrichment, 335
    job enlargement, 335
    job enrichment, 335
    participation and, 329
    telecommuting and, 348
Job duties, 469
Job enlargement, 335
Job enrichment, 335-336
Job fair, 317
Job growth, 138, 266
Job rotation, 335
Job satisfaction
    teamwork and, 233
Job sharing, 325, 482
Job simplification, 335
Job summary, 317
Job task, 318
Job titles, 318
John Brooke & Sons, 499
Johnny's Lunch, 264-265
Johnson, Gary, 272
Johnston Sweeper Company, 65
Joint venture, 54-55, 160
Joint venture partner, 63
Jolie, Angelina, 243
Jordan, Kim, 324
Josephson, Michael, 471
Journal of Commerce, 66
Journal of Management, 347
Joy, 158
Joyner, Dan, Sr., 509
Joyner, Danny, Jr., 509
Juice, 46
Jumps, 179, 517
Junk mail, 31-32
Jupiter Research, 183
Jury awards, 484, 529
Just-in time and lean operations
    layout and, 219, 256, 263
Just-in-time, 123, 243, 349-350
Just-in-time II (JIT II), 364
Just-in-time inventory, 362
Just-in-time (JIT) inventory
    reduce inventory, 269

K
Kaiser Family Foundation and Health Research and
    Educational Trust, 536
Kalitta Air, 125
Karen Neuburger's Sleepwear, 4
Karim, Jawed, 169
Kauffman Foundation, 141, 157-158, 290
Kaufmann, Daniel, 81
Keegan, Michelle, 25
Keegan, Paul, 306-307, 348
Kellogg, Helen, 467
Kennedy, John, 489
Kennedy, John F., 489
Kennedys, 340
Kenya, 127
Kesmodel, David, 25
Ketchum, 75
Key success factors, 281, 512
KFC, 57, 473
King Features Syndicate, 338
King, Lee, 64
Kiss, 506
Kitty Litter, 269
kiwi, 13
Klein, Andy, 175
Kleppe, Nancy, 61
Kleptomaniacs, 374
Klick-Lewis Buick-Chevrolet-Pontiac, 426
Klock, David, 170
Knockoffs, 437
Knowledge Anywhere, 8
knowledge base, 53, 232, 275
Knowledge management system (KMS)
    best practices in, 360
knowledge management systems (KMS)
    learning management systems, 177
Koch Group, 32
Koss Corporation, 368
KPMG, 469

iter, Suzanne, 75
spy Kreme, 277
c, Ray, 265
skal-Wallis one-way ANOVA
  Correction, 359
nta, Paul, 155

111, 381
ich, Kenneth, 307
or
  underutilized, 134
  wages for, 316
or market
  payroll taxes, 72, 271, 444
or movement before 1930
  conspiracy, 449
or movement challenges and
  airline industry, 92, 131
or relations process
  union organizing, 270
or supply
  wages and, 270, 313
or supply and demand
  employee productivity and, 290-291
m, N. Mark, 75
mmers, Ted, 32
nding pages, 210
guage
  abusive, 455, 484
  obsolete, 51, 162, 455
nguage
  of venture capital, 162
  silent language, 75
nham Trademark Act, 452
rson, Polly, 80
tin America
  economies in, 45
  trade mission, 64
w Merchant, 432
w of agency, 259, 423
ws
  antitrust, 53-54, 98, 451
  staffing and, 321-324
  union, 59, 451
  wage and hour, 337
yered financing, 149
yout
  Web page, 218
yout and design
  shoplifting and, 349
yout strategy
  fixed-position layout, 303
yout/design
  for manufacturers, 263
  signs and, 280
  size and, 61, 280
  sound and, 378
yton, Mark, 188
ad underwriter, 170
ader roles
  of managers, 164-165, 313
adership
  by example, 471
  employees and, 309, 506
  entrepreneur's role, 309-310
adership
  peer, 297, 329
  transforming, 297
adership behaviors
  on team performance, 329
aders/leadership
  servant, 347, 474
an
  mapping the process, 230
an manufacturing, 130, 229
an production, 234
an Six Sigma, 262
an systems
  value stream mapping, 229
arning
  lifelong, 326
arning curve effect, 95
ased line networks
  speeds, 30
ase(s)
  fees, 107, 125, 454
aves of absence, 482
ebesch, Jeff, 324

Lectures, 150, 529
Lee, Hau, 262
Lee, Hau L., 262
Lee, Jeanne, 179, 535
Lee, Jim, 498
Lee, Spike, 141
Lee, Young, 13
LEED (Leadership in Energy and Environmental
  Design) principles, 296
legal aspects
  of employment, 293, 443, 482
  of hiring, 345, 443
Legal behavior, 490
legal dispute, 449
Legal issues
  purchasing and, 256
Legal principles, fundamental
  insurable interest, 260
Legal purpose, 425
Legal restrictions, 29
Legal system and human resource management
  quid pro quo harassment, 483
Legal value, 427
Legality, 425
Lego, 376
Legos, 376
Lehnes, Chris, 125
Lenders
  asset-based, 115
  banking institutions, 118
Lenders and investors, 148, 458
Letter of intent, 159
Letters of credit
  amendments, 452
  application for, 205
Levchin, Max, 157
Level of economic development, 58
Levine, Andy, 319
Levinson, J. Conrad, 3
Levinson, Meredith, 348
Levison, Ivan, 25
lex mercatoria, 432
Liabilities
  bank loan, 447
Liability
  joint and several, 436
  lawsuits and, 531
  market share, 114
  motor vehicle, 522
  property damage, 519
  strict, 437
  unlimited, 437
Liaison, 246
Libraries, 15, 318
Library of Congress, 443
Licensee, 57
Licensing
  nonexclusive, 450
  occupational, 449
Licensing arrangements, 49
Lien, 111, 138, 434
Life expectancy, 498
Life insurance companies, 126
Lifeline, 447
Lifelong learning, 326
Lifestyle center, 285
Lifestyle centers, 279
Lifestyle Market Analyst, 267
Lifetime gifting, 515
LIFO (last-in, first-out)
  liquidation, 366
Lift, 73, 111
LightWedge, 255
Limited liability partnerships (LLPs)
  liability insurance for, 529
limited partnerships
  name of, 29
Limited, The, 516
Ling, Barbara, 189
Liquidated damages, 434
list brokers, 31
Literacy, 47, 490
Literacy programs, 490
Literacy rate, 47
Living standards
  and productivity, 290
L.L.Bean, 207
LLCs, 118
Lloyd's, 519-520

Lloyd's of London, 519
Loan balances, 126
Loan guarantee, 116
Loan portfolio, 133
Loans
  intermediate and long-term, 120
  involving international trade, 137
  leveraged, 505-506
  margin, 119
  microloans, 136-137
loans
  SBA-backed, 133
  to employees, 505
Local cable, 16
Local customs, 52
Local governments
  spending by, 114
Local laws and regulations, 276
Local loan development programs, 138
Local newspaper, 4, 270, 314
Localization, 199
Locating customers
  guerrilla marketing, 37, 187, 305
Location
  retail and service businesses, 263
Location, measures of
  median, 274, 529-530
Location strategy, 270
Lock-up agreement, 172
Loechner, Jack, 221
Log files, 108
Logitech, 157
London stock exchange, 180
long tail, 352-353
Long-term contracts, 87, 131
Long-term disability, 524
Long-term investments, 120
Long-term loans, 120
Los Angeles Times, 4, 536
Loss
  chance of, 177, 365
  of use, 442
Loss prevention, 367
Loss-control program, 531
Louis Vuitton, 5, 204, 437
Lowe, Keith, 122
Lowe's, 293
Lukowitz, Edward, 428
Luna, 459
Luxuries, 93, 226
Lyne, Susan, 204-205
Lynn, Jacquelyn, 122, 306, 535

M
MacBooks, 503
Machinery and equipment insurance, 523
MAD, 363
Madagascar, 225
Magazine advertising
  selectivity, 20
Magazine Publishers of America, 40
Magnuson-Moss Warranty Act, 452
Mailbox rule, 427
Main, Jeremy, 80-81
Maine, 269, 467, 529
Maintain Customers form
  labels on, 489
  with title, 258
Major medical insurance
  supplemental, 425
Malcolm Baldrige National Quality Award, 261
Mall of America, 286
Malpractice
  medical, 530-531
Malpractice insurance, 530
Managed care plans, 526
Management
  amoral, 466-467
  filters, 205
  shareholders and, 167
management accounting
  Nonprofits, 324
Management career issues
  dual-career couples, 184
management consulting, 88, 290, 330
Management consulting services, 290
Management development programs
  job rotation, 335
Management planning

business plan, 52, 118, 148, 219, 261, 346, 381, 458, 493, 534
Management programs, 166
management pyramid, 520-521
"Management Science Application" (box)
    Mars, 476, 498
    NASA, 131, 256
Management succession plans
    trusts and, 515
Managerial judgment, 240
managers
    departmental, 328
Managing, dynamics of
    human resource managers, 347
    top managers, 170, 480
Managing quality
    tools of TQM, 232
Mandated benefits, 72
Mandel, Peter, 499
Mango, 13
Manpower, 48
Mansi, Sattar, 498
Manual system, 354
Manuals, 61
Manufacturers
    layout and design, 263
    layout for, 297
    layouts, 263
    site selection, 263
Manufacturer's export agents (MEAs), 53
Manufacturing
    lean, 67, 130, 227-229, 350-351
    lean manufacturing, 130, 229
    world-class, 77, 226-227, 275, 351
Manufacturing companies
    manufacturing costs, 78, 101, 234, 363
Manufacturing cost, 46
Manufacturing costs, 78, 101, 234, 363
Manufacturing processes
    production line, 236
Marc Jacobs, 204
Marco International, 3
Marginal benefits, 448
marginal corporate tax rate (TC)
    financing and, 125
Marine insurance, 523
Marine Midland Bank, 66
Marinelli, 499
Markels, Alex, 155
market access, 48
Market analysis, 63, 282
market capitalization, 177
Market economy
    shortage, 234
Market failure
    incomplete information and, 312
Market forces, 84
Market interest rates, 138
Market niche, 196
market opportunity, 165
Market power
    firms with, 449
Market saturation, 280
market segmentation
    generations, 479
    product usage, 195
Marketability, 169
marketing
    buzz, 13-14, 297
    Classical music, 296
    concentrated, 166, 269
    Concerts, 276
    establishing a brand, 87, 160
    guerrilla, 37, 187, 305
Marketing
    Museums, 208, 276
    promotion strategies, 201
    Stars, 14, 44
    stealth, 37-38
Marketing channel strategy and
    trade relations, 76
Marketing communications budget, 36
Marketing in global firm
    ethical dimensions of, 493
marketing mix
    modifying the, 63
    price in, 69, 93-94
Marketing processes and consumer behavior
    target marketing, 26

marketing services, 23, 326, 475
Marketing Web site, 40, 220
Market(s)
    black, 26, 249, 353, 479, 535
    gray, 536
Markets
    ideas, and creativity, 76
    institutions and, 140
Market(s)
    loan, 113-114, 155, 447
Markets
    market value, 126
    thin, 29
MarketWatch, 155, 494-495
Markon, 100
markup
    additional, 95
    maintained, 99
Markups, 298
Marquez, Jessica, 347
Martin, Justin, 221
Martin, Kip, 191
Martin's, 104
Mashup, 200
Mashups, 200
mass audience, 18
Mass media, 10
MassMutual Financial Group, 499
Mass-production, 302
Master franchising, 59
Mastercard, 107
Matchmaker Trade Delegations Program, 55
Material breach, 431
Material cost, 87
Material costs, 86
Material fact, 430
Material misrepresentation, 451
Mattioli, Dana, 381
McAfee, 192-193
McCafferty, Joseph, 180
McCann-Erickson, 12
McCarthy, Ryan, 40, 99
McCaw, 160
McCaw, Craig, 160
McCormick, 225
McGee, Suzanne, 162
McGraw's Custom Construction, 527
McKee, Steve, 95
McKinsey and Company, 88, 246, 317, 362, 463
McLaughlin, Katy, 279
McNeil Consumer & Specialty
    Pharmaceuticals, 31
McPhee, Lynn, 155
McRae's, 252
Measurable objectives, 329
Measurement, in marketing research
    unit of, 109, 335
Measuring performance, 341
Mecca, 270
Media
    out-of-home, 27-30
    out-of-home advertising, 27-30
    papers, 11
    Publicity, 1-6
    Reviews, 13, 188-189, 348
    rich, 27, 189
Media Awareness Network, 40
Media characteristics
    print media, 10
media (medium)
    urgency and, 20
Media relations
    new media, 194
    traditional media, 12
Media research, 221, 267
Media types
    mass media, 10
Media vehicle, 10
medical costs, 480, 531
medical leave, 530
Meetings, conducting
    participation, 55, 471
Meinhardt, Shelly, 10
Melick, Steven, 123
Mental incapacities, 429
Mentors, 480, 509
Merchandise
    available for sale, 259
    description, 354

fad, 472
    inspection, 233, 369, 436
Merchandise companies
    sales tax, 375
Merchandise inventory, 356
Merchant, 52, 193, 285, 426, 463
merchant account, 216
Merchant's firm offer, 426
Merger, 450, 507
Mergers and acquisitions
    stock exchange, 171
    survival and, 311
Merging, 459
Merry Maids, 528
Mesa, 267, 518
Message
    vehicles, 10
Message boards, 196
messages
    topic of, 16
Me-too products, 93
Metric, 220
Metropolitan areas, 266
Meyer, David, 347
Meyers, Tiffany, 307
Miami, 271, 364, 476
Miami Dolphins, 297
Miami Heat, 271
Miami Herald, 476
Michaud, Laura, 509
Michelin, 278
Mickey Mouse, 34
Microloan Program, 136
Microloans, 136-137
Microsoft
    Bill Gates, 274
    Word, 38
Microsoft Access
    other features, 85
Microsoft Bing, 203
Microsoft Small Business Center, 32
Microsystems, 128, 152
Midland Bank, 66
migration strategies
    principles to guide, 471
Miles, Dudley, 519
Milestones, 145
Miller, Annetta, 535
Minimum objective, 8
Minimum price, 98
Minimum prices, 98
Minor breach, 431
Mint, 166-167
Mirror image rule, 427
Misconduct, 468
Misrepresentation
    innocent, 430
Mississippi, 96, 138, 254, 302
Mitchell, Alana, 434
Mitchell, Will, 434
Mix
    population age, 280
mobile digital platforms
    RFID, 360-361
Mobile entertainment
    games, 451
Mobile phone industry, sporadic price
    discrimination in, 452
Mobius Partners, 515
Mohammed, 97
Mohammed, Rafi, 97
Molinari, Josh, 24
Momentum, 185, 232, 312, 510
Monahan, Bonnie, 467
Monetary damages
    consequential damages, 424
    liquidated damages, 434
Monetary expansion
    coordinated, 171
Monetary policy
    tight, 372
Money
    fiat, 132
    hot, 123, 165, 191, 279, 494, 500
    purchase plans, 168
Money and banking
    credit cards, 64, 106, 115, 187, 372, 464
Money demand
    money management, 166-167

ney laundering, 464
ney market
  rates on, 125, 184
ney supply
  growth rates, 167
ney-back guarantee, 209
onitor Group, 270, 507
onitoring systems, 343
onopolies
  breaking up, 449
onopolistic competition
  firms in, 37
  managerial decision making, 101
onthly Labor Review, 347
ood, 13, 307, 347
oore, Bob, 506
oore, Pam, 193
oral awareness, 466
oral blindness, 469-470
oral hazard
  insurance and, 519
oral management, 466-467
oral managers, 467
oral stance, 464
orality, 472
oran, Gwen, 180
ores, 72
organ Stanley, 171
ori Books, 4
ori, Richard, 4
ortgage
  lenders, 125
otherboard, 335
otion pictures, 443
otivation
  and rewards, 327
  conflicts, 331
  job design, 332
  vision and, 313
ount, Ian, 80-81, 262, 324
ountaineers, 5
ovie(s)
  Audiences, 4
oving averages
  averages, 154, 286
SA, 268
ultilateral trading system, 76
ultiple unit pricing, 97
ulti-State/Catalog Exhibition Program, 55
urdoch, Rupert, 511
usculoskeletal disorders (MSDs), 294
usic
  Classical, 19, 296
usic downloads, 96
usk, Elon, 149
uzak, 307
ycoskie, Blake, 315, 474
ySpace, 201, 323
yths
  of e-commerce, 181-182

adel, Brian, 262
ager, Ross, 501
ail salons, 279
ano, 94
arrative, 40
ASDAQ OMX, 177
ational brand, 176
ational Business Incubation Association, 290
ational Center for Employee Ownership, 505
ational Community Reinvestment Coalition, 134
ational Cooperative Business Association, 241
ational Cyber Security Alliance, 216
ational Environmental Policy Act (NEPA)
  lawsuits, 170, 424-425, 488, 527
ational Institute of Standards and Technology, 261
ational market, 169
ational Market System (NMS), 169
ational Organization for Women, 473
ational origin discrimination
  discrimination against, 293, 321-322, 482
  spouse, 470
ational Public Radio, 6
ational Research Council, 145
ational Retail Federation, 372
ational Rifle Association (NRA)
  ads, 16-17, 180, 188, 314, 473
ational Safety Council, 532

National Science Foundation, 131
National Small Business Association, 115
National Trade Data Bank, 55
national trade policies
  economic development programs, 113
National Venture Capital Association, 165
Natural disasters, 130, 225, 517
Natural Foods, 506
Natural gas, 264
Natural listings, 201-203
Nayar, Vineet, 331
NBC, 441
Negative feedback, 166, 342
Negligence
  defenses against, 429
Negligent design, 436
Negligent hiring, 323
Negligent manufacturing, 436
Neighborhood locations, 283
Neighborhood shopping center, 284
Neighborhood shopping centers, 284
Neil, Dan, 93
Nelson, Bob, 339
nepotism, 502
Nestle, 306
Net assets
  classes of, 446, 516
Net sales, 100
Netnames, 208
Netscape, 155
Netting, 177
Network connections
  building trust and, 467
network television, 16
New Belgium Brewing Company, 324
New digital media
  digital media, 12
New Hampshire, 4, 127, 156, 336, 498
New Line Cinema, 5
New media, 194
New Pig, 207
New Products
  launching, 35, 47, 95, 153, 181, 261, 264, 317, 526
New York Stock Exchange (NYSE)
  transaction volume, 193
New York Yankees, 514
News Corporation, 511
news media, 3
NFL, 450-451
niche markets, 49, 99, 195, 353
Nickelodeon, 286
Nickelodeon Universe, 286
Nielsen
  Nielsen Media Research, 267
Nintendo, 324, 503
Nintendo Wii, 324
Nissan Motor Corporation, 488
Node, 347
Nonaccredited investors, 174
Nondisclosure agreement, 69
Nonperformance, 431
Non-performance
  excuses for, 471
Nonprice competition, 89
Nonprofit public relations
  libraries, 15
  museums, 276
Nonstore-based retailing perspective
  store layout, 256, 297-298
Nontariff barriers, 47-48
Normal costing
  in manufacturing, 101
  simplified, 178
Normal curve, 244-247
Normal distribution
  standard deviation, 245
Normal distributions
  areas under, 246
Normal retirement age, 506
Normally distributed, 244
Norman, Jan, 254, 536
North American Free Trade Agreement (NAFTA)
  origin, 48, 322-323, 453
North Carolina State University, 229, 270
Northeast, 136, 270, 315
Norton, 247
No-safety stock system, 248
Notification, 173, 209, 444, 487
Novotny, Sarah, 336

NOW account, 183
Number
  Serial, 119, 156
Numerical statistical measures
  Summary, 80, 261
Nutrition, 529
Nygard International, 234
Nygard, Peter, 234

O
Oakley, 437
OAS, 494
Obama presidential campaign (1998)
  blog, 14, 306, 535
Oberwager, Brad, 46
Objective criteria, 225
Objective theory of contracts, 425-426
Objective-and-task method, 36
Objectives
  competitor's, 94
Obsolescence, 33, 235, 350-351, 501
Occupational Safety and Health
  fatalities, 307
  hazard, 519
  inspections, 232, 356, 519
  National Institute of, 261
  safe working environment, 444
Occupational Safety and Health Administration
  (OSHA)
  record keeping, 357-358
  Website, 25, 536
Occurrence, 533
Oceania, 50
O'Connell, Vanessa, 306
Octagon, 253
Octagon Research Solutions, 253
OD strategies
  basic types, 202, 352
Odd pricing, 95
Odors, 288
Offer price, 99
Offeree, 426-427
Offeror, 426-427
Offers
  extreme, 199, 267, 428
OfficeTeam, 318
Offline, 220
Offsets, 325
O'Hara, William T., 499
O'Hare Airport, 231
Oil Pollution Act
  of 1990, 456
Oil spills, 66, 456
Old Navy, 299
Older workers, 317
Ombudsman, 489
OMX, 177
O'Neill, Danny, 86
O'Neill, Talmadge, 72
One-time costs, 49
Oneupweb, 207
Online advertising
  e-mail marketing, 24-25, 191, 475
Online auction
  brokers and, 65
Online auction sites, 375
Online companies, 99, 192
Online newsletters, 197
Online order tracking, 209
online presence, 185
Online privacy, 214
Online research, 69, 183
Online sampling techniques
  invitation, 192
Online search, 440
Online security, 186
Online videos, 200
Onysko, Joshua, 277, 476
Open account, 67
Open economy
  imaginary, 425-426
open rate, 23-24, 197
Open system
  organization as, 463
operating budget, 9
Operating costs, 72, 165, 271, 343, 365, 447, 476
Operating profit, 105-106
Operating profit margin, 105
operating reports, 334

Operations control tools
    process control, 232-233
operations management
    service sector, 87
Operations management, operational
    renovations, 368
Operations planning
    product layouts, 302-303
Operations strategy in a global environment
    strategy options, 497
Opinion Research Corporation, 490
Opportunities, identifying
    qualities of, 20
Opportunity cost
    of funds, 95, 124, 148-149, 498
    of investments, 153-154
    of running a business, 332
Opportunity pressures, 470
Optimal decision, 312
Optional-product pricing, 97
Options
    employee stock, 168, 324, 504-505
Order fill rate, 361
Order management
    order processing, 7, 189, 512
Order processing as activity-level model (e-business
        model)
    self-service, 27, 89
Order quantity, 223, 354
Order tracking, 209
Ordering costs, 236-237, 364
Organic chemicals
    in water, 476
Organic listings, 202-203
organization
    agile, 310
Organization
    tall, 48
Organizational atmosphere, 368
Organizational culture
    learning environment, 326
    participative management, 326
    positive culture, 325
    sense of fun, 326
    sense of purpose, 325, 510
Organizational leadership, 509
Organizational policies and procedures, 464
Organizational renewal strategies implementation of
    turnaround, 162, 218
Organizational settings
    top management, 62
Organized crime, 375
Origin, 48, 322-323, 441
Original contract, 433
OSHA, 294
Out of the Book, 473
Outback Steakhouse, 128, 161
Outdoor advertising, 28-29
Outdoor Advertising Association, 28
Outdoor Advertising Association of America, 28
Outlet, 40, 98, 207, 279
Outlet centers, 284
Outlet shopping centers, 279
Outlying areas, 282
out-of-home advertising
    advertising plan, 9
    spectaculars, 29
Outsourcing
    total cost of, 254
    vendors, 242-244
Overfelt, Maggie, 35, 122
Overproduction, 227
Oversight, 114
Ownership plans, 168, 340, 505
Oxygen, 489
Ozone, 456

P

Pace Productivity, 7
Packaging requirements, 65
Page, Larry, 149
page views, 212
Paid listings, 203
Paid search, 203
Pangea Organics, 277, 476
Papa John's, 182, 453
Papa John's Pizza, 453
Par value
    of stock, 167, 234, 354, 515-516

Paramount, 129, 251
Parent, 149, 511
Pareto principle, 353
Pareto, Vilfredo, 352
Pareto's Law, 232, 352-353
parity conditions, international
    prices in, 89-90
Parker Pen, 74
Parker Pen Company, 74
Partial inventory control systems, 355
Participants in international business
    facilitators, 328
Passage of title, 258
Paste
    Values, 63
Patek, 88
Patek Philippe, 88
Patent, 52, 152, 208, 438-439
Patent and Trademark Office, 208, 438
Patent application, 152, 438
Patent law, 440
Paychecks, 526
Pay-for-knowledge programs
    technological innovation, 459
Pay-for-performance compensation systems, 337
Payloads, 65
Paymaxx, 169
payment services, 193
payment terms, 118, 243, 426
Payne, John, 355
Payne, John W., 355
PayPal, 149, 189
Pay-per-click, 23, 197
Pay-per-click ad, 213
Pay-per-click ads, 23
Payroll tax, 367
Pearson, Roy, 529
Pebble Beach, 97
Peer appraisals, 344-345
Peer pressure, 373
Peer ratings, 319
Peer reviews, 344
Pella, 508
Pella Products, 508
Penalties, 25, 108, 368-369, 424, 484, 527
Penetration, 50, 93-94
Penetration pricing strategy, 94
Penetration strategy, 94
Penguin, 364
pension plans
    cash balance, 125
pension trust funds
    governments, 69, 456
Pentilla, Chris, 347
Penttila, Chris, 247, 347-348, 494
People
    land and, 530
People with disabilities, 307, 322
percentage terms, 454
Percentage-of-sales approach, 36
percentages, 299
Pereira, Joseph, 111, 494
Perez, Antonio, 179
Perfect competition
    business decision, 68, 305
Performance
    discharge of, 456
Performance
    rewards for, 232, 339
performance appraisals
    peer appraisals, 344-345
Performance compensation, 337
Performance evaluation
    data analysis tools, 202, 230
Performance evaluations, 508
Performance feedback, 339
Performance gap, 342
Performance Management
    realities of, 480, 513
Performance objectives, 232, 325
Periodic count, 358
Perishability, 288
Perpetual inventory systems, 354
Perry Ellis, 364-365
Person marketing, 256
Personal Auto Policy (PAP)
    liability coverage, 523
Personal bias, 480
Personal guarantees, 118

Personal injury
    endorsement, 25, 306
Personal property
    abandoned, 90, 189, 283, 506
Personal satisfaction, 327
Personal savings, 89, 147
Personal service, 24, 89
Personal services, 431, 524
Personality
    traits and, 320
Personalization, 205
Persuasive messages
    mistakes in, 319
Pew Internet, 200
Pew Internet & American Life Project, 200
Pew Internet and American Life Project, 206
Pew Research Center, 26
Pfeffer, Jeffrey, 347
Pharmaceutical industry
    development costs, 95
Phillips curve
    return of, 24, 95
Phishing
    email, 220
Physical address, 192
Physical barriers, 280
Physical breakdowns, 369
Physical delivery, 434
Physical environment, 47
Physical inventory count, 357-359
Physical proximity, 254
Physical resources, 311
Pier, 284
Pier 1 Imports, 284
Pilferage, 235
Pillsbury, 424
Pillsbury Doughboy, 424
Pinkberry, 13
Pirated software, 437
Pit, 231
Place of delivery, 432
Planes, 162, 265, 311
Planned shopping center
    community shopping center, 284
    developers, 201, 283
    neighborhood shopping center, 284
    open-air, 284-285
Planning
    capital needs, 151
    for capital needs, 151
Planning activities, 364
Plant size, 152
plants, 130, 225, 269, 363, 447
Platt, Gordon, 66
PlayStation, 98
Plotter, 258
Plummer, Daryl, 194
Point of indifference, 282
pointers, 74
Point-of-purchase ads, 27
Poison Prevention Packaging Act, 452
Poland, 126
Policy loans, 126
politeness, 74, 377
Political barriers, 71, 280
Political economy
    of trade, 33, 62, 449-450
pollution
    air, 455-457
    solid waste, 456
    water, 455, 476
Pollution prevention, 455-457
Pollution Prevention Act of 1990, 456
POM for Windows
    inventory problems, 359
Pontiac, 426
pooled retained earnings
    balances, 125-126, 168
Pope, Ivan, 201
population
    extent, 62, 279
    trading area, 275
Population trends, 268
pop-up ad, 22
Portal, 56
Porter, Michael E., 275
POS system, 359
Positive correlation, 474
possession, 258, 434-435

sters, 29
tter, Harry, 443
well, Emily, 507
well, Michael, 507
well's Books, 507
wer
  authority and, 513
  contrast, 294-295
wer center, 284-285
wer centers, 283-284
wer orientation
  by country, 183
Newswire, 459
ada, 5
aching, 272
cision, 257
edictable variability management
  sales and operations planning, 364
eferential trade agreements
  free trade area, 79
  in North America, 285, 506
eferred provider organization (PPO), 526
eferred provider organizations (PPOs), 533
ejudices, 479
elitigation process
  complaint, 8, 164, 254, 342, 448
escription medications, 437
esley, Elvis, 104
estige pricing, 86
evailing wage, 270
ice controls
  minimum prices, 98
ice discrimination
  buyers and, 33, 99, 363, 504
ice elasticity
  coupons and, 90
ice leader, 96
ice lining, 96
ice points, 109-110
ice strategy
  leader pricing, 96
  manufacturers and, 33, 276, 452
  odd pricing, 95
  price lining, 96
  unit pricing, 97
ice support
  of agriculture, 276
ice transparency, 189
ice wars, 89-90
iceline, 96, 189, 438
ice/pricing
  captive-product, 97
  cost-plus, 95
  optional-product, 97
  price leader, 96
ices/pricing
  byproduct, 98
  follow-the-leader, 86
  image and, 89
  impact of credit on, 83
  multiple unit, 97
  odd, 95
  penetration, 50, 93-94
  suggested retail, 98, 241
icewaterhouseCoopers, 161, 498-500
icing
  airline, 92
icing
  by retailers, 83
  prestige, 86
  the market and, 94
  uniform delivered, 96
icing and pricing strategies
  psychology of pricing, 85
icing, international
  setting prices, 88
icing method, 101
icing practices
  prestige pricing, 86
icing strategies
  established products and services, 95
  new product pricing, 93
  service businesses, 105
icing structure, 62, 99
imary sources, 366
ime interest rate, 133-134
ime prospects, 33
ime rate, 114
inceton, 166

Principal
  of loan, 119-120
Print ads, 9
Privacy
  invasion of, 480
  medical records, 482
  surveillance, 377, 493
privacy and information rights
  technological solutions, 380
private companies, capitalizing
  outside investors, 164
private debt
  term loans, 118
Private investors, 128, 148-149
Private sector, 337, 479
Privileges, 471
PRIZM, 305
PRNewswire, 459
Pro bono, 474
Pro forma statements, 144
proactive management, 518
Probability
  Rules, 32, 292, 368-369
Procedures
  sub, 486
Proceeds, 118, 170, 445, 515-516
Process control, 232-233
Process control charts, 233
Process improvement, 230, 329
Process layouts, 303
Process strategy
  strategic fit, 504
  sustainability, 465
Process structure
  in services, 76
Process transactions, 107
processes
  variation in, 233
product
  Films, 71
  invention, 438
Product assortment, 300
product categories, 208, 252
Product class
  compatibility, 275
Product defects
  correction of, 359
Product demand, 352
Product descriptions, 21, 205
product design
  complementary products, 22, 279
Product development and marketing
  promotional strategies, 2, 186
product flow, 303
Product innovation, 166
Product layout, 303
Product layouts, 302-303
Product liability lawsuits, 436-437, 529
Product life cycle (PLC)
  sales and profits over, 10
Product management
  of existing products, 438
product manager, 324
Product pricing, 93
Product reviews, 13, 200
Product strategy
  packaging and labeling, 452
Production
  efficiency in, 87
Production costs
  total costs, 103, 237
production cycle
  production operations, 302
Production inputs, 224
Production line, 236
Production scheduling, 249
Production technology
  radio frequency identification, 359
Productivity
  machine, 303
Products
  defective, 225-226, 435-437
  equivalent, 5, 95, 183, 278
  global markets and, 53
  me-too, 93
  packaging for, 52
  quantity discounts for, 366
  revolutionary, 93, 501
  right to choose, 490

products
  samples of, 121
Product(s)
  tied, 359
  unsafe, 231, 452
Products, developing and pricing
  convenience goods, 298
  pricing tactics, 97-98
  prototype development, 131
  specialty goods, 298
Products/services
  manufacturing layouts, 302
Professional development, 324
Professional ethic, 470
Professional shoplifters, 374
Profit and loss statement, 144
profitability ratios
  Raw material costs, 86
Profit/profitability
  cash and, 164, 361
Profit-sharing plan, 506
Programmer, 68
Project initiation and planning (PIP)
  challenge of, 332
project management
  milestones, 145
  project manager, 175
Project quality
  baseline, 230
Project resources
  RBS, 130-131
Projective techniques
  Completion, 83, 181, 333, 349
  Motivational, 339
  Ranking, 201
Prominence, 21
Promissory estoppel, 427-428
Promoters, 189
Promotion
  Star, 6
Promotion from within, 314
Promotion strategies, 201
Promotion techniques, 93
Promotional activities, 39
Promotional campaign, 2
Promotional products, 98
Proper form, 456
property
  artistic, 443
Property damage, 519
property taxes
  discounts on, 516
  levied, 126
Proprietary technology, 57
Propstra, George, 526
Prosecutors, 464
Protection
  of international trade, 48
Protection of intellectual property, 423
Protocols, 73
Proximate cause, 437
Pryde, Joan, 122
Psychology of pricing, 85
Public acceptance, 468
Public assistance, 455
public companies, 168-169
Public goods
  rival, 91, 190
Public image, 191
Public offering, 149, 205
Public property, 443
Public radio, 6, 459
Public relations
  working in, 176
Public relations agencies
  billing, 140, 455
Public Relations Society of America (PRSA)
  body of knowledge, 509
Public services, 276
public speaking, 4
Public stock sale, 167
Publicly traded, 168
Puffery, 453
Puma, 296
Purchase discounts, 223
Purchase order, 123, 354, 433
Purchase requisitions, 243
Purchaser, 66
Purchasing

electronic data interchange (EDI), 249, 359
Purchasing costs, 184, 364
Purchasing function, 223-225
Pure Food and Drug Act, 452

Q

Quadrille Quilting, 15
Quality
  Control charts, 232-233
  Deming, 226
  quantity and, 59, 269, 452
  SPC, 232
  Statistical quality, 232
  statistical quality control, 232
quality assurance, 506
Quality issues
  of raw materials, 87, 123, 269
Quality levels, 78
Quality of life, 264
Quality of Work, 106, 226, 325
Quality of work life, 226
Quality theory
  quality management and, 232
Questions
  discriminatory, 322-323
  environmentally responsible, 477
  franchisors, 78
QuickBooks, 536
Quid pro quo, 483
Quid pro quo harassment, 483
Quid pro quo sexual harassment, 483
QVC, 18

R

Racine Federated, 518
RADAR, 131, 332, 479
Radicati Group, 23
Radio advertising
  signal, 301, 359
radio frequencies, 359
Radio frequency identification tags (RFID), 359
Railway Labor Act (RLA)
  Act and, 304
Rainmaker Institute, 313
Raleigh, 270, 332
Ralph Brennan Restaurant Group, 522
RAM, 306
Ranch, 514
RAND, 267
Random drug tests, 323, 519
Random number
  seed, 156-157, 290
rate of return
  investors and, 149-150
Rates
  excessive, 71, 142
  reasonable, 125, 190, 225, 276, 513
Rathke, Fran, 467
Rationalization, 368, 469
Ratios
  average collection period, 119
  average inventory turnover, 119
  average payable period, 119
Raw material, 86, 169, 251-252, 264, 334, 360, 424
Raymond Institute, 510
Razor, 92
real estate brokers, 429
Real estate transactions
  appraisals, 121, 342
Real money, 97-98
real property
  contracts involving, 430
  fixtures, 125, 229
  security interest in, 120
Really Simple Syndication (RSS), 200
Reasonable accommodations, 293
rebates, 90, 241
Receivables, 118
Recency, 213
Recession
  recent, 92
Record keeping, 357-358
Recruiting and hiring
  "retired" workers, 317
Recruiting employees for international assignment
  locals, 74
recruiting process, 314
Recruitment and selection process

legal implications, 223
Red Cross, 490
Red Door Interactive, 106
Red flag, 517
Red Owl Stores, 428
Reduced cost, 363
Redundancy, 80
Reeb, David, 498
Reebok, 450
Reese's Pieces, 16
RefCheck Information Services Inc., 323
Refining, 163, 201
Refrigerator Safety Act, 452
Refunds, 374, 495
Regional shopping malls, 284
Regional stock exchanges, 169
Registration statements, 173
Regression projects
  guides, 467
  running, 243, 330, 508
Regulation A, 152
Regulation D, 173-175
Regulation S-B, 152
Regulations
  product safety, 457
Regulatory agencies, 448
Regulatory changes, 121
Regulatory compliance, 169, 449
Regulatory issues
  harassment and, 464
Rehiring, 448
REI, 5
Reid, John, 146
Reifert, Jane, 521
Reilly's law of retail gravitation, 282
Reimbursement, 340, 444
Reingold, Jennifer, 494
Rejections, 7, 320
Relative cost, 10-11, 269, 454
Relative importance, 251, 272, 355
Reliance Industries, 498
Reliance Industries Ltd., 498
Religion
  respect for, 471
Relocation, 306
remarketing, 220
Remedies
  seller's, 434
Reminder ads, 26
Renaissance Capital, 180
Renovations, 286, 368
Reorder point model, 243-244
Reorder points, 243
Repayment schedules, 125
Report format
  data analysis, 306
Requirements analysis phase of SDLC
  changes in requirements, 358
Research
  Tourism, 76
Research and development costs
  capitalization of, 177
Resident buying offices, 53
Resnick, Rosalind, 99, 118, 159
Resource conservation, 455-457
Resource decisions, in multiproject
  environments, 121, 328
Resources
  leveling, 510
  private ownership of, 45
Resources management, 72
Response rates, 23
Responsible citizenship, 471
Restaurant business, 146, 295
Restoration, 132, 428, 522
Retail compatibility, 279
Retail environment, 295, 364
retail industry
  Specialty stores, 284-285, 364
Retail layout, 297-298
Retail strategy
  low-end, 70
Retail, Wholesale, and Department Store
  Union, 59, 127, 272, 451
Retailers
  location criteria for, 263
Retailer(s)
  off-price, 285
Retailers/retailing

chain stores, 89, 241
convenience stores, 280, 353
specialty stores, 284-285, 364
warehouse clubs, 284
Retailing, online, 220-221
Retaliation, 345, 482-483
retention rate, 228, 330
retention rates, 192, 226
Retirement income
  monthly, 108, 116, 524
Retirement planning
  employee stock ownership plans, 340, 505
Return policies, 190
Returns to scale
  decreasing, 250, 270
Reuse, 476
Reuters, 111, 139, 459, 482
Revenue accounting of governmental funds
  licenses and permits, 54
Revenue bonds, 128
Revenue growth, 163, 498
Revolutionary products, 93
Revolving line of credit, 135
Revolving loan funds (RLFs), 138
Reward system, 231, 337, 469
Reward systems, 337
RFID tag, 360
Richard de Bas, 499
Richness, 478
Riedel Glas Austria, 501
Riedel, Maximilian, 501
Right Management, 347
Rights
  recall, 224
Right(s)
  third parties, 455, 484
  to inspect, 230, 434
  to strike, 178, 482
Rihanna, 179
Riken Corporation, 363
RIM, 53
Rising prices, 87
Risk
  burdens of, 519
  comparable, 68
  housing and, 130, 498
  moderate, 130, 277
  owners, 44-45, 91, 114-115, 152, 183, 235, 278,
    310, 462-464, 498-502
  prevalent, 211, 257
  return for, 156
  return to, 159, 210, 235
Risk
  spreading, 532
Risk capital, 152
Risk identification, 518
Risk Management
  global supply chains, 247
Risk management process
  risk identification, 518
Risk management pyramid, 520-521
Risk management strategies, 497
Rite, 122
Rite Aid, 122
Ritter, Jay, 180
Rivals, 195, 226, 264, 359, 535
Rivers, 280
Robert Half International, 317
Roberts, Carlotta, 454
Robillard, Mike, 133
Rolex, 88
Rolling stock, 56
Rolling Stone, 26
Rolls-Royce, 92
Roof Connect, 519
Rosenbaum, Andrew, 75
Rosenberg, Alec, 507
Rosetta Stone, 171
Ross, Charles, 256
Rounds, 153-154
RSS, 179, 200, 495, 535
Ruby Tuesday, 92
Ruiz, Gina, 494
Rule 505 offering, 174
Rule making (agency)
  exempted, 174
Rural areas, 131, 289
Rural Business-Cooperative Service (RBS), 130
Rural development, 136

...shing in, 152
...nes, Sara, 475

...bbaticals, 325
...CS Consulting & Investigative Services Inc., 367
...fety stock, 244-245, 356-358
...fety stock system, 248
...ga, 535
...insbury, 498
...nts, 451
...ladino, Joseph, 97
...le and lease contracts
  modification of, 233
...le for cash plus a note, 504
...les
  conditions of, 46, 454
  receipts, 358, 448
  UCC and, 436
...les channel, 183
...les contracts
  writing requirement, 425
...les function, 39
...les promotion
  sweepstakes, 5
...les salaries, 33
...les warranties, 435-436
...lespersons, 435
...lon, 133, 218
...lvage value, 125
...mple frame
  Internet users, 206, 463
...mple size
  overall, 30, 45, 163, 186, 269-270
  population size and, 280
...mpling techniques
  Statistical, 230
...m's Club, 137
...an Antonio Clippers, 133
...an Francisco Business Times, 145
...an Francisco Chronicle, 146
...an Francisco Giants, 474
...nchanta, Mariko, 75
...nctions, 484
...anders, Colonel, 473
...arbanes–Oxley Act
  Section, 178-179, 219, 426, 529
...avings
  college, 36, 89, 154, 315
  for retirement, 526
...avings account, 116, 526
...avings and loan associations (S&Ls), 126
...avvy, 205, 503
...BAExpress Program, 133
...BIR Program, 132
...canAlert, 215
...canner, 16
...carborough, 1, 43, 83, 113, 147-148, 181, 223, 263,
    309, 349, 423, 461, 497
...cent, 295
...cents, 18, 295
...chreiber, Jeff, 242
...chreibfeder, Jon, 361
...chultz, Howard, 75
...chutte, Ron, 61
...CM, 248-249
...COR, 152
...cotland, 196
...cotsman Ice Systems, 231
...cott Fiore, 9
...cott, Robert E., 141
...creening process, 163, 319, 370
...CTR Systems, 513
...ean John, 18
...earch costs, 353
...earch engine optimization (SEO), 201-202
...earch engine optimization (SEO) strategy, 201
...earch marketing, 201
...easonal merchandise, 19
...eattle Post-Intelligencer, 459, 535
...ection 504 Certified Development Company
    Program, 136
...ectors, 80, 227
...ecure sockets layer (SSL), 216
...ecure sockets layer (SSL) technology, 216
...ecured credit, 123
...ecured loans
  accounts receivable as collateral, 123
  inventory loans, 125

Securities Act of 1933
  registration statements, 173
Securities and Exchange Commission (SEC)
  IPO, 149
  Rule 147, 152
Securities, bank-related
  traded, 168-169
Securities Exchange Act of 1934
  Regulation S, 152
securities regulations
  registration requirements, 173
Seed capital, 154, 204, 290
seed money, 151
SeeWhy, 193
Segmentation
  Importance of, 355
  Usage, 355-357
SELECT statement (SQL) calculations
  ranges, 215, 478
Selective listening, 331
Self-directed work team, 328
Self-esteem
  clothing and, 332
Self-insurance, 518-519
Self-insurance fund, 518
Self-managed work teams
  reward system, 231, 337
Self-sufficiency, 153
Sell-through, 204
Senior citizens, 97
Sensation, 501
Sensory systems
  scents, 295
Sephora, 300-301
September 11, 81, 347
Servant leadership, 347
service businesses
  pricing strategies for, 93
Service charges, 454
Service facility, 289
Service level factors, 246
Service mark, 441
Service retailing
  location in, 131, 277
Service sector
  TQM in, 231
service sectors, 227
Servicemarks, 442
Service(s)
  blueprint, 317
Services
  channels of distribution, 63, 94, 186
services
  international market for, 63
Setup cost, 236
Setup costs, 33, 238
Seven-step strategic management process
  implement the strategies, 313
Seventh Generation, 104
Several liability, 436
Severance pay, 116
Severiens, Hans, 157
Severity, 215, 314, 520-521
Sevin Rosen, 165
Sexual harassment
  assault, 323
  hostile work environment, 486
  quid pro quo, 483
  same sex, 494
Seymour, Kim, 332
ShamWow, 18
Shaping, 509
Shared advertising, 37-38
Shares
  issued, 463, 504
Shares of common stock, 174, 504
Shares of stock, 167-168
shares, of stock, 167-168
Sharma, Amol, 535
Shellenbarger, Sue, 306
Shepherd, Jeremy, 104
Sherman Antitrust Act of 1890, 450, 490
Shipley, Thomas, 523
Shipment contract, 258
Shippers, 65
Shipping costs, 96, 190, 240, 288
Shipping terms, 65-66, 258, 426
Shock, 87
shoplifting, 235, 298, 349

Shopping
  atmospherics, 41
Shopping agents
  second-generation, 361
Shopping carts, 189
Shopping center, 176, 279
shopping malls, 127, 279
Shopping networks, 17-18
Shortages, 224, 317, 355-356
Short-term disability, 524
Short-term interest rates, 179
Shrinkage, 371-372
SHRM, 347-348
Shuttle, 320
Sick leave, 482
SideStep, 174
Sight draft, 67
Signatures
  unauthorized, 215
Silent generation, 206
Silent language, 75
Simmons & Simmons, 67
Simon, Mike, 165
Simple linear regression
  Pitfalls in, 56
sincerity, 14, 342
Singer, 459
Single audit
  applicability, 302
  purposes, 129
Site evaluation
  parking facilities, 283
Site selection, 263
situational interviews, 321
Size
  of competition, 279, 450
Skill variety, 335
Skills simulation
  team development, 329
Skimming, 93-95, 372
Skimming pricing strategy, 94-95
Skimming strategy, 94
Skype, 52, 156
SLAM, 132, 170, 292
Slice-of-life executional framework
  encounter, 88, 464
SlideShare, 220
Sloan School of Management, 353
slots, 19-20
Slow-moving inventory, 365-366
Slow-moving items, 360
Small business
  Small Business Development Center (SBDC), 268
Small Business Administration (SBA)
  anticipated expenses, 100, 346
  certified development company (CDC), 136
  disaster loans, 137-138
  loan programs, 65, 113
Small Business Innovation Research (SBIR), 131
Small Business Innovation Research (SBIR) program,
  131
Small Business Investment Act, 128
Small business lending companies (SBLCs), 129
Small Business Technology Transfer (STTR), 132
Small Business Technology Transfer (STTR) program,
  132
Small Company Offering Registration, 152
Small Company Offering Registration (SCOR), 152
Small firms, 19, 49, 109, 114, 235, 317, 355, 449
Smart phones, 12
Smell & Taste Treatment & Research Foundation, 295
Smith, Adam, 381
Smith, Jack, 89
Smoke, 162
Smoking, 529
Sniffing, 491
Snipperoo, 201
Snodgrass, Paul, 508
Soccer, 336
Social class
  middle class, 47
Social costs
  of accidents, 527
  of crime, 373
Social dilemmas
  business as, 477
  volunteer, 187, 467-468
social entrepreneur, 494
Social entrepreneurs, 468

social networking
    for entrepreneurs, 63, 154, 199, 479
    marketing tool, 182
    to attract customers, 188
    widgets, 201
Social networking and Web
    campaigns and, 24, 474
    viral marketing and, 14
social problems, 468
Social Security
    credits, 277, 343
Socially responsible behavior, 467
Society for Human Resource Management (SHRM)
    guidebook, 348
sockets, 216
Sockets layer, 216
Soft goods, 284
Software
    Green Dam, 463
    intrusion detection, 215
    patches, 529
    reuse, 476
software development, 528
Soldiers, 34
Sole sourcing, 253-254
Solon, 40
Song, 40, 307
Sonoma, 292
Sony PlayStation, 111
sound effects, 20
sourcing debt globally
    market of, 76
South Africa
    business opportunities in, 77
South Carolina, 51, 130, 225, 269, 314, 367, 474
Southdale, 283
Southern Institute for Business and Professional
        Ethics, 470
Space Store, 281
Spangenberg, Eric, 295
Spanyi, Andrew, 230
Special form (HO-3)
    fire in, 520
Special interest groups, 462
Specialties, 27
Specialty retailers, 284-285
Specialty store, 365
Specific risk, 533
Spectrum, 138
Speeches, 459
Spiders, 202
Spiegel, 288
Spill, 138
Spinning, 194
Spin-offs, 163
Spoke, 315
Spokespersons, 4
Sponsored listings, 202
Sports Clips, 133
Sports teams, 157
Sportswear, 360
Spread, 13, 141, 448, 519-520
Spring Street Brewing, 175
Springfield Remanufacturing Corporation, 45, 505
Springfield Remanufacturing Corporation (SRC), 505
Sprout, 476
SPSS Windows
    EXPLORE, 300
SQL (Structured Query Language)
    case in, 451
Stack, Jack, 45, 505
Stamps, David, 75
Standard & Poor's 500 Index, 498
Standard deviation
    of returns, 31
Standard error
    Statistical process control, 232-233
Standard markup, 109
Standard rate, 31
Standard Rate and Data Service, 31
Standards of performance, 341, 511
Stanford University, 212
Stanley Brothers Furniture Outlet, 207
Stanley, Morgan, 171
Star
    Images, 6
Starch, 76, 478
staring, 294
Start-up capital, 133, 148, 315

start-ups
    business plan for, 176
State and Metropolitan Area Data Book, 266
State evaluation matrix, 271-272
State government, 128
State governments, 271
State laws
    environmental protection, 455
Statements
    bank statements, 372
Statements of Financial Accounting Standards (SFAS)
    pledges, 123
States
    business climate in, 268
Static, 16
statistical process control (SPC)
    variables for, 267
Statistical quality
    process control charts, 233
Statistics
    jumps, 179
Statistics of Income, 267
Statute of Frauds
    UCC, 432-436
Statute(s)
    of limitations, 435
Stealing, 99, 216, 322, 367-371
Stealth advertising, 37-38
Stein, Nicholas, 535
Stock
    brokerage houses, 126
    preferred, 163, 504
    repurchases, 125
Stock brokerage houses, 126
Stock exchange, 171
Stock market
    since 1948, 44
Stock option
    scandals, 167, 468
Stock ownership, 168, 324, 504-506
Stock purchase plans, 168
Stockbrokers, 126, 157
Stonyfield Farm, 155
stop-loss insurance, 527
Storage costs, 234
Store design, 300
Store entrance, 299
Store personnel, 373
Store security, 378
Store traffic, 9, 90
Store-based retailing perspective
    storefront, 216, 292-293
stored procedures
    and security, 367-368, 533
Strap, 155
Strategic alliances
    selection of partners, 56
Strategic analysis
    of profitability, 325, 465
Strategic business units (SBUs)
    dogs, 14, 188, 495
Strategic Direction, 341
Strategic management
    key success factors, 512
Strategic planning
    planning process, 165, 510
Strategic planning process, 165
Strategies
    for e-commerce, 191-192
Strategy
    company's customer base, 107
Strategy implementation (Chapter 7) – Management
        and Operations Issues
    Benefits of a diverse workforce, 479
Strategy implementation (Chapter 8) – Marketing,
        Finance, R&D, MIS Issues
    Wellness programs, 528
Strategy (strategies)
    merger and acquisition, 507
streaming media, 29
Strict liability
    chain of distribution, 436
    failure to warn, 437
Strip malls, 284
Strong competitors, 162
Stuart, Elliott, 6
subject line
    attention-getting, 3
Subjective evaluation, 251

Substance abuse problems, 480-481
Substitute products, 84, 225
Suburbs, 283
Subway
    Success, 286-288
Success
    and adaptability, 49, 291
Succession planning
    buy-sell agreement, 515
    estate freeze, 516-517
    estate planning, 498-499
    family limited partnership (FLP), 516
    family-owned business, 534
    lifetime gifting, 515
    sale for cash plus a note, 504
    selling to insiders, 504
    selling to outsiders, 504
Successors, 508
Suggested retail prices, 98
Suicide, 184
Sullenberger, C. B. "Sully", 320
Sullivan, Deidre, 75
Sullivan, John, 340
SUMIF function
    criteria in, 206
Sundia, 46
Sundia Inc., 46
Super Bowl Sunday, 182
Super-regional shopping malls, 284
Supplemental pay benefits
    for executives, 347
Supplements, 464
Suppliers
    long-term relationships with, 253
    payments to, 67, 259
supply chain management and
    purchasing plan, 223
Supply chain management, 224, 350, 503
supply chain management (SCM)
    production scheduling, 249
    supply network, 262, 364
Supply flexibility, 253
Supply network, 262, 364
SurePayroll, 313, 474
Surety insurance, 523
Survey of Buying Power, 267
Surveying, 333
Surveys
    response rate, 32
Survival, 45, 146, 155, 269, 311, 470, 499
Survivor, 220
sustainable growth, 224
Suzuki, 111
Swatch, 30
Swinmurn, Nick, 190
Sycamore Group, 123
Symbols, 5, 199, 441-442
Symphony, 310
Symphony orchestra, 310
Syracuse University, 316
System(s)
    marketing information, 70

T
T1 lines, 271
Tactical decisions, 77
Tag system, 358
Tags, RFID, 359-360
Tailgating,, 317
Taiwan Semiconductor, 257
Talbot's, 284
Taliban, 52
Tan, C. Lu-Lien, 111
tangible assets, 522
Target
    costing, 17, 102, 214
Target customers, 9-11, 61, 85-87, 189, 264-265, 365,
        473
Target service level under a single-period
    inventory system, 228, 354
Target Stores, 375
tariff barriers, 70
task force, 479
Task independence
    rules and, 462
Task significance, 335
Tattoos, 325
Tax burden, 271-272, 514
Tax considerations

location selection, 271
x laws, 280, 515
x payments, 367
x rates
revenues and, 183
x reform, 81
x returns, 121
xes
cigarette, 280
corporate income, 270
excise, 288
gas, 447
individual income taxes, 306
x(es)
lower, 46, 126-128, 264, 336-337, 366, 448, 515
xes
service companies, 287
xes, interest rates
life insurance policies, 126, 524
am focus, 329
am-based management, 328
ams
communication in, 330
chCrunch, 219-220, 306, 353
chnological innovation
coming up with, 437
individuals, 165, 230
chnology
nature of work, 290
chnology services, 164, 324
chnology transfer, 132
chnovative Marketing, 256
chSpace, 289
chTarget, 216
leconferences, 69
lemarketers, 454
lemarketing and Consumer Fraud and Abuse
Protection Act, 454
lephones, 141
levision
Fans, 16, 196
news, 6, 91, 200-201, 279, 494-495
Viewers, 17-18, 188
levision advertising
DVRs, 257
levision test, 470
ender
of delivery, 433-434
ender of delivery, 434
rm life insurance, 126
rm loans, 118
rminals, 37, 250, 351, 485
sla, 172
sla Motors, 149
sts
aptitude, 340
xtiles, 68, 499
HAI, 271
he American Marketplace: Demographics and
Spending Patterns, 267-268
he Cheesecake Factory, 339
he Cleveland Clinic, 275
he Container Store, 334
he Golden Rule, 220, 470
he grapevine, 348
he Limited, 516
he Los Angeles Times, 4
he Roasterie, 86
he Robinson-Patman Act, 452
he Root, 226
he Sense of Smell Institute, 295
he Shops of Saddle Creek, 284
he Tipping Point, 275
heater
Promoting, 20
eater of the mind, 20
heft by employee
embezzlement, 523
hermos, 442
hirty-Minute Photos Etc., 121
homas Global, 252
homas Global Register, 252
homson Financial, 168
hrifty Car Rental, 120
hrifty Car Sales, 120
hurow, Lester, 45
ice, Carol, 145, 535
ickets

Pricing strategy, 95-96
Tiffany, 293, 445
TIGER (Topographically Integrated Geographic
Encoding Referencing), 268
Timberland, 467
Time draft, 67
Timeliness, 19-20
Timely information, 249-250, 336
Times Square, 29, 149
Timiraos, 220
Tindell, Kip, 334
Tischler, Linda, 307
Title
passage of, 258
Title to goods
passage of title, 258
T-Mobile, 166
Toastmasters, 4
Tobacco debate
evidence, 145, 485-486
Tolerance, 371, 469
Tom's of Maine, 467
Top quality, 314
Top-level domain, 208
Topshop, 362-363
Torrini Firenze, 499
Tort, 459
Toshiba, 257
Total costs, 103, 237
Total inventory, 190, 234-235, 357
total quality management (TQM)
employee involvement, 231
Total revenues, 97
total value, 90, 350, 516
Total variable cost, 103
Totalitarianism, as political ideology
communist, 59
Totes, 476
Touch points, 187
Tourism & travel
WTO, 75-76
Toxic substances, 477
Toyota Production System, 228
Trace, 5, 232, 369
trade
in goods, 30, 432
Trade area, 79, 279
Trade area size, 279
Trade associations, 53, 189, 252, 532
Trade Commission Act, 451
Trade discount, 240-241
Trade diversion
in South America, 46
Trade mission, 63-64
Trade missions, 58
Trade Opportunity Program (TOP), 55
Trade practices, 76, 423
Trade relations, 76
Trade restrictions, 47
Trade secrets
protection for, 58, 447
trademark infringement, 441
Trademark protection, 48, 441
Trade-offs
taboo, 73
Trading area
saturated, 57, 275
Trading companies, 53
trading partners, 55
Traditional advertising media, 12, 188
Traditional bank loans, 118
Traditional indemnity plans, 526
Traffic department, 65
Traffic flow, 274
Training
lectures, 529
lifelong learning, 326
on-the-job, 532
Training and development
employee orientation, 481
Training process
results and, 344, 469
Trait systems
performance based, 344
Transactions
swap, 427
Transformation, 233, 272, 324
Transit advertising, 30
Translations, 73, 162, 199

Transport architects, 65
Transportation:
freight forwarders and, 65
rail, 276
truck, 258, 288
transportation infrastructure, 255, 276
Transportation management
density, 47, 280
hazardous materials, 476
Transportation system
terminals, 359
Travel agents, 65
Travelocity, 199
Treasury Department, 114
Treatments, 473, 527
Tree, 41
Trickle Up, 137
Trigger point, 354
Triple bottom line, 465
Triple bottom line (3BL), 465
Troubled Asset Relief Program (TARP), 114
True Value, 473
Trust
knowledge-based, 314
swift, 68
Trust Insurance, 515-516
TRUSTe, 192
Trustee(s)
for bankruptcy, 444-445
trusts
beneficiaries, 515-516
living, 516
resulting, 534
trustee, 515
Truth in Lending Act, 454-455
Tsai, Michelle, 81
Tsao, Harry, 72
Tuberman, Brian, 513
Tuition reimbursement, 340
Tuning, 331
Tunnel, 44, 294
Tunnel vision, 44
Turnaround strategy, 218
turnkey project, 447
TV commercials, 17
TvB, 40
Twain, Mark, 339
Twinkies, 444
Twist, 204, 535
Twisting, 331
Two-bin system, 357-358
Tying, 36, 141, 232, 350, 450
Tying contracts, 450
typographical errors, 198

U

Ugly Betty, 520
Unconditional, 209
Unconscionable contracts, 429
Underhill, Paco, 291-292
Underutilization, 227
Underwood, Ryan, 347
Underwriter, 170-171, 198
Underwriter Laboratories, 198
Unfair trade practices, 452
Unhealthy products, 473
Unica Corporation, 173
Uniform delivered pricing, 96
Uniforms, 34, 273
Union drive and election
fact finder, 40
unions
today's, 73
Unique selling proposition (USP), 1-2
unique visitors, 185
Uniqueness, 15, 77, 88
Unit costs, 110
Unit pricing, 97
United Arab Emirates, 57
United Nations
Charter, 87
United States
Administration (OSHA), 294
airports, 56, 264
Commercial Service, 56
Copyright Office, 443
United States
crime in, 455
Department of Housing and Urban, 130

Development (HUD), 130
Export Assistance Centers, 53-55
goods and services in, 59
ITC, 71
Occupational Safety and Health, 294, 449
wealth in, 507
United States (U.S.)
Central Intelligence Agency, 535
universal product code (UPC)
product code, 354
Universal resource locator (URL), 207
University of Alabama, 123
University of Georgia, 10
University of Michigan, 160
University of New Hampshire, 156, 336
University of North Dakota, 160
University of Phoenix, 494
University of Texas, 292
University of Texas at Austin, 292
University of Utah, 161
University of Washington, 297
University Venture Fund, 160
Unplanned business district
CBD, 282
Unz and Company, 60
Uploading, 203
UPS Capital, 125
Upscale image, 296
upward communication, 330
Upward feedback, 344-345
Urban Decay, 283
Uribe, Jay, 515
URLs, 188
Uruguay, 76
U.S. Department of the Treasury, 114
U.S. government
doing business with, 55
U.S. Patent and Trademark Office (USPTO)
patent process, 440
Usage rate, 239
Useful life, 125
Usury, 429
Usury laws, 429
Utilitarian Principle, 470
Utility
place, 270
popularity, 295
Utilization review, 532

V
Vacant, 274
Vacation schedules, 340
Value pricing, 86
Value stream mapping, 229
Vanity Fair, 40
Vans, 281
Variable expenses, 102
Variety store, 284
Vault, 122
Vendor analysis, 115, 224
Vendor certification, 250-251
Vendor selection, 225
Venture capital firm, 195
Venture capital firms, 128, 150
Venture capital funds, 161
Venture capitalist, 165, 204
venture capitalists, 129, 148
Verbal communication, 319
Verdicts, 482
VeriSign, 192
Vermont, 48, 269, 326, 467
Vertical job loading, 335
Victoria's Secret, 296
Video game consoles, 94
Video games, 16, 249, 302, 443
Viewership, 40
Viewpoint, 8
Vineyard, 499
Viral marketing, 14
virtual companies, 188
Virtual currency, 150
Virtual order fulfillment, 194
Virtual reality, 270
virtuous cycle, 475
Viruses, 215, 523
Visionary objective, 8
Visitor segmentation measurements, 213
Visual control systems, 355
Vogelstein, Fred, 220

Voice over IP (VoIP)
between sites, 189
Volatile, 171, 290
Volcanic eruption, 225
volume increases, 94
Volumes, 70, 114, 214, 264, 523
Vonage, 170
Vérité Coffee, 4
Vuitton, 5, 204, 437
Vuitton, Louis, 5, 204, 437
Vulnerability, 215

W
Wage and salary issues
hourly compensation, 270
Wages
health insurance and, 533
Wales, 196
Walgreen's, 298
Walker, James, 253
Wallpaper, 277
Walls, 272, 523
Walton, Sam, 265
Wang, Vera, 5
Warehouse club, 285
Warehousing management
design considerations, 263
Warming, 455
warning labels, 437, 489
warranties
new car, 453
of title, 432
Warranty of fitness, 436
Warranty of fitness for a particular purpose, 436
Warranty of merchantability, 436
Warranty of title, 435
Washington, George, 440
Washington Post, 99, 381, 536
Washington State University, 295
watchdog groups, 189
Watches, 88, 437-438
Water-quality problems
copper, 499
pollutants, 288, 456
Weather conditions, 131
Weaver, Abby, 24
Web
mashups, 200
Web advertising, 22
Web analytics software, 108, 203
Web browsers, 210
Web designers, 22, 190
Web logs, 202
Web page
hyperlinks, 209
Web pages
cross-selling, 209
up-selling, 209
Web search engines, 188
Web site design
navigation and, 212
WebCPA, 262
Webinars, 56
Webster, 16, 436
Wegman's, 340
Wei, Shang-Jin, 81
Weighted average cost of capital
estimates of, 39
West Edmonton Mall, 284
West Michigan Uniform, 517
West Virginia, 128, 264
Westcott, Scott, 348
Westminster College, 161
Wharton, 41, 192, 381
What-is-affordable method, 35
Wheeler, John, 532
Whirlpool Corporation
global marketing strategy, 55
White Castle, 312
White, D. Steven, 276
White, Steven, 276
Whitford, David, 459
Whole Foods, 128, 176
Whole Foods Market, 128
Whopper Bar, 306
Widgets, 201
Wii, 98, 324
Wilcoxon matched-pairs signed rank
Ties, 298, 356

William Prym GmbH & Company, 499
Williams, Geoff, 80
Williams, Michael, 75
Willingness to accept, 433
Wilson, Amy, 494
Wilson, Sara, 39-41, 93, 179
Wind, 324, 476
Winkler, Connie, 262
Winning Workplaces, 340, 494
Winterberry Group, 32
Wish lists, 208
wizards, 214
Women's Health, 307
Wonder Bread, 444
words and visuals
attracting attention, 20
the visual, 268, 379
work group, 488
Worker productivity, 226, 304
Workers' compensation, 294, 444, 521
Workers compensation
defenses, 331
injury, 137, 489, 527
scope of employment, 443
Workers' compensation coverage, 521
Workers compensation insurance
laws for, 337
Workers' Compensation Laws, 444, 527
Workforce
cultural diversity in, 326, 478
Working Woman, 486
Work-in-process, 229, 303, 350
work-life balance, 326
Work–life balance, 325
workplace
accidents in, 527
Workplace safety and health management
laws governing, 448, 514
World Trade Center, 64
World Trade Center Wisconsin, 64
World Trade Organization (WTO)
and the environment, 187, 423, 463
waivers, 536
World Wide Web
direct stock offerings, 174-175
site design, 124, 186
World Wide Web (Web)
in Great Britain, 58
World Wide Web (WWW)
marketing on, 32
Worrell, David, 111, 122, 180, 262
Wrappers, 476
Written memorandum, 433
Wrongful termination, 488, 530
Wurtzel, Marvin, 230

X
Xuny, 155

Y
Yahoo!
Launch, 152-153
Yahoo! Network, 190
Yerkes, Leslie, 327
YMCA, 324
Young adults, 473, 508
Young entrepreneurs, 151, 187, 274, 475
Young, Shawn, 180
Yugoslavia, 225

Z
Zachary's Chicago Pizza, 507
Zachowski, Zach, 507
Zapping, 17
Zappos, 3, 190-191, 320-321, 353
Zara, 255
ZDNet, 39
Zhang, 81, 146
Zimmerman, Ann, 382
Zip Code Business Patterns, 275
Zip Code Tabulation Areas, 266
Zip Code Tabulation Areas (ZCTA), 266
ZIP codes, 267
Zone pricing, 96
Zoning laws, 276
Zoning ordinances, 288
zoom, 207, 268
ZoomProspector, 266-267